Masterplots

Fourth Edition

Masterplots

Fourth Edition

Volume 1

About a Boy—The Big Rock Candy Mountain

Editor
Laurence W. Mazzeno
Alvernia College

Salem Press
Pasadena, California   Hackensack, New Jersey

Cover photo: James Baldwin (Ulf Andersen/Getty Images)

∞ The paper used in these volumes conforms to the American National Standard for Permanence of Paper for Printed Library Materials, Z39.48-1992 (R1997).

Library of Congress Cataloging-in-Publication Data

Masterplots / editor, Laurence W. Mazzeno. — 4th ed.
v. cm.
Includes bibliographical references and indexes.
ISBN 978-1-58765-568-5 (set : alk. paper) — ISBN 978-1-58765-569-2 (v. 1 : alk. paper)
1. Literature—Stories, plots, etc. 2. Literature—History and criticism. I. Mazzeno, Laurence W.
PN44.M33 2010
809—dc22

2010033931

Fourth Edition
First Printing

PRINTED IN THE UNITED STATES OF AMERICA

Publisher's Note

Masterplots, Fourth Edition is an expanded and updated version of *Masterplots, Second Revised Edition* (1996), which was itself a culmination of the *Masterplots* sets published at intervals since 1949. *Masterplots, Fourth Edition*, in twelve volumes, retains the original purpose of the *Masterplots* concept: providing fundamental reference data, plot synopses where applicable, and critical evaluations of a comprehensive selection of English-language and world literature that has been translated into English. The essays are in alphabetical order by title, and each includes an annotated bibliography to aid readers in further study.

Revision Details

Masterplots, Fourth Edition features 2,220 essays in 12 volumes: 438 essays are newly written (including 14 replacement essays), 98 feature thoroughly revised or replaced plot synopses or critical evaluations; and 1,684 have been previously published but reedited for this new edition as part of the continuing *Masterplots* updating process. (To ensure that *Masterplots* remains comprehensive, no titles from the previous edition were dropped.) This updating process reflects the results of recent research and new critical understandings of the works in question. The 1,684 titles from the 1996 set were carefully reviewed for currency, accuracy, biased language, and quality of critical analysis before inclusion in the fourth edition. In adding new titles, Consulting Editor Laurence W. Mazzeno of Alvernia College and other editors considered classroom curricula at both high school and college levels, as well as the broader context of literary culture both within and beyond North America. Editors added classics that had been previously overlooked and contemporary classics that represent a range of cultural identities and diverse modern experiences.

Although the editors realize that the definition of what constitutes a literary classic or masterwork shifts over time and that the list of possible candidates for inclusion is endless, they have attempted to create a collection of important literary texts drawn from as many sources as are accessible in English. The core of the *Masterplots* collection remains the canon of English and American literature, but it has been significantly augmented with contemporary literature and with works representing a wide range of cultures, peoples, and perspectives. Effort was made to include works by women, representing almost a third of all new titles, and works originally written in a language other than English, with almost a fifth of new titles. The chronological range of the set extends from antiquity to 2007, with a main emphasis on the literature of the nineteenth through twenty-first centuries.

Essay Format and Content

Because *Masterplots* essays are intended to be efficient reference sources, they have been formatted to provide the available factual information about a work at a glance. All essays open with a succinct compilation of carefully researched reference data on the type of work, the author, and the date of first publication and, where applicable, first English translation. The category *Type of work* indicates whether a work of fiction is a novel, short fiction, drama, or poetry; nonfiction genres include autobiography, history, social criticism, travel and nature writing, and philosophy. The *Author* line includes the given name in cases where the writer is known by a pseudonym; pseudonyms under which the writer has published; and the years of birth and, where applicable, death. The *First published* or *First produced* line provides a range of information that depends on the work, including alternative titles under which the work might have been published or produced, or for foreign-language works, the original title; the date of first publication, production, or transcription (in rare cases, where this is greatly at variance with the time of creation, a *First transcribed* date will be given); dates of serial publication; and dates of publication for the individual volumes of multivolume works. For foreign-language works the date of the first English translation (in cases where the title of the first translation differs from that used in this series, the first title is also indicated). For all works of fiction, the opening section also provides information on the *Type of plot*, which indicates the genre of the work, and *Time of plot* and *Locale*, which give the time frame and places in which the story or stories take place. These reference categories can prove useful for comparative and historical literary research. In addition, there is for most works of fiction a section entitled *Principal characters*, which lists the work's main characters, along with brief descriptions.

Also retained from the 1996 *Masterplots* edition is the use of two types of format for the essays, that of the synopsis review and that of the essay review. The synopsis reviews, which treat works that have an identifiable narrative line, provide five categories of information: the opening reference data; *Principal characters*; *The Story* or *The Poem*, a straightforward summary of the plot; *Critical Evaluation*, an incisive, critical analysis that discusses significant aspects of the work's artistry and history; and *Further Reading*, a brief, annotated list of significant English-language secondary sources that are readily accessible to general readers and that provide focused interpretation of the work in question. The essay reviews cover collections of poetry and short stories, as well as nonfiction. In this format, the essay has three subdivisions: the reference data, the analytical essay, and an annotated bibliography. Occasionally, as for some autobiographical and travel writing, an additional category—*Principal personages*—is included. This category features a list and brief descriptions of historical figures mentioned in the work.

For all ancillary works of literature, music, or art referred to throughout the text of the individual essays, the dates of first publication, performance, or creation are provided in parentheses; as a rule, titles, except in the case of some extremely long examples from eighteenth century fiction, are not abbreviated. All historical persons are referred to at first mention by their full name.

Reference Aids

At the beginning of each volume are a list of Contents for that volume as well as a Complete List of Contents for the entire set. Volume 12 ends with several reference tools, including six comprehensive indexes. The *Chronological Index* organizes titles by year of publication or production, the *Geographical Index* groups authors by their countries of origin and activity, the *Title Index* lists essays alphabetically, and the *Author Index* lists authors alphabetically. New to this edition are the *Genre Index*, which groups titles by genre, and the *Themes & Issues Index*, which groups titles by their prominent subject matter to act as a guide for students, teachers, and reading groups. All indexes are cross-referenced with alternative author names, work titles, and related themes and issues. Foreign titles are cross-referenced to their English translations.

Online Access

Salem Press provides access to its award-winning content both in traditional, printed form and online. Any school or library that purchases *Masterplots, Fourth Edition* is entitled to free, complimentary access to Salem's fully supported online version of the content. Features include a simple intuitive interface, user profile areas for students and patrons, sophisticated search functionality, and complete context, including appendixes. E-books are also available. For more information about our online database, please contact our online customer service representatives at (800) 221-1592.

Acknowledgments

Hundreds of scholars and writers contributed their expertise and creativity to the preparation of this work. Their names, close to 700 of them, and academic affiliations appear in the *List of Contributors* section in volume 1. In most cases, bylines are given for whole essays or for specific sections, including those sections that were revised or rewritten for this edition. Salem Press thanks all the scholars and writers who helped compile *Masterplots, Fourth Edition*. Particular thanks go to Consulting Editor Laurence W. Mazzeno.

List of Contributors

Randy L. Abbott
University of Evansville

Michael Adams
City University of New York, Graduate Center

Patrick Adcock
Henderson State University

C. M. Adderley
University of South Florida

V. Addington
Independent Scholar

Karley K. Adney
University of Wisconsin—Marathon County

A. Owen Aldridge
University of Illinois

Amy Alexander
Southwestern Assemblies of God University

M. D. Allen
University of Wisconsin—Fox Valley

Phyllis E. Allran
Guilford Technical Community College

Stephanie M. Alvarez
University of Texas—Pan American

Emily Alward
College of Southern Nevada

Candace E. Andrews
San Joaquin Delta College

Scott Andrews
University of California, Riverside

Raymond M. Archer
Indiana University—Kokomo

Stanley Archer
Texas A&M University

Gerald S. Argetsinger
Rochester Institute of Technology

David B. Arnett
National Sun Yat-sen University

Karen L. Arnold
Columbia, Maryland

Kenneth John Atchity
Atchity Entertainment International

H. C. Aubrey
Portland, Oregon

Charles Lewis Avinger, Jr.
Washtenaw Community College

Sheli Ayers
Kaplan University

Mary C. Bagley
Missouri Baptist College

Jim Baird
University of North Texas

L. Michelle Baker
Shepherd University

JoAnn Balingit
Bancroft Intermediate School

Jane L. Ball
Yellow Springs, Ohio

Nancy G. Ballard
Independent Scholar

Carl L. Bankston III
Tulane University

Judith L. Barban
Winthrop University

Jack Barbera
University of Mississippi

Donna J. Barbie
Embry-Riddle Aeronautical University

Paula C. Barnes
Hampton University

Henry J. Baron
Calvin College

David Barratt
Montreat College

Cordelia E. Barrera
University of Texas, San Antonio

Jane Missner Barstow
University of Hartford

Melissa E. Barth
Appalachian State University

Dana Reece Baylard
Mt. San Jacinto College

Martha Bayless
University of Oregon

Paulina L. Bazin
Nicholls State University

L. Elisabeth Beattie
Elizabethtown Community College

Cynthia S. Becerra
Humphreys College

Pamela Bedore
University of Connecticut

Laurence Behrens
University of California, Santa Barbara

Carol F. Bender
Alma College

Chris Benson
Clemson University

Joe Benson
Greensboro, North Carolina

Richard P. Benton
Trinity College

Steve Benton
East Central University

Jill Stapleton Bergeron
University of Tennessee, Knoxville

Gordon N. Bergquist
Creighton University

Donna Berliner
University of Texas at Dallas

Anthony Bernardo, Jr.
Wilmington, Delaware

Dorothy M. Betz
Georgetown University

Cynthia A. Bily
Adrian, Michigan

Margaret Boe Birns
New York University

Nicholas Birns
Eugene Lang College, The New School

Carol Bishop
Indiana University—Southeast

Robert G. Blake
Elon University

Richard Bleiler
University of Connecticut

Pegge Bochynski
Beverly, Massachusetts

Edra Charlotte Bogle
University of North Texas

Judith Bolch
University of Missouri

Timothy E. Bollinger
Independent Scholar

Sarah A. Boris
Boston University

Brinda Bose
Archer, Florida

Bradley R. Bowers
Barry University

William Boyle
University of Mississippi

Virginia Brackett
Park University

Gerhard Brand
California State University, Los Angeles

Glen Brand
University of Northern Iowa

Carol Breslin
Gwynedd-Mercy College

Chris Breyer
Los Angeles, California

Jennifer Costello Brezina
University of California, Riverside

Peter A. Brier
California State University, Los Angeles

Peter Brigg
University of Guelph

Larry K. Bright
Portland Community College

Ludger Brinker
Macomb College

Wesley Britton
Harrisburg Area Community College

Howard Bromberg
University of Michigan

David Bromige
Sonoma State University

Diane Brotemarkle
Aims Community College

Keith H. Brower
Salisbury State University

James S. Brown
Mansfield University

Stephen G. Brown
University of South Florida

Valerie C. Brown
Northwest Kansas Educational Service Center

Faith Hickman Brynie
Bigfork, Montana

Stefan Buchenberger
Nara Women's University

David D. Buck
University of Wisconsin—Milwaukee

Sally Buckner
Peace College

Jeffrey L. Buller
Florida Atlantic University

Judith Burdan
James Madison University

Susan Butterworth
Salem State College

Ann M. Cameron
Indiana University, Kokomo

Edmund J. Campion
University of Tennessee, Knoxville

Amee Carmines
Hampton University

Kelly C. Walter Carney
Methodist University

Thomas Gregory Carpenter
Lipscomb University

Henry L. Carrigan, Jr.
Northwestern University

Carmen Carrillo
Los Angeles Harbor College

David B. Carroll
California State University, Los Angeles

Emmett H. Carroll
Seattle University

Sharon Carson
University of North Dakota

Ron Carter
Rappahannock Community College

Tara Y. Carter
University of Northern Iowa

Catherine Cavanaugh
College of Saint Rose

Kathleen R. Chamberlain
Emory and Henry College

Vera Chernysheva
Actors Studio Drama School

James Thomas Chiampi
University of California, Irvine

Diana Arlene Chlebek
University of Akron Libraries

Eric H. Christianson
University of Kentucky

C. L. Chua
California State University, Fresno

Jarrell Chua
California State University, Fresno

Alice Chuang
Vanderbilt University

Paul Cockeram
Harrisburg Area Community College

David Coley
Louisiana State University

Julian W. Connolly
University of Virginia

Brett Conway
Hansung University

Alan Cottrell
American International College

Howard Cox
Magnolia Bible College

Christopher E. Crane
United States Naval Academy

Theresa L. Crater
Metropolitan State College of Denver

Amy Cummins
Fort Hays State University

Constance A. Cutler
Independent Scholar

Su A. Cutler
Kalamazoo Valley Community College

Marsha Daigle-Williamson
Spring Arbor University

Richard Damashek
Calumet College of St. Joseph

Anita Price Davis
Converse College

Delmer Davis
Andrews University

Jane Davis
Fordham University

Jo Culbertson Davis
Williams Baptist College

Linda Prewett Davis
Charleston Southern University

Mary Virginia Davis
University of California, Davis

Randee Dawn
Jackson Heights, New York

Frank Day
Clemson University

Dennis R. Dean
University of Wisconsin—Parkside

Mary Jo Deegan
University of Nebraska—Lincoln

Robert Dees
Los Angeles, California

Danielle A. DeFoe
Sierra College

Bill Delaney
Independent Scholar

Francine Dempsey
College of Saint Rose

James I. Deutsch
Smithsonian Institution

Joseph Dewey
University of Pittsburgh—Johnstown

Carolyn Ford Dickinson
Columbia College

Frank Dietz
University of Texas at Austin

Marcia B. Dinneen
Bridgewater State College

Matts G. Djos
Mesa State College

Kim Dolce
Independent Scholar

Cecilia S. Donohue
Madonna University

Terrence R. Doyle
California State University, Long Beach

Theresa E. Dozier
Prince George's Community College

Barbara Drake
Linfield College

Thomas Du Bose
Louisiana State University—Shreveport

Margaret M. Duggan
South Dakota State University

Charles F. Duncan
Clark-Atlanta University

Joyce Duncan
East Tennessee State University

Victor Manuel Durán
University of South Carolina—Aiken

Wilton Eckley
Colorado School of Mines

K Edgington
Towson University

Glenn M. Edwards
University of Southern California

Robert A. Eisner
California State University, Sacramento

Janet M. Ellerby
University of North Carolina, Wilmington

Julie Elliott
Indiana University—South Bend

Robert P. Ellis
Worcester State College

Scott D. Emmert
University of Wisconsin—Fox Valley

Nikolai Endres
Western Kentucky University

Victoria Erhart
Strayer University

Jack Ewing
Boise, Idaho

Kevin Eyster
Madonna University

Thomas H. Falk
Michigan State University

Jo N. Farrar
San Jacinto College

Gisèle C. Feal
State University of New York, Buffalo

James Feast
Baruch College

Thomas R. Feller
Nashville, Tennessee

Lydia E. Ferguson
Clemson University

Christine Ferrari
Monash University

Joseph A. Feustle, Jr.
University of Toledo

John W. Fiero
University of Louisiana at Lafayette

Jack Finefrock
Kenyon College

Mary Peace Finley
Boulder, Colorado

Edward Fiorelli
St. John's University

Sandra K. Fischer
State University of New York, Albany

Bonnie Flaig
Kalamazoo Valley Community College

Nancy Foasberg
City University of New York, Queens College

Robert J. Forman
St. John's University

Lydia Forssander-Song
Trinity Western University

Edward E. Foster
University of San Diego

Jan Kennedy Foster
San Diego, California

Thomas C. Foster
University of Michigan—Flint

Robert J. Frail
Centenary College

Carol Franks
Portland State University

Bonnie Fraser
Independent Scholar

Timothy C. Frazer
Western Illinois University

Thomas B. Frazier
Cumberland College

Michelle Fredette
Loyola University

William Freitas
University of San Diego

Raymond Frey
Centenary College

Rachel E. Frier
University of Maryland

Patricia H. Fulbright
Clark College

Kelly Fuller
Claremont Graduate University

Constance M. Fulmer
Pepperdine University

Robert L. Gale
University of Pittsburgh

Elizabeth M. Galoozis
Bentley University

M. E. Gandy
Bishop State Community College

Ann D. Garbett
Averett University

E. N. Genovese
San Diego State University

Marshall Bruce Gentry
Georgia College and State University

Leslie E. Gerber
Appalachian State University

Bishnupriya Ghosh
Utah State University

Jill B. Gidmark
University of Minnesota

Howard Giskin
Appalachian State University

Beaird Glover
Southaven, Massachusetts

Diana Pavlac Glyer
Azusa Pacific University

Vibha Bakshi Gokhale
Pune, India

Jeffrey K. Golden
University of North Carolina, Wilmington

Sheldon Goldfarb
University of British Columbia

Marc Goldstein
Independent Scholar

M. Carmen Gomez-Galisteo
Universidad de Alcala

Julie Goodspeed-Chadwick
Indiana University—Purdue

Sidney Gottlieb
Sacred Heart University

Karen K. Gould
Austin, Texas

Lewis L. Gould
University of Texas at Austin

Charles A. Gramlich
Xavier University of Louisiana

William E. Grant
Bowling Green State University

Ronald Gray
Grand Junction, Colorado

James Green
Arizona State University

Glenda Griffin
Sam Houston State University

John L. Grigsby
Appalachian Research & Defense Fund of Kentucky

M. Katherine Grimes
Ferrum College

M. Martin Guiney
Kenyon College

James Gunn
University of Kansas

Kenneth E. Hada
East Central University

Angela Hague
Middle Tennessee State University

James L. Hale
Central Washington University

Elsie Galbreath Haley
Metropolitan State College of Denver

Jay L. Halio
University of Delaware

Jan Hall
Columbus, Ohio

Max Halperen
North Carolina State University

Barbara J. Hampton
Independent Scholar

Katherine Hanley
St. Bernard's School of Theology & Ministry

Wells S. Hansen
Milton Academy

Stephen Hanson
Beverly Hills, California

Michele Hardy
Prince George's Community College

Judith E. B. Harmon
Lake Forest College

Natalie Harper
Bard College at Simon's Rock

Gregory Harris
San Francisco, California

Suzan Harrison
Eckerd College

Jack Hart
University of Rio Grande

Stephen M. Hart
University College London

Lodwick Hartley
Independent Scholar

Chris Hartman
Fort Lewis College

Wayne E. Haskin
North Carolina State University

Alan C. Haslam
Sierra College

A. Waller Hastings
Northern State University

David Haugen
Western Illinois University

Vera Lucia de Araujo Haugse
Santa Monica, California

John C. Hawley
Santa Clara University

Mary H. Hayden
California State University, Fullerton

Steve Hecox
Averett University

Terry Heller
Coe College

Joyce E. Henry
Ursinus College

Susan Henthorne
White Pines College

Howard Lee Hertz
Alhambra, California

Angela D. Hickey
Adrian College

John Higby
Appalachian State University

Michael R. Hill
University of Nebraska—Lincoln

Richard A. Hill
Taylor University

Susan E. Hill
University of Northern Iowa

KaaVonia Hinton
Old Dominion University

Rebecca Stingley Hinton
University of Cincinnati, Clermont College

Jen Hirt
Pennsylvania State University, Harrisburg

Matthew Ryan Hoch
Shorter College

Thomas Hockersmith
Little Rock, Arkansas

James L. Hodge
Bowdoin College

Roseanne L. Hoefel
Alma College

Dennis R. Hoilman
University of Osaka

Hal L. Holladay
Bard College at Simon's Rock

John R. Holmes
Franciscan University of Steubenville

Yasuko Honda
Loyola University, New Orleans

Joan Hope
Palm Beach Gardens, Florida

Glenn Hopp
Howard Payne University

Gregory D. Horn
Southwest Virginia Community College

Pierre L. Horn
Wright State University

George F. Horneker
Arkansas State University

Katharine Bail Hoskins
LaVerne College

James Marc Hovde
University of Paris

William L. Howard
Chicago State University

Anne B. Howells
Occidental College

John F. Hudson
West Concord Union Church

Patrick Norman Hunt
Stanford University

E. D. Huntley
Appalachian State University

Mary G. Hurd
East Tennessee State University

Farhad B. Idris
Frostburg State University

Robin L. Imhof
University of the Pacific Library

Earl G. Ingersoll
State University of New York, Brockport

Muriel B. Ingham
San Diego State University

Archibald E. Irwin
Indiana University—Southeast

John Jacob
Northwestern University

Helen Jaskoski
California State University, Fullerton

Shakuntala Jayaswal
Independent Scholar

Jeffry Jensen
Altadena, California

David Johansson
Brevard Community College

Edward Johnson
University of New Orleans

Jeff Johnson
Brevard Community College

Sheila Golburgh Johnson
Santa Barbara, California

Yvonne Johnson
St. Louis Community College, Meramec

Eunice Pedersen Johnston
North Dakota State University

Douglas A. Jones
Andrews University

Jane Anderson Jones
Manatee Community College

Keith Jones
Northwestern College

Richard Jones
Stephen F. Austin State University

Sharon Lynette Jones
Wright State University

Michael Scott Joseph
Rutgers University Libraries

Mitchell Kalpakgian
Simpson College

Mathew J. Kanjirathinkal
Park University

Ludmila Kapschutschenko-Schmitt
Rider University

Daven M. Kari
Vanguard University

Joanne G. Kashdan
Golden West College

Milton S. Katz
Kansas City Art Institute

Susan E. Keegan
Mendocino Community College

Richard Keenan
University of Maryland—Eastern Shore

Heidi Kelchner
University of South Florida

Steven G. Kellman
University of Texas at San Antonio

Richard Kelly
University of Tennessee, Knoxville

Viktor R. Kemper
Western Illinois University

W. P. Kenney
Manhattan College

Howard A. Kerner
Polk State College

Mabel Khawaja
Hampton University

Leigh Husband Kimmel
Indianapolis, Indiana

Paul Kincaid
Folkestone, Kent, England

Henderson Kincheloe
Williamsburg, Virginia

Patricia Ann King
Independent Scholar

Cassandra Kircher
Elon University

Kat Kitts
Fairfield, Ohio

Michael Kleeberg
Ivy Tech Community College

Grove Koger
Boise State University

Stephen W. Kohl
University of Oregon

Elitza Kotzeva
Appalachian State University

Mona Y. Kratzert
Tustin, California

Kenneth Krauss
College of Saint Rose

David L. Kubal
California State University, Los Angeles

Kathryn Kulpa
University of Rhode Island

Linda L. Labin
Husson College

Jon W. La Cure
University of Tennessee

P. Huston Ladner
University of Mississippi

Wendy Alison Lamb
South Pasadena, California

Carole J. Lambert
Boston University

David W. Landrum
Cornerstone College

Mary L. Otto Lang
Wharton County Junior College

David H. J. Larmour
Texas Tech University

Craig A. Larson
Trinidad State Junior College

Eugene Larson
Los Angeles Pierce College

Susan T. Larson
Clemson University

Dorie LaRue
Louisiana State University

Jon Lavieri
East Greenwich, Rhode Island

John M. Lawless
Providence College

William T. Lawlor
University of Wisconsin—Stevens Point

Benjamin S. Lawson
Florida State University

Henry A. Lea
University of Massachusetts—Amherst

Linda Ledford-Miller
University of Scranton

Josephine M. Lee
South Dakota School of Mines & Technology

L. L. Lee
Western Washington University

Michael Levine
Independent Scholar

Jennie MacDonald Lewis
University of Denver

Leon Lewis
Appalachian State University

Thomas Tandy Lewis
St. Cloud State University

Anna Lillios
University of Central Florida

Elizabeth Blakesley Lindsay
Washington State University

Victor Lindsey
East Central University

Thomas Lisk
North Carolina State University

Richard Logsdon
Community College of Southern Nevada

Stanley Vincent Longman
University of Georgia

R. M. Longyear
University of Kentucky

Eileen Lothamer
California State University, Long Beach

Bernadette Flynn Low
Community College of Baltimore County—Dundalk

Janet Luehring
Cherry Valley, Illinois

Eric v.d. Luft
College of Saint Rose Gegensatz Press

Robert M. Luscher
University of Nebraska—Kearney

Carol J. Luther
Pellissippi State Community College

R. C. Lutz
CII Group

Laurie Lykken
Century Community & Technical College

Janet McCann
Texas A&M University

Joanne McCarthy
Tacoma, Washington

Barbara McCaskill
University of Georgia

Sandra C. McClain
James Madison University

Andrew F. Macdonald
Loyola University, New Orleans

Gina Macdonald
Nicholls State University

Roxanne McDonald
Wilmot, New Hampshire

Margaret McFadden-Gerber
Appalachian State University

Ron McFarland
University of Idaho

Robert Kuhn McGregor
Sangamon State University

S. Thomas Mack
University of South Carolina—Aiken

Richard McKirahan
Pomona College

Nancy A. Macky
Westminster College

Peter W. Macky
Westminster College

Joseph McLaren
Hofstra University

John L. McLean
Missouri Valley College

Willis E. McNelly
California State University, Fullerton

Jim McWilliams
Gering, Nebraska

David W. Madden
California State University, Sacramento

Paul Madden
Hardin-Simmons University

Gordon R. Maddison
Broward Community College

Phyllis Mael
Pasadena City College

Maria Theresa Maggi
University of Idaho

Annette M. Magid
Erie Community College

Philip Magnier
Fairfield, Iowa

Mary E. Mahony
Wayne County Community College

Cherie Maiden
Furman University

Melissa Mallon
University of Pittsburgh, Johnstown

Edward A. Malone
Missouri Western State University

Barry Stewart Mann
Alliance Theatre

Lois A. Marchino
University of Texas at El Paso

Eberly Mareci
Marymount Manhattan College

Brian L. Mark
California State University, Fullerton

Jean G. Marlowe
North Carolina State University

Kathryn D. Marocchino
California State University, Maritime Academy

Chogallah Maroufi
California State University, Los Angeles

Catherine Gimelli Martin
Memphis State University

Lee Roy Martin
Church of God Theological Seminary

R. A. Martin
Lausanne Collegiate School

Mirjana N. Mataric
University of Belgrade, Serbia

Beverly J. Matiko
Andrews University

J. Greg Matthews
Washington State University Libraries

Julia Matthews
Albright College

Robert N. Matuozzi
Washington State University

Harry A. Maxson
Wesley College

Charles E. May
California State University, Long Beach

Laurence W. Mazzeno
Alvernia College

Frank Joseph Mazzi
Brentwood School

Kenneth W. Meadwell
University of Winnipeg

Muriel Mellown
North Carolina Central University

David Michael Merchant
Louisiana Tech University

Diana M. Merchant
Austin Peay State University

Siegfried Mews
University of North Carolina, Chapel Hill

Julia M. Meyers
Duquesne University

Walter E. Meyers
North Carolina State University

Vasa D. Mihailovich
University of North Carolina, Chapel Hill

Dodie Marie Miller
Fort Wayne, Indiana

Jane Ann Miller
Dartmouth College

Paula M. Miller
Biola University

Timothy C. Miller
Millersville University of Pennsylvania

Craig A. Milliman
Fort Valley State University

Leslie B. Mittleman
California State University, Long Beach

Michele L. Mock
University of Pittsburgh at Johnstown

Christian H. Moe
Southern Illinois University at Carbondale

Carl Moody
Los Osos, California

Catherine E. Moore
Independent Scholar

Robert A. Morace
Daemen College

Bernard E. Morris
Independent Scholar

Patrick D. Morrow
Auburn University

Sherry L. Morton-Mollo
California State University, Fullerton

Charmaine Allmon Mosby
Western Kentucky University

Roark Mulligan
Christopher Newport University

C. Lynn Munro
Belton, Missouri

Russell Elliott Murphy
University of Arkansas at Little Rock

N. Samuel Murrell
College of Wooster

John M. Muste
Ohio State University

Leslie Pendleton Myers
Independent Scholar

D. Gosselin Nakeeb
Pace University

Richard A. Nanian
Salem State College

Keith Neilson
California State University, Fullerton

William Nelles
University of Massachusetts—Dartmouth

Byron Nelson
West Virginia University

Elizabeth R. Nelson
St. Peter's College

Caryn E. Neumann
Miami University of Ohio

Terry Nienhuis
Western Carolina University

Holly L. Norton
University of Northwestern Ohio

Benjamin Nyce
University of San Diego

George O'Brien
Georgetown University

Rafael Ocasio
Agnes Scott College

Stephen C. Olbrys
University of Indiana

Vina Nickels Oldach
University of Colorado, Colorado Springs

Kenneth Oliver
Independent Scholar

Lawrence J. Oliver
Texas A&M University

Bruce Olsen
Independent Scholar

Brian L. Olson
Kalamazoo Valley Community College

James Norman O'Neill
Bryant College

Max Orezzoli
Florida International University

William Osborne
Florida International University

Cóilín D. Owens
George Mason University

Shannon Oxley
University of Leeds

Geert S. Pallemans
Southern Illinois University at Edwardsville

Lucille Izzo Pallotta
Onondaga Community College

Janet Taylor Palmer
Caldwell Community College & Technical Institute

Sally B. Palmer
South Dakota School of Mines & Technology

Virginia Pannabecker
Arizona State University

Robert J. Paradowski
Rochester Institute of Technology

Matthew Parfitt
Boston University

David B. Parsell
Furman University

David Partenheimer
Truman State University

David Patterson
Oklahoma State University

Jay Paul
Christopher Newport University

Susie Paul
Auburn University at Montgomery

Pamela Pavliscak
University of North Carolina

Craig Payne
Indian Hills Community College

Roberta L. Payne
Louisiana State University, New Orleans

D. G. Paz
University of North Texas

David Peck
Laguna Beach, California

Pamela Peek
Charleston Southern University

Ted Pelton
Buffalo, New York

Susana Perea-Fox
Oklahoma State University

Carl J. Perez
Independence, Missouri

Thomas Amherst Perry
Texas A&M University—Commerce

Thomas D. Petitjean, Jr.
Louisiana State University, Eunice

Marion Petrillo
Bloomsburg University

R. Craig Philips
Michigan State University

Lela Phillips
Andrew College

Allene Phy-Olsen
Austin Peay State University

H. Alan Pickrell
Emory and Henry College

Valerie A. Murrenus Pilmaier
University of Wisconsin—Sheboygan

Mary Ellen Pitts
Rhodes College

J. Scott Plaster
Independent Scholar

Marjorie Podolsky
Pennsylvania State University, Erie—Behrend College

Francis Poole
University of Delaware

Laurence M. Porter
Michigan State University

Stanley Poss
California State University, Fresno

Clifton W. Potter, Jr.
Lynchburg College

Jessie Bishop Powell
American Public University System

John Powell
Oklahoma Baptist University

Luke A. Powers
Tennessee State University

Julie D. Prandi
Illinois Wesleyan University

Andrew B. Preslar
Lamar State College, Orange

Verbie Lovorn Prevost
University of Tennessee at Chattanooga

Cliff Prewencki
Delmar, New York

Victoria Price
Lamar University

Karen Priest
Lamar State College, Orange

Norman Prinsky
Augusta State University

Maureen J. Puffer-Rothenberg
Valdosta State University

Charles Pullen
Queen's University

Josephine Raburn
Cameron University

Gregary J. Racz
Long Island University, Brooklyn

Thomas Rankin
Concord, California

R. Kent Rasmussen
Thousand Oaks, California

Abe C. Ravitz
California State University, Dominguez Hills

John D. Raymer
Holy Cross College

Bruce D. Reeves
Bank of America

Rosemary M. Canfield Reisman
Charleston Southern University

Ann E. Reynolds
Raleigh, North Carolina

Michael S. Reynolds
Santa Fe, New Mexico

Rodney P. Rice
South Dakota School of Mines & Technology

Betty Richardson
Southern Illinois University at Edwardsville

Debora J. Richey
California State University, Fullerton

Janine Rider
Mesa State College

Edward A. Riedinger
Ohio State University

Dorothy Dodge Robbins
Louisiana Tech University

Kenneth Robbins
Louisiana Tech University

Claire J. Robinson
Independent Scholar

Susan M. Rochette-Crawley
University of Northern Iowa

Bernard F. Rodgers, Jr.
Bard College at Simon's Rock

Kim Dickson Rogers
Independent Scholar

Mary Rohrberger
New Orleans, Louisiana

Carl Rollyson
City University of New York, Baruch College

Michele Valerie Ronnick
Wayne State University

Paul Rosefeldt
Delgado Community College

Joseph Rosenblum
Greensboro, North Carolina

Natania Rosenfeld
Duke University

Robert L. Ross
University of Texas at Austin

Daniel V. Runyon
Spring Arbor University

Susan Rusinko
Bloomsburg University

Donelle Ruwe
Northern Arizona University

Murray Sachs
Brandeis University

Chaman L. Sahni
Boise State University

Gregory Salyer
Huntingdon College

Todd Samuelson
Cushing Memorial Library & Archives

Vicki A. Sanders
Gainesville, Georgia

Katherine Sanger
Mercy College

Martel Sardina
Roselle, Illinois

Richard Sax
Lake Erie College

Steven C. Schaber
San Diego State University

James Schiavoni
Hiwassee College

Reinhold Schlieper
Embry-Riddle Aeronautical University

Gary D. Schmidt
Calvin College

Beverly E. Schneller
Millersville University

Noel Schraufnagel
Alcorn State University

Roberta Schreyer
State University of New York, Potsdam

James Scruton
Bethel College

Marc Seals
University of Wisconsin—Baraboo/ Sauk County

Kenneth Seib
Reno, Nevada

John Sekora
North Carolina Central University

D. Dean Shackelford
Concord College

Suzanne Obenauer Shaut
Caldwell Community College & Technical Institute

Emily Carroll Shearer
Middle Tennessee State University

Martha A. Sherwood
Kent Anderson Law Associates

Agnes A. Shields
Chestnut Hill College

Wilma J. Shires
Cisco Junior College

R. Baird Shuman
University of Illinois at Urbana-Champaign

Laura Shumar
Purdue University

Paul Siegrist
Fort Hays State University

Charles L. P. Silet
Iowa State University

Maria Eugenia Silva
Virginia Union University

Armand E. Singer
West Virginia University

Carl Singleton
Fort Hays State University

Amy Sisson
Houston Community College

Jan Sjåvik
University of Washington

Joshua A. Skinner
University of Dallas

Genevieve Slomski
Independent Scholar

David Smailes
Westfield State College

Nick David Smart
College of New Rochelle

Marjorie Smelstor
Kauffman Foundation

Pamela J. Olubunmi Smith
University of Nebraska at Omaha

Clifton M. Snider
California State University, Long Beach

Jean M. Snook
Memorial University of Newfoundland

A. J. Sobczak
Santa Barbara, California

George Soule
Carleton College

Hartley S. Spatt
State University of New York, Maritime College

Maureen Kincaid Speller
University of Kent at Canterbury

Amy Spitalnick
Toluca Lake, California

Holly Sprinkle
Kaplan University

Brian Stableford
Reading, England

James Aaron Stanger
University of California, Riverside

Isabel B. Stanley
East Tennessee State University

Gayle Steck
El Paso Community College

Karen F. Stein
University of Rhode Island

Judith L. Steininger
Milwaukee School of Engineering

Tiffany E. Stiffler
Randolph-Macon Woman's College

Ingo R. Stoehr
Kilgore College

Louise M. Stone
Bloomsburg University

Theresa L. Stowell
Adrian College

Gerald H. Strauss
Bloomsburg University

Geralyn Strecker
Ball State University

Trey Strecker
Ball State University

Michael Stuprich
Ithaca College

James Sullivan
California State University, Los Angeles

Rosemarie Cardillicchio Sultan
Independent Scholar

A. Tatiana Summers
University of Alabama System

David Sundstrand
Association of Literary Scholars & Critics

Charlene E. Suscavage
University of Southern Maine

Catherine Swanson
Austin, Texas

Alice L. Swensen
University of Northern Iowa

Peter Swirski
University of Hong Kong

Glenn L. Swygart
Tennessee Temple University

Susan J. Sylvia
Acushnet, Massachusetts

James Tackach
Roger Williams University

Ann M. Tandy
University of St. Thomas

Thomas J. Taylor
University of Akron

Tom Taylor
Independent Scholar

Charlotte Templin
University of Indianapolis

Nancy Conn Terjesen
Kent State University

Julie Thompson
Petaluma, California

Lou Thompson
Texas Woman's University

Stephanie Lewis Thompson
Kaplan University

Jonathan L. Thorndike
Belmont University

Burt Thorp
University of North Dakota

John G. Tomlinson, Jr.
University of Southern California

Karen Tracey
University of Northern Iowa

Paul B. Trescott
Southern Illinois University

Richard Tuerk
Texas A&M University—Commerce

Linda Turzynski
Rutgers University

Dennis Vannatta
University of Arkansas at Little Rock

Mary Verrill
National American University

Albert Wachtel
Pitzer College

Jaquelyn Weeks Walsh
McNeese State University

Gordon Walters
Independent Scholar

Qun Wang
California State University, Monterey Bay

Shawncey Webb
Taylor University

R. David Weber
University of Southern California

James Weigel, Jr.
Ames, Iowa

Janet Wester
Independent Scholar

Thomas Whissen
Wright State University

Lana A. Whited
Ferrum College

Barbara M. Whitehead
Hampton University

Julia Whitsitt
Lander University

Albert E. Wilhelm
Tennessee Technological University

Thomas Willard
University of Arizona

Philip F. Williams
Arizona State University

Scott G. Williams
University of Texas at Austin

Tyrone Williams
Xavier University

Judith Barton Williamson
Sauk Valley Community College

Michael Witkoski
University of South Carolina

Susan Wladaver-Morgan
Independent Scholar

Pat M. Wong
Palos Verdes Estates, California

Shawn Woodyard
Independent Scholar

Scott Wright
University of St. Thomas

Lisa A. Wroble
Edison State College

Qingyun Wu
California State University, Los Angeles

Robert E. Yahnke
University of Minnesota

Scott D. Yarbrough
Charleston Southern University

Clifton K. Yearley
State University of New York, Buffalo

Mary Young
College of Wooster

Robert B. Youngblood
Washington & Lee University

Laura M. Zaidman
University of South Carolina—Sumter

Gay Pitman Zieger
Santa Fe College

Laura Weiss Zlogar
University of Wisconsin—River Falls

Contents

Contents

Complete List of Titles

Volume 1

Volume 2

Volume 3

Volume 4

Volume 5

Volume 6

Volume 7

Volume 8

Volume 9

Volume 10

Volume 11

Volume 12

Indexes

Masterplots

Fourth Edition

A

About a Boy

Author: Nick Hornby (1957-)
First published: 1998
Type of work: Novel
Type of plot: Bildungsroman
Time of plot: 1993-1994
Locale: London, Cambridge, and Royston, England

Principal characters:
WILL FREEMAN, an independently wealthy man
MARCUS, a twelve-year-old boy
FIONA, his mother, a music therapist
SUZIE, her friend
ELLIE MCCRAE, Marcus's friend
CLIVE, Marcus's father, a social worker
RACHEL, Will's girlfriend, an illustrator

The Story:

Twelve-year-old Marcus and his mother, Fiona, have just moved from Cambridge to London, four years after his parents' divorce. Marcus tries to understand his mother's depression and to adjust to their new location. He discovers that his new school conforms to strict fashion and behavioral styles. Marcus dresses unfashionably and has a habit of drifting off and singing out loud. Although he tries to avoid bullies, he is not successful. In addition, Marcus worries increasingly about his mother's signs of mental illness.

Will Freeman, according to a magazine quiz he has taken, has a "coolness" rating of subzero. His philosophy is to avoid clutter, whether of possessions or of personal responsibilities. Will receives royalties for his father's only hit song, "Santa's Super Sleigh," allowing him to avoid work and providing him with time for fantasies of volunteering. Although he never actually volunteers for a cause, Will finds a new philanthropic endeavor: He becomes involved with Angie, a beautiful single mother. For Will, it is a perfect relationship. The attractive single mother adores him for not being her previous husband and for listening attentively, and she ends the relationship herself just when Will is wondering how to break up and still be considered a nice guy.

To meet more single mothers, Will invents a two-year-old son, Ned, and a former wife, Paula, and attends a meeting of SPAT (Single Parents Alone Together). Will meets Suzie, Fiona's best friend, at the meeting and is invited to a SPAT picnic with Suzie, Marcus, and Suzie's daughter. Bringing Marcus home, they find that Fiona has attempted suicide. While Marcus is in a living nightmare, Will is fascinated by the drama and Marcus's sudden fear that his mother will make another attempt to kill herself.

This encounter provokes one of Will's periodic resolutions to help others, and he offers to spend time with Marcus. After Fiona's suicide attempt, Marcus decides that, although he may not need a father, he and his mother are not safe alone. As a result, Marcus accepts Will's offer on the condition that Fiona can accompany them. Marcus hopes that Will and his mother will get together. Will, a dedicated materialist, and Fiona, an antiestablishment hippie, talk to each other but have no interest in each other romantically. The outing ends, to Will's horror, in a sing-along to Joni Mitchell that causes Will to rethink his volunteerism.

Marcus shows up at Will's apartment one afternoon and invites himself in. Although Will is dubious about what become Marcus's recurring visits to watch *Countdown*, a television quiz show, he fits them into his routine. At one point, Will sees how much Marcus is bullied at school and resolves to help him. Fiona does not approve of Marcus spending time with Will, but Marcus refuses to stop seeing him. Will resists involvement, but his and Marcus's relationship becomes stronger and is furthered when Will tangentially helps Marcus find two fifteen-year-old friends at school, Ellie and Zoe. Will is especially helpful to Marcus in teaching him about popular music, such as the band Nirvana. Ellie is an obsessive fan of the band's lead singer, Kurt Cobain, eschewing her school uniform for a sweatshirt with Cobain's picture on it. A bully herself, Ellie protects Marcus from other school bullies. Marcus is awed by Ellie's strong personality, aggressive nature, and refusal to back down in the face of rules. Ellie's parents are divorced as well, and she and Marcus begin to develop a strong friendship.

On New Year's Eve, Will meets Rachel, a beautiful, intelligent woman who is not interested in him until they connect on the topic of children. Rachel assumes that Marcus is Will's son. Will allows her to believe this, and they agree to get their sons together. In love for the first time, Will is desperate to see Rachel. Marcus agrees to help him (hoping Will can help him further with Ellie, too), although Marcus does not understand why Will cannot just tell Rachel the truth. Eventually, Will does tell Rachel the truth. In the end, this deepens their relationship, although at first Rachel is more circumspect.

When Fiona begins crying again, Marcus asks Will and Ellie for help, but each says that, although Marcus thinks they know things, they cannot help with "real" problems. Will rethinks this statement, however, and he realizes that he is an adult and that he has a responsibility to Marcus, but he is unsure how to help. Upon Rachel's suggestion, Will talks to Fiona, and they arrive at a deeper friendship. Will sees that she will not attempt suicide despite her continuing depression.

Ellie accompanies Marcus to visit his father on the day that Cobain's suicide is made public. She reacts violently to the news, becoming drunk and damaging property; both she and Marcus end up in jail as a result. This episode results in Marcus finally confronting his father and recognizing Ellie's weaknesses, while Ellie is struck by her culpability for her actions when she meets and identifies with the shopkeeper whose window she damaged. The woman seems to Ellie to be much like Ellie herself, only ten years older.

Marcus, Ellie, and Zoe become close friends. Will and Fiona feel that they have lost some of Marcus, who is conforming more to his school's dress styles and common teen interests, but they are happy to see him adjusting to school and building relationships. Will is considering proposing to Rachel. Will and Marcus continue to develop their different relationships, having both arrived at new levels of stability, self-awareness, and maturity supported by their network of friends and family.

Critical Evaluation:

Many critics identify Nick Hornby as reflecting contemporary English middle-class issues concerning social relationships in urban settings. *About a Boy* contains many elements similar to his earlier works, *Fever Pitch* (1992) and *High Fidelity* (1995), such as the relationship of one's identity to one's pastimes and interests. Hornby's personal interests in music and football are highly visible in the novel, as are other autobiographical elements, such as a setting in North London (where Hornby grew up in the 1960's and 1970's), divorce, and the complexity of relationships. Some critics also contend that Marcus's character is inspired by Hornby's son, who has autism. Hornby's straightforward, conversational writing style includes an element of advising the contemporary individual. These stylistic aspects are considered unique and responsible for his large following.

Hornby is among the group of contemporary authors involved with McSweeney's, an independent publisher experimenting with new ways of creating and disseminating accessible literature, reaching out to diverse communities online, in print, and through social programs. In *About a Boy*, Hornby widens his scope, incorporating two protagonists with great superficial age differences to explore and expand traditional conceptions of family and relationships. As a result, *About a Boy* goes beyond a simple coming-of-age story to represent a contemporary literary view of the potential for newly envisioned interaction between individuals and groups, even as many places become increasingly urbanized and traditional definitions of family and community may appear to be dissolving.

A short bildungsroman with a humorous tone, *About a Boy* combines the beginning of the customary journey to maturity of a serious young man who at times seems old with the journey to maturity of a thirty-six-year-old man who acts like a teenager. The book alternates chapters between Marcus's and Will's points of view, emphasizing their interdependent journey toward understanding their own areas of naïveté. Marcus becomes increasingly self-reliant, self-aware, and savvy regarding contemporary popular culture. Will, whose identity is founded on the connoisseurship of possessions, becomes increasingly aware of others and opens himself to the difficulties and benefits of long-term, well-maintained relationships.

Throughout the novel, media and popular culture play an important role, made notable in the ways they are inevitably or by choice part of individuals' and groups' lives. Characters often relate to events, problems, and other people through media or popular culture references. Marcus references television programs and films frequently when attempting to understand events and life. References to media and popular culture within the first two chapters provide contextual definitions of the protagonists' personalities and their positions relative to general middle-class social norms.

Marcus chooses a documentary on fish as a safe film, free of violence or upsetting events, to watch with his mother. This choice, like the magazine quiz through which Will is introduced, reveals each character's outlook on life. Trying to cope with school, Marcus employs a fantasy about being tutored at home like Macaulay Caulkin (a child actor). Will plans his day around popular culture: watching *Countdown* and buying new CDs, his funds generated by royalties from his father's famous Christmas pop song. Ellie defines her life around a rebellion against racist, classist, and sexist traditions. She sees Nirvana and lead singer Kurt Cobain as embodying this rebellion, and she emphasizes her self-expression by daily wearing a Cobain sweatshirt instead of her school uniform.

As the novel develops, these media representations become part of a greater exploration of identity and connections. Marcus, Will, and Ellie are all presented as extremely individualistic and alone in a sea of unreachable individuals. Fiona also displays this sense of isolation and inability to find connections, especially in London. Marcus dresses and acts so differently that even the designated outcasts in his school do not wish to be associated with him. Will is a self-described island. He has lost contact with his only remaining family, a stepbrother and stepsister, and avoids long-term, serious relationships, even friendships. Ellie's aggressiveness and extroverted behavior make her appear to be more involved with others than she really is. She has one good friend, Zoe, before becoming friends with Marcus. The repeated references to Nirvana, along with Ellie's ever-present sweatshirt, make Cobain a representative figure as well. Divorce has affected each of these individuals, including Cobain, as a child or as an adult. As a group, they represent contemporary splintered relationships that generate only partial ties to the communities with which they interact.

As Marcus, Will, Ellie, Fiona, Rachel, and others form relationships with one another, the paths they follow unfold along with a straightforward, contextualized examination of topics such as gender identity, personal responsibility, community development, and representations of social interaction in media forms such as television, film, and music. As noted by critics Jonathan Alexander and Matthew Bannister, the resulting development of these characters' extended family-friend community reveals a breaking up of traditional conceptions of family and social norms. Although none of the characters is homosexual, the lack of insistence on the need for certain structured, narrowly defined familial and social relationships challenges heterosexual stereotypes of such relationships. The emphasis on taking personal responsibility for and action toward building relationships and communities is also supported by the program depicted in Royston, where Ellie meets and connects with the shopkeeper whose store window she damaged. The figure of Cobain as a cultural icon, an embodiment of angst, and a vehicle for self-expression adds a larger, societal dimension to this theme. Cobain's death as described in *About a Boy* is depicted as an event that, despite its tragedy, connects many people in vastly different locations.

Community and family can be defined in different, more or less inclusive ways. Marcus's theory, echoing the saying that there is safety in numbers, stresses that there is a need for, and perhaps a turn toward, finding new and more inclusive ways to define these groups. By expanding and attending to the variety of connections that make up such relationships, one can see these connections as meaningful and necessary for contemporary societies, whose complexity and fragmentation render traditional, less inclusive models insufficient.

Virginia Pannabecker

Further Reading

Alexander, Jonathan. "One Gay Author, One Straight Author, and a Handful of Queer Books: Recent Fiction of David Leavitt and Nick Hornby." *Harrington Gay Men's Fiction Quarterly* 4, no. 2 (2002): 110-120. Examines characters' social relationships concerning themes of openness and extended social communities that are broader than traditionally conceived family units.

Anthony, Andrew. "The Observer Profile: The Boy Done Good." *The Observer*, October 26, 1997. Discusses Hornby's place in English literature and provides an overview of his writing style and themes.

Bannister, Matthew. "'Loaded': Indie Guitar Rock, Canonism, White Masculinities." *Popular Music* 25, no. 1 (2006): 77-95. Although *About a Boy* is not discussed, this article examines identity and gender related to indie guitar rock—the genre of Nirvana, the band referenced frequently in *About a Boy*. Helps explicate the meaning of Nirvana, both to popular culture and to Hornby's novel.

Crawshaw, Steve. "Profile: Nick Hornby—Mad About the Boy." *The Independent* (London), May 26, 2001. Provides an overview of Hornby's work, writing style, and themes. Includes biographical information.

Espen, Hal. "Too Cool for Words." *The New York Times Book Review*, June 28, 1998, p. 13. General overview of Hornby's writing style that also delves into the place of comic novels in contemporary literature and the place of Hornby's work within that genre.

Gerard, Nicci. "Soft Lad." *The Observer*, April 25, 1999. Discusses Hornby's works and influences, both his literary forebears and the biographical experiences that shape his writing.

Murray, Stuart. "Autism and the Contemporary Sentimental: Fiction and the Narrative Fascination of the Present." *Literature and Medicine* 25, no. 1 (Spring, 2006): 24-45. Discusses *About a Boy*, among other novels and films with characters identified either explicitly as autistic or as having autistic characteristics.

Abraham and Isaac

Author: Unknown
First produced: Fifteenth century
Type of work: Drama
Type of plot: Mystery play
Time of plot: Antiquity
Locale: Beersheba

Principal characters:
ABRAHAM
ISAAC, his son
DEUS, God
ANGELUS, the angel
THE DOCTOR, a commentator

The Story:

Abraham, offering a prayer of thanksgiving to God, counts his blessings—his land, his peaceful life, his children—and tells of his delight in his favorite child, Isaac. He stands praying in a field near his home in Beersheba. After the prayer, he calls to Isaac to return to their home.

God, in Heaven, summons an angel and tells him that he intends to test Abraham's steadfastness by asking him to sacrifice Isaac, and he orders the angel to announce his wish to Abraham. Meanwhile, Abraham prays again, asking God what gift or offering might please him most. The angel then appears and tells Abraham that God commands the sacrifice of Isaac as an indication of Abraham's love for the Lord. Abraham immediately experiences great inward conflict. He keeps repeating that Isaac is the most loved of all his children, that he would rather sacrifice anything else of his, including his own life, than to offer up Isaac. At the same time, he is aware that God's will must be obeyed and that the sacrifice, no matter how painful, must be made. Abraham then calls Isaac, who is praying, and tells him that they must perform a sacrifice for the Lord. Isaac declares his willingness to help. Abraham feels his heart breaking as they walk toward Mount Vision to make the sacrifice.

On their arrival at the mountain, Isaac asks why Abraham seems so concerned. The boy begins to quake at the sight of the sharp sword in his father's hand because, aware of his father's acute misery, he guesses that he is to be the offering in the sacrifice to the Lord. Abraham then tries to explain to Isaac that they must follow God's commandment, having no other choice. Isaac prays to his father, asking him to spare his life and wishing his mother to be there to intercede for him. Isaac also wonders what crimes he committed that his life should be demanded by God. Abraham, in his misery, explains that God's will must simply be obeyed. At last, Isaac understands and yields to God's will. He asks, however, that Abraham not tell his mother he was killed. Instead, she is to believe that he went into another land.

Resigning himself to death, Isaac asks for his father's blessing. Abraham gives his blessing, laments further, and proceeds to bind Isaac's hands. Abraham then repeats his hope that he could be sacrificed in Isaac's place, but the brave Isaac reminds him that God must be obeyed and asks that the killing be done quickly. Abraham covers Isaac's face with a cloth and makes ready to lift his sword. Just as Abraham is about to strike Isaac, the angel appears and takes the sword from Abraham's upraised hand. The angel says that Abraham proved his willingness to obey God's command, an act that fully displayed Abraham's mind and heart. Therefore, the angel continues, Abraham will not be compelled to sacrifice his son, but might substitute a young ram, tied nearby, for the offering. Abraham is overjoyed and, after the angel's departure, gives thanks to God for Isaac's deliverance. Isaac welcomes his reprieve, but only after Abraham assures him that God will regard the ram as a worthy substitute. Isaac, at his father's bidding, runs to bring the ram. Returning with it, Isaac expresses his happiness that the beast, rather than he, is to be sacrificed. When Abraham offers up the ram, Isaac still shows a great fear of Abraham's sword and does not wish to look at it.

After the sacrifice, God again speaks to Abraham, acknowledging his goodness and promising that his family will multiply. Abraham then returns with Isaac to their home, recounting on the way his pleasure that his favorite child is spared. Isaac is also grateful, but he mentions his fear and states that he never wants to see the hill again. Abraham and Isaac thank God and show great relief to be returning home together. Abraham praises the gentleness and understanding of his young son.

The play's commentator, the Doctor, then appears on the scene to make explicit the moral of the story: that one should follow God's commandments without quarreling. The Doctor asks how many in the audience would be willing to smite their children if God so commanded. He thinks that several might do so, although the children's mothers would wail and protest. The Doctor then says that God will mend everything for those truly willing to follow his commandments—those who serve God faithfully will be certain to benefit from their loyalty.

Critical Evaluation:

One of the fifteenth century mystery plays performed by guild members in various towns in England, *Abraham and Isaac* tells the biblical story of Abraham's willingness to sacrifice his son. The Brome version of the play is distinguished from others by its greater length and its fuller development of the characters of Abraham and Isaac. The mystery plays, although often simple in both plot and design, helped to provide the background and tradition from which Elizabethan drama later emerged. The play is in verse, sometimes written in five-line stanzas rhyming *abaab*, sometimes in eight-line stanzas with alternate rhymes, these stanzas often ending in a shortened line. Sometimes there is no clear rhyming or stanzaic pattern. It is difficult to determine whether the play was originally written in a more careful poetic pattern, now lost through successive copying and oral repetition, or whether it was originally written in a form close to the present version.

Abraham and Isaac is a type of work that could have been created only in an age of faith. Dealing as it does with the ultimate subject of human duty to God, it depends for its effectiveness on a set of shared assumptions between playwright and audience about the omnipotence and omnipresence of God, humanity's relationship to God, and God's justice. The slightest hint of skepticism or rationalistic questioning of values—for example, asking why God's commandment should be obeyed blindly when it appears so arbitrary and unjust, or how one can be sure that this is truly the word of God—would be fatal. As it is, the playwright handles his subject not only with a perfect consistency of tone but also with great clarity, with dramatic power, and, most important, with considerable insight into the human dimension.

The central issue of the play is made clear at the outset when God says, "I shall assay now his good will,/ Whether he loveth better his child or me./ All men shall take example by him my commandments how to keep." This issue never deviates thereafter. The play is an exemplum, or moral tale, as shown by the Doctor's appearance on stage at the end to reinforce the moral and to make the personal application to the audience explicit. The dramatic power of *Abraham and Isaac* derives largely from the manner in which the degrees of ignorance of father and son become knowledge. The audience, from God's first speech and also from its own knowledge of the Bible, knows the significance of the events to come, making dramatic irony possible. Abraham is ignorant of God's will for an appropriate sacrifice until the angel partially discloses it to him. His knowledge makes him heavy with grief, and so he tries to keep Isaac ignorant of the dire event to come until it is no longer possible to conceal it. When Isaac becomes aware of God's will, he acquiesces immediately, and the plight and subsequent behavior of father and son in their state of partial knowledge become poignant in the extreme. Finally, this partial knowledge of God's purpose is revealed as true ignorance when the angel stays Abraham's hand and informs him of God's real purpose in demanding the sacrifice of Isaac. The full knowledge thus acquired provides characters and audience with new insight not only into God's power and authority but also into his beneficence.

If the play were merely an exemplum, it would no longer interest the reader except on the level of didacticism and as an indication of medieval attitudes toward God. This play, however, is an intensely personal work; the playwright is not simply a dramatic preacher, but a man who shares and makes his audience share the agony of Abraham and Isaac. Abraham's love for his son is one of the first dramatic facts established in this play. The loving father's anguish and near despair as he is torn between his reverence for his God and his love for his son are powerful even on the printed page. Isaac does even more to create audience sympathy. By turns he shows the reader his innocence, his filial love, his devoutness, his trustingness, his anxiety at the sight of Abraham's sword, his fear, his resignation to the will of God, his courage (even exceeding his father's), his mildness under sentence of death, his concern for his mother, his plea for a quick death, and finally his joy at his deliverance. He also displays his lingering fear of the knife and the hill on which he so narrowly escaped slaughter. All of these psychologically sound changes of mood, material for a play of far greater length, are handled with a dramatic skill that is economical, convincing, and moving.

Further Reading

Collier, Richard. "Poetry and Instruction." In *Poetry and Drama in the York Corpus Christi Play*. Hamden, Conn.: Archon Books, 1978. Collier shows that the moral is explicitly drawn in the Abraham and Isaac plays by the Brome play's Doctor, the Chester play's Expositor, and in the dialogue of the York play.

Davidson, Clifford. "The Sacrifice of Isaac in Medieval English Drama." In *History, Religion, and Violence: Cultural Contexts for Medieval and Renaissance English Drama*. Burlington, Vt.: Ashgate, 2002. This collection of essays on medieval English drama includes an analysis of the various Abraham and Isaac plays.

Foster, Verna A. "Early English Tragicomedy: From Providential Design to Metatheatre." In *The Name and Nature of Tragicomedy*. Burlington, Vt.: Ashgate, 2004. Foster analyzes the Brome *Abraham and Isaac*, as well as other medieval mystery plays, describing how they exemplify early English tragicomedy.

Mills, David. "Religious Drama and Civic Ceremonial." In *Medieval Drama*. Vol. 1 in *The Revels History of Drama in English*. New York: Methuen, 1983. Mills discusses how the verisimilitude of the Brome *Abraham and Isaac* threatens the exemplary quality of the drama. He also notes that the play was probably not part of a cycle.

Rendall, Thomas. "Visual Typology in the Abraham and Isaac Plays." *Modern Philology* 81, no. 3 (February, 1984): 221-232. Focuses on the way in which medieval staging underlined the typological overtones in the plays. Rendall points out the parallel staging between the Old Testament and New Testament plays.

Williams, Arnold. "The Literary Art of the Cycles." *The Drama of Medieval England*. East Lansing: Michigan State University Press, 1961. Shows how scriptural exegesis is needed to understand the mystery plays' use of biblical material. As an example of this, Williams notes that the Abraham and Isaac play is one of the types of the sacrifice of the cross.

Woolf, Rosemary. "Types and Prophecies of the Redemption." In *The English Mystery Plays*. Berkeley: University of California Press, 1972. Compares the Abraham and Isaac plays with the Noah and Moses plays of the mystery cycles. Woolf considers the Brome, Chester, and *Ludus Conventriae* Abraham and Isaac plays the most accomplished among the cycles.

Abraham Lincoln

Author: Carl Sandburg (1878-1967)
First published: Abraham Lincoln: The Prairie Years, 1926; *Abraham Lincoln: The War Years*, 1939
Type of work: Biography

Carl Sandburg's six-volume *Abraham Lincoln* is a monumental work on a monumental theme: the life, works, and times of a symbolic American of history and legend. Sandburg sets Abraham Lincoln against a tremendous movement of history as he tells simultaneously, on different levels, the story of a man, a war, an age, and a people. In the end the qualities that set this work apart seem appropriate and significant. Lincoln, that ungainly, complex, humorous, melancholy, and serenely sad man, was also one of the great solitaries.

When *Abraham Lincoln: The War Years* appeared in 1939, more than one reviewer commented on the happy conjunction of the perfect writer and the perfect subject. In Sandburg's case there is more truth in this critical generalization than in most, for he brought to his tremendous task a greater familiarity with the regional and folk aspects of Lincoln's life than anyone had possessed since Lincoln's day. In the late nineteenth century there was still no wide gap between Sandburg's boyhood in Galesburg, Illinois, and Lincoln's young years in the Sangamon River country. Familiar with New Salem, Vandalia, Springfield, and other landmarks of Lincoln's early life, the Swedish immigrant's son had known the men and women of Lincoln's day and had listened to their stories. Poet, fabulist, folklorist, and singer of the American Dream, Sandburg felt in time that the Lincoln story had become a part of himself, not in the sense of blind hero worship but as evidence of the believable reality and fulfilled promise of American life.

More than thirty years of preparation, research, and writing went into the two divisions of *Abraham Lincoln*. At first Sandburg had in mind a history of Lincoln as the prairie lawyer and politician, but as the writer's investigations continued he realized that his book was outgrowing its projected length and purpose. Sandburg's increasing desire to tell all the facts of Lincoln's life as they existed in books already published, in documentary records, and in the memories of men and women finally led him to divide his material into two parts, the first a story of the country boy and lawyer-politician, the second an account of Lincoln in the White House.

Abraham Lincoln: The Prairie Years was published in 1926. In these two volumes Sandburg deals with the more legendary aspects of the Lincoln story: boyhood days and backwoods life; a young man's journeys down the Mississippi River; Lincoln's education, mostly self-taught, in grammar, mathematics, surveying, debate, and law; the years of clerking in grocery stores and working at odd jobs; military service in the Black Hawk War; his relations with Ann Rutledge, Mary Owens, and Mary Todd; his law practice; and his early political career. This material is presented with a wealth of anecdote—stories about Lincoln and by him—so that it resembles at times an anthology of Lincoln lore. This period of Lincoln's life lends itself at times to fabulous or lyric treatment of which Sandburg the poet takes full advantage. There are passages that read like poetry, sentences and paragraphs that celebrate the beauty of nature and the mystery and wonder of life, yet these occasional flights of poetic fancy are held within bounds by realistic portrayal and strict regard for fact. In these volumes Sandburg's Lincoln emerges as a man of the people but no hero in the ordinary sense. Circumstances had shaped him into a man of vision and resource, but he was also a troubled, threatened, doubted man when he left Springfield in 1861 on the eve of his inauguration as president of the United States.

Abraham Lincoln: The War Years was published in four volumes thirteen years later, in 1939. In the meantime Sandburg had traveled widely to gather material from every available source; read extensively in histories, biographies, newspapers, pamphlets, diaries, letters, and handbills; looked at pictures and cartoons; collected memorabilia of every sort; and written steadily while he studied, pondered, and re-created—in effect, relived—Lincoln's life during the American Civil War period. The result, in the opinion of historians and critics, is a biography not likely soon to be surpassed of a person linked inseparably to his country's history and folk imagination.

Sandburg makes no attempt to gloss over the dark years of 1861-1862. Lincoln, who had incurred ridicule by arriving in Washington, D.C., in a military cape and a Scotch plaid cap—in disguise, his enemies jeered—found himself hated in the South, handicapped by his cabinet and the U.S. Congress, and faced with the crisis of Fort Sumter. Having taken over the leadership that William Henry Seward, secretary of state, had tried at first to withhold from the chief executive, Lincoln then proceeded to display a temporizing attitude that history finds hard to explain. His declaration at the end of 1862—"Fellow-citizens, we cannot escape history"—is open to various interpretations. Lincoln was to ride out of the storm of public disfavor. The Emancipation Proclamation, the turn of the tide at Gettysburg, the appointment of Ulysses S. Grant to the high command, and the Gettysburg Address mark what Sandburg calls the "Storm Center" of the war years. Although the midterm elections of 1863 were against Lincoln, and his own party was prepared to abandon him for the sake of political expediency, he won the campaign of 1864 in the face of the bitterest opposition of his enemies and the apathy of his party. From this time on Sandburg shows the tide in full flood—the aggressive final phase of the war, Sherman's march to the sea, the passing of the Thirteenth Amendment, the surrender at Appomattox, and the night at Ford's Theater on April 14, 1865. The end of the story is starkly, movingly, eloquently told with a poet's power of words and the historian's respect for truth.

In handling the massive reportage of *Abraham Lincoln*, Sandburg never pretends to be more than a storyteller, a recorder. After the publication of *Abraham Lincoln: The Prairie Years* critics tried to find a term to describe Sandburg's method as a biographer, since his work could not be judged by any of the accepted schools of writing history. *Abraham Lincoln: The War Years*, with all its vast accumulation of fact piled on fact, detail on detail, gave them the answer. Sandburg's method is the way of the old chronicles and sagas in telling the stories of folk and tribal heroes. This biography is a work that expands within the consciousness of the reader because of its continuous addition and multiplication of concrete and evocative details—battle summaries, character sketches, anecdotes, letters, quotations of every kind—all presented without analysis or interpretation so that in the end they shape themselves to their own pattern and carry their own weight of meaning.

Nothing is too vast or too commonly known to be glossed over without patient attention to every living detail; nothing is too trivial to be included. Never was there such a summoning of witnesses to testify to a person and that person's time. Foreign diplomats, members of the cabinet and the Congress, military men of the North and the South, Leo Tolstoy, Henrik Ibsen, Nathaniel Hawthorne, Mary Chesnut, and hundreds of obscure men and women appear briefly, make their gestures or have their say, and then disappear. Lincoln's enemies make their insults and accusations; his detractors voice their ridicule; his friends speak in his praise. All leave behind them something that adds to the reader's understanding of Lincoln, something more important than the opinions of politicians or the decisive outcomes of battles and accounts of military campaigns in creating the illusion of life.

These details, great and small, are the background setting against which Lincoln casts his shadow. Against this backdrop of history he appears as a man with human weaknesses and failures, just as he appears greater than others in the strength, wisdom, and sad serenity of his last months. "Unfathomable" is the adjective Sandburg most frequently applies to him. Many writers have tried to analyze Lincoln. It remained for Sandburg simply to show the man, letting him speak and act for himself. This also was the method of the anonymous writers of the ancient sagas.

Abraham Lincoln: The War Years, more somber in tone, offers less opportunity than *Abraham Lincoln: The Prairie Years* for bardic song. Occasionally, however, the poet breaks in on the biographer and historian. One such passage occurs after the account of the Gettysburg Address when Lincoln, a wet towel over his tired eyes, was on his way back to Washington, and a moonlit hush had fallen over the battlefield and the new graves. Then in Whitmanesque measures Sandburg speaks his requiem for the buried dead in the silent cemetery as he looks out over the land and into the homes where the son, the husband, or the father is missing from his familiar place and the clocks of time and destiny tick on. Again, at the beginning of the chapter "The Calendar Says Good Friday," he employs another poetic passage to set the mood for coming tragedy. Nowhere, however, is he more moving than in the solemn intensity of the three simple sentences that bring the Lincoln story to its close.

Sandburg's *Abraham Lincoln* is the biography of an American whose true story lends itself to the spirit of legend, a pageant of history, a poet's dream, a national myth. It is a story that is vast and at times contradictory. It is the stubborn, time-defying stuff of life itself, a story in which Sandburg finds in Lincoln's life the meaning of America. *Abraham Lincoln* is a poet's biography only in the sense that every true poet is a biographer providing insights to human experience. Unfortunately, not all biographers are poets. Sandburg, to the reader's enrichment, is the rare writer who is both. If America has an epic, it is this story of a national hero re-created from the testimony of the men and women of Lincoln's time.

Further Reading

Allen, Gay Wilson. *Carl Sandburg*. Minneapolis: University of Minnesota Press, 1972. Brief but useful introduction to Sandburg's life and creative career. Includes references to the poet's biographical studies of Abraham Lincoln.

Callahan, North. *Carl Sandburg: His Life and Works*. University Park: Pennsylvania State University Press, 1987. Provides an overview of Sandburg's career and critical readings of his poems; offers a complete discussion of Sandburg's works on Lincoln.

_______. *Carl Sandburg: Lincoln of Our Literature*. New York: New York University Press, 1970. A critical biography of Sandburg that focuses, in large part, upon the nature of the poet's interest in Abraham Lincoln's life and writings.

Crowder, Richard. *Carl Sandburg*. New York: Twayne, 1964. Excellent overview of Sandburg's life and literary career. The chapters "Lincoln and America" and "The People and the Union" recount and interpret the development of Sandburg's publications on Lincoln. Notes that Sandburg was as interested in Lincoln the myth as he was in the historical personage, which accounts for the unique power of Sandburg's biographical works on the president.

Cullen, Jim. "'A Tree Is Best Measured When It's Down': Carl Sandburg, James Randall, and the Usable Pasts of Abraham Lincoln." In *The Civil War in Popular Culture: A Reusable Past*. Washington, D.C.: Smithsonian Institution Press, 1995. Describes how Sandburg's recollections of Lincoln were shaped by contemporary concerns and perspectives.

Niven, Penelope. *Carl Sandburg: A Biography*. New York: Charles Scribner's Sons, 1991. First-rate critical biography of Sandburg, with a section on "The Lincoln Years." Discusses the nature of Sandburg's interest in and identification with Lincoln. One of the best single works to date on Sandburg and his literary career.

Wooley, Lisa. "Carl Sandburg and Vachel Lindsay: Composite Voices of the Open Road." In *American Voices of the Chicago Renaissance*. DeKalb: Northern Illinois University Press, 2000. Describes how the two poets used language to convey simplicity, democracy, and Americanness—characteristics associated with Chicago's literary renaissance.

Absalom, Absalom!

Author: William Faulkner (1897-1962)
First published: 1936
Type of work: Novel
Type of plot: Psychological realism
Time of plot: Nineteenth century
Locale: Mississippi

Principal characters:
THOMAS SUTPEN, owner of Sutpen's Hundred
ELLEN COLDFIELD SUTPEN, his wife
HENRY and JUDITH, their children
ROSA COLDFIELD, Ellen's younger sister
GOODHUE COLDFIELD, Ellen and Rosa's father
CHARLES BON, Thomas Sutpen's son by his first marriage
QUENTIN COMPSON, Rosa Coldfield's young friend
SHREVE MCCANNON, Quentin's roommate at Harvard

The Story:

In the summer of 1909, as Quentin Compson is preparing to go to Harvard, old Rosa Coldfield insists upon telling him the whole infamous story of Thomas Sutpen, whom she calls a demon. According to Miss Rosa, he brought terror and tragedy to all who had dealings with him.

In 1833, Sutpen came to Jefferson, Mississippi, with a fine horse and two pistols and no known past. He lived mysteriously for a while among people at the hotel, and after a short time he disappeared from the area. He purchased one hundred square miles of uncleared land from the Chickasaws and had it recorded at the land office. When he returned with a wagonload of blacks, a French architect, and a few tools and wagons, he was as uncommunicative as ever. At once, he set about clearing land and building a mansion. For two years he labored, and during all that time he rarely saw or visited his acquaintances in Jefferson. People wondered about the source of his money. Some claimed that he stole it somewhere in his mysterious comings and goings. Then, for three years, his house remained unfinished, without windowpanes or furnishings, while Sutpen busied himself with his crops. Occasionally he invited Jefferson men to his plantation to hunt, entertaining them with liquor, cards, and combats between his giant slaves—combats in which he himself sometimes joined for the sport.

At last, he disappeared once more, and when he returned, he had furniture and furnishings elaborate and fine enough to make his great house a splendid showplace. Because of his mysterious actions, sentiment in the village turned against him. This hostility, however, subsided somewhat when Sutpen married Ellen Coldfield, daughter of the highly respected Goodhue Coldfield.

Miss Rosa and Quentin's father share some of Sutpen's revelations. Because Quentin is away at college, many of the things he knows about Sutpen's Hundred come to him in letters from home. Other details he learns during talks with his father. He learns of Ellen Sutpen's life as mistress of the strange mansion in the wilderness. He learns how she discovered her husband fighting savagely with one of his slaves. Young Henry Sutpen fainted, but Judith, the daughter, watched from the haymow with interest and delight. Ellen thereafter refused to reveal her true feelings and ignored the village gossip about Sutpen's Hundred.

The children grew up. Young Henry, so unlike his father, attended the university at Oxford, Mississippi, and there he met Charles Bon, a rich planter's grandson. Unknown to Henry, Charles was his half brother, Sutpen's son by his first marriage. Unknown to all of Jefferson, Sutpen got his money as the dowry of his earlier marriage to Charles Bon's West Indian mother, a wife he discarded when he learned she was part black. Charles Bon became engaged to Judith Sutpen. The engagement was suddenly broken off for a probation period of four years. In the meantime, the American Civil War began. Charles and Henry served together. Thomas Sutpen became a colonel.

Goodhue Coldfield took a disdainful stand against the war. He barricaded himself in his attic, and his daughter, Rosa, was forced to put his food in a basket let down by a long rope. His store was looted by Confederate soldiers. One night, alone in his attic, he died. Judith, in the meantime, waited patiently for her lover. She carried his letter, written at the end of the four-year period, to Quentin's grandmother. Some time later, Wash Jones, the handyman on the Sutpen plantation, came to Miss Rosa's door with the crude announcement that Charles Bon was dead, killed at the gate of the plantation by his half brother and former friend. Henry fled. Judith buried her lover in the Sutpen family plot on the plantation. Rosa, whose mother died when she was born, went to Sutpen's Hundred to live with her niece. Ellen was already dead. It was Rosa's conviction that she could help Judith.

Colonel Thomas Sutpen returned. His slaves were taken away, and he was burdened with new taxes on his overrun land and ruined buildings. He planned to marry Rosa Coldfield, more than ever desiring an heir now that Judith had vowed spinsterhood and Henry had become a fugitive. His son, Charles Bon, whom he might, in desperation, have permitted to marry his daughter, was dead.

Rosa, insulted when she understood the true nature of his proposal, returned to her father's ruined house in the village. She spent the rest of her miserable life pondering the fearful intensity of Thomas Sutpen, whose nature, in her outraged belief, seemed to partake of the devil himself.

Quentin, during his last vacation, learns more about the Sutpen tragedy and reveals much of the story to Shreve McCannon, his roommate, who listens with all of a Northerner's misunderstanding and indifference. Quentin and his father visit the Sutpen graveyard, where they see a little path and a hole leading into Ellen Sutpen's grave. Generations of opossums live there. Over her tomb and that of her husband stands a marble monument from Italy. Sutpen himself died in 1869. In 1867, he took young Milly Jones, Wash Jones's granddaughter. After she had a child, a girl, Wash Jones killed Thomas Sutpen.

Judith and Charles Bon's son, his child by an octoroon woman who had brought her child to Sutpen's Hundred when he was eleven years old, died in 1884 of smallpox. The boy earlier married a black woman, and they had a son, James Bond. Rosa Coldfield placed headstones on their graves, and on Judith's gravestone she inscribed a fearful message.

In the summer of 1910, Rosa Coldfield confides to Quentin that she feels there is still someone living at Sutpen's Hundred. Together the two go there at night and discover Clytie, the aged daughter of Thomas Sutpen and a slave. More important, they discover Henry Sutpen himself hiding in the ruined old house. He returned, he tells them, four years before, coming back to die. James Bond watches Rosa and Quentin as they depart. Rosa returns to her home, and Quentin goes back to college.

Quentin's father writes to tell him the tragic ending of the Sutpen story. Months later, Rosa sends an ambulance to the ruined plantation house, for she finally determined to bring her nephew, Henry, into the village to live with her so that he could get decent care. Clytie, seeing the ambulance, is afraid that Henry will be arrested for the murder of Charles Bon. In desperation she sets fire to the old house, burning herself and Henry Sutpen to death. Only James Bond, the last surviving descendant of Thomas Sutpen, escapes. No one knows where he went, for he is never seen again. Miss Rosa takes to her bed and dies soon afterward, in the winter of 1910. Quentin tells the story to his roommate because it seems to him, somehow, to be the story of the whole South, a tale of deep passions, tragedy, ruin, and decay.

Critical Evaluation:

Absalom, Absalom! is the most involved of William Faulkner's works, for the narrative is revealed by recollections years after the events described have taken place. Experience is related at its fullest expression; its initial import is recollected, and its significance years thereafter is faithfully recorded. The conventional method of storytelling is discarded. Through his special method, Faulkner re-creates human action and human emotion in their own setting. Sensory impressions gained at the moment, family traditions as powerful stimuli, the tragic impulses—these focus in the reader's mind so that a tremendous picture of the nineteenth century South, vivid down to the most minute detail, grows slowly in the reader's imagination.

This novel is Faulkner's most comprehensive attempt to come to terms with the full implications of the southern experience. The structure of the novel, itself an attempt by its various narrators to make some sense of the seemingly chaotic past, is indicative of the multifaceted complexity of that experience, and the various narrators' relationship to the material suggests the difficulty that making order of the past entails. Each narrator has, to begin with, only part of the total picture—and some parts of that hearsay or conjecture—at his disposal, and each narrator's response is conditioned by individual experience and background. Thus, Miss Rosa's idea of Sutpen depends equally upon her Calvinist background and her failure to guess why Henry Sutpen killed Charles Bon. Quentin's father responds with an ironic detachment, conditioned by his insistence upon viewing the fall of the South as the result of the workings of an inevitable fate. As Quentin and Shreve do, the reader must attempt to coordinate the various partial histories of the Sutpen family into a meaningful whole—with the added irony that the reader must also deal with Quentin's romanticism. In effect, the reader becomes another investigator, one whose concern is with the entire scope of the novel rather than with only the Sutpen family.

At the heart of the novel is Thomas Sutpen and his grand design, and the reader's comprehension of the meaning of the novel depends upon the discovery of the implications of this design. Unlike the chaos of history the narrators perceive, Sutpen's design would, by its nature, reduce human history and experience to a mechanical and passionless process that he could control. The irony of Sutpen's failure lies in the fact that he could not achieve the design precisely because he is unable to exclude such human elements as Charles Bon's need for his father's love and recognition. Faulkner, however, gains more than this irony from his metaphor of design. In effect, Sutpen's design is based upon a formula of the antebellum South that reduces the South to essentials. It encompasses the plantation, the slaves, the wife and family—all the external trappings of the plantation aristocracy that Sutpen, as a small boy from the mountains, saw in his first encounter with this foreign world.

Sutpen, who never really becomes one of the aristocracy that his world tries to mirror, manages, by excluding the human element from his design, to reflect only what is worst in the South. Unmitigated by human emotion and values, southern society is revealed to have at its heart the simple fact of possession: of the land, of the slaves, and of the wife and children. Thus, Faulkner demonstrates that the urge to possess is the fundamental evil from which other evils spring. Sutpen, trying to insulate himself from the pain of rejection that he encountered as a child, is driven almost mad by the need to possess the semblance of the world that denies his humanity, but in his obsession, he loses that humanity.

Once the idea of the design and the principle of possession in *Absalom, Absalom!* is established, Sutpen's treatment both of Charles Bon and Bon's mother is more easily understood. In Sutpen's distorted mind, what is possessed can also be thrown away if it does not fit the design. Like certain other Faulkner characters—Benjy of *The Sound and the Fury* (1929) being the best example—Sutpen is obsessed with the need to establish a perfect order in the world into which he will fit. His first vision of tidewater Virginia, after leaving the timeless anarchy of the mountains, was the sight of perfectly ordered and neatly divided plantations, and, like a chick imprinted by its first contact, Sutpen spends his life trying to create a world that imitates that order. He also seeks to establish a dynasty that will preserve that order. His rejection of Bon is essentially emotionless, mechanical, and even without rancor because Bon's blackness simply excludes him from the design. Similarly, the proposal that Rosa have his child to prove herself worthy of marriage and the rejection of Milly when she bears a female child are also responses dictated by the design. Thus, Sutpen, and all those whose lives touch his, ultimately become victims of the mad design he created. Sutpen, however, is not its final victim: The curse of the design lives on into the present in James Bond, the last of Sutpen's bloodline.

Sutpen's rejection of Charles Bon and the consequences of that rejection are at the thematic center of *Absalom, Absalom!* In the fact that Bon is rejected for the taint of "black blood," Faulkner clearly points to the particularly southern implication of his story. Bon must be seen, on one level, to represent the human element within southern society that cannot be assimilated and will not be ignored. Faulkner implies that the system, which inhumanely denies the human rights and needs of some of its children, dehumanizes all it touches—master and victim alike. In asserting himself to demand the only recognition he can gain from his father—and that only at second hand through Henry—Bon makes of himself an innocent sacrifice to the sin upon which the South was founded. His death also dramatizes the biblical admonition relevant to *Absalom, Absalom!*: A house divided against itself cannot stand.

Sutpen's history is a metaphor of the South, and his rise and fall is southern history written in one person's experience. The Sutpens, however, are not the only victims in the novel. The narrators, too, are the victims of the southern experience, and each of them seeks in Sutpen's history some clue to the meaning of his or her own relationship to the fall of the South. Their narratives seek to discover the designs that will impose some order on the chaos of the past.

"Critical Evaluation" by William E. Grant

Further Reading

Blotner, Joseph. *Faulkner: A Biography*. 2 vols. New York: Random House, 1974. A lengthy biography of William Faulkner's life and work. Shows how *Absalom, Absalom!* evolved to become what Blotner considers Faulkner's most important and ambitious contribution to American literature.

Brooks, Cleanth. "History and the Sense of the Tragic." In *William Faulkner: The Yoknapatawpha Country*. New Haven, Conn.: Yale University Press, 1963. One of the most valuable studies of Faulkner's fiction. Focuses on the author's fictional county and the role it played in his writing.

_______. *William Faulkner: Toward Yoknapatawpha and Beyond*. New Haven, Conn.: Yale University Press, 1978. The appendixes are an especially valuable aid. One essay discusses Brooks's answer to the question of how typical Thomas Sutpen is of the "southern planter." Another focuses on the narrative structure of the novel.

Hobson, Fred, ed. *William Faulkner's "Absalom, Absalom!": A Casebook*. New York: Oxford University Press, 2003. Seven essays about the novel written from the 1970's to the date of publication, including interpretations by Cleanth Brooks, Thadious Davis, and Eric Sundquist. Also features Faulkner's own remarks about the novel.

Leary, Lewis. *William Faulkner of Yoknapatawpha County.* New York: Thomas Y. Crowell, 1973. Chapter 5 describes *Absalom, Absalom!* as disclosing the way history is made and legends develop. Cites examples of how Thomas Sutpen's story emerges as a jigsaw puzzle, as various narrators' contributions finally fit together to disclose a design.

Marius, Richard. *Reading Faulkner: Introduction to the First Thirteen Novels*. Compiled and edited by Nancy Grisham Anderson. Knoxville: University of Tennessee Press, 2006. A collection of the lectures that Marius, a novelist, biographer, and Faulkner scholar, presented during an undergraduate course. Provides a friendly and approachable introduction to Faulkner. Includes a chapter on *Absalom, Absalom!*

Minter, David. *William Faulkner: His Life and Work.* Baltimore: Johns Hopkins University Press, 1980. Provides a context for the writing of *Absalom, Absalom!* Identifies the force of the novel as emerging from entangled relationships among generations of "doomed" families, races, and sexes. Discusses relationships between the narrators' stories and their lives.

Porter, Carolyn. *William Faulkner.* New York: Oxford University Press, 2007. Concise and informative, this resource spans Faulkner's entire life, but focuses on his most prolific period, from 1929 to 1940. It examines his childhood and personal struggles and offers insightful analyses of his major works. *Absalom, Absalom!* is discussed in chapter 3.

Towner, Theresa M. *The Cambridge Introduction to William Faulkner.* New York: Cambridge University Press, 2008. An accessible book aimed at students and general readers. Focusing on Faulkner's work, the book provides detailed analyses of his nineteen novels, discussion of his other works, and information about the critical reception of his fiction.

Volpe, Edmond L. *A Reader's Guide to William Faulkner.* New York: Farrar, Straus & Giroux, 1964. An early treatment of Faulkner's novels, this volume remains valuable. Includes sections on narrative structure and technique as well as on key characters. Contains a genealogy and a helpful chronology of events.

Absalom and Achitophel

Author: John Dryden (1631-1700)
First published: 1681
Type of work: Poetry
Type of plot: Satire
Time of plot: Late seventeenth century
Locale: London

Principal characters:
DAVID, king of Israel
ABSALOM, his illegitimate son
ACHITOPHEL, chief of the rebels

The Poem:

The political situation in Israel (England) had much to do with David's (Charles II's) virility, which, though wasted on a barren queen, produced a host of illegitimate progeny, of which by far the fairest and noblest is Absalom (duke of Monmouth). David's kingly virtues are equally strong but unappreciated by a great number of Jews (Whigs), who, because of a perverse native temperament, want to rebel. Although David provides no cause for rebellion, as the wiser Jews (Tories) point out, a cause is found in the alleged Jebusite (Catholic) plot to convert the nation to the Egyptian (French) religion. The plot miscarries, but it does create factions whose leaders are jealous of David and oppose his reign.

Achitophel (the Earl of Shaftesbury, leader of the Whigs) is the chief of these leaders, and he makes efforts to persuade Absalom to seize the throne. Achitophel is a brilliant wit touched by the madness of ambition. Unwilling to be remembered only for his distinguished career as a judge, he resolves "to ruin or to rule the State," using the king's alleged sympathy for the Jebusites as an excuse for rebellion. Achitophel first uses flattery to win over Absalom, proclaiming that the nation is clamoring for him—a "second Moses." At first Absalom resists, pointing out that David is a wise and just king, and that David's brother (the duke of York) is the legal heir. These halfhearted objections Achitophel meets with sophistry. David's mildness, he claims, deteriorated into weakness; the public good demands Absalom's strength; the rightful heir is planning to murder Absalom; David secretly wants Absalom to be king and will support his claim as heir to the throne. To these specious arguments Absalom succumbs, whereupon Achitophel proceeds to organize all the Jewish malcontents into a single seditious party.

Among these misguided patriots are opportunists, republicans, and religious fanatics. Zimri embodies the fickleness and "extremity" of Buckingham, Shaftesbury's lieutenant in the Whig Party. Shimei represents the Sheriff of London, who betrays the king's interests, and Corah, the notorious Titus Oates, who fabricates many of the details of the Catholic plot.

Absalom makes a tour of the nation, planned by Achitophel to gauge the extent of the people's support for their plan to exclude the legal heir from the throne and to establish Absalom's right to the succession by law. Traveling up and down the land, Absalom craftily represents himself as the people's friend, opposed to Egyptian domination, the Jebusite plot, and a senile king, but powerless to act because of his loyalty to the crown and the lawful succession. The Jews, always easy to delude, proclaim Absalom a new messiah.

The speaker of the poem attacks the Jews' naïve support of Absalom and their willingness to overthrow legally instituted authority. He fears that the government will quickly deteriorate into anarchy if the people are given the power to make and break kings at will by changing the order of the succession.

Next are portraits of David's supporters—the Tory leaders. Barzillai (the duke of Ormond) is lavishly praised as the noblest adherent to David's cause and one of Israel's true heroes. Two members of the clergy, namely Zadoc (the Archbishop of Canterbury) and the Sagan of Jerusalem (the Bishop of London), are commended for their services to the crown. Other loyalists, praised for their services in Sanhedrin (Parliament), include Adriel (the Earl of Mulgrave), Jotham (the Marquis of Halifax), Hushai (Laurence Hyde), and Amiel (Edward Seymour). These loyal chieftains who defy the powerful rebel faction ultimately convince David that concessions to the people will but feed their leaders' ambition, and that Absalom is being used as a tool by the treacherous Achitophel.

David finally reasserts the royal prerogative. Realizing that his enemies interpret his moderation and clemency as signs of weakness and fear, he resolves to show his strength. David, regretting that Absalom will be compelled to suffer, expresses his willingness to forgive at the sign of repentance, but he refuses to condone disloyalty. David denounces the Sanhedrin's attempt to change the line of succession, scorning their deceitful claim that they are trying to protect him from a scheming brother. Finally David states his reluctance to resort to force but declares his readiness to use it to defend the supremacy of established law over both Sanhedrin and king. Heaven claps its thunder in approval of David's words and the new era that they herald.

Critical Evaluation:

John Dryden claimed that *Absalom and Achitophel* was carefully planned to promote political reform. To gain this end, Dryden used satire, the true aim of which he defined as "the amendment of vices by correction." The particular vices he wanted to correct were those of the Whigs of his day, who were seeking to secure the succession of the duke of Monmouth, illegitimate son of Charles II, to his father's throne. Second, realizing that direct satire might defeat its purpose by incurring resentment, Dryden chose to attack the Whigs by casting them as characters in the biblical story of Absalom's revolt against David. Third, to increase his satire's effectiveness, he cast it in verse, "for there's a sweetness in good verse, which tickles even while it hurts."

Written in heroic couplets, *Absalom and Achitophel* is often called Dryden's best poem, and it is one of the most famous political satires ever written. Its direct literary influence reaches from Dryden's contemporaries to Alexander Pope and Charles Churchill in the eighteenth century and to Lord Byron in the nineteenth century. In the poem, Dryden indicates similarities between the biblical story, which tells how the wicked Achitophel urged King David's illegitimate son Absalom to rise up against his father, and events in England between 1678 and 1681, when Anthony Ashley Cooper, Earl of Shaftesbury, a leader of the Whiggish opposition to the king, was accused of persuading James Scott, duke of Monmouth and illegitimate son of Charles II, to rebel against his father.

Perhaps Dryden intended his poem, published in November, 1681, to help in convicting Shaftesbury, on trial for treason for his part in the rebellion. If so, Dryden was not successful: The jury, friendly to Shaftesbury, declared it did not have sufficient evidence for a conviction and acquitted Shaftesbury. Dryden's devastating satire probably helped to create an atmosphere so hostile to the earl that soon after the trial he fled to Holland, where he remained until his death several years later.

The poem is difficult reading for those unaccustomed to satire, unversed in the Bible, and unacquainted with late seventeenth century English history. It presented no problems to readers in Dryden's day, who, vitally interested in contemporary politics and well read in the Bible, were able to correlate

King David's situation with that of Charles II. The Bible not only gave Dryden's satire a ready-made, well-known reference; it also provided heavenly authority for condemning the actions of Shaftesbury, Monmouth, and their allies. It enabled Dryden to use the outcome of the biblical story of David to show that Monmouth's rebellion would be useless and that the king's divinely sanctioned victory would be inevitable.

In the poem, which is 1,031 lines long, the speaker suits the tone to the rhetorical purpose in telling the story of the rebellion. The first part (lines 1-227) begins with a good-humored account of the father-son relationship, in which Absalom (the duke of Monmouth), although illegitimate and therefore unable to succeed to the throne, is David's (Charles II's) beloved son, whose every fault is forgiven. The tone becomes condemnatory when the speaker accuses David of too much leniency. David is too lenient toward his grumbling subjects, the Jews (the English), whom "No king could govern, nor no God could please"; toward the inhabitants of his own city, the Jebusites (the Londoners); and particularly toward their depraved leader, the "false Achitophel" (Shaftesbury). Achitophel is a Satanic tempter who looks for and finds in Absalom a likely victim. Achitophel's appeals to Absalom's ambition (lines 229-302) soon prove convincing. Absalom, of course, fails to realize that "They who possess the prince, possess the laws" applies not only to his mastery of his own father but also to Achitophel's mastery over him. Next (lines 491-681), readers are told how Achitophel collects other malcontents, named in the poem after evil men of the Bible. They include several noblemen, the Lord Mayor of London, the Sheriff of London, members of Parliament, and others important in the opposition to Charles II. First is Zimri, the notoriously indecisive duke of Buckingham, who "in the curse of one revolving moon,/ Was chemist, fiddler, statesman, and buffoon." Dryden was so proud of that jab that he compared his own satiric skill with the artistry of the executioner Jack Ketch, whose deft ax strokes left his victims with their heads still sitting on their necks.

After Absalom is applauded for his hypocritical lament on the necessity of rebellion (lines 682-810), a few alarmed defenders of the king, bearing the names of virtuous men in the Bible, appear to warn the king that he must act to save his throne (lines 816-938). These include such members of the high nobility as the duke of Ormonde and the Marquis of Halifax and churchmen such as the Archbishop of Canterbury.

The climax of the narrative, when the king is about to invoke the law, is intended to evoke the situation in England in the autumn of 1681, when royalists hoped that Charles II would assert his rights (lines 939 and following). The king's soliloquy shows that reluctantly he put aside geniality for sternness. In so doing, he becomes like Zeus the Thunderer and like Jehovah the Judge in condemning the rebels to the fate they themselves have chosen (lines 1005-1011). The poem ends with the speaker's announcement of the simultaneous end of rebellion and disappearance of all discord—an abrupt but appropriate conclusion because it corresponds to the king's decisive action. The ending, with its promise of "a series of new time," is a prophecy that recalls both Greek myths of renewal and Hebrew accounts of how Jehovah made fresh starts possible.

Significant in the historical context is that the ending of the poem is a warning to rebels not to persist. If events in England are really parallel to biblical events, then, as Dryden strongly hints, Monmouth's end will be like that of Absalom, who was killed despite David's pleas that he be spared. Monmouth's fate, it turned out, was like Absalom's. In 1685, soon after the death of his father, Monmouth led an army rebellion against his uncle, James II, the new king. Monmouth was caught, tried, convicted, and executed.

"Critical Evaluation" by Margaret Duggan

Further Reading

Hammond, Paul, and David Hopkins, eds. *John Dryden: Tercentenary Essays*. New York: Oxford University Press, 2000. This collection, published during the tercentenary of Dryden's death, examines some of Dryden's individual works, as well as more general characteristics of his writing. Some of the essays question if Dryden is a classic, explore Dryden and the "staging of popular politics," and describe the disintegration evident in his later writing.

Hopkins, David. *John Dryden*. Tavistock, England: Northcote House/British Council, 2004. Concise and thorough overview of Dryden's life and work. Hopkins demonstrates that Dryden was not only a man of his times but also a writer whose ideas continue to be significant in the twenty-first century.

Lewis, Jayne, and Maximillian E. Novak, eds. *Enchanted Ground: Reimagining John Dryden*. Toronto, Ont.: University of Toronto Press, 2004. Collection of essays that apply twenty-first century critical perspectives to Dryden's work. The first section focuses on Dryden's role as a public poet and the voice of the Stuart court during Restoration; the second explores his relationship to drama and music.

McKeon, Michael. "Historicizing *Absalom and Achitophel*." In *The New Eighteenth Century: Theory, Politics, English*

Literature, edited by Felicity Nussbaum and Laura Brown. New York: Methuen, 1987. Argues that in "*Absalom and Achitophel*, Dryden proposes a model for a new sort of poetry, which draws power and value from the realms of religious faith, political allegiance, and historic factuality while evading subservience to them all."

Rawson, Claude, and Aaron Santesso, eds. *John Dryden, 1631-1700: His Politics, His Plays, and His Poets*. Newark: University of Delaware Press, 2004. Contains papers presented at a Yale University conference held in 2000 to commemorate the tercentenary of Dryden's death. The essays focus on the politics of Dryden's plays and how his poetry is poised between ancient and modern influences.

Schilling, Bernard. *Dryden and the Conservative Myth*. New Haven, Conn.: Yale University Press, 1961. Discusses Dryden's role as spokesman for royalism and as creator of myths that justify and defend kingship. Shows how the myth appears in the structure, style, and content of *Absalom and Achitophel*.

Thomas, Walter K. *The Crafting of "Absalom and Achitophel": Dryden's "Pen for a Party."* Waterloo, Ont.: Wilfred Laurier University Press, 1978. Investigates political conditions in England from 1678 to 1681. Discusses Dryden's responses to them in *Absalom and Achitophel*.

Zwicker, Steven N., ed. *The Cambridge Companion to John Dryden*. New York: Cambridge University Press, 2004. Among these seventeen essays are discussions of Dryden and the theatrical imagination, the invention of Augustan culture and patronage, and Dryden's London and the "passion of politics" in his theater.

The Absentee

Author: Maria Edgeworth (1768-1849)
First published: 1812
Type of work: Novel
Type of plot: Social realism
Time of plot: Early nineteenth century
Locale: England and Ireland

Principal characters:
LORD CLONBRONY, an absentee landlord
LADY CLONBRONY, his affected, ambitious wife
LORD COLAMBRE, their son
GRACE NUGENT, a cousin
MISS BROADHURST, an heiress
ARTHUR BERRYL, Lord Colambre's friend
COUNT O'HALLORAN, an Irish gentleman
SIR TERENCE O'FAY, an impecunious nobleman
LADY DASHFORT, a designing noblewoman
LADY ISABEL, her daughter
MR. MORDICAI, one of Lord Clonbrony's creditors
MR. BURKE, an honest estate agent
NICHOLAS GARRAGHTY, a dishonest estate agent

The Story:

Lord Clonbrony is an absentee landlord who owns large but encumbered Irish estates. He lives in England because his wife, an extravagant, ambitious woman, will have nothing to do with Ireland or the Irish. People of wealth and position laugh at her and the silly determination with which she apes English manners and speech, and they totally ignore Lord Clonbrony. A respected peer in Dublin and a good landlord when he lived on his own estates, he is a cipher in his wife's fashionable world. As a result, he associates with such questionable and dissipated companions as Sir Terence O'Fay. Little is known about their son and the Clonbrony heir, Lord Colambre, except that he is a student at Cambridge and a young man of considerable expectations from a distant relative. A cousin, Grace Nugent, is well thought of because of her beauty and good manners.

Lady Clonbrony is anxious to have her son marry Miss Broadhurst, a young woman of much sense and large fortune. Although Lady Clonbrony and Mrs. Broadhurst do their best to promote the match, the young people, while friendly, are not drawn to each other. Lord Colambre is attracted to Grace's amiability and charm, and Miss Broadhurst respects his feelings for his cousin.

In execution of a commission for Arthur Berryl, a Cambridge friend, Lord Colambre goes to the establishment of

Mr. Mordicai, a coachmaker and moneylender. There he overhears that his father's financial affairs are not in good order. When questioned, Lord Clonbrony admits that his situation is grave but that he relies on Sir Terence, often his intermediary with his creditors, to prevent legal action against him. The father reflects with some bitterness that there would be no need for such expediency if landowners would live on their own estates and kill their own mutton.

Lord Colambre sees for himself the results of reckless borrowing when Sir John Berryl, the father of his friend, is taken suddenly ill. Mordicai, demanding immediate payment of a large debt, attempts to have the sick man arrested and thrown into prison. Only Lord Colambre's presence and firm words of rebuff keep the moneylender from carrying out his intention. Mordicai leaves with threats that Lord Colambre will someday regret his insults. Sir John Berryl dies that night, leaving his family almost penniless.

Deeply concerned for his family's welfare, Lord Colambre decides to visit Ireland to see for himself the state of his father's affairs. Lady Clonbrony uses every possible argument to dissuade her son, and Sir Terence suggests that the young man can best help his father by marrying a woman as wealthy as Miss Broadhurst. When Lord Colambre leaves suddenly for Ireland, his mother, refusing to give up her matrimonial plans for her son, allows her friends to believe that he went to attend to private business in connection with his marriage settlement. Since many people expect him to marry Miss Broadhurst, that story satisfies the Clonbrony creditors for the time being.

Arriving in Dublin, Lord Colambre meets Sir James Brooke, a British official well informed on Irish affairs, and the two men become good friends. The young nobleman, pleased with everything he hears and sees, is unable to understand his mother's detestation of the Irish. He tries to meet Nicholas Garraghty, his father's agent, but the man is away on business. Instead, he is entertained by the agent's sister, a silly, affected woman named Mrs. Raffarty.

He also meets Lady Dashfort, who sees in him a possible husband for her widowed daughter, Lady Isabel. Although he hears no favorable reports of Lady Dashfort or her daughter, he becomes a frequent visitor in their home. At last, interested in securing an alliance for her daughter, Lady Dashfort proposes that he accompany her to Killpatrickstown, where she is going to visit Lord and Lady Killpatrick. It is her intention to show him Irish life at its worst so that he will have no desire to live on the Clonbrony estates after his marriage to Lady Isabel. Aware of his affection for Grace, Lady Dashfort arranges matters so that Lady Killpatrick asks her to exhibit her genealogical table, which was prepared as evidence in a lawsuit. She does so with seeming reluctance, on the grounds that she is ashamed of her remote connection with the scandalous St. Omars. She then reveals that Grace's mother was a St. Omar.

Lord Colambre writes to his mother to ask the truth. She replies that the girl's mother was a St. Omar but that she took the name Reynolds after an affair with a gentleman of that name. When the Reynolds family refused to acknowledge her child, she married Mr. Nugent, who generously gave the daughter his name. The young man realizes that this disclosure puts a barrier between Grace and him.

Through the Killpatricks, Lord Colambre meets Count O'Halloran, who is regarded by his neighbors as an oddity because of his learning, his fondness for animals, and his liking of the Irish. When the count returns the visit, Lady Dashfort takes issue with him because he criticizes the improper conduct of an English officer with whom both are acquainted. Lady Dashfort's lack of good manners and moral sense and the further revelation of Lady Isabel as a malicious flirt show the two women to Lord Colambre in their true light. He decides to leave the Dashforts and continue his tour alone.

Count O'Halloran prevails on Lord Colambre, however, to accompany him to Oranmore. There Lord Colambre finds a family of taste and breeding, interested in affairs of the day and the welfare of their tenants. Stimulated by the example of Lord and Lady Oranmore, he plans to go immediately to his father's estate, but incognito, so that he can observe more accurately the conditions of the tenantry and the conduct of the estate agents.

He finds the village of Colambre neat and prosperous, well looked after by Mr. Burke, the agent. After a dinner with the Burkes, the agent shows him around the estate with evident pride in all he accomplished. He regrets, however, that the absentee owner takes no interest in the land or the tenants, aside from the revenues derived from them. Burke's fears that Lord Clonbrony is displeased with his management are confirmed by the arrival of a letter in which his lordship dismisses the agent and directs him to turn over his accounts to Nicholas Garraghty.

Lord Colambre goes on to Clonbrony, where he learns from a driver that the tenants hate and fear Nicholas Garraghty, the factor, and Dennis Garraghty, his brother and assistant. When his carriage breaks down, Lord Colambre spends the night with Mrs. O'Neill, a widow whose niece was named after Grace Nugent. The next day, the young nobleman is present when Dennis Garraghty refuses to renew a lease promised to Mrs. O'Neill's son Brian. The arrival of Mrs. Raffarty and her identification of Lord Colambre causes Dennis Garraghty to change his mind quickly. Disgusted by the man's methods of doing business and by the unkempt, poverty-stricken appearance of the village, Lord Colambre writes to his father and asked him to have no further dealings with the Garraghtys.

During the voyage back to England, Lord Colambre's ship is delayed by a storm, so that the Garraghtys arrive in London ahead of him. He returns, however, in time to confront the agent and his brother with a report on their transactions. Hearing his son's story, Lord Clonbrony would have dismissed them on the spot if he had possessed the cash necessary to settle their entangled accounts. Lord Colambre then asks his father and Sir Terence for a full accounting of the distressed nobleman's obligations. In return, he proposes to settle the debt with the inheritance he will receive when he comes of age, a date only a few days off, if his father will end all business relations with the Garraghtys and go to Ireland to live. Lord Clonbrony welcomes the proposal, but his wife, when she hears of it, treats the idea with scorn. She is already displeased with her son because he did not press his suit with Miss Broadhurst, who is now to marry his friend, Sir Arthur Berryl. When Lord Colambre expresses pleasure over his friend's good fortune, Lady Clonbrony retires in disgust.

Under persuasion by every member of her family, Lady Clonbrony at last ungraciously agrees to return to Ireland. Meanwhile, Lord Colambre, busy with his father's accounts, discovers that many of the London bills were deliberately overcharged and that Nicholas Garraghty is, in reality, his lordship's debtor, not his creditor, as the agent claims. With ready money sent by Lady Berryl, the former Miss Broadhurst, through her husband, Lord Colambre is able to settle his father's most pressing debts, and Sir Terence is able to reclaim Mordicai's bond at a discount. After Nicholas Garraghty was dismissed in disgrace, Mr. Burke is appointed agent of the Colambre and Clonbrony estates.

On the day he comes of age, Lord Colambre's first duty is to execute a bond for five thousand pounds in Grace's name, to repay her the inheritance that was lent to her guardian years before. The young man's secret regret is that he cannot offer his heart with his cousin's restored property.

Arriving in London, Count O'Halloran calls on Lord Colambre. When the young nobleman confides his true feelings for Grace and tells his friend something of her story, the count recalls Captain Reynolds, whom he knew in Austria. Dying, the officer told of his secret marriage with Miss St. Omar and entrusted to the count a packet of private papers, among them a marriage certificate. The count gave the papers to the English ambassador, and they passed in turn into the keeping of Sir James Brooke, the executor of the ambassador's estate. Acting on this information, Lord Colambre goes to Sir James and obtains the papers, which were never carefully examined. When he presents them to the dead officer's father, old Mr. Reynolds accepts the proof of his granddaughter's legitimacy with delight and declares his intention to make her his heiress. Because Grace never knew of the shadow cast on her birth, Lady Berryl is delegated to tell her the whole story, a task that young woman performs with great delicacy and tact.

Acquainted with the true state of affairs, Lady Clonbrony offers no objections to her son's marriage to Grace. Lord Clonbrony and his wife return to Ireland and there, in due time, Grace becomes Viscountess Colambre, much to the satisfaction of Lady Clonbrony, who sees so happily fulfilled her hopes that her son would marry an heiress.

Critical Evaluation:

The Act of Union of 1800, which brought Ireland under the direct rule of the British, was a significant influence on the conception, execution, and reception of *The Absentee*. Some of the act's direct implications may be gathered from the depiction of the Dublin that Lord Colambre encounters on his arrival in Ireland. The city that had asserted parliamentary independence about twenty years earlier is a shadow of its former self. The prospect of independence was part of the public atmosphere in which Maria Edgeworth grew up. Beyond that, the kind of juridical and administrative independence conceived by the Dublin parliament was one with which Edgeworth's family of enlightened landowners readily identified.

The Act of Union dislocated the landowning class's sense of where their interests lay, dividing their sources of identity between the control they had over their land and the judicial and parliamentary sanction for that control, which was now lodged explicitly in the organizations of the British state. The condition of dislocation was lived out literally by many Irish landlords who spent the rents earned by their land in a manner exemplified by Lady Clonbrony in *The Absentee*. This subset of landlords was known as absentees, and while their absence had been a feature of Irish life long before the Act of Union, the new political order made their dereliction of duty more difficult to overlook.

Edgeworth's sense of the significance of the various problems deriving from the new institutional and administrative arrangements forms the narrative core of *The Absentee*. Because it belongs to the two series of novels and novellas known by their collective title as *Tales from Fashionable Life*, this novel may be considered representative of the so-called silver-fork school of fiction. There is, however, a great deal more explicit cultural and political awareness in *The Absentee* than in most other works of that type. Silver-fork novels concentrate on fashionable life to the virtual exclusion of other concerns. Although it is extremely difficult to depict fashionable life without being aware of its economic and ideological underpinnings, such an awareness is typically merely latent. In the case of *The Absentee*, however, it is Lord Colambre's heightened awareness of the insufficiency of fashionable life that provides both narrative and plot with momentum and moral insight.

Thus *The Absentee* is not merely a search for a responsible agenda for Irish landlords and, by extension, Irish social and economic life. It may also be considered a critique of some of the vulgar consumerist excesses in early nineteenth century England. The freedom without responsibility that Lady Clonbrony exhibits is understandably embarrassing to her son. However, Edgeworth is also careful to note that she perpetrates her spendthrift excesses in order to gain credibility as an equal member of the society putatively enlarged by the Act of Union. The fact that she will never be accepted as an equal by the matrons who patronize her parties makes the point. Parliamentary independence may have been surrendered because of the Act of Union, but Edgeworth shows that there is no need for self-respect to vanish also. Lord Colambre's decision to return to Ireland and to a responsible role there as landlord implies that the situation cannot be rectified by exclusively parliamentary means.

By going to Ireland, Lord Colambre forsakes the metropolis for the rural life, the fashionable for the unprepossessing, the self-denying mimicry of the salon for the self-empowering possibility to learn through experience. The strangeness of Ireland and the fact that Colambre does not bring with him all the moral resources and ideological self-consciousness necessary for him to live the life for which birth and fortune equip him are vital to the didactic purpose that here, as always, underlies Edgeworth's fictional preoccupations. Lord Colambre's experiences in Ireland register the country's distinctive and frequently disturbing difference, and they challenge him to confront that difference.

The importance of his capacity to sustain such a confrontation is not merely to authenticate Lord Colambre by virtue of his personal adaptability to change. In addition, Edgeworth implies that if Colambre can adapt to Irish conditions and intervene in them productively, he will be well on the way to becoming a model landlord. With commitment, control, and maturity, he can redress the social and moral ills of absenteeism. The Act of Union will take its place among the statutes without having impinged on the integrity of the new generation represented by Lord Colambre. As a result, the integrity of relations between landlord and tenant can be restored, an act of union far more significant than its parliamentary counterpart because of the demonstrable social contract that is its premise.

Edgeworth grounds these social and cultural concerns in a series of challenges that Colambre must overcome before he arrives at the appropriately mature identity. Although Edgeworth's significance as a novelist derives in part from the fact that she never shirks the large question, that question is shown here to have an unsuspected number of facets. Among the more noteworthy of these are the state of Irish culture, with which Lord Colambre engages through his acquaintance with Count O'Halloran, and the young lord's emotional integrity, which is exemplified by his relationship with Grace Nugent. The fact that there is a link between these two areas suggests that Edgeworth is aware of the significance of providing Lord Colambre not only with property and moral intelligence but also with an extensive inner life, the existence of which distinguishes him from his hollow and defeated parents. It is the combination of the various elements of Colambre's experiences that distinguishes Edgeworth's *The Absentee*.

"Critical Evaluation" by George O'Brien

Further Reading

Butler, Marilyn. *Jane Austen and the War of Ideas*. New York: Oxford University Press, 1975. Despite its title, this work contains an important chapter on Edgeworth. The overall context of the Napoleonic Era is taken into consideration. The obvious contrast between Edgeworth and Austen, and its consequences for the development of English fiction, result in a stimulating critique of Edgeworth's oeuvre.

_______. *Maria Edgeworth: A Literary Biography*. Oxford, England: Clarendon Press, 1972. The standard biography, providing comprehensive information on all aspects of Edgeworth's life, work, and family. The sources, intentions, and reception of all of Edgeworth's writings are discussed. Contains a thorough account of *The Absentee*'s social, artistic, and political contexts.

Davie, Donald. *The Heyday of Sir Walter Scott*. New York: Routledge, 1961. A pioneering study of Scott's influence on English and European literature. The distinctive place of Edgeworth's fiction in this overview is clearly established. *The Absentee* receives concise and pertinent treatment.

Dunne, Tom. *Maria Edgeworth and the Colonial Mind*. Dublin: National University of Ireland, 1985. An influential study of Edgeworth's work, to which subsequent considerations of Edgeworth's politics and cultural colonialism are indebted. Dunne's discussion is directly relevant to the concerns addressed in *The Absentee*.

Edgeworth, Maria. *The Absentee*. Edited by W. J. McCormack and Kim Walker. New York: Oxford University Press, 1988. Contains a scholarly introduction, bibliography, and explanatory notes. Also reprints material on the connotations of the name Grace Nugent and Edgeworth's notes for an essay on Edmund Burke.

Gilmartin, Sophie. "Oral and Written Genealogies in Edgeworth's *The Absentee*." In *Ancestry and Narrative in Nineteenth-Century British Literature: Blood Relations from Edgeworth to Hardy*. New York: Cambridge University Press, 1998. Explores the importance of the concept of ancestry in Victorian England by examining novels from that era, including an analysis of Edgeworth's *The Absentee*. Includes bibliographical references and an index.

Harden, Elizabeth. *Maria Edgeworth*. Boston: Twayne, 1984. Harden chooses the theme of education around which to organize her survey of Edgeworth's life and works. This approach reveals in broad outline the range of Edgeworth's sympathies and activities. Contains a full bibliography.

Hollingworth, Brian. *Maria Edgeworth's Irish Writing*. New York: St. Martin's Press, 1997. Hollingsworth examines Edgeworth's Irish works, including *The Absentee*, to explore her attitudes toward vernacular language and regionalism. Includes detailed notes and a bibliography.

McCormack, W. J. *Ascendancy and Tradition in Anglo-Irish Literary History from 1789 to 1939*. New York: Oxford University Press, 1985. Contains a section on *The Absentee*, which is appraised in the light of Edgeworth's reading of the writings of Edmund Burke. A pathbreaking contribution to Irish cultural history.

Nash, Julie, ed. *New Essays on Maria Edgeworth*. Burlington, Vt.: Ashgate, 2006. A collection of essays examining Edgeworth's work from a variety of perspectives, including analyses of *The Absentee*.

The Accidental Tourist

Author: Anne Tyler (1941-   )
First published: 1985
Type of work: Novel
Type of plot: Comic realism
Time of plot: Early 1980's
Locale: Baltimore and Paris

Principal characters:
MACON LEARY, an author
SARAH SIDEY LEARY, his wife
ETHAN LEARY, their only child
ROSE, Macon's sister
PORTER and CHARLES, Macon's brothers
JULIAN EDGE, Macon's boss
MURIEL PRITCHARD, a dog trainer
ALEXANDER PRITCHARD, Muriel's son
EDWARD, Macon's dog

The Story:

Sarah and Macon are driving home from a vacation. A year earlier, twelve-year-old Ethan Leary had gone to summer camp in Virginia. One evening, he and another camper had snuck away to Burger Bonanza, where Ethan was senselessly murdered. As Macon drives, Sarah announces that she is leaving him. Macon points out to her that many couples who experience the death of a child separate, but he wants to stay together. Sarah finds Macon too predictable, methodical, and unemotional. Macon thinks Sarah is too spontaneous.

Macon makes a living writing travel books, primarily for businesspeople who, like Macon, hate to travel. They want to pretend they never leave home. Each book's title includes the name of a particular city, for he feels that business travelers go only to cities. In his international books, Macon tells his readers how to travel with very little disruption in their lives, how to find hotels that have American-type service and restaurants that serve American-type food. He tells them where to find American chain restaurants, such as McDonald's, what dishes to order because they are familiar, and where to find restaurants that serve things such as Chef Boyardee ravioli in Rome. He periodically updates his books.

When Sarah leaves him, Macon reorders his life. He starts wearing nothing but sweat suits. He washes his clothes in the bathtub as he showers. He cooks coffee and eggs and pops popcorn in his bedroom for breakfast. He disconnects the clothes dryer's exhaust tube and teaches the cat to use the resulting hole as an exit and entrance to the house. He sleeps in what he thinks of as a body bag made of sheets sewn together.

Macon decides to use the coal shuttle to lower food for his dog, Edward, into the house. For this plan to work, however, Edward must be willing to eat in the basement, and Edward is terrified of the basement. Moreover, when Macon prepares to leave on his first trip to update a book since Sarah's departure, he finds that Edward can no longer stay where he usually has because he has started to bite. Instead, Macon leaves Edward at the Meow-Bow Animal Hospital, where Macon meets Muriel Pritchard, who offers to train Edward.

One day, Macon reconnects the dryer so he can dry his sweat suits. The cat tries to get into the house, making a terrible noise that frightens Edward. Edward knocks Macon over, and Macon breaks his leg. Macon moves into his sister's house and lives with her and his two brothers. On most evenings, they play a card game they call Vaccination. Only the siblings know how to play it. The men's former wives tried to learn how to play, but they could not.

Macon's siblings, like Macon himself, are very concerned with order. His sister Rose alphabetizes all the things in her kitchen, even though it means putting allspice next to ant poison. Macon's brothers, who are divorced and live with Rose, are similarly fussy and orderly. However, Edward causes problems in Rose's house. He attacks visitors and Macon's brothers. One of the brothers wants Edward put to sleep, but Macon refuses because Edward was Ethan's dog. At the insistence of his siblings, Macon calls Muriel to train Edward.

Muriel is chatty and disorganized; Macon is silent and organized. During the lessons, she talks constantly. Macon thinks Muriel is much too hard on Edward. After Edward lunges at Muriel and she hangs him briefly on his leash, Macon tells her not to come back.

On a trip to New York City, Macon goes to a restaurant on top of a skyscraper. He has a panic attack. He phones his sister, but she is not home. Instead, he reaches his brother Charles, who is shut in the pantry because Edward attacks him whenever he tries to leave. Charles wants to call the police to come shoot Edward. Macon insists that Charles not call the police. Macon tries to call Sarah, but she is not home. He finally reaches Muriel, who says she will rescue Charles. Then, Macon's panic attack ends, and he returns to eat his meal. Muriel again starts training Edward.

Macon and Muriel soon become lovers, and Macon moves in with Muriel. Muriel has a son, Alexander, who is seven years old and sickly. After Ethan's death, Macon felt that he could never enjoy sex and never interact joyfully with a young boy again. He finds that he enjoys sex with Muriel, as well as shopping with, playing with, and teaching Alexander.

Nonetheless, when Macon returns from one of his trips, he drives past Muriel's house and returns to his house, where Sarah is now living. He and Sarah reconcile with each other. Then, Macon goes to Paris, France. He finds that Muriel is on the plane with him. When in Paris, he tries to avoid Muriel, but she uses Macon's guidebook and so stays at the same hotel as Macon. They go to some dinners together.

Julian Edge, Macon's publisher, courts Rose. She and Julian get married, but shortly thereafter, Rose moves back into her own house, leaving Julian. Julian asks Macon how he can get Rose back. Macon advises him to ask Rose to put his office in order.

In Paris, Macon hurts his back and is unable to travel to finish the work of updating his guidebook. He calls Julian's office and finds Rose working there. Rose arranges to send Sarah to Paris to travel around the city for Macon and do his updating for him. Macon tells Sarah, truthfully, that he is not involved in Muriel's coming to Paris and does not want her there. After a while, however, he decides that he wants to return to Muriel rather than stay with Sarah. At the end of the book, Macon, with a sore back, gets into a taxi to go to the airport. He stops on the way to pick up Muriel, who is herself trying to get a cab to the airport.

Critical Evaluation:

The Accidental Tourist quickly became a best seller. Many reviewers and critics hailed it as Anne Tyler's best work, even though its publication occurred just three years after that of *Dinner at the Homesick Restaurant* (1982), which had similarly been hailed as her best work. Critics praised Tyler's handling of point of view in *The Accidental Tourist.* The point of view is third-person limited: The narration focuses on Macon, but it is not first-person narrative. Tyler carefully controls point of view throughout the novel.

The Accidental Tourist won the National Book Critics Circle Award for American fiction, an award given by book reviewers to honor the most distinguished works for each year. In 1988, *The Accidental Tourist* was made into a movie starring John Hurt. Geena Davis, who played Muriel, won an Academy Award for Best Supporting Actress for her work in the movie.

In the book, Tyler demonstrates her ability to re-create in fiction the complexity of the American family. Macon hates change. The biggest change for him is the senseless murder of Ethan. Macon reacts to the murder by becoming more withdrawn and more opposed to change. Macon writes travel books but hates to travel. The logo on Macon's travel books is an armchair with wings. This logo symbolizes the books' purpose: They provide a way for someone to travel while giving up none of the security and comfort of home. The logo also stands for Macon himself, who wants to systematize and simplify all things in his life so he can repeat the same actions over and over. He prefers not to travel in any sense of the word but to keep everything static. His attempt to systematize his life ends disastrously when he breaks his leg. While he is in his cast, he wishes it covered his whole body, thus insulating him from the outside world and preventing change. The image he uses for his body's covering makes it resemble a cocoon, however. Thus, he unconsciously implies his need for change, for the kind of rebirth a cocoon represents.

Macon and his siblings display symptoms of obsessive-compulsive disorder. They want everything in its place, and they want life to go smoothly. They want nothing to change, but Rose's putting ant poison next to allspice indicates the dangers this desire presents. When Macon moves back in with his siblings, he fits right into their pattern of life. The Leary brothers are so upset by change that when Rose cooks the Thanksgiving turkey in a new way, they refuse to eat it, believing it is full of bacteria.

The main disrupter of order in Rose's house is Edward, who is unruly and, at times, vicious. He interrupts the serene lives of the Learys, but Macon will not even consider getting rid of his dead son's dog. Because of Edward, Muriel enters Macon's life, providing him with a chance to begin to grow. At the end of the novel, Macon chooses growth over the stagnant life he lived with Sarah and then with his siblings.

The relationship Macon builds with Muriel paves the way for Rose to build a relationship with Julian. Julian is fairly wild. He is a womanizer and a sailor. Macon thinks Julian is interested in Rose only so that he can laugh at the Learys. Eventually, though, he realizes that Julian truly loves Rose. When Rose leaves Julian to return to her brothers, Julian cannot convince her to return to living with him. A sign of Macon's growth occurs when he recognizes some of his family's problems and recommends that Julian win Rose back by asking her to help put his office in order. Macon knows that Rose, with her alphabetized kitchen, will not resist an invitation to make a place more orderly.

Richard Tuerk

Further Reading

Bail, Paul. *Anne Tyler: A Critical Companion.* Westport, Conn.: Greenwood Press, 1998. Chapter 10 discusses *The Accidental Tourist*, including the plot and characters, and it provides a political reading of the work.

Croft, Robert W. *Anne Tyler: A Bio-Bibliography.* Westport, Conn.: Greenwood Press, 1995. Treats works by and about Tyler, including dissertations, theses, and many reviews.

Evans, Elizabeth. *Anne Tyler.* New York: Twayne, 1993. An easily accessible introduction to Tyler and her works through *Saint Maybe* (1991). Treats, among other things, the role of Rose Leary and the Leary family's habit of correcting people's grammar in the context of Tyler's other works.

Jansen, Henry. *Laughter Among the Ruins: Postmodern Comic Approaches to Suffering.* New York: Peter Lang, 2001. Compares Tyler's use of comedy to represent suffering with the similar strategies of Iris Murdoch and John Irving.

Kissel, Susan S. *Moving On: The Heroines of Shirley Ann Grau, Anne Tyler, and Gail Goodwin.* Bowling Green, Ohio: Bowling Green State University Popular Press, 1996. Treats the way Macon Leary opens himself up to possibility through his interactions with others, especially Muriel.

Macpherson, Heidi Slettedahl. *Transatlantic Women's Literature.* Edinburgh: Edinburgh University Press, 2008. Study of novels in which characters cross the Atlantic Ocean and must confront the resulting cultural differences. Includes a chapter on Tyler's representation of characters who reinvent home in foreign locales.

Petry, Alice Hall. *Understanding Anne Tyler.* Columbia: University of South Carolina Press, 1990. A good introduction to Tyler and her works. Chapter 9 treats *The Accidental Tourist*, reading the book as a kind of tragic comedy.

Sweeney, Susan Elizabeth. "Anne Tyler's Invented Games: *The Accidental Tourist* and *Breathing Lessons*." *Southern Quarterly* 34, no. 1 (Fall, 1995): 81-97. Treats Vaccination, the card game the Learys play, as an analogy for Tyler's fiction.

Voelker, Joseph C. *Art and the Accidental in Anne Tyler.* Columbia: University of Missouri Press, 1989. Chapter 8 reads *The Accidental Tourist* in connection with Freud's idea of the death instinct.

The Acharnians

Author: Aristophanes (c. 450-c. 385 B.C.E.)
First produced: Acharnēs, 425 B.C.E. (English translation, 1812); first published, 425 B.C.E.
Type of work: Drama
Type of plot: Satire
Time of plot: 431-404 B.C.E.
Locale: Athens

Principal characters:
DICAEOPOLIS, a peace-loving citizen
AMPHITHEUS, his friend
EURIPIDES, a playwright
LAMACHUS, a general
AMBASSADORS TO THE ALLIES OF ATHENS
THE ACHARNIANS, a chorus of charcoal burners

The Story:

Dicaeopolis, waiting for the assembly to convene, sits musing, making figures in the dust, pulling out his loose hairs, and longing for peace. He is fully prepared to harass and abuse the speakers if they talk of anything but peace with Sparta. Immediately after the citizens gather, his friend Amphitheus begins to complain of hunger because of the wartime diet. He is saved from arrest only by the intervention of Dicaeopolis.

The assembly then listens to a series of fantastic claims made by the pompous ambassadors to Athens's allies, each speech punctuated by a scoffing aside from Dicaeopolis, who knows full well that the entire alliance is wasting away from the effects of the Peloponnesian War. The high point of absurdity is reached when the last of the ambassadors ushers in a few scraggly, miserably dressed troops, introducing them as a Thracian host sent to assist in the war. Dicaeopolis, knowing of the assembly's willingness to adjourn upon the slightest provocation, then brings about the end of the session by claiming to have felt a drop of rain.

Finding himself unable to bring about the end of the war, Dicaeopolis determines to effect a personal, separate peace. Amphitheus, his own ambassador, returns from the enemy with three bottles of wine—the first five years old, the second ten years old, and the third thirty years old. The first two taste vile, but the last is rich with a bouquet of nectar and ambrosia. Drinking it down, Dicaeopolis personally accepts and ratifies a thirty-year peace. The Acharnians, whose vineyards were ravaged by the enemy, having got wind of this traitorous act, arrive in pursuit of Amphitheus just as Dicaeopolis is leaving his house to offer up a ritual prayer to Bacchus in thanks for the peace that allows him to resume once more a normal existence with his wife. Upon hearing his prayer, the Acharnians begin to stone him as he tries in vain to persuade them that peace is good. Threatened with further violence, Dicaeopolis seizes a covered basket of coals and announces that it is an Acharnian child, a hostage, which he will disembowel if he is not permitted to plead his cause. When the Acharnians agree, he asks further to be allowed to dress properly for the occasion.

Dicaeopolis then goes to the house of Euripides to borrow the costume of Telephus, the most unfortunate and pathetic of all the heroes of Euripides' tragedies. The great playwright, in the midst of composing a new tragedy, is hardly in the mood to be disturbed, but Dicaeopolis cannot resist the opportunity to tease him about his wretched heroes and about the fact that his mother sold vegetables. Finally the irate Euripides gives him the miserable costume and turns him out.

The eloquent plea for peace that Dicaeopolis delivers to the Acharnians is so moving that the chorus is divided on the issue. At that moment Lamachus, a general dressed in full armor, arrives on the scene. He declares that nothing can dissuade him from eternal war on the Spartans and their allies. Dicaeopolis counters with a proclamation that his markets are henceforth open to all the enemies of Athens, but not to Lamachus.

Shortly thereafter a starving Megarian appears in Dicaeopolis's marketplace with his two daughters, who agreed with their father that it would be better to be sold than to die of hunger. After disguising them as pigs by fitting them with hooves and snouts, the Megarian stuffs them into a sack and offers them to Dicaeopolis as the finest sows he could possibly offer to Aphrodite. Dicaeopolis, aware of the deception, nevertheless accepts them in exchange for a supply of garlic and salt. The next trader is a fat, thriving Boeotian with a tremendous supply of game birds, animals, and fish. All he asks in exchange is some item of Athenian produce not available in Boeotia. Careful bargaining reveals, however, that the only such item is an informer—a vessel useful for holding all foul things, a mortar for grinding out lawsuits, a light for looking into other people's accounts. At last the bargain is made, and the next meddling informer to enter the marketplace and threaten Dicaeopolis with exposure to the authorities is seized, bound, and carefully packed in hay for the Boeotian to carry home.

Suddenly, General Lamachus is ordered to take his battalions to guard the borders against invasion during the forthcoming Feast of the Cups. At the same time the priest of Bacchus orders Dicaeopolis to prepare for joyous participation in the feast. The chorus wishes them both joy as Lamachus dons his heavy armor and Dicaeopolis dresses in festival clothes, as Lamachus unhooks his spear and Dicaeopolis unhooks a sausage. After the feast Lamachus is carried in, hurt in a fall in a ditch before encountering the enemy, and Dicaeopolis enters, hilariously drunk and supported by two voluptuous courtesans. The blessings of peace are emphasized by the fact that, in the end, Lamachus the militarist is carried off to the surgeon while Dicaeopolis is conducted before the judges to be awarded the wineskin of victory.

Critical Evaluation:

Thematically, *The Acharnians* is the most inclusive of Aristophanes' plays; in it audiences find his powerful wit and satire against militarism and war, his contempt for petty politicians and informers, his delight in earthy sex play, and his spirited spoofing of Euripides—qualities that make it the most personal of Aristophanes' works. When Dicaeopolis speaks directly to the audience, he does so with the voice of Aristophanes, eloquently asserting his intellectual honesty and independence and declaring that he will always fight for the cause of peace and justice. Aristophanes directed the play and acted in it, taking the part of the protagonist.

Presented in 425 B.C.E., *The Acharnians* is the earliest surviving play of Aristophanes, who began his career as a dramatist in 427. The play is set in the sixth year of the Peloponnesian War (431-404 B.C.E.), which was fought by Athens and Sparta. The conflict had already inflicted grave hardship on Athens. Some Athenians apparently wished to pursue the war more aggressively to exact revenge on Sparta. The protagonist of *The Acharnians*, Dicaeopolis, takes a different approach and concludes a private peace treaty with the Spartans. Much of the play depicts the opposition to Dicaeopolis's treaty and the way in which the hero thwarts his opponents and sets about enjoying the rewards of his private peace.

Most plays of Aristophanes are built around some great idea, which is a plan undertaken by the main character to remedy some unsatisfactory political or private situation. This fantastic project is the main character's way of setting things right, and he or she usually encounters strong opposition to the proposal. Overcoming this opposition, the protagonist eventually implements the plan, and the good (or bad) consequences follow. The role of the great idea in *The Acharnians* is somewhat different: Dicaeopolis achieves his object—a private peace treaty with Sparta—very early in the play. For the remainder of the play he rebuffs his opponents and enthusiastically enjoys the benefits of his treaty. The result is an apparently lopsided dramatic structure. Aristophanes bypasses the usual dramatic struggle regarding implementing the plan and indulges instead in broad satire of leading Athenians of his day, such as Cleon, Lamachus, and the poet Euripides. Another consequence of this design is a lingering impression of the protagonist's selfishness. Dicaeopolis's peace treaty is for himself and his family alone. The implicit message is that peace is good for everyone. Through the greater part of the play Dicaeopolis extravagantly enjoys the benefits of his treaty and refuses (with one exception) to share his wineskin of peace with anyone else.

The private nature of Dicaeopolis's peace should also constitute a warning against reading *The Acharnians* simply as a political tract. The central concern of Dicaeopolis is to achieve peace and to end the personal hardships caused by the protracted struggle with Sparta. Although *The Acharnians* may therefore seem to advocate a political program, the dramatist's message is clearly different from that of a political pamphlet. On the one hand, like many Athenians, Aristophanes probably believed that conflict among Greeks was foolish and wasteful. The gist of the argument that Dicaeopolis presents to the chorus is that the causes of the war are trivial. This viewpoint should not be confused with pacifism or opposition to all war, since in the opening scenes of the play there are suggestions of a greater military threat from outside Greece, that is, Persia. There is no evidence that an organized peace movement at Athens existed at the time of the play's first production, and the play generally depicts the war more as a nuisance than as something unjust.

Aristophanes has a reputation for conservatism in politics and social mores. He was, however, no enemy of democracy, only of its abuse in the hands of leaders such as Cleon. After all, it was the famous free speech and democracy of the Athenians that allowed the poet to speak in support of peace with Sparta in the midst of war. As for Aristophanes' championing of old-fashioned virtues, it is to be noted that the Acharnians, who violently oppose Dicaeopolis, represent the older generation and its values. They are staunch advocates of war with Sparta. It is possible that as an artist Aristophanes was primarily interested in depicting the great polarities of Athenian life, such as the old and the new, city and country, and peace and war. The political content of his plays should be understood more as a dramatic opposition of competing ideas than as advocacy of a specific political program.

Parody is one element that gives *The Acharnians* its special appeal, and the objects of parody range from the political and social to the literary and artistic. Using the power of slapstick parody, Aristophanes creates a broad satire of Athenian politics, society, and art. Although the figure of Cleon lurks in the background, it is the soldier Lamachus who is specifically held up for ridicule. He is depicted as the typical braggart soldier and militarist, although the historical Lamachus appears to have been a brave and admirable soldier, who actually helped to negotiate the Peace of Nicias in 421 B.C.E. It is, however, the tragic poet Euripides who is Aristophanes' favorite object of satire. Aristophanes apparently resented the political message of some of Euripides' plays that contain anti-Spartan sentiments, but he also has a literary argument with the dramatist who experimented with technical innovations and depicted new kinds of characters (beggars like Telephus) on the tragic stage. Still, Aristophanes' criticism of Euripides, in this play and elsewhere, shows intimate familiarity with his tragedies. One cannot escape the impression of grudging admiration for the tragic poet's work.

Aristophanes' play won first prize in the dramatic competition of 425 B.C.E., taking precedence over works by the veteran poets Cratinus and Eupolis. Although it will never be known on what explicit basis the judges of the festival made their verdicts, it is probable that the fantasy of Dicaeopolis, with his private peace, was a great success with its Athenian audience.

"Critical Evaluation" by John M. Lawless

Further Reading

Aristophanes. *Acharnians*. Edited and translated by Alan H. Sommerstein. 2d ed. Warminster, England: Aris & Phillips, 1984. Provides scholarly introduction, bibliography, Greek text, facing English translation, and commentary keyed to the translation. Sommerstein's translation supersedes most earlier versions.

Dover, K. J. *Aristophanic Comedy*. Berkeley: University of California Press, 1972. Useful and authoritative study of the plays of Aristophanes. Chapter 6 provides a synopsis of *The Acharnians*, a scholarly discussion of problems of its theatrical production, and an examination of the themes of peace and war. An essential starting point for study of the play.

Harriott, Rosemary M. *Aristophanes: Poet and Dramatist*. Baltimore: Johns Hopkins University Press, 1986. Harriott does not devote an individual chapter to each of Aristophanes' plays but instead discusses each play as it illustrates the central themes and techniques of the playwright's work.

Platter, Charles. "The Return of Telephus: *Acharnians, Tesmophoriazusae*, and the Dialogic Background." In *Aristophanes and the Carnival of Genres*. Baltimore: Johns Hopkins University Press, 2007. Platter uses the theories of literary critic Mikhail Bakhtin to analyze Aristophanes' plays, focusing on how the Greek playwright incorporated multiple genres and styles of speech to create different forms of dialogue for his characters. Includes discussions on *Acharnians* and several other plays.

Silk, M. S. *Aristophanes and the Definition of Comedy*. New York: Oxford University Press, 2002. Silk looks at Aristophanes not merely as an ancient Greek dramatist but as one of the world's great poets. He analyzes *The Acharnians* and the other plays to examine their language, style, lyric poetry, character, and structure.

Spartz, Lois. *Aristophanes*. Boston: Twayne, 1978. A reliable introduction to the comedy of Aristophanes for the general reader. Chapter 2 summarizes the problems of the play and discusses the central themes of peace and prosperity.

Whitman, Cedric. *Aristophanes and the Comic Hero*. Cambridge, Mass.: Harvard University Press, 1964. A standard work on the characterization of the Aristophanic protagonist. Chapter 3, "City and Individual," offers a valuable study of Dicaeopolis and of the motifs and imagery in this play.

Ada or Ardor
A Family Chronicle

Author: Vladimir Nabokov (1899-1977)
First published: 1969
Type of work: Novel
Type of plot: Science fiction
Time of plot: Alternate late nineteenth and early twentieth centuries
Locale: Antiterra, an alternate world on the North American continent

Principal characters:
IVAN "VAN" VEEN, the principal protagonist, a man of wealth and privilege
ADA VEEN, Van's purported cousin, who is actually his sister
DEMENTY "DEMON" VEEN, father of Van and Ada
DANIEL "DAN" VEEN, Demon's ineffectual brother, Ada's putative father
AQUA VEEN, Demon's wife, Van's putative mother
MARINA VEEN, Daniel's wife, Demon's lover, and the mother of Van and Ada
LUCETTE VEEN, daughter of Daniel and Marina

The Story:

Van Veen briefly sees a girl in an antique shop but never speaks to her. Subsequently, he discovers Ada, his cousin, during a summer at Ardis Hall, his ancestral family estate. He falls passionately in love with her. Van soon gives himself over to the physicality of passion, and the two carry on a love affair. During this period, they also discover that the supposed facts about their family are all an elaborate sham and in fact the two of them are full siblings, making the incestuous nature of their relationship far more serious than if they were merely cousins.

Ada is intensely physical and demonstrates an inability to refuse anyone in sexual need. As a result, she becomes involved with two other young men, Phillip Rack and Percy de Prey. When Van discovers her infidelity, he seeks revenge, only to be distracted and wounded by an extraneous soldier named Trapper. As a result, both of his rivals die by other hands, and Van ends up in a rather shallow physical relationship with Percy de Prey's cousin Cordula.

During Van's subsequent youth, he studies psychology and whiles his time away at a chain of brothels called the Villa Venus, the sexual equivalent of a fast-food restaurant. His half sister Lucette declares her love for him despite being courted by one Andrey Vinelander. Van accepts her interest, and they cohabit in an apartment that formerly belonged to Cordula de Prey.

After Dan Veen dies as a result of a hallucinatory episode, Demon Veen effectively orders Van to end his relationship with Ada. Van attempts suicide, but the gun misfires. He then hunts down a former servant, Kim Beauharnais, an amateur photographer who has captured evidence of the affair with Ada and is using it for blackmail. Van beats Kim so savagely that Kim is left blind, a fitting punishment in the tradition of the original Peeping Tom, who was struck blind for spying upon Lady Godiva as she rode nude through Coventry to spare it from the plague.

Ada marries Andrey Vinelander, while Van drowns his grief in travel and debauchery in Europe. When Van encounters Lucette in England, she attempts to seduce him. However, everything goes awry when they watch a movie called *Don Juan's Last Fling* and find that Ada is one of the actresses. Lucette ends up taking an overdose of sleeping pills, throwing herself off the steamship on which they are traveling, and drowning in the Atlantic Ocean.

With Lucette dead, Ada and her husband Andrey go to Switzerland in an effort to locate various secret bank accounts in which Lucette has hidden a considerable fortune. Van meets them and conspires with Ada to free her of Andrey. However, their plan is foiled when Andrey contracts tuberculosis, which leads Ada to decide she cannot abandon him.

Ada and Van remain separated for seventeen years, during which time Van begins to delve into philosophy as well as psychology. He theorizes on the nature of time as personal experience, eventually producing a lecture titled "The Texture of Time." When they are finally reunited in Switzerland, they being to live together as a married couple. When they reach old age, Van develops cancer. He and Ada contrive to commit mutual suicide in a final act of love.

Critical Evaluation:

Ada or Ardor (most commonly known as *Ada*) is presented as the autobiography of Van Veen, begun when he was in his fifties and completed when he is ninety-seven. It consists of five sections, each successively shorter than its predecessor, told in a lush and dreamlike prose. The first section introduces Van's family in their ancestral estate of Ardis Hall, recounting some basic family history (since this is supposed to be a family chronicle) before actually introducing Van and Ada.

The fifth and final section of the work summarizes the entire story, bringing it up to the point of the elderly Van's present. He intersperses it with comments upon world events since his reunion with his beloved Ada in a way that suggests the unpleasant realities of the twentieth century, including the rise of a threatening figure whose name echoes that of Adolf Hitler. Van's story of his last years suggests a disintegration of the comfortable world of his childhood and youth into anxiety, paralleling his own physical decay into the maladies of age, including the cancer that is slowly devouring him from the inside out. When he and Ada commit suicide together, they dissolve into their story and become in a sense immortal.

The novel represents one of the earliest examples of the genre of alternate history, which has since been popularized by such authors as Harry Turtledove and S. M. Stirling. Because Vladimir Nabokov is generally known as a writer of literary fiction, many critics will adamantly deny that *Ada* is a work of alternate history because of the mass-cultural, nonliterary associations of the genre. However, *Ada* contains the critical element of alternate history: It represents a departure from historical events and explores the consequences of that departure, generating a fictional world markedly different from the one familiar to readers.

In Nabokov's work, the Tatar conquest resulted not in submission but in the migration of the Russian people eastward through Siberia into Alaska and Canada. As a result, many of the critical events of Russian history take place in North America, often near important landmarks. For instance, the reforms of Patriarch Nikon result in the mass executions of Old Believers on the shores of Canada's Great Slave Lake.

Unlike Turtledove or Stirling, Nabokov spends relatively little time on the particulars of history and politics in his imagined world. He offers only glimpses of exactly how the Russians interacted with the English settlers as they arrived upon the eastern seaboard or how precisely the combined American-Russian society developed. It is possible for different readers to argue persuasively either that North America north of the Rio Grande is ruled by a czar (although likely under a constitutional monarchy as a result of English influence) or that it is a republic ruled by the political heirs of George Washington and Thomas Jefferson. Only one thing can be said for certain about the political landscape of Nabokov's alternate America—there is no equivalent to the Bolshevik Revolution in Amerussia. If analogues of revolutionaries Vladimir Ilich Lenin and Leon Trotsky exist in that world, they have been coopted by the political establishment.

Similarly, Nabokov devotes relatively little attention to the particulars of how technology has developed differently in his imagined world. Electricity is not used in his society: Its use has been prohibited as a result of a disaster, but the author refuses to discuss the precise nature of the mysterious L disaster. Such matters are only for more mature ears, he warns the reader in a rather Victorian manner, effectively declaring the question closed. Even as he makes this declaration, however, he archly mocks such pruderies through his cheerful wordplay.

Nabokov devotes relatively little attention to the world-building elements that are of such paramount importance to most alternate history authors, because his focus is not upon the great events of history but upon the personal relationships of his protagonists, the Veen family. Thus, a reader learns the particulars of the invention of the dorophone, a sort of hydraulic telephone that enables long-distance communication in a world in which electricity is banned, because it was the work of one of the protagonists' parents. Moreover, the invention itself is presented as part of Aqua's descent into madness, which has profound effects upon Van and Ada Veen.

One of the names given to this alternate world by its inhabitants, Demonia, suggests the orgiastic sexuality often attributed to various beings of the spiritual realms. The sexual athletics of the various characters of the novel may bring to mind the ancient Greek gods and goddesses. Both Aqua and Marina Veen can be seen as water nymphs, who were often the objects of the lusts of the Greek gods. Alternatively, they can be regarded as personifications of the feminine nature of water, simultaneously both life-giving and threatening. Both women die young of mental illness, one sliding into lassitude and the other taking her own life in one short, sharp blow. Given this association of its characters with myth and abstraction, the novel admits of a fantastical reading, in which the characters become larger-than-life beings, symbols of indulgence and its power over the human psyche.

Forbidden love and madness are two major themes in Nabokov's work. While his most famous novel, *Lolita* (1955), deals with pedophilia, *Ada* is the story of the lifelong incestuous relationship of the two protagonists. However, this incest is never represented in a prurient fashion but always artistically and indirectly, in myriad delicate details and through the effect it has upon their relationships with each other and with others. Even when those details create a sense of a repellant society in which pleasure becomes horror, there is a compelling beauty that drives readers to go on.

Just as his fixation with the young Lolita drove Humbert mad in *Lolita*, there is strong textual evidence that his forbidden love for Ada finally drives Van over the edge. In fact, some critics have denied the alternate historical aspect of the novel altogether and have suggested that the fascinating world in which America and Russia have blended into one is the product of Van's fevered imagination and that he is in fact, like Nabokov himself, a Russian émigré living in America. The novel's representation of the real world as a hallucination experienced by the inhabitants of Antiterra is in this reading nothing more than Van's covert acknowledgment of reality even while he seeks to deny it.

Leigh Husband Kimmel

Further Reading

Connolly, Julian W., ed. *The Cambridge Companion to Nabokov.* New York: Cambridge University Press, 2005. Collection of essays offers a good introduction to Nabokov's life and writings. Topics addressed include Nabokov as a storyteller, a Russian writer, a modernist, and a poet, as well as his transition to writing in English.

De la Durantaye, Leland. *Style Is Matter: The Moral Art of Vladimir Nabokov.* Ithaca, N.Y.: Cornell University Press, 2007. While focusing on *Lolita*, this study also looks at Nabokov's other works to discuss the ethics of art in Nabokov's fiction. Asserts that although some readers find Nabokov to be cruel, his works contain a moral message—albeit one that is skillfully hidden.

Dembo, L. S., ed. *Nabokov: The Man and His Work.* Madison: University of Wisconsin Press, 1967. Collection of scholarly essays on Nabokov's literary techniques.

Field, Andrew. *VN: The Life and Art of Vladimir Nabokov.* New York: Crown, 1977. Scholarly biography that relates Nabokov's life experiences to his work as a writer.

Glynn, Michael. *Vladimir Nabokov: Bergsonian and Russian Formalist Influences in His Novels.* New York: Palgrave Macmillan, 2007. Glynn disagrees with other critics who have called Nabokov a Symbolist writer, arguing that he was an anti-Symbolist who was influenced by the philosopher Henri Bergson and by Russian Formalism. Bergson's philosophy revolves around the nature of time and the human experience of it, making his influence on Nabokov particularly important to *Ada*.

Grayson, Jane, Arnold B. McMillin, and Priscilla Meyer, eds. *Nabokov's World.* 2 vols. New York: Palgrave Macmillan, 2002. Collection of essays written by an international group of Nabokov scholars, providing comprehensive discussion of his work. Presents analyses of individual novels as well as coverage of topics such as intertextuality in Nabokov's works and the literary reception of his writings.

Hyde, G. M., ed. *Vladimir Nabokov: America's Russian Novelist.* London: Marion Boyars, 1977. Critical essays focusing on the interaction of Russian and American culture in Nabokov's writing.

Quennell, Peter, ed. *Vladimir Nabokov: A Tribute.* New York: William Morrow, 1980. A collection of reflections upon Nabokov's literary legacy by major literary critics.

Wood, Michael. *The Magician's Doubts: Nabokov and the Risks of Fiction.* Princeton, N.J.: Princeton University Press, 1994. Examines Nabokov's work in the context of the striving for artistic excellence.

Adam Bede

Author: George Eliot (1819-1880)
First published: 1859
Type of work: Novel
Type of plot: Domestic realism and bildungsroman
Time of plot: 1799
Locale: England

Principal characters:
ADAM BEDE, a carpenter
SETH BEDE, his brother
MARTIN POYSER, the proprietor of Hall Farm
MRS. POYSER, his wife
DINAH MORRIS, her niece and a Methodist preacher
HETTY SORREL, another niece
ARTHUR DONNITHORNE, a young squire

The Story:

In the village of Hayslope at the close of the eighteenth century, there lives a young carpenter named Adam Bede. Tall and muscular, Adam is respected by everyone as a good worker and an honest and upright man. Even the young squire, Captain Arthur Donnithorne, knows Adam and likes him, and Adam in turn regards the squire as his best friend.

Adam is, in fact, so good a worker that his employer, Jonathan Burge, the builder, would welcome him as his son-in-law and partner. Adam, however, has no eyes for Mary Burge; his only thoughts are of distractingly pretty Hetty Sorrel, niece of Mrs. Poyser, whose husband, Martin, runs Hall Farm. Hetty, however, cares nothing for Adam. She is interested only in Donnithorne, whom she met one day at her aunt's dairy.

No one in Hayslope thinks Hetty would make a good wife for Adam, least of all Adam's mother, Lisbeth, who will disapprove of any girl who threatens to take her favorite son away from her. Her feelings of dependence upon Adam are intensified after her husband, Matthias Bede, drowns in Willow Brook while on his way home from the village inn.

Adam's brother, Seth, has fallen in love with the young Methodist preacher, Dinah Morris. Dinah is another niece of Mrs. Poyser, as unlike her cousin Hetty as Adam is unlike Seth. Hetty is as soft and helpless as a kitten, but Dinah is firm and serious in all things. One evening, while Dinah and Seth are walking home together from the village green, he proposes marriage. Dinah sadly declines, saying she has dedicated her life to preaching the gospel.

When funeral services for Matthias Bede are held in Hayslope Church on the following Sunday, the thoughts of the congregation are on many events other than the solemn occasion they are attending. Adam's thoughts of Hetty blend with memories of his father. Hetty's thoughts are all of Donnithorne, who has promised to make his appearance. She is disappointed, however, for Donnithorne has already departed with his regiment.

When Donnithorne returns on leave, the young squire celebrates his twenty-first birthday with a great feast to which nearly all of Hayslope is invited. Adam is singled out as a special guest to sit at Donnithorne's table, which makes Adam's mother both proud and jealous, since her son seems to be getting more and more out of her reach.

One August night, three weeks after the Donnithorne party, Adam is returning home from his work on the Donnithorne estate when he sees Donnithorne and Hetty in close embrace. When Adam's dog barks, Hetty hurries away. Donnithorne, embarrassed, tries to explain that he had met the girl by chance and had stolen a kiss. Adam calls his friend a scoundrel and a coward. They come to blows, and Donnithorne is knocked senseless. Adam, frightened that he might have killed the young squire, revives him and helps him to a nearby summerhouse. There he demands that Donnithorne write a letter to Hetty telling her that he will not see her again.

The next day, Donnithorne sends the letter to Hetty in Adam's care, thus placing the responsibility for its possible effect on Adam himself. Adam gives Hetty the letter while they are walking the following Sunday. When she reads the letter in the privacy of her bedchamber, Hetty is in despair. Her dreams shattered, she thinks only of finding some way out of her misery.

In November, Adam is offered a partnership in Mr. Burge's business, and he proposes to Hetty. Mr. and Mrs. Poyser are delighted to find that their niece is to marry the man they so much admire. The wedding has to be delayed, however, until two new rooms can be added to the Bede house. In February, Hetty tells her aunt that she is going to visit Dinah at Snowfield. Though at this point she is engaged to Adam, Hetty is frantic at the knowledge that she is pregnant with Donnithorne's child and runs from everything she knows as she struggles to deal with the consequences of her affair with the squire. As a result, she is determined to find Donnithorne.

When Hetty arrives at Windsor, where Donnithorne is supposed to be stationed, she finds that his regiment has been transferred to Ireland. In complete despair, Hetty roams about, ending up in a strange village in the house of a widow named Sarah Stone, where her child by Donnithorne is born. Confused and frightened, Hetty wanders on, leaving her baby to die in the woods. Later, tortured by her conscience, she returns to find the child gone.

When his grandfather dies, Donnithorne returns to Hayslope to discover that Hetty is in prison, charged with the murder of her child. He does everything in his power to free her. Dinah arrives at her prison cell and prays with her to open up her heart and tell the truth. Finally, poor Hetty breaks down and confesses everything that has happened since she left Hayslope. She had not intended to kill her baby; in fact, she had not directly killed the child. She had, instead, considered taking her own life. Two days later, Donnithorne, filled with shame and remorse, brings a reprieve. Hetty's sentence is commuted to deportation. A few years later, she dies on her way home. Donnithorne suffers from a grave illness and almost dies.

Dinah stays with the Poysers more often after Hetty's exile. Gradually, she and Adam are drawn to each other, but Dinah's heart is still set on her preaching. She leaves Hall Farm and goes back to Snowfield. Adam finds his only satisfaction in toiling at his workbench.

One day, Adam's mother again mentions Dinah and her gentle ways, leading Adam to try to find her. Adam and Dinah eventually marry, have two children, and settle with their children and a doting Uncle Seth.

Critical Evaluation:

One of the major issues in George Eliot's novel *Adam Bede* is a binary opposition in characterization: Adam Bede versus Arthur Donnithorne and Hetty Sorrel versus Dinah Morris. In contrast to Adam's hardworking, staunch personality, Arthur comes from money and, though he does hold a military position, does not have to work. Dinah is similar to Adam in her zest for her cause, preaching, but Hetty's cause is her beauty, about which she obsesses.

From the beginning of the novel, Adam is presented as a hardworking, ethical man who encourages others to behave in similar ways. For example, when the workday draws to an end, Adam's coworkers stop work and begin to collect their belongings before the final toll of the clock. Adam alone continues to work, chastising his mates for their lack of work ethic. His responsibility extends to his family relationships. Though he teases Seth for neglecting to complete his work, he also provides a lesson in proper labor. He continues to mentor Seth by commenting on Seth's interest in Dinah's preaching and its relevance to religious beliefs that Seth had been exposed to prior to her arrival.

Adam's familial responsibility stretches further as his father dies, and he is left with his mother's care. Despite his mother's clinging possessiveness and open dislike of the woman he believes himself in love with, Adam prepares to provide for her needs. His love for Hetty allows for another instance of his constancy. When Adam spies Arthur kissing Hetty and later finds evidence that the kiss has been the least of their relations, he forces Arthur to do the right thing and let Hetty know that there will never be a chance for their relationship to be legally consummated. Later, when Adam is informed of Hetty's imprisonment, he refuses to believe that she could be so wicked and vows to go after Arthur for his part in Hetty's downfall.

When Adam goes to the jail where Hetty is being held, he is horrified by the story presented to him and refuses, even when irrefutable evidence is presented to him, to believe that Hetty would be so selfish and evil. Adam's purity of heart is yet again displayed when he and Hetty talk for the last time and she asks his forgiveness, which he willingly gives. He is continually more concerned about her loss than his own. He is also able to forgive Arthur, and in doing so regrets what he perceives as his own previous shortcomings.

While Adam truly cares for Hetty and wants to marry her, even after she has been involved with another man, Arthur uses her and is willing to let her go to Adam. The only truly selfless action Arthur takes is to get Hetty's sentence changed to exile rather than execution. He feels sorry for the damage he has done to others only after that damage has been done; prior to Hetty's imprisonment, he had never stopped to think about the consequences of his actions. The novel ends with a final opposition: Adam marries Dinah and lives happily, while Arthur remains single and contracts an illness that almost kills him.

Dinah and Hetty present another binary opposition. Dinah's preaching is done out of pure motives. She is interested in the well-being of others, even to the point that she travels to minister to Hetty in jail. She stands next to Hetty when the punishment is handed down. She agrees to marry Adam only when she is sure that the relationship is the best choice. The differences between Hetty and Dinah are as clear as the ones between Adam and Arthur. While Dinah refuses to join into a relationship without clear thought and meditation, Hetty jumps into a relationship with Arthur and then with Adam when Arthur rejects her. In contrast to Dinah's self-sacrifices, Hetty regrets the abandonment of her infant only because of the repercussions on herself. The end of the novel brings a last opposition to the women, as it does the men: Dinah marries Adam and becomes the angel of the house. Hetty dies on her way home from exile, and she becomes no more than a footnote.

The binary contrasts between the four main characters in the novel reinforce several of the major themes. For example, the novel presents an opposition in the theme of marriage and motherhood. Adam's mother, Lisbeth Bede, is selfish and greedy for her son's attention. She is jealous of others who might draw his interest away from her. Her own marriage is so weak that she relies more on her son than on her husband. Hetty, though she accepts Adam's proposal, is never meant to be a wife. She is too self-centered. She agrees to marry Adam, but only because she needs a husband to cover for her pregnancy. Hetty also is an unfit mother, abandoning her newborn child and admitting to a total lack of feeling for her child. She returns to the forest where she left the child because she wants to alleviate her own guilt rather than to care for the child.

Dinah, on the other hand, becomes the consummate wife and mother. She is even gentle enough that Lisbeth encourages Adam's relationship with her. In motherhood, Dinah not only gives up her call to preach but also agrees with new Methodist tenets that deny women the right to share the message in a public venue.

A variety of additional themes reflect contrasts. Adam's industrious occupation in Mr. Burge's woodworking operation brings the issue of a changing nation to light, while Dinah's devoted preaching opens questions about religious belief and change. Political issues also are raised, as the class system is challenged and the king's governmental leadership is questioned. In addition, much criticism of the novel is concerned with the pastoral and the way the novel reflects Eliot's own childhood memories.

Another aspect of the novel is the quest. Though the immediate assumption would be to follow Adam's journey, Hetty's quest is more interesting. The novel traces the psychological journey of Hetty from the protected innocence of childhood dreams to the harsh realities of a woman's choices. From a quest standpoint, then, *Adam Bede* is the story of Hetty's coming of age. Her pregnancy forces the mental child Hetty, who is living in a daydream world, to face the repercussions of the real world and adult problems and actions.

The narrative point of view in the novel is a final critical point. The narrator readily admits that he sees things through a slightly warped mirror and that he shares his observations with his readers based on the abnormalities present in that vision. Thus, the characters are reflected in a limited way: Hetty's physical beauty becomes her most obvious characteristic, Adam's sometimes unbending expectations become the focus of his attention, Dinah's devotion to religion becomes her defining characteristic, and Arthur's irresponsibility becomes his central trait.

"Critical Evaluation" by Theresa L. Stowell

Further Reading

Barrett, Dorothea. *Vocation and Desire: George Eliot's Heroines*. New York: Routledge, 1989. Offers helpful insights concerning conflicts between women's desires for creative fulfillment and culturally defined gender limitations.

Brady, Kristin. *George Eliot*. New York: St. Martin's Press, 1992. Summarizes contemporary reactions to Eliot and explains the historical gender assumptions that Eliot both worked within and tried to reform.

Eliot, George. *Adam Bede*. Edited by Carol A. Martin. New York: Oxford University Press, 2001. This edition of the novel is valuable for several reasons: It is the first edition of the novel based on Eliot's final 1861 revision, and it includes Eliot's journal entry on the real-life origins of the story. The introduction discusses the novel's historical context. Includes comprehensive notes that describe literary and historical allusions in the novel.

Hardy, Barbara. *George Eliot: A Critic's Biography*. New York: Continuum, 2006. An examination of Eliot's life combined with an analysis of her work, which will prove useful to readers with some prior knowledge of her writings. Includes an outline of her works and the events in her life.

_______, ed. *Critical Essays on George Eliot*. New York: Barnes & Noble, 1970. This collection, edited by a pioneer in Eliot studies, helped inspire feminist analyses of Eliot's work. One of the essays is devoted to an analysis of *Adam Bede*.

Jedrsejewski, Jan. *George Eliot*. New York: Routledge, 2007. A comprehensive study of Eliot and her works. Provides a biographical overview as well as feminist, historical, postcolonial, and psychoanalytical criticism of Eliot's writings.

Karl, Fred. *George Eliot: Voice of a Century*. New York: Norton, 1995. A biography that draws on valuable new archival material and feminist criticism, depicting Eliot as an author whose work symbolizes "the ambiguities, the anguish, and divisiveness of the Victorian era."

Levine, George, ed. *The Cambridge Companion to George Eliot*. New York: Cambridge University Press, 2001. Collection of essays analyzing Eliot's work from various perspectives. Includes discussions of her early and late novels as well as studies of Eliot in relation to realism, philosophy, science, politics, religion, and gender.

Marshall, Joanna Barszewska. "Shades of Innocence and Sympathy: The Intricate Narrative Syntax of Gossip, Metaphor, and Intimacy in Eliot's Treatment of Hetty Sorrel." In *Dorothea's Window: The Individual and Community in George Eliot*, edited by Patricia Gately, Dennis Leavens, and Cole Woodcox. Kirksville, Mo.: Thomas Jefferson Press, 1994. Analyzing Eliot's narrative art, this article supports the argument that her treatment of Hetty is more sympathetic than many critics have recognized.

Rignall, John, ed. *Oxford Reader's Companion to George Eliot*. New York: Oxford University Press, 2000. An encyclopedic volume on Eliot that includes information on her pets, her homes, and her literary themes, and that examines the various contexts in which to place her works.

Uglow, Jennifer. *George Eliot*. New York: Pantheon Books, 1987. This critical biography examines in detail the relationship between Eliot's life and her art, offering thoughtful analyses of her fiction within the context of Victorian feminism.

The Admirable Crichton

Author: Sir James Barrie (1860-1937)
First produced: 1902; first published, 1914
Type of work: Drama
Type of plot: Satire
Time of plot: Early twentieth century
Locale: Mayfair, England; a desert island

Principal characters:
THE EARL OF LOAM
LADY MARY,
LADY CATHERINE, and
LADY AGATHA, his daughters
THE HON. ERNEST WOOLLEY, his nephew
WILLIAM CRICHTON, his butler

The Story:

Once every month, the philanthropic Earl of Loam gives expression to his views on human equality by forcing his servants to have tea with him and his family in the great hall of Loam House in Mayfair. It is a disagreeable experience for everyone concerned, especially for his butler, Crichton, who does not share his master's liberal views. Lord Loam alone enjoys the occasion, for he is the only one who remains in his station. He orders his daughters and his nephew about and treats them exactly as he treats his servants on the other days of the month.

Lady Mary, his oldest daughter, is a spirited young woman who resents her father's high-handed methods with his family. Her indignation reaches a climax one day when Lord Loam announces that his three daughters are to have but one maid among them on a yachting trip on which the family is about to embark. Lady Mary is furious, but she assumes that her maid, Fisher, will go along. When Fisher learns that she is expected to look after the two younger sisters in addition to Lady Mary, she promptly resigns, and the two maids attending Catherine and Agatha follow suit. Lord Loam is left without any servants for his projected cruise, for his valet also resigns. Although his pride is hurt deeply, Crichton finally agrees, out of loyalty to his master, to act as his valet on the trip. Moreover, he persuades Tweeny, the housemaid upon whom he casts a favorable eye, to go along as maid to Lord Loam's daughters.

The cruise ends unhappily when the yacht is pounded to pieces during a violent storm in the Pacific, and the party is cast away on a tropical island. All reach shore except Lord Loam. The survivors watched him throw away his best chance at safety in a frantic but vain attempt to get into the lifeboat first.

On the island all try to preserve as much as possible the class distinction that prevailed in England, but the attempt is unsuccessful. Crichton alone knows exactly what he is doing, and it is upon him that the others must depend. Crichton, the servant, becomes on the island the natural leader, and he rules his former superiors with a gentle but a firm hand. For example, he finds the epigrams of the Hon. Ernest Woolley, which seemed so brilliant in England, a bit trying; as a consequence, Crichton adopts the policy of submitting Ernest to a severe ducking whenever he comes forth with an epigram. The aristocrats worry over the rising authority of their former butler and the decline in their own prestige. When

Lord Loam appears, after washing ashore with some wreckage, they urge him to take a stand of authority. Lord Loam's only recourse is to remove his little party to another section of the island apart from Crichton. Hunger, which the aristocrats by their own efforts cannot assuage, brings them meekly back. Crichton becomes the acknowledged leader of them all.

Crichton takes full advantage of his newly acquired authority. Sharing none of the earl's ideas about equality, he finds no necessity to pretend that on the island his former betters are his equals in any sense. Each is kept in his place and required to do his own work according to the needs of the camp.

Under Crichton's rule the aristocrats are happy for perhaps the first time in their lives. The hard physical labor makes something approaching a man out of Ernest, and the task of helping to prepare Crichton's food and waiting on him at the table turns Lord Loam's snobbish daughters into attractive and useful women. Lord Loam, dressed in animal skins, is merely a harmless and rather genial old man with no particular talents, whom everyone calls Daddy. The greatest change occurs in Lady Mary. She alone realizes that in any environment Crichton is superior to them all, and that only the conventions of so-called civilized society obscure that fact. Consequently she falls in love with the butler and does everything in her power to make herself his favorite. Crichton, attracted to the beautiful Lady Mary, considers making her his consort on the island. He indulges in the fancy that in some past existence he was a king and she a Christian slave. When a rescuing ship appears on the horizon, Crichton realizes that his dreams are romantic nonsense. On their return to England he again will be a butler, and she will be Lady Mary.

It is as Crichton expects. After the rescue Lord Loam and his family return to their old habits of thought and behavior. Crichton is again the butler. Ernest writes a book about their experiences on the island and makes himself the hero of their exploits. Crichton is barely mentioned. Lady Mary reluctantly renews her engagement to the rather ridiculous Lord Brocklehurst, whose mother is greatly worried over what happened on the island and not sure that a daughter of Lord Loam is a fit wife for her son.

Lady Mary still recognizes Crichton's superiority and tells him so frankly. Crichton is shocked. Her views may have been acceptable on the island, he says, but not in England. When she expresses the radical view that something might be wrong with England, Crichton tells her that not even from her will he listen to a word of criticism against England or English ways.

Critical Evaluation:

One of the best of Sir James Barrie's comedies, *The Admirable Crichton* contains a more definite theme than Barrie generally put into his plays. His satirical portrait of an English aristocrat with liberal ideas is among the most skillfully executed of this character type. Lord Loam, like many liberals, is a kind of social Jekyll and Hyde, accepting the doctrine of the rights of humanity in theory but holding tightly to his privileges in practice.

The immediate inspiration for *The Admirable Crichton*, as for its successor *Peter Pan* (pr. 1904), was Barrie's relationship with the four sons of Arthur Llewellyn Davies, whom Barrie "adopted" as almost his own. *Peter Pan* was based in the stories Barrie made up for the boys, and *The Admirable Crichton* was based in the make-believe games he played with them, in which fantasies of being cast away on a deserted island played a major part. The games were fueled by his memories of Daniel Defoe's *Robinson Crusoe* (1719) and of such boys' books derived from Defoe's work as Johann Rudolf Wyss's *Der schweizerische Robinson* (1812-1827; *The Swiss Family Robinson*, 1814, 1818, 1820) and R. M. Ballantyne's *Coral Island* (1858). In all these tales the resourcefulness of the heroes invariably allows them to establish a comfortable lifestyle, thereby demonstrating the superior nature of British civilization. The skeptical Barrie probably used the make-believe games to teach the four boys that lighting fires and building huts are not quite as easy as such stories make out—a lesson that Lord Loam learns the hard way.

The title of the play is as ironic as its contents. The reputation—what kind of reputation is a matter of interpretation—of the original Admirable Crichton, a sixteenth century Scots adventurer who died in a brawl at the age of twenty-two, is immortalized in Thomas Urquhart's *Ekskubalauron* (1652), for example. The play's contrasting of the English aristocracy and its servant class is rooted in Barrie's awareness of the difference in outlook between the wealthy but airy-fairy English and the poor but hardheaded Scots. As a Scotsman from a poor background, Barrie was acutely aware of the delusions of the well-off Londoners among whom he had come to live, and the temptation to subject their affectations to the hypothetical test of castaway life proved irresistible. The silliness that moves along the plot is not as casually satirical as it seems; a depth of bitter feeling in it becomes increasingly apparent as the play progresses.

The blue-blooded Lord Loam poses as a believer in the equality of men, although he sets aside only one day a month for the elevation of his servants' status. Crichton, on the other hand, makes an obsession out of knowing his place and insisting that one's rank reflects one's worth. How ironic this insistence is depends on how the part is played—Barrie's notes to the cast are relentlessly sarcastic—but Crichton's keen awareness that worth depends on context indicates that he harbors carefully concealed resentments.

While it is society that determines his worth, Crichton is a dutiful servant, but when the castaways are cut off from society, his true self emerges. When Lady Mary asks him who made up the rule that those who do not work do not eat, he explains that he "seems to see it growing all over the island." Unlike the rules governing London society, it is no arbitrary invention: It is the way things are. This ability to see things as they are and to apply his common sense to them—which fits Crichton for the leader's role on the island—is exactly the same ability that fits him to be a butler in Mayfair. On the island this ability receives the approval of nature. His common sense sends him straight back to his former station when the party returns to Mayfair, but he is determined that it will be a temporary measure. Having lived for a while as his true self, he can no longer be content with a lie.

A last inversion in the plot is Lady Brocklehurst's interrogation of Crichton, who contrives to answer all her questions truthfully while giving a completely false picture of what actually transpired on the island. The result of this deception is that Lady Mary's promise to marry Crichton does not compromise her engagement to the young Lord Brocklehurst. Afterward, Lady Mary asks Crichton whether he despises her for allowing it to remain uncompromised. This question makes a very subtle point. Instead of having Crichton reply to Lady Mary's question, Barrie inserts a gratuitous (and inaccurate) note that "the man who could never tell a lie makes no answer." Shortly thereafter, Lady Mary asks Crichton to tell her that he did not lose his courage; the man who can and did tell several lies calls down the curtain with an assertion that he did not. The author carefully leaves it to the audience members to make up their mind what he means by that remark. He clearly cannot mean that he intends to resume his interrupted courtship of Lady Mary—he just exerted himself to ensure that she can marry Lord Brocklehurst—but perhaps he means that he considers that his obligations to the family are now finally and fully discharged.

Crichton, as an honorable and admirable man, cannot refuse to fire the beacons that enabled his companions to be restored to their place in society, but now that he sees Lady Mary's marriage prospects safely restored, everything is back in its "proper" place—except for him. Whatever his proper place may be, he must leave in order to find it. The audience is likely to wish Crichton good luck—but one does have to bear in mind the fate of the man after whom Crichton is named.

"Critical Evaluation" by Brian Stableford

Further Reading

Birkin, Andrew. *J. M. Barrie and the Lost Boys: The Love Story That Gave Birth to Peter Pan*. New York: Clarkson N. Potter, 1979. Collective biography of Barrie and the Davies family, told primarily through documentary evidence. Discusses the way in which Barrie, playing castaways with the Llewellyn Davies boys, was inspired to write *The Admirable Crichton*.

Blake, George. *Barrie and the Kailyard School*. London: Barker, 1951. Places Barrie's work in its social and literary context.

Chaney, Lisa. *Hide-and-Seek with Angels: A Life of J. M. Barrie*. New York: St. Martin's Press, 2006. Chaney's biography focuses on Barrie's inner life from his childhood in Scotland to his international success, providing details about his work, marriage, and relation with the Davies family, among other subjects. Chapter 13, "A Second Chance," contains information about *The Admirable Crichton*.

Darlington, W. A. *J. M. Barrie*. London: Blackie, 1938. An appreciation of Barrie's work by a noted drama critic.

Dudgeon, Piers. *Captivated: J. M. Barrie, the du Mauriers, and the Dark Side of Neverland*. London: Chatto & Windus, 2008. Recounts how Barrie developed an intense interest in writer George du Maurier and his family, eventually becoming "Uncle Jim" to du Maurier's eight grandchildren. Dudgeon maintains that four of those children were the model for the "lost boys" in *Peter Pan*.

Roy, James A. *James Matthew Barrie: An Appreciation*. London: Jarrolds, 1937. A useful commentary on Barrie's works.

Walbrook, H. M. *J. M. Barrie and the Theatre*. London: F. V. White, 1922. The first detailed survey of Barrie's dramatic work.

Adolphe
A Story Found Among the Papers of an Unknown Writer

Author: Benjamin Constant (1767-1830)
First published: Adolphe: Anecdote trouvée dans les papiers d'un inconnu, 1816 (English translation, 1816)
Type of work: Novel
Type of plot: Psychological realism
Time of plot: Late eighteenth and early nineteenth centuries
Locale: Germany and Poland

Principal characters:
ADOLPHE, the narrator
ELLÉNORE, his lover
COUNT DE P——, Ellénore's earlier lover

The Story:

Having creditably completed his studies in Göttingen in spite of a somewhat dissipated life, Adolphe is expected, after a preliminary period of travel, to take his place in the governmental department of which his father, the minister of a German electorate, is the head. His father has great hopes for his son and is inclined to be lenient about his indiscretions, but because of an inherent timidity shared by father and son—a timidity combined, on the part of the father, with a defensive outward coldness—no real sympathy is possible between the two.

The constraint generated by this relationship has a considerable effect on Adolphe's character, as does a period he spends as the protégé of a much older woman whose strong and unconventional opinions make an indelible impression on him. This period, spent in long, passionately analytical conversations, ends with the woman's death.

Upon leaving the university, Adolphe goes to the court of the small German principality of D——. At first, he is welcomed, but he gradually attracts resentment for his mannered frivolity, alternating with scathing frankness, which stem from his profound indifference to the society of the court. The woman who formed his mind bequeathed to him an ardent dislike of mediocrity and all of its expressions, and he finds it difficult to reconcile himself with the artificiality of society and the necessity for arbitrary convention. Moreover, his only interest at that time is to indulge in passionate feelings that lead to contempt for the ordinary world.

One thing that does impress Adolphe is to see the joy of a friend at winning the love of one of the less mediocre women of the court. His friend's reaction develops in Adolphe not only the regrets connected with piqued vanity but also other, more confused, emotions related to newly discovered aspects of his desire to be loved. He can discover in himself no marked tastes, but soon after making the acquaintance of the Count de P——, Adolphe determines to attempt to establish a liaison with the woman who has shared the count's life for ten years and whose two illegitimate children the count has acknowledged.

Ellénore is a spirited woman from a good Polish family that has been ruined by political troubles. Her history is one of untiring devotion to the count and of constant conflict between her respectable sentiments and her position in society—a position that has gradually become sanctioned, however, through the influence of her lover.

Adolphe does not consider himself to be in love but to be fulfilling an obligation to his self-esteem; yet, he finds his thoughts increasingly occupied with Ellénore as well as his project. Unable to make a verbal declaration, he finally writes to her. His inner agitation and the conviction he sought to express rebound, however, and his imagination becomes wholly entangled when Ellénore refuses to receive him. That convinces him of his love, and he finally succeeds in overcoming her resistance to his suit.

When the count is called away on urgent business, Adolphe and Ellénore bask for a few weeks in the charm of love and mutual gratification. Almost immediately, however, Adolphe begins to be annoyed at the new constraint imposed on his life by this attachment, rewarding though he finds it. The idea that it cannot last calms his fears, and he writes to his father upon Ellénore's urging, asking permission to postpone his return for six months. When his father consents, Adolphe is immediately confronted again by all the drawbacks involved in his remaining at D——. He is irritated at the prospect of prolonging the deceptions required by his affair, of continuing the profitless life he leads under Ellénore's exciting domination, and, above all, of making her suffer by compromising her position. For upon his return, the count has become suspicious.

Adolphe's resentment leads to a quarrel with Ellénore, in which are made the first irreparable statements that, once spoken, cannot be recalled. The quarrel and the forced intimacy that follow it only increase Ellénore's anxiety and ardor, and she decides to break with the Count de P—— when he orders her not to see Adolphe. Adolphe cannot summon the courage to reject her sacrifice, although it causes him great anguish and destroys in a moment the social respect that Ellénore has acquired after years of effort. His sense of duty increases as his love weakens; he is willing to fight a duel at the slightest disparaging remark about her, yet he himself wrongs her in inconsequential social conversation. When the time comes for him to leave, he promises to return, fearing her violent grief. Moreover, he discovers that the arrival of the break he has longed for fills him with keen regret, almost with terror.

Adolphe writes regular letters to her, each beginning with the intention of indicating his coldness but always ending with words calculated to restore her confidence in his passion. At the same time, he relishes his regained independence. When Ellénore understands from Adolphe's letters that it will be difficult for him to leave his father, she decides to join him. He writes to advise her to postpone her coming, but she becomes indignant and hastens her arrival. Adolphe resolves to meet her with a show of joy that conceals his real feelings, but she senses the deception immediately and reproaches him, putting his weakness in such a miserable light that he becomes enraged. In a violent scene, the two turn on each other.

When Adolphe returns to his father's house, he learns that his father has been informed of Ellénore's arrival and has taken steps to force her to leave the town. His father's concern with Adolphe's future is undoubtedly genuine, but it unfortunately takes the form of adherence to the standard values of a corrupt society and can only have the effect of strengthening the bond between the lovers. Adolphe makes hurried arrangements and carries Ellénore off precipitately, smothering her with passion. Always astute, she detects contradictions in his actions and tells him that he has been moved by pity rather than by love—thereby revealing something he would have preferred not to know and giving him a new preoccupation to conceal.

When the two reach the frontier, Adolphe writes to his father with some bitterness, holding him responsible for the course he has been forced to take. His father's reply is notable for its generosity; he repeats everything Adolphe has said and ends by saying that although Adolphe is wasting his life, he will be allowed complete freedom. In the absence of the necessity to defend Ellénore, Adolphe's impatience with the tie becomes even more pronounced. They settle for a time in Bohemia, where Adolphe, having accepted the responsibility for Ellénore's fate, makes every effort to restrain himself from causing her suffering. He assumes an artificial gaiety, and with the passing of time he once again comes intermittently to feel some of his feigned sentiment. When alone, however, his old unrest grips him, and he makes vague plans to flee from his attachment.

At this point, Adolphe learns of a fresh sacrifice that Ellénore has made, the refusal of an offer from the Count de P—— to settle her again in suitable circumstances. Adolphe, grasping at this opportunity, tells her that he no longer loves her; at the sight of her violent grief, however, he pretends that his attitude has been a ruse. Another possibility of escape occurs after Ellénore's father is reinstated in his property in Poland: She is notified that he has died and that she is the sole heir. Because the will is being contested, Ellénore persuades Adolphe to accompany her to Poland. Their relationship continues to deteriorate.

Adolphe's father writes, pointing out that since Adolphe can no longer be considered Ellénore's protector, there is no longer any excuse for the life he is leading. The father has recommended Adolphe to his friend Baron T—— (the minister from their country to Poland) and suggests that Adolphe call on him. When the young man does, Baron T—— assumes the father's role and attempts to separate the lovers. Adolphe spends a night wandering in the country, engaged in confused meditations in which he tells himself that his mind is recovering from a long degradation.

Ellénore makes another futile effort to penetrate the closed sanctuary of his mind, but a new alignment of forces emerges as Adolphe succumbs more and more to the influence of Baron T——. He continues to procrastinate about ending the relationship. When the baron forwards some of Adolphe's incriminating letters to Ellénore, she becomes fatally ill. Adolphe is finally freed by her death, which produces in him a feeling of great desolation.

Critical Evaluation:

In *Adolphe*, Benjamin Constant develops three major themes: the role of society in creating the mores and morals by which a particular society lives and the power of that society in enforcing its code of morality, especially in regard to women; the force of passion; and a man's quest for self-discovery. The first two themes connect the novel to eighteenth century fiction while the third theme anticipates the twentieth century novel, in which self-discovery intensifies into self-realization with the antihero. Constant's novel provides an essential link between the eighteenth century novel that portrays the individual as a member of society and twentieth century fiction that focuses on the individual as a unique creature yet representative of all human beings.

The society of Constant's novel is that of the haute bourgeoisie and nobility of the eighteenth and early nineteenth centuries. It is a patriarchal society, governed by men and affording them the opportunity to achieve power, fame, and importance. Adolphe has shown considerable prominence as a student, and his father believes that he will enjoy success in his life. Achieving this success is to be the focal point of Adolphe's life.

Women in this society serve two purposes: As proper wives they produce children, and those unsuitable as wives exist for the amusement of men. Throughout the novel, Adolphe is aware of this moral code. He seduces Ellénore out of vanity and the desire to prove that he can seduce her. He never considers marrying her, for Ellénore is unacceptable as a wife. The ruin of her family in Poland, her ten-year liaison with the Count de P——, and her two illegitimate children negate any consideration of marriage. Likewise, the Count de P—— has never considered marrying Ellénore.

Through the character of Ellénore, Constant portrays the common conception of a woman's life during the period: that a woman's life is totally on an emotional level, that love to her is synonymous with life. Once she has fallen in love with Adolphe, Ellénore is obsessed with him. She sacrifices everything for him. She destroys her acceptance, though it is a reluctant acceptance, in society as the Count de P——'s mistress, abandons her children, and eventually destroys herself. Her passion for Adolphe is so strong that she cannot live without him; her grief at his rejection of her leads to her illness and eventual death. The motif of an impossible or unwanted love relationship being solved by the woman's death is common in the eighteenth century novel. For example, it appears in Abbé Prévost's *Histoire du chevalier des Grieux et de Manon Lescaut* (1731, 1733, 1753; *Manon Lescaut*, 1734, 1786) and in Jean-Jacques Rousseau's *Julie: Ou, La Nouvelle Héloïse* (1761; *Eloise: Or, A Series of Original Letters*, 1761; better known as *The New Héloïse*). Although the century prided itself on its rationalism, it could not totally reject the power of emotion and of passion, in particular, to control the individual.

This theme of an overwhelming, life-controlling passion is the operating force of *Adolphe*. Ellénore refuses to let Adolphe leave her; she pursues him. Adolphe keeps returning to her. Even though Ellénore inhibits his freedom and his possibility of being successful in society, he cannot leave her. Adolphe wants both to be loved by her and to be free from her. He cannot escape his passion. He attempts to explain his inability to renounce her and walk away as his pity, which is elicited by her suffering and grief. He repeatedly plans to break with her; he assures his father and Baron T—— that the liaison is over. He lies to them and to himself. When she dies, he realizes that he is alone, not loved by any woman. Adolphe leads a disillusioned, pointless life after destroying the woman he has loved. He is a victim of his own passion.

However, Constant goes beyond a mere depiction of fatal passion in his novel. As Adolphe struggles with his vacillation, finds excuses for himself, and analyzes his acts and his emotional reactions, he foreshadows the antiheroes of the twentieth century novel. With his character of Adolphe, Constant focuses on the individual and on personal self-realization. Adolphe becomes painfully cognizant of his ability to harm others, of how any interaction with others contains within it the potential to harm. He is also intensely aware of himself, of his vanity, of his needs. In his attempt to become who he is, to achieve self-realization, Adolphe is the predecessor of Michel in André Gide's *L'Immoraliste* (1902; *The Immoralist*, 1930) and of the existential characters of twentieth century writers such as Albert Camus and Jean-Paul Sartre.

To avoid criticism of the novel as a fictional fantasy, Constant creates an account of how he came to possess the novel's "manuscript" and how it came to be published. With the inclusion of a preface, a letter to the editor, and a response to the letter in the novel's introduction—and with further explanation about why the editor had decided to publish the novel—Constant presents evidence of the tale's veracity.

The manuscript, he writes, was found among the belongings left behind by an unidentified man whom Constant had met at an inn. The manuscript had been discovered in a case found by someone on a local road, which both Constant and the man had traveled. The manuscript was then given to the innkeeper. The innkeeper had Constant's permanent address, but not that of the other man, so he sent the items to Constant. Later, Constant met a man who insisted upon reading the manuscript; upon returning it, the man stated that he knew many of the people mentioned in the manuscript. Constant decided to publish the manuscript as a true account of the misery suffered by the human heart. The first-person narration adds authenticity and substantiates the intimate facts revealed about Adolphe.

Constant uses the motif of movement, as he describes the arrival of letters and the movement of people from one place to another, to give structure to his novel; he also uses this motif to move the action along. Letters reveal information with important consequences for the characters. Moving entails separation and reunion for Adolphe and Ellénore. The motif also reinforces Adolphe's emotional vacillation.

From the time of its first publication, readers and critics of *Adolphe* have viewed the work as an autobiographical novel, a depiction of Constant's life in a fictional form. There are definitely biographical elements in the novel; however, *Adolphe* is more than a fictionalization of a life, it is a detailed look at society and the individual, at passion and its effects, and at the individual as a potentially harmful self-creating being.

"Critical Evaluation" by Shawncey Webb

Further Reading

Coleman, Patrick. *Reparative Realism: Mourning and Modernity in the French Novel, 1730-1830.* Geneva: Librairie Droz, 1998. Examines the feeling of melancholy in *Adolphe* and other pre-Romantic French novels. Coleman maintains that the ideas of the Enlightenment enabled writers to have greater freedom, but also created a sense of anxiety and loss, which is expressed in the works of the time.

Cruickshank, John. *Benjamin Constant.* New York: Twayne, 1974. Still one of the best introductions in English to the wide range of Constant's literary, biographical, political, and religious works. Includes a good chronology and a selected, if dated, bibliography.

Fairlie, Alison. *Imagination and Language: Collected Essays on Constant, Baudelaire, Nerval, and Flaubert.* Edited by Malcolm Bowie. New York: Cambridge University Press, 1981. Approximately one-fourth of this volume consists of essays on *Adolphe*, which Fairlie calls "that most quietly disruptive of all French novels." Treats the book's style, structure, and characterization, as well as its reception by other French novelists, such as Honoré de Balzac.

Matlock, Jann. "Novels of Testimony and the 'Invention' of the Modern French Novel." In *The Cambridge Companion to the French Novel: From 1800 to the Present*, edited by Timothy Unwin. New York: Cambridge University Press, 1997. This essay includes a discussion of *Adolphe*, placing it within the historical context of the French novel between the early nineteenth and late twentieth centuries.

Nicolson, Harold. *Benjamin Constant.* Westport, Conn.: Greenwood Press, 1985. A sympathetic biography by a noted writer and diplomat. Places Constant clearly in the context of his tumultuous period. Based on secondary sources and not reflecting later scholarship.

Rosenblatt, Helen, ed. *The Cambridge Companion to Constant.* New York: Cambridge University Press, 2009. A collection of interpretive essays on the major aspects of Constant's life and work, including *Adolphe*. Provides a good overview for readers new to Constant.

Todorov, Tzvetan. *A Passion for Democracy: Benjamin Constant.* Translated by Alice Seberry. New York: Algora, 1999. A critical biography, in which Todorov describes Constant as the first analyst of democracy and argues that Constant's work deserves a better reception than it has traditionally received.

Winegarten, Renee. *Germaine de Staël and Benjamin Constant: A Dual Biography.* New Haven, Conn.: Yale University Press, 2008. A biography that focuses on Constant's seventeen-year relationship with writer Germaine de Staël. Includes discussion of *Adolphe* and Constant's other literary contributions.

Wood, Dennis. *Benjamin Constant: "Adolphe."* New York: Cambridge University Press, 1987. An essential, sharply focused study. Includes a useful chronology of Constant's life, chapters on *Adolphe*'s biographical and intellectual contexts, and a detailed analysis of the novel's first three chapters. Wood concludes by highlighting the novel's influence on future generations of writers.

Adonais
An Elegy on the Death of John Keats, Author of Endymion, Hyperion, etc.

Author: Percy Bysshe Shelley (1792-1822)
First published: 1821
Type of work: Poetry
Type of plot: Mythic
Time of plot: 1818-1821 and mythic time
Locale: England, Rome, and mythic space

Principal characters:
THE NARRATOR, the speaker of the poem
ADONAIS, a young poet and shepherd
URANIA, the Muse of great poetry
DEATH, a king
THE QUICK DREAMS AND THE LIKE, Adonais's living thoughts, presented as sheep in his flock
THE FRAIL FORM, a mourning poet and shepherd
THE NAMELESS WORM, the serpent that murders Adonais
THE FOND WRETCH, a mourner whom the narrator orders to Rome

The Poem:

The narrator proclaims grief for Adonais and calls upon the Muse Urania to wake and weep for her son, who died before fulfilling his great promise. In Rome, says the narrator, Adonais lies in his death chamber as if he were sleeping, with his flesh as yet uncorrupted. A shepherd-poet, Adonais is survived by his flock of dreams and other poetic thoughts, who mourn the one who fed them. Spring has come, but, as life returns throughout the natural world, sorrow also returns to those who know death. While worms eat corpses, flowers bloom atop the graves. The narrator questions the origin and purpose of humans, who recognize their individual mortality.

In stanza 22, Urania awakes. While she hastens to Adonais from her paradise, the hateful world wounds her feet, but her blood causes everlasting flowers to bloom. In the death chamber, Death vanishes momentarily when Urania arrives, and a glimmer of life returns to the corpse before, roused by Urania's suffering, Death rises to meet her embrace. Exclaiming that she would join Adonais were she not bound to Time, Urania asks why he left his ordinary ways prematurely to face vile animals, such as vultures, and states that, when the sun rises, insects that live just one day flourish, only to die when the sun sets and the eternal stars can be seen.

Starting in stanza 30, Adonais's fellow shepherds arrive from the mountains to mourn him. Most noticeable among them is a solitary figure, powerful in spirit but bleeding and weak in flesh. While that shepherd weeps, he recognizes his own destiny in Adonais's, and, when Urania asks who he is, he suddenly pulls back his hood to reveal his resemblance to Cain, the first vagabond, or to Christ.

Stanza 36 begins a denunciation of the anonymous, poetically deaf serpent that, according to the narrator, poisoned Adonais and will grow still older and die unlamented. Within the denunciation comes the narrator's effort to find joy amid the sorrow of the young poet's death. Adonais's spirit will return to the everlasting fountain of fire from which it came, unlike the serpent's spirit. Leaving invective behind with stanza 40, the narrator declares that Death has died, not Adonais, who has achieved unity with the impersonal Power that animates nature and who has ascended to join other poets who died before they could reach on Earth the greatness that should have been theirs. Adonais will become the guiding spirit of Venus and shine amid the stars.

In stanza 47, the narrator asks who grieves for Adonais and, with one person in mind, calls him foolishly unhappy and urges that he travel to Rome. There, he will find a graveyard beside the decaying city wall, where an ancient pyramidal tomb stands beside more recent graves, including one that holds intensely personal meaning for the unhappy man. The narrator asks why people fear to become like Adonais: Unity abides, unchanging, while multiplicity changes and passes away. When death shatters life's many-hued dome, eternity's white light becomes visible. Finally, the narrator asks himself why he remains in his hopeless life. The eternal light shines on him, the narrator says, removing mortal clouds, and a freshening wind fills his soul's sails and drives him far from the safety of land, while Adonais's soul, an eternal star, guides him through the frightening dark.

Critical Evaluation:

Adonais begins with an epigraph of Greek elegiac poetry attributed to Plato. The epigraph is followed by Percy Bysshe Shelley's preface to the poem proper, which quotes Greek lines from the "Lament for Bion," an ancient poem, possibly by Moschus, on the death of the second century B.C.E. poet who composed a "Lament for Adonis." Later, following a reference to John Keats's death in Rome early in 1821 and his burial there in the Protestant Cemetery, Shelley claims that Keats's pulmonary tuberculosis derived from the harsh, anonymous attack on Keats's long poem *Endymion: A Poetic Romance* (1818) in the *Quarterly Review*. Denouncing the reviewers, Shelley asks how they could favorably treat works by bad writers but act so hostile to *Endymion*, which, regardless of its flaws, deserved far better treatment. As Shelley nears the end of his preface, he again says, in effect, that critical animosity killed Keats. Upon concluding this direct, literal response to the poet's death, he launches into his elegy proper, which is set in mythic time and space.

Through the first two-thirds of its fifty-five stanzas, *Adonais* is a pastoral elegy, revealing the influence of the ancient Greek-speaking poets Bion and (presumably) Moschus, as well as that of Shelley's English predecessors Edmund Spenser, who wrote *Astrophel* (1595), and John Milton, who wrote "Lycidas" (1638). The pastoral tradition appears when Shelley invokes a Muse (one of a set of nine Greek goddesses), presents poets as shepherds, and depicts mourners in procession. Writing in an overtly artificial tradition, Shelley displays genuine emotion and daringly places himself in a line of illustrious forerunners.

The verse form of *Adonais*, the Spenserian stanza, mimics a form created by Spenser that comprises eight lines of iambic pentameter and a ninth line of iambic hexameter (an Alexandrine). Each of the first eight lines of a stanza is built with five metric feet, and each of those feet, with occasional exceptions, consists of a relatively unstressed syllable followed by a relatively stressed one. The ninth line of each stanza has an extra metric foot and thus tends to make a reader pay special attention. In conventional notation, with letters representing rhyming sounds, the tightly binding rhyme scheme of a Spenserian stanza is *ababbcbcc*.

Shelley and Keats had met and talked several times in England but had never become close friends. Keats wanted to keep a distance from Shelley, who was better known than Keats as a poet and came from a higher social class. While living in Italy, Shelley heard in July, 1820, that Keats was ill and invited him to come to Italy. Shelley's letter contained gentle criticism of *Endymion*, and Keats, in his grateful reply to the invitation, responded with polite criticism of Shelley's poetry. Eventually, Keats sailed to Italy, but he never reached Pisa, where Shelley was then living. Instead, Keats died in Rome on February 23, 1821, and was buried in the Protestant Cemetery, near the grave of Shelley's son William.

Shelley started writing *Adonais* soon after he learned on April 11 of Keats's death, and the first copies, from a Pisan printer, appeared on July 12. The copies that Shelley sent to his English publisher sold poorly, and the elegy received two disparaging reviews late in 1821. Most of the critical response since then, however, has been admiring, as was Shelley's own opinion of the work.

With a title conflating Adonis, Aphrodite's slain lover, with *Adonai*, a Hebrew word translated as "Lord," *Adonais* is as much about Shelley as about Keats. The anonymous evaluation of *Endymion* in the *Quarterly Review*, while unpleasant for Keats, did not kill him. Shelley wrongly thought that the older poet Robert Southey had written condemning reviews in the *Quarterly Review*, not only of *Endymion* but also of Shelley's own poetry. The review of *Endymion* was actually written by John Wilson Croker, and that on Shelley's poetry was the work of John Taylor Coleridge.

Feeling kinship with Keats as a victim of the poetic establishment and seemingly foreseeing his own early death, Shelley placed Southey in *Adonais* as the "nameless worm" and portrayed himself as the narrator, as the "frail Form" among the shepherds, and as the "Fond wretch" sent to Rome. An atheist, Shelley brought "Heaven's light" into stanza 52 in not a Christian but a Platonic sense, and immortality in *Adonais* may be no more than a poet's unconscious life through his poems. Whatever the case may be, Shelley's nautical ending of *Adonais*, which alludes to the destroying and preserving breath he celebrated in "Ode to the West Wind" (1820), has long impressed readers as a prophecy of his own drowning on July 8, 1822. His remains now lie near those of Keats.

Victor Lindsey

Further Reading

Bieri, James. *Percy Bysshe Shelley: A Biography*. 2 vols. Newark: University of Delaware Press, 2004-2005. Gives a detailed, psychologically probing account of Shelley and treats the most important of Shelley's relatives, friends, and enemies.

Johnson, Paul. *Intellectuals: From Marx and Tolstoy to Sartre and Chomsky*. 1988. Rev. ed. New York: HarperCollins, 2007. This now classic work portrays Shelley in chapter 2 as a great poet whose love for humanity often failed to lead to kindness toward individuals.

Keats, John. *Keats's Poetry and Prose: Authoritative Texts, Criticism*. Selected and edited by Jeffrey N. Cox. New York: Norton, 2009. Includes *Endymion*, Croker's review as well as several others, Shelley's letter inviting Keats to Italy, and Keats's letter in reply.

Knerr, Anthony D., ed. *Shelley's "Adonais": A Critical Edition*. New York: Columbia University Press, 1984. Presents the relationship between Shelley and Keats, facts about the composition and first printing of *Adonais*, the text of the poem with notes about textual variants in early editions, comments on numerous lines, and a survey of critics' evaluations of *Adonais* from the 1820's to the 1980's.

Shelley, Percy Bysshe. *Shelley's Poetry and Prose: Authoritative Texts, Criticism*. 2d ed. Selected and edited by Donald H. Reiman and Neil Fraistat. New York: Norton, 2002. Includes an editorial introduction to *Adonais*, Shelley's preface, the poem itself, many explanatory footnotes, commentary by Michael Scrivener, and a chronology of Shelley's life.

The Adventures of Augie March

Author: Saul Bellow (1915-2005)
First published: 1953
Type of work: Novel
Type of plot: Picaresque
Time of plot: 1920-1950
Locale: Primarily Chicago

Principal characters:
AUGIE MARCH, the narrator and protagonist
SIMON MARCH, Augie's older brother
CHARLOTTE MAGNUS, Simon's wife
GEORGIE MARCH, Augie's mentally challenged younger brother
WILLIAM EINHORN, Augie's friend and employer
MRS. RENLING, a woman who wants to adopt Augie
THEA FENCHEL, Augie's sometime mistress
STELLA CHESNEY, Augie's wife

The Story:

Born and reared in Chicago, Augie March never knows the identity of his father. Grandma Lausch, who is not related to Augie but boards with the Marches, dominates the household, teaching Augie manners and how to lie to people in authority. As a child, he gets involved in petty crime, stealing from a department store where he works as one of Santa Claus's helpers and participating in a robbery. At Grandma Lausch's insistence, Georgie, Augie's mentally challenged brother, is institutionalized. Grandma Lausch eventually goes to a home for the aged, and Augie's mother goes to a home for the blind.

For a while, Augie does odd jobs for a paraplegic named William Einhorn, whom Augie calls the "first superior man" he knows. Shortly after graduating from high school, Augie attends college at night and works in a downtown clothing store where his brother Simon works. Then he quits his job and school to work for Mr. and Mrs. Renling, selling articles associated with dude ranches to an aristocratic clientele in Evanston, Illinois. Augie learns to ride horses. On Mrs. Renling's summer vacation, Augie accompanies her to Benton Harbor. There, he falls in love with Esther Fenchel, and her sister, Thea, falls in love with him. Esther rejects Augie, and Augie rejects Thea, but Thea vows that she will see him again.

Returning to Evanston, Mrs. Renling decides to adopt Augie, so Augie leaves the Renlings and works at odd jobs in Chicago. He steals books and almost gets caught in an illegal scheme to bring immigrants out of Canada.

Meanwhile, Simon marries Charlotte Magnus, daughter of a wealthy family, and enters the coal business in which her family works, soon getting his own coal yard. Augie works for him. Simon becomes wealthy. Augie becomes engaged to Lucy Magnus, Charlotte's cousin. Helping Mimi Villars, his friend and neighbor, get an abortion, Augie is spotted by one of Lucy's relatives, who tells Lucy's family. Lucy's father forces her to break off her relationship with Augie. Simon fires Augie, saying he wants nothing more to do with him.

Augie works then as a union organizer and starts an affair with Sophie Geratis, a chambermaid in a hotel Augie is trying to organize. While Augie is in bed with Sophie, Thea knocks on his door. Augie leaves Sophie for Thea, whom he comes to believe he loves.

Thea wants Augie to help her train an eagle to hunt giant iguanas in Mexico. Thea provides the money. In Texarkana, they buy the eagle, which they name Caligula. Driving south, they train Caligula. When they reach Thea's house in Acatla, Mexico, they start training the bird with lizards. He does well with little ones, but when a medium-sized one bites him, the eagle becomes furious, killing the lizard but refusing to eat it. The first giant iguana Caligula attacks bites him, and Caligula flies from it. During the encounter, Augie's horse throws him and he fractures his skull. While Augie recovers, Thea sells Caligula and starts hunting snakes.

In Acatla, Augie meets Stella Chesney, who is with a man running from the U.S. Treasury Department. One day the man threatens Stella with a gun. She asks Augie to help her get away from him. Seeing Augie leaving town with Stella, Thea tries unsuccessfully to stop him. The car breaks down in the mountains, and Stella and Augie spend the night together. The next day, Augie lends Stella some money, and she goes to Mexico City. Augie returns to Thea, who breaks up with him.

While Augie is in Acatla, Leon Trotsky, Russian revolutionist and commissar of war who quarreled with Joseph Stalin, the Soviet dictator, comes to see the cathedral. Augie goes to Mexico City, where he gets involved in a plan to pretend he is Trotsky's nephew, so the Russian can travel incognito in Mexico and thus elude Stalin's secret police, who are trying to assassinate him. Trotsky, however, rejects the plan. Augie then returns to Chicago, where he and Simon become friends again. Augie works for a millionaire named Robey and goes to school to become a teacher. He dreams of running a school for foster children and having children of his own.

Then the United States enters World War II. When Augie tries to enlist, he discovers that he has an unhealed inguinal hernia from falling off the horse in Mexico, so he has an operation. He is rejected again by the Army and Navy, so he joins the Merchant Marine. He takes a training cruise on the Chesapeake Bay. On his first liberty, he visits Stella in New York. When he later graduates from Purser's and Pharmacist's Mate School, he and Stella get married. After a two-day honeymoon, Augie ships out on the *Sam McManus*, which is torpedoed. Augie spends many days on a lifeboat with another man from the ship, who wants to go to the Canary Islands, where he can be interned and do research for the rest of the war. He tries to keep Augie from signaling for help. Augie does signal, and they are picked up by a British ship that takes them to Naples.

After six months, Augie returns to New York. During the war he makes three more voyages. After the war ends, he and Stella live in Europe. Stella works in motion pictures. Augie makes large amounts of money doing illicit dealing with a man he meets through Stella. He learns some unpleasant things about Stella's past and discovers that she lies "more than average." He would, he writes, prefer to be in America having children, but Stella refuses to leave Europe. Augie travels around Europe on business and writes his memoirs.

"The Story" by Richard Tuerk

Critical Evaluation:

Saul Bellow's *The Adventures of Augie March* is a novel that must be understood at several levels. Each of these levels is completely meaningful in itself yet unmistakably intertwined with the others.

At the simplest level of reading, the novel is in the picaresque tradition, telling the adventures, often comic, of a rascal born out of wedlock to a charwoman, reared in the poverty of a down-at-the-heels Chicago neighborhood and early addicted to taking life as it comes. Augie March the adult, thus seen, is a ne'er-do-well hanger-on to people of wealth, a thief, and even a would-be smuggler. As a child of poverty, he learns from the adults in his life and from his experience that a ready lie told with a glib tongue and an air of innocence is often profitable. Growing older, he learns that many women are of easy virtue, holding the same loose reins on their personal morality as Augie does on himself. Easy love and easy money seem, at this level, to be Augie's goals in life. Although he may dream of becoming a teacher, take a few courses at the University of Chicago, and read widely in an informal way, Augie stays on the fringes of the postwar black market, where he finds the easy money he needs to live in what he regards as style.

When viewed at the literal level, *The Adventures of Augie March*, like Bellow's earlier fiction, is largely in the naturalistic tradition. In Bellow's choice of setting, in his pessimistic characters, in his use of a wealth of detail, and in the implicit determinism apparent in the careers of Augie, his relatives, and his friends, one notes similarities to the fiction of the giants of the naturalistic tradition in literature and a kinship with the novels of Nelson Algren and James T. Farrell. At times, Augie seems little more than a Jewish boy from Chicago's Northwest Side who is one part Farrell's Studs Lonigan and one part Farrell's Danny O'Neill from Chicago's South Side Irish neighborhood. With Farrell's characters, Augie shares an immigrant background, little or no sense of meaning in life, degrading poverty, and a grossly hedonistic view of life.

Unlike many naturalistic novelists, however, Bellow seeks meaning in facts; he is not confined to the principle that the novelist is simply an objective, dispassionate reporter of life among the lowly, the immoral, and the poverty-stricken as he finds it. He does not permit his character Augie to be merely a creature of his environment, molded by forces outside or within himself, over which he has no control. *The Adventures of Augie March* can be read at a deeper level than environmental determinism. Augie is capable of intellectual activity of a relatively high order, of knowing with what and for what he is struggling. Throughout his life, he learns that other people want to make him over. Grandma Lausch, an elderly Russian Jew of fallen fortunes who lives with the Marches, tries to form the boy, and he rebels. Later Mr. and Mrs. Renling, well-to-do shopkeepers in a fashionable Chicago suburb and Augie's employers, want to make him over, even adopt him, but he rebels. Augie's brother Simon, who achieves wealth and considerable respectability, tries to make a new man of Augie and finds Augie rebellious. Various women in Augie's life, including Thea Fenchel, Augie's mistress (whom he follows to Mexico to hunt iguanas with an eagle), try to recast Augie's character. They, too, fail, because, above all, Augie refuses to be molded into someone else's image of what he ought to be.

Refusing to be cast in any mold suggested by the people about him, Augie wants to become something—but he never seriously accepts any goal. He wants always to be independent in act and spirit, and he does achieve some sort of independence, empty though it is. He wants to be "someone," to fulfill his capabilities, but he never settles on the path to success. By refusing to commit himself to anything, he ends up accomplishing nothing. It is a sad fact of his existence that he comes to be a bit envious of his mentally challenged brother Georgie, who masters some of the elements of shoe repair. Bellow seems to be saying through the character of Augie that it is possible to have a fate without a function, but ironically Augie shows that without a function no one can have a worthwhile fate.

Another view of the novel is that it is social commentary. Most remarkable is the portrayal of the section of American society in which Augie moves. Augie is a Jew; that fact is literally beaten into him by neighborhood toughs, including those among the Gentiles he thinks are his friends, while he is a child. As he grows up, takes jobs, finds friends and confidants, seeks out women to love, Augie moves almost always in the company of Jews. The respectability toward which he is pushed is always that of the Jewish middle class, particularly that of the Jews who have lost their religion and have turned to worshiping success in moneymaking and in a passion for fleshy women, flashy cars, and too much rich food. While in one sense Bellow's novel is one of an adolescent discovering the world, it is a restricted world. Augie seems never to understand the vast fabric of American culture that lies about him. If his is a sociological tragedy, and many readers find it so, it is not a broad American tragedy. Rather, it is the tragedy of a Jewish child who sees only the materialism of Jews who have forsaken their rich tradition and who have found nothing to replace it.

While some readers will readily grasp the tragic elements in *The Adventures of Augie March*, others will grasp more readily the comic aspects. Following as it does in many ways the picaresque tradition, the novel has a wide strain of the comic. Neither Augie nor his creator takes some of the main character's deviations from conventional standards of conduct very seriously. Augie bounds in and out of crime and of sin with scarcely a backward glance. If his loves seem empty and his women unfaithful, Augie accepts that with lighthearted aplomb. Unheroic, weak, and ineffectual, Augie can be viewed as a comic protagonist in a comic work. The comic spirit, however, is used traditionally for satiric and serious purpose. While the comic elements are undeniably woven into the novel, adding to the richness of its texture, one may wonder about their purpose. Does the creator of Augie share his character's belief in the irrational nature of the individual, of society, and of the universe?

Augie seems at times to be a symbol of the irrational, mirrored in the eaglet that Augie and Thea train to hunt. The young bald eagle, fierce in appearance, proves to be an apt pupil: He is marvelously equipped, with powerful wings, beak, and claws, to be an instrument of destruction, and he learns well how to attack a piece of meat tendered by his trainers. Nevertheless, when a live creature, even a tiny lizard, puts up resistance, the eagle defies his nature, turning away and refusing to do what he is capable of doing. Like the eagle, Augie fails, too. Young, handsome, charming, and intelligent, Augie refuses to face life, always seeing it as something someone else wants him to do. When life hits back at him, Augie turns away. He strikes the reader as being without purpose. Like the trained eagle, he exists to exist, to be looked at, and to be fed. That the character sees this as living is perhaps the greatest irony of all. Augie is an antihero; he is not so much comic as pathetic. As a narrator, he realizes, vaguely, that while he denied the traditional goals that others held up for him, he failed to find for himself a worthwhile goal. In trying to live, he found little but a meaningless existence.

Further Reading

Atlas, James. *Bellow: A Biography*. New York: Random House, 2000. Atlas spent ten years working on this book, which some critics consider the definitive biography of Bellow. Atlas is particularly good at finding parallels between the tone of Bellow's novels and his mood at the time he wrote them.

Bach, Gerhard, ed. *The Critical Response to Saul Bellow.* Westport, Conn.: Greenwood Press, 1995. Collection of reviews and essays about Bellow's work that were published from the 1940's through the 1990's, including pieces by Delmore Schwartz, Robert Penn Warren, Alfred Kazin, and Granville Hicks. Contains articles about all of the major novels.

Clayton, John Jacob. *Saul Bellow: In Defense of Man.* 2d ed. Bloomington: Indiana University Press, 1980. Clayton says the novel is about reaching after personal uniqueness and the way each person tries to convince others that he or she has "captured reality."

Codde, Philippe. *The Jewish American Novel.* West Lafayette, Ind.: Purdue University Press, 2007. Codde explains the reasons for the unprecedented success of novels written by Bellow and other Jewish American authors after World War II.

Cohen, Sarah Blacher. *Saul Bellow's Enigmatic Laughter.* Champaign: University of Illinois Press, 1974. Cohen argues that in this "comedy of character," Augie is a kind of Columbus exploring America and Americans. He is "the picaresque apostle" who hears all confessions and forgives all sins.

Cronin, Gloria L. *A Room of His Own: In Search of the Feminine in the Novels of Saul Bellow.* Syracuse, N.Y.: Syracuse University Press, 2001. A feminist interpretation of Bellow. Cronin argues that his male protagonists search for but ultimately destroy the "lost feminine essence" they desire.

Dutton, Robert R. *Saul Bellow.* Rev. ed. Boston: Twayne, 1982. Treats the novel on three levels: as a picaresque, as a "fictional history of American literature," and as a comment on the "contemporary human condition." Augie turns out to be a "fallen angel" and "artist of alienation."

Pifer, Ellen. *Saul Bellow Against the Grain.* Philadelphia: University of Pennsylvania Press, 1990. Pifer describes how Augie travels through "a New World Babylon" on a pilgrimage to discover what is "uniquely meaningful" in his life. He refuses to yield to the authority of people who claim to be authorities and instead seeks his own truth.

Sternlicht, Sanford. "Saul Bellow, *The Adventures of Augie March.*" In *Masterpieces of Jewish American Literature.* Westport, Conn.: Greenwood Press, 2007. This book, aimed at high school and college students, provides analyses of ten works of twentieth century literature written by Jewish Americans, including *The Adventures of Augie March.* Sternlicht places the novel in biographical and historical context and discusses its plot, character development, themes, and narrative style.

Wilson, Jonathan. *On Bellow's Planet: Readings from the Dark Side.* Rutherford, N.J.: Fairleigh Dickinson University Press, 1985. Wilson maintains that Augie's main conflict is internal. For Augie, growing up does not bring him control over the self; instead, he struggles between the will to freedom and the need to be controlled.

Adventures of Huckleberry Finn

Author: Mark Twain (1835-1910)
First published: 1884; revised new edition, 2001
Type of work: Novel
Type of plot: Satire
Time of plot: Nineteenth century
Locale: Along the Lower Mississippi River

Principal characters:
HUCKLEBERRY FINN, a free-spirited boy
TOM SAWYER, his friend
JIM, a black slave
PAP FINN, Huck's father
THE DUKE and THE KING, con men
WIDOW DOUGLAS, Huck's guardian

The Story:

Huckleberry Finn and Tom Sawyer had found a box of gold in a robber's cave. Later, after Judge Thatcher takes the money and invests it for the boys, each receives the huge allowance of one dollar a day. The Widow Douglas and her sister, Miss Watson, take Huck home with them to try to reform him. At first, Huck cannot stand living in a tidy house where smoking and swearing are forbidden. Worse, he has to go to school and learn how to read. He does, however, manage to drag himself to school almost every day, except for the times when he sneaks off for a smoke in the woods or goes fishing on the Mississippi River.

Life is beginning to become bearable to him when one day he notices a boot print in the snow. Examining it closely, he realizes that it belongs to his worthless father, whom he has not seen for more than a year. Knowing that his father will be looking for him when he learns about the money, Huck rushes to Judge Thatcher and persuades him to take the fortune for himself. The judge is puzzled, but he signs some papers, and Huck is satisfied that he no longer has any money for his father to take from him.

Huck's father shows up one night in Huck's room at the Widow Douglas's home. Complaining that he has been cheated out of his son's money, the old drunkard later takes Huck away with him to a cabin in the Illinois woods, where he keeps the boy a prisoner, beating him periodically and half starving him. Huck is allowed to smoke and swear, however, and before long he begins to wonder why he ever liked living with the widow. His life with his father would be pleasant except for the beatings. One day, he sneaks away, leaving a bloody trail from a pig he kills in the woods. Huck wants everyone to believe he is dead. He climbs into a canoe and goes to Jackson's Island to hide until the excitement subsides.

After three days of freedom, Huck wanders to another part of the island, and there he discovers Jim, Miss Watson's black slave, who tells Huck that he ran off because he overheard Miss Watson planning to sell him down South for eight hundred dollars. Huck swears he will not report Jim. The two stay on the island many days, Jim giving Huck an education in primitive superstition. One night, Huck paddles back to the mainland. Disguised as a girl, he calls on a home near the shore. There he learns that his father disappeared shortly after the people of the town concluded that Huck was murdered. Since Jim disappeared just after Huck's apparent death, there is now a three-hundred-dollar reward posted for Jim's capture, for most people believe that he killed Huck.

Knowing that Jackson's Island will soon be searched, Huck hurries back to Jim, and the two head down the Mississippi on a raft they have found. They plan to sell the raft at Cairo, Illinois, and then go on a steamboat up the Ohio River into free territory. Jim tells Huck that he will work hard in the North and then buy his wife and children from their masters in the South. Helping a runaway slave bothers Huck's conscience, but he reasons that it would bother him more if he betrayed a good friend. One night, as they are drifting down the river on their raft, a large steamboat looms before them, and Huck and Jim, knowing that the raft will be smashed under the hull of the ship, jump into the water. Huck swims safely to shore, but Jim disappears.

Huck finds a home with a friendly family named Grangerford, who are feuding with the nearby Shepherdson family. The Grangerfords treat Huck kindly and leave him mostly to himself, even giving him a young slave to wait on him. One day, the slave asks him to come to the woods to see some snakes. Following the boy, Huck comes across Jim, who has been hiding in the woods waiting for an opportunity to send for Huck. Jim repairs the broken raft. That night, one of the Grangerford daughters elopes with a young Shepherdson, and the feud breaks out once more. Huck and Jim run away after the shooting begins and set off down the river.

Shortly afterward, Jim and Huck meet two men who pretend they are European royalty and make all sorts of nonsensical demands on Huck and Jim. Huck is not taken in, but he reasons that it would do no harm to humor the two men to prevent quarreling. The so-called Duke and King are clever schemers. In one of the small river towns, they stage a fake show, which lasts long enough to net them a few hundred dollars. On the third night, just before the scheduled third show, they run off before the angered townspeople can catch them.

From a talkative young man, the King learns about the death of Peter Wilks, who has left considerable property and some cash to his three daughters. Wilks's two brothers, whom no one in the town ever saw, are living in England. The King and the Duke go to the three nieces, Mary Jane, Susan, and Joanna, and present themselves as the two English uncles. They take all the inheritance, put up the property for auction, and sell the slaves. This high-handed deed causes great grief to the girls, and Huck cannot bear to see them so unhappy. He decides to expose the two frauds, but he wants to ensure Jim's safety first. Jim is hiding in the woods waiting for his companions to return to him. Employing an ingenious series of lies, subterfuges, and maneuverings, Huck exposes the Duke and King. Huck flees back to Jim, and the two escape on their raft. Just as Jim and Huck think they are on their way and well rid of their former companions, the Duke and King come rowing down the river toward them.

The whole party sets out again, with the Duke and the King planning to continue their schemes to hoodwink people in the towns along the river. In one town, the King turns Jim in for a reward, and he is sold. Huck has quite a tussle with his conscience. He knows that he ought to help return a slave to the rightful owner, yet on the other hand he thinks of all the fine times he and Jim had together and how loyal a friend Jim is. Finally, Huck decides that he will help Jim to escape.

Learning that Silas Phelps is holding Jim, he heads for the Phelps farm. Mrs. Phelps runs up and hugs him, mistaking him for the nephew whom she is expecting to come for a visit. Huck wonders how he can keep Mrs. Phelps from learning that he is not her nephew. Then to his relief, he learns she has mistaken him for Tom Sawyer. Huck rather likes being Tom for a while, and he is able to tell the Phelpses about Tom's Aunt Polly and Sid and Mary, Tom's half-brother and cousin. Huck is feeling proud of himself for keeping up the deception. Tom Sawyer, when he arrives, tells his aunt that he is Sid.

At the first opportunity, Huck tells Tom about Jim's capture. To Huck's surprise, Tom offers to help him set Jim free. Huck cannot believe that Tom will be a slave stealer, but he keeps his feelings to himself. Huck intends merely to wait until there is a dark night and then break the padlock on the door of the shack where Jim is kept; but Tom says the rescue has to be done according to the books and lays out a highly complicated plan. It takes a full three weeks of plotting, stealing, and deceit to get Jim out of the shack. The scheme results in a chase, however, in which Tom is shot in the leg. After Jim is recaptured, Tom is brought back to Aunt Sally's house to recover from his wound. There, he reveals the fact that Miss Watson died, giving Jim his freedom in her will. Huck is greatly relieved to learn that Tom is not really a slave stealer after all.

When Tom's Aunt Polly arrives unexpectedly, she quickly sets straight the identities of the two boys. Jim is given his freedom, and Tom gives him forty dollars. Tom tells Huck that his money is still safely in the hands of Judge Thatcher, and when Huck moans that his father will likely be back to claim it again, Jim tells Huck that his father is dead; Jim observed him lying in a derelict house they saw floating in the river. Huck is ready to start out again because Aunt Sally says she might adopt him and try to civilize him. Huck thinks that he cannot go through such a trial again after the Widow Douglas's attempts to civilize him.

Critical Evaluation:

Little could Mark Twain have visualized in 1876 when he began a sequel to capitalize on the success of *The Adventures of Tom Sawyer* (1876) that *Adventures of Huckleberry Finn* would come to be regarded as his masterpiece and one of the most significant works in the American novel tradition. His greatest contribution to the tradition occurred when, with an unerring instinct for American regional dialects, he elected to tell the story in Huck's own words. The skill with which Twain elevates the dialect of an illiterate village boy to the highest levels of poetry established the spoken American idiom as a literary language and earned for Twain the reputation, proclaimed for him by Ernest Hemingway, William Faulkner, and many others, as the father of the modern American novel.

Twain maintains an almost perfect fidelity to Huck's point of view in order to dramatize the conflict between Huck's innate innocence and natural goodness and the dictates of a corrupt society. As Huck's story, the novel centers around such major themes as death and rebirth, freedom and bondage, the search for a father, the individual versus society, and the all-pervasive theme of brotherhood. Huck's character reflects a stage in Twain's own development when he still believed human beings to be innately good though increasingly corrupted by social influences that replace their intuitive sense of right and wrong. This theme is explicitly dramatized through Huck's conflict with his conscience over whether or not to turn Jim in as a runaway slave. Huck, on the one hand, accepts without question what he was taught about slavery by church and society. In his own mind, as surely as in that of his southern contemporaries, aiding an escaped slave is both legally and morally wrong. Thus Huck's battle with his conscience is a real trauma for him, and his decision to "go to Hell" rather than give Jim up is made with a certainty that such a fate awaits him for breaking this law of society. Twain compellingly establishes the irony that Huck's "sin" against the social establishment affirms the best that is possible in the individual.

Among the many forms of bondage that permeate the novel—including the widow's attempt to "civilize" Huck, the "code of honor" that causes Sherburn to murder Boggs, and the law of vendetta that rules the lives of the Grangerfords and the Shepherdsons—slavery provides Twain his largest metaphor for both social bondage and institutionalized injustice and inhumanity. Written well after the termination of the Civil War, *Adventures of Huckleberry Finn* is not an antislavery novel in the limited sense that *Uncle Tom's Cabin* (1852) is. Rather than simply attacking an institution already legally dead, Twain uses the idea of slavery as a metaphor for all social bondage and injustice. Thus, Jim's search for freedom, like Huck's own need to escape both the Widow Douglas and Pap Finn, is as much a metaphorical search for an ideal state of freedom as it is a flight from slavery into free-state sanctuary. It is almost irrelevant that Twain has Huck and Jim running deeper into the South rather than north toward free soil. Freedom exists neither in the North nor in the South but in the ideal and idyllic world of the raft and river.

The special world of raft and river is at the very heart of the novel. In contrast to the restrictive and oppressive social world of the shore, the raft is a veritable Eden away from the evils of civilization. It is here that Jim and Huck can allow their natural bond of love to develop without regard for the question of race. It is here that Jim can become a surrogate father to Huck, and Huck can develop the depth of feeling for Jim that eventually leads to his decision to imperil his own soul. While the developing relationship between Huck and Jim determines the basic shape of the novel, the river also works in other structural ways. The picaresque form of the novel and its structural rhythm are based on a series of episodes onshore, after each of which Huck and Jim return to the peaceful sanctuary of the raft. It is onshore that Huck encounters the worst excesses of which "the damned human race" is capable, but with each return to the raft comes a renewal of spiritual hope and idealism.

The two major thrusts of Twain's attack on the "civilized" world in *Adventures of Huckleberry Finn* are against institutionalized religion and the romanticism he believed characterized the South. The former is easily illustrated by the irony of the Widow Douglas's attempt to teach Huck religious principles while she persists in holding slaves. As with her snuff-taking—which is acceptable because she does it herself—there seems to be no relationship between her fundamental sense of humanity and justice and her religion. Huck's practical morality makes him more Christian than the widow, though he takes no interest in her principles. Southern romanticism, which Twain blamed for the fall of the South, is particularly allegorized by the wreck of the steamboat *Walter Scott*, but it is also inherent in such episodes as the feud, where Twain shows the real horror of the sort of situation traditionally glamorized by romantic authors. In both cases, Twain is attacking the mindless acceptance of values that he believed kept the South in its dark age.

Many critics have argued that its juvenile ending hopelessly flaws *Adventures of Huckleberry Finn*; others argue that the ending is in perfect accord with Twain's themes. Nevertheless, all agree that the substance of Twain's masterpiece transcends the limits of literary formalism to explore those eternal verities on which great literature rests. Through the adventures of an escaped slave and a runaway boy, both representatives of the ignorant and lowly of the earth, Twain affirms that true humanity is found in humans rather than institutions.

"Critical Evaluation" by William E. Grant

Further Reading

Blair, Walter. *Mark Twain and Huck Finn*. 1960. Reprint. Berkeley: University of California Press, 1973. An elegantly written classic essay on the writing of *Adventures of Huckleberry Finn*. Still valuable as an exploration of the novel's background of characters and ideas.

Bloom, Harold, ed. *Mark Twain's "The Adventures of Huckleberry Finn."* Updated ed. New York: Bloom's Literary Criticism, 2007. Collection of essays providing numerous interpretations of the novel, including discussions of the novel's realism; Huck, Jim, and the "black-and-white" fallacy; *Huckleberry Finn* and the problem of freedom; and the trouble with whiteness on Twain's Mississippi.

Camfield, Gregg. *The Oxford Companion to Mark Twain*. New York: Oxford University Press, 2003. Collection of about three hundred original essays on individual works, themes, characters, language, subjects that interested Twain, and other topics. Includes an appendix on researching Twain, which lists useful secondary sources, and an annotated bibliography of Twain's novels, plays, poems, and other writings.

Doyno, Victor. Writing *"Huck Finn": Mark Twain's Creative Process*. Philadelphia: University of Pennsylvania Press, 1992. This study of Twain's ideas and works includes a definitive essay on the creation of *Adventures of Huckleberry Finn*.

Emerson, Everett. *Mark Twain: A Literary Life*. Philadelphia: University of Pennsylvania Press, 2000. A complete revision of Emerson's *The Authentic Mark Twain* (1984), this masterful study traces the development of Twain's writing against the events in his life, and provides illuminating discussions of many individual works.

Fishkin, Shelley Fisher. *Was Huck Black? Mark Twain and African-American Voices*. New York: Oxford University Press, 1993. This original and important work demonstrates conclusively that the major sources for *The Adventures of Huckleberry Finn* were African American.

Mensh, Elaine, and Harry Mensh. *Black, White, and Huckleberry Finn: Re-Imagining the American Dream*. Tuscaloosa: University of Alabama Press, 2000. Examines the racial messages in the novel, comparing Twain's depictions of slaves and slaveholders with the historical realities of slavery. Argues that Twain, in the character of Huck, does not question slavery but upholds traditional racial attitudes.

Quirk, Tom. *Coming to Grips with "Huckleberry Finn": Essays on a Book, a Boy, and a Man*. Columbia: University of Missouri Press, 1993. Explores issues in the novel and presents factual contexts for them. Examines Twain's attitude toward race.

Rasmussen, R. Kent. *Bloom's How to Write About Mark Twain*. New York: Bloom's Literary Criticism, 2008. Designed for students, this volume contains a chapter offering clear guidelines on how to write essays on literature, a chapter on writing about Twain, and chapters providing specific advice on individual works, including *Adventures of Huckleberry Finn.*

_______. *Critical Companion to Mark Twain: A Literary Reference to His Life and Work.* 2 vols. New York: Facts On File, 2007. Alphabetically arranged entries about the plots, characters, places, and other subjects relating to Twain's writings and life. The revised edition features extended analytical essays on Twain's major works, an expanded and fully annotated bibliography of books about Twain, and a glossary explaining unusual words in Twain's vocabulary.

_______, ed. *Mark Twain.* Pasadena, Calif.: Salem Press, 2010. This collection of new and reprinted essays addresses realism, humor, and racial issues in *Adventures of Huckleberry Finn.* Several other essays also discuss the novel at length. Of particular interest is Hilton Obenzinger's essay, "'Pluck Enough to Lynch a Man': Mark Twain and Manhood," which explores Twain's adult male characters.

Wieck, Carl F. *Refiguring "Huckleberry Finn."* Athens: University of Georgia Press, 2000. A novel approach to the meaning and influence of Twain's best-known work. Concentrates on certain key words to decipher the text.

The Adventures of Peregrine Pickle

Author: Tobias Smollett (1721-1771)
First published: The Adventures of Peregrine Pickle, in Which Are Included Memories of a Lady of Quality, 1751
Type of work: Novel
Type of plot: Picaresque
Time of plot: Early eighteenth century
Locale: England and the Continent

Principal characters:
PEREGRINE PICKLE, a reckless young man
GAMALIEL PICKLE, his father
GRIZZLE PICKLE, his aunt, later Mrs. Trunnion
COMMODORE HAWSER TRUNNION, an old sea dog and Peregrine's godfather
LIEUTENANT HATCHWAY, the Commodore's companion
TOM PIPES, a companion and servant
EMILIA GAUNTLET, Peregrine's sweetheart

The Story:

Gamaliel Pickle is the son of a prosperous London merchant who bequeaths his son a fortune of no small degree. Later, having lost a part of his inheritance in several unsuccessful ventures of his own, Gamaliel prudently decides to retire from business and to live on the interest of his fortune rather than risk his principal in the uncertainties of trade. With his sister Grizzle, who kept his house for him since his father's death, he goes to live in a mansion in the country.

In the region to which he retires, Gamaliel's nearest neighbor is Commodore Hawser Trunnion, an old sea dog who keeps his house like a seagoing ship and who possesses an endless list of quarterdeck oaths to be used on any occasion against anyone who offends him. Other members of his household are Lieutenant Hatchway, a one-legged veteran, and a seaman named Tom Pipes.

Shortly after he settles in his new home, Gamaliel meets Sally Appleby, the daughter of a gentleman in a nearby parish. After a brief courtship, the two are married. Before long, Gamaliel discovers that his wife is determined to dominate him completely. Sally takes such a dislike to Grizzle that she tries in every way possible to embarrass and humiliate her sister-in-law. During Sally's pregnancy Peregrine, the oldest son of the ill-starred union, Grizzle realizes that she is no longer wanted in her brother's household, and she begins a campaign to win the heart of old Commodore Trunnion.

Ignoring his distrust of women in general, she wins out at last over his obstinacy. The wedding is not without humor; on his way to the church, the Commodore's horse runs away with him and carries him eleven miles with a hunting party. Upset by his experience, he insists that the postponed ceremony be performed in his own house. The wedding night is also not without excitement: The ship's hammocks, in which the bride and groom are to sleep, collapse and drop them to the floor. The next morning, wholly indifferent to her husband's displeasure, Grizzle proceeds to refurnish and reorganize the Commodore's house according to her own notions.

In order to silence his protests, Grizzle pretends to be pregnant. The Commodore's hopes for an heir, however, are short-lived; his wife employs her ruse only to make herself absolute mistress of the Trunnion household. Lacking an heir of his own, the gruff but kindly old seaman turns his attention to young Peregrine, his nephew and godson. Peregrine is an unfortunate child. While he is still very young, his mother takes an unnatural and profound dislike to him, and the boy is often wretched from the harsh treatment he receives. Under the influence of his wife, weak-willed Gamaliel does little to improve the unhappy situation. As a result, Peregrine grows into a headstrong, rebellious boy who shows his high spirits in pranks that mortify and irritate his parents. He is sent away to school, and he rebels against his foolish and hypocritical teachers; at last, he writes to the Commodore to request removal from the school. The Commodore feels pity for the boy and admires his spirit of independence, so he takes him out of school and adopts him as his son and heir.

When Peregrine's pranks and escapades become more than his indulgent uncle can stand, the boy is sent to Winchester School. Pipes accompanies him as his servant. Mindful of his uncle's kindness, Peregrine studies and makes steady progress until he meets Emilia Gauntlet and falls in love with her. Emilia is visiting in Winchester; her home is in a village about a day's journey away. Peregrine's infatuation is so great that soon after she returns home, he runs away from school and takes lodgings in the village in order to be near her. His absence is reported by the school authorities, and Hatchway is sent to look for him. The boy is summoned to visit his uncle, who is alarmed by his heir's interest in a penniless young woman. Peregrine's mother grows even more spiteful, and his father disowns him for his youthful folly. Indignant at the parents' harsh treatment of their son, the Commodore sends Peregrine to Oxford to continue his studies. There he encounters Emilia again and renews his courtship. Hoping to make a good match for his nephew, the Commodore attempts to end the affair by sending Peregrine on a tour of the Continent. Aware of his uncle's purpose in sending him abroad, Peregrine visits Emilia before his departure and vows eternal devotion.

Shortly thereafter, warned by the Commodore that his reckless behavior will lead only to disaster, Peregrine sets out for France. Peregrine is accompanied by Pipes, as his servant, and a mentor who is supposed to keep a check on Peregrine's behavior. All efforts in that direction are fruitless. Peregrine barely sets foot on French soil before he makes gallant advances to Mrs. Hornbeck, the wife of a traveling Englishman. In Paris, he encounters the lady again and elopes with her, an escapade that ends when the British ambassador intervenes to send the lady back to her husband. On one occasion, Peregrine is imprisoned by the city guard. At another time, he fights a duel with a musketeer as the result of an amorous adventure. He quarrels with a nobleman at a masked ball and is sent to the Bastille in company with an artist friend. After Pipes discovers his whereabouts and secures his release, Peregrine is ordered to leave France within three days.

On his way back to England, Peregrine becomes embroiled with a knight of Malta, quarrels with Pipes, and is captivated by a lady he meets in a carriage. Shortly afterward, he loses his carriage companion and resumes his earlier affair with Mrs. Hornbeck. Her husband interposes, and Peregrine is thrown into prison once more. After his release, the travelers proceeded to Antwerp and then to England. His uncle, who retains his affection for his wayward nephew, receives him with great joy.

On his return, Peregrine calls on Emilia, but he finds her indifferent to his attentions. He wastes no time in pining over a lost love but continues to disport himself in London and Bath, until he is called home by the final illness of his uncle. The old Commodore is buried according to his own directions, and he is remembered with great affection and respect by his nephew. His uncle wills a fortune of thirty thousand pounds and his house to Peregrine. After a vain attempt to reach a friendly understanding with his parents, Peregrine leaves the house to the tenancy of Hatchway and returns to London.

As a handsome, wealthy young bachelor, he indulges in extravagance and dissipation of all kinds. After exaggerated reports of his wealth are circulated, he is pursued by matchmaking mothers. Their efforts merely amuse him, but their designs give him entrance into the houses of the fashionable and the great.

Peregrine meets Emilia again and begins the same campaign to win her that were successful with his other light and casual loves. Disappointed in his attempts to seduce her, he takes advantage of the confusion attending a masquerade ball to try to overcome her by force. He is vigorously repulsed, and her uncle forbids him to see Emilia again.

He becomes the friend of a notorious lady who gives him a copy of her memoirs. The woman is Lady Vane, whose affairs with many lovers have created a great scandal in London. Peregrine's friend Cadwallader assumes the character of a fortune-teller and magician. In that way Peregrine is able to learn the secrets of the women who come to consult Cadwallader. Peregrine acquires a reputation as a clever man and a wit, and he uses his knowledge to advance his own position.

Grizzle dies, and Peregrine attends her funeral. On the road, he meets a vulgar young female beggar whom he dresses in fashionable clothes and teaches a set of polite phrases. It amuses him to introduce the beggar into his own fashionable world. When his contemptuous joke is at last exposed, he loses many of his fine friends. Peregrine decides to retrench. He cuts down his foolish expenses and makes loans at a good rate of interest. He is persuaded to stand for Parliament. This decision is taken after he meets Emilia at her sister's wedding, and he begs the sister to intercede for him. His political venture, however, costs more money than he expects. After he loses the election, he is, for the first time in his life, faced with the need for mature reflection on himself and his world.

His affairs go from bad to worse. A mortgage that he holds proves worthless. A friend for whom he endorsed a note defaults. Reduced at last to complete ruin, he tries to earn money by writing translations and satires. He is again thrown into jail after the publication of a satire directed against an influential politician.

His old friends, Hatchway and Pipes, remain loyal to him in his adversity. Each brings his savings to the Fleet prison and offers them to Peregrine, but he refuses to accept their aid. It is his intention to earn money for his release by his writing or else starve in the attempt.

Emilia's brother, Captain Gauntlet, learns that he was promoted to his rank largely through Peregrine's services in the days of his prosperity. Discovering Peregrine's plight, he sets about to relieve his benefactor. Peregrine has an unexpected bit of luck when one of his debtors repays a loan of seven hundred pounds. Emilia inherits ten thousand pounds and offers the money and her hand to Peregrine. Although he is touched by her generosity and forgiveness, he reluctantly refuses to burden her with his debts and degradation.

Peregrine is saved by the death of his father, who dies intestate. Legal heir to his father's fortune, he is able to leave Fleet prison and take immediate possession of his estate. Having settled an allowance upon his mother, who goes to live in another part of the country, Peregrine hastens to ask for Emilia's hand in marriage. With his bride, he settles down to lead the life of a country squire.

Critical Evaluation:

The Adventures of Peregrine Pickle, Tobias Smollett's second novel, has never been as popular as his first, *The Adventures of Roderick Random* (1748), or his last, *The Expedition of Humphry Clinker* (1771). He wished it to be a more polished and panoramic work, with wider appeal, but a variety of circumstances flowed together to frustrate that hope. It met with a mixed reception when it was published in 1751, a response that persists.

Smollett was the most prolific and venturesome of the eighteenth century's novelists. After 1754, when Henry Fielding died and Samuel Richardson published his last work, he was often praised as the most talented novelist in the language. At the same time, he was one of England's foremost political journalists, serving as defender of both prime minister and monarch and directing two major reviews. He also came to be regarded as the most influential historian after David Hume and was easily the most productive, publishing three dozen volumes within a decade. In the 1750's and 1760's, he wrote or edited more than seventy volumes of nonfiction. These interests and the quarrels they fostered help explain the peculiar flavor of *The Adventures of Peregrine Pickle*.

Controversy became Smollett's forte, as a conservative, pugnacious Scot making his way in Whiggish London. For his fiction, he chose two forms that made contention not only possible but also inevitable. The first is a modification of the picaresque—the journey of a roguish outsider through contemporary places and manners. The second is satire—the relentless exposure of fools and knaves. In each new novel, he seeks a different mixture of exotic adventure and harsh ridicule. In *The Adventures of Peregrine Pickle* he creates twice as many characters—226—and covers nearly three times as many pages as he did in the earlier *The Adventures of Roderick Random*, and he balances exotic adventure and contemporary scandal. Peregrine Pickle passes through a three-part series of peregrinations that reveals his hot blood, his thirst for adventure, and his sympathy for the downtrodden. First comes his youth, with ribald stories of life at sea and at school; then comes the panorama of the Grand Tour; finally, there is his life as a fortune hunter in London.

What distinguishes the work, then and now, are the three long, interpolated narratives of contemporary scandal that make up a third of the novel, more than those of any earlier English novel. These insert stories may have been evoked by the growing taste for journalistic narrative. As long as a novel in itself, "Memoirs of Lady Vane"—Frances Vane, a prominent socialite with a taste for the sensual—echoes parts of Peregrine's story, especially his jousts with the money-hungry, and follows John Cleland's tale of Fanny Hill, *Memoirs of a Woman of Pleasure* (1748). The others are those of Daniel Mackercher, who assisted James Annesley in a legal battle with the Earl of Anglesey, and of the Count d'Alvarez, captured and found in bondage in Bohemia. Critics appreciate these digressions in themselves but doubt their contribution to the novel. Similarly, critics applaud the gusto and the originality of the opening part, with its theme of home, family, and surrogates and its gallery of unforgettable characters: Pipes,

Grizzle, Keypstick, Hatchway, and Trunnion. This section is notable for many reasons but especially for the more than fifty pages Smollett uses to introduce the major characters other than Peregrine. Such a modernist device provides a prehistory of the title character, a foretaste of the social and emotional world into which he will grow. Historians of child rearing and education have studied it to advantage.

The second part of the novel, which takes place on the Continent, disappoints many. Neither originality nor precision is as apparent, as Smollett resorts to a lamer form of satire. He surely knew the territory, for during the summer of 1750 he traveled to Paris and the Low Countries, probably gathering material to be used in the novel. There is a Swiftian quality to the relentless exposure of stupidity in this section. However, Peregrine cannot be as successful a moral vehicle as Gulliver, for he is too proud and venal to be a proper judge. He does not long remain an amused spectator of French affectation, for example, but soon becomes an active participant.

Part three regains some of the opening vigor, however, as Peregrine endures the trial by adversity. Scalded by misfortune and despair, he then recuperates by the generosity of friends, by the love of Emilia, and by the inheritance of his father's estate. Many readers doubt Peregrine's deserts; he is granted such rewards rather than earning them. The novel provides more of a dazzling world to examine than a sympathetic hero to admire. Even those who admire the exuberance of that world find their admiration impeded by the length of the interpolated stories that bulk so large in this section. Although they upset the symmetry of the novel, these stories do support its theme. Long and now shorn of their original scandal, Lady Vane's memoirs prove that the behavior of the upper classes can be brutal and immoral. All of the inset pieces reveal the fate of those who would be ruled by their passions rather than by the dictates of moral common sense.

So, too, with their creator. In this novel, Smollett is more troubled and troubling than he was in his first and last fictions. Little is known of his life while composing the novel, but one can presume a measure of disquiet never fully removed. Smollett never possessed the gift of repose, and, in this period, he seems more irascible than ever. This explains his quarrels with more than a dozen contemporary figures whom he challenged, for at least a short while, until he found other opponents. He wanted a direct and unmediated outlet for his antagonisms and soon found one in his work in political reviews.

"Critical Evaluation" by John Sekora

Further Reading

Beasley, Jerry C. *Tobias Smollett: Novelist.* Athens: University of Georgia Press, 1998. An analysis of Smollett's five novels, which Beasley interprets as "exercises in the visual imagination," written by an author who believed the private, interior life could be defined by the externally visible. Chapter 2 focuses on *The Adventures of Peregrine Pickle*.

Brack, O. M., Jr., ed. *Tobias Smollett, Scotland's First Novelist: New Essays in Memory of Paul-Gabriel Bouce.* Newark: University of Delaware Press, 2007. Collection of essays on Smollett's fiction and nonfiction, including a comparison of his work with that of Henry Fielding, an examination of Smollett's contributions to the gothic novel, and proof that he wrote "The Memoirs of a Lady of Quality" in *The Adventures of Peregrine Pickle*.

Buck, Howard S. *A Study in Smollett, Chiefly "Peregrine Pickle."* New Haven, Conn.: Yale University Press, 1925. An early scholarly study that remains valuable. Collates the first and second editions of the novel and explains the many quarrels Smollett included in it.

Evans, David L. "Peregrine Pickle: The Complete Satirist." *Studies in the Novel* 3, no. 3 (Fall, 1971): 258-274. A favorable view, arguing that the novel is not only a satire but also a study of satire, combining the conventions of both forms.

Gibson, William. *Art and Money in the Writings of Tobias Smollett.* Lewisburg, Pa.: Bucknell University Press, 2007. Analyzes some of Smollett's novels and nonfiction writing, focusing on issues of aesthetics, commercialism, luxury, and taste in order to describe how these works provide insights into the eighteenth century art world.

Lewis, Jeremy. *Tobias Smollett.* London: Jonathan Cape, 2003. An appreciative look at Smollett's life and work, written by an acclaimed biographer. Includes bibliography and index.

Smollett, Tobias. *The Adventures of Peregrine Pickle.* Edited by James L. Clifford. New York: Oxford University Press, 1964. Unexpurgated text of the first edition, with good introduction, notes, and bibliography.

Weinsheimer, Joel. "Defects and Difficulties in Smollett's *Peregrine Pickle*." *Ariel: A Review of International English Literature* 9, no. 3 (July, 1978): 49-62. An unfavorable estimate, arguing that the novel fails as satire, as a bildungsroman, and as a combination of the two.

The Adventures of Roderick Random

Author: Tobias Smollett (1721-1771)
First published: 1748
Type of work: Novel
Type of plot: Picaresque
Time of plot: Eighteenth century
Locale: England

Principal characters:
RODERICK RANDOM, an adventurer
TOM BOWLING, his uncle
STRAP, Tom's friend and companion
MISS WILLIAMS, an adventuress
NARCISSA, Roderick's sweetheart

The Story:

Although Roderick Random comes from a wealthy landowning family in Scotland, his early life is beset by vicissitudes. Soon after Roderick's birth, his mother dies. When his father thereupon marries a servant in the household, he is disowned by his own father. Heartbroken and penniless, he disappears, leaving his son Roderick in the care of his grandfather, who is prevailed upon to send the lad to school for the sake of the family reputation.

At school, Roderick, although a great favorite with the boys his own age, is the butt of the masters. His whippings are numerous, for he is used as a whipping boy whenever something goes wrong and the real culprit cannot be determined. In Roderick's fourteenth year, however, there is a change in his fortunes. His mother's brother, Tom Bowling, a lieutenant in the navy, comes to visit his young nephew.

Lieutenant Bowling remonstrates with his nephew's grandfather over his treatment of Roderick, but the old man is firm in his refusal to do anything beyond what necessity dictates for the offspring of the son he disinherited. When the grandfather dies, he leaves Roderick nothing. Bowling sends the lad to the university, where Roderick makes great progress. Then Bowling becomes involved in a duel and is forced to leave his ship. This misfortune cuts off the source of Roderick's funds and makes it necessary for him to leave the university.

Casting about for a means of making a livelihood, Roderick becomes a surgeon's apprentice. He proves to be so capable that before long his master sends him to London with a recommendation to a local member of Parliament, who is to obtain Roderick a place as surgeon's mate in the navy. Securing a place on a man-of-war is a difficult task. To keep himself in funds, Roderick works for a French chemist in London. In the shop, he meets and falls in love with Miss Williams. Much to his chagrin, however, he discovers one day that she is a prostitute trying to better her fortune. Soon afterward, Roderick is accused of stealing and is dismissed by his employer. While he is leading a precarious existence, waiting for his navy warrant, he learns that Miss Williams lives in the same lodging house. He wins her everlasting gratitude by acting as her doctor while she is ill.

One day, while walking near the Thames, Roderick is seized by a press-gang and shanghaied aboard the man-of-war *Thunder*, about to sail for Jamaica. Roderick finds friends on board the ship and is made a surgeon's mate. The voyage to Jamaica is terrible. The commanding officer, Captain Oakhum, is a tyrant who comes very close to hanging Roderick and another surgeon's mate because one of the ship's officers claims he heard them speaking ill of the surgeon and the captain. The captain thinks that Roderick's Greek notebook is a military code, and he threatens again to hang him as a spy.

After seeing action against the Spanish at Cartagena, Roderick secures a billet as surgeon's mate aboard the *Lizard*, a ship returning to England with dispatches. On the way, the captain dies and Lieutenant Crampley, an officer who greatly dislikes Roderick, takes command of the ship. Crampley, a poor officer, runs the ship aground off the Sussex coast. The crew robs and tries to kill Roderick when they reach the shore, but an old woman befriends him, cures him of his wounds, and finds him a place as footman with a spinster gentlewoman who lives nearby.

Roderick spends several months in her service. He finds his way into his employer's goodwill by his attention to his duties and by showing a knowledge of literature, even to the extent of explaining passages from Torquato Tasso's Italian poetry to her. The spinster has a niece and a nephew living with her. Narcissa, the niece, is a beautiful girl of marriageable age to whom Roderick is immediately attracted. Her brother, a drunken, fox-hunting young squire, is determined that she will marry a wealthy knight in the neighborhood.

One day, Roderick prevents the girl's brutal suitor from forcing his attentions on her, beating the man severely with a cudgel. While he deliberates on his next move, he is taken prisoner by a band of smugglers who for their own safety carry him to Boulogne in France. There Roderick finds his uncle, Bowling, and assures him that he will be safe if he returns to England, for the man Bowling believes he killed in a duel is still alive.

Roderick sets out for Paris in the company of a friar who robs him one night and leaves him penniless. Roderick then meets a band of soldiers and enlists in the army of King Louis XIV. He serves at the battle of Dettingen. After the battle, his regiment goes into garrison, and Roderick unexpectedly meets a boyhood companion, Strap, who is passing as Monsieur d'Estrapes and who is friendly with a French nobleman. Strap befriends Roderick and secures his release from onerous service as a private in the French army.

Strap and Roderick scheme for a way to make their fortunes. They finally hit upon the idea of setting up Roderick as a wealthy gentleman. They hope that he will soon marry a wealthy heiress. The two men go to Paris, where Roderick buys new clothes and becomes acquainted with the ways of a man about town. Then they go to London. There Roderick quickly becomes acquainted with a group of young men on the fringe of fashionable society.

Roderick's first attempt to become intimate with a rich woman is a dismal failure, for she turns out to be a prostitute. On the second attempt, he meets Melinda, a young woman of fortune, who wins many pounds from him at cards and then refuses to marry him because he does not have an independent fortune of his own. Finally, one of Roderick's friends tells him of a cousin, Miss Snapper, who is a wealthy heiress. The friend promises to help Roderick in his suit in return for Roderick's note for five hundred pounds, due six months after the marriage.

Roderick agrees to this suggestion and immediately starts out for Bath in the company of the young woman and her mother. On the way, he saves them from being robbed by a highwayman, a deed that establishes him in the good graces of both mother and daughter. At Bath, Roderick squires the young woman about day and night. Although she is crippled and unattractive, her fortune is more important to him than her appearance. Besides, she is an intelligent and witty young woman.

All goes well until Roderick catches sight of Narcissa. Realizing that he is in love with her, he deserts Miss Snapper. Narcissa soon reveals to Roderick that she returns his love. Her brother has no objections because he thinks Roderick is a wealthy man. Unfortunately, Roderick's former sweetheart, Melinda, arrives in Bath and catches the attention of Narcissa's brother. At a ball, she spreads evil reports about Roderick because he left her. The result is that Roderick first fights a duel with Lord Quiverwit, one of Narcissa's admirers, and then sees Narcissa being spirited away by her brother. The only thing that keeps Roderick's hope alive is the fact that he knows Narcissa loves him and that her maid, the Miss Williams whom Roderick long before befriended, is eternally grateful to him and will help him in any way.

Roderick returns to London and again meets his uncle, Bowling, who was appointed to take a merchant ship on a mysterious trip. He proposes to take Roderick with him as ship surgeon, and he gives his nephew one thousand pounds to buy goods to sell on the voyage. He also makes out a will leaving all of his property to Roderick.

The mysterious trip proves to be a voyage to the Guinea Coast to pick up black slaves for the Spanish American trade. The slaves and the cargo, including the goods shipped by Roderick, are sold at a handsome profit. While their ship is being prepared for the return voyage, Roderick and his uncle spend several weeks ashore, where they are entertained by new friends and business acquaintances. One of their acquaintances is a wealthy Englishman known as Don Rodrigo, who invites them to visit him on his estate. During their stay, it is discovered that the man is Roderick's father, who went to America to make his fortune after having been disinherited.

The voyage back to England is a happy one. Roderick is full of confidence, for he made a small fortune from the voyage and has expectations of a large fortune from the estates of his father and his uncle. He immediately proposes to Narcissa, who accepts his offer of marriage despite her brother's opposition. They are married shortly afterward and go to live in Scotland on the Random estate, which Roderick's father buys from his bankrupt elder brother.

Critical Evaluation:

The Adventures of Roderick Random is among the most adventure-ridden episodic novels of the eighteenth century. Innumerable incidents befall Roderick as he, driven by necessity, roams in every conceivable direction on land and sea. It is a novel written in the best picaresque tradition, with a hero who is at once roguish and (up to a point) virtuous, resilient in the face of adversity yet often despairing, honorable in some matters but underhanded in a great many others. He is by turns whimsical, deliberate, sensitive, vengeful, petulant, gracious, and whatever else Tobias Smollett finds occasion for him to be. Structurally *The Adventures of Roderick Random* also fits easily into the picaresque tradition, not only in the obvious influence of Alain-René Lesage's *Gil Blas* (1715-1735), which Smollett translated into English in 1749, but also in its plot deficiencies. There are several such weaknesses—most of them sudden, unconvincing turns in the narrative—that betray the picaresque fondness for overemphasizing action and character.

The novel is marked above all by its glittering wit and caustic social satire. There are many delightful touches in the book (the repartee of Miss Snapper, for example) that show off Smollett's comic skills and these, added to the author's ribaldry, make for highly diverting passages. Perhaps the most engaging parts of the novel are its scenes of London life: the cardsharps, the wags, the floozies and fops, the poverty, the stench, the cruelty. Readers meet every imaginable species of human creature, ranging from prissy lords and lavender-trousered ship captains to lascivious priests and penitent whores. Smollett depicts not just the sins of a sin-worn world but also the need to match good nature with plain animal cunning. Part of the controlling idea in *The Adventures of Roderick Random* is that education is best obtained not in schoolrooms but in living and learning to adapt to harsh realities.

This theme is a favorite of eighteenth century British fiction. Henry Fielding's *The History of Tom Jones, a Foundling*, published just a year after *The Adventures of Roderick Random*, is a well-known reiteration of it. Because Tom, like Roderick, lacks wisdom and self-control (the age would have called it prudence), he is repeatedly victimized by individuals with a crueler nature than his own. In Smollett's book, readers see the same pattern: A young man with a basically good nature (to echo Fielding) is forced into a world of duplicity where his kindness and trust are manipulated by others. The "knavery of the world," as Smollett dubs it, everywhere demands that the hero learn to be worldly-wise; his main difficulty is to do this without losing his fundamental goodness. Often Roderick appears on the verge of such a fate. He is ungracious to his faithful friend Strap, he is at times unconscionably cruel in his schemes for revenge, he gravitates too easily toward unsavory rakes (Banter is a good example), and he himself is at times tainted with affectation. He does, however, remain good at heart and in the end is rewarded with Narcissa much as Tom Jones, having gained prudence, is allowed to possess Sophia.

It can be said that the novel employs its main character as a moral exemplum for preaching and illustrating the traditional values of the age, among them temperance, virtue, fortitude, and honesty. It can also be said that the book's emphasis on sensibility reinforces the efficacy of human goodness, for if the reader is moved to applaud virtue and hate vice, to upbraid the hero's ingratitude despite his attractiveness, then Smollett in large part proves his point.

Even a quick reading of the novel makes it plain how much Smollett relies on the theme of disguise to develop not only the concept of prudence but also a number of other concerns. One notable example is clothing imagery, which abounds in the book in such scenes as Beau Jackson's appearance before the medical examiners. Wildly costumed as an old duffer, Jackson is a literal application of the adage that "the clothes make the man." He is found out, naturally, and thereby Smollett prepares readers for one of the dominant themes of the novel: Pretension, subterfuge, and hypocrisy are all penetrable. An individual with experience and a sharp eye can see through them.

The question as to who that individual may be is usually answered by eighteenth century writers as "the satirist." It is a commonplace observation that the satirist strips away the coverings of things, that after creating disguises for his characters he tears them away in order to reveal what lies beneath. This is unquestionably so in the case of Smollett. The clothing imagery fits well with his satiric purposes, for everywhere his intent is to bare human morals as well as physical nature. An understanding of this commonplace in part elucidates Smollett's dislike of romantic novels and other such writings. His attack on romance in the preface owes much to the satiric spirit that prevailed in the Augustan age, for there are few modes so different in philosophy as the romantic and the satiric. Romances—or "novels" as they were often called in Smollett's day—are in a sense departures from this world; they are fantasies, unrealities, idealizations. Satire, on the other hand, is fully committed to the world as it is; therefore, it both eschews the improbable and dissolves the apparently real in order to plumb life's deepest recesses.

It should also be mentioned that *The Adventures of Roderick Random*, Smollett's first novel, is interesting simply for its biographical and historical inclusions. Smollett was a surgeon and, as is to be expected, the book offers plenty of commentary on eighteenth century medical practices. Like his main character, the author served in the Royal Navy as a surgeon's mate and was present at the disastrous attack on Cartagena (this is discussed at length in the novel); he thus had a firsthand knowledge of seamanship as well as of medicine. The story of Molopoyn, which occurs near the end of the book, is a thinly disguised account of Smollett's endeavors to promote his tragedy, *The Regicide* (1749).

"Critical Evaluation" by David B. Carroll

Further Reading

Beasley, Jerry C. *Tobias Smollett: Novelist*. Athens: University of Georgia Press, 1998. An analysis of Smollett's five novels, which Beasley interprets as "exercises in the visual imagination," written by an author who believed the private, interior life could be defined by the externally visible. Chapter 1 focuses on *The Adventures of Roderick Random*.

Bold, Alan, ed. *Smollett: Author of the First Distinction*.

London: Vision, 1982. Collection of essays designed to reassess and revive Smollett's literary reputation. Deals with his work in the context of his Scottish heritage and tradition. Discusses Smollett's urgency of pace, use of language, and selection of themes.

Bouce, Paul-Gabriel. *The Novels of Tobias Smollett*. Translated by Antonia White. London: Longman, 1976. Begins with brief biography and attempts to show the inclusion of autobiographical elements throughout Smollett's novels. Addresses Smollett as a moralist rather than the usual picaresque designation, but notes the influence of Alain-René Lesage and Miguel de Cervantes on his work.

Brack, O. M., Jr, ed. *Tobias Smollett, Scotland's First Novelist: New Essays in Memory of Paul-Gabriel Bouce*. Newark: University of Delaware Press, 2007. Collection of essays on Smollett's fiction and nonfiction, including a comparison of his work with that of Henry Fielding, an examination of his contributions to the gothic novel, and "Bouce, Celine, and Roderick Random" by Gerald J. Butler.

Bruce, Donald. *Radical Doctor Smollett*. Boston: Houghton Mifflin, 1965. One of the definitive works on Smollett, providing a historical survey of his critical reputation as a novelist. Addresses his use of medicine, sex, crime, and wealth as themes for social criticism. Discusses whether his work should be categorized as picaresque, ultimately describing the author as pessimistic and belligerent.

Giddings, Robert. *The Tradition of Smollett*. London: Methuen, 1967. Discusses Smollett as a standard-bearer of the picaresque tradition and compares him to Henry Fielding. Maintains that Smollett is an evolutionary predecessor for all rogue novels up to the work of John Barth.

Lewis, Jeremy. *Tobias Smollett*. London: Jonathan Cape, 2003. An appreciative look at Smollett's life, written by an acclaimed biographer. Includes bibliography and index.

Spector, Robert Donald. *Tobias George Smollett*. Rev. ed. Boston: Twayne, 1989. Discusses Smollett's five novels as masterpieces of the picaresque form and shows how each led to and perfected the next. Repudiates previous critical analysis of the author.

The Adventures of Tom Sawyer

Author: Mark Twain (1835-1910)
First published: 1876
Type of work: Novel
Type of plot: Adventure
Time of plot: 1840's
Locale: St. Petersburg, Missouri

Principal characters:
TOM SAWYER, the protagonist
AUNT POLLY, his deceased mother's sister
HUCKLEBERRY FINN and JOE HARPER, his friends
BECKY THATCHER, his sweetheart
INJUN JOE, a murderer
MUFF POTTER, the village ne'er-do-well

The Story:

Tom Sawyer lives securely with the knowledge that his Aunt Polly loves him dearly. When she scolds him or whips him, he knows that inside her breast lurks a hidden remorse. Often he deserves the punishment he receives, but there are times when he is the victim of his tattletale half brother, Sid. Tom's cousin Mary is kinder to him. Her worst duty toward him is to see to it that he washes and puts on clean clothes, so that he will look respectable when Aunt Polly takes the children to Sunday school.

When a new family moves into town, Tom sees a pretty, blue-eyed girl with lacy pantalettes. Instantly the fervent love he has felt for Amy Lawrence flees from his faithless bosom, replaced by devotion to this new girl. At Sunday school, Tom learns that her name is Becky Thatcher. She is in school the next day, sitting on the girls' side of the room with an empty seat beside her. Tom comes late to school that morning. When the schoolmaster asks Tom why he is late, the empty seat beside Becky catches his eye. Recklessly he confesses he stopped to talk with Huckleberry Finn, son of the town drunk. Huck wears cast-off clothing, never attends school, smokes and fishes as often as he pleases, and sleeps wherever he can. For associating with Huckleberry Finn, Tom is whipped by the schoolmaster and ordered to sit on the girls' side of the room. Amid the snickers of the entire class, he takes the empty seat next to Becky.

Tom first attracts Becky's attention with a series of drawings on his slate. At length, he writes the words, "I love you," and Becky blushes. Tom persuades her to meet him at lunch.

Sitting with her on a fence, he explains the possibilities of an engagement between them. Innocently, she accepts his proposal, which Tom insists must be sealed by a kiss. In coy resistance she allows Tom a brief chase before she yields to his embrace. Tom's happiness is unbounded. When he mentions his previous tie with Amy Lawrence, however, the brief romance ends, and Becky leaves with a toss of her head.

That night, Tom hears Huck's whistle below his bedroom window. Sneaking out, Tom joins his friend, and the two go off to the cemetery. They are about to try a new method for curing warts. The gloomy atmosphere of the burial ground fills the boys with apprehension, and their fears increase when they spy three figures—Injun Joe, Muff Potter, and Doctor Robinson. Evidently they have come to rob a grave. When the two robbers exhume the body, they begin to quarrel with the doctor about money. In the quarrel, the drunken Potter is knocked out. Then Injun Joe takes Potter's knife and kills the doctor. When Potter recovers from his blow, he thinks he has killed Robinson, and Injun Joe allows him to believe himself guilty. Terrified, Tom and Huck slip away from the scene, afraid that if Injun Joe discovers them he will kill them, too.

Becky has not come to school since the day she broke Tom's heart. According to rumor, she is ill. Tom loses all interest in life, brooding over what he and Huck saw in the graveyard. Convinced that Tom is ill, Aunt Polly doses him with a quack painkiller and keeps him in bed, but he does not seem to recover. When Becky finally returns to school, she cuts Tom coldly. Feeling that there is nothing else for him to do, Tom decides to run away. He meets Joe Harper and Huck Finn, and they go to Jackson's Island and pretend to be pirates. For a few days they are happy on the island and learn from Huck how to smoke and swear. They are beginning to get homesick when they hear a cannon being fired over the river from a steamboat. Then the boys realize that the townspeople are searching for their bodies. This discovery puts a new aspect on their adventure; the people at home think they were dead. Gleeful, Tom cannot resist the temptation to see how Aunt Polly is reacting to his death. He slips back to the mainland one night and into his aunt's house, where Mrs. Harper and Aunt Polly are mourning the deaths of their mischievous but good-hearted children. When Tom returns to the island, he finds Joe and Huck tired of their game and ready to go home. Tom proposes to them an attractive plan which they immediately decide to carry out.

With a heavy gloom overhanging the town, funeral services are held for the deceased Thomas Sawyer, Joseph Harper, and Huckleberry Finn. The minister pronounces a lengthy eulogy about the respective good characters of the unfortunate boys. When the funeral procession is about to start, Tom, Joe, and Huck march down the aisle of the church into the arms of the startled mourners. For a while, Tom is the hero of all the boys in the town. They whisper about him and eye him with awe in the schoolyard. Becky, however, ignores him until the day she accidentally tears a page in the schoolmaster's anatomy book. When the irate teacher demands to know who tore his book, Tom confesses to save Becky from a whipping. Becky's gratitude and forgiveness are his reward.

After Muff Potter is jailed for the murder of the doctor in the graveyard, Tom and Huck swear to each other they will never utter a word about what they saw. Afraid that Injun Joe will murder them in revenge, they furtively sneak behind the prison and bring Muff food and other cheer; but Tom cannot let an innocent man be condemned. At the trial, he appears to tell what he saw on the night of the murder. While Tom speaks, Injun Joe, a witness at the trial, springs through the window of the courtroom and escapes. For days Tom worries, convinced that Injun Joe will come back to murder him. As time goes by and nothing happens, he gradually loses his fears. With Becky looking upon him as a hero, his world is filled with sunshine.

Huck and Tom decide to hunt for pirates' treasure near an old abandoned house. One night, they watch, unseen, while Injun Joe—who returns to town disguised as a mute Spaniard—and a companion unearth a chest of money buried under the floorboards of the house. The two frightened boys flee before they are discovered. The next day, they begin a steady watch for Injun Joe and his accomplice, for they are bent on finding the hidden treasure.

Becky's parents give a picnic for all the young people in town, after which Becky is supposed to spend the night with Mrs. Harper. One of the biggest excitements of the merrymaking comes when the children go into the cave by the river. The next day, Mrs. Thatcher and Aunt Polly learn that Tom and Becky are missing. No one remembers having seen Tom and Becky after the picnickers left the cave. Meanwhile, Tom and Becky lose their bearings and wander through the cave's labyrinthine passages until their last candle burns out beside a freshwater spring. To add to Tom's terror, he discovers that Injun Joe is also in the cave.

Meanwhile, Huck keeps his vigil at Injun Joe's lodgings in town until the disguised murderer emerges. He then follows Injun Joe and his accomplice and overhears them planning to assault the Widow Douglas. After warning a neighbor named Jones in time for the man and his sons to save the widow and chase away her would-be attackers, Huck collapses in a fever. He later recovers to learn that he is a public hero.

After Tom and Becky have been inside the cave for five days, Tom finds a way out—at a spot five miles from the main entrance. He and Becky then miraculously reappear in town, where Tom is again acclaimed a hero. To prevent others from getting lost in the cave, Judge Thatcher installs a heavy iron door at its entrance. When Tom recovers from his exhausting ordeal two weeks later and hears about the iron door, he announces that Injun Joe is inside the cave. Townspeople then rush to the cave, where they find Injun Joe lying behind the new door, dead of starvation.

Using the secret entry that he discovers, Tom later takes Huck back to the cave, where they find the treasure chest hidden by Injun Joe. It contains twelve thousand dollars in gold coins. Huck, who now has an income of a dollar a day for the rest of his life, is informally adopted by the Widow Douglas. He never would have stayed with the Widow or consented to learn her prim, tidy ways if Tom had not promised that he would form a pirate gang and make Huck one of the bold buccaneers.

Critical Evaluation:

Mark Twain, who began his writing career as a frontier humorist and ended it as a bitter satirist, drew on his experiences growing up with little formal schooling in a small Missouri town and on his life as printer's apprentice, journalist, roving correspondent, silver prospector, world traveler, Mississippi steamboat pilot, and lecturer. He was influenced by Artemus Ward, Bret Harte, and Joel Chandler Harris. Beginning with the publication of his short story "Jim Smiley and His Jumping Frog" (1865; later published as "The Celebrated Jumping Frog of Calaveras County") and proceeding through novels and travel books—*The Innocents Abroad* (1869), *Roughing It* (1872), *The Gilded Age* (1873), *The Adventures of Tom Sawyer* (1876), *Life on the Mississippi* (1883), *Adventures of Huckleberry Finn* (1884), *A Connecticut Yankee in King Arthur's Court* (1889), and *The American Claimant* (1892)—Twain developed a characteristic style that, while uneven in its productions, made him the most important and representative nineteenth century American writer. His service as delightful entertainer to generations of American youngsters is equaled by his influence on such twentieth century admirers as Gertrude Stein, William Faulkner, and Ernest Hemingway.

Twain's generally careful and conscientious style was both a development of the tradition of humor of Augustus Baldwin Longstreet and Joel Chandler Harris and a departure from the conventions of nineteenth century literary gentility. It is characterized by the adroit use of exaggeration, stalwart irreverence, deadpan seriousness, droll cynicism, and pungent commentary on the human situation. All of this is masked in an uncomplicated, straightforward narrative distinguished for its introduction of the colloquial and vernacular into American fiction that was to have a profound impact on the development of American writing and shape the world's view of America. Twain, according to Frank Baldanza, had a talent for "paring away the inessential and presenting the bare core of experience with devastating authenticity." The combination of childish rascality and innocence in his earlier writing gave way, in his later and posthumous works, to an ever-darkening vision of man that left Twain bitter and disillusioned. This darker vision is only hinted at in the three Tom Sawyer books—in addition to *The Adventures of Tom Sawyer*, Twain wrote *Tom Sawyer Abroad* (1894) and *Tom Sawyer, Detective* (1896)—and in his masterpiece, *Adventures of Huckleberry Finn*.

Twain's lifelong fascination with boyhood play led to the creation of *The Adventures of Tom Sawyer*, a book of nostalgic recollections of his own lost youth that was dismissed too lightly by some as "amusing but thin stuff" and taken too analytically and seriously by others, some of whom seek in it the complexities of carefully controlled viewpoint, multiple irony, and social satire found in *Adventures of Huckleberry Finn*. Beyond the fact that *The Adventures of Tom Sawyer* is a delicate balance of the romantic and realistic, humor and pathos, innocence and evil, the book defies simple analysis. Twain's opening statement in *Adventures of Huckleberry Finn* is, ironically, more applicable to *The Adventures of Tom Sawyer*: "Persons attempting to find a motive in this narrative will be prosecuted; persons attempting to find a moral in it will be banished; persons attempting to find a plot in it will be shot." The book is purely, simply, and happily "the history of a boy," or as Twain also called it, "simply a hymn, put into prose form to give it a worldly air." It should be read first and last for pleasure, by both children and adults.

As even Twain admitted paradoxically, *The Adventures of Tom Sawyer* is also for those who have long since passed from boyhood: "[It] is not a boy's book at all. It will be read only by adults. It is written only for adults." Kenneth S. Lynn explicates the author's preface when he says that *The Adventures of Tom Sawyer* "confirms the profoundest wishes of the heart." Christopher Morley calls the book "a panorama of happy memory" and had made a special visit to Hannibal because he wanted to see the town and house where Tom lived. During that visit, Morley and friends actually whitewashed Aunt Polly's fence. There can be no greater testimony to the effectiveness of a literary work than its readers' desire to reenact the exploits of its hero.

Tom is the archetypal all-American boy, defining in himself the very concept of American boyhood, as he passes with equal seriousness from one obsession to another: whistling, glory, spying, sympathy, flirtation, exploration, piracy, shame, fear—always displaying to the utmost the child's ability to concentrate his entire energies on one thing at a time (as when he puts the treasure hunt out of his mind in favor of Becky's picnic). Tom is contrasted to both Sid, the "good boy" who loses the reader's sympathies as immediately as Tom gains them, and to the outcast, Huck. In contrast to Huck's self-reliant, unschooled, parentless existence, his passive preference for being a follower, and his abhorrence of civilization, Tom is adventurous, shrewd in the ways of civilization, and a leader. He comes from the respectable world of Aunt Polly and has a literary mind coupled with a conscious romantic desire for experience and for the hero's part, an insatiable egotism that assists him in his ingenious schematizations of life to match his heroic aspirations. The relationship between the two boys may be compared to that between the romantic Don Quixote and the realist Sancho Panza. It was Twain's genius to understand that the games Quixote played out of "madness" were, in fact, those played by children with deadly seriousness. Lionel Trilling summarizes Twain's achievement when he says that "*The Adventures of Tom Sawyer* has the truth of honesty—what it says about things and feelings is never false and always both adequate and beautiful." Twain's book is an American classic, but a classic that travels well as an ambassador of American idealism.

Further Reading

Blair, Walter. "Tom Sawyer." In *Mark Twain: A Collection of Critical Essays*, edited by Henry Nash Smith. Englewood Cliffs, N.J.: Prentice-Hall, 1963. A leading Mark Twain scholar traces autobiographical and literary influences in *The Adventures of Tom Sawyer.* Shows how Twain adapted real people, places, and events into this early novel.

Camfield, Gregg. *The Oxford Companion to Mark Twain.* New York: Oxford University Press, 2003. Collection of about three hundred original essays on individual works, themes, characters, language, subjects that interested Twain, and other topics. Includes an appendix on researching Twain, which lists useful secondary sources, and an annotated bibliography of more than 1,700 of Twain's novels, plays, poems, and other writings.

Emerson, Everett. *Mark Twain: A Literary Life.* Philadelphia: University of Pennsylvania Press, 2000. A complete revision of Emerson's *The Authentic Mark Twain* (1984), this masterful study traces the development of Twain's writing against the events in his life and provides illuminating discussions of many individual works.

Fields, Wayne. "When the Fences Are Down: Language and Order in the Adventures of Tom Sawyer and Huckleberry Finn." *Journal of American Studies* 24, no. 3 (December, 1990): 369-386. A valuable comparison of the two novels. Images of fences place Tom Sawyer within an ordered community, while Huck explores a disordered, insecure world outside the fences.

Fishkin, Shelley Fisher. *Lighting Out for the Territory: Reflections on Mark Twain and American Culture.* New York: Oxford University Press, 1996. A broad survey of Twain's influence on modern culture, including the many writers who have acknowledged their indebtedness to him. Discusses Twain's use of Hannibal, Missouri, in his writings. Charts his transformation from a southern racist to a committed antiracist.

Rasmussen, R. Kent. *Bloom's How to Write About Mark Twain.* New York: Bloom's Literary Criticism, 2008. Designed for students, this volume contains a chapter offering clear guidelines on how to write essays on literature, a chapter on writing about Twain, and chapters providing specific advice on individual works, including *The Adventures of Tom Sawyer.*

_______. *Critical Companion to Mark Twain: A Literary Reference to His Life and Work.* 2 vols. New York: Facts On File, 2007. Alphabetically arranged entries about the plots, characters, places, and other subjects relating to Twain's writings and life. Features extended analytical essays on Twain's major works, an expanded and fully annotated bibliography of books about Twain, and a glossary explaining unusual words in Twain's vocabulary.

Robinson, Forrest G. "Social Play and Bad Faith in *The Adventures of Tom Sawyer.*" *Nineteenth-Century Literature* 39, no. 1 (June, 1984): 1-24. Defends the novel's reputation by asserting that its coherence relies on a dominant character with "a dream of himself as a hero in a world of play."

Twain, Mark. *The Adventures of Tom Sawyer, Tom Sawyer Abroad, and Tom Sawyer, Detective.* Edited by John C. Gerber, Paul Baender, and Terry Firkins. Berkeley: University of California Press, 1980. The definitive, corrected edition of all three Tom Sawyer novels, prepared by the Mark Twain Project at Berkeley. Heavily annotated, with citations to many specialized sources.

Wolff, Cynthia Griffin. "*The Adventures of Tom Sawyer*: A Nightmare Vision of American Boyhood." In *Mark Twain*, edited by R. Kent Rasmussen. Pasadena, Calif.: Salem Press, 2010. First published in *Massachusetts Review* in 1980, this revisionist essay explores the novel's dark undercurrents and demonstrates that the pessimism for which Twain's late writings are well known can also be found in his early fiction.

The Adventurous Simplicissimus

Author: Hans Jakob Christoffel von Grimmelshausen (1621?-1676)
First published: *Der abenteuerliche Simplicissimus*, 1669 (English translation, 1912)
Type of work: Novel
Type of plot: Picaresque
Time of plot: Seventeenth century
Locale: Germany

Principal characters:
SIMPLICIUS SIMPLICISSIMUS, a vagabond
A PEASANT, his foster father
A HERMIT, his real father
A PASTOR
ULRICH HERZBRUDER, Simplicissimus's friend
OLIVER, a rogue

The Story:

Simplicissimus's beginning is one of a child of pure innocence. Since he lives far removed from any other influences except the small, barely sufficient farm near the Spessart forest, he presents himself as nothing short of a simpleton. His main job is looking after the livestock, and when told to look out for the foxes who come to raid the chickens, Simplicissimus mistakes some soldiers for foxes. Since he never saw either a fox or a knight before, he interprets them in the only way he knows how. The soldiers are soldiers of the Thirty Years' War and plunder his family's farm as Simplicissimus escapes into the forest.

Deep in the forest, he meets a hermit. This hermit asks him many questions that Simplicissimus can answer only in the most naïve manner. He cannot even tell the hermit his real name. He states that his father calls him "boy." For two years the boy stays with the hermit and learns from him. The hermit dies and the pastor who gives Simplicissimus supplies is captured by the soldiers. The small town nearby is plundered. Simplicissimus again escapes to the forest but ends up having even his small hut plundered. He is taken as prisoner to the Governor of Hanau. The soldiers questions Simplicissimus, and again he cannot tell his name, nor much of his history. A pastor comes to Simplicissimus's rescue by stating that the pastor saw Simplicissimus in a hermitage with the old man, who happened to be a nobleman disenchanted with the war.

As Simplicissimus's life goes on, he begins his climb in status. He becomes a page, but his simpleton ways are not those of the court. He is at a grave disadvantage. He ends up looking and playing a fool. He comments liberally about society, and during a great feast, he sees men acting with such bad manners he thinks that they are representing themselves as beasts instead of men. The more he sees the more Simplicissimus realizes a fool's ways are better suited for survival than the ways of a courtier.

Again his circumstance change and he becomes a prisoner to the Croats. He learns to serve many masters. He escapes dressed as a girl, but he is destined to serve as a lady's maid. He is then discovered to be male and ends up as a horse boy, at which time he meets his friend Ulrich Herzbruder. Simplicissimus gives Ulrich money to escape, which Ulrich successfully does, and again Simplicissimus's situation changes.

Simplicissimus is beginning to become educated as to the ways of the world. He begins to climb the ladder of success. He goes through the military ranks, and although he plunders, he never takes from the poor, always the rich. He has plenty of wealth and has a reputation as a superior forager, something he was taught by the hermit. Later, Simplicissimus discovers someone attempted to steal his name and reputation and committed crimes in his name, wearing the green garb synonymous with Simplicissimus. Simplicissimus finds and punishes this man. From this time forward, Simplicissimus aspires to become a nobleman, but his fate will not allow it. The Swedes capture him.

During his incarceration with the Swedes, Simplicissimus establishes himself with the ladies. The Swedes, after hearing of his reputation as a soldier, offer him a position in their armies, but Simplicissimus turns them down. The Swedes allow him to roam around the city at will. A young daughter of a colonel attracts Simplicissimus and they marry. Shortly after, Simplicissimus pledges his alliance to the Swedes.

Then his life changes again. On a trip to Cologne the Swedes convince him to go to Paris. There he loses his fortune in a robbery, but he gains many adventures in love. Then Simplicissimus uses a ruse to return to Germany; he impersonates a doctor. He never makes it back to Germany. Instead he is captured and forced to become a soldier in another army. He meets Oliver, who took advantage of his good friend Ulrich. Soldiers kill Oliver, and Simplicissimus travels onward.

Following the war, Simplicissimus visits a Swiss spa and stumbles upon an old man who happens to be his peasant father. Simplicissimus discovers that his peasant father is actually his foster father and that the old hermit of noble birth is his real father. From that time on, he has many adventures, including getting married again only to have his wife die after a year. In the end, Simplicissimus returns to the life of his real father and becomes a hermit.

Critical Evaluation:

Considered an oasis within a desert of medieval German novels, Hans Jakob Christoffel von Grimmelshausen's *The Adventurous Simplicissimus* was a critical flop but was quite influential and extremely popular. Critics often refer to it as the greatest prose work in German literature, and it has influenced many others. Grimmelshausen is said to have been influenced by Henry Neville's *Isle of Pines* (1668).

The actual name of the author of *The Adventurous Simplicissimus* was not discovered until 1838. Grimmelshausen's work possesses autobiographical elements, especially in scenes tied to the Thirty Years' War. The novel is a picaresque most of the time, but in addition it could be interpreted as a bildungsroman. In a picaresque novel the protagonist is someone of low birth. This low status gives a worm's-eye view from which the narrator can comment on, criticize, and assess the different strata of society. The plot is generally loosely organized. The protagonist never fully develops; he remains a rogue and his experiences do not educate him. The bildungsroman describes the complete development of a character. The protagonist of a bildungsroman slowly achieves moral, spiritual, psychological, and social harmony. The bildungsroman is about a character's struggle toward a better life, whereas the picaresque character merely experiences life. *The Adventurous Simplicissimus* has attributes of both types of novel, but on balance it is more picaresque. The protagonist is a rogue, although of noble birth. He tries to fulfill his urge to be noble but does not yearn for it very strongly. Simplicissimus merely experiences and comments upon the various situations happening in his life and never learns much from them.

Grimmelshausen strips his character of familial ties and replaces them with religious ties. All of Simplicissimus's interpretations are religious. The author couples all observances with religious interpretations of action, and in the end the protagonist fulfills the circle as he returns to the life of his father, the hermit. Throughout the work the author has the protagonist complete many circles. Simplicissimus starts out on top of the circle. Then, through his simpleton ways, he falls prey to situations for which he is not prepared.

Janet Luehring

Further Reading

Allen, Ann Taylor. *Satire and Society in Wilhelmine Germany: Kladderadatsch and Simplicissimus, 1890-1914.* Lexington: University Press of Kentucky, 1984. An excellent history and criticism of *The Adventurous Simplicissimus*, with discussion of social problems as related to literature. Includes bibliography.

Bertsch, Janet. "Grimmelshausen's *Der abentheurliche Simplicissimus Teutsch* and *Der seltzame Springinsfeld*." In *Storytelling in the Works of Bunyan, Grimmelshausen, Defoe, and Schnabel*. Rochester, N.Y.: Camden House, 2004. Bertsch examines two of Grimmelshausen's novels, including *The Adventurous Simplicissimus*, as well as works by John Bunyan, Daniel Defoe, and J. G. Schnabel. These works were written between 1660 and 1740, a period of transition between intense religiosity and a growing secularization, and Bertsch demonstrates how these authors' works reflect this societal change.

Glasberg, Ronald. "The Perversions of Folly in Grimmelshausen's *Simplicius Simplicissimus*: Foreshadowing of Nazism." *CLIO: A Journal of Literature, History, and the Philosophy of History* 16, no. 3 (1987): 253-271. A great discussion of *The Adventurous Simplicissimus*, with an especially valuable analysis of its characters.

Horwich, Cara M. *Survival in "Simplicissimus" and "Mutter Courage."* New York: Peter Lang, 1997. A comparison of *The Adventurous Simplicissimus* and Bertolt Brecht's play *Mother Courage and Her Children*, which was based on Grimmelshausen's work. Horwich maintains that the novel and play share a common concern with human survival in a dangerous world.

Menhennet, Alan. *Grimmelshausen the Storyteller: A Study of the "Simplician" Novels.* Columbia, S.C.: Camden House, 1997. A detailed examination of Grimmelshausen's novels about Simplicissimus, in which Menhennet focuses on their common elements, arguing that they are not separate books but part of a coherent cycle. He also demonstrates how they integrate religious and moral concerns with a more secular curiosity and sense of humor.

Negus, Kenneth. *Grimmelshausen*. New York: Twayne, 1974. A wonderful book that notes major influences on Grimmelshausen. Includes a chapter on his sources and his references and a bibliography.

Otto, Karl F., Jr., ed. *A Companion to the Works of Grimmelshausen.* Rochester, N.Y.: Camden House, 2003. A collection of essays analyzing Grimmelshausen's works, including discussions of Grimmelhausen and the picaresque novel, allegorical and astronomical elements in his works, and gender identity in the Simplicissimus cycle.

Richtie, J. M. "Grimmelshausen's *Simplicissimus* and *The Runagate Courage*." In *Knaves and Swindlers: Essays on the Picaresque Novel in Europe*, edited by Christine J. Whitbourn. London: Oxford University Press, 1974. An excellent essay integrating the Thirty Years' War, Grimmelshausen's life, and some of his other works. Includes bibliography.

Wicks, Ulrich. *Picaresque Narrative, Picaresque Fictions: A Theory and Research Guide.* Westport, Conn.: Greenwood Press, 1989. An excellent beginning source. Describes the various aspects of a picaresque novel. Discusses *The Adventurous Simplicissimus* and its themes.

Aeneid

Author: Vergil (70-19 B.C.E.)
First transcribed: c. 29-19 B.C.E. (English translation, 1553)
Type of work: Poetry
Type of plot: Epic
Time of plot: After the Trojan War
Locale: The Mediterranean

Principal characters:
AENEAS, a Trojan hero destined to found the Roman race
DIDO, queen of Carthage, in love with Aeneas
ANNA, her sister
ASCANIUS, son of Aeneas
ANCHISES, father of Aeneas
VENUS, goddess of love and beauty, mother of Aeneas
JUNO, queen of the gods and enemy of the Trojans
CUMAEAN SIBYL, prophet who leads Aeneas to Hades
LATINUS, king of the Latins, whom Aeneas defeats in battle
LAVINIA, his daughter
TURNUS, Latin hero ambitious for the Latin throne and hand of Lavinia
EVANDER, Arcadian king, ally of Aeneas
PALLAS, his son

The Poem:

Aeneas, driven by a storm to the shores of Libya, is welcomed gladly by the people of Carthage. Because Carthage is the favorite city of Juno, divine enemy of Aeneas, Venus has Cupid take the form of Ascanius, son of Aeneas, so that the young god of love might warm the heart of proud Dido, queen of Carthage, and Aeneas will come to no harm in her land. At the close of a welcoming feast, Aeneas is prevailed upon to recount his adventures.

He describes the fall of his native Troy at the hands of the Greeks after a ten-year siege, telling how the armed Greeks entered the city in the belly of a great wooden horse, and how the Trojans fled from their burning city, among them Aeneas, with his father, Anchises, and young Ascanius. Not long afterward, Anchises advised setting sail for distant lands. Blown by varying winds, the Trojans at length reached Buthrotum, where it was foretold that they would have a long and arduous journey before Aeneas would reach Italy. Setting sail once more, they reached Sicily. There Anchises, who was his son's sage counselor, died and was buried. Forced to leave Sicily, Aeneas was blown by stormy winds to the coast of Libya. Here he ends his tale, and Dido, influenced by Cupid disguised as Ascanius, feels pity and admiration for the Trojan hero.

The next day, Dido continues her entertainment for Aeneas. During a royal hunt, a great storm drives Dido and Aeneas to the same cave for refuge. There they succumb to the passion of love. Aeneas spends the winter in Carthage and enjoys the devotion of the queen, but in the spring, he feels the need to continue his destined course. When he sets sail, the sorrowing Dido kills herself. The light of her funeral pyre is seen far out at sea.

Again on the shores of Sicily, Aeneas bids his men refresh themselves with food, drink, and games. First, there is a boat race in which Cloanthus is the victor. The second event is a foot race, won by Euryalus. Entellus engages Dares in a boxing match, which Aeneas stops before the clearly superior Entellus achieves a knockout. The final contest is with bow and arrow. Eurytion and Acestes make spectacular showings, and each is awarded a handsome prize. Following the contests, Ascanius and the other young boys ride out to engage in war games. Meanwhile, the women grieve the lost guidance of Anchises and, at the instigation of Juno, set fire to the ships. Aeneas, sustained by the gods, bids his people repair the damage. Once more, the Trojans set sail.

Finally, they reach the shores of Italy, at Cumae, which is famous for its Sibyl. The Sibyl grants Aeneas the privilege of visiting his father in the underworld. After due sacrifice, Aeneas and the Sibyl begin their descent into Hades. At length, they reach the river Styx and persuade the boatman, Charon, to row them across. Aeneas sees the spirits of many people he knew in life, including the ill-fated Dido. Then they come to the beginning of a forked road. One path leads to the regions of the damned; the other leads to the land of the blessed. Following the latter road, they come at last to Anchises, who shows Aeneas in marvelous fashion the future of Rome and commands him to found his kingdom at the place where he would eat his tables. On his return to the upper regions, Aeneas revisits his men and proceeds to his own abode.

Again the Trojans set sail up the coast of Italy, to the ancient state of Latium, ruled by Latinus. On the shore, they prepare a meal, laying bread under their meat. As they are eating, Ascanius jokingly observes that in eating their bread they are eating their tables. This remark tells Aeneas that this is the place Anchises foretold. The next day, the Trojans come to the city of King Latinus on the Tiber. Latinus was warned by an oracle not to give his daughter Lavinia in marriage to any native man but to wait for an alien, who would come to establish a great people. He welcomes Aeneas as that man of destiny.

A Latin hero, Turnus, becomes jealous of the favor Latinus shows Aeneas and stirs up revolt among the people. Juno, hating Aeneas, aids Turnus. One day, Ascanius kills a stag, not knowing that it is the tame favorite of a native family. From this incident, there grows such a feud that Latinus shuts himself up in his house and ceases to control his subjects. Aeneas makes preparations for battle with the Latins under Turnus.

In a dream, he is advised to seek the help of Evander, whose kingdom on the Seven Hills will become the site of mighty Rome. Evander agrees to join forces with Aeneas against the armies of Turnus and to enlist troops from nearby territories as well. Venus presents Aeneas with a fabulous shield made by Vulcan, for she fears for the safety of her son.

When Turnus learns that Aeneas is with Evander, he and his troops besiege the Trojan camp. One night, Nisus and Euryalus, two Trojan youths, enter the camp of the sleeping Latins and slaughter a great many of them before they are discovered and put to death. The enraged Latins advance on the Trojans with fire and sword and force them into open battle. When the Trojans seem about to beat back their attackers, Turnus enters the fray and puts them to flight. The thought of Aeneas inspires the Trojans to such bravery that they drive Turnus into the river.

Aeneas, warned in a dream of this battle, returns and lands with his allies on the shore near the battlefield, where he encounters Turnus and his armies. Evander's troops are being routed when Pallas, Evander's beloved son, urges them on and himself rushes into the fight, killing many of the enemy before he is slain in combat with Turnus. Aeneas seeks to take the life of Turnus, who escapes through the intervention of Juno.

Aeneas decrees that the body of Pallas should be sent back to his father, with appropriate pomp, during a twelve-day truce. The gods watched the conflict from afar; now Juno relents at Jupiter's command but insists that the Trojans must take the Latin speech and garb before their city can rule the world.

Turnus leads his band of followers against Aeneas, in spite of a treaty made by Latinus. An arrow from an unknown source penetrates Aeneas, but his wound is miraculously healed. The Trojan hero reenters the battle and is again wounded, but he is able to engage Turnus in personal combat and strike him down. Aeneas kills his enemy in the name of Pallas and sacrifices his body to the shade of his dead ally. No longer opposed by Turnus, Aeneas is now free to marry Lavinia and establish his long-promised new nation. This is Rome, the greatest power of the ancient world.

Critical Evaluation:

Publius Vergilius Maro, better known as Vergil, is among the greatest poets Rome produced. His finest work, the *Aeneid*, became the national epic and, when Rome collapsed, it survived to become the most influential book Rome contributed to Western culture. Dante Alighieri drew direct inspiration from book 4 for *The Divine Comedy* (c. 1320), allowing the spirit of Vergil to guide him through the Inferno and up the heights of Purgatory.

Vergil was a modest, retiring man who preferred the seclusion of his country estate to life in the bustling metropolis of Rome. He was much liked and esteemed by important people, including the poet Horace and the Emperor Augustus. He won the patronage of the great, secured the wealth and leisure necessary to write, composed three supreme poems—the *Georgics* (36-29 B.C.E.), the *Eclogues* (42-37 B.C.E.), and the *Aeneid*—and died revered and honored. In his lifetime, he saw the closing years of the civil war that destroyed the Roman Republic and the established Roman Empire under Augustus. To celebrate the Pax Romana and the leadership of Augustus, Vergil wrote the *Aeneid*, his patriotic epic dealing with the mythical Roman past.

According to legend, the Trojan hero Aeneas came to Italy after escaping the fall of Troy and became the ancestor of the Romans through his descendant, Romulus. Vergil took this material and, borrowing his structure from Homer, fashioned an epic. The first part of the poem, dealing with Aeneas's wanderings, resembles Homer's *Odyssey* (c. 725 B.C.E.) in form and content; the second half, which treats Aeneas's war in Latium and its surroundings, imitates in some ways the *Iliad* (c. 750 B.C.E.). Certain poetic devices, such as the repeated epithet, are taken from Homer, as well as the way the gods interfere on behalf of their favorites. However, the *Aeneid* is wholly original in concept, possessing a unique unity of its own.

The originality lies in its presentation of Aeneas, a hero who struggles and fights, not for booty, personal fame, or any existing country but for a civilization that will exist in the distant future, that of Rome and of Augustus. He sacrifices his personal comforts, leaving home after home because of the prodding of his inner sense of destiny. He knows that he is to be the founder of a new nation, but the details are revealed to him gradually in the course of his journeying. Chronologically, the pattern is one of revelation and sacrifice, and each new revelation about his destiny imposes a greater burden of responsibility. The final revelation—when Aeneas descends with the Sibyl into the cavern of death and is shown the coming glory of Rome by his father, Anchises—prepares him spiritually and physically for the greatest fight of his life. Finally, he is something greater than a man. In fulfilling his grand fate, he becomes a monument, an unstoppable force, an instrument of the gods, like the Roman Empire as Vergil visualized it.

When the poem opens and Aeneas and his men are shipwrecked at Carthage, the hero already knows two things: that he has an important mission to accomplish and that his future home lies on the western coast of Italy. This knowledge ensures, on his part, a limited commitment to Dido, who falls completely in love with him, giving herself freely even though it ruins her as a woman and a queen when Aeneas is ordered by Jupiter to sail on to Italy. In the coldness of his parting, the founder of Rome draws upon himself all the wrath of Dido, the founder of Carthage, which points forward to the Punic Wars between those cities.

Aeneas is not hard-hearted, however. He feels pity for those who are crushed in trying to prevent him from accomplishing his aim—Dido, Lausus, the son of Mezentius, even Turnus. The entire epic is weighted with the sadness of mortality. Aeneas's sense of destiny gives him courage, fortitude, patience, determination, and strength; yet it also makes him humorless, overbearing, and relentless. Still, without that inner conviction in the future destiny of his life and of his fellow Trojans, he would be nothing. Pity is the most that a person who knows he is doing right can feel for those who oppose him. Aeneas has a noble character, although somewhat inhuman, and he seems to embody the best traits of the Roman people.

The crux of the *Aeneid* comes, as Dante rightly perceived, in book 4, when Aeneas enters the realm of Death to gain enlightenment about his future. From the fall of Troy, where the ghost of Hector warns Aeneas, to this point, the dead are associated with revelation. In the underworld Aeneas must purify himself ritually, enter the cavern of death, brave all the terrors of hell, meet dead comrades, and finally, with a rite, enter the realms of the blessed to learn the truth about himself and his fate. Like Dante's hell, Vergil's has various places assigned for various acts, sins, and crimes, but punishment there purges the soul to prepare it for the Elysian Fields, from which it may reincarnate.

In this section, Vergil delineates his view of the meaning of life and death. There is a Great Soul that gives birth to all living spirits, which incarnate themselves in flesh as assorted creatures, including people. The desires of these spirits hinder them from living up to their true purpose in bodily form, so that they must be cleansed after death, only to take on flesh again until they learn their rightful end and achieve it. Thus, death purifies and life tests one on the long road to perfection. This occult view is, in Vergil's case, a mixture of Pythagorean reincarnation, Stoic pantheism, and Platonic mysticism. That view gives credence to everything Anchises shows Aeneas about his illustrious descendants and the rising power of Rome. Aeneas sees the souls of the future waiting their turn, and he knows how much responsibility he really bears. Anchises's judgment of Aeneas is a fitting comment on Rome itself:

> But yours, my Roman, is the gift of government,
> That is your bent—to impose upon the nations
> The code of peace; to be clement to conquered,
> But utterly to crush the intransigent!

In these lines, Vergil sums up the particular genius of Rome, together with its greatness and its terrors.

"Critical Evaluation" by James Weigel, Jr.

Further Reading

Cairns, Francis. *Virgil's Augustan Epic*. New York: Cambridge University Press, 1989. An outstanding piece of criticism that opens the poem to the reader. Explains the role of games in the narrative, the significance of numerous characters, and geographical and mythological references. Accessible and pleasant to read.

Conte, Gian Biagio. *The Poetry of Pathos: Studies in Virgilian Epic*. Edited by S. J. Harrison. New York: Oxford University Press, 2007. An interpretation of the *Aeneid* that demonstrates how Vergil reworked poetry by Homer and other early poets to create broad literary and emotional effects. Describes how Vergil in *Aeneid* devises a new form of epic poetry.

Fratantuono, Lee. *Madness Unchained: A Reading of Virgil's "Aeneid."* Lanham, Md.: Lexington Books, 2007. A guide to *Aeneid*, describing Vergil's purpose for writing the epic. Analyzes every scene, as well as every line in some crucial passages. Surveys Vergil studies and provides bibliographies of works about the poet.

Gransden, K. W. *Virgil: The "Aeneid."* 2d ed. New York: Cambridge University Press, 2004. Stresses the character of Aeneas, his moral burdens, his ambition, and his suffering. Useful in understanding Vergil's epic ambition and the political goals of his poem within the context of Augustan Rome.

Henry, Elisabeth. *The Vigour of Prophecy: A Study of Virgil's Aeneid*. Carbondale: Southern Illinois University Press, 1990. An examination of the various temporal perspectives of Vergil's *Aeneid*. Illustrates how recollection of past events and prophetic knowledge of the future create a philosophical vision of fate and divine will which determines heroic action in the epic.

Johnson, W. R. *Darkness Visible*. Berkeley: University of California Press, 1976. Reassesses the temper of the poem, seeing it not as imperial and stately but as pessimistic and skeptical. Controversial among Vergil scholars, but probably the most important book on the *Aeneid* published in the last quarter of the twentieth century.

Lyne, R. O. A. M. *Words and the Poet: Characteristic Techniques of Style in Vergil's "Aeneid."* New York: Oxford University Press, 1989. Occasionally difficult, but excellent stylistic analysis of the *Aeneid*. Especially provocative in its discussion of the technique of epic simile and the way in which epic simile helps the poem define itself as a narrative.

Reed, J. D. *Virgil's Gaze: Nation and Poetry in the "Aeneid."* Princeton. N.J.: Princeton University Press, 2007. Examines how Vergil in *Aeneid* defines, or fails to define, Roman identity. Argues that Roman identity is depicted as "multivalent" and constantly changing, instead of unitary and stable.

Ross, David O. *Virgil's "Aeneid": A Reader's Guide*. Malden, Mass.: Blackwell, 2007. Describes the *Aeneid*'s poetic style and imagery and places it within its historic and social context. Discusses Vergil's depiction of his hero, victims, fate and the gods, Troy, and ancient Rome. A chapter summarizing Vergil's life and works contains information on the *Eclogues* and *Georgics*. The appendix explains how to read and hear poetry written in Latin hexameter.

Rossi, Andreola. *Contexts of War: Manipulation of Genre in Virgilian Battle Narrative*. Ann Arbor: University of Michigan Press, 2004. Argues that Homer's epic poetry is not the only source for Vergil's depiction of battle in *Aeneid*. Demonstrates how Vergil was influenced by other genres, including historiography and ancient tragedy, and how he created a war narrative that allows for multiple visions of reality.

Slavitt, David. *Virgil*. New Haven, Conn.: Yale University Press, 1991. Pays particular attention to the craft of the poem and the personal sensibility of the poet. Comments on and critiques the quality of various English translations of the *Aeneid*.

Aesop's Fables

Author: Aesop (c. 620-c. 560 B.C.E.)
First transcribed: Aesopea, fourth century B.C.E. (English translation, 1484)
Type of work: Short fiction
Type of plot: Fable
Time of plot: Antiquity

The fables attributed to Aesop were actually composed over the course of many centuries. Aesop is a semilegendary figure, about whom various stories have been told. All that can be known with any certainty about Aesop is that he was a Phrygian slave who was later freed by his Greek master because of the wit and charm of his stories. All other details about Aesop's life appear to have been invented after his death. For example, it is said that Aesop served under two masters, Xanthus and Iadmon, on the island of Samos. After being freed by Iadmon, Aesop is reported to have traveled as far as the Lydian city of Sardis, where he became a favorite of King Croesus (c. 600-546 B.C.E.). Another legend reports that the citizens of Delphi were outraged by Aesop's description of them as mere parasites, living off the wealth of others. To punish Aesop for this insult, the Delphians are said to have hidden a golden bowl among his possessions just before he left the city. When the bowl was discovered, Aesop was convicted of theft and executed by being thrown from a cliff. None of these incidents is likely to have occurred. While the historian Herodotus (c. 484-c. 425 B.C.E.) does describe Iadmon as Aesop's master and says that the former slave was murdered by the Delphians, it must be remembered that Herodotus is not always reliable. In the fourth century B.C.E., the comic poet Alexis wrote a play, *Aesop*, now lost. Some of the episodes included in later biographical sketches of the author may actually have been derived from this comic work.

The stories told by the historical Aesop appear to have been a mix of legends, myths, and political parables. Even in antiquity, however, it was the fable—and, in particular, the animal fable—with which Aesop became most closely associated. More than a hundred animal stories are now attributed to him. Aesop himself was probably responsible for few of the tales that bear his name. He never wrote a book. His stories belonged to the oral tradition. Even as late as the Renaissance, numerous moral fables were still being attributed to Aesop. Many of the fables that later ages believed were written by Aesop were actually the work of Demetrius of Phalerum (c. 350 B.C.E.), Phaedrus (c. 15 B.C.E.-c. 50 C.E.), Babrius (second century C.E.), Avianus (c. 400 C.E.), and Jean de La Fontaine (1621-1695). Manuscripts of stories said to have been written by Aesop include legends that vary widely by date, are sometimes composed in Greek and sometimes in Latin, and are arranged not by subject but alphabetically by the first word in the story, hardly a likely categorization system for a storyteller.

In most examples of Aesop's fables, each animal symbolizes a different human virtue or vice. The fox represents cunning, the ass stupidity, the lion ferocity, the ant industry, the grasshopper laziness, the crow vanity, and so on. By placing these creatures in different combinations, the fables comment upon the varieties of human nature and criticize common human foibles. For example, in "The Ass, the Fox, and the Lion," a fox offers to betray his friend the ass to the lion, provided that the lion promises never to harm the fox. The lion agrees to this proposal, and the ass foolishly falls into the trap that the fox prepares. Once the ass is safely ensnared, however, the lion turns and attacks the fox, proving that those who act with treachery are themselves often betrayed.

In a similar tale, "The Lion, the Ass, and the Fox Go Hunting," the same three animals agree to help one another by forming a hunting party. Since each contributes his own particular skills, they are very successful and, at the end of the day, there is a great heap of booty. The ass proceeds to divide the profits into three equal parts and asks the lion which share he would prefer as his own. Instead of answering, the lion simply attacks the ass and gobbles him up. Then the fox proceeds to divide the booty, claiming only a tiny morsel for himself and granting his comrade the "lion's share." "Why did you divide our goods in that way?" the lion asks. "I'm no fool," the fox replies. "I needed no other lesson than the ass's fate."

Frequently, the fox is depicted as using his cleverness to the detriment of others. In "The Fox and the Crow," for example, a crow steals a piece of cheese that she holds in her beak high in the branches of a tree. The fox sees her and begins to flatter her great beauty. "What a pity," the fox concludes, "that a creature with such a beautiful beak and feathers does not have an equally lovely voice!" The crow, out of vanity, wishes to prove the fox wrong and, opening her beak to sing, drops the piece of cheese. The fox leaps on the cheese at once, proving both the shallowness of false flattery and the foolishness of conceit.

At times, however, even cunning is not enough to win the fox what he wants. In "The Fox and the Grapes," for instance, a fox sees a bunch of grapes ripening in the sun high up on a vine. Despite his repeated efforts, the fox is unable to leap high enough to reach the grapes. "Never mind," the fox mutters as he walks away, "the grapes are probably sour anyway." From this story comes the expression "sour grapes," a phrase used to describe a person's denigrating something that the person wants but cannot have. In a similar story, "The Fox and the Bramble," the fox is about to fall from a hedge when he catches hold of a bramble for support. The thorns of the bramble wound the fox severely, and he accuses the bramble of being inhospitable to those in need. "You were foolish," the bramble replies, "to cling to one who usually clings to others." The moral of the story is that no one should expect aid from those who usually seek it.

In the fable of "The Ant and the Grasshopper," a grasshopper is hungry during the winter and begs an ant for a share of the food that it has in its store. "Why did you not do what I did and spend the summer storing up grain?" the ant asks. "Because I preferred to sing all summer," the grasshopper replies. "Well," the ant says as it walks away, "if, instead of working, you sang all summer, then you must dance hungry all winter." The moral of the story is that the person who works hard will be rewarded while the person who wastes time in idleness will suffer when times are lean.

Not all of the stories attributed to Aesop are animal fables. "Zeus, Poseidon, Athena, and Momus" is a traditional Greek myth with the Olympian gods as central characters. Zeus, Poseidon, and Athena decide to have a contest to see which of them can produce the perfect creation. Zeus makes a man, Athena makes a house, and Poseidon makes a bull. The god Momus, who personifies fault-finding and is never happy with anything, is then appointed by the gods to choose the winner of their contest. Momus, however, refuses to award the prize to any of the participants: The man is poorly made, Momus says, because the man does not have a window in his breast so that all can see what is hidden in his heart; the house is poorly made because it has no wheels to roll it away from unpleasant neighbors; and the bull is poorly made because he must lower his eyes when he charges. In frustration at this reply, Zeus drives Momus from Mount Olympus forever, accusing him of being one of those critics who can only find flaws but never create useful things themselves. Other stories by Aesop also deal with other gods from Greek mythology, including Hermes and Heracles.

Even inanimate objects occasionally appear as the subjects of Aesop's fables. In "The Two Pots," for example, a bronze pot and an earthenware pot are carried off by a stream. The bronze pot urges the earthenware pot to remain close to him so that his strength can protect the weakness of the clay pot. "That is just what I am afraid of," the earthenware pot replies. "If I keep my distance from you, we may both be safe. If I get too close to you, your very strength may do me damage." This story suggests that humble people should not associate too closely with the mighty since, when trouble comes, the weak will suffer from having risen above their place.

The typical Aesop's fable seeks, therefore, to make its point through a homely and easily understood parable. Few of the legends attributed to Aesop are much longer than a paragraph. They teach a lesson simply and not through elaborate detail. The author draws character by introducing broad types of personalities rather than by creating highly differentiated individuals. According to tradition, the historical Aesop told stories to comment upon political events of his day. For example, he is said to have created the fable "The Frogs Who Wanted a King" because he wanted to suggest to the Athenians that they were better off under the tyrant Peisistratus (d. 527 B.C.E.) than they would be under a ruler whose faults they did not yet know. The majority of the tales that survive bearing Aesop's name are not political in nature. They deal with general personality types and draw broad conclusions that relate to all people.

Jeffrey L. Buller

Further Reading

Aesop. *Aesopica*. Edited by Ben Edward Perry. Champaign: University of Illinois Press, 1952. A thorough and scholarly collection of Aesopic texts. Contains the fables themselves and texts relating to the life of Aesop. A good place to begin for those who wish to undertake advanced study of the Aesopic canon.

Babrius and Phaedrus. *Babrius and Phaedrus*. Edited by Ben Edwin Perry. Cambridge, Mass.: Harvard University Press, 1975. Original texts and English translations of all Aesopic fables by the authors Babrius and Phaedrus. Includes a valuable historical introduction and a comprehensive survey of all Greek and Latin fables in the Aesopic tradition.

Blackham, Harold John. *The Fable as Literature*. Mineola, N.Y.: Dover, 1985. Blackham does not confine himself to Aesop, but this is one of the best introductory studies of the literary use of fable. Includes an index and a bibliography.

Halliday, William Reginald. *Indo-European Folk-Tales and Greek Legend*. Cambridge, England: Cambridge University Press, 1933. Although somewhat dated, Halliday's discussion of Greek legend and its origin in Indo-European folklore is still a valuable survey of the origins of myth, saga, and fable.

Holzberg, Niklas. "Fable Books in Prose." In *The Ancient Fable: An Introduction*. Translated by Christine Jackson-Holzberg. Bloomington: Indiana University Press, 2002. This chapter in Holzberg's history of the fable in antiquity focuses on two books of Aesop's fables dating from ancient Rome, one written in Latin and the other in Greek.

Keidel, George Charles. *A Manual of Aesopic Fable Literature*. Geneva: Slatkine Reprints, 1974. A useful reference on the sources of Aesopic animal fables from antiquity to 1500.

Patterson, Annabel M. *Fables of Power: Aesopian Writing and Political History*. Durham, N.C.: Duke University Press, 1991. An extensive and highly readable study of Aesop's influence and of the imitations of his fables in English literature during the sixteenth and seventeenth centuries. Discusses the continuing role that Aesop's fables have played in European society.

Zafiropoulos, Christos A. *Ethics in "Aesop's Fables": The Augustana Collection*. Boston: Brill, 2001. Zafiropoulos argues that the fable is a type of ethical reasoning and demonstrates how *Aesop's Fables* provides a guide to proper behavior and attitudes.

The Affected Young Ladies

Author: Molière (1622-1673)
First produced: Les Précieuses ridicules, 1659; first published, 1660 (English translation, 1732)
Type of work: Drama
Type of plot: Comedy of manners
Time of plot: Seventeenth century
Locale: Paris

Principal characters:
LA GRANGE and DU CROISY, young men of Paris
MAGDELON and CATHOS, romantic ladies
THE MARQUIS DE MASCARILLE, La Grange's valet
VISCOUNT JODELET, Du Croisy's valet
GORGIBUS, Magdelon's father and Cathos's uncle

The Story:

Gorgibus brings his daughter Magdelon and his niece Cathos from their country home for a stay in Paris. There La Grange and Du Croisy, calling on them to propose marriage, are greatly disgusted by the affectation displayed by the young ladies, for the girls adopt a manner prevalent everywhere in France, a combination of coquetry and artificiality. With the help of their valets, La Grange and Du Croisy determine to teach the silly young girls a lesson. One of the valets, Mascarille, loves to pass for a wit; he dresses himself as a man of quality and composes songs and verses.

Gorgibus, meeting the two prospective suitors, inquires into their success with his niece and his daughter. The evasive answers he receives make him decide to discuss the affair with the two ladies. He waits for them while they paint their faces and arrange their hair. When they are finally ready to receive him, he is enraged by their silly conversation.

He expected them to accept the two young men, who are wealthy and of good family, but the affected young ladies explain that they spurn suitors who are so direct and sincere. Much to the girls' disgust, the young men proposed at their first meeting. They want lovers to be pensive and sorrowful, not joyful and healthy, as La Grange and Du Croisy are. In addition, a young lady must refuse her lover's pleas in order to make him miserable. If possible, there should also be adventures: the presence of rivals, the scorn of fathers, elopements from high windows. Another fault the girls find with the two young men is that they are dressed simply, with no ribbons or feathers on their clothing. Poor Gorgibus thinks that his daughter and niece are out of their minds, especially when they ask him to call them by other names, for their own are too vulgar. Cathos is to be called Aminte, and Magdelon Polixene. Gorgibus knows one thing after this foolish conversation—either the two girls will marry quickly or they will both become nuns.

Even their maid cannot understand the orders the girls give her, for they talk in riddles. She announces that a young man is in the parlor, come to call on the two ladies. The caller is the Marquis de Mascarille, in reality La Grange's valet.

The girls are enchanted with Mascarille, for he is a dandy of the greatest and most artificial wit. His bombastic puns are so affected that the girls think him the very soul of cleverness. He pretends to all sorts of accomplishments and acquaintances. On the spot, he composes terrible verses and songs, which he sings out of key and in a nasal tone. He claims to have written a play that will be acted at the Royal Theater. He draws their attention to his beautiful dress, complete with ribbons, feathers, and perfume. Not to be outdone, the ladies boast that although they know no one in Paris as yet, a friend promises to acquaint them with all the fine dandies of the city. They are a perfect audience for the silly valet. They applaud each verse, each song, each bit of shallow wit.

The Viscount Jodelet, in reality Du Croisy's valet, joins the group. He claims to be a hero of the wars, in command of two thousand horsemen, and he lets the girls feel the scars left by deadly wounds he received. The two scoundrels are hard put to outdo each other in telling the foolish girls ridiculous tales. When they talk of their visits with dukes and countesses, the girls are fascinated by their good connections. Running out of conversation, the two valets then ask the girls to arrange a party. They send for musicians and other young people in order to have a proper dance. Mascarille, not being able to dance, accuses the musicians of not keeping proper time, and Jodelet agrees with him.

The dance is in full swing when La Grange and Du Croisy appear and fall upon the two impostors, raining blows on them and calling them rogues. Mascarille and Jodelet try to pretend it is all a joke, but their masters continue to beat them. When other servants appear and begin to strip the clothes from the two pretenders, the girls scream in horror. La Grange and Du Croisy berate them for receiving servants better than they receive their masters. They tell the girls that if they love the two scoundrels so well, they must love them without their masters' finery. Taking all the outer apparel from the rogues, La Grange and Du Croisy order them to continue the dance.

Gorgibus, having heard of the scandal on the streets of Paris, soundly berates the pranksters for the disgrace they bring on his house. All Paris, all France even, will laugh at the joke, for the young people at the dance are now spreading the news up and down the streets and in the cafés. Gorgibus is furious with La Grange and Du Croisy for their trick, but he knows the stupid girls deserve the treatment they received. He sends the two valets packing and orders the affected young ladies to hide themselves from the world. Then he curses folly, affectation, and romantic songs, the causes of his horrible disgrace.

Critical Evaluation:

The Affected Young Ladies was first performed only one year after the author's permanent establishment in Paris; it was an enormous success and secured his reputation as the capital's foremost dramatist. The play is significant as a curious blend of the particular and the universal, for it not only ridicules a specific group in the Parisian society of Molière's day but also satirizes human foibles common to every time and place.

In the second quarter of the seventeenth century, there grew up in Paris, in reaction to the prevalent coarseness of manners in French society, a group known as the Précieux. This group centered on the literary salon of Madame de Rambouillet and was devoted to the cultivation of dignified speech and manners and the study, discussion, and patronage of literature. What began as a sort of cultural club, however, evolved in the hands of Madame de Rambouillet's successors into a fad distinguished only by its absurdity. The later Précieux, who met to gossip and act out scenes from popular romantic novels, spoke in a highly affected style that became for a time the rage in salons all over Paris. It is the craze led by this later circle that Molière lampoons in *Les Précieuses ridicules* (which is also frequently translated as *Two Precious Damsels Ridiculed*). Madame de Rambouillet herself, realizing that Molière's barbs were aimed not at her but at her successors, was one of the play's ardent admirers and invited Molière to stage three performances at her home.

Given the specificity of the play's target, it is easy to imagine its success with Molière's contemporaries. They understood all the references and recognized the follies of the characters. They laughed at Cathos's and Magdelon's assumption of romantic pseudonyms ("The names Polixene and Aminte are far more graceful, you must agree") and their avowal to live their lives as romantic heroines; they sympathized with the down-to-earth Gorgibus and his bewilderment in the face of his daughter's and niece's "gibberish" ("No doubt about it; they're over the edge"). If audiences continue to laugh at this play for more than three centuries, the answer lies in the universality of Molière's comedy. The impulse toward preciosity is not exclusively a seventeenth century French phenomenon but rather a constitutional weakness common to all people. Every time and place has its précieux because the desire for distinctiveness and novelty of expression seems to be part of human nature. Thus it is that people laugh at Cathos and Magdelon, at Mascarille and Jodelet, even as they recognize some of their folly and affectation as their own.

Molière found the perfect vehicle for making audiences laugh at human folly in plays such as *The Affected Young*

Ladies. In the development of this style, he drew heavily on two sources: traditional French farce and Italian commedia dell'arte. Using and creatively transforming features from each, he molded the kind of dramatic comedy for which he became famous. Masks, for example, which date back to ancient times and which had been revived in Italian drama, were thereupon adopted by French neoclassicists, who used them to characterize types such as scheming valets, jealous husbands, unscrupulous liars, misers, prudes, braggarts, coquettes, libertines, and pedants. Molière developed his own character types on the basis of old stock figures; two of his most famous types were Sganarelle and Mascarille. He became a master of the device of the mask and developed the art of relying on gesture and posture rather than facial expression to convey meaning. After expanding, modifying, and exploring all the theatrical possibilities of masks, however, Molière went on to do what the commedia dell'arte never attempted: He depicted through his characters all the social relationships and class conditions within French society, exposing the vices of high and low alike with his wit.

In an early play such as *The Affected Young Ladies*, the masks are still of standard farcical types. In the play's original performances, Molière himself played Mascarille, wearing a mask, while Jodelet, a widely popular slapstick comedian, performed under his own name, wearing the white powder mask for which he was famous. The figures of Mascarille and Jodelet—valets who have a talent for parading about, passing for what they are not—represent the folly of affectation and falseness. They are the agents through which Molière ridicules the representatives of the Précieux, Cathos and Magdelon; they are brought to humiliation through their gullible acceptance of the valets' deception. The message in *The Affected Young Ladies* is basically the same as in all of Molière's plays: Excess, whether of vice or virtue, leads to downfall. Molière, a constant and thorough observer of life, early concluded that people who become dominated by a single passion, idea, or obsession lose their common sense. Because the two young ladies in this play have been carried beyond all bounds of reason by their passion for romances, they are easily duped by the valets.

The plot in *The Affected Young Ladies*, as in all of Molière's comedies, is minimal; it is merely a vehicle to allow characters their full comic play, which is the playwright's primary purpose. Molière was a master of all the verbal laugh-getting devices, including double entendre, echo-dialogues, and malapropisms, but above all he was the supreme farceur. Some fine examples of traditional, rollicking French farce in this play include Mascarille's entrance with the sedan-chair bearers, the drubbing of the valets by La Grange and Du Croisy, and Jodelet's stripping of his countless layers of garments. For this reason, a play such as *The Affected Young Ladies* must be seen performed for full effect. Molière's greatness lies in his ability to fuse astute criticism of the follies and absurdities of human behavior with unsurpassed comedy. Ironically, perhaps his greatest and most lasting tribute came from one of his contemporaries who, in a malicious attempt to slander him, called Molière "the first jester of France."

"Critical Evaluation" by Nancy G. Ballard

Further Reading

Backer, Dorothy. *Precious Women*. New York: Basic Books, 1974. A historical study that shows how preciousness (*préciosité*) was an early feminist literary movement. Explains that Molière made fun only of the pretentious and not the truly creative precious writers who were his contemporaries.

Lawrence, Francis L. *Molière: The Comedy of Unreason*. New Orleans, La.: Tulane University Press, 1968. Explores conflicts between rational and irrational characters in Molière's comedies. Examines parody and comic representations of love in *The Affected Young Ladies*.

McCarthy, Gerry. *The Theatres of Molière*. New York: Routledge, 2002. Places Molière's life and work within the context of the French theater of his time. Discusses the productions of some of his plays, including their actors, scenes, and costumes.

Polsky, Zachary. *The Comic Machine, the Narrative Machine, and the Political Machine in the Works of Molière*. Lewiston, N.Y.: E. Mellen Press, 2003. Examines the nature of seventeenth century French comedy by analyzing the works of Molière. Discusses the moralism and political context of Molière's plays and describes the use of speech, voice, and body in their performance.

Scott, Virginia. *Molière: A Theatrical Life*. New York: Cambridge University Press, 2000. Chronicles Molière's life and provides an overview of his plays, placing them within the context of seventeenth century French theater.

Wadsworth, Philip A. *Molière and the Italian Theatrical Tradition*. 2d ed. Birmingham, Ala.: Summa, 1987. Analyzes the profound influence on Molière of Italian actors and playwrights. Discusses the importance of nonverbal gestures and wordplay in *The Affected Young Ladies*.

Walker, Hallam. *Molière*. Rev. ed. Boston: Twayne, 1990. Contains an excellent introduction to Molière's comedies and an annotated bibliography of important critical studies on the playwright. Examines the role of parody and social satire in *The Affected Young Ladies*.

Yarrow, P. J. *The Seventeenth Century: 1600-1715*. Vol. 2 in *A Literary History of France*, edited by P. E. Charvet. London: Ernest Benn, 1967. A general history of seventeenth century French literature that includes one chapter with a very clear introduction to Molière's plays. Yarrow discusses role reversal and the conflict between illusion and reality in *The Affected Young Ladies.*

The Afternoon of a Faun

Author: Stéphane Mallarmé (1842-1898)
First published: L'Après-midi d'un faune, 1876 (English translation, 1936)
Type of work: Poetry

Stéphane Mallarmé's *The Afternoon of a Faun* is first and foremost poetry, but its origins link it to the theater. At the time of its composition, Mallarmé described it as a "heroic interlude," a fragment of a dramatic presentation. In the same letter, however, he also refers to its lines as "verses," and when the text was ready for publication, he submitted it for inclusion in the third collection of *Le Parnasse contemporain* in 1874. Rejected for inclusion in this volume, the poem finally appeared in its own limited edition in 1876.

Mallarmé's subtitle calls the work an "eclogue," a word derived from the idea of a poetic fragment that in later usage came to designate a work with a bucolic setting. While both senses of the word fit the text that follows, that alone does not prepare the reader to understand the first lines on an initial reading.

In the manner of the French classical theater, the faun's speech draws on events that have already begun and translates past action into dramatic discourse. The first line, "These nymphs, I want to perpetuate them," indicates from the initial descriptive adjective a need to refer to circumstances that the faun knows but that the reader must intuit. The French phrase "je les veux perpétuer" uses archaic word order and links the speech to past time, underlining both the dramatic conventions and the mythological persona that define the faun.

As with much of Mallarmé's poetry, the reader must imagine the action. Here, however, Mallarmé supplies more obvious clues than he does in his difficult poems. Idyllic images immediately lead the reader into a reverie resembling that of the faun. Given the reader's participation in the creation of the poem, the experience is all the more likely to touch the reader personally.

The faun apparently just awakens from a dream in which he sees the nymphs. Mallarmé immediately forces the reader to exert his or her interpretive faculties by the use of nontraditional language to describe this experience. When the nymphs appear in "leur incarnat léger," the pale rosy color that might normally be a descriptive adjective takes on the substance of a noun. The faun himself is "drowsy with bushy sleep." The adjective "touffus" may allude to the woodland setting in which the faun sleeps, but its other possible use in describing an involved style of writing suggests the faun's confused state of mind. He asks, after a pause, whether he loves a dream, since the empty woods around him suggest that he is alone. As he reflects on his memory, however, a number of specific details attest to the reality of the experience. There were clearly two nymphs. The first, he recalls, had the cold blue eyes of chastity. The other was defined by the music of her sighs. The faun expands on the musical sound, similar to the tone he can produce on his panpipes, and on the breath that produced it, warm as a summer breeze.

Emboldened by these specific memories, the faun invokes the "Sicilian shores" that his vanity would "pillage" to tell him what actually happened. Here Mallarmé introduces the first of three italicized segments of the poem in which the faun, playing both parts of the still theatrical dialogue, seems to answer his own question. However, the answer remains incomplete. The faun recalls only that he was cutting reeds to play music when he suddenly saw an "animal whiteness" that could have been either swans or naiads.

Then the memory, along with the italics, disappears. The faun remains alone under a hot sun, thinking that his own sexual longing may have inspired the fantasy. As he awakens, presumably returning to the present, he finds himself beneath an "ancient flood of light." The light of the sun, constant over time, represents to him a link with the past and recalls the state in which he had awakened in the first lines of the poem, troubled by a doubt that came from "old night." Both images suggest the hold the past still has upon him. Still contemplating his memories, the faun finds evidence of a kiss in the bite mark of a tooth in his breast. Still he hesitates, knowing that beauty can deceive and that he seems to have confused it with his own "credulous song." Perhaps all that happened is that he had a banal glimpse of the two fleeing creatures.

Even if the vision led to an imagined encounter, the faun knows how to relive the event. He addresses his panpipes, "the instrument of flight," asking them to make the lakes "flower again." The pipes may evoke the flight of the nymphs, but they also enable the faun's imagination to take flight in the sense that the images of the nymphs will bloom through his artistic re-creation. This imaging of the nymphs draws on important analogies between Mallarmé's work and the poems of Charles Baudelaire. In *Les Fleurs du mal* (1857, 1861, 1868; *Flowers of Evil*, 1931), Baudelaire developed a vision of a female figure as muse that both inspired and tormented the poet. Similarly, Mallarmé's faun says that he will "speak at length of goddesses," whom he seems to dominate (he "removes the belts from their shades" to reveal their physical being) at the same time that he allows them to dominate him. In a further association with Baudelaire, the vision of the nymphs reminds the faun of intoxication. He will reveal the intimate picture of them just as he saw light through the empty skins of grapes when he spent a long afternoon "sucking out the brightness" of their apparently intoxicating juice. The fusion of images of bright light, fruits of nature, and the female figures emphasizes the role of woman as muse. She inspires the faun's visions that are linked to his music and provides an analogy to the creation of the poet's songs.

The inspiration provided by the nymphs leads to Mallarmé's second italicized section, much more explicit than the first, in which the faun recalls finding the two nymphs asleep and ravishing them. Nature images in this section reinforce the sensuality of the experience. At first, the faun sees only fragments of the nymphs' bodies as his eye pierces the reeds. Then he runs toward them as toward a mass of blooming roses. More Baudelairean themes occur as he likens the light reflected in their hair to jewels and evokes the secret perfume of the flowers.

Between this and the final italicized section, the faun pauses to reflect on the "wrath of virgins" that he provokes. The nymphs' resistance increases his desire, but apparently they do not resist long, as fear "abandons their innocence." Despite references to their trembling and tears, the passage ends with emotions that are "less sad." The nymphs seem moved by the desire of the faun. Whereas the nymphs awaken to desire, the faun begins to see the harm of his attack.

The final italicized section begins with his reference to "my crime." Devoted to pleasure as he is, however, the faun cannot think of seduction in negative terms. A number of positive references seek to justify his action as he "gaily vanquished their fears" with an "ardent laugh under the happy folds" of the nymphs. He even sees a divine sanction for the seduction in that "the gods had kept their kisses so well mingled."

By the end of this scene a reversal takes place. The nymphs, no longer blushing, are inspired to passion by the faun's advances. However, the encounter ends. The nymphs, whom the faun now describes as his "prey," free themselves, leaving "without pity for the sob still intoxicating" him. The faun may have sought to exploit the nymphs, but he now sees himself as the victim of the emotions he releases. The faun does not remain emotionally engaged for long. Immediately after the italicized memory ends, he looks to the future and to others who will bring him new happiness, "knotting their tresses around the horns on my forehead." Each passionate encounter, far from representing a unique event, forms a part of the lascivious pattern of nature. The faun sees his passion as resembling a ripe pomegranate surrounded by bees that represent "the eternal swarming of desire."

The faun's erotic insouciance echoes the traditions linked to such creatures in classical times. The faun invokes this past tradition as the setting of the festival of nature that will take place on "Etna, visited by Venus." The goddess arrives to touch the mountain's lava with her "naïve heels." Thus she recalls the innocence of the nymphs, but her hovering light, as she barely touches the ground, parallels that often attributed to the muse by the Romantic poets. Ethereal though the nymph may be, the faun sees her as yet another woman because, when sleep finally extinguishes the flame of his desire, he concludes this section with the exclamation, "I hold the queen!" This declaration of possession, almost as if he were referring to the queen in a deck of cards, reasserts the faun's dominance.

The poem asks whether the fatigued sleep is a punishment for the faun's actions, to which he answers that it is not, but that he merely "succumbs to the proud silence of noon" for a midday nap, his mouth open to the sun, the producer of wine. In the last line of the poem, an adieu to the nymphs before the faun goes to sleep, he declares, "I will see the shadow that you become." He will sleep and dream, again, of his vision of the nymphs. The time invoked by this final section seems to conflict with the title of the poem. If, after the major events described, the faun falls asleep in the noon sun, the "afternoon" of the title has not yet begun. The question arises as what the true subject of the poem is. The faun will probably spend the afternoon re-creating the events in his dream. If the afternoon is the true subject, the major importance attaches not to the event but to its re-creation, the element evocative of the composition of the poet.

Dorothy M. Betz

Further Reading

Evans, David. *Rhythm, Illusion, and the Poetic Idea: Baudelaire, Rimbaud, Mallarmé.* Amsterdam: Rodopi, 2004. Analyzes the form and aesthetics in the work of three major nineteenth century French poets, with particular focus on these poets' uses of and ideas about rhythm. Part 3 provides an analysis of Mallarmé's poetry, including *The Afternoon of a Faun*, and the references to this poem are listed in the index.

Fowlie, Wallace. *Mallarmé.* Chicago: University of Chicago Press, 1953. The first part of this study analyzes the dominant themes in Mallarmé's work. In the second part, Fowlie discusses specific texts. Chapter 5 is devoted to a discussion of the genesis of the poem *The Afternoon of a Faun* as well as to a close reading and interpretation.

Gill, Austin. *The Early Mallarmé.* 2 vols. New York: Oxford University Press, 1979. Two chapters in volume 1, discussing Mallarmé's early compositions, focus on his use of the god Pan and provide background to *The Afternoon of a Faun.*

McCombie, Elizabeth. *Mallarmé and Debussy: Unheard Music, Unseen Text.* New York: Oxford University Press, 2003. Mallarmé's poem inspired composer Claude Debussy to create *Prélude à l'après-midi d'un faune* (*Prelude to the Afternoon of a Faun*); Mallarmé had a vision of combining music and poetry. This book points out the similarities between Mallarmé's poetry and Debussy's music and discusses Mallarmé's "musico-poetic" aesthetic.

Shaw, Mary Lewis. *Performance in the Texts of Mallarmé: The Passage from Art to Ritual.* University Park: Pennsylvania State University Press, 1993. In chapter 8, Shaw analyzes *The Afternoon of a Faun* with an emphasis on its theoretical elements. An examination of the evolution of Mallarmé's text reveals the work's distinctly theatrical genesis.

St. Aubyn, Frederic Chase. *Stéphane Mallarmé.* Rev. ed. New York: Twayne, 1989. Discusses *The Afternoon of a Faun* in chapter 5, "The Secret Terror of the Flesh," and provides a close and accurate reading of the text.

Williams, Heather. *Mallarmé's Ideas in Language.* New York: Peter Lang, 2004. Examines Mallarmé's concern with ideas and the way language behaves when it is placed within the constraints of poetry.

Woolley, Grange. *Stéphane Mallarmé: 1842-1898.* Madison, N.J.: Drew University Press, 1981. Begins with a lengthy biographical sketch followed by short essays on various poems. The discussion of *The Afternoon of a Faun* provides information on the poem's sources and critical reception and concludes with a narrative analysis.

Against the Grain

Author: Joris-Karl Huysmans (1848-1907)
First published: À rebours, 1884 (English translation, 1922)
Type of work: Novel
Type of plot: Character study
Time of plot: Late 1800's
Locale: Paris

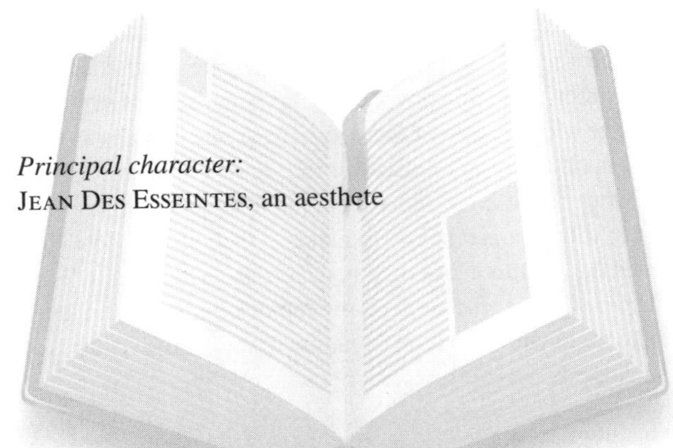

Principal character:
JEAN DES ESSEINTES, an aesthete

The Story:

The Des Esseintes family has a long history. In the Château de Lourps, the portraits of the ancestors show rugged troopers and stern cavalrymen. The family, however, follows a familiar pattern; through two hundred years of intermarriage and indulgence, the men become increasingly effeminate. Now the only remaining Des Esseintes is Jean, who is thirty years old. By a kind of atavism, Jean's looks resemble those of his first grandsire. The resemblance, however, is in looks only.

Jean's childhood was unhappy. His father, living in Paris most of the time, visited Jean briefly at school once in a while when he wished to give moral counsel. Occasionally, he went to see his wife at the château. Jean was always present at those hushed interviews in which his mother took little interest. Jean's mother had a strange dread of light. Passing her days in her shaded boudoir, she avoided contact with the world. At the Jesuit school, Jean became a precocious student of Latin and acquired a fair knowledge of theology. At the same time, he was a stubborn, withdrawn child who refused all discipline. The patient priests let him follow his own bent, for there was little else they could do. Both his parents died while he was young; at his majority, he gained complete control of his inheritance.

In his contacts with the world, Jean goes through two phases. At first, he lives a wild, dissolute life. For a time, he is content with ordinary mistresses. His first love is Miss Urania, an American acrobat. She is strong and healthy; Jean yearns for her as an anemic young girl might long for a Hercules. Nevertheless, Miss Urania is quite feminine, even prudish in her embraces. Their liaison prematurely hastens his impotence. Another mistress is a brunette ventriloquist. One day, Jean purchases a tiny black sphinx and a chimera of polychrome clay. Bringing them into the bedchamber, he prevails on her to imitate Gustave Flaubert's famous dialogue between the Sphinx and the Chimera. His mistress, however, is sulky at having to perform offstage.

After that phase, Jean begins to be disgusted with people. He sees that men reared in religious schools, as he was, are timid and boring. Men educated in the public schools are more courageous but even more boring. In a frantic effort to find companionship, he wildly seeks the most carnal pastimes and the most perverted pleasures.

Jean was never strong, and from childhood he was afflicted with scrofula. Now his nerves are growing weaker. The back of his neck always pains him; his hand trembles when he lifts a light object. In a burst of despairing eccentricity, he gives a farewell dinner to his lost virility. The meal is served on a black table to the sound of funeral marches. The waitresses are nude black women. The plates are edged in black; the menu includes dark bread, meat with licorice sauce, and wine served in dark glasses.

At thirty years old, Jean decides to withdraw from the world. Having concluded that artistry is much superior to nature, he vows that in his retreat he will be completely artificial. He finds a suitable house in a remote suburb of Paris and makes elaborate preparations for his retirement. The upper floor is given over to his two elderly servants, who wear felt coverings on their shoes at all times. He reserves the downstairs for himself. The walls are paneled in leather like book binding, and the only color for ceilings and trim is deep orange. In his dining room, he simulates a ship's cabin and installs aquariums in front of the windows. The study is lined with precious books. With great art, he contrives a luxurious bedroom that looks monastically simple.

Among his paintings, Jean treasures two works of Gustave Moreau that depict Salomé and the head of John the Baptist. He ponders long over the meaning of the scenes. History being silent on the personality of Salomé, Jean decides that Moreau re-created her perfectly. To him, she is the incarnation of woman.

His library is his chief concern. Among the Latin writers, he has no love for the classicists: Vergil, for example, he finds incredibly dull. Nevertheless, he takes great delight in Petronius, who brings to life Roman decadence under Nero. He ardently loves a few of the French sensualists, Paul Verlaine and Charles Baudelaire among them. He also has a small collection of obscure Catholic writers whose refinement and disdain for the world suit his own temperament.

For months, his life is regular and satisfying. He eats breakfast at five and dines at eleven. About dawn, he has his supper and goes to bed. Because of his weak stomach, he is most abstemious in his diet. After a time, his old ailments come back to plague him. He can eat or drink very little, and his nerves pain him. After weeks of torture, he faints. When his servants find him, they call a neighborhood doctor, who can do little for him. At last, Jean seems to recover, and he scolds the servants for having been so concerned. With sudden energy, he makes plans to take a trip to England.

After his luggage is packed, he takes a cab into Paris. To while away the hours before train time, he visits a wine cellar frequented by English tourists and has dinner at an English restaurant. Realizing afresh that the pleasure of travel lies only in the anticipation, he drives himself home that same evening and thus avoids the banality of actually going somewhere. At one stage of his life, Jean loved artificial flowers. Now he comes to see that it would be more satisfying to have real flowers that look artificial. He promptly amasses a collection of misshapen, coarse plants that satisfy his aesthetic needs.

Jean's energy, however, soon dissipates. His hands tremble, his neck pains him, and his stomach refuses food. For weeks, he dreams away his days in a half stupor. Thinking of his past, he is shocked to realize that his wish to withdraw from the world is a vestige of his education under the Jesuits. Finally, he becomes prey to hallucinations. He smells unaccountable odors, and strange women keep him company.

One day he is horrified to look into his mirror. His wasted face seems that of a stranger. He sends for a doctor from Paris. After the physician gives him injections of peptone, Jean returns to something like normal. Then he mistakes a prescription for a dietary supplement for a recipe for an enema. For a while, Jean is entranced with the notion of getting all his sustenance through enemas. One more activity, eating, would therefore be unnecessary.

Then the doctor sends his little artificial world crashing; he orders Jean to leave his retreat and live a normal social life in Paris. Otherwise, his patient will be in danger of death or at least of a protracted illness with tuberculosis. More afraid of his illness than of the stupid world, Jean gives the necessary orders and glumly watches the movers begin their work.

Critical Evaluation:

Against the Grain became the central document of the French Decadents, partly because its elaborate description of Des Esseintes's tastes in art and literature established a frame of reference for Decadent writers and painters and partly because the characterization of Des Esseintes helps to define the Decadent sensibility. The novel instructs the acolytes of the movement in what to read, how to appreciate what they read, and how to pass cynical judgment on the affairs of a world that they are fully entitled to despise. It sends people forth in search of new ways to experience the world, and it offers philosophical arguments to justify all manner of self-indulgent fetishisms. Its most attentive readers were doubtless careful to bear in mind that the whole thing is a joke, but it must be admitted that not everyone noticed that.

In the beginning of the story, Des Esseintes gives up the kinds of activity that most people think of as decadent. He abandons all his mistresses and concludes his experiments in unnatural passion. His experiments with drugs never really go far, because drug-taking only makes him vomit. His one desire is to seek solace in well-furnished isolation. He isolates himself in carefully designed luxury, like a castaway on an island infinitely better in its equipment than that on which Robinson Crusoe found himself. Incidentally, Jean-Jacques Rousseau, the champion of the essential goodness of nature and the human spirit, to whose ideas Huysmans and the Decadents were diametrically opposed, recommended *Robinson Crusoe* (1719) as the only book that a boy needed by way of education.

It is important to notice that Des Esseintes does not see this process of careful isolation as an abandonment of human relationships. He craves contact with the minds of men, as others do, but he desires to refine that contact into a peculiar kind of perfection by restricting his contact to the works of art that are the finest product of human endeavor and the best medium of human communication.

Unlike many who retreat from society, Des Esseintes is not intent upon private communion with God or nature. He acknowledges the contribution made by nature to the hothouse flowers and perfumes of which he is a connoisseur, but insists that they are essentially products of human artifice. He loves the exotic because, for him, exoticism is the ultimate manifestation of human imagination and human artistry. His antipathy to the natural is reflected in antipathy to the realistic; he despises representative works of art, preferring those that attempt to transform and transcend ordinary experience. This is one reason why he retires from the company of human beings. In the flesh, people cannot rise above their essential ordinariness; their artwork offers something more.

The character of Des Esseintes is to some extent a caricature. Some of his tastes and mannerisms are borrowed, tongue-in-cheek, from the most famous of contemporary Parisian men-about-town, Count Robert de Montesquiou. Des Esseintes is also a fantastic self-projection of the author, and there is an unmistakable depth of feeling behind the calculatedly absurd mask. The character's final decision to throw himself into the arms of the Church—not because its doctrines are true but rather because they are fantastic—anticipates the direction the author was to take in real life. Huysmans's account of a man who ardently desires to do everything in stark opposition to the way things are conventionally done is based on his authentic and wholehearted rejection of the tyranny of normality.

Against the Grain never tries to deny that an uncompromisingly Decadent worldview cannot actually work as a practical, or better yet impractical, way of living. Experiments in the building of private utopias are always doomed to failure. The narrative is content to insist that the Decadent's view of life and art is clearer and more logical, aesthetically and morally, than anything that passes for common sense or orthodox faith. The pose that Des Esseintes adopts is not entirely sincere, and it contains a strong element of self-mockery, but its insincerity and irony are the velvet glove that overlies the iron determination of Des Esseintes's condemnation of the world. The moral parables he derives by comparing barmaids with prostitutes, and by throwing crusts of bread to a mob of street urchins, have a sharp satirical bite.

The key to Des Esseintes's entire enterprise is that he is sick, in body, mind, and heart. The treatment of his sickness eventually leads to the most absurd and most brutal of all his inversions of normality, when he begins to take his daily nourishment by enema. His doctor leaves him in no doubt that if he continues to nurture his sickness instead of trying to cure it, he will die. At this point, Des Esseintes capitulates to the tyranny of fate and gives up his experiment. He never surrenders the conviction, however, that his sickness allows him to step outside the world of the commonplace and look back at it objectively, thus giving him a clearer insight into the condition of the world than what is contained in the self-satisfied illusions of healthy, normal people.

Huysmans does not ask or expect his readers to sympathize with Des Esseintes or to accept his conclusions. The text is designed to provide a challenge rather than be a guidebook. It intends to make its readers take a step back from the moral and aesthetic judgments that they take for granted, and to wonder whether such judgments might profitably be inverted. Huysmans scrupulously leaves the verdict open and is careful never to forsake his sense of humor while summing up the evidence.

"Critical Evaluation" by Brian Stableford

Further Reading

Antosh, Ruth B. *Reality and Illusion in the Novels of J.-K. Huysmans*. Amsterdam: Rodopi, 1986. Rejects the opposition of realism and Decadence, which has dominated criticism of Huysmans. Antosh sees Huysmans's work as presenting a tension between the real and the imaginary. Includes an excellent analysis of memory in *Against the Grain*.

Baldick, Robert. *The Life of J.-K. Huysmans*. Oxford, England: Clarendon Press, 1955. Rev. ed. Sawtry, England, Dedalus, 2007. One of the most authoritative biographies of Huysmans available in English. Contains valuable information about the writing of *Against the Grain*. In the new edition, Brendan King has extensively revised and updated Baldick's notes to discuss new developments in Huysmansian studies.

Burton, Richard D. E. "Church Prowling: The Back-to-Front Pilgrimage of Joris-Karl Huysmans (1884-1892)." In *Blood in the City: Violence and Revelation in Paris, 1789-1945*. Ithaca, N.Y.: Cornell University Press, 2001. Burton describes how French history from the start of the French Revolution until the end of World War I was filled with outbursts of political violence. He analyzes works by Huysmans and other French writers to show how this violence is reflected in nineteenth century literature.

Cevasco, G. A. *The Breviary of the Decadence: J.-K. Huysmans's "À rebours" and English Literature*. New York: AMS Press, 2001. Cevasco examines the significant influence of Huysmans's Decadent novel upon English literature, including the works of Oscar Wilde and James Jones. Includes bibliography and index.

Ellis, Havelock. Introduction to *Against the Grain*, by J.-K. Huysmans. Translated by John Howard. Mineola, N.Y.: Dover, 1969. A fascinating reaction to Huysmans's novel from an important English psychologist.

Friedman, Melvin J. "The Symbolist Novel: Huysmans to Malraux." In *Modernism*, edited by Malcolm Bradbury and James McFarlane. Atlantic Highlands, N.J.: Humanities Press, 1978. Defines the Symbolist novel as being more concerned with words than with reality. As such, *Against the Grain* has great significance in the development of the modern novel.

Hafez-Ergaut, Agnès. *Le Vertige du vide: Huysmans, Céline,*

Sartre. Lewiston, N.Y.: Edwin Mellen Press, 2000. A comparison of the work of Huysmans, Louis-Ferdinand Céline, and Jean-Paul Sartre. Hafez-Ergaut maintains that the three French authors are united in their spiritual and philosophical quests and their use of sordid elements to describe the traumatic experiences of modern times.

Lloyd, Christopher. *J.-K. Huysmans and the Fin-de-Siècle Novel*. Edinburgh: Edinburgh University Press, 1990. Defines the fin de siècle period as it applies to literature, and charts in detail the influence of *Against the Grain* on other writers.

Schoolfield, George C. *A Baedeker of Decadence: Charting a Literary Fashion, 1884-1927*. New Haven, Conn.: Yale University Press, 2003. Schoolfield's analysis of thirty-two European and American Decadent novels and novellas begins with an examination of *Against the Grain* in chapter 1 and discusses that novel and Huysmans's other works throughout the book.

The Age of Anxiety
A Baroque Eclogue

Author: W. H. Auden (1907-1973)
First published: 1947
Type of work: Poetry

W. H. Auden was one of the outstanding poets of the twentieth century. He had not only the vision and skill of a major poet but also the necessary luck, or perspicacity, to create poetry that many of his contemporaries felt spoke for them. He spoke their language, he had the "sound" of the 1930's, and he found that sound early. He played a part in shaping the decade because his words and ideas shaped many of the people who influenced the course of events. Auden went on composing poetry for another thirty years and more, but he made his mark when he was barely thirty years old.

Auden was born in 1907 in England, where he continued to live until emigrating to the United States in 1939 just before World War II broke out in Europe. He studied at Oxford, publishing his first book of poems in his early twenties and several more in his next decade. He also published plays, some of which were given radio performance, and he supported himself by teaching school; once in the United States, he took temporary positions at a number of colleges.

Although Auden never stopped challenging his readers, his work began to lose currency during the 1940's. His career peaked early, and while his early success guaranteed him a substantial readership for the remainder of his days, many felt that his career was on a downward slope in later years.

Auden wrote *The Age of Anxiety* right after World War II. Its setting recalls "September 1, 1939," the poem he wrote on the outbreak of that war, which begins

> I sit in one of the dives
> On Fifty-Second Street
> Uncertain and afraid
> As the clever hopes expire
> Of a low dishonest decade.

It is as though the poet were completing a circuit after a hiatus of several years, although there is little other similarity between "September 1, 1939" and *The Age of Anxiety*. The former is driven urgently by the need to respond to the impending cataclysm after Germany invaded Poland. *The Age of Anxiety*, on the other hand, although it, too, is set during World War II, was actually written more than a year after the war's end. The poem contains many passages that are amusing, entertaining, and instructive, but overall the work feels desultory and undermotivated. Many critics agree that it is not among Auden's finer achievements.

To understand the attractiveness of Auden's earlier work, it needs to be seen against the backdrop of its immediate precursors, principal among them the poems of T. S. Eliot, Ezra Pound, H. D., Marianne Moore, and Edith Sitwell among the modernists, and Robert Graves, John Betjeman, and W. B. Yeats among those who opposed the modernist temper. The figure of the long-lived Thomas Hardy, born in 1840 but still writing poems during the 1920's, also looms large in this configuration. Auden took it upon himself to create a poetry that reconciled these various camps.

Auden's innovations were characteristically paradoxical. He kept up with the innovators of the previous generation by returning innovation to traditional measures. He resuscitated many old forms and gave them a contemporary aspect. He was particularly fond of, and adroit with, Anglo-Saxon, or Old English, verse techniques, bringing their heavy alliteration and paucity of articles into play while presenting a modern landscape or theory. *The Age of Anxiety* shows this technique, as in the passage with Auden's rendering of a radio bulletin during World War II:

> *Now the news. Night raids on*
> *Five cities. Fires started.*
> *Pressure applied by pincer movement*
> *In threatening thrust. Third Division*
> *Enlarges beachhead. Lucky charm*
> *Saves sniper. Sabotage hinted*
> *In steel-mill stoppage. Strong point held*
> *By fanatical Nazis. Canal crossed*
> *By heroic marines.*

Auden uses four "n" sounds in the first of these lines, two "f" sounds in the second, three "p" sounds in the third, and so on. He combines the Anglo-Saxon tendency to do without articles, with an up-to-date telegrammatic manner appropriate to news headlines. As in many other poems by Auden, there is a good deal of contemporary slang from the 1940's as well as topical references to such objects as jukeboxes and radios. Auden thus spans the entire history of the English language.

The Age of Anxiety is called a Baroque eclogue; traditionally, an eclogue is a pastoral dialogue between bucolics who are really erudite and sophisticated persons playing at being bucolics. They go—or pretend to go—to the country for refreshment and relaxation, then return to town renewed. Auden's eclogue is Baroque insofar as it resembles a style in art and architecture from the sixteenth, seventeenth, and early eighteenth centuries in Europe, a style marked by strict forms and elaborate ornamentation.

The bucolics in *The Age of Anxiety* are four people who meet in a bar one evening during World War II. They are Quant, an older man and an Irish emigré; Malin, also older and a medical intelligence officer on leave from the Canadian Air Force; Rosetta, who is probably in her thirties, was raised in Britain, and is now a successful buyer for an American department store; and Emble, a young and handsome U.S. sailor. In part 1, the prose part of the prologue, Auden provides a historical frame (World War II) that is also timeless (wartime). During a war, Auden tells us, bar business booms, and "everyone is reduced to the anxious status of a shady character or a displaced person, and becomes a worshiper of chance." They seek out "an unprejudiced space in which nothing particular ever happens"—a bar.

It is All Hallows' Eve. First one character, then the next, speaks to himself or herself his or her thoughts. When the radio delivers a wartime news bulletin, memories of the war revive in the four characters. Rosetta then speaks, permitted to do so by the common topic of the news. The others respond, and shortly they are engaged in a discussion of the present. After another radio bulletin, they decide to share a round of drinks. Malin begins to wax metaphysical—"Let us then/ Consider rather the incessant Now of/ The traveller through time. . . ." The alcohol makes them convivial, and they move from bar stools to a booth.

Part 2, "The Seven Ages," does not have much to do with war but consists of the quartet's various responses to, and reflections upon, human fate as seen through its seven stages: childhood, adolescence, early adulthood, the struggle to succeed, success and recognition, the beginning of senescence, and old age sliding into death. (Of course, the fact of war casts its shadow over the entire recitation.)

Sobered and scared by the picture they have jointly conjured, they turn to Rosetta, the only woman, for consolation, but she can offer only the comfort of the "regressive road to Grandmother's House." Part 2 ends with the bucolics getting drunker, seeking out "that state of prehistoric happiness which, by human beings, can only be imagined in terms of a landscape bearing a symbolic resemblance to the human body." In their separate fantasies, although this is not clear to the reader at the time, they imagine themselves together encountering what ensues.

Part 3, "The Seven Stages," consists of their imaginary wanderings—alone, all together, or in various pairings—across a countryside and through a city, commenting upon the symbolism of the mythic landscapes. The stages of the title are the episodes of this journey but also the settings where their journey plays itself out. Finally, they find themselves facing the last half of the seventh stage, a desert of Joshua trees and giant cacti, and anxiously ask themselves if they are, against all odds, about to succeed in completing this dream quest. Their fears are confirmed: "For the world from which their journey has been one long flight rises up before them now." They come to themselves; the bartender is flicking the lights on and off, as it is closing time. Rosetta invites them back to her place for a snack and a nightcap, and they all accept.

Part 4, "The Dirge," occurs as the quartet shares a cab uptown. It is a stately, highly alliterative poem in dancing measures for whoever spares them from the dangers of the wilderness, of praise and lament "for such a great one who . . . has always died or disappeared."

Part 5, "The Masque," plays out at Rosetta's apartment. Quant and Malin sing; Rosetta and Emble dance, feeling their casual attraction grow. Later, they kiss and exchange vows in stychomythic alternation. After some high-spirited interchanges among the four, Quant and Malin decide that the time comes to depart. Rosetta escorts them to the elevator. When she returns, Emble passes out on her bed. Rosetta—half sad, half relieved—soliloquizes above his sleeping body, to the effect that it is all for the best and that their encounter will remain forever a lovely dream, safe from the slow erosion of suburban reality. In Part 6, "Epilogue," Quant and Malin bid each other goodnight and each goes home alone with his thoughts, returned to his solitary condition.

Auden begins his Baroque eclogue not in some grand European park but in a setting that recalls the bar life of midtown Manhattan, a life Auden knew well. He loved New York, and he became a U.S. citizen (he is often classified as an American poet), but, of course, he remained more British than not. In *The Age of Anxiety*, for example, written six years after he had emigrated, three of his four characters are not native Americans, and the landscapes are often British; moreover, the use of Americanisms accords uneasily with the prevailing English diction.

Through its very pervasiveness, Auden's heavy use of alliteration, which in this work brings along with it a diction that suggests the Anglo-Saxon origins of modern English, overwhelms distinctions between characters. Yet, this is not a play in the dramatic sense of the term, but rather an "entertainment," where the pretense of the actors should be allowed to show.

Part 3 aside—which is confusing and unnecessarily mystifying as characters hop in and out of airplanes, boats, and trains—*The Age of Anxiety* contains many delights for the fans of Auden. The work features many of his familiar devices, his logical reversals, clever puns, philosophical nuggets, and irreverent asides. For the student of verse forms, it offers a wide variety of formal techniques that Auden either revived or invented.

David Bromige

Further Reading

Bloomfield, Barry, and Edward Mendelsohn. *W. H. Auden: A Bibliography, 1924-1969*. 2d ed. Charlottesville: University Press of Virginia, 1972. Excellent and thorough bibliography.

Callan, Edward. *Auden, a Carnival of Intellect*. New York: Oxford University Press, 1983. Full, sound study of Auden's life and works. Callan views Auden as a "professional" poet rather than one seeking constant inspiration. Discusses the wide range of Auden's forms and techniques and defines his "perennial themes" to be consciousness and the human condition.

Carpenter, Humphrey. *W. H. Auden, a Biography*. Boston: Houghton Mifflin, 1981. Gives a detailed account of the poet's life and situates the works in relation to it. Good primary and secondary bibliographies.

Gottlieb, Susannah Young-ah. *Regions of Sorrow: Anxiety and Messianism in Hannah Arendt and W. H. Auden*. Stanford, Calif.: Stanford University Press, 2003. A comparison of the works of the two authors, including an analysis of the meditations on Nazi terror in *The Age of Anxiety* and in Arendt's *Origins of Totalitarianism*. Gottlieb also interprets Auden's "In Praise of Limestone," concentrating on the messianic elements in the work.

Rosen, David. *Power, Plain English, and the Rise of Modern Poetry*. New Haven, Conn.: Yale University Press, 2006. Rosen analyzes works by Auden, T. S. Eliot, and William Butler Yeats, describing how they and other British poets tried to present themselves as persons of power and the moral voices of their communities.

Smith, Stan, ed. *The Cambridge Companion to W. H. Auden*. New York: Cambridge University Press, 2004. Collection of essays about Auden, including discussions of his life and character, the various genres of his work, religion, politics, and his influence upon other writers.

Spender, Stephen, ed. *W. H. Auden: A Tribute*. New York: Macmillan, 1975. Essays by those who knew Auden in England—Stephen Spender, Geoffrey Grigson, John Betjeman, Cyril Connolly, and Christopher Isherwood—and those who knew him principally in America—John Hollander, Chester Kallman, Oliver Sacks, and others.

The Age of Innocence

Author: Edith Wharton (1862-1937)
First published: 1920
Type of work: Novel
Type of plot: Social realism
Time of plot: Late nineteenth century
Locale: New York City

Principal characters:
NEWLAND ARCHER, a young attorney
MAY WELLAND, his fiancé
COUNTESS ELLEN OLENSKA, her cousin

The Story:

Newland Archer, a handsome and eligible young attorney engaged to lovely May Welland, learns that the engagement will be announced at a party to welcome his fiancé's cousin, Countess Ellen Olenska. This reception for Ellen constitutes a heroic sacrifice on the part of the many Welland connections, for her marriage to a ne'er-do-well Polish count did not improve her position so far as rigorous and straitlaced New York society is concerned. The fact that she contemplates a divorce action also makes her suspect, and, to cap it all, her rather bohemian way of living does not conform to what her family expects of a woman who made an unsuccessful marriage.

Archer's engagement to May is announced. At the same party, Archer is greatly attracted to Ellen. Before long, with the excuse that he is making the cousin of his betrothed feel at home, he sends her flowers and calls on her. To him she seems a woman who offers sensitivity, beauty, and the promise of a life quite different from the one that he expects after his marriage to May. He finds himself defending Ellen when the rest of society is attacking her contemplated divorce action. He does not, however, consider breaking his engagement to May but constantly seeks reasons to justify what is to the rest of his group an excellent union. With Ellen often in his thoughts, May's cool beauty and correct but unexciting personality begin to suffer in Archer's estimation.

Although the clan defends her against all outsiders, Ellen is often treated as a pariah. Her family keeps check on her, trying to prevent her from indulging in too many bohemian acts, such as her strange desire to rent a house in a socially unacceptable part of town. The women of the clan also recognize her as a dangerous rival, and ruthless Julius Beaufort, whose secret dissipations are known by all, including his wife, pays her marked attention. Archer finds himself hating Beaufort very much.

Convincing himself that he was seeing too much of Ellen, Archer goes to St. Augustine to visit May, who is vacationing there with her mother and her hypochondriac father. In spite of her cool and conventional welcome and her gentle rebuffs to his wooing, her beauty reawakens in him a kind of affection, and he pleads with her to advance the date of their wedding. May and her parents refuse because their elaborate preparations cannot be completed in time. Archer returns to New York. There, with the aid of the family matriarch, Mrs. Manson Mingott, he achieves his purpose, and the wedding date is advanced. This news comes to him in a telegram sent by May to Ellen, which Ellen reads to him just as he is attempting to advance the intimacy of their relationship. Archer leaves Ellen's house and finds a similar telegram from May to him. Telling his sister Janey that the wedding will take place within a month, he suddenly realizes that he is now protected against Ellen and himself.

The ornate wedding, the conventional European honeymoon that follows, and May's assumption of the role of the proper wife soon disillusion Archer. He realizes that he is trapped, that the mores of his society, helped by his own lack of courage, have prepared him, like a smooth ritual, for a rigid and codified life. There is enough intelligence and insight in Archer, however, to make him resent the trap. On his return to New York, he continues to see Ellen. The uselessness of his work as junior attorney in an ancient law firm, the stale regimen of his social life, and the passive sweetness of May do not satisfy that part of Archer that sets him apart from the rest of his clan.

He proposes to Ellen that they go away together, but Ellen, wise and kind, shows him that such an escape would not be a pleasant one, and she indicates that they could love each other only as long as he does not press for a consummation. Archer agrees. He further capitulates when, urged by her family, he advises Ellen, as her attorney and as a relative, not to get a divorce from Count Olenska. She concurs, and Archer again blames his own cowardice for his action. The family faces another crisis when Beaufort's firm, built upon a framework of shady financial transactions, fails, ruining him and his duped customers. The blow causes elderly Mrs. Mingott to have a stroke, and the family rallies around her. She summons Ellen, a favorite of hers, to her side. Ellen, who was living in Washington, D.C., returns to the Mingott house to stay. Archer, who had not seen Ellen since he had advised her against a divorce, begins seeing her again. Certain remarks by Archer's male acquaintances, along with a strained and martyrlike attitude that May adopts, indicate to him that his intimacy with Ellen is known among his family and friends. The affair comes to an end, however, when Ellen leaves for Paris, after learning that May is to have a baby. It is obvious to all that May triumphs, and Archer is treated by his family as a prodigal returned. The rebel is conquered. Archer makes his peace with society.

Years pass. Archer dabbles in liberal politics and interests himself in civic reforms. His children, Mary and Dallas, are properly reared. May dies when Archer is in his fifties. He laments her passing with genuine grief. He watches society changing and sees the old conservative order give way, accepting and rationalizing innovations of a younger, more liberal generation.

One day, Archer's son, Dallas, about to be married, telephones him and proposes a European tour, their last trip together. In Paris, Dallas reveals to his father that he knew all about Ellen, and he arranges to visit her apartment. When they arrive, however, Archer sends his son ahead, to pay his respects, while he remains on a park bench outside. A romantic to the end, incapable of acting in any situation that makes demands on his emotional resources, he sits and watches the lights in Ellen's apartment until a servant appears on the balcony and closes the shutters. Then he walks slowly back to his hotel. The past is the past; the present is secure.

Critical Evaluation:

Edith Wharton's *The Age of Innocence* is probably one of her most successful books because it offers an inside look at a subject the author knew very well, that is, New York society during the 1870's. That was her milieu, and her pen captures the atmosphere of aristocratic New York as its inhabitants move about in their world of subtleties, innuendoes, and strict adherence to the dictates of fashionable society. Wharton describes those years for herself as "safe, guarded, and monotonous." Her only deviations as a young adult were the frequent journeys abroad and summers in Newport. Her marriage to Edward Wharton, a prominent Bostonian, assumed the same character as her own early life until it became apparent that he suffered from mental illness and would have to be hospitalized. During World War I, Wharton worked for the Allies and received the French Cross of the Legion of Honor for her work with the Red Cross in Paris. Most critics agree that her best years as a novelist were from 1911 to 1921, during which time she produced *Ethan Frome* (1911), a grim New England study, and *The Age of Innocence*, for which she was awarded the Pulitzer Prize.

Wharton's most successful theme (like that of her friend Henry James) was the plight of the young and innocent in a world that was more complicated than that for which they were prepared. Newland Archer and Ellen Olenska found the society of New York intricate and demanding and, as such, to be an impediment to their personal searches for happiness and some degree of freedom. *The Age of Innocence* is a careful blending of a nostalgia for the 1870's with a subtle, but nevertheless inescapable, criticism of its genteel hypocrisies and clever evasions.

With respect to Wharton's style, it can be generalized that she is not a particularly daring writer nor an experimenter in form. Rather, she writes in a comfortable, fixed, formal style that is closely layered. In some instances, her narrative becomes heavy, and the intricate play and counterplay of the characters' motives can lose all but the most diligent reader. The author's presence is never forgotten, and the reader feels her control throughout the story, as the narrative view is quickly established from the beginning. Wharton's characters are portrayed through their actions. Since *The Age of Innocence* so carefully fits a historical niche, its scope is limited and its direction narrow. That is not to say that the drama is limited or lacking. On the contrary, in detailing such a small world, the drama is intense, even if it is found beneath a sophisticated, polished surface.

Three figures are projected against the historical background of New York society. May Welland, the beautiful betrothed of Archer, is completely a product of the system she seeks to perpetuate. Archer observes, after their marriage, that May and her mother are so much alike that he sees himself being treated and placated just as Mr. Welland is by his wife and daughter. There is no doubt that May will never surprise Archer "by a new idea, a weakness, a cruelty or an emotion."

Ellen, on the other hand, frees herself from the restraints of society by her experiences abroad and through her subsequent separation from her husband, the Polish count. Madame Olenska not only is more cosmopolitan but also is a character of more depth and understanding than the other women in the novel. She suggests by her presence as well as by her past experiences a tragic and emotionally involved element in the story. Ellen definitely does not conform to the rules of accepted behavior. She moves in a cloud of mystery that makes her an intriguing personality to those who observe her, if even only to criticize. As soon as she and Archer are aware of their feelings for each other, Archer tries to convince Ellen, in a halfhearted way, that one cannot purchase freedom at the expense of another. He gives her an idea by which to live and, in so doing, destroys his opportunity to find freedom for himself.

Archer is, in many ways, a typical Wharton masculine figure. He is a man set apart from the people he knows by education, intellect, and feeling, but is lacking the initiative and courage to separate himself physically from the securities of the known. The movement of the plot in *The Age of Innocence* is established by the transition from one position to another taken by Archer in his relations with May and with Ellen. Archer's failure to break the barriers of clan convention leads him to an ironic abnegation, for in the last pages of the novel readers see Archer retreating from the opportunity to meet with Ellen—an opportunity his eager son Dallas is quick to arrange. Dallas is anxious to meet Ellen, because he heard from his mother, shortly before she died, that Archer had given up the thing he had most wanted (namely, Ellen) for her. It is sad to see that Archer, the object of two loves, is never able to satisfy or to be satisfied by either. The tragedy in the novel rests with May. It is she who appears to be the most innocent and naïve, yet, in the end, she is perhaps the most aware of them all. She suffers quietly through the years, knowing that her husband's true desires and passions are elsewhere. Dallas's generation observes the whole situation out of context, as "prehistoric." He dismisses the affair rather casually, because his contemporaries have lost that blind adherence to social custom that the Archers, the Wellands, and the rest knew so well.

The novel is an incisive but oblique attack on the intricate and tyrannous tribal customs of a highly stratified New York society. Wharton's psychological probing of the meaning and motivation behind the apparent façade of her characters' social behavior shows her to be of the same school of fiction as her friend Henry James. The method is that of James, but Wharton's style is clearer and less involved. The novel is the work of a writer for whom form and method are perfectly welded, and the action results inevitably from the natures of the characters. *The Age of Innocence* is a novel of manners that delineates a very small world with great accuracy. Under the surface of wealth, readers see a world of suffering, denial, and patient resignation—a situation that deserves more attention and reflection than one might give at first reading.

"Critical Evaluation" by Constance A. Cutler

Further Reading

Ammons, Elizabeth. *Edith Wharton's Argument with America*. Athens: University of Georgia Press, 1980. An insightful study that chronologically traces Wharton's evolving point of view and her complaints with American society from the female perspective. Extremely well-written and particularly useful for feminist issues, the text covers all of Wharton's works.

Bell, Millicent, ed. *The Cambridge Companion to Edith Wharton*. New York: Cambridge University Press, 1995. Collection of essays, including a critical history of Wharton's work, discussions of Wharton and race and the science of manners, and "The Social Subject in *The Age of Innocence*" by Pamela Knights.

Bloom, Harold, ed. *Edith Wharton's "The Age of Innocence*." Philadelphia: Chelsea House, 2005. Collection of essays providing numerous interpretations of the novel. Includes an analysis of Wharton's fiction published from 1912 through 1920, a comparison of Wharton's novel with Henry James's *The Portrait of a Lady*, and "Archer's Way" by John Updike.

Farwell, Tricia M. *Love and Death in Edith Wharton's Fiction*. New York: Peter Lang, 2006. An insightful look at Wharton's beliefs about the nature of love and the way they reflect her philosophical views, namely those of Plato and Charles Darwin. Wharton's own shifting feelings on the role of love in life are revealed in conjunction with the shifting role that love played for her fictional characters.

Fryer, Judith. *Felicitous Space: The Imaginative Structures of Edith Wharton and Willa Cather*. Chapel Hill: University of North Carolina Press, 1986. An important inquiry into the meaning of actual and imagined spaces in the works of the two women writers. Explores Wharton's anthropological knowledge in the structure and characterizations of *The Age of Innocence*.

Haytock, Jennifer. *Edith Wharton and the Conversations of Literary Modernism*. New York: Palgrave Macmillan, 2008. Although Wharton denied she was a modernist writer, Haytock argues that Wharton's fiction contained elements of modernism, as demonstrated by her writing style and the cultural issues she addresses.

Lee, Hermione. *Edith Wharton*. New York: Knopf, 2007. An exhaustive study of Wharton's life, offering valuable insights and pointing out interesting analogies between her life and her fiction.

Lewis, R. W. B. *Edith Wharton: A Biography*. New York: Harper & Row, 1975. A Pulitzer Prize-winning biography, enormously detailed. Begins with a discussion of Wharton's English and Dutch colonial ancestors and traces her life and artistic development.

McDowell, Margaret. *Edith Wharton*. Boston: Twayne, 1976. An excellent introduction to Wharton's life and work. Interprets *The Age of Innocence* as a satirical portrait of a society that Wharton also respected. Includes an annotated bibliography of secondary sources.

Vita-Finzi, Penelope. *Edith Wharton and the Art of Fiction.* New York: St. Martin's Press, 1990. A close look at Wharton's sources of inspiration and imagination, which then turns to her method in practice. The appendix contains extracts of Wharton's notebook, chapter summaries, and excerpts from typed drafts.

Wolff, Cynthia Griffin. *A Feast of Words: The Triumph of Edith Wharton.* New York: Oxford University Press, 1977. An exceptional psychological study of Wharton's life and artistic career that complements the Lewis biography. *The Age of Innocence* is read as Wharton's most significant bildungsroman, tracing Newland Archer's struggle to mature.

The Age of Reason

Being an Investigation of True and Fabulous Theology

Author: Thomas Paine (1737-1809)
First published: part 1, 1794; part 2, 1795
Type of work: Religious philosophy

In *The Age of Reason*, Thomas Paine is driven by the same impulses that energize such earlier works as the pamphlet *Common Sense* (1776) and a series of papers gathered under the title *The American Crisis* (1776-1783). In *Rights of Man* (1791-1792) he expresses his hatred of enslavement and his belief that all people have the natural right to be free of all tyranny—physical, mental, and spiritual. Benjamin Franklin once said, "Where liberty is, there is my country." Paine replied, "Where liberty is not, there is mine." This idealistic altruism motivated him to give his writings to the world without hope of financial remuneration.

In approach and style, *The Age of Reason* is similar also to the earlier works. The author is direct, candid, and simple; he appeals to common sense and presents what to him is overwhelming evidence for his arguments. The author is at times ironic, jeering, or sarcastic. He never writes down to his audience or forgets for whom he is writing.

It is one of the ironies of the literary and theological world that *The Age of Reason*, which, although written to express the author's doubts regarding traditional religion, was intended primarily to save the world from atheism, brought against Paine the charge of atheism. Paine, in *The Age of Reason*, seeks to combat atheism. As a result of this book, the great reputation he earlier enjoyed as one of the prime movers in the Revolutionary War was blackened. Paine became feared throughout America because of his alleged atheism.

Paine's doubts about conventional religion were deep. John Adams said that Paine had them in 1776, and Paine says in *The Age of Reason* that he had entertained such ideas for many years. Paine's ideas grew out of his idealistic view that the human condition could be better. They were strengthened by the influences of his Quakerism; by his Newtonian bent toward science; by the examples of classical antiquity in the teachings of such people as Aristotle, Socrates, and Plato and the great society in which they lived; and by the revelations of research into Eastern religions. Paine was one of the early comparative religionists.

The Age of Reason is subtitled *Being an Investigation of True and Fabulous Theology.* In the dedication to his "Fellow-Citizens of the United States of America," Paine insists that the views he is about to express are his alone, and he reaffirms his belief in the right of all to form their own opinions, for to deny the right of all to their own beliefs leads to slavery. He will, therefore, he says, examine all aspects of life, especially religion, with reason.

Paine's own position is made clear from the start. He believes in one God, and, like all Newtonians, he professes the Deistic hope for happiness in another world because, contrary to the Calvinistic doctrines that he detests, Deism affords a happiness not found in other religions. Paine states explicitly that he does not believe in the creeds professed by any churches, for his own mind is his tabernacle. All national institutions of faith and dogma have been instituted to rule over the lives of people, he opines.

The universal purpose of churches—to beguile or to deceive the people—is strengthened by another characteristic churches have in common: the pretense of some special mission from God communicated to certain individuals, for example, Moses to the Jews, Jesus Christ to the Christians, Mahomet to the Turks. These revelations must be accepted on faith because there is never a pragmatic truth to grant their validity.

Paine has no criticism of Jesus, who was, Paine feels, a virtuous and amiable man. Jesus, Paine notes, wrote nothing about his so-called special mission on Earth. Thus, all accounts about him were written by others, many long after his death. For this reason they are open to suspicion. That Jesus existed is an unquestionable historical fact, and that he preached morality is certain. That he claimed to be the Savior of the world, however, is suspect. Further, most of the writings about Jesus as Savior, the bases of Christianity, differ very little from the writings of other mythologies. Such writings, written by limited and particular human minds, calumniate the wisdom of the Almighty.

Paine examines in detail the whole structure of Christianity. He investigates the books of the Old Testament. He seizes upon the Apocrypha, rejected by those who established the biblical canon, and concludes that all books were chosen arbitrarily; had others been chosen or rejected, the present basic structure of Christianity would have been altered. The books that were chosen are filled with "obscene" stories, "voluptuous debaucheries," and "cruel and torturous executions" that constitute a "history of wickedness that has served to corrupt and brutalize mankind." Paine detests these stories, as he despises all cruelty. The Proverbs, attributed to Solomon, are inferior to the proverbs of the Spaniards and are less wise and economical than those of Benjamin Franklin. Here, as elsewhere, Paine demonstrates his great respect for the wisdom and general goodness of Franklin, who was instrumental in getting Paine to come to America in 1774.

The New Testament, Paine claims, is likewise spurious. Had Jesus been truly the Savior of humanity, he surely would have arranged to have this knowledge transmitted to the world during his lifetime. He was in fact a Son of God only in the way all people are children of God, and the falsehoods about his divinity were written after his death. Like scholars interested in comparative mythologies, Paine notes that it is curious that all leaders of religions come from obscure or unusual parentage: "Moses was a foundling; Jesus was born in a stable; Mahomet was a mule driver."

Having destroyed the sanctity of the Bible as a basis of religion, Paine asks if there is no word of God, no revelation. A Deist, his response is without equivocation. The true theology is nature, and the "word of God is the Creation we behold," and only in the Creation are united all of humanity's "ideas and conceptions of a word of God." To Paine, God is a first cause. Here, with an adroitness and wit more characteristic of his earlier works, he turns the Christian's own assertions against him. The Christian "system of faith," he says, seems to be a "species of atheism," a kind of "denial of God," for it believes in a man rather than in the true God and interposes "between man and his Maker an opaque body, which it calls a Redeemer." All such beliefs run counter to Deism, the belief in one Deity who is wise and benign.

The Christian belief in miracles brings forth from Paine his bitterest tirades, almost as fiery and heated as they were in his earlier works. Mysteries, he says, run counter to true religion. He jeeringly examines the miracle of the whale swallowing Jonah and concludes that although it approaches the marvelous, it would have been much more marvelous if Jonah had swallowed the whale. He derides especially the "most extraordinary" of all miracles of the New Testament, that of Satan flying Jesus to the top of a high mountain and promising him all the kingdoms throughout the world. Paine wonders why both then did not discover America; he questions whether "his sooty highness" was interested only in kingdoms.

One of Paine's more amusing refutations of biblical lore is found in part 2. His book is clearly serious in intent, but he delights in poking fun wherever possible. He attacks the wisdom of Solomon as claimed in Ecclesiastes. Paine affirms that Solomon should have cried out that "All is vanity," for with seven hundred wives and three hundred concubines, how could any man in retrospect conclude anything else? Then Paine contrasts Solomon with Franklin, whom he glorifies almost to deification; he claims that Franklin is wiser than Solomon, for his "mind was ever young, his temper ever serene; science, that never grows gray, was always his mistress."

Between the writing of part 1 and part 2 Paine spent eleven months in a French prison. Believing that part 1 had been written in too great haste without a Bible handy for reference, Paine attempts in part 2 to buttress his former statements with details. He directs part 1 against the "three frauds, mystery, miracle, and prophecy," and he intends to blast revelation in part 2, for although all things are possible with God, he is against the use of "pretended revelation," which is "the imposition of one man upon another." He believes that most of the wickedness, the greatest cruelties, and the miseries that have broken the human race originated in the hoax called revelation. Whereas Deism teaches without any possibility of deceit, Christianity thrives on deceit. Religion becomes form instead of fact, "of notion instead of principle," and morality is replaced by faith, which had its beginnings in a "supposed debauchery."

Part 2 attacks the Bible as an imperfect collection of words, not as a statement of religion. Except in details, in more evidence, and in more direct examination and refutation, part 2 advances Paine's thesis little beyond its points in part 1. Paine ends part 2, as he generally ends his works, with a challenge to the reader. He shows, he says, that the Bible is filled with "impositions and forgeries," and he invites readers to refute him if they can. He hopes that his ideas will cause readers to think for themselves, for he is certain that when opinions are allowed to thrive in a free air "truth will finally and powerfully prevail."

Paine's style and technique are uniquely his. He is candid in approach and unrelenting in carrying out his thesis. His style is simple, honest, direct, and free of all cant and reverence. His subject matter and his approach led to his being accused of being unscientific and vulgar. When it was first announced that Paine was going to write on the subject of religion, many Americans approved. As the work appeared, reprinted far and wide in newspapers, approval turned to disapprobation. His reputation was so blackened that after his return to the United States in 1802 he found himself virtually without friends. Paine's pen was always his most important weapon, but the reputation that his earlier writings created was what *The Age of Reason* destroyed.

Further Reading

Aldridge, Alfred Owen. "*The Age of Reason*." In *Man of Reason: The Life of Thomas Paine*. London: Cresset, 1960. Provides an excellent summary of the argument developed in *The Age of Reason*. Describes the work's publication history and critical reception.

Davidson, Edward H., and William J. Scheick. *Paine, Scripture, and Authority: "The Age of Reason" as Religious and Political Idea*. Bethlehem, Pa.: Lehigh University Press, 1994. Discusses Paine's subversiveness and notes how *The Age of Reason* appears to authorize a world order that depends on the traditions it criticizes.

Foner, Eric. *Tom Paine and Revolutionary America*. Updated ed. New York: Oxford University Press, 2005. An updated edition of the book originally published in 1976. Examines Paine's political and social ideas and describes the new form of political writing in which he expressed these concepts.

Larkin, Edward. "The Science of Revolution: Technological Metaphors and Scientific Methodology in *Rights of Man* and *The Age of Reason*." In *Thomas Paine and the Literature of Revolution*. New York: Cambridge University Press, 2005. Treats Paine as a literary figure, describing how his writings "translated" eighteenth century political theories into a language that was accessible to the public.

Nelson, Craig. *Thomas Paine: Enlightenment, Revolution, and the Birth of Modern Nations*. New York: Viking, 2006. Nelson argues that *The Age of Reason* is not an expression of Paine's atheism but advocates eighteenth century Deism and is part of the "mainstream Anglo-American religious discourse" of its time.

Popkin, Richard H. "*The Age of Reason* Versus *The Age of Revelation*: Two Critics of Tom Paine, David Levi, and Elias Boudinot." In *Deism, Masonry, and the Enlightenment*, edited by J. A. Leo Lemay. Newark: University of Delaware Press, 1987. Shows how Paine's humanistic Deism was opposed to orthodoxy.

Wilson, Jerome D., and William F. Ricketson. "Reaction to Organized Religion." In *Thomas Paine*, edited by Patricia Cowell. Boston: Twayne, 1989. Describes the historical and social contexts of *The Age of Reason* and notes how the essay stands as a remarkable example of classic eighteenth century Deism.

Agnes Grey

Author: Anne Brontë (1820-1849)
First published: 1847
Type of work: Novel
Type of plot: Domestic realism
Time of plot: Mid-nineteenth century
Locale: England

Principal characters:

AGNES GREY, a young governess
EDWARD WESTON, a curate and later Agnes's husband
MARY GREY, Agnes's sister
RICHARD GREY, Agnes's father
MRS. GREY, Agnes's mother
MRS. MURRAY, the owner of Horton Lodge, and Agnes's second employer
ROSALIE MURRAY, Mrs. Murray's older daughter
MATILDA MURRAY, Mrs. Murray's younger daughter
MR. HATFIELD, the rector at Horton and Rosalie's suitor
SIR THOMAS ASHBY, later Rosalie's husband
HARRY MELTHAM and MR. GREEN, Rosalie's other suitors
NANCY BROWN, an old widow at Horton
MRS. BLOOMFIELD, the owner of Wellwood, and Agnes's first employer
TOM BLOOMFIELD, her oldest child
MARY ANN BLOOMFIELD, her older daughter
FANNY BLOOMFIELD, her younger daughter
UNCLE ROBSON, Mrs. Bloomfield's brother

The Story:

Mrs. Grey, a squire's daughter, offends her family by getting married only for love to a poor parson in the north of England. She bears him six children, but only two, Mary and Agnes, survive. Nevertheless, the Greys are happy with their humble, educated, pious life in their small house and garden. Mr. Grey, never wholly at his ease because his wife was forced to give up carriages and fine clothes in order to marry him, attempts to improve their fortunes by speculating and investing his patrimony in a merchant's sea voyage. However, the vessel is wrecked, everything is lost, and the Greys are soon left penniless. In addition, Mr. Grey's health, never robust, begins to fail perceptibly under the strain of his guilt for bringing his family close to ruin. Mary and Agnes, reared in the sheltered atmosphere of a clergyman's household, have spent their time reading, studying, and working in the garden. When the family situation becomes desperate, however, Mary tries to sell her drawings to help with the household expenses, and Agnes, the younger daughter, decides to become a governess.

Overcoming the qualms her family feels at the idea of her leaving home, Agnes finds employment and, on a bleak and windy autumn day, arrives at Wellwood, the home of the Bloomfield family. She is received coldly by Mrs. Bloomfield and told that her charges, especially Tom, a seven-year-old boy, are noble and splendid children. She soon finds that the reverse is true. Tom is an arrogant and disobedient little monster whose particular delight is to pull the legs and wings off young sparrows. Mary Ann, his six-year-old sister, is given to temper tantrums and refuses to do her lessons. The children are frightened of their father, a peevish and stern disciplinarian, and the father, in turn, blames Agnes when the children frequently get out of control.

Agnes finds it impossible to teach the children anything because all her efforts to discipline them are undermined by Mrs. Bloomfield, who believes that her angels are always right. Even four-year-old Fanny lies consistently and is fond of spitting in people's faces. For a time, Agnes is heartened by Mr. Bloomfield's mother's visit, but the pious old lady turns out to be a hypocrite who sympathizes with Agnes verbally and then turns on her behind her back.

Matters become a great deal worse with the visit of Uncle Robson, Mrs. Bloomfield's brother, who encourages young Tom to torture small animals. One day, after he collects a whole brood of young birds for Tom to torture, Agnes crushes them with a large stone, choosing to kill them quickly rather than to see them suffer a slow, cruel death. The family thinks she deprived Tom of his normal, spirited pleasure. Shortly after this incident, she is told that her services are no longer required; the Bloomfields believe that she did not discipline the children properly or teach them very much.

Agnes spends a few months with her family at home before taking up her next post. She finds the Murrays, the owners of Horton Lodge, more sophisticated, wealthier, and less bleak and cruel than the owners of Wellwood; but they are still hardly the happy, pious, warm family that Agnes hoped to encounter. Her older charge, Rosalie, is sixteen years old, very pretty, and interested only in flirting and in eventually making the most suitable marriage possible; her younger charge, Matilda, fourteen years old, is interested only in horses and stables. Although they treat her with politeness, neither girl has any respect for the learning and piety that Agnes offers. If Agnes's work is less unpleasant than it was at Wellwood, it is equally futile.

After living at Horton Lodge for nearly a year, Agnes returns home for a month for her sister's wedding. During this time, the Murrays give Rosalie a debutante ball, after which she exercises her charms on the young men at Horton. When Agnes returns, she is shocked to find Rosalie flirting with all the men and summarizing the marital possibilities of each with a hardened and materialistic eye. In the meantime, a new curate comes to Horton. Edward Weston is a sober and sincere churchman, neither climbing nor pompous like the rector, Mr. Hatfield. Mr. Weston and Agnes, attracted to each other, find many opportunities to meet in their sympathetic visits to Nancy Brown, an old widow who is almost blind. At first, Rosalie finds Mr. Weston both dogmatic and dull, but Agnes finds him representative of the true piety and goodness that she believes are the qualities of a clergyman. Rosalie, continuing to play the coquette, first conquers the unctuous rector, Mr. Hatfield, and then after he proposes and is quickly rejected, she turns her charms on Mr. Weston. Although Agnes is fiercely jealous of Rosalie's flirtation, she never really acknowledges her own growing love. Finally, Rosalie accepts Sir Thomas Ashby; his home, Ashby Park, and his fortune are the largest in the vicinity of Horton.

Shortly after Rosalie's marriage, before Agnes has the opportunity to see much of Mr. Weston, she is called home by the death of her father. She and her mother decide to start a school for young ladies in the fashionable watering place of A——. Although Agnes returns to Horton Lodge for another month, she does not see Mr. Weston before she resignedly leaves to rejoin her mother. Although the school begins to prosper after a few months, Agnes still seems weary and depressed, and she welcomes an invitation from Rosalie, now Lady Ashby, to visit Ashby Park. She finds Rosalie disappointed in her marriage to a grumbling, boorish man who ignores her and who, after a honeymoon on the Continent, forbids her the frivolous pleasures of London and European society. Agnes also learns from Rosalie that Mr. Weston left Horton a short time before.

A few days after Agnes returns to her mother and the school, she is walking along the waterfront one morning when she unexpectedly encounters Mr. Weston. He secured a position as a minister in a nearby village. He promptly begins calling on Agnes and her mother, who soon comes to hold him in high esteem. One day, while walking with Agnes to the top of a high hill, Mr. Weston proposes marriage. As husband, father, clergyman, and manager of a limited income, he is in later years the perfect mate for virtuous and worthy Agnes.

Critical Evaluation:

Written around 1846, *Agnes Grey* expresses ideas on women and their capacity for a life based on reason similar to those of Mary Wollstonecraft in *A Vindication of the Rights of Woman* (1792). Its feminism predates that of the novels by Charlotte Brontë, Elizabeth Gaskell, and George Eliot, yet only recently has it come to be recognized as a notable achievement, distinguished for its pervasive realism, its significant themes, and its innovative literary techniques.

The work of Anne Brontë, long dismissed as insipid compared to that of her sisters Charlotte and Emily, is in fact simply different in kind from theirs. In *Agnes Grey*, Brontë eschews sensational events and strong passions in favor of a restrained portrayal of actual life. The opening sentence, "All true histories contain instruction," suggests both her goal and her method: a demonstration, through sustained realism, of the heroine's spiritual and moral growth. Drawing heavily on her own experiences, Brontë convincingly presents the governess' s life and the factors that often made it unbearable. She takes for her heroine and hero ordinary people struggling to cope in difficult situations. Numerous details of travel, weather, food, customs—all the circumstances of Victorian life—increase the verisimilitude.

The underlying theme, that women are rational beings who should be accorded the means and opportunities for independence and fulfillment, is expressed primarily in Agnes's life story. Seeking employment, Agnes accepts the only occupation available to middle-class women, and she embarks on her career as a governess exhilarated by the prospect not merely of earning money but also of broadening her horizons. Her excited optimism, however, is naïve, based on ignorance of the world. The novel concerns her education and growth toward maturity. Despite her trials as a governess, she perseveres, determined to adopt a logical, rational approach to her unruly charges. She enlarges her understanding of human nature, making shrewd character evaluations and learning to penetrate hypocrisy. Although she suffers many humiliations, she gains self-assurance, and, at certain points, she openly challenges authority.

At Horton Lodge, she makes further progress toward understanding others and learning to control herself. Her consistent attempts to inculcate firm moral principles in her charges eventually win her some measure of respect. Moreover, even in situations that emphasize her social inferiority, she remains cognizant of her own worth and moral superiority. Love for Mr. Weston does not diminish her self-control and judgment. Pained as she is by Rosalie's flirtation with him, she never loses her composure in public; she steadily attempts to view her situation with reason and objectivity.

Finally, at the school she establishes with her mother, she achieves a position in which she is a decision maker instead of a subordinate. Here, while she does not overcome what appears to be a hopeless love, she gains command of her feelings and experiences an upsurge of energy, physical well-being, and a sense of freedom. It is a confident, self-reliant woman who strolls along the sands at the dawn of a new day and unexpectedly meets Mr. Weston. Their declaration of love, denuded of glamour and the trappings of romance, is the prelude to a union that is an equal partnership, founded on sincere feelings, mutual respect, and shared moral principles.

These feminist themes are reinforced by the other female portraits. Agnes's mother is an accomplished woman, possessed of spirit and energy. She defies her parents in her marriage, and she defies convention in her determination to support herself after her husband's death. She is the opposite of the gentle but ineffective Mr. Grey, and if she has a fault, it is that of trying to control too much in the home, a fault occasioned by the narrow sphere in which she is forced to exercise her considerable organizational abilities.

By contrast, Mrs. Murray and Rosalie reveal the emptiness and misery experienced by women who have no meaningful activity. Mrs. Murray's life is centered on parties, fashion, and unfortunate matchmaking for her daughters. Rosalie is the victim of such a lifestyle. Not trained or disciplined, she is guided by her ambitious mother into a bitterly unhappy marriage to Sir Thomas Ashby, and when Agnes visits her at Ashby Park, Rosalie's situation underlines the advantages that the poorer, but more purposeful, woman possesses.

A secondary theme concerns the corrupting effects of the economic system. The novel presents different gradations of wealth, ranging from the Bloomfields, who acquire their money from trade, to the Murrays, who represent the country gentry, to the Ashbys, who belong to the titled aristocracy. At all levels, the pernicious consequences of the leisured life of the moneyed classes are shown. The cruelty and viciousness of Mr. Robson and Tom Bloomfield are only the most obvious instance. Mr. Bloomfield's snobbery, the Murray daughters' mockery of the cottagers, Mr. Hatfield's ingratiating ways with the rich and neglect of his poorer parishioners, and Sir Thomas Ashby's dissipation are all the result of an economic system that fosters idleness, self-indulgence, and lack of good judgment.

Brontë's innovations, however, extend beyond themes to narrative technique. The first-person female narration recounts experiences and opinions very close to the author's own. While author and female narrator are not identical, the link between them establishes an entirely female perspective enhanced by direct address to the "Reader." This original manipulation of female point of view adds authenticity and conviction.

Equally significant is the style. Lucid and restrained, the style never draws attention to itself but presents persons and events with an air of controlled objectivity. The cool, unimpassioned voice of the female narrator is perfectly adapted to the theme of a woman's rational nature. Yet, the quiet tone is enlivened by a mild and sometimes comic irony. Agnes is skilled in deflating human affectation and gently mocking human foibles. Typical is her quiet response to Rosalie's query about whether her sister's husband is rich, handsome, and young: "Only middling," comes the calm reply.

In comparison with most Victorian novels, *Agnes Grey* is subdued. However, if it lacks the dramatic, it also avoids the melodramatic, the sensational, and the sentimental. In its sober way, it gives a telling picture of women in Victorian England and utilizes a technique and style consonant with that subject. It deserves recognition as a significant contribution to nineteenth century feminism.

"Critical Evaluation" by Muriel Mellown

Further Reading

Bell, A. Craig. *The Novels of Anne Brontë*. Braunton, England: Merlin Books, 1992. A critical study providing a general introduction to Brontë's work. Includes discussion of the novels' sources, style, structure, and characters.

Chitham, Edward. *A Life of Anne Brontë*. Malden, Mass.: Blackwell, 1991. This biography reexamines sources of previous biographies and guards against indiscriminate use of novels and poems for the purpose of biographical study. Explains the composition of *Agnes Grey* and distinguishes its autobiographical and fictional elements.

Eagleton, Terry. *Myths of Power: A Marxist Study of the Brontës*. Anniversary ed. New York: Palgrave Macmillan, 2005. A significant reading by a major Marxist critic, originally published in 1975. Analyzes social implications of *Agnes Grey* and its triadic structure of pious heroine, morally lax upper-class man, and principled hero. Maintains that the novel connects social and economic issues with moral principles and inculcates bourgeois virtues of piety, plainness, duty, and sobriety.

Jay, Betty. *Anne Brontë*. Tavistock, Devon, England: Northcote House/British Council, 2000. Reevaluates Brontë's novels and poetry from the perspective of feminism and other twentieth century critical theories.

Langland, Elizabeth. *Anne Brontë: The Other One*. Totowa, N.J.: Barnes & Noble, 1989. One of the best book-length critical studies of Anne Brontë. Examines Brontë's innovations in theme and technique, identifies her literary precursors, and analyzes the relationships between the novels of all three Brontë sisters. Treats *Agnes Grey* as a novel of female development and stresses its feminist principles and realism.

Meyer, Susan. "Words on 'Great Vulgar Sheets': Writing and Social Resistance in Anne Brontë's *Agnes Grey*." In *The Brontës*, edited by Patricia Ingham. London: Longman, 2003. Meyer's analysis of the novel is one of the essays that examine the Brontë sisters' work from the perspective of feminism, Marxism, postcolonialism, and other twentieth century interpretations.

Nash, Julie, and Barbara A. Suess, eds. *New Approaches to the Literary Art of Anne Brontë*. Burlington, Vt.: Ashgate, 2001. Collection of essays, the majority of which offer various interpretations of *Agnes Grey* and *The Tenant of Wildfell Hall*.

Scott, P. J. M. *Anne Brontë: A New Critical Assessment*. Totowa, N.J.: Barnes & Noble, 1983. Analyzes themes and characters with particular emphasis on moral issues and on Agnes's learning to cope with the realities of life. Includes close reading and explication of a number of passages.

Torgerson, Beth E. *Reading the Brontë Body: Disease, Desire, and the Constraints of Culture*. New York: Palgrave Macmillan, 2005. Examines how the Brontë sisters' literary depictions of illness and disease reflect Victorian attitudes and their personal experiences. Includes analyses of *Agnes Grey* and *The Tenant of Wildfell Hall*.

Ajax

Author: Sophocles (c. 496-406 B.C.E.)
First transcribed: Aias, c. 440 B.C.E. (English translation, 1729)
Type of work: Drama
Type of plot: Tragedy
Time of plot: Trojan War
Locale: Phrygia

Principal characters:
AJAX, a Greek warrior
ODYSSEUS, a Greek leader
TECMESSA, Ajax's female captive
TEUCER, Ajax's half brother
EURYSACES, son of Ajax and Tecmessa

The Story:

Odysseus, chosen by Greek leaders in the Trojan War to replace the dead Achilles as the chief warrior of the Greek forces, paces up and down before the tent of Ajax, who was slighted by the selection of Odysseus. The goddess Athena, appearing above the tent, tells Odysseus that Ajax, covered with blood, is in his tent. Her words confirm Odysseus's suspicions that it is indeed Ajax who slaughtered all of the Greeks' livestock and their shepherd dogs. Athena explains that she cast a spell over Ajax, who, in his hurt pride, vowed to murder Menelaus and Agamemnon, the Greek commanders, as well as Odysseus. Under her spell Ajax committed the horrible slaughter in the belief that the animals he slew were the hated leaders who opposed his election to the place of the late Achilles.

When Tecmessa, Ajax's Phrygian captive, reveals to his followers what the great warrior did, they lament his downfall and question the dark purposes of the gods. Certain that Ajax will be condemned to die for his transgressions, his warriors prepare to retire to their ships and return to Salamis, their homeland.

Ajax, recovered from the spell, emerges from his tent and clearly reveals to his friends that he is a shamed and broken man. Sick in mind at the thought of the taunts of Odysseus, he wishes only to die. Even in his abject misery, however, he is sure that had Achilles personally chosen his successor he would have named Ajax. The despairing man tries to find some means of escape from the consequences of his deed. The alternative to death is to return to Salamis and his noble father, Telamon, but he knows that he can never shame Telamon by facing him. His friends, alarmed at his deep gloom and sensing tragedy, advise him to reflect; Tecmessa urges him to live for her sake and for the sake of their little son, Eurysaces. At the mention of the name of his beloved son, Ajax calls for the boy. Solemnly he gives Eurysaces his great shield and directs that the child be taken to Salamis, so that he might grow up to avenge his father's disgrace. After dismissing Tecmessa and his son, he remains in his tent alone to clear his troubled thoughts. His followers, meanwhile, resume their lament over their disgraced leader.

Apparently reconciled to his fate, Ajax emerges at last from his tent and declares that he is ready to recognize authority, to revere the gods, and to bury his sword with which he brought disgrace and dishonor upon himself. His decision, he says, was dictated by his affection for Tecmessa and Eurysaces. This apparent change brings forth cheers of rejoicing from his countrymen; they thank the gods for what appears to be Ajax's salvation.

In the meantime, the Greeks taunt Teucer, Ajax's half brother, for his kinship with one demented. Calchas, the Greek prophet, warns Teucer that unless Ajax is kept in his tent a full day, no one will again see Ajax alive, since the proud warrior twice offended the goddess Athena in the past. Ajax, however, already left his tent in order to bury his sword. Teucer and the men of Salamis, in alarm, hasten in search of their leader.

Ajax plants his sword, a gift from Hector, the great Trojan warrior, hilt down in the earth. After he asks the gods to inform Teucer of his whereabouts so that he might receive a proper burial, he falls upon his sword. Heavy underbrush partly conceals his body where it lies.

Tecmessa is the first to discover her dead lord; in sorrow she covers him with her mantle. Teucer is summoned. Tecmessa and the men of Salamis cannot refrain from mentioning the dire part played by Athena in the tragedy of Ajax and the pleasure Menelaus and Agamemnon will feel when they hear of Ajax's death. Fearing foul play, Teucer orders Tecmessa to bring Eurysaces immediately. Teucer is in a dilemma. He knows that the Greeks detest him because of his kinship with Ajax. He fears also that Telamon will suspect him of being responsible for Ajax's death, so that he might be Telamon's heir.

While Teucer ponders his own fate, Menelaus appears and tells him that Ajax cannot receive proper burial because he was a rebel, offensive to the gods. Teucer maintains that Ajax was not subject to Spartan Menelaus, nor to anyone else, for he came to Troy voluntarily at the head of his own men from Salamis; therefore he deserves burial. Seeing that Teucer holds firm, Menelaus goes away. Teucer digs a grave while Tecmessa and Eurysaces stand vigil over the body. The men of Salamis sing a dirge over their dead leader.

Agamemnon, king of Mycenae, appears and rebukes Teucer, the son of a slave, for his audacity in defying the will of Menelaus. Agamemnon insults the memory of Ajax by saying that he was stronger than he was wise. Teucer, bitterly recalling Ajax's many heroic deeds in behalf of the Greek cause, reminds Agamemnon of the many blots on the escutcheon of the Atridae, Agamemnon's royal house. Teucer defends his own blood by pointing out that although his mother, Hesione, was a captive, she was nevertheless of noble birth.

Odysseus resolves the dispute by declaring that no Greek warrior should be denied burial. He himself hates Ajax, but he admits that Ajax was both noble and courageous. He shakes hands with Teucer in friendship, but Teucer, lest the gods be offended, refuses his offer to assist in the burial. Thus Ajax, whose pride brought him to an early death, receives proper burial and the death ceremonies of a warrior hero.

Critical Evaluation:

The problem of individual versus group prerogative is masterfully presented in this play. One finds it tempting to sympathize with Ajax for his devotion to his consort and his son, the love and admiration he commands from his followers, and the courage he displays before the walls of Troy. It is inevitable, however, that his ungovernable pride should bring about his ruin. His downfall is one of the most touching and disturbing in literature.

Ajax is considered the earliest of Sophocles' plays that have survived, first produced about 442 B.C.E. The playwright was in his middle fifties at that time and had already had a successful dramatic career of about twenty-five years. Thus *Ajax* was the work of a fully mature writer, and one who had considered life deeply. Whatever problem the play may present structurally, its strengths are remarkable.

Sophocles is the most accomplished poet among the three great Athenian dramatists. His style is marked by smoothness, simplicity, and clarity. It is at once beautiful and lofty, and it has an august dignity that Aeschylus and Euripides could not equal. With Sophocles, even the most intense passions are revealed in a stately, logical, well-polished manner that can be surprisingly moving. For all the formality of his poetry, it never impresses one as being artificial. He created the classical style of writing, and he remains unsurpassed in it.

An accomplished athlete, an honored public dignitary, and the most successful tragedian of the Periclean Age, Sophocles lived to be ninety with his full creative and intellectual vigor intact. His good luck did not blind him to the suffering of others. His extant plays explore the problem of human misery with a rare honesty and thoroughness. He saw Athens reach its finest moment in the Persian Wars and then devolve into a ruthless imperial power embarking on a suicidal war. He knew very well the instability of life, and how greatness can be the source of calamity.

Ajax is a case in point. Next to Achilles, Ajax is the most formidable fighter in the Greek army at Troy. A huge, headstrong bull of a man, his pride is bitterly offended when the Greeks vote to give Achilles' armor to Odysseus. To avenge himself he tries to massacre the Greeks but instead madly butchers their livestock in a god-induced frenzy. Thus, in one night he turns from a hero into an outcast and a laughingstock. The humiliation is too much for him, and he commits suicide. This is the heart of the story, but what is interesting is the way Sophocles develops it.

The key to Sophocles' treatment of the legend is balance. The action moves by antithesis, by the juxtaposition of opposites, in the revelation of Ajax's character and heroism. At the end of the play the audience arrives at a complete assessment of this tragically flawed man, and the impersonal verdict is that he is to be buried as a hero rather than left to rot like a renegade. The decision is close, for Sophocles shows Ajax at his very worst, in total degradation.

At the beginning, when Athena calls Ajax from the tent to reveal his shame to Odysseus, Ajax is insane. He is vindictively slaughtering and tormenting helpless animals in his delusion. Odysseus is appalled and touched by pity. Athena is merciless, however, because Ajax in his own mind is savagely murdering the Greeks. Ajax himself is pitiless in his wounded pride.

When his sanity returns, his pain is excruciating because he fails to kill his enemies and because he makes a fool of himself. He thinks of himself as a hero, and public disgrace is unbearable. As he talks to his soldiers, or to Tecmessa and Eurysaces, he shows himself to be self-centered, hard, concerned only with his damaged honor. However, this portrait is relieved by the pity and the love these dependent people feel for him. An ignoble man cannot command such loyalty.

The audience is further softened to his plight when he seems piously resolved to live with his shame out of concern for Tecmessa and his son. Then the audience realizes he is simply putting on an act to avoid a scene. He is still intent on suicide. Beyond that, the audience learns the reason for Athena's hostility to Ajax. He deliberately affronts her in his arrogant pride by twice refusing her assistance, desiring all the glory for himself. Athena, then, operates by the same vengeful morality. She, however, merely supervises Ajax's destruction—it is actually his own pride that forces him to commit suicide. He is proud to the last, calling upon Zeus to ruin his enemies and arrange a means of burial.

Sophocles goes further and points up the desolation caused by Ajax's stubborn vanity and death. Tecmessa, Teucer, and the Salaminian warriors are utterly bereft of comfort: friendless, unprotected, subject to ridicule, and exiled from home. Ajax betrays them all in his inhuman pride.

This situation makes the debate over Ajax's right to burial doubly forceful, because Teucer is defending a man who violates every human trust, a man who cut him off from his own father. Menelaus's argument that Ajax put himself before the good of the community has special validity in this context. Ajax even put himself before the gods. Teucer's assertion that, on the other hand, Ajax prevented a complete defeat of the Greek army is also true. He is a hero no matter how monstrous he became. Neither the Atridae nor Teucer is allowed to make the final judgment. The Atridae want Ajax unburied out of vindictiveness, while Teucer wants him buried out of brotherly loyalty. Neither is impartial. It is Ajax's enemy, Odysseus, who decides that Ajax is to have a decent burial. Odysseus, who was capable of pity when Ajax was mad, is also capable of forgiving him in death. In this way, Ajax receives his burial by sheer grace.

Sophocles demonstrates in this play the hairbreadth line between criminality and heroism. The very pride that motivates the hero to surpass everyone else can also degrade him into the vilest bestiality. Heroes do not feel the demands of others; they live by some imperious demand within their own breast. Heroes can call forth extraordinary loyalty from their followers—a loyalty that persists after heroes betray their followers—but heroes can also conjure up terrible hatred in their pride. At the last it is grace alone that pronounces the verdict. *Ajax* is a profound and moving study of the nature of the hero.

"Critical Evaluation" by James Weigel, Jr.

Further Reading

Beer, Josh. *Sophocles and the Tragedy of Athenian Democracy.* Westport, Conn.: Praeger, 2004. Analyzes Sophocles' plays within the context of Athenian democracy in the fifth century B.C.E., focusing on the political issues in the dramas. Examines Sophocles' dramatic techniques and how they "revolutionized the concept of dramatic space." Chapter 4 discusses *Ajax*.

Garvie, A. F. *The Plays of Sophocles*. Bristol, England: Bristol Classical, 2005. Concise analysis of Sophocles' plays, with a chapter devoted to *Ajax*. Focuses on Sophocles' tragic thinking, the concept of the Sophoclean hero, and the structure of his plays.

Hesk, Jon. *Sophocles: "Ajax."* London: Duckworth, 2003. A companion to the play, placing it within the context of Sophoclean heroism and Athens's masculine culture. Discusses the characters of Ajax and Tecmessa, the play's depiction of deception and suicide, language and form, and the drama's critical reception.

Kirkwood, Gordon MacDonald. *A Study of Sophoclean Drama*. Ithaca, N.Y.: Cornell University Press, 1958. Reprint. 1994. Analyzes Sophocles' structures and methods of dramatic composition. Compares the plays of Sophocles, focusing on the characters, irony, illustrative forms, use of diction, and oracles in each. Excellent coverage of *Ajax*.

Morwood, James. *The Tragedies of Sophocles*. Exeter, England: Bristol Phoenix Press, 2008. Analyzes each of Sophocles' seven extant plays, with chapter 2 devoted to *Ajax*. Discusses several modern productions and adaptations of the tragedies.

Ringer, Mark. *"Electra" and the Empty Urn: Metatheater and Role Playing in Sophocles*. Chapel Hill: University of North Carolina Press, 1998. Focuses on elements of metatheater, or "theater within theater," and ironic self-awareness in Sophocles' plays. Analyzes plays-within-plays, characters who are in rivalry with the playwright, and characters who assume roles in order to deceive one another. Chapter 3 focuses on *Ajax*.

Scodel, Ruth. *Sophocles*. Boston: Twayne, 1984. Focuses on the historical and mythological significance of the character of Ajax. Discusses the plot and compares it to Homer's *Iliad*. Provides information on Sophocles' seven plays. Includes a chronology of Sophocles' life, a bibliography, and an index.

Seale, David. *Vision and Stagecraft in Sophocles*. Chicago: University of Chicago Press, 1982. An excellent starting point. Distinguishes Sophocles from other playwrights of his time and demonstrates his influence on later ones. Considers the theatrical technicalities in many Sophoclean plays, including *Ajax*. Includes an extended explanation and notes regarding *Ajax*.

Segal, Charles. *Tragedy and Civilization: An Interpretation of Sophocles*. Cambridge, Mass.: Published for Oberlin College by Harvard University Press, 1981. Compares *Ajax* to the other plays by Sophocles in terms of structure and theme. Traces and explains the plot.

Woodard, Thomas, ed. *Sophocles: A Collection of Critical Essays*. Englewood Cliffs, N.J.: Prentice-Hall, 1966. A collection of essays, including writings by Friedrich Nietzsche, Sigmund Freud, and Virginia Woolf. Draws connections between *Ajax* and later literary works.

The Albany Cycle

Author: William Kennedy (1928-)
First published: 1975-1983; includes *Legs*, 1975; *Billy Phelan's Greatest Game*, 1978; *Ironweed*, 1983; *The Albany Cycle*, 1985 (includes *Legs*, *Billy Phelan's Greatest Game*, and *Ironweed*); *Quinn's Book*, 1988; *Very Old Bones*, 1992; *The Flaming Corsage*, 1996
Type of work: Novels
Type of plot: Psychological realism
Time of plot: 1930's
Locale: Albany, New York, and environs

Principal characters:
JACK DIAMOND, a gangster, known as Legs
MARCUS GORMAN, his lawyer
ALICE, Jack's wife
MARION (KIKI), Jack's mistress
BILLY PHELAN, a young man
MARTIN DAUGHERTY, a journalist
PATSY MCCALL, the political boss of Albany
FRANCIS PHELAN, Billy's father, a hobo
HELEN ARCHER, Francis's companion
ANNIE PHELAN, Francis's wife

The Story:

Albany was a wide-open town in the 1930's. The capital of the state of New York, it was also the wholly owned property of the corrupt and apparently omnipotent Democratic machine headed by Patsy McCall. Although the notorious gangster Jack "Legs" Diamond concentrated most of his criminal activities outside the city itself, it was a fitting place for him to be shot to death, as he was at 67 Dove Street early in the morning of December 18, 1931.

In 1948, however, Marcus Gorman still is not sure that Diamond is dead. Marcus was Diamond's attorney and, at the time of the shooting, had just won him an acquittal on a charge of kidnapping. In the months leading up to these events, Marcus, after a casual meeting with Diamond in a speakeasy in the summer of 1930, found himself drawn more and more into the gangster's orbit. At first, Marcus's personal and professional relationship with Diamond remained within clearly defined boundaries. Marcus was able to avoid any complicity in the criminal life of his client. Diamond, however, was the object of a national obsession. It was hard for Marcus, a lapsed Catholic whose hierarchy of values was shaky to begin with, to resist this man who so fascinated a nation.

Marcus knew, for example, that sailing to Europe with Diamond could compromise an attorney's professional standing, but he went. On the voyage, he resisted the proposal that he carry stolen jewels, and when Diamond, accepting Marcus's decision, cast the stones in the ocean, Marcus was impressed. Diamond seemed to be a man of integrity; he continued to respect the boundaries defined by Marcus. Diamond also had flair; throwing those valuable jewels over the side was a grand gesture.

Marcus either underestimated Diamond or overestimated himself. Before long, Marcus was wearing a money belt; the money it concealed was money Diamond stole from other gangsters. It was not surprising that by the time of the kidnapping trial, Marcus's defense strategy included constructing a false alibi for a client of whose guilt he had no doubt. Like the women who loved Diamond—Alice, his wife, and Kiki, his mistress—and like the country that was fascinated by him, Marcus was.

Looking back seventeen years after Diamond was fatally shot, Marcus is still not convinced the gangster is dead. Was he simply transformed from the mortal man of flesh and blood to the mythic man of collective memory and imagination?

Diamond was a force, a man who could take on a place like Albany, to some extent even shape it. His kind were few. More commonly, the people of Albany were shaped by the place and its institutions. The most powerful of these, even more powerful than the Church in this largely Irish Catholic community, was the local Democratic machine, dominated by Patsy McCall. A young man like Billy Phelan might think that McCall's organization played no significant role in his life. Billy had a genius for games; his bowling score of 299 was celebrated in the local press by Martin Daugherty, an eminent local journalist. Billy was not involved in politics. When McCall's nephew was kidnapped, suspicion fell on Morrie Berman, a friend and occasional backer of Billy, and Billy was summoned into the presence of McCall himself. Billy was a man who played by the rules and beyond them, and he knew that the rules by which he lived meant he could never betray a friend, no matter what the circumstances. For his refusal to become McCall's instrument, Billy found himself declared an unperson, unable even to buy a drink in his own town.

Martin Daugherty had troubles of his own. He found it hard to accept his son Peter's decision to enter the priesthood, and he also was working out the still-unresolved tensions of his relationship with his own father, including the complex relationship he had with his father's mistress. The two conflicts were emotionally related. Coming to terms with his father's memory, which involved going to bed with his father's mistress, enabled Martin to accept with a better grace the decision of his son. Another column by Martin made McCall lift the curse on Billy. In managing to survive while remaining true to his code, Billy played his greatest game.

During this already difficult time, Billy's life was complicated by the return to Albany of his wandering father, Francis Phelan. Once a major-league ballplayer, Francis was now a bum who hoped to earn a little money voting for the Democratic machine, at five dollars a vote, on election day.

Francis lived with violence. A rock he threw with a ballplayer's skill at the head of a scab in a strike years before killed the man and sent Francis into hiding; he killed again in his time on the road; and he would be forced to kill one more time during this visit to Albany. Scarring him more deeply than any of these killings was the accidental death of Gerald, his infant son. The infant, slipping from Francis's grasp, broke his neck. Guilt and shame led Francis to abandon his family.

Over the course of three days sacred in the Christian calendar—Hallowe'en (All Saints' Eve), All Saints' Day, and All Souls' Day—Francis worked his way toward a kind of redemption. The process began with a visit to the cemetery where Gerald was buried. From the grave, Gerald told Francis that he would have to perform acts of expiation for abandoning his family, even though he would not recognize his acts as expiatory. When these acts were complete, Gerald promised, Francis would stop trying to die because of Gerald.

During those days, Francis worked as a gravedigger and rag collector. He looked after his fellow hoboes, Rudy and Helen, to the best of his ability. He shared what he had with others. Above all, he faced the family he abandoned. For Billy, acceptance of his father was easy. Billy's sister Peg resisted longer; old resentments had to be overcome. Annie, Francis's wife, had long since moved beyond forgiveness. She welcomed him. What Francis could never have imagined, but somehow was not surprised to learn, was that Annie never told anyone that it was he who was holding Gerald when the accident occurred.

When Francis had to kill once more, in defense of another hobo's life, he could take refuge in the Phelan home. Was this the fantasy he carried with him as, a fugitive once more, he rode a freight out of Albany? Either way, Francis comes home.

Critical Evaluation:

The idea of referring to the three novels *Legs, Billy Phelan's Greatest Game*, and *Ironweed* by the collective title of *The Albany Cycle* was apparently not the idea of William Kennedy; reportedly, it was a marketing device devised by an editor at Viking, Kennedy's publisher. Nevertheless, it is true to his perception early in his career that Albany, the city in which he grew up, would become his great subject. His first novel, *The Ink Truck* (1969), is set in Albany, although not in the 1930's. *Quinn's Book* (1988), although set in the nineteenth century, places much of the action in Albany. In *Very Old Bones* (1992), Kennedy returns to the period and some of the characters, including several Phelans, of the earlier *The Albany Cycle*. There is no place, Kennedy realizes, that he will ever know as he knows Albany. He further understands that he is the sort of writer for whom the sense of place is crucial. Abstract novels of psychological analysis do not interest him. His interest in place, specifically in Albany, is by no means primarily sociological. Rather, he wants to explore how the inner lives of human beings are shaped by the experience of living in a particular time and a particular place. Because all people are shaped by such forces, Kennedy's examination of these particulars as they manifest themselves through highly individual characters is equally an examination of what may be most universal in human experience.

The protagonist of *Legs*, the first novel of *The Albany Cycle*, is a historical figure who operated around Albany and was finally shot to death there in 1931. Kennedy thoroughly researched Jack Diamond's life, and, as far as the external events are concerned, the novel does not deviate significantly from the established facts. A documentary account of a killer's life, however, is not the author's goal. His Diamond transcends the historical record to enter the realms of legend and myth. Why, Kennedy asks, are people so fascinated with Diamond and with others like him? An important structural pattern is the seduction and moral collapse of Marcus Gorman. Since he is not predominantly evil, but a man of middling moral stature, Gorman's inability to resist Diamond's charisma symbolizes the hold a man such as Diamond can have on the imagination of ordinary, moderately decent people. Some critics have felt that the author, not merely the character, was seduced by Diamond. These critics argue that Kennedy, fascinated by Diamond as some kind of life force, fails to place him within a coherent moral vision. Kennedy would respond that, by watching a character such as Diamond go to extremes of charisma and cruelty, one may be stimulated to explore one's own hierarchies of value.

Billy Phelan, protagonist of the second novel, *Billy Phelan's Greatest Game*, is a character whose hierarchies of value bring him close to destruction at the hands of Patsy McCall, the political boss of Albany. Kennedy modeled this character on Dan O'Connell, who was Albany's political boss for more than forty years. The key event in Kennedy's plot, the kidnapping of McCall's nephew, is based on the kidnapping of O'Connell's nephew in the 1930's. Once again, Kennedy is anything but a documentarian. He wants to explore the consequences for the self of living in the shadow of a corrupt and omnipotent political machine. This is the most political novel of the three, but Kennedy's primary concern is with the inner life.

Some critics have found that *Billy Phelan's Greatest Game* fails as a novel because its parts, although often impressive in themselves, do not cohere. The secondary plot involving Martin Daugherty may seem extraneous to the main plot focusing on Billy. In fairness to Kennedy, his purposes require that the reader know Albany in order to know Billy. Whether the secondary plot provides the sort of knowledge that best illuminates Billy, however, remains a legitimate critical question.

Ironweed, the third novel of *The Albany Cycle*, is, for many critics, the finest novel in the trilogy, perhaps the most impressive achievement of Kennedy's career. Although *Ironweed* was initially rejected by publishers on the grounds that it was depressing, that readers did not care about bums, even that real bums were not as eloquent as Kennedy's creations, the novel's publication won its author not only widespread critical acclaim but also an audience. Excited by *Ironweed*, readers discovered the simultaneously reissued earlier novels, which had hitherto been relatively neglected.

As is customary with Kennedy, the strength of this novel rests on its powerful evocation of place, but it is even more impressive in its exploration of the soul of its protagonist, Francis Phelan. As he confronts the past and its many pains, Francis moves toward a redemption that is presented entirely without sentimentality. His circumstances have altered only slightly. As before in his life, he is being pursued for killing a man, but he confronts his demons and takes his own measure as a man. Above all, against the odds, he survives, not only physically but also spiritually.

As the third novel of *The Albany Cycle*, *Ironweed* illuminates the first two in a number of ways. Francis becomes a touchstone for understanding Diamond and Billy, and Francis's struggles deepen one's sense of the Albany presented in the other novels. One consequence is that the earlier novels improve in the light of *Ironweed*. Features that were troublesome now find their place in the larger whole. The structural problems of *Billy Phelan's Greatest Game* no longer seem so important. The moral ambiguities of *Legs* become acceptable as part of a more inclusive design. Ultimately, *The Albany Cycle* adds up to a whole greater than the sum of its parts.

W. P. Kenney

Further Reading

Edinger, Claudio. *The Making of "Ironweed."* New York: Penguin Books, 1988. A detailed look at the 1987 film made from the third novel of *The Albany Cycle* and the process of its production. Kennedy himself wrote the script, and the book illuminates a number of aspects of the novel, as does a viewing of the film itself.

Gillespie, Michael Patrick. *Reading William Kennedy*. Syracuse, N.Y.: Syracuse University Press, 2002. An introductory overview of Kennedy's work, placing it within the context of the Albany culture that shapes his characters and plots. Each of the six novels in *The Albany Cycle* is analyzed in a separate chapter.

Kennedy, William. *Conversations with William Kennedy*. Edited by Neila C. Seshachari. Jackson: University Press of Mississippi, 1997. Contains twenty-four interviews with Kennedy conducted between 1969 and 1996 in which he discusses, among other subjects, the process of writing his novels. Demonstrates the seriousness with which Kennedy pursues his work and his artistic growth.

________. *O Albany! Improbable City of Political Wizards, Fearless Ethnics, Spectacular Aristocrats, Splendid Nobodies and Underrated Scoundrels*. New York: Viking Press, 1983. In this combination of memoir and journalism, Kennedy recounts the history of his hometown—and the city that has been the source of much of his fiction. Includes maps and vintage photographs of Albany.

________. *Riding the Yellow Trolley Car*. New York: Viking Press, 1993. The first section of this collection of pieces by Kennedy includes many of the author's reflections on the novels that make up *The Albany Cycle*. The fifth section contains his account of the making of the film *Ironweed*.

Lynch, Vivian Valvano. *Portraits of Artists: Warriors in the Novels of William Kennedy*. Lanham, Md.: International Scholars, 1999. Detailed examination of Kennedy's work, emphasizing its Irish and American themes. Devotes a separate chapter to each of Kennedy's novels through *The Flaming Corsage*.

McCaffery, Larry, and Sinda Gregory. *Alive and Writing: Interviews with American Authors of the 1980's*. Urbana: University of Illinois Press, 1987. Includes a probing, engaging interview with Kennedy. Provides a concentrated supplement to the materials in *Riding the Yellow Trolley Car.*

Michener, Christian. *From Then into Now: William Kennedy's Albany Novels*. Scranton, Pa.: University of Scranton Press, 1998. Analyzes the novels in *The Albany Cycle* individually as well as assessing the work as a whole. Michener argues that the novels are united by their characters, who embark on heroic quests to redeem themselves by accepting the truth of their past lives.

Reilly, Edward C. *William Kennedy.* Boston: Twayne, 1991. Introduction to Kennedy's life and works for the general reader. Broadly useful critical study. Includes bibliography.

Van Dover, J. K. *Understanding William Kennedy.* Columbia: University of South Carolina Press, 1991. Asserts that Kennedy moves toward his true subject in the process of writing *The Albany Cycle*. Heavy emphasis on the role of place in Kennedy's work.

Alcestis

Author: Euripides (c. 485-406 B.C.E.)
First transcribed: Alkēstis, 438 B.C.E. (English translation, 1781)
Type of work: Drama
Type of plot: Tragicomedy
Time of plot: Antiquity
Locale: Pherae, in ancient Greece

Principal characters:
APOLLO, god of the sun
ADMETUS, the king of Pherae
ALCESTIS, his wife
THANATOS, Death
HERCULES, son of Zeus and friend to Admetus

The Story:

Phoebus Apollo has a son, Asclepius, who in time becomes a god of medicine and healing. Asclepius transgresses divine law by raising a mortal, Hippolytus, from the dead, and Zeus, in anger, kills Apollo's son with a thunderbolt forged by the Cyclops. Apollo then slays the Cyclops, a deed for which he is condemned by Zeus to leave Olympus and to serve for one year as herdsman to Admetus, the king of Pherae in Thessaly.

Some time after Apollo completes his term of service, Admetus marries Alcestis, the daughter of the king of Iolcus, Pelias. On his wedding day, however, he offends the goddess Artemis and so is doomed to die. Apollo, grateful for the kindness Admetus showed him in the past, prevails on the Fates to spare the king on the condition that when his hour of death comes, they accept instead the life of whoever will consent to die in his place.

None of Admetus's kin cares to offer himself in his place, but Alcestis, in wifely devotion, pledges herself to die for her husband. The day arrives when she must give up her life. Concerned for the wife of his mortal friend, Apollo appeals to Thanatos, who comes to take Alcestis to the underworld. Thanatos rejects his pleas, warning the god not to transgress against eternal judgment or the will of the Fates. Apollo declares that there is one powerful enough to defy the Fates who is even then on his way to the palace of Admetus. Meanwhile Alcestis prepares for her approaching death. On the day she is to die, she dresses herself in rich funeral robes and prays before the hearth fire to Vesta, goddess of the hearth, asking her to be a mother to the two children she is leaving behind, to find a helpmate for the boy and a gentle lord for the girl, and not to let them follow their mother's example and die before their time. After her prayers, she places garlands of myrtle on each altar of the house and at each shrine prays tearlessly, knowing that death is coming. In her own chamber she weeps as she remembers the happy years she and Admetus lived together. Her children find her there, and she says her farewells. The house is filled also with the sound of weeping servants, grieving for the mistress they love. Admetus too weeps bitterly, begging Alcestis not to leave him. While he watches, however, her breath grows fainter, and her cold hand falls languidly. Before she dies, she asks him to promise that he will always care tenderly for their children and that he will never marry again.

At that moment, Hercules arrives at the palace of Admetus, on his way to slay the wild horses of Diomedes in Thrace as the eighth of his twelve labors. Admetus conceals from Hercules the news of Alcestis's death so that he might keep the son of Zeus as a guest and carry out the proper rites of hospitality. Hercules, ignorant of what took place before his arrival in Pherae, spends the night carousing, drinking wine, and singing, only to awaken in the morning to discover that Alcestis died hours before he came and that his host purposely deluded him in order to make his stay in Pherae as comfortable as possible. In gratitude for Admetus's thoughtfulness and in remorse for having reveled while the home of his friend was deep in sorrow, he determines to ambush Thanatos and bring Alcestis back from the dead.

Since no labor is too arduous for the hero, he sets out after Thanatos and Alcestis. Overtaking them, he wrestles with Thanatos and forces him to give up his victim. Then he brings Alcestis, heavily veiled, into the presence of sorrowing Admetus and asks the king to protect her until Hercules returns from Thrace. When Admetus refuses, Hercules insists that the king at least peer beneath the woman's veil. Great is the joy of Admetus and his household when they learn that the woman is Alcestis, miraculously returned from the grave. Pleased with his efforts, doughty Hercules continues his travels, firm in the knowledge that with him goes the undying gratitude of Admetus and the gentle Alcestis.

Critical Evaluation:

Alcestis, the earliest extant tragedy by Euripides, was written when the dramatist was in his forties. It is therefore the work of a fully matured man. First staged in 438 B.C.E., the play is in part a product of Athens's Age of Pericles, that period between the end of the Persian Wars and the onset of the Peloponnesian War. This play shares some of the piety and optimistic confidence of that golden era when Athens reached its greatest power and achieved its finest cultural successes, including the great tragedians Aeschylus, Sophocles, and Euripides.

In *Alcestis*, Euripides reworks an old legend that had earlier been dramatized by the tragic poet Phrynichus. The work bears Euripides' inimitable stamp in the keen psychological portraiture, in the rare mixture of comic and tragic elements, and in the deus ex machina ending. Presented as the fourth drama in a tetralogy, which is traditionally a satyr-play, *Alcestis* is best described as a tragicomedy.

The opening confrontation between Apollo and Thanatos, or Death, sets forth the opposition that is the play's main underlying theme. Apollo is a radiant god, the representative of light, health, and life, whereas Thanatos is a dark, dismal underworld divinity with an awesome power over all living creatures. Both deities have a claim on Admetus and Alcestis, yet because they belong to different supernatural spheres a compromise between them is impossible. However, Apollo, with his prophetic gift, foresees a resolution in the arrival of Hercules, who will rescue Alcestis from Death.

From that point on, the action proceeds on purely human terms. All the characters are recognizable as persons, with private attitudes, emotions, and choices. Euripides reveals the feelings of Alcestis, a woman who freely sacrifices her life so that her husband may live; of Admetus, who asks for and accepts such a sacrifice; of the child of such a marriage; of Admetus's old father, Pheres, reviled by his only son for refusing to lay down his life; and of Hercules, who accepts hospitality from the grieving Admetus, drunkenly amuses himself, and then wrests Alcestis from Death to redeem his honor. These are not mere puppets of Fate but men and women acting of their own volition. They are, however, torn between life and death—between Apollo and Thanatos—by the choices they make.

Alcestis chooses the heroic role in laying down her life for Admetus. She knows well what she will leave behind: the joy of her marriage bed, her small children, and the pleasures of living. Her sacrifice is all the greater because she is also aware of the terrors of death. She loves her husband, but Alcestis is also thinking of her children and of what will happen to them if the kingdom passes to a stranger. Her final restoration dramatically suggests the biblical paradox that whoever loses his life for love's sake will gain new life.

Admetus suggests the complementary paradox, that whoever seeks to save his life will lose it. He turns weak in the face of death and chooses to let another die for him. His remorse while his wife is still alive is sheer sentimentality, for at heart he is an egoistic coward. However, when she is dead, he must confront his ignoble shame and live a deathlike existence of perpetual mourning.

His moment of self-recognition occurs in the bitter meeting with his father, Pheres. Admetus blames Pheres for Alcestis's death, because the old man chose to live when he might have died for his son. Pheres exhibits the same cowardice that afflicts Admetus, but he speaks the truth when he condemns Admetus and declares that no one should ask another to die in his place. Pheres, in clutching life, loses the only thing that matters to him—the respect of his son—and so his life becomes a curse.

If Admetus damns his father, he also damns his children to a motherless desolation and damns himself. He performs one generous act by admitting Hercules as a guest and disguising the cause of his mourning. It is dramatically necessary that Hercules be ignorant of Alcestis's death so that he makes a drunken fool of himself. Euripides ingeniously retains the sober mood of the play in this scene, for Hercules in his intoxicated solemnity discourses on death's inevitability.

This leads to Hercules' discovery of the truth and of his own shame. To every man in this play there comes a moment when he must face personal shame. In Hercules' case, shame motivates him to a noble act. The final scene, where Hercules restores Alcestis to Admetus, is perfectly integrated with the pattern of the whole play and with the themes of sacrifice, loss, and redemption.

The view of life behind this drama is psychologically coherent. It shows the heroic nature of a total sacrifice, the base nature of asking and accepting such a gift, and the path of salvation through a full realization of personal degradation and through acts of unsolicited generosity. Hercules, in entering Admetus's home, becomes involved in his degradation and must save himself by this same path. Baseness is a form of death, Euripides seems to say, but redemption is life, true life. In *Alcestis*, Euripides revives an old myth in a way that probes the basis of human experience.

"Critical Evaluation" by James Weigel, Jr.

Further Reading

Bloom, Harold, ed. *Euripides: Comprehensive Research and Study Guide*. Philadelphia: Chelsea House, 2003. Includes a biography of Euripides and a plot summary, list of characters, and six critical essays providing various interpretations of *Alcestis*.

Euripides. *Alcestis*. Edited by Desmond J. Conacher. Warminster, England: Aris & Phillips, 1988. Contains the Greek text and an English translation. Conacher's introduction sets the play in context and discusses problems of interpretation. The commentary emphasizes structure and themes.

Grube, G. M. A. *The Drama of Euripides*. London: Methuen, 1941. A general treatment of Euripides, still highly regarded. Contains chapters on the structural elements of Euripides' plays, the chorus, the gods, and contemporary issues; also provides penetrating analysis of individual plays, including *Alcestis*.

Luschnig, C. A. E. *The Gorgon's Severed Head: Studies in "Alcestis," "Electra," and "Phoenissae."* New York: Brill, 1995. Examines three plays from various periods in Euripides' career and concludes that all three demonstrate his use of innovative dramatic techniques and traditional stories, his depiction of characters who create themselves and each other, and his treatment of gender issues. The chapters on *Alcestis* focus on the two main characters of Alcestis and Admetus.

Morwood, James. *The Plays of Euripides*. Bristol, England: Bristol Classical, 2002. Morwood provides a concise overview of all of Euripides' plays, devoting a separate chapter to each one. He demonstrates how Euripides was constantly reinventing himself in his work.

Mossman, Judith, ed. *Euripides*. New York: Oxford University Press, 2003. Collection of essays, some providing a general overview of Euripidean drama, others focusing on specific plays. Includes "Euripides' *Alkestis*: Five Aspects of an Interpretation" by R. G. A. Buxton.

Pickard-Cambridge, Arthur W. *The Dramatic Festivals of Athens*. Rev. ed. Oxford, England: Clarendon Press, 1968. A magisterial work, closely based on ancient sources, treating the religious festivals at which tragedy and comedy were performed. Includes chapters on the actors, costumes, chorus, audience, and guilds of performers.

Wilson, John R., ed. *Twentieth Century Interpretations of Euripides' "Alcestis."* Englewood Cliffs, N.J.: Prentice-Hall, 1968. A useful collection of ten critical essays on *Alcestis* that were originally published between 1940 and 1965, as well as ten "Points of View," brief, thought-provoking extracts from larger works.

Wohl, Victoria. "Mourning and Matricide in Euripides' *Alcestis*." In *Intimate Commerce: Exchange, Gender, and Subjectivity in Greek Tragedy*. Austin: University of Texas Press, 1998. A feminist study of *Alcestis* and plays by Aeschylus and Sophocles in which Wohl demonstrates how the female characters fail to become active subjects.

The Alchemist

Author: Paulo Coelho (1947-)
First published: O Alquimista, 1988 (English translation, 1993)
Type of work: Novel
Type of plot: Fable and Magical Realism
Time of plot: Undetermined
Locale: Andalusia, Spain; Africa; Egypt

Principal characters:
THE ALCHEMIST, a spiritual messenger
SANTIAGO, a sheepherder
MELCHIZEDEK, the king of Salem
THE ENGLISHMAN, a spiritual messenger

The Story:

In Andalusia, Spain, a shepherd boy, Santiago, decides to sleep in an abandoned church that has no roof but has a sycamore tree growing from within. Aside from a herd of sheep, Santiago's only property is a jacket and one book, which he uses as a pillow. The next morning, he begins his journey to the village where he plans on selling his sheep's wool.

Stopping briefly in Tarifa, Santiago visits a fortune-teller for help in interpreting a recurring dream. In the dream, he is in a field with his sheep when a child appears. The child takes Santiago's hands and transports him to the Egyptian pyramids, telling him along the way that there is a hidden treasure there. At this point in the dream, Santiago awakens. The soothsayer advises him to travel to the pyramids to find this treasure.

While reading his book, Santiago meets an old man, professing to be Melchizedek, the king of Salem. The king encourages Santiago to seek his Personal Legend, and he explains that when a person wants something, that desire arises from the Soul of the World. Melchizedek tells Santiago that the treasure he is looking for is near the Egyptian pyramids and that he will have to follow the omens to find it. The old man gives him two stones, Urim and Thummim, to consult in case he has trouble interpreting the signs.

Santiago sells his flock and travels through Tangier, Africa, where he is swindled out of his money. Upset, he asks the two stones if he will find the treasure. In reply, the stones fall to the earth. Santiago interprets this as a positive sign, reaffirming his faith. Resuming his travel, he happens upon a crystal shop and offers to work in exchange for food. Intent on returning home some day, Santiago asks to continue working at the shop to earn the money to buy a flock of sheep, and the merchant agrees. Santiago earns the needed money to return home, though he decides instead to resume his journey to the pyramids.

On his way to the pyramids, Santiago meets an Englishman in search of an Arab alchemist living in Al-Fayoum. The alchemist is said to possess exceptional powers. As the boy is holding Urim and Thummim, the Englishman produces two similar stones from his pocket, which Santiago interprets as a favorable omen. The Englishman and Santiago board a caravan that is crossing the desert, but the ride is arduous because tribal wars have been waged. They arrive safely at an oasis and begin their stay as guests there until the threat of war is over.

While at the oasis, Santiago sees a hawk, prompting a vision of an army attacking the oasis. Because the oasis is a safe zone, he doubts his own vision, yet he tells the camel driver, who instructs him to notify the chieftain. The chieftain declares that everyone shall carry arms. He then promises that for every ten enemies Santiago kills, Santiago will receive a piece of gold. If Santiago does not use a weapon by the end of the following day, one will be used against him. He accepts whatever fate God will bestow upon him.

After the meeting, Santiago is faced with a powerful desert messenger, the alchemist, who demands to know why he read the omen that the hawk delivered. Santiago replies that he was meant to save the oasis. The next morning the oasis is attacked, but the intruders are killed. In payment, Santiago receives fifty gold pieces. The alchemist agrees to guide Santiago to the treasure the next evening, and on their seventh day of travel, tells Santiago that if he listens to his heart, he will find the treasure. Santiago remembers the proverb, "the darkest hour of the night came just before the dawn."

Before long, the alchemist and Santiago are caught and taken to a nearby military camp. The alchemist gives the chief Santiago's gold coins and tells him that the boy is an alchemist. When asked what the boy can do, he replies that he could destroy their camp by becoming the wind. Santiago is afraid, but the alchemist instructs him not to let his fear overtake him.

On the third day, the boy brings his captors to a cliff. He then asks the desert for help in producing wind. The desert agrees, but tells him to also ask the wind, who directs Santiago to ask Heaven for help. The boy agrees, but says he needs the wind to make a sandstorm to block the sun so he will not be blinded. The chief is enthralled as the sand begins to whirl about. Santiago realizes that his soul is one with God and that he can perform miracles. Along with the alchemist, Santiago is released.

Shortly after, the alchemist and Santiago enter a monastery near the pyramids. The alchemist turns lead into gold to show the boy that it is possible to reach one's Personal Legend. He splits the gold into four parts: one for himself, one for the monk, one for the boy, and the last to be held in trust at the monastery in case Santiago needs it in the future.

The boy travels on alone and, as he listens to his heart, is told to beware of the place that will bring him to tears. Finally, at the top of a dune, he sees the pyramids. The boy weeps as he begins to dig. Soon, several war refugees approach him for money. They search his bag and find the alchemist's gold piece; thinking he uncovered it in the sand, they force him to dig for more. When none is found, they beat him. At last, the boy tells the refugees that he did not find the gold in the sand; he then tells them of his journey and the treasure. The leader calls Santiago a fool and confesses that he, too, had a dream that told him to travel in search of treasure. His dream had directed him to a ruined church in Spain, where a treasure is buried within a sycamore tree's roots. The leader tells Santiago that he himself had not been not stupid enough to travel all this way because of a dream. After he leaves, the boy realizes where the treasure has always been.

Some time later, the boy arrives at the abandoned church. He digs with a shovel at the sycamore's roots. He marvels at God's strange way of showing him where the treasure is and realizes that the alchemist intentionally left the bit of gold at the monastery so he could afford to return home. He hears the alchemist's voice on the wind telling him that he never would have seen the beauty of the pyramids had he simply been told where the treasure is buried. Santiago finds a chest of gold coins, precious stones, and other items and realizes that life is generous to those who follow their Personal Legend.

Critical Evaluation:

Written in less than one month in 1987, Paulo Coelho's *The Alchemist* was inspired by the short tale "The Ruined Man Who Became Rich Again Through a Dream" from the classic Arabic short-story cycle *The Arabian Nights' Entertainments*, also known as *The Thousand and One Nights* (fifteenth century). This tale has been adapted by many authors because of the powerful message it delivers about discovering that one's treasure does not need to be pursued; it can be found at home.

For *The Alchemist*, Coelho adapts four principles from the tale: the personal quest, the awareness of omens, the soul of the world, and the idea of listening to one's heart as a guide. The novel also mentions *The Thousand and One Nights* when Santiago and the Englishman see many wells, colored tents, and date trees upon approaching the oasis. The Englishman acknowledges that the view looks like a scene from the classic story.

In this semiautobiographical work, Coelho's own experiences are mimicked in Santiago's journey to find his Personal Legend. At the age of sixteen, Santiago leaves the monastery against his father's wishes, in favor of seeking his true dream of traveling. Like Santiago, Coelho had left his Jesuit schooling and Roman Catholicism in favor of his own journey. When his parents realized that writing was his dream, they sent him to a psychiatric hospital, where he underwent electroconvulsive therapy.

Coelho followed this period of hospitalization with stints as a hippie, a songwriter, and a dabbler in black magic. He also spent time in jail, where he was tortured by the Brazilian government for participating in subversive activities. At this point in his life, Coelho took a pilgrimage on the Santiago de Compostela in Spain, where the revelations that followed brought him back to the Catholic religion and fostered an interest in simplicity. He surmised that people find their spirituality through self-fulfillment rather than through stifled individual freedom. Coelho made a full circle in his journey.

Similarly, Santiago finds his treasure in the physical place where he began his journey: the dilapidated church in Andalusia, Spain. It is no coincidence that both Coelho and Santiago have epic journeys that begin in Spain and that the main character's name, Santiago, mimics the pilgrim's trail that Coelho traveled. When Coelho began this novel, the only aspect he was certain of was that Santiago, like himself, would end in the place he started.

Coelho's rebellion ultimately helped him to identify his path in life and to develop the survival skills necessary to overcome conflict. Santiago also develops these strengths along his own journey. On three separate occasions, all of his money is stolen. The first time he weeps from despair, then he chooses to have faith. The second time, he questions the alchemist's judgment in handing over his earnings; again, he still has faith. Finally, the war refugees steal his money and beat him severely. Through this experience, he understands how he can achieve his personal goal. Ultimately, Santiago prevails.

From his personal experiences, Coelho develops a number of thematic topics for *The Alchemist*. The fable delivers the moral lesson about realizing your dreams and listening to your heart. Santiago dreams of traveling instead of living in a monastery, and he follows his heart by leaving. When pursuing his dream, he is warned by the alchemist that fear should not be an option because paralysis inhibits life's progress. Eventually, Santiago also discovers that when he listened, his heart had directed him toward his Personal Legend. Coelho is making a statement against conformity and rigidity.

Coelho also uses his voice to examine the debate of fate versus free will. For example, King Melchizedek retells the story of appearing before a miner who had been ready to abandon his Personal Legend. The old king then transformed himself into a stone to attract the miner's attention and aid him in finding the precious stone he was seeking. The king is a manifestation of God, as is the gypsy (Roma) who identifies Santiago's dream without needing to be told. Fate is controlling Santiago's destiny.

Stylistically, Coelho uses simplistic language, making his text accessible to the reader. He avoids complex metaphor and idioms, yet employs symbolism that alludes to spiritual guidance. The hawk leads Santiago to have a vision that enables him to save the oasis from attack, and a scarab beetle indicates the spot where Santiago will weep and then dig for treasure before the pyramids.

The Alchemist references the book of Exodus in the Old Testament in the mention of the two stones, Urim and Thummim, which were said to be divination tools held within the breastplate worn by the high priest. Melchizedek, who gives Santiago the stones, opens his cape and reveals a gold breastplate covered with precious stones, which ultimately convinces Santiago that he is a king. He gives Santiago the stones and tells him they will help him read omens when he is indecisive. In the Old Testament, Melchizedek is the king of Salem.

The Alchemist is not only a fable but also a work of Magical Realism, evoking a realistic setting as well as magical and mysterious events. The work connects to socially relevant topics and employs mythical and fablelike happenings. The characters are often endowed with supernatural abilities, such as when Santiago converses with the natural elements when trying to turn himself into the wind.

Over time, *The Alchemist* has become a modern classic, and Coelho is now one of the most widely read of Latin American authors. He has changed the lives of many readers by encouraging them to rediscover themselves through personal journeys. The novel has inspired a symphony and theatrical adaptations, and the rights to the novel were purchased in 2008 by American film producer Harvey Weinstein.

Susan J. Sylvia

Further Reading

Coelho, Paulo. "The Beyond Is Accessible to Those Who Dare." *UNESCO Courier* 51, no. 3 (March, 1998): 34-37. This interview with Coelho focuses on his thoughts about the spirituality of and themes in *The Alchemist*. It also addresses how some of his own life influenced his feelings about how and what to write. Also addresses why people should pursue their goals.

_______. "The Coming of Age of a Brazilian Phenomenon." Interview by Glauco Ortolano. *World Literature Today* 77, no. 1 (2003): 57-59. Coelho discusses his writing technique and the motivations behind his works. A brief but helpful article.

Hart, Stephen M. "Cultural Hybridity, Magical Realism, and the Language of Magic in Paulo Coelho's *The Retrieve*." *Romance Quarterly* 51, no. 4 (Fall, 2004): 304-312. Although focused on a different Coelho novel, this essay examines the evolution of the genre of Magical Realism and its application to his works. Also discusses how Coelho's works reflect Magical Realism.

Morais, Fernando. *Paulo Coelho*. New York: HarperCollins, 2009. This biography includes a time line of Coelho's life with facts that detail how he rediscovered his faith and immersed himself in a life of simplicity.

Weeks, Linton. "Paulo Coelho: At Peace with the Inexplicable." *The Washington Post*, September 27, 2004. This newspaper article addresses Coelho's popularity with his readers and gives specifics regarding his life experiences. In particular, Weeks examines Coelho's personal growth as a writer.

The Alchemist

Author: Ben Jonson (1573-1637)
First produced: 1610; first published, 1612
Type of work: Drama
Type of plot: Comedy of manners
Time of plot: Early seventeenth century
Locale: London

Principal characters:
FACE, a butler
SUBTLE, a swindler posing as an alchemist
DOL COMMON, their partner
LOVEWIT, owner of the house, and Face's master
SIR EPICURE MAMMON, a greedy knight
DAME PLIANT, a young widow

The Story:

Master Lovewit leaves the city because of plague. His butler, Jeremy, known as Face to his friends of the underworld, invites Subtle, a swindler posing as an alchemist, and Dol Common, a prostitute, to join him in using the house as a base of operations for their rascally activities. Matters fare well for the three until a dispute arises between Face and Subtle over authority. Dol, seeing their moneymaking projects doomed if this strife continues, rebukes the two men and cajoles them back to their senses.

No sooner have Face and Subtle become reconciled than Dapper, a gullible lawyer's clerk given to gambling, calls, by previous arrangement with Face. Dapper wants to learn from the eminent astrologer, Doctor Subtle, how to win at all games of chance. In the hands of the two merciless rascals, Dapper is relieved of all his ready cash, in return for which Subtle predicts that Dapper will have good luck at the gaming tables. In order to gull Dapper further, Subtle tells him to return later to confer with the Queen of Fairy, a mysterious benefactress who can promote Dapper's worldly success.

Abel Drugger, an ambitious young druggist who was led on by Face, is the next victim to enter the house. To his delight, he learns from Subtle, who speaks mostly in incomprehensible pharmaceutical and astrological jargon, that he will have a rich future.

Next arrives Sir Epicure Mammon, a greedy and lecherous knight, with his friend Pertinax Surly, a man versed in the ways of London confidence men. Having been promised the philosopher's stone by Subtle, Mammon has wild visions of transforming all of his possessions into gold and silver, but he is completely taken in by the duplicities of Subtle and Face. Subtle further arouses Mammon's greed by describing at length, in the pseudoscientific gibberish of the alchemist-confidence man, the processes that led to his approximate achievement of the mythical philosopher's stone. Surly, quick to see what is afoot, scoffs at Subtle and at the folly of Mammon.

During the interview, Dol appears inadvertently. Mammon catches sight of her and is fascinated. Thinking quickly, Face tells Mammon that Dol is an aristocratic lady who, being mad, is under the care of Doctor Subtle but who, in her moments of sanity, is most affable. Before he leaves the house, Mammon promises to send to the unprincipled Subtle certain of his household objects of base metal for the purpose of having them transmuted into gold.

The parade of victims continues. Elder Ananias of the Amsterdam community of extreme Protestants comes to negotiate for his group with Subtle for the philosopher's stone. Subtle, with Face as his assistant, repeats his extravagant jargon to the impressionable Ananias, who, in his greed, declares that the brethren are impatient with the slowness of the experiment. Subtle, feigning professional indignation, frightens Ananias with a threat to put out forever his alchemist's fire.

Drugger reappears to be duped further. Subtle and Face are delighted when he tells them that a wealthy young widow took lodgings near his, and that her brother, recently come into an inheritance, journeyed to London to learn how to quarrel in rakish fashion. The two knaves plot eagerly to get brother and sister into their clutches.

Ananias returns with his pastor, Tribulation Wholesome. The Puritans manage to wink at moral considerations as Subtle glowingly describes the near completion of the philosopher's stone. Prepared to go to any ends to procure the stone, Ananias and Tribulation contract to purchase Mammon's household articles, which, Subtle explains, he needs for the experiment; the proceeds of the sale will go toward the care of orphans for whom Subtle says he is responsible.

Subtle and Face also plot to sell these same household articles to the young widow, who, having just moved to London, is probably in need of such items. In the meantime, Face meets in the streets a Spanish don—Surly in clever disguise—who expresses a desire to confer with Subtle on matters of business and health.

Dapper returns to meet the Queen of Fairy. At the same time, Drugger brings to the house Master Kastril, the angry young man who wants to learn to quarrel. Kastril is completely taken in. Subtle, promising to make him a perfect London gallant, arranges to have him instructed by Face, who poses as a city captain. Kastril is so pleased with his new acquaintances that he sends Drugger to bring his sister to the house.

Kastril having departed, Dol, Subtle, and Face relieve Dapper of all of his money in a ridiculous ritual in which Dapper is to see and talk to the Queen of Fairy. During the shameless proceedings, Mammon knocks. Dapper, who was blindfolded, is gagged and hastily put into a water closet at the rear of the house. Mammon enters and begins to woo Dol, whom he believes to be a distracted aristocrat. Face and Subtle, in order to have the front part of the house clear for further swindles, shunts the amorous pair to another part of the house.

Young Kastril returns with his widowed sister, Dame Pliant; both are deeply impressed by Subtle's manner and rhetoric. When the Spanish don arrives, Subtle escorts Kastril and Dame Pliant to inspect his laboratory. By that time, both Subtle and Face are determined to wed Dame Pliant. Face introduces the Spaniard to Dame Pliant, who, in spite of her objections to Spaniards in general, consents to walk in the garden with the don.

In another part of the house, Dol assumes the manner of madness. Subtle, discovering the distraught Mammon with her, declares that Mammon's moral laxity will surely delay completion of the philosopher's stone. Following a loud explosion, Face reports that the laboratory is a shambles. Mammon despondently leaves the house, and Subtle simulates a fainting spell.

In the garden, Surly reveals his true identity to Dame Pliant and warns the young widow against the swindlers. When, as Surly, he confronts the two rogues, Face, in desperation, tells Kastril that Surly is an impostor who is trying to steal Dame Pliant away. Drugger enters and, being Face's creature, insists that he knows Surly to be a scoundrel. Ananias comes to the house and all but wrecks Subtle's plot by talking indiscreetly of making counterfeit money. Unable to cope with the wily rascals, Surly departs, followed by Kastril.

Glad to be rid of his callers, Subtle places Dame Pliant in Dol's care. They are thrown once more into confusion when Lovewit, owner of the house, makes an untimely appearance. Face, quickly reverting to his normal role of Jeremy, the butler, goes to the door in an attempt to detain his master long enough to permit Subtle and Dol to escape.

Although warned by his butler that the house is infested, Lovewit suspects that something is amiss when Mammon and Surly return to expose Subtle and Face. Kastril, Ananias, and Tribulation confirm their account. Dapper, having managed to get rid of his gag, cries out inside the house. Deciding that honesty is the only policy, Face confesses everything to his master and promises to provide him with a wealthy young widow as his wife, if Lovewit will have mercy on his servant.

In the house, meanwhile, Subtle concludes the gulling of Dapper and sends the young clerk on his way, filled with the belief that he will win at all games of chance. Subtle and Dol then try to abscond with the threesome's loot, but Face, back in Lovewit's good graces, thwarts them in their attempt. They are forced to escape empty-handed by the back gate.

Lovewit wins the hand of Dame Pliant and, in his good humor, forgives his crafty butler. When those who have been swindled demand retribution, they are finally convinced that they have been defrauded as a result of their own selfishness and greed.

Critical Evaluation:

The Alchemist marks the peak of Ben Jonson's artistic career. Despite a somewhat muddled denouement, the play is a masterpiece of construction. As far as is known, the plot is original with Jonson. In this play, Jonson the artist supersedes Jonson the moralist: A highly entertaining and dramatic satire on human greed, *The Alchemist* displays none of the sermonizing that marks, to some extent, Jonson's other plays.

For those interested in learning how to take in the gullible, Jonson's *The Alchemist* is a fundamental text. "Cony-catching" was a popular practice in Elizabethan England, and Jonson, an intimate of London's jails, taverns, theaters, and places of even less repute, reveals in this play the techniques involved in several of the most amusing and lucrative ploys. His protagonist, it should be noted, is not punished for his misdeeds.

The complexities of life in London during the Elizabethan era, coupled with limited general scientific understanding, help account for the widespread faith in astrology and alchemy of the time. This faith in such branches of knowledge helped make them leading gimmicks for swindles. Commerce thrived and new continents were explored, but people were not far from believing in the dragons slain by King Arthur's knights. Many believed also that the dawning age of science would discover a "philosopher's stone" that would transmute dross into gold. Jonson's London, the London of *The Alchemist*, was growing and glittering and slightly hysterical, and cozening was easy, widespread, and immensely successful.

The critical response to the play has been intriguing. Samuel Taylor Coleridge, presumably impressed by the play's adherence to the classical unities, praised it as having one of the three best plots in literature, the other two being Sophocles' *Oidipous Tyrannos* (c. 429 B.C.E.; *Oedipus Tyrannus*, 1715) and Henry Fielding's *Tom Jones* (1749). Several modern commentators have contended that, although *The Alchemist* does cleave to the classical ideals, it is not a proper comedy, has no plot at all, and consists merely of a series of linked incidents. Romantic and Victorian critics particularly, understandably enchanted by Jonson's contemporary and diametric opposite, William Shakespeare, were put off by Jonson's classical forms, his satiric manner, and his coarseness. They also disliked his unemotional tone, controlled plots, and intellectual detachment. Although *The Alchemist* lacks none of these features, they do not render it deficient.

The classical ideals are so well met in *The Alchemist* that the play is, in its own way, a small classical masterpiece. Jonson observes unity of time, in that the dramatic situation is enacted in the same amount of time that it would take in real life. Unity of place is maintained because the scene, Lovewit's house in the Friars, is specific and limited. The discrete beginning, middle, and inevitable conclusion of the play provide for unity of action. The characters are "types" who behave consistently, doing nothing unexpected, and thus the ideal of decorum, the paramount classical precept, is met: Jonson's prostitute is bawdy, his churchmen sanctimonious.

Faithfulness to classical concepts, however, is not the only virtue of *The Alchemist*. A talented actor as well as a writer of poetry, masques, criticism, and tragic and comic plays, Jonson was a masterful manipulator of theatrical effects. The opening argument of *The Alchemist*, presented in antic verse, catapults the play headlong into a rollicking, boisterous, bawdy life of its own. The simple yet ingenious plot provides for the multiplicity of incident dear to the Renaissance heart; costume, disguise, and transmutation of identity are similarly exploited.

The internal development is more complex than some critics suggest. The characters are introduced in approximate order of their social status and rapacity. As these advance, so does the degree of cozening inflicted by Face and Subtle, and this progression reinforces the cohesiveness of the play. Although the fates of the characters are not contingent, since all are frauds or dupes, they interact in complex and amusing ways. These interactions, which become so dense that eventually Face and Subtle have their victims cozening each other, engender organic unity and dramatic tension simultaneously. As the play advances, the number of characters on stage increases, the pace quickens, and the scenes grow shorter. The climax is predictable but impressive, the entire proceeding animated by a genuine and hearty spirit.

Despite its qualifications as a well-wrought, clever, and entertaining play in the classical mode, *The Alchemist* owes much of its literary interest and charm to Jonson's rhetorical flourishes. The underworld slang and alchemical jargon used by the protagonists lend color and authenticity. Double entendres and simultaneous dialogue, which originated with Jonson, add to the effect. Most impressive, perhaps, is the way Subtle and Face use a debased eloquence in perpetrating their frauds. One of Subtle's elegant, highly rhetorical, pseudo-rational arguments, for example, seems unequivocally to establish the propensity of all metals to turn into gold. Surly's calm and earnest reasoning with Dame Pliant, on the other hand, seems but a pale counterfeit of Subtle's spirited equivocation.

The Alchemist dramatizes what might happen when moral order is suspended by plague in London. Lovewit, representing responsible society, jettisons civic responsibility and flees the city, leaving behind only knaves and fools. Although the reader is reminded early that order will be restored eventually, society in the hands of the unscrupulous degenerates into chaos. The servant supplants the master, science is overthrown by alchemy, reason is toppled by rhetoric, nature's secrets are transcended, and moral order is subverted as churchmen become swindlers.

Jonson's vehicle, satire, was quite popular in Elizabethan England, and in *The Alchemist* its effect is intensified by the plague in the background. Jonson intends to be instructive, even if it means instructing by ridicule. The classicist in him wants to restore to England some of the glory of Augustan Rome. To this end, Jonson adheres in his works to Cicero's famous dictum, "a copy of life, a mirror of custom, a representation of truth." Accordingly, he anchors his play in contemporary London and reflects the speech, behavior, and attitudes of its citizens. The Renaissance saw a shift in emphasis from the world of the Church to the world of experience, but while Jonson set an extremely worldly stage, his morality was severe and almost medieval. His moral values, clear from the first scene on, are constantly reiterated as *The Alchemist* indicts vain and wishful thinking and directs the mind to the contemplation of virtue. It is a sign of Jonson's genius that he does it unequivocally and entertainingly.

"Critical Evaluation" by Michael Levine

Further Reading

Barton, Anne. *Ben Jonson: Dramatist*. New York: Cambridge University Press, 1984. In addition to its introduction to *The Alchemist*, this book offers an essential discussion of the meaning and use of names and naming in

Jonson's plays—an almost obsessive interest of Jonson's throughout his work—in the context of Western discussions of language from Plato to historian William Camden, Jonson's contemporary and teacher.

Bowers, Rick. *Radical Comedy in Early Modern England: Contexts, Cultures, Performances*. Burlington, Vt.: Ashgate, 2008. Applies the theories of Mikhail Bakhtin and other philosophers to analyze early modern English comedies, describing the types of humor employed in these plays and how they satirize political, religious, and medical authority. Chapter 8 discusses *The Alchemist* and several of Jonson's other plays.

Butler, Robert. *"The Alchemist" Exposed*. London: Oberon, 2006. Butler goes behind the scenes of a National Theatre production of *The Alchemist*, chronicling how director Nicholas Hytner, the actors, and other crew members interpret the play and discover how Jonson's seventeenth century play remains relevant to twenty-first century audiences.

Donaldson, Ian. *Jonson's Magic Houses: Essays in Interpretation*. New York: Oxford University Press, 1997. Donaldson, a Jonson scholar, provides new interpretations of Jonson's personality, work, and literary legacy. Chapter 6 focuses on *The Alchemist*.

________. "Language, Noise, and Nonsense: *The Alchemist*." In *Seventeenth Century Imagery*, edited by Earl Miner. Berkeley: University of California Press, 1971. Focused discussion of the thematic significance of the play's concern with language, including meaningless language. Places the play in the context of seventeenth century ideas about language.

Harp, Richard, and Stanley Stewart, eds. *The Cambridge Companion to Ben Jonson*. New York: Cambridge University Press, 2000. Collection of essays about Jonson's life and career, including analyses of his comedies and late plays, a description of London and its theaters during Jonson's lifetime, and an evaluation of his critical heritage.

Loxley, James. *A Sourcebook*. New York: Routledge, 2002. An introductory overview of Jonson's life and work, particularly useful for students. Part 1 provides biographical information and places Jonson's life and work within the context of his times; part 2 discusses several works, including *The Alchemist*; part 3 offers critical analysis of the themes in his plays, the style of his writing, and a comparison of his work to that of William Shakespeare.

McEvoy, Sean. *Ben Jonson, Renaissance Dramatist*. Edinburgh: Edinburgh University Press, 2008. McEvoy analyzes all of Jonson's plays, attributing their greatness to the playwright's commitment to the ideals of humanism during a time of authoritarianism and rampant capitalism in England. Chapter 6 focuses on *The Alchemist*.

Martin, Mathew R. *Between Theater and Philosophy: Skepticism in the Major City Comedies of Ben Jonson and Thomas Middleton*. Newark: University of Delaware Press, 2001. Martin provides deconstructionist and other modern critical interpretations of *The Alchemist* and several other Jonson plays.

Alcools

Poems, 1898-1913

Author: Guillaume Apollinaire (1880-1918)
First published: Alcools: Poèmes, 1898-1913, 1913 (English translation, 1964)
Type of work: Poetry

The son of a Polish adventurer and an Italian officer, Guillaume Apollinaire spent most of his childhood in Monaco and the South of France. By 1899, when he was nineteen, he had come to Paris, where he became one of the most remarkable leaders of the young intellectual movements in the capital. In one way or another he contributed to Fauvism, to cubism, and even to Surrealism. He helped, moreover, to establish the reputation of the painter Henri Rousseau.

Apollinaire's *Alcools*, a collection of poems published in 1913, contains works that span the years 1898 to 1913. There is little thematic or formal unity within this collection, and the title expresses the poet's thirst for vivid sensation and experience as well as his remarkable impressionability.

The rather long poem "Zone" was not Apollinaire's original selection as the first in the 1913 collection. Its themes and aesthetic are scarcely characteristic, but perhaps an explanation may be sought in the very element of surprise, which is an essential part of Apollinaire's poetic technique.

"Zone" and several other pieces in *Alcools* may justifiably be compared with cubist paintings by artists such as Robert Delaunay. There is the same prismatic view of the world, the juxtaposition of apparently disparate elements, and the attempt to offer several views from different angles simultaneously. A contrapuntal or polyphonic effect in "Zone," as in other pieces, is furthered by Apollinaire's complete suppression of punctuation from the collection. This effect introduces a constant element of ambiguity and necessitates a careful reading, and often a rereading, which helps to immerse the reader in the atmosphere of the poem. Apollinaire, when he uses punctuation, shows himself to have a faulty knowledge of it; he was later to become skilled in not using it. The reader has the impression of helping to re-create the poem when he or she reads it.

The opening lines of "Zone" situate its mood, if not its true time or location. The poem is ostensibly a lament for excessive devotion to the past, and Apollinaire's introduction of the Eiffel Tower, automobiles, and precise, proper names is pointedly topical. There is, however, a much deeper theme and unity in the form of the poet's quest. Unhappy in love, he searches in vain for some consolation. The mood remains nostalgic, even unhappy. Walking through Paris, the poet has the impression that he is cast in the role of unhappy lover, and this unhappiness develops into a pattern, a consciousness of a life lived in frenzy and waste. With a technique similar to that of the flashback in the cinema, the language dissolves into a series of images as the poet reviews the places he visited. Viewing himself as object, then speaking as the subject of the description, passing from second to first person, then combining the two, the poet achieves a remarkable fusion of past and present, the overall effect of which is a sense of complete failure.

Apollinaire's influence on the later Surrealist movement cannot be doubted. "Zone," like many other pieces, suggests the presence of beauty and poetry as a latent quality in the most unconventional objects. Street scenes in Paris with cafés and streetcars, the Eiffel Tower, police thrillers: These are a few of the manifestations of the French scene in Apollinaire's day around which he shaped his poetry.

The Surrealist poet André Breton was later to assert that poetry is contained within objects that up to his time had been held to be alien to art. Apollinaire would have agreed. He does not hesitate to intersperse snatches of conversation with a nostalgic lament or part of a popular song. In at least one poem, "The Pretty Redhead," Apollinaire's stated ambition is no less enormous than that of Breton and indeed could easily find a place inside one of the Surrealist manifestos.

It would be quite wrong to cast Apollinaire simply as a poet-explorer or a virtuoso playing with words. Many critics would even claim that his essential talent is lyrical, and it is true that there is a peculiar poignancy about his laments for love lost or for the passage of time, two of the permanent subjects of poetry.

In "Mirabeau Bridge," Apollinaire offers the reader the simplest of situations: a bridge over the Seine, with someone looking into the water. Though the external description is slight, almost everything in the poem suggests movement, and the flow of the river evokes the moods of love and of the passing of time. When the poet tries to establish a parallel between the bridge and the lovers, to suggest a possible permanence in love, the attempt fails. Love is shown to disappear, like the waters of the river.

The third piece in *Alcools* is a long poem in several movements entitled "The Song of the Ill-Beloved." In it Apollinaire displays his ready acceptance of the world and his openness and receptiveness to it, as well as his vulnerability. The poem is often ambiguous. It has love as its theme, but love made noticeable through its absence and the poet's memory of it rather than through any form of fulfillment. The opening stanza prepares the reader for the mysterious, unreal atmosphere of the poem, similar to that conjured up in the thrillers of the period. In the image of a young hoodlum appearing in the fog of a London evening Apollinaire creates an aura of mystery that makes anything seem possible. He communicates a sense of immediacy, so that each description comes vividly to life. For each mood, each idea, the poet immediately offers an image. A memory is no sooner called up than it fills the poem, temporarily changing its direction. There is, however, a single thread running through the poem, a strain of melancholy involving a return to present reality from memories of springtime and love. The final stanza reasserts the poet's awareness of his role as the one who captures memories and sings them, who makes of his experience a pattern, a ritual, a song that can be passed on to others.

Better, perhaps, than any other poet in the early twentieth century, Apollinaire is able to translate the eclectic, anxious consciousness of his time, which combines the awareness of tradition and the desire for change. In Apollinaire, the Romantics' rediscovery of the dual nature of human beings—angel and beast, body and soul, the *homo duplex* of Christian terminology—gives way to a more complex concept. Apollinaire reveals the *homo multiplex*, the human beings of manifold aspirations and moods that often coexist simultaneously. The apparent disorder of this consciousness is reflected in the poems.

Further Reading

Bates, Scott. *Guillaume Apollinaire*. New York: Twayne, 1967. A detailed, exhaustive study of Apollinaire's poetic art, tracing characteristic themes and sources.

Cornelius, Nathalie Goodisman. *A Semiotic Analysis of Guillaume Apollinaire's Mythology in "Alcools."* New York: Peter Lang, 1995. Cornelius closely analyzes several of the poems, using semiotics, or the study of signs and symbols, to discover a structure for the seemingly random use of allusions, myths, and neologisms.

Davies, Margaret. *Apollinaire*. Edinburgh: Oliver & Boyd, 1964. A well-grounded life-and-works study in the British tradition, rich in documented anecdote if somewhat short on literary analysis. Davies examines in detail the "riddle" of Apollinaire's paternity, a major theme in his literary art.

Saul, Scott. "A Zone Is a Zone Is a Zone: The Repeated Unsettlement of Guillaume Apollinaire." In *Understanding French Poetry: Essays for a New Millennium*, edited and coauthored by Stamos Metzidakes. 2d ed. Birmingham, Ala.: Summa, 2001. This analysis of Apollinaire's work is included in a collection of essays that examine French poetry from the Middle Ages to the present in order to determine why French verse has been overshadowed by artistic and critical prose.

Shattuck, Roger. *The Banquet Years*. Rev. ed. New York: Vintage Books, 1968. A pioneering work of cultural history. Although trained as a scholar of literature, Shattuck ranges freely and knowledgeably across disciplinary boundaries in search of the modernist spirit and its origins, concentrating on the figures of Henri Rousseau, Alfred Jarry, Apollinaire, and Erik Satie. Treats both Apollinaire's poetry and his role as critic and publicist of modern art.

Stamelman, Richard Howard. *The Drama of Self in Guillaume Apollinaire's "Alcools."* Chapel Hill: University of North Carolina Department of Romance Languages, 1976. Offers insightful commentary and criticism in clear, often memorable prose.

Steegmuller, Francis. *Apollinaire: Poet Among the Painters*. New York: Farrar, Straus, 1963. Written by one of the best-known and most effective English-language translators of Apollinaire, Steegmuller's volume complements Shattuck's discussion of Apollinaire as poet and art critic. Also provides a useful re-creation of artistic life in turn-of-the-century Paris.

Aleck Maury, Sportsman

Author: Caroline Gordon (1895-1981)
First published: 1934
Type of work: Novel
Type of plot: Social realism
Time of plot: Late nineteenth and early twentieth centuries
Locale: Virginia, Tennessee, Mississippi, and Missouri

Principal characters:
ALECK MAURY, a southern sportsman
JAMES MORRIS, his uncle
VICTORIA, his aunt
JULIAN, his cousin
MR. FAYERLEE, the owner of Merry Point
MRS. FAYERLEE, his wife
MOLLY FAYERLEE, their daughter and Aleck's wife
RICHARD and SARAH or SALLY, Aleck and Molly's children
STEVE, Sarah's husband

The Story:

Aleck Maury's love for hunting and fishing begins in childhood. At the age of eight, Aleck goes coon hunting with Rafe, a black handyman at the Maury household. Not long after, a mill owner named Jones takes the boy fishing and encourages his lifelong love for that sport. Aleck is always happiest when he is out in the fields. One of five children, he is reared by his oldest sister after his mother dies. Until he is ten years old, he is educated at home by his father, who puts great stress upon the classics and teaches his children nothing else.

At the age of ten, Aleck goes to live at Grassdale with his Uncle James and Aunt Victoria Morris and their son, Julian. There, his education is broadened under the tutelage of Aunt Victoria, a learned woman. Aleck's life at Grassdale is pleasant, centering chiefly on sport.

When Aleck graduates from the University of Virginia, he has a classical education but no plans for making a living. He tries several jobs. He clears out a dogwood thicket for a set sum of money; he works on a construction project on the Missouri River, in the city engineer's office in Seattle, and as a day laborer on a ranch in California. While working at the ranch, he contracts typhoid fever and is sent back east, as far as Kansas City, to stay with some relatives there. At last, through the efforts of his family, Aleck becomes a tutor at Merry Point, the home of Mr. Fayerlee, near Gloversville, Tennessee.

Aleck, living with the Fayerlees, becomes the local schoolmaster for the children of most of the landowners in the area. Aleck's first interest, however, is not in the school or the students he teaches but in the possibilities for fishing and hunting.

During his stay with the Fayerlees, Aleck falls in love with Molly Fayerlee, and in 1890, they are married. They continue to live with the Fayerlees, and Aleck continues to teach school. During his first year of marriage, Aleck acquires the pup Gyges, a small but thoroughbred bird dog. He trains Gy from a puppy and becomes greatly attached to him. The next fall, Aleck's son, Richard, is born. Two years later, Sarah, nicknamed Sally, is born. They all continue to live at Merry Point.

When Richard is seven, Aleck is offered the presidency of a small seminary in Mississippi, and over the protestations of the Fayerlee family, the Maurys leave Merry Point. On the way, while spending the night in Cairo, Aleck loses Gy. The dog is never heard of again. They continue their journey to Oakland and the seminary. When Aleck arrives, he finds that the school is running smoothly under the able direction of Harry Morrow, his young assistant, who is interested in administration rather than teaching. A few months after arriving at Oakland, Aleck acquires an untrained two-year-old pointer named Trecho from his friend, William Mason. Once again Aleck starts the slow, arduous training of a good hunting dog.

When Richard is fifteen, Aleck tries to interest him in the joys of his life, hunting and fishing, but his son, although a splendid swimmer and wrestler, has little interest in his father's fondness for field and stream. That summer, Richard, while swimming in the river with a group of his companions, drowns. The boy had been Molly's favorite, and his loss is almost more than she can bear. Aleck thinks it would be best for all concerned to leave for different surroundings.

He decides after some correspondence with friends that he will start a school in Gloversville, and the family moves back there. Settled in the small Tennessee town, Aleck finds much time for fishing and hunting. He meets Colonel Wyndham and from him learns a great deal about casting, flies, and the techniques to be used for catching various fish. Finally, he begins to grow tired of the same pools and the same river, and it is with pleasure that he accepts Harry Morrow's offer of a job on the faculty of Rodman College at Poplar Bluff, Missouri, of which Morrow is president.

Aleck's main reason for accepting the position is the possibility it offers for fishing in the Black River. Thus once again, after ten years in Gloversville, the Maury family is on the move to newer fishing grounds. Sally, however, does not accompany them but goes to a girls' school in Nashville. The faithful Trecho is also left behind, destroyed at the age of twelve because of his rheumatism.

At Rodman, Aleck has only morning classes, a schedule that leaves him free to fish every afternoon. This pleasant life—teaching in the morning, fishing in the afternoon—continues for seven years. Then Molly dies after an emergency operation. Mrs. Fayerlee and Sally arrive too late to see her alive. The three of them take her body back to be buried in the family plot at Merry Point.

Aleck returns to Poplar Bluff and continues teaching there for several years, but he at last resigns his position and goes to live at Jim Buford's, near Gloversville, where he spends the next two years restocking Jim's lakes with bream and bass. Later, he decides to go to Lake Harris in Florida to try the fishing, but he finds it disappointing because of the eel grass, which keeps the fish from putting up a fight. About that time, he receives a letter from Sally, who has married and gone touring abroad with her husband. The letter informs him that she and her husband are soon to return home and that they hope to find a quiet place in the country on some good fishing water, where Aleck will go to live with them. Aleck writes and suggests that they start their search for a house near Elk River.

Four weeks later, he meets Sally and Steve at Tullahoma, only to learn that his daughter and husband, who arrived the day before, have already discovered a place they would like to own. They tell him it is the old Potter house, close to the river. When Aleck sees the big clapboard house, however, all his dreams about a white cottage disappear, and when he looks at the river, he decides that it would probably be muddy about half the year. Seeing his disappointment, Steve and Sally promise to continue looking for a more ideal house, but at the end of the day's search, they decide that they still like the old Potter house the best. That night Aleck boards a bus bound for Caney Fork, the place where he really wants to live, and he goes to stay at a small inn located there. The fishing is always good at Caney Fork.

Critical Evaluation:

Caroline Gordon's second novel, *Aleck Maury, Sportsman*, marks her first experiment with a first-person narrator. Seventy-year-old Alexander Gordon Morris Maury reminisces about his life, from his lonely childhood in Virginia to the solitary future he envisions on Caney Fork in Tennessee. The narrative, divided into eight chapters, seems episodic because in each chapter the focus is on Aleck's hunting and fishing experiences, with the accounts of his family life relegated to a comparatively minor role. Gordon's original title was "The Life and Passion of Aleck Maury," and she always preferred the title of the English edition, *Pastimes of Aleck Maury: The Life of a True Sportsman.*

Gordon claimed her father provided the background material for this novel, as she induced him to tell her stories about his hunting and fishing experiences. Aleck and his family are closely modeled upon the Gordon family. Aleck's name reflects his similarity to James Maury Morris Gordon, Caroline Gordon's father. Classically educated by an inattentive father, Aleck is hired to tutor the children of the large Fayerlee clan, all of whom live at or near Merry Point, a family estate similar to Merrimont, the Meriwether estate near Clarksville, Tennessee. Aleck marries Douglas Fayerlee's daughter Molly, just as James Gordon married Nancy Minor Meriwether. Their first child, a handsome, blond son named Dick, is his mother's favorite, as Caroline Gordon's older brother, Morris Meriwether Gordon, was Nancy's special pet. The second child, a daughter named Sarah but called Sally, inherits her father's dark coloring and "Maury features." The novel's final chapters gently poke fun at the intellectual Sally and her scholar husband, Stephen Lewis, obvious parallels to Caroline Gordon and Allen Tate.

At the time of the novel's debut, its popularity was attributed to its vivid accounts of hunting and fishing, and Gordon was criticized for the almost photographic detail of her descriptions. *Aleck Maury, Sportsman* can be read solely for its description of fishing and hunting in the early twentieth century South. Before long, however, critics discerned the author's impressionistic style and the novel's symbolism. Interpretation then focused upon Aleck Maury as a modern epic hero, resembling Ulysses in his restless search for new experiences and fresh challenges, but also possessing Aeneas's single-minded dedication to fulfilling his destiny and Davy Crockett's capacity for boasting about his skills and accomplishments. Such criticism customarily links Gordon with the southern agrarians in her use of the hunt as a ritual that establishes order and meaning in a chaotic world.

Initially, Aleck's perseverance appears heroic, and for much of his life, he seems to find sacramental value in his sport. As an eight-year-old boy on his first hunt, he experiences a mystic "delight" when he looks into the golden, glowing eyes of a possum just before its death. His life is devoted to recapturing that excitement in new hunting grounds and fishing holes. Aleck does not measure success in terms of career advancement; he chooses to be a teacher because that occupation leaves his afternoons free for fishing. The only possessions he values are his hunting dogs, his guns, and his fishing rod.

According to the sportsman's code, death in the hunt is heroic. For his favorite dog, Aleck provides the ideal death in the field: a shot through the head while the dog is on point. This code also demands that Aleck respect the birds he shoots and the fish he catches. He believes that he must thoroughly know his prey in order to take full pleasure in the life-and-death struggle. Thus, he devotes his life to studying these creatures, and generally he can anticipate their behavior, but he prefers to fish alone because he is unwilling to share his hard-won knowledge with others.

Gradually, however, Gordon demonstrates the limitations of the sportsman's code, and Aleck's failures of comprehension are seen to be an integral part of the novel's meaning. In middle age, Aleck receives a symbolic warning: His vision becomes unreliable, and he has difficulty seeing his targets. Still, he rarely considers the effects of time. The ritual deaths of birds and fish allow Aleck to ignore his own mortality until Molly dies. He then must confront death as the ultimate enemy, and for two years he merely "goes through the motions" of fishing, becoming increasingly aware that his lifestyle is as obsolete as the classical Greek and Latin he teaches. For the first time he suspects that, though he may heroically battle time's changes, probably time, in the form of the modern world, ultimately will defeat him. Actually, despite the fact that *Aleck Maury, Sportsman* ends with a temporary victory as Aleck escapes to his newest fishing hole, a later short story, "The Presence," portrays the elderly Aleck forced to watch younger men enjoy the sports in which he can no longer participate.

Aleck draws emotional sustenance from what critic Louise Cowan calls "the secret life of joy and danger" in the rituals of his sport: Hunting provides him an escape from stress when Molly is in labor and from grief when Richard dies. Nevertheless, pursuit of his sport isolates him from his family, whom he repeatedly uproots as he pursues new fishing grounds. Aleck never manages to live up to Molly's expectations, and he cannot understand a son whom he cannot teach to hunt, fish, or read Latin. Finally his preference for Caney Fork separates him even from Sally. In fact, Aleck needs the emotional distancing his sporting rituals provide; he comments that keeping in touch with family and friends becomes too painful for him.

Ultimately, then, Aleck's sporting code proves inadequate. First, it fails to link him with society. Although Aleck admires legendary hunters and fishermen, he scorns the group ritual of the fox hunt, calling it an immature form of the sport. Thus, he becomes the solitary man, lacking any tie with his personal or regional past. Moreover, Aleck's code is not strong enough to counterbalance the inherent selfishness of his nature. For example, when he wants a boat to travel up the Black River, he abandons his own principles and catches spawning bream to pay the rental fee. Likewise, he treats his superior casting skill as a subject for gloating; deciding that he deserves an excellent line more than Harry Morrow does, he steals Morrow's one-hundred-foot black enameled fly line.

Thoroughly grounded in the classical tradition, Gordon bases her critical stance upon Aristotelian principles of unity. As she explains in *How to Read a Novel* (1957), she considers form important: For her, complication and resolution are essential plot elements, and the author's role is to impose form upon complex human experience. In *Aleck Maury, Sportsman*, the title character's experiences as a sportsman constitute the complication, and the resolution is the reader's recognition that Aleck's life was pleasant but ultimately inconsequential. Gordon adheres to her belief that a novel must present the complexity of life, as she portrays a character who seems both self-effacing and self-centered. Lamenting the absence of heroism in the modern world, Gordon turns to the classics to highlight humanity's archetypal patterns. Ultimately, then, the key to Aleck's character may be pride, the tragic flaw he shares with the heroes of Greek tragedy.

"Critical Evaluation" by Charmaine Allmon Mosby

Further Reading

Boyle, Anne M. *Strange and Lurid Bloom: A Study of the Fiction of Caroline Gordon*. Madison, N.J.: Fairleigh Dickinson University Press, 2002. Discusses Gordon's efforts to attain her own voice and respect as a fiction writer and explores the racial and sexual themes of her works. Includes notes and index.

Brinkmeyer, Robert H., Jr. "The Key to the Puzzle: The Literary Career of Caroline Gordon." In *Three Catholic Writers of the Modern South*. Jackson: University Press of Mississippi, 1985. Discusses *Aleck Maury, Sportsman* in terms of Gordon's emphasis upon the classical literary tradition.

Cowan, Louise. "Aleck Maury, Epic Hero and Pilgrim." In *The Short Fiction of Caroline Gordon: A Critical Symposium*, edited by Thomas H. Landess. Dallas, Tex.: University of Dallas Press, 1972. Interpretation of Aleck as an Odysseus figure, in the novel and especially in the short stories.

Fraistat, Rose Ann C. *Caroline Gordon as Novelist and Woman of Letters*. Baton Rouge: Louisiana State University Press, 1984. Consideration of Aleck as an example of Gordon's lifelong concern with the artist's role, which, she thought, was to create a code of honor that can combat society's disintegration.

Jonza, Nancylee Novell. *The Underground Stream: The Life and Art of Caroline Gordon*. Athens: University of Georgia Press, 1995. A good, updated biography of Gordon. According to Jonza, Gordon assumed the persona of a traditional southern belle who became an artist with the benevolent help of her husband, writer Allen Tate; Jonza examines the causes and effects of this self-mythologizing. Includes bibliographical references and an index.

McDowell, Frederick P. W. *Caroline Gordon*. Minneapolis: University of Minnesota Press, 1966. Discussion of *Aleck Maury, Sportsman* as an account of an outwardly uneventful life that is actually the story of "a Ulysses figure, always seeking the new and untried."

Makowsky, Veronica A. *Caroline Gordon: A Biography*. New York: Oxford University Press, 1989. A feminist interpretation of *Aleck Maury, Sportsman* as a balance between a man's potential for heroic action and "his tendency to desert it all at a whim and leave women to suffer the consequences."

Stuckey, W. J. "The Sportsman as Hero." In *Caroline Gordon*. New York: Twayne, 1972. Sympathetic appraisal of Aleck Maury as a candid and reliable narrator, set apart from other people by his exceptional responsiveness to nature. Praises the novel's lightly ironic tone, dramatic structure, and comic resolution.

Trefzer, Annette. "Gendering the Nation: Caroline Gordon's Cherokee Frontier." In *Disturbing Indians: The Archaeology of Southern Fiction*. Tuscaloosa: University of Alabama, 2007. Trefzer examines works by Gordon and other Southern Renaissance writers, focusing on their depiction of Native Americans in the colonial South. Includes notes, bibliography, and index.

The Alexandria Quartet

Author: Lawrence Durrell (1912-1990)
First published: 1962; includes *Justine*, 1957; *Balthazar*, 1958; *Mountolive*, 1958; *Clea*, 1960
Type of work: Novels
Type of plot: Psychological realism
Time of plot: Before and during World War II
Locale: Alexandria, Egypt

Principal characters:
L. G. DARLEY, an Anglo-Irish schoolteacher and an aspiring writer
JUSTINE HOSNANI, Darley's second lover and wife of Nessim
NESSIM HOSNANI, a Coptic banker and conspirator
NAROUZ HOSNANI, his younger, harelipped brother, a religious fanatic
S. BALTHAZAR, a Jewish doctor and mystic
DAVID MOUNTOLIVE, a British diplomat
CLEA MONTIS, a golden blond painter, Darley's third lover
MELISSA ARTEMIS, a pale, sick Greek dancer and prostitute, Darley's first lover
PAUL CAPODISTRIA, an ugly, rich lecher and a conspirator
PERCY PURSEWARDEN, an erudite, ironical English writer
LIZA PURSEWARDEN, the writer's blind sister
MEMLIK PASHA, the Egyptian minister of the interior

The Story:

Justine. A young Anglo-Irish writer, L. G. Darley, reflects on his life in Alexandria, Egypt, around the time of World War II, and on his three great loves: Melissa, Justine, and Clea. Darley resides on a Greek island, writing and gaining perspective on his love affairs.

He first recalls Melissa, a poor cabaret dancer who sometimes engaged in prostitution. They begin their love affair as "fellow bankrupts": He is a writer who cannot write, and she is a dancer with no talent. They have nothing in common, except that they have both been through Alexandria's "winepress of love."

While living with Melissa, Darley meets his second great love, Justine, who attends one of his lectures on Alexandria's famous poet, Constantine Cavafy. Justine, "solitary student of the passions and the arts," is a modern incarnation of Cleopatra. She captivates men with her esoteric searchings into the nature of knowledge and with her magnificent body. After the lecture, Justine invites Darley to her home, so that he can meet her husband, Nessim, a fabulously wealthy Coptic banker, who also shares in her metaphysical speculations.

Although Darley respects Nessim, he cannot refrain from falling into an affair with Justine. She rules his mind to such an extent that Darley seeks insight into her nature from the novel *Moeurs*, written by Justine's ex-husband, Arnauti. In *Moeurs*, Arnauti created an emotionally complex character like Justine, who was sexually abused by an uncle. Arnauti fails to unravel Justine's secrets, and Darley, too, is tormented by the decline in Justine's affections and by his belief that Nessim learns of the affair. Tensions reach a climax at a duck shoot that Nessim arranges at Lake Mareotis. Darley fears that he will be murdered by the jealous husband. Instead, another body is found floating in the lake. The corpse turns out to be Capodistria, the relative who abused Justine. When the hunters return to shore, they discover that Justine fled. Darley feels as if the whole city crashes around his ears. Later, Darley hears through Clea that Justine is working on a Jewish kibbutz in Palestine and that Capodistria is still alive.

Darley takes a job teaching English at a school in Upper Egypt for two years and keeps in only limited contact with Melissa, who is in a clinic to cure her tuberculosis. Melissa dies before Darley can see her for a last time. He agrees to adopt her child, who is the issue of Melissa's brief liaison with Nessim after Justine's departure.

By the end of the novel, Darley draws closer to Clea, a lovely artist who is recovering from a lesbian affair with Justine. Together Clea and Darley analyze the events that have transpired, recalling the wisdom of their enigmatic literary friend, Percy Pursewarden, who recently committed suicide.

Balthazar. On the Greek island, Darley completes his manuscript, presumably *Justine*, and mails it to his friend, Balthazar. Balthazar knows the secrets of his fellow Alexandrians. After reading Darley's book, Balthazar travels to the island to set Darley straight and present him with his own commentary—the Interlinear—penned between the lines of Darley's manuscript. The Interlinear provides Darley with new information regarding the characters about whom he wrote. One revelation is that Justine's true love is Pursewarden. Darley is stunned, forced to take a new perspective on his reality, an essential task for one who aspires to be a writer. After Balthazar departs, Darley picks up an old photograph and stares at the images of his friends. He is ready to begin the torturous process of reassessment by examining the many facets of his friends' personalities.

There is a wild carnival attended by Narouz Hosnani, Nessim's brother. Narouz, a rough-hewn religious fanatic, manages the family's country estate. He attends the carnival because he hopes to see his great secret love, Clea, who loathes him. Instead, he murders a man, in the guise of Justine, who made lecherous advances to him.

This volume closes with a letter that Pursewarden writes to Clea just before his suicide. He proposes "a new way of living with joy" and calls for relationships based on loving-kindness.

Mountolive. The British ambassador to Egypt is David Mountolive. The omniscient narrator chronicles Mountolive's life—how he began his diplomatic career in Egypt as a guest at the Hosnani estate and rose through the ranks to become ambassador. The Hosnanis, particularly Leila, Nessim and Narouz's mother, give the young Mountolive his education in Egyptian mores. Mountolive falls in love with Leila and carries on a passionate affair with her out of sight of her disabled husband. When he is posted elsewhere, they stay in touch through letters. With the passage of years their ardor fades. Their meeting, after Mountolive was appointed ambassador, is a disaster. He is repulsed by how much she aged, and she is disappointed in his lack of character.

More knowledge is gained regarding Justine's true affections. She is, in fact, Nessim's devoted wife. She shares Nessim's political goal: to conspire against British interests in Palestine. She becomes involved with Darley and Pursewarden, both minor functionaries in the British legation, in order to spy for Nessim. The plot falls apart when Melissa inadvertently stumbles onto its details and informs Pursewarden during the one night of passion they shared. He, in turn, faces a dilemma, torn between his friendship with Nessim and his official duties. His suicide appears to be a way out of the quandary; before dying he lets both Nessim and Mountolive know that he uncovered the conspiracy.

Retribution arrives swiftly. Nessim was bribing the minister of the interior, Memlik, to overlook his activities, but learning of the plot, Mountolive forces Memlik to suppress it. Memlik decides to spare Nessim and sends his agents to kill the other leader, Nessim's fanatical brother, Narouz. Narouz suffers an agonizing death. His last request is to see Clea again. She reluctantly goes to his deathbed but arrives too late.

Clea. Darley leaves his island retreat to return to Alexandria and is nervous about seeing Justine again. She is much changed. The collapse of the conspiracy made her a recluse, and a slight stroke diminished her beauty. Darley realizes he has grown beyond her narcissistic type of loving. He is more in tune with the gentle Clea, who, like him, is struggling to become an artist. Clea and Darley begin a love affair amid the shelling of World War II.

Inexplicably, Clea and Darley drift apart. They decide to separate, but, before doing so, they go on one last excursion. Accompanied by Balthazar, they travel by boat to a nearby island. As Clea is swimming underwater, Balthazar accidentally releases a harpoon which goes through Clea's hand and pins her underwater. Darley springs to save Clea's life by hacking off her hand.

Although the two separate, they seem likely to reunite. Both resolve their artistic problems: Darley is able to start writing, and Clea is painting extraordinary canvases with her artificial hand. She writes to Darley that she is "serene and happy, a real human being, an artist at last." Darley, too, feels as if "the whole universe" has given him "a nudge."

Critical Evaluation:

Beginning with the publication of Lawrence Durrell's first serious novel, *The Black Book*, in 1938, perceptive readers recognized his innovative genius. T. S. Eliot praised *The Black Book* as "the first piece of work by a new English writer to give me any hope for the future of prose fiction." *The Alexandria Quartet* marks a turning point in the development of the twentieth century novel. In its pages, modernism makes the transition into postmodernism. Modernist concerns with the privileged role of art, the mythic quest, and the hero's search for meaning give way to postmodern concerns: indeterminacy, relativity, and the hero's unstable ego.

The Alexandria Quartet is experimental in style and metaphysical in content, so readers are often confused by the lack of narrative structure. Durrell is a meticulous craftsman; the novel is based on what he calls an n-dimensional structure, based in turn on Albert Einstein's theory of relativity. The theory of relativity, Durrell believed, accurately defines the reality of time. Einstein destroyed the old Victorian material universe. Science shattered any coherent view of the cosmos, Durrell points out in the preface to *Balthazar.* Modern literature therefore offers no unities either. The book's relativity in its point of view is a reflection of the central advance made in human understanding in the twentieth century. Thus, the first three novels of *The Alexandria Quartet* present three dimensions of space, and the last novel, *Clea*, moves the story ahead in time. How the reader should, ideally, read such a novel is illustrated by a cartoon, which appeared around the time of *The Alexandria Quartet*'s publication. A man is shown reading *The Alexandria Quartet* by means of a machine that allows him to read all four volumes simultaneously.

In addition to incorporating relativistic ideas into his novel, Durrell suggests that Sigmund Freud destroyed the idea of the stable ego. Describing such a personality in fiction or in love is complicated by the fact that many perspectives can be taken on the subject. Balthazar points out this notion to Darley: "Each psyche is really an ant-hill of opposing predispositions. Personality as something with fixed attributes is an illusion—but a necessary illusion *if we are to love!*"

By focusing on love relationships in *The Alexandria Quartet*, Durrell addresses issues raised by Freud and Einstein. The central topic of the novel is an investigation of modern love. Durrell believed that "the sexual act becomes identified with all knowledge." In other words, eros is the "motive force" in humans. Eros awakens the "psychic forces latent in the human being." Durrell's characters are interesting in their own right, but they are also metaphysical pawns in the search for metaphysical knowledge. Such knowledge must take into account the cosmology of the age: Personality is not fixed, and space and time are relative. Thus, Darley's adventures in love are the key elements in his progression toward greater self-awareness and knowledge not only of himself but also of the world around him.

His first lover, Melissa Artemis, encounters him at his lowest point of self-awareness. They meet at a party. Melissa has passed out, from exhaustion and from the ingestion of Spanish fly. Darley takes her home and nurses her back to health. They begin a relationship based on the fact that they are "fellow bankrupts," without a "taste in common."

During this period with Melissa, Darley gives a lecture on Constantine Cavafy. After the lecture, a beautiful society woman approaches him with questions. This woman is Justine, who becomes his second great love. Justine is married to the immensely wealthy Coptic Christian banker Nessim Hosnani. Darley is instantly intrigued by the dark Justine, who has the remarkable ability to expel "people from their old selves." Darley is willing to be led and follows after Justine, despite the fact that he meets her husband and strikes up a friendship with him. When Justine abruptly leaves both of them, Darley is forced to reevaluate the relationship and himself; this act increases his awareness of self and others.

Darley seeks solace in his third and most important relationship, with the painter Clea Montis, who also suffered through a sexual relationship with Justine. Darley and Clea work together as they attempt to determine the right way to live as artists and as human beings. Rejecting the ego-dominated, narcissistic concerns of their past lives, they try to live a more tender existence, which their mentor, Pursewarden, claims exists in the "primal relation between animal and plant, rain and soil, seed and trees, man and God."

Before Clea and Darley reach this state of being, however, they must pass through a terrible trial. When Clea is accidentally shot by a harpoon, Darley must suddenly transform himself from a man sunk in passivity to a man of action. In saving Clea's life, he transforms himself as well. By the end of *The Alexandria Quartet*, his self-awareness and confidence allow him to take his place in the community of authors.

Durrell's goal in the novel is twofold: First, he attempts to address the major philosophical questions regarding the nature of reality and the right way to live and love, and second, he shows that there is an ideal spiritual realm in which to live. Durrell believes in an existence that abandons selfish cravings and ambitions and that enters a state of oneness with the universe. His characters begin their journeys in Alexandria but metaphorically become reflections of their age.

Anna Lillios

Further Reading

Begnal, Michael H., ed. *On Miracle Ground: Essays on the Fiction of Lawrence Durrell*. Cranbury, N.J.: Bucknell University Press, 1990. In a transcript of a 1986 lecture, Durrell explains his life and art. Other essays in this volume give mythological, Buddhist, and narratological perspectives on *The Alexandria Quartet*.

Diboll, Michael V. *Lawrence Durrell's "Alexandria Quartet" in its Egyptian Contexts*. Lewiston, N.Y.: Edwin Mellen Press, 2004. Examines the influence of Egyptian history and resurgent nationalism on the tetralogy, focusing on the interaction of time, place, and exile on the literary imagination. Diboll maintains that *The Alexandria Quartet* is the most important novel of the mid-1950's.

Durrell, Lawrence. *A Key to Modern British Poetry*. Norman: University of Oklahoma Press, 1952. In the context of the book's subject, Durrell presents the philosophical, artistic, and scientific ideas that underlie *The Alexandria Quartet*.

Friedman, Alan Warren. *Lawrence Durrell and the Alexandria Quartet: Art for Love's Sake*. Norman: University of

Oklahoma Press, 1970. Shows that love presents "an endless potential for variations on a theme."

_______, ed. *Critical Essays on Lawrence Durrell*. Boston: G. K. Hall, 1987. Contains a comprehensive selection of essays on Durrell's work. Included are early reviews of *The Alexandria Quartet*.

Kaczvinsky, Donald P. *Lawrence Durrell's Major Novels: Or, The Kingdom of the Imagination*. London: Associated University Presses, 1997. An excellent discussion of Durrell's seminal works, including *The Alexandria Quartet*. Kaczvinsky describes how these novels feature artist-heroes who come into contact with a debilitating culture and place.

Pine, Richard. *Lawrence Durrell: The Mindscape*. New York: St. Martin's Press, 1994. A book-length study of Durrell's work, based on his diaries and notebooks.

Rashidi, Linda Stump. *(Re)constructing Reality: Complexity in Lawrence Durrell's "Alexandria Quartet."* New York: Peter Lang, 2005. Uses the linguistic theories of M. A. K. Halliday to analyze the four novels.

Steinberg, Theodore L. *Twentieth-Century Epic Novels*. Newark: University of Delaware Press, 2005. Analyzes *The Alexandria Quartet* and other novels whose contents and themes, particularly the essence of heroism, define them as epic.

Weigel, John A. *Lawrence Durrell*. Boston: Twayne, 1989. A good summary of Durrell's life and work. Selected bibliography.

Alias Grace

Author: Margaret Atwood (1939-)
First published: 1996
Type of work: Novel
Type of plot: Historical realism
Time of plot: 1828-1972
Locale: Kingston, Ontario, Canada

Principal characters:

GRACE MARKS, a young servant imprisoned for murder
JAMES MCDERMOTT, a stable hand hanged for murder
THOMAS KINNEAR, a wealthy gentleman farmer and Grace and McDermott's employer, who is murdered by McDermott
NANCY MONTGOMERY, a housekeeper and a lover of Kinnear, who is murdered by McDermott
SIMON JORDAN, a young doctor specializing in mental illness
MARY WHITNEY, Grace's close friend and coworker
JAMIE WALSH, a flute-playing farmhand and Grace's future husband
JEREMIAH, a peddler and magician

The Story:

Grace Marks, a talented seamstress who loves to quilt, was born poor in 1828 in the north of Ireland to a drunken failure of a father and a mother overborne by poverty. Grace is one of nine children. In 1843, she had been convicted, along with the bad-tempered, violence-prone stable hand James McDermott, of murdering their employer, the wealthy gentleman farmer Thomas Kinnear. Also killed was Kinnear's pregnant lover, Nancy Montgomery, who had been jealous of Grace.

McDermott makes Grace complicit in the murder by threatening her. They flee to the United States but are soon apprehended and returned to Ireland. They are tried and then found guilty. McDermott receives the death penalty and is hanged. Grace, fifteen years old at the time of the crime, receives a sentence of life imprisonment. Grace breaks down in prison and is remanded to a mental hospital. After eight years there, she is released as a model inmate and allowed to work as a skilled housemaid for a wealthy prominent woman, Mrs. Palmer. Grace is now twenty-three years old.

Simon Jordan, a young doctor who is sympathetic to the new medical preoccupation with mental illness, is interested in Grace's case, one of the most famous of the time. He meets with Grace repeatedly and gains some of her confidence, though doctors generally terrify her, and for good reasons.

Grace has blocked her memory of the trauma so deeply that neither Dr. Jordan nor hypnosis unearths the truth. Grace herself quite likely does not know. She becomes so dissociated that she speaks during hypnosis as if she is her good friend and coworker Mary Whitney, who had died after a botched abortion. The question of the degree of Grace's involvement in the murder or Kinnear and Montgomery is never answered.

Enlightened liberal opinion personified by a local parson, the Reverend Verringer, and his allies believes Grace is the victim of a miscarriage of justice, given her youth, her mental fragility, and the ambiguities of the trial (McDermott had told one story, Grace several others). Verringer and the others enlist Dr. Jordan in their cause. He works with Grace from May to August in 1859, but then confesses failure. Grace remains an enigma. An itinerant peddler named Jeremiah, who has many names and faces and who also is a mesmerist and magician, attempts to aid Grace by urging her to leave town with him; she cannot respond.

Dr. Jordan gives up his attempts to understand Grace. He travels briefly to Switzerland to participate in a mental clinic, returns to the United States, enlists with the Unionists in the American Civil War, and is wounded and loses his memory. In 1872, Grace is pardoned. She had been in prison for twenty-eight years and ten months. She is taken to New York State and soon marries Jamie Walsh, her sweet-tempered admirer from long ago at Kinnear's farm. The marriage had been arranged without her knowledge by her supporters. The new couple settles on a farm outside Ithaca, New York.

It turns out that Grace had written a letter to Dr. Jordan many years ago, a letter she had never sent to him. In the letter, she summarizes her life but does not clarify the central question of her guilt or innocence. Grace continues to quilt.

Critical Evaluation:

Alias Grace, a demanding, lengthy, historical novel, is Margaret Atwood's ninth work of long fiction. The book derives from the story of an actual person named Grace Marks, a nineteenth century Irish immigrant to Canada who had been accused of being an accomplice in the murder of her employer and his housekeeper-mistress. The case was one of the most notorious and widely publicized of its time.

Atwood initially came to know of the event after reading a contemporary account in an autobiographical work by Canadian writer Susanna Moodie, *Life in the Clearings Versus the Bush* (1853). Atwood was so taken by the story that she wrote a long poem, "The Journals of Susanna Moodie" (1970), which is a re-creation of and commentary on Moodie's work.

In Moodie's account, Grace is the instigator. She wants Thomas Kinnear as her lover and, thus, persuades James McDermott to kill Nancy Montgomery, her rival. McDermott realizes Grace has set him up and kills Kinnear in a rage. Atwood thought about the story for years before writing her own version. A major feminist author, Atwood wanted to set straight the record of injustice and female oppression, or at least to explore fully the enigma of Grace, who claims to have no memory of the murders.

Atwood's novel combines historical accuracy with an account of Grace's heart and mind. In the novel's chronological twists and turns and its multiple stylistic shifts, Atwood presents an elaborate spelunking expedition into the depths of the complicated story to render visible the tale's darkness. Chronologically, the above plot summary of the novel merely suggests how adroitly Atwood manages her story. Stylistically, it is a classic demonstration of the Russian literary critic Mikhail Bakhtin's influential theory of the dialogic imagination, also called heteroglossia, a technical term for "other languages." Bakhtin was not a full-fledged Marxist, but his theory carries a political implication that denies implicitly the hegemonic ascendancy of one class over another. This is highly relevant for Atwood's story of the servant girl nearly helpless before the power of the state and the established order it represents and enforces, though she does acquire supporters eventually.

In *Alias Grace*, the sections about Grace are told in the first person. The shrewd, laconic, and demotic clarity of Grace's plainspokenness cuts through the evasions and the inhibited and genteel voices of the Victorian upper-middle-class women whose ascendancy is unquestioned, least of all by them. In addition to the Victorian voices, the range of stylistics in the novel includes the rough-hewn pseudo folk ballad at the beginning, which tells the story of Grace and the others. The novel also includes excerpts from contemporary newspapers and rules for punishment of offenses in Grace's prison, epigraphs from a number of writers (including Emily Dickinson, William Morris, and Henry Longfellow), and Victorian definitions of hysterics. There also are many letters by educated characters, including those of Dr. Jordan's mother, the epitome of the fearful Victorian matron who shudders at troublesome reality and averts her eyes from it. Her letters are tours de force of deadpan mimicry. Style in the novel is never window dressing. It is the heart and kernel of the reality the novel seeks to evoke. In *Alias Grace*, the medium is the message.

The story's message, however, is ambiguous, as can be surmised from the babel of contending voices. It is far from clear that Grace was an accomplice in the crime, much less a willing one, even much less the instigator. Did she counterfeit madness? Did she conceal from herself the traumatic truth? Was she milking the cow or working in the garden when McDermott attacked Montgomery? Why did McDermott put his shirt on the dead Kinnear? Montgomery was pregnant, but was Grace pregnant, too? The only certainty is that Grace, a pretty and talented young woman born into a life of drudgery and deprivation, had experienced an ineluctable confrontation with a destiny that was Grecian in its insistence on the utter impossibility of evading that destiny. Like novelist Thomas Hardy's character Tess, class and circumstances conspire to move Grace inevitably to tragedy, though Atwood grants Grace surcease from her travails at the end of the story.

Stanley Poss

Further Reading

Bloom, Harold, ed. *Margaret Atwood*. Philadelphia: Chelsea House, 2000. A collection of essays by literary critics that provides analyses of Atwood's major novels, including *Alias Grace*. Includes a brief biography, a chronology of Atwood's life, and an informative editor's introduction.

Cooke, Nathalie. *Margaret Atwood: A Biography*. Toronto, Ont.: ECW Press, 1998. Although this is not an authorized biography, Atwood answered Cooke's questions and allowed her access, albeit limited, to materials for her research. A substantive work.

Howells, Coral Ann. *Margaret Atwood*. New York: St. Martin's Press, 1996. A lively critical and biographical study that elucidates issues that have energized all of Atwood's fiction: feminist issues, literary genres, and her own identity as a Canadian, a woman, and a writer.

_______, ed. *The Cambridge Companion to Margaret Atwood*. New York: Cambridge University Press, 2006. This collection of twelve excellent essays provides critical examination of Atwood's novels, including *Alias Grace*, as well as a concise biography of the author.

Wilson, Sharon Rose, ed. *Margaret Atwood's Textual Assassinations: Recent Poetry and Fiction*. Columbus: Ohio State University Press, 2003. This collection of scholarly essays examines Atwood's work, with a focus on her writings published since the late 1980's. Includes discussion of the novel *Alias Grace* and others.

Wisker, Gina. *Margaret Atwood's "Alias Grace": A Reader's Guide*. New York: Continuum, 2002. A brief but comprehensive reader's guide to Atwood's *Alias Grace*. A good place to start for students new to Atwood's fiction.

Alice's Adventures in Wonderland

Author: Lewis Carroll (1832-1898)
First published: Alice's Adventures in Wonderland (1865) and *Through the Looking-Glass: And What Alice Found There* (1871, but dated 1872)
Type of work: Novel
Type of plot: Fantasy
Time of plot: Victorian era
Locale: The dream world of an imaginative child

Principal characters:
ALICE
THE WHITE RABBIT
THE DUCHESS
THE QUEEN OF HEARTS

The Story:

Alice is quietly reading over her sister's shoulder when she sees a White Rabbit dash across the lawn and disappear into its hole. She jumps up to rush after him and finds herself falling down the rabbit hole. At the bottom, she sees the White Rabbit hurrying along a corridor ahead of her and murmuring that he will be late. He disappears around a corner, leaving Alice standing in front of several locked doors.

On a glass table, she finds a tiny golden key that unlocks a little door hidden behind a curtain. The door opens upon a lovely miniature garden, but Alice cannot get through the doorway because it is too small. She sadly replaces the key on the table. A little bottle mysteriously appears. Alice drinks the contents and immediately begins to grow smaller, so much so that she can no longer reach the key on the table.

Next, she eats a piece of cake she finds nearby, and soon she begins to grow to such an enormous size that she can only squint through the door. In despair, she begins to weep tears as big as raindrops. As she sits crying, the White Rabbit appears, moaning that the Duchess will be angry if he keeps her waiting. He drops his fan and gloves, and when Alice picks them up, she begins to grow smaller. Again she rushes to the garden door, but she finds it shut and the golden key once more on the table out of reach.

Then she falls into a pool of her own tears. Splashing along, she encounters a mouse who stumbled into the pool. Alice tactlessly begins a conversation about her cat Dinah, and the mouse becomes speechless with terror. Soon the pool of tears is filled with living creatures—birds and animals of all kinds. An old Dodo suggests that they run a Caucus Race to get dry. Asking what a Caucus Race is, Alice is told that the best way to explain it is to do it, whereupon the animals run themselves quite breathless and finally become dry. Afterward, the mouse tells a "Tail" to match its own appendage. Alice is asked to tell something, but the only thing she can think of is her cat Dinah. Frightened, the other creatures go away, and Alice is left alone.

The White Rabbit appears once more, this time hunting for his gloves and fan. Catching sight of Alice, he sends her to his home to get him a fresh pair of gloves and another fan. In the Rabbit's house, she finds the fan and gloves and also takes a drink from a bottle. Instantly, she grows to be a giant size and is forced to put her leg up the chimney and her elbow out the window to keep from being squeezed to death.

She manages to eat a little cake and shrink herself again. As soon as she is small enough to get through the door, she runs into a nearby wood where she finds a caterpillar sitting on a mushroom. The caterpillar is very rude to Alice, and he scornfully asks her to prove her worth by reciting "You Are Old, Father William." Alice does so, but the words sound very strange. Disgusted, he leaves her, after giving her some valuable information about increasing or decreasing her size. She breaks off pieces of the mushroom and finds to her delight that she can become taller by eating from the piece in her left hand, shorter by eating from the piece in her right hand.

She comes to a little house among the trees. There a footman, who looks very much like a fish, presents to another footman, who closely resembles a frog, an invitation for the Duchess to play croquet with the Queen. The two amphibians bow to each other with great formality, tangling their wigs together. Alice opens the door and finds herself in the chaotic house of the Duchess. The cook is stirring a large pot of soup and pouring plenty of pepper into the mixture. Everyone is sneezing except the cook and a Cheshire cat, which sits on the hearth grinning. The Duchess holds a sneezing, squalling baby and sings a blaring lullaby to it. Alice, in sympathy with the poor child, picks it up and carries it out into the fresh air, whereupon the baby gradually turns into a pig, squirms out of her arms, and trots into the forest.

Standing in bewilderment, Alice sees the grinning Cheshire cat sitting in a tree. He is able to appear and disappear at will, and after exercising his talents, he advises Alice to go to a tea party given by the Mad Hatter. The cat vanishes, all but the grin. When that, too, finally disappears, Alice leaves for the party.

There, Alice has to deal with the strangest people she has ever seen—a March Hare, a Mad Hatter, and a sleepy Dormouse. All are too lazy to set the table afresh, and dirty dishes from preceding meals lie next to clean ones. The Dormouse falls asleep in its teacup, the Mad Hatter tells Alice her hair needs cutting, and the March Hare offers her wine and then tells her there is none. They ask her foolish riddles that have no answers, and then they ignore her completely and carry on a ridiculous conversation among themselves. She escapes after the Dormouse falls asleep in the middle of a story he is telling.

Next, she finds herself in a garden of rose trees. Some gardeners appear with paintbrushes and begin to splash red paint on a white rose. Alice learns that the Queen ordered a red rose to be planted in that spot, and the gardeners are busily and fearfully trying to cover their error before the Queen arrives. The poor gardeners, however, are not swift enough. The Queen catches them in the act, and the wretched gardeners are led off to be decapitated. Alice saves them by shoving them down into a large flower pot, out of sight of the Queen.

A croquet game begins. The mallets are live flamingos, and the balls are hedgehogs which think nothing of uncurling themselves and running rapidly over the field. The Duchess corners Alice and leads her away to the seaside to introduce her to the Mock Turtle and the Gryphon. While engaged in a Lobster Quadrille, they hear the news of a trial. A thief stole some tarts. Rushing to the courtroom where a trial by jury is already in session, Alice is called upon to act as a witness before the King and Queen of Hearts, but the excited child upsets the jury box and spills out all of its occupants. After replacing all the animals in the box, Alice says she knows nothing of the matter. Her speech infuriates the Queen, who orders that Alice's head be cut off. The whole court rushes at her, and Alice defiantly calls them nothing but a pack of cards. She awakens from her dream as her sister brushes away some dead leaves blowing over Alice's face.

Critical Evaluation:

One summer afternoon in 1862, the Reverend Charles Lutwidge Dodgson, his Oxford friend, and three little girls set out on a boat trip. Somewhere along the way, *Alice's Adventures in Wonderland* was created. Although it was not the first story that Dodgson had told the daughters of Henry George Liddell, the dean of Christ Church in Oxford, it was one that immediately captivated Alice Liddell, the prototype for the fictional seven-year-old heroine. Her later requests for Dodgson to "write it down" led to his becoming one of the world's favorite authors; his work was eventually translated into more than forty-five languages and became part of the heritage of most literate people growing up in Western culture.

Dodgson, who transposed his first two names into the pen name Lewis Carroll, was a shy and seemingly conventional Oxford mathematician who could relate most easily with children, particularly young girls. Later ages regarded his seemingly innocent affinity for children as the sign of a possible neurosis and an inability to grow up. Alice Liddell was only one of many young girls who shared with him the secret world of childhood in which he spent much of his adult life.

Carroll's attraction to fantasy expressed itself in many ways, among them his love of whimsical letters, gadgets, theatricals, toys, and, of course, fantasy stories. The Alice stories were first prepared for Alice Liddell in a handwritten manuscript and initially given the title *Alice's Adventures Under Ground*; the book was published in its present form in 1865 and was an almost immediate popular success. Adding to its originality were the illustrations by Sir John Tenniel (for his model, he did not use the real Alice, who, unlike the pictured child, had short dark hair and bangs).

The book—which was followed in 1871 by the even more brilliant sequel, *Through the Looking-Glass and What Alice Found There*—has always been enjoyed on several levels. It is a children's story, but it is also a book full of interest for adults and specialists such as mathematicians, linguists, logicians, and Freudians. It may be the suggestion of a philosophical underpinning that gives the work its never-ending appeal for adults.

Viewed as children's literature, the book offers its young readers a charming new outlook that dispenses with the moralistic viewpoint then so prevalent. Alice is neither continuously nice nor thoroughly naughty; she is simply a curious child whose queries lead her into strange situations. In the end, she is neither punished nor rewarded. A moral, proposing that she do this or that, is absent. Indeed, Carroll pokes fun at many of the ideas with which Alice, a well-bred English child, was imbued. The Mock Turtle, for example, chides the sacred subject of learning by terming the branches of arithmetic Ambition, Distraction, Uglification, and Derision. Children who read the book are permitted to see adults quite unlike the perfect beings usually portrayed. It is the story's adults rather than Alice who are rude, demanding, and ridiculous.

As a work for the specialist, *Alice's Adventures in Wonderland* touches on many puzzles that are subsequently even more thoroughly presented in *Through the Looking-Glass and What Alice Found There*. The playfulness with language, for example, involves puns, parodies, and clever phrasing but does not deal as fully with the basic nature of language as does its sequel. Even in *Alice's Adventures in Wonderland*, however, Carroll's casual amusement with words often has deeper meaning. When he parodies the well-known poems and songs of his day, he is clearly questioning their supercilious platitudes. When he makes a pun (the Gryphon tells the reader that boots and shoes under the sea are "done" with whiting rather than blacking and are, of course, made of soles and eels), Carroll asserts the total logic of illogic. When he designs a Cheshire cat, he is taking a common but unspecific phrase of his time—"Grin like a Cheshire cat" referred either to inn signs in the county of Cheshire depicting a grinning lion or to Cheshire cheeses modeled in the shape of a smiling cat—and turning it into a concrete reality. Logicians also find a multitude of tidbits. The Cheshire cat "proves" it is not mad by adopting the premise that if a dog is not mad, anyone who reacts in ways opposite to a dog must be so. The March Hare offers a nice exercise in logic and language with his discussion of taking "more" versus taking "less" and his challenge as to whether "I mean what I say" is the same as "I say what I mean."

For mathematicians, Carroll presents the Mad Hatter's watch, which tells the day of the month rather than the hour. The watch does not bother with the hour, since from the center of the earth, the sun would always look the same, whereas the moon's phases would be visible. For the Freudians, the book is also a mass of complicated mysteries. Freudians see significance in most of the characters and incidents, but the fall down the rabbit hole, the changes in size, the great interest in eating and drinking, the obnoxious mature females, and Alice's continual anxiety are some of the most revealing topics, all of them possibly suggesting Carroll's neuroses about women and sex.

The larger philosophical questions raised by Alice center on the order of life as readers know it. Set in the context of the dream vision, a journey different from a conscious quest, the book asks whether there is indeed any pattern or meaning to life. Alice is the curious innocent who compares favorably with the jaded, even wicked, grown-ups. Always sensible and open to experience, she would seem the ideal messenger of a true concept, yet her adventures hint that there is only the ridiculousness of logic and reality and the logic of nonsense. Readers see that Wonderland is no more incomprehensible—and no more comprehensible—than Victorian England, that the Mad Duchess lives next door, and that, as the Cheshire cat says, "We're all mad here."

Alice brings to Wonderland certain acquired concepts and a strong belief in order. When Wonderland turns her views askew, she can withstand only so long, then she must rebel. The trial, which is the last refuge of justice in the real world, is the key factor in Alice's rejection of Wonderland, for it is a trial of Wonderland itself, with many of the earlier creatures reassembled to assert forcefully that expectations and rules are meaningless. Like the child of the world that she is, Alice (and Carroll) must deny the truth that there is no truth. She must shout "Nonsense" to it all. As one critic pointed out, she rejects "mad sanity in favor of the sane madness of the ordinary existence." The reader faces the same confusion and, frightened by what it implies, must also rebel, though with laughter.

"Critical Evaluation" by Judith Bolch

Further Reading

Blake, Kathleen. *Play, Games, and Sport: The Literary Works of Lewis Carroll.* Ithaca, N.Y.: Cornell University Press, 1974. Wittily argues that the *Alice* books create a world of games spinning out of control. Firmly establishes their author in a Victorian context.

Bloom, Harold, ed. *Lewis Carroll's "Alice's Adventures in Wonderland."* New York: Chelsea House, 2006. Collection of essays about the novel, including discussions of Alice's identity, elements of folklore and fairy tales, and the treatment of love and death. Contains a bibliography and an index.

Carroll, Lewis. *The Annotated Alice: Alice's Adventures in Wonderland and Through the Looking-Glass.* Edited by Martin Gardner. New York: Clarkson N. Potter, 1960. Gardner's notes in the margin alongside the text help to clarify jokes and conundrums and explain contemporary references.

_______. *More Annotated Alice: Alice's Adventures in Wonderland and Through the Looking-Glass.* Edited by Martin Gardner. New York: Random House, 1990. Based on letters from readers of the original *The Annotated Alice* as well as on new research, this sequel supplements rather than revises the first book. Reprints for the first time Peter Newell's illustrations and includes Newell's essay on visually interpreting *Alice in Wonderland.*

Guiliano, Edward, ed. *Lewis Carroll: A Celebration.* New York: Clarkson N. Potter, 1982. A collection of fifteen essays, most referring to the *Alice* books, written to commemorate the 150th anniversary of Carroll's birth. Provides many photographs and illustrations, including Carroll's original renderings for *Alice in Wonderland.*

Jones, Jo Elwyn, and J. Francis Gladstone. *The Alice Companion: A Guide to Lewis Carroll's Alice Books.* New York: New York University Press, 1998. Full of information, a commentary on the people and places that make up Carroll's and Alice Liddell's world in mid-nineteenth century Oxford, and a sourcebook of the extensive existing literature on this period in Carroll's life.

Kelly, Richard. *Lewis Carroll.* Boston: Twayne, 1977. A broad critical survey of Carroll's work. Emphasizes the humor in the *Alice* books.

Phillips, Edward, ed. *Aspects of Alice: Lewis Carroll's Dreamchild as Seen Through the Critics' Looking-Glasses, 1865-1971.* New York: Vanguard Press, 1971. A wide-ranging and often entertaining omnibus. Includes a comprehensive bibliography.

Reichertz, Ronald. *The Making of the Alice Books: Lewis Carroll's Uses of Earlier Children's Literature.* Montreal: McGill-Queen's University Press, 1997. Analyzes children's literature from the seventeenth through nineteenth centuries. Argues that Carroll combined the formality and the themes of earlier books with his narrative imagination to create an original form of children's literature.

All Fall Down

Author: James Leo Herlihy (1927-1993)
First published: 1960
Type of work: Novel
Type of plot: Bildungsroman
Time of plot: Late 1950's
Locale: Cleveland, Ohio

Principal characters:
CLINTON WILLIAMS, a boy
RALPH WILLIAMS, his father
ANNABEL WILLIAMS, his mother
BERRY-BERRY, his older brother
ECHO O'BRIEN, a girl loved by Clinton and destroyed by Berry-Berry
SHIRLEY, a young prostitute

The Story:

Clinton Williams is fourteen years old. His brother, Berry-Berry, is away "on his travels," begun shortly after his twenty-first birthday. The Williams family recently moved into a house in a different section of Cleveland. Clinton is afraid that Berry-Berry will not be able to find the new house if he should return, and as a gesture of quiet protest he stays away from school for fifty-seven consecutive days. In the daytime, he loafs in the Aloha Sweet Shop, recording in his notebooks everything he sees or overhears. At home he eavesdrops on his parents' conversations, which he records in his journals as well, along with copies of letters he opens on the sly. During the time he is skipping school, he fills twenty-five notebooks. His entries are naïve, funny, boring, and revealing. His romantic view of Berry-Berry is the first interest of Clinton's life. The second is his tremendous curiosity about people and the nature of experience, explaining his effort to put down everything he knows and learns in order that he might solve some of life's mysteries.

In many ways, Clinton is his father's son. Ralph Williams was a politically active liberal before he was trapped by marriage and a family. Theoretically he is in business, but he spends most of his time in the cellar with a jigsaw puzzle in front of him and a bottle of bourbon within reach. He simplifies his life to two convictions: that Christ founded the Socialist Party and that Berry-Berry will turn out all right in the end. His wife, Annabel, is nervous, querulous, and tearful, constantly wishing for Berry-Berry's return without ever realizing that he hates her.

The memory of the absent son is all that holds the strange family together. Ironically, Berry-Berry is unworthy of his family's love and their hopes for his return. A bum, a pimp, and a sadist, he turns up first in one section of the country, then in another, in jail and out, either living off one of his women or else calling on his family for money to get him out of his latest escapade. Most of these facts are unknown to Clinton, however, during the time he is working in an all-night eating place and saving his money for the day when he might join his brother. The opportunity comes when Berry-Berry writes, asking his father for two hundred dollars to invest in a shrimping venture in Key Bonita, Florida. Ready to offer the money, Clinton takes a bus to Key Bonita, to find on his arrival that Berry-Berry already skipped town after mauling one of his lady loves. This knowledge comes to Clinton during the night he spends with a prostitute, and the realization of his brother's true nature is almost more than he can bear. He returns home, falls ill, and even contemplates suicide. He is saved when he falls shyly in love with Echo O'Brien, older than he and the daughter of one of his mother's friends, who comes to visit in Cleveland.

Berry-Berry returns and all is forgotten, or at least forgiven, and the Williamses are reunited by love. Berry-Berry makes a play for Echo. His parents hope that the affair will cause Berry-Berry to settle down at last. Clinton accepts the fact of Echo's romance with his brother out of gratitude for the atmosphere of family happiness. Berry-Berry, however, cannot be reclaimed from the moral rot that infects him. Refusing to accept responsibility for Echo's pregnancy, he callously discards her, and Echo commits suicide. Clinton at first intends to kill his brother, but in the end, he decides that Berry-Berry's knowledge of his own corruption is punishment enough. Berry-Berry takes to the road again. Clinton begins writing in his notebooks once more, with the difference that, he believes, he has grown up.

Critical Evaluation:

The route by which one travels from the cradle to the grave is no broad highway but a road with many ups and downs, sudden turnings, and strange byways. To many modern novelists, no route is more interesting or significant than the downward road to wisdom. In much modern fiction, the beginning of knowledge is the loss of innocence.

The fable of innocence confronted by evil and gaining a sad kind of wisdom in the encounter is the theme of James Leo Herlihy's *All Fall Down.* The fact that its youthful hero makes a long journey in the geography of his own soul puts him into some rather interesting literary company: Huck Finn on his raft, Holden Caulfield exploring an adult world of hypocrisy and sham, Frankie Addams willing herself into becoming a member of the wedding. Although *All Fall Down* is a book that invites comparisons, to note them is not to say that Herlihy is in any way imitative. Quite the opposite: His ability to present the emotional adventures of youth as a difficult passage between childhood and maturity and to tell the story as if it had never been written before is striking proof of his imaginative force and dramatic control.

Clinton Williams, his hero, is a boy as freewheeling in his character as J. D. Salinger's Holden Caulfield in *The Catcher in the Rye* (1951), but in a vastly different way. Caulfield is an uncomplicated realist whose quickness of mind enables him to identify pretense wherever he finds it. Clinton, on the other hand, grows up pursuing an illusion, the glamour that his romantic imagination creates around his older brother, whom Caulfield would have recognized at once. Ironically, while Caulfield the realist suffers a nervous breakdown as a result of his disillusioning experiences, Clinton the romantic experiences emotional liberation through his painful epiphany. Although Clinton wants to be a writer, he cannot produce anything but verbatim transcriptions of other people's speech and correspondence, because he has not yet learned how to synthesize his experience. This bildungsroman, or coming-of-age novel, mainly concerns Clinton's liberation from bondage to his illusions. This liberation comes through his insight into his brother Berry-Berry's true character. There is a strong suggestion that Clinton's adoration of Berry-Berry has homosexual overtones and that the story, like Herlihy's *Midnight Cowboy* (1965), is really about the disenchanted protagonist's attaining the freedom to form a wholesome heterosexual relationship when he finds an appropriate love object.

Ralph Williams, Clinton's father, who was a political activist and dynamic personality in his youth, seems to have been emasculated by a dull marriage and his effort to maintain middle-class respectability. He deals in real estate but does not do well at it, because of his anticapitalist sentiments and his chronic depression. He is a heavy solitary drinker. He feels despised and rejected because both Clinton and Annabel have directed all their love toward the rebellious, charismatic Berry-Berry. In this carefully orchestrated novel, Ralph stands in sharp contrast to Berry-Berry, who has no respect for convention or middle-class morality.

Clinton's mother, Annabel, a drab, unimaginative housewife, has an unhealthy emotional attachment to her older son. There is a strong suggestion that she may have even had an incestuous relationship with Berry-Berry. At any rate, he loathes and fears her. She is the most symbolic of all the characters in the novel; she represents Herlihy's unfavorable view of American middle-class women in general. Annabel's unwholesome possessiveness is largely responsible for Berry-Berry's cruelty toward women and his dread of forming a permanent relationship with a woman. Clinton escapes the same destructive influence, because most of his mother's affection is directed at his older brother, who can be regarded as a victim as well as a victimizer.

Berry-Berry, Clinton's handsome, predatory older brother, is about twenty-three years of age when most of the events of the novel take place. His unusual first name suggests beriberi, which is a serious and often fatal disease. Psychologists would diagnose him as a psychopath, a totally self-centered person who is incapable of realizing that other people have feelings or exist as independent entities. Like most psychopaths, Berry-Berry can be very likable and can project an illusion of human sympathy and affection. It is precisely because he is totally lacking in normal human emotions that he is so fascinating to women: He learns to mimic affection and sympathy through a natural flair for imitation common to psychopathic personalities. Although Berry-Berry is not the hero or the viewpoint character in this cleverly constructed novel, he is the sun around whom all the other characters revolve—or a "disease" with which all the other characters are infected.

Echo is a virgin in her early thirties. She lived a sheltered life as her disabled mother's nurse and constant companion; she remained sweet and innocent. She is clearly heading for tragedy because of her alarmingly childlike trust in the essential goodness of everyone she encounters. Her wholesomeness provides a striking contrast to the sickness of the members of Clinton's dysfunctional family. Her first name, Echo, suggests that she possesses the instinctive responsiveness, the authentic ability to relate to other people, that Berry-Berry only projects through mimicry. She is a mirror in which the other characters view their own hypocrisy and unworthiness. Most important, she is the catalyst directly responsible for the change in the relationship between Clinton and Berry-Berry.

Shirley is a young prostitute who introduces Clinton to sex and begins the boy's long process of disillusionment with Berry-Berry by telling him cold facts about his older brother's parasitical and sadistic behavior. This gentle, generous young woman serves as the novel's only concrete example of the kind of women Berry-Berry habitually exploits.

All Fall Down is a story expertly told, dramatically convincing, and oddly comic. For his novel's epigraph, Herlihy uses a passage from Sherwood Anderson's *Winesburg, Ohio* (1919), the section telling of people who seize upon some particular truth, try to make it their truth only, and become grotesques as a result. The quotation is relevant to Herlihy's novel, for the book is, on one level, a story of grotesques. For a long time, the Williamses have lived apart and according to their own concerns. It is not until they share love that they really come alive. The use of the grotesque also is in keeping with the modern view that its image, antiromantic and antitragic alike, provides the most effective means of expressing both the irrationality of things and the moral evil that is also the devouring, obsessive evil of modern society, the isolation of the loving and the lonely. Herlihy sees moral isolation as one of the conditions of being, but he does not make it, as some of his contemporaries have done, a reason for fury or despair. His novel ends on a note of hope.

Further Reading

Hicks, Granville. "Within the Shadow of Winesburg." *Saturday Review* 43 (August 6, 1960): 14. Compares Herlihy to his "literary ancestor" Sherwood Anderson, who drew his material from grotesques and social misfits. Mentions other Anderson followers, such as John Steinbeck, William Saroyan, and Erskine Caldwell.

"James Leo Herlihy: Obituary." *The Times* (London), November 20, 1993. Reviews Herlihy's career, including the success of *All Fall Down*, and explains how his novels eventually were eclipsed by the successful film adaptation of *Midnight Cowboy*.

Levin, Martin. "Young Man on the Lam." *The New York Times Book Review*, August 21, 1960. Complimentary and influential review of *All Fall Down*. Compares it to a Tennessee Williams play with its mixture of "incest, infantile regression, impotence, and sadism overlaid with quaintness."

"Odd but Human." *Time*, August 15, 1960, 76. Compares Clinton Williams to J. D. Salinger's Holden Caulfield. Defines the theme of *All Fall Down* as the universal need for love. Asserts that the characters are odd, but important because of their kinship with humanity.

Pratley, Gerald. *The Cinema of John Frankenheimer.* New York: A. S. Barnes, 1969. Chapter 6 of this study of the filmmaker who directed the 1962 film adaptation of *All Fall Down* presents Frankenheimer's interpretation of the story and his analysis of the characters' motivations.

Quirk, Lawrence J. *The Films of Warren Beatty.* Secaucus, N.J.: Citadel Press, 1979. Contains an analysis of the 1962 screen adaptation of *All Fall Down*. The screenplay was written by William Inge, and the cast included Karl Malden, Eva Marie Saint, Brandon De Wilde, and Angela Lansbury. Includes illustrations.

All Fools

Author: George Chapman (c. 1559-1634)
First produced: 1604; first published, 1605
Type of work: Drama
Type of plot: Comedy
Time of plot: Sixteenth century
Locale: Italy

Principal characters:
RINALDO, a young gentleman
VALERIO, his friend
GOSTANZO, Valerio's father
MARC ANTONIO, Rinaldo's father
FORTUNIO, Rinaldo's brother
CORNELIO, a jealous husband
GRATIANA, Valerio's wife
BELLANORA, Valerio's sister, loved by Fortunio
GAZETTA, Cornelio's wife

The Story:

Gostanzo fancies himself a man of true worldly wisdom. He loves money, relishes his neighbor's misfortunes, and is unhampered by any petty scruples about honesty. Aware of the temptations that might lead a young man to become a wastrel, he takes great care in rearing his son Valerio. He lectures the boy on the importance of thrift and, to teach him responsibility, makes him an overseer.

Valerio is also a man of worldly wisdom. He puts on the

appearance of industry and innocence in front of his father, and he is well acquainted with the gentlemanly activities of dicing, drinking, and wenching. He accumulates, as the result of these pursuits, a respectable number of debts. To cap his sins, he marries Gratiana, a woman with beauty but no dowry. Fortunio is a young man of quite different character. Without parading his virtue, he leads an upright life and is a dutiful son. In love with Valerio's sister Bellanora, he is not permitted to court her because Gostanzo is seeking a wealthier son-in-law. Fortunio's brother Rinaldo, having experienced the fickleness of women, is through with love and now devotes himself exclusively to conning others.

One day, when Rinaldo, Fortunio, Valerio, and Gratiana are together talking, they sight Gostanzo coming their way, and all but Rinaldo rush off. In answer to Gostanzo's questions, Rinaldo says that Gratiana is the wife of Fortunio, who dares not tell his father of the marriage; Gostanzo believes the lie. Although he promises to keep it secret, he nevertheless reveals it the minute he is alone with Marc Antonio, the father of Fortunio and Rinaldo. Acting on Rinaldo's suggestion, Gostanzo recommends that Fortunio and Gratiana be installed in his home. Marc Antonio accepts this offer, not because he is angry with his son, but because Gostanzo convinces him that Fortunio is in danger of falling victim to greater evils. With the restraining influence of the strict Gostanzo and the good example of Valerio, he might still be saved.

Rinaldo's scheming thus enables Valerio and his wife to live in the same house, and it also gives Fortunio a chance to pursue his courtship of Bellanora. When Gratiana is brought to Gostanzo's home, the old man tells Valerio to kiss her, but the crafty youth feigns shyness. The father, gratified by this manifestation of a strict upbringing, congratulates himself on being a much better parent than the easygoing Marc Antonio.

Later, however, Gostanzo finds Valerio embracing and kissing Gratiana. The old man, still not suspecting the true state of affairs, thinks merely that his son is a fast learner. He decides that, to avoid mischief, Gratiana and Fortunio will have to leave his house. When he tells Rinaldo of this development, Rinaldo suggests that his father be told that Gratiana is really Valerio's wife and that Marc Antonio now take her into his house. Rinaldo further advises that, in order to make the ruse effective, Valerio be permitted to visit her there. The plan meets with the ready assent of Gostanzo, who, being gulled, is happy in the thought that he will be gulling Marc Antonio.

Meanwhile, Rinaldo, encouraged by his success in this project, is directing his genius to a new endeavor, a plan intended to gull Cornelio, an inordinately jealous husband who is an easy mark for a trickster and whose wife, Gazetta, complains that he brings home gallants and then upbraids her for being in their company. Rinaldo's accomplice in his scheme is Valerio, who is angry at Cornelio for making fun of his singing. Valerio has little difficulty in awakening the jealousy in Cornelio. With the help of a page who defends Gazetta on the grounds that women's wantonness is a result of weakness and not design, he so infuriates Cornelio that the jealous husband attacks and wounds his wife's supposed lover.

When Marc Antonio is told that Valerio, not Fortunio, is married to Gratiana, he makes merry with Gostanzo for his blind pride. The latter, unable to tolerate gloating other than his own, declares that the plot was contrived for entertainment. When they meet Valerio, Gostanzo feigns extreme anger with him and threatens to disown his son. Valerio, playing the penitent, protests his devotion to his father and avows his love of Gratiana. Gostanzo, believing the whole affair a joke, dissembles an appearance of being softened and gives his blessing to the match.

Cornelio, meanwhile, procures a notary and is proceeding with the divorce of his wife. A nosebleed, which he takes as an omen, causes him to suspend action just as he is preparing to sign the final papers. After the notary leaves, a friend explains to him that he was tricked into his jealousy by Rinaldo and Valerio. Cornelio resolves to repay them with a deception of his own.

When Cornelio finds Rinaldo, he tells this master trickster that Valerio was arrested for debts. Since Valerio was dodging the officials for some time, Rinaldo believes the lie and, having gone on bond for Valerio, he believes that some immediate action is unnecessary. At Cornelio's suggestion, he takes Gostanzo with him to the Half Moon Tavern, where Cornelio says Valerio is being held before being taken to prison. Valerio is at the tavern, but not as a captive. Instead, he is engaged in his usual pursuits of drinking and playing dice.

When Gostanzo sees his son's true nature and also learns that Valerio really is married to Gratiana, he threatens, this time in earnest, to disown the boy and to settle his estate on his daughter. This plan is rejected when he discovers that Bellanora married Fortunio. The old man, frustrated in his efforts to control events, decides to accept them. Finally, when Cornelio reveals that his jealousy was feigned in order to restrain his wife's high spirits, the reconciliations are complete and happiness reigns in the Half Moon Tavern.

Critical Evaluation:

The English poet and critic Algernon Charles Swinburne considered *All Fools* to be George Chapman's best comedy. Having proven successful with sophisticated and popular audiences, it was notably revived for performance before King James I on New Year's Eve night, 1604. *All Fools* remains one of Chapman's most skillfully constructed plays, with well-rounded, realistically established characters and a plot that transcends the contrivance of much of Jacobean comedy.

All Fools is based on elements taken from three separate plays by the Roman dramatist Terence, a favorite source of playwrights of the Elizabethan and Jacobean period. The main plot, contrasting two fathers, Gostanzo and Marc Antonio, and their two sons, Valerio and Rinaldo respectively, is adapted from the comedy *Heautontimorumenos* (163 B.C.E.; *The Self-Tormentor*, 1598). Substantial additional material is also taken from two other plays by Terence, *Adelphoe* (160 B.C.E.; *The Brothers*, 1598) and *Eunuchus* (163 B.C.E.; *The Eunuch*, 1598). In addition, Chapman freely adds to his plot, introducing figures of contemporary satire such as the notary and the doctor, in order to skewer the types so prevalent in the comedies of the period.

Chapman does more than simply translate and adapt the classical Roman comedies. He substantially revises and expands his original sources, making the major individual characters more rounded and providing them with additional motivations. While this has the effect of making the comedy more believable and substantial, it also allows Chapman to introduce a moral dimension to the play that is lacking in Terence.

The stock figures of the Roman comedy are guided by simple and often base motivations, in particular lust and avarice. Chapman's characters, on the other hand, are imbued with the wealth of the Christian and humanist traditions, which makes them more honorable, attractive, and sympathetic. For example, Rinaldo, younger brother of Fortunio, is based on the scheming slave who sets into motion and then continues through his machinations the dizzying round of events in *The Self-Tormentor*. In the Roman play, the slave is an essentially stock character rather than an individual; he is an amoral trickster, witty and clever, whose purpose is to advance the plot in a fairly predictable fashion. In *All Fools*, on the other hand, Rinaldo is elevated to the status of family member. He is an accomplished scholar and has a complex moral code that, while it allows him to fool others, allows him to fool his family in the service of love and affection. His tricks allow the pair of lovers to live together despite the disapproval of their fathers. In Chapman's play, there is a substance to Rinaldo that, ultimately, has a moral basis. He is much more than a trickster, and if he is at times a con man, he is usually in the service of morally laudable goals.

This same higher degree of motivation in Chapman's play is also seen in Valerio, Rinaldo's friend. Although Valerio initially appears to other characters and to the audience as only a dandy, given to music, poetry, dancing, and flirting, he also comes to express, in his speeches and in his actions, a sincere neo-Platonic idealism. Valerio believes that devotion to love is a ladder by which human beings can transcend their mortal limitations and gain greater knowledge and excellence.

Chapman makes outstanding use of language and theatrical staging in establishing these characters and presenting the action of the play. In Terence's original, the humor is derived mainly from the plot, which is complex to the point of confusion and complicated beyond either rationality or realism. By grounding his comedy on sympathetic characters, Chapman makes the multiple tricks and deceptions practiced in the play understandable, humorous, and believable. At the play's end, for example, Gostanzo, Valerio's father, learns at last that Valerio is really married to Gratiana and Fortunio is wed to Bellanora. Gostanzo's learning that what he believed throughout the play is actually false is a comedic revelation that leads to a final thematic and moral development. Gostanzo realizes that he is unable to control the young lovers; he must simply accept them with the full measure of his love. Such an ending transcends the moral frame of Terence's original drama and raises Chapman's play to a different level.

As typical with Chapman, the language of *All Fools* is flowing and fluent, easy to grasp. Some critics have objected to this quality in Chapman's other plays, noting that while his verse carries the sense of meaning remarkably well, it lacks any outstanding or distinctive touches. Such, however, is not the case with *All Fools*, for the play, although set in Italy, makes extensive use of Elizabethan figures of speech. These bring a strength and sense of immediacy to the dialogue that is sometimes lacking in Chapman's other dramas. Chapman displays an impressive command of the possibilities of colloquial speech of his times. Ultimately, it is the combination of all of these qualities of characterization, plotting, staging, and language that raises *All Fools* to its acknowledged level as being among the best, if not the best, of Chapman's comedies.

"Critical Evaluation" by Michael Witkoski

Further Reading

Bradbrook, M. C. "George Chapman." In *British Writers*, edited by Ian Scott-Killert. New York: Charles Scribner's Sons, 1979. Fine overview of Chapman and his work. Presents a measured view of his plays.

Braunmuller, A. R., and Michael Hattaway, eds. *The Cambridge Companion to English Renaissance Drama*. New

York: Cambridge University Press, 2003. Chapman's plays are discussed in several places in this collection of essays, and these references are listed in the index.

Lewis, C. S. *English Literature in the Sixteenth Century, Excluding Drama*. Oxford, England: Clarendon Press, 1954. The discussion of Chapman, while relatively short, is excellent and evaluates him as a writer of his times rather than an isolated figure.

Sanders, Andrew. *The Short Oxford History of English Literature*. New York: Oxford University Press, 1994. Concise and to-the-point. Useful for gaining an appreciation of Chapman's career and achievements.

Spivack, Charlotte. *George Chapman*. Boston: Twayne, 1967. Introductory survey of Chapman's life and writings, with a generous and sympathetic study of *All Fools*. Includes bibliography.

All for Love
Or, The World Well Lost

Author: John Dryden (1631-1700)
First produced: 1677; first published, 1678
Type of work: Drama
Type of plot: Tragedy
Time of plot: First century B.C.E.
Locale: Alexandria, Egypt

Principal characters:
MARK ANTONY, one of the Roman triumvirate
VENTIDIUS, his faithful general
DOLABELLA, Antony's friend
OCTAVIA, Antony's wife
CLEOPATRA, queen of Egypt
ALEXAS, Cleopatra's eunuch

The Story:

After his humiliating defeat at Actium, Mark Antony retires to Alexandria, Egypt, where he remains in seclusion for some time in the temple of Isis. He avoids meeting his mistress, Cleopatra, the queen of Egypt, whose cowardice largely caused the defeat. Meanwhile the Romans, under Octavius, Maecenas, and Agrippa, have invaded Egypt, where, having laid siege to Alexandria, they calmly await Antony's next move. Serapion, a patriot and a priest of Isis, becomes alarmed at a sudden rising of the Nile and by prodigious disturbances among the royal tombs; these events seem to presage disaster for Egypt.

Ventidius, Antony's trusted and highly successful general in the Middle East, comes at this time to Alexandria to aid his commander. Alexas, Cleopatra's loyal, scheming eunuch, and Serapion try to encourage citizens and troops with a splendid birthday festival in Antony's honor. Ventidius, in Roman fashion, scorns the celebration. He tells Antony's Roman soldiers not to rejoice, but to prepare to defend Antony in his peril. Antony, clearly a ruined man, at last comes out of his seclusion. While he curses his fate and laments the day that he was born, Ventidius, in concealment, overhears the pitiful words of his emperor. Revealing his presence, he attempts to console Antony. Both men weep; Antony marvels that Ventidius can remain faithful to a leader who brought a large part of the Roman Empire to ruin through his love for Cleopatra.

Ventidius offers to Antony his twelve legions, which are stationed in Lower Syria, but his stipulation that these legions will not fight for Cleopatra plunges doting Antony into renewed gloom. When Ventidius mentions the name of Cleopatra lightly, Antony takes offense and curses the general as a traitor. After this insult Antony, his mind filled with misgivings, guilt, and indecision, hastens to assure Ventidius of his love for him. He promises to leave Cleopatra to join the legions in Syria.

The word that Antony is preparing to desert her leaves Cleopatra in a mood of anger and despair. Meanwhile Charmion, her maid, goes to Antony and begs the Roman to say farewell to her mistress. Antony refuses, saying that he does not trust himself in Cleopatra's presence. Not daunted by this refusal, Alexas later intercepts Antony as he marches out of Alexandria. The eunuch flatters the Romans and presents them with rich jewels from Cleopatra. As Antony is with difficulty clasping a bracelet around his arm, Cleopatra makes her prepared appearance. Antony bitterly accuses her of falseness and of being the cause of his downfall. The two argue. In desperation, Cleopatra tells Antony that as her friend he must go to Syria, but that as her lover he must stay in Alexandria to share her fate. Antony wavers in his determination to leave when Cleopatra tells him that she spurned Octavius's offer of all Egypt and Syria if she would join his forces, and he elects to stay when she represents herself as a weak woman left to the mercy of the cruel invaders. Antony declares, in surrendering again to Cleopatra's charms, that Octavius could have the world as long as he had Cleopatra's love. Ventidius is overcome with shame and pity at Antony's submission.

Cleopatra is triumphant in her renewed power over Antony, and Antony seems to have recovered some of his former magnificence when he is successful in minor engagements against the troops of Octavius. While Octavius, biding his time, holds his main forces in check, Ventidius, still hopeful of saving Antony, suggests that a compromise might be arranged with Maecenas or with Agrippa.

Dolabella, the friend whom Antony banishes because he fears that Cleopatra might grow to love the young Roman, comes from Octavius's camp to remind Antony that he has obligations toward his wife and two daughters. Then Octavia and her two young daughters are brought before Antony, Octavia, in spite of Antony's desertion, still hopes for reconciliation with her husband. When Antony accuses her of bargaining with her brother Octavius, Octavia, undismayed, admits that Octavius is prepared to withdraw from Egypt at the news that a reconciliation has been effected between his sister and Antony. Octavia's calm dignity affects Antony greatly, and when his two small daughters embrace him, he declares himself ready to submit to the will of Octavia. Cleopatra, entering upon this family reunion, exchanges insults with the momentarily triumphant Octavia.

Still afraid to face Cleopatra for the last time, Antony prevails upon Dolabella to speak his farewell to Cleopatra. Dolabella, aspiring to Cleopatra's favors, accepts the mission with pleasure. Alexas, knowing of Dolabella's weakness and ever solicitous of the welfare of Egypt, advises Cleopatra to excite Antony's jealousy by pretending to be interested in Dolabella. After Ventidius and Octavia secretly overhear the conversation between Dolabella and Cleopatra, Ventidius, now unwittingly a tool of Alexas, reports to Antony Cleopatra's apparent interest in the young Dolabella. Octavia confirms his report, and Alexas suggests to the raging Antony that Cleopatra is capable of perfidy. Antony's passionate reaction to this information convinces Octavia that her mission is a failure and she returns to the Roman camp. Antony, meanwhile, accuses Cleopatra and Dolabella of treachery. Ignoring their earnest denials, he banishes them from his presence.

Cleopatra, cursing the eunuch's ill advice, attempts unsuccessfully to take her own life with a dagger. Antony ascends a tower in Alexandria harbor to watch an impending naval engagement between the Egyptian and Roman fleets. To his horror he sees the two fleets join and the entire force advance to attack the city. Antony realizes now that his end is near; furthermore, his heart is broken by the belief that Cleopatra is responsible for the treachery of the Egyptian fleet. When Alexas brings false word that Cleopatra retired to her tomb and took her life, Antony, no longer desiring to live, falls on his own sword. The faithful Ventidius kills himself. Cleopatra comes to the dying Antony and convinces him, before he dies, that she remained steadfast in her love for him. Then, to cheat Octavius of a final triumph, she dresses in her royal robes and permits herself to be bitten by a poisonous asp. Her maids, Iras and Charmion, kill themselves in the same manner. Serapion enters to find Cleopatra joined with her Antony in death.

Critical Evaluation:

John Dryden, the premier poet of his age, is honored primarily as a satirist and controversialist in the political and religious skirmishes of the Restoration. It was in drama, however, that he honed the fine poetic skills of his later poems. Between 1667 and 1678, he wrote a series of comedies and tragedies that provided him with the opportunity to develop the authority and control that distinguish his major poetry. Dryden was never a truly successful comic dramatist, perhaps because the prospect of a foolish or flawed man's getting better than he deserved was at odds with Dryden's essentially satiric sensibility. He did, however, create a series of memorable tragedies, including *Aureng-Zebe* (1675) and *Tyrannic Love: Or, The Royal Martyr* (1669), which set the norm for heroic drama in the period.

The Restoration was an exciting period in the history of the drama, with the introduction of women playing female roles. The heroic drama, the dominant serious form, is an exaggerated and stylized presentation of themes of epic proportions. Large heroes and heroines confront dastardly villains with a great deal of bombastic rhetoric, usually in heroic couplets. Through his tragedies, Dryden had been building toward a greater control of the excesses of the genre and, in *All for Love*, he abandons the couplet for blank verse and manages his highly romantic subject matter with distance and restraint.

All for Love is a retelling of the story of Antony and Cleopatra, but, despite Dryden's great admiration for Shakespeare, it is in no sense an adaptation of Shakespeare's version. Dryden's play lacks the panoramic sweep of Shakespeare's *Antony and Cleopatra* (pr. c. 1606-1607, pb. 1623), which ranges broadly over the civilized world. As a devotee of a more rational kind of theater based on a strict interpretation of Aristotle, Dryden is much more concerned about the unities of time, place, and action. The whole drama unfolds in Alexandria and is narrowly limited to the period after the defeat of Antony at the battle of Actium.

The play does not have a climax in the usual sense of the term. The climax of a drama is ordinarily a focal point toward which the conflicts and complications build. It is true that in some Shakespearean plays the climax is early, as in *Macbeth* (pr. 1606, pb. 1623), in which the murder of Duncan is accomplished in the second act so that the audience may concentrate on the consequences of Macbeth's crime. Dryden goes a step further. If *All for Love* has a climax at all, it occurs before the beginning of the action on stage. The play traces the complex chain of results of the battle of Actium, which changes the course of history, seals the fate of Antony, and dooms Egyptian civilization.

Such a context is the natural element of Restoration heroic drama: a hero larger than life, worthy of the grandest exploits, is thrust into a moribund civilization. Heroic drama of the Restoration is fashioned by a poetics of the terminal. The overreacher, the hero who monumentally represents all that is best in a nation and who tests the justice and the restraining limits of the universe, is gone from the moral universe of the Restoration. Instead, the audience has heroes, noble beyond reproach, who are cast into a twilight world, the world of the terminus, or end. Dryden's images of sunsets and twilight reinforce the impression of finality. The optimism of Renaissance drama is replaced, if not by despair, at least by resignation to a world in decline. Antony challenged the world, but that time is now past. He is left to examine his passions in a series of after-the-fact confrontations.

New attitudes about what is efficacious social behavior emerge from the Restoration's predilection for order and stability. The heroic drama is a transposition of the daring hero into a more subdued context. Dryden's play may be considered a reflection of the time in which he lived in its lack of belief in the social utility of the hero. Dryden establishes a new kind of tragedy that recognizes the limitations of the hero and searches out what is beyond.

Unlike Shakespeare, Dryden does not use setting as a premise for characterization. Dryden takes pains to remove his characters from the particularities of any specific time or place, to isolate them in a world free of extraneous distractions. In this context Antony, his great exploits over, is free to confront himself. It is probably a limitation of the dramatic form that these complications seem to be thrust externally upon Antony, but the fact remains that he must face a series of trials, each of which is designed to challenge another facet of his sorely burdened moral identity. As Antony faces his troubles, he is no more a passionate drunkard than he is any longer the potent hero. He is not a weak man. The conflict is no longer a simple dichotomy of passion and responsibility; rather, it is a matter of Antony, through the blandishments of Ventidius and Cleopatra, trying to decide who he is by discovering where his true loyalties lie.

It is typical of this oddly muted tragic world that its passions are manipulated and stage-managed by the eunuch Alexas. Octavius, the hero in the ascendant, never appears on stage. It is Antony's descent from godhead to humanity, rather than the drama of war, that is the source of the special tragedy of *All for Love*. Antony's experience brings him to a self-perception and an understanding of passion, loyalty, and power that are beyond the hero at the height of his success. Heroic perception of this diminished sort is the appropriate insight for an age of reason and skepticism.

"Critical Evaluation" by Edward E. Foster

Further Reading

Hammond, Paul, and David Hopkins, eds. *John Dryden: Tercentenary Essays*. New York: Oxford University Press, 2000. This collection, published during the tercentenary of Dryden's death, examines some of Dryden's individual works, as well as more general characteristics of his writing. Some of the essays question if Dryden is a classic, explore Dryden and the "staging of popular politics," and describe the dissolution evident in his later writing.

Hopkins, David. *John Dryden*. Tavistock, England: Northcote House/British Council, 2004. Concise and up-to-date overview of Dryden's life and work. Hopkins demonstrates that Dryden not only was a man of his times; he also continues to have significant ideas to express to a twenty-first century audience.

Kirsch, Arthur. "*All for Love*." In *Twentieth Century Interpretations of "All for Love,"* edited by Bruce King. Englewood Cliffs, N.J.: Prentice-Hall, 1968. Discusses the play's relationship to heroic tragedy. Maintains that in the play, heroism is replaced by sentimentality and domesticity. The introduction by Bruce King is also illuminating.

Lewis, Jayne, and Maximillian E. Novak, eds. *Enchanted Ground: Reimagining John Dryden*. Toronto, Ont.: University of Toronto Press, 2004. Collection of essays that apply twenty-first century critical perspectives to Dryden's work. The first section focuses on Dryden's role as a public poet and the voice of the Stuart court during Restoration; the second explores his relationship to drama and music. Includes Richard Kroll's essay "The Political Economy of *All for Love*."

Milhous, Judith, and Robert D. Hume. "*All for Love*." In *Producible Interpretation: Eight English Plays, 1675-1707*. Carbondale: Southern Illinois University Press, 1985. Examines the play in terms of staging. Provides discussion that includes the nature of its tragedy, character analysis, rhythm, settings, time, costumes, casting, and effects.

Novak, Maximillian E. "Criticism, Adaptation, Politics, and the Shakespearean Model of Dryden's *All for Love*." In *Studies in Eighteenth-Century Culture*, edited by Roseann Runte. Vol. 7. Madison: University of Wisconsin Press, 1978. Discusses the relationship of *All for Love* to Shakespeare's *Antony and Cleopatra*. Explores how, where, and why Dryden made his play different from Shakespeare's.

Rawson, Claude, and Aaron Santesso, eds. *John Dryden, 1631-1700: His Politics, His Plays, and His Poets*. Newark: University of Delaware Press, 2004. Contains papers presented at a Yale University conference held in 2000 to commemorate the tercentenary of Dryden's death. The essays focus on the politics of Dryden's plays and how his poetry was poised between ancient and modern influences.

Waith, Eugene. "The Herculean Hero." In *Twentieth Century Interpretations of "All for Love,"* edited by Bruce King. Englewood Cliffs, N.J.: Prentice-Hall, 1968. Examines Antony's character. Claims that he is a "Herculean hero" because he is brave, generous, passionate, and indifferent to public opinion.

Zwicker, Steven N., ed. *The Cambridge Companion to John Dryden*. New York: Cambridge University Press, 2004. Among these seventeen essays are discussions of Dryden and the theatrical imagination, the invention of Augustan culture and patronage, and Dryden's London and the "passion of politics" in his theater.

All Hallows' Eve

Author: Charles Williams (1886-1945)
First published: 1945
Type of work: Novel
Type of plot: Allegory
Time of plot: October, 1945
Locale: London

Principal characters:

LESTER FURNIVAL, a dead young wife
RICHARD FURNIVAL, her husband
EVELYN MERCER, her dead friend
BETTY WALLINGFORD, another friend
LADY SARA WALLINGFORD, Betty's mother
JONATHAN DRAYTON, Betty's artist fiancé, friend of Richard
SIMON THE CLERK, the leader of a religious group

The Story:

To Lester Furnival, standing on Westminster Bridge at twilight, the lights of the city and the drone of a friendly plane overhead are symbols of the peace, a return to the natural order of life. Lester slowly becomes conscious, however, of a silence that is unnatural. Lester realizes that she is dead.

A vital and passionate young woman killed in a plane crash, she first finds herself alone in the city with Evelyn, the friend who is killed with her. She realizes that theirs was never a true friendship. As the two dead women try to establish a genuine relationship in the afterlife, they become involved in the affairs of the living. Lester's husband Richard has an artist friend, Jonathan, who is in love with Betty, a school friend whom Lester and Evelyn never liked. Betty is completely dominated by her mother, Lady Wallingford, who is a disciple of a mysterious faith healer who calls himself Simon the Clerk.

Lady Wallingford and Betty call to see a portrait of Father Simon commissioned from Jonathan. A Christian, Jonathan, without realizing it, reveals in the portrait the essence of evil, which Simon represents. Lady Wallingford, infuriated, calls off Betty's engagement to Jonathan and takes Betty away. Jonathan calls on Richard for help. The conflict between mother and lover for possession of Betty becomes the conflict between the God of love and the power of darkness for the human soul.

Surrounded by a band of zealous converts, preaching to a mesmerized audience in his shabby back-street headquarters, Simon is the reembodiment of Simon the Magus, the Jew who rejected Christ. Simon is, in fact, the Antichrist. Exploiting the devotion of Lady Wallingford, he conceives Betty to be his agent and fears that his power over the daughter is threatened by her love for Jonathan. Simon decides that the time comes for the final magical operation that will separate her human soul from her body and substitute his will in its place. He is thwarted by love in action. At each crisis, he makes a mistake, because his magic powers cannot perceive what love can do. When Simon goes to Betty's bedroom to perform the final operation of magic, Lester is there, having gone to ask Betty's forgiveness for rejecting her friendship. Betty's forgiveness of Lester releases Lester's spirit; Lester's love sustains Betty and becomes Betty's substitute to receive Simon's magic. Lester is already dead, so Simon's magic has no effect on her, and Betty is released from his spell to rebel against her mother and rejoin Jonathan. The defeated Simon then turns his attention to the wretched soul of Evelyn, who sought his aid to regain her power of persecuting Betty. Lester tries to rescue Evelyn, as she rescued Betty, by joining her within Evelyn's miserably deformed physical body, which Simon creates for her with his magic powers. Simon attempts to control Evelyn's body and use it to trap Betty, Jonathan, and Richard. Lester, however, exercises a greater control through the power of love and warns them in time for them to expose Simon and bring his work and his house to ruins.

The climax of the action takes place on a gray, rainy Halloween, All Hallows' Eve, when the deformed body, containing the souls of Lester and Evelyn, moves through the streets of London and keeps a rendezvous at Jonathan's flat. The engaged couple invites the bereaved Richard to join them for dinner. When Lester wants to warn Richard of the approach of the magical body, she thinks of the telephone. Having begged two pennies from a passerby, she goes into a telephone booth opposite the Charing Cross underground station. When Richard comes to the phone, he hears Lester's voice as clearly as he saw her form several times in the last few days. She gives him the message that they have to wait at the flat until the old woman comes. Instead of going out to dinner, they spread a meal of bread, cheese, cold cuts, and wine, and thus prepare themselves for the crisis of All Hallows' Eve. After meeting, the three living friends take the deformed body with them in a taxi through the rainy midnight streets of London to the darkened house where Simon and Lady Wallingford are stalled in their last desperate act of magic. Love triumphs over evil; Lester disappears in a blaze of white light.

Critical Evaluation:

Charles Williams's last novel is set in the locale he knew best, central London, but in a time that he did not live to appreciate: the first autumn of the peace after World War II. The novel removes the barrier between the natural and the supernatural worlds. Lester is the central character in a drama that illustrates Williams's mystical and imaginative interpretation of Christian doctrine. The plot traces the triumph of love over evil during Lester's period of purgatory. She is a modern version of the figure of Beatrice, the spiritual guide of Dante's *The Divine Comedy* (1802). Her love for her husband, which survives her death, leads to his conversion, to the defeat of evil, and to her own salvation. The story combines natural and supernatural elements with a realism that is not merely a matter of literary technique but also an expression of Williams's belief that the material and the spiritual, and the temporal and the eternal, are equally real. This tenet of faith is basic to the creative imagination for Williams. The novel is not intended as a fantasy or as an allegory; the novel form is used simply for its traditional purpose of revealing life's reality. Williams believes that a person who loves can bear another's burdens in a way that he considers physical as well as spiritual. This ability involves not simply praying for the burdened one but also loving that one so deeply that the burden of suffering is transferred from the loved one to the person who loves. As the human form of Christ on the cross suffers for all humanity, so the central character of this story saves a victim by substituting herself.

From the moment when Lester finds herself alone on Westminster Bridge to the climax of her disappearance from Simon's house, there is always a strong sense of London as the background to the action. At first, Lester sees only the city, but as her spirit develops, she hears all the familiar noises of people and traffic, feels the pavement under her feet, and smells the river and the October rain.

The literalness of London sights, sounds, and locations is not merely a device to root the supernatural story in the natural world. For Williams, London is an image of the City of God, the Holy City, the community of the saints. When the city is first mentioned, the term indicates the ancient borough of London, site of St. Paul's, as distinguished from Holborn, where Simon's headquarters are. Through Lester's developing spiritual perception, however, the spiritual reality of the eternal city is revealed. Its identity is hinted to mortal eyes on the fateful afternoon when Lady Wallingford and Betty call to look at Jonathan's portrait of Simon. Lady Wallingford is equally antagonized by another painting that Jonathan and Richard consider the best that Jonathan did, a painting of a part of London after a raid, a scene of desolation bathed in living light.

This city, emerging from war and night, is the setting in which Richard meets his wife again with a deeper understanding of their love. At the end of the novel, Jonathan and Betty give Richard the painting, and Lester disappears into light. Although the plot of the novel centers on the conflict over Betty, considerable thematic interest is focused on the dead Lester and the living Richard as they move through the city, at first absolutely separated, then gradually reunited as each comes to understand the reality of love, and finally separated when the understanding is complete. These two characters are developed with a psychological depth, dramatic sensitivity, and humor that make them as fully credible as the protagonists of a more traditional novel. Jonathan and Betty are less fully delineated and are seen more from the outside, through the eyes of their friends, than from the inside. The dead Evelyn is no longer a human personality but merely the epitome of egocentric peevishness, which was her dominant trait.

In descending scale, Simon and Lady Wallingford are agents of evil, as much puppets as the bodies that Simon can create. These differing degrees of characterization reflect Williams's belief that only love can make a human being whole. Jonathan and Betty, in their initial stages of love, cannot be as fully developed as Lester and Richard are. In characterization, as in every aspect of the novel, Williams's story is perfectly integrated with his doctrine. Final assessment of his achievement requires the resolution of a basic dilemma: whether the credibility of the story makes the doctrine convincing or whether the credibility of the story depends on conviction about the doctrine.

Further Reading

Ashenden, Gavin. *Charles Williams: Alchemy and Integration*. Kent, Ohio: Kent State University Press, 2008. Examines the influence of Williams's interest in neo-Rosicrucianism on his novels and poetry.

Dunning, Stephen M. *The Crisis and the Quest: A Kierkegaardian Reading of Charles Williams*. Carlisle, Cumbria, England: Paternoster Press, 2000. Uses the philosophy of Søren Kierkegaard to analyze the crisis between Christianity and hermiticism in Williams's work and to chronicle his attempts at resolution.

Eliot, T. S. Introduction to *All Hallows' Eve*, by Charles Williams. Grand Rapids, Mich.: Wm. B. Eerdmans, 1981. Eliot was an important literary friend of Williams.

Fredrick, Candice, and Sam McBride. "Women as Mythic Icons: Williams and Tolkien." In *Women Among the Inklings: Gender, C. S. Lewis, J. R. R. Tolkien, and Charles Williams*. Westport, Conn.: Greenwood Press, 2001. Williams and the other two authors were members of the Inklings, a group of male intellectuals that met at Oxford, England, during the 1930's and 1940's. This book examines the role of women in the three authors' lives, their attitudes toward women, and the depiction of women in their work.

Howard, Thomas. *The Novels of Charles Williams*. New York: Oxford University Press, 1983. Discusses Christian doctrines of forgiveness and judgment as portrayed in *All Hallows' Eve*.

Reilly, R. J. *Romantic Religion: A Study of Barfield, Lewis, Williams, and Tolkien*. Athens: University of Georgia Press, 1971. Reprint. Great Barrington, Mass.: Lindisfarne, 2007. Examines the theological and philosophical ideas of a group of writers and intellectuals now known as the Oxford Christians. Devotes a chapter to Williams.

Sibley, Agnes. *Charles Williams*. Boston: Twayne, 1982. Contains a summary and insightful commentary on *All Hallows' Eve*, as well as a useful bibliography.

Williams, Charles. *The Image of the City, and Other Essays*. Edited by Anne Ridler. New York: Oxford University Press, 1958. Williams expounds his theories; in addition, the critical introduction contains a brilliant analysis of his major themes.

All Men Are Brothers

Author: Shi Naian (c. 1290-1365)
First transcribed: Shuihu zhuan, earliest version, c. thirteenth century; fuller text versions by sixteenth century (English translation, 1933)
Type of work: Novel
Type of plot: Adventure
Time of plot: Thirteenth century or earlier
Locale: China

Principal characters:
SHIH CHIN, the Nine Dragoned
LU TA, later LU CHI SHEN, the Tattooed Priest
LING CH'UNG, the Leopard Headed
CH'AI CHIN, the Little Whirlwind
YANG CHI, the Blue-Faced Beast
CHU T'UNG, the Beautiful Bearded
LEI HENG, the Winged Tiger
CH'AO KAI, the Heavenly King
WU YUNG, the Great Intelligence
KUNG SUN SHENG, Dragon in the Clouds
SUNG CHIANG, the Opportune Rain
WU SUNG, the Hairy Priest
WANG THE DWARF TIGER
TAI CHUNG, the Magic Messenger
LI K'UEI, the Black Whirlwind
LU CHUN I, the Jade Ch'Lin

The Story:

To escape the persecution of evil Commander Kao, a military instructor flees to the border. On the way, he instructs a village lord's son, Shih Chin, in warlike skills. Later, Shih Chin becomes friendly with the robbers of Little Hua Mountain. Discovery of this alliance forces Shih Chin to flee. He falls in with Captain Lu Ta, who, after killing a pig butcher who was persecuting a young woman, escapes capture by becoming priest Lu Chi Shen. His violence and intemperance, however, force the abbot to send him to another temple. On the way, he makes peace between a village lord and the robbers of Peach Blossom Mountain.

Shih Chin joins the robbers of Little Hua Mountain. Lu Chi Shen goes on to his temple, where he becomes a friend of military instructor Ling Ch'ung. Commander Kao's son lusts for Ling Ch'ung's wife, so Ling Ch'ung is falsely accused of murder, branded, and exiled to Ch'ang Chou. His guards are prevented by Lu Chi Shen from carrying out their secret orders to kill Ling Ch'ung. Again on his way, Ling Ch'ung is hospitably received by Lord Ch'ai Chin.

In Ch'ang Chou, Ling Ch'ung accidentally escapes a death trap and kills his three would-be assassins. Again, he encounters Ch'ai Chin, who sends him to take refuge in Liang Shan P'o, a robbers' lair headed by the ungracious Wang Lun. Warrior Yang Chi, after killing a bully, is branded and sent to be a border guard. His skill delights Governor Liang of Peking, who keeps and promotes him and even selects him to transport rich birthday gifts to Liang's father-in-law. To rid the way of robbers, Chu T'ung and Lei Heng are sent out ahead of the party that is carrying the treasures. Lei Heng captures drunken Liu T'ang and takes him to Lord Ch'ao Kai, but the lord arranges his release upon privately discovering that Lei Heng has come to seek him; Lei Heng brings the news of the birthday gifts, which he, Ch'ao Kai, and a teacher, Wu Yung, then plot to steal. Magician Kung Sun Sheng and the three Juan brothers join them.

The plotters cleverly drug Yang Chi and his disguised soldiers and steal the treasure. In despair, Yang Chi leaves the others, who resolve to pin the blame on him. Yang Chi falls in with Lu Chi Shen; they go to Double Dragon Mountain and, overcoming the robber chief who refuses to admit them, become the leaders of the band.

When Ch'ao Kai is discovered to have been one of the robbers, plans are made to catch him, but with the aid of scribe Sung Chiang and robber-catcher Chu T'ung, Ch'ao Kai and the others escape to Liang Shan P'o. Ling Ch'ung kills the ungracious Wang Lun, and Ch'ao Kai is made the chief. Ling Ch'ung discovers that his wife has killed herself to escape the advances of Commander Kao's son. The robbers vanquish two groups sent against them.

Sung Chiang's connection with the robbers is discovered by his unfaithful mistress. Enraged at her blackmail threats, he kills her and escapes to Ch'ai Chin's village. There he meets Wu Sung, who is on his way to see his older brother after a long absence.

Wu Sung kills a tiger and is greatly celebrated. He is of heroic size; his brother is puny and small. The latter's wife tries unsuccessfully to seduce Wu Sung. In Wu Sung's absence, she takes a lover and, with his help, kills her husband. Wu Sung returns and kills the pair. Although generally pitied, he is branded and exiled.

After an eventful journey, Wu Sung defends his jailer's son against a usurper and so offends the tyrant that he plots with General Chang to accuse Wu Sung falsely of a crime. Wu Sung kills the plotters and joins those at Double Dragon Mountain.

While on a visit to military magistrate Hua Yung, Sung Chiang is captured by the robbers of the Mountain of Clear Winds, but they recognize and welcome him. One of them, lustful Wang the Dwarf Tiger, captures the wife of a civil magistrate, Liu Kao. Hoping to please Hua Yung, Sung Chiang persuades Wang to release her. Later the woman, a troublemaker, identifies Sun Chiang as one of the robbers. Sung Chiang and Hua Yung escape to the Mountain of Clear Winds, and Liu Kao is killed.

General Ch'ing Ming comes against these robbers and is captured. Their plot to force him to join their band is successful. Liu Kao's wife is recaptured and executed. Sung Chiang promises to get a wife for the disappointed Wang the Dwarf Tiger. The whole band decides to join those at Liang Shan P'o, but Sung Chiang is summoned home for the burial of his father. The report of his father's death, however, turns out to be a trick to keep Sung Chiang from turning outlaw. Persuaded to stand trial for his mistress's murder, he is branded and exiled. The trip is very eventful, involving many near escapes in encounters with robbers who later prove friendly. At his destination, Sung Chiang becomes a friend of his jailer, Tai Chung, who possesses magic enabling him to walk three hundred miles a day. Another friend, violent but loyal Li K'uei, causes much trouble, which Sung Chiang is able to smooth over. One day, Sung Chiang becomes drunk and writes revolutionary verses on a wall. Tai Chung, sent to a distant city to get execution orders, goes instead to Liang Shan P'o, where a letter is forged, freeing Sung Chiang. A mistake made in the seal, however, also results in Tai Chung's death sentence. Both are freed from the execution grounds by the robbers. All go back to Liang Shan P'o, enlarging their group with additional robbers recruited along the way.

Sung Chiang sets out to bring his father and brother to the robbers' lair. He is miraculously saved from capture by a temple goddess who gives great prophecies. The robbers take the Sung family to their lair. Kung Sun Sheng and Li K'uei go out to get their old mothers. On his journey, Li K'uei kills a false robber who pretends to be himself, but the impostor's wife escapes. On the return journey, Li K'uei's mother is killed by tigers. Li K'uei kills the tigers, but when he goes to receive the reward money, the impostor's wife identifies him, and he is captured. Another of the band frees him, however, and they return to Liang Shan P'o.

Shih Hsiu opens a meat shop with the help of official Yang Hsiung. Shih Hsiu discovers adultery between Yang Hsiung's wife and a priest. They kill the adulterers and escape. Later, they fall in with a thief, Shih Ch'ien, who causes a row and is captured in the village of Chu. In Liang Shan P'o, the robbers plan warfare against the Chu village; the others are, at last, victorious. Li K'uei, ignoring a pact between the robbers and the Hu village, kills all the members of the Hu household except the female warrior, the Ten-Foot Green Snake, who had previously been captured by the robbers. Later, she joins the robbers and marries Wang the Dwarf Tiger.

Robber catcher Lei Heng, after killing a courtesan, is allowed to escape to Liang Shan P'o by robber catcher Chu T'ung, who is, consequently, exiled. He pleases the magistrate, however, who wants Chu T'ung to look after his little son. By killing the little boy, the robbers force Chu T'ung to join them.

Li K'uei and Ch'ai Chin go to right a wrong; Ch'ai Chin is captured, and the robbers attempting to free him are repelled by their enemies' magic. Kung Sun Sheng, now a hermit, is summoned; his magic finally enables the robbers to overcome the enemy and free Ch'ai Chin.

A fresh advance planned by Commander Kao against the robbers results in many useful additions to Liang Shan P'o when enemy leaders are captured and persuaded to change allegiance. The robbers of Double Dragon, Peach Blossom, and Little Hua mountains, after some difficulties of capture and escape, join those at Liang Shan P'o.

A stolen horse intended for Sung Chiang has been stolen again by the Chun family. Instructor Shi Wen Kung, who now possesses the horse, boasts that he will destroy the robbers. While leading his men, Chief Ch'ao Kai is mortally wounded. Before he dies, he asks that whoever captures Shi Wen Kung be named the new chief. A long period of mourning follows.

Rich and respected Lu Chun I is enticed to Liang Shan P'o in the hope that he will join them. Returning, he is arrested and imprisoned as a robber. His steward, now in possession of his wife and goods, plots to have Lu Chun I killed. Many events follow, including the near death of Sung Chiang, but finally the city is taken. The prisoners are freed and the adulterers killed. Lu Chun I refuses Sung Chiang's offer to make him the chief.

The robbers capture additional soldiers sent against them and add many of the leaders to their ranks. Ch'ao Kai's death is finally avenged in the conquest of the Chun family and of Shi Wen Kung, whose actual captor is Lu Chun I, who still refuses to become the chief. Since all the robbers wish Sung Chiang to remain the leader, he prepares a test. He and Lu Chun I each lead a group against one of the two cities remaining to be taken. The first to take his city will be the chief. After some reverses, Sung Chiang is successful. He then goes to the aid of Lu Chun I, who has been twice vanquished by warrior Chang Ch'ing. This general, finally overcome, is persuaded to join the outlaws. Sung Chiang receives a heavenly message in the form of a miraculous stone tablet that lists all thirty-six greater and seventy-two lesser chieftains who make up the robber band. All swear undying loyalty, wishing to be united forever, life after life.

Critical Evaluation:

The stories that make up the plot of *All Men Are Brothers* originated many years before the novel as a whole was composed and probably have some basis in fact. There are many more versions of this novel than of other Chinese novels. This may be the result of the vastness of its scope and characterization, or the suitability of the novel to shorter versions. The translation of the shortest version runs to more than twelve hundred eventful pages. One hundred eight named chieftains form the band at the close of the book. The plot outline given above conveys only a little of the extraordinary bloodthirstiness of these "good fellows," who slaughter entire households of their enemies, who occasionally indulge in cannibalism, and whose reasons for becoming outlaws are not always noble. The characters, however, are vividly portrayed, the story is always interesting, and all is presented with the greatest realism and vigor. Long attributed to Shi Naian, the novel, many scholars claim, may be the work of Luo Guanzhong or of another author whose identity is unknown.

All Men Are Brothers was translated into English in 1933 by noted author Pearl S. Buck. Buck, the daughter of American missionaries and the wife of a missionary, was familiar with the Chinese people and culture. Buck titled her translation *All Men Are Brothers* because she thought the literal translation of the title ("water margin novel") was too remote for the sensibilities of Western readers. Her title comes from the *Analects* of Confucius and is intended to capture the novel's human spirit.

Readers may wish to distinguish individual bandits from others by means of the vividness of their characterizations and the uniqueness of their stories, but readers should not expect to keep the identities of the myriad bandits straight, beyond some exceptional personalities and incidents. Perhaps not every leader of the bandit gang is meant to be identifiable; the text, unlike the average Western novel, contains many inconsistencies, errors, and improbabilities. For example, none of the more than one hundred chieftains dies in the numerous fights and battles before the assembly at the end.

Perhaps, to Western sensibilities, these imperfections flaw the novel as a conscious literary creation. Given the early date of this novel, and the fact that it is probably a compilation of the work of multiple storytellers, weaving fiction in and out of some probable historical events, complications, errors, and improbabilities are to be expected. Also, Chinese readers have exhibited tolerance for error, incongruity, implausibility, and lack of completeness, especially when vitality, energy, spirit, and underlying psychological truthfulness are as evident as they are in *All Men Are Brothers*. The truth of a Chinese novel lies more in its insight into and sympathy with its characters than in its crafted, careful exposition. Portraying a world of emotions, sensibilities, feelings, and actions is often, to the Chinese reader, in opposition to, or subtly at odds with, a strictly factual, totally explainable, plausible world.

Broad generalizations are often used to discuss this complicated, highly episodic, and well-peopled novel, but few generalizations can be accurate for the novel as a whole, beyond that of a compendium of Robin Hood-like, best-loved bandit stories, renowned in Chinese literature for their variety, inventiveness, dramatic surprise, and knowledge of human nature. Even these generalizations are not always applicable to the text: The bandits often have little socially redeeming value, help only themselves, and often are unnecessarily violent.

Despite the fact that the novel was probably composed after a period of storytelling, its incidents and moods are surprisingly consistent and uniform in narrative structure. They are also almost always captivating, enlivening, thrilling, adventurous, spontaneous, and varied, with much of the appeal of the unseen endings of modern Western mystery stories.

Seen at various times as a textbook for outlaws and an actual sourcebook for the nicknames of real bandits, it has also been seen by some as a political metaphor for the actions of Chinese Communists after 1949 and by others as a glorification of peasant revolutionaries. It could be argued that nearly any use or misuse could be made of a novel so large and various as *All Men Are Brothers*. This work, however, has a unique popularity in Chinese literature, transcending use or even explanation of a band of bandits who see themselves as mostly generous-spirited but who have been forced by the oppressions of life and government into banditry and outlaw life and now glorify a marginal life in the boundaries of the safe swamps that they make their hideout, headquarters, and refuge. That so much life, liveliness, inventive incident, and devilish and repugnant charm should issue from the least likely, and perhaps least deserving, of characters is one of the great unexplainable fascinations of this highly popular novel.

"Critical Evaluation" by Jack Finefrock

Further Reading

Buck, Pearl S. *The Chinese Novel*. New York: John Day, 1939. Buck's 1938 Nobel Prize lecture discusses the vividness of characterization in *All Men Are Brothers*, the folk mind, and the freedom and flexibility of the Chinese novel. Includes discussion of Buck's philosophy of translation and a brief examination of the instincts of Chinese fiction.

Hsia, C. T. *The Classic Chinese Novel: A Critical Introduction*. 1968. Reprint. Ithaca, N.Y.: East Asia Program, Cornell University, 1996. Discusses the importance of Shi Naian's book as one of six major Chinese novels. Provides general discussion and excellent commentary on the novel, with well-selected quotations from the text.

Irwin, Richard Gregg. *The Evolution of a Chinese Novel: "Shui-hu chuan."* Cambridge, Mass.: Harvard University Press, 1953. Discusses the novel in its most complete form and in shorter forms and translations. The conclusion offers helpful chapter-by-chapter plot summaries.

McGreal, Ian P., ed. *Great Literature of the Eastern World: The Major Works of Prose, Poetry, and Drama from China, India, Japan, Korea, and the Middle East*. New York: HarperCollins, 1996. Chapter titled "*The Water Margin*" discusses Shi Naian's life and the major themes of his novel. Provides a critical evaluation of the novel as well as bibliographies of Shi Naian's works in English translation and of secondary sources about him.

Plaks, Andrew H. *The Four Masterworks of the Ming Novel*. Princeton, N.J.: Princeton University Press, 1987. Contains a chapter on the deflation of heroism in *All Men Are Brothers*. Argues that the models in the novel can serve for serious historical writing, although the characters are largely products of the imagination and not true historical figures.

Rolston, David L., ed. *How to Read the Chinese Novel*. Princeton, N.J.: Princeton University Press, 1990. Collection of essays provides a good general introduction to Chinese fiction criticism. Includes a chapter on how to read *All Men Are Brothers*.

Wang, Jing. *The Story of Stone: Intertextuality, Ancient Chinese Stone Lore, and the Stone Symbolism in "Dream of the Red Chamber," "Water Margin," and "The Journey to the West."* Durham, N.C.: Duke University Press, 1992. Presents a thorough discussion of the stone symbolism in *All Men Are Brothers* (translated here as *Water Margin*) and the relationship of this symbolism to intertextuality, myth, and religion.

All My Sons

Author: Arthur Miller (1915-2005)
First produced: 1947; first published, 1947
Type of work: Drama
Type of plot: Psychological realism
Time of plot: Mid-twentieth century
Locale: An American town

Principal characters:
JOE KELLER, a middle-aged businessman
KATE, his wife
CHRIS, their son
ANN DEEVER, a former neighbor
GEORGE, her brother

The Story:

The night Ann Deever returns to her old neighborhood to visit Chris Keller and his family, a tree in their backyard blows over in a storm. The tree was planted as a memorial to the older Keller son, Larry, a fighter pilot who was lost in World War II. The morning after the storm, family members and neighbors gather in the yard to chat, to read the newspaper, and to discuss Ann's return.

Ann's father, who was Joe Keller's partner in a wartime business, is in the penitentiary for having allowed cracked cylinder heads to be shipped, which caused the deaths of twenty-one pilots. (Joe was jailed, too, but was later exonerated for his part in the incident.) After the neighbors leave and while Ann is still inside the Keller house eating breakfast, Joe and Chris—a father and grown son who obviously admire each other—discuss Larry's tree falling and the effect it will have on Kate, the mother. Chris also tells his father that he asked Ann to visit because he wants to ask her to marry him; Joe responds that his mother will not like the news because she still thinks of Ann as Larry's girl. Chris explains that if he is to stay with the family business, he will need his father's support in convincing Kate that Larry is not coming back from the war and that Ann and he have the right to be happy.

When she enters the backyard, Kate tries to downplay the significance of Larry's destroyed tree, but she notes the coincidence of Ann's return. She reminds the two men that she is sure Larry is not dead and that Ann must share that sentiment. Chris tries to reason with her, but she insists that it is possible that Larry is still alive. She mentions that a neighbor is working out Larry's horoscope to establish whether or not Larry's plane crash could have occurred on one of Larry's "lucky" days.

Once Ann joins the Keller family in the yard, the talk turns to old times and ultimately to Larry. Ann makes it clear that she is not waiting for Larry, but Kate tells her that she should listen to her heart, "because certain things have to be, and certain things can never be." Their talk also turns to Ann's father in prison, and Ann reveals that her sympathy for him came to an end once she heard of Larry's crash. Joe explains that Steve—Ann's father—is not a bad man, just the type of weak man who buckles under pressure. Joe goes on to say that in spite of Steve's claim that he, Joe, approved the damaged shipment, he would be willing to let Steve come back to the business, not as a partner but as a worker. Ann marvels at Joe's magnanimity, and Chris agrees that he is "a great guy."

After the group makes plans to go out for a celebratory dinner, Chris and Ann talk seriously. Chris explains his feelings for her, and Ann assures him that she wants to marry him. Chris also confides his guilt in having survived the war, explaining that in combat he realized his responsibility for others. He wonders whether there is any meaning to all the suffering and destruction and whether his actions and participation in his father's business since the war are admirable or self-serving.

Ann's brother George calls after having visited their father in prison, and he announces that he needs to see the Kellers. He does not say why, and Joe begins to worry that he might want to stir up old trouble. In anticipation of George's return, Kate makes his favorite grape drink and tells her husband: "Be smart now, Joe. The boy is coming. Be smart."

Ann challenges Chris's complete acceptance of his father's innocence, and Chris asks: "Do you think I could forgive him if he'd done that thing?" Later that afternoon, George arrives. He tells Chris and Ann that his father charged Joe with having given him the go-ahead to ship the defective cylinder heads and with lying about his role in the crime when he claimed to have been home, sick in bed.

Chris and Ann are able to calm George, and once Kate greets him and reminds him of all the good times in the old neighborhood, George accepts the Kellers' dinner invitation. Joe appears in the backyard and greets George, and eventually the conversation turns to Joe's remarkable good health. Kate offhandedly mentions that he has not been sick a day in his life. Joe interjects with a reminder that he had the flu during the war, but George catches the Kellers in the discrepancy and he openly charges Joe with having let his father take the blame.

George storms out, and Chris confronts Joe, asking him what he did with the 120 cracked engine heads. Joe explains that a slowdown in production would have been costly for the business and that he let the shipment go, but he did not think that the defective parts would be installed. He concludes by saying that he did it for Chris. Chris yells back at him and pounds on his father's chest before he leaves.

At two o'clock the following morning, Kate and Joe discuss the situation and wonder what their son will do with their secret. Ann enters the backyard where they sit and says that she will do nothing about Joe but that Kate must accept that Larry is dead so that she and Chris can marry. Kate balks and Joe goes into the house. Ann produces a letter from Larry written on the day he crashed, in which he tells of knowing about his father's part in the shipment of defective engine parts and that it is his intention to crash his plane.

When Chris returns, he announces that he is going to leave home and asks his parents what they are going to do to make the situation right. Joe, still unable to comprehend, asks why he is considered "bad," to which Chris responds, "you're no worse than most men but I thought you were better. I never saw you as a man. I saw you as my father."

Chris reads Larry's letter aloud to his father and asks him if he understands his moral obligation. Just before going back into the house, Joe haltingly admits that the deaths of the twenty-one pilots are his responsibility: "they were all my sons." A few minutes later, inside the house, Joe shoots himself.

Critical Evaluation:

Regarded by critics as Arthur Miller's first successful play, *All My Sons* presents a narrow slice of American middle-class life. The play's context is limited: A manufacturer sells defective parts to the military and then covers up his crime by forcing his partner to take the blame. The ensuing situation, however, is where the scope of the play enlarges, culminating in the moment when the American Everyman must take a moral stand.

The drama's spatial confines underscore the theme of the play. The Kellers' backyard is enclosed by hedges and arbors and offers only a glimpse into the adjoining neighbors' yards. The focus is on the individual family and its moral limitations. While the story's premise is specific, the everyday, down-home setting of a backyard in a middle-class neighborhood in a nameless American town offers the audience a common ground of experience.

A major theme of *All My Sons* is that of responsibility. Before the play's action begins, Joe Keller ducked moral responsibility by allowing cracked cylinder heads to be shipped out of his factory. He covers up and blames his partner, but he is able to justify his actions as a consequence of his obligation to his family. At the end of the play, he accepts responsibility for his crime only after his dead son Larry's letter indicts him.

Kate Keller, too, bears responsibility for the cover-up, but she participates in it primarily as a way to keep Larry alive in her mind. If she acknowledges Joe's guilt, she will have to acknowledge that Larry crashed. Kate represents the intuitive and the irrational. Her responsibility to her family defies—and defines—moral obligation.

The son Chris is the idealist who must come to grips with his parents' human weaknesses. It can be said that in idolizing his father he sets up a barrier to the truth and to exploring the notion of his father's guilt, a possibility that must have occurred to him. Chris feels a larger responsibility. Where Joe has his family in mind, Chris sees something bigger than family. It is Chris's responsibility to make his father see that larger arena. In doing so, he brings about his father's ultimate acceptance of responsibility and his father's decision to take his own life in expiation for his crime.

All My Sons also addresses the material aspect of the American Dream and its effects on the soul. When Joe says that he acted as he did for Chris and his family, he represents the tension between the need to succeed materially and the responsibility of behaving ethically. Because the American economy flourished as a result of World War II, a sense of guilt could be overpowering. Chris lives this tension, and by the end of the play Joe, too, is forced to confront it. The sentiments of the play are rooted in a prewar era, but the emotional power defines the angst of postwar American society.

All My Sons, which prepares the way for Miller's masterpiece, *Death of a Salesman* (1949), continues a tradition in twentieth century American drama that was established by Eugene O'Neill in *Ah, Wilderness!* (1933) and *Long Day's Journey into Night* (1956), and by Thornton Wilder in *Our Town* (1938). In these plays, as in Miller's *All My Sons*, the authors explore the complex dynamic between individual responsibility and family relationships.

Douglas A. Jones

Further Reading

Abbotson, Susan C. W. *Critical Companion to Arthur Miller: A Literary Reference to His Life and Work.* New York: Facts On File, 2007. Includes a biography and dictionary-style entries about Miller's works and related subjects, such as the concepts, people, places, and genres in his plays. The entries about his works provide synopses, critical commentary, initial reviews, and performance histories.

Bigsby, Christopher. *Arthur Miller: A Critical Study.* New York: Cambridge University Press, 2005. Bigsby, who has written extensively about Miller, provides in-depth examinations of all of Miller's work, including a chapter on *All My Sons.*

Bloom, Harold, ed. *Arthur Miller.* New ed. New York: Bloom's Literary Criticism, 2007. Collection of critical essays about Miller's work, including "*All My Sons* and Paternal Authority" by James A. Robinson.

Carson, Neil. *Arthur Miller.* 2d ed. New York: Palgrave Macmillan, 2008. Provides critical analyses of all of Miller's work, including a chapter on *All My Sons.*

Huftel, Sheila. *Arthur Miller: The Burning Glass.* New York: Citadel Press, 1965. The chapter dedicated to *All My Sons* provides a significant overview of the play along with a careful analysis of the main and peripheral characters. The influence of Henrik Ibsen, the Norwegian dramatist, on Miller is discussed, as is *All My Sons* in relation to Miller's adaptation of Ibsen's play *An Enemy of the People* (1882).

Mason, Jeffrey D. *Stone Tower: The Political Theater of Arthur Miller.* Ann Arbor: University of Michigan Press, 2008. Argues that Miller is essentially a political playwright and that *All My Sons* examines political issues in personal terms.

Miller, Arthur. Introduction to *Arthur Miller's Collected*

Plays. New York: Viking Press, 1957-1981. Miller devotes many pages to *All My Sons*, explaining that it is a social play of relationship and responsibility. He discusses the inspiration for the drama and gives context for the play's underlying philosophies.

Stambusky, Alan A. "Arthur Miller: Aristotelian Canons in the Twentieth Century Drama." In *Modern American Drama: Essays in Criticism*, edited by William E. Taylor. DeLand, Fla.: Everett/Edwards, 1968. The first part of this chapter discusses classical tragedy and Miller's adherence to the literary archetype. Stambusky argues that *All My Sons* falls short of tragedy in plot development, dialogue, and characterization.

Wood, E. R. Introduction to *All My Sons*, by Arthur Miller. London: Heinemann, 1971. Probes the relationship between commerce and war. Explicates the play's dramatic qualities and the three main characters' motivations and actions.

All Quiet on the Western Front

Author: Erich Maria Remarque (1898-1970)
First published: Im Westen nichts Neues, 1928, serial; 1929, book (English translation, 1929)
Type of work: Novel
Type of plot: Historical realism
Time of plot: World War I
Locale: France and Germany

Principal characters:
PAUL BÄUMER, a young German soldier
ALBERT KROPP,
MÜLLER, and
FRANZ KEMMERICH, his comrades and former classmates
TJADEN,
HAIE WESTHUS, and
DETERING, German soldiers
STANISLAUS KATCZINSKY, the group's leader
HIMMELSTOSS, a training instructor
KANTOREK, a teacher of literature
GÉRARD DUVAL, a French soldier

The Story:

Paul Bäumer is a young enlisted soldier. His classmates in school had been cajoled into joining the service by a teacher. Classmate Josef Behm, who had resisted enlistment, ironically is the first to die. For Bäumer, resources in the field are more important than people. With his comrades, he has access to plentiful food because those soldiers for whom the food was meant are now either in the hospital, wounded in combat, or in mass graves. The situation is worth rejoicing over.

World War I is characterized by trench warfare. Soldiers hold their own lines while periodically attempting to take the trenches of the other side or to avoid having their own trenches taken. Franz Kemmerich dies of gangrene after his leg is removed. His soft boots go to Müller, who had eyed them even before Kemmerich died. Müller is shot in the belly by a tracer bullet, and his boots go to Bäumer, who, in turn, promises them to Tjaden if he dies before him. The boots matter, and the death of individuals does not.

Kantorek, the comrades' former literature teacher and now their comrade, refers to Bäumer's generation as the iron youth; reality consists of death and suffering. Schoolbooks report events at a political level, where emperors need to make a name for themselves by an impressive war or two and where the ideals of a country must seek fulfillment. Reality, on the other hand, dehumanizes and trivializes, and turns humans into hospital and medical classifications: belly-shot cases; spinal injuries; head shots; amputees; jaw-shot cases; gas diseases; shots into noses, ears, and necks; blindness injuries; lung shots; hip injuries; joint shots; kidney hits; testicle shots; belly hits; dripping puss; open intestines; and the bomb craters within the psyches of soldiers.

Bäumer is on furlough, and an acquaintance points out to him that he fails to see the larger connections. The acquaintance advises Bäumer to stop the trench warfare, to kick out the fellows on the other side, and to get this thing over with. Bäumer's mother's concern is with the sufficient supply of food to the soldiers. His father wants to hear heroic tales. These requests all lead to Bäumer's alienation from life at home. He wonders whether he should tell the folks back home about finding gassed enemy soldiers in their trenches, blue-faced and poses betraying how they looked before the gas extinguished their lives. Home front and war front present such stark contrasts that Bäumer cannot integrate them into one experience. As the war's madness increases in reality, home fades into alienation for Bäumer.

An older comrade, Detering, experiences this cognitive dissonance differently. Hearing that cherries are ripe, this farmer simply leaves the battlefield. The reality of home wins over the reality of battle. He is not deceptive, for he does not escape to another country; he simply attempts to go to his home in Germany. He runs into military police and—because judges at courts-martial do not grasp such cognitive dissonances—will suffer execution, in all probability.

Another key experience is the enemy. After his furlough, Bäumer spends some time guarding Russian POWs. He reflects on this experience, thinking how someone's order had made the Russians his enemies; another order could turn them into friends. He sees the Russians as people, in a vision that would make wars impossible.

Having just returned from furlough, Bäumer volunteers to reconnoiter enemy territory. Lost in the dark and unclear about the proper directions, he ducks into a bomb crater. With shots and the sounds of attacking enemy troops, he cannot move, and he hopes to be rescued by his own side's counterattack. However, the German side does not advance, and an enemy soldier jumps into the bomb crater. Bäumer had anticipated this event and had gone through the procedures several times in his mind: Stab the soldier quickly, effectively, and with little noise. He proceeds to enact that scenario successfully, but he then faces a dying French soldier, whom he tries to succor—without success. The young soldier dies.

Bäumer sees the soldier's identification and learns that he is Gérard Duval, typesetter. Bäumer swears that, for the sake of that young person from the other side, he will return to tell all about the sheer madness of war. This resolution fades when he returns to his own side later.

No soldier is able to make sense of the war as a rational enterprise, and most are convinced that someone is getting wealthy by it. However, the soldiers do not know where to place agency for the war; even the visiting emperor seems caught in the chain of events, unable to control them. Corporal Himmelstoss's name, broken down, is rather telling, evoking some sense to the acts of war: *Stoss* means "thrust," something the enemy might engage in. *Gegenstoss* means "counterthrust," something one might engage in when one responds to an enemy's thrust. *Himmelstoss* means "heaven thrust."

The soldiers' superior, Stanislaus "Kat" Katczinsky, and Bäumer are in the hospital. They hear a man singing hymns until his death rattle shuts him up—so much for self-administered extreme unction. The two go to a Catholic hospital, Kat because he is feverish and Bäumer because he simulates fever so the two can remain together. Early in the morning, the nuns pray in the hallway, leaving the doors open to the sickrooms. The soldiers scream for closed doors, for stopping the prayers, and for permission to continue sleeping. Bäumer finally pitches a bottle into the hallway, splintering the glass into hundreds of shards. This stops the prayers; it also starts an inquiry into the identity of the culprit. Josef Hamacher takes the blame because, he says, he has a *Jagdschein* (a hunting license—a certificate of mental illness). With such a diagnosis, he claims to be able to do anything without repercussion.

Other episodes show the clash of values in an insane world. Berger, a soldier, seeks to euthanize an injured dog. Berger dies in the attempt. Young recruits appear at the front to die; a single pilot shoots a couple of battalions of these young soldiers, unprepared as the youth are. Soldiers are suffering bloody colic while factory owners in Germany become wealthier.

The war becomes increasingly one-sided as German soldiers are outgunned and overpowered by newly arriving tanks. They also are outdone by fresh, well-fed U.S. and British troops and are hunted by a great number of enemy planes, which outnumber German planes five to one.

Large-scale enmities are lost in the small-scale use of people. Officers have brothels to keep them happy; soldiers find French women who are so hungry that they sell sex for food. Civilization and values break down ubiquitously, but these breakdowns define normalcy. Mittelstaedt, the trainer of conscripted Kantorek, the literature teacher, delights in abusing Kantorek to get even for in-school insults. Himmelstoss is abusive as a training sergeant because his abuse ensures that he will not be sent to frontline duty—until he manages to have the son of a political leader among his recruits, a recruit who ensures that Himmelstoss is sent to the front. There, he runs into Bäumer and his comrades, who are all itching to get even with Himmelstoss by abusing him in various ways.

Eventually, Bäumer's classmates, all of his comrades, are all killed, and only he remains. Bäumer, too, soon dies. His body is on the ground, appearing to sleep, but Bäumer is dead. It appears that he had not tortured himself for very long. His face has a collected expression as though he is almost content with the way things had turned out. He had finally died, as much from despair as from gunshot. He had died on a day when military reports had indicated that on the western front all is quiet, that there is "nothing new" (*nichts neues*) to report. Another death is not extraordinary.

Critical Evaluation:

Erich Maria Remarque's narrative in *All Quiet on the Western Front* is written entirely in the present tense, which conveys urgency and immediacy. The reader does not know why the war is being fought because only Paul Bäumer's thoughts are known; his is a particular perspective that is absent from schoolbooks and historical accounts. This perspective increases readers' compassionate understanding for the unfair situations faced by all soldiers on all sides of war.

The situation is augmented by propaganda. Some historical accounts of the war claim that German soldiers had skewered and eaten Belgian babies. Propagandists can do no better than pitch people against each other with the myth that they are seeking each other's destruction. Remarque has his main character make sense of his experiences by working through the episodes of his life to attempt to create order from the experiential chaos. The fundamental immorality of war is the blatant use of people to achieve goals they themselves do not understand or identify with.

Propaganda evaporates under the onslaught of the stark reality in which the soldiers find themselves. At one point, Bäumer wonders how a shorn head can become more important than four volumes of philosopher Arthur Schopenhauer's work, a significant allusion if one recalls that Schopenhauer had considered the spirit of the world divided against itself and preying upon itself in war. For Schopenhauer, the world itself is mad with wars.

Remarque's novel takes a very important place in antiwar literature that includes work by Wilfred Owen, Siegfried Sassoon, Kurt Vonnegut, Thomas Hardy, Wolfgang Borchert, and Ken Saro-Wiwa. In addition, *All Quiet on the Western Front* has been adapted into an American film of the same name.

Revised by Reinhold Schlieper

Further Reading

Barker, Christine R., and R. W. Last. *Erich Maria Remarque*. New York: Barnes & Noble, 1979. An accessible biography, with a great deal of material that is relevant to *All Quiet on the Western Front*. Good, brief coverage of the novel's popular and scholarly reception.

Bloom, Harold, ed. *Erich Maria Remarque's "All Quiet on the Western Front."* Philadelphia: Chelsea House, 2001. Collection of essays about the novel, including discussions of Remarque and other men of feeling, the critical reception of the novel, and comparisons of Remarque's book with other war novels.

Firda, Richard Arthur. *"All Quiet on the Western Front": Literary Analysis and Cultural Context*. New York: Twayne, 1993. Contains much biographical information, as well as solid discussion of the novel. Includes a useful annotated bibliography.

Gordon, Haim. *Heroism and Friendship in the Novels of Erich Maria Remarque*. New York: Peter Lang, 2003. Focuses on Remarque's depiction of ordinary people who are capable of performing acts of heroism and of establishing genuine friendships in even the harshest of circumstances. Includes a bibliography and references.

Gutiérrez, Peter. *The Story Behind Erich Maria Remarque's "All Quiet on the Western Front."* Chicago: Heinemann Library, 2007. This helpful guide to Remarque's famous novel is written especially for younger readers. Part of the History in Literature series.

Murdoch, Brian. *The Novels of Erich Maria Remarque: Sparks of Life*. Rochester, N.Y.: Camden House, 2006. Examines Remarque's entire body of writing, including his lesser-known novels, paying attention to recurring themes and motifs. Portrays Remarque as an artist, shedding light on his personal life and his reputation as a playboy.

Pfeiler, Wilhelm K. *War and the German Mind: The Testimony of Men of Fiction Who Fought at the Front*. 1941. Reprint. New York: AMS Press, 1966. An excellent, if dated, study of German World War I novels. The chapter on *All Quiet on the Western Front* treats the novel in the context of contemporary war novels. Especially good on political background and reception.

Taylor, Harley U., Jr. *Erich Maria Remarque: A Literary and Film Biography*. New York: Peter Lang, 1989. Four brief chapters supply a basic, journalistic treatment of the novel and the fascinating story of the 1930 American film based on it. Contains a useful chronology.

Tims, Hilton. *Erich Maria Remarque: The Last Romantic*. New York: Carroll & Graf, 2003. A biography that focuses primarily on the events of Remarque's life, including his many relationships with women. Contains notes and references, a bibliography, and an index.

Wagener, Hans. *Understanding Eric Maria Remarque*. Columbia: University of South Carolina Press, 1991. Treats all of Remarque's works, with one chapter devoted to a thorough analysis of *All Quiet on the Western Front*. A basic biographically and historically grounded presentation.

All That Fall

Author: Samuel Beckett (1906-1989)
First produced: 1957, radio play; first published, 1957
Type of work: Drama
Type of plot: Absurdist
Time of plot: Twentieth century
Locale: County Dublin, Ireland

Principal characters:
MADDY ROONEY, a woman in her seventies
DAN ROONEY, Maddy's husband
MISS FLITE, a lady in her thirties

The Story:

It is a fine summer Saturday in Boghill, a community in rural Ireland. In most respects, it is an ordinary day. Trains are expected to run on time. Things have remained unchanged in the enigmatic home of the widow that Maddy Rooney passed on her way to the railroad station to meet her husband Dan, who is returning at midday from work. This is a time when it is customary to work a five-and-a-half-day week. Everything that Maddy learned about the condition of the spouses and dependents of those she encounters on her walk to the station remains, painfully, unchanged.

Yet, in other respects, it is by no means an ordinary day. One difference is that a race is to be held locally. Although this event is not greeted with a great deal of exuberance by Mrs. Rooney and the majority of the other characters, including Mr. Slocum, the clerk of the course, it does alleviate the boredom of the station-hand, Tommy. Each of the old, familiar acquaintances Mrs. Rooney meets in the course of her walk to the station offers to give her a helping hand. Although well meant, these offers vary only in the degree of their preposterousness. Today, as on every other day, it is enough for Mrs. Rooney to try to keep her feet on the ground. Therefore, in response to the offers of assistance, she insists on her desire to make every effort to maintain her elementary means of locomotion. The offers range from a ride on Christy's manure cart to a ride in Mr. Slocum's car. Mrs. Rooney accepts the latter offer, but its results prove as humiliating as if she had taken the former. Her walk to the station, however, is not taken up by questions of transportation alone. On her way, Mrs. Rooney muses in a fashion that is alternately desultory and fretful about various experiences and perceptions. The most prominent of these is the death of her daughter Minnie.

Her journey does not quite end once she arrives at the station. She also needs assistance to climb the stairs to the platform. It is when she asks for help, however, that it turns out not to be readily forthcoming. Eventually, Miss Flite helps her. Although she suspected while she made her way to the station that something is amiss, it is only when she gets there that her suspicions are confirmed. Her husband's train is delayed. Such a state of affairs is previously unknown. In due course, however, the train arrives, and Dan Rooney alights, accompanied by his guide, Jerry, a necessary presence because of Dan's blindness. The weather changes for the worse as the Rooneys make their way home, and the miserable conditions overshadow the conversation between husband and wife. Their conversation covers many topics, including Dan's thoughts on his retirement, particularly relevant as his birthday falls on this very day. Their homeward path takes them past the church at which they regularly worship. Here they note with uncharacteristic amusement the text for Sunday's sermon: "The Lord upholdeth all that fall and raiseth up all those that be bowed down."

As they walk along, Maddy is also quite interested to discover the cause of the train's delay, but Dan remains rather uncommunicative about that. Oddly, however, just as the stormiest interludes of their conversational exchanges seem to have passed, they are hailed by Jerry. He was sent after them by the stationmaster in order to return to Mr. Rooney something he dropped. It is a child's ball. To satisfy her curiosity about the late arrival of the train, Maddy asks Jerry if he can tell her anything. Jerry replies that the delay was caused by a child falling out of a carriage and under the wheels of the train. Nothing further is said, but the impression irresistibly remains that this accident is Mr. Rooney's doing, and that perhaps there is little difference in either his or his wife's mind that such an act is to be meaningfully differentiated from the early, and presumably unjustifiable, death of their daughter.

Critical Evaluation:

First broadcast by the British Broadcasting Corporation on January 13, 1957, *All That Fall* is Samuel Beckett's first and, arguably, most substantial radio play. Quite apart from the insights it provides into this controversial and significant author's overall output and imaginative vision, the play also represents a comparatively rare conjunction of an avant-garde artist and a mass medium. As such, it represents both a milestone in the history of radio drama—a literary form taken much more seriously in European artistic circles than in American—and in the diversification of Beckett's aesthetic range.

What ultimately gives the play substance is the same distinctive approach that distinguishes all this artist's works: the manner in which it challenges—and even satirizes—the medium through which it is being produced. Yet, on a superficial level, the play seems to be a departure for Beckett. Despite its unprepossessing name, the setting of Boghill bears a recognizable relationship to Foxrock, the community in county Dublin, Ireland, where Beckett grew up. This relationship is to some degree strengthened by the proximity of a racecourse in the play. Foxrock is quite close to the premier racing venue of Leopardstown. Although commentators have strongly discouraged neat and exclusive identifications of Beckett characters with real-life counterparts, Beckett's father did commute to the city by train. Protestantism looms large in a number of the characters' existences, including the Rooneys', and Beckett's background was Protestant.

Another distinctive feature of *All That Fall* is that it is an uncharacteristically populist work for Beckett. While the range of characters is comparatively narrow, it suggests a more common social world and the roles, mannerisms, and equipment used in order to represent oneself within it. These roles—the stationmaster, the clerk of the racecourse, and so on—are clearly identified. Other nominally realistic features of the play include weather, sound effects, a superficially conventional sense of time, and a marked use of colloquial and idiomatic English as it is spoken in Ireland. Like all Beckett plays, *All That Fall* also appears to be structured in terms of the Aristotelian unities of time, place, and action.

At the same time, however, the play subverts these ostensibly reliable, and essentially commonplace, elements. The name of Boghill is an oxymoron. Two types of terrain are contained in it, each of which, in its own distinct and opposite way, makes forward movement difficult. While the name may indeed convey Irish resonances, its evocative relationship to the Rooneys' progress seems more to the imaginative point. This relationship may be further appreciated by considering the familiar Irish name Rooney, with its echoes of "ruin," which is commonly pronounced in Ireland as "rune." The second syllable of the Rooney name acts as a diminutive of those echoes, muffling them and diminishing them lest they provide too facile an interpretative opening. These minor facets of the work both are and are not what they seem. Perhaps the most significant instance of this is the play's Christian dimension. While the Rooneys may attend church, and while Maddy might be subjected to various parodic instances of Good Samaritanism on her way to the station, their acquaintance with the Christian message may be more a matter of habit than of profundity, as their blasphemous laughter at the phrase from the Psalms that gives the play its name suggests.

The play's minor characters act as a chorus which articulates the opposite of the dual perspective embodied by the Rooneys. Unlike the chorus in Greek tragic drama, however, these characters do not act in concert, nor are they intended to function as mediators between action and audience. On the contrary, the state of privileged knowledge that such functioning implies is the very opposite of the quality of consciousness embodied by a Christy or a Mr. Slocum. Each of the minor characters represents a point on a scale of ineffectuality, the highest point of which is denoted by Maddy and Dan. This highest point may also, without contradiction, be termed the lowest point. It is the point of maximum pain, denoted by Maddy in her inability to confine her discourse to mundane pleasantries and connoted by Dan in his blindness. Compared to them, the other characters are nothing if not one-dimensional. While a case may be made for the Aristotelian unities being observed, the fact that the most important action—the death of the child—takes place outside the dramatic framework of the play seriously compromises any such case. It is not clear what kind of action the death is, since Dan's involvement with it is, to say the least, obscure. The time of the accident is not clear. The place of the accident is unfixed in two senses: The train is moving, and the event has to be viewed in the context of that emptiness in which all falls take place.

Rather than develop a plot line in which variously conflicting interests collide and are resolved, the conflict of *All That Fall* exists between the irreconcilable duality of its various elements. The nature of this duality extends to the conditions under which the play is produced, and the work exploits many of the apparent contradictory production values of radio drama. Thus, for example, the play places an emphasis on sensory experience—particularly hearing and seeing—which is unusual for a Beckett drama. Paradoxically, the naturalistic detail of the sensory material evokes for the audience an imaginary landscape. This paradox in turn draws attention to the gap that exists between audience and performance, a gap that is obviously endemic to radio plays. The play's formal and aesthetic reality is based on what transpires in the emptiness between the radio and the listener. The integrity of that emptiness is what the play addresses.

Despite the scrupulous integration of its formal elements, *All That Fall* is far from being a hollow organizational exercise. Like all of Beckett's works, the formal order serves ultimately to crystallize that which cannot be ordered. Dan's mathematical summation of his work and days cannot allay the uncertainty of whether he will be alive when Jerry comes to fetch him for another week's work. Open as Maddy is to her own awareness of the vicissitudes of existence, she cannot hear that the music coming from the widow's house—the "Death and the Maiden" quartet by Franz Schubert—has themes that are unnervingly close to her own home. The discrepant representation of Christian ideas in the play does not reduce the relevance of such motifs as pilgrim and Via Dolorosa. As though to demonstrate that form is finally negated by its own requirements, the two deaths that underlie the play's pedestrian and repetitive action—those of Minnie and of the child—take place outside the course of the day.

"Critical Evaluation" by George O'Brien

Further Reading

Bair, Deirdre. *Samuel Beckett: A Biography.* 1978. Reprint. New York: Simon & Schuster, 1993. Although Beckett was often reluctant to talk about himself, he cooperated with Bair for this biography. It provides a full, helpful version of his life, and to know his life is to understand his art. The criticism of the specific texts is often limited, but Bair is very good at putting the work in conjunction with his very odd life.

Cronin, Anthony. *Samuel Beckett: The Last Modernist.* London: HarperCollins, 1996. A fully documented and detailed biography of Beckett, describing his involvement in the Paris literary scene, his response to winning the Nobel Prize, and his overall literary career.

Fletcher, John. *About Beckett: The Playwright and the Work.* London: Faber & Faber, 2003. Fletcher's introductory study explains why Beckett's plays are both significant and enduring, providing insights based upon his long-standing relationship with the playwright and his interviews with actors and directors.

Fletcher, John, and John Spurling. *Beckett the Playwright.* Rev. ed. New York: Hill and Wang, 1985. A helpful introductory study of all of Beckett's dramatic works, with a chapter on *All That Fall.* Discussion focuses on the work's motifs of love and loss and on the wit of its complicated verbal play.

Kenner, Hugh. *A Reader's Guide to Samuel Beckett.* London: Thames and Hudson, 1973. Kenner comments clearly and simply on the individual texts and is an essential companion for anyone determined to get Beckett to make some kind of sense. Beckett's work will never be completely clear, but with Kenner, it sometimes makes sense, if only for the moment, which is all Beckett wanted.

Knowlson, James. *Damned to Fame: The Life of Samuel Beckett.* New York: Simon & Schuster, 1996. Knowlson, Beckett's chosen biographer, provides a meticulously detailed book, containing much new material, as well as detailed notes and a bibliography.

McDonald, Rónán. *The Cambridge Introduction to Samuel Beckett.* New York: Cambridge University Press, 2006. Chapter 3 of this concise overview of Beckett's life and work includes a discussion of *All That Fall.*

McWhinnie, Donald. *The Art of Radio.* London: Faber & Faber, 1969. McWhinnie produced the first broadcast of *All That Fall.* In addition to his general thoughts about radio as an artistic medium, he provides detailed information regarding the play's production; of particular interest are the insights regarding the challenges of Beckett's script.

Worth, Katharine. *Samuel Beckett's Theatre: Life Journeys.* New York: Clarendon Press, 1999. A look at the production history and psychological aspects of Beckett's plays. Includes information about *All That Fall* and its adaptation for television.

Zilliacus, Clas. *Beckett and Broadcasting.* Abo, Finland: Abo Akademi, 1976. The definitive account of Beckett's artistic and professional involvement with radio and television. Beckett's thoughts about the various productions of his broadcast works are included. Detailed accounts of the productions are provided, including some illuminating commentary on the use of sound effects in *All That Fall.*

All the King's Men

Author: Robert Penn Warren (1905-1989)
First published: 1946
Type of work: Novel
Type of plot: Social realism
Time of plot: Late 1920's and early 1930's
Locale: Southern United States

Principal characters:
JACK BURDEN, a journalist and political lackey
WILLIE STARK, a political boss
SADIE BURKE, his mistress
ANNE STANTON, a social worker
ADAM STANTON, her brother
JUDGE IRWIN, unintimidated by Stark

The Story:

When Governor Willie Stark tries to intimidate old Judge Irwin of Burden's Landing, the judge stands firm against the demagogue's threats. As a result, Willie orders Jack Burden to find a scandal in the judge's past that could ruin the elderly man.

Jack met Willie back in 1922, when Willie, the county treasurer, and Lucy Stark, his schoolteacher wife, were fighting against a corrupt building contractor who was constructing the new schoolhouse. Sent by his newspaper, *The Chronicle*, to investigate, Jack found that both Willie and Lucy lost their jobs but were still fighting graft. Two years later, when the fire escape of the school collapsed during a fire drill, Willie became a hero.

He thereupon ran for governor in the Democratic primary race, in which there were two factions. Jack covered the campaign. Because it was expected to be a close race, someone from one side, that supporting Harrison, proposed that Willie be used as a dummy candidate to split one group of rural voters who supported MacMurfee. Tiny Duffy and others convinced Willie that he could save the state. By then, Willie was a lawyer and politically ambitious. Supporting him was Sadie Burke, a clever, energetic woman with political skill. Inadvertently she revealed Harrison's plan to Willie. Crushed at this news, Willie rallied and offered to campaign for MacMurfee, who was elected. Willie practiced law until 1930; he then ran for governor with the assistance of Sadie Burke, who became his mistress, and Tiny Duffy, who was Willie's political jackal.

Meanwhile, Jack quit his job on *The Chronicle*. Reared by a mother who remarried after Ellis Burden deserted her, Jack became a faithless, homeless cynic who practiced his profession without believing in its higher aims. He, in his youth, played with Anne and Adam Stanton, the children of the governor. Adam was now a famous surgeon, and Anne, still unmarried, was a welfare worker. Jack was in love with Anne, but time placed a barrier between him and the girl with whom he fell in love during the summer after he came home to Burden's Landing from college. He was twenty-one then, she seventeen. Even then, however, Jack's youthful cynicism damaged him in Anne's eyes. When Jack went to work for Governor Willie Stark, Jack's mother was deeply pained and Judge Irwin was disgusted, but Jack cared little for their opinions.

By 1933, Willie was on the verge of losing his wife, who could no longer tolerate her husband's political maneuvers and his treatment of their son, Tom. Willie assured Jack that Lucy knew nothing about Sadie Burke. Lucy remained with Willie through his reelection, in 1934, and then retired to her sister's farm. She appeared with Willie in public only for the sake of his reputation.

When Jack begins to dig into Judge Irwin's financial transactions during the time when he was attorney general under Governor Stanton, he learns that the government sued a power company for a large sum. The company bribed the attorney general by firing one of its men and giving the highly paid job to Irwin. Later, the man who was fired, Littlepaugh, committed suicide after writing the facts in a letter to his sister. Miss Littlepaugh tells Jack the story.

Willie Stark's six-million-dollar hospital project makes it necessary to use the scandal Jack uncovered. Willie tells Jack that he wants Adam Stanton to head the new hospital. It would, Jack knew, be a ridiculous offer to the aloof and unworldly young doctor, but he makes an effort to convince Adam to take the post. Adam flatly refuses. A few days later, Anne sends for Jack. She, too, wants Adam to take the position. Jack shows Anne the documents proving that Judge Irwin accepted a bribe and that Governor Stanton attempted to cover up for his friend. Knowing that Adam would want to protect his father's good name, Anne shows the evidence to him, after which he agrees to head the hospital.

Later, Jack wonders how Anne knew about the plans for the hospital, because neither he nor Adam told her. Jack's suspicions are confirmed when Sadie Burke, in a torrent of rage, tells him that Willie is betraying her. Jack knows then that Anne is the cause. Disillusioned, he packs a suitcase and drives to California. Once he completes the journey to the

West and back, Jack has his torment under control and goes back to work for Willie.

One of MacMurfee's men tries to bribe Adam to select a man named Larson as the builder of the medical center. Adam, outraged, decides to resign, whereupon Anne phones Jack for the first time since he learned of her affair with Willie. Anne and Jack decide to persuade Adam to sign a warrant against the man who tried to bribe him. Jack warns Anne, however, that as a witness she will be subject to public scrutiny of her relationship with Willie, but she says she does not care. Jack asks her why she is associating with Willie. She says that after learning about Governor Stanton's dishonesty in the past, she does not care what happens to her. Later, Jack persuades Adam not to bring suit.

After Willie's political enemy, MacMurfee, tries to blackmail him because of a scandal concerning Tom Stark, Willie orders Jack to use his knowledge to make Judge Irwin throw his weight against MacMurfee's blackmail attempt. When Jack goes to Burden's Landing to confront Judge Irwin with the evidence that he obtained from Miss Littlepaugh, the old man shoots himself. In the excitement following the suicide, Jack's mother tells him that he caused his father's death. Belatedly, Jack discovers the reason for Ellis Burden's desertion. In his will, Judge Irwin leaves his estate to his son, Jack Burden.

There seems to be only one way left to handle MacMurfee. Willie decides to give the building contract for the hospital to MacMurfee's man, Larson, who in turn will suppress the scandal about Tom. Duffy makes the arrangements. Tom is a football hero. One Saturday during a game, his neck is broken. Adam reports that Tom will remain paralyzed for life. When he hears this, Willie tells Duffy that the hospital deal is off. He breaks things off with Sadie Burke and Anne and turns back to Lucy.

Duffy, driven too far by Willie, telephones Adam and tells him that Anne is responsible for his appointment. Adam knows nothing of his sister's relationship with the governor. He goes to her apartment to denounce her. After that, in the hall of the state building, Adam shoots Willie and is killed immediately afterward by Willie's bodyguard.

Piece by piece, the tangled mess of Jack's life begins to take on new meaning. He separates himself from every particle of his past with the exception of two people: his mother, whose devotion to Judge Irwin over all the years reveals a new personality to Jack's eyes, and Anne, whom he marries.

Critical Evaluation:

One of the richest and most powerful of twentieth century American novels is Robert Penn Warren's *All the King's Men*. In its pages can be traced a multitude of fascinating subjects ranging from politics to religion, from sociology to philosophy. There is an equally wide scope to the thematic questions posed by the work. The novel's complexities arouse various responses in its readers. Some, for example, praise it as Christian, while others revile it as nihilistic on exactly the same grounds. The book is generally regarded as the masterpiece of a novelist who is also a respected poet, critic, and professor.

Warren, a Kentucky native, has a special affinity for the South, and much of his work suggests the traditions and problems of this region. *All the King's Men*, while exploring issues that are universal as well as regional, has an unmistakable southern flavor in areas other than mere setting. An immediate query regarding this Pulitzer Prize-winning book usually touches on the relationship of Willie Stark and Huey Long. Governor of Louisiana from 1928 to 1931, Long led a career that parallels what Warren designs for Stark, and Long presented a similarly powerful and paradoxical personality. The product of a poor background, Long became a lawyer at twenty-one after completing the three-year Tulane University course in eight months. Three years later, aggressive and determined, he sought and won the one state office open at his age, a seat on the Railroad Commission. An unorthodox champion of the little man, Long in his 1924 race for governor was unsuccessful when he tried to remain moderate on the Ku Klux Klan issue. His 1928 try for the office was a triumph, however, and at thirty-five, the outspoken country boy was a governor who almost single-handedly ruled the state. Using patronage as his lever, Long talked the legislature into a thirty-million-dollar bond issue to finance farm roads, hospitals, free schoolbooks, and other programs popular with the poor but infuriating to his opponents. Like Stark, Long soon found himself impeached and charged with bribery, plotting the murder of a senator, misusing state funds, and various other crimes, some of which this strange mixture of demagogue and selfless public servant no doubt had committed. However, his promises and threats kept Long in office after a sufficient number of senators signed a round robin promising not to convict him no matter what the evidence.

Long's career, which included the unprecedented move of becoming a U. S. senator while still serving as governor, and having plans to seek the presidency, was halted by assassination. In a 1935 scene almost re-created in *All the King's Men*, a man stepped from behind a pillar at the Capitol and shot once. Felled by sixty-one bullets from Long's bodyguards, the assassin, Dr. Carl A. Weiss, died within seconds. Thirty hours later, Long, the "Kingfish," was also dead. Weiss's motivations were never satisfactorily explained, but some claimed that he was angry because Long's maneuvering had cost his father a judgeship.

Despite the overwhelming similarities between Long and Stark, Warren denied having attempted merely to create a fictional counterpart of a political figure. He admitted, however, that the "line of thinking and feeling" in the book did evolve from the atmosphere of Louisiana he encountered while teaching at Louisiana State University, an atmosphere dominated and directed by Long's tenure as governor.

Central to the book is the primary theme of human beings' search for knowledge; all other facets are subordinate to and supportive of this theme. Knowledge includes both objective and subjective comprehensions, with the end goal being self-knowledge. "Life is Motion toward Knowledge," as Warren writes in *All the King's Men*. Elsewhere, the author asserts that the right to knowledge is the human being's "right to exist, to be himself, to be a man." Humans define themselves through knowledge, and the book's pivotal incident demands accumulation of knowledge. Jack, assigned to "dig something up" on the judge, does indeed uncover the judge's dishonor, but the information precipitates a far greater understanding.

For each of the characters, it is a lack of knowledge or an incomplete knowledge that constitutes the chief problem, and those who eventually blunder forward do so only when they see what has previously been hidden from them. The narrator, Jack Burden, is, for example, allegedly telling Willie Stark's story. The reader, however, senses that as he relates the events, Jack is clarifying their meaning mostly for his own benefit. The product of an aristocratic background, Jack in essence eschews knowledge throughout most of the story, for he exists in a vacuum, refusing to be touched or to feel. At moments of crisis, he seeks oblivion in The Great Sleep or by adhering to a belief in The Great Twitch: "Nobody has any responsibility for anything." He is a man of reflection only until those reflections become painful.

Willie seems to be the book's most knowing character. However, his knowledge is questioned, at first only occasionally, then fully. Unlike Jack, who drops his idealism for inertia, Willie is always a man of action, though that action is sometimes based on only partial knowledge. His innocence, lost by the knowledge that he has been betrayed, is replaced by a willingness to use evil if it is necessary for his purposes. He can justify blackmail or protection of a crook on this basis. For a time, Willie maintains and understands the balance between good and evil, but "obsessed with the evil in human nature and with his power to manipulate it," he is drawn completely onto the side of this dark force.

Jack ignores both ideals and the world; Willie ignores the ideals. The third important character, Adam Stanton, ignores the world. Make good out of evil, says Willie, for the bad is all you have to work with. Horrified by such a philosophy, Adam denies that honor, purity, and justice can commingle with evil. When his preconceptions of the state of the universe prove false, he repudiates not his ideas but the universe. He is the man of ideas untainted by fact or action; thus, his knowledge is also faulty and weak, a situation that leads him to tragedy.

Through his investigation of the judge, Jack inadvertently stumbles on the greater truth for himself and for the novel. He discovers his true father, but, even more important, he learns what he is: an imperfect being who must accept imperfection in himself and others and lovingly make what he may out of that state. He learns that human beings cannot be separated from other human beings, that no action or idea exists alone, that past, present, and future are entangled in the web. He realizes what Willie initially knew, then forgot, but reclaimed at the end of the novel. When he tells Jack that all might have been different, Willie implies that his fate might have been different had he remembered that both good and evil exist and influence each other, but that they are not the same.

Closely aligned with the knowledge theme is the Humpty Dumpty motif. The title hints at multiple meanings, for on one level Willie is the king (the boss), and the characters "all the king's men." However, even greater significance arises when Willie is interpreted as Humpty Dumpty, who falls to his doom and cannot be repaired. In this view, the king is God, and the king's men represent humankind. The fall becomes "The Fall" because Willie ruins himself by his knowledge of evil unbalanced by a corresponding ability to overcome its effects. Jack too could be interpreted as Humpty, but one whose breakage is not irrevocable because his understanding and knowledge of evil ultimately correspond to an appropriate conception of the nature of good.

"Critical Evaluation" by Judith Bolch

Further Reading

Bohner, Charles. *Robert Penn Warren*. Rev. ed. Boston: Twayne, 1981. A good general introduction to Warren's writings. Views the novel as the story of Jack Burden's philosophical growth. By examining the past, Jack comes to recognize the paradoxical nature of human isolation and simultaneous kinship through the oppressions of sin that bind all humankind.

Chambers, Robert H., ed. *Twentieth Century Interpretations of "All the King's Men."* Englewood Cliffs, N.J.: Prentice-Hall, 1977. One of the best collections of criticism on the novel. Discusses such topics as point of view, character studies, significance of the title, the centrality of the Cass Mastern episode, and Jack Burden's search for a father.

Grimshaw, James A., Jr. *Understanding Robert Penn Warren*. Columbia: University of South Carolina Press, 2001. Comprehensive introduction to Warren's work, analyzing his fiction, poetry, and drama. Discusses the nature of his protagonists and common themes, such as history, time, truth, responsibility, and love. The references to *All the King's Men* are listed in the index.

Guttenberg, Barnett. *Web of Being: The Novels of Robert Penn Warren*. Nashville, Tenn.: Vanderbilt University Press, 1975. An existentialist reading of Warren's novels. Asserts that the greatness of *All the King's Men* results from Warren's decision to make Jack Burden the narrator of and a chief participant in Willie Stark's story.

Hendricks, Randy. *Lonelier than God: Robert Penn Warren and the Southern Exile*. Athens: University of Georgia Press, 2000. Focuses on the theme of exile in Warren's work and how that theme relates to his ideas about regionalism, race, and language.

Justus, James H. *The Achievement of Robert Penn Warren*. Baton Rouge: Louisiana State University Press, 1981. Examines the entire body of Warren's work and in that context views *All the King's Men* as both a moral fiction and a political novel.

Madden, David, ed. *The Legacy of Robert Penn Warren*. Baton Rouge: Louisiana State University Press, 2000. Collection of essays interpreting Warren's work, including discussions of Warren as a mentor and a moral philosopher, Warren and Thomas Jefferson, the function of geography as fate in his writings, and "Medusa, the Movies, and the King's Men" by Deborah Wilson.

Perkins, James A., ed. *The Cass Mastern Material: The Core of Robert Penn Warren's "All the King's Men."* Baton Rouge: Louisiana State University Press, 2005. In chapter 4 of *All the King's Men*, Jack Burden learns about a distant relative named Cass Mastern. Warren wrote a short story and a play about this character, and Perkins argues that the Mastern episode is crucial to understanding *All the King's Men* and the mystery of Jack's paternity.

Watkins, Floyd C., and John T. Hiers, eds. *Robert Penn Warren Talking: Interviews 1950-1978*. New York: Random House, 1980. Contains brief but valuable comments by Warren on the relationship of *All the King's Men* to the dramatic versions, the significance of the epigraph, and various other aspects of the novel.

Woodell, Harold. *"All the King's Men": The Search for a Usable Past*. New York: Twayne, 1993. Argues that the novel is not about a political tyrant, and that Jack Burden, not Willie Stark, is the central figure in the book. Maintains the novel is about the struggle between the conservative Old South, which Jack has inherited, and the progressive New South, as symbolized by Willie, and that Jack ultimately is able to reconcile the two.

All's Well That Ends Well

Author: William Shakespeare (1564-1616)
First produced: c. 1602-1603; first published, 1623
Type of work: Drama
Type of plot: Comedy
Time of plot: Sixteenth century
Locale: France and Italy

Principal characters:
THE KING OF FRANCE
BERTRAM, the Count of Rousillon
THE COUNTESS OF ROUSILLON, his mother
HELENA, the Countess's ward
PAROLLES, a scoundrel, Bertram's follower
A WIDOW OF FLORENCE
DIANA, her daughter

The Story:

Bertram, the Count of Rousillon, is called to the court to serve the king of France, who is ill of a disease that all the royal physicians have failed to cure. In the entire country the only doctor who might have cured the king is now dead. On his deathbed he bequeaths to his daughter Helena his books and papers describing cures for all common and rare diseases, among them the one suffered by the king.

Helena is now the ward of the Countess of Rousillon, who thinks of her as a daughter. Helena loves young Count Bertram and wants him for a husband, not a brother. Bertram considers Helena only slightly above a servant, however, and will not consider her for a wife. Through her knowledge of the king's illness, Helena at last hits upon a plot to gain the spoiled young man for her mate, in such fashion as to leave him no choice in the decision. She journeys to the court and, offering her life as forfeit if she fails, gains the king's consent to try her father's cure on him. If she wins, the young lord of her choice is to be given to her in marriage.

Her sincerity wins the king's confidence. She cures him by means of her father's prescription and, as her boon, asks for Bertram for her husband. The young man protests to the king, but the ruler keeps his promise, not only because he gave his word but also because Helena won him over completely.

When the king orders the marriage to be performed at once, Bertram, although bowing to the king's will, will not have Helena for a wife in any but a legal way. Pleading the excuse of urgent business elsewhere, he deserts her after the ceremony and sends messages to her and to his mother saying he will never belong to a wife forced upon him. He tells Helena that she will not really be his wife until she wears on her finger a ring he now wears on his and carries in her body a child that is his. He then states that these two things will never come to pass, for he will never see Helena again. He is encouraged in his hatred for Helena by his follower, Parolles, a scoundrel and a coward who will as soon betray one person as another. Helena reproaches him for his vulgar ways, and he wants vengeance on her.

Helena returns to the Countess of Rousillon, as Bertram commands. The countess hears of her son's actions with horror, and when she reads the letter he writes her, restating his hatred for Helena, she disowns her son, for she loves Helena like her own child. When Helena learns that Bertram says he would never return to France until he no longer has a wife there, she sadly decides to leave the home of her benefactress. Loving Bertram, she vows that she will not keep him from his home.

Disguising herself as a religious pilgrim, Helena follows Bertram to Italy, where he goes to fight for the duke of Florence. While lodging with a widow and her daughter, a beautiful young girl named Diana, Helena learns that Bertram seduced a number of young Florentine girls. Lately he turned his attentions to Diana, but she, a pure and virtuous girl, will not accept his attentions. Then Helena tells the widow and Diana that she is Bertram's wife, and by bribery and a show of friendliness she persuades them to join her in a plot against Bertram. Diana listens again to his vows of love for her and agrees to let him come to her rooms, provided he first gives her a ring from his finger to prove the constancy of his love. Bertram, overcome with passion, gives her the ring, and that night, as he keeps the appointment in her room, the girl he thinks is Diana slips a ring on his finger as they lie in bed together.

News came to the countess in France and to Bertram in Italy that Helena died of grief and love for Bertram. Bertram returns to France to face his mother's and the king's displeasure, but first he discovers that Parolles is the knave everyone else knows him to be. When Bertram holds him up to public ridicule, Parolles vows he will take revenge on his former benefactor.

When the king visits the Countess of Rousillon, she begs him to restore her son to favor. Bertram protests that he really loves Helena, though he did not recognize that love until after he lost her forever through death. His humility so pleases the king that his confession of love, coupled with his exploits in the Italian wars, wins him a royal pardon for his offense against his wife. Then the king, about to betroth him to another wife, the lovely and wealthy daughter of a favorite lord, notices the ring Bertram is wearing. It is the ring given to him the night he went to Diana's rooms; the king in turn recognizes it as a jewel he gave to Helena. Bertram pretends that it was thrown to him in Florence by a high-born lady who loved him. He says that he told the lady he was not free to wed, but that she refused to take back her gift.

At that moment, Diana appears as a petitioner to the king and demands that Bertram fulfill his pledge to recognize her as his wife. When Bertram pretends that she is no more than a prostitute he visited, she produces the ring he gave her. That ring convinces everyone present, especially his mother, that Diana is really Bertram's wife. Parolles adds to the evidence against Bertram by testifying that he heard his former master promise to marry the girl. Bertram persists in his denials. Diana then asks for the ring she gave him, the ring which the king thinks to be Helena's. The king asks Diana where she got the ring. When she refuses to tell on penalty of her life, he orders her taken to prison. Diana then declares that she will send for her bail. Her bail is Helena, now carrying Bertram's child within her, for it was she, of course, who received him in Diana's rooms that fateful night. To her Diana gave the ring. The two requirements for becoming his real wife being now fulfilled, Bertram promises to love Helena as a true and faithful husband. Diana receives from the king a promise to give her any young man of her choice for her husband, the king to provide the dowry. Thus the bitter events of the past make sweeter the happiness of all.

Critical Evaluation:

William Shakespeare's *All's Well That Ends Well* is among his plays that defy easy genre classification and are often grouped under such categories as dark comedy and problem play. Though more comic than tragic, these plays contain troublingly dark aspects or resolutions whose very glibness causes unease. Some of these plays received very little attention until the twentieth century, when the unflagging interest in Shakespeare caused critics to turn to the less familiar works in his canon. The modern interest in these more difficult plays is also quite natural because modern literature often focuses on uncertainty, ambiguity, irony, unstable characters, and mixed moods. Those aspects of Shakespeare's plays that may have puzzled his contemporaries and repelled even his greatest fans invite creative attention from modern readers and audiences.

Among such plays, *All's Well That Ends Well* presents several distinctive problems of interpretation. The history of the critical reception of this play, though covering many other aspects, identifies fairly clearly three key subjects of controversy: the active character of Helena, the surprisingly ungracious character of Bertram, and the bed trick to which the heroine turns in order to win back her reluctant husband, a trick that raises grave questions about the moral center of the play.

One way that scholars have tried to ease their discomfort about issues in the play is to consider the folk tradition underlying the plot. Several have noted that tales of women who endured much hardship for love and of wives who were sorely tested were extremely popular. Stories about women who manipulated events in order to get what they wanted often presented such women in a favorable light. That Shakespeare might have wanted to preserve this point of view for those in his audience not familiar with the folk tradition seems likely, given his depiction of the older characters in the play. Unlike traditional comedies, where the older people are obstructions to the younger ones, in *All's Well That Ends Well*, Helen has the support of the countess and of the king. Such support serves two purposes. Within the plot, it allows Helena to concentrate her efforts on winning Bertram, and the approval of the older characters places Helena in a positive light, subtly persuading the audience to accept her desires and actions favorably.

These differences from other comedies give rise to controversies in interpretation. On one hand, Helena can be seen as the agent of a double healing action in the play. She effects the physical cure by healing the king and then spiritually "cures" Bertram of his immaturity and brings about his acceptance of responsibility as an adult male. This interpretation is not far from the love-conquers-all scenario found in most romantic comedies. It may be considered merely a pleasant change that the woman, rather than the man, is the active pursuer who resorts to doing all that is necessary to achieve her desire. The basic underlying plot of traditional comedy remains intact.

A closer scrutiny of this, however, reveals that the gender change creates a much messier play. Innumerable questions about Helena's motivations and behavior come to mind. In the first act alone, Helena mentions several times, in her soliloquy and in speaking to the countess, that she is deeply conscious of the class difference between Bertram's position in society and her own. Nevertheless, she decides to try to win him anyway. Having used her personal knowledge and skill inherited from her physician father to get Bertram, only to find that he does not want her, she then exacerbates her initial mistake in judgment by continuing to pursue him. She lies to those who care about her, pretending to take a pilgrimage when she is actually on her way to find Bertram in Italy. When she gets there, she is willing to pay to degrade herself to substitute for Diana. Though it is quite conventional for comic characters—and, more often, their servants—to resort to all manner of guile and deception to overcome obstacles, it seems troubling to some critics over the years that it is a woman who determines the man she wants and then sets out to get him by any means available.

The object of all her travails is another source of unease in the play because Bertram is such an unattractive male character. Granted that his position in the beginning is pitiable, since he is forced by the king into a marriage he does not want, his subsequent actions seem both reprehensible and inconsistent. He behaves in a hateful manner, taunting Helena with two impossible tasks, running away to war, and abandoning his mother, estate, and country to escape his wife. He seduces young women, and then, as in the case of Diana, denies responsibility for his behavior, casting aspersions on their characters. His repentance and newfound love for Helena upon hearing of her death are, at the very least, patently insincere and, at best, a mysteriously sudden and inconsistent change of heart. This young man, with so few discernible attractive personality traits, seems to have little but noble birth to recommend him. Helena's determination to have him anyway is sometimes interpreted to mean that she is a social climber. This motivation links her to Parolles, one of Shakespeare's great comic creations, morally questionable but theatrically vital to the comic atmosphere of the play. This viewpoint alone makes the play unusual, for though other characters in Shakespeare's plays have attempted to move up in class, Helena is the only one who succeeds, to general approval.

From being a simple comic tale of sturdy and faithful love surviving all obstacles, the meaning of *All's Well That Ends*

Well thus begins to shift and waver, starting with the ambivalence of the title. The play can only ironically be said to end well, when the heroine tricks the hero into staying with her. That the hero cannot distinguish between Diana, the woman he ostensibly desires, and Helena, the wife he rejects, is unromantic, at the very least. Instead of sounding like a simple exclamation of relief that troubles have been successfully endured, the title can take on a more morally ambiguous shade: that all—including the means—is justified by the end.

The concept that merit, as in the case of Helena's independent and courageous spirit, counts as much as or more than the inherited position of Bertram seems startlingly modern. That and the combination of comic and puzzling characterizations make *All's Well That Ends Well* one of Shakespeare's more thought-provoking plays.

"Critical Evaluation" by Shakuntala Jayaswal

Further Reading

Barker, Simon, ed. *Shakespeare's Problem Plays: "All's Well That Ends Well," "Measure for Measure," "Troilus and Cressida."* New York: Palgrave Macmillan, 2005. Collection of essays providing a range of late twentieth century interpretations of the three plays. The chapters regarding *All's Well That Ends Well* discuss the chivalric quest; political effects of gender and class; subjectivity, desire, and female friendship; love; and disease, desire, and representation in this work.

Clark, Ira. *Rhetorical Readings, Dark Comedies, and Shakespeare's Problem Plays*. Gainesville: University Press of Florida, 2007. Examines *All's Well That Ends Well* and two other "problem plays," or plays that ostensibly are comedies but lack clear resolutions. Analyzes the most prominent rhetorical features of these plays, including rhetorical devices that were commonly used in Elizabethan literature.

Cole, Howard C. *The All's Well Story from Boccaccio to Shakespeare*. Urbana: University of Illinois Press, 1981. A unique source for tracing the different versions of the basic story, starting with Giovanni Boccaccio's *Decameron* (1348-1353). Detailed discussions include a chapter on Shakespeare's handling of the tale.

Greenblatt, Stephen. *Will in the World: How Shakespeare Became Shakespeare*. New York: Norton, 2004. Critically acclaimed biography in which Greenblatt finds new connections between Shakespeare's works and the Bard's life and engagement with Elizabethan society.

Lawrence, William Witherle. "*All's Well That Ends Well*." In *Shakespeare's Problem Comedies*. London: Macmillan, 1931. One of the earliest, and most influential, studies to connect the play with the narrative and dramatic traditions preceding it. Explains the basic folktale underlying the plot.

Marsh, Nicholas. *Shakespeare: Three Problem Plays*. New York: Palgrave Macmillan, 2003. Examines the unresolved issues in *All's Well That Ends Well* and two other plays by analyzing excerpts from their texts, pointing out multiple interpretations of young men, women, politics and society, and fools. Places the plays in relation to Shakespeare's life and oeuvre. Provides historical and cultural context and analyses by five literary critics.

Parker, Patricia A. "Dilation and Inflation: *All's Well That Ends Well*, *Troilus and Cressida*, and Shakespearean Increase." In *Shakespeare from the Margins: Language, Culture, Context*. Chicago: University of Chicago Press, 1996. This study of Shakespeare's use of wordplay examines how the concept of increase, in terms both of economics and of "increase and multiply," is the preoccupation of *All's Well That Ends Well*. Describes how the play reflects concerns about various forms of inflation in the late sixteenth and early seventeenth centuries.

Waller, Gary. *All's Well, That Ends Well: New Critical Essays*. New York: Routledge, 2007. The essays provide a range of interpretations, including discussions of the "marriage" of tragedy and comedy, female theatricality, absent fathers, religion, and Helena and the fairy bride tradition in the play. Waller's introduction examines the work's critical and theatrical emergence from an "unfortunate comedy" to an "infinitely fascinating play."

Zitner, Sheldon P. *All's Well That Ends Well*. New York: Harvester Wheatsheaf, 1989. An excellent critical introduction to many aspects of the play. Considers the stage history, critical reception, sources, and the main critical issues of the play. A good starting point for study.

Almanac of the Dead

Author: Leslie Marmon Silko (1948-)
First published: 1991
Type of work: Novel
Type of plot: Impressionistic realism
Time of plot: Twentieth century, especially the 1980's
Locale: Southwestern United States and Mexico

Principal characters:
ZOEME, the guardian of tribal secrets
ZETA, her granddaughter, a drug smuggler
LECHA, her granddaughter, a psychic
FERRO, Lecha's son
PAULIE, Ferro's former lover
STERLING, a Laguna Pueblo Indian, banished from tribal lands
SEESE, Lecha's assistant
DAVID, Seese's former lover
BEAUFREY, David's former lover
MENARDO, a security expert
ALEGRIA, his second wife, an architect
TACHO, his chauffeur, and a twin
MAX BLUE, a New Jersey mafia boss
LEAH BLUE, his wife
SONNY, their older son
EDWARD TRIGG, a businessman
RAMBO-ROY, a transient working for Edward
CLINTON, a transient working with Rambo-Roy
EL FEO, Tacho's twin brother, a leader of dispossessed Indian groups
ANGELITA, a Mayan campaigner for reclamation of tribal land
BARTOLOMEO, a Cuban political agitator

The Story:

Tucson, Arizona, is "home to an assortment of speculators, confidence men, embezzlers, lawyers, judges, police and other criminals." It is also the home of "addicts and pushers," and they all have been coming here since "the 1880's and the Apache Wars." It is now the 1980's, one hundred years later, and unrest is increasing in South and Central America. The U.S. government is sending drugs and arms south across the U.S.-Mexico border to support right-wing regimes.

Meanwhile, refugees are fleeing north, crossing into the United States legally if they can, but by whatever means if they cannot. Transients, too, are drawn to Tucson because of its proximity to the border, and huge encampments of people with nowhere else to go have formed around the city. Tucson is a crossroads: Sooner or later, many people will pass through on their way to somewhere else; Tucson is a stepping-stone to a different life.

Sterling, a Laguna Pueblo Indian, had fallen asleep on the bus to Phoenix and ended up in Tucson instead. Exiled from the pueblo for reasons that are not entirely clear to him, but which are possibly related to his detachment from tribal affairs, he eventually finds work as a gardener on the ranch owned by Zeta and Ferro, and works alongside Ferro's former lover, Paulie, a security expert. Sterling chooses to overlook that they are clearly conducting illegal business and focuses on the positive elements of his new situation. When Zeta's twin sister, Lecha, arrives, bringing with her Seese, a young white woman who has lost her baby, the relative peace of the ranch, and Zeta's drug-smuggling racket, is threatened.

Lecha is a psychic who specializes in finding dead bodies. Seese has come to her because she fears her baby is dead. Lecha seems unwilling to help Seese but strings her along, employing her as her personal assistant. Lecha alleges she has terminal cancer, although it is not clear whether this is a cover for her drug addiction or vice versa. She has returned home without warning, convinced that the moment has come for her and Zeta to transcribe the notebooks bequeathed to them by their grandmother, Zoeme.

Zoeme is an indigenous Mexican woman much feared by the rest of her family, not least because over the years they have attempted to conceal their Indian ancestry, whereas Zoeme flaunts her ancestry. The notebooks, the Almanac of the Dead, are ancient, powerful objects, and Lecha has become convinced that they foretell a change in the world order, marking the moment when the downtrodden Indian populations will rise up and take control of their destiny.

South of the border, Menardo's security company has become a front for arms dealing. His business has been successful until now, but he is struggling to keep up with the mysterious contacts from the U.S. government who are encouraging him to move bigger weapons. Menardo is proud of how he has built his business, but he is terrified by the thought that the local aristocrats will discover that he has Indian ancestry. Dimly perceiving his own disloyalty to his ancestry, he keeps an Indian chauffeur, Tacho, who plays on his employer's superstitious fears.

Unknown to anyone, Tacho has a connection to the rebel leaders, El Feo and Angelita, also known as La Escapia, who are building a huge rebel army, manipulating various groups sympathetic to their cause to gather a war chest. Chief among these is Bartolomeo, a Cuban Marxist with clear ideas of what the revolution should achieve, but only too willing to sacrifice the truth for an ideology that writes the Indians' struggles out of existence.

Others are gathering in Arizona, looking for rich pickings. Max Blue, who has mafia connections in New Jersey, has moved to Tucson with his family, all of whom are finding ways to make money. Sonny has become involved in gunrunning and drug smuggling, establishing a connection with Menardo, while Max's wife, Leah, has, through her real estate dealing, come into contact with Edward Trigg, a paraplegic determined to walk again. He attempts to fund research through dealing in real estate and through organ harvesting and blood donation, taking advantage of the presence of a huge local transient population, unaware that two of their leaders, Rambo-Roy and Clinton, are building the transients into an army of the dispossessed.

Seese remains unaware that her partner, David, did not steal her child, as he remains unaware that she did not steal the child from him. Both are being manipulated by a former lover, Beaufrey, who is in turn in thrall to Serlo, a man obsessed with genetic purity who is conducting research of his own on how to maintain the "aristocratic" blood that indicates those eligible to rule.

Zeta's smuggling racket is under attack, but she has long been stockpiling weapons; aware that government agencies are trying to sabotage the grassroots liberation and environmental movements, she is now ready to support them in a violent struggle if necessary. Menardo insists that Tacho shoot him to test a bulletproof vest he has been given, unaware that the vest is deliberately faulty; he is shot and dies. Tacho takes this opportunity to slip away and join his brother, El Feo, and take up his role as the vessel of the Macaw Spirits; the twin brothers lead a march north. Menardo's wife, Alegria, attempts to cross the border into the United States, and although robbed and abandoned, she survives by sheer force of will and is finally found and rescued.

Meanwhile, many of the liberation groups have met at the International Holistic Healers' Convention to exchange views, and it is clear that there already is a divergence of opinion—some arguing for peaceful campaigning via the ballot box, and others prepared for armed insurrection. All groups believe that the time has come for change.

Sterling secretly returns home to pueblo lands. Having previously remained at a distance from his community and its beliefs, he has finally come to understand the significance of the appearance of the giant stone serpent on tribal lands and is waiting for the arrival of the twin brothers and their followers from the south.

Critical Evaluation:

For many critics, the greatest difficulty with Leslie Marmon Silko's *Almanac of the Dead* is its sheer size, including its large number of characters. Silko has constructed an intricate network of connections between the different groups of characters to demonstrate the complexity of the issues that the indigenous populations of the Americas face, and to show that the different groups have much in common, regardless of how various their superficial problems.

Although the novel is set in the turbulent years of the 1980's, when the United States had sought to destabilize left-wing governments and had given covert support to right-wing groups—and had supported mining and logging interests that wanted to seize land in the care of indigenous peoples—Silko is keen to make the point that these are simply recent manifestations of a situation that began hundreds of years ago, with the arrival of Europeans. The arrival of the Europeans was prophesied, but she notes that the disappearance of "all things European" also was prophesied. Many of the characters in *Almanac of the Dead* believe that this time has arrived.

The almanac carried by Lecha and Zeta, and received by them from Zoeme, is a fictional version of the Popol Vuh

(c. sixteenth century), a collection of mythological narratives and genealogies from Guatemala that, among other things, includes tales of the Hero Twins, embodied in the present day in brothers Tacho and El Feo. Silko's use of the Popol Vuh has been criticized, in part for the clumsiness of her representation of the collection. Her focus on the U.S.-Mexico border represents a widespread belief that the cultures of southern United States tribes draw on the cultural practices of Mesoamerican tribes as much as they do on northern tribes. With this focus, it might appear that she does indeed marginalize the experience of the northern Native American and First Nations peoples. Lecha's visit to an Alaskan Nation village, for example, seems more like a sop than a considered engagement with the very real border issues between the United States and Canada. In Canada, the free movement of tribal peoples, although sanctioned, is very often hindered.

Similarly, the portrayal of the International Holistic Healers' Convention, a front for campaigning groups to meet, inadvertently privileges southern customs over northern, and while it is clearly also meant to satirize Euro-American attitudes to indigenous customs, it is perhaps too successful in that it often seems to demean that which it intends to support. Similarly, Silko's attempts to link the black American experience with those of other Native American groups points to a presumably unintentional attempt at universalizing that takes little account of how different those experiences have been for individual groups. The reader is frequently left with a sense of Silko's having reduced extremely complex issues to their bare bones, stripping them of nuance to squeeze everything into the novel. The novel also has been criticized for its portrayal of gay and lesbian characters, who are, with one exception, uniformly unpleasant and villainous.

Nevertheless, Silko's novel is bold in its intention and adventurous in its scope. That it stumbles in its execution says as much about the complexity of the issues with which it attempts to deal as it does about Silko's ability to address them.

Maureen Kincaid Speller

Further Readings

Barnett, Louise K., and James L. Thorson, eds. *Leslie Marmon Silko: A Collection of Critical Essays*. Albuquerque: University of New Mexico Press, 1999. These essays cover the entire range of Silko's work through *Almanac of the Dead*, offering biographical information on Silko as well as an extensive bibliography of primary and secondary sources and a helpful bibliographical essay.

Brigham, Ann. "Productions of Geographic Scale and Capitalist-Colonialist Enterprise in Leslie Marmon Silko's *Almanac of the Dead*." *Modern Fiction Studies* 50, no. 2 (Summer, 2004): 303-331. Focuses on the concept of space in the novel. Brigham argues that the novel re-envisions space through a Native American lens: Space is "expansiveness rather than expansion."

Fitz, Brewster E. *Silko: Writing Storyteller and Medicine Woman.* Norman: University of Oklahoma Press, 2004. Fitz analyzes *Almanac of the Dead* and several of Silko's short stories, focusing on the relationship between the written word and the oral storytelling tradition of Silko's family and Laguna culture.

Salyer, Gregory. *Leslie Marmon Silko*. New York: Twayne, 1997. A critical study of Silko's work, describing how her fiction has been influenced by her Laguna background and by Native American stories. Includes a bibliography and an index.

Almayer's Folly
A Story of an Eastern River

Author: Joseph Conrad (1857-1924)
First published: 1895
Type of work: Novel
Type of plot: Social realism
Time of plot: Late nineteenth century
Locale: Dutch East Indies

Principal characters:
ALMAYER, an unsuccessful trader of Dutch ancestry
MRS. ALMAYER, his Malay wife
NINA, his half-caste daughter
DAIN MAROOLA, Nina's Malay lover
LAKAMBA, rajah of Sambir, and Almayer's enemy

The Story:

By marrying Lingard's adopted Malay daughter, Almayer inherits that prosperous merchant's business and his plans for amassing a huge fortune in gold from rich mines up the Pantai River. Almayer and his wife have one daughter, Nina, a beautiful girl, who was sent to Singapore and for ten years was educated as a European. She returns home to Sambir unexpectedly at the end of that time, for she cannot bear to be treated as a half-caste in a white community. Unsuccessful in business, Almayer nurses dim hopes that he can find a gold mine and, his fortune made, take Nina to Amsterdam to spend his last days in prosperous retirement.

News that the English are to seize control of the Pantai River causes Almayer to begin building a new house in his compound, not far removed from the one in which he is living. He wants a house fine enough to receive the British. When the project is abandoned and the Dutch are left in nominal power, Almayer stops work on his new house. A company of Dutch seamen christens the structure "Almayer's Folly."

Lakamba, the native rajah, has a compound across the river from Almayer's home. There he lives with his women, his slaves, and his principal aide, Babalatchi. Lakamba keeps close watch on Almayer as he leaves for several days at a time with a few of his men. After a time, Almayer gives up his trips and settles down to empty daydreams on his rotten wharf. His native wife despises him.

Nina's presence in Sambir offers another problem for Almayer, for the young men of the settlement are eyeing her with interest. One day, Dain Maroola, the handsome son of a Malayan rajah, comes sailing up the river in a brig to trade with Almayer. After conversations with Lakamba and long conferences with Almayer, Dain gets the gunpowder he seeks. Meanwhile, he falls passionately in love with Nina. One night, she comes into the women's room in her father's house and discovers her mother counting out the money Dain is giving her in payment for Nina. Mrs. Almayer was arranging meetings between Nina and Dain and giving them warning at the approach of Almayer. Mrs. Almayer wishes her daughter to remain native. She has a deep distrust of white men and their ways.

Dain goes away, promising that he will return to help Almayer in locating the hidden gold mine. When he does return, he sees Almayer for just a moment and then hurries to see Lakamba. He tells the rajah that his brig fell into the hands of the Dutch and that he narrowly escaped with one slave. Most of his men were killed, and in a day or two, the Dutch will be up the Pantai looking for him.

After this interview, Lakamba tells Babalatchi he must poison Almayer before the arrival of the Dutch. Now that Dain knows where the gold treasure is located, Almayer is no longer needed. If allowed to live, he might reveal his secret to the white men.

The next morning, the body of a Malay is found floating in the river. The corpse is beyond recognition, but it wears an anklet and a ring that belonged to Dain. Almayer is overcome with grief, for Dain was his last hope of finding the gold. The Dutch officers who come looking for Dain tell how he escaped. As the Dutch approach his brig, the gunpowder it carries ignites and blows up the boat, killing two of the Dutch. Almayer promises his visitors that after they dine he will deliver Dain into their hands.

Meanwhile, Babalatchi is telling Lakamba the true story of Dain. Nina was waiting for the young Malay on the night of his conference with Lakamba, and she took him to a secluded clearing farther up the river. He is now hiding there. The corpse that floated down the river is that of his slave, who died when the canoe overturned. Mrs. Almayer suggested that Dain put his anklet and ring on the body and let it float down the river. Lakamba and Babalatchi plan Dain's escape from his Dutch enemies. Knowing that Dain will not leave without Nina, Babalatchi and Mrs. Almayer plot to get her away from Almayer, who is drinking with the Dutch. After some persuasion, Almayer leads his guests to the grave of the man recovered from the river. The Dutch take the anklet and ring as proof that Dain is dead. Then they leave for the night.

Nina, willing to go with Dain, feels an urge to see her father once more before she leaves, but her mother will not let her go into the house where her father lies in a drunken sleep. Nina goes to the clearing where Dain is hiding. Soon afterward, a slave girl awakens Almayer and tells him of Nina's whereabouts. Almayer is panic-stricken. He traces Nina to Dain's enclosure and begs her to come back to him, but she will not. She does not want to run the risk of insults from white people. With Dain she will be a ranee, and she will be married to a Malay, a brave warrior, not a lying, cowardly white man. Almayer threatens to send his servant to tell the Dutch of Dain's hiding place.

While they argue, Babalatchi approaches and cries out that the slave girl revealed Dain's hiding place to the Dutch, who are now on their way to capture the young Malay. Babalatchi, astounded when Dain announces that he will stay with Nina, leaves them to their fate. After he leaves, Almayer says he will never forgive Nina, but he offers to take the two to the mouth of the river. In heavy darkness, the fugitive lovers escape their pursuers.

On an island at the mouth of the river Dain, Nina, and Almayer await the canoe that will take the lovers to Lakamba's hidden boat. After the two have gone, Almayer covers up Nina's footprints and returns to his house up the river. His compound is deserted.

Mrs. Almayer and her women go to Lakamba for protection, taking Dain's gift of money. Almayer finds the old rusty key to his unused office. He goes inside, breaks up the furniture, and piles it in the middle of the room. When he comes out, he throws the key into the river and sits on his porch until the flames began to billow from his office. He burns down his old house and lives out the rest of his days in "Almayer's Folly." Eventually, he begins the practice of smoking opium in an effort to forget his daughter, Nina. By the time he dies, the opium gives his eyes the look of one who indeed succeeded in forgetting.

Critical Evaluation:

In *Almayer's Folly*, his first novel, Joseph Conrad blends together several of the characteristic themes that would pervade his later and more powerful works: the conflict between two mutually uncomprehending civilizations, Western and Eastern; the fearsome and nearly unconquerable power of human sexuality, especially as embodied in the female; and his harsh, dismal belief that all human beings are condemned to live out their lives in isolated worlds of individual illusion. In this early work, Conrad is also exploring and refining his distinctive methods of presenting these themes through setting, characterization, and style. Since *Almayer's Folly* can be seen as a precursor to such later tales as *Heart of Darkness* (1899) and *Lord Jim* (1900), it has the double value of being an important work in itself and the first step in Conrad's development as one of English literature's most powerful writers.

The conflict between European and Eastern cultures underlies the novel. Sambir, the setting for the tale, is the prize in an interlocking series of conflicts for power between forces ranging from the imperial to the domestic. Nominal control of Sambir is disputed between the Dutch, who initially claim the territory as part of their possessions, and the British, who as the more dynamic and progressive imperial power seem poised to exert their influence over the deceptively sleepy tropical site. It is in response to what he perceives as an imminent change of rule that Almayer begins construction of the house that, never completed, becomes a "new ruin" and is dubbed "Almayer's Folly." Almayer's house fits the traditional architectural sense of the word "folly," in that it is an expensive but useless building that serves no practical purpose. More significant, however, is Almayer's true folly: that he neglects the true politics of Sambir, which center not on distant empires but on local domestic concerns. The rajah of Sambir, Lakamba, is Almayer's implacable enemy not least because he believes that the European knows of a rich source of gold. Lakamba commands Almayer's native wife to leave him by playing on the disgust she feels at her white husband's sloth and failure. Almayer, convinced of his innate superiority—after all, he is a European—hardly notices, much less combats, his decline. In this sense, he prefigures Kurtz of *Heart of Darkness*, who becomes more savage than the natives among whom he lives.

Almayer is betrayed twice by women close to him. His wife and his half-caste daughter, Nina, both abandon him and reject European ways for the native Malay culture. Through his dense, highly rhetorical prose, Conrad heavily implies that this rejection is more than cultural; it is in large part a condemnation of Almayer's inadequate sexuality, bound by centuries of European repression and therefore incapable of the natural expression found among the Malay people, characters such as Nina's lover, Dain Maroola.

The distinctive trait of all the major figures in *Almayer's Folly* is self-delusion; no one, European or Malay, truly understands his or her situation or character. All of them are to some extent exiles. Lakamba, although he is a powerful figure on the local scene, is only a pawn in the larger game of the great powers. He has been marginalized and made, to a great degree, irrelevant—the politician's final exile.

Almayer is cut off from his European heritage by distance and from his own dreams by his indolence and lack of ability; at the end of the novel, through the destructive powers of opium, he exists only in a dream world, truly isolated. His wife, on the other hand, has been exiled from her native culture through her marriage to Almayer; she can end her isolation only by betraying her husband and fleeing to his archenemy, Lakamba. Nina, Almayer's daughter, is perhaps the most pitiful exile of all. A half-caste, she will never be accepted as European (although she is educated as one in Singapore), yet her return to her Malay roots is accomplished only by renouncing her father and all his dreams and escaping into the jungle with Dain Maroola.

These themes, which occur repeatedly in Conrad's writings, are expressed in an early and sometimes fumbling form of the narrative style that became uniquely his. When the novel opens, the reader is forced to navigate through a series of flashbacks and interior monologues until the outlines of the situation and story begin to resolve themselves. In a sense, this pattern is a structural representation of the moral confusion in which the characters find themselves, but it is also a foreshadowing of Conrad's technique in works such as *Lord Jim*, where the plot progresses in a psychological rather than chronological fashion.

The Eastern setting of *Almayer's Folly* becomes—another typical Conrad trait—almost a character itself. The dangerously lush and exotic landscape is more than a backdrop to the actions of the human characters, and the setting becomes partly an expression, partly a cause, of the characters' actions. In such a location, all emotions, especially the more primal ones, are intensified and natural inclinations are emphasized and exaggerated. Sambir is an early version of the nonhuman, even demonic landscape that Conrad creates in *Heart of Darkness*, and the river in *Almayer's Folly*, the Pantai, is an early study of the Congo River that winds through the later story. In Conrad's prose, tropical vegetation comes to represent both the primal force of life and life's inevitable and implacable decay.

Stylistically, the novel is characteristic of Conrad in its heavy reliance on adjectives and a tendency toward rhetorical excess. The descriptions of the Malay landscape and the portraits of the novel's characters are often lengthy and involved, most often with the purpose of establishing a psychological and artistic frame in which the story and its meaning can take shape. At times convoluted in its syntax, the language of *Almayer's Folly*, like its setting, mirrors the complex, complicated, and often self-contradictory nature of its characters and their motivations and actions. It was with this novel that Conrad staked out territory that remained very much his own throughout his works.

"Critical Evaluation" by Michael Witkoski

Further Reading

Hampson, R. G. *Joseph Conrad: Betrayal and Identity*. New York: St. Martin's Press, 1992. In the chapter "Two Prototypes of Betrayal: *Almayer's Folly*," the author examines the psychologies of the major characters and the tension created within them by their ideal selves at war with their actual personalities.

Karl, Frederik R. A. *Reader's Guide to Joseph Conrad*. Rev. ed. New York: Farrar, Straus & Giroux, 1969. An introduction that provides a clear review of the essential features of *Almayer's Folly* and its place in the Conrad canon.

Peters, John G. *The Cambridge Introduction to Joseph Conrad*. New York: Cambridge University Press, 2006. An introductory overview of Conrad, with information on his life, all of his works, and his critical reception.

Robert, Andrew Michael. *Conrad and Masculinity*. New York: St. Martin's Press, 2000. Uses modern theories about masculinity to analyze Conrad's work and explore the relationship of masculinity to imperialism and modernity. *Almayer's Folly* is discussed in the chapter entitled "Masculinity, 'Race' and Empire: *Almayer's Folly*, *An Outcast of the Islands*."

Schwarz, Daniel R. *Conrad: "Almayer's Folly" to "Under Western Eyes."* Ithaca, N.Y.: Cornell University Press, 1980. An excellent discussion of Conrad's psychology during the period he conceived and composed the novel. Schwarz also discusses the connections and relationships between *Almayer's Folly* and *An Outcast of the Islands* (1896).

Sherry, Norman. *Conrad's Eastern World*. New York: Cambridge University Press, 1966. Places the novel within the context of Conrad's early and continuing interest in settings and plots involving the Far East. Helpful in understanding the nuances of Malayan politics and culture.

Stape, J. H., ed. *The Cambridge Companion to Joseph Conrad*. New York: Cambridge University Press, 1996. Collection of essays discussing Conrad's life and analyzing his work, including discussions of the Conradian narrative, Conrad and imperialism, Conrad and modernism, and Conrad's literary influence. The many references to *Almayer's Folly* are listed in the index.

Alton Locke
Tailor and Poet

Author: Charles Kingsley (1819-1875)
First published: 1850
Type of work: Novel
Type of plot: Social realism and bildungsroman
Time of plot: 1840's
Locale: London and Cambridge, England

Principal characters:
ALTON LOCKE, a poor tailor, poet, and political radical
SAUNDERS "SANDY" MACKAYE, a philosopher and bookseller
JOHN CROSSTHWAITE, a tailor
JEMMY DOWNES, a poor, drunk, Irish weaver
LORD LYNEDALE, a paternalistic aristocrat
ELEANOR STAUNTON, his wife
GEORGE LOCKE, Alton's ambitious, conscienceless, middle-class cousin
LILLIAN WINNSTAY, Alton's vain, selfish, and beautiful love interest
DEAN WINNSTAY, her father, dean of Cathedral D—

The Story:

Alton Locke is a poor, cockney (working-class), retail-tradesman's son. His father had invested all his money in a small shop that failed; by contrast, Alton's uncle has prospered and now owns several grocery stores. Desperately poor, Alton's widowed mother asks the uncle to find Alton a position as a tailor's apprentice.

The tailor's establishment is Alton's first experience of the world outside his mother's strict Baptist household. The workroom is closed, stinking, and filthy, and most of the other tailors are gross, vulgar, and irreverent. Alton is, however, drawn to a coworker, John Crossthwaite, who is more thoughtful than the others. Locke wants to improve himself by reading. Having exhausted his mother's few narrow Calvinist theological tomes, he discovers a used-book shop. The shop owner, Saunders "Sandy" Mackaye, befriends him, lends him books, and gives him a place to live after his mother evicts him for reading secular books.

One morning, Alton is summoned to his uncle's office for an interview, during which he meets his cousin George, who is about to enter Cambridge University. Together, they visit an art gallery, where Alton sees the beautiful Lillian Winnstay along with her father, Dean Winnstay, and her cousin Eleanor Staunton. Alton instantly falls in love with Lillian and spends the following year looking for her in London and feeling bitter toward the gentlemen who can visit her because of their rank in society. His frustration finds release in poetry. At first, he writes mannered, Byronic trash until, under Sandy's guidance, he finds his voice in poetry that describes the lives of the poor workers of London.

Meanwhile, Alton's employer, wanting to increase his profit margin, changes his business focus to the so-called show-trade—cheap, flashy, ready-to-wear clothing—and orders his employees to do piecework at home for much lower wages. Crossthwaite organizes a protest, which Locke joins, but they lose their jobs when Jemmy Downes, one of their number, reports them to their employer. Angered at this injustice, and under Crossthwaite's influence, Alton joins the Chartist movement, which advocates the vote for workers. Mackaye thinks that Alton is too young to become involved in politics; he advises him to visit his cousin George in Cambridge, and to ask him for help in finding a publisher for his poetry.

Alton's stay at Cambridge is memorable for several reasons: He comes to know his cousin better and is at last introduced to the people he had seen at the gallery so long before. To obtain security, George has decided to become a Church of England priest, despite preparation and having been brought up a Baptist. Being self-centered, George makes little effort to help Alton, but he does introduce him to Lord Lynedale, another Cambridge student. Lynedale respects Alton's abilities, despite the difference in rank between the two men, and he is interested in improving the agricultural workers on his family estates and helpful in finding a publisher. He introduces Alton to Dean Winnstay, who arranges for publication of the poetry. The dean, however, asks Alton to omit certain crucial passages that he considers politically subversive. Alton agrees, as it is the only way to see his work in print. Through the dean, Alton meets Eleanor Staunton. Eleanor is sympathetic to the plight of the working classes and argues that workers and Anglican clergy should be reconciled.

Feeling guilty about having betrayed his poetry, Alton returns to London and begins to make his living with hack writing for the popular press, especially for Feargus O'Flynn's *Weekly Warwhoop*, while waiting for his book of poetry to appear in print. When at last it does, Alton resumes contact with his upper-class acquaintances. He learns that his cousin George is pursuing ordination and plans to marry Lillian, and that Eleanor and Lynedale have married, but that the latter had died in an accident.

Alton also continues his Chartist activities, and although O'Flynn turns against him because of his success as a compromised poet and because of his upper-class connections, Alton pleads to represent the London Chartists at an agricultural workers' rally. He finds the rally is to be held near D—, the town where the Winnstays live. When the rally turns into a riot, Alton is arrested, tried, and sentenced to three years in prison. For three years, he remains infatuated with Lillian, tormented by the sight of her house from his cell. He also is tormented by knowledge that his cousin George is pursuing her, too, as he becomes a successful clergyman of the new and fashionable High Church.

Alton is released just in time to help present the People's Charter (a petition calling for enactment of the Chartist movement's democratic goals) to Parliament on April 10, 1848. Mackaye has long warned Alton and Crossthwaite that the Chartist movement is too influenced by rogues and demagogues such as O'Flynn and that the charter itself is filled with false signatures. With his dying breath, he predicts that the attempt to present it will prove a disaster. Meanwhile, Crossthwaite and Alton dream of revolution and prepare for street fighting. When April 10 arrives, Mackaye is proven correct. The Chartist leaders, fearing arrest, flee the rally; the London workers ignore the presentation; and the meeting breaks up in disarray. As Alton, despairing, walks the streets, he meets the betrayer Downes, now living in poverty. Downes's wife and children, dead of fever and starvation, lie covered by the coats they had been sewing. Alton calls for help, but it comes too late to prevent Downes from committing suicide.

Alton's despair deepens into illness and delirium. Nursed back to health by Eleanor and Crossthwaite, Alton becomes convinced through long discussions with Eleanor that the Bible is the true charter, that workers should earn their rights by reforming their characters, and that class cooperation rather than class conflict is the prerequisite for bringing God's kingdom to pass. Alton also learns that the coats that had shrouded Downes's family had infected George and Lillian, killing the former and destroying the latter's beauty.

As he comes to learn of Eleanor's charitable activities among the London poor, Alton realizes that he had loved the wrong woman, but he finds an opportunity for redemption. Mackaye has bequeathed him money on condition that he and Crossthwaite emigrate for seven years. Eleanor cannot go with them, for her health is declining, so Alton and the Crossthwaite family set sail for Texas. The night their ship arrives on the American shore, Alton dies. His last written words are a poem, calling for a day of hope between workers and the upper classes.

Critical Evaluation:

Charles Kingsley was a remarkable Victorian. An Anglican clergyman, he is often associated with the founding of Christian Socialism and also of "muscular Christianity." He was a social reformer but also an academic, serving for some time as a professor of modern history at Cambridge University. He also wrote articles on scientific subjects, rather like character Dean Winnstay, who in some ways represents these aspects of Kingsley himself. Kingsley is now better known as a novelist who wrote social realism as well as children's fantasy, including *The Water-Babies* (1863).

Kingsley's *Alton Locke* is solidly rooted in the historical events of the 1840's. In 1848, Kingsley had made a tour of Jacobs Island in Bermondsey, one of the worst of London's slums, and had made it the basis of both *Yeast* (1848, serial; 1851, book), his first novel of social criticism, and *Alton Locke*. Kingsley also drew on his social observations for his description of working conditions among London tailors. Before writing *Alton Locke*, he published an inflammatory and powerful pamphlet, "Cheap Clothes and Nasty" (1850), which describes the tailors' trade in the London sweatshops.

The Chartist movement of the 1840's also provides background for the novel. Chartism took its name from the People's Charter, a petition to the British parliament that called for universal suffrage for men, the secret ballot, and other political reforms, all of which would have turned Great Britain into a democracy with working-class participation in government. The Chartist movement ended in a somewhat anticlimactic attempt to deliver the People's Charter to Parliament on April 10, 1848. Kingsley used real-life characters for *Alton Locke*. Feargus O'Flynn and the *Weekly Warwhoop* represent the Chartist leader Feargus O'Connor and his *Northern Star*. Alton Locke himself is based on two Chartist tailors: Thomas Cooper, who was likewise a poet, and Walter Cooper, who had converted to Anglicanism. Sandy Mackaye is a type of Thomas Carlyle, the Scottish social reformer, who had influenced writer Charles Dickens as much as he had Kingsley.

Alton Locke is told in the first person and thus has in its writing all the contradictions found in Alton's own character. In many ways the novel is a bildungsroman, a story of one person's development—spiritually, culturally, and as a writer. Kingsley takes the Victorian theme of self-help, the rising of the poor self-educated person, to some degree of attainment, but he refuses to follow the Victorian optimistic stereotype, so well typified in *John Halifax, Gentleman* (1856), Dinah Maria Mulock's best seller. Alton can get only so far, especially because of his political views, and in the end, he is diseased and dies young and unfulfilled.

Ironically, Kingsley does produce a self-help antihero, Alton's alter ego, his cousin George Locke. George knows that the best means for advancement for a working-class lad is to jump on the new High Church bandwagon. Without any real convictions, though very intelligent, he marries above his station and looks all set for a respected post in the church hierarchy. He has worked hard for it, but he has done this at the cost of losing any convictions and integrity. Kingsley refuses to reward this, and George is killed off before Alton, this time by typhus, which emanates from the unsanitary parts of London. The theme of disease as punishment for social ills is later used by Dickens in his *Bleak House* (1852-1853, serial; 1853, book).

The portrayal of Alton is intense. Although Kingsley gives Alton the same perceptions and experiences of the London poor, Alton never becomes Kingsley's mouthpiece. Rather, Alton has to go through many stages of political thinking before he can reach Kingsley's Christian Socialism. To do this, Alton voices various forms of radicalism associated with the decade: It is through his dialogues with Dean Winnstay, Eleanor, and above all, Sandy, that his own thinking is matured.

The dialectic form of Alton's development is never merely intellectual. He is allowed personal emotions, from hope to despair, especially in his infatuation with Lillian Winnstay but also in the hopelessness of the means of protest available to him. Near the end, Alton's fever and its long dream sequence take the reader into almost fantasy writing, as Kingsley portrays his own evolutionary views.

Inevitably, *Alton Locke* is classified as belonging to the condition-of-England subgenre of the social novel. Here it finds affinities with Benjamin Disraeli's *Conningsby: Or, The New Generation* (1844) and *Sybil: Or, The Two Nations* (1845) in the alliance recommended between the working class and the upper class. Both writers feel the bourgeoisie has betrayed the lower classes and has exploited them, especially by using the laissez-faire theories of economic science. The upper classes, including the Anglican clergy, have the means and power to legislate for social improvements, thereby winning the respect and cooperation of all thinking workers. In this cooperation, the "mob" will be restrained, much unlike the French Revolution.

Kingsley has been criticized for allowing the dialectic to overwhelm the fiction. The fiction has its own weaknesses, for example, in the use of obvious melodramatic devices. However, these were common devices even with great novelists of the time, like Dickens and George Eliot. What saves the novel from such weaknesses is Kingsley's clear human sympathies, his own descriptive abilities, and the tensions and contrasts he structures into the social and intellectual fabric of the text. *Alton Locke* also is a Christian novel, not only in its portrayal of Alton's long coming to faith but also in its integrity as expression of Kingsley's deeply held beliefs, born out of personal experience, suffering, and open-mindedness to the voices of the day.

D. G. Paz; revised by David Barratt

Further Reading

Beeson, Trevor. "The Novelist: Charles Kingsley, Chester and Westminster." In *The Canons: Cathedral Close Encounters*. London: SCM Press, 2006. An account of Kingsley's life, ecclesiastical career, and social and religious significance. Part of a collection surveying the canons of literature and the Church of England.

Chitty, Susan. *The Beast and the Monk: A Life of Charles Kingsley*. London: Hodder & Stoughton, 1974. An innovative biography that draws on unpublished documents and illuminates the place of physical love in Kingsley's thinking and private life. The chapter on *Alton Locke* discusses the London scenes that inspired Kingsley to write the novel.

Horsman, Ernest Alan. *The Victorian Novel*. Vol. 13 in *The Oxford History of English Literature*, edited by John Buxton and Norman Davis. New York: Oxford University Press, 1990. An authoritative survey discussing minor as well as major novelists. Includes a good bibliography of secondary works for further reading. Horsman compares Kingsley's *Alton Locke* with the works of novelist Elizabeth Gaskell.

Kaufmann, Moritz. *Charles Kingsley: Christian Socialist and Social Reformer*. Whitefish, Mont.: Kessinger, 2009. A biographical approach to Kingsley's work, bringing out his commitment to the Christian and reformist ideas expressed in *Alton Locke*.

Klaver, Jan Marten Ivo. *The Apostle of the Flesh: A Critical Life of Charles Kingsley*. Boston: Brill, 2006. Comprehensive intellectual biography of Kingsley, placing his life and work within the broader context of the social, religious, and historical developments that occurred during his lifetime.

Martin, Robert Bernard. *The Dust of Combat: A Life of Charles Kingsley*. New York: W. W. Norton, 1960. This standard biography of Kingsley focuses more on his public life than on his private thoughts. Includes an extensive analysis of the background of social observation that led to *Alton Locke*.

Rapple, Brendan A. *The Rev. Charles Kingsley: An Annotated Bibliography of Secondary Criticism, 1900-2006*. Lanham, Md.: Scarecrow Press, 2008. An annotated bibliography of selected works about Kingsley's writings, life, and activities.

Uffelman, Larry K. *Charles Kingsley*. Boston: Twayne, 1979. A brief, clear overview of Kingsley's works. In the chapter devoted to the three novels of social criticism, Uffelman relates the characters in *Alton Locke* to figures in British life during the 1840's.

Williams, Raymond. *Culture and Society, 1780-1950*. 1960. Reprint. New York: Columbia University Press, 1983. A classic analysis of modern British culture from a Marxist perspective. The chapter on *Alton Locke* focuses on the conflict among different conceptions of Chartism.

Always Coming Home

Author: Ursula K. Le Guin (1929-)
First published: 1985
Type of work: Novel
Type of plot: Science fiction
Time of plot: The future
Locale: Kesh

Principal characters:
STONE TELLING, a young woman of the Sinshan tribe
WILLOW, her mother
TERTER ABHAO, her father
PANDORA, the first woman, according to Greek mythology
THE VALLEY PEOPLE, a near-utopian society in California
THE CONDOR PEOPLE, a warlike society
STONE LISTENING, Stone Telling's husband

The Story:

The tribes of Kesh, a country in what is now California, live a fairly rustic existence, but they have access to a variety of technological apparatuses. One apparatus, an interplanetary computer called The Exchange, provides information to anyone who knows its programming language, TOK. Additionally, the tribes have battery-powered flashlights and motorized boats, and tribal supplies are carried by train from town to town.

The Valley People live in a virtual utopia, holding sacred seasonal ceremonies and existing in cooperation with the land. The Condor People, a warlike group that once had been nomadic, live in a central city and worship a single deity, the Condor. Where Valley women are completely free and equal, Condor women live in cloistered harems and are not permitted to learn how to write. Where Valley People share communal leadership, the Condor answer to one man and hold slaves who were not born to Condor families. Where the Valley People are rural, the Condor People are urban and consider the Valley folk rustic.

One story emerges as central to understanding the differences between Valley and Condor folk. Blue Owl of the Blue Clay Tribe in the Sinshan Valley lives with her mother and grandmother, thinking she is "half a person" because she does not know her father. When she is nine years old, her father, Terter Abhao, a Condor Person from the north whose name means "kills," arrives with his army to spend time in the valley. After he leaves, Blue Owl's mother, Willow, who had thought he had come to stay, changes her own name back to her childhood name of Towhee and withdraws from the family. In Valley culture, this reclaiming of an old name is considered going against nature and liable to be dangerous to the changed person. Thus, when Terter Abhao returns when Blue Owl is fourteen years old, his daughter begs him to take her with him and asks him to rename her.

Blue Owl and Terter ride to Terter's home city. Blue Owl, now Ayatu, learns that Condor women lead conscripted lives, and she now regrets her decision to leave her mother's people. She finds the city stifling and, as her father loses favor in the eyes of the Condor, finds her family losing importance. She is assigned a servant who teaches her how to survive in the harem and who comes with her when she is married off as a second wife, a pretty wife, to another family. Ultimately, she has a daughter and, before he rides to his own death in a canyon, Terter helps Ayatu and her servant and daughter escape from the Condor People.

Ayatu then chooses her own name, Woman Coming Home, and teaches her servant and daughter how to be free. She returns to find little changed in the Valley, but agrees that her story is important, since no other Valley folk have ever gone to live among the Condor and returned. She records her biography with The Exchange. She cares for her somewhat delusional mother, Towhee, who has turned even more inward, possibly because she went back to her old name. Woman Coming Home helps her friend establish herself in this new culture. When Towhee dies, Woman Coming Home renames her mother Ashes and participates in her ritual cremation.

Woman Coming Home meets a Valley man, and they become lovers. Because of her experiences among the Condor, she is initially unwilling to marry, but she ultimately consents, and the two enjoy a peaceful existence with her daughter; they have no children as a couple. A friend marries one of Woman Coming Home's cousins, and the two families ultimately move to separate homes. Woman Coming Home changes her name to Stone Telling, and her husband changes his name to Stone Listening. She begins telling her story to researchers from another place and possibly another time, maybe the present.

Critical Evaluation:

Always Coming Home, Ursula K. Le Guin writes in her preface to the novel, is a possible archaeology of the future, and the story unfolds through narration, poetry, pictures, and drama. To shape Kesh's culture in *Always Coming Home*, Le Guin displays her signature Taoist principles, in which oneness with the world is a significant driver of plot and characterization. In the valley, all life is interdependent, and each entity relies on all others to be whole. Rather than use the yin and yang that Taoism uses to symbolize balance, Le Guin uses a double spiral, with two arms moving outward from a central hinge. Towns are shaped like this double spiral, with sacred places on one arm, a common area in the center hinge, and living and working spaces along the other arm. She also draws on American Indian beliefs to create valley lore; the Coyote, a central figure in much American Indian folklore, is a sacred figure in the valley.

Le Guin's Pandora, from Greek mythology, addresses the reader directly and poses philosophical conundrums. In mythology, Pandora had disobeyed the gods and had opened a jar, releasing all human evils and retaining only hope. In Le Guin's tale, Pandora is an external force, a visitor who marvels at the valley people, sometimes with jealousy, sometimes with spite. Uneasy with the valley, she nonetheless values it and constantly examines it. She engages in a dialogue with one character, an archivist, about the utopian nature of the valley. Though the archivist insists the valley is not a utopia, Pandora argues that it is, and she suggests that, ironic though it may seem, only through a utopian lens can reality be properly evaluated.

Children serve a similar purpose throughout the work, disrupting the world in ways that help readers connect with the work. These forces, while they interrupt the story, serve as bridges to readers and help keep the novel from becoming too difficult to follow—the novel moves from short poems to short dramas to short stories, without offering a central character other than Stone Telling. This stylistic technique, however, is also one of the book's primary strengths.

Shaking readers loose from traditional narrative patterns invites them to participate in the dialogue more directly. It allows a glimpse inside the writer's mind, encouraging readers to imagine this future world in contrast to their own. Le Guin insists that this future is only a possible future, and thus only a possible history of the future. Indeed, the work is set so far in the future that nuclear apocalypse is long past and nuclear wastelands are once more habitable, though chemically polluted areas still remain. San Francisco, for example, has sunk into the ocean, and the waters of the bay now cover the remains of the city. In one short story, characters marvel that where they now ride in the water in boats, homes once stood.

Stone Telling's story enhances reader understanding of the conflict between the Condor and the Valley peoples, illustrating the differences between the two groups that some of the shorter pieces treat as common knowledge. In turn, the poetry, drama, and folklore surrounding the sections of Stone Telling's tale draw out concepts she does not need to explain, such as how The Exchange works or why trains, but not automobiles, still exist. This interdependence is a crucial facet of the work, as it reflects both the Taoist and American Indian principles expressed in the valley's religions and in Le Guin's body of literature as a whole.

Always Coming Home displays several unique tendencies that are now common in fiction. The novel is the first to use interactive media as an important part of the story. Todd Barton composed music to accompany the words of Le Guin, who had written several valley songs; the music was released on cassette tape and sold with the 1985 edition of the book. Early reviewers expressed astonishment, insisting that it was lucky the book stood alone, because readers would not want to use (and pay for) added content. Similarly, the artwork of Margaret Chodos (now Chodos-Irvine) is included in the novel as examples of Keshian art. Interactive media are now commonly included with books, in the form of compact discs and digital files. Indeed, novels themselves have become interactive, as readers and writers can interact and change stories through the Web. The success of *Always Coming Home* marks its connection with a real future that had been, in 1985, only a possibility.

Jessie Bishop Powell

Further Reading

Bernando, Susan M., and Graham J. Murphy. *Ursula K. Le Guin: A Critical Companion.* New York: Greenwood Press, 2006. A good starting place for those interested in Le Guin's works. Offers detailed analyses of her literary style and a transcript from a 2005 interview with the novelist. Includes a brief biography and an essay concerning Le Guin's place in the "literary genealogy of science fiction."

Cadden, Mike. *Ursula K. Le Guin Beyond Genre: Fiction for Children and Adults.* New York: Routledge, 2005. Examines Le Guin's influential role in the development of popular and literary fiction. Discusses how her work often transcends its assigned genre. Includes the chapter "*Always Coming Home*: Childhood, Children's Stories, and the Child Reader."

Dooley, Patricia. "*Always Coming Home*." Review of *Always Coming Home*, by Ursula K. Le Guin. *Library Journal* 110, no. 15 (September 15, 1985): 93. One of the first reviews of the work. Shows the contemporary public response, in terms of both its unusual configuration and the then-unprecedented use of interactive technology.

Hostetler, Margaret. "Was It I That Killed the Babies? Children as Disruptive Signifiers in Ursula K. Le Guin's *Always Coming Home*." *Extrapolation* 42, no. 1 (Spring, 2001): 10. Explores children as nearly alien forces who often exist in contradiction to the order of things in Le Guin's novel.

Kelso, Sylvia. *Ursula K. Le Guin.* Vashon Island, Wash.: Paradoxa, 2008. Although slightly more difficult to obtain than some Le Guin criticisms, this work offers a comprehensive examination of the author's career and philosophies, especially as these relate to her writing.

Oziewicz, Marek. *One Earth, One People: The Mythopoeic Fantasy of Ursula K. Le Guin, Lloyd Alexander, Madeleine L'Engle, and Orson Scott Card.* Jefferson, N.C.: McFarland, 2008. Argues that the works of fantasy authors, including Le Guin, have socially transformative power, giving expression to a worldview based on the supernatural or spiritual.

Reid, Suzanne Elizabeth. *Presenting Ursula K. Le Guin.* New York: Twayne, 1997. A critical biography aimed at young adults. Provides a good introduction to Le Guin's fiction and examines how the events of the author's life have helped to shape her work.

Rochelle, Warren. *Communities of the Heart: The Rhetoric of Myth in the Fiction of Ursula K. Le Guin.* Liverpool, England: University of Liverpool Press, 2001. Analyzes Le Guin's construction of myth and her use of mythological themes in her work.

Amadeus

Author: Peter Shaffer (1926-   )
First produced: 1979; first published, 1980
Type of work: Drama
Type of plot: Fantasy
Time of plot: 1783-1823
Locale: Vienna

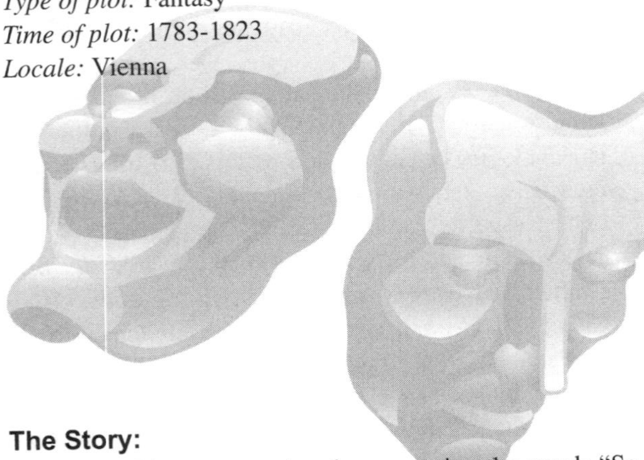

Principal characters:
ANTONIO SALIERI, Imperial court composer of Vienna, rival of Mozart
WOLFGANG AMADEUS MOZART, genius composer from Salzburg
CONSTANZE MOZART, wife of Mozart
LEOPOLD MOZART, father of Mozart
JOSEPH II, emperor of Austria-Hungary
KATERINA CAVALIERI, previous mistress of Salieri, seduced by Mozart
COUNT ORSINI-ROSENBERG, a patron of musical arts
EMANUEL SCHICKANEDER, an impresario of the Volkstheater, friend of Mozart
COUNT COLLOREDO, archbishop of Salzburg, original patron of Mozart

The Story:

Heard whispers open the play, repeating the words "Salieri" and "Assassin." A seated man's silhouette is seen with its back toward the audience. The man is Salieri, retired court composer to the Habsburg emperor Joseph II; he is sitting in his apartment in Vienna. Turning around in his wheelchair, he narrates a confession to the audience, asking it to be his confessor.

Salieri recollects his first meeting with the adult Mozart, even though he had been familiar with the wunderkind Mozart's music when Mozart toured Europe as a child prodigy, accompanied by his father Leopold. As Salieri muses on Mozart's music, he reminisces about how Mozart epitomized what Salieri wanted to be: divinely gifted. Instead, Salieri was a mediocre composer, just as history has judged him. Salieri knows too well that the emperor has a tin ear and that Salieri's politicking rather than musical talent gained him his court appointment.

Mozart arrived in Vienna seeking commissions from the court, where Salieri jealously guarded Vienna's music scene as if it were his own personal fiefdom. As much as he at first worshiped Mozart's music as a connoisseur from a distance, Salieri was stunned when he met Mozart as an adult and realized Mozart was as irreverent as Salieri was reverent.

Mozart himself interrupts Salieri's confession, crudely chasing a girl into the room, at times on all fours, throwing her onto the floor and cavorting with her under the table. His excited speech is filled with playful gutter language, and he acts almost as if he is about to remove the girl's clothes and make a conquest of her on the spot, although she also appears fairly willing. It is only when his music is heard offstage that Mozart runs off to conduct a performance that the court musicians have started without him. Salieri finds Mozart's music as beautiful as he finds Mozart himself repulsive and childish. The girl is Constanze, whom Mozart marries against his authoritarian father's will.

In court, Mozart also makes impromptu variations on one of Salieri's vapid march themes, greatly enlivening the music, to Salieri's frustration. Salieri's anger at Mozart can only grow after the gifted young man seduces Salieri's young mistress, Katerina Cavalieri, and even she finds Mozart far more interesting than the ageing Salieri. However, Mozart's marriage to Constanze is mostly a disaster in Salieri's eyes, as Salieri mocks that he understands her husband's music far better than does Constanze herself.

Count Orsini-Rosenberg, a Viennese courtier, soon intervenes on Salieri's behalf in intrigues to keep the emperor's attention away from Mozart's opera *Le nozze di Figaro: Ossia, La folle giornata* (1786; *The Marriage of Figaro: Or, The Day of Madness*). Mozart has to deal with a court for which he is ill prepared, especially since Mozart is clearly childish in his business and political pursuits, all too often withdrawn from society to compose when he could be performing, and living far more extravagantly than his means.

Salieri pretends to help Mozart, while all the time he is conspiring to hinder Mozart in every possible way, often successfully. Constanze Mozart comes to Salieri for help with a bundle of Mozart's manuscripts, trying to stave off their financial ruin because Mozart is busy composing profoundly colorful operas such as *Die Zauberflöte* (1791; *The Magic Flute*) for Emanuel Schickaneder, an opera librettist and popular Viennese impresario. Salieri reads the musical scores Constanze brings and cannot help but grudgingly admire the beauty of Mozart's music as he hums or picks out the unsurpassed melodies history remembers well. His admiration turns to astonishment, however, when his examination of the musical scores reveals that they were hastily written without any changes or errors, as if they arrived perfectly complete from Mozart's head dictated to his pen. Such a compositional process is incomprehensible to Salieri, who repeatedly rewrites his own scores, unsuccessfully editing out as much of their banality as possible. This realization that, despite his childish buffoonery, Mozart appears blessed with divine musical inspiration drives Salieri half mad with bitter jealousy, and he blames God for his mediocrity, as if God were taunting him with Mozart's genius.

In 1791, Salieri pretends to be a masked apparition of Leopold Mozart and commissions Wolfgang to write a requiem. Salieri intends to steal the music from the soon-to-die Mozart, but his plans are frustrated when the *Requiem Mass in D Minor*, a moving funerary monument for all time, is kept from him and becomes known as Mozart's final work of genius.

Salieri finally attempts half-heartedly to cut his own throat, but he mangles even his own suicide attempt, and Viennese society ultimately deplores him all the more for doing everything in mediocrity. Mozart died at age thirty-five in 1791, not from poison but from a complex of medical ills while living in manifest poverty resulting from financial mismanagement. His growing reputation as a tragic genius was strengthened by his burial as a pauper in an unmarked grave. Salieri, however, hovers round Vienna until 1825, barely recognized by society as anything but a dated musical hack whose music was listenable only in his own time.

Critical Evaluation:

Amadeus is not a traditional biography- or period-centered realist play. Peter Shaffer himself calls his play a fantasy. The narrative frame of Salieri recollecting and relating his mercurial relationship with Mozart as a confession to the audience is an invention by Shaffer that functions to drive the plot. The invention incorporates rumors that have circulated for centuries, as even around 1800 intrigues surrounding Mozart's death included rumors of a murder plot. Salieri's jealousy of Mozart was evidently known well enough for people to suspect him of poisoning his rival. The implication of Salieri in Mozart's death was often popular, as the Russian poet Alexander Pushkin even wrote a dialogue, *Motsart i Salyeri* (pr., pb. 1832; *Mozart and Salieri*, 1920), naming Salieri as Mozart's murderer.

Even though it is only one of the better-known of the composer's middle names, the very title *Amadeus* is almost the crux of the play. Amadeus can mean "loved by God," and this name becomes the springboard that Shaffer develops into obsession: Salieri has loved God from youth onward and has devoted his entire life to serving God, whereas Mozart, who behaves as a crude fool, seems blessed by God with an incomparable gift. Salieri's obsession with Mozart, then, grows not merely out of simple jealousy but also out of a sense of injustice because Mozart inexplicably seems to have been granted divine talents that Salieri believes should rightfully be his. This perception is heightened as a narrative device since the play unfolds as a series of flashbacks to events that occurred decades earlier, when Mozart was still alive. The interplay between Salieri and Mozart—who changes in Salieri's eyes from a musical genius worthy of worship to an incorrigible buffoon whom Salieri grows to hate—becomes the central tension of the drama.

Public reaction to the play was mixed, as it was to a 1984 film adaptation. Many musical professionals walked out of the theaters, believing Shaffer's work was a travesty that caricatured the life of one of art's greatest geniuses. The play primarily relies on imagined music, whereas the film incorporates Mozart's scores throughout. What many who panned *Amadeus* failed to see, however, was that the play does not represent the historical Mozart; instead, it represents Salieri's memory of Mozart, a caricature created by the rival composer to justify his jealous hatred and remind himself of his own mediocrity. Thus, the play portrays Mozart as a composer who wrote almost effortlessly at one go, whereas Salieri wrote with great effort and endless revisions and corrections, because that is how it seems to Salieri.

One inescapable question Shaffer seems to ask throughout *Amadeus* is, would the historical Salieri have ever wondered how his own vapid music—despite its superficial elegance—could survive, regardless of his long service to God and the imperial court, in the face of Mozart's timeless genius? A realization that one's work would be lost to history might drive many people vindictively mad, as it drives Salieri mad in Shaffer's play. The sad juxtaposition of the genius Mozart and the journeyman Salieri in *Amadeus* may not portray the former composer as positively as his aficionados would prefer. However, the absurd, irreligious jester represents a stark contrast to Salieri, who appears to be simply diabolical in the play and is treated more as a conflicted and religious man of stricken conscience in the film version.

Both the play and the film were enormous box office successes, bringing Mozart's music to a far wider audience. Indeed, the film was a blockbuster and won five Academy Awards, including Best Picture and Best Actor. Where the play makes minimal use of Mozart's music, the film's soundtrack incorporates majestic performances of that music wherever appropriate. One great irony of the drama Shaffer fully intended is that Mozart was shown even in caricature as one of history's most loved composers, however vastly unappreciated he was at times in his own life. Salieri, however, would ultimately be as forgotten as his music, despite all his machinations and intrigues to keep Mozart from the musical world Salieri wanted to control. Even in this Salieri failed. Who would not fail contriving to suppress Mozart's incomparable music? To a degree, each audience is gradually led by Shaffer's blunt thesis to realize that most people are jealous of genius and, faced with a rival like Mozart, would probably act much like Salieri.

Patrick Hunt

Further Reading

Bilir, Seda, and Marcia Vale. *Character Conflicts in Peter Shaffer's "The Royal Hunt of the Sun," "Equus," and "Amadeus."* Ankara: Atilim University Graduate School of Social Sciences, 2007. Reads three of Shaffer's most significant plays through the lens of the conflicts he creates between characters.

Edelstein, David. "Amadeus." *Village Voice*, September 25, 1984, p. 63. Examines the decision to recast Salieri's confession in the film adaptation, from a confession to the audience to one to a priest.

MacMurraugh-Kavanagh, Madeleine K. *Peter Shaffer: Theatre and Drama*. New York: Macmillan, 1999. Overview of the playwright's work, its influences, and its significance.

Tibbets, John. "Faces and Masks: Peter Shaffer's *Amadeus* from Stage to Screen." *Literature/Film Quarterly* 32, no. 3 (2004): 166-174. Chronology of adapting first a London, then a Broadway play for the screen and the facile, gifted collaboration between Shaffer and Milos Forman, emphasizing their dual contributions that made the adaptation a major Academy Award-winning film.

Amadís of Gaul

Author: Vasco de Lobeira (c. 1360-c. 1403)
First published: Amadís de Gaula, 1508 (English translation, 1619)
Type of work: Novel
Type of plot: Romance
Time of plot: First century
Locale: France, England, and the rest of Europe

Principal characters:
AMADÍS OF GAUL
KING PERIÓN, his father
PRINCESS ELISENA, his mother
GALAOR, another son of King Perión
LISUARTE, king of Great Britain
BRISENA, his queen
ORIANA, their daughter
URGANDA, an enchantress
ARCALAUS, a magician

The Story:

Not many years after the passion of Christ, there lives in Lesser Britain a Christian king named Garinter. His older daughter is married to the king of Scotland. The younger daughter, Elisena, finds none of her suitors attractive until the day her father brings home King Perión of Gaul, whom Garinter watched defeat two powerful knights and kill a lion. The scheming of Elisena's attendant, Darioleta, allows the young people to meet secretly in the royal garden. King Perión departs ten days later without knowing the results of their nights of love.

When Elisena's son is born, Darioleta conceals her mistress's indiscretion by putting him into an ark, along with his father's sword and ring, and a parchment declaring the boy to be "the timeless Amadís, son of a king." She sets the ark afloat in the river beside the palace; it drifts out to sea, where it is found by a knight, Gandales, who is on a voyage to Scotland. Gandales, who rears the foundling with his son Gandalin, calls the boy "Child of the Sea."

Gandales, riding through the woods when the boy is three years old, rescues Urganda, an enchantress who is being pursued by a knight. The grateful witch, after prophesying that the adopted boy will become the flower of knighthood, the most honorable warrior in the world, promises to aid him should he ever need her help.

When the boy is seven years old, King Languines of Scotland and his queen see him and offer to bring him up at court. Five years later, King Lisuarte and Queen Brisena pause in Scotland on their way to claim the throne of England. They ask permission to leave behind their daughter Oriana until conditions are safe. King Languines appoints the "Child of the Sea" to be her squire.

The two children fall deeply in love with each other, but they dare not let others know of their feelings. To be worthy of Oriana, Amadís determines to be knighted, and when King Perión visits Scotland to seek help against his enemy, King Abies of Ireland, Oriana asks her father's old friend to knight Amadís. The young knight then rides away in search of fame through adventures.

Urganda meets him in the forest and gives him a lance with which he rescues King Perión from Irish knights. Although neither is aware of the blood relationship between them, Amadís swears always to aid King Perión in time of danger. Then follows a series of fantastic and extraordinary adventures, among them the encounter with haughty Galpano, whose custom is to stop and rob all who pass through his realm. Amadís defeats the bully and his two brothers, although he is so severely wounded in the battles that he has to be nursed back to health by a friendly noble.

Meanwhile, King Perión marries Elisena. Although they lament their lost son, they take pleasure in a second son, Galaor. When King Abies sends an expedition against Gaul, Amadís overcomes the Irish champion. In the celebration festivities at King Perión's court, the identity of Amadís is discovered through the ring he wears, and King Perión proudly acknowledges his long-lost son.

Amadís remains melancholy, thinking himself unworthy to aspire to wed the daughter of the king of England. He does briefly visit her at Vindilisora (Windsor), only to be called away to rescue his brother Galaor. That summons is a trick of the enchanter Arcalaus, who casts a spell over the knight and disarms him. When the villain appears in the armor of Amadís and riding his horse, Oriana almost dies. Only the timely news of further feats of arms by Amadís tells her that he is still alive, and so she is restored to health.

Tireless in his villainy, Arcalaus causes King Lisuarte to disappear and abducts Oriana. Amadís and his brother, knighted by Amadís, rescue the princess, but in the absence of the king, the traitor Barsinan tries to seize Brisena and usurp the throne. Dressed in rusty armor, Amadís defeats the rebel, and when Oriana's father reappears, twelve days of feasting follow. Amadís, however, is no nearer to winning the hand of his beloved despite his great service to the king.

Continuing to seek knightly fame, Amadís and his friends sail for Firm Island, settled by Apolidón, son of the king of Greece, who took refuge there after eloping with the daughter of Emperor Siudan of Rome. On Firm Island is an enchanted arch through which only faithful lovers can pass. Beyond it is a marriage chamber guarded by invisible knights. After his arrival in that land, Amadís receives a note from Oriana, who believes the lying charges of unfaithfulness made against him by a malignant dwarf. She signs herself as a damsel pierced through the heart by the sword of Amadís.

His overwhelming grief upon reading the note and his withdrawal, under the name of Beltenebros (Fair Forlorn One) to the hermitage at the Poor Rock, convince Oriana that she wronged him. There is nothing she can do, however, to right matters, for King Lisuarte gives her in marriage to the emperor of Rome.

When a fleet from Rome takes her away, Amadís, calling himself the Greek Knight, defeats it and returns Oriana to her father, asking only that she be protected against further misalliances. King Lisuarte decides to punish such effrontery by an attack on Firm Island, a decision that ranges the knights of the world on two sides. King Lisuarte enlists the help of the emperor of Rome. Amadís visits the emperor of Constantinople and sends a messenger to the king of Bohemia. Arcalaus hates both Amadís and King Lisuarte and encourages King Aravigo to march with his army and prey on both sides.

When the hosts assemble for the battle, King Gasquilán of Sweden sends a personal challenge to Amadís to meet him in single combat between the lines. The king's overthrow is the signal for a general onslaught that lasts for two days, until at last the death of the emperor of Rome disheartens and routs his army.

Out of affection for Oriana, Amadís does not pursue the defeated host, but King Aravigo takes the opportunity to plunder the followers of King Lisuarte. A hermit, who was trying to bring about peace among the combatants, sends the youthful Esplandían to take the news of King Lisuarte's distress to Amadís. The hero marches at once to the rescue of King Lisuarte, a kindness that wipes out the enmity between them. The marriage of Oriana and Amadís is solemnized on Firm Island. Afterward, the couple pass under the Arch of True Love into the magic bridal chamber.

Critical Evaluation:

A single original to this text has been lost. What most modern English readers have is an abridged 1803 translation by the poet Robert Southey of a Spanish work published in Saragossa in 1508 by Garcia Rodríguez de Montalvo. Southey's work superseded an earlier English translation by Anthony Munday, dating from the Elizabethan era, while Montalvo claimed to have derived his version from a work by the Portuguese writer Vasco de Lobeira. This attribution is dubious because Vasco de Lobeira was active in the latter part of the fourteenth century, and the earliest references to the text date from the first half of that century.

If the work did originate in Portugal, a more probable author might be Juan Lobeira, who was active in the latter part of the thirteenth century and who is credited elsewhere with the composition of a song whose Spanish translation can be found in the Montalvo version, although Vasco de Lobeira might conceivably have done a later version of it. There is no way of knowing for sure where the original version of the story was written down, by whom, or when. Montalvo does tell his readers, however, that in translating Lobeira's work he has considerably modified its supposedly outmoded style, and modern commentators believe that the fourth volume of his version consists of material added by him.

In its form and content *Amadís of Gaul* is an imitation of the tradition of French chivalric romances concerning the exploits of Charlemagne and his knights, which expanded to take in such figures as Alexander the Great and the English King Arthur and such motifs as the quest for the Holy Grail. As in many such romances, the protagonist, Amadís, begins in "Lesser Britain" (Brittany), at the interface of Anglo-Norman and Gallic culture. Amadís, the son of Perión of Gaul, is brought up on the barbarous fringe of the Norman sphere of influence but must eventually seek his fortune on a hypothetical island that has been settled by a prince of Greece and the daughter of the emperor of Rome. In this manner the plot bridges the whole spectrum of imagined European traditions and values (tacitly extended to include the eastern domains of Constantinople and Bohemia). The central figure, Amadís, symbolizes, among other things, the union of all Christendom. His natural nobility must perforce be hidden under various guises—most notably that of the Green Knight—but it nevertheless causes him to remain absolutely faithful to his ideal, Oriana. Primarily a romantic ideal, Oriana is also a political and spiritual ideal.

Montalvo's version of the story is important in several ways. As a robust product of a vernacular language it embodies something of the spirit of the Renaissance. It was enormously popular not only as an adventure story but also as a guide to morals and manners, and it made a substantial contribution to the sense of cultural rebirth that boosted progressive ideas and ideals. It also wrought a subtle but vital revision of the medieval mythology of courtly love, in which the women idealized by knights were traditionally the wives of their liege-lords and thus permanently unattainable. The substitution of a marriageable heroine changed the story's ideal ending and thus its whole direction. The most perfect knights of traditional romance were those who remained utterly chaste; the ultimate prize of beholding the Holy Grail was withheld from any who had ever harbored a lustful thought. Montalvo refuses to indulge such fervent asceticism; the symbolic Arch of True Love that permits Amadís and the conveniently eligible Oriana passage into their bridal chamber grants a significant license to physical passion. This conclusion probably did not exist in the accounts of Amadís's adventures that circulated before Montalvo's, and it may mark the story as it exists currently as a true product of the early sixteenth century.

Although the supernatural plays a muted role in Montalvo's story—at least by comparison with later tales of adventure penned by his many imitators—the mode of its operation contrasts with the pious supernaturalism of the grail romances, more closely resembling the fanciful supernaturalism of the French romances featuring the conveniently pre-Christian Alexander. *Amadís of Gaul* cannot be regarded as a wholeheartedly secular work, but much of Amadís's knight errantry is conducted in a forthright spirit of adventure that finds a Christian conscience relatively unburdensome. This aspect of the work is probably not original to Montalvo, but it is nevertheless significant of an important shift in values.

The genre for which *Amadís of Gaul* served as an archetype flourished during the sixteenth century, and it became one of the most popular forms of literature ever. Its ruthless satirization in Miguel de Cervantes' *El ingenioso hidalgo don Quixote de la Mancha* (1605, 1615; *Don Quixote de la Mancha*,1612-1620) signified that it had become ridiculous. Although the genre of chivalric romance faded away throughout Europe in the seventeenth century, certain key elements of it retained their potency and continued their evolution. *Amadís of Gaul* provided a vital steppingstone in the evolution of the modern mythology of romantic love, and modern "romantic fiction" still retains within its formula that final passage through the arch of true love to the bridal chamber. Even more spectacularly, the revived genre of "heroic fantasy" brought back into favor exactly the kind of plot that *Amadís of Gaul* lays out, with an astonishing abundance of misplaced heroes embarking upon lengthy quests, beset by all manner of magical and monstrous perils before they finally achieve their proper station in a confused world. The strong similarities between these modern genres and a work that few modern writers have read are testimony to the sturdiness of the literary traditions. The survival of such forms of literature is tribute to the extent to which modern culture is rooted in the intellectual achievements of the Renaissance.

"Critical Evaluation" by Brian Stableford

Further Reading

Damiani, Bruno M. "Amicitia and Amor: Toward an Analysis of Love and Sexuality in *Amadís de Gaula*." In *Hispanic Essays in Honor of Frank P. Casa*, edited by A. Robert Lauer and Henry W. Sullivan. New York: Peter Lang, 1997. Collection of critical essays interpreting *Amadís of Gaul* and other literary works written during the Golden Age of Spain.

Green, Otis H. *Spain and the Western Tradition*. 4 vols. Madison: University of Wisconsin Press, 1963. A discussion of *Amadís of Gaul* in the context of the mythology of courtly love appears in volume 1 on pages 104-111.

Moorcock, Michael. *Wizardry and Wild Romance: A Study of Epic Fantasy*. London: Victor Gollancz, 1987. Chapter 1 discusses *Amadís of Gaul* as the primary ancestor of the modern genre of fantasy.

Northup, George Tyler. *An Introduction to Spanish Literature*. 3d rev. ed. Chicago: University of Chicago Press, 1960. Describes the origins of chivalric romance, discussing the authorship and influence of *Amadís of Gaul*.

Place, Edwin B., and Herbert C. Behm. *Amadís of Gaul: A Romance of Chivalry of the Fourteenth Century Presumably First Written in Spanish*. 2 vols. 2d ed. Lexington: University Press of Kentucky, 2003. A full English translation of the work from the earliest available source; the introduction offers an introduction to the original edition of the text, published in 1974, as well as an introduction to the new edition.

Rothstein, Marian. *Reading in the Renaissance: Amadís de Gaule and the Lessons of Memory*. Newark: University of Delaware Press, 1999. Examines the French version of *Amadís of Gaul*, which enjoyed great popularity when it was published in 1540 but was virtually ignored twenty years later. Explains the reason for the work's rise and fall and what this shift in popularity says about the habits of Renaissance readers.

Williams, Grace S. "The *Amadís* Question." *Revue Hispanique* 21 (1909): 1-167. A comprehensive discussion of the origins of the story and its various versions.

The Amazing Adventures of Kavalier and Clay

Author: Michael Chabon (1963-   )
First published: 2000
Type of work: Novel
Type of plot: Historical realism
Time of plot: 1939-1954
Locale: Prague; New York City and Long Island, New York; Antarctica

Principal characters:
SAMUEL KLAYMAN, comic-book writer and editor
JOSEF KAVALIER, Samuel's cousin and creative partner
ROSA SAKS, Josef's lover and Samuel's wife
THOMAS KAVALIER, Josef's younger brother
BERNARD KORNBLUM, an escape artist and Josef's teacher
SHELDON ANAPOL, a publisher, Samuel and Josef's employer
GEORGE DEASEY, Samuel and Josef's editor
TRACY BACON, an actor and Samuel's lover
TOMMY KLAYMAN, Rosa and Josef's son

The Story:

Samuel Klayman is in his Brooklyn bedroom one night in 1939 when his mother introduces him to his cousin, Josef Kavalier, newly arrived from Prague, who will be staying with them, having escaped Europe and the Nazis. Samuel is initially suspicious of Josef, but agrees to try to help him obtain employment at the company where he works, Empire Novelties.

The son of two Jewish doctors, Josef had become interested in the art of escape and studied with Bernard Kornblum, a famous escape artist. To safeguard him, Josef's parents arranged to send him out of the country, but he was thrown off the train because of a change in regulations. In desperation, he begged Kornblum to help him flee. Kornblum had already contracted to arrange the shipment to Vilna of Rabbi Loew's golem (a giant clay man said to come to life to protect Jews) in order to protect it, and he agreed to secrete Josef with the golem, allowing him to escape.

The morning after Josef's arrival, Samuel awakes to find him drawing on a comic panel and is very impressed by his work. Josef reveals that he studied for two years at Prague's Academy of Fine Arts. Samuel asks Josef to draw a portfolio to show his employer, Sheldon Anapol. The cousins meet with Anapol and propose that they create a new hero similar to Superman. Anapol agrees to entertain the idea if they can come up with a good sample comic. They leave to begin work and Samuel reminisces about his father, the "Mighty Molecule," a strongman on the vaudeville circuit who abandoned the family during Samuel's childhood. He returned when Samuel was a teenager and promised to take him along on the circuit, but left in the middle of the night and died soon afterward.

Samuel and Josef go to the apartment where several of Samuel's artist friends live; they all begin creating characters for the sample comic. Samuel and Josef create The Escapist, whose real name is Tom Mayflower. Mayflower trains with a famous escape artist and takes over his role as helper of the innocent when the older man is killed. They present their work to Anapol, suggesting that he start a company called Empire Comics. Anapol agrees to finance the project, but only if his employee George Deasey is editor. He asks Josef to change the cover art for the first issue, which shows The Escapist punching Adolph Hitler. Josef refuses to compromise, feeling that the anti-Nazi artwork is an important element in his quest to bring attention to the plight of Jews in Europe. Anapol agrees to let them keep the cover, and Empire Comics is born.

The Escapist is a huge success, and Anapol becomes extremely wealthy, while Samuel and Josef earn good salaries. Now known as Joe Kavalier and Sammy Clay, the team creates many successful characters, with Samuel writing the stories and Josef providing the art. Josef is continually trying to get his family out of Prague. He learns that his father has died, prompting him to consider joining the Canadian air force. Eventually, he rejects this plan and redoubles his efforts to save his mother and brother.

Distraught, Josef breaks into the office of the Aryan-American League, run by Carl Ebling, an anti-Semite. Ebling catches him, but he escapes. Ebling later places a fake bomb in the Empire Comics offices, prompting an evacuation of the Empire State Building, though Josef refuses to leave. Deasey, a disillusioned Columbia University graduate who feels comics are beneath him, but who nevertheless needs the money and admires Josef, warns the partners that Anapol is selling The Escapist as a radio serial. He advises them to press Anapol for more money.

Josef begins a relationship with Rosa Saks, whom he meets at a party given by her father, Longman Harkoo. At Harkoo's party, Josef saves Salvador Dali's life and Samuel witnesses two men kissing romantically, which surprises and intrigues him. Rosa introduces Josef to Hermann Hoffman, who runs the Transatlantic Rescue Agency, dedicated to rescuing Jewish children from Europe. Josef enlists Hoffman's help in rescuing his brother Thomas. Josef and Samuel create a new female comic character named Luna Moth and attempt once again to get more money from Anapol. Deasey again intervenes to tell them that Anapol is being sued by Superman's creators. They use this information to convince Anapol to give them a small profit-sharing deal in exchange for their (untruthful) testimony that The Escapist was not based on Superman.

Samuel spends his newfound wealth, but Josef saves his money to help Hoffman charter a ship to transport a group of Jewish children, including his brother, from Europe. They also meet the actors playing their characters in the radio serial; Tracy Bacon, who plays The Escapist, shows an interest in Samuel. Josef begins to appear at bar mitzvahs as a magician, "The Amazing Cavalieri." During one performance, Carl Ebling attempts to kill him with a planted bomb, but Josef recognizes him and defuses the bomb.

Samuel is working as a civilian air spotter in the Empire State Building, when Tracy Bacon arrives one night and kisses him; they eventually begin a love affair. The State Department refuses visas to the Jewish refugee children waiting to cross the Atlantic in the TRA ship, and Harkoo calls Eleanor Roosevelt to seek her intervention. With her help, the ship sets sail, but it is sunk by a German submarine; all aboard are killed. Josef learns of his brother's death at a performance, and Rosa finds out as she is painting a mural in the room that was to be Thomas's. Samuel is visiting the home of a wealthy gay friend of Tracy, which is raided by the police at the behest of the maid, Carl Ebling's sister. Samuel is forced to provide sexual favors to an FBI agent and is traumatized by the experience. Josef leaves the next day to join the Navy, and Samuel learns that Rosa is pregnant with Josef's child.

The narrative shifts to Antarctica, where Josef has been posted by the Navy as a radioman. One night, he is awakened and realizes all the men and dogs in the shelter with him are dead. Only he and John Shannenhouse, a pilot posted at the station, remain alive. A stove vent in the facility was faulty, and it caused the men to die of carbon monoxide poisoning. It is winter, and it is impossible for Josef and Shannenhouse to leave the station until the heavy ice surrounding it thaws in the spring.

Shannenhouse begins to work on the sea plane, and Josef spends his time listening obsessively to radio traffic. They eventually learn of a German geologist also marooned in Antarctica, and they plan to kill him. Shannenhouse completes the plane repairs, and they take off, in defiance of orders. Shannenhouse suffers a burst appendix and dies, causing the plane to crash. Josef survives the crash but is shot in the leg by the German. They scuffle and Josef shoots and kills him. Though he thought this would satisfy his rage, in reality he is bereft.

The final section of the book finds Samuel and Rosa married and living in Long Island, raising Rosa and Josef's son, Tommy. Samuel is employed by Pharaoh House comics, after unsuccessful attempts at several other professions. Bacon became an Army Air Corps pilot and was killed in the Pacific theater during the war. A letter appears in the newspaper stating that The Escapist will jump from the Empire State Building. Police question Samuel; he explains that Josef never returned from the Navy and they do not know his whereabouts. Eventually, they learn that Tommy wrote the letter in an attempt to draw out Josef, whom he has been secretly seeing. Josef had contacted him, having seen him in a magic shop and recognized him.

Josef appears and attempts to bungee jump off the building, but he falls on a ledge and is injured. Josef moves in with Samuel and Rosa; Samuel discovers the epic comic based on the golem that Josef has created during his absence. Samuel expresses a desire to publish the comic, and Josef eventually buys Empire Comics, which Anapol is selling after killing off The Escapist. Samuel is publically exposed as homosexual when he is called to testify before a congressional committee on the effects of comics on American youth. Tommy eventually discovers that Josef is his real father, and Samuel leaves for Los Angeles to live openly as a gay man, leaving Josef, Rosa, and Tommy together as a family.

Critical Evaluation:

Michael Chabon's work has been well received both critically and popularly since his first novel, *The Mysteries of Pittsburgh* (1988); his third novel, *The Amazing Adventures of Kavalier and Clay*, won the 2001 Pulitzer Prize in fiction. Chabon's work has been praised for many factors, primarily his intricate, believable characterizations and highly developed, artistic prose.

The Amazing Adventures of Kavalier and Clay brings together Chabon's most important themes: the search for identity, the persistent need for humans to escape (from society's strictures, family expectations, and even themselves), and the importance of art in dealing with human identity and emotions. It deals with these themes by using comic book artists and characters to represent the need for escape, literally and figuratively. Josef Kavalier studies to be an escape artist and uses the skills learned from his teacher to literally escape the Nazis. He then becomes obsessed with helping his family escape, though his attempts all fail. He escapes his anger over his brother's death by joining the Navy and escapes from the mother of his child because he cannot imagine his own happiness.

Samuel Klayman is also in the constant process of attempting escape, as he tries to leave his mother, his boring life in Brooklyn, and his growing realization of his own homosexuality—he even escapes from his identity by adopting the pen name Sammy Clay. Though he is in love with Tracy Bacon, Samuel escapes from the train that is to take them to Los Angeles because he cannot bear the stigma of homosexuality. After he marries Rosa and helps her raise Josef's son, he views his suburban life in Long Island as a kind of prison. Even Tommy, Rosa's son, contrives to escape from his boring days at school to visit Josef in Manhattan.

Creating art is represented in the novel as a crucial method used by the characters to express their inner longings; their most popular character is called "The Escapist." The Escapist shares characteristics of both Josef and Samuel and exists in the comic pantheon that includes other characters who are created by Jewish authors and who are seen as representing the immigrant experience. The most famous of these is Superman. Josef's anger at the Nazis is expressed in his art, and he refuses to compromise on this. As Josef comes to terms with his rage and guilt, he writes an epic comic based on the golem. The comic draws strongly on his Jewish origins and thus represents his acceptance of his identity. Samuel's final escape to Los Angeles to live an openly gay life shows his acceptance of his true self also.

The Amazing Adventures of Kavalier and Clay most directly explicates Chabon's core themes—and resolves them—when it most clearly represents art as a healing force. It also represents comics as important cultural touchstones that are deeply meaningful and transformative, rather than just shallow and superficial. The novel intricately and lavishly describes the comic-book art produced by Josef and its place in Jewish American culture and history. It thus simultaneously comments on and transforms that history, using fictional works of art to comment upon the actual role of art in life.

Vicki A. Sanders

Further Reading

Chabon, Michael. "Michael Chabon: A Writer With Many Faces." Interview by Byron Cahill. *Writing* 27, no. 6 (April/May, 2005): 16-19. Cahill interviews Chabon about his various influences and his writing process.

Glaser, Amelia. "From Polylingual to Postvernacular: Imagining Yiddish in the Twenty-First Century." *Jewish Social Studies* 14, no. 3 (Spring/Summer, 2008): 150-164. Discusses Chabon's use of Jewish identity and Jewish language in several of his novels.

Myers, D. G. "Michael Chabon's Imaginary Jews." *Sewanee Review* 116, no. 4 (Fall, 2008): 572-588. Dissects the ways in which Chabon uses Jewish characters to explore the lives of those in the actual Jewish diaspora and the concept of Jewishness as an identity.

Punday, Daniel. "Kavalier and Clay, the Comic-Book Novel, and Authorship in a Corporate World." *Critique* 49, no. 3 (Spring, 2008): 291-302. Points out ways in which the contemporary novel wrestles with the idea of the self and being an author in the contemporary industrial economy, as well as ways in which the novel examines owning one's work.

Singer, Marc. "Embodiments of the Real: The Counterlinguistic Turn in the Comic-Book Novel." *Critique* 49, no. 3 (Spring, 2008): 273-289. Provides a history of some modern critical theories as they relate to the novel, offering the view that it fits into a pattern of using comic-book characters to deal with the problems of language and metaphor in new ways.

The Ambassadors

Author: Henry James (1843-1916)
First published: 1903
Type of work: Novel
Type of plot: Psychological realism
Time of plot: c. 1900
Locale: Paris

Principal characters:
MRS. NEWSOME, a wealthy American widow
CHADWICK "CHAD" NEWSOME, her son and an American expatriate
LAMBERT STRETHER, his friend
MARIA GOSTREY, an acquaintance of Strether
COMTESSE DE VIONNET, a woman in love with Chadwick Newsome
MRS. POCOCK, Chadwick's married sister
MAMIE POCOCK, Mrs. Pocock's husband's sister

The Story:

Lambert Strether is engaged to marry Mrs. Newsome, a widow. Mrs. Newsome has a son, Chadwick, called Chad, whom she wants to return home from Paris and take over the family business in Woollett, Massachusetts. She is especially concerned for his future after she hears that he is seriously involved with a Frenchwoman. In her anxiety, she asks Strether to go to Paris and persuade her son to return to the respectable life she planned for him. Strether does not look forward to his task, for Chad ignored all of his mother's written requests to return home. Strether also does not know what hold Chad's mistress might have over him or what sort of woman she might be. He strongly suspects that she is a young girl of unsavory reputation. Strether realizes, however, that his hopes of marrying Mrs. Newsome depend upon his success in bringing Chad back to America, where his mother can see him married to Mamie Pocock.

Leaving his ship at Liverpool, Strether journeys across England to London. On the way he meets Miss Gostrey, a young woman who is acquainted with some of Strether's American friends, and she promises to aid Strether in getting acquainted with Europe before he leaves for home again. Strether meets another old friend, Mr. Waymarsh, an American lawyer living in England, whom he asks to go with him to Paris. A few days after arriving in Paris, Strether goes to Chad's house. The young man is not in Paris, and he temporarily gave the house over to a friend, Mr. Bilham. Through Bilham, Strether gets in touch with Chad at Cannes. Strether is surprised to learn of his whereabouts, for he knows that Chad would not dare to take an ordinary mistress to such a fashionable resort.

About a week later, Strether, Miss Gostrey, and Waymarsh go to the theater. Between the acts of the play, the door of their box opens and Chad enters. He is much changed from the adolescent college boy Strether remembers. He is slightly gray, although only twenty-eight years old. Strether and Chad are pleased to see each other. Over coffee after the theater, the older man tells Chad why he came to Europe. Chad answers that all he asks is an opportunity to be convinced that he should return. A few days later, Chad takes Strether and his friends to a tea where they meet Mme and Mlle de Vionnet. The former, who married a French count, turns out to be an old school friend of Miss Gostrey. Strether is at a loss to tell whether Chad is in love with the comtesse or with her daughter Jeanne. Since the older woman is only a few years the senior of the young man and as beautiful as her daughter, either is possibly the object of his affections. As the days slip by, it becomes apparent to Strether that he himself wants to stay in Paris. The French city and its life are much calmer and more beautiful than the provincial existence he knew in Woollett, and he begins to understand why Chad is unwilling to go back to his mother and the Newsome mills.

Strether learns that Chad is in love with Mme de Vionnet, rather than with her daughter. The comtesse was separated from her husband for many years, but their position and religion make divorce impossible. Strether, who is often in the company of the Frenchwoman, soon falls under her charm. Miss Gostrey, who knew Mme de Vionnet for many years, has only praise for her and questions Strether as to the advisability of removing Chad from the woman's continued influence. One morning Chad announces to Strether that he is ready to return immediately to America. The young man is puzzled when Strether replies that he is not sure it is wise for either of them to return and that it would be wiser for them both to reconsider whether they would not be better off in Paris than in New England.

When Mrs. Newsome, back in America, receives word of that decision on the part of her ambassador, she immediately sends the Pococks, her daughter and son-in-law, to Paris along with Mamie Pocock, the girl she hopes her son will marry. They are to bring back both Strether and her son. Mrs. Newsome's daughter and her relatives do not come to Paris with an obvious ill will. Their attitude seems to be that Chad and Strether have somehow drifted astray, and it is their duty to set them right. At least that is the attitude of Mrs. Pocock. Her husband, however, is not at all interested in having Chad return, for in the young man's absence, Mr. Pocock controls the Newsome mills. Mr. Pocock further sees that his visit was probably the last opportunity he will have for a spirited time in the European city, and so he is quite willing to spend his holiday going to theaters and cafés. His younger sister, Mamie, seems to take little interest in the recall of her supposed fiancé, for she is interested in Chad's friend, Mr. Bilham.

The more Strether sees of Mme de Vionnet after the arrival of the Pococks, the more he is convinced that the Frenchwoman is both noble and sincere in her attempts to make friends with her lover's family. Mrs. Pocock finds it difficult to reconcile Mme de Vionnet's aristocratic background with the fact that she is Chad's mistress. After several weeks of hints and genteel pleading, the Pococks and Mamie go to Switzerland, leaving Chad to make a decision whether to return to America. As for Strether, Mrs. Newsome advises that he be left alone to make his own decision, for the widow wants to avoid the appearance of having lost her dignity or her sense of propriety.

While the Pococks are gone, Strether and Chad discuss the course they should follow. Chad is uncertain of his attitude toward Mamie Pocock. Strether assures him that the girl is already happy with her new love, Bilham, who tells Strether that he intends to marry the American girl. His advice, contrary to what he thought when he sailed from America, is that Chad should remain in France with the comtesse, despite the fact that the young man cannot marry her and will, by remaining in Europe, lose the opportunity to make himself an extremely rich man. Chad decides to take his older friend's counsel.

Waymarsh, who promised his help in persuading Chad to return to America, is outraged at Strether's changed attitude. Miss Gostrey, however, remains loyal, for she fell deeply in love with Strether during their time together in Paris. Strether, however, realizing her feelings, tells her that he has to go back to America alone. His object in Europe was to return Chad to his mother. Because he fails in that mission and will never marry Mrs. Newsome, he cannot justify to himself marrying another woman whom he meets on a journey financed by the woman he at one time intended to marry. Only Mme de Vionnet, he believes, can truly appreciate the irony of his position.

Critical Evaluation:

In Henry James's *The Ambassadors*, plot is minimal; the story line consists simply in Mrs. Newsome's sending Lambert Strether to Europe to bring home her son, Chad. The important action is psychological rather than physical; the crucial activities are thought and conversation. The pace of the novel is slow. Events unfold as they do in life: in their own good time. Because of these qualities, James's work demands certain responses from the reader, who must not expect boisterous action, shocking or violent occurrences, sensational coincidences, quickly mounting suspense, or breathtaking climaxes: These devices have no place in a Henry James novel. Rather, the reader must bring to the work a sensitivity to problems of conscience, an appreciation of the meaning beneath manners, and an awareness of the intricacies of human relationships. Finally, and of the utmost importance, the reader must be patient; the power of a novel like *The Ambassadors* is only revealed quietly and without haste. This is why, perhaps more than any other modern author, James requires rereading—not merely because of the complexity of his style, but also because the richly layered texture of his prose contains a multiplicity of meanings, a wealth of subtle shadings.

In *The Ambassadors*, which James considered his masterpiece, this subtlety and complexity are partially the result of his perfection of the technique for handling point of view. Departing from traditional use of the omniscient narrator, James experiments extensively with the limited point of view, exploring the device to discover what advantages it might have. He finds that what is lost in panoramic scope and comprehensiveness, the limited viewpoint more than compensates for in focus, concentration, and intensity. It is a technique perfectly suited to an author whose primary concern is with presenting the thoughts, emotions, and motivations of an intelligent character and with understanding the psychological makeup of a sensitive mind and charting its growth.

The sensitive and intelligent character through whose mind all events in the novel are filtered is Strether. The reader sees and hears only what Strether sees and hears; all experiences, perceptions, and judgments are his. Strictly adhered to, this device proves too restrictive for James's purpose; therefore, he utilizes other characters—called confidants—who enable him to expand the scope of his narrative without sacrificing advantages inherent in the limited point of view. The basic function of these "listening characters" is to expand and enrich Strether's experience. Miss Gostrey, Bilham, Waymarsh, and Miss Barrace—all share with him attitudes and insights arising from their widely diverse backgrounds; they provide him with a wider range of knowledge than he could ever gain from firsthand experience. Miss Gostrey, Strether's primary confidant, illustrates the fact that James's listening characters are deep and memorable personalities in their own right. Miss Gostrey not only listens to Strether but also becomes an important figure in the plot, and as she gradually falls in love with Strether, she engages the reader's sympathy as well.

Strether interacts with and learns from the environment of Paris as well as from the people he meets there; thus, the setting is far more than a mere backdrop against which events in the plot occur. To understand the significance of Paris as the setting, the reader must appreciate the meaning that the author, throughout his fiction, attached to certain places. James was fascinated by what he saw as the underlying differences in the cultures of America and Europe and, in particular, in the opposing values of a booming American factory town such as Woollett and an ancient European capital such as Paris. In these two places, very different qualities are held in esteem. In Woollett, Mrs. Newsome admires practicality, individuality, and enterprise, while in Paris, her son appreciates good food and expensive wine, conversation with a close circle of friends, and leisure time quietly spent. Woollett pursues commercialism, higher social status, and rigid moral codes with untiring vigor; Paris values the beauty of nature, the pleasure of companionship, and an appreciation of the arts with studied simplicity. Thus, the implications of a native of Woollett, such as Strether, going to Paris at the end of his life are manifold; it is through his journey that the theme of the novel is played out.

The theme consists of a question of conscience: Should Strether, in his capacity as Mrs. Newsome's ambassador, be faithful to his mission of bringing Chad home once he no longer believes in that mission? That he ceases to believe is the result of his conversion during his stay in Paris. He is exposed to a side of life that he had not known previously; furthermore, he finds it to be good. As a man of noble nature and sensitive conscience, he cannot ignore or deny, as Mrs. Newsome later does, that life in Paris has vastly improved Chad. Ultimately, therefore, he must oppose rather than promote the young man's return. The honesty of this action not only destroys his chance for financial security in marriage to Chad's mother but also prevents him from returning the love of Miss Gostrey. Although Strether's discovery of a different set of values comes too late in life for his own benefit, he at least can save Chad. The lesson he learns is the one he passionately seeks to impart to Bilham: "Live all you can; it's a mistake not to. It doesn't so much matter what you do in particular, so long as you have your life. . . . Don't, at any rate, miss things out of stupidity. . . . Live!"

If, in reading *The Ambassadors*, readers' expectations are for keenness of observation, insight into motivations, comprehension of mental processes, and powerful characterizations, they will not be disappointed. If James demands the effort, concentration, and commitment of his readers, he also—with his depth and breadth of vision and the sheer beauty of his craftsmanship—repays them a hundredfold.

"Critical Evaluation" by Nancy G. Ballard

Further Reading

Bell, Millicent. *Meaning in Henry James*. Cambridge, Mass.: Harvard University Press, 1991. Examines James's novels in reference to narrative theory. The analysis of *The Ambassadors* focuses on narrative techniques and shows the relationship between narrative and meaning.

Coulson, Victoria. *Henry James, Women, and Realism*. New York: Cambridge University Press, 2007. Examines James's important friendships with three women: his sister Alice James and the novelists Constance Fenimore Woolson and Edith Wharton. These three women writers and James shared what Coulson describes as an "ambivalent realism," or a cultural ambivalence about gender identity, and she examines how this idea is manifest in James's works, including *The Ambassadors*.

Edel, Leon. *Henry James: A Life*. Rev. ed. New York: Harper & Row, 1985. A classic biography. Places *The Ambassadors* in the context of James's biography, showing its place in James's life and in his stylistic development. Good for those interested in biographical criticism.

Freedman, Jonathan, ed. *The Cambridge Companion to Henry James*. New York: Cambridge University Press, 1998. A collection of essays that provides extensive information on James's life and literary influences and describes his works and the characters in them.

Fussel, Edwin Sill. *The French Side of Henry James*. New York: Columbia University Press, 1990. A good analysis of James's novels set wholly or partly in France. Discussion of *The Ambassadors* shows the importance of place to the theme in James's work. Explains specific French concepts and images in the novel.

Hocks, Richard A. *"The Ambassadors": Consciousness, Culture, Poetry*. New York: Twayne, 1997. A detailed examination of the novel, including analyses of James's narrative technique, his treatment of the philosophical dilemma of freedom versus determinism, and how the novel reflects his theories about literature.

Krook-Gilead, Dorothea. *Henry James's "The Ambassadors": A Critical Study*. New York: AMS Press, 1996. A close reading of the novel, examining its theme, style, plot, relationships among its characters, and mixture of the tragic and comic elements.

Kventsel, Anna. *Decadence in the Late Novels of Henry James*. New York: Palgrave Macmillan, 2007. Kventsel interprets *The Ambassadors* and two other novels from the perspective of fin-de-siècle decadence. Includes bibliography and index.

Pippin, Robert B. *Henry James and Modern Moral Life*. New York: Cambridge University Press, 2000. A look at the moral message James sought to convey through his writings. Pippin interprets several of James's works, including *The Ambassadors*.

Wagenknecht, Edward. *The Novels of Henry James*. New York: Frederick Ungar, 1983. Excellent basic study of James's novels. The chapter on *The Ambassadors* presents an enlightening reading of the novel and places it at the highest point of James's achievement.

Amelia

Author: Henry Fielding (1707-1754)
First published: 1751
Type of work: Novel
Type of plot: Domestic realism
Time of plot: 1740's
Locale: England

Principal characters:
CAPTAIN WILLIAM BOOTH, a soldier
AMELIA, his wife
ELIZABETH HARRIS, her sister
SERGEANT ATKINSON, her foster brother
DR. HARRISON, Booth's benefactor
MISS MATTHEWS, a woman of the town
COLONEL JAMES, Booth's former superior

The Story:

One night, the watchmen of Westminster arrest Captain William Booth, seizing him as he is attempting to rescue a stranger being attacked by two ruffians. The footpads secure their own liberty by bribing the constables, but Booth is brought before an unjust magistrate. His story is a straightforward one, but because he is penniless and shabbily dressed, the judge dismisses his tale and sentences him to prison. Booth is desperate; there is no one he knows in London to whom he can turn for aid. His plight is made worse by his reception at the prison. His fellow prisoners strip him of his coat, and a pickpocket steals his snuffbox.

He is still smarting from these indignities when he sees a fashionably dressed young woman being escorted through the gates. Flourishing a bag of gold in the face of her keepers, she demands a private room in the prison. Her appearance and manner remind Booth of Miss Matthews, an old friend of questionable background whom he did not see for several years; but when the woman passes him without a sign of recognition, he believes himself mistaken.

Shortly afterward, a guard brings him a guinea in a small parcel, and with the money, Booth is able to redeem his coat and snuffbox, but he loses the rest of the money in a card game. Booth is once again penniless when a keeper comes to lead him to Miss Matthews, for it is indeed she. Seeing his wretched condition as he stands by the prison gate, she sent him the guinea. Reunited under these distressing circumstances, they proceed to relate the stories of their experiences. Miss Matthews tells how she is committed to await sentence for a penknife attack on a soldier who seduced her under false promises of marriage.

Booth, in turn, tells this story. He met Miss Amelia Harris, a beautiful girl whose mother at first opposed her daughter's marriage to a penniless soldier. The young couple eloped but were later reconciled with Amelia's mother through the efforts of Dr. Harrison, a wise and kindly curate. Shortly before a child was to be born to Amelia, Booth's regiment was ordered to Gibraltar. Reluctantly he left Amelia in the care of her mother and her older sister, Elizabeth. At Gibraltar, Booth earned the good opinion of his officers by his bravery. Wounded in one of the battles of the campaign, he became very ill. Amelia, learning of his condition, left her child with her mother and sister and went to Gibraltar to nurse her sick husband. Then Amelia, in her turn, fell sick. Wishing to take her to a milder climate, Booth wrote to Mrs. Harris for money, but in reply he received only a rude note from Elizabeth. He hoped to get the money from his army friend, Major James, but that gentleman was away at the time. Finally, he borrowed the money from Sergeant Atkinson, his friend and Amelia's foster brother, and went with his wife to Montpelier. There the couple made friends with an amusing English officer named Colonel Bath and his sister.

Joy at the birth of a second child, a girl, was dampened by a letter from Dr. Harrison, who wrote to tell them that old Mrs. Harris was dead and that she left her property to Amelia's sister. The Booths returned home, to be greeted so rudely by Elizabeth that they withdrew from the house. Without the help of Dr. Harrison, they would have been destitute. Harrison set Booth up as a gentleman farmer and tried to help him make the best of his half-pay from the army. Booth, however, made enemies among the surrounding farmers because of several small mistakes. Dr. Harrison was traveling on the Continent at the time, and in his absence, Booth was reduced almost to bankruptcy. He came to London to try his fortunes anew. He preceded Amelia, found modest lodgings, and wrote her of his location. At this point, the latest misfortune landed him in prison. At the end of Booth's story, Miss Matthews sympathizes with his unfortunate situation, congratulates him on his wife and children, and pays the jailer to let Booth spend the next few nights with her in her cell.

Booth and Miss Matthews are shortly released from prison. The soldier wounded by Miss Matthews completely recovers and drops his charges against her. Miss Matthews also secures Booth's release, and the two are preparing to leave prison when Amelia arrives. She comes up from the country to save him, and his release is a welcome surprise. The Booths establish themselves in London. Shortly afterward, Booth meets his former officer, now Colonel James, who in the meantime marries Miss Bath and grows quickly tired of her. Mrs. James and Amelia resume their old friendship. Booth, afraid that Miss Matthews will inform Amelia of their affair in prison, tells Colonel James of his difficulties and fears. The colonel gives him a loan and tells him not to worry. Colonel James is also interested in Miss Matthews, but he is unable to help Booth by his intercession. Miss Matthews continues to send Booth reproachful, revealing letters, which might at any time be intercepted by Amelia.

While walking in the park one day, the Booths meet Sergeant Atkinson. He joins their household to help care for the children, and soon he starts a mild flirtation with Mrs. Ellison, Booth's landlady. Mrs. Ellison proves useful to the Booths; a lord who also comes to visit her advances money to pay some of Booth's debts. Meanwhile, Miss Matthews spitefully turns Colonel James against Booth. Colonel Bath, hearing his brother-in-law's poor opinion of Booth, decides that Booth is neither an officer nor a gentleman and challenges him to a duel. Colonel Bath strongly believes in a code of honor, however, and when Booth vanquishes him in the duel without serious injury, the colonel is so impressed by Booth's gallantry that he forgives him and brings about a reconciliation between James and Booth.

During this time, Mrs. Ellison tries to arrange an assignation between Amelia and the nobleman who gave Booth money to pay his gambling debts. Amelia is innocently misled by her false friends. The nobleman's plan to meet Amelia secretly at a masquerade, however, is thwarted by another neighbor, Mrs. Bennet. This woman, who is a boarder in Mrs. Ellison's house, also met the noble lord, encountering him at a masquerade and drinking the drugged wine he provided. To prevent Amelia's ruin in the same manner, Mrs. Bennet comes to warn her friend. Then she informs Amelia that she recently married Sergeant Atkinson, whom Amelia thought to be in love with Mrs. Ellison. Amelia's joy at learning of the plot, which she now plans to escape, and of the marriage is marred by the news that Booth is again in prison for debt, this time on a warrant of their old friend Dr. Harrison.

Amelia soon discovers that Dr. Harrison was misled by false rumors of Booth's extravagance and jailed him to stop his rash spending of money. Learning the truth, Dr. Harrison allows Booth to be released from prison.

On the night of the masquerade, Amelia remains at home but sends Mrs. Atkinson dressed in her costume. At the dance, Mrs. Atkinson is able to fool not only the lord but also Colonel James. There are many complications of the affair, and almost every relationship is misunderstood. Booth falls in with an old friend and loses a large sum of money to him. Again, he becomes worried about being put in jail. Then he becomes involved in a duel with Colonel James over Miss Matthews, whom Booth visited only at her insistence. Before the duel can take place, Booth is again imprisoned for debt, and Dr. Harrison is forced to clear his name with Colonel James. Finally James forgives Booth, and Miss Matthews promises never to bother him again.

Called by chance into a strange house to hear the deathbed confession of a man named Robinson, Dr. Harrison learns that Robinson was at one time a clerk to a lawyer named Murphy who made Mrs. Harris's will. He learns also that the will, which left Amelia penniless, is a false one prepared by Elizabeth and Murphy. Dr. Harrison has Robinson write a confession so that Amelia can get the money that is rightfully hers. Murphy is quickly brought to trial and convicted of forgery.

Booth's troubles are now almost over. He and Amelia return home with Dr. Harrison to confront Elizabeth with their knowledge of her scheme. Elizabeth flees to France, where Amelia, relenting, sends her an annual allowance. Booth's adventures finally teach him not to gamble, and he settles down with his faithful Amelia to a quiet and prosperous life blessed with many children and the invaluable friendship of Dr. Harrison and the Atkinsons.

Critical Evaluation:

As Henry Fielding states in his introduction to *Amelia*, he satirizes nobody in the novel. Amelia, the long-suffering wife of every generation, is charming and attractive; the foibles of her husband still ring true; and Dr. Harrison is a man any reader would like to know. Some of the interest of the novel lies in Fielding's accurate presentation of prison life and the courts. Having been a magistrate for many years, he is able to present these scenes in a most realistic way, for aside from presenting the virtuous character of Amelia, Fielding wanted to awaken his readers' interest in prison and legal reform. The novel lacks the extravagant humor of his earlier novels, but the plot presents many amusing characters and complex situations.

Amelia is intended to appeal to a psychological and social awareness rather than to an intellectual consciousness. Between the publication of *The History of Tom Jones, a Foundling* (1749) and *Amelia*, the nature of Fielding's moral feelings deepened and with it the means and techniques by which he expressed his ethical purposes. Impressed by the social problems he encountered daily in the world around him, he felt the need to promote virtue and to expose the evils that infected England. He abandoned his satirical comic mode and such traits as impartiality, restraint, mockery, irony, and aesthetic distance. Instead, he adopted a serious, sentimental, and almost consciously middle-class tone.

The characters in *Amelia* give strong indications of Fielding's intensified moral purposes. They are more fiery and vehement and clearly intended to embody his beliefs more so than was the case in his earlier works. Abandoning the aesthetic distance between himself and his characters, he seems, in *Amelia*, to live and act directly in them. This results in a new kind of immediacy and closeness between the novel's characters and the writer's psychological concerns. The cost of this immediacy is the rejection of almost all formal conventions of characterization. The description of the heroine is typical of this. On a number of occasions, she is described by the emotions that are reflected in her face or by her physical reactions to situations that bring pain or joy; but in contrast to Fielding's elaborate descriptions of the beauty of the heroines of his earlier works, Amelia's beauty is never delineated. Rather, her beauty is embodied in the qualities she represents. The same might be said for the other characters in the novel. Fielding is more concerned with the moral makeup of each one than in their physical appearance. In *Amelia*, the author does not segregate the reader and the characters, who reveal themselves to the reader through their own words and deeds. The characters thereby appear as individuals rather than types.

The central theme of Fielding's portrait of a marriage concerns not so much the issue of adultery as it does the tragic irony of marital distrust that accompanies it. Although Booth's infidelity with Miss Matthews strains the marriage and seems disgusting when contrasted with Amelia's steadfast loyalty, what almost destroys the marriage is that Booth, throughout most of the novel, cannot bring himself to confess his adultery out of fear and pride. He does not trust in his wife's understanding and love for him. Amelia, who is beset almost from the beginning of her marriage by amorous advances, fails to confide to her husband the real motive behind James's pretense of friendship because she fears Booth will lose his temper and attack James. Husband and wife, therefore, work unconsciously to the detriment of their marriage because they will not trust in each other.

In *Amelia*, the reader cares more about the heroine, but the action turns on Booth. It is on the adequacy or inadequacy of Booth that the novel succeeds or fails for the reader. Amelia is the stable character. Booth constantly poses the problems of marriage, while she endures and solves them. Booth's ordeal reflects Fielding's own increasing despair with social conditions. The grim social picture of this novel is Fielding's solemn warning that society may destroy itself on the larger plane, as it very nearly destroys the Booths on the smaller plane. The placement of a woman of Amelia's moral character within a society that preys on her effectively points up the evils of that society in relation to the constant moral Christianity of the heroine. It is Fielding's most emphatic statement of Christian morality through the treatment of the subject within marriage. The loss of faith in individual morality, as portrayed in this novel through the assaults on Amelia's virtue and the setbacks suffered by Booth, is easily transferred from the plane of individuals to reflect criticism of society as a whole.

Amelia was published to much rancor and ridicule on the part of the majority of critics. The characters were reviled as being low and the situations as too sordid. Enemies gleefully pounced on Fielding's oversight in failing to mend his heroine's broken nose. Earlier victims of Fielding's satire, notably Samuel Richardson, author of *Pamela* (1740-1741), were gleeful over the adverse reception of this novel and joined in denouncing it. The novel's later success was based on the gradual recognition of the work as a serious denunciation of, as Fielding himself said, "glaring evils of the age."

"Critical Evaluation" by Patricia Ann King

Further Reading

Battestin, Martin C. *A Henry Fielding Companion*. Westport, Conn.: Greenwood Press, 2000. A comprehensive reference book covering Fielding's life and work. Includes sections on where he lived, his family, literary influences, his works, themes, and characters. Bibliography and index.

Dircks, Richard J. *Henry Fielding*. Boston: Twayne, 1983. An introduction to Fielding, with an emphasis on the major novels, including *Amelia*. Includes brief but useful biographical information, a chronology, and an annotated bibliography. With few notes and references, and a clear, accessible style, this is a good tool for students.

Fraser, Donald. "Lying and Concealment in *Amelia*." In *Henry Fielding: Justice Observed*, edited by K. G. Simpson. Totowa, N.J.: Barnes & Noble, 1985. Shows how Fielding uses lying, deception, and concealment as both a theme and a device to force the reader to pay close attention to details and explanations within the story.

Johnson, Maurice O. *Fielding's Art of Fiction: Eleven Essays on "Shamela," "Joseph Andrews," "Tom Jones," and "Amelia."* Philadelphia: University of Pennsylvania Press, 1961. Three of the essays in this study deal directly with *Amelia*, which Johnson sees as a moral work exalting the "good life." Little biography or historical context, but excellent explications of specific passages and structural effects.

Pagliaro, Harold E. *Henry Fielding: A Literary Life*. New York: St. Martin's Press, 1998. An excellent, updated account of Fielding's life and writings, with chapter 3 devoted to his novels and other prose fiction. Includes bibliographical references and an index.

Paulson, Ronald. *The Life of Henry Fielding: A Critical Biography*. Malden, Mass.: Blackwell, 2000. Paulson examines how Fielding's literary works—novels, plays, and essays—all contained autobiographical elements. Each chapter of the book begins with an annotated chronology of the events of Fielding's life; also includes a bibliography and index.

Rawson, Claude, ed. *The Cambridge Companion to Henry Fielding*. New York: Cambridge University Press, 2007. A collection of essays commissioned for this volume, which includes an examination of Fielding's life, major novels, theatrical career, journalism, Fielding and female authority, and Fielding's style, among other topics. Chapter 7 is devoted to an analysis of *Amelia*.

_______. *Henry Fielding, 1707-1754: Novelist, Playwright, Journalist, Magistrate, a Double Anniversary Tribute*. Newark: University of Delaware Press, 2008. A collection of essays by Fielding scholars designed as a tribute to the two-hundred-fiftieth anniversary of his death in 1754 and the tercentenary of his birth in 1707. The essays cover all aspects of Fielding's life and work.

Smallwood, Angela J. *Fielding and the Woman Question:*

The Novels of Henry Fielding and Feminist Debate, 1700-1750. New York: St. Martin's Press, 1989. Argues that Fielding's novels, including *Amelia*, actively engage in the eighteenth century debate about gender roles. As important as his concern with national politics is Fielding's concern with sexual politics.

Wright, Andrew. *Henry Fielding: Mask and Feast.* Berkeley: University of California Press, 1965. Explores the relationships in Fielding's work between art and life, with a strong focus on the influence of comic theater. Wright looks at three Fielding novels and considers *Amelia* as a domestic epic.

The American

Author: Henry James (1843-1916)
First published: serial, 1876-1877; book, 1877
Type of work: Novel
Type of plot: Psychological realism
Time of plot: Mid-nineteenth century
Locale: Paris

Principal characters:
CHRISTOPHER NEWMAN, an American
MR. TRISTRAM, a friend
MRS. TRISTRAM, his wife
M. NIOCHE, a shopkeeper
MLLE NIOCHE, his daughter
MADAME DE BELLEGARDE, a French aristocrat
CLAIRE DE CINTRÉ, her daughter
MARQUIS DE BELLEGARDE, her older son
VALENTIN DE BELLEGARDE, her younger son
MRS. BREAD, her servant

The Story:

In 1868, Christopher Newman, a young American millionaire, withdraws from business and sails for Paris. He wants to relax, to develop his aesthetic sense, and to find a wife. One day, as he wanders in the Louvre, he makes the acquaintance of Mlle Nioche, a young copyist. She introduces him to her father, an unsuccessful shopkeeper. Newman buys a picture from Mlle Nioche and contracts to take French lessons from her father.

Later, through the French wife of an American friend named Tristram, he meets Claire de Cintré, a young widow, daughter of an English mother and a French father. As a young girl, Claire was married to Monsieur de Cintré, an evil old man. He soon died, leaving Claire with a distaste for marriage. In spite of her attitude, Newman sees in her the woman he wishes for his wife. An American businessman, however, is not the person to associate with French aristocracy. On his first call, Newman is kept from entering Claire's house by her elder brother, the Marquis de Bellegarde.

True to his promise, M. Nioche appears one morning to give Newman his first lesson in French. Newman enjoys talking to the old man. He learns that Mlle Nioche dominates her father, who lives in fear that she will leave him and become the mistress of some rich man. M. Nioche tells Newman that he will shoot his daughter if she does. Newman takes pity on the old man and promises him enough money for Mlle Nioche's dowry if she will paint more copies for him.

Newman leaves Paris and travels through Europe during the summer. When he returns to Paris in autumn, he learns that the Tristrams were helpful; the Bellegardes are willing to receive him. One evening, Claire's younger brother, Valentin, calls on Newman and the two men find their opposite points of view a basis for friendship. Valentin envies Newman's liberty to do as he pleases; Newman wishes himself acceptable to the society in which the Bellegardes move. After the two men become good friends, Newman tells Valentin that he wishes to marry his sister and asks Valentin to plead his cause. Warning Newman that his social position is against him, Valentin promises to help the American as much as he can.

Newman confesses his wish to Claire and asks Madame de Bellegarde, Claire's mother, and the Marquis for permission to be her suitor. The permission is given, grudgingly. The Bellegardes need money in the family. Newman goes to the Louvre to see how Mlle Nioche is progressing with her copying. There he meets Valentin and introduces him to the young lady. Mrs. Bread, an old English servant of the

Bellegardes, assures Newman that he is making progress with his suit. He asks Claire to marry him, and she accepts. Meanwhile, Valentin challenges another man to a duel in a quarrel over Mlle Nioche. Valentin leaves for Switzerland with his seconds. The next morning, Newman goes to see Claire. Mrs. Bread meets him at the door and says that Claire is leaving town. Newman demands an explanation. He is told that the Bellegardes cannot allow a commercial person in the family. When he arrives home, he finds a telegram from Valentin stating that he is badly wounded and asking Newman to come at once to Switzerland.

With this double burden of sorrow, Newman arrives in Switzerland and finds Valentin near death. Valentin guesses what his family did and tells Newman that Mrs. Bread knows a family secret. If he can get the secret from her, he can make the family return Claire to him. Valentin dies the next morning. Newman attends the funeral. Three days later, he again calls on Claire, who tells him that she intends to enter a convent. Newman begs her not to take this step. Desperate, he calls on the Bellegardes again and tells them that he will uncover their secret. Newman arranges to see Mrs. Bread that night. She tells him that Madame de Bellegarde killed her disabled husband because he opposed Claire's marriage to M. de Cintré. The death was judged natural, but Mrs. Bread has in her possession a document proving that Madame de Bellegarde murdered her husband. She gives this paper to Newman.

Mrs. Bread leaves the employ of the Bellegardes and comes to keep house for Newman. She tells him that Claire is in the convent and refuses to see anyone, even her own family. The next Sunday, Newman goes to mass at the convent. After the service, he meets the Bellegardes walking in the park and shows them a copy of the paper Mrs. Bread gave him.

The next day, the Marquis calls on Newman and offers to pay for the document. Newman refuses to sell. He will, however, accept Claire in exchange for it. The Marquis refuses. Newman finds he cannot bring himself to reveal the Bellegardes' secret. On the advice of the Tristrams, he travels through the English countryside and, in a melancholy mood, goes to some of the places he planned to visit on his honeymoon. Then he goes to America. Restless, he returns to Paris and learns from Mrs. Tristram that Claire became a nun.

The next time he sees Mrs. Tristram, he drops the secret document on the glowing logs in her fireplace and tells her that to expose the Bellegardes now seems a useless and empty gesture. He intends to leave Paris forever. Mrs. Tristram tells him that he probably did not frighten the Bellegardes with his threat, because they knew that they could count on his good nature never to reveal their secret. Newman instinctively looks toward the fireplace. The paper is burned to ashes.

Critical Evaluation:

One of Henry James's achievements is that he developed the international novel. *The American*, his first major book, portrays a typical post-Civil War American and delineates his differences from Europeans. Although ultimately a tragic story, *The American* uses irony and humor in its depiction of some of the incongruities between the two cultures.

The hero's name strongly hints at James's purpose. Christopher Newman, the reader is told, is named after the explorer Christopher Columbus. Thus, as he returns to Europe for the culture and civilization that he has not had time to pursue in his moneymaking career, this new man becomes a discoverer in reverse. Whereas Columbus brought the Old World to the New World, Newman is a representative of the New World who seeks to discover the Old World.

Besides visiting museums, Newman seeks a wife who embodies culture. In his pursuit, he strikes against rigid European traditions. The new man is confronted with the old ways. Those old ways include the exercise of unearned privilege. Newman underestimates the power and prejudice of his French adversaries. In his New World innocence, he does not anticipate their sinister machinations. He achieves some small victories and attracts the approbation of the finest Europeans—Mrs. Bread, Valentin de Bellegarde, and the incomparable Claire de Cintré—but ultimately Newman discovers something that he did not experience in America. He is denied an opportunity to reap the rewards of his own endeavors. Through no fault of his own, but rather through the injustice of others, he loses the prize for which he has longed.

Part of the frustration the American experiences is that, with his native capaciousness, he believes that he can incorporate into his own character the best of other cultures and so improve himself. Indeed, Valentin and Claire, brother and sister of the old Bellegarde family, are willing to join Newman's wide embrace. Their good natures are stronger than their aristocratic prejudices. James, however, does not allow the best members of the Bellegarde family to prevail. He ends the novel unhappily. In answer to the objections of his editor, William Dean Howells, James explained that a happy ending would have been unrealistic and would have been pandering to his readership. Claire and Christopher would have been, in James's words, "an impossible couple."

In exploring the contrasting outlooks of the democratic Americans and the aristocratic Europeans, James utilizes humor. This novel is sometimes reminiscent of Mark Twain's

The Innocents Abroad (1869), a hilarious account of Americans in Europe and the Middle East. James's boorish Mr. Tristram, for example, wonders whether the pictures hanging in the Louvre are for sale. Subtler irony lies in Newman's failure to realize that his having manufactured washtubs jeopardizes his efforts to win the approbation of the French aristocracy. Like Twain, James was keenly aware of differing cultural values and their humorous potential.

James's biographer suggests that the portrait of Newman as a national type is filled with ambiguity. Newman could not have met with James's total admiration. He is too obtuse and self-satisfied with his material success, and he has the audacity to believe that he can buy culture, including a cultured wife. The new man has fine qualities and deplorable ones. He does not deserve the wrong he receives, but does he really deserve to gain the hand of Claire?

Some romantic elements in the novel were deplored by critics and by James himself later in his career. The mystery of Monsieur Bellegarde's death, the implications of foul play lying behind the medieval walls of the Bellegardes' home, and the horrible prospect of Claire's impending "burial" in a convent are all melodramatic. James became, in spite of this beginning, one of the major figures of the realistic movement. His attention was on verisimilitude, as his choice of a common man for a protagonist and his interest in the pragmatic philosophy of the protagonist attest. Usually regarded as inferior to masterpieces such as *The Ambassadors* (1903) and *The Portrait of a Lady* (1880-1881), *The American* nevertheless exhibits many of the qualities that made James one of the major novelists of his time.

"Critical Evaluation" by William L. Howard

Further Reading

Cargill, Oscar. *The Novels of Henry James*. New York: Hafner Press, 1971. An analysis of the sources of the novel, including writer Ivan Turgenev, French theater, and James's own inspiration. Defines the international novel in which a character possessing one set of cultural values is confronted with a different set of values.

Coulson, Victoria. *Henry James, Women, and Realism*. New York: Cambridge University Press, 2007. Examines James's important friendships with three women: his sister Alice James and the novelists Constance Fenimore Woolson and Edith Wharton. These three women writers and James shared what Coulson describes as an "ambivalent realism," or a cultural ambivalence about gender identity, and she examines how this idea is manifest in James's works, including *The American*.

Freedman, Jonathan, ed. *The Cambridge Companion to Henry James*. New York: Cambridge University Press, 1998. An essay collection that provides extensive information on James's life and literary influences and describes his works and the characters in them.

James, Henry. *The American*, edited by Gerald Willen. New York: Thomas Y. Crowell, 1972. Includes the text of the later, revised version of the novel, a preface by James, the ending from the original version of the novel, a letter from James to his editor William Dean Howells, and ten interpretative essays by different critics on subjects as diverse as point of view, romantic elements, the revision, and the American self-image depicted in the novel.

Lee, Brian. *The Novels of Henry James: A Study of Culture and Consciousness*. New York: St. Martin's Press, 1978. Argues that James was interested in the concept of consciousness and its response to culture. Thematically, *The American*, with its confrontation between an innocent American and sophisticated Europeans, opposes moral consciousness and social consciousness. Lee notes James's later assessment of his novel: that it violated the reader's sense of how things really happen.

Long, Robert Emmet. *Henry James: The Early Novels*. Boston: Twayne, 1983. Places *The American* in the context of James's early career. Provides basic information about the novel's magazine serialization, James's subsequent revision, and the novel's influences. Discusses the roles of romance, melodrama, and realism.

Person, Leland S. *Henry James and the Suspense of Masculinity*. Philadelphia: University of Pennsylvania Press, 2003. Examines several of James's works, including *The American*, to describe how he challenged traditional concepts of heterosexual masculinity, depicting characters with alternate sexual and gender identities.

Powers, Lyall H. *Henry James: An Introduction and Interpretation*. New York: Holt, Rinehart and Winston, 1970. Discusses the theme, nomenclature, humor, gothic elements, and characterization regarding Christopher Newman.

American Buffalo

Author: David Mamet (1947-)
First produced: 1975; first published, 1975
Type of work: Drama
Type of plot: Social criticism
Time of plot: One Friday in the 1970's
Locale: Chicago

Principal characters:
DONNY DURBROW, owner of Don's Resale Shop
WALTER "TEACH" COLE, a friend of Donny
BOBBY, Donny's gofer at the shop
FLETCHER, a poker player and Donny's friend

The Story:

One Friday morning in Don's Resale Shop, Donny and Bobby are talking; Donny is upset because Bobby abandoned his post in the store when he was supposed to be watching someone. While Bobby apologizes, Donny imparts some wisdom about running a business, referring to Fletcher, a winning poker player, who embodies the critical savvy people can learn only on the street. It is evident that Donny cares about Bobby as a friend and his mentor.

Shortly, Walter Cole, called Teach, enters the shop ranting about a trivial misunderstanding with Ruthie and Grace, some poker friends, over a recent breakfast; to assuage Teach's fury, Donny suggests that Bobby run to the Riverside restaurant to pick up breakfast for the three of them. In Bobby's absence, the two discuss last night's poker game, and Teach expounds on the necessary distinction between business and friendship. During the exchange, Teach picks up some old knickknacks from the counter and complains that if only he had kept all the things he threw out, he would be a wealthy man.

Bobby reenters the shop with breakfast, but he has forgotten Donny's coffee. Before heading back to the restaurant to retrieve the coffee, Bobby tells Donny that he saw the guy they are looking for leaving the restaurant with a suitcase. Teach wants to know about the man with the suitcase. Donny first hesitates but then tells Teach that the man had recently taken advantage of him by purchasing a buffalo nickel for less than what it is worth. Donny wants revenge and plans to steal the nickel from the man, then resell it at a higher price to another collector.

Teach warns against involving Bobby, alluding to Bobby's history of drug use, and argues that Donny is blinded by his sense of loyalty, which angers him. Donny assures Teach that Bobby is clean, but Teach insists he himself is the better person for the job. Bobby reenters the shop with the coffee, and Teach verbally bullies him, trying to make him look incompetent to Donny. Bobby, oblivious, asks Donny for some money for the nickel job up front; Donny agrees to give Bobby the cash, but tells him to forget about the job.

Bobby leaves, and Teach and Donny discuss their plans for the theft, talking with certainty about how they will get in but uncertain where the coins will be located. Teach suggests they take more than just the coins for their trouble. Donny, worried they might need help, decides to bring in Fletcher, which makes Teach feel slighted; in the end he agrees. They plan to meet again later that night.

Later that evening, Donny tries to contact Teach and Fletcher, irritated by their tardiness. Bobby enters and tells Donny that he needs money; he wants to sell a buffalo nickel that he has acquired. Distracted, Donny tells him he wants to consult his coin book first. Teach enters, sees Bobby, and demands an explanation. To get Bobby to leave, Donny orders Teach to give him some money and promises Bobby they will talk tomorrow. Bobby leaves.

Teach is defensive and suspicious, asking Donny about Fletcher's whereabouts and about Bobby's nickel; eventually, Donny settles him and they continue working on the robbery plan, deciding they should call the target's house to make sure he is not there; it appears he is not.

Donny continues to make calls in search of Fletcher, while Teach explicates a cutthroat version of free enterprise. Teach is suspicious of Fletcher and suggests they do the job without him, but Donny disagrees; they continue in heated discussion about the theft. The longer they wait, however, the more aggressive Teach becomes. Finally, Teach declares he is going to the target's house himself, and then reveals a gun, which he explains he needs in case something goes wrong. There is a sudden knock on the door, but it is only Bobby.

According to Bobby, Fletcher has been mugged and is in the hospital. Bobby then says that he has business to take care of, and turns to leave; Teach stops him, disbelieving his story. Bobby cannot tell them exactly where Fletcher has been taken, so Teach continues his interrogation and asks where Bobby got the nickel. Donny begins to side with Teach, thinking perhaps Bobby went ahead with the deal himself. The men grow more combative, and Bobby pleads that he is telling the truth. Suddenly, Teach picks up some junk from nearby and hits Bobby in the head.

Donny, having lost all softness toward Bobby, tells him he brought the hit on himself and demands he tell them where Fletcher is. The phone rings; it is Ruthie, who says Fletcher is at Columbus Hospital. Donny confirms with a phone call. Meanwhile, Bobby begins to bleed out of his ear, and Donny concedes there will be no job tonight. Bobby, whimpering, explains that he bought the nickel for Donny in a coin store earlier today. Donny's feelings of compassion for Bobby return, but Teach insists that hitting Bobby was for his own good. Donny yells at Teach to leave.

Teach calls Donny a fake, accusing him of taking the side of a junkie. Furious, Donny advances on him, beating him. In the background, Bobby admits that he never saw the coin buyer earlier. After this news, Teach trashes Donny's store in a rage. After the destruction, Donny stands stunned. Teach asks if he is mad at him, and Donny replies no, telling Teach to get his car and take Bobby to the hospital. Teach leaves, and Donny helps Bobby to his feet and apologizes; Bobby returns the apology, blaming himself. Donny consoles him, saying he did "real good."

Critical Evaluation:

American Buffalo was first produced in 1975 in Chicago and was David Mamet's first drama to gain critical attention. Although receiving mixed reviews, the play commenced a brief Broadway run in 1977, winning Mamet the New York Drama Critics Circle award. *American Buffalo* lays the thematic foundations for Mamet's future works, including the Pulitzer Prize-winning and Tony Award-winning *Glengarry Glen Ross*, which explores the corrupt ethics of American business and their effects on the individual.

American Buffalo presents a disturbing portrait of American culture, exposing the capitalistic agendas that drive the corruption of American industry, and of how individuals are led astray by the failure of the American Dream. Each character—Donny, Teach, and Bobby—strives for economic success and some position of power. Ultimately, the play questions what occurs when business and self-interest take precedence over moral responsibility to the public good.

Don's Resale Shop, located in the South Side of Chicago, becomes an allegory for the world of business, a system in which all three characters become trapped. Donny's business is selling junk from America's past. At one point, Teach fondles some items collected from 1933, presumably from the Chicago World's Fair. The objects are at once reminders of a time of possibility and progress for the United States, also of a time of extreme poverty and hardship—the Great Depression. A similar dichotomy functions in the lives of the three central characters, who invest in the illusion of progress and free enterprise, but who will never realize that potential.

The buffalo nickel upon which the action centers is itself a symbol of the corruption of American business, simultaneously signifying the prosperity of an expanding nation and also revealing the more sinister aspects of manifest destiny—the oppression and near annihilation of the American Indian peoples. Here, Teach's ruthless definition of free enterprise applies: "the freedom of the individual to embark on any . . . course that he sees fit." America indeed embarked on a course, without regard to the cost.

The cost of American business, according to *American Buffalo*, is morality. After selling a buffalo nickel for ninety dollars, Donny feels exploited; thus the purchase of the coin feels like a robbery, not only of the nickel but also of Donny's pride and masculinity, which Donny must steal back to regain. For Donny, this is a matter of business, and business means "people taking care of themselves." He takes pride in imparting these lessons to Bobby, emphasizing that all it takes to run a business is "common sense, experience and talent." Unfortunately, all three central characters lack these qualities, which dooms them to perpetual entropy.

Though the characters see themselves as streetwise entrepreneurs, they know little about succeeding in a capitalistic world. Donny instructs Bobby in business, although he has little practical knowledge of it. He is the owner of his own shop, yet the shop is little more than a storage space for forgotten junk. Bobby admires Donny as a mentor and aims to please him, yet he lacks follow-through and confidence to act. Teach is crippled by his suspicions and his inability to communicate. He attempts to hide his incompetence behind vocabulary, but his discourse is confused, contextually inappropriate, and void of substance. These three characters do a lot of talking, but their words signify nothing and initiate no action; they therefore fall prey to confusion and distrust, which not only destroys their "business" plan but also destroys their relationships.

Inasmuch as the play is about business, it is also about male friendship, examining the universal need for human contact. Personal alliances are betrayed in pursuit of self-interests. *American Buffalo* questions those remainders of friendships that are forgone in pursuit of personal greed, and offers no easy answers.

The central betrayal occurs between Bobby and Donny, two men who have formed a compassionate bond. It is evident that Donny cares for the young man; however, Donny is easily manipulated and betrays his young protégé. Teach first discredits Bobby's ability to do the job, and then Donny's loyalty to Bobby is further eroded when Teach convinces him that Bobby has deceived them by committing the crime himself. The ultimate treason occurs, however, when Donny allows—even condones—Teach's violent attack on Bobby. Learning the truth, however, Donny is ashamed; at this moment, he calls off the theft. In putting business before friendship, Donny has risked his best comrade, and in so doing has betrayed himself.

Teach, too, although far less sympathetic than Donny or Bobby, is desperate to form personal connections; he is incapable of ever truly understanding friendship or trusting others, yet he longs for approval. This is perhaps most evident in his attempt to displace Bobby as Donny's "business" partner. At several points in the play, Teach expresses his hurt feelings: when Ruthie slights him at breakfast, when Donny suggests they bring in Fletcher for the theft, and when Donny calls off the job, after which Teach feels betrayed, loses control, and destroys Donny's shop. Despite his violent acts, Teach still needs Donny's acceptance; Teach's bravado is at last squelched and he is reduced to being a foolish, needy child.

Dysfunctional as the three characters may be, in the end they are, in a way, a family. The play ultimately illuminates how easily human relationships can be fractured by greed and selfishness, qualities so easily bred in a nation that still hungers for the American Dream.

Danielle A. DeFoe

Further Reading

Bigsby, C. W. E. "American Buffalo." In *David Mamet*. London: Methuen, 1985. An analysis of *American Buffalo* as social criticism, examining the play as an illustration of the failure of capitalism and the corruption of American business.

Bigsby, Christopher, ed. *The Cambridge Companion to David Mamet*. New York: Cambridge University Press, 2004. An accessible overview of Mamet's work. Chapter 2 explores the influence of corrupt business ethics on the formation of personal relationships in *American Buffalo*.

Bloom, Harold. *David Mamet*. Philadelphia: Chelsea House, 2004. A collection of essays discussing the dominant themes of Mamet's work. *American Buffalo* is referenced throughout and is contextualized in comparison to other works.

Dean, Anne. "American Buffalo." In *David Mamet: Language as Dramatic Action*. Rutherford, N.J.: Fairleigh Dickinson University Press, 1990. A thorough investigation of how Mamet's characters employ language, specifically as a means of survival.

Dennis, Carrol. "Business." In *David Mamet*. New York: St. Martin's Press, 1987. Discusses how *American Buffalo* and *Glengarry Glen Ross* critique an American society built on business.

Dietrick, Jon. "Real Classical Money: Naturalism and Mamet's *American Buffalo*." *Twentieth Century Literature* 52, no. 3 (2006): 330-345. Explores Mamet's naturalism as it applies to the anxieties of a money-based economy.

Kane, Leslie. "The Comfort of Strangers." In *Weasels and Wise Men: Ethics and Ethnicity in the Work of David Mamet*. New York: St. Martin's Press, 1999. Discusses ethnicity, specifically Jewish identity, and how it informs the actions of Mamet's characters.

Zeifman, Hersh. "Phallus in Wonderland: Machismo and Business in David Mamet's *American Buffalo* and *Glengarry Glen Ross*." In *David Mamet: A Casebook*, edited by Leslie Kane. New York: Garland, 1992. Investigates the male exclusivity of American business mirrored in Mamet's work. Part of a collection of twelve critical essays and two interviews.

The American Commonwealth

Author: James Bryce (1838-1922)
First published: 1888; final revised edition, 1922-1923
Type of work: Social criticism

James Bryce served in several capacities that qualified and trained him to write on American political and social institutions. A professor of history at Oxford and a member of Parliament, he also served in numerous political posts and was ambassador to the United States from 1907 to 1913. His monumental work *The American Commonwealth* grew out of five visits to the United States and extensive reading about the country.

The book is a shrewd analytical study of the American scene designed for a European audience and obviously written by a man who was prejudiced in favor of America. In Bryce's opinion, regardless of the many flaws and weaknesses (especially on the local and state levels) in the American political system and institutions, the sum total of American hopes and aspirations created a system of rule that was the best to date, one that offered hope to the world.

The American Commonwealth is divided into six parts. The first concerns the national government, the Constitution, the presidency, the two houses of Congress, the federal courts, the federal system of government, and the relations of the federal government with the state governments. Bryce emphasizes the organic growth of the American political system. He believes that the happy combination of events and thinking that resulted in the system, and especially in the Constitution, stemmed from the fact that the predominant race in America in the eighteenth century was Anglo-American. This race was directly responsible for the Constitution, which, though by no means a perfect instrument, merits the veneration that Americans generally bestow on it. Bryce believed that the greatness of the Constitution derives from the fact that there is nothing new about it, that like all good political documents and all things that deserve to win and hold the obedience and respect of citizens, it has its roots deeply planted in the past and grew slowly through changing periods of history. The men who drew up the Constitution were practical politicians who wanted to walk the paths trod by former successful governments. The path was made easy and its progress assured by the fact that in America during those days there were no reactionary conspirators threatening the nation. The most remarkable feature of the American governmental system, Bryce believes, is the preeminence of the Constitution and the fact that the Constitution can be altered only by the people.

The creation of a president to head the American government was fortuitous. In outlining his role and power, the Framers of the Constitution, fearing the monarchical system and a strong centralized government, nevertheless modified existing offices of leaders; that is, they created the office as one that enlarged the role of the state governor, whose office resembles that of the British king but on a smaller and improved scale. There are many disadvantages to this office and the method of electing its holder, but in practice the responsibility of the position and the realization that the president represents the nation as a whole sobered and controlled the holders of the office. With a few exceptions, the presidency was not filled by men of brilliance. The office does not demand intellectual brilliance; rather, it demands common sense and honesty.

In fact, political offices in America are not filled by outstanding citizens, few of whom take up a career in politics. Even the Senate and the House of Representatives are not constituted of the nation's best minds, although the Senate draws to itself the best talent in politics and establishes its authority in the American political system by its dignity and six-year tenure in office. It faithfully fulfills the intentions of the Founders of the nation in resisting change and yielding to it only gradually.

In comparison to the Senate, the House of Representatives is chaotic and lacks the dignity and the power of the upper chamber. It also lacks the men of ability claimed by the other chamber, but what it lacks in these aspects it makes up for in the worthiness of its purpose and its real accomplishments.

Those who drafted and signed the American Constitution were especially wise in establishing such complex legal institutions. Bryce believes that few American institutions warrant closer study than the intricate system of the judiciary, which deserves great admiration because it operates smoothly and contributes to the peace and prosperity of America. The weaknesses in the American legal system, in fact, flow not from their makeup but from human frailties.

The second part of *The American Commonwealth* discusses state and local governments. The state constitutions in general grew out of the royal charters, but in being changed and rewritten they cast out the worst aspects of their models. A state constitution is a law passed directly by the people at the polls and is an example of popular sovereignty directly exercised. As such, it has few parallels in modern Europe. State governments are more subject to local pressures than is the federal government, and they are more widely influenced by political parties. Some of the weaknesses of the state governments are exaggerated in lower local groupings, especially in city governments. Universal suffrage has many serious weaknesses, and all become evident and important in a city, where foreign immigrants swell the population. Though there are obviously serious problems in the American city, probably no other system of government could have been devised that would have worked as well, and American cities have made progress in solving their problems.

Part 3 concerns itself with "Political Methods and Physical Influences." It is a detailed study of the American political machinery, nominating conventions, and public opinion and its power. Bryce considers that of all American experiments in politics, the most worthy of serious study is this governing by public opinion, which towers above all other aspects of American political life as a source of power. However, it is a power used well: Individuals are reckless, but the mass of people is restrained. As a result, public opinion becomes gradually more temperate, mellow, and tolerant.

The very size, strength, and potential of the United States give Bryce great pause for contemplation. Can a nation so immense in size, so varied in population, and so gifted in wealth remain one nation and control itself? Given his own tentative and conservative disposition, Bryce hesitates to answer his own question, but his conclusions almost assert themselves. His prophecies are in fact somewhat optimistic. Never before, he claims, has a nation had such golden opportunities for defensive strength and material prosperity. He concludes that America will probably remain unified in government and in speech as well as in character, ideas, and action.

In all aspects *The American Commonwealth* is exhaustive. One of its great strengths derives from the background of its author. Deeply read in European and other governments, Bryce gives his study of the American government an unusual breadth and depth, which inform the reader profoundly. His book becomes essentially a study in comparative government and therefore remains as informative today as at the time of its composition. Only in the study of some of the detailed aspects of American government—in cases where the institutions he describes or aspects of those institutions have been changed by custom, act of legislature, or amendment—is the work dated. In general, Bryce's comments on the American character and his belief that America is the nation pointing toward the future constitute stimulating and interesting reading.

Further Reading

Ions, Edmund S. *James Bryce and American Democracy, 1870-1922.* New York: Humanities Press, 1970. A British scholar uses Bryce's personal papers to trace his interaction with the United States. Contains much useful information about the writing and impact of *The American Commonwealth* and Bryce's subsequent career as ambassador between 1907 and 1913.

Keller, Morton. *Affairs of State: Public Life in Late Nineteenth Century America.* Cambridge, Mass.: Belknap Press, 1977. A late twentieth century historian looks at the period that Bryce's book examined. Useful for a comparative perspective on what Bryce wrote.

_______. "James Bryce and America." *Wilson Quarterly* 12 (Autumn, 1988): 86-95. Keller considers Bryce's work a century after it was written and finds it "a vivid, affectionate, informed portrait" of the United States and its government during the 1880's. One of the best short analyses of Bryce's contribution to the study of American culture.

Seaman, John T., Jr. *A Citizen of the World: The Life of James Bryce.* London: Tauris Academic Studies, 2006. Chapter 6 of Seaman's biography is devoted to a discussion of *The American Commonwealth.*

Shaughnessy, D. F. "Anatomy of the Republic: On Bryce's Americans." *Encounter* 73 (July-August, 1989): 31-37. An interesting analysis of Bryce's view of the United States and the accuracy of his assessments. Shaughnessy argues that Bryce's judgments held up very well and that his comments about American political institutions retain contemporary relevance.

The American Notebooks

Author: Nathaniel Hawthorne (1804-1864)
First published: 1932
Type of work: Diary

In *The American Notebooks* Nathaniel Hawthorne reviews such topics as isolation, sin, the degeneration of families, and the subjugation of one person to another, common themes in his work. Hawthorne was one of the originators of the American short-story form, and he was a leading novelist of nineteenth century American letters. He began the observations, story ideas, and character sketches that make up *The American Notebooks* in 1835, when he was an unknown college graduate living in isolation in Salem, Massachusetts. The last entry of the notebooks is that of June, 1853, by which time Hawthorne had traveled in the northeastern United States and had married and had children. By then Hawthorne had also published his most successful works. *The American Notebooks* shows Hawthorne's development as a writer; as such, it is an invaluable contribution to an understanding of his literary development. Some of the collection's entries contain ideas that are important in his most famous fictional works.

The American Notebooks follows chronological order, tracing Hawthorne's development over a period of eighteen years. The individual entries, however, are quite random in their makeup and contain adages, animal folklore, and biblical references that captivated Hawthorne. Observations of people whom he saw in the streets of nineteenth century Salem, Boston, and North Adams, Massachusetts, are mixed with flights of fancy that occurred to Hawthorne as he labored at his writing. Quotations from early eighteenth century newspapers and church books chronicle Hawthorne's lifelong interest in New England history. In this sense, the notebooks provide not only a glimpse of Hawthorne's close observation as a writer but also a picture of New England in the early-to-mid-nineteenth century.

The production of his novels, essays, and tales took up much of the winter months in Hawthorne's adult life; the notebook entries were made mainly during the summer months as he traveled to and from Boston, out to western Massachusetts, and through the towns of Maine. The freer time of summer may account for the relatively unfocused form of the notebooks; however, the unfocused form shows the creative imagination of Hawthorne at work.

When he began *The American Notebooks*, Hawthorne was a recent graduate of Bowdoin College. He confounded his family by returning to the family home in Salem to use his time to read and practice the craft of writing. These early entries show Hawthorne at work on descriptions of long nature walks; these entries reflect his sadness, preoccupations, and fantasies. A particular entry notes an idea for a story—never to be produced—of "the fantasy of a man taking his life by instalments, instead of at one payment,—say the years of life alternately with ten years of suspended animation." This was an odd but fitting idea for an artist who would later write novels that fused the fantastic with the mundane and the real. The early entries also hint at the major themes that Hawthorne would actively explore for all of his writing life. He records entries on decaying, degenerate families, and he makes notes on the evil in every human heart. He also plants the seeds for future fiction on the diseases of the soul.

By July, 1837, however, the notebooks begin to tell a different story. Hawthorne went on an extended summer visit to Horatio Bridge, a Bowdoin College classmate who lived in bachelor's quarters in Augusta, Maine. In these early entries, Hawthorne records his walks through the streets of Augusta and his visits to the Irish and Nova Scotian shantytowns with his friend Bridge. Hawthorne makes detailed observations of the houses with sod roofs and an Irishwoman washing her clothes in a river. Hawthorne was still an unknown author with one book, *Twice-Told Tales* (1837), to his credit when he wrote the long descriptive passages of fishing for sturgeon, drinking brandy and rum in a dimly lit store, and riding to Augusta past mowers pausing along the roadside with their scythes. Hawthorne was emerging from his years of solitary living in Salem, however, and was contemplating a new stage in life.

In the second phase of *The American Notebooks*, Hawthorne demonstrates his capacity to link thematic interests to the places he sees in geographical landscapes. On a trip to view the Maine mansion of General Henry Knox, the secretary of war in President George Washington's cabinet, Hawthorne links his preoccupation with the degeneration of families over time with the house that he carefully observes: His notebook chronicles his thought that in less than forty years since the mansion was built, "now the house is all in decay." This observation underscores his obsession with the decline of the fortunes of a family, represented by the decay of a mansion. As a writer primarily interested in ideas such as sin, the estrangement of the individual from society, and the degeneration of families over time, Hawthorne appears to have used the notebooks to review those themes: Repeatedly, he sketches characters and places that illustrate his ideas; equally important, he uses the notebooks to set out his ideas regarding the conflicts of life.

The American Notebooks also records some of the changes that took place in Hawthorne's life. By 1841, he had experimented with different ways of life. He resided at Brook Farm, a utopian agricultural commune in Massachusetts. Then he married in 1842 and took up residence at the Old Manse in Concord, Massachusetts. There he was able to have a relationship and important conversations with Ralph Waldo Emerson, the Transcendentalist American philosopher and writer. Although Hawthorne does not record the conversations, *The American Notebooks* contains invaluable descriptions of Emerson. Hawthorne characterizes Emerson—and, perhaps, Emerson's Transcendentalist philosophy—as "that everlasting rejector of all that is, and seeker for he knows not what." For his part, Emerson valued Hawthorne's friendship, while placing little value on his writing. Equally important to Hawthorne's development were his discussions with the writers Henry David Thoreau, Margaret Fuller, and others.

In contrast with the journal entries of earlier years, which reflect solitude and preoccupation with sin and death, his later journals, while never completely leaving those issues aside, do record a different side of Hawthorne as a man who exchanges ideas with his contemporaries in the fields of literature and art and as a husband who revels in his newfound home life and marriage. In the entries of the early 1840's, Hawthorne compiles descriptions of his home in his notebooks; these descriptions later served as material for some of his essays. In one such entry he notes: "My business is merely to live and to enjoy; and whatever is essential to life and enjoyment will come as naturally as the dew from Heaven."

These entries, filled with the daily activities of his two children born at this time, and Hawthorne's obvious enjoyment of them, gave Hawthorne material for *The Scarlet Letter* (1850); some of the elaborate descriptions of their childhood play served as background material for that novel, especially in the characterization of little Pearl. These entries also give the reader a broader perspective of a more settled, cheerful, indeed rapturous Hawthorne as a recorder of his children's lives.

The record of his son's laughter is interspersed with story ideas that reflect a darker reality. In part, *The American Notebooks* serves to record the dual nature of life as Hawthorne saw it. One story idea written by Hawthorne during the 1840's reflects the duality this way: "In a grim, weird story, a figure of gay, laughing, handsome youth, or young lady, all at once, in a natural, unconcerned way, takes off its face like a mask, and shows the grinning bare skeleton face beneath." Such individual entries show Hawthorne's mixture of fantasy with reality in his work and in his notebooks. Fantasy is always an important element throughout the notebooks; these entries convey Hawthorne's lifelong obsession with the darker sides of life.

Recurrent themes, story ideas, tantalizing conflicts, and character sketches, many of which appeared later in his fiction, provide a rich canvas of ideas in the notebooks. One entry notes the following: "The life of a woman, who, by the old colony law, was condemned always to wear the letter A, sewed on her garment, in token of her having committed adultery." This refers to a law passed in the New England colonies in 1696; its record in the notebooks shows the seed of an idea to which Hawthorne would return much later in his writing of *The Scarlet Letter.* In that novel, Hawthorne's heroine, Hester Prynne, must struggle with a community that condemns her for the act of adultery. Isolated and punished, she is sentenced to wear an *A* on her chest as an eternal announcement of her crime. Throughout *The American Notebooks*, Hawthorne struggles with the themes of guilt, redemption, and sin.

A final entry in June, 1851, after Hawthorne completed his major works, including *Twice-Told Tales*, *The Scarlet Letter*, *The House of the Seven Gables* (1851), and *The Blithedale Romance* (1852), ends on a curious, tantalizing note. In this last entry, Hawthorne records having burned great quantities of his letters and personal papers in preparation for an extended journey to England. He writes, "What a trustful guardian of secret matters is fire! What should we do without fire and death!" This entry surely alerts the reader to the fact that *The American Notebooks* is not intended as a completely candid and factual chronicle of Hawthorne's personal life. Indeed, many personal milestones of his life are left out. Hawthorne makes no effort to review the contents of *The American Notebooks*, which were an important professional resource for him as a writer, and which have preserved an intimate portrait of his creative, keen, and active mind.

Further Reading

Bell, Millicent, ed. *Hawthorne and the Real: Bicentennial Essays*. Columbus: Ohio State University Press, 2005. Collection of essays, commemorating the bicentennial of Hawthorne's birth, that explore his connection to the "real" world and how he expressed this relationship in his writing. Includes discussions of Hawthorne and politics, slavery, feminism, and moral responsibility.

Hawthorne, Julian. *Hawthorne and His Circle*. New York: Harper & Row, 1903. Reminiscences and notes by his son on the times recounted in *The American Notebooks*. An illuminating second look at the individuals and ideas chronicled by Nathaniel Hawthorne.

Hawthorne, Nathaniel. *The Heart of Hawthorne's Journals*. Edited by Newton Arvin. Boston: Houghton Mifflin, 1929. Contains entries in Hawthorne's journals that extend beyond the time period of *The American Notebooks*. Notes Hawthorne's journal observations up to his time in England in 1866.

Matthiessen, F. O. *American Renaissance: Art and Expression in the Age of Emerson and Whitman*. New York: Oxford University Press, 1941. Critical interpretation of the mid-nineteenth century and Hawthorne's place in it. The treatment of Hawthorne and his relation to American fiction is of particular merit for the reader of *The American Notebooks*.

Mellow, James R. *Nathaniel Hawthorne in His Times*. Boston: Houghton Mifflin, 1980. A complex and comprehensive investigation into Hawthorne's development as a major writer of nineteenth century America. Essential to an understanding of the historical context behind *The American Notebooks*.

Person, Leland S. *The Cambridge Introduction to Nathaniel Hawthorne*. New York: Cambridge University Press, 2007. An accessible introduction to the author's life and works designed for students and general readers. It places Hawthorne within the context of the political and philosophical developments of his times and provides a brief survey of Hawthorne scholarship.

Stewart, Randall, ed. *The American Notebooks*. New Haven, Conn.: Yale University Press, 1932. Examines Hawthorne's notebooks as they appear in manuscript form in the Pierpont Morgan Library. Points out the recurrent themes and character types in Hawthorne's notebooks. Offers extensive historical notes on persons and places discussed in the notebooks.

Wineapple, Brenda. *Hawthorne: A Life*. New York: Knopf, 2003. A meticulously researched, evenhanded analysis of Hawthorne's often contradictory life proposing that much of Hawthorne's fiction was autobiographical. Includes more than one hundred pages of notes, a bibliography, and an index.

American Pastoral

Author: Philip Roth (1933-)
First published: 1997
Type of work: Novel
Type of plot: Social criticism
Time of plot: 1940-1995
Locale: New Jersey

Principal characters:

NATHAN ZUCKERMAN, the narrator, a well-known writer
SEYMOUR "SWEDE" LEVOV, a successful Jewish American businessman
DAWN DWYER LEVOV, his wife
MEREDITH "MERRY" LEVOV, their militant radical daughter
JERRY LEVOV, Swede's younger brother
LOU and SYLVIA LEVOV, Swede's immigrant parents
BILL and JESSIE ORCUTT, friends of Swede and Dawn
RITA COHEN, Merry's purported friend, a fellow 1960's radical
SHEILA SALZMAN, Merry's speech therapist

The Story:

Nathan Zuckerman is growing up in the tight-knit, Jewish Weequahic section of Newark, New Jersey, in the 1940's. His childhood friendship with Jerry Levov allows Zuckerman access to Jerry's older brother, the godlike Seymour "Swede" Levov, a miraculous, mythical, high school athletic hero. Seymour has been nicknamed Swede because of his Nordic blonde hair, blue eyes, and fair complexion. Later, Zuckerman learns through gossip of Swede's life after childhood: He graduated from college in 1948, served in the Marines, then worked in and eventually took over his father's Newark glove factory. Over the opposition of his father, Swede has married a gentile, Irish American beauty queen,

Dawn Dwyer. The couple has one daughter, Meredith ("Merry"), and is living in a beautiful historic home in rural, upper-middle-class New Jersey.

In 1985, Zuckerman, now a well-known author, meets Swede by chance at a Mets game. Ten years later, he receives a letter from Swede asking for help in writing a memorial tribute to his deceased father. Zuckerman, curious about the troubles that may have befallen the legendary Swede, meets him for lunch, where Zuckerman learns only that Swede has three wonderful sons and has apparently remarried.

Shortly thereafter, at their forty-fifth high school reunion, Zuckerman encounters Jerry, who explains that Swede has recently died of prostate cancer and details the tragic derailment of Swede's life. Jerry divulges that Swede once owned a historic stone house in pastoral Old Rimrock, New Jersey, and appeared to be living the perfect American life. Then, one morning during the era of Vietnam War protests, his obese, stuttering, adolescent daughter Merry bombed the village post office and killed a beloved doctor picking up mail. According to Jerry, Swede, who had never before questioned his perfect American dream world, suddenly found his life turned completely upside down. It is Jerry's theory that Swede's never-ending desire always to do the right thing has killed him.

Intrigued, Zuckerman begins to contemplate the stoic Swede and tries to understand how this once-mythical figure fell from grace. Realizing he has simplified and idealized Swede's life, Zuckerman begins to retell Swede's story, reinventing and reimagining his all-American life, picking up the story after Merry's bombing of the post office.

In Zuckerman's posthumous narration, Merry has disappeared, and the distraught Levovs search fruitlessly for her. Suddenly, Rita Cohen, a purported emissary from Merry, appears at the glove factory to taunt Swede and swindle money. Five years pass, and during this time Swede, who has been permanently traumatized, struggles to determine what wounded Merry, derailing her development. He considers his own inappropriate kiss on the mouth of the stammering child, her psychiatrist's theories, her mother's anxiety, her struggles for fluency, her flirtation with Dawn's Catholicism, her adolescent self, her attitude toward bourgeois values, and her anger at the Vietnam War and the "system." Swede feels responsible for Merry's behavior and ruminates on his repeated conversations and interventions with the militant adolescent. Meanwhile, Dawn has a psychiatric breakdown and finally recovers after an expensive face-lift.

Swede receives a note from Rita stating that Merry is now living in the most derelict section of Newark. Father and daughter meet on a blighted street corner. Merry has converted to Jainism, an ancient Indian religion that prescribes a nonviolent life. She is emaciated, decrepit, and filthy, but astoundingly has lost her stutter. She leads him to the hovel she inhabits, where she admits to bombing the post office, fleeing to her speech therapist's house, blowing up three more people, living in communes, and being raped. Merry says she has now denounced selfhood and begs her father to go. Swede becomes distraught, but, unable to help his daughter, he returns to Old Rimrock, his idyllic life shattered.

When Swede returns home after meeting Merry, he begins preparing for a large dinner party planned earlier. It is the summer of the 1973 Watergate hearings, and Swede's father, Lou, is watching television. In a manner reminiscent of Merry, Lou spits out vitriolic abuse against President Nixon. During the chaotic dinner party, Swede's innocence is further shattered when he discovers that his wife is having an affair with their neighbor, Bill Orcutt. He also discovers to his horror that Merry's speech therapist, Sheila Salzman, a woman with whom he had a brief fling in the aftermath of the bombing, had secretly harbored Merry after the bombing, when it still might have been possible to stop her before others were killed. The novel closes with the inebriated Jessie Orcutt physically attacking Lou Levov, who is trying to supervise her erratic behavior.

Critical Evaluation:

Winner of the 1998 Pulitzer Prize in fiction, *American Pastoral* is the first novel in Philip Roth's American trilogy, and, like the other works—*I Married a Communist* (1998) and *The Human Stain* (2000)—it examines a significant post-World War II decade in American history. In *Reading Myself and Others* (1975), which presents Roth's philosophy of writing, he states that whereas World War II weakened social and class constraints, the Vietnam War demythologized America. In *American Pastoral*, Roth presents a disastrous meeting between the benign national myth that every American can achieve joyful plentitude and the inexorable, insidious reality of that era.

The 1960's were a particularly turbulent time that rapidly dispensed with President John F. Kennedy's vision of America as Camelot. They culminated in radical racial and antiwar demonstrations and ended in tragic disillusionment. The story line of *American Pastoral* traces that trajectory and its social consequences, thereby establishing the significance of the novel. The American immigrant's dream—if one excels, works hard, and is honorable, one will achieve success along with all one's dreams—is the myth that Roth debunks.

Critics have either hailed or assailed Roth for what they see as the politically conservative viewpoint of his novel, but he has been critical of the backlash of conservatism that the violent 1960's stimulated, and some critics argue that Roth's sympathies do not lie only with Swede. In fact, *American Pastoral* has inspired many interpretations. Questions arise as to why Roth wrote about the 1960's in the 1990's, but he actually began a different version of the novel in the early 1970's.

Throughout his American trilogy, Philip Roth uses a fictional narrator, Nathan Zuckerman, to reconstruct meditatively the stories being told. Zuckerman is Roth's mechanism for both distancing himself as author and sabotaging truth. In *American Pastoral*, Roth extends this technique by having Zuckerman imagine Seymour (Swede) Levov awakening to self-reflection, while Zuckerman remains in the background. Swede's ponderings are disjointed as he searches his memories for a transgression that he can blame for the tragedy his life has become. The postmodern narrative begins with Swede's death and ends midstream, around the time of the Watergate hearings in 1973. There are ellipses in the story—Merry's demise, Swede's remarriage—but this information becomes diminished because the intensity of the storyline focuses on Swede's life up to the time his daughter destroyed it along with the village post office. Through the unreliability of his narrative line, Roth suggests that truth cannot be determined.

To demythologize American culture, Roth uses a tragic hero, Swede, and, for emphasis, parodies John Milton by dividing the novel into three sections ("Paradise Remembered," "The Fall," and "Paradise Lost"). Swede, as befits a hero, receives a very sympathetic portrayal in this story. A gym teacher christens the fair-complexioned, Viking-like Seymour "Swede" and so differentiates him from the other, typically dark-complexioned, Jewish Seymours at Weequahic High. The good boy, an all-American athlete, grows into a good, successful man. His only trespass seems to be marrying an Irish American girl, but she also is from poor immigrant stock, and neither one is religious. Why does this golden pair have a child like Merry Levov? Some critics believe that Roth has finally turned to an examination of Jewish identity problems, and some find a religious moral in the story, but Roth's insistence on the intrusiveness of history and the randomness of events makes these readings questionable.

Through the character of Merry Levov, Roth foregrounds the extremism of sixties youth but also explores other themes, including the downfall of venerable American values, the lies of upward mobility and assimilation, the dashed hopes of parents, the influence of outside forces on youth, and the chasm between generations. Although the anti-Vietnam War movement was a mixture of radical and nonviolent political visions, Merry embodies its violent rage. Much like a collage artist, Roth chooses the pieces that fit best in his work, so at the peak of activity by Students for a Democratic Society (SDS) in 1968, Merry explodes her bomb, exiles her family from their perfect American dream life, and makes redemption impossible for her father.

Comedy with a grave underside is a mark of Roth's work. Swede presents a contrast with other Roth heroes. Many, such as Alexander Portnoy of *Portnoy's Complaint* (1969) and Mickey Sabbath of *Sabbath's Theater* (1995), rage and rebel, but all Roth's heroes share a life of suffering. Unlike Swede, Jerry and Lou, his brother and father, are characters with uncompromising viewpoints and are susceptible to emotional tirades. This genealogy might suggest that Swede, rather than Merry, is the aberration in the family, but Jerry and Lou can also be viewed as contrasting and humorous figures who promote sympathy for Swede. In his novels, Roth demonstrates that the incongruities, absurdities, and inexplicability of everyday life can best be dealt with through humor, so the other Levovs provide the humorous levity to the novel that the tragic hero cannot.

American Pastoral, published some forty-seven years after Roth's first novel, marked a turning point in the focus of his subject matter. Roth, observing the historical, political, social, and cultural forces that mold the notion of American identity, placed his individual protagonists at the mercy of such forces. Many critics consider his later works to be more substantial than his earlier ones. Since Roth has won every literary prize short of a Nobel Prize, however, critics tend to focus more on the connectedness of all his works, working to see them as a coherent whole. Identity has always been an issue for Roth. *American Pastoral* examines the hopes, dreams, and tragedies of Americans struggling for national identity in the tumultuous latter half of the twentieth century.

Debora J. Richey and Mona Y. Kratzert

Further Reading

Brauner, David. *Philip Roth*. New York: Manchester University Press, 2007. Evaluates Roth's works written between 1979-2004, their style, and issues in their critical interpretation; assesses the American trilogy from the standpoint of Roth's concern with social issues.

Halio, Jay L., ed. *Turning Up the Flame: Philip Roth's Later Novels*. Newark: University of Delaware Press, 2005. Contains three chapters on *American Pastoral* that consider identity, utopia, and feminism in the novel.

Parrish, Timothy, ed. *The Cambridge Companion to Philip Roth*. New York: Cambridge University Press, 2007. A comprehensive introduction to Roth's themes and works. Roth critic Mark Shechner considers *American Pastoral* from the standpoint of Jewish American identity.

Royal, Derek Parker, ed. *Philip Roth: New Perspectives on an American Author.* Westport, Conn.: Praeger, 2005. An excellent chronological survey of all Roth's novels, edited by the founder and president of the Philip Roth Society. These original essays also contain plot summaries. The bibliography includes an extensive listing of primary sources.

Safer, Elaine B. *Mocking the Age: The Later Novels of Philip Roth.* Albany: State University of New York Press, 2006. Explores the relation of humor to theme and form in Roth's later novels. Includes a chapter on each novel in the American trilogy.

Shostak, Debra. *Philip Roth: Countertexts, Counterlives.* Columbia: University of South Carolina Press, 2004. Makes extensive use of Roth's personal papers and considers the relation of Roth's texts to one another by theme rather than by chronology.

The American Scholar

Author: Ralph Waldo Emerson (1803-1882)
First published: 1837, as *An Oration Delivered Before the Phi Beta Kappa Society, Cambridge*
Type of work: Essay

Ralph Waldo Emerson's *The American Scholar* calls for cultural and intellectual independence and combines a rejection of industrialization with a nuanced diagnosis of modern alienation. The essay exhibits Emerson's striking aphoristic formulations, and although the figurative language is sometimes elliptical, its subversive message reverberates through American cultural life and influences thinkers and writers around the world.

The essay, which introduces many of Emerson's core intellectual themes, first was delivered as an address on August 31, 1837, in Cambridge, Massachusetts. It was published first as a pamphlet and reissued in 1849 as part of Emerson's collection *Addresses and Lectures*. With the essay's publication, Emerson became one of the foremost public intellectuals in the United States.

Emerson begins the essay with a sketch of the social fragmentation caused by work. Equated with their occupational function, people become tool-like, with a corresponding social arrangement that reinforces this state of affairs. He views this deformation as inherent in the mercantile and manufacturing culture then emerging in the United States. This social fragmentation not only inhibits human potential; in the extreme case of chattel slavery, its soul-destroying consequences are dehumanizing.

In vivid contrast to this lapsed condition, Emerson posits a vital aboriginal state that is characterized by a kind of cosmic consciousness. In this sense his examination of the American scholar is a reformation project, an idealized portrait of intellectual life rooted in the liberated humanity of the individual thinker. In practice this means an outright rejection of conformity and groupthink, including the uncritical acceptance of established creeds and dogmas. For Emerson, systems and institutions promote mental timidity. They diminish the value and intensity of direct experience while undermining the self-reliant agency necessary for authentic engagement with the world.

Emerson then reviews the primary educative influences on what he calls Man Thinking: nature, history, and life as action or praxis. The essay treats nature as endless depth, a mirror image of the mind and the soul. The innate tendency of the mind, says Emerson, is to classify seemingly disparate natural phenomena into tendencies, facts, and laws. Moreover, nature and reason reciprocally form and illuminate one another. In this and other ways, Emerson's thought exhibits a curious blend of Platonism and pragmatism. As natural philosophy, *The American Scholar* also hints at Charles Darwin's theory of evolution.

The section on history focuses on books as the primary repositories of the past. Books represent humankind's best attempt to distill and preserve the essence of the human condition. Nonetheless, says Emerson, books pose a grave threat to intellectual self-reliance if the creativity and energy used to make them are congealed through misuse. One form of misuse is canonization. Another is the focus on books as aesthetic or material artifacts. Another misuse of books is to use them as purveyors of the status quo. For Emerson, books are tools to inspire and provoke the reader to enlarge and vitalize his or her life. Their ultimate value is instrumental: Properly used, the best books inspire self-trust because they comment on larger concerns, connecting the reader to deep human possibilities and perennial themes. In contemporary terms (and echoing Francis Bacon), Emerson would say that books and knowledge "empower." This is especially true if they contribute to the reader's autonomy.

Emerson's remarks on worldly action are relevant to his ideas on human potential. The scholar immerses him- or herself in the world rather than fleeing it. The world is an occasion to gain valuable knowledge through focused, mindful participation. In advancing such ideas in *The American Scholar*, Emerson knew that he was countering nineteenth century (and later) stereotypes of people who work primarily with their mind. Although action is itself material to be used for self-knowledge, purposeful action deepens perception and awareness. Distilling value from adversity or the dreariest circumstances results from the creative power to transform all experience into valuable spiritual resources. Emerson emphasizes the mutually reinforcing fusion of thought and action in its most obvious manifestation—the character (and speech) of the self-reliant intellectual. He finds affirmation for this concept in nature by way of a principle he calls polarity.

A central theme in *The American Scholar* is the striving for wholeness. Since this private aspiration is linked with an individualist ethic and often clashes with social norms and public institutions, Emerson's project would seem to require a powerful will. In this regard, his ideas resemble the nineteenth century school of thought known as voluntarism, except that Emerson would finally reject this perspective as one-sided. Nonetheless, the harmonization of will, intellect, and soul is difficult, perhaps the chief impediment to the full realization of self-reliance and self-trust.

Emerson concludes *The American Scholar* with a description of the scholar's prospects and duties. These duties presuppose certain qualities—freedom, courage, openness, attentiveness, a resolute awareness of the moment—essential for undertaking the task of living and thinking at the highest intensity. However, the abstract, almost visionary argument in this section suggests certain ironies and inconsistencies. Historical figures and trends are used to illustrate and summarize major themes even as Emerson accentuates the atemporal dimensions of his project. A radical individualist philosophy rooted in self-cultivation and instinct becomes, in part, a studied denunciation of eccentricity. Emerson seeks a robust embrace of the universal as a necessary conduit to larger forces and laws, but certain traditions might matter if they promote the scholar's slow path to self-realization. Emerson celebrates everyday life and vernacular culture even as he diminishes the role of the masses in effecting significant historical change.

In the end, Emerson's espousal of self-reliant individualism in *The American Scholar* is an unwavering rejection of whatever blunts creative human potential. Wherever circumstances threaten the value of autonomy, the outspoken message of *The American Scholar* will offer encouragement, providing a clear alternative to debilitating conformity and spiritual alienation.

Robert N. Matuozzi

Further Reading

Buell, Lawrence. *Emerson*. Cambridge, Mass.: Harvard University Press, 2003. An informal but learned study that views Emerson's ideas and writing through a broad cultural prism. Buell shows why Emerson's philosophical concerns make him perennially interesting to individual readers and intellectual movements. He also offers a useful account of Emerson's multifaceted global influence.

Kateb, George. *Emerson and Self-Reliance*. Rev. ed. Lanham, Md.: Rowman & Littlefield, 2002. An examination of Emerson's notion of self-reliance that emphasizes democratic individuality. Although Emerson's texts propose self-reliance as a complex array of tensions and perspectives, Kateb's analysis emphasizes self-reliance as a therapeutic strategy to deal with the world and as a basis for self-fashioning.

Porte, Joel. *Representative Man: Ralph Waldo Emerson in His Time*. 1979. Reprint. New York: Columbia University Press, 1988. An unconventional, subtle biography of Emerson that considers him a primary cultural expression of his era. Particularly good at weaving a close reading of various texts with illustrative biographical events. Emerson comes into focus through his own words and through the observations of George Santayana, Henry James, Gertrude Stein, and Oliver Wendell Holmes, among others.

Richardson, Robert D. *Emerson: The Mind on Fire*. Berkeley: University of California Press, 1995. An outstanding, thoroughly researched intellectual biography of Emerson that examines his life and ideas in social and cultural context. In a series of short chapters, Richardson traces the key books and writers that shaped Emerson's thought. He also provides a detailed account of Emerson's close acquaintances and friendships. A fluent synthesis of interpretation and biographical narrative.

Sacks, Kenneth S. *Understanding Emerson: "The American Scholar" and His Struggle for Self-Reliance*. Princeton, N.J.: Princeton University Press, 2003. Describes the circumstances surrounding Emerson's 1837 Phi Beta Kappa oration, including that the speech was delivered after the person originally selected to give the oration declined. Discusses the clash of values and ideas between the Transcendentalists and Harvard-Unitarian culture. Argues that the speech was Emerson's attempt to forge an intellectual identity by overcoming his own apprehensions about himself and his ideas.

Wider, Sarah Ann. *The Critical Reception of Emerson: Unsettling All Things*. Rochester, N.Y.: Camden House, 2000. Carefully charts the varied critical reception of Emerson's works through an array of ideological and literary lenses. Examines Emersonian themes such as self-reliance, power, individualism, and idealism; Emerson's style; his views on science, politics, culture, and aesthetics; and his status as thinker, philosopher, and icon.

An American Tragedy

Author: Theodore Dreiser (1871-1945)
First published: 1925
Type of work: Novel
Type of plot: Naturalism
Time of plot: Early twentieth century
Locale: Kansas City, Missouri; Chicago; Lycurgus, New York

Principal characters:
CLYDE GRIFFITHS, the protagonist
ROBERTA ALDEN, his mistress
SAMUEL GRIFFITHS, Clyde's wealthy uncle
GILBERT GRIFFITHS, Samuel's son
SONDRA FINCHLEY, a society girl whom Clyde loves

The Story:

When Clyde Griffiths was still a child, his religious-minded parents took him and his brothers and sisters around the streets of various cities, where they prayed and sang in public. The family was always very poor, but the fundamentalist faith of the Griffithses was their hope and mainstay throughout the storms and troubles of life. Young Clyde was never religious, however, and he always felt ashamed of the life his parents were living. As soon as he was old enough to make decisions for himself, he went his own way.

At age sixteen, he gets a job as a bellboy in a Kansas City hotel. There the salary and the tips he receives astonish him. For the first time in his life he has money in his pocket, and he can dress well and enjoy himself. Then a tragedy overwhelms the family. Clyde's sister Hester, or "Esta," runs away, supposedly to be married. Her elopement is a great blow to their parents, but Clyde does not brood over the matter. Life is too pleasant for him; more and more, he enjoys the luxuries that his job provides. He makes friends with the other bellhops and joins them in parties that revolve around liquor and women. Clyde soon becomes familiar with drink and brothels.

One day, he discovers that his sister is back in town. The man with whom she ran away deserted her, and she is penniless and pregnant. Knowing his sister needs money, Clyde gives his mother a few dollars for her. He promises to give her more; instead, he buys an expensive coat for a girl in the hope that she will yield herself to him. One night, he and his friends go to a party in a car that does not belong to them. Coming back from their outing, they run over a little girl. In their attempt to escape, they wreck the car. Clyde flees to Chicago.

In Chicago he gets work at the Union League Club, where he eventually meets his wealthy uncle, Samuel Griffiths. The uncle, who owns a factory in Lycurgus, New York, takes a fancy to Clyde and offers him work in the factory. Clyde goes to Lycurgus. There his cousin, Gilbert, resents this cousin from the Midwest. The whole family, with the exception of his uncle, considers Clyde beneath them socially and will not accept him into their circle. Clyde is given a job at the very bottom of the business, but his uncle soon makes him a supervisor.

In the meantime, Sondra Finchley, who dislikes Gilbert, invites Clyde to parties that she and her friends often give. Her main purpose is to annoy Gilbert. Clyde's growing popularity forces the Griffithses to receive him socially, much to Gilbert's disgust. In the course of his work at the factory, Clyde meets Roberta Alden, with whom he soon falls in love. Since it is forbidden for a supervisor to mix socially with an employee, they have to meet secretly. Clyde attempts to persuade Roberta to give herself to him, but the girl refuses. At last, rather than lose him, she consents and becomes his mistress. At the same time, Clyde is becoming fascinated by Sondra. He comes to love her and hopes to marry her and, thus, acquire the wealth and social position for which he yearns. Gradually, Clyde begins breaking dates with Roberta in order to be with Sondra every moment that she can spare him. Roberta begins to be suspicious and eventually discovers the truth.

Roberta also discovers that she is pregnant. Clyde goes to drugstores for medicine to terminate the pregnancy, which does not work. He attempts to find a doctor of questionable reputation. Roberta goes to see one physician, who refuses to perform an operation. Clyde and Roberta are both becoming desperate, and Clyde sees his possible marriage to the girl as a dismal ending to all his hopes for a bright future. He tells himself that he does not love Roberta, that it is Sondra whom he wishes to marry. Roberta asks him to marry her for the sake of her child, saying she will go away afterward, if he wishes, so that he can be free of her. Clyde will not agree to her proposal and grows more irritable and worried.

One day he reads an item in the newspaper about the accidental drowning of a couple who went boating. A plan begins to form in his mind. He tells Roberta that he will marry her and persuades her to accompany him to an isolated lake resort. There, as though accidentally, he lunges toward her. She is hit by his camera and falls into the water. Clyde escapes, confident that her drowning will look like an accident, even though he planned it all carefully. He was careless, however, and letters that he and Roberta wrote are found. When her condition becomes known, he is arrested. His uncle obtains an attorney for him. At his trial, the defense builds up an elaborate case in his favor. Yet, in spite of his lawyer's efforts, he is found guilty and sentenced to be electrocuted. His mother comes to see him and urges him to save his soul. A clergyman finally succeeds in getting Clyde to write a statement—a declaration that he repents of his sins. It is doubtful that the religious statement is sincere. Clyde dies in the electric chair, a young man driven to betrayal, murder, and his own destruction by desire for luxury and wealth.

Critical Evaluation:

Theodore Dreiser is one of the primary practitioners of American naturalism, a school of writing that, like its counterpart in France, seeks to convey realistically and almost clinically the effects of social conditions on individual lives. All of Dreiser's characteristics are most clearly reflected in *An American Tragedy*, the masterpiece of an author who had earlier published three important novels: *Sister Carrie* (1900), *Jennie Gerhardt* (1911), and *The Financier* (1912, 1927). In this book, Dreiser the naturalist asserts the doctrine that the individual is struggling endlessly to survive in an uncaring world. The individual is also a victim of heredity, environment, and chance, all of which leave one with little room for free choice. Dreiser's theory of life is largely mechanistic, and for *An American Tragedy*, he invented the term "chemism" to explain the chemical forces that he believed propel people to act the way they do. Humanity, according to Dreiser, is a "mechanism, undevised and uncreated and a badly and carelessly driven one at that." Such a poor creature is Clyde Griffiths, the central character of *An American Tragedy*. The book, which is full of scientific imagery, shows readers how Clyde is driven to his final destruction.

Dreiser chooses to concentrate an individual's struggle against one particular force: society and its institutions. In each of the novel's three sections, Clyde strives not against a malign God or a malevolent fate but against the unyielding structure of his culture. In other times, people have defined themselves by other touchstones (religion, honor, war), but Clyde can answer his craving for meaning in only one way. To matter in America means, in the book's terms, to be masterful, to have material goods and status. Clyde's America tempts him with its powerful businesses, its glittering social affairs, and its promises that anyone who is deserving can share in its riches. That is a false promise; the American tragedy is the gap between the country's ideals and its reality.

Doomed to failure in his quest, Clyde, whose story has been called a parable of the American experience, cannot be blamed for desiring what he sees all about him. He cannot be blamed for the weaknesses and handicaps that ensure his end. Immature and shallow, offering a "gee" on all occasions, uneducated and poor, Clyde is willing to compromise in any necessary fashion in order to become materially successful. His lack of moral or intellectual distinction, when coupled with the intensity of his desires, makes him representative of a culture in which achievement is gauged by material and social success. In the novel (inspired by a 1906 murder case involving Chester Gillette, who killed an inconveniently pregnant girlfriend for reasons much like those in the book), Clyde's attorney calls him a "mental as well as a moral coward—no more and no less," but he later adds that Clyde cannot help this state.

The list of what created Clyde includes poor parents who were as inept as he. Impractical and ineffectual, the Griffithses offer him only their God, who, as Clyde can plainly see, bring them none of the things he or they want. Religion is one obstacle Clyde can and does overcome when he ignores his parents' protests and responds instead to his environment and inner urgings. His adaptability is exploited in the hotels in which he works, places where luxury alone is vital, and kindness and honesty mere trifles. When, in the second part of the novel, Clyde finds himself in Lycurgus, he once again gravitates helplessly toward the surrounding values. Named after the Spartan who initiated that society's rigid rules, Lycurgus is just as tantalizing as the hotels. It is a "walled city" that, as one of the novel's major symbols, allows outsiders to peek at its glories but rarely permits them to enter its gates. Clyde, fascinated and overwhelmed, abandons the simple pleasures he finds with Roberta and attempts to climb its walls.

Whenever Clyde struggles free of his environmental influences, he is frustrated by the accidents and coincidences that haunt him. He unwillingly leaves Kansas City because of the car accident, and he leaves Chicago because of a seemingly happy encounter with his uncle. His chance meeting with Sondra begins their relationship, and Roberta's unplanned pregnancy obstructs his dreams. Even his murder scheme is derived from a chance newspaper article, and the murder itself, in a sense, happens by accident, for Clyde, in a failure of nerve, allows rather than forces Roberta's drowning.

Other characters in the novel are equally victims of the roles in which they find themselves. While many of them are compellingly presented, their main importance is to provide background and stimuli for Clyde. He rarely sees others as people but rather as either impediments (his family, Roberta) or as exciting objects (Sondra); the reader too (in an act of complicity that Dreiser's narration skillfully elicits) is for the most part interested in the other characters in the same ways that Clyde is. The book belongs almost entirely to the decidedly unsympathetic Clyde.

In *An American Tragedy*, Dreiser, a former newspaperman and editor of women's publications, watches Clyde's world and its foibles and is moved by humanity's helplessness. He shows readers how useless moral judgment is in solving such dilemmas as the existence and acts of Clyde. Dreiser insists, as he does in all of his works, that all that people may expect of one another is compassion for common plights. Although he offers little encouragement, Dreiser does hint that perhaps the human condition may improve. The final scene—"Dusk, of a summer night"—closely resembles the opening. A small boy once again troops reluctantly with a group of street missionaries—the Griffithses. However, Mrs. Griffiths responds to Esta's child as she had never done to Clyde. She gives the child money for an ice cream cone. This child, she promises herself, will be different.

"Critical Evaluation" by Judith Bolch

Further Reading

Bloom, Harold, ed. *Theodore Dreiser's "An American Tragedy."* New York: Chelsea House, 1988. One of America's leading literary critics updates Jack Salzman's 1971 collection of essays (see below).

Cassuto, Leonard, and Clare Virginia Eby, eds. *The Cambridge Companion to Theodore Dreiser.* New York: Cambridge University Press, 2004. A collection of twelve essays focusing on the novelist's examination of American conflicts between materialistic longings and traditional values. Includes essays on Dreiser's style, Dreiser and women, and Dreiser and the ideology of upward mobility. The numerous references to *An American Tragedy* are listed in the index.

Gerber, Philip L. "Society Should Ask Forgiveness: *An American Tragedy*." In *Theodore Dreiser Revisited.* Boston: Twayne, 1992. A structural analysis that also examines Dreiser's sources, his progression through early drafts, and the novel's effect on his career. Includes an annotated bibliography.

Gogol, Miriam, ed. *Theodore Dreiser: Beyond Naturalism.* New York: New York University Press, 1995. Ten essays interpret Dreiser from the perspectives of new historicism, poststructuralism, psychoanalysis, feminism, and other points of view. Gogol's introduction advances the argument that Dreiser was much more than a naturalist and deserves to be treated as a major author.

Juras, Uwe. *Pleasing to the "I": The Culture of Personality and Its Representations in Theodore Dreiser and F. Scott Fitzgerald.* New York: Peter Lang, 2006. Juras examines how the two authors depicted the newly emerging concept of personality, defined as the outward presentation of self, in their work. Includes a discussion of *An American Tragedy.*

Lehan, Richard. "*An American Tragedy*." In *Theodore Dreiser: His World and His Novels.* Carbondale: Southern Illinois University Press, 1969. Discusses Dreiser's identification with Clyde Griffiths, particularly his fundamentalist religious background and the techniques Dreiser uses to mitigate Clyde's culpability.

Loving, Jerome. *The Last Titan: A Life of Theodore Dreiser.* Berkeley: University of California Press, 2005. This engrossing survey of the author's life and work is a welcome addition to Dreiser scholarship. Focuses on Dreiser's work, including his journalism, discussing the writers who influenced him and his place within American literature.

Orlov, Paul A. *"An American Tragedy": Perils of the Self Seeking "Success."* Lewisburg, Pa.: Bucknell University Press, 1998. A book-length interpretation of *An American Tragedy.* Orlov examines the novel's historical context, critical reception, sources, handling of time and place, elements of naturalism, and the theme of betrayal in order to attain success.

Pizer, Donald. "American Literary Naturalism: The Example of Dreiser." In *Realism and Naturalism in Nineteenth-Century American Literature.* Rev. ed. Carbondale: Southern Illinois University Press, 1984. One of the foremost authorities on naturalism in American literature defends Dreiser against critical antagonism toward naturalism and illustrates the principles of determinism in *An American Tragedy.*

Salzman, Jack, comp. *The Merrill Studies in "An American Tragedy."* Westerville, Ohio: Charles E. Merrill, 1971. A critical casebook on the novel, containing essays on topics such as naturalism, materialism, and Dreiser's sources for the novel.

Amores

Author: Ovid (43 B.C.E.-17 C.E.)
First transcribed: c. 20 B.C.E. (English translation, c. 1597)
Type of work: Poetry
Type of plot: Erotic
Time of plot: Augustan Age
Locale: Rome

Principal characters:
THE LOVER, the speaker of the poems
CORINNA, the beloved of the speaker

The Poem:

Book 1. The speaker, prepared to sing of heroic deeds, arms, and war, is struck by Cupid's arrow. He turns to the poetry of love. The speaker tosses sleepless at night, enthralled by love and suffering. He prays that the lady will favor him; he in return will immortalize her in verse. A monologue addressed to the lady explains how at a party she can dupe her husband and send signals to the speaker.

The first assignation of the lovers, on a sultry summer afternoon, takes place. There follows a sorrowful complaint as the speaker spends a long solitary night outside the locked door of Corinna's house. Next he feels guilt and remorse for a moment of anger in which he dishevels her hair. He overhears a conversation between Corinna and Dipsas, a bawdy old hag who gives the lady cynical advice on milking her lovers of gold and gifts. The speaker scolds his lady for her cupidity and tries to persuade her that love can only be given, never sold. He sends a letter to her, in hopes of a meeting, and feels despair when it is returned with a refusal.

Next, the lovers spend a night together, and the speaker complains of the inexorable coming of day, when they will have to part. A crisis happens: From too-frequent applications of the curling iron, Corinna's hair falls out. The poet chides and commiserates with her.

Book 2. Opening with a stout denial that he will be a better poet if he tries more serious subjects, the speaker harangues Corinna's guard about how easy and profitable he might find it to smuggle the speaker past the door and into her house. A similar plea is made to her eunuch. The speaker boasts about his ability to love any woman in town; but as if for punishment, the next poem relates his agonies when he suspects a rival.

Accused of dallying with Corinna's slave girl, the speaker denies the charge vehemently, with injured dignity, and in the next poem chides the slave for having blushed at the accusation, proving it true. A general complaint to Cupid comes next, on the theme that love is hell but heaven too. The lover boasts to a friend of his great capacity for lovemaking; he hopes he might die in bed.

When Corinna goes on a voyage, the lover bemoans their separation, charges the seas to be calm, the winds favorable, the trip safe and short. The lover then experiences another successful meeting with his love. Immediately following, the lover discovers Corinna performed an abortion on herself and endangered her life, and the poet is shocked and worried. She recovers and he gives her a ring as a love token.

Another separation occurs. The lover, visiting his native village, Sulmo, misses Corinna deeply. The poet explains how hard it is to write seriously when Cupid laughs and the ladies distract him. In poetry, he predicts, love will triumph over war. The last poem of book 2 advises Corinna's husband during an imagined meeting. Since forbidden fruits are sweetest, the poet will have the husband be jealous and watchful of his wife, to make the cuckolding more satisfying.

Book 3. The affair is on the wane. The muse of tragedy calls to the poet for a great work, but he asks for a short delay while he finishes his *Amores*. The poet discovers that Corinna's vows of love are broken. He is bitter and blames himself for ever having believed her protestations. At last he decides to let her lie if she must, but let her not swear false vows by his eyes.

Addressing the husband, the poet points out how silly it is to set guards on his wife: The faithful wife does not need them and the unfaithful wife will always find ways to get around them. Next is an account of a dream the poet has of a bull deserted by a heifer. A seer interprets this as a forecast that Corinna will leave the poet. The speaker, however, is still eager for her. On his way to visit her, he is blocked by a flood-swollen stream, which he curses and rages at in his thwarted desire.

Matters continue to go wrong: Once with her, he finds, ironically, that he is impotent, and he rages even more mightily at himself. The lady is furious, thinking he wore himself out with other women. She smiles on a new lover, and the poet, neglected, is left to wonder how she can prefer a parvenu and a soldier to him, a great poet.

The following poem is in a more serious tone. It is a funeral elegy on the death of a poet and friend, Tibullus. Next comes a poem in autumnal mood in praise of Ceres, goddess of the harvest, and of lament for his unhappy love affair. The poet tries unsuccessfully to renounce his love for the false Corinna. She is too beautiful, and he has to love her. Wryly he realizes that it is his celebration of Corinna in poetry that spreads her fame and attracts other men to her. He says they should have known he exaggerates, and that she cannot be perfect, as he paints her.

In a last confrontation with his cruel lady, the poet begs her at least to pretend she still loves him, even though he knows she is deceiving him. Let her deny that she strayed, he argues, so that he can continue to persuade himself that she loves him. In the last poem the poet announces that he gave up writing love poetry. He is ready to turn to a grave and serious subject. He hopes that all his writing will immortalize him.

Critical Evaluation:

Ovid read publicly from his *Amores* in 25 B.C.E., when he was about eighteen, and they proved immediately popular in Augustan Rome, despite, or perhaps because of, Augustus's efforts to promote morality, particularly marital fidelity, at court. The tradition of romantic and erotic elegies had been established by Catullus, who died c. 54 B.C.E., and Propertius, who died no later than 2 C.E. Ovid's elegies are often examined in the context of the work of these two predecessors. The poems of Propertius in particular are often compared to those of Ovid, who appears to have imitated and in some cases parodied Propertius. In general, Ovid undermines serious, romantic love in favor of fun.

Typical marriages for free and literate Roman patricians or aristocrats, those most likely to be Ovid's audience, were arranged. Adulterous relationships for both husband and wife appear to have been the rule rather than the exception. The male speaker in the forty-nine poems that make up the three books of the *Amores* takes this condition for granted and assumes his audience will be sympathetic. It is not surprising, therefore, that the first-person speaker and the mistress (sometimes Corinna and other times apparently not) are playful and promiscuous.

Most critics now agree that there was no model in Ovid's life for Corinna, who appears by name in about one-fourth of the poems, but Ovid gives her realistic features. She has auburn hair, as readers discover in 1.14, in which her hair is ruined by being restyled, and she is attended by various servants. She appears to be married, although she could be a concubine.

The speaker is a poet from Sulmo (as was Ovid) who believes in the power of his art to win and sustain the affections of his mistresses. More specifically in several "programmatic" poems (1.1, 1.15, 2.1, 2.18, 3.1, 3.8, 3.15) the poet argues his confidence in the elegy as opposed to either tragedy or epic when it comes to assuring his fame. This argument constitutes one theme of the *Amores*. In effect Ovid argues for poems other than those that are filled with pathos or profundity. In 2.1, he says he would like every young man who is in love to be able to recognize his symptoms in these poems, "and ask himself in amazement 'How does this poet know/ about me and my personal problems?'" Perhaps this is the goal of most poets.

The perspective throughout is distinctively male. Not

well-off financially, the speaker depends on his art and its appeal to his mistress's vanity (her desire for eternal fame) to get by. As a lover he is at odds with men of affairs, whether businessmen or soldiers, but he makes use of their language in the process of presenting his case. For example, in 1.9, he argues that all lovers are soldiers, and they must use military tactics to avoid the guards and night patrols set out by sleeping husbands.

Of course the lover is jealous and suspicious, but the cause may have less to do with his mistress's infidelity than with his own. In 2.7, for example, he uses metaphors drawn from the law in describing himself as a defendant unjustly accused of an affair with his mistress's hairdresser, Cypassis. He insists no true gentleman would carry on with a mere maid, but in the next poem he smooth-talks Cypassis with an argument from Homer, pointing out that, after all, "Achilles adored his maid Briseis." Clearly, the fun of the *Amores* requires the setting aside of conventional moral and ethical standards, and perhaps of the rules of logic as well.

It could be said that the premise of the *Amores* is hedonistic, that the poems are founded upon the simple human drive to avoid pain and seek pleasure, even at great cost. Certainly the languid sexuality of 1.5, and the morning song 1.13, in which the lover pleads with the sun not to rise, are examples. In 2.15 he imagines himself as his girlfriend's ring slipping inside her dress and fondling her breast, and in 3.4 he pleads to her husband to be more alert and more possessive, as the challenge will make their affair more exciting. The speaker's most embarrassing moment is celebrated in 3.7, when he confesses his inability to achieve an erection, despite the professional efforts of his mistress (not Corinna, in this case, as he mentions her for having "inspired" his "record" of nine times "in one short night").

One might argue that in the *Amores* Ovid offers comic relief to a society that tended to be stifling in its commitment to business and affairs of state and increasingly puritanical in its moral outlook. As studies of supposedly proper Victorians have revealed, repressive societies tend to force sexual play underground, not to eradicate it. Some critics have suggested that Ovid himself, who was married three times, may not have enjoyed the self-indulgent escapades of his speaker, but the poems remain an invitation to erotic love. In 2.4 the speaker says he offers no excuse for his "weak character" or lack of discipline, for he loves all types of women: "I admire a girl in make-up for what she is/ and a girl without for what she could be."

There is a price to be paid for the unleashing of the libido, however, and occasionally Ovid reveals it. For example, in 1.7 he shows remorse for having beaten his mistress, and in 2.13 and 2.14 he shows his concern when she nearly dies after a self-inflicted abortion and then anger over the act itself. The third book of the *Amores* involves a sort of cooling off, as Ovid prepares his audience for other kinds of poetry. Poems such as 3.6, on rivers, and 3.10, on sexual abstinence practiced during the feast of Ceres, concern mythological tales rather than personal erotic adventures. The third book also includes a moving elegy to the poet Tibullus (3.9) and a dream allegory (3.5) that most critics think is not Ovid's work.

Poems 3.11 through 3.15, the last five of the book, include an angry farewell to the bondage of love, a lament that the speaker loses Corinna because his poems made her too popular, an account of the legend of his wife's hometown, and a plea to his mistress to deceive him if she does not really love him. The poet, who is supposed to be the master of illusions, now begs to be deluded.

"Critical Evaluation" by Ron McFarland

Further Reading

Boyd, Barbara Weiden. *Ovid's Literary Loves: Influence and Innovation in the "Amores."* Ann Arbor: University of Michigan Press, 1997. Boyd disagrees with other scholars who maintain the *Amores* are an imitation or parody of Roman elegiac poetry, particularly the work of Propertius. She points out the nonelegiac and non-Propertian aspects of the poems, as well as their extended similes, irony, and narrative structure.

DuQuesnay, I. M. le M. "The Amores." In *Ovid*, edited by J. W. Binns. London: Routledge & Kegan Paul, 1973. Conjectures on Corinna and comments on style and technique. Sees the speaker as parody not really directed at Propertius but at Ovid and notes that Ovid takes playful jabs at Augustan society.

Hardie, Philip. *The Cambridge Companion to Ovid*. New York: Cambridge University Press, 2002. Collection of essays examining the historical contexts of Ovid's works, their reception, and the themes and literary techniques of his poetry. The numerous references to *Amores* are listed in the index.

Knox, Peter E., ed. *Oxford Readings in Ovid*. New York: Oxford University Press, 2006. Collection of twenty influential scholarly essays published since the mid-1970's that provide a range of interpretations of Ovid's poetry. Two of the essays discuss *Amores*: "Reading Female Flesh: *Amores* 3.1" by Maria Wyke and "The Death of Corinna's Parrot Reconsidered: Poetry and Ovid's *Amores*" by Barbara Weiden Boyd.

Lyne, R. O. A. M. *The Latin Love Poets*. New York: Oxford University Press, 1980. The chapter on Ovid's *Amores* reflects on the kind of society that reads the poems, on the character of Corinna, and on connections with poems by Propertius and Tibullus. Notes Ovid's antiromantic wit, playful cynicism, and opposition to "the moral earnestness of Augustan Rome," arguing that what Ovid believed in was fun and poetry.

Mack, Sue. *Ovid*. New Haven, Conn.: Yale University Press, 1988. Notes the conventionality of the lover, the mistress, and the situations in the poems. Finds that Ovid distinguishes between poet and persona and creates a "constantly changing interaction between himself and the audience."

Morgan, Kathleen. *Ovid's Art of Imitation*. Leiden, the Netherlands: E. J. Brill, 1977. Examines Ovid's "creative imitation" and parody of Propertius in the *Amores*. Contains a useful bibliography of works on the *Amores*.

Amoretti

Author: Edmund Spenser (c. 1552-1599)
First published: 1595
Type of work: Poetry

Edmund Spenser's sonnet sequence, the *Amoretti* (meaning "little love gifts" in Italian), ranks among the most notable of the collections produced during the golden age of English poetry, also the heyday of the English sonnet. Beginning in fourteenth century Italy with Petrarch's tributes, in sonnet form, to his beloved Laura, the sonnet cycle describing the lover's pangs and the inamorata's remote beauty quickly became a poetic standard. The introduction of this poetic form to England is generally credited to Sir Thomas Wyatt, who brought it from France and adapted it to the English taste and tongue. Although the prestige of the sonnet had begun to decline by the time Spenser produced his sequence, no notable poet of the period could afford to ignore the sonnet or the sonnet cycle. As had William Shakespeare and Sir Philip Sidney before him, Spenser used the sonnet cycle as part of his claim to literary fame.

The *Amoretti* differs from Sir Philip Sidney's *Astrophel and Stella* (1591) sequence and from Shakespeare's sonnets in ways that have too often led to comparisons unfavorable to Spenser. Not only does Spenser use a more labored rhyme scheme (adapted from the French), but also his subject matter is subtler and less dramatic. Shakespeare and Sidney address their rhymes to amorous objects presented in a highly fictionalized and formalized context. Spenser, on the other hand, blends traditional elements of idealization of the love object with elements of the actual courtship of his future wife. For this reason, the *Amoretti* wavers somewhere between the dramatic outpourings of emotion typical of Shakespeare and the elegantly crafted tributes to the lady's charms typical of Sidney. As a result, Spenser's reader must look beneath the "artificial" elements of the sonnets to see their "natural" appeal. They record the vagaries of real courtship, with all its alternating moments of doubt, despair, hope, tenderness, elation, and joy sketched with characteristic Spenserian delicacy and tact.

This delicacy may create problems for the reader who demands more straightforward vigor; it can best be appreciated by noting how the sonnets' unusual rhyme scheme produces a graceful modulation between and within lines. Although each of Spenser's sonnets closes with a ringing couplet, traditional in the sonnet in English, its scheme as a whole is tighter and subtler than that of the more ordinary form. Ending each quatrain with the rhyme that will begin the next, Spenser achieves a remarkably smooth, graceful, and highly unified effect. While some critics have criticized this rhyme scheme as overly artificial, it is very well suited to the fine modulation of emotions expressed by a forty-year-old poet seeking the hand of a beautiful and socially superior young lady. Similarly, while the character of this lady tends toward the ideal, Spenser ably sketches the personality of a real woman. His Elizabeth Boyle is not the inaccessible mistress of Petrarchan tradition, nor is her lover its traditional victim. Each partner to this courtship exhibits strengths and weaknesses, each ultimately being referred back to the perfecting grace of God. Spenser's sonnet sequence is a remarkable achievement: It is one of the first fully realized attempts in lyric poetry to represent an actual, rather than an ideal, human relationship. The *Amoretti* creates one of the earliest and greatest tributes to the Protestant virtues of married love and domestic tranquillity.

The sequence also is unique in charting a real-time sequence, the period between late 1592 and June 11, 1594, the day on which Spenser's wedding was finally solemnized, and which his famous *Epithalamion* (1595) celebrates. The New Year's Days of 1593 and 1594 are observed in the sequence, as are the occasions of Easter, the couple's betrothal, and their separation for a brief period before their wedding. Along with these time markers, many purely conventional elements are included, as in the first sonnet, a traditional dedication to love, to poetry, and to the muse. Characteristic of Spenser, this classical theme is Christianized by the poet's asking his book to testify to "that angels blessed look,/ My souls long lacked food, my heavens bliss." However, instead of merely borrowing the language of religion to praise the ecstatic "bliss" of the lady's beauty, the poet uses it to consecrate the institution of holy matrimony, which will in turn prepare the couple for their heavenly home. This theme is reiterated with new emphasis in sonnet 3, in which the poet speaks of his beloved's beauty as having kindled heavenly fire:

> In my frail spirit, by her from baseness raised:
> That being now with her huge brightness dazed,
> Base thing I can no more endure to view;
> But looking still on her, I stand amazed
> At wondrous sight of so celestial hue.

Even in this sonnet, however, some customary aspects of the poet's praise are apparent. Drawing upon the Neoplatonic conception of the relationship among light, beauty, and virtue, the poem praises a conventionally fair lady, a golden-haired ideal of Elizabethan loveliness. More than a compendium of Christian virtues, then, she is also celebrated for her classically aristocratic "virtue" of pride. In sonnet 5, Spenser associates her pride not only with nobleness of spirit and mind but also with chastity:

> For in those lofty looks is close implied
> Scorn of base things, and disdain of foul dishonor;
> Threatening rash eyes which gaze on her so wide,
> That loosely they ne dare to look upon her.
> Such pride is praise, such portliness is honor.

This theme continues with variations throughout the sequence. The poet also argues that women are like trees even while he laments the suffering that their "hardness" inflicts upon him. His protests of the suffering caused him by the hardness and remoteness of the love object rank among the most conventional devices of the *Amoretti*. Comparing his lady's eyes to blinding darts or beams capable of inflicting life or death, he eventually grows outraged in sonnet 10 at "the huge massacres which her eyes do make"; at how, in sonnet 11, a warrior takes him hostage without ransom; and at how like a huntress she seeks to despoil his poor "hart." The pun on the human heart and the tender "hart," or deer (with an additional pun on "dear"), is conventional. Such techniques date back to Petrarch, although Spenser uses them with a characteristically personal emphasis. For example, he begins sonnet 15 with a traditional metaphor of love as a form of journey, courtship as a labor of exploration, and his beloved as a precious mine: her lips are rubies, her teeth pearls, her skin ivory, her hair gold, and her hands silver. Rather than extending the metaphor and making this blazon or ceremonial poetic device culminate in an ultimate jewel or setting, the poet unexpectedly declares that her true worth is as immeasurable as the invisible beauty of "her mind." A series of metaphors that are concrete and particular culminate not in a summary of the concrete and particular aspects of the loved one's beauty but rather in an abstraction. Spenser's characteristically Protestant emphasis falls on the inner self, the invisible realm of human and divine perfection.

This mixing of Petrarchan convention and a more individual approach persists throughout the sequence, with the innovative approach ultimately triumphing. As the poet's love prospers, so does the originality of his inspiration. This triumph is foreshadowed by Spenser's continual refusal, even in despair, to regard his beloved as merely the trite goddess of lyric tradition. What he wants is a companion and a virtual equal. Although her feminine beauty is a predictably perfect blend of "Nature and Art," its true purpose is not only to humble her suitors but also to "train and teach" her lover, in sonnet 21, with "such art of eyes I never read in books." Spenser combines the literal eye of beauty with the metaphoric "mind's eye" of Platonic tradition. Spenser's vision of the lady amplifies her human completion: Neither her beauty nor her pride can be reduced to earthly treasures of art or nature; both must be seen as spiritual treasures, on earth as in heaven. This thought, lacking in the Petrarchan tradition, constitutes Spenser's most remarkable contribution. Even when lamenting the lady's cruelty, the speaker continually encourages her to examine and refine her motives. In sonnet 30, for example, his comparison of her to ice and of himself to fire is resolved into a kind of "miracle" in which each becomes capable of taking on the properties of the other.

Once the lady graciously accepts him (this is also a significant departure from convention), both lady and lover are free to develop their personal characteristics in a new context. The turning point in the sequence and the courtship appropriately concurs with the arrival of the new year in sonnet 62. The passing of the solstice and the "storms and tempests" of winter in sonnet 63 are sealed with a kiss as sweet as all the gentle blooms of spring in sonnet 64. Some doubts remain in her heart, however, so the poet reassures his lady that her miraculous gift will increase rather than diminish her liberty: She will free them both to each other. The most successful sonnets of the sequence surround this turning point, which culminates with Spenser's praise of the "lord of life," whose example, at Eastertide in sonnet 68, teaches the lovers the lesson of rebirth by means of self-sacrifice. Marriage is celebrated as a "sweet prison" of freedom and "eternal peace" in sonnet 71.

The final sonnets of the *Amoretti* rank among the most elevated and moving examples of the Renaissance sonnet tradition. They sometimes merely rewrite Petrarch by way of Wyatt (the metaphor of the huntsman, for example, in sonnet 67), but examples of the sonnets' considerable originality (which, in the poet's time, was not as important in poetry as it has been since the Romantic era) include the poet's personal admiration, in sonnet 71, of his love's "drawn work." He characteristically interprets her drawing as signifying the reign of an "eternal peace." His celebration of her "thrice happy" name in sonnet 74 and his denunciation in sonnet 85 of a gossip who threatens their relationship are other examples of Spenser's original use of personal experience in actual courtship. Interspersed with these personal reflections are some of Spenser's loftiest spiritual sonnets, such as sonnet 79. Perhaps the most successful sonnet of the sequence incorporates the mundane and the lofty. Sonnet 75 begins with the poet's unsuccessful attempt to write Elizabeth's name on the sand. The tide erases her name and speaks to the poet, mocking him for his efforts. The sonnet ends with a meditation on how in the poet's praise of her "virtues rare," "Our love shall live, and later life renew." Conventional as this theme is, Spenser's complex reflection on the tides of time and of human life produces a timeless work of art.

Catherine Gimelli Martin

Further Reading

Dasenbrock, Reed Way. "The Petrarchan Context of Spenser's *Amoretti*." *PMLA* 100, no. 1 (1985): 38-50. Makes a comprehensive statement of the case for the originality and vigor of the *Amoretti*. Includes bibliography.

Gibbs, Donna. *Spenser's "Amoretti": A Critical Study*. Aldershot, England: Scolar Press, 1990. Excellent sourcebook on the poetic structure, personas, and philosophical background of the *Amoretti*, as well as its current critical reception. Thorough bibliography and index.

Hadfield, Andrew, ed. *The Cambridge Companion to Spenser*. New York: Cambridge University Press, 2001. Collection of essays providing an overview of Spenser's life and work. Some of the essays discuss the relevance of Spenser, his life and career, the historical contexts of his work, his use of language, and his literary influence. The references to *Amoretti* are listed in the index.

Lethbridge, J. B., ed. *Edmund Spenser: New and Renewed Directions*. Madison, N.J.: Fairleigh Dickinson University Press, 2006. Reprints a collection of papers originally delivered at a conference about Spenser. Includes discussions of the Spenserian stanza, Spenser's relationship to Ireland, and the trend toward a new historical criticism of his work.

Lewis, C. S. *The Allegory of Love: A Study in Medieval Tradition*. New York: Oxford University Press, 1967. A classic study of the *Amoretti* in the context of Western culture's evolving ideas about love and marriage.

McCabe, Richard A. *Spenser's Monstrous Regiment: Elizabethan Ireland and the Poetics of Difference*. New York: Oxford University Press, 2002. Analyzes how Spenser's experiences of living and writing in Ireland challenged his ideas about English nationhood. Assesses the influence of colonialism on the themes, imagery, language, and structure of his poetry.

Martz, Louis L. "The *Amoretti*: "Mostly Goodly Temperature." In *Form and Convention in the Poetry of Edmund Spenser*, edited by William Nelson. New York: Columbia University Press, 1961. A generally sympathetic treatment of the *Amoretti* from the perspective of the sonnets' emotional and literary development.

Spiller, Michael R. G. "The Elizabeth Sonnet Vogue and Spenser." In *The Development of the Sonnet: An Introduction*. London: Routledge & Kegan Paul, 1992. An invaluable and highly perceptive guide to the place of the *Amoretti* in the sonnet tradition.

Amphitryon

Author: Plautus (c. 254-184 B.C.E.)
First produced: Amphitruo, c. 185 B.C.E. (English translation, 1694)
Type of work: Drama
Type of plot: Farce
Time of plot: Heroic Age
Locale: Thebes

Principal characters:
AMPHITRYON, a Theban general
ALCMENA, his wife
JUPITER and MERCURY, Roman gods
SOSIA, Amphitryon's slave

The Story:

Amphitryon, a Theban, joins the army of Thebes to fight against the Teloboans. When he leaves for the wars, his wife Alcmena, daughter of Electryon, is pregnant. Nevertheless, in the absence of Amphitryon, Jupiter falls in love with Alcmena and decides that he must enjoy her favors. Disguising himself as Amphitryon, Jupiter appears to Alcmena as her husband, just returned from a battle with the Teloboans. Alcmena is unable to recognize the impostor and welcomes Jupiter as her husband. Because Jupiter wishes to enjoy Alcmena as long as possible, he has the sun, moon, and stars remain fixed, and so the night he spends with Alcmena is long enough for her to conceive and be ready to bring forth a child by Jupiter at the same time she gives birth to the child by her husband.

In the meantime Amphitryon's ship returns to Thebes. It is still night, so Amphitryon's slave, Sosia, fearfully walking the streets of the sleeping town, tries to console himself with the pleasantness of the news he is bringing to its citizens. He thinks how well his master, Amphitryon, handled the war with the Teloboans, how the enemy refused to arbitrate the dispute over lands, how the battle was joined, and how Amphitryon was awarded the golden cup of Pterela as a token of the valor displayed in the battle.

While Sosia soliloquizes, Mercury, disguised as Sosia, is listening to every word. Mercury assumes the disguise to aid his father, Jupiter, in the latter's scheme to make love to Alcmena. As Sosia comes through the streets to Amphitryon's house, Mercury, in the guise of Sosia, is guarding the house and the inmates against any disturbance. When Sosia sees Mercury he is afraid, but he goes up to the door and tries to enter. Mercury, as Sosia, tells him to be gone and beats him with his fists. When Sosia cries out that he is a slave named Sosia who belongs to the household, he receives another drubbing.

Sosia, confused, then asks the stranger who he is. Mercury replies that he is Sosia, a slave of the household. Looking closely, Sosia sees that the person in front of him is dressed and looks exactly like himself. When Sosia goes on to ask questions about the household, Mercury answers each one satisfactorily. Sosia asks about his own conduct during the battle; Mercury replies that he was drinking. Knowing that the answer is correct and sure that someone stole his identity, Sosia runs off to the ship, leaving Mercury to chuckle over the ruse that will prevent Amphitryon from spoiling Jupiter's night with Alcmena.

Eventually Jupiter takes leave of Alcmena, after telling her that he must return to his army, lest the men become bitter because their leader absents himself while they cannot. When she grows sad at the thought of his departure, the god, to propitiate her, gives her the golden cup of Pterela that Amphitryon received as a token of merit in the war. As he leaves, Jupiter orders the night to move on in its regular course.

Amphitryon is furious when Sosia returns to the ship. He thinks that the slave must be mad or, at the very least, drunk, and he refuses to believe that anyone could have stolen the identity of Sosia, as the slave declares. Amphitryon, anxious to discover what is happening, sets out for his home immediately, taking Sosia with him. By the time the real Amphitryon and Sosia arrive at the house, Jupiter and Mercury were departed. Alcmena is surprised to see her husband return in so short a time. She fears that he is simply testing her fidelity.

Amphitryon, greeting his wife as a husband would after an absence of months, is unable to understand what Alcmena means when she rebukes him for leaving her a short time before on a pretext of returning to his army. When she tells Amphitryon that he spent the night with her, Amphitryon becomes suddenly and decidedly angry. Then she mentions the golden cup of Pterela, which she received from Jupiter during his visit in disguise. Amphitryon declares she cannot have the cup, for he has it under seal in his possession. When Amphitryon opens the chest in which he put the cup, however, it is missing; the gods stole it to give to Alcmena.

In spite of the evidence produced to show that it is he who was with his wife, Amphitryon is exceedingly angry and accuses his wife of losing her honor by breaking her marriage vows. Alcmena, entirely innocent of any such intent and still believing that her husband visited her earlier, is hurt and furious at the charges he makes. Amphitryon, wishing to be fair but wanting to get to the bottom of the matter, goes to get Alcmena's kinsman, Naucrates, who was with him all night on board the ship. He also tells Alcmena that he will divorce her unless she can prove her innocence.

Alcmena is upset at the charges heaped upon her by Amphitryon and makes plans to leave the house. Jupiter, sorry for the trouble he caused, prepares to help her. He appears to Alcmena in disguise and softens somewhat her anger against Amphitryon. Speaking as Amphitryon, he apologizes for the charges made against Alcmena's honesty and virtue.

Amphitryon is unable to find Naucrates and returns to his home. Warned by Mercury, Jupiter appears as Amphitryon, and a riotous scene, with both men seeming to be Amphitryon, follows, an argument broken off when word comes that Alcmena is about to give birth to a child. As Amphitryon prepares to leave, Jupiter strikes him unconscious with a thunderbolt. With Jupiter's aid Alcmena painlessly gives birth to two sons, one by Amphitryon and the other by Jupiter. One child is so active that he can hardly be held on his cot to be bathed, and the waiting-women report that within a few minutes of his birth the baby strangled two large snakes that entered the room. The voice of Jupiter calls out to Alcmena and tells her that the lusty lad, Hercules, is his and the other child Amphitryon's.

After the waiting-women leave, Jupiter himself appears to Amphitryon and tells the husband what happened. When he warns Amphitryon not to be harsh toward his wife for producing a child by a god, Amphitryon, faced with no other choice, promises to obey all that the god commands.

Critical Evaluation:

When the Roman writers adapted Greek comedies, as Plautus almost certainly did in the case of this play, they eliminated the chorus completely, thereby making the action continuous. They also made song and dance an integral part of the play, much like contemporary musical comedies. Tradition says that Plautus learned stagecraft early in life, put his earnings into trade, went bankrupt, had to work in a flour mill, and there began writing his comedies, of which more than a hundred were attributed to him. Twenty have survived, and from these readers can see that Plautus was very experienced in stage technique. He knew the value of timing, of comic repetition, of puns, of double entendre, of idiomatic speech, and of varying his poetic meters. His humor was suggestive rather than lewd. He was a master at simply being funny. In reading his plays it is essential to visualize the action as taking place on the stage in front of a backdrop of a house or two. Imagination is necessary to re-create the humor of Plautus. Otherwise, his jokes seem stale, particularly in translation. His plays were performed outdoors at public festivals in a carnival atmosphere, and they had to compete with other entertainments. The audiences were restive, unsophisticated, and straitlaced in that period of Roman history. Under such conditions a dramatist had to be continuously interesting, and a comic dramatist had to be amusing at all costs. Plautus knew his audience thoroughly. He took the threadbare formulas of Greek New Comedy and inspirited them with his own vivacity.

Amphitryon is the only extant Roman comedy to treat Greek mythology. The story derives from a myth in which Zeus (Jupiter) lengthened a night into seventy-two hours and, disguised as Amphitryon, made love to Amphitryon's wife Alcmena. The supreme god did this in order to engender the great hero Herakles (Hercules). In this play, however, the effect is to make Jupiter appear as an insatiably lecherous and a troublemaking bully who would do anything to satisfy his whims. He and Mercury are rogues playing a rather nasty practical joke on three decent people. It is a joke that gets out of hand and threatens to become tragic when Amphitryon intends to divorce Alcmena for adultery. However, Jupiter unravels the mystery, restoring an equilibrium, when he has enough amusement at their expense. Thus the play blends two of Plautus's favorite plots—the comedy of mistaken identity and the comedy of deliberate deception.

The structure is surprisingly well done for Plautus, who usually took few pains to construct a sound plot. He makes excellent use of dramatic irony in the confusions of the human characters balanced against the knowledge of the divine characters, which the audience shares. The audience is given an Olympian viewpoint from which to witness the befuddlement of human beings as they encounter their exact duplicates and are bettered at every turn. Much of the humor lies in the way Plautus exposes the discrepancy between perplexed humans and clear-sighted, interfering immortals. It is very funny when Sosia comes to doubt his own identity, having been displaced in his household by another Sosia who is identical in every respect. He thinks he has somehow twinned himself. The joke is still good later when Amphitryon and Jupiter ask Blepharo the pilot to decide who is the real Amphitryon. The theme of twins, the doppelgänger, is carried through right to the end, when Alcmena gives birth to twins, one of human and the other of divine origin.

The play becomes serious, however, when Alcmena is accused of adultery because she finds no difference between Amphitryon and Jupiter playing Amphitryon. Her husband comes to seem like an utter lunatic vacillating wildly between tenderness and incomprehensible jealousy. She genuinely loves Amphitryon and is deeply hurt by his accusations. Plautus gives a sympathetic portrayal of her as the duped wife. Amphitryon, although he loves Alcmena, seems like a proud, hot-tempered stuffed shirt who deserves, to an extent, his humiliation at Jupiter's hands. Plautus lifts both of these characters above the farcical level to reveal two people tricked and thwarted by the gods. Their love endures these buffetings.

Amphitryon had a great influence on modern drama throughout the Western world, and there are numerous translations, adaptations, and imitations. Such great dramatists as John Dryden, in England, and Molière, in France, made use of its theme and structure. A production of the story as adapted by Jean Giraudoux was successful as a stage play under the title *Amphitryon 38* (1929).

"Critical Evaluation" by James Weigel, Jr.

Further Reading

Anderson, William S. *Barbarian Play: Plautus' Roman Comedy.* Toronto, Ont.: University of Toronto Press, 1993. Anderson focuses on Plautus's "deconstruction of Menander," or the ways in which Plautus alters elements in his source to make his plays Roman instead of Greek. Includes good notes, a thorough index, and a comprehensive bibliography.

Fraenkel, Eduard. *Plautine Elements in Plautus.* Translated by Tomas Drevikovsky and Frances Muecke. New York: Oxford University Press, 2007. This is the first English translation of a German study initially published in 1922. Fraenkel, an influential twentieth century classicist, provides an analytical overview of Plautus's plays, including their motifs of transformation and identification, mythological material, dialogue, and the predominance of the slave's role.

Hunter, R. L. *The New Comedy of Greece and Rome.* New York: Cambridge University Press, 1985. Lucid discussion of forms, motifs, and themes in New Comedy, with numerous references to Plautus and *Amphitryon.* Extensive notes and a bibliography.

Leigh, Matthew. *Comedy and the Rise of Rome.* New York: Oxford University Press, 2004. Analyzes the comedies of Plautus and Terence, placing them within the context of political and economic conditions in Rome during the third and second centuries B.C.E. Discusses how audiences of that time responded to these comedies.

Plautus. *Amphitryo: Text and Commentary.* Translated by Anne Mahoney. Newburyport, Mass.: Focus/R. Pullins, 2004. In addition to the Latin text of the play and Mahoney's commentary, this edition features an introduction, in English, discussing the play's history, grammar, and poetic meter and a supplement, written in the fifteenth century, to substitute for the scenes lost in the original.

Sandbach, F. H. *The Comic Theatre of Greece and Rome.* London: Chatto & Windus, 1977. Both the chapter "Drama at Rome" and the chapter devoted to Plautus provide excellent overviews. Insists that Plautus was less dependent on Greek sources than is generally assumed. Essential Greek and Roman terms are defined in a glossary, which includes a thorough discussion of meter. Includes a brief bibliography and illustrations.

Segal, Erich. *Roman Laughter: The Comedy of Plautus.* Harvard Studies in Comparative Literature 29. Cambridge, Mass.: Harvard University Press, 1968. Shows how Plautus's works reflect Roman culture and literary traditions. References to *Amphitryon* appear throughout the text and the notes. Carefully indexed.

_______, ed. *Oxford Readings in Menander, Plautus, and Terence.* New York: Oxford University Press, 2001. Includes essays on Plautus and the public stage, the response of Plautus's audience, and traditions, theatrical improvisation, and mastery of comic language in his plays. Two of the essays analyze *Amphitryon*: "Theatrical Significance of Duplication in Plautus' *Amphitruo*" by Florence Dupont and "*Amphitruo*, *Bacchae*, and Metatheatre" by Niall W. Slater.

Amphitryon 38

Author: Jean Giraudoux (1882-1944)
First produced: 1929; first published, 1929 (English translation, 1938)
Type of work: Drama
Type of plot: Mock-heroic
Time of plot: Antiquity
Locale: In and about Amphitryon's palace, Thebes

Principal characters:
JUPITER, master of the gods
MERCURY, a god
AMPHITRYON, a general of Thebes
ALKMENA, his wife
SOSIE, their servant
LEDA, queen of the Spartans

The Story:

Basking on a cloud and spying on Alkmena, Jupiter and Mercury make plans for the seduction of Alkmena as if preparing for a tasty banquet. In order to remove Amphitryon from his bedchamber, Mercury suggests that Jupiter have the Athenians declare war on Thebes. Amphitryon, a stalwart general of the Theban army, will hurry to engage the enemy. Mercury can then take the place of Sosie, a servant, and tell Alkmena that Amphitryon will momentarily desert the battle and return to her bed that night. Jupiter can impersonate Amphitryon and partake of the delectable Alkmena. They begin to carry out their plan.

Jupiter arrives before the palace of Alkmena amid a great clanging noise, for he forgot the laws of gravity in his descent. With the help of Mercury and with some difficulty, Jupiter transforms himself from his state as a god to that of a mortal.

Mercury already prepared the faithful wife for the return of Amphitryon, to whom she promised fidelity or suicide if she knowingly deceives him. Jupiter whets his appetite for love by demanding admission to her bed as a lover, not as a husband. It is not enough to love within the union of marriage—the added fillip is to be the tantalizingly illegal husband-seducer. With guileless logic, Alkmena swears fidelity to her vows and refuses to open her gates and admit the false husband to her chambers as a lover. As her husband, however, he gains easy entry through the gates, which have been unlocked all the while.

Mercury thoughtfully holds back the dawn until Jupiter consummates the union, and he takes the precaution of informing the universe that Jupiter made another mortal conquest so that the proper celestial eruptions will signify the seduction. He also practices a caprice of his own and has the real Amphitryon leave the battle and return to Alkmena the next day. This is only fair, since Jupiter, as is his practice, will reveal his true identity to Alkmena with the coming of dawn and take leave of her in a burst of ego-satisfying, celestial glory.

Mercury and Jupiter, however, have underestimated the power of Alkmena. Alkmena, because she is a woman, is more than a match for Jupiter. When dawn finally arrives, she is on her patio placidly eating breakfast fruit, while Jupiter, the traditional ravisher of innocent womanhood, lolls in the drowsy sensuality of her bed. When he joins her, he tries to reveal his true identity, but he is thwarted at every turn by Alkmena's charming and unclouded humanistic approach to divinity. She possesses a clarity and lack of religious fervency that perhaps resembles naïveté, although in truth her attitude is more indicative of admirable simplicity and faithfulness in the gods.

Jupiter, having satisfied his desires, and knowing that if his true identity is revealed Alkmena will kill herself and his unborn child, wishes to stroke his holy ego by paying a formal celestial visit to Alkmena, thereby legalizing their secret union. Mercury makes the official proclamation of the impending visit, and Leda, Queen of Sparta, who has some previous knowledge of heavenly unions, pays a call on Alkmena. Leda describes her encounter with the heavenly swan.

Alkmena, having discovered that Leda longs for another encounter with Jupiter, persuades the queen to take her place in the bedchamber. Jupiter will visit her in the form of Amphitryon, for he has a habit of appearing in the form most desired by his earthly mates. Leda agrees, and the real Amphitryon arrives. He is mistaken for Jupiter and is sent into the palace. Only when Jupiter himself appears to Alkmena does she realize her mistake.

The resolution of the provocative situation is brought about by the resourceful Alkmena. She asks if perhaps Jupiter would forgo the celestial visit for which she is so evidently unprepared and remain only friends with her. Jupiter quickly agrees to this strange relationship and assures the suspicious Alkmena that he never visited her before—as her lover. Jupiter then gives his blessing to Alkmena and Amphitryon and bids them name their unborn child Hercules. As an afterthought, he offers to be "godfather" to the child.

Critical Evaluation:

Jean Giraudoux began his writing career with the Paris newspaper *Le Matin*, for which he wrote many stories. It was a job that introduced him to a number of figures in the literary world. Next, he launched a career as a novelist, but it was not until 1928, with the performance of his play *Siegfried*, that his name became widely known. He followed up this success a year later with a greater one when *Amphitryon 38* was presented. Popular as these plays were, however, Giraudoux was not taken seriously by the intellectual audience until the production of his 1935 play, *Tiger at the Gates*. The major theme concerns the inevitability of war, and the possibility of another war with Germany was much on the minds of Giraudoux's French audience—of people throughout the world—in 1935.

Giraudoux's other employment, as an inspector general of diplomatic posts abroad, did not prevent him from continuing to turn out plays and novels, and his drama *Electra* (1937), as the title suggests, continued his practice of using ancient Greece for the setting, a distancing device to help his audience see themselves more clearly. In his 1939 play, *Ondine*, he availed himself of a German legend concerning a water nymph.

A number of Giraudoux's plays and stories were published and presented posthumously. Critical acclaim waxed throughout the 1950's and later, and Giraudoux's plays have been performed many times in all parts of the world. His major theme, the reconciliation of the ideal with the real, has proven popular in decades of rapid social change, decades that have required continual readjustment on the part of those who have had to live through them. One of his favorite devices—putting contemporary sentiments and expressions in the mouths of figures from ancient legends—provides the pleasures of incongruity. This device is well illustrated by *Amphitryon 38*. The number presumably signifies that the author is aware of the fact that many writers before him have made use of this legend, although there may have been more or fewer than thirty-seven precursors. Gods and mortals alike give the impression that they are acting in roles, rather than being themselves; they take themselves either too seriously or not quite seriously enough; they insist too much on their identities, or they are too offhand with them. They may bear the names and wear the costumes of the gods and heroes of ancient Greece, but they appear to suffer some impairment of memory about who they are and how they should act. Another way of saying this is to point out that they appear to be what they are in truth: contemporary people dressed up as, and pretending to be, ancient Greeks. This incongruity encourages readers to think that, superficial (and amusing) distinctions aside, the ancients were not much different from people today, and there is a human nature whose relationship to the cosmos and to the divine transcends social change. Another effect of this technique is to bestow some of the dignity of the old myths upon the contemporary world, turning what would otherwise be a 1920's drawing-room comedy into something loftier, an embodied disquisition upon man, woman, and the divine. Giraudoux's interest in the institution of marriage drives the drama. For a man of his day, Giraudoux was something of a feminist, and Alkmena evinces his feminism. It is necessary to exempt her character from most of the preceding generalities. Seriousness has its home in her, in this play. None of the other characters can match her for depth and variety. She is not without flaws, but these only serve to enhance her credibility; for example, having persuaded Jupiter not to insist on making love with her, she worries that she is losing her sex appeal. Beside her, even Mercury, a glib and witty figure, and certainly Amphitryon and Jupiter, look flat and two-dimensional.

The play concerns the irrational forces that bring about passionate love and lust and that cause wars to be fought, won, and lost. The gods rule over these—or are people's creations, on whom people lay the blame for their irrationality. As mere mortals, what can people do when taken over by divine madness? What can people do, as sometimes rational creatures, to regulate their lives, to spare pain to themselves and to others, to live at one with the cosmos? The answers mostly lie with Alkmena. She has none of Leda's giddy lust and vanity; Alkmena would rather not lie with Jupiter. She does not wish for immortality; she has no envy of the gods. She loves her husband, and she wants only their faithfulness to each other. If, nevertheless, she commits adultery with Jupiter, and she contrives affairs so that Amphitryon is adulterous with Leda, and if she is pregnant with Hercules, Jupiter's son, still, none of these deeds or results are within her capacity to prevent or avoid. In this way, Giraudoux's play exudes an air of forgiveness, of tolerance and acceptance. Mortals have limits, and ignorance and forgetfulness can prove to be happy failings. Deceit, where it offers and intends no harm, may be preferable to the truth; it can certainly be kinder.

"Critical Evaluation" by David Bromige

Further Reading

Korzeniowska, Victoria B. *The Heroine as Social Redeemer in the Plays of Jean Giraudoux*. New York: Peter Lang,

2001. Focuses on Giraudoux's female characters, describing the gender politics in his plays and his heroine's roles in both the domestic and public spheres. Places his heroines within the context of the French idealization of women during the interwar years.

Lemaître, Georges. *Jean Giraudoux: The Writer and His Work*. New York: Frederick Ungar, 1971. Usefully incisive analysis of many of the plays; particularly sound on *Amphitryon 38*.

LeSage, Laurent. *Jean Giraudoux: His Life and Works*. University Park: Pennsylvania State University Press, 1959. A basic study of Giraudoux. Good on the relationship of technique and style to content.

Raymond, Agnes. *Jean Giraudoux: The Theatre of Victory and Defeat*. Amherst: University of Massachusetts Press, 1966. Political analysis of the plays, including their relationship to war.

Reilly, John H. *Jean Giraudoux*. Boston: Twayne, 1978. One of the better studies in the Twayne series, this book examines each work, whether dramatic or literary, in chronological order. Offers an engaging discussion of the role that predestination plays in *Amphitryon 38*. Discusses the harmful effects of the ideal upon humans, and the possibly beneficent effects of deceit. Notes the influence of the German playwright Heinrich von Kleist's play *Amphitryon* (1807), in turn based on Molière's *Amphitryon* (1668).

Amsterdam

Author: Ian McEwan (1948-)
First published: 1998
Type of work: Novel
Type of plot: Comedy
Time of plot: Late 1990's
Locale: London and the Lake District, England; Amsterdam

Principal characters:
MOLLY LANE, a photographer who dies after a long illness
GEORGE LANE, her husband, a wealthy publisher
CLIVE LINLEY, a composer, her former lover
VERNON HALLIDAY, newspaper editor, her former lover
JULIAN GARMONY, a conservative British foreign secretary
ROSE GARMONY, his wife, a surgeon

The Story:

At a crematorium near London, family, friends, and lovers of Molly Lane are gathered to mark her death after her long, painful struggle with cancer. Her husband, George Lane, had decided to postpone a formal memorial service, in part because he is not ready to deal with Molly's former lovers, exchanging knowing glances and comparing notes during the service. Among the mourners are former lovers Clive Linley, a composer, and Vernon Halliday, a newspaper editor, who are both deeply moved by Molly's death; she was only forty-six years old.

Because Clive is no longer married nor in a long-term relationship, he is especially horrified that he could one day face unbearable suffering from something like terminal cancer without a friend or lover to help him escape his pain by accelerating his death. He persuades Vernon to become that friend in need, and the two agree to a sort of suicide pact. It is not their intention to join each other in dying, but merely to do whatever is possible to shorten the other's life if that person is dying of a terminal disease.

George discovers among his wife's personal belongings an envelope of photographs she took of Julian Garmony, the ultraconservative British foreign secretary, rumored to be considering the prime ministry. In the photographs, Garmony is shown as a cross-dresser. George gives Vernon the photographs, anticipating that Vernon will print them in his newspaper, the *Judge*, which is seeing a decline in circulation. This decline could be reversed by news of a high-ranking member of Her Majesty's government cavorting in drag, imitating the seductive smile of a woman making herself sexually available. Vernon has a reputation for embarrassing public figures, having earned it through Pate-gate, the exposure of a U.S. president who used taxpayers' money to buy a toupee. Eventually, it becomes clearer that Lane is plotting to get even with Garmony (yet another former lover of Molly) through this newest scandal; it is possible he is seeking vengeance against Vernon as well. Given the more liberal climate of the 1990's, the devious George anticipates that public sentiment may well turn against Vernon for exposing Garmony's kinky pastime.

Meanwhile, Clive, the composer, who is approaching the

end of his career, has been commissioned to write another piece of music, already talked about as his "millennial symphony." At Molly's funeral gathering, Clive is pressed into being introduced to Julian, who asks how the composition is coming and adds that the commission had been decided at the cabinet level, where he supported it. Given the public pressure, Clive wants to compose something similar to Ludwig van Beethoven's monumental *Ninth Symphony*, a massive expression of the mastery of Beethoven's art. Clive hopes that his own creation will bring to fruition all he has written before, and help to find him a place in the pantheon of great twentieth century composers. He has completed much of the composition but needs a theme for the finale. Deciding that a change of venue might stimulate his creative imagination, he visits the Lake District of northwest England, a lovely vacation spot similar to the Finger Lakes of upstate New York.

One day while out for a walk, Clive has his moment of inspiration and feels he is close to grasping his central theme. He encounters what he first thinks is a married couple having a disagreement; soon, however, he sees that the woman is struggling to fight off a rapist. After a moment of hesitation, Clive abandons the woman to her struggle and finds a flat rock to use as a desk to write out this elusive theme.

Clive makes the mistake of sharing this experience with his friend, Vernon, who later informs him that the man he saw attacking a woman in the Lake District was the Lakeland rapist, who has been preying on women hikers. This particular woman had escaped her attacker. However, because Clive refused to intervene or even to report the incident to the police, the rapist attacked another woman two days later. Fortunately, the rapist was soon arrested. Vernon threatens to report Clive, a witness to the earlier attempted rape, to the police if Clive refuses to do his moral duty. Vernon himself is hardly an embodiment of morality, being embroiled in an effort to publicly embarrass Julian. Before Vernon even got the racy photographs, he had been served with a court injunction to not publish them. However, Vernon succeeds in getting the injunction lifted. His staff shares Clive's initial response to the photos: that it would be unethical to reveal what Molly and Julian intended to remain private.

In a brilliant preemptive strike, Rose Garmony, Julian's wife, calls a press conference and lies to the media to save her husband's reputation. She asserts that he had revealed his cross-dressing to her early in their relationship, and that she had decided to overlook it as a harmless eccentricity. Holding the racy photographs for the media cameras to record, she focuses on Vernon's effort to blackmail her husband, damning the editor for having the "moral stature of a *flea*." Public sympathy is for Julian, and Vernon's reputation is ruined, along with his career. Clive sends Vernon a postcard criticizing his friend's behavior, and the "war" is on. Vernon reports his friend to the authorities, and Clive's creative efforts are further disrupted when the police pursue him as a material witness to the rapist's crime.

Clive and Vernon each come to believe that the other is showing all the symptoms of a terminal disease, and they make plans to visit Amsterdam. The city has liberal attitudes toward prostitution, recreational drug use, and even euthanasia, which will make it easy to find a doctor to assist in their suicides. The plan is for both Vernon and Clive to hire a doctor to help the two kill themselves and, thereby, fulfill their earlier suicide pact.

George and Julian have a bizarre conversation while they await their flight to Amsterdam to retrieve the bodies of Clive and Vernon and have them returned to England. George tells Julian he admires him for surviving the affair of the photographs, adding that a lesser man would have committed suicide. Presumably, this is exactly what Clive had intended in passing the envelope of photos to Vernon. Now that Vernon is dead, along with Clive—apparently an unexpected bonus for George—the time may finally be right to conduct a memorial service for his dead wife.

Critical Evaluation:

Amsterdam was received with mixed reviews. Although it has brilliant plotting, the story focuses on the nastiness in human behavior. Few readers are likely to feel great pain in witnessing, for example, Vernon Halliday's decline and fall. As the editor of a respectable newspaper, he resorts to the tactics of the tabloids to increase sales. He is so convinced that his views are right that he attempts to destroy the reputation of a politician who does not share his liberal views. Vernon deludes himself into thinking that his exposure of Julian is for the good of the country and not for his own satisfaction in discrediting and humiliating another person.

Clive Linley is a more problematical character, in large part because he is an artist. Society is not simply more tolerant of the shortcomings of artists, who are often expected to be different; society tends to revere those whose art may last forever. William Faulkner, arguably one of America's greatest novelists, was asked by an interviewer whether he thought writers have to make sacrifices: Faulkner said that "If a writer has to rob his mother, he will not hesitate; the *Ode on a Grecian Urn* is worth any number of old ladies." *Amsterdam* demonstrates the dangers of this view, especially for those artists, like Clive, who work alone and can easily lose a sense of perspective. Clive, for example, deludes himself into believing that his music will not be understood, much less appreciated, unless he produces a monumental symphony comparable to Beethoven's *Ninth*.

Amsterdam also was controversial for its depiction of tolerant and lenient liberal attitudes, especially those of the Dutch. While the Netherlands may have had the best of intentions for those persons hoping to end their lives because of terminal illnesses, few expected Amsterdam would become the euthanasia capital of the world. Perhaps even worse, McEwan's *Amsterdam* discredits the convention that one cannot get away with murder. Clive and Vernon, it could be argued, killed each other.

The power of George Lane's vengeance may have not been limited to the deaths of Clive and Vernon. Critic Robert E. Kohn asserts that Clive eased Molly's pain through euthanasia, but a closer reading indicates Clive was merely imagining what he might have done if Molly had been his wife. The point is that neither Clive nor George performed euthanasia; indeed, there is a distinct possibility that George resisted the impulse to accelerate Molly's death, less because his love for her was so great he could not bear to lose her, and more because he felt the agony of cancer was punishment for her casual attitudes toward marital fidelity.

Amsterdam earned for Ian McEwan the Booker Prize in 1998, but not without controversy. Some believe the novel was too slight to be awarded the prize. After the award announcement, Douglas Hurd, the chair of the Booker Prize committee and himself a former Conservative Party foreign secretary, revealed that the committee's decision to award the prize to McEwan had been a compromise. He said that *Amsterdam* was given the prize by default because there were no "overwhelming masterpiece[s]" among the short-listed novels. To further the irony, McEwan's next and perhaps best novel, *Atonement* (2002), lost the competition because McEwan had recently won the prize for *Amsterdam*. McEwan's next novel, *On Chesil Beach* (2007), was favored for the Booker Prize as well but, once again, controversy kept the prize from him. Reviewers and bloggers attacked the work for being not a novel but a novella. Few, if anyone, seemed to notice that it was just about the length of *Amsterdam*.

Earl G. Ingersoll

Further Reading

Chetrinescu, Dana. "Rethinking Spatiality: The Degraded Body in Ian McEwan's *Amsterdam*." *British and American Studies* 7, no. 2 (2001): 157-165. A focus on illness and the human body in McEwan's *Amsterdam*.

Childs, Peter, ed. *The Fiction of Ian McEwan: A Reader's Guide to Essential Criticism*. New York: Palgrave Macmillan, 2006. An excellent resource for students of McEwan, providing excerpts from books, articles, and reviews examining his work.

Head, Dominic. *Ian McEwan*. New York: Manchester University Press, 2007. A study of McEwan's aesthetics and themes, including those in *Amsterdam*.

Ingersoll, Earl G. "City of Endings: Ian McEwan's *Amsterdam*." In *Waiting for the End: Gender and Ending in the Contemporary Novel*. Madison, N.J.: Fairleigh Dickinson University Press, 2007. This chapter focuses on "endings"—death, sexual climax, the ends of musical compositions and novels—in McEwan's *Amsterdam*. Part of a study examining how gender is associated with the theme of endings in the contemporary novel.

Malcolm, David. *Understanding Ian McEwan*. Columbia: University of South Carolina Press, 2002. This critical study covers McEwan's work up to *Amsterdam*. Each chapter is organized around what Malcolm sees as the five key issues in McEwan's work: textual self-consciousness, feminism, rationalism and science, moral perspective, and the "fragmentariness" of his novels.

Roger, Angela. "Ian McEwan's Portrayal of Women." *Forum for Modern Language Studies* 32, no. 1 (1996): 11-26. This article deals with the key issue of gender in McEwan's fiction. Roger argues that women in McEwan's fiction are always constructed from a male point of view.

Walkowitz, Rebecca L. "Ian McEwan." In *A Companion to the British and Irish Novel, 1945-2000*, edited by Brian W. Shaffer. Malden, Mass.: Blackwell, 2005. A biographical essay on McEwan in a literary companion examining British and Irish novelists writing from the end of World War II through the end of the twentieth century.

Anabasis

Author: Saint-John Perse (1887-1975)
First published: Anabase, 1924 (English translation, 1930)
Type of work: Poetry

Type of plot: Allegory
Time of plot: Indeterminate
Locale: The East

Principal characters:
THE SPEAKER, the poet
THE LEADER, an unidentified man who tells the story
THE STRANGER, an unidentified man
THE WOMEN, a group of young women met by the Leader and his troops

The Poem:

In the opening song, the Leader, unidentified, describes the foaling of a colt under bronze tree leaves. A passing Stranger places bitter berries in the Speaker's hands. The Speaker's exclamations evoke far-off provinces, the call of a trumpet, and winged movement. From the bronze tree comes a great noise, forces of life and death expressing themselves, as the Stranger beckons to roads leading to unknown destinations.

In canto 1, the Leader recounts how, with honor and dignity, he founded his law and built a primitive society in a coastal region, not yet knowing the name of the sun but realizing the potential of humanity to dream of achieving glory. The Leader declares that he will spend one more year among his followers, not because he wishes to trace towns along the sloping landscape but because he desires to live in the community he created. The Leader communicates the aspirations of his people, spiritual and eternal, to strive to discover the unknown, to uncover the cosmic forces that feed humanity's desires. He repeats his intent to stay for one more year among his own, although recognizing that his glory is upon the seas.

In canto 2, the Leader and his followers walk along slopes covered in the linen of the Greats, exposed to the air. The Leader speaks of a man's desire for a woman and her daughter, a primordial impulse liberated by a sea breeze that blows inland, scattering the linen like a priest torn into pieces.

In canto 3, at barley harvest, the Leader recounts how visiting foreign dignitaries ate at a table at his door. The Assayer of Weights and Measures, with the remains of insects and bits of straw in his beard, returns after surveying the flora and fauna of the region. A society that is no longer nomadic is being founded. Illuminated by the Sun's power, the natural order is challenged by the newly organized forces of civilization. The Leader speaks of the danger of illusion, of questioning the reality of things. As a man of action, the Leader condemns idle contemplation of one's sadness and begins to specify the members of this new society: princes, ministers, captains, priests, grammarians, and tailors. Finally, the Leader, enveloped by the strong smells of the world around him, condemns the contemplation of death in the present.

The founding of the City, built of stone and bronze, is described by the Leader in canto 4. No longer surrounded by encampments on the hills, the unidentified port city receives tall ships laden with grain. However, in the midst of the bustling activity, a dead ass floats in the port's dead water, a sign of the stagnation and destruction that might befall this civilization. Blacksmiths, mules, bankers, the druggist's wares, festivals, and tumults are contrasted to those who, keeping watch on the hillside, refuse to become part of the City. A dealer in flasks like his father, a sole man strides forth toward the beginning of the desert.

Following the foundation of the City, the Leader feels the need of solitude and the desire to depart in canto 5. Squadrons of stars beckon to him, and at dawn the Stranger of the opening song reappears, and the colt, born in the opening song, nuzzles its chin into the hands of a child. The sudden presence of the Stranger, embodiment of transcendental forces, suggests the imminent departure of those wishing to continue their nomadic discoveries.

The Leader, now a powerful military governor, enjoys omnipotence and triumph against invading forces. In canto 6, a call to the horsemen, now dismounted among the crops, is heard. Future expeditions to impoverished, weakened countries are near at hand.

The Leader describes the ephemeral nature of civilization. In canto 7, all is transient; of this the Leader is acutely aware. Like camels, hills march in silence toward this civilization, kneeling at the plains as a beckoning force. Evoking deserts, they invite nomadic wanderings. Voices proclaim the erection of protecting walls as the shadow of a great bird, a symbol of life and movement, pass over the Leader's face.

Canto 8 recounts the long march of humanity, begun once again. Nomads' laws and visions of swaying grass and horsemen on the move: These are the fundamental elements of this voyage whose Leader remains an eternal wanderer, committed to the quest, not for personal glory but for the progress of civilization.

Moving westward through the desert in canto 9, having forsaken the temporal nature of his own society, the Leader is addressed by one of a group of young women who greet the expedition and announce great blessings. The woman speaks of the vine of the womb, the fecundity of the female body, and earthly pleasures. A union between men and women creates a new order.

In the final canto, the tenth, this new union is celebrated. Sacrifice of colts on the tombs of children, purification of widows, consecration of monuments and flags, and a general rebuilding of this formerly ruined society are the first activities. Diverse vocations are enumerated to show the array of duties and interests among the citizens, from the toll gatherer to the man with the falcon to he who dwells in a country of great rains to the man learned in science. Finally, the Leader, who incarnated the conquering spirit of humanity, remained conscious of the call from faraway lands in dream, of the eternal beckoning from exotic, fertile countries.

In the song that closes *Anabasis*, the Leader and his horse stop by a tree full of turtledoves. The young colt of the introductory song is carried forward by time toward maturation. The Leader, supremely fulfilled, whistles sweetly and wishes peace to the dying.

Critical Evaluation:

In 1960, Saint-John Perse, career diplomat and poet, received the Nobel Prize in Literature. In 1916, he had been posted to the French legation in Peking and, during his China years, which lasted until 1921, traveled in Korea, Manchuria, Mongolia, and the Gobi Desert. The composition of *Anabasis* dates from this period. He is said to have written this work, his best known, in a Taoist temple overlooking the caravan routes leading to the northwest. T. S. Eliot published his English version of the poem, the first English translation of it, in 1930.

Perse explained that the poem, whose title means "military expedition" in the tradition of such mighty military leaders as Alexander the Great, depicts the loneliness of action and the breadth of human potential. A prose poem, it is allegorical; the action is seen through the deeds and words of the nameless Leader, who recites the text. Leader of a nomadic people, he remains faceless throughout the entire work, revealing his innermost thoughts as he speaks but never identifying his ancestry or the elements of his personal life. A similar lack of detail is noticed in all the other characters as well as in the time and place of the poem. Perse's travels in Asia inspired the sweeping images he depicts of nomadic movement and conquest, although the geographical setting, apart from references to maritime and desert areas, is without identifying detail. The historical period is depicted with equal ambiguity for, although the peoples evoked in *Anabasis* live in a relatively complex society, as seen in allusions to agriculture, architecture, blacksmithing, and libraries, a precise time frame in world history is not conveyed to the reader. Perse's objective is to capture the essence of human action in the process of realization and, in doing so, compensate for the lack of precise spatial and temporal references by creating sweeping epic verses that carry the reader along with the Leader on his conquests and discoveries.

Perse's encyclopedic vocabulary, the use of somewhat obscure words—anabasis, for example—is characteristic of his unique style. While his vocabulary conveys extreme precision, and in the contexts of botany and zoology is almost scientific in its specificity, the structure of individual cantos in *Anabasis* is often elliptical and sometimes difficult to follow. Perse does not guide the reader by means of a simple, straightforward style. Rather, his complex images at times produce cryptic meanings that do not always reveal themselves to the reader but that add to the mystery that emanates from the poem. The characters, for example, receive little realistic differentiation, allowing them to convey more than individual personalities; they express the essence of pioneers, adventurers, and nomads. More important than the characters themselves is the ultimate action of the poem: the foundation and organization of a society. The captivating rhythm of *Anabasis* is built on symmetries, alliterations, assonances, and internal rhymes that carry the reader along in the same majestic and expansive movements that characterize the anabasis. Human movement is, therefore, at the core of the poem's imagery. The use of language is often elliptical, reflecting the idea of movement and omitting linking elements that follow a standard language usage that renders a text easily understandable. Perse's style, lyric and evocative, follows an internal logic different from standardized usage, but that conveys, for example, the urgency of movement or an act in progress.

Skillful translations of *Anabasis* exist in Russian, Italian, and German. The fact that the poem is so widely read is testimony to the manner in which its grandeur captivates the reader through the portrayal of humanity's collective history, of its epic aspirations to establish modern civilization, and of its constant yearning to surpass the here and now. The universal appeal of Perse's work is undoubtedly the presence of allegory and symbolism, elements that unite people in a shared cultural experience that transcends time and space.

Saint-John Perse is the poet of humanity's struggle to surpass itself. His gift of poetic language achieves its apotheosis in complex and exotic images: "Like milch-camels, gentle beneath the shears and sewn with mauve scars, let the hills march forth under the scheme of the harvest sky." His poetry functions as myth in a modern world, paradoxically subject to fragmentation and disunity, for it expresses a vision of history that reminds one of the cohesive influence of collective action, of our past, and of a future that will forever loom on the horizon of the human imagination.

Kenneth W. Meadwell

Further Reading

Galand, René. *Saint-John Perse*. New York: Twayne, 1972. A complete general introduction to Perse's poetry. Includes a concise study of *Anabasis*, as well as a short, annotated bibliography of the major critical studies, mostly in French, of his work.

Gallagher, Mary. "Seminal Praise: The Poetry of Saint-John Perse." In *An Introduction to Caribbean Francophone Writing: Guadeloupe and Martinique*, edited by Sam Haigh. New York: Berg, 1999. Analyzes the "highly complex connection" between the Caribbean and Perse's poetry.

Knodel, Arthur. *Saint-John Perse: A Study of His Poetry*. Edinburgh: Edinburgh University Press, 1966. An excellent study of all of Perse's poetry. Includes some biographical details and in-depth analyses of *Anabasis*.

Little, Roger. *Saint-John Perse*. London: Athlone Press, 1973. A brief overview of Perse's work, including some comments on *Anabasis*. Includes a short biographical sketch.

Mehlman, Jeffrey. "Saint-John Perse: Discontinuities." In *Émigré New York: French Intellectuals in Wartime Manhattan, 1940-1944*. Baltimore: Johns Hopkins University Press, 2000. Chronicles the lives of Perse and other French writers who spent World War II living in exile in New York City.

Rigolot, Carol. *Forged Genealogies: Saint-John Perse's Conversations with Culture*. Chapel Hill: University of North Carolina, Department of Romance Languages, 2001. Rigolot likens reading Perse's poetry to "eavesdropping on a telephone conversation in which only one side is audible." She analyzes his use of dialogue in his poetry, focusing on his conversations with a range of historical figures. Chapter 3 focuses on *Anabasis*.

Anabasis

Author: Xenophon (c. 431-c. 354 B.C.E.)
First transcribed: Kyrou anabasis, between 394 and 371 B.C.E. (English translation, 1623)
Type of work: History

Principal personages:
XENOPHON, the narrator
CYRUS, son of King Darius of Persia
ARTAXERXES, the older son of Darius
TISSAPHERNES, a Persian general
CLEARCHUS, a Spartan exile, a general under Cyrus
CHIRISOPHUS, a Spartan mercenary captain
AGASIAS, a Stymphalian captain in the Greek army
PROXENUS, a Theban mercenary general under Cyrus

The Story:

After the death of King Darius of Persia, his son Artaxerxes takes possession of the throne. Cyrus, the younger son, with the support of his mother, Parysatis, begins to build up an army to wrest control of Persia from his brother. By pretending to need troops to fight the Persian general Tissaphernes and the Pisidians, Cyrus acquires armies from the Peloponnese, the Chersonese (under the Spartan exile Clearchus), the Thessalians (under Aristippus), the Boeotians (under Proxenus), the Stymphalians (under Sophaenetus), and the Achaeans (under Socrates, the mercenary).

Cyrus marches from Sardis to Tarsus, gathering the elements of his army. At Tarsus the troops under Clearchus refuse to move forward, arguing that they were not hired to fight against the king. Clearchus deals with the mutiny by first enlisting the loyalty of the men to himself (by pretending he will stay with them and not with Cyrus) and then by supporting Cyrus's claim that the enemy is not the king but Abrocomas, one of the king's commanders.

By marches averaging fifteen miles a day Cyrus brings his army from Tarsus to Issus, the last city in Cilicia, where he is joined by ships from the Peloponnese. The march continues through the gates of Cilicia and Syria without opposition.

When Cyrus arrives at the city of Myriandrus, Xenias the Arcadian and Pasion the Megarian desert the army. Cyrus refuses to pursue or punish them, declaring that they served him well in the past.

The army moves on to the Euphrates and the city of Thapsacus. Here the word is finally given to the Greek soldiers that the campaign is to be against King Artaxerxes. At first the soldiers refuse to go further without more pay, but when Menon leads his forces across the Euphrates in order to set a good example and to win Cyrus's favor, and when Cyrus promises to give each soldier additional pay, the Greeks cross the river in force on foot. Since the Euphrates is usually too high for such a passage, the army is encouraged by this good sign.

When they reach the Arabian desert, Cyrus forces the troops on long marches in order to bring them to water and fodder. He keeps discipline by ordering important Persians to help with the wagons when the road is difficult. A quarrel between the soldiers of Menon and of Clearchus is halted by Cyrus's warning that they will all be destroyed if they fight among themselves.

Orontas, a Persian under Cyrus, attempts to transfer his army to the king's forces, but Cyrus learns of the plan by intercepting a letter from Orontas to the king. At a trial held in Cyrus's tent Orontas is condemned to death. He is never seen again.

Cyrus moves through Babylonia and prepares for battle with King Artaxerxes, but when the king's forces fail to take a stand at a defensive ditch, Cyrus proceeds with less caution.

The two armies meet at Cunaxa, and the Greeks put the opposing Persian forces to flight. Cyrus, with six hundred Persian cavalry, charges the center of the Persian line in order to reach the king, but after wounding King Artaxerxes, Cyrus is killed by a javelin blow. The cavalrymen with Cyrus are killed, except for the forces under Ariaeus, who hastily retreats.

While the main Greek armies under Clearchus and Proxenus are pursuing the Persians, the king's troops break into Cyrus's camp and seize his mistresses, money, and property. Tissaphernes then joins the king's force and attacks the Greeks, but again the Greeks put the Persians to flight.

Phalinus, a messenger from King Artaxerxes, attempts to force Clearchus to surrender, but the Spartan, regarding the Greeks as victors, refuses. The Greeks then ally themselves again with Ariaeus, who was second to Cyrus, and pledge their support of him. When Ariaeus refuses to attempt further battle against the king, the joint decision is to take a longer route back, putting as much distance as possible between their forces and the king's army.

The Greeks begin their march and by accident come close to the king's army, frightening it into retreat. A truce is then arranged, and the king transfers supplies to the Greeks. Finally a treaty is made that provides safe conduct for the Greek army, with Tissaphernes as escort.

Many of the Greek leaders suspect Tissaphernes of treachery, but Clearchus, reassured by a conference with the Persian general, goes to Tissaphernes with four of his generals and twenty of his captains in order that those who were slandering the Persian commander can be named. Then, at a signal from the treacherous Tissaphernes, the Persians massacre the captains and take the generals as prisoners. The generals—Clearchus, Proxenus, Monon, Agias, and Socrates—are taken to the king and beheaded. Ariaeus is discovered to be involved with Tissaphernes in this act of treachery.

After the capture of the generals, Xenophon, who accompanied the Greek army at the urging of his friend Proxenus, bolsters the courage of the Greeks and urges that new generals and captains be appointed. The army responds to this decisive act of leadership.

Mithridates, a Persian commander who was with Cyrus, returns to the Greeks and pretends to be friendly, but he suddenly attacks them and is driven back. The Greeks are then pursued by Tissaphernes and harassed by attacks from the Carduchi as they cross the mountains to Armenia. Hearing that Tiribazus, the governor of Western Armenia who promised the Greeks safe passage, plans to attack them, the Greek generals order a raid on Tiribazus's camp and then quickly resume the march across snow-covered plains. The soldiers suffer from snow blindness and frostbite.

To encourage the soldiers, Xenophon often works and marches with the men. He arranges to procure guides from the Armenians and conceives the idea of capturing the mountain pass beyond the Phasis River by climbing it at night. Chirisophus and Xenophon are the principal leaders of the march.

In the country of the Taochi the Greeks are delayed by an attack from a fortification out of which large boulders are rolled down a hill, but when the stones are exhausted and as the opposing forces—including women and children—begin to leap from the walls, the Greeks take possession. Finally, after fighting the Chalybes, the Greeks come within sight of the sea on their arrival at Trapezus.

Chirisophus is sent to secure ships, and the Greeks, now

numbering eighty-six hundred troops of their original ten thousand, go on plundering expeditions for supplies. When Chirisophus is delayed, the available ships are loaded with the sick and wounded and with women, children, and baggage, while the rest of the army continues by land. After battling their way through the country of the barbarous Mossynoici, the Greeks arrive in the Euxine. There Xenophon considers founding a city, but he rejects the idea when the others oppose him. Some of the generals are critical of Xenophon's disciplinary measures, but he is able to defend himself against their charges.

The Greeks buy food and also plunder supplies from the Paphlagonians. During their stay in that territory the captains go to Xenophon and ask him to be commander-in-chief of the army, but after reflection and sacrifices to the gods he decides that it would be better both for himself and for the army if the command were either kept divided or given to some other man. When Chirisophus is elected commander-in-chief, Xenophon willingly accepts a subordinate position.

By this time the Greeks have enough ships to carry all of their men, and they sail along the Paphlagonian coast from Harmene, the port of Sinope, to Heraclea, a Greek city in the country of the Maryandyni. The army then splits into three parts because of a disagreement about demanding supplies from Heraclea. The Arcadians and Achaeans, who favor the demand, form one body; Chirisophus, no longer in supreme command, heads a second body of troops; and Xenophon commands the remainder. The Arcadians land in Thrace and attack some villages. When they get into difficulties, they are rescued by Xenophon and his force. At Port Calpe the three armies are reunited.

Many Greeks are killed by the Bithynians while hunting for supplies, but the Greek forces finally achieve victory. A quarrel involving Cleander, the Spartan governor of Byzantium, and Agasias, a Greek captain who rescued one of his men from arrest by Dexippus, a traitorous Greek acting on Cleander's order, is settled by Xenophon's diplomacy.

Eventually the army crosses the straits from the East to Byzantium. After some difficulty with Anaxibius, a Spartan admiral at Byzantium, the Greeks join forces with King Seuthes of Thrace and participate in numerous raids on Thracian villages for supplies. When King Seuthes withholds pay from the Greeks, Xenophon is blamed, but after a long inquiry, during which Xenophon is accused of being too much concerned with the welfare of the ordinary soldier, King Seuthes finally gives the Greeks the money due them.

Xenophon then leads the army out of Thrace by sailing to Lampsacus, marching through the Troad, and crossing Mount Ida to the plain of Thebes. When the army reaches Pergamon in Mysia, Xenophon conducts a partially successful raid against the Persian Asidates. He then turns the Greek army over to Thibron, the Spartan commander, who uses the Greeks to war against Tissaphernes and Pharnabazus, a Persian governor.

Critical Evaluation:

Anabasis is Xenophon's personal account of one of the most amazing marches in history, the march of a Greek army numbering ten thousand men from Babylon to the Black Sea. Xenophon played a leading role in the march and was, in effect, supreme commander of the army, although he refused the actual title. This account of the Persian expedition begins with the recital of Cyrus's effort to wrest the Persian throne from his brother Artaxerxes, but its principal part is concerned with the march from Babylon after the death of Cyrus at the battle of Cunaxa.

For centuries, *Anabasis* has been recognized as a stirring piece of historical narrative but dismissed as lacking in intellectual substance because of what some have seen as Xenophon's overzealous self-justification. Unquestionably, the portrait of Xenophon the military leader that emerges from the text is exceedingly flattering. The tone often shows great objectivity and restraint, but the stirring record of the Greeks rising to the many challenges they faced in struggling to survive against both military and political obstacles can hardly be called impartial. Unfortunately, the propagandistic qualities of the story have often overshadowed the literary and intellectual merits of a work important in its own right.

One must remember, however, that historiography had a different meaning for the Greeks than it does for later scholars. Like most historians of antiquity, including his predecessor and model Thucydides, Xenophon takes great liberty with speechmaking, inventing lengthy speeches to place in the mouths of characters who represent various types Xenophon respects or reviles. One has a sense, however, that he represents the major actions he describes with great accuracy, and his analysis of motives sets his story apart from mere chronicles. Xenophon also examines larger moral and social issues important to his countrymen. Through his presentation of character and motive, and through his careful structuring of events to present his readers clear parallels that highlight comparisons and contrasts, Xenophon elevates his narrative to an analysis of moral qualities, revealing something of the nature of his society and its values. In *Anabasis*, Xenophon offers a valuable lesson to readers about the impact of practicing virtue, especially in times of crisis.

Revised by Laurence W. Mazzeno

Further Reading

Anderson, J. K. *Xenophon*. New York: Charles Scribner's Sons, 1974. Complete and scholarly study of Xenophon's life and works. Judges *Anabasis* as the work of a reporter, not a historian. A list of important dates, twelve pages of plates, suggestions for further reading, and concise footnotes enrich this study.

Fox, Robin Lane, ed. *The Long March: Xenophon and the Ten Thousand*. New Haven, Conn.: Yale University Press, 2004. Twelve essays provide various interpretations of *Anabasis*, including discussions of sex and gender, the religious dimension, the depiction of the army, and displacement and identity in the work. Another essay examines when, how, and why Xenophon wrote *Anabasis*.

Livingstone, R. W., ed. *The Pageant of Greece*. Oxford, England: Clarendon Press, 1923. Reprint. 1953. A history of the literature and culture of classical Greece, with a broad introduction followed by excerpts from the major writers and commentary on them. Characterizes Xenophon as "a man of action" and praises his "natural, unaffected style."

Nussbaum, G. B. *The Ten Thousand: A Study in Social Organization and Action in Xenophon's "Anabasis."* Leiden, the Netherlands: E. J. Brill, 1967. A scholarly study that addresses basic questions about military organization. Separate sections examine the common soldiers, the captains, the generals, and the assembly; others treat the public and the leadership.

Rood, Tim. *The Sea! The Sea! The Shout of the Ten Thousand in the Modern Imagination*. New York: Duckworth Overlook, 2005. Examines the cultural influence of *Anabasis* in Europe and America during the past two hundred years. Discusses literary works by Heinrich Heine, Percy Bysshe Shelley, and James Joyce, travel and adventure literature, magazine articles, romantic novels, plays, and films that adapt Xenophon's work.

Waterfield, Robin. *Xenophon's Retreat: Greece, Persia, and the End of the Golden Age*. Cambridge, Mass.: Harvard University Press, 2006. Attempts to round out Xenophon's account of Cyrus's Persian campaign by providing additional details of military logistics, the lives of Greek and Persian soldiers, motivations for the war, and other aspects of the battle. Compares Cyrus's experiences in Persia with present-day developments in the Middle East.

Xenophon. *The Persian Expedition*. Translated by Rex Warner. New York: Penguin Books, 1972. Excellent paperback edition, with a map and an informative introduction by George Cawkwell. A six-page glossary of names is useful, as is the comprehensive index. The complicated historical context is spelled out in detail.

Anatomy of Criticism
Four Essays

Author: Northrop Frye (1912-1991)
First published: 1957
Type of work: Literary criticism

Anatomy of Criticism, a book that is similar to an anatomical chart depicting parts and functions of the human body, proposes a holistic system for reading and understanding literary works. Northrop Frye wrote *Anatomy of Criticism*, which consists of four interrelated essays, to explore the nature of literature and how it functions as an art form. His ultimate objective is to direct literary criticism toward a comprehensive system of theories, principles, and techniques, and away from personal reactions and ideological interpretations.

One essay in the book, "Historical Criticism: Theory of Modes," posits that literature can be divided into five categories, or fictional modes. These modes correspond to the range of the protagonist's power of action. Stories about gods belong to the mode of myth, and stories about extraordinary human beings with supernatural powers belong to the mode of romance or legend. Stories about extraordinary human beings subject to the powers of nature and the constraints of society belong to the mode of high mimetic, and stories about ordinary people belong to the mode of low mimetic. Stories about powerless people belong to the ironic mode.

These five fictional modes can be either tragic or comic depending on whether the protagonist fails or succeeds at the end of the story. Thus, there are complementary patterns in each mode (for example, a dying god in which nature is destroyed in contrast to a resurrected god in which nature is restored). Furthermore, a narrative in the five modes may emphasize either plot or theme. The purpose of plot-oriented or fictional literature is to entertain, whereas the objective of thematic literature is to educate the reader.

The second essay, "Ethical Criticism: Theory of Symbols," provides perspectives called phases for classifying and interpreting symbols. The literal and descriptive phases are antithetical. Literal writing creates its own meaning inside the text itself and creates verbal patterns for aesthetic delight. In contrast, descriptive language objectively depicts some external reality outside the text.

The formal phase focuses on the use of symbols in a single work. The arrangement of symbols may have a concrete and specific meaning or ambiguous and multiple meanings. Accordingly, literary works can be plotted along a continuum ranging from allegory to paradox. Furthermore, symbols create verbal patterns and designs with aesthetic significance, like a melody in music. Frye views a literary work as a creation of the imagination, providing a reader with a vision and spiritual freedom beyond mere facts.

In the mythical phase, the symbol is an archetype, that is, a recurrent image in the whole of literature. Like words, archetypes are a fundamental means of communication. In this function, archetypes are known as conventions. Besides nature, writers derive their material from other works of literature. Writers imitate, adapt, or reject techniques, images, and forms established through time or tradition. The study of an archetype in a poem leads to a study of it in poetry, then to a study of the role of poetry in civilization. Archetypes are adaptable building blocks that writers use to represent the values and the state of society. Moreover, archetypes reveal the universal aspects of human life.

The anagogic phase is the domain of the imagination, an infinite and eternal world, without natural and social bounds. The metaphor best expresses anagogic meaning because it can transcend logic by presenting two separate entities as identical in the way the Trinity represents the Father, the Son, and the Holy Spirit as one. Like the Trinity, individual literary works form a unified body of literature. Thus, one part is an aspect and representation of the whole.

The third essay, "Archetypal Criticism: Theory of Myths," distributes archetypal images into categories called apocalyptic, demoniac, and analogical. Apocalyptic imagery expresses fulfilled human desire at its highest level, or Heaven. In opposition, demoniac imagery expresses the greatest threats to human desire, or Hell. Between Heaven and Hell lies analogical imagery of human experience. Writers adapt or displace apocalyptic and demoniac imagery to fit the credibility requirements of one of the literary modes: romance, realism, or the ironic. For romance, the imagery is of innocence. For realism and the ironic, the imagery is of experience.

Another approach to archetypal criticism revolves around plot. Literature can be categorized as comic, tragic, romantic, or ironic. The comic plot is analogous to spring because problems are miraculously resolved and a new and lively world emerges. Historically, comic characters and plots have remained consistent. For example, a young couple thwarted by a harsh father figure is the standard comic situation. Comedy has phases distinguishable by the change of society at the end of the story, ranging from no change, escape, a better world, or disintegration.

Romance is associated with summer because the world is in full bloom or idealized, and the protagonist possesses maximum human powers. Romance is an adventure story, a quest for the epitome of a cultural value. Conflict underlies romance. Good and evil are clearly delineated. The protagonist prevails in his or her quest. Even death becomes a resurrection. Romance has phases matching the sequence of birth to death (for example, the mysterious birth of the hero).

Tragedy is associated with autumn because the bountiful fruits of nature are destroyed by the inexorable change of seasons. Tragedy creates a sense of loss because a life of great potential ends in ruin. The tragic hero is at the top of the wheel of fortune about to plummet into catastrophe. He or she is greater than normal human beings but no match for such forces as God and fate. In some fashion, the tragic hero disturbs this higher order and must sacrifice his or her life as punishment or nemesis.

Irony and satire are associated with winter because they represent the cold and lifeless aspects of life. Irony and satire destroy conventions, illusions, ideals, and values. The world of experience consumes the smaller world of rational thought. In irony and satire, the heroic is mocked or absent. The different phases of irony and satire depict human life in its decline from the foolish to the macabre. Even more than tragedy, irony and satire expose the malevolent forces in human life to be avoided.

The essay "Rhetorical Criticism: Theory of Genres" defines four literary genres: epos, fiction, drama, and lyric. Each genre is distinguishable by how it is presented. In epos, the author directly speaks to a listener, while in fiction, words are in print and read. In drama, actors perform language before an audience, and in lyric, a speaker converses with him- or herself.

In addition to these relationships between a writer and audience, genre is distinguishable by its rhythm. In epos, language is recurrent; the accent, meter, and sound pattern are regular and repetitive. In this respect, epos is akin to music. In contrast, the language of prose fiction is continuous; sentences represent the pattern of thought without metrical breaks. In other words, prose is shaped by semantics. In drama, language conforms to decorum; the words must match the characters and their situation. The author's own voice is silent. In lyric, language is associative; the writer freely associates sounds and images in an irregular and unpredictable fashion. Metaphors combine such oppositions as sensation/reflection and abstract/concrete. Dream images predominate because they are more suggestive than descriptive. Moreover, the lyric expresses the mystery of primordial human experience as a mediation or revelation.

From the modes, phases, and plots delineated in the three essays of *Anatomy of Criticism*, Frye constructs a comprehensive circular scheme for categorizing the numerous specific forms of drama, lyric, epos, and prose. Even though Frye describes exemplars for each form, he emphasizes that most literary works combine elements from various forms. The Bible is a prime example of such a composite work, termed "encyclopedic form." Frye argues that the Bible is the most influential work in Western literature in part because it is a comprehensive myth.

Frye postulates that literature and the humanities share a common verbal structure. Therefore, literary criticism should play a central role in interpreting any text. Furthermore, both literature and literary criticism should contribute to a general liberal education that enables a person to see contemporary social values in the context of culture as a whole and to perceive the unity of human knowledge and experience.

David Partenheimer

Further Reading

Balfour, Ian. "Anatomy as Criticism." In *Northrop Frye*. Boston: Twayne, 1988. Chapter 2 of this study of Frye is a readable summary, explication, and defense of *Anatomy of Criticism*.

Calin, William. "Northrop Frye's Totalizing Vision: The Order of Words." In *The Twentieth-century Humanist Critics: From Spitzer to Frye*. Buffalo, N.Y.: University of Toronto Press, 2007. A thorough study that examines Frye's literary theories, namely *Anatomy of Criticism*, as a work by the "last great humanist critic," Frye. Considers Frye to have no equal in significantly influencing literary studies in the twentieth century.

Denham, Robert. *Northrop Frye and Critical Method*. University Park: Pennsylvania State University Press, 1978. A comprehensive explication of *Anatomy of Criticism*, with invaluable illustrations, especially for the essay "Theory of Genres."

_______, ed. *Northrop Frye's Notebooks for "Anatomy of Criticism."* Buffalo, N.Y.: University of Toronto Press, 2007. An annotated collection that provides an "intimate picture of Frye's working process." The notebooks to *Anatomy of Criticism* were compiled between the late 1940's and 1956 and detail how Frye attempted to structure the larger work.

Hamilton, Albert. *Northrop Frye: Anatomy of His Criticism*. Buffalo, N.Y.: University of Toronto Press, 1990. A scholarly examination of *Anatomy of Criticism* and its place in the corpus of Frye's criticism.

Ricoeur, Paul. "*Anatomy of Criticism* or the Order of Paradigms." In *Centre and Labyrinth: Essays in Honour of Northrop Frye*. Buffalo, N.Y.: University of Toronto Press, 1983. A scholarly summary of *Anatomy of Criticism*, with discussion of opposing literary perspectives.

Rockas, Leo. "The Structure of Frye's *Anatomy*." *College English* 28 (1967): 501-507. A commentary on the flaws of selected arguments in *Anatomy of Criticism*. Dated but still useful.

The Anatomy of Melancholy

Author: Robert Burton (1577-1640)
First published: 1621
Type of work: Psychology

In the seventeenth century, ideas and theories, old and new, clamored for attention and consideration; rational thought and science had not yet begun to classify, assimilate, accept, and reject the great mass of learning that had accumulated over the centuries since ancient times. More than that, each scholar attempted, in that age before specialization, to master all human knowledge. Such was the age in which Robert Burton, who styled himself Democritus, Jr., wrote *The Anatomy of Melancholy*, which in many ways exemplifies the times in which it was written.

Burton was more than an educated man; he gave his life to learning, and much of his vast hoard of erudition found its way into his book. Ostensibly a study on melancholy, his work, before it was finished, absorbed into its pages most of the learning of Burton's time, either through his examination of everything he could associate with melancholy or through his many digressions.

The Anatomy of Melancholy is difficult to categorize. Its organization is complex, almost incoherent. An outline for each of the three "partitions" of the book, complicated though each is, does not indicate all that Burton manages to cram into the pages. The device seems really to be Burton's way of following a pseudoscientific convention, a style of his times. Perhaps the best way to categorize the book is to regard it as an informal and heterogeneous collection of essays on human dissatisfaction with the universe, as people of the seventeenth century understood the universe, and on ways in which that dissatisfaction could be cured. In that sense, at least, the book is a treatise on psychology, although the digressions Burton makes are so numerous and involved that the reader sometimes wonders whether the author may not have lost his way.

Burton assuredly has no special theme or thesis he is attempting to prove. One critic has said that all *The Anatomy of Melancholy* proves is that a seventeenth century classical education could produce an astounding amount of recondite learning. Burton presents no set of principles, scientific or otherwise, to be proved, but he does bring to his work a tremendous zest for learning. This sense of gusto often puts the contemporary reader at a disadvantage, for Burton lards his paragraphs heavily, perhaps no English writer more so, with tags of Latin prose and poetry. Too few contemporary readers have enough knowledge of Latin to enable them to read tags in that language. The quotations are from countless authorities, many of them long since forgotten. A typical page, for example, cites Leo Afer, Lipsius, Zuinger, Seneca, Tully, Livy, Rhasis, Montaltus, Celsus, and Comesius. This host of references, allusions, and quotations makes Burton's style seem heavy. Actually, he writes in the tradition of Francis Bacon, studiously striving for a plain, even colloquial and racy, style. Like Bacon, too, he frequently begins a topic with an allusion, an anecdote, or a quotation as a springboard and from such a start often moves to whimsy and humor.

Sections of *The Anatomy of Melancholy* are famous for various reasons. The opening letter, a foreword to the reader, is well known for its satirical tone and its catalog of the follies of humanity. Humor and whimsy account for the popularity of the sections on marriage and bachelorhood, on the "love of learning or overmuch study," and on the nature of spirits. The last "partition," ostensibly on melancholy growing out of love and religion, has many short synopses of world-famous stories. One contemporary critic has shown that if Elizabethan literature had somehow been lost during the intervening centuries, scholars could reconstruct a good bit of its nature from a study of *The Anatomy of Melancholy* alone.

The pervading tone of the book is satirical, but Burton's satire is always realistic, reflecting the point of view of an objective, even detached, observer of human folly. He begins the first "partition" with a contrast between people as they were in the Garden of Eden and people as they have been since the Fall. The result of human transgression, according to Burton, is that humanity has since suffered a universal malady, a melancholy that affects mind and body. Since he regards the individual as a whole, from a humanistic point of view, he proceeds to mingle sympathetically both religion and science. Much of the learning and many of the notions and theories that found their way into the book are nowadays of historical interest only, such as the analysis of the four bodily humors, the discussion of the understanding and the will (as the seventeenth century used those terms), and the discussion of the nature of angels and devils. Still amusing, however, are his discussions of old age, diet, heredity, exercise, and constipation. While admitting that none is a panacea, Burton offers various cures for melancholy, including prayer, practice of the arts, the study of geography, coffee, traditional games, and moderate amounts of wine and other drink.

Like many another learned man in history, the writer often found himself discoursing on subjects on which there is perhaps no answer. Thus it is in his critique on marriage, which he delivers under the heading of "Cure of Love-Melancholy," that Burton, who himself never married, first quotes twelve reasons in favor of marriage, taking them from Jacobus de Voragine. Those arguments in favor of marriage include statements that a wife is a source of comfort and assistance in adversity, that she will drive away melancholy at home, that she brings an additional supply of the "sweet company of kinsmen," and that she enables a man to have fair and happy children. Immediately following these arguments, Burton adds an equal number of his contrary arguments. He suggests that a wife will aggravate a man's misery in adversity, will scold a man at home, bring a host of needy relatives, and make him a cuckold to rear another man's child. At the last, all Burton can say is that marriage, like much of life, is filled with chance: " Tis a hazard both ways I confess, to live single or to marry."

A sound observer of human nature, Burton also shows sympathetic understanding for his fellow beings. Living in an age when religious beliefs maintained a strong hold on men's and women's emotions, reinforced by fears of Satan and by Calvinistic doctrines of predestination and the depravity of humanity, Burton advocates that people afflicted by religious melancholy turn from contemplation of the more awful aspects of God and religion to such aspects of God as his infinite mercy and love. Burton also advocates recreation of an honest sort as an antidote to too much religion. In this, as in other ways, Burton stands out as being ahead of his time.

Further Reading

Chapple, Anne S. "Robert Burton's Geography of Melancholy." *Studies in English Literature, 1500-1900* 33, no. 1 (Winter, 1993): 99-130. Examines the influence of the contemporary proliferation of maps and charts, for which Burton had a natural affinity, on the *Anatomy*, a work that Burton compared to an explorer's task in its examination of uncharted territories.

Dewey, Nicholas. "Robert Burton's Melancholy." *Modern Philology* 68 (1971): 292-293. Notes the early shift in the preferred abbreviation of the title, from *Melancholy* to *Anatomy*. Dewey sees this shift as a move away from scholarly interest in the psychological and toward antiquarian delight in miscellaneous learning.

Gowland, Angus. *The Worlds of Renaissance Melancholy: Robert Burton in Context*. New York: Cambridge University Press, 2006. Interprets the *Anatomy* within the context of Renaissance philosophy, describing Burton's work as the culmination of that era's medical, philosophical, and spiritual inquiry into melancholy.

Reid, Jennifer I. M. *Worse than Beasts: An Anatomy of Melancholy and the Literature of Travel in Seventeenth and Eighteenth Century England*. Aurora, Colo.: Davies, 2005. Analyzes the derogatory portrayal of foreigners in *The Anatomy of Melancholy, Gulliver's Travels* by Jonathan Swift, and other travel literature of the seventeenth and eighteenth centuries.

Renaker, David. "Robert Burton's Tricks of Memory." *PMLA* 87 (1972): 391-396. Examines the means by which Burton was able to quote, though often inaccurately, from memory or from sketchy notes. Renaker examines the errors.

Schmelzer, Mary Murphy. *'Tis All One: "The Anatomy of Melancholy" as Belated Copious Discourse*. New York: Peter Lang, 1999. Describes how Burton became frustrated when he modeled his book on Erasmus's theory of "copious discourse" and chose instead to base the book on observation and experience rather than on theory or pure logic. This decision, Schmelzer argues, demonstrates the change in the intellectual climate of Western Europe at the beginning of the seventeenth century.

And Quiet Flows the Don

Author: Mikhail Sholokhov (1905-1984)
First published: Tikhii Don, 1928-1940 (partial English translations, 1934 as *And Quiet Flows the Don*; 1940 as *The Don Flows Home to the Sea*; complete English translations, 1942 as *The Silent Don*; 1967 as *And Quiet Flows the Don*)
Type of work: Novel
Type of plot: Historical realism
Time of plot: 1913-1918
Locale: Tatarsk, Russia

Principal characters:
GREGOR MELEKHOV, a Cossack
PIOTRA, Gregor's brother
NATALIA, Gregor's wife
AKSINIA ASTAKHOVA, Gregor's mistress
BUNCHUK, a revolutionary leader

The Story:

The Melekhov family lives in the small village of Tatarsk, in the Don River basin of czarist Russia. Gregor, the oldest son, has a love affair with Aksinia, wife of his neighbor, Stepan Astakhov. Stepan is away serving a term in the army. In an effort to make his son settle down, Gregor's father arranges a marriage with Natalia Korshunov. Gregor never loves Natalia, and their relationship is a cold one. Soon Gregor goes openly to Aksinia, and the affair becomes the village scandal.

When he hears the gossip, Gregor's father whips him. Humiliated and angry, Gregor leaves home. With Aksinia, he becomes the servant of the Listnitsky family, well-to-do landowners who live outside the village of Tatarsk. When Aksinia bears him a daughter, Gregor's father relents enough to pay a visit before Gregor leaves for the army.

In the meantime, Gregor's wife, Natalia, tries to commit suicide because Gregor does not return her love. She goes back to her own home, but the Melekhovs ask her to come to them. She is glad to do so. When Gregor returns to Aksinia on his first leave from the army, he discovers that she was unfaithful to him with Eugene Listnitsky, the young officer-son of his employer. Aksinia's daughter dies, and Gregor feels nothing but anger at his mistress. He fights with Eugene and whips Aksinia. Then he returns to his own home, and there he and Natalia are reconciled. During the time he served in the army, Natalia bore twins, a boy and a girl.

In the war against the Central Powers, Gregor distinguishes himself. Wounded, he is awarded the Cross of St. George, and so he becomes the first Chevalier in the village. While in the army, he meets his brother, Piotra, and his enemy, Stepan Astakhov, who swore to kill him. Nevertheless, on one occasion, Gregor saves Stepan's life during an attack.

Discontent is growing among the soldiers. Bolshevik agitators begin to talk against the government and against a continuation of the war. In Eugene's company, an officer named Bunchuk is the chief agitator. He deserts before Listnitsky can hand him over to the authorities.

Then the provisional government of Kerensky is overthrown, and a Soviet Socialist Republic is established. Civil war breaks out. The Cossacks, proud of their free heritage, are strongly nationalistic and want an autonomous government for the Don region. Many of them join the counterrevolutionists, under such men as Kornilov. Many return to their homes in the Don basin. Gregor, joining the revolutionary forces, is made an officer of the Red Army.

Meanwhile, the revolutionary troops in Rostov are under attack. Bunchuk, the machine gunner, is prominent in the battle and in the administration of the local revolutionary government. He falls in love with a woman machine gunner, Anna Poodko, who is killed during an attack. The counterrevolutionary troops are successful, and the Red Army troops retreat.

Gregor returns to the village and resumes the ordinary life he led before the war. News soon comes that revolutionary troops are advancing on the village. When his neighbors prepare to flee, Gregor refuses to do so. Stories of burning, looting, and rape spread throughout the countryside. A counterrevolutionary officer attempts to organize the villagers against the approaching enemy troops. He names Gregor as commander, but the nomination is turned down in anger because the people in the village know that Gregor sympathizes with the Reds and fought with them. Instead, Gregor's brother Piotra is named commander.

The village forces march out, and Gregor goes with them. When they arrive at their destination, they find that the revolutionary troops are already defeated and that the leaders were captured. When Gregor asks what will happen to them, he is told they will be shot. Then Gregor comes face-to-face with Podtielkov, his old revolutionary leader. When his former leader accuses him of being a traitor and opportunist, all of Gregor's suppressed feelings of disgust and nationalism burst forth. He reminds Podtielkov that he and other Red leaders ordered plenty of executions, and he charges that Podtielkov sold out the Don Cossacks. The revolutionists die prophesying that the revolution will live. Gregor goes back to his Cossack village.

Critical Evaluation:

And Quiet Flows the Don is the first of Mikhail Sholokhov's four-part work, and it is largely for this novel that Sholokhov won the Nobel Prize in Literature in 1965. Its title in the original means simply "the quiet Don," and it was published in English in two volumes (in 1934 and in 1940) under two different titles: *And Quiet Flows the Don*, containing the first two parts, and *The Don Flows Home to the Sea*, containing the latter two parts.

The novel is of truly epic proportions. It starts sometime in the first decade of the twentieth century in the Don region of rural Russia and follows the fortunes of the Melekhov family through peacetime, World War I, and the revolution and civil war in Russia, concluding with the victory of the Bolsheviks in that civil war. Within that broad framework, the entire life of a nation within a nation—the Don Cossacks—is depicted: at peace and war, at work and play, through joys and sorrows, weddings, births, love, hatred, death, murder, even incest. The historical, sociological, and ethnographical aspects of the novel are not to be underestimated, although *And Quiet Flows the Don* is not truly a historical novel. Many events, places, and names are historical, to be sure, but there are also fictitious events and characters that make the novel a fictional creation.

As a result of circumstances beyond their control, the Cossacks were called upon toward the end of World War I to decide their future in a situation beyond their understanding. They lived a secluded life for centuries, always regarding Moscow with suspicion and disapproval. Their only bond with the rest of Russia was their inexplicable love and veneration for the czar; when they had to live without him after his abdication, they were left adrift. Although Russians themselves (but mixed with other nationalities, especially those from Asia), they considered the outside world as intruding. Not well informed about the world's happenings and yet forced to participate in them, they were thrust into turbulent events and made numerous mistakes. Nevertheless, a gritty survival instinct kept them afloat. When the years-long upheaval ended, they found themselves bidding farewell to a life they had been living for centuries and adapting to a new life under the Bolsheviks, facing an uncertain future. No one exemplifies the fate of the Cossacks better than the protagonist of the novel, Gregor Melekhov.

At the beginning of the novel Gregor is a carefree, playful youth, whose only desire is to work on the farm and get as much as possible out of life, including amorous pleasures. After years of fighting for causes he does not fully understand, he loses almost all members of his family and faces an uncertain future himself. During those years he changes his allegiance from the czarist army to the revolutionaries, to the Whites, to the separatist Cossacks, back to the revolutionaries or Reds, to the outlaws, and finally comes to terms with the Bolsheviks. He thus becomes a hero in search of himself. Throughout these ordeals, Gregor possesses an uncanny sense of right and wrong, and every time he changes sides he follows his conscience. Although an uncommonly brave and fierce soldier, he is happiest working on his land in peace. He is not the positive hero of the kind required by the official Soviet literary standard in the 1920's and 1930's, because he does not "see the light" at the end and "change for the better." He cannot be called an antihero either, because of his basically healthy and constructive outlook. The closest classification is that of a Greek tragic hero, his tragic flaw being ignorance of the forces shaping his life—a flaw he shares with his entire nation.

Sholokhov succeeds in eschewing potentially didactic, politically overloaded subject matter through genuine artistry. His straightforward realism is sprinkled with poetic outbursts, especially when describing nature. His closeness to nature is expressed also in the employment of all senses when describing human action. Nearly all the action in the novel occurs on the surface of the narration; there is little symbolism, and philosophical themes, if present, are implied. The author keeps himself in the background, creating superb characters and letting them speak and act. The powerful dramatic quality of the action is underscored by the extraordinary time in history of the setting and the excessive amount of fighting and killing throughout the book. The relationship between Gregor and his neighbor's wife, Aksinia, adds love to the story. The striking objectivity in the presentation of the Russian Revolution makes *And Quiet Flows the Don* one of the outstanding novels of twentieth century literature.

"Critical Evaluation" by Vasa D. Mihailovich

Further Reading

Clark, Katerina. "Socialist Realism in Soviet Literature." In *The Routledge Companion to Russian Literature*, edited by Neil Cornwell. New York: Routledge, 2001. Includes discussion of two of Sholokhov's novels, *And Quiet Flows the Don* and *Virgin Soil Upturned*, placing them within the broader context of Soviet social realism.

Ermolaev, Herman. *Mikhail Sholokhov and His Art*. Princeton, N.J.: Princeton University Press, 1982. One of the best studies of Sholokhov and his works by a native scholar trained in the West. *And Quiet Flows the Don* is treated extensively, especially the historical events and sources and Sholokhov's use of them.

Hallet, Richard. "Soviet Criticism of *Tikhy Don*, 1928-1940." *The Slavonic and East European Review* 46, no. 106 (1968): 60-74. A brief but substantive treatment of Sholokhov's difficulties in publishing the novel because the Soviet authorities disliked his objective presentation of the revolution.

Klimenko, Michael. *The World of Young Sholokhov: Vision of Violence*. North Quincy, Mass.: Christopher, 1979. A useful study of Sholokhov's early works, with emphasis on *And Quiet Flows the Don.*

Medvedev, Roy. *Problems in the Literary Biography of Mikhail Sholokhov.* Translated by A. D. P. Briggs. New York: Cambridge University Press, 1977. A former Russian dissident discusses the controversy about the accusations of Sholokhov's plagiarism in writing *And Quiet Flows the Don.*

Muchnic, Helen. "Mikhail Sholokhov." In *From Gorky to Pasternak*. New York: Random House, 1961. Extensive essay on Sholokhov, the first part of which is devoted to *And Quiet Flows the Don.*

Mukherjee, G. *Mikhail Sholokhov: A Critical Introduction.* New Delhi: Northern Book Centre, 1992. A bilingual study, in both English and Russian. Analyzes Sholokhov's works, considering them within the context of Soviet literature and ideology. Discusses Sholokhov's critical reception.

Murphy, Brian, V. P. Butt, and H. Ermolaev. *Sholokhov's "Tikhii Don": A Commentary.* 2 vols. Birmingham, England: Department of Russian Language and Literature, University of Birmingham, 1997. A detailed discussion of the novel.

Simmons, Ernest J. *Russian Fiction and Soviet Ideology: Introduction to Fedin, Leonov, and Sholokhov.* New York: Columbia University Press, 1967. Simmons, a leading American scholar of Russian literature, evaluates Sholokhov within an ideological and political context.

Stewart, D. H. *Mikhail Sholokhov: A Critical Introduction.* Ann Arbor: University of Michigan Press, 1967. A solid introduction to Sholokhov, with emphasis on *And Quiet Flows the Don.*

And Then There Were None

Author: Agatha Christie (1890-1976)
First published: 1939, as *Ten Little Niggers*
Type of work: Novel
Type of plot: Detective and mystery
Time of plot: 1930's
Locale: An island off the coast of Devon, England

Principal characters:

ANTHONY JAMES MARSTON, wealthy playboy
MR. THOMAS ROGERS, elderly butler
MRS. ETHEL ROGERS, housekeeper and wife of Thomas
GENERAL JOHN GORDON MACARTHUR, retired World War I officer
EMILY CAROLINE BRENT, an elderly unmarried woman
JUSTICE LAWRENCE WARGRAVE, retired judge
DR. EDWARD GEORGE ARMSTRONG, successful London surgeon
WILLIAM HENRY BLORE, former policeman, now a private detective
PHILIP LOMBARD, former military man, mercenary, and adventurer
VERA ELIZABETH CLAYTHORNE, former governess

The Story:

Eight strangers are invited by a mysterious person named U. N. Owen to a luxurious mansion on an island off the coast of Devon. Waiting for them on the island are the housekeeping couple, Mr. and Mrs. Rogers. After dinner, the group hears a recording in which a disembodied voice exposes each of them as a murderer whose crime has has gone undetected and unpunished. Playboy Tony Marston is accused of driving recklessly and causing the deaths of two young people; Mr. and Mrs. Rogers are accused of murdering their aged employer by withholding medication from her; General Macarthur is accused of arranging for the death of a fellow officer; Emily Brent is blamed for the death of her maidservant; Justice Wargrave is blamed for sentencing a possibly innocent man to death; Dr. Armstrong is accused of killing a patient; former policeman William Blore is accused of knowingly sending an innocent man to prison, where he died; soldier of fortune Philip Lombard is accused of allowing native Africans to die of starvation; and former governess Vera Claythorne is blamed for the drowning death of a boy in her care.

The guests defend themselves, determined to preserve their status as acceptable members of English society. Lombard justifies the deaths of the natives in modern, social Darwinist terms, citing the law of self-preservation and the superiority of the Anglo-Saxon race, while Blore asserts that he was simply doing his job. Armstrong admits his guilt, but uses his inebriated condition as an excuse. Marston insisted the deaths of the two young people were accidental.

Marston soon dies from drinking cyanide-laced whiskey. Justice Wargrave immediately takes command, suggesting one of the group is in fact "Mr. Owen," who is toying with them sadistically. Comparing notes, they realize that none of them knows their host and that his name, U. N. Owen, translates into "unknown." Shaken, the guests further reflect on the accusations against them. Rogers admits that he and his wife inherited money from the woman from whom they withheld medicine; his wife's nervous demeanor further confirms their guilt. General Macarthur breaks down, admitting that the young man he sent to his certain death was his wife's lover.

Ten figurines are arranged on the mansion's dining room table, representations of the characters in a nursery rhyme that is also framed and hung in each guest's bedroom. This nursery rhyme, originally "Ten Little Niggers," was changed to "Ten Little Indians" in the American edition of the novel. In the twenty-first century, some editions changed the rhyme once more to "Ten Little Soldiers." In each case, the rhyme features the deaths of ten little boys, counting the number of boys who remain alive at the end of each verse. The rhyme ends when all ten are dead, "and then there were none."

Vera Claythorne notes the similarity between Marston's poisoning and the death of the first boy in the rhyme, who chokes to death. The next day, the group discovers that Ethel Rogers has died from an overdose of sleeping pills, matching the second little boy's death by "oversleeping." The survivors also find that only eight china figurines are left on the table; they begin to fear that there will be successive murders, each one matching the next verse in the rhyme.

A violent storm prevents anyone from coming to or leaving the island. As the pressure builds, Emily admits that a maidservant she had dismissed because she was pregnant and unmarried had subsequently committed suicide. A mood of fear and suspicion intensifies. General Macarthur, increasingly passive and penitential, is found dead; the next day, Rogers is also found dead. Each death conforms to the manner of death of the next little boy in the nursery rhyme. Each time, a figurine disappears.

Confessions and deaths continue to accumulate. Blore admits to Lombard that he had indeed caused an innocent man to be sent to jail. Emily Brent is found dead from an injection of poison that conforms to the "bee sting" death of the fifth little boy in the rhyme. That evening, the judge is discovered dead of a gunshot to the head, corresponding to the sixth little boy in the rhyme. Soon after, Armstrong disappears. The next day, Vera confesses that she deliberately let the boy she was looking after swim out too far and drown so that her lover could inherit the boy's money.

Vera and Lombard find Blore felled by a bear-shaped clock thrown from a window, a death that conforms to the "bear hug" from which the eighth little boy dies. Neither of them was in a position to commit this crime. When the missing Dr. Armstrong's body washes up on the shore, however, Vera and Lombard are each irrationally convinced that the other is the murderer. The quick-witted Vera seizes Lombard's gun and shoots him. She returns to the house, finds a noose waiting for her, and understands that she is meant to die as the tenth boy did in the nursery rhyme. Emotionally exhausted and pushed to the brink of madness, Vera hangs herself.

The discovery of the bodies on the island baffles the police until a letter in a bottle is found by a fishing trawler and sent to Scotland Yard. It is a manuscript by Justice Wargrave, who confesses that he lured his victims to the island to punish them in a way that the law could not. He convinced the gullible Dr. Armstrong to help him fake his death, later murdering him by throwing him off a cliff into the sea. After making sure Vera would commit suicide, the terminally ill Wargrave hastened his death by shooting himself in the head in exactly the same manner in which he appeared to have been shot earlier. His gloating confession reveals a sociopathic temperament hiding behind his cloak of judicial respectability.

Critical Evaluation:

Agatha Christie examines the psychology of the island's guests, as each deteriorates under the pressure of guilt and grave danger. At first, the guests hide their guilt not only from others but also from themselves. This is possible because their crimes are perceived as accidental and unintentional; a number are also passive-aggressive. Vera Claythorne, General MacArthur, Mr. Blore, Emily Brent, Mr. and Mrs. Rogers, and Philip Lombard all deny any active agency in the deaths they are said to have caused. Instead, each could be said to have betrayed a trust by failing to act. For instance, Vera failed to stop the boy she looked after from swimming too far from shore; Mr. and Mrs. Rogers withheld needed medication; Emily Brent failed to demonstrate compassion for her maidservant; Mr. Blore and General Macarthur hid their crime under the rubric of duty.

While these characters maintain a show of innocence, however, their guilt emerges less consciously, through dreams or memories that undermine their self-assurance and certainty. Thoughts of their victims trouble a number of the guests. Emily feels haunted by the spirit of her servant; for Vera, the smell of the sea seems to summon the spirit of the drowned boy. These episodes point to the way in which guilt, even if denied by the rational faculties, can make its presence felt in other ways. Vera is tormented by her unbidden fantasies and memories to such an extent that she is no longer in her right mind by novel's end. She readily cooperates with the suggestion of the nursery rhyme, hanging herself on the noose the judge has provided.

Related to the psychology of the guilty is the theme of exposure. The isolated island mansion is modern, flooded with light, indicating a venue in which all will be revealed. Each guest exposes a side far from rational and decent. Bestial metaphors suggest that, under duress, each has reverted to a primitive law of the jungle, participating in a war of all against all. This disturbing Darwinist vision is first articulated by Philip Lombard as a justification for his crime, but as the characters are reduced to their instincts for self-preservation, the originally paradisaical island becomes a hellish jungle.

The law of the jungle does momentarily reward the intellectually and physically agile Vera, who murders Lombard with his own gun. The hardened mercenary Lombard, whose conviction of racial superiority had justified his abandonment of native Africans, also believed that he was superior to any woman, at first dismissing the idea of female mastermind behind the murders. Lombard lives to see Vera outsmart him, but Vera's humanity, not her Darwinian survival instinct, prevails—she has utterly disintegrated psychologically under the pressure of her nerve-racking situation and the promptings of her own guilty conscience. Far from triumphant, she becomes the final victim of Justice Wargrave.

A brilliant psychologist himself, the judge in the end discloses his own character and motive. The artfully composed letters and the mysterious recorded voice of Mr. "Unknown" are two early indications that the mansion's visitors are being subjected to the manipulations of a "mastermind." As an experienced judge, Wargrave is able to turn all the guests against one another and to enlist the most useful of them as an ally.

In his manuscript, Wargrave admits that he became a judge because sentencing criminals to death allowed him to exercise his sadistic impulses free of the qualms of conscience. Wargrave does not simply execute his guests, however. Each victim plays a part in the judge's ruthless theatrical reinvention of the punitive nursery rhyme. He characterizes himself as a creative genius, seeing his success at controlling the fates of his guests as an artistic achievement. The nursery rhyme allows the judge to become a playwright and stage manager, with each guest assigned a role. The rhyme further produces an uncanny inevitability; the executions are carried out as if they were the product of an inexorable godlike mechanism.

The judge confesses that he sees himself as an avenging deity, replacing both human and divine justice in favor of his own. He acknowledges this through the symbolism of his bullet wound, which, he explains, is the "mark of Cain," misreferencing the biblical story in which God set a mark of protection upon the unscrupulous Cain when he took the law into his own hands, murdering his brother, Abel. This reference may recall Emily Brent's warning to Lombard that, in causing the deaths of Africans, he had murdered men he should understand as his brothers. While both Lombard and Justice Wargrave demonstrate a depraved indifference to the taking of life, Wargrave's cold, prideful, sadistic glee is such that he goes well beyond Lombard's mercenary logic to a psychology that suggests the diabolical.

One of Christie's most famous, most highly praised, and most ingenious novels, *And Then There Were None* demonstrates darker and more unsettled aspects of Christie's mystery fiction. There is no romance or recovery at the end of the novel and no pure detective figure who can restore innocence and peace of mind. The novel is instead a study of criminal psychology and of the human personality under pressures of guilt, fear, and anxiety.

Margaret Boe Birns

Further Reading

Bargainnier, Earl F. *The Gentle Art of Murder: The Detective Fiction of Agatha Christie*. Bowling Green, Ohio: Bowling Green State University Popular Press, 1980. Examines *And Then There Were None* in a survey of setting, character, plot, narrative strategies, and themes; finds the novel most effective in its shifting of suspicion and its examination of guilt.

Light, Alison. *Forever England: Femininity, Literature, and Conservatism Between the Wars*. New York: Routledge, 1991. *And Then There Were None* is included in this highly regarded study of Christie's fiction between World War I and World War II. Discusses the issue of the original title.

Miller, D. A. *The Novel and the Police*. Berkeley: University of California Press, 1988. This groundbreaking new historicist study of Victorian detective fiction is crucial for understanding Christie's later foray into the genre. It establishes the relationship between public and private life at the heart of the genre, a relationship at the center of Christie's works, in which every character seems to harbor a secret.

Osborne, Charles. *The Life and Crimes of Agatha Christie*. New York: St. Martin's Minotaur, 2002. Discusses *And Then There Were None*, integrating aspects of Christie's biography and personality, with emphasis on the nursery rhyme and on the novel's composition. Includes illustrations.

Palmer, Scott. *The Films of Agatha Christie*. London: Batsford, 1993. Useful discussion of five different film adaptations of Christie's *And Then There Were None*.

Wagstaff, Vanessa, and Stephen Poole. *Agatha Christie: A Reader's Companion*. London: Aurum Press, 2004. Includes a summary of *And Then There Were None* that features background information and color photographs of the island that inspired the setting.

York, Richard. *Agatha Christie: Power and Illusion*. New York: Palgrave Macmillan, 2007. Brilliant, groundbreaking study that includes *And Then There Were None* in an insightful examination of Christie's mythic elements; narrative strategies; and explorations of illusion and reality, modern times, and the nature of evil.

Andersen's Fairy Tales

Author: Hans Christian Andersen (1805-1875)
First published: Eventyr, 1835-1872 (as *The Complete Andersen*, 1949; as *Fairy Tales*, 1950-1958; as *The Complete Fairy Tales and Stories*, 1974)
Type of work: Short fiction
Type of plot: Fairy tales
Time of plot: Indeterminate
Locale: Denmark

Principal characters:
KAREN, the owner of the red shoes
THE UGLY DUCKLING
THE SNOW QUEEN
KAY, a little boy
GERDA, a little girl
THE SHEPHERDESS, a china figure
THE CHIMNEYSWEEP, her lover
THE EMPEROR
A TIN SOLDIER
A POOR SOLDIER

The Stories:

The Red Shoes. Karen is such a poor little girl that she has to go barefoot in winter. An old mother shoemaker feels sorry for her and makes Karen a clumsy pair of shoes out of pieces of red felt. When Karen's mother dies, the girl wears the red shoes to the funeral. An old lady, seeing Karen walking forlornly behind her mother's coffin, pities her and takes the child home. The old lady thinks that the red shoes are ugly, and she burns them.

One day, Karen sees the queen and the little princess. The princess is dressed all in white, with beautiful red morocco shoes. When the time comes for Karen's confirmation, she needs new shoes. The old lady, almost blind, does not know that the shoes Karen picks out are red ones just like those the princess wore. During the confirmation, Karen can think of nothing but her red shoes.

The next Sunday, as Karen goes to her First Communion, she meets an old soldier with a crutch. After admiring the red shoes, he strikes them on the soles and tells them to stick fast when Karen dances. During the service, she can think only of her shoes. After church, she starts to dance. The footman has to pick her up and take off her shoes before the old lady can take her home.

At a ball in town, Karen cannot stop dancing. She dances out through the fields and up to the church. There an angel with a broad sword stops her and tells her she will dance until she becomes a skeleton, a warning to all other vain children.

Karen dances day and night until she comes to the executioner's house. There she taps on the window and begs him to come out and cut off her feet. After he chops off her feet, they and the little red shoes dance off into the forest. The executioner makes Karen wooden feet and crutches and teaches her a psalm, and the parson gives her a home. Karen thinks she suffers enough to go to church, but each time she tries she sees the red shoes dancing ahead of her and is afraid. One Sunday, she stays at home. As she hears the organ music, she reads her prayer book humbly and begs help from God. Then she sees the angel again, not with a sword but with a green branch covered with roses. As the angel moves the branch, Karen feels that she is being carried off to the church. There she is so thankful that her heart breaks, and her soul flies up to heaven.

The Ugly Duckling. A mother duck is sitting on a clutch of eggs. When the largest egg does not crack with the rest, an old matriarchal duck warns the setting fowl that she should leave that egg alone; it will probably turn out to be a turkey. The egg, however, finally cracks, and out of it comes the biggest, ugliest duckling ever seen in the barnyard. The other ducklings peck it and chase it and make it so unhappy that it feels comfortable only when it is paddling in the pond. The mother duck is proud only of the very fine paddling the ugly duckling does.

The scorn heaped on his head is so bitter that the ugly duckling leaves home. He spends a miserable winter in the marsh. When spring comes, he sees some beautiful white swans settle down on the water. He moves out to admire them as they come toward him with ruffled feathers. He bends down to await their attack, but as he looks in the water he sees that he is no longer a gray ugly duckling but another graceful swan. He is so glad then that he never thinks to be proud, but he smiles when he hears some children say that he is the handsomest swan they have ever seen.

The Snow Queen. A very wicked hobgoblin invents a mirror that reflects everything good as trivial and everything bad as monstrous; a good thought turns into a grin in the mirror. His cohorts carry it all over the earth and finally up to heaven to test the angels. There many good thoughts make the mirror grin so much that it falls out of their hands and splinters as it hits the earth. Each tiny piece can distort as the whole mirror did.

A tiny piece pierces Kay through the heart, and a tiny grain lodges in his eye. Kay was a happy little boy before that. He played with Gerda in their rooms high above the street, and they both admired some rosebushes their parents planted in boxes spanning the space between their houses. With the glass in his eye and heart, however, Kay sees nothing beautiful, and nothing pleases him.

One night, Kay goes sledding in the town square. When a lady all in white drives by, he thinks that she is so beautiful that he hitches his sled behind her sleigh as she drives slowly around the square. Suddenly, her horses gallop out of the town. The lady looks back at Kay and smiles each time he tries to loosen his sled. Then she stops the sleigh and tells Kay to get in with her. There she wraps him in her fur coat. She is the Snow Queen. He is nearly frozen, but he does not feel cold after she kisses him nor does he remember Gerda.

Gerda does not forget Kay; at last, she runs away from home to look for him. She goes to the garden of a woman learned in magic and asks all the flowers if they have seen Kay, but the flowers know only their own stories. She meets a crow who leads her to the prince and princess, but they have not heard of Kay. They give her boots and a muff and a golden coach to ride in when they send her on her way. Robbers stop the golden coach. At the insistence of a little robber girl, Gerda is left alive, a prisoner in the robbers' house. Some wood pigeons in the loft tell Gerda that Kay went with the Snow Queen to Lapland. Since the reindeer tethered inside the house know the way to Lapland, the robber girl sets him free to take Gerda on her way.

The Lapp and the Finn women give Gerda directions to the Snow Queen's palace and tell her that it is only through the goodness of her heart that Kay can be released. When Gerda finds Kay, she weeps so hard that she melts the piece of mirror out of his heart. Then he weeps the splinter from his eye and realizes what a vast and empty place he was in. With thankfulness in her heart, Gerda leads Kay out of the snow palace and home.

The Shepherdess and the Sweep. In the middle of the door of an old wooden parlor cupboard is carved a ridiculous little man with goat's legs, horns on his head, and a beard. The children call him Major-general-field-sergeant-commander-

Billy-goat's-legs. He always looks at the china figure of a Shepherdess. Finally, he asks the china figure of a Chinese man, who claims to be her grandfather, if he can marry the Shepherdess. The Chinese man, who can nod his head when he chooses, nods his consent. The Shepherdess is engaged to the china figure of a Chimneysweep. She begs him to take her away. That night, he uses his ladder to help her get off the table. The Chinese man sees them leave and starts after them.

Through the stove and up the chimney go the Shepherdess and the Chimneysweep. When she sees how big the world is, the Shepherdess begins to cry, and the Chimneysweep has to take her back to the parlor. There they see the Chinaman broken on the floor. The Shepherdess is distressed, but the Chimneysweep says the Chinaman can be mended and riveted. Although the family has the Chinaman riveted so that he is whole again, he can no longer nod his head. When the Major-general-field-sergeant-commander-Billy-goat's-legs asks again for the Shepherdess, the Chinaman cannot nod, and so the Shepherdess and the Chimneysweep stay together and love each other until they are broken to pieces.

The Emperor's New Clothes. A foolish Emperor loves clothes so much that he spends all the kingdom's money to buy new ones. Two swindlers, who know the Emperor's weakness, come to town with big looms. They tell the people that they weave the most beautiful cloth in the world but that it has a magical property: If someone unworthy of his post looks at it, the cloth becomes invisible.

The Emperor gives the pair much gold and thread to make him a new outfit. The swindlers set up their looms and work far into the night. Becoming curious about the materials, the Emperor sends his most trusted minister to see them. When the minister looks at the looms, he sees nothing; thinking of the magical property of the cloth, he decides that he is unworthy of his post. He says nothing to the swindlers and reports to the Emperor, praising the colors and pattern of the cloth as the swindlers described it.

Others, looking at the looms, see nothing and say nothing. Even the Emperor sees nothing when the material is finished and then is made into clothes, but he also keeps silent. He wears his new clothes in a fine procession. All the people, who also know of the cloth's supposed property, call out that his new clothes are beautiful—all the people except one little boy, who says that the Emperor does not have on any clothes at all.

Then there is a buzzing along the line of march. Soon everyone is saying that the Emperor wears no clothes. The Emperor, realizing the truth, holds himself stiffer than ever until the procession ends.

The Steadfast Tin Soldier. A little boy has a set of twenty-five tin soldiers made out of the same tin spoon. Since there is not quite enough tin, one soldier has only one leg, but he stands as solidly as those with two legs. The one-legged soldier stands on a table and looks longingly at a paper castle, at the door of which stands a paper dancer who wears a gauze dress. A ribbon over her shoulder is held in position by a spangle as big as her face.

One morning, the little boy puts the one-legged soldier on a windowsill. When the window opens, the soldier falls three stories to the ground. There he stays, head down between two stones, until some boys find him. They make a paper boat for the soldier and sail it down the gutter. After a time, the boat enters a sewer. Beginning to get limp, it settles deeper into the water. Just as the soldier thinks he will fall into the water, a fish swallows him.

When the fish is opened, the soldier finds himself in the same house out of which he fell. Soon he is back on his table looking at the dancer. For no reason, the boy throws him into a roaring fire. Suddenly, a draft in the room whisks the dancer off the table and straight to the soldier in the fire. As the fire burns down, the soldier is melted to a small tin heart. All that is left of the dancer is her spangle, burned black.

The Tinder Box. A soldier is walking along the high road one day when a witch stops him and tells him that he can have a lot of money if he will climb down a hollow tree and bring her up a tinder box. Thinking that is an easy way to get money, he ties a rope around his waist and the witch helps him to climb down inside the tree. He takes along the witch's apron, for on it he will place the dogs that guard the chests of money. The first dog, with eyes as big as saucers, guards a chest full of coppers. The soldier places the dog on the apron, fills his pockets with coppers, and walks on.

The next dog, with eyes as big as millstones, guards silver. The soldier places the dog on the apron, empties his pockets of coppers, and fills them with silver. The third dog has eyes as big as the Round Tower. He guards gold. When the soldier places the dog on the apron, he empties his pockets of silver and fills them, his knapsack, his cap, and his boots with gold. Then he calls to the witch to pull him up.

When she refuses to tell him why she wants the tinder box, he cuts off her head and starts for town. There he lives in splendor and give alms to the poor, for he is good-hearted.

He hears of a beautiful princess who is kept locked up because of a prophecy that she would marry a common soldier. Idly he thinks of ways to see her. When his money runs out and he has no candle, he remembers that there is a piece of candle in the tinder box. As he strikes the box to light the candle, the door flies open and the dog with eyes like saucers bursts in, asking what the soldier wants. When he asks for money, the dog brings it back immediately. Then he finds that he can call the second dog by striking the box twice, and the third dog by striking it three times. When he asks the dogs to bring the princess, she is brought to his room.

The king and queen have him thrown into prison when they catch him. There he is helpless until a little boy to whom he calls brings the tinder box to him. When the soldier is about to be hanged, he asks permission to smoke a last pipe. Then he pulls out his tinder box and strikes it once, twice, three times. All three dogs come to rout the king's men and free the soldier. The people are so impressed that they make the soldier king and the princess his queen.

Critical Evaluation:

Hans Christian Andersen was a dreamy little boy whose thoughts were very much like those of many of the characters in his fairy tales. When his father died and his mother remarried, he asked to go to Copenhagen to make his fortune. A soothsayer told his mother that her son would be Denmark's pride, so she let him go. When he tried to enter the theater, he had little success. Some influential men, however, realized that he was a poet and helped him until his publications began to attract attention. By the time Andersen died, he was Denmark's most beloved countryman. His tales may be fantastic, encompassing many moods, but they merely reflect his own character, which was equally fantastic, though lovable.

The 168 tales written by Andersen may be classified in two general groups. The first group comprises the traditional European folktales retold by Andersen and includes selections such as "Little Claus and Big Claus," "The Wild Swans," and "The Three Little Pigs." These are excellent versions in which the spirit of the source is maintained while the tale is enhanced by the author's gift for storytelling. The majority of the tales, however, belong to the second group, composed of Andersen's original stories; among these one finds a great variety, ranging from stories imitative of the folktale style, to moral allegories, to stories that seem to foreshadow modern fantasy tales. Despite their diversity, however, all of Andersen's tales are marked by common features in both their content and their style.

To a greater or lesser degree, almost all the tales directly reflect the author's personal experiences. Perhaps the most striking example of this is "The Ugly Duckling," which may be read as both a literal and a spiritual autobiography. Similarly, Karen in "The Red Shoes" directly parallels the young Andersen, who at his confirmation was more thrilled with his leather shoes, so new that they squeaked, than with the religious ceremony. In addition to occasional fictionalized accounts of the author's past, readers find a multitude of tales that are more subtly sprinkled with the author's childhood experiences and with the rich lore and colorful traditions of Odense, the provincial town in Denmark where he was reared. The appearance of benevolent grandmothers in so many of the stories, for example, reflects Andersen's own kindly grandmother, who not only gave the boy sympathy and support but also fed his imagination with peasant tales and reports of the eerie happenings in the insane asylum near which she worked. The many portraits of witches in the fairy tales owe their vividness to the author's terrifying memories of the local "witches" for whom his mother sent when he was ill; towns such as Odense in the early nineteenth century were still steeped in medieval beliefs, and mothers of peasant background might still trust in a witch's potion rather than turn to a doctor's prescription to cure their children. Still other tales in the collection are built around recollected daydreams rather than the actual experiences of the author. Such is the case in the beautiful story "The Nightingale," inspired by Andersen's fanciful habit as a boy of singing in the evening to the emperor of China, reputed by the peasants to reside directly under the Odense River.

Perhaps the single most important feature of Andersen's tales is the meaning or significance with which they are charged; a tale is rarely told solely for the sake of a catchy or an entertaining plot. This certainly is not to say that the plots are dull—they are never that—or that the stories are heavily didactic, but rather that all of Andersen's work is illuminated (unobtrusively, for the most part) by a moral outlook on life. Sometimes this outlook takes the form of sharp social criticism, as in "The Emperor's New Clothes," which satirizes the pompousness and vanity of court life through its portrait of the unscrupulous weavers, the ridiculous emperor, and the hypocritical courtiers. Similarly, "The Swineherd" attacks the artificial and materialistic values that blind people to the true worth of things. Occasionally, a tale will be particularly frightening in its harsh presentation of a moral lesson; "The Red Shoes," in which a girl's amputated feet go dancing off, leaving her a cripple in punishment for her vanity over a new pair of shoes, is an especially grim and severe illustration. This type of story, however, is the exception rather than the rule; for the most part, Andersen's humor is gentle rather than scathing, and his moral viewpoint is characterized by its subtlety and sensitivity, its kindliness and concern for others.

One distinctive device that Andersen developed as a highly effective way of presenting his ideas is the transformation of inanimate objects into creatures with personalities. Perhaps most memorable is the steadfast tin soldier whose struggles to remain fearless through all of his trials for the sake of his beloved paper ballerina exemplify the spirit of true devotion. In "The Old Streetlamp," Andersen uses a worthy (and very human) old lamppost to weave a symbolic tale about how fear of death robs the soul of its tranquillity and about how hope leads to inner peace. Interspersed with these tales peopled by tin soldiers and lampposts, drops of water and darning needles, candles and inkstands, are others containing the more traditional talking animals and trees, which are also used to convey various themes. "The Three Little Pigs" illustrates the superiority of brains over physical strength; in "The Buckwheat," a wise old oak tree weeps over a proud stalk of wheat that is destroyed because he refuses to take advice from his neighbors.

Andersen's ability to create such vivid and sympathetic characters, be they humans, animals, or objects, is the result of his exceptional handling of dialogue. His interest in dialogue began early in his childhood, when, with the aid of a polyglot dictionary, he wrote whimsical stories in which each character spoke a different language. By the time he came to write the fairy tales, his characters all spoke the same language, but he had mastered the secret of revealing their personalities and motives through their speech. Rather than describing what a character is like, Andersen lets the characters expose themselves. Therefore, in "The Shepherdess and the Sweep," the Shepherdess shows both her frivolity and petulance—"I'll never be happy until we are out in the big, wide world"—and her flightiness and shallowness: "I followed you faithfully out into the world, and if you love me the least bit you'll take me right home." The Chimney-sweep's speech shows him to be sensible yet devoted: "Have you thought how big [the wide world] is, and that we can never come back here?"

Andersen saves his descriptive passages for presenting scenery and landscape, and at this, too, he is masterful. He reproduces with loving detail the inside of a humble cottage kitchen or brings a towering mountain range before the reader's eyes with equal skill. In this excerpt from "The Ice Maiden," one of the longer tales, the author's descriptive power is at its best:

> Often the clouds hang around the towering peaks like thick curtains of smoke, while down in the valley dotted with brown wooden houses, a ray of the sun may be shining brightly, throwing into sharp relief a brilliant patch of green, until it seems transparent.

Toward the end of his life, Andersen made the statement, "I have imagined so much and had so little." He was referring in part to his frequent romantic attachments to women who eventually married other men and to his long life spent as a bachelor. Still, coming from a man beloved by his fellow Danes, whose friendship was valued by great writers of his age, and whose society was sought after by nearly all the courts of Europe, the words "so little" seem incongruous. With the "so much," however, those who have read Andersen's tales may call the phrase an understatement.

"Critical Evaluation" by Nancy G. Ballard

Further Reading

Blegvad, Erik. *Hans Christian Andersen: From an Artist's Point of View.* Washington, D.C.: Children's Literature Center, Library of Congress, 1988. Critique of Andersen's fairy tales from a noted Danish illustrator. Describes visual qualities of Andersen's tales that are rarely noted. Based on a lecture, this book is casual about references; the reader needs some familiarity with Andersen's works.

Bloom, Harold, ed. *Hans Christian Andersen.* Philadelphia: Chelsea House, 2005. Collection of essays about Andersen's life and work. Some of the essays discuss the heroes and heroines in the fairy tales, Andersen and the European literary tradition, and "Hans Christian Andersen's Fairy Tales and Stories: Secrets, Swans, and Shadows."

Dahl, Svend. *A Book on the Danish Writer, Hans Christian Andersen, His Life and Work.* Copenhagen: Berlingske Bogtr., 1955. An introductory approach to Andersen's life and work. Includes coverage of his story themes and relates them to events in his life.

Gronbech, Bo. *Hans Christian Andersen.* Boston: Twayne, 1980. Treats Andersen's fairy tales in depth, primarily as literary compositions. Extensive bibliographical references.

Mortensen, Finn. *A Tale of Tales: Hans Christian Andersen and Danish Children's Literature.* Minneapolis: Center for Nordic Studies, University of Minnesota, 1989. Considers the original quality of some of the writer's best-known tales and their importance to the national literature.

Nojgaard, Morten, et al., eds. *Telling of Stories, Approaches to a Traditional Craft: A Symposium.* Odense, Denmark: Odense University Press, 1990. Conference proceedings that include essays looking at Andersen's fairy tales from the perspective of the storyteller. Selected tales are examined from the point of view of drama, audience, voice, and cultural notions of continuity and disruption.

Wullshläger, Jackie. *Hans Christian Andersen: The Life of a Storyteller.* New York: A. A. Knopf, 2001. An extensively researched biography, portraying Andersen as a self-pitying and desperate man whose life was far darker than his fairy tales.

Zipes, Jack David. *Hans Christian Andersen: The Misunderstood Storyteller.* New York: Routledge, 2005. Zipes examines the relationship of Andersen's work to the development of literature, particularly the fairy tale. His analysis of Andersen's work focuses on the tales, describing how they have been misunderstood and misinterpreted over time.

Andersonville

Author: MacKinlay Kantor (1904-1977)
First published: 1955
Type of work: Novel
Type of plot: Historical realism and war fiction
Time of plot: October, 1863, to April, 1865
Locale: Camp Sumter, Georgia

Principal characters:
IRA CLAFFEY, a Georgia plantation owner
LUCY CLAFFEY, his daughter
VERONICA CLAFFEY, his wife
HARRY ELKINS, a Confederate army doctor
HENRY WIRZ, the Swiss-born commandant of the prison camp
NATHAN DREYFOOS, a Union army prisoner of war
CORAL TEBBS, a Confederate army veteran

The Story:

In mid-autumn, 1863, Confederate army surveyors arrive near the southern Georgia plantation of Ira Claffey to begin construction of a military prison camp. Claffey is told that the facility, planned to encompass about twenty-seven acres, will house ten thousand prisoners of war. There will be no barracks, only an open enclosure bound by a series of fences.

Amid the chaos of the closing months of the American Civil War, the camp swells to close to fifty thousand prisoners. Quickly, as cattle cars of captured Union army soldiers keep arriving, conditions in the camp degenerate: Disease, starvation, insect infestations, impure water from a stream that flowed through the camp, and a lack of adequate medical care contribute to an appalling death rate. The camp is run by Confederate captain Henry Wirz, a cold-blooded bureaucrat plagued by his own demons (most notably a painful wounded hand) who feels hopelessly alone (he is Swiss-born, and his heavy accent underscores his isolation). Overwhelmed by the responsibilities of running the sprawling camp, Wirz fears most the possibility of a camp uprising, as its population steadily grows. Indeed, his fears are justified as a contingent of desperate prisoners valiantly attempts to tunnel out of the camp.

New prisoners arrive every week, including Eben Dolliver, an Iowa farmboy and bird lover who is driven to killing a swallow by twisting its neck and then eating it raw, and Father Peter Whalen, who ministers to the scores of dying and tries to maintain a sense of God's presence. Other prisoners include Tom Gusset, an Ohio harness maker who, at the age of fifty-eight, is among the oldest prisoners and who manages to stay physically sound until he gradually loses his mind, overwhelmed by the misery in the camp. He hallucinates that he is back home with his family, holding animated conversations with his children and his neighbors; he is carted off to die in the camp hospital. Another prisoner is Nazareth Stricker, a Pennsylvania soldier who lost a hand at the Battle of Gettysburg. He escapes from the camp one day only to confront Coral Tebbs, a Confederate veteran who had lost a leg at the same battle.

Plantation owner Claffey observes from a distance the camp's steadily deteriorating conditions. He is a noble, generous, long-suffering, and learned person given to philosophical contemplations on humanity and history. He has already lost two sons in the war, but his love of the Confederacy does not blind him to its failings. He recognizes the horrors of the camp built on his land—underscored by the nauseating stench that comes to hang about the plantation. He lovingly cares for his wife, Veronica, who is slowly losing her mind over the death of their sons. Their beautiful daughter, Lucy, who herself had lost her fiancé in the war, is falling in love with Dr. Harry Elkins, a distant cousin who had accepted the thankless position as physician for the camp. Elkins keeps Claffey informed of conditions at the camp, leading Claffey to petition the Confederate command to help ameliorate the conditions. However, his efforts prove futile.

As the months grind away and conditions grow worse, a sharp conflict arises among the prisoners. A group of hardcore thugs, who had for the most part enlisted in the Union army to avoid prison, start to terrorize the other prisoners. Calling themselves the Raiders, they steal what little the captured soldiers had brought to the camp and use intimidation and violence to create a formidable power structure within the prison. The Raiders are challenged by a group of idealistic prisoners, led by the intellectual and worldly Nathan Dreyfoos. The idealists refuse to allow the hellish conditions in the camp to destroy their humanity and their sense of right and wrong. They round up the Raiders and hang them, but not before they hold a trial that (ironically) works to preserve the highest ideals of civilization and justice. Conditions continue to deteriorate. As food stocks run out, prisoners are driven to eating their own feces to survive. Water runs out. Diseases, including cholera, dropsy, scurvy, dysentery, and malaria, are rampant. Union soldiers finally arrive to liberate the camp just weeks before the Confederate surrender at Appomattox; the Union soldiers find the grimmest of conditions at the camp.

In the days following the end of the war, and after news of U.S. president Abraham Lincoln's assassination reaches the South, Claffey walks amid the grounds of the abandoned stockade. He contemplates the implications of the South's lost crusade. His daughter, now married to Elkins, is certain she is pregnant—Claffey senses her joy and hopes that she is indeed pregnant. Still, he struggles to find philosophical meaning in the abomination of the camp. He acknowledges the moral evil of slavery, although he describes the appalling conditions in Northern factories as de facto economic slavery.

Finally, Claffey gets beyond the war and its issues—it is the thousands of dead from Andersonville who now weigh on his conscience. He hopes that the story of their lives and their deaths will not be lost to history. He decides, as he heads back to his own ruined plantation, that the only hope rests in the country rising from the ashes of the war and, by avoiding incendiary extremism, rededicating itself to the work of rebuilding the union. As he turns from the ruins of the camp, birds soar toward the rising Sun.

Critical Evaluation:

Given MacKinlay Kantor's ambition to re-create with encyclopedic detail the infamous Confederate prisoner-of-war (POW) prison and the deaths of more than thirteen thousand Union army soldiers, *Andersonville*, not surprisingly, can be a daunting read of close to eight hundred pages. The novel's narrative structure is on the grand scale of nineteenth century historical novels, like the work of Leo Tolstoy, with their multiple plot lines and hundreds of named characters. The most immediate achievement of *Andersonville* is the sheer visceral impact of Kantor's account.

Drawing on nearly six years of investigations into the conditions of the POW prison near Anderson (now Andersonville), Georgia, Kantor delivers with unblinking journalistic fidelity the appalling reality of the camp. He had been a career newspaper reporter and also had written about, before *Andersonville*, prison camps of the Civil War: *Arouse and Beware* (1936), for example, recounts conditions at the Confederate camp at Belle Isle, Virginia. What separates the earlier account from *Andersonville*, however, is Kantor's experiences as a reporter during World War II.

As Kantor would explain to interviewers concerned about the impact of reading about such shocking horrors, he was compelled to write about Andersonville after being assigned to cover the Allied liberation of Buchenwald, a notorious German concentration camp where thousands of Jews were killed. He came to believe that the fullest story of war, indeed the only honest account of history, had to include accounts of horrific inhumanity. Thus, the narrative of *Andersonville* is presented without emotional coloring—the narrative voice describes with care and precision the horrors as the numbers of prisoners escalates. Kantor dispenses with quotation marks in dialogue, unnerving at first read but part of his attempt to make the experience of the prison immediate without the niceties of conventional prose.

Despite its graphic nature and epic scale, the novel was a best seller for more than two years and won the 1957 Pulitzer Prize for fiction, a testimony to Kantor's belief that the story of the Civil War, the pivotal trauma for the United States, had been incomplete without the story of Andersonville. In fact, his novel became part of the national commemoration that would mark the approaching centennial of the Civil War.

In addition, *Andersonville* contributes to the genre of historical realism generally and to war fiction specifically. The novel positions the reality of death as central to historical presentation. A comparison helps. In terms of sales and cultural impact, *Andersonville* most resembles Margaret Mitchell's novel *Gone with the Wind* (1936) from the generation before World War II. While Mitchell's novel certainly depicts disease, violence, and death, it is far from the scale of Kantor's narrative. There is an undeniable grimness to reading Kantor's narrative—characters introduced seldom last more than one or two chapters, as the camp's death toll steadily rises. The reader witnesses the lengths to which the prisoners attempt to survive. Kantor graphically describes prisoners picking through fecal matter to salvage food scraps, describes the physical effects of scurvy and diarrhea, recounts the primitive conditions in the camp hospital, and details the mechanics of a hanging, as a group of prisoners execute the Raiders.

The narrative redefines the conservative tradition of decorum in historical realism by exposing the grimmest elements of war with unrelenting honesty. That said, the largest part of the narrative is given over to rescuing from anonymity the Union casualties of Andersonville. Chapter to chapter, readers are introduced to new characters, inmates who, given the appalling death rate in the camp, quickly disappear from the story. However, Kantor makes each prisoner vivid and gives each one dignity and depth by creating a background through childhood stories, recollected war experiences, or heartbreaking reminiscences of love and family left behind. In many cases, Kantor actually researched the names of the dead (the novel is appended by an extensive bibliography).

As a narrative, Kantor's work, with its highly experimental combination of historic figures and fictional characters, audaciously upends the long-held assumption that fact and fiction cannot blur. Historical fiction traditionally has focused on invented characters with historic personages making brief and generally clichéd cameo appearances. In *Andersonville*, Kantor explores the psychology of many of the camp's dominant individuals and shapes into narrative immediacy the actual soldiers who died there. He also juxtaposes the real figures with fictional characters, leaving unclear which characters are real and which are fictional. In mingling fact and fiction, Kantor anticipates by more than a decade narrative experiments in creative nonfiction, or New Journalism, by writers such as Tom Wolfe, Norman Mailer, Truman Capote, Joan Didion, E. L. Doctorow, and Don DeLillo.

Kantor's anticipation, however, was hardly deliberate. He did not perceive writing as an experiment in form, and his account of the camp is not an expression of some abstract theory of narration. Rather, Kantor wanted to tell a story. His defining achievement in *Andersonville* is his profound love of storytelling, giving humanity and dignity to the otherwise forgotten Union dead. In a career that spanned nearly six decades and produced more than thirty novels in a variety of genres—from detective fiction to children's books—Kantor saw historical realism primarily as the opportunity to tell stories, to use real events to create the intricacy of character, to realize everyday objects into potent and resonant symbols, and ultimately to test the dynamic of morality itself—that is, to test how real-time events can generate insight, even wisdom. It is the grandness of the storytelling art, that faith in narrative, that is the enduring achievement of *Andersonville*.

Joseph Dewey

Further Reading

Cullen, Tim. *The Civil War in Popular Culture: A Reusable Past.* Washington, D.C.: Smithsonian Institute Press, 1995. A landmark examination of the literature of the American Civil War. Includes a discussion of *Andersonville*, specifically of the relationship between fiction and history and how Kantor uses stereotypes of Civil War fiction.

Kantor, Tim. *My Father's Voice: MacKinlay Kantor Long Remembered.* New York: McGraw-Hill, 1988. A highly readable Kantor biography that includes an account of his background as a war correspondent, his career-long love of the history of the Civil War, and the effect of his experience at Buchenwald on the evolution of *Andersonville*.

Marvel, William. *Andersonville: The Last Depot.* Chapel Hill: University of North Carolina Press, 2006. An important study of the legacy of the prison camp that separates facts from the considerable accumulation of distortions, many of them part of Kantor's fictional account, which have altered the perception of the camp in history.

Ransom, John L. *John L. Ransom's Andersonville Diary.* New York: Berkley Books, 1994. A classic firsthand account of the prison camp by a survivor. This work was used by Kantor as a key resource in writing his novel of Camp Sumter in Georgia.

Sachsman, David B., S. Kittrell Rushing, and Roy Morris, Jr. *Memory and Myth: The Civil War in Fiction and Film from "Uncle Tom's Cabin" to "Cold Mountain."* West Lafayette, Ind.: Purdue University Press, 2007. Places Kantor's *Andersonville* within a broad context of novels and films that have shaped the contemporary perception of the Civil War era. Deals specifically with issues of romanticizing the war and ignoring its brutality. Uses Kantor's novel as a critical corrective to idealized readings of the war.

Andria

Author: Terence (c. 190-159 B.C.E.)
First produced: 166 B.C.E. (English translation, 1598)
Type of work: Drama
Type of plot: Comedy
Time of plot: Second century B.C.E.
Locale: Athens

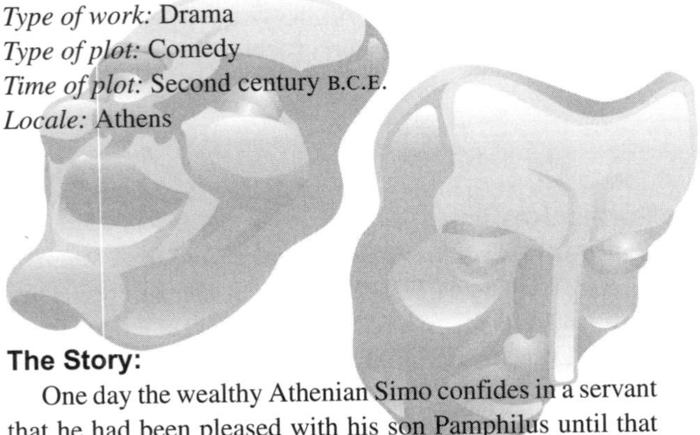

Principal characters:
SIMO, a wealthy Athenian
PAMPHILUS, Simo's son
DAVUS, a slave of Pamphilus
CHREMES, another wealthy Athenian, friend of Simo
GLYCERIUM, beloved of Pamphilus, originally named Pasibula and eventually revealed to be a daughter of Chremes
PHILUMENA, another daughter of Chremes
CRITO, a traveler from Andros
CHARINUS, a suitor for the daughter of Chremes

The Story:

One day the wealthy Athenian Simo confides in a servant that he had been pleased with his son Pamphilus until that very afternoon, when Simo discovered that his son was in love with Glycerium, the sister of a courtesan who has recently died. Simo, who wishes to marry his son to Philumena, the daughter of his friend Chremes, sees in his son's love for Glycerium a threat to his plans.

Later Simo encounters his son's slave, Davus, and threatens him with severe punishment. Simo is afraid that Davus, a clever fellow, will help Pamphilus thwart his father's plans for his future. Davus immediately sees that some scheme will have to be put into action quickly before the love between Pamphilus and Glycerium ends in marriage. Glycerium is already pregnant by Pamphilus.

Pamphilus's own scheme is to acknowledge the expected infant and then claim that Glycerium is actually an Athenian whose father was shipwrecked on Andros and that she was reared by the family of the courtesan as a foster child. Davus laughs at the story and says that no one will believe it.

Pamphilus, warned that his father wants him to marry that day, is greatly troubled. He is put at ease, however, when Davus hears that the approaching marriage to Philumena has been refused by the young woman's father. Chremes has also learned of the affair between Pamphilus and the courtesan's sister. Davus tells Pamphilus to agree to the marriage for the time being. Before long, he reasons, some way out of the predicament will be found.

Charinus meets Davus and Pamphilus and tells them that he is in love with Philumena. Pamphilus says he had no desire to marry the woman and that Charinus is welcome to her. Not knowing the true reason for Pamphilus's assent, Charinus is thrown into despair later when he hears Pamphilus (following Davus's advice) agree to marry Chremes' daughter.

Later, while Pamphilus's father, Simo, and Davus stand before the door of Glycerium's residence, they hear the servants send for a midwife. Simo is angry, thinking that Davus is trying to trick him into believing that Glycerium is having a child by his son. A short time later Glycerium is delivered of a baby boy. When Simo hears the news, he still thinks Davus is trying to trick him and refuses to believe what he has heard.

Meanwhile, Pamphilus waits patiently, believing that no marriage with Chremes' daughter has been arranged. While he waits, however, Simo meets Chremes on the street, and they agree once more to marry their children to each other. When Davus reports the latest development to Pamphilus, the young man is furious. It now seems certain he will never be able to marry the woman he loves. Glycerium, from her confinement bed, sends for Pamphilus to learn what progress he is making in his plans to marry her.

Davus, to prevent the marriage between Pamphilus and Philumena, has Glycerium's maidservant lay the infant on a bed of verbena in front of Simo's door. Chremes comes up the street and sees the child. Davus, pretending that he does not see Chremes, begins to argue with Glycerium's servant. During the argument the fact that the child is the son of Pamphilus and Glycerium is shouted aloud. Chremes storms into Simo's house to withdraw his offer of marriage between Pamphilus and Philumena.

Soon afterward Crito, a cousin of the dead courtesan, comes looking for the house of his dead cousin. As soon as he finds it, he asks the maidservant if Glycerium ever found her parents in Athens. Davus, looking after Pamphilus's interests, overhears the conversation and enters the house.

When Davus leaves the house a few minutes later, he meets Simo, who orders the slave chained and thrown into a dungeon. While Chremes and Simo are talking over the delayed wedding, Pamphilus also leaves the house. After some argument, the young man convinces his father that Crito has proof that Glycerium is an Athenian, and Pamphilus will have to marry her because they have had a child. Pamphilus reenters the house where Glycerium is lodged and emerges presently with Crito.

Chremes immediately recognizes Crito as an acquaintance from Andros. Simo is finally convinced that Crito is an honorable man from that island. Crito then tells how Phania, a citizen of Athens, was shipwrecked on Andros and died there. With the man had been a little girl, whom Phania, as he lay dying, said was his brother's daughter. Chremes then interrupts Crito's story to exclaim that Glycerium must be his own daughter, because Phania had been his brother. When Chremes asks what the girl's name was, Crito says that her name had been changed to Glycerium from Pasibula, which Chremes' recognizes as the name of his long-lost daughter.

Everyone congratulates Chremes on finding his child. Pamphilus reminds his father that there is no barrier to the marriage, since Glycerium, too, is a daughter of Chremes and, according to the law, Pamphilus would have to marry her as her seducer. Chremes, overjoyed, declares that he will give a dowry of ten talents to the bride.

Davus is freed from the dungeon, and Pamphilus tells him all that has occurred. While they speak, Charinus enters, happy that Philumena, the other daughter of Chremes, is now free to be his bride. The father gives ready consent to Charinus's suit and says that his only objection had been a desire to have his family united with Simo's. In addition, he promises that Charinus will receive a large dowry as well as a wife.

Critical Evaluation:

Although *Andria* was Terence's first play, it shows those characteristics for which this dramatist was noted throughout his career. As in all his plays, the action is closely knit, with no digressions, and the comedy is of a more serious turn than popular slapstick humor. The language is natural.

The plot was not new. Terence admits in his prologue that he adapted his drama from two plays by Menander, a Greek dramatist who wrote in the fourth century B.C.E. The story turns, as it does in so many Greek and Latin comedies, on the theme of mistaken identity. The modern reader will be inclined to compare the play to William Shakespeare's *The Comedy of Errors* (pr. c. 1592-1594, pb. 1623), which in turn was freely adapted from Plautus's *Menaechmi* (pr. second century B.C.E.; *The Menaechmi*, 1595). Modern authors have not ceased to adapt from Terence's *Andria*: It was the basis of Sir Richard Steele's *The Conscious Lovers* (pr. 1722, pb. 1723) and Thornton Wilder's novel *The Woman of Andros* (1930).

As Terence's first play, produced in 166 B.C.E., when the author was in his early twenties, *Andria* heralds the direction and concerns of the playwright's later work. Like each of Terence's dramas, this is adapted from the Greek New Comedy, Menander in particular. Among critics there is wide variance of opinion as to how much Terentian comedy owes to the original sources, and since the original sources have been lost, there is no way of settling the dispute. It seems likely, however, that the tone and the use of the double plot are distinctly those of Terence.

If one compares Terence to his only predecessor whose plays have survived, Plautus, there is striking dissimilarity in these two comic playwrights, even though both adapted from Menander and his contemporaries. Plautus is preeminently a man of the stage, ebullient, funny, always ready to sacrifice the logic of plot for the sake of humor and interest. Terence is more the writer than the playwright; a careful craftsman, he is concerned with polished style, character delineation, and a smooth and elegant plot. If he lacks Plautus's vivacity, he is always agreeably humane.

Terence's career itself was remarkable. Born in North Africa, he was brought to Rome as a slave while still a child. His master, Terentius Lucanus, educated him and eventually freed him, which allowed Terence to develop his interest in drama. He was admitted into the aristocratic circle of the Scipios, who were interested in disseminating Greek culture in Rome. As a youthful member, he achieved early success with his plays and encountered the envious spite of the elderly dramatist Lucius Lanuvinus, whom he took pains to answer in his prologues. His career was cut short at about the age of twenty-eight, when he mysteriously disappeared on a trip to Greece. Tradition says that he was lost at sea.

The dramas of Terence, then, are the work of a young man, and they reflect the interests and assumptions of youth. The two primary subjects with which he deals are romance and the relations of sons and fathers, both of these being related in his plots. Generally, his stories center on a double love affair, each of which is thwarted or clandestine usually because of fatherly opposition, and each tends to be resolved satisfactorily. Often there is a clever slave who complicates matters by his deceptions, acting on behalf of one of the young men and against the will of the father.

In *Andria* readers see Terence's initial development of this subject matter. Later works would handle the double plot with greater virtuosity, but this play is fresher and livelier and shows considerable maturity. The reader finds natural, idiomatic dialogue, use of the neat maxim, and appealing, if misguided, characters. *Andria* is the first romantic comedy to come down to modern readers from antiquity and is a precursor of Shakespearean comedy. One thinks of all the double romances in Shakespeare's comedies, and one is struck by the similarities to Terence.

The basic problem in *Andria* is that of getting Simo to consent to Pamphilus's marriage to Glycerium, when Simo has become intent on having his son marry Chremes' daughter, Philumena. The difficulty is that Simo, a forceful old man, believes what he wishes to believe, and he interprets what he sees in terms of his self-delusion. Thus, he pretends a forthcoming marriage between Pamphilus and Philumena to test his son's feelings, but also because he wants it to occur in actuality, since Philumena has birth, wealth, and status, whereas Glycerium has none of these. Threatening the slave Davus, Simo gets support in his mistake, which results in an actual marriage-to-be. This is a calamity for both Pamphilus, who loves Glycerium, and Charinus, who loves Philumena. Having lied successfully, Davus is forced to tell the truth to extricate Pamphilus, and no matter what Davus does, Simo refuses to believe him, insisting obsessively on the marriage. The trouble becomes grave when Simo disowns his son for visiting Glycerium. Everything is settled, however, by a deus-ex-machina ending in which Glycerium's parentage, citizenship, status, and wealth are established. In this plot Simo is the center of the action. His character determines the fates of Davus, Pamphilus, Charinus, and Glycerium. Finally, it is his wish to have his son marry well that must be appeased by the arbitrary ending.

The other characters, while peripheral to Simo, are clearly delineated. Chremes is a sensible old man who wants his daughter to marry happily, in contrast to the deluded Simo, who wants his son to marry, even if unhappily. Pamphilus has a passionate nature like his father, and he ardently cares for Glycerium. Charinus, on the other hand, is theatrical, and one has the impression that his love is make-believe, founded on a desire to marry into status and money. Davus at first secures his own safety by lying and getting Pamphilus to pretend compliance to Simo, but when that backfires, he risks and receives punishment in order to reveal the truth. None of these characters, not even the stubborn ones, is unsympathetic.

In *Andria* age must be respected, no matter how mistaken a father may be. As Terence continued to write, it increasingly becomes youth that must be served, although Terence felt that some restraints must be exercised on the whims of young men. *Andria* has influenced many writers, who borrowed its plot without dissimulation. A great borrower himself, Terence would have felt honored.

"Critical Evaluation" by James Weigel, Jr.

Further Reading

Butler, James H. *The Theatre and Drama of Greece and Rome*. San Francisco: Chandler, 1972. Discusses Terence's defense of the plays he wrote; Terence's works were better received after his lifetime and severely criticized during it. Discusses *Andria* in the context of other works by Terence. Compares the plays of Terence to those of Plautus.

Copley, Frank O. "Terence." In *Latin Literature: From the Beginnings to the Close of the Second Century A.D.* Ann Arbor: University of Michigan Press, 1969. Describes the circumstances in which *Andria* was written and how it was first presented to playwright and critic Caecilius.

Dutsch, Dorota M. *Feminine Discourse in Roman Comedy: On Echoes and Voices*. New York: Oxford University Press, 2008. Analyzes the dialogue of female characters in Terence's plays, noting its use of endearments, softness of speech, and emphasis on small problems. Questions if Roman women actually spoke that way.

Hadas, Moses. *A History of Latin Literature*. New York: Columbia University Press, 1952. Examines how *Andria* was created from two plays of Menander, a classical playwright. Gives a helpful plot line and offers criticism of *Andria*. Discusses circumstances in which the play was presented and produced.

Leigh, Matthew. *Comedy and the Rise of Rome*. New York: Oxford University Press, 2004. Analyzes the comedies of Plautus and Terence, placing them within the context of political and economic conditions in Rome during the third and second centuries B.C.E. Discusses how audiences of that time responded to these comedies.

Segal, Erich, ed. *Oxford Readings in Menander, Plautus, and Terence*. New York: Oxford University Press, 2001. Includes essays on the originality of Terence and his Greek models and on dramatic balance in *Andria*.

Terence. "A Poet Defends Himself: *Andria* I-27." In *Ancient Literary Criticism: The Principal Texts in New Translations*, edited by D. A. Russell and M. Winterbottom. Oxford, England: Clarendon Press, 1972. Discusses Terence's prologue of *Andria*. Claims Terence uses this prologue for literary defense—Terence often used his prologues to defend his works and not merely for an introduction to the plot.

Andromache

Author: Euripides (c. 485-406 B.C.E.)
First produced: c. 426 B.C.E. (English translation, 1782)
Type of work: Drama
Type of plot: Tragedy
Time of plot: About a decade after the Trojan War
Locale: The temple of Thetis in Thessaly

Principal characters:
ANDROMACHE, Hector's widow and slave to Neoptolemus
HERMIONE, the wife of Neoptolemus and daughter of Menelaus
MENELAUS, the king of Sparta
PELEUS, Neoptolemus's grandfather
MOLOSSUS, the son of Andromache and Neoptolemus
ORESTES, Agamemnon's son
THETIS, a goddess and the dead wife of Peleus
CHORUS OF PYTHIAN MAIDENS

The Story:

After the death of Hector and the fall of Troy, Andromache is given as a special prize to Neoptolemus, son of Achilles. As his slave and concubine, she bears a son, Molossus, thereby arousing the jealous wrath of Hermione, Neoptolemus's barren wife. Fearing Hermione's hatred and sensing her doom, Andromache seeks sanctuary in the sacred grounds of the temple of Thetis, after secretly sending her son to a neighbor for safekeeping.

Hermione appears at the temple and accuses Andromache of seeking to oust her, taunting her for bearing a son to Hector's slayer and threatening her with death. Andromache protests that as an aging woman and a helpless slave she would be mad to compete with Hermione and that she herself gracefully accepted Hector's illegitimate children rather than let herself be corrupted by jealousy. Hermione, unmoved by these arguments, leaves the temple, promising to find the bait that would lure Andromache from her sanctuary.

Hermione is true to her word, for soon afterward Menelaus arrives, leading Molossus by the hand. The Spartan king warns Andromache that he will kill the boy on the spot if she does not emerge and offer up her own life instead. Andromache argues with him, pointing out that murder will surely pollute his reputation and that Neoptolemus will never condone the death of his only son. Menelaus is adamant, however, and Andromache emerges from the sanctuary to learn that both she and her son are marked for slaughter. Before the order for execution can be carried out, the aged Peleus appears and, in response to Andromache's supplication, commands that her bonds be loosened. Peleus, furious with Menelaus, denounces Spartan cowardice and treachery; he orders the king to leave Thessaly at once and to take his barren daughter with him. Menelaus, however, announces that he is leaving with his army only in order to vanquish a city hostile to Sparta, after which he will return to confront Neoptolemus himself and settle the matter of his daughter's status in Thessaly.

After everyone leaves the temple, a distraught Hermione enters carrying a sword with which she intends to commit suicide. When her nurse wrests the sword from her, Hermione, in great anguish, laments the horrible deed she plotted and speaks of her fear that Neoptolemus will banish her. Suddenly Orestes appears, claiming that he is merely passing through on his way to the oracle at Dodona. Hermione throws herself at his feet. Orestes was once betrothed to Hermione and always loved her, and he now reveals that he comes to carry her off and is prepared to murder her husband, even if the deed involves sacrilegious treachery. Hermione's taunts at Andromache ironically are now turned upon herself.

After the desperate pair flees, Peleus appears, but before he can question the chorus about the fearful rumors he hears, a messenger brings the sad news that his grandson, Neoptolemus, is dead; he was murdered and mutilated by Orestes and his brigands while praying to the gods in the temple of Phoebus. Neoptolemus's body is then carried in on a bier. The bereaved old Peleus laments the end of his line now that the only son of his only son is dead. Throwing his scepter on the ground, the grieving king resolves to grovel in the dust until his death. At that moment the dim form of the divine Thetis, the goddess who was once his wife, appears, hovering in midair. She commands her husband to cease his mourning and take the body of Neoptolemus to be buried at the Pythian altar as a reproach to the Spartans. She further commands that he take Andromache and Neoptolemus's son to Helenus, whom Andromache will marry so that the line of Peleus can continue. After this mission, Peleus himself will be converted into a god and live with Thetis in the halls of Nereus forever. Peleus consents, moralizing that every prudent man should take heed to marry a wife of noble stock and give his daughter to a good husband.

Critical Evaluation:

Critics have focused their attention on a central problem in *Andromache*: The subject of the drama completely disappears midway through the play. The action falls basically into three stages that are connected only by the slenderest of threads. In the first stage, Andromache provides the focus, as her life and that of her small son are imperiled by Hermione's jealous hatred; in the second, Hermione, beside herself with fear after her plot fails, is rescued by her old lover, Orestes. In the last stage, after Neoptolemus is brutally murdered by Orestes, his aged grandfather Peleus mourns his death until his divine mate, Thetis, appears to comfort him.

Some critics complained of the discontinuous plot structure, but others proposed that the play's episodic plot is compensated for by a unity of theme and characterization. It is suggested, for example, that *Andromache* is a bitter attack on the Spartan national character, particularly on its arrogance, treachery, and ruthlessness. This theory is certainly supported in the first two parts of the play when Andromache, generalizing from the individual wrongs committed against her, denounces all Spartans as liars and cheats, and Hermione's vengefulness and Menelaus's cowardly bullying and bragging nature seem to confirm her judgment. The interpretation is much less convincing, however, when applied to the last portion of the play, since it is never made clear that Orestes is meant to represent Spartan villainy. Other readings see the play variously as a denunciation of slavery, as a dramatization of the political failure of Greek alliances, and as a warning against forced or inadvisable marriages.

Perhaps more convincing than these views, as well as more consistent with the values Euripides expressed in his other dramas, is the interpretation of *Andromache* as a portrayal of the tragedy of war. The theme of war—its trivial causes, its horrible course, and its disastrous aftermath—is everywhere present. Although the Trojan War ended ten years earlier, it continues to dominate the lives of the characters, either directly or indirectly. Andromache combines within herself all the tragic ills suffered by victims of war: She is not only widowed and orphaned but enslaved in the enemy's land. Menelaus, who represents the victors, is shown as worthless and self-serving; leaving the fighting and dying to men such as Achilles, he returns to strut about and reap a hero's reward. Even Orestes, who was not personally involved in the war, is presented as someone whose character is warped by the evil circumstances surrounding the conflict. The Trojan War, as with all wars, produces a multitude of wounds and wrongs. For this reason, the cruel characters of *Andromache* are intent on revenge: Hermione against Andromache; Orestes against his lost betrothal to Hermione; Menelaus against his enemies. Even the kind-hearted Peleus rages against the Athenian enemy, Sparta. In the wake of the ravages of war, friendships are violated, sympathies are forbidden.

Just as *Andromache* was noted for highlighting the tragic effects of the Trojan War, modern critics comment on its characterizations from a feminine perspective. Daniel Junkins, who translated the play in 1998, imagines Andromache as the "fullest female presence"—dignified, expressive, self-contained, serene. Wesley Smith notices the play's focus on the nature of women, contrasting heroic female virtues with cowardly male traits. The martial boasting of the Trojan War is left behind; what remains are the social and domestic issues only hinted at in the Homeric epic. In ancient times Euripides was reputed to be both a misogynist and a feminist, but perhaps he is best considered a realist in probing the nature of male and female relations. The chorus consists of women from Pythia who describe the role and the plight of the female characters. The relationship among Neoptolemus, Hermione, and Andromache is itself an investigation into the nature of marriage and a commentary on the concubinage tolerated in Greek society. As the Greek wife, Hermione would be expected to be portrayed in a favorable light, but in this play the subjugated Trojan Andromache retains the royal virtues she possesses as the wife of Hector. Euripides' sympathies extend even to the lowly female slave whose life is endangered. The critic Loukas Papadimitropoulos finds a unifying theme of the drama to be its various marriages. The Trojan War began over a violation of marriage. Andromache's dignity is reminiscent of her noble and fertile marriage to Hector. Hermione absurdly accuses Andromache of destroying her barren marriage to Neoptolemus, which is savagely and treacherously destroyed by Orestes. The play ends with Peleus's exalted marriage to Thetis. It is in the consequences of war, the consideration of the feminine character, and the displays of marriage that this often unappreciated play reaches its grandeur.

"Critical Evaluation" by Bruce D. Reeves; revised by Howard Bromberg

Further Reading

Aldrich, K. M. *The "Andromache" of Euripides*. Lincoln: University of Nebraska Press, 1961. A detailed analysis of the play. Aldrich makes an argument for the work's unity of plot and of theme.

Allan, William. *The "Andromache" and Euripedean Tragedy.* New York: Oxford University Press, 2000. A thorough analysis of the play, which the author argues deserves a greater degree of critical appreciation than it has received historically.

Euripides. *Andromache.* Translated by Michael Lloyd. 2d ed. Warminster, England: Aris & Phillips, 2005. The text of the play is written in Greek, with the English translation on facing pages. The introduction by Lloyd places the work in its historical and literary context, while his commentary clarifies allusions and references and provides other information that enhances understanding of the play.

Grube, G. M. A. *The Drama of Euripides.* London: Methuen, 1941. A learned, traditional, close reading of the play. Accepts the anti-Spartan tone of the work at face value and sees the characters as lively but not subtle.

Kitto, Humphrey Davy Findley. *Greek Tragedy: A Literary Study.* 1939. Reprint. New York: Routledge, 2002. A classic study of classical tragedy. Argues that *Andromache* is unified in theme but not in plot and that Hermione, Menelaus, and Orestes embody negative Spartan qualities of "arrogance, treachery, and criminal ruthlessness." Expresses admiration for the work's action and characterization.

Kovacs, Paul David. *The "Andromache" of Euripides.* Chico, Calif.: Scholars Press, 1980. Argues against the view that Euripides' tragedies are antiheroic and that they attack traditional attitudes. Instead, Kovacs sees *Andromache* as conventional and close to Sophocles' view of the tragic. Kovacs also disputes the claim that Euripides sides with the Sophists in this play.

Morwood, James. *The Plays of Euripides.* Bristol, England: Bristol Classical, 2002. Morwood provides a concise overview of all of Euripides' plays, devoting a separate chapter to each one. He demonstrates how Euripides was constantly reinventing himself in his work.

Papadimitropoulos, Loukas. "Marriage and Strife in Euripides' *Andromache*." *Greek, Roman, and Byzantine Studies* 46 (2006): 147-158. Finds that the familial relations between the characters is what gives *Andromache* its thematic unity

Vellacott, Philip. *Ironic Drama: A Study of Euripides' Method and Meaning.* New York: Cambridge University Press, 1975. Sees *Andromache* as an indictment of cruelty to women and the horrors of war. Vellacott rejects the view that the play's early episodes are irrelevant to the outcome, maintaining instead that these scenes are essential.

Andromache

Author: Jean Racine (1639-1699)
First produced: Andromaque, 1667; first published, 1668 (English translation, 1674)
Type of work: Drama
Type of plot: Tragedy
Time of plot: Shortly after the end of the Trojan War
Locale: Epirus

Principal characters:
ANDROMACHE, the widow of Hector and the captive of Pyrrhus
PYRRHUS, the king of Epirus and the son of Achilles
HERMIONE, the affianced bride of Pyrrhus and the daughter of Helen
ORESTES, the spurned suitor of Hermione and son of Agamemnon
PYLADES, Orestes's friend and companion

The Story:

Orestes, son of the Greek leader Agamemnon, journeys to Epirus to tell Pyrrhus, king of Epirus, that the Greeks are fearful of Astyanax, the young son of Hector and Andromache. It is believed that Astyanax might someday try to avenge the fall of Troy. Because of the Greeks' fear, Orestes had been sent to Epirus to request that Pyrrhus put Astyanax to death.

Pyrrhus has fallen in love with Andromache, however, and, at first, afraid of losing her love, he refuses to grant the request. To Orestes, who has long loved Hermione, betrothed of Pyrrhus, the news of Pyrrhus's love for Andromache is welcome. Orestes thinks he sees in the situation a chance for him to win Hermione for his wife. Orestes' friend Pylades is amazed, for Orestes had previously sworn that his love for

Hermione had degenerated into hate because she had spurned him.

Pyrrhus refuses to kill Astyanax or turn the child over to the Greeks, so Orestes threatens him. Pyrrhus swears that he will make Epirus a second Troy before he permits the death of Astyanax. Pyrrhus, hoping that his decision will lead her to forget her dead husband, tells Andromache what he has done, but she makes no response to his overtures. Angered, Pyrrhus tells her that unless she marries him the child will die.

Meanwhile, Hermione, spurned by Pyrrhus, is trying to decide whether she loves or hates the king, and whether she wants to flee with Orestes. When Pyrrhus, rebuffed by Andromache, goes to her, they decide that they are still in love. Reconciled to Hermione, Pyrrhus promises to love only her and to give Astyanax to the Greeks.

Hermione, however, changing her mind, prepares to flee with Orestes to inflict punishment on Pyrrhus, after Orestes tells her that Pyrrhus has renewed his suit of Andromache. Pyrrhus returns while they are speaking and announces that he is ready to give the boy to the Greeks because Andromache has again spurned his love and aid.

Convinced that Pyrrhus has decided to marry Hermione only to keep her from her Greek lover, Orestes plots to flee with the girl. Pylades, his friend, agrees to help in the abduction. When Hermione meets Orestes, she speaks only of her approaching marriage to Pyrrhus, whom she still loves. While they talk, Andromache enters the room and begs Hermione to protect Astyanax, whom Pyrrhus has determined to kill. Andromache reminds Hermione that Hector had championed Helen, Hermione's mother, when the Trojans wished to murder her. Hermione refuses to listen and scorns Andromache's request.

Andromache then pleads with Pyrrhus, but Pyrrhus tells her that her plea comes too late. At last, when Andromache vows to kill herself, her vow and tears move the vacillating Pyrrhus, who once again tells her that he will marry her instead of Hermione and champion the boy against the Greeks. Andromache, however, refuses to save her son by marrying her captor and former enemy. After a conference with her waiting-woman, she decides to consult her husband's ghost. The result of that conference is a decision to marry Pyrrhus, thus bringing Astyanax under Pyrrhus's protection, and then to kill herself.

Hermione, furious when she learns that on the following day Pyrrhus intends to marry Andromache, sends for Orestes and tells him that she wants his help in avenging herself on the king. Without promising herself to Orestes, she asks him to kill Pyrrhus during the wedding ceremony.

At first Orestes demurs. Not wishing to become an assassin, he wants to declare war on Pyrrhus and earn glory on the battlefield. At Hermione's urging, however, he finally agrees to the murder. She tells him that it will be easy to commit the crime because the king's guards have been sent to watch over Astyanax and none has been ordered to guard the nuptial ceremonies. She finally adds that after the murder she will become Orestes' bride.

After Orestes leaves, Pyrrhus visits Hermione once more. Hermione, hoping that the king has changed his mind again, sends her serving-woman to tell Orestes not to act until he has further word from her. Pyrrhus, however, has come to tell her only that he intends to marry Andromache, come what will. Hermione vows she will have revenge. (This is her message to Orestes.) Finally, Orestes arrives to inform her that the deed had been done; Pyrrhus died at the hands of Orestes' soldiers.

Hermione, turning on Orestes, declares that she disowns such savagery and will have no more to do with him because he has killed the man she loves. When Orestes argues with her that she persuaded him to commit the murder for her sake, her only defense is that she was distraught at having her love spurned by Pyrrhus and that Orestes should not have listened to her. She rushes out of the room.

Pylades arrives with the Greek warriors to warn Orestes that if they are to escape the wrath of Pyrrhus's subjects, they must take ship and sail away from Epirus at once. The people, they say, are obeying Andromache as their queen. Hermione, too, is dead; she ran into the temple and threw herself on Pyrrhus's body, after stabbing herself. Hearing that news, Orestes turns mad and faints in his agony. His men quickly take him away and make their escape from Epirus.

Critical Evaluation:

Andromache, with its interplay of human passions, its frenzied picture of love turning to fierce jealousy, then to hatred, and finally to madness and crime, began the main cycle of Jean Racine's dramas. Although his earlier plays, *La Thébaïde: Ou, Les Frères ennemis* (pr., pb. 1664; *The Theban Brothers*, 1723) and *Alexandre le Grand* (pr. 1665, pb. 1666; *Alexander the Great*, 1714), established Racine's reputation as a dramatist, *Andromache* is clearly a more sophisticated and mature work.

The French theater of the seventeenth century accepted, on what it thought was the authority of Aristotle, the three unities of time, place, and action. Racine was especially adept at writing a play that adhered to this rule, and he followed the three unities in the composition of *Andromache*. The play takes place in the palace of Pyrrhus at Epirus (unity of place).

Pyrrhus must decide whether or not to give Astaynax to the Greeks; this decision depends on Andromache's acquiescence or refusal to marry him. Andromache's decision will decide her son's fate, as the Greeks will kill him. Pyrrhus's decision has major importance for Hermione, who will either be rejected or become his bride. Thus the play's action is unified around Pyrrhus's decision and radiates out in a circular pattern always governed by the central problem of Pyrrhus's decision (unity of action).

The action is easily contained in twenty-four hours (unity of time). A classical tragedy demands a subject matter taken from antiquity; contemporary events are unacceptable. Racine strictly follows this rule. The rules of French classical tragedy also require that plays be written in Alexandrine verse, a twelve-syllable verse with the caesura (pause) after the sixth syllable. Racine is an absolute master of this verse form.

Although Racine had already written other successful plays, such as *Alexander the Great*, *Andromache* is his first play that portrays the fatalistic aspect of passion. The deterministic philosophy present in the Greek legends and plays from which Racine took the subjects of his plays already had been part of Racine's way of thinking. Having been orphaned and having spent three years of his early life at Port Royal with the Jansenists, Racine had been imbued with a sense of fatalistic destiny, of sin and damnation. His characters, especially girls and women, are caught in a devastating destiny from which they cannot escape. In his plays, Racine portrays their suffering and agony in their state of hopelessness. In *Bérénice* (pr. 1670, pb. 1671; English translation, 1676) and *Phèdre* (pr., pb. 1677; *Phaedra*, 1701), Racine continues to perfect his portrayal of the agony of fatalistic passion. This concentration upon fatalistic passion makes Racine's female characters the central characters of his plays.

The center of the action in *Andromache* is the question of Pyrrhus's decision in regard to Astyanax. However, Pyrrhus's decision is dependent upon Andromache's decision to marry him or not. Thus, Andromache actually stands at the center of the action. It is also Andromache, not Pyrrhus, who is faced with the tragic dilemma. If she refuses to marry Pyrrhus, her son will die; if she marries Pyrrhus, she will have married the son of Achilles, the man who had killed her husband, Hector, and will consequently degrade and betray the memory of Hector. Although all four of the main characters—Pyrrhus, Andromache, Orestes, and Hermione—are victims of a fatalistic passion, it is Andromache's decision that will determine the denouement of the play. Hermione, desperately in love with Pyrrhus, is helpless to prevent the marriage of Andromache and Pyrrhus; although he may win Hermione by killing Pyrrhus, Orestes cannot eradicate her passion for Pyrrhus. Racine's play presents a complex intertwining of suffering, violence, and death, the inevitable results of fatalistic passion.

Racine's female characters face the most difficult decisions and control the action of the play. Although, given the deterministic orientation of the play's subject matter and the overwhelming role of fate in the action, the control that the women exercise is really an illusion created both for them and for the audience. It is, however, this illusion of control that gives the play its interest and intensity. Andromache's decision will decide the fate of her son. Her marriage to Pyrrhus will save him; her refusal will cause his death. However, her acceptance of marriage will destroy her loyalty to the memory of her dead husband. Andromache believes that she can save her son and maintain her loyalty to Hector's memory by committing suicide after the marriage. Fate has it otherwise, as Pyrrhus is murdered by Orestes' soldiers. Andromache is recognized as the queen and now must call for vengeance for Pyrrhus's murder.

Hermione's situation is different. She is being forced into the role of the rejected woman. She cannot influence Pyrrhus's decision. With the character of Hermione, Racine portrays the psychology of the woman discarded by the man she loves. Hermione's love turns to hatred, and she desires vengeance; yet she recoils from the vision of Pyrrhus's death. Hermione cannot escape her love for Pyrrhus. There is no satisfactory solution for her in life. Fate also takes control from Hermione as Orestes' soldiers murder Pyrrhus. At the end of the play, she joins Pyrrhus in death.

Racine's play is totally dependent upon verbal expression; it is a play of psychological analysis rather than of physical action and happenings. In keeping with the rules of unity and the *bienséances* (decorum and proprieties) demanded by the genre, none of the action, such as the murder of Pyrrhus, is actually done on stage; it is recounted by one of the characters. What is actually presented on the stage is the agony of the individual characters struggling with their unwanted destinies. Racine delves into the souls of his characters and then verbally portrays their emotional and mental struggles.

This focus on verbal expression rather than physical action makes the confidant one of the most essential characters in Racine's tragedies. The confidant is a maidservant in the case of the female characters and may be either a manservant or a very close friend in the case of the male characters. The confidants serve two purposes: They provide trusted and loyal listeners and give the audience access to the thoughts of the main characters. In addition, the confidants bring crucial information to the main characters and thus move the action along.

With Racine, French classical tragedy reaches its point of perfection. Although playwrights of the eighteenth century had continued to write classical tragedies, none of these plays equal the works of Racine.

Racine's work has been critical to the continuing development of French literature. An exceptional psychological poet, his analysis of his characters and portrayal of their inner lives provide the foundations for the psychological portrayals found in the works of French writers such as Guy de Maupassant, Colette, and André Gide.

"Critical Evaluation" by Bruce D. Reeves; revised by Shawncey Webb

Further Reading

Campbell, John. *Questioning Racinian Tragedy.* Chapel Hill: University of North Carolina Press, 2005. Examines individual tragedies, including *Andromache*, and questions if Racine's plays have common themes and techniques that constitute a unified concept of Racinian tragedy.

Cloonan, William J. *Racine's Theatre: The Politics of Love.* University, Miss.: Romance Monographs, 1977. Examines the profound unhappiness of the four principal characters in *Andromache*. Explores the destructive nature of Pyrrhus's egotistical desire to dominate Andromache, and examines the violence and irrational behavior of Orestes and Hermione.

Desnain, Véronique. *Hidden Tragedies: The Social Construction of Gender in Racine.* New Orleans, La.: University Press of the South, 2002. Analyzes *Andromache* and four other plays from a feminist perspective. Argues that the strength of Racine's plays are not their universality but their emphasis on gender differences, with different standards imposed on men and women.

France, Peter. *Racine's Rhetoric.* Oxford, England: Clarendon Press, 1965. An insightful analysis that examines Racine's skill in using classical rhetorical devices to create many effective psychological tragedies. Discusses the portrayal of passion and solitude in *Andromache.*

Racevskis, Roland. *Tragic Passages: Jean Racine's Art of the Threshold.* Lewisburg, Pa.: Bucknell University Press, 2008. Examines *Andromache* and Racine's other secular tragedies, demonstrating how these works construct space, time, and identity. Argues that the characters in these plays are in various stages of limbo, suspended between the self and the other, onstage and offstage, life and death, and that the plays emphasize this predicament of being "in-between."

Turnell, Martin. *Jean Racine: Dramatist.* London: Hamish Hamilton, 1972. Contains a good introduction to Racine's eleven tragedies and also includes a lengthy, but dated, bibliography of major critical studies on Racine. The chapter on *Andromache* examines representations of love and violence and the psychological complexity of its four principal characters.

Angela's Ashes
A Memoir

Author: Frank McCourt (1930-2009)
First published: 1996
Type of work: Memoir
Type of plot: Autobiographical
Time of plot: 1930-1949
Locale: New York City; Toome, Dublin, and Limerick, Ireland

Principal personages:
FRANK MCCOURT, the narrator
ANGELA SHEEHAN MCCOURT, his mother
MALACHY MCCOURT, his father
MALACHY,
MICHAEL, and
ALPHONSUS (ALPHIE), his younger brothers
EUGENE,
OLIVER, and
MARGARET, his deceased siblings
MARGARET SHEEHAN, his maternal grandmother
PAT "THE ABBOT" SHEEHAN, his uncle
AGGIE KEATING, his aunt
PA KEATING, his uncle
LEMAN GRIFFIN, Angela's cousin

The Story:

Frank McCourt's parents emigrate to New York separately in the late 1920's, looking for work. McCourt's father, Malachy McCourt, was from Toome, County Antrim, Ireland, and his mother, Angela Sheehan, was from Limerick. They had five children while living in New York: Francis (Frank; b. 1930), Malachy (b. 1931), Eugene and Oliver (b. 1932), and Margaret (b. 1935).

The family experiences hardship in New York because their father is unemployed and constantly drunk, and they are starving. Frank notes a distinct difference in the temperament of his father and in the climate of the house generally when his father brings home wages, a rare event. Margaret dies unexpectedly, and Angela goes into a deep depression. The family returns to Ireland and, since they are unwelcome among the McCourts in Toome and the Irish Republican Army (IRA) in Dublin, they go to Limerick, where Grandma Margaret Sheehan helps Angela find and temporarily pay for a furnished room for them all.

Soon after returning to Limerick, Angela loses the baby that she is carrying, Malachy goes on the dole, and they receive public assistance. Oliver dies, and the family moves to a new flat. Frank and Malachy attend Leamy's National School. Angela is severely depressed, and Malachy tends to the children. Eugene dies of pneumonia six months after Oliver, and the McCourt family moves to a flat that is directly beside the only lavatory serving the entire lane. At Christmas, they have a pig's head for dinner.

Michael is born in 1936. Representatives of the St. Vincent de Paul Society come to investigate whether the family has a genuine need for assistance. They determine that the situation is deplorable at the McCourt house.

On Frank's First Communion Day, he is excited for the Collection, where he will be able to go to all of his relatives and collect money as gifts. He is very ill after Mass and misses the Collection, but is still able to see a film. Malachy, Sr., decides that Frank needs to learn the Latin Mass and teaches it to him so that he can be an altar boy, but the church turns Frank away. Angela has another boy named Alphonsus (Alphie) in 1940. Malachy drinks away the baby's baptismal present money, and Frank feels torn about his feelings for his father when he is sober versus when he is drunk.

Immediately after being confirmed, Frank contracts typhoid fever and spends three and a half months in the hospital. There, he meets a girl named Patricia Madigan, who later dies of diphtheria, and she introduces him to Shakespeare. When Frank goes back to school, he is put in his younger brother Malachy's class until he writes a composition titled "Jesus and the Weather," which allows him to return back to his proper class. Frank begins to talk of going to America when he is older.

Things are changing in the lanes because of World War II. English factories need workers, and Angela will not have more babies, so Malachy goes to England to work but does not send money back home. They are penniless and again must go on public assistance.

Frank has an eye infection and returns to the hospital for a month. When he is released, Angela goes into the hospital with pneumonia. The children stay with Aunt Aggie and Uncle Pa until Malachy briefly returns and Angela gets out of the hospital. Malachy sends a money order for three pounds from England, but that is the last time he sends money to his family. The family again goes on relief, and Frank is humiliated to see his mother begging at the priest's house for a scrap of food.

Frank gets a short-lived job with Mr. Hannon on the coal float and earns the respect of the boys at school. Malachy comes home at Christmas, stays a few days, and never returns. Destitute, Angela and the boys go to live with Angela's cousin, Laman Griffin, who dislikes the boys and begins an affair with Angela. Frank's teacher, Mr. O'Halloran, tells Angela that Frank should continue his education at high school and attend a university, but the Christian brothers will not accept him and he never attends high school.

Frank reaches puberty and is preoccupied with his body. He gets into a fight with Laman Griffin, who strikes him. Frank then lives with Uncle Pat, who has a house to himself since Grandma recently died. Aunt Aggie, in an uncharacteristic act of kindness, buys Frank new clothes and shoes for work. Frank earns one pound a week at as a telegram boy and saves up money from each check to fund passage to America. Angela and the boys move into Uncle Pat's house, and Frank begins to support the family.

On the job, Frank loses his virginity to Theresa Carmody, who later dies of tuberculosis and leaves Frank heartbroken. He then meets Mrs. Finucane and works for her at night as a letter-writing debt collector. Malachy is absent when Frank turns sixteen, so Uncle Pa buys him his first pint of ale. Frank gets drunk and slaps Angela because of Laman Griffin. The next day, he confesses his sins to a Franciscan friar, who tells him that God forgives him but he needs to forgive himself.

Frank works for Eason's and Mrs. Finucane until he is almost nineteen. By this time, Angela is working for an old man and Malachy, Jr., shovels coal with Uncle Pa. Mrs. Finucane dies, and Frank helps himself to some of her money. With it, he finally has enough money to leave, so Frank books passage on the *Irish Oak*, arrives in America, and agrees with a shipmate that America is a great country.

Critical Evaluation:

A teacher at the prestigious Stuyvesant High School in Manhattan before writing *Angela's Ashes*, Frank McCourt became a phenomenon when the book was published in 1996. His memoir won the 1997 Pulitzer Prize for biography or autobiography, the American Booksellers Book of the Year award, and the *Los Angeles Times* Book Prize, among others. A film adaptation was released in 1999. McCourt's other books, *'Tis* (1999), *Teacher Man* (2005), and *Angela and the Baby Jesus* (2007), were well received but not as assiduously embraced as *Angela's Ashes*. McCourt also authored two musical reviews, *A Couple of Blaguards* (pr. 1984; cowritten with Malachy McCourt, Jr.) and *The Irish and How They Got That Way* (pr. 1997). He died in 2009.

A characteristic element of *Angela's Ashes* is the voice of the narrator, who provides a brutally honest depiction of a family in crisis. McCourt's story begins from the vantage point of a four-year-old boy, and, as he ages, he utilizes more sophisticated observational skills and vocabulary, always in the present tense, to display his growing worldview. This narrative device is reminiscent of the technique used by James Joyce in *A Portrait of the Artist as a Young Man* (serial 1914-1915, book 1916), but it is typically one that is not sustained through the entirety of an autobiographical narrative. By the final chapter, the memoir's viewpoint is that of a young man keenly aware of nuance, with a highly developed sense of humor and a clear understanding of hypocrisy in his society.

McCourt's use of language, with its musical quality and picturesque imagery, creates a landscape unique to the book. He interweaves both comedy and tragedy with Irish language constructions, particularly the dialects and phrases of Northern Ireland and Limerick, to make readers participants, rather than observers, in the action.

Written as a series of remembrances, the anecdotes making up *Angela's Ashes* have no cohesive plot line to tie them together, but they gain some unity from the developing maturity of the narrative voice. While the book focuses on the ravages of savage poverty in Limerick, another equally important theme is Frank's belief in the American Dream—the idea that one can change one's fate through hard work—and his determination to realize it. Other pervasive ideas are the failed example of manhood as perpetuated by Frank's father, the need for respect of his mother, and the notion of a seemingly inadequate self confronting others. The publication of *Angela's Ashes* coincided with a new spirit of openness in Irish society, particularly in regard to the abuses of the past, and helped augur a new era that welcomed the voices of those previously silenced.

Valerie Murrenus Pilmaier

Further Reading

Lynch, Patricia A., Joachim Fischer, and Brian Coates, eds. *Back to the Present, Forward to the Past: Irish Writing and History Since 1798*. New York: Rodopi, 2006. Includes three scholarly essays on *Angela's Ashes*, constituting one of the largest collections of scholarly articles on the book in one source.

O'Brien, George. "The Last Word: Reflections on *Angela's Ashes*." In *New Perspectives on the Irish Diaspora*, edited by Charles Fanning. Carbondale: Southern Illinois University Press, 2000. Double-layered study of the importance of "having the last word," both as a goal of characters within McCourt's memoir and as a goal of McCourt himself in writing it.

Phelan, James. *Living to Tell About It: A Rhetoric and Ethics of Character Narration*. Ithaca, N.Y.: Cornell University Press, 2005. This study of narrative by a leading scholar of narrative theory includes a chapter on unreliable and restricted narration in *Angela's Ashes*.

Potts, Donna. "Sacralizing the Secular in Frank McCourt's *Angela's Ashes*." *Studies: An Irish Quarterly Review* 88 (Autumn, 1999): 284-294. Suggests that the young McCourt rejects the repressive Catholicism surrounding him in favor of a religious zeal for America and all things American.

Robinson, Fred Miller. "The One Way Out: Limerick and *Angela's Ashes*." *New Hibernia Review / Iris Éireannach Nua: A Quarterly Record of Irish Studies* 4, no. 2 (Summer, 2000): 9-25. Provides a fascinating study of Limerick, contrasting the town at the turn of the twenty-first century to its situation at the time that McCourt and his family lived there. Provides helpful background information about the Limerick mores that Frank had to reject to make it to America.

Angels and Insects
Two Novellas

Author: A. S. Byatt (Antonia Susan Drabble, 1936-)
First published: 1992; includes *Morpho Eugenia* and *Conjugial Angel*
Type of work: Novellas
Type of plot: Historical
Time of plots: 1860-1863 and 1875
Locale: Bredley Hall and Margate, England

Principal characters:
WILLIAM ADAMSON, an entomologist
EUGENIA ALABASTER, an Alabaster daughter
EDGAR ALABASTER, Eugenia's brother
THE REVEREND HARALD ALABASTER, Eugenia's father
LADY GERTRUDE ALABASTER, Eugenia's stepmother
ROWENA ALABASTER, Eugenia's sister
MATTY CROMPTON, governess to the younger Alabaster children
SOPHY SHEEKHY, a medium
LILIAS PAPAGAY, Sophy's benefactor
CAPTAIN ARTURO PAPAGAY, Lilias's lost husband
ARTHUR HENRY HALLAM, a poet
ALFRED, LORD TENNYSON, a poet
CAPTAIN RICHARD JESSE, a séance attendee
MRS. EMILY TENNYSON JESSE, Captain Jesse's wife, who had been engaged to Hallam
MR. HAWKE, a minister and spiritualist
MRS. HEARNSHAW, a séance attendee and a grieving mother

The Story:

Morpho Eugenia opens with entomologist William Adamson watching a ball hosted by his benefactors, the Alabasters. Adamson watches the ball as his mind jumps back to the last ten years he spent collecting natural items as well as traveling about South America and the eventual shipwreck that lost most of his collection. He dances with Eugenia Alabaster and is entranced by her delicate beauty, but he also notes her unhappiness. Adamson learns that Eugenia's fiancé, Captain Hunt, has recently committed suicide.

Eugenia's father, the Reverend Harald Alabaster, who has

in the past purchased Adamson's collections of exotic butterflies, moths, and other insects, offers to provide Adamson the job of sorting his extensive collection of specimens. Despite wanting to go on another expedition to South America, Adamson accepts the job because he is penniless, and because the reverend promises to fund Adamson's next trip.

Adamson dislikes sorting through the reverend's disarrayed collection, but he is happy to be part of the Alabaster household to catch glimpses of Eugenia. He falls in love with her but hesitates to tell her because of their class difference, which makes marriage unlikely. When Eugenia's younger sister, Rowena, becomes engaged, the Alabaster family worries about Eugenia's already fragile emotional state, given that she should be married before her younger sister.

Adamson converts the reverend's conservatory to a butterfly garden by carefully collecting butterfly and moth pupae. When they hatch and surround Eugenia, Adamson proposes. To Adamson's surprise, the reverend consents and ignores the class difference between Adamson and his daughter, as long as Adamson agrees to engage in intellectual discussion on the topics of creationism and human origins. Adamson finds these debates monotonous because he disagrees with the reverend's religious beliefs.

Adamson and Eugenia's marriage begins a repetitive cycle in which Eugenia is seen only briefly by Adamson and disappears into what Adamson calls the "world of women" during her pregnancies and periods of confinement after the birth of each child. To fill the time and abate the loneliness, Adamson begins spending time in the schoolroom with the younger Alabaster children and their caretaker, Matty Crompton.

While working to create an indoor insect community, Matty and Adamson write a book chronicling the lives of the local ant population and soon develop a friendship. Matty also publishes her own collection of short stories.

Adamson is called to the house one afternoon by a servant who claims that Eugenia needs him. When he enters Eugenia's bedroom, Adamson witnesses her having an incestuous relationship with her brother, Edgar. Eugenia explains that her relationship with Edgar stems back to childhood, and that despite trying to end the relationship when she became engaged to Captain Hunt, the relationship had continued. After learning about the incest, her then-fiancé, Captain Hunt, had committed suicide. Adamson now doubts that he is the father of his children, all of whom favor the Alabaster side of the family in physical appearance.

After confiding to Matty about Eugenia and Edgar's relationship, Adamson discovers that Matty and the servants already know about it. In hopes of traveling to South America, Matty has already booked passage on a boat for her and Adamson to leave together. After some reluctance to take her, Adamson agrees. He leaves the Alabaster home without taking any compensation from the family. He feels a profound sense of freedom. Before leaving, he tells Eugenia that she must find a way to live with the consequences of having sex with her brother.

Conjugial Angel begins with séances led by the medium Sophy Sheekhy. In attendance are Sophy's benefactor Lilias Papagay, Captain Richard Jesse and Mrs. Jesse, Mr. Hawke, and Mrs. Hearnshaw, who all hope to communicate with dead loved ones. Grief has shaped and directed the lives of all of the women who attend the séances. Mr. Hawke's attendance is out of spiritual and intellectual interest based on his devotion to the teachings of the Swedish philosopher, theologian, and scientist Emanuel Swedenborg.

At one séance, Mrs. Hearnshaw receives a spiritual message, and the attendees determine that the message is from her five daughters, all of whom had died shortly after birth. The message reveals that Mrs. Hearnshaw is pregnant with a sixth child, a child that the spirits of her dead children claim will live. The spirits even provide a name for the new baby. Mrs. Hearnshaw has not yet told her husband of her new pregnancy, and the group eagerly attempts communication with the spirit world again.

The second spiritual message is received as segments of Alfred, Lord Tennyson's poem *In Memoriam* (1850). The group assumes the messages are directed at Mrs. Jesse, whose dead fiancé, English poet Arthur Henry Hallam, is the subject of Tennyson's poem. The group interprets the message as an accusation from Hallam that Mrs. Jesse had been unfaithful to him by marrying Captain Jesse after Hallam's death.

After receiving this message, Mrs. Jesse is overcome with guilt about her marriage to Captain Jesse. Hallam's family has maintained friendship and financial support of Mrs. Jesse, even after Hallam's death. Despite having waited nine years to marry Captain Jesse, she has been labeled as insensitive and unappreciative. She struggles with her fear of loneliness. She also has begun to realize that Tennyson's grief over Hallam's death had been stronger and longer lived than her own grief.

At the end of the séance, Mr. Hawke escorts Mrs. Papagay and Sophy home. Once there, Mr. Hawke begins to propose to Mrs. Papagay, who has been expecting the proposal. Mrs. Papagay still loves her assumed-to-be-deceased husband, Captain Arturo Papagay, who had been lost at sea. A marriage to Mr. Hawke would remedy her loneliness and her financial problems. Mr. Hawke, however, botches the proposal by falling on Mrs. Papagay, and he leaves awkwardly before she can respond.

Alone in her room at Mrs. Papagay's home, Sophy enters a trance and is joined by the suffering spirit of poet John Keats. She comforts the anguished spirit and recites poetry. She sees a vision of a hand buttoning a nightshirt, and the story switches to the perspective of Tennyson. Now an old man wrestling with his feelings for Hallam, Tennyson relives his emotions and tries to understand the deep connection he had with Hallam. Tennyson tries to convince himself that he had felt only a keen sense of friendship and had not been romantically attracted to Hallam, despite referring to himself as Hallam's widow and acknowledging that his attachment and feelings had been returned by him.

The group assembles for the next séance. Sophy receives a message for Mrs. Jesse from a spirit assumed by everyone to be Hallam. The spirit claims that he and Mrs. Jesse will be united in death. Mrs. Jesse furiously rejects this idea, surprising Captain Jesse, who has always felt that Mrs. Jesse does not love him as much as she had loved Hallam. Mrs. Jesse moves past her grief and guilt over her marriage by rejecting the idea that she will be joined to Hallam after death, and decides to end the séance.

On the way back to their home, Mrs. Papagay and Sophy are followed by an unidentified man. They stop and are joined by Captain Papagay, alive and well despite being presumed dead. Sophy pictures each of her séance attendees moving past their grief, noting that sometimes, literally, there is life after death.

Critical Evaluation:

In *Morpho Eugenia*, A. S. Byatt weaves into the story of the secret lives of Victorian England an intellectual dialogue that represents the most important debates of the period. Through the character of the Reverend Alabaster, the debate between creationism and evolution is highlighted by the ways Victorians faced the issue, which affected every fiber of social, religious, intellectual, and scientific life. Byatt presents this controversy through the eyes of the Victorians while still making the debate current and relevant to the development of the novella's central characters and themes.

Byatt captures the obsessive desire of Victorians to collect and possess the natural world. Adamson's entomological interest becomes an analogy of Adamson's own life in the home of the Alabasters. Matty Crompton serves as the voice of feminism in the novella. Independent and determined to live her life the way she wants rather than the way she is told, Matty is an interesting contrast to Eugenia, who claims that her behavior with her brother had been an attempt to break social rules for acceptable behavior. Matty succeeds in breaking through the social repression, while Eugenia's attempt to do so is at the expense of Adamson and Captain Hunt.

Conjugial Angel thematically centers on experimentation. The characters participate in a séance and attempt to reconcile their traditions with their experimentations. Mrs. Papagay, Tennyson, and Mrs. Jesse are all at different stages in their struggles between their own desires and their need to conform socially and sexually. Mrs. Papagay and Mrs. Jesse exemplify this contrast, raising feminist issues in the text.

The novella questions life after death and the existence of a spiritual affinity between two people. By examining these questions, Byatt once again mingles an important Victorian intellectual debate into her storytelling. The séances serve not only as narrative techniques but also as imaginative depictions of the Victorian interest in spiritualism, the occult, and the afterlife.

Conjugial Angel also is a memoriam to Tennyson, just as Tennyson's *In Memoriam* memorializes Arthur Hallam. Byatt's fiction also can be read as simultaneously Victorian, postmodern, and contemporary, raising important questions of genre.

Holly Sprinkle

Further Reading

Adams, Ann Marie. "'Reader, I Memorialized Him': A. S. Byatt's Representation of Alfred, Lord Tennyson in *The Conjugial Angel*." *LIT: Literature, Interpretation, Theory* 19, no. 1 (2008): 26-46. Explains the role of Alfred, Lord Tennyson, as both character and poet in Byatt's *The Conjugial Angel*.

Alfer, Alexa, and Michael J. Noble, eds. *Essays on the Fiction of A. S. Byatt*. Westport, Conn.: Greenwood Press, 2001. For the advanced student of Byatt. This volume includes at least one essay on each of her major works. Includes an index and a select bibliography.

Kelly, Kathleen Coyne. *A. S. Byatt*. New York: Twayne, 1996. Part of a well-established series of introductions to literary figures, this volume includes a chronology, an annotated bibliography, a biographical sketch, and a commentary on Byatt's individual works, including the novellas in *Angels and Insects*.

Levenson, Michael. "*Angels and Insects*: Theory, Analogy, Metamorphosis." In *Essays on the Fiction of A. S. Byatt: Imagining the Real*, edited by Alexa Alfer and Michael J. Noble. Westport, Conn.: Greenwood Press, 2001. Discussion of the prominent themes of the work. Part of a collection of essays exploring Byatt's fictional works as types of realism.

Pearce, Margaret. "*Morpho Eugenia*: Problems with the Male Gaze." *Critique: Studies in Contemporary Fiction* 40, no. 4 (1999): 399-411. An explanation of the issues of gender and feminism raised by the male narrator who presents himself as the center of the story.

Reynolds, Margaret, and Jonathan Noakes. *A. S. Byatt: The Essential Guide*. New York: Random House, 2004. Provides a close reading of Byatt's novels and novellas, a well-developed interview with Byatt, and a thorough discussion of themes and techniques.

Shuttleworth, Sally. "Writing Natural History: *Morpho Eugenia*." In *Essays on the Fiction of A. S. Byatt: Imagining the Real*, edited by Alexa Alfer. Westport, Conn: Greenwood Press, 2001. An examination of the role that naturalism plays in *Morpho Eugenia*. Part of a collection of essays exploring Byatt's fictional works as types of realism.

Williamson, Andrew. "'The Dead Man Touch'd Me from the Past': Reading as Mourning, Mourning as Reading in A. S. Byatt's *The Conjugial Angel*." *Neo-Victorian Studies* 1 (2008): 110-137. Explores the séance as a motif that correlates spirituality with reading and writing.

Angels in America
A Gay Fantasia on National Themes

Author: Tony Kushner (1956-   )
First produced: Part One: Millennium Approaches (1991), *Part Two: Perestroika* (1992); first published, *Part One* (1992), *Part Two* (1993; revised, 1996)
Type of work: Drama
Type of plot: Political
Time of plot: 1985-1990
Locale: New York

Principal characters:
PRIOR WALTER, a man living with AIDS
LOUIS IRONSON, Prior's lover, a Marxist
ROY M. COHN, a conservative attorney
JOE PITT, chief clerk of a Federal Appeals Court, and a Mormon
HARPER PITT, Joe's wife
HANNAH PITT, Joe's mother
BELIZE, a nurse and a former drag queen
MR. LIES, a travel agent
THE ANGEL

The Story:

Conservative attorney Roy M. Cohn offers court clerk Joe Pitt a job in Washington, D.C., with the U.S. Justice Department, but Joe has to discuss the job offer with his wife, Harper. Often consumed by fantasies and fears, Harper hides in her home. When she wants to travel, a travel agent named Mr. Lies magically appears to her and offers to take her anywhere she wants. After Joe returns home, he and Harper fight about going to Washington. They also fight about her emotional problems and about the secrets he keeps from her.

Prior Walter reveals to his lover, Louis Ironson, that he has a cancerous lesion, a sign of advancing complications from acquired immunodeficiency syndrome, or AIDS. Prior jokes about it, but he fears that Louis might leave him. In truth, Louis does not know if he can stay with Prior to watch him die. One day, Joe finds Louis crying in the men's room at the Brooklyn Federal Courthouse. Louis thinks Joe is gay and is surprised when Joe denies it.

Prior and Joe's wife, Harper, are in each other's dreams. In the dreams, Prior tells Harper that her husband is gay, and Harper tells Prior that deep inside, he is free of disease. For the first time, Prior hears a mysterious angelic voice call to him. Later, Harper asks her husband, Joe, if he is gay, but Joe insists he fights all his "indecent" desires. His behavior is correct, and that is all that matters.

Told that he, too, has AIDS, Roy threatens to destroy his doctor if he says "Roy Cohn is a homosexual." For Roy, "homosexual" does not mean what it seems to mean. It does not explain who has sex with whom; rather, it describes one's status and one's power. Homosexuals have no clout, but Roy has clout. He could talk to the president or the president's wife at any time. Roy has sex with men, but he reasons that because he is not homosexual, he does not have AIDS. The doctor advises Roy that an experimental drug called AZT might help him, but the drug has a two-year waiting list. Roy will have to call the president for help.

Prior becomes violently ill, and Louis, hysterical, takes him to the hospital. Afraid, Louis leaves him there. Joe tells Roy about his marital problems. Roy, who reveals that he is dying, passes this wisdom to Joe. Roy says that love is a trap, that responsibility is a trap, and that Joe should not be afraid to live alone.

Roy, who has been threatened with disbarment, wants Joe to take a job at the Justice Department so that he might protect Roy from his enemies. Roy's enemies include the fancy lawyers with corporate clients who need the goodwill of the department. If he worked at the department, Joe could pressure these lawyers to leave Roy alone. Joe knows that this is unethical. An angry Roy tells Joe that ethics does not matter in the world of politics.

Joe and Louis fall in love. They feel that they are caught between their duty to love and their duty to themselves. Both fear and want freedom. They are children of the age: selfish, greedy, loveless, and blind. They become lovers, and Louis leaves Prior, saying he has to be free. Joe tells Harper that he has no sexual feelings for her. Harper, who is now heartbroken, asks Mr. Lies to take her to Antarctica.

Late at night, Joe calls his mother, Hannah Pitt, who lives in Utah, and tells her he is gay. Angry, she tells him to go home to his wife. Hannah sells her house and travels to New York. In a vision, two of Prior's dead ancestors tell him that he has been chosen by the Angel. He then sees a huge book drop from the heavens and, more and more, feels doomed, as if something is following him.

Roy calls Joe a sissy when he refuses the Washington job. Joe wants to be nice, but he has to choose between being nice and being effective, as Roy had been in getting spy Ethel Rosenberg executed for treason. As Roy collapses in pain, the ghost of Ethel Rosenberg appears to watch him suffer. Roy rages at her, refusing to give in.

With great fanfare, the Angel appears to Prior. God, fascinated by humanity's ability to evolve, change, and progress, had become bored with angels and had abandoned Heaven on the same date as the San Francisco earthquake of 1906. Prior is to tell humanity to stop moving and changing, so that God might perhaps return.

Harper's fantasy of Antarctica eventually ends and, back in reality, she is rescued by Hannah Pitt. Hannah, after being lost in the Bronx, has found Harper's apartment.

A hospitalized Roy insults a nurse, Belize, but she fights back. Belize gives Roy medical advice, and when Roy asks why he should trust Belize, the nurse answers that unlike Roy's doctors, Belize knows that Roy is gay. When Roy gets his AZT, he shares it with Belize, but only after goading the nurse into insulting him.

At a local Mormon center, Prior and Harper watch a diorama of a pioneer Mormon family. The father looks just like Joe. When they see Louis enter the diorama and take Joe away with him, Harper and Prior feel they are going crazy. Harper asks the Mormon woman in the diorama how people change; she answers that God slits them open, squeezes their insides, and leaves them to heal themselves.

At Jones Beach, Louis tells Joe about gay life and sex before AIDS. Although Joe says he loves Louis, Louis misses Prior and Joe feels guilty about Harper. Louis admits that he never accounts for love in his theories. Joe suggests that being selfish is sometimes the most generous thing one can do.

Louis asks Prior for forgiveness, but Prior refuses. Angry that Louis has abandoned him and betrayed him with a Mormon Republican, Prior tells Louis to come back when he has visible wounds. Roy, remembering the Bible stories his mother told him, gives Joe his blessing. When Joe confesses his homosexuality, Roy orders him to go back to his wife and never speak of it again.

Belize tells Louis that Joe is Roy's protégé. Louis cannot accept it: Roy is, to Louis, the most evil man in the world. Belize hates Louis' idealistic notions about America. For him, Roy Cohn is America: terminal, crazy, and mean.

Hannah has no sympathy for her son. Joe has been running away all his life, and he is still running. Joe and Harper try to reconcile, but Joe cannot hide his sexuality. Harper knows that she will leave Joe. Meanwhile, Joe tries to return to Louis, but Louis, who has researched the legal decisions Joe has written, attacks him for the immoral way he manipulates the law. Joe tries to defend his politics but finally becomes so angry that he beats Louis.

The ghost of Ethel Rosenberg brings Roy the news of his disbarment. Having long hated him, Ethel relishes his defeat. Roy, pretending to be delirious, tricks Ethel into singing him a Yiddish song. Mocking her, Roy claims victory even as he dies.

Prior, on Hannah's advice, wrestles the Angel. When he wins, the Angel takes him to Heaven, to the council of angels. Prior tells them that humanity cannot stop changing, for that is what living things do. He cannot bring God back. Prior believes that if God does come back, then humanity should sue him for abandoning them and for all the horrible things that had happened in the terrible twentieth century. Although the angels say that the future will be terrible, Prior wants more life. Humanity is addicted to life, no matter how painful.

Belize insists that Louis say the Kaddish for Roy, that their enemy be forgiven. Louis does not know the Hebrew prayer, but Ethel gives him the words. Roy, in the afterlife, offers to defend God, who is being sued, although God is guilty and has no case. Prior wakes up wondering if all that has happened is a dream. Louis again asks if he could come back, even though he has failed at love. Prior loves Louis but can never take him back.

Harper, on a flight to San Francisco, has a vision. She sees the souls of the dead rising, hands clasped together, forming a protective shield for the earth. Four years later, Prior, Louis, Belize, and Hannah are in Central Park in New York City, beneath the statue of the angel Bethesda. Prior is still living with AIDS. Many have died, but gays are not going away, nor will they die secret deaths anymore.

"The Story" by Chris Breyer

Critical Evaluation:

In 1993, when Tony Kushner's epic eight-hour, two-part play *Angels in America* opened on Broadway, the issues it explores—the AIDS epidemic in the United States, conservative political control of Washington, D.C., and society's acceptance of homosexuality—were hot issues, at the fore of the cultural zeitgeist. In revisiting this play in the new millennium, which Kushner had imagined in part 1 of the play (called "Millennium Approaches"), the first question has to be, does the work hold up or is it somehow a literary piece forever tied to the time in which it debuted?

Angels in America still speaks powerfully into the twenty-first century. Its themes still resonate: Even though AIDS has faded from the center of discussion, especially in the United States, the disease remains epidemic worldwide. The 2008 election of a liberal U.S. president, Barack Obama, had awakened a new kind of attack-dog conservatism, which is embodied in the play's right-wing character Roy M. Cohn. Furthermore, even though several states had legalized same-gender marriage in the first few years of the new millennium, many Americans still view homosexuals with ambivalence at best, and hostility at worst.

The deeper questions raised by *Angels in America* are untethered from time and place as well. Does human love last, or are humans naturally selfish, moving on to the next lover when times get hard? Can enemies be forgiven, even the worst ones? Is politics really all just about naked power and greed? What should one make of God, the main "character" of the play, even if his (or her?) performance is unspoken and uncredited? Is God really absent from the heavens, and are the various real and metaphorical plagues visited upon the earth the result of God's wrath and disappointment or merely the chaotic vagaries of a neutral universe and of scientific law?

Angels in America remains relevant and powerful. The play was adapted for an HBO television miniseries in 2003, directed by Mike Nichols. The script was adapted by Kushner, and the play had a stellar cast that included Al Pacino, Meryl Streep, and Emma Thompson. It received numerous critical awards. In 2004, an opera based upon the play opened in France. The character of the Angel perfectly sums up the challenge of any major literary work standing up to the passage of time. The Angel's problem with humans is that they are forever moving forward: evolving, destroying, learning, and changing; these actions literally shake up Heaven. Even though the millennium, which Kushner so ominously warns of, is now here, *Angels in America* remains one of the most ambitious, provocative, political, astonishing, and moving works of drama created in the twentieth century.

The play still matters. It works because it skillfully uses deeply familiar biblical and human motifs that speak to the human condition. Times may change but mere mortals do not, and the questions about life and death and Heaven, Hell, and redemption go on. In one of the play's most powerful scenes, Joe Pitt—the closeted gay law clerk who also is a Republican and Mormon—tries to explain to his wife, Harper, his struggles to come to terms with his real self, his authentic self, buried deep within, and his fear of what God will do when that core is discovered. Joe remembers from his childhood a picture of Jacob from the Bible, wrestling with the angel. Joe says,

> The angel is not human and it holds nothing back. So how could anyone human win, what kind of a fight is that? It is not just. Losing means your soul thrown down in the dust, your heart torn out from God's. But you can't not lose.

It is these battles with angels that form the heart of the play: Prior Walter, who is dying of AIDS, is literally wrestling the Angel back to Earth because he does not want to be a prophet; Joe wrestles with the angels of his inner "demonic" (in his eyes) desires for men; Cohn wrestles with the angel of death.

Angels take the guise of human characters, too. Prior's best friend, nurse Belize, is a sharp-tongued former drag queen who comforts his dying friend and even finds the grace to forgive Cohn his national and personal sins. The same female actor who portrays the Angel also plays Prior's nononsense AIDS-clinic nurse, the only one left who will tenderly touch his disease-ravaged body, if only for a physical examination.

Though Joe's mother, Hannah, can be a steel-spined Mormon zealot, she also rescues and shelters her shell-shocked daughter-in-law, Harper, and sells her house in Utah to move to the Big Apple and find her son Joe. Compassion abounds in these rich characters.

Dreams—real, imagined, surreal—also occupy the play's landscape, like the biblical dreams that spoke to Joseph and Mary and Jacob and so many other ancient "angel wrestlers." Harper's Valium-induced dream takes her to Antarctica to escape her sexless marriage to Joe. Prior dreams throughout the play's first part, as the Angel slowly but steadily approaches, its flapping wings heard in the distance as he lays half-awake in a fever-drenched sleep. Ghosts abound, too. Prior's namesake ancestors appear to herald the arrival of the Messenger. Roy meets the ghost of Ethel Rosenberg, the Communist Jewish subversive he helped convict for treason in the 1950's—the Joseph McCarthy era in the United States. Rosenberg was put to death, along with her husband, Julius, in part because of Cohn's unethical prodding of the trial judge; now, she comes back to watch Roy face his death sentence.

It is a telling to note that *Angels in America* appears in literary critic Harold Bloom's monumental book *The Western Canon: The Books and Schools of the Ages*, a 1995 compendium of the most significant works of world literature and thought from 2000 B.C.E. to the end of the twentieth century. Kushner is one of only a handful of American playwrights whose work is cited by Bloom—Kushner's is the final name cited, a coda to the list. The millennium had approached and has arrived, "midwifed" literarily and dramatically in part by *Angels in America*. As the Angel says at the conclusion of her grand entrance at the end of the play's first part, "Greetings, Prophet!/ The Great Work begins:/ The Messenger has arrived."

"Critical Evaluation" by John F. Hudson

Further Reading

Bloom, Harold, ed. *Tony Kushner*. Philadelphia: Chelsea House, 2005. A collection of essays, many of which provide interpretations of *Angels in America*. Includes discussions of Kushner's philosophy of history as reflected in this play, *Angels in America* as epic theater and as medieval mystery, and the intersection of gay and Jewish identity in the drama.

Bras, Per K. *Essays on Kushner's Angels*. Winnipeg, Man.: Blizzard, 1996. This collection of essays and an interview with the playwright discuss the affects of productions of *Angels in America* in regions and nations outside the United States, including Scandinavia, England, and Australia.

Brustein, Robert. "On Theater: *Angels in America*." *The New Republic*, May 24, 1993. One of the finest theater critics in the United States provides an excellent overview of *Angels in America*.

Clum, John. *Still Acting Gay: Male Homosexuality in Modern Drama*. New York: St. Martin's Griffin, 2000. An expanded version of Clum's earlier book, *Acting Gay: Male Homosexuality in Modern Drama* (1992), which is an analysis of the depiction of gay life and homosexual characters in American and British drama. Includes a lengthy and laudatory discussion of *Angels in America*.

Fisher, James. *The Theater of Tony Kushner: Living Past Hope*. New York: Routledge, 2001. Fisher, a theater scholar, examines *Angels in America* and Kushner's other plays, discussing their themes and techniques, how they reflect Kushner's progressive politics, and the playwright's place in American and world theater.

________. *Understanding Tony Kushner*. Columbia: University of South Carolina Press, 2008. Examines the themes and techniques of *Angels in America* and Kushner's other plays, his adaptations of other playwrights' works, and his own screenplays. Fisher argues that Kushner is a "sociopolitical dramatist" in the tradition of Henrik Ibsen, George Bernard Shaw, and Bertolt Brecht.

Geis, Deborah R., and Steven F. Kruger, eds. *Approaching the Millennium: Essays on "Angels in America."* Ann Arbor: University of Michigan Press, 1997. The essays provide a variety of interpretations of Kushner's play, discussing its depiction of Roy Cohn and of Anglo-Saxon characters, its treatment of race, the filming of the play, and several productions of the drama.

Olson, Walter. "Winged Defeat." *National Review*, January 24, 1994, 71-73. A revealing discussion of how Kushner tries to combine Marxism, mysticism, and transgression in his work.

Osborn, M. Elizabeth, Terrence McNally, and Lanford Wilson. *The Way We Live Now: American Plays and the AIDS Crisis*. New York: Theatre Communications Group, 1990. Plays by a variety of contemporary playwrights including Susan Sontag, Harvey Fierstein, and Kushner demonstrate how the performing-arts community has been devastated by the AIDS crisis.

Posnock, R. "Roy Cohn in America." *Raritan* 13, no. 3 (Winter, 1994): 64-77. A study of how Kushner uses the real history of Roy Cohn in *Angels in America*.

Angle of Repose

Author: Wallace Stegner (1909-1993)
First published: 1971
Type of work: Novel
Type of plot: Historical realism
Time of plot: 1860-1970
Locale: California, the Dakotas, Colorado, Idaho, and Mexico

Principal characters:
LYMAN WARD, the narrator
ELLEN HAMMOND WARD, Lyman's estranged wife
RODMAN WARD, their son
SUSAN BURLING WARD, Lyman's grandmother
OLIVER WARD, Susan's husband
AUGUSTA DRAKE HUDSON, Susan's close friend
THOMAS HUDSON, Augusta's husband
ADA HAWKES and ED HAWKES, Lyman's neighbors and caregivers
SHELLY RASMUSSEN, daughter of Ada and Ed

The Story:

Fifty-eight-year-old Lyman Ward is a history professor at the University of California, Berkeley, where his research won for him a Bancroft Prize. Following his retirement, Lyman, partially disabled since he lost a leg to a bone disease, moves to Grass Valley, California. He lives in Zodiac Cottage, which was built and inhabited for many years by his paternal grandparents, Oliver and Susan Burling Ward. There he finds the letters from which he reconstructs the story of his grandparents' lives.

Oliver, a self-taught engineer and a cousin of Henry Ward Beecher, drops out of Yale after two years because of failing eyesight. He meets Susan at a reception in Brooklyn; shortly thereafter, he leaves for California, seeking his fortune. Susan, a twenty-one-year-old art student who mixes freely in New York's artistic and literary society, corresponds with Oliver but is not romantically attached to him.

Her lifelong friend is Augusta Drake, with whom Lyman suggests his grandmother may have had a lesbian relationship during the first five years of their friendship. Susan, not actively seeking a husband, develops a strong platonic attachment to Thomas Hudson, the brilliant editor of *Scribner's* and later *The Century*. Thomas, Susan, and Augusta become an inseparable trio. Then Thomas and Augusta marry. Their marriage leaves Susan feeling excluded.

Coincidentally, Oliver returns after half a decade in the West and spends a week with Susan and her family in Milton, New York. During that week, Susan falls in love with and decides to marry Oliver, agreeing to join him in the West for a short sojourn before they return to the East to live permanently.

Two weeks after they marry in Milton, Oliver returns to California, where he works as a mining engineer in New Almaden. He prepares a house for Susan, spending so much money on renovation that he has nothing left to send her for the railroad tickets she needs to get herself and her servant, Lizzie, across the continent. Susan pays for the tickets, setting out for what becomes a lifelong adventure.

Oliver's work is extremely demanding. He has a knack for invention but lacks the business acumen to profit from such inventions as hydraulic cement or flood control valves, which he develops, fails to patent, and loses to opportunists. Early in their marriage, Oliver sometimes lives apart from Susan because the places where he works lack suitable accommodations for her.

Susan continues to draw and to write, regularly selling her work to significant publishers in the East, always nurturing the dream of returning to Eastern society. Susan remains ever the Eastern snob; Oliver remains the kindly, gentle, unassuming engineer and inventor. When Susan is thirty-seven years old and Oliver thirty-five, their marriage crumbles. Infatuated with Oliver's assistant, Frank Sargent, Susan conspires to go into the Idaho countryside with him, saying that she is taking five-year-old Agnes for a walk. She does not pay sufficient attention to Agnes, whose lifeless body is found floating in a canal. The day after Agnes's funeral, Frank Sargent commits suicide.

Grief-stricken, Oliver leaves for work in Mexico, while Susan remains in Idaho. After two years, the two are reunited, but Oliver never forgives Susan's infidelity. Through more than half a century, they live together with forbearance rather than love, never touching each other. Susan remains the snob she always was, the celebrity she receives for her writing feeding her sense of superiority. Oliver continues to be the gentle, patient man he always was. Oliver dies at the age of eighty-nine. Susan, ninety-one years of age, dies two months later.

Lyman Ward is a distinguished historian who comments darkly about the Berkeley of the revolutionary 1960's. A disability forces his early retirement. Ellen, his wife, is unable to cope with Lyman's disability and runs off with his surgeon and divorces her husband. Rodman, Lyman and Ellen's only child, is a sociology professor at the University of California at Santa Cruz. He has little respect for history and is unimpressed by Lyman's academic accomplishments. His chief goal is to get his father into a nursing home.

Lyman not only resists Rodman's pressures but also calculatedly documents his routine activities so that Rodman has no grounds for declaring him incompetent. Ada and Ed Hawkes live on the property with their daughter, Shelly Rasmussen, who dropped out of Berkeley. The Hawkeses and Shelley attend to Lyman's needs. Lyman, living alone, asserts his independence in every possible way. One night, Lyman has a nightmarish dream in which Ellen returns and attempts to care for him. She and Shelly fight over who will give him his bath, a nightly ritual usually performed by Ada who, in the dream, is suddenly hospitalized.

Critical Evaluation:

In the late 1940's, Wallace Stegner, professor of creative writing at Stanford University, arranged for the university's library to acquire the papers of American writer and illustrator Mary Hallock Foote. Foote lived from 1847 until 1938, roughly the period during which Susan Burling Ward lived, and, like Susan, married a self-educated mining engineer. Using the Foote papers as his base, Stegner wrote the Pulitzer Prize-winning novel *Angle of Repose*.

The novel, although detailed and based on much fact, is essentially a fiction. Stegner, as a creative artist, felt free to distort history to his own artistic ends. The book is realistic and, because it is based on history, can be labeled historical realism.

Recognized as a preeminent writer about the West, Stegner is sometimes compared to William Faulkner, because both use locale to express universal truths that extend far beyond their compressed geographies: Stegner, the West; Faulkner, the South and his fictional Yoknapatawpha County. Stegner, however, ranges farther geographically than Faulkner usually did; the story in *Angle of Repose* centrally involves three parts of California, as well as Colorado, Idaho, and Mexico.

Angle of Repose is, to a large extent, a study in contrasts between East and West. One major distinction between the two is that of scale, as Stegner demonstrates in the scene in which Susan, on an outing along the Hudson River with Oliver, falls in love with him. Susan leans over a precipice to see a waterfall; Stegner notes that at about the same time, John Muir is doing the same thing to look at Yosemite Falls in California. He comments that Muir has much farther to look and that the rush of water is much greater than what Susan is looking at.

In building this contrast, Stegner sets up the sort of dichotomy that, throughout the novel, defines Susan, an Easterner who, despite living for seventy years in the West, can never be a Westerner. Perhaps the vastness of scale intimidates her, forces her retreat into herself, into her world of words and drawings.

The most salient East-West distinction Stegner makes, however, is that the West lacks the sense of community and tradition the East has. There is, in the West, a sense always of moving on, of impermanence.

Susan is the more distinguished of Lyman's grandparents. Oliver, however, emerges as the admirable character. He lacks Susan's imagination and abilities, although he has his own abilities firmly grounded in the world that he inhabits. The differences between the two probably are what first attracted them to each other, Stegner implies, but these differences also eventually drive them into their own separate worlds. Stegner uses the geological term "angle of repose," the slope at which rocks cease to roll, as a metaphoric description of their relationship. Their angle of repose, however, is merely an unhappy accommodation.

The story Stegner tells might have been told in half the space he uses for its unraveling. Had he compressed it, however, he would have compromised the novel's relaxed, episodic quality. In this book, which spans the period from 1860 to 1970, he explores the complex theme of how people interact with each other over time. He also explores how people deal with their wounds. When Oliver and Susan lose their daughter, the pain is too great for them to speak of her again within the family. Although Lyman's father never speaks of his lost sister, he expends considerable time and great energy perfecting a hybrid rose that he names "The Agnes Ward." Through this device, Stegner shows that, although people refrain from talking about the injuries that haunt their souls, the memory of these injuries remains with them.

Tied into this theme is the novel's final, surrealistic dream, in which Ellen comes to Zodiac Cottage. This chapter brings together many of the novel's disparate threads, answering some questions the rambling narrative poses and suggesting, however feebly, that perhaps people do, with difficulty, finally achieve their angles of repose.

Ellen presumably comes to effect some sort of reconciliation with Lyman. Lyman, however, is no longer a part of Ellen's life, Ellen no longer a part of his. He constructs quite carefully the society he wants and needs: the Hawkeses,

Shelly, and Al Sutton, his old friend from junior high school. When Ellen intrudes into this society, she threatens the structure that Lyman devises and that suits him well. His dream becomes a nightmare as he is left alone with Ellen, who finally fixes his meal because Ada suffers an arrhythmia that requires Ed and Shelly to take her to the hospital. Al has long since departed.

After dinner, when the subject of Lyman's bath is raised, Shelly returns, planning to bathe Lyman. She goes into the bathroom with him, draws a hot bath, takes off her blouse (her pendulous breasts transfix him), and then proceeds to strip him. Lyman becomes an object in a struggle between his former wife and his caregiver, thereby revealing his subconscious fears generated by his son's desire to control his father's life.

R. Baird Shuman

Further Reading

Benson, Jackson J. *Down by the Lemonade Springs: Essays on Wallace Stegner.* Reno: University of Nevada Press, 2001. Collection of essays by a Stegner biographer (below). The essays include examinations of Stegner's fiction, the writer as an environmentalist, and Stegner's friendship with poet Robert Frost. Chapter 10 provides an introduction to *Angle of Repose.*

_______. *Wallace Stegner: His Life and Work.* New York: Viking Press, 1996. A biography that argues against pigeonholing Stegner as a Western writer. Focuses largely on the people and events that most influenced Stegner's art, including Robert Frost and Bernard DeVoto; covers Stegner's teaching career and his influence on such writers as Ken Kesey, Edward Abbey, Wendell Berry, and Larry McMurty.

Burrows, Russell. *Reading Wallace Stegner's "Angle of Repose."* Boise, Idaho: Boise State University Press, 2001. Provides a brief introductory overview of the novel.

Fradkin, Philip L. *Wallace Stegner and the American West.* New York: Alfred A. Knopf, 2008. A detailed, astute biography, describing how Stegner transformed the failure of his father's homestead and other incidents of his father's life into his fiction about the American West.

Lewis, Merrill, and Lorene Lewis. *Wallace Stegner.* Boise, Idaho: Boise State College, 1972. A brief overview of Stegner's life and work.

Meine, Curt, ed. *Wallace Stegner and the Continental Vision: Essays on Literature, History, and Landscape.* Washington, D.C.: Island Press, 1997. A collection of papers presented at a 1996 symposium in Madison, Wisconsin. Includes essays on Stegner and the shaping of the modern West, the art of storytelling, history, environmentalism, politics, and bioregionalism.

Proffitt, Steve. "Wallace Stegner: An Interview." *Los Angeles Times*, June 7, 1992. This interview, published a year before Stegner's death, focuses on some of the writer's most central concerns. Reveals a great deal about Stegner's approach to the West as a literary setting.

Rankin, Charles E., ed. *Wallace Stegner: Man and Writer.* Albuquerque: University of New Mexico Press, 1996. A collection of essays by various critics on Stegner's life and art. Includes discussion of Stegner as a Western humanist; Stegner, the environment, and the West; and *Angle of Repose* as literary history.

Robinson, Forrest G., and Margaret G. Robinson. *Wallace Stegner.* Boston: Twayne, 1977. Offers an extended analysis of *Angle of Repose* and interesting insights into Stegner's creative production generally. Includes a useful chronology and well-constructed index.

Stegner, Wallace, and Richard W. Etulain. *Conversations with Wallace Stegner on Western History and Literature.* Rev. ed. Salt Lake City: University of Utah Press, 1990. Stegner discusses his life and his writing, as well as his views on literature and history.

Animal Dreams

Author: Barbara Kingsolver (1955-)
First published: 1990
Type of work: Novel
Type of plot: Psychological realism
Time of plot: Late 1980's
Locale: Grace, Arizona

Principal characters:
COSIMA "CODI" NOLINE, a young woman
HOMER NOLINE, her father
HALIMEDA "HALLIE" NOLINE, her younger sister
CARLO, Codi's lover
EMELINA DOMINGOS, Codi's friend
LOYD PEREGRINA, Codi's high school boyfriend
DOÑA ALTHEA, leader of the Stitch and Bitch Club

The Story:

After fourteen years away, Codi Noline reluctantly returns to her hometown of Grace, Arizona, to attend to her father, Homer. Homer is a practicing physician, but he seems to be losing his memory. Codi has unpleasant and incomplete memories of her life in Grace. She has always felt like an outsider in the town and has been estranged from her father. One of her memories concerns the loss of her mother when Codi was three and her sister Hallie was a baby. She seems to recall seeing a helicopter come too late to rescue her dying mother, even though she was not present at the time. Another unpleasant memory centers on Codi's pregnancy and miscarriage while she was in high school. She has never told anyone about this incident, not even Loyd, the father of the miscarried child.

Codi has arranged to stay in her high school friend Emelina's guesthouse instead of with her father. She has been hired to teach biology in her old high school, and she plans to be in Grace for only a year. She is concerned about Hallie, who has gone to Nicaragua to serve as an agricultural adviser in spite of reports about rebels called the Contras who are violently opposing the government there.

Codi reports for her first day of teaching and introduces the students to the skeleton in the biology lab. Later, she takes the class to the river to collect water samples so they can study the river's organisms under their microscopes, but they discover that there is nothing alive in the water. A local copper-mining company has been trying to extract metals from the mine's waste and has been releasing water used in the process into the river, causing it to become highly acidic. The poisoned water also affects the orchards in a nearby canyon. Codi files an affidavit about the polluted water at the courthouse because the Environmental Protection Agency has begun to investigate the mine.

In the meantime, Loyd, who is Apache but is also related to the Pueblo and the Navajo, has reconnected with Codi. He now has a job with the railroad. One day, he takes her to the ruins of a Pueblo village that is several hundred years old. He tells Codi he has changed since high school, and he apologizes for his past ill treatment of her.

Homer continues to practice medicine, but he increasingly confuses past and present. He tells Codi that he is taking medicine to slow the memory loss from his Alzheimer's disease and that he will retire when he is no longer effective. Homer was aware that Codi was pregnant in high school, but he said nothing to her. After her miscarriage, however, when she asked for some aspirin, he gave her something for pain and for cramping. Only in his thoughts does he admit his love for his children.

Codi maintains a correspondence with Hallie, who has arrived safely in Nicaragua. Hallie is working hard and fitting into Nicaraguan society. She occasionally mentions Contra attacks in the area and is dismayed to learn that the Contras are supported by the U.S. government.

The ladies of a local social group, the Stitch and Bitch Club, ask Codi to explain the environmental damage to the river. The men of the town are considering a lawsuit against the company, but such a suit would likely take years; in the meantime, the town would die. The ladies decide to hold a fund-raiser and to publicize the pollution. They make several dozen peacock piñatas to sell in Tucson. Codi writes a town history, a copy of which is attached to each piñata. The sale is a huge success. Eventually, the piñata project is covered in several magazines, as well as in a CBS news broadcast.

Codi becomes more involved with Loyd. He takes her to a cockfight to see his roosters battle. She realizes that he is very skilled with his birds but is repulsed by the roosters' fighting to the death. Loyd decides to give up cockfighting. At Christmas, he takes Codi to meet his mother and her family at the Santa Rosalia Pueblo, where they watch the traditional kachina singing and dancing. Codi sees a picture of Loyd's twin brother, who was killed when he was fifteen.

After the trip, Codi learns that Hallie has been kidnapped

by the Contras. She writes and telephones everyone that she thinks might be able to do something but to no avail. She becomes angry in her classroom as she tries to make her students understand the general threats to the environment and the specific problems in Grace.

A folk-art expert who has seen the news coverage of the piñatas comes to talk to the Stitch and Bitch Club. He suggests that the ladies try to get the town placed on the National Register of Historic Places. This designation will protect the town from polluters and can be accomplished more quickly than a lawsuit. The money raised by selling the piñatas will be enough to pay for the necessary documentation of the town's history.

Codi has gradually learned that, contrary to Homer's assertion that they had no family in Grace, her mother was descended from one of the Gracela sisters who founded the town. She also discovers that Homer changed his name from "Nolina" to "Noline" to distance himself from a trashy ancestor in Grace and that he lied to his children when he told them that the family had moved to Grace from Illinois. Codi also learns the details of her mother's death. She tells Homer that she left medical school when she lost her nerve while helping with a premature birth. She also tells him about her miscarriage and learns that he already knew about it.

At last, Codi hears that Hallie has been killed by the Contras. People in town urge Codi to stay in Grace, but she carries through on her plan to leave at the end of the school year after arranging for her father's care. She boards an airplane to Colorado to be with Carlo, but the plane has mechanical trouble and is forced to return to the airport. This incident frightens Codi and forces her to realize that she wants to return to Grace. She goes back and holds a memorial service for Hallie, and she finally tells Loyd about the miscarriage.

Two years after her father's death, Codi and Loyd are a couple, and she is pregnant. She decorates her father's grave on the Day of All Souls and then walks up the canyon to the place where the medical helicopter came for her mother. She knows that her memory of seeing it was true.

Critical Evaluation:

Barbara Kingsolver attempts in her fiction both to entertain and to effect change in the world. *Animal Dreams*, like most of her novels, addresses political, social, and environmental issues; it can be categorized as ecofiction. In 2000, Kingsolver was awarded the National Humanities Medal, the nation's highest honor for service through art.

Kingsolver began writing the novel by asking herself a question: What causes one person to become engaged with the world while another one is not? She explores the answer through the contrasting lives of Codi and Hallie. The contrasting experiences of the two sisters shape the choices they make. *Animal Dreams* focuses on Codi, who has been estranged from her father, her hometown, and the larger arena of political and social issues. Codi has a negative view of herself, but she gradually makes connections that allow her to become more confident. Codi narrates most of the novel's twenty-eight chapters in the first person, while Hallie's voice is heard in her letters. Seven of the chapters are narrated in the third person and filtered through Homer's perspective.

Codi has a distant relationship with her father. His high standards and protective actions do not satisfy Codi's need for emotional support, and they serve to undermine her self-confidence. Homer cannot verbalize his love for his daughters. Codi's secret miscarriage also separates her from her father and contributes to her sense of failure. Her decision not to complete medical school is another source of her lack of self-worth. By the end of the novel, however, Codi has managed to discuss dropping out of medical school with Homer and has learned about some secrets that he himself kept. She is able to let go of her negativity.

Codi has always felt like an outsider in Grace because Homer encouraged her and Hallie to think of themselves as more intelligent than the others in town and because she believed she had no family there. When Codi discovers her true origins, however, she realizes that she has been surrounded by family all the time.

Although Codi admires Hallie's commitment to make the world better, she is uninterested in larger issues. Gradually, however, she becomes involved in the fight against the mining company. She recognizes the importance of environmental concerns and that the town's heritage is her heritage too.

Codi's gradual reconnection to her father and her community repair her sense of self-worth. Instead of leaving Grace after her year of teaching as she had planned, Codi realizes that she wants to stay because she has found her home at last. She is finally able to commit to Loyd, and their relationship will bring with it a network of Native American connections. In the final chapter, Codi's pregnancy represents the fact that she can now look forward with hope.

In contrast to Codi, Hallie is confident, optimistic, and idealistic. Codi observes that she and Hallie actually grew up in different situations: Hallie never knew their mother and always had Codi there as her older sister; in addition, she did not have Codi's sad secret to deal with. Codi admires Hallie and contrasts herself unfavorably with her younger sister. After receiving one of Codi's hero-worshiping letters, however, Hallie replies by scolding Codi and telling her to get over her feelings about herself and to think about what her actions say about her. For Hallie, people's actions determine what kind of characters they have. This philosophy helps Codi move forward, and she repeats it to her father when he wonders if he has been of any use to the town. Similarly, Loyd echoes Hallie's idea when he tells Codi, "If you want sweet dreams, you've got to live a sweet life."

Kingsolver treats environmental and political issues through her characters' involvement with those issues. Hallie goes to Nicaragua at a time when the United States government was supporting the right-wing Contra army in its attacks on Nicaragua's leftist Sandinista government and its citizens. The novel is dedicated to Ben Linder, an American engineer who was killed by the Contras in 1987. Hallie opposes the U.S. support of the Contras.

Back in Arizona, Codi discovers a copper-mining company's poisoning of the river. While Hallie treks to another country to help improve its agriculture, Codi finds that there is plenty to do closer to home. Both sisters' actions show that individuals should oppose powerful forces. In Codi's case, neither she nor the Stitch and Bitch ladies seem to have any power when compared to the mining company, yet their persistent efforts bring about change. Kingsolver's optimism comes through in the idea that actions are significant in themselves. Even though Hallie's efforts are cut short, she acts. Without such action, change will never be possible.

Carol J. Luther

Further Reading

DeMarr, Mary Jean. *Barbara Kingsolver: A Critical Companion*. Westport, Conn.: Greenwood Press, 1999. Chapter 4 succinctly covers the sources, structure, settings, character development, and themes of *Animal Dreams*.

Jacobs, Naomi. "Barbara Kingsolver's Anti-Western: Unraveling the Myths in *Animal Dreams*." *Americana: The Journal of American Popular Culture* 2, no. 2 (Fall, 2003). Argues that Kingsolver through her work proposes a different view of the Western's conventions of heroism, violence and death, and community.

Rubenstein, Roberta. "Home Is (Mother) Earth: *Animal Dreams*, Barbara Kingsolver." In *Home Matters: Longing and Belonging, Nostalgia and Mourning in Women's Fiction*. New York: Palgrave, 2001. Sees the novel as a story of quest and return home. Explores Kingsolver's synthesis of Western and Native American mythology.

Smiley, Jane. "In One Small Town, the Weight of the World." *The New York Times Book Review*, September 2, 1990. Praises Kingsolver's ability to present her characters' states of mind.

Snodgrass, Mary Ellen. *Barbara Kingsolver: A Literary Companion*. Jefferson, N.C.: McFarland, 2004. Arranged alphabetically by name and topic. Each entry has suggestions for further reading. Topics include cooperation, ecofeminism, Noline genealogy, Carlo, All Souls' Day, and the pueblo. A useful supplement.

Stevenson, Sheryl. "Trauma and Memory in Kingsolver's *Animal Dreams*." *Lit: Literature Interpretation Theory* 11, no. 4 (February, 2001): 327-350. Interprets the novel as a survivor's story of recovery from trauma.

Wagner-Martin, Linda. *Barbara Kingsolver*. Philadelphia: Chelsea House, 2004. Chapter 7 characterizes Codi's struggles, mentions the political themes in the novel, and comments about the text's comparison of humans and animals.

Animal Farm

Author: George Orwell (1903-1950)
First published: 1945
Type of work: Novel
Type of plot: Satire
Time of plot: Mid-twentieth century
Locale: England

Principal characters:
MR. JONES, a human, owner of Manor Farm
OLD MAJOR, a pig, the first to speak of rebellion
BOXER, a cart horse
MOLLIE, a white mare
BENJAMIN, a donkey
MOSES, a tame raven
SNOWBALL, a pig, coleader in the rebellion, with
NAPOLEON, a pig, later ruler of Animal Farm
SQUEALER, a pig, a brilliant talker

The Story:

Old Major calls a meeting as soon as Mr. Jones goes to sleep. Jones, who is cruel to his animals, is drinking excessively of late. When all the animals are gathered, Major begins to speak. He had a dream in which he remembers the song *Beasts of England* from his distant past. He teaches it to the others and tells them they should rise up to defeat Jones and do their work for themselves, for their own benefit. He says that all men are evil and that all animals are good and equal.

Three days after telling his dream, Major dies. Snowball, Napoleon, and Squealer develop Major's teachings into a system called Animalism. The rebellion comes quickly and suddenly after Jones was drinking in town. When he returns home, the animals run him and the other humans off the farm. The animals can hardly believe their good fortune. Napoleon leads them back to the barn, where everyone is served extra food to celebrate.

In preparation for the rebellion, the pigs learned to read and write. One day, the pigs write the seven commandments of Animalism on the wall of the barn. It is realized that, since the rebellion, the cows have not been milked. The pigs manage to do it, but the five buckets of milk vanish while the other animals are out working.

The animals set forth to harvest the hay crop. They do this faster than it was ever done, but the pigs do not do any actual work, they hold a supervisory position. Boxer, the cart horse, is the hardest worker and the quickest to follow the rules set up by the pigs. "I will work harder" is his maxim and his motto; under any difficult circumstance, he always repeats it. Benjamin, the donkey, is the only animal that is unchanged since the rebellion. He works in the same obstinate way that he always has, doing his share and no more. Napoleon and Snowball oppose each other at every juncture at which decisions are made. Snowball begins committees for the adults while Napoleon takes puppies away from their parents, to educate them and to keep them in a special loft of the barn where no one else is allowed to go.

Jones and other humans attempt to take back Animal Farm but they are unsuccessful. In the battle, Snowball leads the forces and is wounded by a shotgun. Snowball manages to rid Jones of his gun, and Boxer kicks a boy. This is named the "Battle of the Cowshed" and is a success for the animals.

The winter draws near and at the meetings held every Sunday, Napoleon and Snowball still oppose each other. No matter what is in question, they always hold different views. Snowball is a brilliant speaker at the meetings and wins support through his eloquent speeches, while Napoleon is better at drumming up support for himself in sly conversations between the meetings. Napoleon trains the sheep to bleat "Four legs good, two legs bad" at crucial moments in Snowball's speeches, which serves to negate anything of relevance that Snowball might say.

The worst argument is the one over the windmill. Snowball wants the animals to build a windmill because with it, and the electricity it would provide, the animals will only have to work three days a week. Napoleon is against it, saying they should spend their time producing more food. Benjamin is the only one who does not side with either Snowball or Napoleon. Windmill or no windmill, he says, life will go on as it has always gone on—that is, badly. At the meeting at which the question of the windmill will be decided, Snowball gives an eloquent speech and Napoleon says nothing. Snowball looks sure to win. Then Napoleon's puppies come forth, now as large and treacherous dogs, and they drive Snowball off the farm.

Napoleon establishes himself as leader, with the pack of dogs reinforcing his position. He says there will be no more meetings and no more debates. He and other pigs will decide everything. Three weeks later, Napoleon uses Snowball's plans for the windmill and issues the order that work on the windmill is to begin.

To get necessary supplies, Napoleon begins dealing with people. The other animals feel uneasy about it but can do nothing as Napoleon seems above reproach and his guard dogs assure his position completely. The pigs move into Jones's house and begin sleeping in the beds. This is in direct opposition to one of the seven commandments, so the pigs begin changing the commandments in order to fit their increasing status as masters of the farm. The windmill becomes the top priority, and whenever problems arise, they are always blamed on Snowball, who is supposedly lurking near the farm and causing every problem that exists. Food grows scarce. Napoleon tells the animals that he will begin selling eggs to humans again, and the hens are required to lay eggs for this purpose. The hens believe this is murder of their chicks and refuse, but Napoleon stops their food rations until they comply with his demands. Soon after the hens' attempted refusal to comply with Napoleon, there is a mass murder, in which Napoleon's dogs kill every animal that ever spoke against him. Squealer upholds the actions of Napoleon and convinces all the remaining animals that their lives are much better than they ever have been.

The seven commandments are abolished and the only slogan left is this: "All animals are equal but some animals are more equal than others." The pigs discover alcohol and clothes and invite humans over to inspect the farm. The people find it in excellent running order. The pigs look and act like people and treat the animals more horribly than Jones had.

Critical Evaluation:

Animal Farm was written soon after George Orwell resigned from the British Broadcasting Corporation (BBC) in 1943, while he worked as the literary editor for the *Tribune*, in London. He had not written a novel during the three years he was with the BBC and was having an extremely hard time writing at all, with World War II in full force. *Animal Farm* was completed in four months. It was one year later that he found someone who would publish it and almost another year before it was finally offered to the public. *Animal Farm* and the book he wrote following it, *Nineteen Eighty-Four* (1949), are Orwell's most highly acclaimed works.

An anti-Soviet satire, the book was ahead of its time. The U.S.S.R. was fighting with the allied forces in World War II, and the book was seen as an attack on the U.S.S.R. and Joseph Stalin. After World War II, the book was published. The political situation was different then, and *Animal Farm* appeared just as the Cold War was beginning.

Orwell called *Animal Farm* "the first . . . in which I tried, with full consciousness of what I was doing, to fuse political purpose and artistic purpose into one whole." *Animal Farm* was a huge success as soon as it was published. It was established as a modern classic almost immediately. A very short book, written simply and fluently, it is a drastic departure from anything else Orwell had or would produce.

Animal Farm abounds with allegory, beginning with Old Major, who recalls Karl Marx. Every character and event may be seen as symbolic of historical Russian figures and events between the years 1917 and 1943. Orwell said the book's purpose was "the destruction of the Soviet myth." The flag raised by the animals, with hoof and horn, is similar to the Russian flag of hammer and sickle. Napoleon is generally likened to Stalin, and the countenance and actions of Snowball are thought to resemble those of Leon Trotsky. The name Snowball recalls Trotsky's white hair and beard, and possibly, too, that he crumbled under Stalin's opposition. The event in which Snowball is chased away from the farm is similar to the expulsion of Trotsky from Russia in 1929. The book is written with such sophistication and subtlety, however, that a reader unaware of Russian history might very well see it as an animal story only. Moreover, reading the book strictly to find reference to Russian history misses an important point: Orwell said the book "is intended as a satire on dictatorship in general." The name of the ruling pig, "Napoleon," is a reminder that there have been dictators outside Russia. Not Stalin in particular, but totalitarianism is the enemy Orwell exposes.

The problem Orwell addresses is how to combine power with ideals. How do the oppressed who rise above their oppressors manage to keep from becoming like the oppressors? With this book, Orwell gives an instance of the slave coming to resemble the master after overthrowing him. There is not a happy ending. From the beginning of the story, the dogs are against the rats, thus foreshadowing an animal government in which social justice will not be acquired.

Beaird Glover

Further Reading

Bloom, Harold, ed. *George Orwell's "Animal Farm."* Philadelphia: Chelsea House, 1999. Collection of critical essays, including discussions of Orwell and Marxism, the making of *Animal Farm*, the novel as a twentieth century beast fable, and an assessment of the novel fifty years after its initial publication.

Bowker, Gordon. *Inside George Orwell*. New York: Palgrave Macmillan, 2003. Presents the "human face" of Orwell, describing his inner emotional life and its relationship to his political activities and ideas. One of the better books about Orwell published in the centenary year of his birth.

Gardner, Averil. *George Orwell*. Boston: Twayne, 1987. Gives information on Orwell at the time of writing *Animal Farm* and a chapter-by-chapter synopsis of meaning and symbols as they apply to Russian history. Includes some of the criticism that *Animal Farm* received at its publication.

Hammond, J. R. *A George Orwell Companion*. New York: St. Martin's Press, 1982. Features photographs of Orwell spanning his career and gives an extended reference to characters and events of *Animal Farm* as they compare to Russian history. Considers the evolution of Orwellian philosophy through his novels and essays.

Hitchens, Christopher. *Why Orwell Matters*. New York: Basic Books, 2002. Hitchens emphasizes Orwell's criticism of Nazism and Stalinism—philosophies he never softened his view of in order to sell books. Hitchens argues that Orwell's analysis of those two governmental systems continues to apply in the early twenty-first century.

Kalechofsky, Roberta. *George Orwell*. New York: Frederick Ungar, 1973. Has an extended section on *Animal Farm* focusing on the corruption of the seven commandments of animalism and compares the themes of *Animal Farm* as similar to those of *Nineteen Eighty-Four*.

Meyers, Jeffrey. *Orwell: Wintry Conscience of a Generation*. New York: W. W. Norton, 2000. A well-researched biography that provides a balanced look at Orwell's life and work. Meyers vividly describes the contrast between Orwell the writer and Orwell the man.

_______. *A Reader's Guide to George Orwell*. Totowa, N.J.: Littlefield, Adams, 1977. Gives a detailed account of the political allegory of *Animal Farm*, specifically with regard to Russian history.

Rodden, John, ed. *The Cambridge Companion to George Orwell*. New York: Cambridge University Press, 2007. Collection of essays providing an overview of Orwell's works and literary influence. Morris Dickstein's piece, "*Animal Farm*: History as Fable," analyzes this novel.

Saunders, Loraine. *The Unsung Artistry of George Orwell: The Novels from "Burmese Days" to "Nineteen Eighty-Four."* Burlington, Vt.: Ashgate, 2008. Saunders reappraises all of Orwell's novels, arguing that the novels published in the 1930's deserve as much credit as the subsequent *Animal House* and *Nineteen Eighty-Four.* Analyzes the influences of writer George Gissing and of 1930's politics on Orwell's work and examines his depiction of women.

Williams, Raymond. *George Orwell*. New York: Viking Press, 1971. Includes several quotes from Orwell and describes the criticism he received for *Animal Farm*. Explains the difficulties Orwell encountered in trying to find a publisher.

Anna Christie

Author: Eugene O'Neill (1888-1953)
First produced: 1921; first published, 1923
Type of work: Drama
Type of plot: Social realism
Time of plot: Early twentieth century
Locale: New York City and Provincetown harbor

Principal characters:
CHRIS CHRISTOPHERSON, captain of a barge
ANNA, his daughter
MAT BURKE, a stoker
MARTHY OWEN, a prostitute

The Story:

Old Chris Christopherson looks upon the sea as the symbol of a malignant fate. True, he is now skipper of the coal barge *Simeon Winthrop*, but in his younger days he was an able seaman and boatswain on the old windjammers and visited every port in the world. As far back as he knew, the men of his family in Sweden followed the sea. His father died aboard ship in the Indian Ocean, and two of his brothers drowned. The curse of the sea is not confined to the men in the family. After the news of her husband's and her sons' deaths, Chris's mother died of a broken heart. Unable to bear the loneliness of being a sailor's wife, his own wife brought their young daughter, Anna, to America to live with some cousins on a farm in Minnesota. Anna's mother died, and the girl is being brought up by her relatives.

Chris did not see his daughter for almost twenty years. One day while he is having a drink at Johnny the Priest's saloon near South Street in New York City, he receives a postcard from St. Louis telling him that Anna is on her way to New York. This news throws Chris into something of a panic, for living on the barge with him is a middle-aged prostitute named Marthy. Chris decides to get rid of the woman. Being a kind-hearted soul and genuinely fond of Marthy, he dislikes the idea of turning her out, but Marthy says that Chris always treated her decently, and she will move on to someone else. When Marthy catches a glimpse of Chris's daughter, she is shocked. Anna is twenty years old and pretty in a buxom sort of way, but her painted face and cheap showy clothes are telltale evidence of what she is—a prostitute. Marthy wonders what Chris's reaction is going to be.

In his eyes, however, Anna is the innocent child he always imagined her to be, and he is even hesitant about ordering wine to celebrate their reunion. Life on the barge is an entirely new experience for Anna. She comes to love the sea and to respond to its beauty with the same intensity with which her father responds to its malignance. With the soothing effect of her new environment, and the presence of her father's gentleness and simplicity, Anna begins to lose some of her hardness and to build some faith in men.

One night, while the *Simeon Winthrop* is anchored in the outer harbor of Provincetown, Massachusetts, Chris hears cries for help. He pulls aboard the barge four men who have been drifting for five days after the wreck of their ship. One of the men, an Irishman named Mat Burke, takes an immediate fancy to Anna, and even in his weakened condition he makes it clear that he intends to have Anna for his own. Mat represents everything in life that Chris hates. In the first place, he was a stoker on a steamship, an occupation the old windjammer sailor regards as beneath contempt. Second, Mat follows the sea and so is connected in the old Swede's mind with inevitable tragedy. Last, and most important from Chris's viewpoint, Mat is obviously in love with Anna and wants to take her away from him. To Anna, on the other hand, Mat represents all that she has always wanted in life. At first she is naturally suspicious of his Irish glibness, but she soon begins to see that underneath his voluble exterior there are some genuine convictions, a basic core of integrity that gives her a sense of security as well as, in the light of her own past, a gnawing fear.

Her father and Mat are mortal enemies from the start. This conflict reaches its climax one day in the cabin when Chris, goaded on by the Irishman's taunts, comes at Mat with a knife, intending to kill him. Anna comes in as Mat overpowers the old man. She realizes that they are fighting over her as if she were a piece of property that must belong to one or the other.

This situation is so close to her previous experience with men that she makes them both listen to a confession of the truth about herself, of which apparently neither of them has been aware. She informs her father that his romantic picture of her idyllic life on the Minnesota farm is untrue from beginning to end, that she was worked relentlessly by her relatives, and that at sixteen she was seduced by one of her cousins. At last she went to St. Louis and entered a bawdy house, where her experience with men did not differ greatly from what she knew on the farm. She informs Mat that for the first time in her life she realizes what love might be. Mat, having neither intelligence nor imagination enough to appreciate Anna's sincerity, angrily calls her names and leaves the barge in disgust. Chris follows him, and the two men proceed to get drunk. Anna waits on the *Simeon Winthrop* for two days, hoping that Mat will return. Finally she prepares to go to New York and resume her old profession.

Her father is the first to return with the news that to save her from going back to the old life he has signed on the *Londonderry*, a steamer to Cape Town, Africa, and made arrangements for his pay to be turned over to Anna. When Mat returns, Anna feels sure he came back merely to kill her. He is bruised and bloody from waterfront fights. He, too, signed on the *Londonderry*, and the irony of her father and Mat on the same boat strikes Anna as funny. Finally she makes Mat see that she hates the men who have bought her and that all she wants is the assurance of one man's love.

Chris is glad that Anna and Mat are reconciled and are going to be married and be happy, for he now realizes that much of Anna's past misery is his own fault. At the same time, however, he wonders what tricks the malignant sea will play on Anna and Mat in the future.

Critical Evaluation:

Anna Christie, which won a second Pulitzer Prize for Eugene O'Neill in 1922, was produced in an earlier version as *Chris*, about a veteran seaman reduced to the role of coal bargeman, who frequented O'Neill's favorite saloon. The final title of the play indicates O'Neill's shift of emphasis during numerous rewrites from the crusty old sea dog to his daughter Anna. Originally conceived of as a young woman carefully raised in England, Anna emerges as the title character in *Anna Christie*, a former prostitute tormented by her past. A realistic drama, with symbolic overtones, the play focuses upon the dynamics of the love-hate relationships of the three central figures, Chris, Anna, and Mat, the Irish sailor tossed into their lives.

From one perspective, the plot of *Anna Christie* concerns the regeneration of a hardened prostitute as a result of her giving and receiving love, but this somewhat simplistic story is provided complexity through the development of the characters. As O'Neill has created them, they are human beings of passion and energy, people struggling against the forces of an impersonal universe.

The product of a brutal upbringing, Anna, a woman who is strong physically and mentally, mistrusts all men, and her dreams of love, home, and a sense of belonging are pitifully simple and small. Alienated and outcast, her position links her with the central figures of two of O'Neill's other early plays, Brutus Jones in *The Emperor Jones* (pr. 1920) and Yank in *The Hairy Ape* (pr. 1922). Like them, she is a victim of circumstances beyond her control. Unlike them, she is honest with herself and eventually is compelled to be honest with her father and lover. In the third act her outburst about the truth of her past is a proclamation of self not unlike Nora's declaration in Henrik Ibsen's *Et dukkehjem* (1879; *A Doll's House*, 1880). In essence, she demands recognition and acceptance for herself. She may have sold herself to men in the past, but she refuses to be owned by them in the present. In contrast, Chris and Mat are weak and insensitive men. Chris is immature and deluded; he avoided responsibility as a father by sending Anna away as a child. He avoids responsibility for his woman Marthy by forcing her away when Anna arrives. He further tries to escape a truthful relationship with Anna by shipping out at the end of the play. Unwilling to examine his own motives, Chris hates and fears "dat ole davil" sea and blames it for all his misfortunes. Still, his efforts to protect Anna, although misguided, are understandable and human.

Mat, supremely confident in his youth and physical strength, as well as superstitious in his Catholicism, does not listen to Anna's doubts or see her misgivings, believing that the power of his love will overcome whatever obstacles she might voice. Jealous of each other, both men would prefer to maintain the illusion that Anna is an innocent young woman in need of their masculine protection and guidance. Despite the fact that their sexual behavior as sailors has been equally promiscuous, the revelation of her sordid past hurts and enrages them, driving them off on two-day binges. Their sudden conversion to tolerance at the end of the play has concerned critics and audiences.

Certain elements, carefully integrated, lift the play above the realistic level. O'Neill uses the sea symbolically, as he does many times in his works, to represent the forces of life that are ineffable, uncontrolled, and sometimes cruel. Contrasted with the sea is the land. On land, there is the harshness of the farm of Anna's childhood, and the house she entered that brought her disease, and even Johnny the Priest's saloon, which is unfriendly to women of her kind. The vastness and power of the sea exhilarate Anna, who has been landlocked all her life. On the barge she feels cleansed, happy, as though she has found a home. Chris mistrusts the sea as Anna mistrusts men. He sees himself as its victim. The sea has deprived him of wife and family, and he fears losing Anna to its spell. On the other hand, Mat, rescued by the barge, believes that the sea has brought him to Anna, and that the will of God operates within it. The sea is life, and the characters, however they respond to it, are at its mercy.

Another symbolic element is the fog, which represents the mystery of life and which sometimes clouds human understanding. Chris fears the fog for its ability to confuse and mislead; he considers it the worst of the tricks the sea can play. The fog of the first two acts allows Anna to be soothed and freed from the guilt of her past. When the fog lifts and the sun shines in act 3, she finds the strength to enlighten the men with the truth. When the fog returns at the end of the play, it carries a sense of foreboding for the future of the three characters.

Critics have faulted the last act, citing the neatness of the resolution as contrived, "a compromise with integrity." In its sense of inevitability, the play seems to promise a tragic ending. O'Neill responded that it is "just the sort of compromise those characters would have arranged for themselves in real life." In a letter he jokingly claimed that he had told his characters to die, but they insisted on living, which is "what most of us have to do." Another point of view sees the ending as far from happy, as the fog swirls in and old Chris mutters about the fog: "You can't see vhere you vas going, no. Only dat ole davil, sea—she knows!" Moreover, Anna is left landlocked and alone.

Written in the early 1920's, when O'Neill was producing startling experimental plays, *Anna Christie* appears to represent a return to more conventional drama for him. However, in the depth of the character delineation and the subtle integration of the symbolic material, O'Neill demonstrates his continued progress as a playwright.

"Critical Evaluation" by Joyce E. Henry

Further Reading

Bloom, Steven F. *Student Companion to Eugene O' Neill.* Westport, Conn.: Greenwood Press, 2007. Includes a brief biographical sketch, a discussion of O'Neill's literary heritage, and a chapter providing critical analysis of *Anna Christie.*

Bogard, Travis. *Contour in Time: The Plays of Eugene O'Neill.* Rev. ed. New York: Oxford University Press, 1988. Argues for viewing the O'Neill canon as the playwright's autobiography. Contains a detailed comparison of the final version with earlier versions of *Anna Christie.*

Estrin, Mark W., ed. *Conversations with Eugene O'Neill.* Jackson: University Press of Mississippi, 1990. A fascinating collection of interviews with the playwright arranged chronologically from 1920 to 1948. Contains many of O'Neill's comments about the characters and creation of *Anna Christie.*

Floyd, Virginia. *The Plays of Eugene O'Neill: A New Assessment.* New York: Frederick Ungar, 1985. Contains chapters analyzing each of O'Neill's plays. Argues that *Anna Christie* is a failure of character and plot.

Gelb, Arthur, and Barbara Gelb. *O'Neill.* Rev. ed. New York: Perennial Library, 1987. A monumental biography of almost one thousand pages with several sections of photographs. An excellent reference for details of the playwright's life and plays.

Houchin, John H., ed. *The Critical Response to Eugene O'Neill.* Westport, Conn.: Greenwood Press, 1993. A collection of critical opinions, including reviews of productions from periodicals and scholarly essays, three of which focus upon *Anna Christie.* The diversity of perspectives is useful.

Johnson, Katie N. "The Repentant Courtesan in *Anna Christie* and the Lesbian Prostitute in *The God of Vengeance*." In *Sisters in Sin: Brothel Drama in America, 1900-1920*. New York: Cambridge University Press, 2006. Analyzes the depiction of prostitutes in O'Neill's work and a play by Sholem Asch.

Törnqvist, Egil. *Eugene O' Neill: A Playwright's Theatre*. Jefferson, N.C.: McFarland, 2004. Demonstrates how O'Neill was a controlling personality in the texts and performances of his plays. Describes his working conditions and the multiple audiences for his works. Examines the titles, settings in time and place, names and addresses, language, and allusions to other works in his dramas.

Voglino, Barbara. "Feminism versus Fatalism: Uncertainty as Closure in *Anna Christie*." In *"Perverse Mind": Eugene O'Neill's Struggle with Closure*. Madison, N.J.: Fairleigh Dickinson University Press, 1999. Focuses on nine plays written at different periods of O'Neill's career in order to demonstrate how the failed endings of the early works developed into the successful closures of his later plays.

Anna Karenina

Author: Leo Tolstoy (1828-1910)
First published: 1875-1877 (English translation, 1886)
Type of work: Novel
Type of plot: Social realism
Time of plot: Nineteenth century
Locale: Russia

Principal characters:
ANNA KARENINA
ALEXEI KARENIN, her husband
COUNT VRONSKY, her lover
STEPAN OBLONSKY, her brother
KITTY SHTCHERBATSKY, Stepan's sister-in-law
KONSTANTINE LEVIN, Kitty's beloved

The Story:

Anna Karenina, the sister of Stepan Oblonsky, comes to Moscow in an attempt to patch up a quarrel between her brother and his wife, Dolly. There she meets the handsome young Count Vronsky, who is rumored to be in love with Dolly's younger sister, Kitty. Konstantine Levin, of an old Muscovite family, is also in love with Kitty, and his visit to Moscow coincides with Anna's. Kitty refuses Levin, but to her chagrin she receives no proposal from the count. Indeed, Vronsky has no intention of proposing to Kitty. His heart goes out to Anna the first time he lays eyes on her, and when Anna returns to her home in St. Petersburg, he follows her.

Soon they begin to be seen together at soirées and at the theater, apparently unaware of gossip that circulates about them. Karenin, Anna's husband, becomes concerned. A coldly ambitious and dispassionate man, he believes that his social position is at stake. One night, he discusses these rumors with Anna and points out the danger of her flirtation, as he calls it. He forbids her to entertain Vronsky at home and cautions her to be more careful. He is not jealous of his wife, only worried over the social consequences of her behavior. He reminds her of her duty to her young son, Seryozha. Anna says she will obey him, and there the matter rests.

Anna, however, is unable to conceal her true feelings when Vronsky is injured in a racetrack accident. Karenin upbraids her for her indiscreet behavior in public. He considers a duel, separation, and divorce but rejects all these courses. When he finally decides to keep Anna under his roof, he reflects that he is acting in accordance with the laws of religion. Anna continues to meet Vronsky in secret.

Levin returns to his country estate after Kitty refuses him, and he busies himself there in problems of agriculture and peasant labor. One day, he goes into the fields and works with a scythe along with the serfs. He believes that he is beginning to understand the old primitive philosophy of their lives. He plans new developments, among them a cooperative enterprise system. When he hears that Kitty is not married after all and that she was ill but will soon be returning to Moscow, he resolves to seek her hand in marriage once more. Secretly, he knows she loves him. His pride, as well as hers, keeps them apart. Accordingly, Levin makes the journey to Moscow with new hope that soon Kitty will be his wife.

Against her husband's orders, Anna sends for Vronsky and tells him that she is pregnant. Aware of his responsibilities to Anna, he begs her to petition Karenin for a divorce so that she will be free to marry him. Karenin informs her coldly that he will consider the child his and accept it so that the world should never know his wife's disgrace, and he refuses to think of going through shameful divorce proceedings. Karenin reduces Anna to submission by warning her that he will take Seryozha away if she persists in making a fool of herself.

The strained family relationship continues unbroken. One night, Karenin plans to go out, and Anna persuades Vronsky to come to the house. As he is leaving, Karenin meets Vronsky on the front steps. Enraged, Karenin tells Anna that he has decided to get a divorce and that he will keep Seryozha in his custody. Divorce proceedings, however, are so intricate, the scandal so great, the whole aspect of the step so disgusting to Karenin that he cannot bring himself to go through with the process. As Anna's confinement draws near, he is still undecided. After winning an important political seat, he becomes even more unwilling to risk his public reputation.

At the birth of her child, Anna becomes deathly ill. Overcome with guilt, Vronsky attempts suicide but fails. Karenin is reduced to a state of such confusion that he determines to grant his wife any request, since he thinks she is on her deathbed. The sight of Vronsky seems to be the only thing that restores her. After many months of illness, she goes with her lover and her baby daughter to Italy, where they live under strained circumstances. Meanwhile, Levin proposes once more to Kitty; after a flurry of preparations, they are married.

Anna and Vronsky return to Russia and go to live on his estate. It is now impossible for Anna to return home. Although Karenin did not go through with divorce proceedings, he considers himself separated from Anna and is everywhere thought to be a man of fine loyalty and unswerving honor, unjustly imposed upon by an unfaithful wife. Sometimes Anna steals into town to see Seryozha, but her fear of being discovered there by her husband cuts these visits short.

After each visit, Anna returns bitter and sad. She becomes more demanding toward Vronsky, with the result that he spends less time with her. She takes little interest in her younger child. Before long, she convinces herself that Vronsky is in love with another woman. One day, Anna cannot stay alone in the house. She finds herself at the railway station, and she buys a ticket. As she stands on the platform gazing at the tracks below, the thunder of an approaching train roars in her ears. Suddenly, she remembers a man run over in the Moscow railroad station on the day she and Vronsky met. Carefully measuring the distance, she throws herself in front of the approaching train.

After Anna's death, Vronsky joins the army. He changes from a handsome, cheerful man to one who welcomes death; his only reason for living was Anna. For Levin and Kitty, life becomes a round of increasing daily work and mundane routine, which they share with each other. At last, Levin knows the responsibility wealth imposes upon him in his dealings with the peasants. Kitty helps him to handle his responsibility. Although there are many questions he can never answer satisfactorily to himself, he is nevertheless aware of the satisfying beauty of life—its toil, leisure, pain, and happiness.

Critical Evaluation:

After Leo Tolstoy first conceived of *Anna Karenina* it took him seven years to finish the novel, the last four of which were spent in the task of writing. According to his wife Sonia's diary, the idea of writing a novel about adultery first occurred to Tolstoy in 1870. It was not until three years later, however, as Tolstoy remarked in a letter to a friend, that the impetus to begin work on the book was provided by Tolstoy's rereading of a fragment in Alexander Pushkin's *Povesti Belkina* (1831; *The Tales of Belkin*, 1947). Tolstoy attributed the inspiration to a line that conjured in his imagination the scene of a reception in fashionable society—the scene manifests itself as Princess Betsy Tvershaya's party. Pushkin's influence, however, was perhaps greater than Tolstoy realized, for, in some aspects of character and appearance, Anna Karenina resembles Pushkin's protagonist Zinaida Volsky. Nevertheless, Tolstoy's work on the novel proceeded at an agonizingly slow pace, leaving the writer endlessly frustrated by what he described as a "block" that hampered his progress. Although the opening chapters appeared in 1875—the novel was first published in installments—the last chapters did not find their way into print until 1877. Tolstoy's perfectionism was such that he would allow nothing less than his best writing to be published, regardless of the personal anguish that the constant rewriting caused him.

The epigraph to *Anna Karenina*—a quotation from Romans 12:19, "'Vengeance is mine: I will repay,' saith the Lord"—is suggestive of its theme, for Tolstoy, like his contemporary Fyodor Dostoevski, was deeply concerned with sin (or crime), guilt, punishment, and atonement. Moreover, the epigraph implies, along with its express prohibition of human retribution, that judgment, too, is a divine prerogative. It thus furnishes a key to Tolstoy's treatment of characters in the novel. He does not, for example, explicitly praise or condemn Anna, since such a value judgment would usurp a godly privilege. This is also true of the other characters. Tolstoy does not evaluate, he describes. However, it is difficult to avoid drawing some conclusions because the plot revolves around adultery, an offense with both social and theological ramifications. Nevertheless, Tolstoy maintained that his intent was to show that all the adverse consequences of evil ultimately originated with God. In this context, then, Anna's ostracism from polite society, for example, would have to be understood as a manifestation of God's will—an interpretation consonant with Tolstoy's mystical religious beliefs. There is no doubt that Anna sinned, and society's punishment of her appears to confirm God's guilty verdict. No matter how extenuating the circumstances, Tolstoy seems to say, God's punishment of sinners is inexorable.

In developing this theme in *Anna Karenina*, Tolstoy minimizes the purely secular interest that society has in suppressing adultery as an act disruptive of the social order, although this aspect of the problem has been dealt with by other novelists writing about adultery. Two examples will suffice here. In *The Scarlet Letter* (1850), Nathaniel Hawthorne depicts Hester Prynne's adultery as both a crime against society and a sin against God. Although Hester admits she is a sinner, she will not concede that she is a criminal. Thus, the spiritual strength that she derives from her admission of sinful guilt enables her to cope with her social isolation and ultimately to survive. However, Hawthorne, despite portraying Hester in a sympathetic light, does not clearly exonerate her, for he sees value in society's standards, too. In effect, he declines to choose between the two. In *Madame Bovary* (1857), however, Gustave Flaubert presents Emma's adulteries strictly as transgressions against society; theological considerations are virtually nonexistent. Obsessed with romantic fantasies, Emma has no conception of the real-life strictures of society. Her multiple infidelities carry her deep into debt with gifts for her lovers and with clothing, perfumes, and cosmetics for herself. When she is at last forced to accept the reality that she cannot pay her creditor, she is overwhelmed with guilt, remorse, despair, and the fear of discovery. She then takes arsenic and dies quickly but painfully, unable to face the punishment society is certain to exact. Flaubert thus underscores both the power and the primacy of society's norms.

These three well-known novels about adultery—*The Scarlet Letter*, *Madame Bovary*, and *Anna Karenina*—differ in their emphases, but their treatment of adultery is essentially similar. On one hand, the emphasis in *The Scarlet Letter* is on the tension between the values of established society (religious and social) and individual values; in *Anna Karenina*, it is on the immanence of spiritual values and God's will. On the other hand, all three novels disapprove of adultery, although their reasons vary according to their biases.

In *Anna Karenina*, Tolstoy wrote a moving story of human emotional needs conflicting with the dominant social mores of the time. Given Tolstoy's religious mysticism combined with his incipient socialism, this elemental conflict could be resolved in no other way. The crucial factor in the equation revolves around what is usually characterized, euphemistically, as "the Russian soul," a quality lacking in Hawthorne and Flaubert. This nearly ineffable quality amalgamates religious mysticism and nationalism into almost divine zeal, the pressures of which eventually drive Anna to suicide, since her sense of betrayal of moral imperatives is nevertheless acute for her having betrayed them. She is thus uniquely representative of "the Russian soul." As such, she symbolizes Tolstoy's genuinely Russian insistence upon the marrying of eternal verities with modern conditions. For this reason, many critics believe that *Anna Karenina* stands not second to but equal with *Voyna i mir* (1866-1869; *War and Peace*, 1886) in Tolstoy's corpus, offering a profound insight into the relationship between the individual and the surrounding society.

"Critical Evaluation" by Joanne G. Kashdan

Further Reading

Bloom, Harold, ed. *Leo Tolstoy*. New York: Chelsea House, 1986. Contains essays by R. P. Blackmur and Barbara Hardy. The former explores the way Tolstoy exposes his characters to ambiguity, studies their society and its manners, and discusses the nature of Anna's tragedy. The latter emphasizes Tolstoy's vivid realism, his superb handling of the flow of time, and the intricate and deft way he populates his novels with characters. Includes chronology and bibliography.

Jones, Malcolm, ed. *New Essays on Tolstoy*. New York: Cambridge University Press, 1978. In "Problems of Communication," Jones explores Tolstoy's amazing sense of physical presence and gesture and how previous critics have treated it.

Knapp, Liza, and Amy Mandelker, eds. *Approaches to Teaching Tolstoy's "Anna Karenina."* New York: Modern Language Association of America, 2003. Provides analysis of the novel by noted Tolstoy scholars. Includes discussions of the novel's setting; the history of its serial publication; body, sexuality, adultery, and the woman question in the novel; Tolstoy's antiphilosophical philosophy; and *Anna Karenina* in the literary traditions of Russia and the West.

Knowles, A. V., ed. *Tolstoy: The Critical Heritage*. Boston: Routledge & Kegan Paul, 1978. Contains contemporary Russian reviews of the novel from 1875 to 1877. Includes a bibliography and an appendix with Russian literary and historical references.

McLean, Hugh. *In Quest of Tolstoy*. Boston: Academic Studies Press, 2008. McLean, a professor emeritus of Russian at the University of California, Berkeley, and longtime Tolstoy scholar, compiled this collection of essays that examine Tolstoy's writings and ideas and assess his influence on other writers and thinkers. Includes discussions of the young Tolstoy and women and of Tolstoy and Jesus, Charles Darwin, Ernest Hemingway, and Maxim Gorky.

Morson, Gary Saul. *"Anna Karenina" in Our Time: Seeing More Wisely*. New Haven, Conn.: Yale University Press, 2007. Examines the ethical, philosophical, and social issues with which Tolstoy grapples in the novel, demonstrating how he challenges traditional conceptions of romantic love, social reform, modernization, and the nature of good and evil.

Orwin, Donna Tussig, ed. *The Cambridge Companion to Tolstoy*. New York: Cambridge University Press, 2002. Collection of essays, including discussions of Tolstoy as a writer of popular literature, the development of his style and themes, his aesthetics, and Tolstoy in the twentieth century. Barbara Lönnquist provides an analysis of *Anna Karenina*.

Rowe, William W. *Leo Tolstoy*. Boston: Twayne, 1986. Chapter 5 treats the novel as Tolstoy's finest and traces how he developed the idea for it. Provides a detailed discussion of the novel's structure, as well as separate sections on different themes and literary techniques, such as Anna's "guilt," Levin and Kitty, and foreshadowing. Includes chronology, notes, and bibliography.

Wilson, A. N. *Tolstoy*. London: H. Hamilton, 1988. A full-scale biography. Chapter 12 delves into the gestation and development of *Anna Karenina*, its structural cohesiveness, and its scenes of intimacy. Includes notes and bibliography.

Anna of the Five Towns

Author: Arnold Bennett (1867-1931)
First published: 1902
Type of work: Novella
Type of plot: Domestic realism
Time of plot: Late nineteenth century
Locale: The Potteries, England

Principal characters:
EPHRAIM TELLWRIGHT, a miser
ANNA, his older daughter
AGNES, his younger daughter
HENRY MYNORS, Anna's suitor
WILLIE PRICE, a man in love with Anna
BEATRICE SUTTON, Anna's friend

The Story:

Ephraim Tellwright is a miser, one of the wealthiest men in any of the Five Towns, a group of small industrial towns joined by a single road. He is a former Methodist lay preacher and teacher, concerned more with getting congregations in sound financial shape than with their souls. Although he married money and makes more money from rentals and foreclosures, he lives in the most frugal way possible and gives his two daughters nothing but the barest essentials. Both of his wives have died, the first giving him his daughter Anna and the second producing Agnes. Tellwright is usually taciturn. As long as his meals are on time, no money is wasted, and the house is never left alone and unguarded, he pays little attention to his daughters. Anna loves her father, even though she can never feel close to him. Agnes, much younger, follows her sister's lead. The two girls are unusually close, having no one else in their lives.

On Anna's twenty-first birthday, her father calls her into his office and tells her that she is inheriting almost fifty thousand pounds from her mother's estate. He invested the original sum wisely, and it grew to a fortune. Anna, who never owned one pound to call her own, cannot comprehend an amount so large. Accustomed to letting her father handle all business affairs, she willingly gives him control of her fortune. The income from the stocks and rentals is deposited in the bank in her name, but she gives her father her checkbook and signs only when she is instructed to do so. The money makes little difference in Anna's life; it simply stays in the bank until her father tells her to invest it.

One result of the money, however, creates unhappiness for Anna. Among her properties is a run-down factory owned by Titus Price, who is also a Methodist and superintendent of the chapel's Sunday school. Because Price is continually behind in his rent, Tellwright forces Anna to keep demanding something on account. Knowing that the property will never rent to anyone else, the old miser never puts Price out but keeps hounding him for as much as the man can pay. Anna usually has to deal with Willie Price, the son, and she always leaves the interview with a feeling of guilt. Although the sight of Willie's embarrassment leaves her unhappy, she always demands his money, because she is afraid to face her father without it.

A teacher in the Sunday school in which Anna teaches is Henry Mynors, already at the age of thirty a pillar in the chapel and a successful man in the community. Anna is attracted to him, and she tries to join in his religious fervor but cannot quite bring herself to repent or to accept God publicly at the revival meetings. She feels that repentance should be a private matter. Henry is clearly in love with her. When the townspeople say that he is interested mainly in her money, Anna refuses to believe the gossip. Henry begins to call on her occasionally, combining his courtship with business with Tellwright. The miser persuades Anna to invest some of her money in Henry's business after first arranging for a large share of the profits and a high interest.

After Anna comes in to her fortune, she is invited for the first time to the house of Mrs. Sutton, the town's social leader. Mrs. Sutton's daughter Beatrice and Anna becomes friends. Rumors spread that Beatrice and Henry were once engaged. The Suttons take Anna and Henry to the Isle of Man on a vacation, and Anna thinks there can never again be such luxurious living. It was necessary for her to take ten pounds of her own money to get clothes for the trip, but her father berated her violently when she told him what she did. Her time spent with Henry and the Suttons, however, helps her forget his anger. When the vacation is marred by Beatrice's serious illness, Anna wins a permanent place in the Suttons' affection by her unselfish and competent nursing.

After Beatrice recovers, Anna and Henry return home. Before they leave the island, Henry proposes to Anna, and she accepts. Later her father gives his consent, because Henry knows the value of money. Young Agnes is enchanted by the romantic aspects of the courtship, and Anna is happy in her quiet love for Henry. The joy of her engagement, however, is immediately clouded by the news that old Mr. Price hanged himself. Anna feels that she and her father are to blame, because they hounded him for his rent. Henry assures her that Mr. Price was in debt to many people and that she need not feel guilty. Nevertheless, Anna worries a great deal about the suicide and about Willie, for whom she has quite maternal feelings.

Later, Willie confesses to her that a bank note he gave in payment was forged. The confession seems to reduce Willie to nothing. Anna realizes that he and his father were driven to desperation, and she tries to protect Willie and Mr. Price's reputation by taking the forged note from her father's office. When she tells her father that she burned the note, he is furious with her and never forgives her.

Because Willie is planning to make a fresh start in Australia, Henry arranges to rent the Price house, intending that he and Anna will live there after they are married. Although Anna is sure she can never be happy in a house the miserable Prices owned, she is docile and lets Henry make all the arrangements. When Anna tells her father that she needs one hundred pounds to pay for her linens and her wedding clothes, Tellwright denounces her as a spendthrift. Handing over the checkbook, he tells her not to bother him again about her money. Henry, pleased at the turn of events, is full of plans for the use of Anna's fortune.

It becomes known that before his death, Mr. Price defrauded the chapel of fifty pounds. Anna tries to keep the information from Willie, but someone tells him just as he is ready to leave for Australia. When he tells Anna good-bye, he looks like a whipped child. As Anna looks into his eyes for the last time, she realizes suddenly that he loves her and that she loves him. She lets him go, however, because she feels bound by her promise to Henry. She was dutiful all her life; it is too late for her to change.

Willie is never heard from again. Had anyone in Five Towns happened to look into an abandoned pitshaft, the mystery of Willie would have been solved. The meek lad found his only way to peace.

Critical Evaluation:

Anna of the Five Towns, Arnold Bennett's second novel, was the first that established the identity of the Five Towns, that area of the West Midlands devoted to the pottery industry and usually known as the Potteries. This was where Bennett had been brought up and where he entered his father's law business until moving to London. The Five Towns, as he called them (there are actually six or seven), served as the setting for many of his subsequent and more famous novels, even though he never returned to live in the area.

The novel can to some extent be seen as a regional novel, as are Thomas Hardy's Wessex novels and some of George Eliot's works. Like Eliot's *Adam Bede* (1859), *Anna of the Five Towns* has a Midlands setting further defined by the various Methodist communities that flourished there in the mid- and late nineteenth century. Unlike Eliot's rural novel, however, *Anna of the Five Towns* can also be classified as an industrial novel. Bennett describes the details of the pottery manufacture knowledgeably, and he contrasts the best and worst practices in the works of Titus Price and Henry Mynors. This contrast echoes the larger contrast between Price's son, Willie, who works in his father's ramshackle workshop, and Henry, whose efficiency in everything he does is exemplified in his modern factory.

In its Midlands setting, chapel culture, and industrial descriptions, *Anna of the Five Towns* also anticipates the novels of D. H. Lawrence. Like Lawrence, Bennett stresses the ugliness of industrialized urbanization, the ruination of the countryside, and the circumscribed, barren lives of many of the working class. Bennett, however, unlike Lawrence, does not attempt poetry in his style but veers toward the documentary. One feels there is some civic pride left in Bennett, just as civic pride continued among the inhabitants of the Potteries later in the century. More important, Bennett does not point toward a counterculture; spiritual life, insofar as it is still possible, is to be found in traditional interior modes of Christian self-examination as defined by the practices and traditions of Methodist spirituality.

In some ways, therefore, *Anna of the Five Towns* could also be called a religious novel: not in the traditional sense of the Victorian religious novel, but as a result of Bennett's taking the religious practices, beliefs, and spirituality of his characters seriously and analyzing them in a sympathetic way. Here again, Bennett is more akin to Eliot than to Hardy or Lawrence. Some critics have suggested that Bennett exposes the confining and even repressive atmosphere of nonconformity, but this is surely a prejudiced reading. Certain characters, among them Titus Price and Ephraim Tellwright, are exposed as hypocrites, yet their failings are portrayed in human terms. They are not the fault of Methodism. Ephraim's backsliding is part of his self-chosen dessication of spirit. He is based, if anything, on Honoré de Balzac's *Eugénie Grandet* (1833).

The faith of other characters, however, is genuine: Mrs. Sutton's is particularly attractive, but even Henry's is perfectly genuine. His Christian life may seem too perfect, but this is made to seem so by Bennett to underline Anna's unease with him and to explain why in fact she fell in love with Willie. His tentativeness and confessed failure awake maternal protectiveness in her, an emotion that had survived the dessication of the Tellwright household.

In fact, Bennett has described very accurately not only the industrial state of the Potteries at the latter end of the nineteenth century, but also the state of nonconformist Protestantism, when the fires of the evangelical spirit were being replaced by duty and good works as an unspoken piety. Anna's spiritual odyssey mirrors this exactly: Unable to respond to the fervor of the revival meetings, she consciously chooses good works, obedience, and duty, and this she believes includes marriage to Henry, the epitome of the good Christian leader. Anna's choice is one of powerlessness. In feminist terms, she trades the control of father for that of husband. Although the situation may be sanctioned by religion, Bennett does not see it as having been caused by it. The irony is that neither Anna's religion nor her money ever becomes a source of empowerment for her. She remains the poor little rich girl.

The literary success of *Anna of the Five Towns* lies in its being above all a novel of character. It is written from within Anna's experience and consciousness, and the inner psychological movements of her growth are as delicately described by Bennett as Hardy delineates Tess's development in *Tess of the D'Urbervilles* (1891). Anna's sympathies are those that remain with the reader, which is why her miserly and manipulative father retains some shreds of humanity and never becomes a Dickensian caricature. The scene in which Anna, on her twenty-first birthday, is presented with a list of documents to sign as the induction into her wealth is memorable because of the ambiguities of tone and sympathy with which the author surrounds this rite of passage. Bennett wisely understates the ironies of her shabby dress and yet polite treatment by moneyed society; he is more concerned with Anna's conscience and its dilemma. She technically owns the ramshackle Price works, and it is she who demands the rent, yet she is almost powerless not to do so, and so feels her guilt. The gesture of tearing up the forged note is poignant, as is, in its futility, the final, unused gift of a bank draft to Willie.

The novel's ending is, from the point of view of character, an anticlimax. Greater happiness could have been accorded to Anna, but Bennett is always a realist. Although she will have no great sorrows in her future life, she will have to rely on just those few memories of joy, epitomized in the Isle of Man holiday, to feed her spirit. Bennett is the sympathetic novelist of ordinary people, and *Anna of the Five Towns* a truly democratic novel.

Bennett's style and structures are economic and prefigure the growing economy of the twentieth century modernist novel, as opposed to the sprawling Victorian one. There is always sufficient detail to describe home, church, town, and factory; a sufficient variety of incidents within Anna's circumscribed life; and sufficient dialogue to balance the narrative. Everything unnecessary is pared away, however. The plot revolves around Henry's courtship of Anna, but as this is understated in itself, it allows Bennett a leisurely pace. His economies are not those of the miser but of the good housekeeper. The "slice of life" method of the French realists is the most powerful literary model, and what emerges is a novella.

"Critical Evaluation" by David Barratt

Further Reading

Anderson, Linda R. *Bennett, Wells, and Conrad: Narrative in Transition*. London: Macmillan, 1988. Concentrates on the period 1890-1919 and concludes that each novelist was responding to a major redefining of the idea of the novel and of its relationship to reality. Also explores Bennett's refusal to distinguish between serious and popular literature. Analyzes *Anna of the Five Towns* in detail. Selected bibliography and index.

Bauer, H. P. "Spiritual Maternity and Self-Fulfillment in Arnold Bennett's *Anna of the Five Towns*." In *The Anna Book: Searching for Anna in Literary History*, edited by Mickey Pearlman. Westport, Conn.: Greenwood Press, 1992. A historical, critical discussion of *Anna of the Five Towns* in a collection of essays about fictional characters named Anna.

Drabble, Margaret. *Arnold Bennett*. New York: Alfred A. Knopf, 1974. The most readable of the biographies on Bennett. Helps relate the complicated nexus that held him to the Five Towns, even when physically and culturally far removed. Contains a bibliography and index, including a full list of Bennett's published works.

Koenigsberger, Kurt. "Elephants in the Labyrinth of Empire: Arnold Bennett, Modernism, and the Menagerie." In *The Novel and the Menagerie: Totality, Englishness, and Empire*. Columbus: Ohio State University Press, 2007. Koenigsberg traces the relationship of zoos and other animal collections to the narratives in domestic English novels, including those of Bennett. Koenigsberger maintains that writers drew upon menageries as a means of representing the dominance of the British empire in the daily life of England.

Lucas, John. *Arnold Bennett: A Study of His Fiction*. London: Methuen, 1974. A general overview of his fiction that includes a substantial section on *Anna of the Five Towns*. Praises Bennett's handling of Anna's relationship with Willie Price.

McDonald, Peter D. "Playing the Field: Arnold Bennett as Novelist, Serialist, and Journalist." In *British Literary Culture and Publishing Practice, 1880-1914*. New York: Cambridge University Press, 1997. Examines the publishing careers of Bennett, Joseph Conrad, and Sir Arthur Conan Doyle in order to demonstrate the radical transformation of British literary culture in the years between 1880 and 1914.

Squillace, Robert. *Modernism, Modernity, and Arnold Bennett*. Lewisburg, Pa.: Bucknell University Press, 1997. Squillace argues that Bennett saw more clearly than his contemporaries the emergence of the modern era, which transformed a male-dominated society to one open to all people regardless of class or gender. Detailed notes and a bibliography acknowledge the work of some of the best scholars.

Stone, Donald. "The Art of Arnold Bennett: Transmutation and Empathy in *Anna of the Five Towns* and *Riceyman Steps*." In *Modernism Reconsidered*, edited by Robert Kiely. Cambridge, Mass.: Harvard University Press, 1983. A comparative study of Bennett's two novels in the context of twentieth century English literature. Includes bibliographic references.

Annals

Author: Tacitus (c. 56-c. 120)
First transcribed: Ab excessu divi Augusti, c. 116 C.E. (English translation, 1598)
Type of work: History

Principal personages:
TIBERIUS, Augustus Caesar's stepson and successor
GERMANICUS or NERO CLAUDIUS DRUSUS, Tiberius's brother
AGRIPPINA (MAJOR), Germanicus's wife and Caligula's mother
DRUSUS, Tiberius's son
DRUSUS, Germanicus's son
CALIGULA, Tiberius's successor
CLAUDIUS, Caligula's uncle and his successor
MESSALINA, Claudius's first wife
AGRIPPINA (MINOR), Claudius's niece and second wife
BRITANNICUS, Claudius's son, killed by Nero
NERO, Agrippina's son and Claudius's successor
POPPAEA, Nero's wife
AELIUS SEJANUS, Tiberius's favorite
PISO, leader of a conspiracy against Nero

By an accident of fate, works of Cornelius Tacitus are the only surviving histories of his day; all the writings of his contemporaries and immediate predecessors are lost. It may be that the fates were guided by standards of literary aesthetics rather than historical accuracy. Tacitus's facts and interpretations have from time to time been severely criticized, but he has always been admired for his lucid, morally charged narrative style. The *Annals* are not only a skillful prose account of a half century of Roman history but also a compassionate evaluation of the horrors of imperial despotism. In fact, the earliest extant manuscript is entitled *Ab excessu divi Augusti* (although in book 4, the writer refers to his work as *Annals*).

Tacitus saw in Roman history a gradual decline from a primitive golden age when no laws were necessary to times when laws became a necessity and, finally, an abominable evil. As the *Annals* proceed from the reign of Tiberius to those of Claudius and of Nero (a section dealing with Caligula is lost, as are the last books), the tyranny becomes more cruel, the populace and patricians become more submissive, the opportunists and informers become more despicable, and the dwindling number of virtuous people become more helpless. In these matters, Tacitus is by no means taciturn; in fact, so great are the horrors depicted in the *Annals* that until the atrocities of modern politics and war recapitulated them on a horrendously magnified scale, Tacitus's readers were inclined to view his account as grossly exaggerated, beyond the possible depths to which human nature could sink.

Tacitus is modest about his aims, though the grave irony of his remarks should not go unnoticed:

> The matter upon which I am occupied is circumscribed, and unproductive of renown to the author—a state of undisturbed peace, or only interrupted in limited degree, the sad condition of affairs in the city, and a prince indifferent about extending the bounds of the empire. Not unprofitable, however, will it be to investigate matters which, though unimportant in a superficial view, frequently give the first impulse to events of magnitude. . . . I have only to record the mandates of despotism, incessant accusations, faithless friendships, the ruin of innocence; the one unvarying repetition of causes terminating in the same event, and presenting no novelty from their similarity and tiresome repetition. (4, 32-33)

In general, Tacitus presents not a sustained history but a chronological depiction of selected events—some thoroughly detailed over several chapters and others sketched in lightly, continually referred to but not described extensively in any one place. It has been conjectured that the original *Annals* consisted of three hexads, the pattern employed by Vergil, Statius, Polynus, and Cicero, but there is no concrete evidence that there were two books written after book 16, and the loss of books 7-10 prevents scholars from being absolutely certain that those books fitted with books 11-12 to constitute a middle hexad. At any rate, the *Annals*, as they now stand, can be conveniently arranged by subject matter—the reign of Tiberius is the concern of the first six books, of Claudius in books 11-12, and of Nero in the final four books.

This is not to say that the focus of attention is concentrated on the three emperors. In dealing with Tiberius, for example, Tacitus devotes the opening forty-nine chapters to the first year (more space than to any other year of the entire history), beginning with the jockeying for power after the death of Augustus. Since Tiberius never led troops in battle after he became emperor, the narrative shifts to Tiberius's son Drusus (chapters 16-30) quelling the Pannonian mutiny and to Germanicus (most of chapters 31-71) campaigning on the Rhine. These two men, possible heirs to the throne, were the objects of the intrigues of the utterly unscrupulous Aelius Sejanus, Tiberius's favorite. Jealous of Germanicus's successes, Tiberius had him recalled and sent east as king in Armenia, where he died in 19 C.E., probably at the hands of Piso under orders from Tiberius. Piso's trial ended abruptly with his unexplained murder, although Tacitus hints that Tiberius arranged that as well. Drusus, then, dominated the sons of Germanicus as heir apparent, but Tiberius openly preferred Sejanus—"a stranger was called in as coadjutor in the government; nay, how little was wanting to his being declared colleague." Sejanus, "whose heart insatiably lusted for supreme domination," then dispatched Drusus with a slow poison that made him appear a victim of disease and set out to marry Livia, his widow and the sister of Germanicus. There remained, however, Agrippina, widow of Germanicus, and her three sons. Sejanus contrived open enmity between Agrippina and Tiberius and skillfully arranged for the emperor to retire to Capri from Rome in 27 C.E. There, while Sejanus plotted his rise to power, Tiberius "indulged his cruel and libidinous disposition . . . in the secrecy of a retired situation." One of the most tantalizing lacunae of the *Annals* deals with Agrippina's hopeless struggle for the rights of her sons and the final conflict between Sejanus and the emperor, a struggle leading to Sejanus's execution.

The first hexad ends with Tiberius at the age of seventy-eight, at which age he had outlived all the intriguers who surrounded him and relinquished "nothing of his libidinous excesses." His end was dramatic, and Tacitus relishes the irony. Assured by Tiberius's physician that his death was imminent,

> Caligula in the midst of a great throng of persons, paying their gratulations, was already going forth to make a solemn entrance on the sovereignty, when suddenly a notice came, "that Tiberius had recovered his sight and voice, and had called for some persons to give him food to restore him." The consternation was universal: the concourse about Caligula dispersed in all directions. . . . Caligula himself stood fixed in silence—fallen from the highest hopes, he now expected the worst. Macro [Caligula's right-hand man], undismayed, ordered the old man to be smothered with a quantity of clothes. (6, 51)

The dramatic technique is magnificent. Caligula is left as a monstrous legacy to Rome. The extant history resumes in book 11 with Claudius's succession to the purple. The new emperor is depicted as a cut above his predecessors: He dignified the theater, augmented the alphabet, restrained predatory creditors, increased the senate, and incorporated new provinces into the Empire. Intrigues, however, continued to flourish, centering upon Claudius's wife Messalina, who was concerned at the way in which freedmen (especially Narcissus and Pallas) had gained power. Messalina, knowing she was about to be murdered by Claudius's agents, committed suicide: "Tidings were then carried to Claudius 'that Messalina was no more'; without inquiring whether by her own or another's hand, [he] called for a cup of wine and proceeded in the feast." Tacitus brilliantly achieves a sense of horror at the moral corruption of the Roman Empire with just such detail and understatement. Book 12 opens with the contest among the freedmen concerning the choice of a new wife for Claudius. Pallas prevailed with his suggestion of Agrippina, despite the fact that she was the daughter of Claudius's brother Germanicus. The horrendous narrative continues to delineate debauchery and chaos. Nero destroyed the emperor's son Britannicus, and Agrippina afterward poisoned Claudius in order to secure the succession for her own son, Nero. Book 13 tells of Agrippina's struggles for power, first against the freedwoman Acte and then against Poppaea, Nero's wife—murders and counter-murders and abortive palace revolts that went on while Nero engaged in his orgiastic debauches. Book 14 opens with Poppaea's vigorously dramatic reproach against Nero for his cowardice in not destroying his mother, who had desperately clung to life and power by incestuously lavishing her own body on her son. Tacitus handles Nero's attempts on Agrippina's life with almost grotesque comedy. First, she was put to sea in a faulty vessel, but she swam ashore while another woman, hoping to save herself by claiming to be the emperor's mother, was slain. Finally, brute force was resorted to and she was slain in bed: "to the centurion, as he was drawing his sword to dispatch her, she presented her womb, and with a loud voice, 'Strike your sword into my belly,' she cried, and was instantly dispatched." Thus, Tacitus vivifies an important dramatic scene with a stroke of realism.

Nero, struck with remorse and apparently unaware of the extent to which Roman society had degenerated to his own low level, feared to return to the capital. Matricide during the Republic would have seemed the destruction of morality's basis, the family. Nero's entry into Rome, however, was triumphant, and he thenceforth "abandoned himself to all his inordinate passions which, though insufficiently controlled, had been somewhat checked by his reverence for his mother, such as it was." Throughout his career "Nero wallowed in all sorts of defilements, lawful and unlawful: and seemed to leave no atrocity which could add to his pollution," including one that Tacitus describes with great disgust—a mock-marriage "with all the solemnities of wedlock" to a homosexual. The height of Nero's inhuman cruelty was the great fire of Rome, in which he madly reveled and from which he gained enormous profits. The most sustained episode of the final books concerns the conspiracy in 65 C.E. of Piso and eighteen other leaders to assassinate Nero and set up Piso as emperor.

Piso gave no promise of better government, since he was almost as addicted to sensuous pleasure as Nero himself, but some change was obviously necessary. The conspiracy had difficulty settling on a method, and before it could get underway the plot was inadvertently revealed when Epicharis, a freedwoman, attempted to solicit one of Nero's naval officers, Volusius Proculus, who alerted Nero. One of the rare cases of personal virtue was Epicharis's refusal to betray the conspirators, despite the horrible torture she endured. In their haste the conspirators betrayed themselves, and in panic Nero began wholesale slaughters. Chapters 37-70 constitute a steady series of death scenes—Epicharis, Seneca, Subrius Flavus, Lucan (who died reciting his verses), and others—each presented with vivid detail. Piso, though urged to stir up a popular revolt, chose to sever his veins and "left a will full of odious flattery to Nero, in tenderness to his wife, a depraved woman and void of every recommendation but personal beauty."

The deaths of those close to Nero continued. Poppaea died "by a fit of passion in her husband, who gave her a violent blow with his foot when she was pregnant; for I cannot believe he poisoned her as some have stated." Her funeral was sumptuous; she was embalmed with spices rather than cremated as was the custom, but her death was "rejoiced at by those who recollected her . . . lewdness and cruelty." An account of the last two years of Nero's life is missing. The *Annals* end in mid-sentence, which indicates that this section was lost.

Such are the main lines of Tacitus's history, but the text abounds in frequent digressions tracing in close detail the fortunes of the Roman Empire and its provinces and outposts. This is done so vividly that some authorities suggest that Tacitus must have had a host of reliable sources in the form of autobiographies and diaries. The *Annals*, however, are in sum clearly the personal document of a writer with sincerity, intelligence, courage, and enormous artistry. In a very real sense, Tacitus was an existentialist in his manner of understanding the replacement of traditional morality with corruption. Convinced that human effort is absurd, he was sustained by a faith in human solidarity and unity in suffering. The gravity of his tragic vision is relieved by a deeply felt compassion for suffering, and he has left in the *Annals* one of the greatest histories of all time.

Further Reading

Davies, Jason P. *Rome's Religious History: Livy, Tacitus, and Ammianus on Their Gods*. New York: Cambridge University Press, 2004. Examines how Tacitus and the two other ancient writers depicted the role of religion in their accounts of Roman history.

Luce, T. J., and A. J. Woodman, eds. *Tacitus and the Tacitean Tradition*. Princeton, N.J.: Princeton University Press, 1993. Anthologizes important criticism by leading Tacitus scholars. Comments on the historian's influence as well as his achievement.

Mellor, Ronald. *Tacitus*. London: Routledge & Kegan Paul, 1993. An essential work. Portrays Tacitus as a moralist and psychologist whose observations of imperial Rome are of permanent relevance. Discusses how the portraits of the various emperors reflect Tacitus's biases and partialities.

Momigliano, Arnaldo. *Essays in Ancient and Modern Historiography*. Middletown, Conn.: Wesleyan University Press, 1977. An authoritative study that places Tacitus within the tradition of historiography.

O'Gorman, Ellen. *Irony and Misreading in the "Annals" of Tacitus*. New York: Cambridge University Press, 2000. Analyzes the language and style of *Annals*, placing the work within the context of Roman politics and theories of history in the first and second centuries C.E.

Paterculus, Velleius. *The Tiberian Narrative, 2.94-131*. Edited by A. J. Woodman. New York: Cambridge University Press, 1977. Comprehensive treatment of the portrait of Tiberius. Stresses the measure of qualified admiration within Tacitus's general contempt for the emperor.

Santoro L'Hoir, Francesca. *Tragedy, Rhetoric, and the Historiography of Tacitus' "Annales."* Ann Arbor: University of Michigan Press, 2006. Examines how Tacitus's historical work incorporated the themes, vocabulary, and poetic imagery of Attic and Roman tragedy.

Syme, Ronald. *Tacitus*. Oxford, England: Clarendon Press, 1958. Still an excellent sourcebook for the general reader. The most ambitious attempt to correlate Tacitus's history with documentary evidence on ancient Rome.

Annie Allen

Author: Gwendolyn Brooks (1917-2000)
First published: 1949
Type of work: Poetry

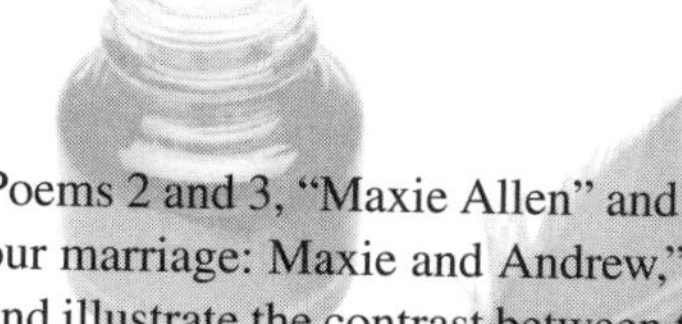

With the publication of her second book of poetry, *Annie Allen*, Chicago poet Gwendolyn Brooks became the first African American to win a Pulitzer Prize. The blackness-nourishing collection is arranged in three parts: "Notes from the Childhood and the Girlhood," "The Anniad" (which includes the long poem of that title and two short works as "Appendix to the Anniad"), and "The Womanhood." As the titles imply, each section of the book corresponds to a stage in the life of Annie Allen.

Brooks is securely anchored in the African American literary tradition. The poet's expertise with technical poetic forms is overshadowed only by her abiding and evident joy in words. Her work attests to an admiration for poet Langston Hughes, whose sharp comic irony matches her own. In the early 1940's, at their Chicago apartment located in the "very buckle of the Black belt," as Brooks describes it, she and her husband Henry Blakely gave a party for Hughes. Not long after, in 1945, Brooks's first book of poems, *A Street in Bronzeville*, was published by Harper & Row. Four years later, *Annie Allen* emerged to glowing reviews for its linguistic brilliance. While her first book emphasizes community consciousness, the second focuses on self-realization; the central character, Annie, moves from the security of her parents' home into city life, marriage, and motherhood. From her kitchenette above a real-estate agency, of which she says, "If you wanted a poem you had only to look out of a window," Brooks creates the three-part poem that explores the artistic sensibility of a black woman not unlike herself.

Annie Allen begins with a dedication poem: "Memorial to Ed Bland," a soldier killed in World War II. Brooks and Bland were members of a Chicago poetry-writing workshop conducted by Inez Cunningham Stark. This first poem presents Brooks's central theme of an artistic life cut short and unfulfilled. Its structure underlines the truncated testimonial with lines of varying length and irregular rhymes and rhythms.

The first part, "Notes from the Childhood and the Girlhood," contains eleven poems. Beginning with "the birth in a narrow room," Brooks describes Annie's genesis in a "western country" and her early years of prancing with "gods and fairies," a romantic sensibility that permeates her life in the years before she sadly realizes "How pinchy is my room!" Poems 2 and 3, "Maxie Allen" and "the parents: people like our marriage: Maxie and Andrew," portray Annie's parents and illustrate the contrast between their stable, humble lives and her dreams of "something other." Halfway through the rhymed couplets of "Maxie Allen," however, Annie's mother shares some of her daughter's dissatisfaction with the moderate, dull life that convinces them to settle for chicken and "shut the door."

Annie's innocent kindness comes through clearly in "Sunday chicken" (poem 4), eleven lines with three rhyming tercets and a concluding couplet. She dislikes killing the lovely "speckle-gray," "wild white," and "baffle-brown" chickens, comparing such actions to cannibalism. Poems 5 and 6 expose Annie once again to death and for the first time to white racism. Ironically, both poems have musical connections. In "old relative," structurally identical to poem 4, Annie grieves for the death of an elderly uncle and a resulting restriction on playing her favorite songs for the week-long mourning period. "[D]owntown vaudeville" introduces Annie to a black performer in a show attended by hostile whites:

> What was not pleasant was the hush that coughed
> when the Negro clown came on the stage and doffed
> His broken hat. The hush, first. Then the soft
> concatenation of delight and lift,
> And loud. The decked dismissal of his gift. . . .

If the first six poems in part 1 reflect Annie's childhood, poems 7 through 11 establish her as an adolescent dreamer hoping for a "gold half-god" to rescue her. Brooks believes in the power of the imagination and uses the ballad stanza in "the ballad of late Annie" and "throwing out the flowers" to introduce a mythical quality to the collection. Her flights of fancy, however, are always tempered by harsh reality. The theme of life truncated is reiterated once more in the final stanza of "throwing out the flowers":

> Forgotten and stinking they stick in the can,
> And the vase breath's better and all, and all.
> And so for the end of our life to a man,
> Just over, just over and all.

Despite such ominous foreshadowing, the first part of *Annie Allen* ends with two positive affirmations and hints of the heroic "Anniad" to follow. In "pygmies are pygmies still, though percht on Alps," Annie celebrates the excellence and independence of pygmies who can see better and laugh at all the giants wallowing below. Poem 11, "my own sweet good," implies Annie's appreciation of her goodness and worth; yet it ends with her anticipation of a golden promise from a dimpled gold god.

Part 2, "The Anniad," is a forty-three-stanza mock heroic celebrating Annie's everyday life in a technically grand style. Unusual for modern poetry, the mock heroic provides Brooks with a means of social criticism that does not seem to take itself too seriously. "The Anniad" begins with

> Think of sweet and chocolate,
> Left to folly or to fate,
> Whom the higher gods forgot,
> Whom the lower gods berate;
> Physical and underfed Fancying on the featherbed
> What was never and is not.

She dreams of a knight who will rescue her from her parents' home. By the end of "The Anniad" Annie has been courted, married, separated from her husband during the war, has suffered his infidelity, and has reconciled with him, and, finally, she is deserted permanently. Her "knight" loves neither her color nor her womanhood. He sees her as a mere trophy and "Leads her to a lowly room./ Which she makes a chapel of./ Where she genuflects to love."

"The Anniad's" self-conscious form and grandeur structurally convey Annie's satirical, lifesaving wit and imagination, while its content carries the daily frustrations, pain, and struggle. This contrast and resulting tension echo the earlier conflict between Annie's internal emotional complexity and her restrictive, "pinchy" room. When her "tan man" returns from war, he, like other black men, suffers from a lack of respect; he rejects her and pursues affairs with exotic, light-skinned women. While Annie tends the children at home, he revels with "wench and whiskey," trying to escape the overseas disease, tuberculosis, that stalks and finally kills him. The final stanza is a sad salute to Annie's survival and imagination:

> Think of almost thoroughly
> Derelict and dim and done.
> Stroking swallows from the sweat.
> Fingering faint violet.
> Hugging old and Sunday sun.
> Kissing in her kitchenette
> The minuets of memory.

The "Appendix to the Anniad" contains two poems, "leaves from a loose-leaf war diary" and "the sonnet-ballad," each challenging the romantic illusions created by "The Anniad." The first begins coldly with the line "thousands-killed in action" and goes on to suggest that to endure the horror of war and death ("untranslatable ice") people need superhuman powers. In the second stanza of the first poem, Brooks admits that the thought of heaven is no solace now. Instead, she longs for a return to life with all its sensual exuberance, "lips, lax wet and warm,/ Bees in the stomach,/ sweat across the brow. Now." Perhaps the second poem is most poignant, written without fantasy or myth, asking one simple postwar question: "oh mother, mother, where is happiness?"

"The Womanhood," Brooks final section of *Annie Allen*, returns to the ordinary yet important aspects of black life. Its first five-part poem, "the children of the poor," is a mother's dramatic monologue:

> People who have no children can be hard:
> Attain a mail of ice and insolence:
> Need not pause in the fire, and in no sense
> Hesitate in the hurricane to guard.

Brooks clearly echoes the frustration of women who want to help children survive in a hostile world but feel powerless: "What shall I give my children? who are poor,/ who are adjudged the leastwise of the land." She questions the power of prayer in part 3 and advises in part 4 that children be taught first to fight and then to fiddle. Other poems in this section express concern for children's physical and psychological safety. "Life for my child is simple and is good" shows daily dangers like "fingering an electric outlet" and simple joys like "throwing blocks out of a window," while "the ballad of the light-eyed little girl" tells of sweet Sally who starved her pet pigeon and then had to bury him "down and down."

The poems following "The Anniad" depart from the mock heroic's traditional rhyme and meter, employing free verse and irregular line breaks to illustrate Annie's move from romantic idealism to a clear-eyed response to social and racial injustice. Brooks confronts these issues gently but firmly in "I love those little booths at Benvenuti's" wherein an "old oaken waiter" looks amusedly at a group of whites who have ventured into a restaurant in Bronzeville expecting to be entertained. She reminds the reader "Nobody here will take the part of jester," a far cry from "downtown vaudeville" in the early part of the book.

One of Brooks's most powerful and black-affirming poems is "Beverly Hills, Chicago," faintly echoing the poetic style of T. S. Eliot in its narrative distance and its list of objects and events. Annie's satirical remark, "We say ourselves fortunate to be driving by today" implies a clear sense of racial injustice, for she goes on to describe the privileged lives of the white-haired white people who live in the posh neighborhood with their "golden gardens":

> We do not want them to have less.
> But it is only natural that we should think we have not
> enough.
> We drive on, we drive on.
> When we speak to each other our voices are a little gruff.

Perhaps Brooks was prompted to include the beautiful poem "truth" immediately after "Beverly Hills, Chicago" because it reflects accurately the night years spent in the shade of white society. Brooks implies that blacks have waited too long to see the sun: "What if we wake one shimmering morning to/ Hear the fierce hammering/ Of his firm knuckles/ Hard on the door?" Of course, her implication is that the shock would be too much. The next poem, simply numbered "XI," refers to the "enormous business"of racism and inequality that makes blacks wonder "if one has a home."

The long poem "intermission" uses images of light and dark to convey Annie's self-affirming attitude, a sharp contrast to her earlier romantic desire for a gold god. In the third part of this poem, she reflects, "there is silver under/ the veils of the darkness./ But few care to dig in the night/ For the possible treasure of stars." In the final poem of the book, Brooks calls for black and white unity: "Rise./ Let us combine. There are no magics or elves/ Or timely godmothers to guide us./ We are lost, must/ Wizard a track though our own screaming weed." Reading the entire collection brings the understanding that in *Annie Allen* Brooks undertook a struggle and a journey with life and with words. Like her character Annie, she carries many lesions from her experience, but she experiences some triumph, too.

Carol F. Bender

Further Reading

Bloom, Harold, ed. *Gwendolyn Brooks*. Philadelphia: Chelsea House, 2005. Contains a biography and several essays examining Brooks's poetry, including "The Satisfactions of What's Difficult in Gwendolyn Brooks's Poetry" by Brooke Kenton Horvath and "Gwendolyn Brooks: Beyond the Wordmaker the Making of an African Poet" by Haki R. Madhubuti.

Brooks, Gwendolyn. *Conversations with Gwendolyn Brooks*. Edited by Gloria Wade Gayles. Jackson: University Press of Mississippi, 2003. Compilation of interviews conducted during three decades in which Brooks discusses, among other topics, how she creates her poetry and the position of the poet in a humane society.

_______. *Report from Part One*. Detroit, Mich.: Broadside Press, 1972. An essential work for students of Brooks, this autobiography illuminates her early years as a writer and traces the publication of *Annie Allen*. The appendix contains useful authorial notes on poems.

Burr, Zofia. "Reading Gwendolyn Brooks Across Audiences." In *Of Women, Poetry, and Power: Strategies of Address in Dickinson, Miles, Brooks, Lorde, and Angelou*. Urbana: University of Illinois Press, 2002. Burr argues that the "canonization" of Emily Dickinson has created the assumption that all women's poetry is private and personal. She attempts to dispel this assumption by examining the "political work" of Brooks and other twentieth century women poets.

Evans, Mari. *Black Women Writers (1950-1980)*. Garden City, N.Y.: Doubleday, 1984. Three essays on Brooks's work, one written by Brooks herself. Excellent biographical chart and selected bibliographies.

Kent, George E. *A Life of Gwendolyn Brooks*. Lexington: University Press of Kentucky, 1990. Completed shortly before Kent's death in 1982, this book provides an authoritative and sympathetic account of Brooks's life and work to the time of her mother's death in 1978. Kent devotes a good portion of the book to the details surrounding the publication of *Annie Allen*. An afterword by D. H. Melhem advances the story to 1987.

Melhem, D. H. *Gwendolyn Brooks: Poetry and the Heroic Voice*. Lexington: University Press of Kentucky, 1987. A biocritical study that traces Brooks's development to 1987 and includes an extended analysis of *Annie Allen*. Contains a bibliography of works by Brooks.

Mootry, Maria K., and Gary Smith, eds. *A Life Distilled: Gwendolyn Brooks, Her Poetry and Fiction*. Urbana: University of Illinois Press, 1987. An indispensable collection of critical essays on Brooks. An essay by Claudia Tate is devoted to *Annie Allen*; one by Gary Smith examines the "children of the poor" sonnets. The editor's introduction and the essays in the first section of the book provide a general assessment of Brooks's achievement.

Shaw, Harry B. *Gwendolyn Brooks*. Boston: Twayne, 1980.

Shaw's examination of Brooks's work gives special attention to four themes: death, the fall from grace, the labyrinth, and survival. Contains a biographical sketch, an annotated bibliography, and a chronology of the poet's life to 1978.

Wright, Stephen Caldwell, ed. *On Gwendolyn Brooks: Reliant Contemplation*. Ann Arbor: University of Michigan Press, 1996. Compilation of reviews and essays about *Annie Allen* and Brooks's other works of poetry, fiction, children's literature, and nonfiction.

Annie John

Author: Jamaica Kincaid (Elaine Cynthia Potter Richardson, 1949-)
First published: 1985
Type of work: Novel
Type of plot: Narrative
Time of plot: British colonial rule
Locale: Antigua

Principal characters:
ANNIE JOHN, a smart girl
MOTHER OF ANNIE, a homemaker
FATHER OF ANNIE, a carpenter
MA CHESS, Annie's grandmother
MISS CATHERINE, one of Annie's schoolteachers
GWEN and THE RED GIRL, Annie's friends at school

The Story:

Ten-year-old Annie John is in Sunday school, remembering when she first observed death. A little girl Annie knew had died in her mother's arms. Annie starts to obsess about death, and she fears its nearness in her own life.

Annie is now twelve years old, and she is going to a new school, one sponsored by the Anglicans. She is wearing a new uniform, and her clothes no longer match those of her mother. Annie wants to fit in with the other girls, and she finds the best way to fit in is to beat them at marbles. The affections and opinions of peers take on a new importance for Annie.

A rift begins between herself and her mother, especially after Annie's loss of innocence in catching her parents making love one day. The rift widens as Annie begins to withhold information from her mother about her school friends, such as Gwen and the Red Girl. Annie's mother still reacts lovingly toward her, but Annie does not trust the facade. Annie is earning a bad reputation at school among the teachers because she does not do what she is supposed to do, even though she is a top student. She is not happy learning only what she is taught, and wants to know more. Her grades begin to fall. Also, she tries to hide that she plays and wins at marbles by hiding them under the house, and her mother never finds them. Annie gets away with much mischief and meanness toward others, troubles that eventually go away.

Annie develops a high fever and gets very sick. It takes months for her to recover and return to school, even with the help of family, friends, neighbors, and her teacher, Miss Catherine. During her illness she demonstrates incredible raving; she has lucid dreams, which she remembers and describes. Her intense raving, however, also leads her to destroy some cherished family photographs.

Annie graduates from secondary school, but her secret actions and hate for her mother continue until the day she leaves the island. She takes a boat bound for Barbados, planning to continue to England to be trained as a nurse. After the usual Sunday breakfast, her mother and father walk with her through the village to the jetty, to see her safely aboard the boat. Her father is speechless, but her mother gives her a warm, tearful sendoff, indicating that she will love Annie forever.

Critical Evaluation:

Annie John is the story of a girl who grows up in a small village in Antigua, with a focus on Annie's relationship with her mother. The plot of the novel is based on author Jamaica Kincaid's own childhood in Antigua, although *Annie John* is not an autobiography. The protagonist, Annie John, appears to readers slowly, as if Kincaid is hiding something. Annie's last name is revealed even later in the novel. This method of revealing names slowly reflects the way children learn important details, over time.

Annie describes each distinct age in her life—organized by Kincaid as one year per chapter—as she advances in the school system, notices changes in her body as she grows, and learns about family, humanity, and life in general. Her learning leads to a loss of innocence, the end of a friendship, a strained relationship with her mother, and other experiences. Annie develops a pattern of meanness toward others, including playmate Sonia, a friend whose mother suddenly dies. Instead of displaying sympathy, Annie reacts to her friend's mother's death by refusing to speak with Sonia. This negative, obstinate pattern of behavior continues through the story.

The entire novel takes place in the past, as though Annie is looking back on her youth and remembering short bursts from the time. Because the novel includes no years, months, or dates, the story has a sense of timelessness; the ebb and flow of time runs forward and backward like the tides of the nearby sea. Annie's age and level of schooling, even the aging of her mother's hands, are benchmarks of time passing. Those benchmarks are in chronological order.

The novel is interspersed with smaller stories about Annie and her relationships with others, who return to the novel's "present" and then fade back into the general remembered story. The brief stories within stories, which jump back and forth in time, include actual accounts from Annie's past. One such account is the story of cousin John, whose death led his mother to wear black for the rest of her life. Some stories are only imagined or are clearly indicated as dreams. Some stories are surreal, such as when Annie is delusional from a high fever.

Despite Annie's attempts to distance herself from her mother, certain themes, such as love between mother and daughter, are revealed through parallelisms: mother and daughter have the same appearance, speak similarly, and react to things in similar ways. Annie also follows a life path similar to that of her mother, having left home after quarreling with her parents. Repeatedly, Annie describes herself as a shadow, holding close to her mother's skirts when she was younger, and having the same hair or eyes. When the two say good-bye before Annie leaves Antigua for Barbados, each says the same, last word at the same second. They are so close emotionally, they appear to be one person.

Other symbols of parallelism recur in the novel. For example, the trunk that Annie's mother brought from Dominica stores items from Annie's infancy—even embroidered diapers—handmade by her mother. Annie declares that as a reward for completing school and coming of age, she wants a new trunk. She gets her mother's trunk, leaves home, and never returns, in the same way her own mother left her home island when she was young with the same trunk.

In a larger context, Annie rebels against her parents, and especially her mother, because they represent the status quo of a stable, colonized society. Annie resists her mother's training and preparation for marriage and adulthood, for continuing the same, predictable life under British domination in Antigua. Annie's misbehavior and inattention at school also is a form of rebellion against coercion and enforced colonial mind control. Furthermore, obeah medicine, and not Western medicine, cures her horrible fever.

Annie John traces the entire growth of a girl's awareness of her own power to take control of her life and to begin to find her place in the world as an independent woman. Although the reader leaves Annie on board a ship that has yet to sail, the instructional discipline, support, and love Annie has had from her family and village point in the direction of a future where she will thrive on her own terms.

Jan Hall

Further Reading

Bouson, J. Brooks. *Jamaica Kincaid: Writing Memory, Writing Back to the Mother.* Albany: State University of New York Press, 2005. Examines Kincaid's life, including her relationship with her mother, the influence of her homeland of Antigua, and her conflicting relations with her father and brother.

Braxton, Joanne M. *Black Women Writing Autobiography: A Tradition Within a Tradition.* Philadelphia: Temple University Press, 1989. This selective overview analyzes autobiographies by women of color, starting with early slave narratives. Braxton distinguishes unique aspects of this type of autobiography, including the role of the "angry mother" and freedom, as recurring themes, to establish it as a genre in its own right. Also discusses parallels in plot, themes, and characters among autobiographies by women of color and fictional works by Kincaid.

De Abruna, Laura Nielsen. "Jamaica Kincaid's Writing and the Maternal-Colonial Matrix." In *Caribbean Women Writers*, edited by Mary Condé and Thorunn Lonsdale. New York: St. Martin's Press, 1999. Discusses Kincaid's presentation of women's experience, her use of postmodern narrative strategies, and her focus on the absence of the once-affirming mother or mother country that causes dislocation and alienation.

"Jamaica Kincaid." In *Notable African American Writers.* 2 vols. Pasadena, Calif.: Salem Press, 2006. A comprehensive article on the life and work of writer Kincaid, including the novel *Annie John.* A good place to start. Includes an annotated bibliography. Part of the Magill's Choice series.

Kincaid, Jamaica. *My Brother.* New York: Noonday Press, 1997. Kincaid provides an emotionally truthful, nonfiction account of her brother's death from AIDS-related complications, delving into the experience of his death as it happened. She also discusses her relationships with her Antiguan family and history, tying these relations to her own literary and writing life.

Paravisini-Gerbert, Lizabeth. *Jamaica Kincaid: A Critical Companion*. Westport, Conn.: Greenwood Press, 1999. Presents biographical information as well as detailed analyses of individual novels by Kincaid, including *Annie John* and *The Autobiography of My Mother*.

Another Country

Author: James Baldwin (1924-1987)
First published: 1962
Type of work: Novel
Type of plot: Social realism
Time of plot: Mid-twentieth century
Locale: New York and France

Principal characters:
RUFUS SCOTT, a musician
IDA SCOTT, Rufus's sister
VIVALDO MOORE, an aspiring writer
ERIC JONES, an actor
RICHARD SILENSKI, a writer
CASS SILENSKI, Richard's wife

The Story:

Rufus Scott, an African American musician, is in a desperate condition. He not only has no money but also he has fallen out of contact with his friends and his family. He was out of touch for about a month and a half. Moreover, the most foreboding aspect of Rufus's condition is his total despair. This despair results primarily from his complete alienation from those who were formerly close to him. As Rufus wanders the streets of New York, he remembers his relationships with people he loves. He realizes that his love is often mixed with hostility. For example, months earlier, he met a white southern woman named Leona at a party. During the party, their affair began. Rufus realizes that part of what he wanted from his relationship with Leona was to take out on her his rage against white people. This relationship is somewhat of a pattern with Rufus. He also had an affair with a white southern actor named Eric Jones. In his present desperate state, Rufus realizes how he abused both Eric and Leona, ultimately driving them away with his racist taunts and physical and psychological humiliation. Consequently, Rufus realizes that he used Eric's and Leona's love for him to abuse them and thereby vent his anger and frustrations. He alienates himself from everyone to whom he was once close. His once-close friend, aspiring writer Vivaldo Moore, who became fed up with Rufus's inflicting his problems on him and others, Rufus also drives away. After reflecting on his relationships and realizing how isolated he is, Rufus kills himself by jumping off the George Washington Bridge.

Meanwhile, Ida, Rufus's sister, is trying to find him. She goes to the home of Richard Silenski, a newly successful novelist, and his wife, Cass. Vivaldo is also present. One of Ida's chief characteristics—her anger against whites—becomes clear. She accuses Rufus's friends of not caring about what happened to him, as all of them are white. Vivaldo feels especially guilty, recalling how he failed to show up for his last scheduled meeting with Rufus. After Richard suggests checking with hospitals and the morgue, Rufus's friends learn the truth: Rufus is dead.

Ida's relationship with Rufus's circle of friends—Vivaldo, Richard, and Cass—continues. Vivaldo becomes attracted to Ida and the two become lovers, even though Ida, like Rufus, feels a simultaneous attraction to and repulsion from whites. Further complicating things is that Ida, an aspiring singer, decides to have an affair with white television producer Steve Ellis. Ida, believing that whites look upon black women as promiscuous, decides to try to exploit this myth for the benefit of her career. She becomes involved with Ellis at the same time that she has a love affair with Vivaldo. Ida, Ellis, and Vivaldo become part of a triangle that mixes affection with hostility.

In addition to his affair with Ida, Vivaldo has other complications in his life. First, he was never completely sure of his sexual orientation. He recalls being part of a gang that attacked a gay man, although he himself is sometimes attracted to men. Also, before meeting Ida, he made frequent trips to

Harlem to have sex with black women, something that made him feel exploitative, racist, and weak. He knows he was merely seeking thrills in his relationships with these women and using them to try to hide from the emptiness of his own life. Complementing his indecisive feelings about his sexuality is Vivaldo's equally murky status as a writer. Vivaldo notes that he feels as distant from his characters as he does from himself. His novel will not crystallize in his imagination. In his relationship with Ida, in his former relationships with black women, in his confusion about his sexual orientation, and in his inertia as a writer—in fact, in his very identity—Vivaldo lives in a state of indecision and ignorance.

Eric Jones, once part of Rufus's circle, is currently an actor living in France. Eric plans to return to New York to look for acting jobs. This means he will be separated temporarily from his male lover, Yves, with whom he has a committed relationship. Eric's impending return to the United States brings back memories of his coming-of-age in the South and accepting his sexual orientation as a young white man who is in love with a black man. In contrast to Vivaldo, Eric accepts his sexuality, even though he knows that much of society condemns his love for the black man, Henry. He also recalls his love and abuse at the hands of Rufus. Eric realizes that in spite of the pain he experiences—in romantic relationships and at the hands of society—he needs to accept himself and to reject society's bigoted categorizations of gay men. On Eric's return to New York, he becomes the catalyst for important realizations by many in his circle of friends. For instance, in Cass's relationship with Eric, she realizes the emptiness of her seemingly successful life as the wife of a successful novelist—who is also an unloving husband. In addition, Vivaldo realizes that while he loves Eric as a friend, his sexual orientation makes him need women in general and Ida in particular. Hence, Eric is an important vehicle for his friends' self-analysis.

The characters' coming to face themselves has important effects. In Vivaldo's case, for instance, he and Ida finally discuss the problems in their relationship, as Vivaldo is now ready to face the truth about many aspects of his life. They discuss their problems, including Ida's relationship with Ellis, which fails to get her the career break she wants. The affair also results in her experiencing the humiliating disrespect of the black musicians with whom she works. They know of her plans to advance her career by having an affair with Ellis. After Eric plays an instrumental part in the lives of others, he resumes his concentration on his own life with the impending arrival of Yves in New York. The novel ends with key characters confronting painful truths about their identities and their lives.

Critical Evaluation:

James Baldwin has been widely acclaimed as America's greatest essayist as a result of his works *Notes of a Native Son* (1955) and *The Fire Next Time* (1963), among others. His novels also play a central role in American literary history. Like Ralph Ellison's *Invisible Man* (1952) and Baldwin's *Giovanni's Room* (1956), *Another Country* is an important landmark in the departure of African American literature from the tradition of the protest novel, best embodied by Richard Wright's *Native Son* (1940). The chief feature of the protest novel is a critique of race relations; in contrast, the aforementioned novels make a critique of society that goes beyond a condemnation of racism. *Another Country* examines such issues as personal responsibility, the formation of identity, and the need for honest self-reflection. Moreover, one can argue that a chief clue to Baldwin's interests in *Another Country* is contained in his early essay "Everybody's Protest Novel" in *Notes of a Native Son*. Particularly illuminating to readers of *Another Country* is the part of the essay that contains an attack on *Notes of a Native Son*. Baldwin states that the main tragedy in the life of the protagonist, Bigger Thomas, is that he accepts racists' labeling of him as subhuman, thus causing Baldwin to object that "the failure of the protest novel lies . . . in its insistence that it is his categorization alone that is real and cannot be transcended." One could argue that in *Another Country* Rufus Scott's similar acceptance of conventional, prejudiced views of him is exactly why he commits suicide at the end of the first part of the book. The focus on him in the early part of the book would lead many readers to believe that he is the main character of the novel. That he is not may be seen as a subtle commentary on *Notes of a Native Son*. Rufus's death dramatizes Baldwin's belief in the destructive and life-negating consequences of internalization, self-condemnation, and self-alienation as represented in such characters as Rufus and his literary ancestor, Bigger Thomas. Rufus's death also jolts the reader into the realization that *Another Country* is not a protest novel, or the same kind of protest novel as *Notes of a Native Son*. Stylistically and thematically, *Another Country* broadens the scope of African American literature beyond the genre of the protest novel.

Another important aspect of *Another Country* is Baldwin's insistence that love, sexuality, and identity are intertwined and demand honest self-acceptance from the individual. Baldwin's statement in *The Fire Next Time* is essential for the reader to understand the centrality to Baldwin's vision of the aforementioned ideas. Baldwin writes: "Love takes off the masks we fear we cannot live without and know we cannot live within." One can say that this dilemma is represented in such characters as Eric and Vivaldo, whose sexuality is unmasked in their relationships and who must struggle for self-acceptance. They must accept what is revealed to them about themselves in their romantic and sexual relationships. Eric accepts his homosexuality. Vivaldo, more ambiguous than Eric, toward the end of the novel purports to accept his need for women in his romantic life. In Baldwin's presentation of the theme of love and the self-illumination it brings, another key idea of his works becomes apparent: honesty. To paraphrase a statement in *Another Country*, Baldwin makes clear in this novel and in other works that one must be honest with oneself about the life one has in order to attain the life one desires. In sum, truth, self-examination, and self-insight are intertwined in Baldwin's vision in *Another Country* and in his other works, novels, essays, and dramas.

Another important aspect of *Another Country* bears mentioning. *Giovanni's Room* and *Another Country* were among the first novels by a major American writer to deal frankly with the theme of homosexuality. Scholars on Baldwin have noted that American literature had treated the topic of homosexuality in a veiled way, sometimes as a subplot of a novel (for example, Wallace Thurman's *The Blacker the Berry*, 1929). Baldwin presents homosexuality frankly, which caused some critics at the time of the novel's publication to chastise him for the frankness of his themes and language. This aspect of the novel's reception makes clear how the novel was ahead of its time. Many readers would not find the novel shocking, though it is complex and honest in the portrayal of the importance of sexuality to one's sense of identity. *Another Country* is a very timely novel in that Baldwin uses it to grapple with issues that had not previously been given prominence in African American literature.

Another Country is an important American novel. Baldwin's complex vision provides a critique of individuals in particular and of society in general. Furthermore, for readers interested in examining central aspects of Baldwin's major thematic concerns in his fiction and in his essays, *Another Country* is essential reading. The novel presents essential psychological issues about the formation and acceptance of identity. This thematic issue makes the novel engrossing; Baldwin ably presents the psychological growth, or lack thereof, of his characters. Baldwin also makes clear how central love is in one's psychological growth. The novel makes it evident that one cannot love others until one understands and accepts oneself. Baldwin thus shows his concern for the growth of the individual and for how that individual can connect in a meaningful way with society. This connection is essential. As in the case with Rufus, self-alienation and isolation lead to death, in Baldwin's vision. Although Baldwin's *Another Country* is not in the genre of protest literature, Baldwin still uses the novel to make clear his concerns for society. *Another Country* engages central questions about life, and takes a central place in American literature.

Jane Davis

Further Reading

Bloom, Harold, ed. *James Baldwin*. New York: Chelsea House, 1986. This collection of critical essays on Baldwin includes two major discussions of *Another Country* by Charles Newman and Roger Rosenblatt. Newman's essay, "The Lesson of the Master: Henry James and James Baldwin," discusses the problem of identity in the novel and the use of Rufus to make the white characters explore the inadequacy of their lives. Rosenblatt's essay, "Out of Control: *Go Tell It on the Mountain* and *Another Country*," focuses on the tensions among the characters, including the whites' guilt regarding Rufus's death and Eric as a liberating character. In his introduction, Bloom sees Baldwin as a prophet whose essays are more important than his fiction.

_______. *James Baldwin*. Updated ed. New York: Chelsea House, 2007. This updated edition includes essays by Henry Louis Gates, Jr., Mario Puzo, and Irving Howe. Two of the essays focus on *Another Country*: " 'Making Love in the Midst of Mirrors': *Giovanni's Room* and *Another Country*" by Carolyn Wedin Sylvander and "The Exorcising Medium: Another Country" by Trudier Harris.

Boyd, Herb. *Baldwin's Harlem: A Biography of James Baldwin*. New York: Atria Books, 2008. Boyd's biography focuses on Baldwin's experiences in Harlem and his relationships with other residents of the New York City neighborhood, including writers Countee Cullen and Langston Hughes and civil rights activist Malcolm X.

Campbell, James. *Talking at the Gates: A Life of James Baldwin*. New York: Viking Press, 1991. This biography, by a man who knew Baldwin personally, is especially interesting because it draws on the Federal Bureau of Investigation files kept on Baldwin. Campbell deals frankly with Baldwin's bisexuality. Included are sixteen pages of photographs.

Harris, Trudier. *Black Women in the Fiction of James Baldwin*. Knoxville: University of Tennessee Press, 1985. Though Harris's long chapter on *Another Country* deals mainly with Ida Scott, it nevertheless offers a full, interesting interpretation of the novel, with good attention to main themes of race, gender, and sexuality.

McBride, Dwight A., ed. *James Baldwin Now*. New York:

New York University Press, 1999. Collection of diverse essays that seek to reevaluate Baldwin's works and interpret them from new perspectives. Most of the essays provide a broad view of Baldwin's writings, but the piece by James A. Dievler, "Sexual Exiles: James Baldwin and *Another Country*," focuses on this novel.

Macebuh, Stanley. *James Baldwin: A Critical Study.* New York: Third Press, 1973. Intriguing discussion on love as the chief social theme of the novel and of Rufus as a major influence on the characters.

O'Daniel, Therman B. *James Baldwin: A Critical Evaluation.* Washington, D.C.: Howard University Press, 1977. Contains essays on Baldwin as novelist, essayist, short-story writer, playwright, and scenarist, as well as a section on his "raps" and dialogues. Eugenia W. Collier's essay, "The Phrase Unbearably Repeated," examines Baldwin's use of music in *Another Country* to express the novel's themes, advance characterization, convey the need for love, and show the characters' emotions.

Pratt, Louis H. *James Baldwin.* Boston: Twayne, 1978. A useful introduction to Baldwin's life and works, including a discussion of *Another Country.* Contains a chronology and an annotated bibliography.

Sylvander, Carolyn W. *James Baldwin.* New York: Frederick Ungar, 1980. This introductory study includes a chronology, a biographical sketch, and chapters on major aspects of Baldwin's career. Chapter 5 summarizes and evaluates *Another Country.*

Zaborowska, Magdalena J. *James Baldwin's Turkish Decade: Erotics of Exile.* Durham, N.C.: Duke University Press, 2008. Chronicles the decade Baldwin spent in Istanbul and how this experience affected his writing, particularly the creation of *Another Country.* Includes more than fifty photographs.

Antigone

Author: Jean Anouilh (1910-1987)
First produced: 1944; first published, 1946, in *Nouvelles Pièces noires* (English translation, 1946)
Type of work: Drama
Type of plot: Tragedy
Time of plot: Antiquity
Locale: Thebes

Principal characters:
ANTIGONE, the younger daughter of Oedipus and Jocasta
CREON, the brother of Jocasta, acting king of Thebes
THE CHORUS, played by a single actor/narrator
HAEMON, the son of Creon, engaged to Antigone
ISMÈNE, Antigone's older sister

The Story:

King Oedipus dies in exile, leaving the kingdom of Thebes to his two sons, Eteocles and Polynices, who are supposed to take turns as rulers. Instead, the two brothers fight over the prize; civil war ensues, and in the end both of them are dead, each by the other's hand. Creon, surviving brother of the incestuous queen Jocasta, has assumed the role of king so as to restore order in Thebes, proclaiming a state funeral for his former ally Eteocles while ordering that the body of Polynices be left to rot in the sun as a negative example to his supporters. Antigone, the younger daughter of Oedipus and Jocasta, defies Creon's edict by digging a grave for Polynices, an act of treason punishable by death.

Elaborating on this basic plot of the ancient Greek play by Sophocles *Antigonē* (441 B.C.E.; *Antigone*, 1729), twentieth century playwright Jean Anouilh begins his version with narration by the Chorus (initially known as the Prologue, performed by a single actor in Anouilh's play). Like the Chorus in Sophocles' version and other classical dramas, Anouilh's narrator provides background information and running commentary to complement the action. The play is performed in modern dress (the narrator, for example, wears a dinner jacket) with occasional deliberate anachronisms, such as the mention of nightclubs and sports cars.

Antigone, fully aware of the consequences of her deed, has already buried Polynices and is preparing herself for death, gradually separating herself from Creon's son Haemon, from her sister Ismène, from the elderly nursemaid who has cared for her since childhood, and even from her dog, to be left in the nursemaid's care. Creon, upon learning from his guards that Polynices has been buried, at first suspects political subversives but soon is forced to accept the fact of Antigone's guilt. Ever the pragmatic politician, Creon considers trying to cover up Antigone's crime, knowing the political troubles that will result from her martyrdom. Creon is prepared to have the guards who know of Antigone's guilt put to death in order to ensure their silence. Antigone, however, brought face-to-face with her uncle, refuses to participate in a cover-up. She will not remain silent about her actions, insisting on her right to give her kin proper burial, even if the punishment she faces for doing so is death.

During their extended conversation, Creon tries to reason with Antigone, urging her to renounce her crime and assuring her of total indemnity so that she can go on to marry Haemon as planned and, presumably, to lead a happy life. Antigone, however, will have none of Creon's proffered happiness, preferring to die rather than to take part in her uncle's political scheme. As in the Sophocles play, religion is the motive of Antigone's determination, since burial is a prerequisite to the afterlife. In Anouilh's version, however, the discussion centers on the generation gap between Antigone and her uncle, pitting youthful idealism against experience and pragmatism. Still attempting to change Antigone's mind, Creon argues that the burial of Eteocles is no more than a matter of politics, of the need to choose one official hero among two scoundrels. Each brother, in fact, had plotted his father's assassination and had planned to sell Thebes to the highest bidder; what is more, the two bodies were in such condition that it was impossible to tell the brothers' remains apart.

Creon, for one, does not care which was which, so long as the burial serves his political purpose. In accepting the throne, Creon agrees to accept matters as they are, not as they should be. Antigone, in refusing Creon's pragmatic offer of compromise, in effect refuses to accept things as they are, insisting rather on how they should be. She forces Creon to proceed with her execution. Although at the last minute she seems to doubt her resolve, she ultimately allows herself to be thrown in a pit, where she hangs herself with her belt. She is soon joined by Haemon, who, keeping Creon at bay with his sword, lies down beside her and stabs himself to death. Haemon's mother, Creon's wife Eurydice, dies a similar death upon learning what has happened to her son. Creon is thus left alone to look after his kingdom, attended by the guards and soldiers who had arrested Antigone.

Critical Evaluation:

Starting in the early 1930's, thanks mainly to the plays of Jean Giraudoux (1882-1944), the topical rewriting of classical myth and drama became more the rule than the exception on the serious Paris stage, offering edification and entertainment in approximately equal portions. As the Greek writers had shown their inventiveness within rigid constraints of plot, so the French playwrights of the period between World Wars I and II impressed their audiences with thoughtful, often witty variations on the familiar myths that most audience members had studied in school. Jean Anouilh, who came of age as a playwright during the decade of Giraudoux's prominence, achieved his first major success with *Le Voyageur sans bagage* (pr., pb. 1937; *Traveller Without Luggage*, 1959), a dark comedy that, despite its contemporary setting, carries strong references to the Oedipus legend. By the time he addressed himself to Antigone, in the midst of World War II and the Nazi occupation of France, Anouilh had already treated the myth of Orpheus and Eurydice rather successfully on the stage, as he was later to do with that of Jason and Medea. In later years, as French taste moved away from the reworking of classical myth, Anouilh would move in other directions, yet without ever forsaking the characteristic themes of youth and age, and realism and idealism, to be found in *Antigone*.

Among the more memorable and durable examples of its subgenre, outlasting even the better efforts of Giraudoux, *Antigone* proved controversial throughout the 1940's and into the 1950's because of Anouilh's ambiguous portrayal of Antigone and Creon. For the initial spectators in 1944, there was little doubt that Antigone represented the indomitable, if weakened, spirit of free France, and Creon the expediency that involved collaboration with the Germans, if need be, in order to keep the country running. It seemed difficult to tell, however, which of the two characters is more sympathetically portrayed. There were those, for example, who saw Antigone's willful martyrdom as meaningless, outweighed by Creon's devotion to duty and to the maintenance of order. Such persons argued that Creon was the one with the most to lose, which in a sense he does. Somewhat to his consternation, Anouilh, among the more resolutely theatrical of dramatists, found himself suddenly ranked with such contemporary thinker-playwrights as Albert Camus and Jean-Paul Sartre, who both, unlike himself, were aligned with the political left. Anouilh, by contrast, preferred to think that his art lifted him above politics, a most difficult position to maintain in France during World War II and after. As if in reaction, Anouilh, for some years after *Antigone* was first performed, went out of his way to avoid any possible identification with thoughtful or literary theater, thus leaving himself open to a countercharge of playing to the crowds.

Ironically, more than a half century after its initial productions, *Antigone* has proved to have survived the allegorical interpretations that seemed obvious to audiences during World War II, emerging instead as one of the more eloquent expressions of the generation gap to be found in the body of world theater. More closely related in theme and tone to Anouilh's earlier and later plays than was once commonly supposed, *Antigone* derives much of its dramatic strength from the author's unobtrusive, almost inadvertent lyricism, especially in those scenes in which Antigone evokes, for Ismène, the nursemaid, and Haemon the beauties of the life and world that Antigone is about to forsake. Certain critics have heard in those lines a recollection of Emily's return from the dead in Thornton Wilder's *Our Town* (pr., pb. 1938), an intertextual impression underscored by resemblances between Wilder's Stage Manager and the Chorus in *Antigone*. In any case, Antigone's lyrical speeches anticipate, and contrast with, the searing, searching rhetoric of her confrontation with Creon, in which she accuses him of selling out and in which she refuses any part of a world in which Haemon might grow to resemble his father. Of interest also, by way of comic relief tinged with social significance, is Anouilh's portrayal of Creon's guards as typical French soldiers with French names, by turns fawning and ferocious, who return to playing cards as soon as their part in the action is over.

During a long and generally distinguished career spanning more than fifty years and nearly as many performed plays, Anouilh consistently rejected traditional classifications, such as comedy and tragedy, for his efforts, preferring such personal, ironic categories as black plays, pink plays, and grating plays, the last designed to set one's teeth on edge. Like the earlier *Traveller Without Luggage*, *Antigone* was labeled as a black play rather than a tragedy; in the absence of any substantial theory or criticism written by Anouilh, certain speeches of the Chorus in *Antigone* are often—and perhaps correctly—assumed to represent the author's views on tragedy as too convenient, too comforting to represent real life. The Chorus's presence, as well as his lightly ironic approach to the action that he narrates, sets the concept of tragedy into a kind of relief, subject to the spectator's objective scrutiny as the familiar plot proceeds to run its course. Tragedy, suggests Anouilh through the Chorus, is for kings and princesses, while the rest of the world must contend with the more sordid details of reality.

David B. Parsell

Further Reading

Bishop, Tom. "Anouilh's *Antigone* in 1970." In *From the Left Bank: Reflections on the Modern French Theater and Novel*. New York: New York University Press, 1997. This analysis of the play is included in a collection of essays about French avant-garde theater and literature written by Bishop, a professor of French literature at New York University.

Della Fazia, Alba. *Jean Anouilh*, Boston: Twayne, 1969. An introductory overview of Anouilh's life and theater.

Falb, Lewis W. *Jean Anouilh*. New York: Frederick Ungar, 1977. A generally reliable overview of Anouilh's plays, prepared fairly late in his career. Somewhat more authoritative on the earlier works than on the later ones. Includes a good discussion of *Antigone*.

Fleming, Katie. "Fascism on Stage: Jean Anouilh's *Antigone*." In *Laughing with Medusa: Classical Myth and Feminist Thought*, edited by Vanda Zajko and Miriam Leonard. New York: Oxford University Press, 2006. Fleming analyzes Anouilh's play within the context of 1940's France and in comparison to Sophocles' version of the Antigone story. She maintains that Anouilh's play is a "pointed departure" from Sophocles' drama, in which the lead character is a "feminist icon."

Harvey, John. *Anouilh: A Study in Theatrics*. New Haven, Conn.: Yale University Press, 1964. Situates Anouilh's major work within the world dramatic tradition, showing how even in *Antigone*, playability takes precedence over ideas. A generally useful discussion of Anouilh's approach to stagecraft.

Howarth, William D. *Anouilh: Antigone*. London: Edward Arnold, 1983. Prepared for a British student audience, Howarth's volume provides useful background on Anouilh's career, the Antigone theme in world literature, and historical context of the play's first performances.

McIntyre, H. G. *The Theatre of Jean Anouilh*. London: Harrap, 1981. Although relatively brief, perhaps the most useful study of Anouilh's entire dramatic output, finding continuity and consistency where other critics have not. Interpretation of *Antigone* shows Creon as the more exemplary character without stressing implications of the war allegory.

Porter, Burton F. "The Good and the Right: Anouilh's *Antigone* and Tolstoy's *Anna Karenina*." In *The Head and the Heart: Philosophy in Literature*. Amherst, N.Y.: Humanity Books, 2006. Porter examines the philosophic content of *Antigone* and other selected works of literature.

Pronko, Leonard C. *The World of Jean Anouilh*. Berkeley: University of California Press, 1961. Perhaps the strongest early study of Anouilh in English, prepared as Anouilh turned fifty, with his future direction still to be determined. Good analysis of *Antigone*.

Antigone

Author: Sophocles (c. 496-406 B.C.E.)
First produced: c. 442 B.C.E.
Type of work: Drama
Type of plot: Tragedy
Time of plot: Antiquity
Locale: Thebes

Principal characters:
ANTIGONE, a young woman
CREON, self-appointed king of Thebes, and Antigone's uncle
THE CHORUS, Thebean elders
ISMENE, Antigone's older sister
HAEMON, son of Creon, engaged to Antigone

The Story:

King Oedipus has died in exile, leaving the Kingdom of Thebes to his two sons, Eteocles and Polynices. The king had decreed that his two sons are supposed to take turns as rulers; they agree, initially. After Eteocles refuses to step down after one year, the two brothers fight over the prize. Polynices attacks Thebes, leading to civil war, and in the end both brothers are dead, each by the other's hand. Creon, their uncle, assumes the role of king. He gives a state funeral to Eteocles but orders that the body of Polynices be left to rot in the sun as an example to his supporters.

Antigone, Oedipus's daughter, meets her sister Ismene at the gates to Creon's palace in Thebes. Antigone feels duty bound to bury her brother Polynices despite Creon's edict and asks her sister for help. Ismene refuses, arguing that as women they should not go against the decisions of men, especially those of the king.

The Chorus is summoned to the palace. Creon informs the Chorus that he claims the throne and that Polynices is to be left unburied. However, Antigone has stealthily sprinkled Polynices' body with a layer of dirt, giving her brother a symbolic burial. A guard runs to Creon and reports the attempted burial. Creon is furious and accuses the guard of being involved. One of the elders says it is the work of a god, but Creon disagrees. He threatens to torture and kill the guard unless he captures the real perpetrator. The Chorus sings about the wonder of humanity, but for the city to be safe, humanity should both honor civil law and revere the gods.

The guards brush the dirt off Polynices' body and then hide, looking to ambush whoever tries to rebury him. Antigone soon arrives and tries to bury Polynices again, but is caught by the guards. She is brought before Creon, where she readily confesses. They argue over her actions and his decree. Creon tries to reason with Antigone, urging her to renounce her crime and assuring her of total indemnity so that she can go on to marry Haemon as planned and, presumably, to lead a happy life. Antigone, however, will have none of Creon's proffered happiness, preferring to die rather than to take part in her uncle's political scheme. Creon decrees that she must die. Ismene is brought in and questioned. She demands that she share the guilt. Antigone argues with her.

Creon's son Haemon argues with his father, trying to convince him to relent. Creon remains stubborn and Haemon threatens to die with Antigone. Creon decrees Antigone to be entombed alive. Antigone mourns her fate and the curse on her family. The Chorus is divided in loyalty between Antigone and Creon. Antigone defends her actions and asks the gods to punish Creon. The Chorus reminds the audience of others who suffered because they tried to subvert the gods' will.

The blind prophet Tiresias tells Creon that he has angered the gods and that Creon is to blame for the people's prayers going unanswered. A sickness plagues Thebes, and neighboring cities bear Thebes ill will. Creon accuses the prophet of being paid to upset him. Tiresias calls Creon a tyrant and warns him that he will lose his son. This troubles Creon, and he asks the Chorus for council. They advise him to yield and release Antigone. Creon agrees and leaves. The Chorus then asks Dionysus to help Thebes.

A messenger arrives and relates to the Chorus what happened at the tomb. The messenger says that Creon and his men went to bury Polynices and to release Antigone, only to discover that she had killed herself. Haemon, weeping over her body, then kills himself before their eyes. Eurydice overhears the messenger. Creon arrives and openly accepts responsibility for the deaths of Antigone and Haemon. A second messenger arrives and tells him that his wife, too, has committed suicide. Creon prays for death. The Chorus delivers one of the moral lessons of the tragedy: Obedience to the laws of the gods comes first.

Critical Evaluation:

The Oedipus myth was well known even in Sophocles' day, so his audience already knew what would happen at the end of *Antigone*. The contrast between what the audience knows and what the characters know sets up the tension, the dramatic irony. However, Sophocles uses dramatic license and adds events that are not found in any previous account of the myth, including the quarrels between Antigone and Ismene, Antigone's two attempts to bury Polynices, Antigone's betrothal to Haemon, the entombment of Antigone, Tiresias's argument with Creon, and the suicides. These added events serve to intensify the play.

Although the last play in the Oedipus trilogy, *Antigone* was written first. The play won for Sophocles first prize at the Dionysia festival. It is still a popular play, with many stage and screen adaptations, including Jean Anouilh's famous stage production *Antigone* (pr. 1944, pb. 1946; English translation, 1946), placing the story in a World War II setting, and Amy Greenfield's 1990 stark, interpretive dance-film version (*Antigone—Rites of Passion*).

The conflicts within the play, represented by the conflicts between Antigone and Creon, are powerful human struggles that are still relevant today: the state versus the individual, the state versus family, the state versus the church, the old versus the young, and man versus woman. Although the Chorus delivers the moral of obedience to the laws of the gods before all else, the moral is not a tidy conclusion. Many questions remain unanswered, many conflicts unresolved. For example, when is family more important than the state? In ancient Greece, it was the duty of women to bury family members. Leaving Polynices unburied was a violation of not only the laws of the gods but also the laws of the family. In addition, Creon was willing to put his own niece, and his son's fiancé, to death. After a brutal civil war, however, restoring order is the responsibility of the king. When, and to what extent, do the laws of the gods and of the state override the laws of the family?

Connected to the above themes is the theme of choices and consequences. The characters in the play have free will to choose, but the consequences of their choices are guided by fate—determined by the gods. To what extent, however, do the characters truly have free will? Antigone's conscience is pressured by the demands of family tradition and obedience to the gods, while Creon is tasked with preserving law and order. How much is each bound by their position in society, or by their conscience? Both Antigone and Creon stick stubbornly to what they feel are logical choices—but they are limited in their knowledge and cannot foresee all the consequences of their choices. Too often they stubbornly refuse to listen to council, which tries to guide them in their choices. Had Antigone and Creon listened more, the tragedies may have been averted, but each would have had to sacrifice some pride as well as give up a little of who they are.

Antigone is a complex play, one that defies ready interpretation. It is a study of human actions, with complex emotions. Each character represents a moral ideal, a moral argument, and the play becomes a great debate. The two major debaters in the play, Antigone and Creon, are both destroyed at the end, leaving the debate with no clear winner. *Antigone* demands its audience to continue the debate.

David Michael Merchant

Further Reading

Butler, Judith. *Antigone's Claim*. New York: Columbia University Press, 2002. Butler presents a feminist critique of *Antigone* and examines the political and philosophical implications of Antigone's resistance to the state. Collected from her lectures on *Antigone*.

Hong, Bonnie. "Antigone's Laments, Creon's Grief: Mourning, Membership, and the Politics of Exception." *Political Theory* 37, no. 1 (February, 2009): 5-43. Hong discusses the politics of lamentation in *Antigone*, analyzing the conflicts between a family's need for mourning and the state's political needs.

Reed, Valerie. "Bringing Antigone Home?" *Comparative Literature Studies* 45, no. 3 (September, 2008): 316-340. Examines the theme of family versus state in *Antigone*, concentrating on what home means, literally and conceptually, to Antigone.

Sophocles. *Antigone*. Translated by Richard Emil Braun. New York: Oxford University Press, 1990. This exceptional translation comes with an informative introduction, notes, an appendix, and a glossary that student researchers will find useful.

Steiner, George. *Antigones: How the Antigone Legend Has Endured in Western Literature, Art, and Thought*. New York: Oxford University Press, 1986. A very good overview of the play's influence on Western culture.

Walsh, Keri. "*Antigone* Now." *Mosaic: A Journal for the Interdisciplinary Study of Literature* 41, no. 3 (September, 2008): 1-13. Walsh examines the reception of *Antigone* and gives a good overview of various critical approaches to the work. Also discusses the role of mourning in the play.

The Antiquary

Author: Sir Walter Scott (1771-1832)
First published: 1816
Type of work: Novel
Type of plot: Fiction of manners
Time of plot: Late eighteenth century
Locale: Scotland

Principal characters:
JONATHAN OLDBUCK OF MONKBARNS, the antiquary
LOVEL, an illegitimate son of unknown parents
SIR ARTHUR WARDOUR, a baronet and Oldbuck's friend
MISS ISABELLA WARDOUR, his daughter
EDIE OCHILTREE, a beggar
HECTOR M'INTYRE, Oldbuck's nephew
THE EARL OF GLENALLAN, the present head of a powerful family
DOUSTERSWIVEL, a magician

The Story:

When old Jonathan Oldbuck of Monkbarns first meets young Lovel, he is impressed by the young man's good manners and conduct, but he is mystified by the little he can learn of Lovel's past. It is obvious that Lovel is not the boy's real name and that there is something in his history of which he is ashamed.

From his good friend Sir Arthur Wardour, Oldbuck at last learns that the young man is the illegitimate son of unknown parents. Although a benefactor has settled a large estate on him, he lives in solitude and disgrace because of his questionable ancestry. To make matters worse, he is in love with Sir Arthur's daughter, Isabella. Although the girl loves him, she will not accept him because she knows her father will not permit an alliance with a man of unknown and illegitimate origins. Even after Lovel saves her life and that of her father when they are trapped by the tides, she gives him no more than the thanks due him for his bravery.

Sir Arthur is in serious financial straits, in debt to dozens of tradesmen and friends, among them Oldbuck. To restore his fortune, he has fallen into a plot prepared by Dousterswivel, an evil magician who has promised his aid in finding valuable minerals on Sir Arthur's property. Sir Arthur, forced to put up money before Dousterswivel will work his magic, has already borrowed one hundred pounds from Oldbuck, who accurately suspects that Dousterswivel is a crook.

Before the magician can attempt to work his magic, Oldbuck's nephew, Captain Hector M'Intyre, comes home for a visit. A hotheaded young man, he accuses Lovel of lying about the little he has told of his past. Hector challenges Lovel to a duel, and although Lovel does everything he can to prevent it, the duel is fought. Having apparently wounded Hector fatally, Lovel is forced to flee the country on a boat provided by a friend. Hector recovers, but Lovel does not hear the news until much later. He has been aided in his flight by Edie Ochiltree, a beggar who knows all the secrets of the countryside. While Edie is hiding Lovel in a cave, they overhear Dousterswivel trying to convince Sir Arthur to put up more money to find buried treasure in the cave.

When Sir Arthur asks Oldbuck for another hundred pounds to give to Dousterswivel so that he can get the treasure from the cave, Oldbuck insists that they themselves go to the cave and dig for the treasure. Although the magician tries to prevent the excursion, Oldbuck will not be denied. Everyone present is completely surprised when, after much digging, old Edie the beggar sticks a pick into the ground and hits a chest. When the chest is opened, the bewildered spectators find a fortune in coin; Sir Arthur is saved from disaster. Edie tricks Dousterswivel into digging for hours for more treasure that Edie says is also buried in the cave. In addition, he arranges with a friend to have a specter appear and frighten the magician.

About the same time, an old woman in the neighborhood sends for the wealthy and powerful earl of Glenallan. Before she dies, she wants to clear her conscience of a terrible wrong she has done the earl. When he was a young man, he was in love with a girl whom his mother hated. The earl had secretly married the girl before his mother, in a spiteful attempt to break up the romance, told her son that the girl was his own sister. Because of certain letters and the perjured testimony of servants, including the old woman telling the story, the earl had believed his mother's story. The young woman had taken her own life, but before she died, she had given birth to a male child. A servant had whisked the child away, and the old woman did not know whether he had lived or died. The earl, who had lived a life of misery because of the horrible crime he thought he had committed in marrying his own sister, was joyful at the old crone's information, though he grieved at the useless death of his wife. He tells the story to

Oldbuck and asks his help in determining whether the child lived.

While Oldbuck and the earl of Glenallan are investigating, news comes that the French are about to raid the Scottish coast. Hector, who is now fully recovered from the wound suffered at Lovel's hands, prepares to gather troops and meet Major Neville, an officer in charge of local defense. Lovel has not been heard from since the duel, and there are rumors that he died at sea. Then old Edie brings the news that the ship carrying Lovel has put in to shore and that all aboard are safe. From his remarks to Oldbuck, the old gentleman learns that the money found in the cave on Sir Arthur's land was buried there by Lovel and Edie after they overheard the conversation between Dousterswivel and Sir Arthur. Lovel, hearing of Sir Arthur's financial difficulties, has chosen that way of helping Isabella's father to avoid embarrassing the old gentleman by offering him money outright.

When Major Neville appears to take charge of the garrison, everyone is amazed to see that he is in reality Lovel. He brings word that there will be no battle. A watchman has mistaken a bonfire for a signal that the French are coming. As they all stand talking, the earl of Glenallan notes the young man's marked resemblance to his dead wife. Through old papers and the words of old servants of the Glenallan family, the earl learns that Lovel is without doubt his son. While a baby, the boy was cared for by the earl's brother and, unknown to the earl, he had inherited his uncle's fortune.

Lovel is restored to his rightful place, and within a month he and Isabella are married. From that time on, they all live in peace, prosperity, and joy.

Critical Evaluation:

Sir Walter Scott's *The Antiquary*, the third in the Waverley series, is the novel most nearly contemporary to the author's own time. Although it is a love story, it is also a novel of manners. Scott admitted that, when necessary, he sacrificed the plot in order to describe more clearly the manners of the characters, particularly those of the lower social classes. His characterizations of the Scottish peasants are much more vivid than those of the upper classes.

The Antiquary met with unprecedented sales when it first appeared in 1816. Scott remarked that "it has been more fortunate than any of [the other novels] . . . for six thousand went off in the first six days." It reached a fifth edition within two years and was translated during ensuing years into at least seven languages.

In spite of its being a potpourri of gothic elements—supernatural escapades among abbey ruins at night, scheming tricks of a charlatan magician, romantic rescues up sheer cliffs from a wild and sudden high tide, and the usual genteel and static hero and heroine falling at the end into marriage as well as vast inherited wealth—the novel succeeds for other, more significant reasons. Its lasting value is based on the scenes of Scottish village life and of the lower classes and their colorful dialogue. These scenes have wit and pathos and provide a sane balance to the contrived, unreal plot in which the upper-class characters are involved. The links between the two levels of the tale are the antiquary Jonathan Oldbuck of Monkbarns (who possesses many of Scott's interests and much of his learning) and the wandering beggar Edie Ochiltree. These two characters move back and forth between the fishing village and country people and the nobility and their estates, providing connections between the two different worlds of the novel.

Scott draws the background of *The Antiquary* from the historical religious opposition of Catholics and Covenanters and the political conflict between England and France. These issues, however, form only a backdrop and do not affect the suspense and tension of the novel. Scenes such as that in the Fairport post office, where the village gossips speculate about the newly arrived mail, or the pathetic gathering of the Mucklebackit family in their cottage after their son Steenie's drowning are remarkable because of their vividness. Such scenes constitute the core of the novel, its color and its poetry. Moreover, Scott brings the characters in these scenes alive, perhaps because he draws them from individuals he knew from boyhood. Action and meaning belong to old Elspeth crooning her eerie ballads, Edie Ochiltree maintaining his pride and religious feeling though merely an "auld" beggar, Maggie haggling with Monkbarns over the price of fish, and Mucklebackit Senior trying to cope with his grief. Scott declared *The Antiquary* to be a novel of lower-class manners; as such, it succeeds.

Further Reading

Daiches, David. "Scott's Achievement as a Novelist." In *Scott's Mind and Art*, edited by A. Norman Jeffares. New York: Barnes & Noble, 1970. Clear analysis of Scott's depiction of character in *The Antiquary*, finding the portrayal of the merchant class more sympathetic than that of the nobility. Discusses the novel's unusual use of comic atmosphere.

D'Arcy, Julian Meldon. *Subversive Scott: The Waverley Novels and Scottish Nationalism*. Reykjavík, Iceland: Vigdís Finnbogadóttir Institute of Foreign Languages, University of Iceland Press, 2005. Demonstrates how the novels contain dissonant elements, undetected manifestations of Scottish nationalism, and criticism of the United Kingdom and its imperial policy. Chapter 3 examines *The Antiquary*.

Irvine, Robert P. "The State, the Domestic, and National Culture in the Waverley Novels." In *Enlightenment and Romance: Gender and Agency in Smollett and Scott*. New York: Peter Lang, 2000. Analyzes the fiction of Scott and Tobias Smollett within the context of the emergence of the social sciences and the dominance of novels written by female writers in the eighteenth century. Describes how the authors adapted the feminine romance and the domestic novel to assert control over the narrative structure of their novels.

Johnson, Edgar. *Sir Walter Scott: The Great Unknown*. 2 vols. New York: Macmillan, 1970. Extensively researched biography that explores Scott as a man and as a writer. Praises *The Antiquary*'s rich portrayal of life in Scotland and discusses the need to understand the past in order to live in the present. An excellent introductory source.

Millgate, Jane. *The Making of a Novelist*. Toronto, Ont.: University of Toronto Press, 1984. Good introductory source that analyzes character and theme in *The Antiquary*. Discusses the novel's structure and the importance of Oldbuck as a central figure. Compares the novel's treatment of past and present with Scott's novel *Guy Mannering* (1815).

Robertson, Fiona. *Legitimate Histories: Scott, Gothic, and the Authorities of Fiction*. New York: Oxford University Press, 1994. Analyzes Scott's Waverley novels within the context of eighteenth and nineteenth century gothic literature. Examines the novels' critical reception. Devotes a chapter to *The Antiquary*.

Shaw, Harry E, ed. *Critical Essays on Sir Walter Scott: The Waverley Novels*. New York: G. K. Hall, 1996. Collection of essays published between 1858 and 1996 about Scott's series of novels. Includes journalist Walter Bagehot's 1858 article about the Waverley novels and discussions of Scott's rationalism, storytelling and subversion of the literary form in his fiction, and what his work meant to Victorian readers.

Sutherland, John. *The Life of Walter Scott: A Critical Biography*. Malden, Mass.: Blackwell, 1995. Interesting literary analysis that characterizes *The Antiquary* as a middle-aged man's story, with Oldbuck a fictionalized portrait of Scott himself. Praises plot development in the first two volumes but asserts that the third demonstrates rushed, conventional plotting.

Wagenknecht, Edward. *Sir Walter Scott*. New York: Continuum, 1991. Provides clear analysis of setting and character in *The Antiquary*, finding the novel most effective in its portrayal of the lower classes. Discusses the importance of the character of Elspeth.

Antony and Cleopatra

Author: William Shakespeare (1564-1616)
First produced: c. 1606-1607; first published, 1623
Type of work: Drama
Type of plot: Tragedy
Time of plot: c. 30 B.C.E.
Locale: Egypt and parts of the Roman Empire

Principal characters:
MARK ANTONY,
OCTAVIUS CAESAR, and
LEPIDUS, triumvirs who ruled Rome
ENOBARBUS and EROS, Antony's friends
SEXTUS POMPEIUS, the leader of the party opposed to Octavius Caesar
CLEOPATRA, the queen of Egypt
OCTAVIA, Caesar's sister and Antony's wife
CHARMIAN and IRAS, Cleopatra's attendants

The Story:

After the murder of Julius Caesar, the Roman Empire is ruled by the noble triumvirs Mark Antony, Lepidus, and Octavius (Caesar's nephew). Antony, given the Eastern sphere to rule, goes to Alexandria and there he sees and falls passionately in love with Cleopatra, queen of Egypt. She is the flower of the Nile, but she is also the mistress of Julius Caesar and many others. Antony is so enamored of her that he ignores his own counsel and the warnings of his friends.

As long as he can, he also ignores a request from Octavius Caesar that he return to Rome. Sextus Pompeius, son of Pompey the Great, and a powerful leader, is gathering troops to seize Rome from the rule of the triumvirs, and Octavius Caesar wishes to confer with Antony and Lepidus. At last the danger of a victory by Sextus Pompeius, coupled with the news that his wife Fulvia is dead, forces Antony to leave Egypt and return to Rome.

Because Antony is a better general than either Lepidus or Octavius, Pompeius is confident of victory as long as Antony stays in Egypt. When Pompeius hears that Antony is returning to Rome, he is reduced to hoping that Octavius and Antony will not mend their quarrels but continue to fight each other as they did in the past. Lepidus does not matter, since he sides with neither of the other two and cares little for conquest and glory. Pompeius is disappointed, however, for Antony and Octavius join forces in the face of common danger. To seal their renewed friendship, Antony marries Octavia, Octavius's sister. Pompeius's scheme to keep Antony and Octavius apart fails, but he still hopes that Antony's lust for Cleopatra will entice him back to Egypt. To stall for time, he seals a treaty with the triumvirs. Antony, accompanied by his new wife, goes to Athens to deal with matters relating to the Roman Empire. There word reaches him that Lepidus and Octavius had waged war in spite of the treaty they signed and that Pompeius was killed. Octavius next seizes Lepidus on the pretext that he aided Pompeius. Now the Roman world has but two rulers, Octavius and Antony.

Antony cannot resist the lure of Cleopatra. Sending Octavia home from Athens, he hurries back to Egypt. By so doing, he ends all pretense of friendship between him and Octavius. Both prepare for a battle that will decide who is to be the sole ruler of the world. Cleopatra joins her forces with Antony's. Antony's forces are supreme on land, but Octavius rules the sea and lures Antony to fight him there. Antony's friends and captains, particularly loyal Enobarbus, beg him not to risk his forces on the sea, but Antony is confident of victory, and he prepares to match his ships with those of Octavius at Actium. In the decisive hour of the great sea fight, however, Cleopatra orders her fleet to leave the battle and sail for home. Antony, too, leaves the battle, disregarding his duty toward his honor, and because he sets the example for desertion, many of his men go over to Octavius's forces.

Antony sinks in gloom at the folly of his own actions, but he is drunk with desire for Cleopatra and sacrifices everything, even honor, to her. She protests that she did not know that he would follow her when she sailed away, but Antony has reason to know she lies. However, he cannot tear himself away.

Octavius sends word to Cleopatra that she may have anything she asks for if she will surrender Antony to him. Knowing that Octavius is likely to be the victor in the struggle, she sends him a message of loyalty and of admiration for his greatness. Antony, who sees her receive the addresses of Octavius's messenger, rants and storms at her for her faithlessness, but she easily dispels his fears and jealousy and makes him hers again. After his attempt to make peace with Octavius fails, Antony decides to march against his enemy again. At this decision, even the faithful Enobarbus leaves him and goes over to Octavius, thinking Antony has lost his reason as well as his honor. Enobarbus is an honorable man, however, and shortly afterward he dies of shame for having deserted his general.

On the day of the battle, victory is in sight for Antony despite overwhelming odds. Once again, though, the Egyptian fleet deserts him. With the defeat of Antony, Octavius becomes master of the world. Antony is like a madman and thinks of nothing but avenging himself on the treacherous Cleopatra. When the queen hears of his rage, she has word sent to him that she is dead, killed by her own hand out of love for him. Convinced once more that Cleopatra was true to him, Antony calls on Eros, his one remaining follower, to kill him so that he can join Cleopatra in death. However, Eros kills himself rather than his beloved general. Determined to die, Antony falls on his own sword. Even that desperate act is without dignity or honor, for he does not die immediately and can find no one who loves him enough to end his pain and misery. While he is lying there, a messenger brings word that Cleopatra still lives. He orders his servants to carry him to her. He dies in her arms, each proclaiming eternal love for the other.

When Octavius Caesar hears the news of Antony's death, he grieves. Although he fought and conquered Antony, he laments the sorry fate of a great man turned weakling and ruined by his lust. He sends a messenger to assure Cleopatra that she will be treated royally, that she should be ruler of her own fate. The queen learns, however, as Antony warned her, that Octavius will take her to Rome to march behind him in his triumphant procession, where she, a queen and mistress to two former rulers of the world, will be pinched and spat upon by rabble and slaves. To cheat him of his triumph, she puts on her crown and all her royal garb, places a poisonous asp on her breast, and lies down to die. Charmian and Iras, her loyal attendants, die the same death. Octavius Caesar, entering her chamber, sees her dead, as beautiful and desirable as in life. There is only one thing he can do for his onetime friend and the dead queen: He orders their burial in a common grave, together in death as they wished to be in life.

Critical Evaluation:

In his tragedies, William Shakespeare rose to dramatic heights seldom equaled. *Antony and Cleopatra* surely belongs to the greatest of his tragedies for its staggering scope, which covers the entire Roman Empire and the men who ruled it. Only a genius could apply such beauty of poetry and philosophy to match the powerful events: A man born to rule the world is brought to ruin by his weaknesses and desires; deserted by friends and subjects, he is denied a noble death and must attempt suicide, but bungles even that. The tragedy is grimly played out, and honor and nobility die as well as the man.

In *Antony and Cleopatra*, Shakespeare did not bind himself with the Aristotelian unities. He moves swiftly across the whole of the civilized world with a panorama of scenes and characters, creating a majestic expanse suitable to the broad significance of the tragedy. The play is Shakespeare's longest. It is broken up into small units, which intensify the impression of rapid movement. Written immediately after Shakespeare's four great tragedies—*Hamlet, Prince of Denmark* (pr. c. 1600-1601, pb. 1603), *Othello, the Moor of Venice* (pr. 1604, pb. 1622), *King Lear* (pr. c. 1605-1606, pb. 1608), and *Macbeth* (pr. 1606, pb. 1623)—it rivals them in tragic effect though it has no plot that Aristotle would recognize. Shakespeare took the story of *Antony and Cleopatra* from a translation of Plutarch but refashioned it into a complex rendering of a corruption that ennobles as it destroys. The play may lack the single, poignant representative character of the great tragedies, but it extends its significance by taking the whole world for its canvas.

As a tragic figure, Antony leaves much to be desired. His actions are little more than a series of vacillations between commitment to a set of responsibilities that are his by virtue of his person and office and submission to the overpowering passion that repeatedly draws him back to Cleopatra's fatal influence. His nobility is of an odd sort. He commands respect and admiration as one of the two omnipotent rulers of the world, but the audience is only told of his greatness; they do not see it represented in any of his actions. In fact, he does not really do anything until his suicide—and that he does not do efficiently. His nobility is attested by his past deeds and by his association with the glories of Rome, and Shakespeare frequently reminds the audience of it, but Antony does not demonstrate this quality in the play.

There is another impediment to Antony's tragic stature: He is too intelligent and aware of what he is doing. As Mark Van Doren has noted, he lives "in the full light of accepted illusion." He is not duped; Cleopatra is not Antony's Iago. There is no self-deception; Antony does not pretend that his love for Cleopatra is more than it is.

That love, however, is sufficiently great to endow Antony with the nobility he salvages. It is not simply that he is a hero brought to disgrace by lust, although that much is true. Viewed from another angle, he is a hero set free from the limits of heroism by a love that frees him from a commitment to honor, allowing him instead to give his commitment to life. Of course, his liberation is also his humiliation and destruction. Both noble and depraved, both consequential and trivial, Antony finds new greatness in the intense passion that simultaneously lays him low.

Cleopatra is an equally complex character, but her complexity is less the result of paradox than of infinite variation. Throughout the first four acts she lies, poses, cajoles, and entices, ringing manifold changes on her powers to attract. However, she is not a coarse temptress, not a personification of evil loosed upon a helpless victim. As her behavior in the last act reminds the audience, she is also an empress. Cleopatra, too, is swept along by overwhelming passion. She is not only a proud queen and conniving seducer but a sincere and passionate lover. Despite her tarnished past, her plottings in *Antony and Cleopatra* are dignified through the underlying love. Like Antony, she is not the sort of character who challenges the universe and transcends personal destruction. Rather, her dignity lies somewhere beyond, or outside, traditional heroism.

The complexity of Cleopatra is most apparent in the motivation for her suicide. Certainly one motive is the desire to avoid the humiliation of being paraded through Rome by the victorious Octavius Caesar. If that had been all, however, she would be nothing more than an egoistic conniver. More important, she is also motivated by her sincere unwillingness to survive Antony. The two motives become intertwined, since the humiliation of slavery will also extend to Antony, whose failures leave her vulnerable and taint his reputation. This mixture of motives is a model of the way in which the two lovers are at once each other's undoing and salvation. Their mutual destruction springs from the same love that provides both with their antiheroic greatness. Love is lower than honor in the Roman world, but it can generate an intensity that makes heroism irrelevant. Antony is too intelligent, Cleopatra too witty, and their love too intricate for ordinary tragedy.

The structure of the plot departs from the tragic norm. There is almost none of the complication and unraveling that are expected in tragedy. Rather, the action moves in fits and starts through the forty-two scenes of the play. Although the action of the play must extend over a long period of time, the quick succession of scenes suggests an unsteady hurtling toward the fatal conclusion. The helter-skelter quality is reinforced by the language of the play. Few speeches are long and there are many abrupt exchanges and quick, wide-ranging allusions. Shakespeare often uses feminine endings and spills the sense over the ends of lines in a metrical reflection of the nervous vitality of the play. Thus, plot and language spread the drama over the entire world and hasten its progress toward the inevitable conclusion.

"Critical Evaluation" by Edward E. Foster

Further Reading

Bloom, Harold, ed. *Modern Critical Interpretations: William Shakespeare's "Antony and Cleopatra."* New York: Chelsea House, 1988. Bloom's concise anthology of major Shakespeare criticism of the 1970's and 1980's judiciously samples postmodernist, new historicist, feminist, and deconstructionist discussions of *Antony and Cleopatra*. The essays by Jonathan Dollimore, Linda Bamber, and Laura Quinney are especially useful.

Charney, Maurice. *Shakespeare's Roman Plays*. Cambridge, Mass.: Harvard University Press, 1961. Chapter 3, the centerpiece of Charney's influential book, brilliantly analyzes the imagery of *Antony and Cleopatra*. Charney gives particular attention to the imagery that clusters around the Egypt-Rome polarity, thereby constituting it as a complex central theme.

Deats, Sara Munson, ed. *Antony and Cleopatra: New Critical Essays*. New York: Routledge, 2005. Some of the essays examine the visual language, passion and politics, modern staging, gambling, politics of food, and sleep, epic, and romance in *Antony and Cleopatra*. Deats provides a survey of the critical reception of stage and screen performances.

Escolme, Bridget. *Antony and Cleopatra: A Guide to the Text and Its Theatrical Life*. New York: Palgrave Macmillan, 2006. A handbook focusing on the challenges of staging the play. Analyzes the text, early productions, subsequent stage and film productions, and the historical and cultural contexts in which the play was produced.

Granville-Barker, Harley. *Prefaces to Shakespeare*. Vol. 1. Princeton, N.J.: Princeton University Press, 1946. Granville-Barker's prefaces remain timeless monuments to a golden age of Shakespearean scholarship and theatrical performance. His preface to *Antony and Cleopatra* offers valuable insights into staging and characterization from the perspective of an influential stage director and critic.

Hall, Joan Lord. *Antony and Cleopatra: A Guide to the Play*. Westport, Conn.: Greenwood Press, 2002. An overview of the play, examining its textual history, contexts and sources, dramatic structure, and themes. Analyzes the characters of Antony and Cleopatra and provides information about various critical approaches to the work.

Miles, Geoffrey. "'Infinite Variety': *Antony and Cleopatra*." In *Shakespeare and the Constant Romans*. New York: Oxford University Press, 1996. Examines the depiction of constancy in *Antony and Cleopatra* and Shakespeare's other Roman plays. The Romans considered constancy a virtue, and Miles traces the development of this ethical concept from ancient Rome through the Renaissance. He then analyzes the ambiguity of this virtue in Shakespeare's depiction of the inconstant Antony.

Riemer, A. P. *A Reading of Shakespeare's "Antony and Cleopatra."* Sydney: Sydney University Press, 1968. A monograph-length, lucid introduction to the background of the play and its plot, characterization, and dramatic structure. Contains a useful chapter that discusses important criticism of the play during the early and mid-twentieth century.

Traversi, Derek. *Shakespeare: The Roman Plays*. Stanford, Calif.: Stanford University Press, 1963. In chapter 3 of this classic study, Traversi offers a methodical, analytical commentary on *Antony and Cleopatra*. He sees the play as a profound work of art that in its spaciousness, episodic form, and morally ambivalent valuations of Rome and Egypt escapes traditional definitions of tragedy.

Apologia pro Vita Sua

Author: John Henry Newman (1801-1890)
First published: 1864
Type of work: Autobiography

This long essay, also known as *History of My Religious Opinions* (1870), is the famous reply written by John Henry Newman in answer to the attack upon him by Charles Kingsley. The years 1833-1841 had seen the publication of *Tracts for the Times*, to which Newman had been a contributor; these tracts, which gave their name to the Tractarian or Oxford Movement, were the spearhead of the great theological controversy of the middle years of the century. Newman and his friends were eager to return the Anglican church to something like its position during past centuries; they valued tradition and hierarchy and wished to return to the severe, authoritarian faith of the past, from which they believed the Church of England had lapsed. They were the High Church party; and some idea of the rift that was created within the Church can be gleaned from Anthony Trollope's Barchester novels. In 1845, Newman left the Anglican church for the Roman; two years later he was ordained priest in that communion.

In January, 1864, Kingsley, an Anglican clergyman of what was known as the Broad Church party and a popular novelist, attacked Newman in a magazine article, in which he stated that "Truth, for its own sake, has never been a virtue with the Roman clergy. Father Newman informs us that it need not, and on the whole ought not to be." To this article, Newman replied in a pamphlet in February of that year, whereupon Kingsley wrote yet another pamphlet entitled "What, then, does Dr. Newman mean?" in which he accused Newman of having "gambled away" his reason, of having a "morbid" mind, and of not caring about "truth for its own sake." It was in answer to this pamphlet that Newman wrote *Apologia pro Vita Sua*.

Newman divides the work into chapters, each dealing with a crucial period in his life. The first gives the story of his youth and his education up to his thirty-second year, by which time he was a Fellow of Oriel College, Oxford, and had been ordained in the Anglican church. By his own account, he is an extraordinarily precocious lad who is preoccupied at a very early age with religious questions. He resembles, indeed, the hero of his own novel *Loss and Gain* (1848)—which phrase might be applied as a description of his career. Later readers may smile at Newman's decision, reached at the age of fifteen, that celibacy is the only course for him, yet his prodigious intellect shines through the account of his youth. He tells of his reading, but the decisive influences are his friends Hurrell Froude and the older John Keble. It is Froude, with his love for tradition and for the external beauty of the Roman church, who begins to soften Newman's insular dislike of that institution.

The year 1830 is a momentous one for Newman. The revolution that deposed Charles X of France distresses him; the Whig victory in England distresses him even more. He has a violent dislike of liberalism, which seems everywhere triumphant, and the Tractarian Movement is largely a counterattack. Newman claims that the movement began to stir as far back as 1828, when he was vicar of St. Mary's, Oxford; but the date of its beginning is usually set in July, 1833, when Keble preached a famous sermon at Oxford against the errors of the Whig government in Church policy. In *Tracts for the Times*, Newman and his friends state their position. As Newman sees it, the Whigs must be opposed and the Church of England returned to the position of authority it had held during the early seventeenth century. He considers himself as belonging to neither the High nor the Low Church party; he is merely anti-Liberal. He explains his position as based on dogma (he has no use for "religion as a mere sentiment" but thinks there must be positive beliefs), a visible church with sacraments and rites and the episcopal system, and anti-Romanism. Such is the general point of view of the Oxford Movement. Newman, incidentally, has very little to say about ritual, which is usually associated with the High Church position. He is interested in theology, not liturgies.

Newman admits frankly that in the vast amount of writing he did during these years he did attempt to refute many of the tenets of Romanism. What he is seeking for himself is a basis in reason for his beliefs; for the Anglican church, he is seeking a theology of its own that would make it more than a *via media*, or "middle way." These investigations lead him to a consideration of the common heritage of Romanism and Anglicanism and to the question of how much of the Roman belief can be accepted by an Anglican. He begins to be convinced that in English history the real objection to Rome had been political rather than theological, and that Romanism and Anglicanism are, after all, not so far apart as is generally believed. Inevitably, he begins to differentiate between Roman dogmas, which he can accept, and Roman practice, which he often cannot. He confesses that, for a long time, the stumbling block had been the Roman veneration of the Virgin and prayers to the saints. He is obviously, however, drawing closer to Rome.

It is tract 90, published in 1841, that brings the storm on Newman's head and leads to his final break with the Church of England. In this tract, he examines whether the Thirty-Nine Articles, on which the Church rests, are capable of a Roman interpretation. Immediately he was accused of everything from "traducing the Reformation" to planning to build a monastery near Oxford. He was feeling grave doubts about Anglicanism, derived mainly from his reading on the abstruse doctrines of the Monophysites. When he could no longer conscientiously maintain his clerical position, he resigned his living of St. Mary's in September, 1843. As he explains, he had spent the years from 1835 to 1839 trying, in his writings, to benefit the Church of England at the expense of the Church of Rome and the years from 1839 to 1843 trying to benefit the Church of England without prejudice to the Church of Rome. In 1843, he begins to despair of the Church of England.

The years between 1843 and 1845 are spent in retirement. Newman had reached the crossroads but is still unable to make the ultimate decision. He has already retracted the "hard things" he had said against Rome, the things he had felt compelled to say in defense of the Anglican church. He makes a point of seeing no Roman Catholics; his struggle is purely an inward one. Though he still believes that the Church of England is a branch of the true Church, though he still deplores the "Mariolatry" of Rome, he is convinced that Rome is more in accord with the early Church. His horror of liberalism also plays its part; he very genuinely believes that the spirit of liberalism is the spirit of Antichrist. As he now sees the situation, on one hand there is liberalism leading inevitably to atheism, and on the other, there is Anglicanism leading to Rome. He still remains in lay communion with the Church of England during this difficult period, but more and more often he asks himself: "Can I be saved in the English Church?" When he is convinced that the answer is negative, he makes the great decision and is received into the Roman communion in 1845. Two years later, he is ordained priest.

In the concluding section of his essay, Newman defends himself against the insults hurled at him after his conversion. It was said that by submitting to Rome he had abdicated his power of personal judgment and that he was now compelled to accept dogmas that might be changed at any moment. His reply is that the Roman doctrines are not difficult for him, and that historically the Church has not suppressed freedom of intellect. He believes that an infallible Church had been intended by the Creator to preserve religion—especially in an age of increasing skepticism. Lastly—and this is the most famous part of the essay—he advances the idea that a conflict between authority and private judgment is beneficial to the person whose ideas are being tested.

Though *Apologia pro Vita Sua* won for Newman a resounding victory over Kingsley, the work is not easy reading. The difficulty does not lie in the style, for no one writes more clearly and simply than he, but in the fact that he was writing for readers who were familiar with Church history and theological problems. Readers who lack the knowledge to grasp many of his arguments find the text impenetrable. Moreover, Newman's dilemma becomes more difficult to understand in later times. Nevertheless, the *Apologia pro Vita Sua* remains a powerful and sincere work. Some have seen in Newman, as Kingsley must have done, only a man whose habit of mind made him take refuge in an authoritarian Church that would solve his spiritual problems for him. Others would say that Newman's faith and intelligence serve as mutual checks, informing and enhancing each other.

Further Reading

Arthur, James, and Guy Nicholls. *John Henry Newman*. London: Continuum, 2007. Overview of Newman's life and work. Includes intellectual biography, critical exposition of his work, and discussion of his work's reception, influence, and continued relevance.

Barros, Carolyn A. *Autobiography: Narrative of Transformation*. Ann Arbor: University of Michigan Press, 1998. Analyzes *Apologia pro Vita Sua* and autobiographies by several other prominent Victorians, describing how these authors relate tales of major transformations in their lives.

Harrold, Charles Frederick. *John Henry Newman: An Expository and Critical Study of His Mind, Thought, and Art*. New York: Longmans, Green, 1945. Authoritative and detailed. Chapter 12 discusses the Newman-Kingsley controversy and *Apologia pro Vita Sua*. Lengthy bibliography and index.

Houghton, Walter E. *The Art of Newman's "Apologia."* New Haven, Conn.: Yale University Press, 1945. Focuses on the artistic qualities of the work rather than on its historical or theological aspects. In-depth concentration on Newman's "principles of biography" and prose style. Includes diagrams of stylistic analysis.

Martin, Brian. *John Henry Newman: His Life and Work*. New York: Oxford University Press, 1982. An accessible and useful work for the beginning student. Discusses *Apolo-*

gia pro Vita Sua throughout, but particularly in chapter 8, "Literature and Religion." Examines the book's influence on Newman's contemporaries.

Newman, John Henry. *Apologia pro Vita Sua*. Edited by David J. DeLaura. New York: W. W. Norton, 1968. A valuable source and overview. Contains the text of *Apologia pro Vita Sua*, as well as basic texts of the Newman-Kingsley debate. Two further sections offer critical essays and early reactions to the work.

Rule, Philip C. *Coleridge and Newman: The Centrality of Conscience*. New York: Fordham University Press, 2004. Compares works by Newman and Samuel Taylor Coleridge in which the two men argued that God exists as the moral conscience of humankind. Chapter 3 discusses *Apologia pro Vita Sua* and Coleridge's *Biographia Literaria* (1817).

Strange, Roderick. *John Henry Newman: A Mind Alive*. London: Darton Longman & Todd, 2008. Introductory overview of Newman's life and thought designed for students and general readers.

Ward, Wilfrid. *The Life of John Henry, Cardinal Newman: Based on His Private Journals and Correspondence*. 2 vols. New York: Longmans, Green, 1912. Early but definitive biography of Newman. Includes a thorough discussion of the background, sources, and effect of *Apologia pro Vita Sua*.

The Apostle

Author: Sholem Asch (1880-1957)
First published: 1943
Type of work: Novel
Type of plot: Historical
Time of plot: First century C.E.
Locale: Roman Empire

Principal characters:
SAUL OF TARSHISH, later known as Paul
JOSEPH BAR NABA OF CYPRUS, Saul's friend, an early convert
REB ISTEPHAN, a famous Jewish preacher
SIMON BAR JONAH, called Peter
REB JACOB, Joseph's son

The Story:

It is seven weeks after the crucifixion of Yeshua (Jesus) of Nazareth by Pontius Pilate. All the poor of Jerusalem, who found in Yeshua their Messiah, go into hiding, but the word is spreading. Little by little the story is told: of Yeshua who came back after his death and of the Messiah who appeared to his disciples. The matter is hotly argued on all sides. The pious Jews cannot believe in a Messiah who was killed; the Messianists devoutly affirm their faith.

Saul of Tarshish and Joseph bar Naba come upon a street preacher, a rustic Galilean, who tells with great conviction of Yeshua's return after he was entombed. Cries of belief and of repugnance interrupt his talk. Saul himself speaks with great bitterness against this Messiah, for he has no patience with the gentle Yeshua who was crucified.

The agitation rapidly spreads. One of the most vigorous upholders of Yeshua is Reb Istephan. He has a gift for moving people's souls, and more and more Jews become persuaded. Joseph bar Naba knew Yeshua in his lifetime, and when Joseph hears Reb Istephan, he is convinced. Joseph becomes a Messianist. This conversion disgusts Saul, and in sorrow and bitterness, he turns away from his friend Joseph.

Then a dramatic incident takes place. Simon, the first of Yeshua's disciples, heals Nehemiah the cripple in the name of the Nazarene. Many are impressed by the cure, but others resent Simon's use of the Messiah's name. As a result, his enemies have their way, and Simon is imprisoned by the High Priest to await trial. Then another miracle happens. Simon and his follower Jochanan, who were securely locked in a dungeon, are the next morning again walking the streets. It is said that they passed directly through the stone walls—with the help of Yeshua.

The resentment against the wild Galileans grows among the rulers, while the humble folk follow Simon with trust. The High Priest again brings Simon to trial, but Simon speaks so well in defense of his doctrine that he is freed. Now the tumult increases. The ignorant folk, seeing Simon released, conclude that there is official sanction for the new cult; hence, more join the followers of Yeshua.

Saul is greatly incensed. He believes that the Messiah is yet to come and that the disciples are corrupting Jerusalem.

He goes to the High Priest and secures an appointment as official spy. In his new job, Saul tracks down the humble Messianists and sentences them to the lash. Growing in power, Saul the Zealot finally takes Reb Istephan prisoner for preaching the new faith. With grim pleasure, Saul leads the way to the stoning pit and watches Istephan sink beneath the flung rocks. As he dies, the preacher murmurs a prayer forgiving his tormentors. Saul is vaguely troubled.

Then the Messianists are much heartened. Yeshua's younger brother, Reb Jacob ben Joseph, comes to Jerusalem to head the humble cult, and Saul can do little against this pious and strict Jew. By chance, the High Priest hears of more Messianists in Damascus. Saul volunteers to investigate and hurries to his new field. En route, however, a vision appears to him in which Yeshua says, "Saul, Saul, why dost thou persecute me?" Saul then recognizes Yeshua as his Lord, and, as he is commanded, he goes on to Damascus, although he is still blinded by the heavenly apparition. A follower of the new religion baptizes him and restores his sight. The penitent Saul hurries away from the haunts of man. In all, he waits seven years for his mission.

Finally, as he prays in his mother's house, the call comes. Joseph bar Naba asks Saul to go with him to Antioch to strengthen the congregation there. At last, Saul is on the way to bring the word of the Messiah to others. He leaves for Antioch with Joseph and the Greek Titus, Saul's first convert.

Simon founds the church at Antioch among the Greeks. The perplexing question is, could a devout Jew even eat with the Gentiles, let alone accept them into the church? In Jerusalem, Jacob holds firmly to the law of the Torah: Salvation is only for the circumcised. Simon vacillates. In Jerusalem, he follows Jacob; among the Greeks he accepts Gentiles fully. Joseph is sent by the elders of Jerusalem to Antioch to apply the stricter rule to the growing Messianic church.

Saul at first meets with much suspicion. The Messianists remember too well Saul the Zealot who persecuted them. Little by little, the apostle wins them over. Yeshua appears to Saul several times, and he is much strengthened in the faith. At last, Saul finds his true mission in the conviction that he is divinely appointed to bring the word of Yeshua to the Gentiles. He works wonders at Antioch and builds a strong church there, but his acceptance of Gentiles costs him Joseph's friendship. As a symbol of his new mission, Saul becomes Paul and begins his years of missionary work.

Paul goes to all the Gentiles—to Corinth, to Ephesus, to Cyprus. Everywhere, he founds a church, sometimes small but always zealous. Lukas, the Greek physician, goes with him much of the time. Lukas is an able minister and a scholar who is writing the life of Yeshua.

The devout Jews in Jerusalem are greatly troubled by this strange preacher who accepts the Gentiles. Finally, they bring him up for trial. Paul escapes only by standing on his rights as a Roman citizen. As such, he can demand a trial before Caesar himself. Paul goes to Rome as a captive, but he rejoices, for he knows the real test of Christianity will be in Rome. Simon is already there, preaching to the orthodox Jews.

The evil Nero makes Paul wait in prison for two years without a hearing and, even then, only the intervention of Seneca frees the apostle. For a short time, Simon and Paul work together, one among the Jews and the other among the Gentiles. They convert many, and the lowly fervently embrace the promise of salvation.

To give himself an outlet for his fancied talents as an architect, Nero burns Rome and plans to rebuild a beautiful city. The crime, however, is too much, even for the Romans. To divert suspicion from himself, Nero blames the Christians. He arrests thousands of them and, on the appointed day, opens the royal carnage. Jews and Christians, hour after hour, are gored by oxen, torn by tigers, and chewed by crocodiles. At the end of the third day, many Romans can no longer bear the sight, but still Nero observes the spectacle. It is so strange: The Christians die well, and with their last breaths, they forgive their persecutors.

Simon, a Jew, is crucified afterward; Paul, born a Roman citizen, is beheaded. Gabelus, the gladiator who accepted Christianity, goes with them to the execution. The deaths of Simon and Paul, however, are, in reality, the beginning. The martyrdom of the early Christians is the foundation stone of the Christian church.

Critical Evaluation:

During the four decades between his first ventures into short fiction and the publication of his novel *Der Man fun Notseres* (1943; *The Nazarene*, 1939), Sholem Asch established himself as the most important Yiddish writer of his time, as well as a spokesperson and a crusader for his people. Although *The Nazarene* was a best seller, it roused a storm of protest among Jews. Certainly, Asch's timing was unfortunate. Asch's story of the life of Christ appeared when Jews were facing the most widescale persecutions in their history. It is hardly surprising that many embattled Jews viewed the book as evidence that Asch had left the faith and was urging others to follow his example or, alternatively, that he was an unprincipled opportunist, aiming at high sales among Christian readers or, perhaps, a Nobel Prize.

Asch was stunned by such accusations. His dedication to Judaism was as strong as ever. Moreover, the subject of *The*

Nazarene did not mark a new departure in Asch's interests. As early as 1906, he had planned to write a book about Jesus, whom he regarded as one of the outstanding Jews in history. With this goal in mind, he had been collecting materials on primitive Christianity for some thirty years; during his numerous trips to the Holy Land, the subject had never been far from his mind. Asch's purpose in writing *The Nazarene*, *The Apostle*, and *Mary* (1949), the story of Jesus's mother, was not to glorify Christianity at the expense of Judaism, but to show his readers how deeply Christianity was rooted in Judaism and to remind them that adherents of the two faiths share the same ethical systems and worship the same God. In this way, he hoped, he could bring about a reconciliation between Christians and Jews.

Although most of his Jewish critics did not see it at the time, thematically, Asch's Christological novels are no different from his earlier works. Asch had always emphasized spiritual values. His heroes had always been Jewish leaders, often rabbis, who devoted themselves to God. Asch often revealed his impatience with legalistic technicalities, especially when they served to separate human beings from their God, and he deplored factionalism, which so often sprang from an emphasis on the letter, rather than the spirit, of the law. Because of convictions like these, as well as his profound knowledge of those distant times, Asch respected the founders of the Christian church, including Jesus; Paul and the other apostles; and Mary, the mother of Jesus. As a deeply religious Jew, he understood these other devout Jews, even though he himself had no interest in adopting their faith.

In *The Apostle*, Saul is introduced as a person with just one aim in life: to serve his God. By nature, he is a fanatic. He cannot admit anything in his life that might distract him from his purpose. Therefore, he rejects the useful, respectable life his parents had intended for him, as a learned rabbi with a wife and a family. In order to avoid the sins of the flesh, he not only avoids women, but, from time to time, he even embraces the ascetic rules of the Nazarites; to avoid the sins of the intellect, Saul continually scrutinizes his ideas and those of others for any taint of heresy.

Ironically, Saul does not experience any uncertainties about his spiritual well-being until after he has become a Christian. From that time on, he is in constant conflict with himself. On one hand, he is as strong-willed as ever. On the other hand, he is mindful of Jesus's insistence on submitting to suffering rather than inflicting suffering upon others.

When Saul, or Paul, is sent to spread the gospel among the Gentiles, he does not feel threatened by paganism. It is clear that the pagan gods are dead. They serve merely to prop up the authority of the state or provide occasions for dissolute behavior. The Gentile world is more than ready for a faith that has some substance and offers some hope. What disturbs Paul is that the Gentiles who accept his news with such joy face rejection from his own people, the Jewish leaders of the new church, who insist that the only way into Christianity is through Judaism. For male Gentiles, that means circumcision. Paul understands that to Greeks, imbued with the ideal of physical beauty, circumcision is abhorrent. Because Christ always stressed the spirit, not the law, Paul is infuriated by the legalistic quibbling of the men in Jerusalem, who are making it difficult for him to fulfill his mission.

Unfortunately, Paul's increasing hostility toward the Jewish Christians has been misinterpreted as a reflection of Asch's own views, perhaps of some antipathy toward Judaism. In reality, although epic in scope and crowded with characters, *The Apostle* is primarily a character study. In Paul, Asch sees a great man, whose single-minded passion for God gives him the strength to do great deeds, while his inability to compromise produces conflicts with others and within himself. Paul's life illustrates how intolerance can damage an individual, while the history of the infant church shows how inflexibility can threaten an institution.

Both Christianity and Judaism continue to be troubled by factionalism. In Asch's novel, however, Paul finally learns to subdue his will and, in submission, he becomes whole. By thus identifying Paul's most important achievement as a spiritual one, Asch offers further proof of the kinship between Judaism and Christianity. As *The Apostle* shows, both great faiths are based on the assumption that human life is, above all, a spiritual matter.

"Critical Evaluation" by Rosemary M. Canfield Reisman

Further Reading

Madison, Charles A. *Yiddish Literature: Its Scope and Major Writers*. New York: Frederick Ungar, 1968. Explains why Asch wrote his trilogy, in particular, the story of Paul, who has been regarded by many Jews as the founder of Christian anti-Semitism. A good discussion of a difficult subject.

Morgentaler, Goldie. "The Foreskin of the Heart: Ecumenism in Sholem Asch's Christian Trilogy." *Prooftexts: A Journal of Jewish Literary History* 8, no. 2 (May, 1988): 219-244. Explores the attitudes that underlie Asch's works, including *The Apostle*. Asserts that *The Apostle* is flawed by Asch's manipulation of history and Pauline theology to reflect his own beliefs.

Siegel, Ben. *The Controversial Sholem Asch: An Introduc-*

tion to His Fiction. Bowling Green, Ohio: Bowling Green University Popular Press, 1976. The first critical biography of Sholem Asch written in English. Siegel finds *The Apostle* to be vivid, but less effective than the other two works in the trilogy, and also dated. Includes a chronology, extensive notes, and useful bibliography.

Stahl, Nanette, ed. *Sholem Asch Reconsidered*. New Haven, Conn.: Beinecke Rare Book and Manuscript Library, 2004. Collection of lectures delivered at a conference held at Yale University in 2000, in which Yiddish literary critics reevaluated Asch's work. Two of the essays focus on his Christological novels *The Apostle* and *The Nazarene*.

"Talmud for the Acts." *Commonweal* 38, no. 24 (October 1, 1943): 588-589. A favorable review of *The Apostle*, reflecting contemporaneous Christian opinion. Admits that the book is fictional and sometimes not consistent with Catholic doctrine, but recommends it highly.

Appointment in Samarra

Author: John O'Hara (1905-1970)
First published: 1934
Type of work: Novel
Type of plot: Naturalism
Time of plot: 1930
Locale: Pennsylvania

Principal characters:
JULIAN ENGLISH, a car dealer
CAROLINE, his wife
HARRY REILLY, a rich man
AL GRECCO, the bootlegger's handyman

The Story:

Julian English is thirty years old, a congenial seller of cars and popular with the country club set. He has the right connections with Ed Charney, the local bootlegger, and consequently is always well supplied with liquor. He and Caroline have been married four years. Both natives of Gibbsville, they have an assured social position and no children.

Just before Christmas, they go to a party at the country club. As usual, Julian has too much to drink. He sits idly twirling his highball and listening to Harry Reilly's stories. Harry is a rich Irish Catholic and definitely a social climber. Julian dislikes Harry, although Harry loaned him twenty thousand dollars the previous summer to bolster his Cadillac agency. That loan does not give Harry the right to make passes at Caroline, Julian thinks darkly. Harry tells stories in paragraphs. He always pauses at the right time. Julian keeps thinking how fitting it would be if he stopped the stories by throwing his drink in Harry's face. Julian grows bored. On impulse he does throw his drink in Harry's face. A big lump of ice hits Harry in the eye.

On the way home, Julian and Caroline quarrel furiously. Julian accuses his wife of infidelity with Harry, among others. Caroline says that Julian always drinks too much and chases women as well. More important, Harry has a mortgage on the car agency and a good deal of influence with the Catholics, and he is a man who can hold a grudge.

Al Grecco is a little man who, as Ed Charney's handyman, has a certain standing in the town. He likes Julian because Julian is the only one of the social set who is really friendly. Al grew up on the wrong side of the tracks. Before he was finally sentenced to a year in prison, he was arrested several times. When he got out, he worked in a poolroom for a while until his boss died. The widow wanted Al to stay on as manager, but he went to work for Charney. Now he delivers bootleg booze, runs errands, and keeps an eye on Helene Holman, the torch singer at the Stage Coach, a country inn owned by Charney. Helene is Charney's girl, but Charney knows that if she is not carefully watched, she might, out of sheer goodheartedness, extend her favors to other men.

On Christmas Day, Julian wakes up with a hangover. As is his custom, he quarrels with the cook. At Caroline's suggestion, he goes to Harry's house to apologize. Although Harry's sister is sympathetic, she brings down word that Harry will not see him; he has a black eye and is still perturbed.

Julian's father and mother come for Christmas dinner. The father, a staid, successful surgeon, is always looking for evidence of moral weakness in Julian, for his own father committed suicide after embezzling a fortune. He is afraid that the English inheritance is stained. Dinner is a trying occasion.

Caroline and Julian have supper at the club. The usual crowd is there. Julian is unmercifully ribbed in the locker room. In a dismal mood, he sits drinking by himself while he waits for a chance to see Father Creedon and asks him to patch up his incident with Harry. The old priest is sympathetic and makes light of the affair. After agreeing that Harry is a bore, he promises to send Julian some good Irish whiskey.

Charney is a good family man who spends Christmas Day with his wife and son. He intends to go out to the Stage Coach only in the evening. Then his son becomes suddenly ill. It looks as if he will have to stay home. Mindful of Helene's weaknesses, he telephones Al to go out to the inn to keep watch on her. It is Christmas night and she will be drinking too much. Al does not care for the assignment, but he dutifully goes out to the inn and sits down with Helene.

The country club set begins to drift in. Froggy Ogden, who is Caroline's one-armed cousin, is the oldest man there; he seems to feel a responsibility for Julian, who is still drinking. In a spirit of bravado, Julian dances several times with Helene, even though Al warns him of Charney's anger. Finally, carried away by the music and too many drinks, Julian and Helene leave the dance floor. Caroline and Froggy find Julian in a stupor in the back of a sedan and take him home.

The day after Christmas, Caroline goes to her mother and announces her intention to divorce Julian. Her mother finds it difficult to listen to her daughter. Caroline thinks of herself as a heroine in an old-fashioned melodrama. She is determined not to go back to Julian. After meeting him on the street and quarreling with him again, she cancels the big party that they were to have given that very evening.

As he backs out of the garage with a case of Scotch, Al decides to kill Charney. When Charney phoned him, Al tried to excuse his lack of vigilance: He protested that he allowed Helene only to dance. Charney, in a rage, said some things that Al cannot accept.

Determined to look businesslike, Julian goes to his office at the automobile agency. He sits importantly at his desk and writes figures on a piece of scratch paper. The only conclusion he can reach is that he needs more money. One of his salesmen comes in to try to lay down the law. He asserts that Julian's difficulties are being gossiped about in the little town of Gibbsville. The offense to Charney is particularly grave: He is a good friend to the agency and helps them sell cars to other bootleggers.

Julian leaves the office in no cheerful mood. He wanders into his club for lunch. Since it is the day after Christmas, the dining room is deserted except for some elderly lawyers and Froggy. Avoiding his wife's cousin, Julian sits down in a far corner of the room. After picking up his plate, Froggy follows him and begins to reproach him for his conduct with the torch singer. He tells Julian he always distrusted him and warned Caroline about his conduct many times. When Froggy invites him outside to fight, Julian refuses because he cannot hit a one-armed man. Froggy becomes more insulting, and the lawyers come to their table to intervene. Julian is intensely angered when they seem to side with Froggy. Turning quickly, he hits one of the lawyers in the mouth and dislodges his false teeth.

Julian goes home and falls asleep. About ten o'clock, a society reporter awakens him when she comes to get a story about the canceled party. After several drinks, he tries to seduce her but with no success. As soon as she leaves, Julian goes to the garage, closes the door, and starts the motor; his death is pronounced a suicide by the coroner.

Critical Evaluation:

John O'Hara is supreme in the art and craft of the short story. Perhaps because of his newspaper background, he is able to condense a tale to its fundamentals and produce tightly crafted and powerful short fiction. With his ear for speech and eye for effect, he is in two or three sentences able to bring to life a character from nearly any walk of life. This gift also marks his novels, in particular perhaps his first novel, *Appointment in Samarra*.

One of O'Hara's shortest and best-structured novels, *Appointment in Samarra* is the story of hubris in a modern setting. It takes place in 1930, after the crash of 1929 but before people understood just how bad the Depression would become. The hero of the novel, Julian English, has social status but destroys himself by not living up to it. Julian has two problems: people and alcohol, and both are revealed to be part of the inner problems that ultimately ruin him. There is much discussion in the book of who "belongs" and who does not, which clubs count in Gibbsville, what preparatory schools and colleges matter, and where one should be seen or not be seen. The laborer, mobster, and society man all think constantly about their position on the social ladder. Julian thinks about it too much.

The novel presents an accurate picture of a broad cross section of Gibbsville society. Observing different kinds of people, from the secretary in the automobile agency and the ex-convict working for the gangland boss to the society matron, O'Hara achieves a new kind of fictional reporting, in the best sense of the term. The humor and fast pace of the novel and the clean, sure style give it a surface slickness that is almost misleading, for it is not a superficial novel. There is depth behind the meretricious glitter and hard-boiled sensual flavor. The book's racy language and sexual candor continue the pathbreaking trend begun only a short time earlier by Ernest Hemingway. The characters are concerned with superficialities, but that does not make them superficial. O'Hara is able to capture, especially in his dialogue, the nuances of tone that reveal the hidden depths.

Julian English, the central figure of the novel, is the most complex and interesting of the characters. He seems to burn with a compulsion toward self-destruction, yet however drunk he gets, part of his mind warns him when he is about to do something dangerous. Like many intelligent people, he observes himself as he moves through life. Yet, he recklessly plunges ahead, throwing the drink in Harry Reilly's face, dancing and going out to the car with Helene Holman at the roadhouse, getting deliberately drunk so that he will not care what happens. By the time he quarrels with Froggy Ogden at the club and fights with the lawyers in the dining room, he has given up hope and is as contemptuous of himself as he is of them. Rational action has ceased to have any meaning for him. Julian is a direct forerunner of the existential heroes of Jean-Paul Sartre and Albert Camus a decade later, who were influenced by O'Hara and Hemingway and other writers of the American "hard-boiled" school of writing, and he toys with his fate with an almost objective curiosity. "If I do this," he seems to think, "will I get away with it?" Of course, he knows somewhere deep inside that he will not, that nobody ever gets away with anything. He is filled with "tremendous excitement" when he realizes that "he is in for it." Perhaps, as he contemplates his "unknown, well-deserved punishment," he is even slightly masochistic in his longing for pain and destruction.

Julian's fatalism, and the fatalism that permeates the novel (and gives it its title), seem to be influenced in part by the novels and stories of Hemingway and F. Scott Fitzgerald. However, O'Hara, while lacking the poetic vision and poetic style of Fitzgerald, avoids the hard-boiled prose of Hemingway and adds a poignant ruthlessness of his own. With economy and artistry, O'Hara draws the painful and engrossing portrait of a complex, fascinating, and doomed individual.

An inevitable progression, gaining in momentum like a ball rolling down a steep hill, takes over Julian's fate. It will take a miracle to halt the inevitable doom that awaits him at the end, and as Julian knows, miracles do not happen for people like him. His death is early foreshadowed by the suicide of his grandfather. His own father frequently expresses fears that Julian's character is as weak as that of his grandfather, and Julian comes to believe that he has a defective character and is doomed by it. This belief numbs him and renders him helpless before the onrush of events.

Appointment in Samarra rises above O'Hara's other long works of fiction because it makes more of an attempt to deal with ideas and values. Often, the author's technique of recording action with the detachment of a photographer fails to establish a moral frame of reference; the reader does not know what the author's attitude toward the characters and events is. In this work, however, the character of Julian is portrayed in compelling vitality. Also adding to the immediacy is O'Hara's custom of surrounding his dramatic action with historical exposition and long descriptions of the period: of its fashions, its horses and clubs, its automobiles, and the other transitory items that date a moment in history. In *Appointment in Samarra*, the precise documentation of social strata contributes to the story's realistic effect.

"Critical Evaluation" by Bruce D. Reeves

Further Reading

Bruccoli, Matthew J. *The O'Hara Concern: A Biography of John O'Hara*. Pittsburgh, Pa.: University of Pittsburgh Press, 1995. A complete biography of O'Hara, first published in 1975 and written with the cooperation of O'Hara's widow. Discusses the sources and background of *Appointment in Samarra* and argues that O'Hara is a major writer. Includes a good bibliography.

Eppard, Philip B., ed. *Critical Essays on John O'Hara*. New York: G. K. Hall, 1994. Contains both reviews and essays about O'Hara's work, including analyses of *Appointment in Samarra*. Other essays discuss O'Hara's relationship to naturalism, his short stories, and his view of society, politics, the family, and small towns. Includes a comprehensive introductory chapter on O'Hara's career and the reception of his novels.

Grebstein, Sheldon N. *John O'Hara*. New York: Twayne, 1966. The earliest and one of the most balanced book-length assessments of O'Hara's controversial career. Identifies the forces at work in *Appointment in Samarra* as fate, society, free will, self-knowledge, sex, and money.

Long, Robert Emmet. *John O'Hara*. New York: Frederick Ungar, 1983. A useful short study. Concludes that O'Hara is not a major writer, but calls *Appointment in Samarra* his "most nearly perfect novel."

Schwarz, Benjamin, and Christina Schwarz. "John O'Hara's Protectorate." *The Atlantic Monthly*, March, 2000. A discussion of O'Hara's writing career, including information about the style and themes of his work and his depiction of his hometown, Pottsville, Pennsylvania, as the town of Gibbsville in his novels and stories. The authors maintain that O'Hara is one of the greatest social novelists of twentieth century America.

Wolff, Geoffrey. *The Art of Burning Bridges: A Life of John O'Hara*. New York: Knopf, 2003. A warts-and-all portrait of O'Hara. Wolff recounts the many incidents of O'Hara's bad behavior, including his alcoholism, bullying, and rages against women, editors, and critics. However, Wolff argues that these character flaws should not detract from O'Hara's literary reputation, citing *Appointment in Samarra* as among his best work. Includes photographs, bibliography, and index.

The Apprenticeship of Duddy Kravitz

Author: Mordecai Richler (1931-2001)
First published: 1959
Type of work: Novel
Type of plot: Satire and bildungsroman
Time of plot: 1940's
Locale: Montreal

Principal characters:
DUDDY KRAVITZ, an ambitious teenager
MAX KRAVITZ, his father, a cab driver
LENNIE KRAVITZ, his brother, a medical-school student
SIMCHA KRAVITZ, his grandfather
BENJAMIN "BENJY" KRAVITZ, his uncle, a factory owner
YVETTE DURELLE, his lover, a waitress
VIRGIL ROSEBORO, a young epileptic employed by Duddy
JERRY "BOY WONDER" DINGLEMAN, a local gangster

The Story:

Duddy Kravitz is a motherless, prankish teenager in a high school in which most of the students come from Montreal's St. Urbain Jewish ghetto. Duddy is the leader of a school gang, the Warriors, who bully other children, especially the students at the neighboring yeshiva, a Jewish religious school. He also is the instigator of a campaign of telephone harassment of the school's goy, or non-Jewish, instructors, especially John MacPherson, an ineffectual teacher and an alcoholic who despises the boy. Duddy causes the death of Macpherson's disabled wife when she leaves her bed to answer one of Duddy's harassing phone calls. Duddy is perpetually haunted by guilt and remorse.

Duddy's stern but loving grandfather Simcha counsels him, saying that "a man without land is nobody." This maxim becomes the driving force in Duddy's ambition to become a success through the acquisition of money. He soon begins engaging in dubious commercial schemes.

A particularly negative influence on Duddy's moral development is his weak father, Max, who moonlights as a pimp and who idolizes a local gangster called Jerry (the Boy Wonder) Dingleman. Duddy is also demoralized by the ridicule heaped on him by his father and his uncle Benjy, who focus their attention on the eldest Kravitz son, Lennie, a promising medical student who is sure to raise the family's fortunes.

Pretensions and crassness define Duddy's social environment. His St. Urbain neighborhood is filled with folly, and his high school is a place of shallow education and anti-Semitism.

After graduation Duddy works at a summer resort. He is subjected to emotional and physical harassment from a group of fellow waiters, snobbish college boys led by a malicious law student, Irwin Shubert, who masterminds a phony roulette game to rob Duddy of his entire summer wages. However, Duddy has become a favorite employee of the resort's boss and clientele, who contribute to restitute his earnings. Irwin is forced to return the boy's losses at roulette. Duddy plans to use this doubling of his earnings as an investment to purchase land around a nearby lake shown to him by Yvette Durelle, a young French Canadian waitress at the resort who has become his lover. Duddy's new life ambition is to acquire this property, settle his beloved grandfather on a farm, and build a lucrative resort.

Duddy is faced with both success and failure in his attempts to raise money; he wants to acquire plots of land around the lake at St. Agathe. Because he is still legally a minor, he uses Yvette as an agent to purchase titles to the various properties. As she become more involved with Duddy as his lover and as his Girl Friday, or secretary, she grows more disillusioned about his marital intentions and his skewed sense of morality in his financial ventures.

Duddy's ambitions and commercial activities grow more frantic and outlandish as he pursues his obsession with money. The most outlandish is his project of filming bar-mitzvahs and weddings of his acquaintances. He then attempts to sell the movies as commemorations to the celebrating families. To this end he employs the services of a has-been alcoholic film director, Friar, who produces hilarious anthropological re-creations of what he considers strange Jewish rituals.

While the films are a hit with Duddy's customers, Friar proves to be an unreliable partner. Duddy soon seeks new ways to make money. He coerces his father to introduce him to Dingleman, who refuses to loan him money. Instead, the gangster takes Duddy to New York and then uses him as an unwitting courier to smuggle drugs to Montreal. During this trip, he meets Virgil Roseboro, who agrees to help him import pinball machines from the United States to sell in Canada at inflated prices.

Meanwhile, the Kravitz family is in an uproar when Lennie disappears. Duddy takes on the responsibility of searching for his brother, who has fled to Toronto after performing an illegal abortion for one of the girls in his new set of wealthy goy friends. Duddy befriends the girl's father, Calder, a wealthy industrialist, and persuades him not to have Lennie charged with the crime. However, as Duddy's debts begin to overwhelm him, Virgil appears with the exported pinball machines. A new moneymaking scheme helps Duddy acquire nearly half of the land that he covets.

Duddy's fortunes seem to be on the rise. He employs Virgil to drive a truck for distributing movies to resorts for his successful movie-rental business. He expands his social circle and even starts dating to search for a respectable (and wealthy) Jewish woman to be his wife; he just wants to exploit Yvette, not marry her.

Crises soon abound. Uncle Benjy gets terminal cancer, and Duddy, ever loyal to the family, seeks out Benjy's wayward wife, Ida, to return her to Montreal. Benjy tries to reconcile with Duddy, whom he has always despised as a materialistic *pusherke* (a pushy Jew), but the boy refuses his overtures. During this crisis, Virgil has an epileptic fit driving the truck and is disabled in an accident. Yvette blames Duddy for the incident and leaves him, taking Virgil to her home in St. Agathe. Duddy, overwhelmed once again by guilt and remorse, plunges into a serious depression, which becomes a full-blown breakdown after Benjy dies.

Virgil writes Duddy a letter, leading Duddy to seek out Yvette and reconcile with her. While at St. Agathe, Duddy reads a posthumous letter from Benjy. After Duddy sees his beloved lake, his hopes rebound. Finally, when he discovers that Dingleman has used him as a drug courier and is now competing with him to purchase the same lake property, Duddy's chase after money is refueled.

Duddy frantically approaches everyone he can to raise enough money to buy the last parcel of lake property. He even foolishly attempts to blackmail Dingleman over the drug-smuggling affair. After unsuccessfully trying to persuade Virgil to loan him money from a family inheritance, Duddy uses forgery to steal money from the bank account of Virgil, who has a stroke after he discovers the theft. After a final confrontation with Duddy, Yvette leaves him.

Duddy takes the Kravitz family to see his new lake property. Lennie is impressed, and Max is ecstatic, even when he is appalled at Duddy's rude behavior toward Dingleman, who shows up to congratulate his rival on acquiring the land. However, Grandfather Simcha, whom Duddy most wants to please, refuses the boy's gift of a farm because Yvette has revealed to him his grandson's crime against Virgil.

Duddy seeks out Yvette, who rejects him with heart-felt loathing, leading him to see himself as betrayed, not the betrayer. At a restaurant where the family celebrates, Max creates a myth around the new Boy Wonder, his Duddy, who is lifted from despondency to euphoric pride in his ill-gotten wealth and power.

Critical Evaluation:

The Apprenticeship of Duddy Kravitz is Mordecai Richler's most popular and critically acclaimed work of fiction, written early in his career. Upon its publication in 1959, the novel created a sensation in Canada's literary world because of its explicit language, controversial thematic content, and hilarious, even bawdy, form of satire. At the time, the work was reviled as coarse and cynical, but it was praised as well for rejuvenating the Canadian comic novel. In terms of Richler's literary career and in the development of Canadian literature the book is considered a seminal work for its examination of aspects of Jewish life that are a source of value and a focus of trenchant criticism.

The novel is divided into four parts and traces Duddy's transition into independent adulthood over a period of several years. Except for one flashback, the narrative is linear and uncomplicated and includes several set pieces which detail specific events that become the targets of Richler's satire.

In many ways, *The Apprenticeship of Duddy Kravitz* embodies the major concerns that Richler had focused upon throughout his writing career. He wished to recapture a truthful vision of his past, especially his youth in the St. Urbain community. He also attempted to make a case for the ostensibly unsympathetic person. Finally, Richler had regarded the moral basis of his works as the most important aspect of his task as a writer, and he had strived to use his skill as a satirist for this purpose.

Richler uses a well-known form of fiction, the bildungsroman (novel of formation) to trace Duddy's development from adolescence to adulthood and adapts this genre to illustrate how the boy's social and physical environments mold his character, especially his moral development. In the St. Urbain Jewish ghetto, family, money (and its antithesis—poverty), and politics are important influences on the boy's life. Thus, the characters who influence Duddy most intensely are evaluated in these terms and have either negative or positive effects on his progress toward maturation. In this respect, his family plays a crucial role in his early life. His grandfather Simcha reinforces Duddy's sense of family in a positive way, whereas his father, Max, proposes a negative model of making money through his idolization of the local gangster, Jerry (the Boy Wonder) Dingleman. Once Duddy leaves St. Urbain, even the positive influence exerted by characters such as Yvette and Virgil cannot sufficiently redirect the boy's moral outlook.

Richler portrays Duddy's character development and fate in terms of a divided nature and thus maintains a level of sympathy for his protagonist even when he acts reprehensibly. In the middle of episodes where he becomes a grasping hustler, emulating the Boy Wonder, Duddy can also rescue and help relatives in his role as a responsible and devoted family man. By describing how the boy is ridiculed by his own family, persecuted at school, and harassed at the resort by snobbish fellow waiters, Richler carefully lays the groundwork for an understanding of the callousness and ruthlessness demonstrated by Duddy in his later life.

Guiding much of the direction of Duddy's apprenticeship is the touchy issue of the relations between Jews and goys—a topic Richler courageously thrusts before his readers whether they are prepared or not for such an exploration. The trenchant satire he uses to target both the Jewish and the goy characters in *The Apprenticeship of Duddy Kravitz* underscores the truth that villainy, stupidity and cruelty are endemic to all races, ethnicities, and nationalities. With his relentless criticism of life in the Montreal Jewish ghetto, and with his descriptions of anti-Semitism as an attitude between Jews themselves as well as between Jew and goy, Richler was often described as a self-hating Jew by critics who were outraged by his honesty. Ultimately, the humor, complexity, and truth of his portrayals in *The Apprenticeship of Duddy Kravitz* won for him wide audiences and critical approval that acknowledged the importance of the work in broadening the language and subject matter of the Canadian novel.

Diana Arlene Chlebek

Further Reading

Kramer, Reinhold. *Mordecai Richler: Leaving St. Urbain.* Montreal: McGill-Queen's University Press, 2008. A thoroughly researched scholarly biography that incorporates never-before published material from the Richler archives as well as interviews with family members and friends. Analyzes the importance of Jewish culture and "Canadianness" in Richler's writing.

Pollock, Zailig. "Duddy Kravitz and Betrayal." In *Perspectives on Mordecai Richler*, edited by Michael Darling. Toronto, Ont.: ECW Press, 1986. Analyzes the novel in terms of Duddy's character and moral values, particularly his adherence to the code of the St. Urbain Street community.

Posner, Michael. *The Last Honest Man: Mordecai Richler, an Oral Biography.* Toronto, Ont.: McClelland & Stewart, 2004. Recounts Richler's life through interviews with family members, friends, colleagues, editors, drinking and snooker companions, and others who discuss their experiences with and impressions of the author.

Ramraj, Victor J. *Mordecai Richler.* Boston: Twayne, 1983. This work presents a succinct overview of Richler's life and writings. The analysis of *The Apprenticeship of Duddy Kravitz* focuses on the artistry of Richler's character portrayals.

Woodcock, George. *Introducing Mordecai Richler's "The Apprenticeship of Duddy Kravitz": A Reader's Guide.* Toronto, Ont.: ECW Press, 1990. An insightful and detailed analysis of the novel. Covers its significance and its critical reception. Also provides a close textual reading of the work.

The Arabian Nights' Entertainments

Author: Unknown
First published: Alf layla wa-layla, fifteenth century (English translation, 1706-1708)
Type of work: Short fiction
Type of plot: Folklore
Time of plot: Legendary past
Locale: India, China, Persia, and Arabia

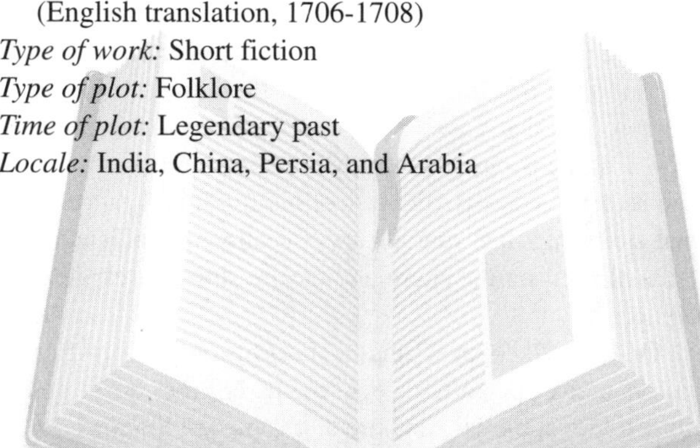

Principal characters:
SHAHRIAR, the emperor of Persia and India
SCHEHERAZADE, his bride
THE FISHERMAN
THE KING OF THE BLACK ISLES, half man, half marble
SINDBAD THE SAILOR, a wanderer from Baghdad
THE SULTAN OF INDIA
HOUSSAIN,
ALI, and
AHMED, his sons
PERIEBANOU, Ahmed's wife
ALI BABA, a woodcutter in Persia
CASSIM, his brother
MORGIANA, his slave
ALADDIN, a good-for-nothing boy in China

The Stories:

Convinced by the treachery of his brother's wife and his own that all women are unfaithful, Shahriar, the emperor of Persia and India, vows that he will marry a new wife every day and have her executed the next morning. Only Scheherazade, wise as well as beautiful, has the courage to try to save the young women of Persia. On the night of her marriage to Shahriar, she begins to tell him a tale that fascinates him so much that he stays her death for one night so that he can learn the end of the story. Eventually, Scheherazade tells him stories for one thousand and one nights. Then, convinced of her worth and goodness, he lets her live and makes her his consort.

One tale Scheherazade tells is "The History of the Fisherman and the Genie": A poor fisherman draws from the sea in his nets a strange box with a seal on top. When he pries off the top, a huge genie appears and threatens him with death, offering the poor man no more than his choice in the manner of his death. The fisherman begs for his life because he did the genie a favor by releasing him, but the genie declares that he vowed death to the man who opened the box. Finally, the fisherman exclaims that he cannot believe anything as huge and as terrible as the genie could ever have been in a space so small. Dissolving into a cloud of smoke, the genie shrinks until he can slip back into the box, whereupon the fisherman clamps on the lid. Throwing the box back into the sea, he warns all other fishermen to beware if it should ever fall into their nets.

Another story is "The History of the Young King of the Black Isles": A fisherman catches four beautiful fish, one white, one red, one blue, and one yellow. They are so choice that he takes them to the sultan's palace. While the fish are being cooked, a beautiful girl suddenly appears and talks to the fish, after which they are too charred to take to the sultan. When the same thing happens two days in a row, the sultan is called. After asking where the fish came from, he decides to visit the lake. Nearby, he finds a beautiful, apparently deserted palace. As he walks through the beautiful halls, he finds one in which a king is sitting on a throne. The king apologizes for not rising, explaining that his lower half is marble.

He is the king of the Black Isles. When he learned that his queen was unfaithful to him, he nearly killed her black lover. In revenge, the queen cast a spell over her husband, making him half marble. She whipped him daily and then had him dressed in coarse goat's hair over which his royal robes were placed. At the same time, while tending her lover, who remained barely alive, she changed her husband's town and all its inhabitants into the lake full of fish.

The king tells the sultan where the queen's lover is kept. There the sultan goes, kills the lover, and puts himself in the black man's place. The queen, overjoyed to hear speaking the one she kept from death for so long, hastens to do all the voice commands. She restores the king to his human form and the lake to its previous state as a populous town. The four colors of fish indicate the four different religions of the inhabitants.

When the queen returns to the sultan, whom she mistakes for her lover, he kills her for her treachery. He takes the king of the Black Isles home with him and rewards the fisherman who led him to the magic lake.

Shahriar is vastly entertained by "The History of Sindbad the Sailor": A poor porter in Baghdad, resting before the house of Sindbad, bewails the fact that his lot is harder than that of Sindbad. Sindbad overhears him and invite the porter to dine with him. During the meal, he tells of the hardships he suffered to make his fortune.

On his first voyage to India by way of the Persian Gulf, Sindbad's ship is becalmed near a small green island. The sailors climb onto the island, only to find that it is really a sea monster, which heaves itself up and swims away. Sindbad is the only man who does not get back to the ship. After days of clinging to a piece of driftwood, he lands on an island where some men are gathered. They lead him to a maharajah, who treats Sindbad graciously. When he is there for some time, Sindbad's ship comes into port, and he claims his bales of goods, to the astonishment of the captain, who thinks he saw Sindbad killed at sea. Then Sindbad sails home in the ship in which he set out.

The porter is so impressed with the first tale that he comes again to hear a second. On his second voyage, Sindbad is left asleep on an island where the sailors rested. There he finds a huge roc's egg. He waits, knowing that the parent bird will return to the nest at dusk. When it comes, he uses his turban to tie himself to the bird's leg. In the morning, the bird flies to a place surrounded by mountains. There Sindbad frees himself when the bird descends to pick up a serpent. The place seems deserted, except for large serpents. Diamonds of great size are scattered throughout the valley.

Sindbad remembers that merchants are said to throw joints of meat into the diamond valley, and big eagles carry the joints to their nests close to shore. At the nests, the merchants frighten away the birds and recover diamonds that stick to the meat. Sindbad collects some large diamonds. With his turban, he fastens a piece of meat to his back and lies down. An eagle picks him up and carried him to its nest. When he is dropped into a nest, the merchant who claims the nest is indignant and accuses Sindbad of stealing his property. When Sindbad offers him some choice diamonds, the merchant is glad to take the adventurer back to civilization in return.

On his third voyage, Sindbad is wrecked on an island inhabited by cannibal dwarfs and huge black creatures, each with only one eye in the middle of its forehead. Sindbad and his friends blind one black giant, but two others help the blind one to chase the sailors. The giants and a large serpent overtake them, and only Sindbad is lucky enough to escape.

On his fourth voyage, Sindbad sails from a port in Persia. He and his friends are shipwrecked on an island inhabited by cannibals, who fatten the sailors before killing them. Sindbad refuses food, grows too thin to interest the cannibals, and finally finds his way to the shore. There he meets men who take him to their kingdom. To please the king, Sindbad makes a fine saddle. In appreciation, the king marries Sindbad to a beautiful girl. In that country, a man or woman is buried alive if the spouse dies. When Sindbad's wife dies, he is put in a tomb with a small amount of bread and water. As he eats the last of his food, he hears an animal snuffling, then running away. Following the sound, he finds himself on the shore and hails a ship that carries him home.

On his fifth voyage, Sindbad uses his own ship. After his sailors break open a roc's egg, the parent rocs hurl tremendous stones at the ship and break it to pieces. Sindbad comes under the power of the Old Man of the Sea and escapes only after making the old man so intoxicated that he loses his death grip on Sindbad. Again, Sindbad finds a ship to take him home, and he does much profitable trading on the way.

On the sixth voyage, all of his companions succumb on a beautiful but lifeless coast. Expecting to die, Sindbad builds a raft that he puts in an underground river to drift where it will. When he reaches the kingdom of Serendib, he has to be revived. He finds the country exceedingly rich and the people kind. When he asks to leave, the king sends him home with rich presents for Sindbad's ruler, the Caliph Harun-al-Rashid of Baghdad.

Sindbad makes his seventh and final voyage to take gifts from the caliph to the king of Serendib. He carries them safely, but his return trip is delayed when corsairs seize his ship and sell the sailors into slavery. Sindbad is sold to an ivory merchant and is ordered to shoot an elephant a day. Annoyed at Sindbad's persistence, an elephant picks him up and takes him to an elephant burial ground, to which Sindbad and his owner return many times to gather ivory. As a reward, the merchant sends Sindbad home with rich goods.

Another diverting tale is "The History of Prince Ahmed": Houssain, Ali, and Ahmed, sons of the sultan of India, are all in love with the Princess Nouronnihar, their father's ward. To determine who should be the bridegroom, the sultan sends them out to find the most extraordinary things they can. Whoever brings back the rarest object will win the hand of the princess.

Houssain finds a magic carpet that will transport him wherever he wished. Ali finds an ivory tube containing a glass that will show any object he wishes to see. Ahmed finds an artificial apple, the odor of which will cure any illness.

The three princes meet before they journey home. As they display their gifts, Houssain, looking through the tube, sees the princess apparently at the point of death. They all jump on his magic carpet and are whisked to her bedroom, where Ahmed uses his magic apple to revive her. The sultan cannot determine which article is the most unusual, for all were of use to effect the princess's recovery. He suggests an archery contest. Ali shoots farther than Houssain, but Ahmed's arrow cannot be found. The sultan decides in favor of Ali. Houssain retires to become a dervish. Instead of attending the wedding, Ahmed goes in search of his arrow, which he finds at the foot of a mountain, much farther away than he could have shot. Looking around, he finds a door into the mountain. When he passes through the door, he finds a fairy called Periebanou, who pleases him so much that he marries her.

When Ahmed goes to visit his father, he refuses to discuss where or how he lives, but he appears to be so rich that the courtiers grow jealous and persuade the sultan that it is dangerous to have his son so powerful a neighbor. The sultan asks Ahmed to perform unreasonable tasks, made possible only by Periebanou's help; but while Ahmed is fulfilling one request Periebanou's brother becomes so annoyed with the sultan that he kills him. Ahmed becomes sultan and afterward deals kindly with his brothers.

Scheherazade also pleases her lord with "The History of Ali Baba and the Forty Thieves": Ali Baba is a Persian woodcutter. One day, to hide from a band of strange horsemen, he climbs a tree under which they halt. When the leader cries, "Open, Sesame!" to a rock nearby, a door opens through which the men carry their heavy packs. After the men leave, Ali Baba uses the secret word to investigate the cave. He finds such riches there that the gold he takes can never be missed.

He and his wife are content with that amount, but his brother Cassim, to whom he tells his story, is greedy for more wealth. Without telling Ali Baba, Cassim goes to the cave. He was so excited by the gold that he forgets the password and cannot get out. When the robbers find him, they murder him.

The robbers try to find Ali Baba, intending to kill him and so keep the secret of their hoard. The leader brings his men, hidden in oil jars, to Ali Baba's house, but a beautiful slave, Morgiana, goes in search of oil, discovers the ruse, and kills the bandits. Soon after, the robber captain, disguised as a merchant, enters the house, but again Morgiana comes to her master's rescue, seeing through the robber's disguise and killing him.

To reward Morgiana, Ali Baba not only makes her a free woman but also gives her to his son in marriage. After that, Ali Baba is the only one who knows the secret of the cave. He uses the hidden wealth in moderation and passes the secret on to his children.

No less pleasing is "The History of Aladdin: Or, The Wonderful Lamp": Aladdin is a youthful vagabond who lives in China. An African magician, sensing that Aladdin will suit his plans and pretending to be the boy's rich uncle, takes him to a secret place to get a magic lamp. Passing through halls stored with treasures, Aladdin fills his gown with so many things that he cannot give the magician the lamp at the moment he wants it, whereupon the magician seals him up in the earth. By chance, Aladdin rubs a ring the magician gave him. A genie appears and escorts him home.

When Aladdin shows his mother the lamp, she tries to clean it to sell. As she rubs, another genie appears from whom Aladdin asks food. The food appears on silver trays that Aladdin sells one by one to a peddler who swindles him. When an honest jeweler stops Aladdin one day and asks to buy the silver, Aladdin begins to realize the great riches he has at his disposal, enough to win him the sultan's daughter as his wife.

Because the grand vizier wants his own son to marry the princess, he suggests that the sultan make many outrageous demands on Aladdin before he can be considered a suitor. The genies produce slaves, costumes, jewelry, gold, and chargers in such profusion, however, that the sultan gladly accepts Aladdin's suit. Overnight, Aladdin has the genie build a magnificent palace next to the sultan's.

Life goes smoothly until one day, when Aladdin is away, the African magician persuades the princess to trade the old lamp for a new one. Then the magician transports the great palace to Africa. When Aladdin comes home, the sultan threatens him with arrest but allows him forty days in which to find the palace and the princess. Rubbing his ring by chance and summoning its genie, Aladdin asks to be carried wherever his palace is. The princess is overjoyed to see him. After he kills the magician by a ruse, he orders the genie of the lamp to transport the palace back to China. There, after disposing of the magician's brother, who followed them, Aladdin and the princess live happily ever after.

Critical Evaluation:

The Arabian Nights' Entertainments is the title usually used in English to designate a group of tales more properly called *The Thousand and One Nights*. These stories, adapted and formalized by bazaar storytellers, had their origins in many lands throughout the East and were handed down by word of mouth for hundreds of years. Some present interesting parallels. In the story of "The Three Sisters," a baby is put in a basket to float down a river, a circumstance reminiscent of the biblical account of Moses in the bulrushes. In Sindbad's various journeys by sea, there are similarities to the wanderings of Ulysses as related by Homer; in one instance, there is a close parallel to the Cyclops story. Some of the characters have been drawn from history, but whether their source is folklore, religious tradition, or history, the tales have a timeless quality that has appealed from legendary times to the present to authors of every kind. Most scholars believe that the collection took its present form in Cairo in the fifteenth century; it was introduced to the Western world in a translation by Antoine Galland, published in Paris in 1704. Traditionally, there were a thousand and one stories told by Scheherazade to her emperor-husband, but in extant manuscripts the tales are not always the same. Practically all modern editions contain only a small portion of the complete collection. Those most frequently reprinted have become minor classics of the world's literature.

The older title of the work refers to the implied dramatic situation in which Scheherazade tells part of a story to Shahriar every night for the famous number of nights so as to forestall her death on the following morning. The tales are embedded in a frame-story, in the tradition of Giovanni Boccaccio's *Decameron* (1349-1351; *The Decameron*, 1620) and Geoffrey Chaucer's *Canterbury Tales* (1387-1400). Like the *Canterbury Tales*, *The Arabian Nights' Entertainments* includes some tales that are enriched by the situation of their framework. One of Scheherazade's first tales to her new husband and king, for example, is much more striking given the backdrop of Shahriar's repeated vow to kill his wife in the morning. "The History of the Fisherman and the Genie" also involves a powerful character, the genie, who vows to kill. In both cases, the vow is directed against one who has performed an act of charity or love. When the fisherman chastises the rebottled genie, predicting Allah's certain vengeance on him for killing, the humble man is in fact a mask through which Scheherazade is speaking to Shahriar.

"The History of the Young King of the Black Isles" alludes to Shahriar's motivation for his vow, which is rooted in his painful experience with an unfaithful wife; the fact that his brother's case parallels his indicates that the societies in which this book took form were preoccupied with a sense of inadequacy in sexual competition with blacks.

This racial, psychosexual problem amounts to the thematic focus of that story. The young king has likewise discovered his wife's infidelity and is greatly disturbed at her preference for a black lover. Throughout the story, black and white are pointedly juxtaposed. The king is described as extremely pale with only the smallest touch of black, a mole. His palace is black, perhaps an omen of his catastrophe. On the first two occasions of the spoiled fish (they are blackened), a fair lady comes out of the wall to upset the pan; on the third occasion, it is a black giant who performs the same act. The fact that the young king is turned to stone below the waist is part of the allegory, signifying his impotence upon having his male ego destroyed by his wife's preference for the slave. The sympathy and vengeance provided by the sultan are obviously designed to soothe Shahriar.

With "The History of Sindbad the Sailor," a smaller frame-story within the larger, readers come to the end of selections that contain pointed allusions to Shahriar's life and problems. All that can be said of the remaining selections' relationship to the framework is that they contain within their allegorical forms a wisdom about the ways of the world, which at one and the same time accords with Scheherazade's great learning and would no doubt impress Shahriar so much as to purge him of his unfortunate vision of all women as faithless and blind in their lust.

Sindbad, a wealthy man, tells his seven tales to a poor porter of the same name. The purpose of telling the tales is to justify the wealth of the rich Sindbad to the envious poor Sindbad. In each story, the wealth is justified by a different example of perils endured by the storyteller. Each of the seven stories follows a narrative pattern in which Sindbad sets out to sea to make money, loses everything in a catastrophe, undergoes a frightening experience (usually underground), escapes by means of his wits, and, finally, emerges with far greater riches than would ever have been possible by ordinary trading. The most frightening part of each episode is invariably a close brush with death or a descent into the mythic world of the dead. Sindbad returns from each descent with treasures commensurate with the risks he has taken.

In "The History of Prince Ahmed," there is the familiar motif of trials undergone for the hand of a princess. In this case, however, there are two princesses, one mortal and one fairy. Ahmed and his brothers vie for the mortal princess, unaware of the fairy princess's love for Ahmed and of her having planned every detail of their adventures. The allegory involves Ahmed's being led unwittingly (and unwillingly) past the mortal princess and inexorably to the fairy princess (who is more beautiful and wise). The story points to the superiority of spiritual riches over material wealth. The sultan is depicted as foolish (and so deserving of his ultimate overthrow) when he ignores the superiority of Ahmed's magic apple, when he disqualifies Ahmed's archery for his arrow's being unrecoverable by ordinary mortal means, and when he demands material wealth of Ahmed.

"The History of Ali Baba and the Forty Thieves" depicts Ali Baba as a man who prospers through his lack of greed. He is contrasted with his brother Cassim in this; Cassim apparently marries for money, while Ali Baba marries a poor woman and is a woodcutter. When Ali Baba learns the magic formula for opening the door to wealth, he takes only as much as will not be missed. Cassim's greed, by contrast, causes him to become so excited by the wealth that he forgets the magic word and is killed. It is significant that Cassim, when he is trapped in the cave, has the entire treasure and, having it, has death along with it. When the threat of death for Ali Baba resolves with the death of the thieves, the hero draws so temperately on his secret cache that it supports his family for many generations. (The fact that Ali Baba's life and fortunes are preserved by a clever woman, Morgiana, would not be lost on Shahriar.)

The next story, too, is an example of riches obtained by a successful descent into the underworld. In "The History of Aladdin: Or, The Wonderful Lamp," Aladdin is a naïve young man who is unaware of the great material value of the gold and silver trays and considers the food they carry to be of greater importance. This sort of naïveté is the stuff of which wisdom is made, making him truly worthy of the sultan's daughter and of the powerful lamp.

It is helpful in understanding and enjoying *The Arabian Nights' Entertainments* to keep in mind the parallel symbolism of wealth, power, and beautiful women. All are symbolic of spiritual fulfillment. The omnipresence of the three in this book is one clear indication of the work's purpose: to teach a moral lesson as well as to entertain. It is a storehouse of wisdom couched in the terms all cultures know best, the terms of sight, smell, and touch and of the delightful forms those sensations take in the imagination.

"Critical Evaluation" by John J. Brugaletta

Further Reading

Bettelheim, Bruno. *The Uses of Enchantment: The Meaning and Importance of Fairy Tales*. New York: Vintage Books, 1977. Bettelheim offers detailed interpretations of the frame story and of the Sindbad stories and "The History of the Fisherman and the Genie." Compares them to Western fairy tales. Lacks a historical perspective but is nevertheless a good demonstration of the psychoanalytic approach to *The Arabian Nights' Entertainments*.

Carpenter, Humphrey, and Mari Prichard. *The Oxford Companion to Children's Literature*. New York: Oxford University Press, 1984. Includes major entries on Aladdin, Ali Baba, and Sindbad as well as references to the collection as a whole. Provides the stories' histories and their incorporation collectively and individually into Western children's literature.

Hamori, Andras. *On the Art of Medieval Arabic Literature*. Princeton, N.J.: Princeton University Press, 1974. Hamori explores links between the tales of two of the collection's story cycles based on theme and literary motif and demonstrates the tales' moral purpose connected to classical Islamic teaching about man's place in the universe.

Irwin, Robert. *The Arabian Nights: A Companion*. London: Allen Lane, 1994. An excellent source, which provides a variety of approaches and materials for study. Discusses translation, composition, and compilation of *The Arabian Nights' Entertainments*, explains medieval Islamic life as the context of the tales, and makes comparisons to literary analogues in Arabic and other cultures.

Ouyang, Wen-chin, and Geert Jan van Gelder, eds. *New Perspectives on "Arabian Nights": Ideological Variations and Narrative Horizons*. New York: Routledge, 2005. Collection of essays focusing on how selected stories in *The Arabian Nights' Entertainments* have been transformed in different historical eras and in various cultures, genres, and media.

Pinault, David. *Story-Telling Techniques in the "Arabian Nights."* New York: Brill, 1992. Detailed study of the tales' narrative structure, arguing for the persistence of oral methods of composition in the literary work as it exists, and analyzing the thematic and linguistic connections among the tales.

Yamanaka, Yuriko, and Tetsuo Nishio, eds. *The Arabian Nights and Orientalism: Perspectives from East and West*. London: I. B. Tauris, 2006. The essays in this collection analyze the various motifs in the tales and describe how they have been interpreted in a variety of cultures, from medieval Europe to modern Japan. Some of the essays discuss the evolution of illustrations for the tales, the image of Scheherazade in English and French traditions, and the Japanese perspective of Orientalism in the tales.

The Arbitration

Author: Menander (c. 342-c. 291 B.C.E.)
First produced: Epitrepontes, after 304 B.C.E. (English translation, 1909)
Type of work: Drama
Type of plot: Comedy of manners
Time of plot: Fourth century B.C.E.
Locale: A suburb of Athens

Principal characters:
CHARISIUS, a young Athenian
PAMPHILA, his wife
SMICRINES, the miserly father of Pamphila
ONESIMUS, Charisius's slave
CHAERESTRATUS, Charisius's friend and neighbor
SYRISCUS, a charcoal burner
DAVUS, a goatherd
HABROTONON, a pretty, harp-playing slave
SOPHRONA, a nurse

The Story:

Pamphila, the daughter of a respected but miserly Athenian citizen, is raped by a drunken young man of ordinarily good behavior during the night festival of the Tauropolia. The only clue she has to his identity is a signet ring that he leaves in her possession. A short time later, Pamphila is married to the young man, an Athenian named Charisius; Smicrines, her father, provides a good dowry for his idealistic but rather priggish son-in-law. Pamphila, who soon begins to love her husband, gives birth to her child during his absence and, acting on the advice of her nurse Sophrona, exposes the infant and leaves with the baby a pouch containing assorted tokens, including the ring. Charisius, learning of the birth from his servant Onesimus, decides that the child cannot be his. Instead of repudiating Pamphila, however, he leaves home and begins to waste his substance in rich feasts given at the home of his friend Chaerestratus, who lives next door. Pamphila is distracted because the husband she loves deserts her for the company of hired dancing girls and harp players.

That is the way matters stand when Smicrines comes to investigate reports of Charisius's conduct; he hears that his son-in-law is spending every night for a hired harp player a sum sufficient to feed a slave for a month. Just before his arrival a conceited, loud-mouthed cook named Carion, on his way to prepare a meal in the house of Chaerestratus, vainly questions Charisius's servant Onesimus about his master; the cook also wants to know why Charisius neglects his wife and pays twelve drachmas a night to be entertained by the lovely harp-playing slave Habrotonon. While Carion and Onesimus are talking, the musician is delivered by her master. The slave dealer manages to persuade the bemused Charisius that he owes money for several previous nights' entertainment. Charisius pays, but wily Onesimus recovers the overpayments for himself.

When Smicrines appears, Onesimus manages to befuddle the anxious, angry father with the story that it is Chaerestratus who is giving the parties and that Charisius attends only to protect his friend's possessions and good name. After Smicrines goes into his son-in-law's house, two of Chaerestratus's tenants appear to pay their rent. They are Davus, a goatherd, and Syriscus, a charcoal burner accompanied by his wife carrying a baby. While they wait they argue over another matter. A month earlier, Davus came upon a baby exposed in the hills. His first impulse was to adopt the foundling, but then, having calculated the cost of rearing a child, he began to think of returning the infant to the place where he found it. Syriscus thereupon offered to adopt the baby in place of his own child, who had just died. When Syriscus found that Davus intended to keep the trinkets left beside the baby, he claimed them because they might someday help to identify the child's parents. Davus refused to give up the tokens, but he agreed to let someone else decide the matter. Smicrines, reappearing from the house of Charisius, is persuaded to listen to the story and give his decision. Deciding that the trinkets ought to go with the baby, he orders Davus to give Syriscus the pouch.

While Syriscus and his wife are looking over the contents of the pouch, Onesimus recognizes the signet ring that his master lost at the time of the Tauropolia festival a year before. The slave borrows it to show his master, then hesitates because to return it would be to accuse Charisius of having fathered the abandoned baby. Habrotonon comes along about that time, sees the ring, hears the story, and concocts a scheme of her own. She will learn the truth by wearing the ring and seeing if Charisius recognizes it. In that case, she will claim that she was the girl he raped and so rescue the child from the life of a slave. Onesimus knows very well that her chief purpose is to win her own freedom.

Smicrines reappears, determined to demand the return of his daughter and her dowry. The neighbors try to dissuade him by saying that everything will turn out all right. As the party ends, broken up by Habrotonon and her claim that the child is hers, Onesimus infuriates the miserly Smicrines by congratulating him on bringing happiness to everybody by his arbitration.

Pamphila begs her father not to meddle with her marriage; she has no desire for another husband, she declares. If Charisius is infatuated with a harpist, that is only a temporary estrangement. At her father's announcement, however, that her husband's current love is the mother of his child, Pamphila faints.

Regaining consciousness, she accuses her nurse Sophrona of causing all the trouble by preventing her confession to Charisius after the birth of the child. While they argue, Habrotonon happens by and recognizes Pamphila as the girl who was Charisius's companion one year earlier. She tells the patrician so when he comes to keep his promise to arrange for her freedom. At first, he regards the story as another of her lies. To save himself, Onesimus also accuses her of having invented the story. Habrotonon maintains stoutly that it is true, and she declares that she would rather see the child looked after properly than win her own freedom.

Chaerestratus, who always admired the lovely slave, begins questioning her about her own early history, but she remembers nothing of her infancy, not even her name. Then the sight of a small silver cup with an indecipherable inscription among the trinkets of Syriscus causes her to comment that she once possessed a similar cup. Smicrines, seeing the cup for the first time, identifies it as having once belonged to his oldest daughter, who was kidnapped by the slave traders during the siege of the city some years before. Sophrona, recognizing the harp player as Smicrines' long-lost daughter Clearista, stirs the girl's recollection by using her baby name of "grasshopper."

Chaerestratus, who loved the girl from the first, now asks to marry her, and when he shows miserly Smicrines how he can get his daughter back without spending money in court trials, he gets both the girl and her father's blessing. Rascally Onesimus, instead of getting the beating he deserves, is probably given his freedom.

Critical Evaluation:

If Aristophanes was the greatest writer of the Old Comedy in fifth century Athens, Menander was certainly the finest practitioner of the New Comedy that flourished there a century later. The difference between these two kinds of theater is vast. The bawdiness and the fearless political and personal satire gave way, in the face of Macedonian military might, to the more timid and bourgeois comedy of manners, in which characters tend to be stock types. The poetic meters are simpler and the language is more colloquial. The chorus has been cut to a bare minimum, usually appearing as a band of revelers bearing no relation to the plot, and their songs are generally omitted from the manuscripts. New Comedy found its subject matter in domestic life and the complications of romance. It exploited sentiment, was given to moralizing, and used complex and improbable plots. Usually it lacked the exuberant vigor that marked the Old Comedy.

This theatrical development may be due, at least in part, to the fact that New Comedy was churned out at a prodigious rate. Menander himself was credited with having written more than a hundred plays, although he was not much older than fifty when he died. Dramatists vied with one another to give their plots ingenious twists as they reworked the same subject matter and the same stereotyped characters. Menander managed to individualize his characters more than his contemporaries, and he gained an international reputation in his lifetime. The Roman playwrights Plautus and Terence adapted Menander's comedies to suit Latin audiences. Through them Menander became the precursor of later Western drama and a direct ancestor of William Shakespeare and Molière.

Menander's own predecessor was the tragedian Euripides, who dealt with the theme of the foundling in *Iōn* (c. 411 B.C.E.; *Ion*, 1781) and possibly other plays. It was a theme that would form a substantial part of the New Comedy. Euripides also handled romantic material that New Comedy writers adapted to their purpose, and he treated commonplace people in a way that suggested new developments in the theater. Further, Euripides developed a near colloquial diction that anticipated the later comedy. However, later dramatists eliminated the divine interventions that Euripides had staged, to concentrate on the element of coincidence in the resolution of human problems. It seems altogether fitting that Menander was buried beside Euripides.

The Arbitration is one of two plays by Menander to have survived nearly intact. Of the rest, there are no more than fragments and snippets. Even this would not be extant if papyrus manuscripts had not been found in Egypt late in the nineteenth century. As a result, the names of eighty of his plays have been ascertained, which show the extent to which the Roman dramatists borrowed from him.

In *The Arbitration*, Menander blends two common themes of New Comedy writing, those of the frustrated romance and of the foundling. He makes skillful use of dramatic irony by manipulating the plot so that the audience is fully aware of a situation to an understanding of which the characters must slowly grope their way. It is only when the characters grasp what the audience already knows that the solution to the problem occurs. The suspense lies in the author's devices to delay the solution. The audience is led logically into a maze where the end is what was stated in the prologue and where a lot of cleverness has been spent in making the maze as complex as possible. It is clear from the outset that Charisius is the sole cause of the misery afflicting him and his wife Pamphila. The end of the play is not extant, but it is certain that Charisius must recognize his guilt and beg Pamphila's forgiveness before the comedy can end.

If the plot is more or less a pat formula, the characters are something more than pure types. Although they conform to stage patterns—Smicrines (small) is the tight-fisted father; Habrotonon (pretty thing) is the mistress with the heart of gold; Onesimus is the rascally servant; and Pamphila (wholly lovable) is the forgiving wife—they transcend their patterns in the natural way Menander has them react to their circumstances. Habrotonon's greatest desire is to gain her liberty, for which she resorts to deception, but when the welfare of a helpless infant is at stake, she is willing to expose her deception and sacrifice her liberty. This sacrifice is not made with great theatrical flourish but rather as an intrinsic part of her character. Menander even takes pains to individualize Davus the goatherd and Syriscus the charcoal-burner in the arbitration scene, where Smicrines unwittingly judges the fate of his own grandson.

The world of *The Arbitration* is one in which commoners are depicted as having dignity, in which slavery is altogether undesirable, and in which the most unlikely people might turn out to have respectable backgrounds. This is a sharp change from the aristocratic outlook of earlier Greek drama. The theme of the foundling, here developed in Pamphila's infant and in Habrotonon, mirrors a democratic view of society, not so much in politics but in morality. It stresses that everyone, regardless of his or her social position, has a right to be treated with consideration. Even though Menander had privileges of birth, wealth, and fame, he subscribed to this outlook wholeheartedly, and *The Arbitration* is illuminated by it.

"Critical Evaluation" by James Weigel, Jr.

Further Reading

Arnott, W. Geoffrey. *Menander, Plautus, Terence*. New York: Oxford University Press, 1975. Chapter on Menander discusses techniques in *The Arbitration* and other plays, placing the dramatist in the historical context of Greek dramatic art. Remarks on his use of traditional methods of dramaturgy to achieve comic effects.

Goldberg, Sander. *The Making of Menander's Comedy*. Berkeley: University of California Press, 1980. Comprehensive study of the dramatist's works. A chapter on *The Arbitration* provides careful explication of the plot and highlights Menander's various dramatic techniques.

Gomme, A. W., and F. H. Sandbach. *Menander: A Commentary*. London: Oxford University Press, 1973. Extensive, detailed, scholarly notes elucidating characters and scenes in *The Arbitration* and other plays. Comments on textual problems and highlights structural techniques used by the playwright.

Handley, E. W. "Conventions of the Comic Stage and Their Exploitation by Menander." In *Oxford Readings in Menander, Plautus, and Terence*, edited by Erich Segal. New York: Oxford University Press, 2001. One of four essays that analyze the elements of Menander's comedy. Other essays discuss his depiction of love, marriage, and prostitution.

Hunter, R. L. *The New Comedy of Greece and Rome*. New York: Cambridge University Press, 1985. Uses *The Arbitration* as a principal example to illustrate techniques used by Menander and his contemporaries when they created their plots, analyzed relationships between the sexes, interjected philosophical issues into their plays, and used earlier works as sources for their dramas.

Traill, Ariana. "The Women of the *Epitreppontes*." In *Women and the Comic Plot in Menander*. New York: Cambridge University Press, 2008. Describes how Menander transformed the tragic theme of human ignorance into the comic premise of mistaken identity in *The Arbitration* and other plays. Focuses on mistaken identity, discussing how the mistakes the male characters make about the female characters reflect the mens' emotional needs.

Webster, T. B. L. *Studies in Menander*. 2d ed. Manchester: Manchester University Press, 1960. Extensive commentary on the various extant fragments of the original play. Remarks on the insights this work provides into the playwright's chief concerns as a comic dramatist.

Arcadia

Author: Sir Philip Sidney (1554-1586)
First published: 1590, as *The Countess of Pembroke's Arcadia*; revised, 1593 and 1598
Type of work: Novel
Type of plot: Pastoral
Time of plot: Antiquity
Locale: Arcadia, Greece

Principal characters:
PRINCE PYROCLES, son of the king of Macedon
PRINCE MUSIDORUS, the duke of Thessalia, and Pyrocles' friend
BASILIUS, the duke of Arcadia
GYNECIA, his wife
PAMELA and PHILOCLEA, their daughters
PHILANAX, an Arcadian general, and Basilius's friend
DAMETAS, Basilius's chief herdsman
MOPSA, his daughter
EVARCHUS, the king of Macedon

The Story:

Basilius is the powerful duke of Arcadia, a quiet and peaceful province of Greece. He rules his faithful subjects happily and well. Overcome by an ungovernable curiosity to learn what the future holds for his family—Gynecia, his wife, and their beautiful daughters Pamela and Philoclea—he consults the Oracle at Delphos. There he is told that his older daughter, Pamela, will be stolen from him and that his younger daughter will engage in an unsuitable love affair and his wife will commit adultery. Also a foreign ruler will sit upon his throne—all within a year.

Basilius repeats the prophecy to his friend Philanax, whom he has left in charge of the country while he, in an effort to escape the destiny foretold by the Oracle, has taken his wife and daughters into a secluded part of the country to live for the year. Basilius lives in one of two lodges with his wife and Philoclea; in the other, he puts Pamela under the care of Dametas, a rude shepherd of whose honesty Basilius has a high opinion.

Shortly after the duke's retirement, two young princes, Pyrocles and Musidorus, arrive in Arcadia. Reared together in close friendship, these young men of great courage, personal beauty, and integrity have been swept ashore at Lydia after experiencing a shipwreck and many strange adventures as well as performing many daring and honorable acts.

Pyrocles sees a picture of Philoclea, learns of her enforced retirement, and falls in love with her. Determined to see the princess face-to-face, he tells Musidorus of his love and of his plan to disguise himself as a chivalric Amazon and to approach Philoclea in woman's guise. For a name, he takes that of his lost lady Zelmane.

After a lengthy debate, in which Musidorus attempts to convince his friend of the folly of love, Pyrocles still remains firm in his intention; and the two princes travel to the place of the duke's retirement with Pyrocles in his disguise as an Amazon. While Musidorus waits in a nearby wood, Pyrocles, now Zelmane, sits down and sings a melancholy song that awakens Dametas, who hastens to the duke's lodge to tell him of a strange woman who has arrived in the vicinity.

Basilius, upon seeing Pyrocles in his disguise, falls in love with the supposed Amazon. His true identity still unsuspected, Pyrocles is introduced to the duke's family and invited to remain with them for a while. Soon, a young shepherd appears. He is Musidorus, who has fallen in love with Pamela on sight and has assumed a disguise of his own. Musidorus, under the name Dorus, is taken by the chief herdsman as a servant after telling his contrived tale of having been sent by a friend to serve Dametas.

Zelmane saves Philoclea from a savage lion, but in doing so, the duke's wife, Gynecia, discovers him to be a man. She immediately falls in love with him. Dorus, meanwhile, saves Pamela from a bear. Before long, both princesses become enamored of the disguised princes.

The Arcadian shepherds, as is their custom, meet and exchange poetic songs for their own entertainment and that of the duke's family and his guests. The songs, often accompanied by dancing, chiefly concern the gods and the human passions. This occasion only increases the intensity of the tangle of love relationships that have so rapidly developed.

After the pastoral festival, Gynecia and Basilius both declare their love for Zelmane, and Philoclea is puzzled greatly by the strange passion she feels for the person she has thought a woman. In the meantime, Dorus pretends to be in love with Mopsa, Dametas's daughter, to be near Pamela, who in this manner becomes aware of his affection for her. He also manages to reveal his true station to her by means of subtle stories and poems.

Pyrocles, distressed by the advances of Basilius, reveals his true identity to Philoclea, who at first embraces him joyously but then becomes ashamed of her sudden show of affection. Gynecia, suspecting this attachment, is overcome with jealousy. While Gynecia, having sent Philoclea home from a meeting with Pyrocles, is starting to tell the disguised prince of the depth of her love, they are attacked by some roving ruffians. With the aid of some shepherds, Pyrocles, Basilius, and then Dorus drive off the attackers.

The citizens of a nearby Arcadian village, meantime, enraged by the duke's seeming unconcern about his country, rise in protest. In an impassioned speech, Pyrocles convinces them of their error and stirs in them a renewed loyalty to Basilius. This triumph is celebrated by another pastoral entertainment, largely taken up with a poetic debate between Reason and Passion. The poems, dances, and stories increase the depth of the emotions felt by the royal party.

Dorus then tells his friend of his moderate success with Pamela, whom he has urged to flee with him to Thessalia. Pyrocles, sharing Dorus's sorrow over their separation, decides to press his suit of Philoclea and to rid himself of the importunate demands of Basilius and Gynecia. When they renew their entreaties, Pyrocles, still in his disguise and fearing to deny them outright, gives them hopeful but obscure answers.

Meanwhile, Dorus, having tricked Dametas and his family into leaving the lodge, has escaped with Pamela to a forest on the way to Thessalia. There they are attacked by a band of ruffians. The false Zelmane, hard pressed by Gynecia's declarations, is forced to pretend a deep passion for her, a situation that so distresses Philoclea that she keeps to her room in the lodge in profound sorrow. To be free to execute a plan to be alone with Philoclea, Pyrocles moves from the lodge to a dark cave not far away. He then takes the duke and his wife aside separately and makes an assignation with each at the same time in the cave.

Gynecia, who has dressed like Zelmane, meets Basilius in the cave; she is not recognized by her husband. Ashamed of her actions, she embraces him lovingly. Back at the lodge, Pyrocles, now in his own person, creeps into Philoclea's room and, after a brief time, wins her over and stays the night.

Dametas, realizing that he has been tricked, begins a search for Pamela. Entering the duke's lodge by a secret entrance, he discovers Philoclea and Pyrocles asleep. He leaves hastily to inform the local citizens of the treachery. Gynecia, angered at her husband's praise of Zelmane, reveals her identity in the cave. Basilius, ashamed, repents his weakness, pledges renewed love to his wife, and drinks a long draught from a cup of a mysterious beverage standing close by. The liquid is a potion, believed by Gynecia to be a love philter, which the duchess had brought to give to Zelmane. After drinking it, Basilius falls to the ground and appears to die. After the duke's death is discovered, Philanax and his troop of soldiers imprison Gynecia, Pyrocles, and Philoclea.

The rogues who had attacked Dorus and Pamela, the remnant of the rebellious band that had earlier caused much trouble, overwhelm the lovers and capture them. While in captivity, Musidorus reveals his actual name and rank. A short time later, some of Philanax's soldiers are sent to search for Pamela and come upon the band and their prisoners. Recognizing the princess, the soldiers return the entire group to Philanax, who puts the lovers under restraint.

There is now a great turmoil, and many opinions and beliefs are exchanged as to the real guilt in the death of the duke and the disgrace of the princesses. Hearing that Evarchus, the king of Macedon, has arrived in Arcadia to visit the duke, Philanax persuades him to be the judge in the trial of the five people involved. Gynecia admits her guilt and begs to be executed. Then Evarchus, not recognizing his son and his nephew because they have been away for such a long time, condemns the two princes to death and the princesses to milder punishments. Even after learning the true identity of the young men, Evarchus refuses, from a deep sense of justice, to alter his verdict.

At this point Basilius, who had swallowed only a powerful sleeping potion, awakens. The young lovers and the duchess are promptly forgiven. Basilius ponders on how accurately the Oracle's prophecy has been fulfilled and how happily events have turned out. The princes and their loves soon wed and assume the high stations for which their rank fits them.

Critical Evaluation:

Arcadia was popular and influential in Sir Philip Sidney's own time and for a century afterward. William Shakespeare, ten years younger than Sidney, adapted elements of *Arcadia* for use in *King Lear* (pr. c. 1605-1606, pb. 1608). Other Elizabethan authors adapted portions of *Arcadia* for the stage.

However, the work imitated by Elizabethans is only one of three distinct versions; known as the *New Arcadia*, it constitutes a significant revision of Sidney's earliest effort, the *Old Arcadia*. Sidney's friend Fulke Greville published the *New Arcadia* in 1590, four years after the author's death. In 1593 there appeared *The Countess of Pembroke's Arcadia*, named after Sidney's sister and concatenating the *New Arcadia* with portions of the earliest version. Meanwhile, the earliest, or old, version was lost until 1907 and not published until 1926.

Changing literary expectations and scholarly focus invite a comparison of the critical responses to *Arcadia* in Sidney's time and in the twentieth and twenty-first centuries, though one must bear in mind that the *Old Arcadia* was not available to Elizabethan critics. Indeed, the current availability of multiple versions has led many contemporary critics to focus on a comparison of the old and new *Arcadia*s.

Why did Sidney undertake a revision? Although he dedicated the original version to his beloved sister, he spoke slightingly of that version and the haphazard manner of its composition, calling it "this idle work of mine." It may have been genuine dissatisfaction that led him to begin the extensive but uncompleted revision.

The *Old Arcadia*, which ends with Basilius waking and Pyroceles and Musidorus saved from punishment, is a pastoral romance in five books with eclogues interspersed. The new version belongs to the epic genre and introduces many new characters in episodic digressions from the main plot. To both Elizabethan and latter-day critics, the change in genre implies a more serious purpose in the new version, but its very complexity, with the parts threatening to overwhelm the whole, has confused some modern readers and led critics such as T. S. Eliot and F. L. Lucas to denounce it as contrived and tedious. On the other side, though both versions display Sidney's extraordinary wit, the *New Arcadia* shows an advance in rhetorical skill over the old. The prose is often clearer and, like a modern novel, introduces perceptive psychological insights. Also, the characters rather than the author deliver much of the moral instruction presented in the *New Arcadia*—a technique used in modern fiction, but also (given the verbal adroitness of his characters) in keeping with the tenet of instruction through entertainment in his *Defence of Poesie* (1595; also known as *An Apologie for Poetry*).

The *New Arcadia* also makes greater use of simile and metaphor, in accordance with Sidney's intention of creating an epic prose poem. His rhetorical figures, while sometimes far-fetched, still avoid the overwrought euphuistic style derided even in Sidney's own day.

Sidney abandoned the revision, however, possibly because he could not mesh the literary genres of the two versions. Generic mixing, or contamination, was forbidden by most Renaissance literary theorists, including Sidney in his *Defence of Poesie*. The *Defence of Poesie*, composed between the old and new *Arcadia*s, may also explain why, in the revision, Sidney ceases to portray royal personages as sometimes behaving like buffoons. The *Defence of Poesie* attacks plays that "be neither right Tragedies, nor right Comedies; mingling in kings and clowns . . . with neither decencie, nor discretion."

Despite the differences between the two *Arcadia*s, one shared theme—an instructive basis for comparison—concerns the disparity between the Platonic ideal and the real. In both *Arcadia*s, the ideal is represented by the closed system of the pastoral world, while the everyday world continually threatens to invade this closed system.

The invasion of a closed system by worldly reality is a common subject of Elizabethan literature. In Shakespeare's *Love's Labour's Lost* (pr. c. 1594-1595, pb. 1598), for example, male characters set up a small academy where no women are to be admitted and hence no traumatic love entanglements can occur. Almost immediately, it becomes obvious that the arrangement cannot be maintained. Similarly, in the *Old Arcadia*, Basilius flees to a pastoral corner of his country with his family to avoid a prophesied series of disasters, only to encounter the dreaded disasters in this supposed refuge. Moreover, as in *Love's Labour's Lost*, the principal characters of the *Arcadia*s begin by railing against love and attempting to fortify their world against it. However, the real world defies all efforts to keep it out of the closed system, and eventually those characters who railed most vehemently succumb, themselves, to love's force.

Love is not the only invasive force against closed systems. The very needs of the political state invade Basilius's attempts to escape them in the idealized Arcadia. For, ironically, in Sidney's work, Arcadia is the name of the political state that Basilius rules, and also the name of the idealized refuge to which he escapes. There is a real-world Arcadia located in southern Greece, reported extensively by ancient historians such as Polybius (c. 203-120 B.C.E.). In literature, Arcadia has served as an idyllic pastoral setting since Heliodorus of Emesa's *Aethiopica* (third century C.E.). In Elizabethan literature the Arcadian convention continues, primarily as an adaptation of poetic themes in Vergil's *Eclogues* (43-37 B.C.E.; also known as *Bucolics*; English translation, 1575), celebrating a peaceful, harmonious life in nature.

In Sidney's work, the stability of the country ruled by Basilius is threatened by his abandonment. Given his impulsive flight, the peaceful literary Arcadia becomes a satiric target when held up to the literal place of the same name. Conversely, the "real" Arcadia demonstrates how far the real world falls short of the literary ideal.

In terms of complexity and of moral aims, the *Arcadia*, especially the new version, is Sidney's most ambitious work. As a work of moral instruction, the *Arcadia* may have been written partly to counter arguments in favor of the proposed "French marriage"—an offer of matrimony from a French nobleman to Queen Elizabeth I. As opponents (including

Sidney) believed that a French marriage—whether for reasons of passion or of politics—would constitute an abandonment of the sovereign's duties to her people, so the Arcadian king's headlong flight—first into illusory security and then into heedless romance—results in political disharmony, illicit love, and in the *New Arcadia*, rebellion by the populace bereft of its leader.

Sidney's treatment of these themes had helped make his work admired and imitated in his own age. On the other hand, although the *Arcadia* is not a novel in the modern sense, Sidney, especially in the *New Arcadia*, anticipates the uses of perspective and psychological insight in modern fiction.

"Critical Evaluation" by Thomas Rankin

Further Reading

Berry, Edward. *The Making of Sir Philip Sidney.* Toronto, Ont.: University of Toronto Press, 1998. A combination of biography, literary criticism, and social history, in which Berry describes how Sidney created himself as a poet by depicting himself in some of his characters, including Philisides in both the old and new versions of *Arcadia*.

Davis, Walter. "A Map of Arcadia: Sidney's Romance in Its Tradition." In *Sidney's "Arcadia,"* by Walter Davis and Richard Lanham. New Haven, Conn.: Yale University Press, 1965. A thorough study of the work's complex background in Greek, Latin, and Spanish pastoral romance.

Lanham, Richard. "The Old *Arcadia*." In *Sidney's "Arcadia,"* by Walter Davis and Richard Lanham. New Haven, Conn.: Yale University Press, 1965. Analyzes Sidney's use of language and other elements of his prose style in relation to classical modes of rhetoric.

Levao, Ronald. *Renaissance Minds and Their Fictions: Cusanus, Sidney, Shakespeare.* Berkeley: University of California Press, 1985. A brilliant discussion of the *Old Arcadia* and how Sidney's narrative refuses to allow readers any stable reference point for judging the characters' moral dilemmas.

Mitchell, Marea, and Dianne Osland. *Representing Women and Female Desire from "Arcadia" to "Jane Eyre."* New York: Palgrave Macmillan, 2005. Examines English novels written in a 250-year-period to describe their depiction of constraints on female passion, femininity, sexual politics, and love. Argues that *Arcadia* provides a sympathetic portrayal of "designing women."

Raitiere, Martin N. *Faire Bitts: Sir Philip Sidney and Renaissance Political Theory.* Pittsburgh, Pa.: Duquesne University Press, 1984. Places Sidney's work in the context of Continental Protestant politics and elucidates his intellectual relations with his close friend, French political theorist Hubert Languet.

Robertson, Jean, ed. *The Countess of Pembroke's Arcadia (The Old Arcadia).* Oxford, England: Clarendon Press, 1973. The first modern scholarly edition of the *Old Arcadia*. Robertson's introduction provides an excellent starting point for study of the work.

Schneider, Regina. *Sidney's (Re)writing of the "Arcadia."* New York: AMS Press, 2008. Traces the development of *Arcadia* through its various revisions to describe how Sidney transformed the work from a collection of poems to a comprehensive prose narrative. Analyzes multiple versions of the text from biographical, historical, and narratological perspectives. Describes the influence of international Renaissance literary theories on Sidney's revisions. Argues that Sidney developed new ways of storytelling that influenced the subsequent development of the novel.

Stewart, Alan. *Philip Sidney: A Double Life*. London: Chatto & Windus, 2000. This biography discusses the handsome, well-born, and talented Sidney as a person belittled in England by Elizabeth I, while he was acclaimed for his writing and statesmanship on the Continent.

Worden, Blair. *The Sound of Virtue: Philip Sidney's "Arcadia" and Elizabethan Politics*. New Haven, Conn.: Yale University Press, 1996. Places *Arcadia* within the context of the political, historical, and religious events of its era to demonstrate that the work is a serious commentary on Elizabethan politics.

Areopagitica

Author: John Milton (1608-1674)
First published: 1644
Type of work: Essay

John Milton's classic defense of freedom of the press and religious liberty is his response to an ordinance of Parliament of June 14, 1643, requiring among other things that all books receive an official censor's approval prior to publication. Milton sees this act as a renewal of Stuart tyranny and of the Star Chamber decree of 1637, which had also denied freedom of the press. When this decree was abolished in 1640, a flood of political and religious pamphlets had followed, and for three years freedom of the press had prevailed in England. Milton views such intellectual and polemic activity as being healthy for the nation, and he deeply regrets the renewal of state control over printing. In his view, such control reflects the growing tendency of the Presbyterian Parliament to impose uniform religious practices on England and to oppose all political opposition. Milton's own *Doctrine and Discipline of Divorce* (1643), which supported more liberal divorce laws, had been printed without permission, and Parliament had sought to discover the author of this unlicensed work. In form, *Areopagitica* is a classical oration addressed to Parliament although it is not intended for oral delivery. Milton draws the title from a speech of Isocrates to the court of the Areopagus in Athens.

In the long opening section, Milton establishes a favorable view of the author and of the Parliament he is addressing. He characterizes Parliament as a strong defender of liberty that has already restored much lost freedom to the nation. Liberty, he adds, can exist only when complaints can be aired openly and considered wisely. He writes to Parliament equally as a passionate lover of liberty and as an ardent supporter of Parliament; beyond that he writes as a learned scholar representing the learned individuals of England.

The first argument in favor of freedom of the press begins with a long historical survey of this issue. Milton demonstrates that Greece and Rome valued this freedom highly and recognized atheism and libel as the only two reasons for censorship. Under the Christian Roman emperors, moreover, only following transcription were books examined, accepted, or judged heretical. Only with the Council of Trent and the Inquisition, "the most antichristian council and the most tyrannous inquisition that ever inquired," were books no more "as freely admitted into the world as any other birth." Milton points out to Parliament that the sources of its legislation are the tyrannical Council of Trent and the forces of tyranny that Parliament itself had once overthrown in the name of liberty.

Those who agree that the source of censorship is bad may still insist that it produces good results. To this contention Milton replies with his second major argument, that moral evil or good is a matter of rational choice and that virtue rests in temperance, in choosing between good and evil. God, Milton argues, left to the individual the exercise of a power of choice so that those who can distinguish between good and evil and who abstain from evil are the true Christians. Real virtue must face trial, must constantly be tested; to prohibit books, therefore, is to prohibit the testing of virtue and the confirming of truth. Censorship denies the efficacy of reason. To know evil through books and to reject it are necessary conditions for human virtue.

Proponents of censorship argue that circulating evil books produces undesirable results, including dissemination of evil thoughts among citizens, unnecessary exposure to temptation, and vain employment of time. Milton answers that all religious disputation would then have to be forbidden, for even the Bible and the church fathers often relate blasphemy, and, he continues, ignorant people are most often led astray not by learned books but by teachers of false doctrine who, even without books, are able to spread their doctrines. Prohibiting books, on the other hand, destroys learning and the ability to dispute evil; in addition, a good person may derive good even from evil while an evil one will be a fool with even the best book. As for unnecessary temptations and vain employment of time, since good people may find false doctrine useful in learning the truth, and bad people cannot be prevented forcibly from acquiring evil knowledge, censorship fails to perform its end.

Thus Milton leads to his third crucial argument, that censorship itself is an impractical gesture because it cannot accomplish its task of removing the sources of evil. Milton admits that Plato allowed censorship, but he adds that Plato also forbade music and dancing. Plato saw how impractical it was to forbid books alone, for to shut one gate against evil and leave open others is a fool's endeavor.

Another impracticality of censorship arises from the machinery required to carry out such a plan. Many hours would be required to read and approve all works ever published or yet to be published. Such a machinery would necessarily grow to resemble the abhorred Inquisition. Sects may flourish despite such efforts because they may persevere through oral tradition, as Christianity itself once did. Finally, how could the quality of the censor be ensured? Only a learned person should have this job, yet the tedium of reading so many books of little value would soon drive away all qualified individuals, leaving the job open to the base and ignorant. No matter what the quality of the censor, the very nature of the job ensures that only received knowledge, those truths already known and accepted by the age, would be allowed to pass.

Thus Milton passes to his next central argument, that censorship would bring harmful consequences. Censorship would discourage learning and the search for truth, dispossess scholars of respect, and undermine regard for the common people's ability to judge for themselves.

Milton's argument concludes with his fourth and most complex point, that licensing publications not only weakens the authority of the truth that England already possesses but also actively hinders the acquisition of new and higher truths. Milton's travels in Europe had shown him the horrible consequences of the Inquisition's suppression and given him perspective on the relative freedoms permitted in England, but he sees that licensing in England would merely substitute the abuses of pre-Reformation England for a new tyranny of presbyters. Truth, he feels, must never stagnate; it must be believed and understood, not simply accepted from external authority. Without questioning and examination, doctrine becomes a matter of outward conformity.

Censorship is an obstacle to acquiring new and unknown truths, and although England through its reformation had advanced somewhat, she must not rest content with half measures. England will be able to boast of the light of her truth and present knowledge only by realizing that truth is given in order to pursue new wisdom. England must search "what we know not by what we know." England's great outburst of learning signifies that God regards the nation with special favor, indicating God's readiness to initiate some great new reformation. It would be wrong to use the terms "sect" or "schism" for this fervent search for wisdom that God inspires among England's people.

Milton believes that it is a good sign to see exercise of rational faculties in the midst of external threats to England's safety; such practice argues a healthy political body and confidence in the safe government Parliament provides, and it demonstrates the large portion of freedom allotted citizens by Parliament's mild yoke. Parliament cannot make English citizens less eager for knowledge and wisdom, Milton states, without first destroying their liberty. Of such tyranny Parliament once relieved this nation.

What is more likely to prohibit truth than the prohibition of new ideas? Because truth most often appears suspect to eyes accustomed only to received opinion, complacent disregard for the new frustrates further discovery of truth. Times such as these readily produce false prophets and true. However, it is impossible to know whether they speak wisely unless they are heard. Defending such truth as is now possessed, people may find themselves persecuting new truths.

It does not matter, Milton avers, that false doctrine may exist under such freedom, for "Strong Truth" can conquer all error in "free and open encounter." If everyone was more charitable, people could tolerate and leave to individual conscience things that are indifferent and not fundamentally at odds with the "unity of Spirit" that truly binds everyone. Imposing strict conformity in matters best left to individual conscience converts truth to base outward conformity.

Further Reading

Campbell, Gordon, and Thomas N. Corns. *John Milton: Life, Work, and Thought*. New York: Oxford University Press, 2008. Insightful and comprehensive biography written by the editors of the *Oxford Milton* that is based in part on new information about seventeenth century English history. Sheds light on Milton's ideas and the turbulent times in which he lived.

Dowling, Paul M. *Polite Wisdom: Heathen Rhetoric in Milton's "Areopagitica."* Lanham, Md.: Rowman & Littlefield, 1995. Dowling challenges the conventional wisdom that *Areopagitica* is an expression of Milton's Puritanism; he argues that the work defends the freedom to philosophize.

Duran, Angelica, ed. *A Concise Companion to Milton*. Malden, Mass.: Blackwell, 2007. Collection of essays analyzing Milton's works, including discussions of his legacy and a survey of more than three hundred years of Milton criticism. The references to *Areopagitica* are listed in the index.

Hanford, James Holly, and James G. Taaffe. *A Milton Handbook*. 5th ed. New York: Prentice-Hall, 1970. A wealth of information about Milton's life, works, and critical reputation. Offers synopses of individual works and comprehensive critical assessments. An excellent beginning source for the general reader and student.

Kranidas, Thomas. "Polarity and Structure in Milton's *Areopagitica*." *English Literary Renaissance* 14 (1984):

175-190. A careful analysis of style and argumentative prose, especially informative on Milton's use of sources. Views Milton as a champion of Greek intellectual freedom, unlike the English prelates associated with historical religious repression and with the Roman Catholic Church.

Milton, John. *The Prose of John Milton*. Selected and edited by J. Max Patrick. Garden City, N.Y.: Doubleday, 1967. Includes the complete text of *Areopagitica*. Extensive introduction to the tract provides a critical analysis, an evaluation of previous scholarship, and a useful bibliography. Heavily annotated.

Whitaker, Juanita. "'The Wars of Truth': Wisdom and Strength in *Areopagitica*." *Milton Studies* 9 (1986): 7-38. Traces the themes of wisdom and strength in the tract and argues that Milton relates both to books, a principal metaphor of the argument. By promoting intellectual freedom, books contribute to political and civic strength.

Ariel

Author: Sylvia Plath (1932-1963)
First published: 1965; revised as *Ariel: The Restored Edition*, 2004
Type of work: Poetry

The poetry collection *Ariel* established Sylvia Plath as one of the most famous confessional poets of the twentieth century. Like Anne Sexton, her contemporary, and other confessional poets, including Robert Lowell, Plath wrote about taboo subjects such as depression, mental and emotional instability, and familial and domestic problems. Her poems challenged Cold War mentality and the mid-twentieth-century expectations of conformity, often lending themselves to psychoanalytic interpretations.

Plath's intense poems deconstruct the boundaries between public and private selves, and most of the poems in *Ariel* are understood by readers and scholars to be autobiographical. However, it is important to understand that the personas of the *Ariel* poems are fabricated; the "I" of the poems is only loosely autobiographical. Plath carefully distances herself from the speaker of the poems in direct ways. For example, in perhaps the best-known poem, "Daddy," Plath positions the victimized speaker as a Jew and her vampire father as a Nazi; furthermore, the poem is replete with references to the Holocaust. Plath, however, was not Jewish and her father was neither a fascist nor a vampire. This poem, like Plath's others, should be read as authentic in its emotional intensity and in its depictions of psychological states, rather than as strictly autobiographical.

The art of *Ariel*, including its use of controversial Holocaust metaphors and allusions, creates a poetry that captures the trauma and suffering of the poems' speakers and that communicates the horrors of living in a suffering female body. *Ariel* has especially fascinated feminist scholars because of its denunciation of patriarchal power, brutality, and violence. The poems in *Ariel* are political in terms of their emphasis on personal identity and subjectivity. The collection pivots on issues pertaining to female agency and freedom (or lack thereof). Additionally, the collection displays the hallmarks of confessional poetry, thus making the personal political: In the poems, Plath reshapes the personal and recasts it to make it political by connecting the pain or the issue at hand to larger social problems. Typically, confessional poetry treats issues that are private, sometimes even shocking or unsavory to readers. Still, the most anthologized poems by Plath come from *Ariel* and have, in fact, influenced how the confessional poetry movement of the 1960's was understood.

Among the most widely read poems of the collection are, in order of their presentation in the standard edition, "The Applicant," "Lady Lazarus," "Tulips," "Ariel," "Daddy," "Fever 103°," and "The Arrival of the Bee Box." Of these, "Lady Lazarus," "Ariel," and "Daddy" are, arguably, the standouts. "Lady Lazarus" combines elements of "Ariel" and "Daddy" in its treatment of the suicidal and traumatized speaker who resists patriarchal power in her attempt to reclaim her life. The Holocaust is used as an extended metaphor to connote the extensive victimization endured by the "I" of the poem. However, the corporeal references are more insistent than in Plath's other poems: The body of the speaker is decaying and dying both from repeated suicide attempts and from the insistent (male) gaze of the people in a crowd, people who want to gawk at the speaker in a metaphorical "big strip tease." In other words, the speaker's valuable and yet vulnerable body is on display in a dangerous and damaging way, and yet no one intervenes. The only interventions are the persona's failed attempts at killing herself: She returns from the dead like the biblical Lazarus. The speaker grows increasingly hostile and angry as the poem progresses, culminating in the turn that makes up the last five stanzas. As the speaker reveals that she has nothing left to show, she warns her readers to beware: "Out of the ash/ I rise with my red hair/ And I eat men like air."

"Ariel" presents a cryptic but vivid portrayal of the suffering female body. The poem opens with an inactive subject in the dark, and the reader learns that the speaker is female and will, ultimately, immolate herself. From the darkness and inactivity she is hauled through the air by hooks and compelled to follow an arrowlike trajectory that involves her body disintegrating before she flies, suicidal, into the sun, the "cauldron of morning." This cauldron, ironically, promises a new and bright beginning for the suffering speaker. In the process of losing her skin and body, the persona appears to be both driven by an outside force and yet in control, by the end, of her life. Although it is not clearly expressed, the transformed speaker seems to gain agency and freedom, albeit at great cost to herself.

"Daddy" invokes a father figure who is both individual and collective: Daddy is the abusive father and, later, the husband of the persona or speaker of the poem. He is the embodiment of all brute, domineering, and misogynistic men. The persona is entrapped by him metaphorically, and this position points to her emotional and psychological dependence on him. In psychoanalytic terms, the poem can be interpreted as the desire by the persona, who may harbor an Electra complex, to be a healthy, whole, and independent self; so, she must renounce her dead father by metaphorically killing him in verse.

Allusions to the Holocaust abound in "Daddy" as well; the speaker positions herself as a suffering Jew being taken to a concentration camp. The Holocaust references are powerful and controversial, as Plath appropriates the hideous imagery to highlight the traumatic legacies that the persona is confronting in the poem. Plath also creates a sing-song tone and rhythm to highlight the perversity of the persona's situation: What has been done to the persona emotionally and psychologically are crimes, and the false brightness of the rhymes and the title of the poem underscore this aspect. Indeed, the poem displays an intergenerational cycle of violence. At various points, the speaker identifies Daddy as a fascist, a devil, and a vampire who loves to torture her. Near the end of the poem, Daddy transforms into the speaker's husband, also couched as a vampire who diminishes the speaker's life and harms her. However, in a heroic turn in the last stanza, the speaker powerfully condemns Daddy and declares that she is through with him and, by extension, all that he represents.

As dark as the majority of the poems are in this collection, there are bright respites. For example, two poems are written about the children Plath had with poet Ted Hughes. "Morning Song" and "Nick and the Candlestick" are sweet in their conceits or extended metaphors. Although there still remains the myth that *Ariel* is Plath's death wish, the restored edition of *Ariel*, brought out with the help of her daughter, shows that Plath intended the last poem of the collection to be "Wintering," a hopeful poem that finishes the cycle of what are called the bee poems in *Ariel*: "The Bee Meeting," "The Arrival of the Bee Box," "Stings," and "The Swarm." The speaker in "Wintering" ponders the future in the last stanza: "Will the hive survive, will the gladiolas/ Succeed in banking their fires/ To enter another year?/ What will they taste of, the Christmas roses?/ The bees are flying. They taste the spring." This optimistic ending counters the more pessimistic ending of the last poem, "Words," in the standard edition, in which the last lines suggest that the speaker is resigned to her fate: "From the bottom of the pool, fixed stars/ Govern a life." There has been much controversy about the order and omission of poems in the standard, posthumous edition of *Ariel*, compiled by Hughes, because they differ from the way Plath had organized the collection before her suicide.

The searing feminist critique, the volatile poetic speakers or personas, the technical mastery, and the confessional subject matter of *Ariel* have intrigued readers since its publication. This interest can be seen in the references to Plath and to the *Ariel* poems in popular culture, and it is supported by the steady production of academic scholarship on Plath's work. As a result, *Ariel* still speaks to human anxieties, fears, and hopes about life, living, and the world, and it remains a touchstone in American poetry.

Julie Goodspeed-Chadwick

Further Reading

Bassnett, Susan. *Sylvia Plath: An Introduction to the Poetry.* 2d ed. New York: Palgrave Macmillan, 2005. Concentrates on close readings of Plath's texts, rather than on the cult of her personality and suicide. Chapters include "God, Nature, and Writing" and "Writing the Family."

Gil, Jo. *The Cambridge Introduction to Sylvia Plath.* New

York: Cambridge University Press, 2008. A brief but comprehensive introduction to Plath's life and work. Includes discussion of *Ariel*, the critical reception to her work, and analyses of the cultural contexts—including the domestic sphere and suburbia—in which she lived and wrote.

_______, ed. *The Cambridge Companion to Sylvia Plath*. New York: Cambridge University Press, 2006. This essay collection features critical and recent discussions on Plath's work and life and on the background and contexts pertinent to *Ariel*. Although some of the essays are dense, this volume provides a serviceable selection of scholarship on Plath.

Hungerford, Amy. *The Holocaust of Texts: Genocide, Literature, and Personification*. Chicago: University of Chicago Press, 2003. Chapter 1 provides an overview of the ways Plath has been read and discusses whether her controversial allusions to the Holocaust are ethical or appropriate.

Kroll, Judith. *Chapters in a Mythology: The Poetry of Sylvia Plath*. 2d ed. Stroud, England: Sutton, 2007. First published in 1976, this book is one of the first to concentrate on the complexity of Plath's work, rather than on the circumstances of her life and death. Discusses books and artwork that influenced Plath, including mythological and psychological sources.

Plath, Sylvia. *Ariel: The Restored Edition*. New York: HarperPerennial Modern Classics, 2005. This edition of *Ariel* follows Plath's vision for the order of the poems and restores a dozen poems that had been cut from the original manuscript. Especially noteworthy is this edition's foreword by Frieda Hughes, Plath's daughter, which situates *Ariel* within the family's history and contextualizes the collection within Plath's life and literary output.

Der arme Heinrich

Author: Hartmann von Aue (c. 1160/1165-c. 1210/1220)
First transcribed: c. 1195 (English translation, 1931)
Type of work: Poetry
Type of plot: Didactic
Time of plot: Late twelfth century
Locale: Germany

Principal characters:
HEINRICH VON AUE, a Swabian knight
A PEASANT GIRL

The Poem:

Heinrich von Aue, a Swabian knight, is a fortunate man. Wealthy and of noble birth, he is known throughout the land for his high standard of honor. His goal is to fulfill his obligations as a knight; nothing but purest virtue and upright truth mark his life. Suddenly, however, his life is blighted by disaster: Heinrich becomes a leper. As in the case of Job in ancient times, his physical appearance deteriorates rapidly, but he does not have the patience of Job. All his life seems a curse to him, and his pride has left him without friends. His cheerfulness vanishes, and he detests even the light of day. Only the hope of a cure for his terrible disease keeps him alive.

Trying to find a cure for his malady, he seeks out the most famous doctors in all Europe. The school of Montpellier is known for its able doctors, but when he goes there, he learns that they know of no medicine to heal him. Disappointed, he travels to Salerno, where he talks to other skilled physicians. At last he meets a master who tells him that there is a cure, yet the cure is of such a nature that it will be impossible to achieve; therefore, the doctor prefers not to talk about it. In desperation, Heinrich begs the doctor to reveal his remedy. After some hesitation the physician yields and tells the knight that he can be cured by the heart's blood of a virgin who will willingly, out of love for him, submit to a fatal operation.

Heinrich realizes the hopelessness of his situation and returns sadly to Swabia. All his worldly belongings he gives to the poor and to the monks. Of his land and estates, he keeps no more than a clearing in a wood where a poor but contented peasant lives with his family. Heinrich decides to join them in their house in the wood, and the peasant and his family do all they can to ease the suffering of the leprous man. They love the knight and are concerned for his health because they realize that they will never find such a good master again. The peasant's young daughter, in particular, is deeply moved by Heinrich's suffering.

One day, the peasant asks why the doctors have been unable to help. Heinrich tells him of the visit to Salerno and describes the impossible cure of which the doctor spoke. The young daughter overhears this tale. That night she awakens her parents with her tears. The next night she decides that she wants to be the virgin who can save their master's life. Her parents are horrified when they hear her request, and her father threatens physical punishment if she dares to mention the subject again. They listen in amazement as their daughter begs with heart-moving words to be allowed to gain the eternal life that would be assured her. She speaks also of the uncertainty her earthly life offers and of the catastrophe that could befall the whole family if their master should die and a harsh ruler scourge the countryside. At last she is able to convince her parents that her service to God and her master would be the most honorable thing she could do. Sorrowfully they give their consent to her intended sacrifice.

Very early the next morning she tells the unbelieving Heinrich of her willingness to help cure him. He warns her that she should not talk lightly about such a subject and assures her that she will soon forget her impulsive idea. After the parents confirm the seriousness of their daughter's wish, Heinrich takes a long time to consider her offer. Finally, he, too, yields to her pleas.

Beautiful clothes and furs and a fine horse are bought for the young woman, and she and Heinrich set out on their journey to Salerno. When the doctor there hears from Heinrich that the young woman is willing to sacrifice herself in that fashion, he doubts the knight's words and takes the girl aside to implore her to speak the truth by telling him whether she is ready of her own free will to face so horrible a fate. Impressed by her sincerity and beauty, the doctor declares that he would be much happier not to take her heart's blood. Still the woman remains steadfast and begs the doctor to proceed with the operation at once.

Sitting in a neighboring room, Heinrich hears the doctor sharpening his knife. The knight peers through a small hole in the wall and sees the girl tied to a table. For the first time he realizes how beautiful she is, and he bitterly accuses himself of trying to circumvent the judgment of God by sacrificing the girl's beauty to his ugliness. At the very last moment, before an incision is made, he is able to stop the doctor. Although the young woman implores him not to be weak and even calls him a coward and a man without the courage of a true knight, Heinrich disregards her insults and leaves with her for home.

During the return journey, the grace of God touches Heinrich, and his leprosy disappears, for he and the peasant girl passed the test given to them by God. Heinrich looks younger and handsomer than ever before. The rumor of his miraculous cure spreads throughout the countryside, and Heinrich's vassals come to meet the travelers three days before they arrive at their destination. The happy parents are the first to meet them, and all thank God for her deliverance and the knight's cure. In spite of the peasant girl's low birth, the council of knights agrees that the hand of God surely chose her to become Heinrich's wife. All in the land, rich and poor, rejoice when she and Heinrich are wed. After a long and happy life, they both enter the eternal kingdom of God.

Critical Evaluation:

Hartmann von Aue was one of the foremost German poets of the Middle Ages, and he is known to have been admired by his contemporary Gottfried von Strassburg for the clarity and purity of his "crystalline words." Beyond that encomium, information on Hartmann is limited to brief self-descriptions, as the one that begins *Der arme Heinrich*, in which he speaks of being a well-educated knight who can read several languages. It is known approximately when his works were written, but his birth and death dates are uncertain, as is the location of the "Aue" where he was born. Several different towns lay claim to him, all with some justification. As with most medieval works, the original manuscript of *Der arme Heinrich* has been lost, and the work survives in only three complete manuscripts from the fourteenth century. Manuscript A, the best, was destroyed in Strassburg in 1870 in the war between the Germans and the French. Manuscripts Ba and Bb, presumably copies of that source, are preserved in Heidelberg and Genf-Cologny, Hungary. There are also three fragments of the work, manuscripts C, D, and E (manuscript E, which contains verses 29 to 255, was discovered in 1965; its pages had been used to insulate organ pipes).

The reason for Hartmann's emphasis in the opening lines on his ability to read is that medieval audiences were interested above all in authenticity. Many of the famous German epics, including *Erek, Iwein, Parzifal*, and *Tristan*, are reworkings of British Arthurian legends as presented to European audiences by the French poet Chrétien de Troyes, and Hartmann's *Gregorius* is based on the Oedipus legend. Audiences first and foremost wanted to know the source of the story. It is all the more unusual, therefore, that no source has been found for the story of *Der arme Heinrich*. Since the main character, Heinrich, is said to come from the same "Aue" as the author, Hartmann, critics have speculated that Hartmann may have had a personal reason for writing this poem, namely to present in a positive light the marriage of one of his ancestors to a member of a lower class, a marriage that, without mitigating circumstances, would have defied the feudal class system. It is generally agreed that *Der arme Heinrich* is one of Hartmann's later works, written when his reputation was sufficiently established to allow his departing from convention.

Heinrich's sin, symbolically punished by the contraction of leprosy, is presumption, *superbia*. He believes that he deserves his health, wealth, and the respect of others because he is a good man. However, in concentrating on worldly pleasures—which Hartmann emphasizes by the repeated use of the adjective "worldly" in the opening pages—Heinrich is flouting the primary moral imperative of the Middle Ages, that of pleasing first God and then the world: "got unde der werlde."

People in medieval times were all too aware of the transience of worldly success and happiness. In their literature, the world is frequently personified as "Frau Welt," who when seen from the front is a seductively beautiful woman, but when seen from the back is rotting and riddled with worms. Heinrich's leprosy serves as a constant reminder of the ugly side of the world.

The conclusion of *Der arme Heinrich* has often been compared to a fairy tale. Heinrich's leprosy is cured, his youth and wealth are restored to him, he marries the girl, and the two of them live a long and happy life. However, these are merely the external manifestations of the actual miracle, which is that of insight. For most of the story, Heinrich's way of thinking is worldly. He thinks he can buy favors: from the surgeon for a huge sum of money, from God for his gifts to the poor, and from the young woman for his gifts of ribbons and trinkets. He calculates his actions according to what others will think of him. Initially, he is afraid to accept the girl's offer not because it will cost her her life, but because he will look foolish in the eyes of others if the attempt fails. The miracle consists of his decision to stop the surgeon regardless of what others might say and to place his life entirely in the hands of God. Only when Heinrich has submitted fully to the will of God is he able to experience the grace of God.

The young woman, though nameless, plays easily as important a role as Heinrich in the work, for she is his counterpart. Heinrich needs to concentrate more on pleasing God, but the girl needs to concentrate more on pleasing the world, so that both of them in the end attain the medieval virtue of *mâze*, or moderation. Whereas the girl might at first appear to be saintly, her premature renunciation of the world is morally flawed, for her motive is not selfless. In believing that God will be obliged to reward her for her sacrifice by making her a queen in heaven, she is trying to force his hand.

The critic Ernst Rose has explained her death wish as a fearful overreaction against her awakening sexuality, a reaction that is not surprising given the fact that the man she loves is hideously deformed by leprosy. John Margetts makes even more explicit the sexual nature of the relationship between Heinrich and the girl by explaining Hartmann's brilliant use of double entendre in the scene where the girl lies bound and naked on the surgeon's table. Modern psychology has provided precise terminology for the human feelings accurately described in literature since the beginning of written record. The interpretation of *Der arme Heinrich* is enhanced by an understanding of the sexual element that is undeniably present. Heinrich's repeated reference to the girl as his *gemahel*, or wife, is evidence that he did not think of her as a child.

Der arme Heinrich is a short but intricately written tale that supports many levels of interpretation. The significance in the work of the number three, for example, is unmistakable. Like the Holy Trinity, three represents perfection and completion. The girl's parents consent to her sacrifice on the third day, but Hartmann gives the reader a numerological sign that their decision is too hasty by noting that the discussions leading up to the decision lasted only two nights.

"Critical Evaluation" by Jean M. Snook

Further Reading

Fisher, Rodney W. "Hartmann's *Arme Heinrich*: The Classical Mediaeval Dilemma of *Ere*." In *Die Ehre als literarisches Motiv*, edited by August Obermayer. Dunedin, New Zealand: University of Otago, 1986. Fisher suggests metaphorical significance for the scene in Salerno, comparing Heinrich knocking on the door to Christ knocking at the door of the human heart.

Gentry, Francis G., ed. *A Companion to the Works of Hartmann von Aue*. Rochester, N.Y.: Camden House, 2005. Collection of essays, including discussions of Hartmann's theological milieu, gender and love in his epic romances, and the literary reception of his works in medieval times. *Der arme Heinrich* is analyzed in Rüdiger Krohn's essay "A Tale of Sacrifice and Love: Literary Way Stations of the *Arme Heinrich* from the Brothers Grimm to Tankred Dorst."

Hasty, Will. *Adventures in Interpretation: The Works of Hartmann von Aue and Their Critical Reception*. Columbia, S.C.: Camden House, 1996. Traces the critical reception of Hartmann's works from the Enlightenment to the postmodern era, with chapter 6 focusing on *Der arme*

Heinrich. Also devotes a chapter to a discussion of Hartmann's life and a chronology of his work.

Jackson, W. H. *Chivalry in Twelfth-Century Germany: The Works of Hartmann von Aue*. Rochester, N.Y.: D. S. Brewer, 1994. Places Hartmann's work within a social, cultural, and historical context. Jackson maintains that knighthood is the major theme of Hartmann's writings.

Margetts, John. "Observations on the Representation of Female Attractiveness in the Works of Hartmann von Aue with Special Reference to *Der arme Heinrich*." In *Hartmann von Aue: Changing Perspectives*, edited by Timothy McFarland and Silvia Ranawake. Göttingen, Germany: Kümmerle, 1988. Draws on research into colloquial German vocabulary to demonstrate double entendre in the scene with the girl awaiting the surgeon's knife. Concludes that a sadomasochistic element is found in all of Hartmann's works, perhaps reflective of a repressive society.

Pincikowski, Scott E. *Bodies of Pain: Suffering in the Works of Hartmann von Aue*. New York: Routledge, 2002. Analyzes how Hartmann uses both the physical body and the body of medieval court and society to symbolically create a distinctly medieval sense of pain.

The Armies of the Night

History as a Novel, the Novel as History

Author: Norman Mailer (1923-2007)
First published: 1968
Type of work: Novel
Type of plot: New Journalism
Time of plot: October, 1967
Locale: Washington, D.C., Virginia, and New York

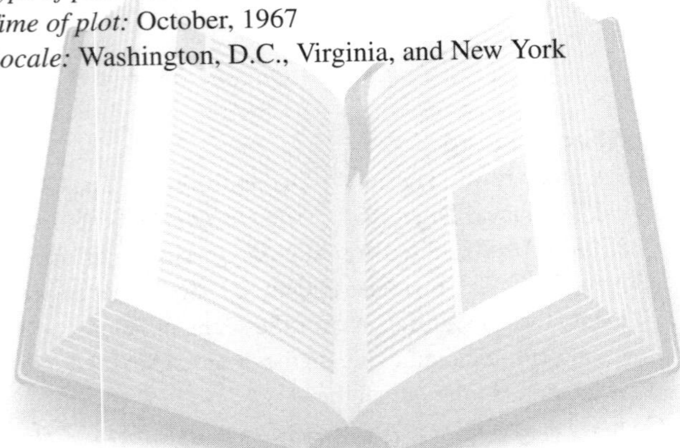

Principal characters:

NORMAN MAILER, the author, a prominent novelist
MITCHELL GOODMAN, an author and political activist
EDWARD DE GRAZIA, a lawyer and friend of Mailer
DAVID DELLINGER, coordinator of the march on the Pentagon
ROBERT LOWELL, a prominent American poet
DWIGHT MACDONALD, a prominent American critic
WILLIAM SLOANE COFFIN, JR., a Yale University chaplain
BENJAMIN SPOCK, a pediatrician and antiwar activist
WALTER TEAGUE, a Leninist organizer jailed with Mailer
HIRSCHKOP, chief counsel for the demonstrators
SCAIFE, U.S. commissioner who presides over Mailer's arraignment
BEVERLY BENTLEY, Mailer's fourth wife

The Story:

On a September morning in 1967, Norman Mailer received a phone call from Mitchell Goodman, an old friend and a political activist, urging his participation in a demonstration the following month against the continuing Vietnam War. Mailer reluctantly agreed and, two days before the scheduled rally at the Pentagon, flew to Washington, D.C., from his home in New York.

Thursday evening, before going on to an assembly at the Ambassador Theater, Mailer attended a cocktail party at the home of a liberal academic couple. Discomfited by their bland benevolence, Mailer, who spent his time conversing with Dwight Macdonald, Robert Lowell, and Edward de Grazia, further offended the host by declining her food and walking away with her copy of his novel *Why Are We in Vietnam?* (1967). Arriving at the Ambassador Theater, where he was supposed to serve as master of ceremonies, Mailer first headed for the unlit men's room, where, spotted by a reporter for *Time* magazine, he inadvertently urinated onto the floor. On stage at last, furious that the proceedings had begun without him, Mailer wrested control of the microphone from de Grazia. Tipsy and inspired, he delivered an elaborate monologue about Vietnam and America in a manner that both engaged and enraged his audience.

On Friday, Mailer went to the Church of the Reformation

for a ceremony in which thirty to forty young men affirmed their refusal of military service. In the company of people he found too nice and too principled, Mailer then walked a mile and a half to the Justice Department, where he, William Sloane Coffin, Jr., Mitchell Goodman, Benjamin Spock, Robert Lowell, and others gave speeches, and 994 draft cards were turned in to officials.

Following Saturday breakfast with Lowell and Macdonald, Mailer joined a crowd variously estimated at between 25,000 and 225,000 that was assembling near the Washington Monument. He was piqued at not being asked to speak, but after speeches by numerous others, the throng proceeded across the Arlington Memorial Bridge toward the Pentagon in order to manifest opposition to the continuing war in Vietnam. Mailer was followed by a crew from the British Broadcasting Corporation, which was making a documentary about him. In the north parking lot, Mailer, seeking symbolic arrest and early release so that he could rejoin his wife in time for a party that evening in New York, was one of the first to cross the military police lines. Apprehended by a U.S. marshal and placed in a van for removal to the lockup, he had a hostile confrontation with a neo-Nazi also arrested during the demonstration. Mailer and dozens of other, mostly young, protesters were imprisoned in the U.S. post office in Alexandria, Virginia.

While impatiently awaiting arraignment, Mailer telephoned his wife, Beverly Bentley, an actress and a southerner whose military father reminded him of some of the U.S. marshals. The prisoners were transported again, to a government workhouse twenty miles away, in Occaquam, Virginia. When a Leninist named Walter Teague lectured fellow prisoners on political tactics, Mailer, who considered himself a "Left Conservative," grew testy and helped defeat Teague's proposal that the imprisoned protesters send a collective letter critical of national mobilization leadership.

Mailer spent an uncomfortable night in custody and was not called to court until the following afternoon. He was represented by Hirschkop, chief counsel for the demonstrators, who argued strenuously with U.S. commissioner Scaife in order to keep his client from having to spend an additional night in jail. Pleading *nolo contendere*, Mailer was assessed a sentence of thirty days but was released on his own recognizance pending appeal and returned home to New York.

After reading distorted accounts of the demonstration and of his own role in it in *Time* magazine and in *The Washington Post*, Mailer began to write his own version in two parts—a novelistic history of himself over four days, followed by a collective history consisting of his own ruminations on the historical context and the significance of the entire event. After recounting his personal experiences as a witness to and participant in the October, 1967, antiwar march, Mailer provided a more detached explanation of the context for the growing opposition to Pentagon policies. Criticizing the misperceptions and distortions of mainstream journalism, he offered an alternative overview of just what happened before, during, and after the incidents he described in the first section of his book. His experience culminated in the creation of *The Armies of the Night*, a hybrid of history and fiction that, for all of its critique of social disorder, concluded with a paean to America.

Critical Evaluation:

The Armies of the Night is not only a brilliant product of the countercultural ferment of the late 1960's but also an enduring attempt to challenge the categorical limits of nonfiction, which it shares with contemporary works by Truman Capote, Tom Wolfe, Joan Didion, Hunter Thompson, and others. With his first book, *The Naked and the Dead* (1948), a work of fiction that drew on his combat experiences in the Pacific theater of World War II, Mailer was hailed as the most promising novelist of his generation. *Barbary Shore* (1951), *The Deer Park* (1955), *An American Dream* (1965), and *Why Are We in Vietnam?* did not fulfill the promise. Twenty years after his debut as a novelist, Mailer began to distinguish himself by endowing reportage with the power of imaginative fiction, by offering up dazzling verbal displays that bear the authority of actuality.

The Armies of the Night, Mailer's rendition of a 1967 march against the Pentagon, was soon followed by *Miami and the Siege of Chicago* (1969), an account of the Republican and Democratic national conventions of 1968, *Of a Fire on the Moon* (1970), a report on the American space program, *The Prisoner of Sex* (1971), Mailer's take on the women's movement, and *The Executioner's Song* (1979), the story of condemned murderer Gary Gilmore. Immersing himself in such salient issues of the day as the Vietnam War, electoral politics, feminism, sports, homicide, and aerospace, Mailer applied his novelistic gifts to depicting and ruminating over contemporary characters and events that he did not invent.

The Armies of the Night recounts its own genesis, in the inspired aftermath of a condensed, intense experience. The narrative derives power by concentrating its plot in a few abundant days and confining its composition to a few inspired weeks. Mailer began writing, rapidly, soon after returning from Washington that October, 1967, and the first fragment of his account, titled "The Steps of the Pentagon," appeared in print as early as March, 1968, in *Harper's Magazine*. The completed book, published a few months later, begins with an excerpt from *Time* magazine and concludes the first of its two sections with a report from *The Washington Post*. Much of the work stands in counterpoint to the reductive vision of reality that journalism, a dialect of what Mailer calls "technologese," would promulgate. Mailer, who flippantly makes himself the principal protagonist of the momentous events in Washington, sees himself in proud battle against totalitarianism, a depersonalizing power evident not only in a government that is conscripting young American men to devastate the people and places of Southeast Asia but also in the regimentation of the liberal opposition. Mailer, who calls himself a Left Conservative, flaunts a flamboyant style and self to defeat the enemies of linguistic nuance and personal freedom. He mocks his own reputation and ambition while nevertheless affirming his distinctive powers of observation.

Compounding the comic arrogance of presuming to position himself at the epicenter of opposition to the war, Mailer refers to himself with a mock humble third-person pronoun "he" and at times with the grandiloquent epithet "The Novelist."

The Armies of the Night is stocked with Mailerisms, ostentatious phrases that dramatize the strain of literary creation and of individual life in the age of the corporation. Mailer playfully offers up virtuoso narrative set pieces, such as the liberal academic cocktail party, the assembly at the Ambassador Theater, and the hearing with a federal commissioner. He delights in cameo appearances by dissident celebrities such as Robert Lowell, Dwight Macdonald, and Benjamin Spock. As master of ceremonies at the Ambassador Theater, Mailer the protagonist dazzles, hectors, and beguiles his audience; as narrator, he delights in brazen epic similes featuring comparisons so prodigious as to leave the reader indignant and in awe. Mailer's self-conscious performance on stage as master of ceremonies, offering up an amalgam of charm and insult, is a miniature version of his activity as author. He celebrates and ridicules his own exhibition, whether on the stage of the Ambassador Theater or in the pages of *The Armies of the Night*.

Book 1 of *The Armies of the Night* purports to be "History as a Novel" and book 2 "The Novel as History." The design of the work suggests a remarkable work of friction—between private and public realities, between Mailer and an impersonal system, between invention and chronicle. Mailer's point is that the first section, the longer and the more compelling of the two, is, though anecdotal, idiosyncratic, jocular, and blatantly subjective, as reliable as the dispassionate, analytic section, an abstract meditation on the significance of the demonstration against the Department of Defense. Like conventional journalism, conventional history is inadequate for the mission of spiritual liberation that Mailer undertakes in marching against the machinery of war and, even more, in writing about that march.

The Armies of the Night begins with preparations for a coordinated defiance of authority and concludes with a paean of love to America. Like Walt Whitman, Mailer would be the epic bard who can speak for and to the entire nation, and his hybrid book, dedicated to a southern wife whom he equates with the nation he embraces, is a self-conscious effort to alert his society about the dangers of suppressing the self. Convinced that jarring figures of speech affirm an author's liberty and the vitality of democracy, Mailer offers a tonic shock to the system, a repressive society that had become inured to the death it was inflicting. *The Armies of the Night* is an exuberant bravura performance, both a raucous call to arms and a passionate farewell to them.

Steven G. Kellman

Further Reading

Bailey, Jennifer. *Norman Mailer: Quick-Change Artist*. New York: Barnes & Noble, 1979. Particularly attentive to Mailer's creation of personae, Bailey analyzes *The Armies of the Night* as his finest achievement in fictional journalism.

Bufithis, Philip H. *Norman Mailer*. New York: Frederick Ungar, 1978. In a lucid survey of Mailer's career, Bufithis pays particular attention to Mailer's characterization of himself and to the presence of Walt Whitman, Ralph Waldo Emerson, and Ernest Hemingway in *The Armies of the Night*. Bufithis praises the book as unmatched in drama, energy, and wit since Benjamin Franklin's *Autobiography*.

Kazin, Alfred. "The Trouble He's Seen." In *Critical Essays on Norman Mailer*, edited by J. Michael Lennon. Boston: G. K. Hall, 1986. Kazin's extended and enthusiastic review places Mailer's book within the context of his career and of American literature.

MacFarlane, Scott. "*The Armies of the Night* (1968): Meta-Journalism, Insta-History." In *The Hippie Narrative: A Literary Perspective on the Counterculture*. Jefferson, N.C.: McFarland, 2007. A constructivist view of the novel, focusing on how it reflected the zeitgeist of the hippie counterculture.

Manso, Peter. *Mailer: His Life and Times*. New York: Washington Square Press, 2008. An exhaustive biography based on more than two hundred interviews, some of which provide multiple versions of the events in Mailer's life.

Merrill, Robert. *Norman Mailer.* Boston: Twayne, 1978. Focusing on the unique structure of what he argues is Mailer's most enduring work, Merrill examines its protagonist's experience as a rite of purification.

Solotaroff, Robert. *Down Mailer's Way.* Urbana: University of Illinois Press, 1974. Noting the work's parallels to Henry Adams, Solotaroff offers insightful analysis of the style and the distance between author and protagonist in *The Armies of the Night.*

Weingarten, Marc. *The Gang That Wouldn't Write Straight: Wolfe, Thompson, Didion, and the New Journalism Revolution*. New York: Crown, 2005. Discusses *The Armies of the Night* and other works of the 1960's new journalism, placing these works within the context of advocacy journalism and of the turmoil of their era.

Arms and the Man
An Anti-Romantic Comedy

Author: George Bernard Shaw (1856-1950)
First produced: 1894; first published, 1898, in *Plays Pleasant and Unpleasant*
Type of work: Drama
Type of plot: Comedy
Time of plot: 1885-1886
Locale: Bulgaria

Principal characters:
RAINA PETKOFF, an attractive young Bulgarian lady
CATHERINE, her mother
MAJOR PAUL PETKOFF, her father
MAJOR SERGIUS SARANOFF, her fiancé
CAPTAIN BLUNTSCHLI, a Swiss mercenary serving in the army
NICOLA, the Petkoffs' manservant
LOUKA, a young servant woman, Nicola's fiancé

The Story:

Raina is in her bedroom on the second floor of the Petkoff house in a small town in Bulgaria when her mother enters to tell her that Sergius has just led the Bulgarians to victory in battle with the Serbs. Raina rejoices; her idealistic expectations of war and soldiers are met. Louka enters to tell them that the army orders them to lock all the doors and windows while enemy stragglers are being pursued. Catherine and Louka leave. Shots are heard outside and a man stumbles into the room. He is a Serbian artillery officer, exhausted, nervous, and hungry. When soldiers appear at the door, demanding to search the room, Raina on impulse hides the man and tells them no one else is there.

Raina and the man talk. She expresses her contempt for his being a coward and for his stuffing his pockets with chocolate instead of ammunition. He tries to explain to her the realities of battle and identifies her portrait of Sergius as the man who led the charge that won the battle; the Bulgarians won only because the Serbians had the wrong-size ammunition. The man describes Sergius as a romantic fool who won by doing the professionally wrong thing. Raina objects strongly to this, but when the man decides to leave, Raina says she will save him and goes in search of her mother; they return to find him fast asleep on the bed.

Four months later, Nicola and Louka are arguing in the Petkoffs' garden. Nicola wants Louka to be more polite to the Petkoffs because he intends to set up a shop and is counting on the Petkoffs as his principal customers. Major Petkoff returns from the war and is greeted by his wife, Catherine. Sergius is shown in. Bitter because the army refuses to promote him, he declares his intention to resign. Sergius and Petkoff speak of a tale they heard of a Swiss officer being rescued by two Bulgarian women. At this point, Raina leaves, and when Louka enters, Sergius attempts to flirt with her. Louka tells him that she knows a secret about Raina and a strange man. When they are alone, Raina and Catherine discuss the Swiss soldier. Raina leaves and Louka announces a Captain Bluntschli, who comes to return a coat Raina and Catherine loaned him. Catherine begs him not to reveal who helped him. Petkoff appears and asks Bluntschli to stay to help with some transportation matters. When Raina enters, she manages to cover up her surprise at seeing Bluntschli.

After lunch that day, Petkoff and Sergius are in the library, writing orders for troop movements. Petkoff wants his comfortable old coat and Catherine says it is in the closet (where she put it after getting it back from Bluntschli). Nicola returns with the coat and all leave except Raina and Bluntschli, who discuss lies, gratitude, and the differences between practicality and the false ideals of romanticism. Bluntschli sees through her pretense of noble ideals and Raina admits that he found her out. Raina tells Bluntschli that she put a photograph of herself in the pocket of the coat, but Bluntschli never found it. He receives mail that was collected for him, among which is the news that his father is dead and left him a number of big hotels.

In a discussion between Louka and Nicola, Nicola suggests that it would be best if Louka and Sergius marry and become his valued customers. Sergius enters and, after Nicola leaves, flirts again with Louka; he is still disillusioned about life and by his own inability to measure up to his ideals. Louka tells him that Raina is sure to marry Bluntschli, so when Bluntschli enters, Sergius challenges him to a duel. Bluntschli agrees and, being a practical man, chooses machine guns. Raina enters and wants to know why they are going to fight; she suspects what has been going on with Louka and has become disenchanted with Sergius, who concludes that life is a farce and that there is now no need for a duel. Raina says that Sergius should fight Nicola, since he is Louka's fiancé, information that disillusions Sergius even more.

When Petkoff enters and wants his coat again, Raina helps her father put it on and takes the opportunity to slip the photograph out of the pocket. Her father already found the picture, however, and wants to know the meaning of the inscription, "Raina, to her Chocolate Cream Soldier: a Souvenir." Thereupon, Bluntschli reveals that he is the chocolate cream soldier; Louka and Sergius become engaged; and Bluntschli laments that despite his practicality he always had a romantic streak—he returned the coat in person, hoping to see Raina again. When he discovers that Raina is really twenty-three, not seventeen, as he supposed, he proposes to her and is accepted. As Bluntschli leaves, Sergius supplies the final comment: "What a man! Is he a man!"

Critical Evaluation:

Arms and the Man, subtitled *An Anti-Romantic Comedy*, is most obviously an attack on the false ideals of warfare and the soldier's profession. Late nineteenth century British society, especially the aristocratic element, tended to see war as a noble undertaking and soldiers as brave, courageous, fearless, and honorable. Many military melodramas of the period upheld these ideals, but they were performed for a civilian audience. As George Bernard Shaw has Bluntschli make clear, soldiers themselves do not think this way. Although far from being a pacifist, Shaw demands that war be seen honestly: War makes men tired and hungry, afraid and nervous. In the person of Bluntschli and in his comments about battle, Shaw establishes the opposition with the archromantics of the play, Raina and Sergius. The satire of the play is aimed at the poetic view of war and soldiers and at the commonplace conjunction between soldiers, aristocracy, and love, the staples of the standard military melodrama of the period. When Raina chooses for her mate the practical, professional, middle-class Bluntschli, Shaw breaks the pattern in which only the brave deserve the fair.

Shaw's dramatic approach in *Arms and the Man* makes deliberate use of many of the oldest, stagiest of devices, ranging from the titillating circumstance of the strange man in the lady's boudoir to the appearance of an incriminating letter or photo. Shaw is reputed to have said that one cannot be too stagy on the stage. His main characters are taken from the stock military melodramas of the time: the noble soldier, the cowardly soldier, the beautiful lady, the comic servant. Shaw turns these stock characters to his own use, however: The beautiful lady does not end up in the arms of the noble soldier; the cowardly soldier is not really cowardly, just practical; the comic servant proves to be a man of considerable practical wisdom.

The key elements of the play are really contained in Sergius and Raina, rather than in Bluntschli. Bluntschli never changes in the course of the play; he is the standard against which the others are measured. Raina learns to divest herself of her impossible ideals, ideals that have no relation to real life, and thus becomes a fit partner for the cool and efficient Bluntschli. Sergius believes that he is to be despised because he finds himself unable to match his ideals. Sergius never does come to see the lesson taught by Bluntschli—that the problem is not an inability to live up to ideals but an acceptance of impossible ideals as reasonable and real.

From this point of view, *Arms and the Man* is a classic statement of the antiromantic view of life. Its commentary is not only directed at the military, however, for the play also presents a version of that common Shavian theme: the professional versus the amateur. The difference between the professional and the amateur is fundamentally one of attitude. Sergius's attitude marks him as an amateur. Romantic idealism makes folly of life because it is unreal and impossible to attain.

Shaw presents his ideas by using the old device of creating a closed unit—the Petkoff household—and then thrusting an outsider into its midst. The members of the Petkoff household had been perfectly content to live in their small dreamworld (which the Bulgarian backwoods setting helps to emphasize), until their routines and values are suddenly called into question by the appearance of Bluntschli, who represents the "reality" of the outside world.

Shaw achieves the humor of the play with the old device of the descent from the sublime to the ridiculous: For each of Raina's and Sergius's noble utterances, Bluntschli has a deflating answer or response. This is not merely a device to provoke laughter; rather, the repeated puncturing of poses lies at the heart of the play. The audience may laugh at Sergius and Raina, but both the audience and the characters are made to realize that it is their fake ideals and poses that are being called into question. The human inability to live up to ideals is a staple of comedy, but Shaw elevates it from a simple comic device to a means of questioning a set of philosophical beliefs.

Arms and the Man is an important play for Shaw because it is the first of his plays to be a public success. In this play, Shaw makes his first fairly direct attack upon false idealism, an attack aimed not so much at conscience as at attitudes. Certainly, the play elicits more laughter than any of Shaw's other plays, either before or after. In contrast to the other plays, the laughter in *Arms and the Man* tends to be more agreeable to many because Shaw uses so many of the traditional devices of comedy.

The play is also important because it marks the shift from Shaw's earlier propagandistic plays on social topics to more benign-seeming attacks on the romantic, idealistic follies of humankind. The social reformer of the earlier plays has shifted methods, though not goals, realizing that he must change attitudes before he can appeal to consciences. Whether propagandist or anti-idealist, however, Shaw does not simply want idle laughter. He maintains that it is easy to make people laugh—he wants to make people think.

Gordon N. Bergquist

Further Reading

Alexander, Nigel. *A Critical Commentary on Bernard Shaw's "Arms and the Man" and "Pygmalion."* London: Macmillan, 1968. A detailed critical exposition. Includes an introduction on "The Play of Ideas," discussion questions, and recommendations for further reading.

Bergquist, Gordon N. *The Pen and the Sword: War and Peace in the Prose and Plays of Bernard Shaw.* Salzburg, Austria: University of Salzburg, 1977. A detailed examination of the depiction of soldiers and war in Shaw's plays and of Shaw's thought on the military and related issues.

Carpenter, Charles A. *Bernard Shaw and the Art of Destroying Ideals: The Early Plays.* Madison: University of Wisconsin Press, 1969. A clear exposition of Shaw's methods in attacking idealism in *Arms and the Man* and other plays.

Crompton, Louis. *Shaw the Dramatist.* Lincoln: University of Nebraska Press, 1969. An excellent consideration of the social, philosophical, and historical background of *Arms and the Man.*

Dukore, Bernard F. *Bernard Shaw's "Arms and the Man": A Composite Production Book.* Carbondale: Southern Illinois University Press, 1982. Covers Shaw's directions and advice for four different productions of *Arms and the Man.* Includes Shaw's directorial notes, manuscript changes, and costume designs. Invaluable for preparing an actual staging of the play.

________. *Shaw's Theater.* Gainesville: University Press of Florida, 2000. Focuses on the performance of Shaw's plays and how *Arms and the Man* and other plays call attention to elements of the theater, such as the audience, characters directing other characters, and plays within plays. Includes a section on "Bernard Shaw, Director," and another section in which Shaw describes how a director should interpret *Pygmalion* for theatrical production.

Holroyd, Michael. *Bernard Shaw: The Search for Love.* New York: Random House, 1988. In this first volume of his standard and indispensable biography of Shaw, Holroyd relates Shaw's life and thought to his works.

Innes, Christopher, ed. *The Cambridge Companion to George Bernard Shaw.* New York: Cambridge University Press, 1998. Collection of scholarly essays examining Shaw's work, including discussions of Shaw's feminism, Shavian comedy and the shadow of Oscar Wilde, his "discussion plays," and his influence on modern theater. The references to *Arms and the Man* are listed in the index.

Pagliaro, Harold E. *Relations Between the Sexes in the Plays of George Bernard Shaw.* Lewiston, N.Y.: Edwin Mellen Press, 2004. Demonstrates how the relationship between men and women is a key element in Shaw's plays. Notes a pattern in how Shaw depicts these relationships, including lovers destined by the "life force" to procreate; relations between fathers and daughters, and mothers and sons; and the sexuality of politically, intellectually, and emotionally strong men.

Arrowsmith

Author: Sinclair Lewis (1885-1951)
First published: 1925
Type of work: Novel
Type of plot: Social realism
Time of plot: Early twentieth century
Locale: Elk Mills, Winnemac; West Indies

Principal characters:
MARTIN ARROWSMITH, a medical-research scientist
LEORA ARROWSMITH, his wife, a nurse
MAX GOTTLIEB, an immunologist
GUSTAF SONDELIUS, a research scientist
TERRY WICKETT, Martin's friend
ALMUS PICKERBAUGH, a public-health reformer

The Story:

Martin Arrowsmith is the descendant of pioneers who lived in the Ohio wilderness. He is growing up in the raw, midwestern red-brick town of Elk Mills. A restless, lonely boy, he spends his odd hours in old Doc Vickerson's office. The village practitioner is a widower with no family of his own, and he encourages Martin's interest in medicine.

Martin, now twenty-one years old, is a junior preparing for medical school at the sprawling University of Winnemac. In medical school, he is most interested in bacteriology, research, and the courses of Professor Max Gottlieb, a noted German biologist. After joining a medical fraternity, he makes many lifelong friends. He also falls in love with Madeline Fox, a shallow pseudointellectual who is doing graduate work in English. To the young man from the prairie, Madeline represents culture. They soon become engaged.

Martin spends many nights in research at the laboratory, and he becomes the favorite of Gottlieb. One day, Gottlieb sends him to Zenith City Hospital on an errand. There, Martin meets an attractive nurse named Leora Tozer; they are soon engaged. Martin finds himself engaged to two women at the same time. Unable to choose between them, he asks both Leora and Madeline to lunch with him. When he explains his predicament, Madeline stalks angrily from the dining room and out of his life. Leora remains, finding the situation amusing. Martin feels that his life has really begun.

Through his friendship with Gottlieb, Martin becomes a student instructor in bacteriology. Leora is called home to North Dakota. Her absence, trouble with the college dean, and too much whiskey lead Martin to leave school during the Christmas holidays. Traveling like a tramp, he arrives at Wheatsylvania, the town where Leora lives. In spite of the warnings of the dull Tozer family, Martin and Leora are married. Martin goes back to Winnemac alone. A married man now, he gives up his work in bacteriology and turns his attention to general study. Later, Leora joins him in Mohalis.

Upon completion of his internship, Martin sets up an office in Wheatsylvania with money supplied by his wife's family. In the small prairie town, Martin makes friends of the wrong sort, according to the Tozers, but he is fairly successful as a physician. He also makes a number of enemies. Meanwhile, Martin and Leora move from the Tozer house to their own home. Martin and Leora's first child is born dead, and they know they will never have another child.

Martin again becomes interested in research. He hears that Swedish scientist Gustaf Sondelius is to lecture in Minneapolis, so he travels there to hear Sondelius's presentation. Martin becomes interested in public health as a means of controlling disease. Back in Wheatsylvania, still under the influence of Sondelius, he becomes acting head of the department of public health. Martin, in his official capacity, finds that a highly respected seamstress is also a chronic carrier of typhoid; he sends her to the county home for isolation. As a result, he becomes generally unpopular. He therefore welcomes the opportunity to join Almus Pickerbaugh of Nautilus, Iowa, as the assistant director of public health, at a considerable increase in salary.

In Nautilus, Martin finds that Dr. Pickerbaugh is a public-spirited evangelist with little knowledge of medicine and little interest in the scientific control of disease. Martin spends his time writing health slogans in doubtful poetic meter, lecturing to clubs, and campaigning for health through the programs Better Babies Week, Banish the Booze Week, and Tougher Teeth Week. He gradually becomes influenced by the flashy, artificial methods used by his superior. Although he tries to devote some time to research, the young doctor finds that his job takes all of his time.

While Pickerbaugh campaigns for election to the U.S. Congress, Martin investigates the most sanitary and efficient dairy of the town. He finds that the dairy is spreading disease through a streptococcus infection in the udders of cows. Against the advice of Pickerbaugh, Martin closes the dairy and makes many enemies for himself. Despite his act, however, he is made Nautilus's acting director of public health when Pickerbaugh is elected to Congress.

In his new capacity, Martin hires a competent assistant so that he can have more time for research in bacteriology. Martin is asked to resign, though, after he sets fire to a block of tenements infested with tuberculosis. For the next year, he works as staff pathologist of the fashionable Rouncefield Clinic in Chicago. He then publishes a scientific paper that brings him to the attention of his old friend and professor, Gottlieb, now located at the McGurk Institute of Biology in New York. Martin is glad to accept the position Gottlieb offers him.

At the McGurk Institute, Martin devotes his whole time to research, with Gottlieb as his constant friend and adviser. He works on staphylococcus germs, producing first a toxin, then an antitoxin. Under the influence of Gottlieb and Terry Wickett, Martin's colleague at McGurk, Martin discovers the X Principle, a bacterial infection that might prove to be a cure for disease. Although Martin wants to postpone publication of his discovery until he is absolutely certain of its value, the directors of the institute insist that he make his results public at once. Before his paper is finished, however, it is learned that the same principle has already been discovered at the Pasteur Institute, where it is called a bacteriophage. After that disappointment, Martin begins work on the possibility of preventing and curing bubonic plague with the phage, as the new antitoxin is called.

Meanwhile, Dr. Sondelius arrives at the McGurk Institute. He becomes so interested in Martin's work that he spends most of his time helping his young friend. When a plague breaks out on St. Hubert, an island in the West Indies, Martin and Sondelius are asked to help in the fight against the epidemic. Accompanied by Leora, they sail for the island of St. Hubert. Before leaving, Martin promises Gottlieb that he will conduct his experiment by deliberately refusing to treat some of the plague cases with phage. In this way, the effects of the treatment can be tabulated against a control group.

The plague spreads daily on the tropical island. Sondelius is stricken, and he dies. Martin is often away from his laboratory as he travels between villages. During one of his trips, Leora lights a half-smoked cigarette that she finds on a table in his laboratory. The tobacco has been saturated with germs from an overturned test tube. Leora dies of the plague before Martin's return.

Martin forgets to be the pure scientist. He gives the phage to all who ask for it. Although his assistant continues to take notes to carry on the research, Martin is no longer interested in the results. When the plague begins to abate, he goes back to New York. There, lonely and unhappy, he marries Joyce Lanyon, a wealthy young widow whom he had met on St. Hubert. The marriage, however, is not a success. Joyce demands more of his time, which he is unwilling to take from his research; he feels ill at ease among her rich and fashionable friends.

Martin is offered the assistant directorship of the McGurk Institute, but he refuses the position. In spite of Joyce's protests, he goes to join his old friend and colleague Wickett at a rural laboratory in Vermont, where they intend to run experiments, searching for a cure for pneumonia. At last, Martin believes, his work and his life are really beginning.

Critical Evaluation:

In significant ways, *Arrowsmith* is a groundbreaking work both as an American novel and as a Sinclair Lewis novel. Never before had an American novel celebrated the work of a scientific researcher—novels that had treated the medical field had focused on doctors and nurses, both heroic and villainous. Indeed, medical research largely had been seen as dull work, its pioneering figures methodical eggheads or misanthropic cranks whose dense and theoretical work was inaccessible to the larger culture.

With *Arrowsmith*, Lewis portrays a young idealistic researcher torn between the pragmatic realities of the practice of medicine and his own irrepressible curiosity about all things medical and his own unwavering commitment to curing disease through lonely hours of tedious experimentation. Martin Arrowsmith speaks passionately of science as a religion. The followers of science are modern revolutionaries unwilling to accept anything but truth, surrounded by the temptation of easier occupations and simpler views of the universe; they are harried by the superstitious, the conservative, and the ignorant. A medical researcher, even one as selfless as Martin, was a most improbable hero of an American novel—his position so unique that a generation of prominent medical researchers, many of them eventual Nobel laureates, would later claim that reading Lewis's novel had inspired them to follow the profession.

Far more important, perhaps, is how *Arrowsmith* appears to so clearly break with the kind of novel that, by 1926, the American reading public had expected from Lewis. Because Lewis's novels do not translate easily into a contemporary idiom (his characters can seem two-dimensional, his dialogue stilted, his passages of description overwhelming) and because contemporary readers often find Lewis's textured novels unapproachable and even tedious, it is difficult to appreciate his position in American culture at the time of *Arrowsmith*'s publication. His previous novels—notably *Main Street: The Story of Carol Kennicott* (1920) and *Babbitt*, published two years later—had made him the most prominent (and controversial) public figure in American letters. His novels were immense sellers, and he was himself widely quoted, frequently photographed, and both praised and vilified for his unblinking (and often meanspirited) satires of the narrow and pretentious lives of small-town America, including the fictional town Elk Mills, in the fictional state of Winnemac.

Arrowsmith is different. Martin is hardly held up to the withering Swiftian satire of Lewis's earlier central characters. Arrowsmith is a conscientious and gifted researcher, a quixotic character who dreams only of helping humanity, whose compassionate heart finds expression in his relentless pursuit of medical research. He distances himself along the way from a gallery of contemptible figures who see in medical research only paths to easy money and financial security or who get entangled in petty rivalries with other researchers; these figures find irresistible the siren call of fame and celebrity. Not surprisingly, whereas Lewis's earlier incendiary novels had generated fiercely divided critical reaction, the response to *Arrowsmith* was nearly unanimous in its praise. The novel would win Lewis the Pulitzer Prize for fiction—although he declined the award, disparaging the award's requirement that winning novels investigate only the wholesome aspects of American life—and its publication positioned him favorably to win the Nobel Prize in Literature four years later.

Lewis does not forsake his signature caustic satire. Taking the measure of the burgeoning field of medical research, as Martin makes his way from small-town doctor to public-health official to research institute fellow, Lewis (whose father had been a country doctor) savages the quacks who maintain their practices through manipulating their patients' misplaced trust; the research institute administrators who hold fund-raising and public relations campaigns in greater esteem than the difficult and time-consuming work of careful research; the public-health officers who are enthralled by the gamesmanship of power politics; the egocentric researchers and medical-school professors who spend enormous energies in undercutting the work and reputation of colleagues; the medical technicians who sell panaceas to a gullible public; researchers who pursue grant money with fraudulent data and questionable research; and supremely those in the medical field who see in it only a way to make money. Such a formidable array of miscreants gives *Arrowsmith* its modern cachet—the vast enterprise of medical research today is still fraught by the mercenary, the egocentric, and the inept.

In addition, *Arrowsmith* evidences Lewis's characteristic realism. As a doctrinaire realist, Lewis, who spent more than three years researching the novel and drew on the help and guidance of the internationally renowned microbiologist and writer Paul de Kruif for verisimilitude, crafts the novel with detail about medical education, medical practice, and laboratory research; this gives Martin's pursuit of the cure for the plague the feel of a documentary. It is this realism that further enhances *Arrowsmith*'s contemporary appeal—although Lewis had no way of anticipating the complicated field of medical ethics that confronts modern medical researchers. In *Arrowsmith*, he sets out the basic dilemmas of such research: tension between pure research and mercenary interests, between cold rationalism and heart-felt compassion, and between short-term and long-term benefits.

These are not simple issues. Because Lewis is not interested in the satiric undercutting of his main character, Martin emerges as a far more complex character than earlier Lewis central figures. Indeed, he is a decidedly ambiguous character. His dealings with women, for instance, are unsettling—his cavalier treatment of Madeleine Fox, his inadvertent exposure of his adoring wife to the plague, and his abandonment of his second wife (and his child) are problematic. His later, emotional decision to immunize all the sick on St. Hubert seriously jeopardizes the value of his research. He is lured too deeply and too often by the comforts of materialism. At times he is stubborn, cavalier in his response to criticism, slow to react, and given to uncomplicated hero-worship of his mentor Max Gottlieb. Are readers to admire him or despise him? Part of the reader's answer revolves around personal commitments to abstract "good" or immediate practical benefits. One may nonetheless view Martin as profoundly influenced by his mentors and professional colleagues; he does indeed strive for the best his fellows represent. If he falls short, Lewis would have readers believe that Martin's intentions are nevertheless worthy of respect.

The ending of the novel, however, is unambiguous and unmistakably optimistic. Ultimately, *Arrowsmith* endorses a theme that has been intrinsic to the American imagination since Henry David Thoreau and Mark Twain: the rejection of society through the withdrawal of the heroic individual from a cultural environment too corrupt to appreciate that heroism. Unlike the characters Carol Kennicott (*Main Street*) or George Babbitt (*Babbitt*), Martin does not surrender to the complacencies and compromises of Lewis's provincial middle-class world. In the end, Martin abandons not only his second wife and his infant child but also the lucrative promise of the institutional life of medical research, to set up a small laboratory in the remote backwoods of Vermont with a colleague. There, far from the disappointments of social responsibilities, the hypocrisies of public life, and the ugly compromises of careerism, Martin prepares, at midlife, to begin what he sees as the real work of his life: pure research into the vital fields of chemotherapy and immunology. Martin's life is now a celebration of simplicity, dedication, and honesty. He is finally free.

Revised by Joseph Dewey

Further Reading

Bucco, Martin, ed. *Critical Essays on Sinclair Lewis*. Boston: G. K. Hall, 1986. Begins with early interviews and includes contemporary critics. Some of the essays discuss *Arrowsmith*, including one essay describing how the novel had developed from Lewis's unfinished book about labor.

Grebstein, Sheldon Norman. *Sinclair Lewis*. Boston: Twayne, 1962. Includes an excellent chapter on the heroic Arrowsmith in the context of American society. Sees the novel as more artistic and inspired than its predecessors.

Griffin, Robert J., ed. *Twentieth Century Interpretations of "Arrowsmith."* Englewood Cliffs, N.J.: Prentice-Hall, 1968. A book-length study of *Arrowsmith* containing early reviews and important essays by leading Lewis scholars.

Hutchisson, James M. *The Rise of Sinclair Lewis, 1920-1930*. University Park: Pennsylvania State University Press, 1996. Focuses on Lewis's career in the 1920's, when he wrote *Arrowsmith* and the other novels that earned him the Nobel Prize in Literature. Hutchisson examines the techniques Lewis used to create his novels, devoting chapter 3 to an analysis of *Arrowsmith*.

_______, ed. *Sinclair Lewis: New Essays in Criticism*. Troy, N.Y.: Whitston, 1997. Includes Hutchisson's piece "*Arrowsmith* and the Political Economy of Medicine," as well as essays on many of Lewis's other novels and an annotated bibliography of Lewis studies from 1977 through 1997.

Lingeman, Richard R. *Sinclair Lewis: Rebel from Main Street*. New York: Random House, 2002. A critical biography that includes analysis of Lewis's novels. Lingeman provides a detailed description of Lewis's unhappy life.

Parrington, Vernon Louis. *Sinclair Lewis: Our Own Diogenes*. 1927. Reprint. Ann Arbor, Mich.: UMI, 2004. A study of Lewis that discusses his role as the "bad boy of letters." Looks at Lewis's disillusionment through his novels *Arrowsmith* and *Babbitt*. A good example of critical thinking of the 1920's. This facsimile reprint is edited by Glenn Hughes.

Schorer, Mark. *Sinclair Lewis: An American Life*. New York: McGraw-Hill, 1961. Dated but indispensable. Includes an examination of *Arrowsmith* from its beginnings to its critical reception. Discusses the men and women who were the prototypes for the characters in *Arrowsmith*.

The Art of Fiction

Author: Henry James (1843-1916)
First published: 1884
Type of work: Literary criticism

Henry James's "The Art of Fiction" remains one of the most influential statements on the theory of the novel. The essay concisely assesses the condition of the genre up to his own time and accurately anticipates the direction of its future development. Much as Edgar Allan Poe did for the short story a generation earlier, James establishes the novel as a serious artistic genre, identifies its unique characteristics, and lays out the fundamental principles for its critical analysis. Prior to that time, the novel was treated as an inferior literary form, considered at best as light entertainment and at worst as pandering to escapism and immorality; in either case, it was generally regarded as unworthy of serious critical analysis.

The catalyst for James's essay was a lecture by novelist-historian Walter Besant, "Fiction as One of the Fine Arts," delivered in 1884. James came across the essay when it was published later that same year as "The Art of Fiction," and he adopted the same title for his response, published in *Longman's Magazine* in September, 1884. The essay created enough of a stir to draw out additional comments on the discussion (including one from Robert Louis Stevenson, which led to a strong friendship between Stevenson and James). The following year, Besant's and James's articles were published together as a book.

Besant's original essay presents three main arguments. First, narrative fiction is a fine art in its own right and should be valued with the arts of painting, sculpture, music, and poetry. Second, the novel is governed and directed by general laws, which may be laid down and taught with as much precision and exactness as the laws of harmony, perspective, and proportion that guide the other fine arts. Third, mastering these rules is necessary, but not sufficient, for success: The novelist also must have powerful artistic talent. James agrees with Besant about the importance and aesthetic interest of the novel and about the high degree of artistic ability demanded by the form, but doubts the existence of general rules or laws that could govern its composition or evaluation. He gathers his various objections together under one main criticism of Besant's approach: Besant is mistaken in his attempt to develop precise criteria for what makes a good novel. In James's view, the only purpose of the novel is to represent life; other than this, the "only obligation to which in advance we may hold a novel . . . is that it be interesting."

James diplomatically concedes that most of Besant's principles are on the surface impossible to disagree with. These principles include the following: the novelist must write from experience, characters should be clearly outlined, the story is the most important element, and a novel should have a conscious moral purpose. However, James then argues that the vagueness of these principles also makes them impossible to positively agree with. Besant's notion of writing from experience, for example, includes such injunctions as advising a lower middle-class writer to avoid introducing scenes among the upper classes. James argues that experience is much more complicated than membership in a socioeconomic class; he conceives of experience as the product of an acute and always highly individual artistic sensibility. The consciousness of the gifted novelist is compared to a huge spider web of fine silken threads suspended in the chamber of consciousness, catching every airborne impression in its tissue.

For James, true experience consists fundamentally of mental impressions, and it is the intensity and directness with which the novelist registers, and then represents, these myriad impressions of life that matter, not simply the quantity of material at hand. For the sensitive and receptive mind "upon whom nothing is lost," accidents of residence or social scale are trivial; what matters is the imaginative power to take hints and fleeting observations and to guess the unseen from the seen, to infer the complete pattern from a fragment. Only exact truth to detail can provide the air of reality, the "solidity of specification" in representing lived experience that is the supreme virtue of the novel, but no one can tell the writer exactly how to achieve it through the mysterious process of selection, synthesis, and arrangement that constitutes the novelist's treatment of that material.

James agrees with Besant that characters should be rendered clearly, but asks if that task is best accomplished by description, through dialogue, or by means of incidents. In James's organic view of form, these categories are artificial and inseparable in practice, as incidents and dialogue function to illustrate character, and the characters dictate our reaction to the incidents and dialogue. He extends his questioning of categories to such traditional distinctions as that made between the romance and the novel, distinctions he finds similarly unhelpful.

James's critique of the importance of the story follows the same pattern of deconstructing implicit oppositions. He concedes that a novel must consist of adventures, but then stipulates that these may be adventures of consciousness, internal and psychological rather than external and purely physical. As to the conscious moral purpose of a novel, he again shifts the ground by pointing up the vagueness of Besant's terms and emphasizing the practical difficulty of setting out to paint a moral picture. James extends his argument by returning to his initial premise: Good novels are works of fine art and, thus, should be evaluated by their formal execution, not their morals. Morality will take care of itself unconsciously, in James's view, precisely because of the high artistic challenges posed by the novel.

> [T]he deepest quality of a work of art will always be the quality of the mind of the producer. . . . No good novel will ever proceed from a superficial mind; that seems to me an axiom which, for the artist in fiction, will cover all needful moral ground.

James's conclusion, expressed as advice to young novelists, is to be true to their own artistic vision, to reject public opinion and critical dogma because the essential condition of the genre is its inclusiveness and freedom. James's insistence that there could be no limits on subject matter, and that stylistic technique and the representation of consciousness must be central concerns of critical discussion and evaluation, seems visionary in hindsight, blazing the trail for the narrative innovations to come from such modernist writers as James Joyce, Virginia Woolf, and William Faulkner.

"The Art of Fiction" does not present a complete overview of James's thinking about the novel, which, taken as a whole, constitutes the invention of the discipline of narrative theory. A notable omission in the essay is any discussion of point of view, one of his most original and important contributions to narrative analysis. His ideas on point of view developed later in the prefaces written for the New York editions of his novels.

In a letter to Stevenson, James characterized "The Art of Fiction" as "simply a plea for liberty." The essay stands as the most concise and durable general statement of James's philosophy of literature.

William Nelles

Further Reading

Daugherty, Sarah B. *The Literary Criticism of Henry James*. Athens: Ohio University Press, 1981. Surveys all of James's literary criticism, devoting chapter 9 to a thorough analysis of "The Art of Criticism."

Davidson, Rob. *The Master and the Dean: The Literary Criticism of Henry James and William Dean Howells*. Columbia: University of Missouri Press, 2005. A comparative study of the criticism of James and fellow American novelist William Dean Howells. Focuses on the two writers' aesthetic concerns, their attitudes toward the market and readers, and their beliefs on the moral value of fiction.

Edel, Leon. *Henry James: 1882-1895, The Middle Years*. 1962. Reprint. New York: Avon Books, 1978. The third volume of Edel's classic study on James's life and work provides a full biographical context for James's "The Art of Fiction" essay.

Hale, Dorothy J. "Henry James and the Invention of Novel Theory." In *The Cambridge Companion to Henry James*, edited by Jonathan Freedman. New York: Cambridge University Press, 1998. Reassesses the standard critical history of James's essay, especially by showing the strong similarities between his theory of fiction and that of Mikhail Bakhtin, two approaches that critics have considered incompatible and opposed.

Jones, Vivien. *James the Critic*. New York: St. Martin's Press, 1985. Jones discusses "The Art of Fiction" throughout this survey of James's literary criticism, and addresses the essay in detail in chapter 3.

Miller, James E., Jr., ed. *Theory of Fiction: Henry James*. Lincoln: University of Nebraska Press, 1972. Collects all of James's writings on the theory of fiction, covering the period from 1865 to 1915. Includes "The Art of Fiction" and a substantial introduction to James's theories.

Schwarz, Daniel R. "James's Theory of Fiction and Its Legacy." In *A Companion to Henry James Studies*, edited by Daniel Mark Fogel. Westport, Conn.: Greenwood Press, 1993. Places "The Art of Fiction" within the contexts of James's time, his own corpus, and modern theoretical debates.

Veeder, William, and Susan M. Griffin, eds. *The Art of Criticism: Henry James on the Theory and the Practice of Fiction*. Chicago: University of Chicago Press, 1986. Includes the full text of "The Art of Fiction" and brief but authoritative sections that usefully survey its biographical, bibliographical, and critical backgrounds. Features a comprehensive bibliography of James's criticism of fiction.

Art of Love

Author: Ovid (43 B.C.E.-17 C.E.)
First transcribed: Ars amatoria, c. 2 B.C.E. (English translation, 1612)
Type of work: Poetry

The Poem:

The poet-narrator says that *Art of Love* is a set of entertaining and lighthearted instructions for successfully undertaking the game of love. Seduction rather than deep emotional attachment or marriage, the narrator says, is the poem's theme.

Rome is full of beautiful young women, so, the narrator says, one looking for love need only go where the women are. The narrator indicates that the likeliest places to meet potential lovers are temples, law courts, the forum, the theater, the races, the public baths, and dinner parties. Timing is important. Beware of occasions on which clever women will demand gifts. Once found, the woman must be enticed to look favorably on the lover.

Be confident, the narrator says, for all women want to be loved. Even if they do not want a lover, they will appreciate attention. Win over the lady's maid to advance your cause. A man should seduce the maid first, if he thinks doing so may help. He should write many letters promising his beloved anything. He should plead eloquently and persist through constant refusals. The narrator next offers advice on personal hygiene and fashion in dress. He tells of the usefulness of wine in warming hearts, and he explains how to handle a lady's husband. Weeping and pallor may gain a lady's pity, but timidity will never gain her favor. The man must take the initiative, and the woman will be glad of an excuse to give in. In short, a man should be adaptable and quick to seize any opportunity to win favor.

The narrator gives advice for holding a woman's love once it is won. Magic spells and potions will not work. To be loved, a man must be lovable. Physical beauty is good, but it fades in time. The mind and spirit must be cultivated. He advises lovers to learn tact, tolerance, gentleness, eloquence, and humility. Never fight with a woman, for making up requires expensive gifts. Bear with her rages and unreasonableness. Let her win at games. Share her opinions and do all possible services for her. If a woman is ill, a man should be constantly in attendance.

A man should praise a woman elaborately and constantly. He should not let her find out about his other mistresses, unless he does so deliberately to make her jealous. If he knows she has other lovers, he should pretend not to know. He should not behave like a jealous husband. Never call attention to her imperfections or her age. Finally, a man should learn the proper techniques in bed so that both partners may have the maximum of pleasure. The narrator acknowledges that women also deserve some instruction in the art of love. He advises young women to taste love's delights now, before they grow too old to be desired by lovers.

The narrator offers detailed advice about improving one's appearance and dress and how to enhance one's basic type. He also discusses cleanliness and cosmetics. A woman must learn to laugh, walk, talk, dance, and sing gracefully, play games well (but not too well), study some literature, and develop an even and pleasing temper. Women should make themselves available to lovers by appearing in public places frequently. Beware of false or mercenary men, and do not believe everything a man says. Cultivate each man for his own particular talents and be especially pleasant to poets, for they can make a woman immortal in their verse.

A woman should not make it too easy for her lover, and should learn how to deceive her husband when necessary. She should not be violently jealous. She should make elaborate vows of love. Women, too, must learn to make love. Feign ecstasy, the narrator tells women, even if you do not feel it. Be subtle and mysterious and desirable.

Critical Evaluation:

Art of Love is among Ovid's most skillfully composed elegiac poems, and the novelty of its topic renders the poem a masterpiece of poetic invention. Belonging to the early part of Ovid's career, this poem would become at once a foundation of Ovid's fame and a cause of his life's greatest tragedy.

Ovid was born into an equestrian family in Sulmo (modern Sulmona) in 43 B.C.E. His family financed his education in Rome, where he excelled in rhetoric. After his studies were complete, Ovid remained in Rome and practiced law, but he found most pleasure and success in the composition of poetry. Ovid's poems were well received, so in his late twenties he abandoned other pursuits to dedicate himself to his art.

Ovid's first known work is *Amores* (c. 20 B.C.E.; English translation, c. 1597), a first-person description of the poet's love life written in elegiac couplets; it was published in about 16 B.C.E. and subsequently revised. He followed *Amores* with *Art of Love*. With this poem, his reputation as a leading poet at Rome was firmly established.

During the next few years, the volume of Ovid's literary output was phenomenal. Scholars debate the particulars of the sequence in which he composed and revised his works, but the main outline is clear. In addition to *Art of Love* and *Amores*, many of Ovid's other well-known works were composed in the period from about 12 B.C.E. to 8 C.E. These works include *Heroides* (English translation, 1567), a series of letters from, and in the latter books to, famous female characters from literature; *Remedia amoris* (*Cure for Love*, 1600), which provides advice on how a lover might end a love affair; and *Medicamina faciei* (*Cosmetics*, 1859).

In the early years of the first century C.E., Ovid became engrossed in his longest work, *Metamorphoses* (c. 8 C.E.; English translation, 1567). *Metamorphoses* comprises fifteen books of dactylic hexameters detailing famous stories of miraculous changes brought on by love in ancient myths. At the same time, Ovid also began work on *Fasti* (English translation, 1859), a description of the meanings of the significant dates in the Roman calendar, a work that he was destined never to complete.

Perhaps it was partly as a consequence of the fame that Ovid achieved as a love poet that he fell into disfavor with Emperor Augustus and was exiled from Rome in 8 C.E. Mystery still surrounds the reasons for Ovid's exile, but scholars have generally agreed that the poet was implicated in a scandal affecting the imperial household. Ovid does not reveal the precise reasons for his exile in his poems, but he does mention that one of the causes was *Art of Love*. Presenting himself to the public as a teacher of seduction would have rendered it difficult for him to rehabilitate his character once imperial opinion had turned against him.

From exile in Tomi (the modern city of Constanta, Romania) on the coast of the Black Sea, Ovid published poems that he hoped would garner popular favor and result in his recall from exile; this, however, was not to be. Ovid died in Tomi around the year 17 C.E. The poems Ovid wrote in Tomi are different from those that he had written in Rome. He abandoned *Fasti*, which he had been composing before his exile, to write *Tristia* (after 8 C.E.; *Sorrows*, 1859) and *Epistulae ex Ponto* (after 8 C.E.; *Letters from Pontus*, 1639). In these haunting elegiac works, Ovid continues to develop his craft by writing reflections on the barren emotional, social, and artistic landscape of a life in exile.

Art of Love, then, belongs to the early part of Ovid's career, a time characterized by energy, high spirit, and invention. Further, with this poem and *Amores*, Ovid successfully defines a distinct new genre of elegiac composition, that of the Augustan erotic elegy. The elegiac meter, characterized by an alternation of a shorter pentameter line with the longer dactylic line used in epics, already had a long history in Greek and Latin before Ovid first set his hand to the meter. Ovid read with care the Greek and Romans elegists who preceded him, especially Catullus, Tibullus, and Propertius.

Ovid's broad knowledge of Greek and Latin literature is evident throughout his poems. Perhaps the seed for *Art of Love* can be traced to a poem of Tibullus, in which the poet describes the god Priapus as giving him a lecture on love. However, it is Ovid's ability to pay homage, to echo, but never to imitate—yet always to excel—his models that continues to delight readers into the twenty-first century. It is this invention for which Ovid's work is best known, for *Art of Love* cannot be read as practical advice. Instead, the poet's ability to weave commonplace observations about love into a brilliant poetic whole allows the poem to elevate its subject. Ovid's success in using the elegiac genre to establish an emotional connection to his readers not only by talking about his love life but also by advising readers on theirs, remains a cornerstone of his achievement.

Ovid's spirit at its lightest and most entertaining is on display in *Art of Love*. In particular, pith, wit, and balance characterize the work. Many of Ovid's couplets are self-contained aphorisms expressed with subtle art. In some cases, one line of the couplet answers another. In other cases, the first half of one line is balanced by the second half. Whether Ovid employs in his couplets a frame of question and answer or thesis and antithesis, or any other balancing architecture, he always succeeds in creating a memorable or surprising turn of phrase. The themes of love and seduction are universal, but Ovid positions *Art of Love* firmly in the Augustan Rome that he so loved and of which he would be so cruelly deprived.

The references to places and the social scenes in *Art of Love* are so vivid and appealing on the one hand and amusing on the other, that some sections of the poem read almost as though they belong to the satirical tradition. Just as Ovid comments on *Art of Love*, so does he comment on the Roman context that provided many opportunities for the practice of seduction. Ovid also draws unselfconsciously from his varied readings to incorporate clever allusions to the literature that precedes him. In many cases, examples of how women behave are drawn from the actions of female characters in famous Greek and Latin literature. These references often present the old stories in a new and more urbane light, divorcing them from traditional or moralistic interpretations.

Art of Love has exerted considerable literary influence through the ages, but not without becoming the target of occasional moral censure. However, even those who would censure *Art of Love* as a reflection, if not an encouragement, of a society preoccupied with seduction must admit that the poem in its proper context excels—in artistry and genius—all other compositions of a similar nature.

"Critical Evaluation" by Wells S. Hansen

Further Reading

Gibson, Roy, Steven Green, and Alison Sharrock, eds. *The Art of Love: Bimillennial Essays on Ovid's "Ars amatoria" and "Remedia amoris."* New York: Oxford University Press, 2006. Ovid scholars provide differing interpretations of his didactic love poems, analyzing their poetic, erotic, and political elements and describing the ancient, medieval, and modern reception of the two works.

Hardie, Philip. *The Cambridge Companion to Ovid*. New York: Cambridge University Press, 2002. Collection of essays examining the historical contexts of Ovid's works, their reception, and the themes and literary techniques of his poetry. Numerous references to *Art of Love* are listed in the index.

Mack, Sara. *Ovid*. New Haven, Conn.: Yale University Press, 1988. A survey of Ovid's literary career, with a lengthy chapter on the love poetry. Asserts that Ovid creates a foolish speaker who uses his folly as a satire on Augustan values. Regards *Art of Love* as an assertion of poetic independence.

Myerowitz, Molly. *Ovid's Games of Love*. Detroit, Mich.:

Wayne State University Press, 1985. Discusses how love, like art, balances emotion and reason: Neither is natural, and both are influenced by conventions. Love is a paradigm for the process of human culture, which liberates through a celebration of play but is constantly threatened by forces of nature.

Sharrock, Alison. *Seduction and Repetition in Ovid's "Ars Amatoria" 2*. New York: Oxford University Press, 1994. Connects the arts of love and poetry. Demonstrates that Ovid shows how one keeps the interest of the beloved and the reader. Examines Ovid's attitudes toward art and audience.

The Art of Poetry

Author: Horace (65-8 B.C.E.)
First published: Ars poetica, c. 17 B.C.E. (English translation, 1640)
Type of work: Poetry

To Horace, this poem was the last of his epistles, but almost at once his contemporaries began referring to it as *The Art of Poetry*, and by "poetry" they meant any field of literary composition. Horace addresses it to his friend Lucius Calpurnius Piso, famous for his battles in Thrace, and to his two sons. Apparently the older son yearns for a career as a dramatist or an epic poet. While not a formal treatise or an abstract discussion, like the similarly named composition of Aristotle, the 476 lines of this unsystematic letter in verse influenced Joachim du Bellay in writing the manifesto of the Pleiad, and a century later inspired Nicolas Boileau's *L'Art poétique* (1674) and Alexander Pope's *An Essay on Criticism* (1711). Some of Horace's suggestions, like the classical five-act division of the drama, are no longer important, but today's writers still can learn much from the rest of the poem. The double purpose of literature, a mingling of "the useful with the sweet," has been quoted through the centuries in every literary movement.

One would be amused rather than impressed, begins Horace, by the painting of a creature with a horse's body and a man's head, with limbs from every sort of animal, adorned with feathers from a variety of birds. However, poets combine just such outlandish elements, adding "purple patches" where they are entirely out of place in order to give color and brilliance to pompous openings in portions of their writing. Therefore, he begins *The Art of Poetry* with a plea for simplicity and unity.

Addressing Piso and his sons directly, Horace confesses that most poets are misled by what looks like truth. When striving for brevity, the poet becomes unintelligible. Attempts to write smoothly result in the loss of vigor and spirit. Aiming at grandeur, the poet becomes bombastic. Only when he or she is guided by art can a writer avoid some errors without committing worse ones. The remedy, therefore, is to select subjects equal to one's ability and to use appropriate language. Old words, properly used, seem new; new words, borrowed from the Greeks, may also have a place. People are admired for making over nature when they build harbors or drain marshes. Usage, then, should maintain or change the material and rules of speech.

Homer, according to Horace, shows the writer how to handle the deeds of kings and the sad tales of war. No one is sure who invented the elegiac couplet, but Archilochus devises the iambus, used in tragic and comic drama; and since it was born of rage, it is designed to record action. According to tradition, the Muses gave the lyric for singing about victories, lovers, and joyful banquets. All these meters have their specific uses, and the poets would do well to employ them only in their appropriate places, though sometimes a writer of comedy may borrow from other forms of poetic art or an author of tragedies set aside sesquipedalian words in favor of shorter ones to touch the audience's hearts.

Horace continues by defining feeling as the true test of literary worth, for beauty of writing is not enough. Unless a writer feels, he or she cannot make the audience feel. One style of writing goes with a gloomy face; another sort goes with an angry one or a playful one. Nature first makes one reveal one's feelings physically; then, with the tongue for an interpreter, she voices the emotions of the heart. There is also a difference in language between the gods and humanity, between old and young, between merchants and farmers, between Colchians, Assyrians, and Thebans.

Either follow tradition or be consistent in one's inventions, Horace advises. Achilles on the stage must be hot-tempered, appealing to the sword rather than to the law. Follow tradition and make Medea haughty, Ino tearful, and Ixion perjured. If the writer presents original characters, they must be consistent. They should not be too bombastic or promise too much out of prudent fear that the mountain in labor will bring forth no more than a ridiculous mouse.

If the writer wishes the applause of an audience, he or she must paint accurately the characteristics of the four ages of humankind. The young boy is unsettled and changing; the beardless youth is fond of horses and dogs, boastful, scornful of advice; in middle age, people are ambitious but cautious; and the elderly are surrounded by discomfort. One should not, in Horace's opinion, attribute the wrong qualities to a stage of human life.

Touching lightly on the rules laid down by classical dramatists, Horace believes in the superiority of showing action rather than telling about it. He does add that there are things too horrible to be seen. He comments on the number of actors—only three—and the place of the chorus. He comments on the rules and restraints of satyric drama. Then, after an appeal that Greek, not Roman, tastes be followed in selecting verse forms, he embarks on a history of the theater.

Slightly confused, he gives Thespis credit for inventing the tragedy, yet he describes him as traveling in a cart to put on plays in which the faces of actors are stained by dregs of wine. Then comes Aeschylus, with the invention of the raised stage, the mask, and the buskins. Old comedy follows, soon to degenerate into license, and the chorus loses its role of criticism of the characters.

Roman playwrights, he continues, tried all forms of drama, but most were not successful because they were careless. Horace adjures his student reader to condemn any literary composition that has not been erased and amended. Even genius cannot discard rules. Characterizing himself, he says that he is too lazy to be a genius; he will perform his duty and criticize.

Answering the question of what to write, Horace declares that knowledge is the basis of good writing and that moral philosophy will supply matter. Life and manners should also occupy a writer's attention. The purposes of the poet should be to benefit and to entertain. "He has received the votes who has mingled the useful and the sweet, by instructing and delighting the reader at the same time."

Horace continues to advise hopeful poets that people do not always expect perfection from a poet. Some faults can be pardoned, for even Homer fails at times, though usually he excels in his craft. Continued carelessness, however, is unforgivable, and eternally second-rate material cannot be tolerated. A person who cannot play the game should keep off the field unless he craves the jeers of the spectators. He advises Piso's son that, if he should write anything, he should let the censor of plays see it and then show it to his father and to Horace himself. Afterward, he should keep it in his desk for nine years. What one has not published, one can always destroy.

The final eighty lines of the poem deal with generalities. In the early days, says Horace, Orpheus represented the dignity of poets who, by their wisdom, distinguished between public and private property, divine and earthly things, lore and law. By their songs, they won honor. Homer and Tyrtaeus inspired men to battle; oracles guided men by their verses. It is still a question for debate whether a poet is born or made, but without both art and study even a genius will fail.

The best of writers need criticism, but they should avoid mere flatterers. One good critic used to mark, for improvement and reworking, lines in poems submitted to him, and if the would-be poet defended his mistakes, the critic had no more to do with him. The honest critic puts black marks before poor verses as Aristarchus did to Homer. Self-willed poets will not like such treatment, comments Horace, but in that case they are not worth trying to save. They are probably mad, each one, like a bear clawing at an innocent bystander. Such poets will be one's death, reading one their poetry.

Further Reading

Armstrong, David. "The Addressees of the *Ars Poetica*: Herculaneum, the Pisones, and Epicurean Protreptic." *Materiali e Discussioni* 31 (1993): 185-230. Armstrong sheds fresh light on old problems. In particular, he discusses the specifics of the Epicurean use of free speech as therapy and its function as a model for Horace's *The Art of Poetry*.

Brink, Charles O. "Cicero's *Orator* and Horace's *Ars Poetica*." *Ciceroniana* 2 (1975): 97-106. An informative article clarifying the relation, function, and sources of the two works.

_______. *Horace on Poetry*. New York: Cambridge University Press, 1963-1982. The most comprehensive work on *The Art of Poetry*. Its three volumes explore the sources of the poem and offer an edition of and extensive commentary on the text, accompanied by discussion of the poem's literary milieu. An annotated edition of Horace's other literary epistles complements his views on poetry.

Frischer, Bernard. *Shifting Paradigms: New Approaches to Horace's "Ars Poetica."* Atlanta: Scholars Press, 1991. Reexamines the problems of genre, addressees, and date of *The Art of Poetry*, reaching the innovative, but eccentric, conclusion that the poem is meant as a parody of pedantic criticism and not as a serious poetic treatise.

Harrison, Stephen, ed. *The Cambridge Companion to Horace*. New York: Cambridge University Press, 2007. Critical overview of Horace's life and work. Some of the essays discuss Horace and ancient Greek and Hellenistic poetry, Horace and Roman literary history, and Horace and Augustus, while others explore the themes and style of his work. Chapter 10 is devoted to an examination of *The Art of Poetry*.

Hills, Philip D. *Horace*. London: Bristol Classical Press, 2005. An introductory overview of Horace's life, times, work, and literary influence. Chapter 7 features an examination of *The Art of Poetry*.

Oliensis, Ellen. *Horace and the Rhetoric of Authority*. New York: Cambridge University Press, 1998. Examines how Horace created a public self-image in his work. Oliensis argues that Horace shaped his poetry so he could promote his authority and remain deferential to his patrons, while taking account of the jealousy of rival poets and the judgment of posterity. Chapter 5 focuses on *The Art of Poetry*.

The Artamonov Business

Author: Maxim Gorky (1868-1936)
First published: Delo Artamonovykh, 1925 (English translation, 1927)
Type of work: Novel
Type of plot: Family
Time of plot: c. 1863-1917
Locale: Russia

Principal characters:
ILYA ARTAMONOV, the father
PYOTR ARTAMONOV, his oldest son
NIKITA ARTAMONOV, his hunchbacked son
ALEXEY ARTAMONOV, an adopted son
NATALYA BAIMAKOV, Pyotr's wife
ULIANA BAIMAKOV, the widow of the late mayor and Ilya's mistress
ILYA, Pyotr's first son
YAKOV, Pyotr's second son
TIKHON VYALOV, a yardkeeper for the Artamonov factory

The Story:

About two years after the liberation of the Russian serfs, Ilya Artamonov arrives with his two sons, Pyotr and Nikita, and Alexey, his nephew and adopted son, in the little town of Dromov along the Vataraksha River. Ilya serves as a bailiff to a prince, and the nobleman recommends him highly to the authorities. Without giving the mayor of Dromov, Evgeny Baimakov, a chance for objections, Artamonov announces that he plans to build a linen factory and that he believes the mayor's daughter Natalya would be a good wife for his oldest son. Disregarding the resentment his dictatorial behavior provokes in the town, Artamonov goes ahead with plans for the factory and preparations for Pyotr's marriage. The mayor, who dies before the wedding, advises his wife Uliana to let Artamonov have his way. Pyotr's marriage to the mayor's daughter and the prospect of employment for many citizens do not, however, reduce the enmity felt toward the intruders.

When Uliana becomes Ilya's mistress, she decides to live with the Artamonovs on the other side of the river, where the factory is located. Ilya tries to be a strict but humane superior to his men. Among his workers, Tikhon Vyalov is the ablest, although he begs not to be promoted because he does not want to supervise others. Meanwhile, Nikita, the hunchback, falls in love with Natalya, and when he overhears an unkind remark she makes about him, he tries to hang himself. The attempt fails, and Nikita enters a monastery.

The factory develops rapidly under Ilya's direction. Pyotr is the second in charge. Alexey is unhappy at the factory and wants to join the army, but Ilya refuses to give him permission to enlist.

When Natalya bears her first child, the baby dies after only five months. Another girl, Elena, follows. Then a much-desired son, also named Ilya, is born. Alexey marries a woman nobody in the family likes or understands.

During the transportation of a heavy steam boiler, Ilya senior suffers a hemorrhage and dies soon afterward. As time passes, Pyotr's only true happiness is his son. Against his wife's wishes, he lets Ilya attend a good secondary school away from Dromov. While Pyotr devotes his time almost exclusively to the factory, Alexey makes the necessary business trips to trade fairs and to Moscow. Although Natalya gives birth to a second boy, Yakov, Ilya remains Pyotr's favorite.

Despite all efforts to prepare Ilya as Pyotr's successor as the factory director, his son shows a completely different attitude. He likes to talk to Vyalov, the philosopher among the workers, whom Pyotr despises, and he also forms a close friendship with an uneducated child of a worker. After completing his schooling, Ilya announces his desire to become a historian. His father objects because he still wants Ilya to take over the factory. Ilya refuses and leaves Dromov without receiving any financial assistance from his father. Thereafter, Pyotr becomes an unhappy man; his wife cannot please him, and he tries to find distraction with a local prostitute.

Often Pyotr has difficulty in controlling his temper, and one day he accidentally kills Ilya's former playmate. Vyalov, too, irritates him with philosophizing whenever he has a question to ask. Hoping to find some spiritual guidance, Pyotr finally decides to visit his brother Nikita in the monastery. Nikita explains that he failed in his efforts to become a good monk. Although he considers himself unworthy, the monastery values him highly because he is able to give visiting pilgrims some comfort with patient ears and empty phrases.

When Pyotr fails to find peace of mind with Nikita, he attends a trade fair in a nearby city. Alexey told him so many exciting stories about city life that he hopes to find distraction there. After a series of extended drinking sprees and orgiastic behavior with prostitutes, he is finally discovered by Alexey, who hears from a friend of the family about Pyotr's disgraceful behavior. Back home, Pyotr hears rumors that his son has become a member of a revolutionary extremist party. He also detects unusual new ideas in Alexey's son Miron. Only his younger son, Yakov, seems unconcerned about the new ideas that are spreading among workers. Yakov is not good-looking; however, Pyotr considers his interests, mainly women, more normal than all the ideas expressed by the others, ideas that he believes are a threat to the factory.

The rapid growth of the factory brings a large settlement of workers to Dromov, along with many hardship cases. Pyotr tries to show his interest in his workers by building a new hospital or arranging a big party for them.

Alexey dies suddenly. A telegram is sent to summon Nikita, but he has left the monastery. Only Vyalov knows his address. After the funeral, Nikita and Vyalov are seen together frequently. Pyotr's feelings grow against all people who do not think primarily of the factory, and when Nikita dies four days before the outbreak of World War I, he has no kind word for his dying brother.

When Pyotr grows too old for most of the factory work and Yakov takes over in his place, Yakov also becomes concerned over the growing signs of unrest among the workers. One worker, who spies for him in the factory, becomes his oppressor. Early in the war, many workers are drafted. Some return, crippled, to the factory. Yakov's fear of being killed by his workers increases rapidly. He plans to go away with his mistress Pauline, a woman of easy virtue and expensive tastes. Trying to avoid suspicion, he lets Pauline leave Dromov first. His own plan is to meet her in Moscow with all the money he can raise, but he never arrives in Moscow. Reports reach Dromov that he has been robbed, killed, and thrown from the train.

Pyotr, who tried to ignore all rumors about uprisings and a new way of life for the workers, lives in a state of semicoma and asks constantly the whereabouts of Ilya and Yakov. He fails to realize what is going on around him until, one day, he feels a sharp sense of hunger and realizes that he is in his garden house. Outside he sees a soldier. When Pyotr calls for his wife, only Vyalov comes. He explains that Pyotr is a prisoner.

At first, Pyotr thinks Vyalov is jeering at him. Later, he believes that he was taken prisoner because someone learned the truth about the death of Ilya's former playmate. Vyalov tries in vain to inform him about the revolution that took place and to explain that he is still alive only because of Ilya's influence. Pyotr thinks Vyalov is mad. When Natalya arrives with a cucumber and a piece of bread, Pyotr considers himself insulted that she dares offer him such meager food when he is so hungry. Angrily, he throws away the food and with abusive words asks her to leave him alone.

Critical Evaluation:

In 1901, Maxim Gorky began to think about writing a novel tracing several generations of a Russian bourgeois family. It was more than twenty years before he actually published this work. In 1916, the publication of the novel was announced, only for Gorky to postpone writing it until after the October Revolution. Not until 1925, while living in Italy, did Gorky actually complete the novel, which depicts the beginning of industrial development in Russia, its brief fluorescence, and its downfall under the blows of the Bolshevik Revolution.

A former serf, Ilya Artamonov, the founder of the dynasty, is a typical representative of the newly born Russian merchant class. He builds a linen factory in a small provincial town of Dromov despite the hostility and apprehension of the townspeople. Energetic and self-confident, he neither looks back nor wastes his time. He goes forward, destroying all obstacles to his goal, and becomes the richest factory owner in his district. When Ilya dies, his sons take over and expand the business. Ultimately, however, the pattern is one of decline. Partly this is because of his sons' lack of vision, but mainly it is because of the impending revolution. Pyotr, as the oldest son, heads the factory, but he lacks Ilya's enthusiasm or passion for work. He carries on the business as a heavy duty but does not really understand the purpose of his hard work. Although the factory prospers, Pyotr's alienation from his wife, children, and brothers grows. Trapped by the routines of life, unable to comprehend the political changes around him, he finds consolation in drinking and debauchery. His brother Nikita spends most of his life in the monastery, telling beautiful lies to pilgrims who seek his advice. When he discovers that there is nothing spiritual or sacred even in the monastery, he returns home to die.

Unlike his brothers, Alexey is full of energy and new ideas. He is interested in art and education, in the political and social life of the country. Always on the run, he is a real capitalist, a proprietor who believes in the power of millions of Russian men and in the possibility of creating a new Russian capitalist economy. His son Miron is also totally absorbed in the political and social issues of the day. He plans not only to become head of the business but to play an important political role in the renewed bourgeois Russia. Like other Russian bourgeois liberals, he tries to turn Russian history in a new direction, toward industrialization, progress, and culture. Father and son symbolize the new Russian intelligentsia. They hold the future of Russia in their hands but are too weak and selfish to protect the country from the coming socialist revolution. The factory business born at the beginning of the novel dies with the arrival of the new era. The last pages of the book sound like an apocalypse—the end of the Artamonovs and their business, the end of all progressive beginnings. The finale is shocking. Pyotr is dying, hungry, in his garden house, and the Red Army soldiers are patrolling his house. Only because his oldest son Ilya is a Bolshevik is Pyotr still alive. Gorky ends his novel with a revolution that brings neither triumph nor happiness, only bitterness and sadness.

Extraordinarily laconic yet amazingly full of depth, this novel imbues each detail with significance. Gorky describes with love and care the old Russian wedding ceremony, with its traditions and rituals, brilliantly depicts several holiday celebrations and sprees at yearly merchant fairs, and sprinkles throughout Russian proverbs, sayings, and folk poetry. The action of the novel develops at different speeds. The first half of the book describes seven years of Ilya's activities, which lay the foundation of his family business. The second half depicts the following forty-seven years in which not only the Artamonov dynasty but also the whole country flourishes and then collapses. Gorky masterfully uses real historical events of the first Russian Revolution of 1905, World War I, and the Revolution of 1917 as a background for portraying individual characters. He distances himself from the passing events and his heroes. Instead, it is the yardkeeper Tikhon Vyalov who survives all three generations of the Artamonovs as an independent witness and a secret judge. Ilya's grandchildren are born and then, like his sons, leave the stage; new characters appear, but Tikhon is still there. He watches everything, remembers everything, evaluating life and giving philosophical comments on the passing events. He is a symbol of the Russian people, a folk sage never precise about anything, who speaks in riddles and is an enigma himself.

Soviet critics praised *The Artamonov Business* for its truthful depiction of the growth of political activity of Russian working people and their fight against the bourgeoisie. They placed the novel among the best works in the traditions of Socialist Realism. With the collapse of Communism and the Soviet empire, new Russian critics have rejected Gorky, blaming him for his direct call for terror and violence and for his justification of repression. The critical extremes of exaggerated praise and then equally exaggerated attacks are based on changing philosophical loyalties. Such criticism ignores the truly complex and contradictory personality of a great writer who was against any form of oppression and violence, who was for democracy and progress, who tried to depict life as it was and to understand what was going on in his beloved Russia. *The Artamonov Business* is a great proof of Gorky's quest to find the truth and to depict life as it was, with all its turmoil and injustice. The reader only has to look with open eyes devoid of political prejudice to see Gorky's honest attempt to capture social, political, and human complexities.

"Critical Evaluation" by Paulina L. Bazin

Further Reading

Clark, Katerina. *The Soviet Novel: History as Ritual*. 3d ed. Bloomington: Indiana University Press, 2000. Clark's chronicle of the development of the Socialist Realist novel includes information about Gorky, his pronouncements on fiction, and *The Artamonov Business*.

Cornwell, Neil, ed. *The Routledge Companion to Russian Literature*. New York: Routledge, 2001. Chapters 15 and 16 provide information about Gorky's contributions to the Russian novel.

Levin, Dan. *Stormy Petrel: The Life and Work of Maxim Gorky*. New York: Appleton-Century, 1965. One of the best interpretations of Gorky's life and literary activity. Chapter 34 gives a brief and very precise analysis of *The*

Artamonov Business as a bitter statement about the Bolshevik Revolution of 1917.

Ovcharenko, Alexander. *Maxim Gorky and the Literary Quests of the Twentieth Century.* Moscow: Raduga, 1985. Provides a detailed analysis of Gorky's literary work. Chapter 3 gives a comprehensive analysis of *The Artamonov Business*, the history of its creation, and the effect it had on world literature.

Scherr, Barry. *Maxim Gorky.* Boston: Twayne, 1988. Gives a brief biography of Gorky and literary analysis of his short stories, novels, plays, autobiographical writings, and essays on literature. Examines Gorky's depiction of historical changes in Russia by comparing *The Artamonov Business* with Gorky's last novel, *The Life of Klim Samgin* (1927-1936). A detailed bibliography is included.

Troyat, Henri. *Gorky.* Translated by Lowell Blair. New York: Crown, 1989. Views Gorky as a writer of the Russian Revolution and the founder of Socialist Realism. Makes brief reference to Gorky's literary canon, including *The Artamonov Business.*

Weil, Irwin. *Gorky: His Literary Development and Influence on Soviet Intellectual Life.* New York: Random House, 1966. An appreciation and evaluation of the social context and artistic merits of Gorky's works, including a brief and comprehensive analysis of *The Artamonov Business.*

Yedlin, Tova. *Maxim Gorky: A Political Biography.* Westport, Conn.: Praeger, 1999. Yedlin's biography focuses on Gorky's political and social views and his participation in the political and cultural life of his country. Includes bibliography and index.

As I Lay Dying

Author: William Faulkner (1897-1962)
First published: 1930
Type of work: Novel
Type of plot: Psychological realism
Time of plot: Early twentieth century
Locale: Mississippi

Principal characters:
ADDIE BUNDREN, a dying old woman
ANSE BUNDREN, her husband
CASH,
DARL,
JEWEL, and
VARDAMAN, their sons
DEWEY DELL, their daughter

The Story:

Addie Bundren is dying. She lies in a bed in the Bundren farmhouse, looking out the window at her son Cash as he builds the coffin in which she is to be buried. Obsessed with perfection in carpentry, Cash holds up each board for her approval before nailing it in place. Dewey Dell, Addie's daughter, stands beside the bed, fanning her mother. In another room, Addie's husband, Anse, and two sons, Darl and Jewel, discuss the boys' plans to make a trip to sell a wagonload of lumber. Addie wishes to be buried in Jefferson, the town where her relatives lie, and Anse is afraid that the boys might not get back in time to carry her body to the Jefferson graveyard. He finally approves the trip, however, and the boys set out.

Addie dies while the two brothers are gone and before Cash can finish the coffin. When it is obvious that she is dying, Dr. Peabody is summoned, but he comes too late to help the sick woman. Vardaman, the youngest boy, arrives home with a fish he caught, and his mother's death somehow becomes entangled in his mind with the death of the fish. Because Peabody is there when she dies, Vardaman thinks the doctor killed her.

Meanwhile, a great rainstorm arises. Jewel and Darl are delayed on the road by a broken wagon wheel. Cash works through the rain to finish the coffin. At last it is complete, and Addie is placed in it, but the crazed Vardaman, who once almost smothered in his crib, tries to let his mother out by boring holes through the top of the coffin.

After Jewel and Darl return, neighbors gather at the Bundren house for a funeral service conducted by Whitfield, the minister. Whitfield was once Addie's lover and fathered Jewel, the son she seemed to favor.

Following the service, the family starts out for Jefferson, but the rainstorm so swells the river that the bridge is damaged and it cannot be crossed by wagon. After trying another bridge, which is also washed out, they drive to an old ford near the first bridge. Anse, Dewey Dell, and Vardaman get across the river on the ruins of the bridge. Darl and Cash then attempt to drive the wagon across at the ford, with Jewel leading the way on his spotted horse, his one great possession. When the wagon is nearly across, a floating log upsets it. Cash breaks his leg and nearly dies, and the mules drown; the coffin falls out and has to be dragged to the bank.

Anse refuses to borrow mules, insisting that he must own the team that carries Addie to the grave. He makes a trade in which he offers, without Jewel's consent, to give the spotted horse as part payment. When Jewel learns what his father did, he rides off, apparently abandoning the group. Later, they discover that he put the spotted horse in the barn of Snopes, who is dickering with Anse. The family thus gets new mules, and the trip continues.

By the time they arrive in Mottson, a town on the way to Jefferson, Addie has been dead for so long that buzzards are following the wagon. They stop to buy cement to strengthen Cash's broken leg, but the locals insist that the wagon move on. The Bundrens, however, buy the cement and treat Cash's leg before they move forward. While they are in the town, Dewey Dell goes to a drugstore to buy medicine that will abort the child she is carrying; she became pregnant by a man with whom she worked on the farm. The druggist refuses to sell her the medicine.

Addie has been dead for nine days and still is not buried. The family spends the last night before their arrival in Jefferson at the house of Mr. Gillespie, who allows them to put the malodorous coffin in his barn. During the night, Darl sets fire to the barn. Jewel rescues the coffin by carrying it out on his back. Anse later turns Darl over to the authorities, who send him to the asylum in Jackson.

Lacking a spade and shovel to dig Addie's grave, Anse stops at a house in Jefferson and borrows the tools. The burial finally takes place. Afterward, Dewey Dell again tries to buy her medicine at a drugstore. One of the clerks pretends to be a doctor, gives her some innocuous fluid, and tells her to come back that night for further treatment. The further treatment takes the form of a seduction in the basement of the drugstore.

Cash's broken leg, encased in cement, becomes so infected that Peabody says Cash might not walk for a year. Before starting on the trip home, Anse buys himself a set of false teeth that he has long needed. He then returns the borrowed tools. When he gets back to the wagon, he has acquired not only the new teeth but also a new Mrs. Bundren, the woman who lent him the tools.

Critical Evaluation:

Considered by many critics to be the greatest American fiction writer, William Faulkner was awarded the Nobel Prize in Literature in 1949, after a prolific career that included the production of nineteen novels and two volumes of poetry. Although his formal education had been limited, Faulkner read prodigiously, including the Greek and Roman classics, the Bible, and the works of William Shakespeare, the English Romantics, Joseph Conrad, James Joyce, and T. S. Eliot. After relatively undistinguished early attempts in poetry and prose, Sherwood Anderson advised Faulkner to concentrate on his "own postage stamp of native soil." This led to the saga of Yoknapatawpha County, a partly true regional history, based on Oxford, Mississippi, that merged imperceptibly into a coherent myth. Faulkner begins the saga with *Sartoris* (1929) and continues it in *The Sound and the Fury* (1929) and *As I Lay Dying*.

In the Yoknapatawpha novels, Faulkner places himself in the forefront of the avant-garde with his intricate plot organization, his bold experiments in the dislocation of narrative time, and his use of the stream-of-consciousness technique. His stylistic view of time is affected by his sense that past events continue into the present. As he once said, "There is no such thing as *was*; if *was* existed, there would be no grief or sorrow." These stylistic characteristics are undergirded by the development of a complex social structure that enables Faulkner to explore the inherited guilt of the southern past, the incapacity of the white aristocracy to cope with modern life, the relations between classes, and the relations between blacks and whites.

Starkly realistic, poignantly symbolic, grotesquely comic, and immensely complicated as an experiment in points of view, *As I Lay Dying* ranks with Faulkner's greatest novels. The relative simplicity of its style, characterized by staccato-like sentences and repetitive dialogue, enhances the tragicomic effect.

The novel's theme, in the very widest terms, is humanity's absurdly comic insistence on distinguishing between being and not-being. Peabody describes death as "merely a function of the mind—and that of the ones who suffer the bereavement." The theme is stated most clearly in the single chapter narrated from Addie's viewpoint: "I could just remember how my father used to say that the reason for living was to get ready to stay dead a long time." Addie has long since considered Anse dead, because she realizes that he, like most humans, cannot distinguish between the "thin line" of words that float upward into nothingness and the terrible reality of "doing [that] goes along the earth, clinging to it."

Nineteen of the fifty-nine chapters are narrated from

Darl's viewpoint, making him the primary *persona* of the novel. His reference to his family's conglomerate madness sets the tone: "In sunset we fall into furious attitudes, dead gestures of dolls." The novel proceeds in a jerky, doll-like movement, as the narration passes through the viewpoints of fifteen different characters. Although Darl might be called the primary narrator, he is not the only interesting one. Vardaman, with ten chapters, displays a mentality reminiscent of Benjie's in *The Sound and the Fury*, showing the crazy events connected with the burial through the eyes of a confused and simple-minded child. The third chapter from his viewpoint consists of a single sentence: "My mother is a fish." Only three chapters present Anse's viewpoint, but that is enough to show that he is a bizarre combination of Darl's imagination, Vardaman's insanity, Cash's stubborn practicality, and Dewey Dell's earthiness.

Faulkner achieves his greatest artistic success with the least intrinsically interesting character, Cash. The first of the five chapters from Cash's viewpoint is an artistic coup. Until this point, the reader has repeatedly heard the steady buzzing of Cash's saw as he prepares his mother's coffin. Even through the rain and through the night, Cash will not cease his labor. In chapter 18, Cash speaks at last, saying "I made it on the bevel." Faulkner presents the carpenter's methodical mind in a straightforward list of his job-related preoccupations, beginning with "1. There is more surface for the nails to grip" and ending with "13. It makes a neater job." Cash's second chapter is a nine-line warning to his impatient father and brothers that the coffin is not "on a balance" in the wagon. After the tragedy in the river results from their ignoring his warning, Cash offers his laconic commentary in a chapter of only three lines. He remarks again that the coffin "wasn't on a balance" and does not even mention that his own leg has been broken. Cash's single-minded craftsmanship and superhuman patience become a reflection of the author's own technique.

"Critical Evaluation" by Kenneth John Atchity

Further Reading

Bleikasten, André. *Faulkner's "As I Lay Dying."* Translated by Roger Little. Rev. ed. Bloomington: Indiana University Press, 1973. A lucid and comprehensive analysis that provides an excellent starting point for serious study. Discusses Faulkner's manuscript and typescript and includes two facsimile pages.

Blotner, Joseph. *Faulkner: A Biography.* 2 vols. New York: Random House, 1974. An enormously detailed work. Begins with discussion of Faulkner's ancestors and traces the writer's development from precocious poet to preeminent novelist.

Cox, Dianne L., ed. *William Faulkner's "As I Lay Dying": A Critical Casebook*. New York: Garland, 1985. Contains a dozen essays examining such topics as the novel's chronology, language, and narrative design. Interesting individual chapters focus on the novel's debt to the Cubist movement and to the works of T. S. Eliot. Includes an extensive annotated checklist of criticism.

Marius, Richard. *Reading Faulkner: Introduction to the First Thirteen Novels*. Compiled and edited by Nancy Grisham Anderson. Knoxville: University of Tennessee Press, 2006. A collection of the lectures that Marius, a novelist, biographer, and Faulkner scholar, presented during an undergraduate course. Provides a friendly and approachable introduction to Faulkner. Includes a chapter on *As I Lay Dying*.

Porter, Carolyn. *William Faulkner.* New York: Oxford University Press, 2007. Concise and informative, this resource spans Faulkner's entire life, but focuses on his most prolific period, from 1929 to 1940. It examines his childhood and personal struggles and offers insightful analyses of his major works. *As I Lay Dying* is discussed in chapter 2.

Towner, Theresa M. *The Cambridge Introduction to William Faulkner.* New York: Cambridge University Press, 2008. An accessible book aimed at students and general readers. Focusing on Faulkner's work, the book provides detailed analyses of his nineteen novels, discussion of his other works, and information about the critical reception for his fiction.

Tredell, Nicholas. *William Faulkner: The Sound and the Fury, As I Lay Dying*. Cambridge, England: Icon Books, 1999. Traces and explains the changing critical reception for both novels from 1929 through the 1990's. The introduction places the novels within the context of Faulkner's life and work.

Vickery, Olga W. *The Novels of William Faulkner.* Baton Rouge: Louisiana State University Press, 1959. A classic treatment of the Faulkner canon, still relevant despite years of subsequent scholarship. Asserts that the heart of *As I Lay Dying* is not the fulfillment of the burial promise but rather Addie herself and her effect on the Bundren family.

Volpe, Edmond L. *A Reader's Guide to William Faulkner.* New York: Noonday Press, 1964. An excellent beginner's source for discussion of Faulkner's works. Analyzes structure, themes, and characters and includes a useful appendix that clarifies the often-confusing chronologies and scene shifts of Faulkner's complex novels.

As You Like It

Author: William Shakespeare (1564-1616)
First produced: c. 1599-1600; first published, 1623
Type of work: Drama
Type of plot: Comedy
Time of plot: Middle Ages
Locale: Forest of Arden, France

Principal characters:
THE BANISHED DUKE
FREDERICK, his brother and usurper of his dominions
OLIVER, the older son of Sir Rowland de Boys
ORLANDO, the younger son of Sir Rowland de Boys
ADAM, a servant to Oliver
TOUCHSTONE, a clown
ROSALIND, the daughter of the banished duke
CELIA, the daughter of Frederick

The Story:

The elder and lawful ruler of a French province is deposed by his younger brother, Frederick. The old duke, driven from his dominions, flees with several faithful followers to the Forest of Arden. There he lives a happy life, free from the cares of the court and able to devote himself at last to learning the lessons nature has to teach. His daughter, Rosalind, remains at court as a companion to her cousin Celia, the daughter of the usurping Duke Frederick. The two girls are inseparable, and nothing her father says or does would make Celia part from her dearest friend.

One day, Duke Frederick commands the two girls to attend a wrestling match between the duke's champion, Charles, and a young man named Orlando, who is a special object of Duke Frederick's hatred because he is the son of Sir Rowland de Boys, who was one of the banished duke's most loyal supporters. Before Sir Rowland dies, he charges his oldest son, Oliver, with the task of looking after his younger brother's education, but Oliver neglects his father's charge. The moment Rosalind lays eyes on Orlando she falls in love with him, and he with her. She tries to dissuade him from an unequal contest with a champion so much more powerful than he, but the more she pleads the more determined Orlando is to distinguish himself in his lady's eyes. In the end he completely conquers his antagonist and is rewarded for his prowess by a chain from Rosalind's neck.

When Duke Frederick discovers his niece's interest in Sir Rowland's son, he immediately banishes her from the court. Rosalind disguises herself as a boy and sets out for the Forest of Arden, accompanied by Celia and the faithful Touchstone, the jester. Orlando finds it necessary to flee because of his brother's harsh treatment. He is accompanied by the faithful servant Adam, an old man who willingly turns over his life savings of five hundred crowns for the privilege of following his young master.

Orlando and Adam set out for the Forest of Arden, but before they have traveled very far they are both weary and hungry. While Adam rests in the shade of some trees, Orlando wanders into that part of the forest where the old duke is and comes upon the outlaws at their meal. Desperate from hunger, Orlando rushes upon the duke with a drawn sword and demands food. The duke immediately offers to share the hospitality of his table, and Orlando blushes with shame over his rude manner. He will not touch a mouthful until Adam is fed. When the old duke finds that Orlando is the son of his friend, Sir Rowland de Boys, he takes Orlando and Adam under his protection and makes them members of his band of foresters.

Rosalind and Celia also arrive in the Forest of Arden, where they buy a flock of sheep and proceed to live the life of shepherds. Rosalind passes as Ganymede, Celia, as her sister Aliena. They encounter real Arcadians—Silvius, a shepherd, and Phebe, a dainty shepherdess with whom Silvius is in love. The moment Phebe lays eyes on the disguised Rosalind, she falls in love with the supposed young shepherd and will have nothing further to do with Silvius. Disguised as Ganymede, Rosalind also meets Orlando in the forest and twits him on his practice of writing verses in praise of Rosalind and hanging them on the trees. Touchstone displays the same willfulness and whimsicality in the forest that he showed at court, even in his love for Audrey, a country girl whose sole appeal is her unloveliness.

One morning, as Orlando is on his way to visit Ganymede, he sees a man lying asleep under an oak tree. A snake is coiled about the sleeper's neck, and a hungry lioness crouches nearby ready to spring. He recognizes the man as his own brother, Oliver, and for a moment he is tempted to leave him to his fate. Then he draws his sword and kills the two animals. In the encounter, he himself is wounded by the lioness. Because Orlando saves his life, Oliver repents and the two brothers are joyfully reunited.

His wound having bled profusely, Orlando is too weak to visit Ganymede, and he sends Oliver instead with a bloody handkerchief as proof of his wounded condition. When Ganymede sees the handkerchief, the supposed shepherd promptly faints. The disguised Celia is so impressed by Oliver's concern for his brother that she falls in love with him, and they make plans to be married on the following day. Orlando is overwhelmed by this news and a little envious, but when Ganymede comes to call upon Orlando, the young shepherd promises to produce the lady Rosalind the next day. Meanwhile Phebe comes to renew her ardent declaration of love for Ganymede, who promises on the morrow to unravel the love tangle of everyone.

Duke Frederick, enraged at the flight of his daughter, Celia, sets out at the head of an expedition to capture his elder brother and put him and all his followers to death. On the outskirts of the Forest of Arden he meets an old hermit who turns Frederick's head from his evil design. On the day following, as Ganymede promised, with the banished duke and his followers as guests, Rosalind appears as herself and explains how she and Celia posed as the shepherd Ganymede and his sister Aliena. Four marriages takes place that day with great rejoicing between Orlando and Rosalind, Oliver and Celia, Silvius and Phebe, and Touchstone and Audrey. Frederick is so completely converted by the hermit that he resolves to take religious orders and straightway dispatches a messenger to the Forest of Arden to restore his brother's lands and those of all his followers.

Critical Evaluation:

William Shakespeare takes most of the plot of *As You Like It* from a popular novel of the period, Thomas Lodge's *Rosalynde* (1590). What he adds is a dramatic characterization and wit. The play, a splendid comedy on love and life, is compounded of many elements, the whole set to some of Shakespeare's loveliest poetry. *As You Like It* more than fulfills the promise of its title. Its characters are, for the most part, wonderfully enamored of love, one another, and themselves. The play has freshness and vitality and, although adapted from an older story full of artifice, suggests a world of spontaneity and life.

As You Like It is often called a pastoral comedy because it employs the conventions of pastoral literature. Beginning in the third century B.C.E. and popular in the late sixteenth century, pastoral literature enabled poets, novelists, and dramatists to contrast the everyday world's fears, anxieties, disloyalties, uncertainties, and tensions with the imagined, mythical world where peace, longevity, contentment, and fulfillment reigned. Each age develops its own manner of describing lost happiness, far removed from the normal toil of human existence; the pastoral was the dominant vision in the late sixteenth century.

In the pastoral, the mythic, lost world is set in a simple, rural environment, which then becomes the image of all things desirable to honest people. *As You Like It* is typical of this convention and contains two contrasting worlds: the world of the court and the rural world—in this case the Forest of Arden. The court is inhabited by corrupt men such as Duke Frederick and Oliver. It is not significant that the gentle banished duke, Orlando, Rosalind, and Celia also once resided there. Rather, as the play develops, the court is the natural home of the wicked and ambitious. The audience is not shown the degeneration of Duke Frederick and Oliver; they are naturally wicked, and the court is their proper milieu.

The elder duke, Orlando, Rosalind, and Celia, on the other hand, are naturally good and the forest is their natural milieu. If the court represents elaborate artifice, ambition, avarice, cruelty, and deception, the forest represents openness, tolerance, simplicity, and freedom. Rather than developing complex characters such as Hamlet, who like most humans has good and bad characteristics, pastorals apportion good and bad traits to separate characters, an allocation that imposes a necessary artifice upon the play and colors all actions, from falling in love to hating to helping a brother. A play such as *As You Like It* does not present natural behavior. On the other hand, by his adroit use of the conventions and artifice, Shakespeare achieves a remarkable exploration of love and its attendant values.

In the opening scene, Orlando, who has been denied an education and kept like an animal by his brother, is seen to be naturally good and decent. Talking to his brother Oliver, Orlando says, "You have train'd me like a peasant, obscuring and hiding from me all gentleman-like qualities. The spirit of my father grows strong in me, and I will no longer endure it: therefore allow me such exercises as may become a gentleman. . . ." Oliver, as naturally wicked as Orlando is naturally decent, says, "for my soul—yet I know not why—hates nothing more than he." Logic has no necessary place in this world. Love, however, does.

Love is a natural part of the pastoral world. Practically at first glance, Rosalind and Orlando are in love. Shakespeare's magic in *As You Like It* is to take the contrived love that is the expected part of the pastoral convention and make of it a deeply felt experience that the audience can understand. Shakespeare manages this not only through the extraordinary beauty of his language but also through the structure of his play.

As You Like It is full of parallel actions. Orlando and Rosalind meet and immediately fall in love. Silvius and Phebe are in love. Touchstone meets Audrey in the forest, and they fall in love. At the end of the play Celia meets the reformed Oliver, and they fall in love just as quickly as Rosalind and Orlando did at the beginning of the play. The love match at the play's end nicely sets off the love match at the beginning.

Each love pairing serves a particular purpose. The focus of the play is primarily upon the Rosalind-Orlando match. Rosalind is the more interesting of the pair, for while she recognizes the silliness of the lover's ardor, she is as much a victim as those she scorns. In act 4, while disguised as a boy, she pretends to Orlando that his Rosalind will not have him. He says, "Then . . . I die." Her response pokes fun at the expiring love: "No, faith, die by attorney. The poor world is almost six thousand years old, and in all this time there was not any man died in his own person, videlicet, in a love-cause. . . . Men have died from time to time and worms have eaten them, but not for love." She can toy with Orlando in her disguise as Ganymede, yet she is completely dominated by her strong passion, which is a part of the love experience. Rosalind's and Orlando's passion, however, is more refined than the passion the others experience.

Touchstone, in his quest for Audrey, exemplifies the earthier side of love. He at first wants to marry her out of church so that he can, once he tires of her, claim their marriage is invalid. The kind of love he represents is physical passion. The Phebe-Silvius pairing shows yet another face of love, that of the typical pastoral lover hopelessly in love with a fickle mistress. He sighs on his pillow and breaks off from company, forlornly calling out his mistress's name. Touchstone's and Silvius's kinds of love are extreme versions of qualities in Rosalind's love. In the comedies Shakespeare often uses this device of apportioning diverse characteristics to multiple characters rather than building one complete character. Without Touchstone, love in the play might have been too sentimental to take seriously. Without Silvius, it might have been too crude. With both, love as exemplified by Rosalind and Orlando becomes a precious balance of substance and nonsense, spirituality and silliness.

Curious things happen in *As You Like It*. Good men leave the honorable forest to return to the wicked court. Wicked men who enter the forest are converted in their ways. At the end of the play, Oliver, who comes to the Forest of Arden to hunt down his brother Orlando, gives his estate to Orlando and marries Celia, vowing to remain in the forest and live and die a shepherd. Duke Frederick comes to the Forest of Arden in order to kill his brother. Meeting "an old religious man" in the forest, Duke Frederick "was converted/ Both from his enterprise and from the world." He, too, gives up his estate and his crown to his brother. The forest, the pastoral world, has the power to transform.

Why, then, do the elder duke, Orlando, and Rosalind elect to return to the court, home of wickedness? They do so because *As You Like It* is ultimately not a fairy tale but an expression of humanly felt experiences. The forest is a cleansing and regenerative experience, a place to which to retire to renew simplicity, honesty, and virtue. It is not, however, a permanent retreat. Good men stained by labor and trouble in their everyday world in the end must participate in that world. If they retreat to the pastoral world to renew themselves, they must return in the end to the community to take on the responsibilities all must face.

"Critical Evaluation" by Brian L. Mark

Further Reading

Bednarz, James P. "Shakespeare in Love: The Containment of Comical Satire in *As You Like It*." In *Shakespeare and the Poets' War*. New York: Columbia University Press, 2001. Analyzes the play within the context of Shakespeare's debate with rival Ben Jonson about the social function of drama and the role of the dramatist. Describes how *As You Like It* was a response to Jonson's *Every Man out of His Humour*.

Halio, Jay L., ed. *Twentieth Century Interpretations of "As You Like It."* Englewood Cliffs, N.J.: Prentice-Hall, 1968. Includes essays by Helen Gardner, John Russell Brown, Marco Mincoff on Thomas Lodge's *Rosalynde* as the source of *As You Like It*, and Halio on time and timelessness in Arden. Contains an introduction and bibliography.

Hunt, Maurice. *Shakespeare's "As You Like It": Late Elizabethan Culture and Literary Representation*. New York: Palgrave Macmillan, 2008. Describes how the play presented issues of interest to Elizabethan audiences and to Shakespeare himself, such as concepts of time, gentlemanly behavior, and transvestism. Compares the play to Edmund Spenser's *The Faerie Queene*.

Knowles, Richard. "Myth and Type in *As You Like It*." *English Literary History* 33 (1966): 1-22. Discusses the many mythical allusions in *As You Like It* that make the literal action reverberate beyond itself. Hercules is the dominant mythological figure, whom by analogy Orlando resembles. Biblical overtones are also discussed.

Leggatt, Alexander. *Shakespeare's Comedy of Love*. London: Methuen, 1974. Leggatt shows how the forest scenes provide an imaginative freedom to explore ideas and play roles. Partisan laughter against any one character in the play is discouraged, for the audience is reminded of the partiality of any single perspective.

Lynch, Stephen J. *"As You Like It": A Guide to the Play.* Westport, Conn.: Greenwood Press, 2003. An overview of the play, examining its textual history, contexts and sources, dramatic structure, and themes. Discusses the play in performance and provides information about various critical approaches to the work.

Mills, Perry. *Shakespeare: "As You Like It."* New York: Cambridge University Press, 2002. Guidebook designed for advanced level students of English literature. Provides a commentary on the text; discusses the play's historical, cultural, and social contexts and use of language; offers a survey of critical interpretation.

Shakespeare, William. *As You Like It*. Edited by Harold Bloom. New York: Bloom's Literary Criticism, 2008. In addition to the text of the play, this edition provides more than eighty pages of introductory and explanatory material, including discussions of the play's date; sources; themes of love, metamorphoses, and doubleness; the character of Rosalind; and the play in performance.

Smallwood, Robert. *"As You Like It."* London: Arden Shakespeare, in association with the Shakespeare Birthplace Trust, 2003. Analyzes how different directors, scenic designers, and actors have interpreted and adapted the play for productions mounted by the Royal Shakespeare Company since 1945. Includes photographs of company productions.

Young, David. *The Heart's Forest: A Study of Shakespeare's Pastoral Plays*. New Haven, Conn.: Yale University Press, 1972. Young reviews the pastoral tradition and its salient characteristics, so important in this play, and shows how Shakespeare explored and exploited the medium of pastoral drama in *As You Like It* and other plays. Argues that a deliberate self-consciousness pervades *As You Like It*, whose atmosphere of artifice and hypothesis is fostered by extensive use of "if," and whose major theme is self-knowledge.

Ash Wednesday

Author: T. S. Eliot (1888-1965)
First published: 1930
Type of work: Poetry

After the 1922 publication of *The Waste Land* had established his reputation as a major poet, T. S. Eliot wrote one important poem, "The Hollow Men" (1925), which seemed at that time to be a postlude to its predecessor but which now appears more as a prelude to *Ash Wednesday*. In any case, it should be read as a connecting link between the two longer poems. Its theme is the emptiness of modern intellectualism, which amounts only to "Shape, without form, shade without colour,/ Paralysed force, gesture without motion." It is another aspect of the Waste Land, desiccated and meaningless, inhabited only by the empty and futile hollow men.

Ash Wednesday marks an important point in the author's poetic development, for it sprang directly from his acceptance of the Anglo-Catholic faith. This biographical aspect of the poem, even more than its theme, influenced its reception by Eliot's former admirers and caused a schism among them that was unexpectedly revealing about the pre-World War II mind.

The tone of the poem is the humility appropriate to *Ash Wednesday*, the first day of the penitential season of Lent; its theme is the dilemma of human beings who want to believe and yet cannot bring themselves to do so because of their dry, sterile intellectualism. This theme is stated in the first of the six parts: the poet, turning his irony upon himself, describes this characteristically twentieth century predicament of a man caught in the web of his own intellectualizing who can yet know that he must

> pray that I may forget
> These matters that with myself I too much discuss
> Too much explain,

and that at this stage of religious experience the proper prayer is

> Teach us to sit still.

Throughout this opening section sound the echoes of the Penitential Office, "Turn thou us, O good Lord, and so shall we be turned," and of Guido Cavalcanti's sixteenth century poem, "In Exile at Sarzana."

The second part of *Ash Wednesday* is based on a reminiscence of the Valley of Dry Bones described by Ezekiel, whose language it echoes. Eliot once said in a lecture that the three white leopards could be taken as representing the World, the Flesh, and the Devil. They have fed on the body of the speaker, but Ezekiel was told to prophesy that these bones should live again, that "I [the Lord] shall put my spirit in you, and ye shall live, and I shall place you in your own land." There is also the figure of the Lady, who seems to play a role analogous to that of Dante Alighieri's Beatrice as an intermediary; she is dressed in white, the color of Faith. The speaker, having been stripped of everything, has learned resignation, but through the intercession of the Lady and the prophecy of Ezekiel he has found hope.

The third section, with its description of the spiral stairway, obviously recalls Dante's winding ascent of the Purgatorial Mount. There seems to be no direct connection with any particular canto of the *Purgatorio* of Dante's *La divina commedia* (c. 1320; *The Divine Comedy*, 1802), only a linking of the journey of purgation with the penitential spirit of Lent. There is also the glimpse through the window of a scene suggestive of sensual pleasure that distracts the pilgrim from his journey. Dante is again recalled in the fourth section, this time by the Earthly Paradise and the Divine Pageant at the end of the *Purgatorio*. Again there are echoes: of St. Paul's *Epistle to the Ephesians* and of the "Salve Regina."

For the fifth section, Eliot makes use of a sermon by Lancelot Andrews that he had already quoted in an essay on the Bishop: "the Word of an Infant? The Word and not be able to speak a word?"—an elaborate play upon the word (speech), the Word (the Logos, the most abstruse of Christian doctrines), and the Word made Flesh.

The last section, doubling back on the opening lines of the poem, suggests a scene in a confessional ("Bless me father") during which the beauty of the natural world intrudes into the mind of the speaker and distracts him from his proper meditation. Thus the world seeks to draw human beings back to itself. The poem ends, appropriately, with words taken (with one slight change) from the Penitential Office for Ash Wednesday in the Book of Common Prayer: "And let my cry come unto Thee."

Eliot's *Ash Wednesday* deals with various aspects of a certain stage in religious experience: "Lord, I am not worthy"; it is a poem of spiritual exile, as Cavalcanti's was one of physical exile. The dweller in the Waste Land who "cannot drink/ there, where trees flower, and springs flow" must find his way back through penitence with the humble prayer: "Suffer me not to be separated."

This is a simpler poem than *The Waste Land*, though Eliot uses many of the same technical devices of ellipsis and echoes. *Ash Wednesday* rises to heights of verbal beauty unequaled in any other contemporary verse. Its reception, however, was curious and not without irony. To many readers of the 1920's, Eliot had become a voice for the disillusionment of the now famous "lost generation"—a statement that he himself characterized as "nonsense." The year 1930, with its Marxian enthusiasm for proletarian literature, probably saw the high point of the secular humanism of the twentieth century; Bertrand Russell's *A Free Man's Worship* (1923) was dominant. It was among the adherents of this way of thought that Eliot's greatest admirers were to be found. His becoming a member of the Anglican Church and writing a poem with a deeply religious theme was to them a grievous shock. Some flatly refused to believe in his sincerity, and many considered his membership in the Church of England a pose, a kind of romantic, aesthetic Catholicism. To others, to whom religion was a retreat from reality, a "failure of nerve," he was a lost leader, a writer whose significant work had ended with "The Hollow Men." However, there is some truth to the claim that the publication of *Ash Wednesday* marked the beginning of the intellectual swing in Western thought from the left to the right, with the consequent decline of the secular humanist attitude.

Further Reading

Ackroyd, Peter. *T. S. Eliot: A Life*. New York: Simon & Schuster, 1984. A very readable biography that treats Eliot's life as an integral part of his work. Also examines the critical reception of *Ash Wednesday* and its relationship to Eliot's other works, as well as the writer's indebtedness to the Bible and Dante.

Beasley, Rebecca. *Theorists of Modernist Poetry: T. S. Eliot, T. E. Hulme, Ezra Pound*. New York: Routledge, 2007. An overview of the origins, aesthetics, and theories of modernist poetry as exemplified by the work of Eliot and his two contemporaries. In addition to analyzing individual poems, Beasley discusses the modernist critique of democracy, the importance of World War I in the development of the new poetics, and the modernist conception of an ideal society.

Cooper, John Xiros. *The Cambridge Introduction to T. S. Eliot*. New York: Cambridge University Press, 2006. An introductory overview to Eliot's life and work, focusing on his poetry. Chapter 3 includes an eight-page discussion of *Ash Wednesday* and the *Ariel* poems.

Gardner, Helen. *The Art of T. S. Eliot*. New York: E. P. Dutton, 1950. Chapter 5 offers a fine analysis of *Ash Wednesday* as a transitional work reflecting Eliot's emerging understanding of Christianity. Gardner analyzes this poem in the context of Eliot's other prominent poems such as *The Waste Land* and *Four Quartets*.

Gordon, Lyndall. *T. S. Eliot: An Imperfect Life*. New York: W. W. Norton, 1999. An authoritative, thoroughly researched biography that concedes Eliot's many personal flaws as well as describing his poetic genius.

Hinchliffe, Arnold P. *"The Waste Land" and "Ash Wednesday": The Critics Debate*. Atlantic Highlands, N.J.: Humanities Press International, 1987. A useful review of the critical reception of these two poems since their publication. A fine introduction to the works' major critics and their positions, along with a succinct and helpful bibliography.

Moody, A. David, ed. *The Cambridge Companion to T. S. Eliot*. New York: Cambridge University Press, 1994. Collection of essays, including discussions of Eliot's life; Eliot as a philosopher, a social critic, and a product of America; and religion, literature, and society in Eliot's work. Also features the essay "*Ash-Wednesday*: A Poetry of Verification" by John Kwan-Ferry.

Raine, Craig. *T. S. Eliot*. New York: Oxford University Press, 2006. In this examination of Eliot's work, Raine maintains that "the buried life," or the failure of feeling, is a consistent theme in the poetry and plays. Chapter 1, "The Failure to Live," contains an explication of *Ash Wednesday*.

Smith, Grover Cleveland. *T. S. Eliot's Poetry and Plays: A Study in Sources and Meaning*. 2d ed. Chicago: University of Chicago Press, 1974. A standard critical work on Eliot's poetry. Includes a detailed exploration of Eliot's clever use of allusions and quotations to express his spiritual and philosophical concerns.

Southam, B. C., ed. *T. S. Eliot: "Prufrock," "Gerontion," "Ash Wednesday," and Other Shorter Poems: A Casebook*. London: Macmillan, 1978. A collection of excerpts from the analyses of prominent critics. Contains five essays on *Ash Wednesday*.

Ashes

Author: Stefan Żeromski (1864-1925)
First published: *Popioły*, 1904 (English translation, 1928)
Type of work: Novel
Type of plot: Historical
Time of plot: 1796-1812
Locale: Poland and Spain

Principal characters:
RAPHAEL OLBROMSKI, the protagonist
CHRISTOPHER CEDRO, his friend
HELEN, Raphael's beloved
PRINCE GINTULT, a nobleman
ELIZABETH, the prince's sister
NARDZEVSKI, Raphael's uncle

The Story:

When he is very young, Raphael Olbromski pays a short visit to the secluded estate of his uncle, Nardzevski, who is fond of his nephew and initiates him into the art of hunting. The fierce old man is a firm adherent to the values of feudal times and treats his peasants as serfs. Casper, his huntsman, is his only intimate. Raphael's visit comes to a sudden end at the arrival of an Austrian official who lectures Nardzevski severely on not having paid the new taxes and for his treatment of his peasants. The old man has no intention of submitting to the Austrians. To emphasize his defiance, he practices his pistol marksmanship in the dining hall. He also orders his steward to summon all the peasants in the morning and arrange for a public flogging of a miscreant. Raphael never learns what happened afterward, because early in the morning he is bundled into a sleigh and sent home.

A great sleighing party one winter attracts all the gentry. Raphael, mounted on a spirited horse, follows Helen's sleigh closely. The party stops to dance at Raphael's house, and his aristocratic father stages a big celebration. During the affair, Raphael manages to tell Helen that he will come to her window some evening at midnight. The party lasts for two days, but Raphael misses much of it because he sleeps in a drunken stupor.

At school, Raphael is no student, but he is a leader. One evening, he and his friend Christopher Cedro steal a rowboat and go out into the ice-packed Vistula. When they try to land, the thin shore ice breaks, and the boys are soaked. As they go on toward school, they sink into a bog. They are nearly frozen before Raphael takes decisive measures. He tears off his wet clothes and those of the weakened Christopher, and the boys pummel each other to get warm. Then, quite naked, they run back to school, where they are caught as they try to slip inside. Christopher falls ill with fever, and Raphael, as the leader, is chastised. When the beadle tries to carry out the punishment, however, Raphael draws a knife, wounds the beadle, and escapes.

When Raphael arrives home in disgrace, his father imprisons him in a small room and forbids the family to speak to him. Later, he has to spend months working with the peasants. One night, Raphael takes a fine mare from the barn and rides through a storm to Helen's house. When a watchman comes upon them in an outbuilding, Helen gets back to her bedroom safely, but Raphael barely escapes the fierce watchdogs.

A storm comes up, and Raphael is followed by four wolves. When his horse stumbles, the wolves are on him. Three bring down the horse; Raphael kills the fourth with his hands. Gravely wounded, he is found by an old peasant, who takes him home. When he recovers, his family casts him out and sends him to live with his older brother Peter, whom they had cast out years before.

Peter, in poor health from war wounds, lives quietly. Raphael spends delightful months in idleness until the arrival of Prince Gintult, his brother's old comrade. Peter and the prince exchange angry words about the treatment of peasants, however, and as the result of the quarrel, Peter has a hemorrhage and dies.

Having lost his home and melancholy with memories of Helen, who has been taken out of the country, Raphael goes to stay with the prince. In the noble household, Raphael is half family, half guest. The prince gives him money for clothes, and others give him errands to run. Raphael is attracted to the prince's sister Elizabeth, a haughty young girl. One day, while they are riding in a group, Elizabeth's horse runs away. Raphael rescues her and makes the mistake of kissing her as he holds her in his arms. She slashes his face with her whip.

The prince suddenly departs on a voyage to Venice and Paris, after paying Raphael's lodging in a school for a year. Raphael studies fairly well and spends his time profitably. When he is forced to return home, his stern father outfits him in work clothes, and for four years he works on the farm. His release comes with an offer of a position from Prince Gintult.

In Warsaw, Raphael serves as secretary to the prince, who is writing a vague philosophical treatise on Freemasonry. In order to continue the work on the secret lodge, Raphael is taken into an order of the Masons; soon afterward, he is accepted in society. Through the lodge, he meets Helen again.

Raphael and Helen flee to the country to enjoy their love. One night, they sleep in a cave in the mountains. Although Raphael is armed, brigands overpower him as he sleeps and bind him while they attack Helen. She escapes their clutches at last and jumps off a cliff.

While he is searching for Helen's body and tracking the brigands, Raphael is arrested by a patrol. He does not dare give his correct name or mention Helen for fear of defiling her memory. While in prison, he has a long siege of fever. More than a year passes before he is released.

Penniless and tramping aimlessly about the country, Raphael falls in with his old friend Christopher. The reunited friends spend happy months on Christopher's estate. Then a soldier who has been with Napoleon for twelve years fires their imagination, and Raphael and Christopher decide to leave that Austrian-dominated part of Poland and join the emperor. Aided by Elizabeth, who is now married and living near the border, they make a daring escape across the frontier.

As an enlisted man, Christopher crosses Europe with Napoleon and takes part in the Spanish campaign. His most vivid impressions are those of the Siege of Saragossa, where he distinguishes himself for valor and saves a young girl from soldiers who have sacked a convent and raped the nuns. He is thrilled when Napoleon abolishes the Inquisition. After being wounded, he sees the emperor at close hand.

Raphael sees action in Poland, where the Austrian legions are too strong for Napoleon's forces. Once the Poles are preparing to demolish a church held by the enemy. Prince Gintult, fighting as a civilian, attempts to save the church by interfering with the cannoneers, and Raphael helps him. For his deed, the prince is cut down by an officer's sword. In the confusion, Raphael carries the wounded nobleman away to his father's house.

When the fighting dies down, Raphael is discharged. He goes to live at his uncle's old estate, and for a time he is happy there. He rebuilds the barns demolished by the soldiers, clears land, and begins building a house. Just as he is finishing, Christopher arrives. Invalided out of the army but well again, he is impatient for action. Reluctant to leave his home, Raphael objects at first; finally, however, he agrees to accompany his friend. In the middle of August, 1812, the Polish Corps is united with the Grand Army, and Raphael returns to serve the emperor. At Orsha, Napoleon reviews his hordes of Polish, Dutch, Italian, and German soldiers.

Critical Evaluation:

The plot of *Ashes* is romantic and fanciful, although often embellished with a realistic covering of details and description. At times it suggests the picaresque tales of Henry Fielding and other eighteenth century novelists, but it also has a lushness and romanticism that are more German than English. The idealistic hero of this novel, Raphael Olbromski, questions the meaning of existence; certainly, in the course of his life, he has reason to doubt the purpose of human suffering. Yet he has an idealism centered in his love for Helen and in his patriotism.

Raphael is essentially passive, letting others work on him; his actions are unpremeditated and often foolish. His father, the prince, the brigands, and others send him hither and thither, changing the course of his existence, and because he has no particular ambitions, he obeys or yields to these forces. He is, for example, led to join the Masons, but through no convictions of his own. He is impressionable, impetuous, and naïve, and he often gets into trouble, as when he and Christopher return to school naked, when he runs away, when he kisses Elizabeth after rescuing her, and when he and Helen flee together. More than once, his character and his adventures come close to straining the reader's credulity.

Stefan Żeromski possesses a gift for describing action. The novel is filled with excellently drawn scenes, including the hunting scene that opens the book, the scene of the sleighs rushing between estates during holiday festivities, the scene of riding through snow on Baska to Helen's house, and the scene of Raphael and Baska chased by wolves. The characterization, too, is often fine; Żeromski can in a single detail encompass a whole personality, as in his description of the superior half-smile always on the faces of Prince Gintult and his sister, Elizabeth.

Raphael is torn between the shallow society of the cities and the life of the country. He is educated but not dedicated to books or intellectual pursuits, preferring to hunt and roam about in the woods and fields. For a long time, he exists on the fringes of the great world, barely aware of the momentous happenings occurring elsewhere. Then he is caught up in the wheel of history, and when his fortunes become so low that they cannot sink any lower, his old friend Christopher Cedro appears to save him.

Raphael tries to rebuild his uncle's old estate, but again history and Christopher carry him away, and once more his fate is determined by forces outside himself. Perhaps Żeromski is suggesting through the life of his protagonist that it is futile for people to struggle against the forces of destiny and history.

Much of this work is in the German Romantic tradition. Żeromski describes nature in great detail and devotes long sections to philosophical speculations engendered by contemplation of nature. The tragic love affair of Helen and Raphael and the frequent unconnected sequences of action are reminiscent of the works of Johann Wolfgang von Goethe. By contrast, the scenes that describe some of the Napoleonic campaigns are precise and realistic. *Ashes* ranks high as a historical novel, and Żeromski has been acknowledged as a master of the genre.

Further Reading

Czerwinski, E. J., ed. *Dictionary of Polish Literature*. Westport, Conn.: Greenwood Press, 1994. A survey of Żeromski's career, explaining his role in the Young Poland movement and commenting on the impact of his novels. Cites *Ashes* as one of his best, in which he speaks to his countrymen about their heroism during the Napoleonic era.

Eile, Stanislaw. "Stefan Zeromski and the Crisis of Polish Nationalism." In *The Literature of Nationalism: Essays on East European Identity*, edited by Robert B. Pynsent. New York: St. Martin's Press, 1996. Describes Żeromski's involvement in and reaction to the Polish nationalist movement.

Kridl, Manfred. *A Survey of Polish Literature and Culture*. Translated by Olga Sherer-Virski. New York: Columbia University Press, 1956. Considers Żeromski the chief spokesperson for the Young Poland movement of the late nineteenth century. Provides a lengthy discussion of several important novels, including *Ashes*. Examines the structure of the book and comments on the significance of a number of themes.

Krzyżanowski, Julian. *A History of Polish Literature*. Translated by Doris Ronowicz. Warsaw: Polish Scientific, 1972. Outlines Żeromski's literary career and discusses the sociological influences that inspired much of his fiction. Notes that the novelist criticizes the Polish people during the Napoleonic period.

Kuk, Zenon M. "Tolstoy's *War and Peace* and Żeromski's *Ashes* as Historical Novels." *Folio: Essays on Foreign Languages and Literatures* 14 (December, 1982): 1-7. Comparative study of two novels about the Napoleonic Wars, explaining how each uses materials from history to create fiction with a didactic purpose.

Miłosz, Czesław. *The History of Polish Literature*. 2d ed. Berkeley: University of California Press, 1983. Sketches the novelist's career and comments briefly on his major fiction. Remarks on the significance of his choice of the Napoleonic era as the subject of *Ashes*. Notes his strengths in handling his story compassionately and in dealing with the historical tradition, but faults him for having "a penchant for melodrama."

The Aspern Papers

Author: Henry James (1843-1916)
First published: 1888
Type of work: Novel
Type of plot: Psychological realism
Time of plot: Late nineteenth century
Locale: Venice

Principal characters:
NARRATOR, a young literary scholar
JULIANA BORDEREAU, a very old woman, once the mistress of Jeffrey Aspern
TITA BORDEREAU, her spinster niece

The Story:

In the 1880's, a young American literary scholar hears that a woman who long ago was the mistress of the famous American poet Jeffrey Aspern is still alive, living in Venice. It is rumored that this old woman, Juliana Bordereau, has a cache of Aspern's papers, mostly letters. Frantic to lay his hands on the papers, the young man vows to do whatever it takes to get hold of them. Unfortunately, Juliana, who is said to be close to death, never receives visitors.

Even though there is no proof that the papers even exist, the young scholar decides to try to gain entrance to Juliana's villa as a lodger. "Hypocrisy, duplicity are my only chance," he declares. "I'm sorry for it, but there's no baseness I wouldn't commit for Jeffrey Aspern's sake." He manages to convince Tita, the niece, that he is a writer who needs solitude. Tita then presents him to Juliana who, after listening to his lies, agrees to let him stay, but at an exorbitant price.

Weeks go by without the scholar getting any closer to the papers. At times he suspects that the women are on to him and are only out for the money. Meanwhile, there develops between him and the women a cat-and-mouse game in which the women tantalize him with vague hints as to the existence of the papers while he tries to conceal his motive for being there.

The more he persuades himself that the papers exist, the more determined he is to get to them, and the more difficult the women make it. Although he is not in the least attracted to Tita, he works hard to ingratiate himself with her. Slowly he brings the conversation around to certain rare items Juliana might possess. When he finally admits that, yes, he is a Jeffrey Aspern scholar, Tita runs out of the room. Oddly enough, a day or so later Juliana asks to see him, but nothing is said about his interest in Aspern or the existence of any papers. Instead Juliana seems more interested in pushing him on Tita.

The scholar and Tita have dinner together during which Tita reveals that Juliana does, after all, have a lot of Aspern's papers. Fearing that Juliana might destroy them, the scholar asks Tita to help him save them, and she promises to do what she can. In the days that follow, there is more game playing as Juliana dickers for higher rent while she hints at an eventual reward. "She was such a subtle old witch," thinks the young man at one point as she offers to sell him a small oval portrait of Aspern. When he feigns ignorance of the man's identity, she mocks him.

One day Tita comes to the young man and says her aunt is ill and probably dying. She then tells him that Aspern's papers have been removed from a green trunk and stuffed between Juliana's mattresses only to be removed again and stuffed in an ornate secretary just outside Juliana's bedroom. As he is passing by that room late one evening, the scholar cannot resist checking out the contents of the secretary. At that very moment, Juliana appears, her eyes blazing and calling him a "publishing scoundrel!"

Shaken, the scholar leaves the villa the next morning, but returns sometime later to learn that Juliana died. Tita tells him she now has the papers and hints that he can have them if he will marry her. Again he flees the villa, but eventually his passion for the papers overcomes any scruple and he returns prepared to agree to Tita's bargain. It is too late; in revenge for his rejection, Tita announces that she destroyed all the papers, "one by one." "It took a long time," she says cruelly, "there were so many."

Earlier Tita gave the scholar the tiny portrait of Aspern that Juliana tried to sell him for a thousand pounds. The scholar accepts it at face value, never suspecting that it might be worthless. At the end of the story, after being rejected by Tita, the scholar sends her a thousand pounds, telling her he sold the portrait. In reality, however, he keeps it for himself and thus never knows how duped he was all along.

Critical Evaluation:

The term "vampirism" has been used to label those characters in Henry James's fiction who will stop at nothing to get what they want. Often it is a psychological sort of vampirism in which one person bullies another into submission. In *The Aspern Papers*, the vampirism is more substantive. The young scholar wants something that belongs to someone else—the papers—and he schemes to get them regardless of the consequences to their owner, the aging and infirm Juliana Bordereau, or to her penniless niece, Tita. In his ruthless quest for these papers, he is not above lying, dissembling, flattering, even stealing. At the same time he lies to himself, rationalizing his duplicity, justifying his strategies as necessary in an effort to rescue valuable materials from a selfish old woman who does not appreciate their value.

As is the case with so much of James's fiction, no character in *The Aspern Papers* is above reproach. It is clear from the first encounter that the scholar has met his match in the crafty old Juliana when she charges him an outrageous rent, which he pays without batting an eye. At that moment, both recognize that they are adversaries, but Juliana has the upper hand because she has the papers (or so she lets him believe). She uses her age and eccentricity to her advantage. Likewise, Tita, though slow to catch on, soon enough sees how, by letting herself be used, she can play both ends against the middle. She becomes the go-between, deceiving both the scholar and her aunt. When her scheme backfires, she takes revenge on the scholar by telling him she has burned the papers. It is exquisitely cruel revenge, all the more so if it is a lie and there never were any papers.

The irony is bitter in this story, for it is quite possible that time, energy, and cunning are expended over papers that either do not exist or do not amount to much. Tita's renunciation of the scholar—after she has burned her bridges—is a moment of the most hollow triumph, for in winning the game with the scholar, she has lost even more than he has.

Much has been made of James's keen dramatic sense, and it is nowhere more evident than in *The Aspern Papers*. At select moments along the way, there are climactic scenes at the end of which a curtain seems to fall. There is, for example, the highly theatrical scene in which Juliana catches the scholar as he is about to pilfer the papers. Then there is the scene in which Tita drives the scholar away with her thinly veiled proposal of marriage. The most dramatic scene occurs when Tita, in a chilling turn, renounces the man who has rejected her and boasts of how methodically she destroyed the papers and how long it took because there were so many.

The moral world James's characters inhabit is a warped one in which perceptions are distorted and traditional values perverted. To begin with, there is the question of obsession. It is clear that the scholar and Juliana share a common obsession with Jeffrey Aspern. In her case, it has made her a mean-spirited recluse whose dependency on Tita has robbed her niece of a life of her own. Even more selfish and inconsiderate is the scholar whose interest in Aspern the poet has degenerated into his interest in Aspern the celebrity. He, too, is willing to exploit Tita in his determination to possess the papers.

There is also the curious question of renunciation, a common theme in the works of James. Ordinarily, renunciation is an act of contrition, but for Tita it becomes an act of revenge against a man who trifles with her affections and against an old woman who drains Tita's lifeblood to sustain the memory of an ancient passion. Tita destroys her inheritance when she destroys the papers. Thus, James presents the seemingly noble act of turning one's back on evil as an even subtler manifestation of evil.

It would be a mistake, no matter how serious the subject matter, to overlook the humor in *The Aspern Papers*. The characters in this story are not dealing in matters of great importance. The letters, if they do exist, could be mere drivel; at best, they would probably do little except add to the gossip surrounding a legendary literary figure. To the scholar, the papers are valuable, not because of what they contain (after all, he has not yet seen them), but merely because they exist (if, indeed, they do). He expends a ridiculous amount of time, money, and guile in the pursuit of something so uncertain and, as far as the world is concerned, unimportant. He cuts a ridiculous figure as he loses at his own game and never really realizes how much he has lost. Tita may play a monstrous joke on him, but she too is more a comic than a tragic figure when the joke turns out to be on her.

Ultimately, the key to the brilliance of this story is to be found in James's decision to have the scholar narrate his own story. In "telling on himself," so to speak, the scholar reveals how naïve he is; he learns nothing from his experience. Instead, he remains a poor judge of what is going on. This is why, at the end, the scholar can only stare at the (probably worthless) picture of Aspern and write to Tita, "When I look at it, I can scarcely bear the loss—I mean of the precious papers."

In writing this story, James reveals the shameful side of scholarship. The novel condemns the use of any means, no matter how devious, to exploit the famous, especially invading their privacy and violating their personal effects. The irony is that James knew it would probably happen to him after he was gone (it did).

Thomas Whissen

Further Reading

Bell, Millicent. "*The Aspern Papers*: The Unvisitable Past." In *Meaning in Henry James*. Cambridge, Mass.: Harvard University Press, 1991. Insightful examination of James's own "second thoughts" about *The Aspern Papers* as revealed in a preface written twenty years later for a revised edition. Bell's examination of James's revisions is particularly enlightening.

Dewey, Joseph, and Brooke Horvath, eds. *"The Finer Thread, the Tighter Weave": Essays on the Short Fiction of Henry James*. West Lafayette, Ind.: Purdue University Press, 2001. Includes Jeanne Campbell Reesman's essay "'The Deepest Depths of the Artificial': Attacking Women and Reality in *The Aspern Papers*."

Edel, Leon. *Henry James: A Life*. Rev. ed. New York: Harper & Row, 1985. An original and pertinent work of biographical criticism by an acclaimed James scholar.

Flannery, Denis. *Henry James: A Certain Illusion*. Brookfield, Vt.: Ashgate, 2000. An analysis of the concept of illusion in James's works, including *The Aspern Papers*.

Freedman, Jonathan, ed. *The Cambridge Companion to Henry James*. New York: Cambridge University Press, 1998. A collection of essays that provides extensive information on James's life and literary influences and describes his works and the characters in them.

Hocks, Richard A. *Henry James: A Study of the Short Fiction*. Boston: Twayne, 1990. Contains a challenging exposition of critic Dennis Pahl's "deconstruction" of *The Aspern Papers*, relatively free of critical jargon. Good discussion of the story's "framing device."

Neider, Charles, ed. *Short Novels of the Masters*. New York: Holt, Rinehart and Winston, 1966. A reliable introduction to the novella—sensible, concise, and literate.

Otten, Thomas J. *A Superficial Reading of Henry James: Preoccupations with the Material World*. Columbus: Ohio State University Press, 2006. Otten argues that physical surfaces—such as items of clothing and furniture—are a significant element in James's work, making it impossible to determine "what counts as thematic depth and what counts as physical surface." Chapter 5 provides an analysis of *The Aspern Papers*.

Perosa, Sergio. "Henry James: *The Aspern Papers*." In *Leon Edel and Literary Art*, edited by Lyall H. Powers. Ann Arbor: University of Michigan Press, 1988. A unique perspective from an Italian professor of Anglo-American literature.

The Assistant

Author: Bernard Malamud (1914-1986)
First published: 1957
Type of work: Novel
Type of plot: Social realism
Time of plot: 1930's
Locale: Brooklyn, New York

Principal characters:
MORRIS BOBER, a sixty-year-old immigrant Jewish grocer
IDA BOBER, his wife
HELEN BOBER, their twenty-three-year-old daughter
FRANK ALPINE, a young Italian man, a drifter

The Story:

Morris Bober, a sixty-year-old Jewish immigrant and the owner of a small Brooklyn grocery store, is slowly being driven out of business by a fancy delicatessen-grocery recently opened around the corner. Rising at six on a cold, windy autumn morning to sell a three-cent roll to a sour-faced Polish woman, Morris begins his daily routine of drudgery and frustration. Working long hours in a dreary store, Morris barely makes a living for himself, his wife Ida, and his daughter Helen, who desires to go to college and live a meaningful life. Every afternoon Morris escapes the gloom of the store by retreating to his upstairs apartment for a nap, his "one refreshment" for the day.

Morris is a decent man in an indecent and abusive world. He is a commercial failure surrounded by success. The harder he works, the less he seems to have. He extends credit indiscriminately, even in cases where he knows he will never be repaid. If he could serve the people who still do business at his store he would. Morris will not ignore the needs of another human being. He says it is the least one man can do for another.

Two holdup men appear one night near closing time. Unwilling to believe that the thirteen dollars in Morris's cash drawer could be his entire take for the day, one of the men pistol-whips him. Sick of his meager existence and filled with self-disgust, Morris bitterly denounces the years of failure and the false hope of success in America. He feels a profound sense of isolation and sadness. He wants more for his wife and daughter, yet he is unwilling to compromise his ideals.

A young Italian drifter named Frank Alpine enters the store. He is one of the men who robbed Morris earlier. Frank worships the gentleness and goodness of Saint Francis. He begins to hang around the store, helps Morris in small ways, and finally asks to be taken in as an assistant in order to gain experience. When Morris stumbles across Frank, who is asleep in the cellar, and learns that Frank has lived for a week on a daily bottle of milk and two rolls stolen from the doorstep each morning, he gives in and hires Frank. Ida is distrustful of having a Gentile in her house, but when Morris's head wound reopens, Frank takes it upon himself to run the store while Morris recovers. Business picks up as the Gentiles in the neighborhood feel more comfortable with one of their own behind the counter.

Ida is suspicious that Frank is up to no good and fearful that he will try to seduce her daughter. Her fears are realized when Frank first spies on Helen naked in the bathroom, and later on when he tries to lure her to his room. Helen, despite strong doubts, finds herself falling in love with Frank, but refuses his sexual advances. She seeks a good man to escape the tragedy of the past, and Frank resolves to be the kind of person Helen wants him to be.

Helen wants to be more self-disciplined and tells Frank he needs to be also. Frank empties stolen cash from his wallet into the register and finds joy that he now has control over his life. A moment later, however, after Helen calls for him to meet her that evening in the park, Frank takes back a dollar from the register in order to bring Helen home in a cab. The theft is discovered by Morris and, despite Frank's pleas, Morris exiles Frank from the store.

That evening Frank goes to the park vowing to show his love to Helen. She arrives ahead of him. Ward Minoque, the man who earlier robbed and beat her father, attempts to rape her. She is saved from rape by Frank's intervention, is then raped by him, and curses him as an "uncircumcised dog!"

During Frank's exile, the Bobers' fate becomes worse. They discover that the previous increase in trade is attributable not so much to their assistant as to the illness of the grocer around the corner. The delicatessen closes, but a new, larger, self-service store opens that will surely drive Morris into bankruptcy. At this point, Morris "accidentally" leaves the gas to his bedroom heater turned on while forgetting to light it and is taken to the hospital. Frank saves his life, returns, and again takes over the store, explaining to Ida that he owes something to Morris.

When Morris returns, Frank confesses to him that he is one of the men who robbed him. Morris surprisingly replies that he already knows this, but that he cannot forgive Frank for stealing from the store after he was taken in. Morris sends Frank away once again. Not long after, Morris dies of pneumonia after shoveling the spring snow from the sidewalk for the few customers he has left. At the funeral, Frank tumbles awkwardly into the grave and climbs out again, symbolically reborn.

Frank comes to take over the store again and declares he is a changed man. He works at an all-night coffee shop and returns to the store every morning in time to sell the Polish woman her roll. Declaring his love for Helen, he offers to finance her college education. Helen accepts and realizes that something in him has changed. She thanks him for running the store and supporting the family. One day in April Frank has himself circumcised and feels both "enraged and inspired" by the pain between his legs. "After Passover he became a Jew."

Critical Evaluation:

Bernard Malamud's second novel, *The Assistant*, was an immediate success and within a few years of its publication attained the status of an American classic. Based upon his own experience working behind the counter in his immigrant father's grocery store, this novel establishes Malamud as a major American writer. Along with Saul Bellow and Philip Roth, Malamud is the third Jewish American writer whose ascendance in American literature results from portraits of the Jew as a persuasive symbol of Everyman. The problem of marginality, of alienation and living on the edge, is central to the Jewish experience, and in their fiction these authors present an ambiguous, complex universe in which Everyman is trying to survive.

Influenced by existentialism, Malamud uses Jewishness as an ethical symbol. In his works, the Jew becomes the metaphor for the universal good person who must endure great suffering while striving to withstand the dehumanizing pressures of the world. Malamud's central metaphor of Jewishness is the prison (the grocery store in *The Assistant*), a perfect symbol for the human and, most particularly, the Jewish condition.

A predominant theme in modern Jewish prose, Malamud's in particular, is that when one strives to accommodate oneself to the world, one loses oneself in the process. In his portrait of Morris Bober in *The Assistant*, Malamud is concerned with self and its standing quarrel with an aggressively materialistic American culture. Malamud reverses the traditional American success story, as Morris and later Frank succeed morally only by virtue of their failure in society.

Morris possesses an ancient identity, and his relationship to this identity determines his moral and ethical development. At one point in the novel, Morris tells Frank that the

"Jewish Law" is the basis of his behavior. Later, at Morris's burial, the rabbi dignifies Morris's life by stating that he was "a true Jew" who lived "the Jewish experience" and "with a Jewish heart." Morris suffers and endures, "but with hope."

Malamud's use of Jewish humor and irony helps to explain his conflicting beliefs of optimism and pessimism and the balanced interplay of hope and despair in his art. Morris is a schlemiel, a character from Yiddish folk literature who is repeatedly knocked down by fortune but who always struggles to his feet to try his luck again. Hoping for the best but expecting the worst, Morris is constantly aware of the absurdity of his situation and his actions in the face of an unlucky fate. Malamud believes that "all men are Jews" because all people have the possibilities to be good. In a world of chaos and suffering, this moral code brings sanity and significance to one's life.

In *The Assistant*, Frank has the possibility of redemption. When Morris dies, the unwitting saint father makes way for the saint-elect prodigal son, the first life creating the pattern and possibility for the second. In continuing Morris's life, Frank fulfills the possibilities of the grocer's actual son, who died while still a child. In suffering for Morris and accepting responsibility, Frank achieves his own redemption, becoming at last an honest and good man. Although his struggle to survive and escape the tragedy of the past is, at the end of the novel, just beginning, Frank has the possibility to be human, to create meaning in life. His purification through pain and suffering and his struggle for rebirth through selfless love and ethical behavior represents Malamud's hope that people can prevail.

Malamud is an intensely moral writer who once said it was the writer's responsibility "to keep civilization from destroying itself." Malamud has consistently emphasized that he bases his writing on a belief in the nobility of the human spirit and that only readers who respect human beings can respect his work. His humane sensibility encompasses both human pain and human potential. He writes in defense of human beings. The humor and irony, tragic vision, and possibility for profound human decency that Malamud weaves throughout *The Assistant* stand as a testament to that defense.

In revealing the mystery of humankind in this brilliant work, Malamud shows faith and a sense of awe for the human capacity to endure. Malamud's work reflects his despair at the futility of humane values in the face of contemporary reality, yet he continues to fill his fictional world with love and beauty, compassion and hope, and to affirm life in spite of its ambiguities.

Milton S. Katz

Further Reading

Alter, Isaka. "The Good Man's Dilemma: *The Natural*, *The Assistant*, and American Materialism." In *Critical Essays on Bernard Malamud*, edited by Joel Salzberg. Boston: G. K. Hall, 1987. Focuses perceptively on the social criticism in Malamud's fiction that most critics generally ignore.

Avery, Evelyn, ed. *The Magic Worlds of Bernard Malamud*. Albany: State University of New York Press, 2001. A wide-ranging collection of essays on Malamud and his writings, including personal memoirs by members of his family and friends and analyses of some of his works. Chapter 8, "Zen Buddhism and *The Assistant*: A Grocery as a Training Monastery," discusses this novel.

Bloom, Harold, ed. *Bernard Malamud*. New York: Chelsea House, 2000. A collection of essays assessing the entire spectrum of Malamud's works. Includes a chronology of his life and a bibliography.

Cappell, Ezra. "Reflecting the World: Bernard Malamud's Post-Holocaust Judaism." In *American Talmud: The Cultural Work of Jewish American Fiction*. Albany: State University of New York Press, 2007. Cappell analyzes the fiction of Malamud and other American Jewish writers to examine how this fiction is linked to religious texts and traditions. He argues that these writers can be viewed as creating a new form of Jewish rabbinic scripture. The chapter on Malamud includes information on *The Assistant*.

Codde, Philippe. *The Jewish American Novel*. West Lafayette, Ind.: Purdue University Press, 2007. Malamud's novels are among those considered in this study of American Jewish novels that enjoyed unprecedented success in the post-World War II period, with Codde describing the reasons for this success.

Davis, Philip. *Bernard Malamud: A Writer's Life*. New York: Oxford University Press, 2007. The first full-length biography. Davis chronicles the events of Malamud's life, describes his writing methods, and connects the events of his life to his work. He also provides literary analysis of Malamud's novels and other fiction. References to *The Assistant* are listed in the index.

Freedman, William. "From Bernard Malamud with Discipline and Love (*The Assistant* and *The Natural*)." In *Bernard Malamud: A Collection of Critical Essays*, edited by Leslie A. Field and Joyce W. Field. Rev. ed. Englewood Cliffs, N.J.: Prentice-Hall, 1975. Analyzes how Frank Alpine, through submitting to the will of Morris Bober and his own conscience, undergoes a spiritual and psychic conversion. Frank is transformed from an "uncircumcised dog" to a "man of stern morality."

Helterman, Jeffrey. *Understanding Bernard Malamud*. Columbia: University of South Carolina Press, 1985. A highly readable guide. Chapter 3 discusses the themes, use of language, points of view, structure, and symbolism of *The Assistant*. The annotated bibliography is especially useful.

Hershinow, Sheldon J. *Bernard Malamud*. New York: Frederick Ungar, 1980. Offers a comprehensive analysis of *The Assistant*, discussing the themes of suffering and redemption, how Malamud relates to the American Dream of success, his use of Jewish humor and irony, and the skillful use of language in the novel.

Richman, Sidney. *Bernard Malamud*. Boston: Twayne, 1966. Chapter 3 provides an excellent, detailed analysis of *The Assistant*. The author concludes that *The Assistant* brought to literature a sense of awe for humanity's capacity to endure and for humanity's enigmatic powers of creation.

L'Assommoir

Author: Émile Zola (1840-1902)
First published: 1877 (English translation, 1879)
Type of work: Novel
Type of plot: Naturalism
Time of plot: Second half of the nineteenth century
Locale: Paris

Principal characters:
GERVAISE, a laundress
COUPEAU, her husband, a roofer
LANTIER, her lover and the father of her first two children
ADÈLE, Lantier's mistress
GOUJET, a neighbor secretly in love with Gervaise
NANA, the daughter of Gervaise and Coupeau
VIRGINIE, Adèle's sister

The Story:

Gervaise is waiting all night for her lover, Lantier, to come back to their quarters in Paris. When he finally comes home, he treats her brutally and does not display the least affection toward Claude and Étienne, their two children. He stretches out on the bed and sends Gervaise off to the laundry where she works.

When she was thirteen years old, Gervaise left her country town and her family to follow Lantier; she was only fourteen years old when Étienne was born. Her family was cruel to her, but until recently Lantier treated her kindly. Gervaise knows that Lantier was under the influence of both the dram shop and of Adèle, a pretty prostitute.

Gervaise is rather pretty, but she has a slight limp which, when she is tired, becomes worse; the hard life she lives also marks her face, although she is only twenty-two. She would be perfectly happy working hard for her own home and a decent life for her children, but all she has ever known is endless hardship and insecurity.

At the laundry she finds some relief in confiding her story to Madame Boche, an older woman who becomes her friend. Suddenly the children come running in with word that Lantier has deserted the three of them to go away with Adèle and that he took with him everything they own.

Gervaise's first thought is for her children, and she wonders what will become of them. Soon, however, she is roused to anger by the insults of Virginie, Adèle's sister; Virginie came to the laundry for the sadistic pleasure of watching how Gervaise would take the triumph of her rival. Gervaise is quite frail and much smaller than Virginie; nevertheless, she jumps toward her, full of rage. A struggle follows, in which the two women use pieces of laundry equipment and wet clothes to beat each other. Surprisingly, Gervaise, who gives all of her strength, comes out victorious. Virginie never forgives her.

Madame Fauconnier, proprietress of a laundry, gives Gervaise work in her establishment. There she earns just enough money to provide for herself and her children. Another person interested in Gervaise is Coupeau, a roofer who knows all the circumstances of her unhappy life. He would like for her to live with him. Gervaise prefers to devote herself entirely to her two small boys; but one day, when Coupeau proposes marriage to her, she is overcome by emotion and accepts him.

The situation is not very promising at first because the couple has no money. Coupeau's sister and brother-in-law, who are as miserly as they are prosperous, openly disapprove of his marriage. Slowly, perseverance in hard work make it possible for Coupeau and his new family to lead a decent life and even to put a little money aside. Gervaise has quite an excellent reputation as a laundress, and she often dreams of owning her own shop. A little girl, Nana, is born to the couple four years later. Gervaise resumes working soon afterward.

This good fortune, however, cannot last. While Coupeau is working on a roof, Nana diverts his attention for a split second and he falls. Gervaise, refusing to let him be taken to the hospital, insists on caring for him at home. Coupeau somehow survives, but his recovery is very slow. Worse, inactivity has a bad effect on him. He has no more ambition, not even that of supporting his family. He also goes more and more often to the dram shop.

Meanwhile, Gervaise is preparing to give up her dream of a little shop of her own when Goujet, a neighbor secretly in love with her, insists that she borrow the five hundred francs he offers her as a gesture of friendship. She opens her shop and soon has it running successfully.

Goujet's money is never returned. Instead, the family's debts keep progressively increasing, for Coupeau remains idle and continues drinking. Gervaise, accustomed to a few small luxuries, is not as thrifty as she once was. Actually, she still feels quite confident that she will be able soon to meet her obligations; she has a very good reputation in the whole neighborhood.

At this point, Virginie returns, pretending that she has forgotten the fight in the laundry. At first, Gervaise is a little startled to discover that her old enemy is going to be her neighbor once more. Unprejudiced, however, she has no objection to being on friendly terms with Virginie.

Then Lantier comes back. When Gervaise hears from Virginie that he deserted Adèle and is seen again in the neighborhood, Gervaise is badly frightened. However, her former lover makes no attempt to see her and she forgets her fears.

Lantier waits to make a spectacular entrance. He chooses to appear in the middle of a birthday party hosted by Gervaise. Most unexpectedly, Coupeau, who by that time is continuously drunk, invites him in. During the weeks that follow, the two men become drinking companions. Later on, Lantier suggests that he might live and board with the Coupeau family. Gervaise's husband, in a state of degeneration, welcomes the idea.

Although the agreement is that Lantier is to pay his share of the expenses, he never keeps his promise, and Gervaise finds herself with two men to support instead of one. Furthermore, Lantier completely takes over the household and runs it as he pleases. Still a charming seducer, he is extremely popular with the women of the neighborhood.

Gervaise herself begins to degenerate. Disgusted by her husband, she cannot find the strength to refuse the embraces of her former lover. Before long her work suffers from such a state of affairs, and she eventually loses the shop. Virginie buys it and, at the same time, wins the favors of Lantier.

Meanwhile, Nana, almost grown up, is placed as an apprentice in a flower shop. When she decides to leave home for the streets, Gervaise gives up all interest in life and joins Coupeau in the dram shop. After he finally dies of delirium tremens, she tries walking the streets, but nobody will have her, wretched as she is. Goujet's timid efforts to help her are useless. Completely worn out by all the demands that were made on her, she dies alone.

Critical Evaluation:

L'Assommoir is the seventh in a series of twenty novels written by Émile Zola about several generations of the Rougon-Macquart family. It is one of the first such generational series and is carefully shaped by the author according to his controversial ideas for a novel that would parallel, he hoped, the objective observation he admired in the natural sciences. His notion was to treat his characters something like guinea pigs in a world that he would create for them. Narrative impartiality and objectivity were paramount.

Not surprisingly, a public that had loved the romantic version of the poor offered them in Victor Hugo's *Les Miserables* (1862) was outraged by the squalor that Zola describes in *L'Assommoir.* The raw language and the clear parallels that the author draws between his characters and barnyard animals disgusted many readers, who found such a depiction threatening to their belief that the human soul raises men and women above the frailties of their bodies. *L'Assommoir* also indicts readers who imagine the poor are ennobled by horrible living conditions.

Zola defended the book as the first novel about working-class people that does not lie about their daily lives. He claimed that the characters in *L'Assommoir* are not evil but ignorant and victimized by the crushing work that fills their days. Pointing to the collapse of Gervaise and the others, he described the novel as morality in action, implicitly teaching his readers a lesson in the consequences of alcohol, lethargy, jealousy, and irresponsibility.

Many find the novel quite painful to read, since the downfall of several of its well-meaning characters is relentless and even cruel. The narration and characterization are truly compelling, more like a classic Greek tragedy than a soap opera, and many readers find the experience one they never forget. Gervaise—with her limp, her youthfulness, her determination, her hard work, and her resilience in the face of great odds—wins over most readers, who cheer her success against Virginie and her initial financial good sense. Zola does all that can be expected of an author to offer readers a sympathetic character. This makes her destruction all the more painful. At the same time, he shows the less admirable side of her character—her self-destructive desire to please—and plots its effect in her disastrous decisions. She and Coupeau do not have enough character or self-definition to resist their environment; instead, they allow themselves to be shaped by it.

Except for the wedding party's interesting trip to the Louvre museum, the novel takes place exclusively within a very cramped space around Montmartre cathedral in Paris. Part of Zola's purpose in the novel is to demonstrate that the imperial grandeur that Louis Napoleon brought to Paris, the result of tearing down old tenements and replacing them with more expensive housing and broad boulevards, displaced the poorer elements of society and crowded them too closely together. The result, he shows in this novel and others of the series, is a kind of reverse evolution—a resurgence of the animal nature in his characters. The devolution accelerates under the influence of peer pressure, drunkenness, and physical abuse (the book's title can also be translated "bludgeon").

Zola was greatly influenced by Charles Darwin's notion of evolution and genetic inheritance and by the social Darwinism that applied biological principles to social theory. Zola's experiment in this novel is a demonstration of the depressing consequences of the survival of the fittest, since in the inhuman world of the nineteenth century Parisian poor, immoral characters such as Lantier and Virginie seem better suited to fight their way to victory. In later novels in the series, Zola charts the history of Gervaise's daughter, Nana, whose prostitution brings her more raw success than her mother's hard work and affability ever achieved. As weak as Gervaise may ultimately appear to be, however, her final decision to refuse Goujet's love raises the melodrama to the level of tragedy. She has come to know her own limitations, and, loving Goujet as he loves her, she decides to go to her death alone rather than drag him down as well. The reader is left to decide whether the fittest deserve to survive.

Many critics consider *L'Assommoir* and *Germinal* (1885) the best of the novels in the Rougon-Macquart series because they most successfully wed Zola's experimental techniques to his naturalism. These were the elements that Henry James so admired in Zola's work and that influenced the American naturalists (such as Frank Norris, Theodore Dreiser, Steven Crane, and Upton Sinclair). This is saying much, because the Rougon-Macquart series is considered the finest of his productions.

Zola was not as interested in portraying psychological states as in presenting the physical world in which his characters lived and in which their personalities took shape. In *L'Assommoir*, as in his other novels, the buildings, the gutters, the machines, take on an importance and prominence that had been missing in much earlier fiction. Rather than have his characters discuss the philosophy behind their existence, he "embodied" the ideas in the environment in which he placed his creations. It is of utmost importance to Zola that Gervaise and Coupeau were born in a particular place, to parents with a particular history, and that they ended up echoing each other's characteristics in the way that—inevitably—would drag them down. Their heredity, their historical moment, and their environment determine the choices that are presented to them and determine the decisions they make in response.

"Critical Evaluation" by John C. Hawley

Further Reading

Baguley, David, ed. *Critical Essays on Émile Zola*. Boston: G. K. Hall, 1986. A collection tracing the history of critical responses to Zola, including the poet Algernon Charles Swinburne's famous condemnation of *L'Assommoir*.

Berg, William J., and Laurey K. Martin. *Émile Zola Revisited*. New York: Twayne, 1992. Focuses on *The Rougon-Macquart* series, using textual analysis and Zola's literary-scientific principles to analyze each of the twenty novels.

Brooks, Peter. "Zola's Combustion Chamber." In *Realist Vision*. New Haven, Conn.: Yale University Press, 2005. Zola's novels are among the works of literature and art that are examined in this study of the realist tradition in France and England during the nineteenth and twentieth centuries.

Brown, Frederick. *Zola: A Life*. New York: Farrar, Straus and Giroux, 1995. A detailed and extensive biography of Zola that discusses his fiction and the intellectual life of France, of which he was an important part. Shows how Zola's naturalism was developed out of the intellectual and political ferment of his time; argues that this naturalism was a highly studied and artificial approach to reality.

Gallois, William. *Zola: The History of Capitalism*. New York: Peter Lang, 2000. Interprets *The Rougon-Macquart* novels as a history of capitalism, drawing connections between Zola's novels and the work of economists and sociologists Karl Marx, Max Weber, and Émile Durkheim. Includes bibliography and index.

Haavik, Kristof Haakon. "*L'Assommoir*: A World of Death." In *In Mortal Combat: The Conflict of Life and Death in*

Zola's "Rougon-Macquart." Birmingham, Ala.: Summa, 2000. Argues that life and death "are bitterly opposed forces" in *The Rougon-Macquart* series, and the "epic struggle" between them is the "central unifying thread" of the series.

King, Graham. *Garden of Zola: Émile Zola and His Novels for English Readers*. New York: Barnes & Noble, 1978. Describes *L'Assommoir*'s compulsive readability, a result of its rise-and-fall structure. Discusses the reception of the novel, its imagery, and much else.

Lethbridge, Robert. "Reading the Songs of *L'Assommoir*." *French Studies: A Quarterly Review* 45, no. 4 (October, 1991): 435-445. Describes the twenty songs in the novel and their context in the plot, showing the upsetting hybridity of the narration: Zola invites the reader ironically to observe the peasants, yet at the same time excludes the reader with the songs.

_______. "A Visit to the Louvre: *L'Assommoir* Revisited." *Modern Language Review* 87, no. 1 (January, 1992): 41-55. Demonstrates in detail what the characters notice and avoid in their visit to the Louvre. Shows the mutually self-defining distinction between verbal and pictorial cultures.

Nelson, Brian, ed. *The Cambridge Companion to Émile Zola*. New York: Cambridge University Press, 2007. Collection of essays, including discussions of Zola and the nineteenth century, his depiction of society, sex, and gender, and Zola's utopias. Includes a summary of Zola's novels, a family tree of the Rougon-Macquarts, a bibliography, and an index.

Astrophel and Stella

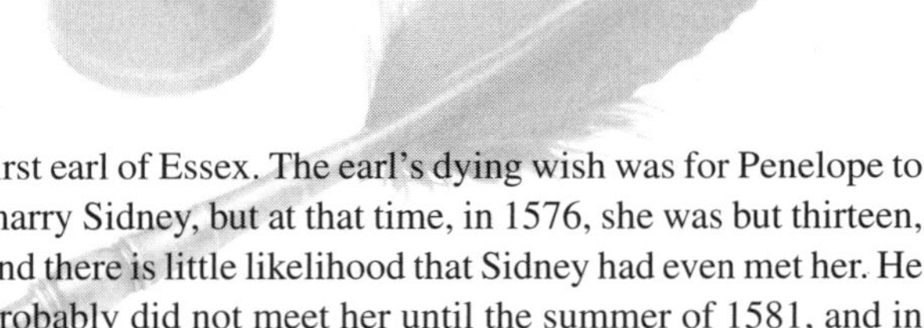

Author: Sir Philip Sidney (1554-1586)
First published: 1591
Type of work: Poetry

Although an imitation of the much earlier Italian sonnets of Francesco Petrarca (1304-1374), better known as Petrarch, Sir Philip Sidney's sonnet sequence *Astrophel and Stella* helped create the vogue for that genre in late Elizabethan England. It was the first great Elizabethan sonnet sequence, predating William Shakespeare's by at least a decade. For the student of Sidney's life and poetry, it has additional interest for its autobiographical implications, reflecting Sidney's vain attempt to woo Penelope Devereux (1563-1607).

Born to an influential noble family, Sidney considered his most important role in English letters to be that of a patron rather than a poet. His support of poets Edward Dyer, Fulke Greville, and Edmund Spenser (whose *The Shepheardes Calender* of 1579 was dedicated to Sidney) expressed his conviction that the English language could rival French and Italian in poetic beauty, a conviction he expressed in his posthumously published *Defence of Poesie* (1595). Sidney's poetry was well known among Elizabethan noblemen but not published until after his death.

Although it is easy to exaggerate the autobiographical element in the *Astrophel and Stella* sonnets, there is little doubt about the identity of the two main characters of the title. "Stella" is Penelope Devereux, the beautiful daughter of the first earl of Essex. The earl's dying wish was for Penelope to marry Sidney, but at that time, in 1576, she was but thirteen, and there is little likelihood that Sidney had even met her. He probably did not meet her until the summer of 1581, and in November of that year she married Robert, third Baron Rich.

By bestowing the pseudonym "Stella" on the object of his sonnets, Sidney was following the pattern in amorous poetry set by Petrarch, who in his sonnets celebrated his beloved under the name of "Laura." However, with the name Stella, Sidney attains further significance, for as well as being a female name it is the Latin word for "star." The speaker of the sonnets, then, the lover of Stella, is aptly named Astrophel, or "star-lover" in Greek; moreover, the "phil" coyly echoes Sidney's first name. There is no doubt about associating Astrophel with Sidney: Sonnet 30 indicates that Astrophel's father is governor of Ireland, as was Sidney's, and sonnet 65 describes Astrophel's coat of arms, which is clearly that of the Sidney family. (Similarly, the Devereux coat of arms is described as Stella's in sonnet 13.)

Sidney's sonnets, like Petrarch's, form a "sequence," a group of sonnets each of which is an artistic whole, yet which together develop a pattern of ideas. This pattern is not a "story" or "plot," for the form is not narrative, but a development of character or emotions. Each sonnet explores a slightly different aspect of the love between Astrophel and his Stella, and from one sonnet to another their situation changes. Throughout the sequence, Stella is already married to another (an indication, though not proof, that they were all written after November, 1581); what changes is her treatment of Astrophel. Properly scornful of his advances at first, she gradually relents, giving him a kiss in sonnet 74. Interspersed with the 108 sonnets are eleven "songs" in various meters, the last of which includes Stella's voice (which does not appear in the sonnets) debating with Astrophel. By that point—only four sonnets follow this last song—Stella regrets having given her heart to Astrophel, and he is constrained to leave.

Sidney shows amazing structural inventiveness in these sonnets and varies their rhyme schemes considerably. Petrarch's sonnets display the complex rhyming pattern that a rhyme-rich language such as Italian makes possible: It is basically a two-part pattern, in which the first eight lines form a single unit (octave) and rhyme *abbaabba*, and the last six lines form another unit (sestet) and rhyme variously but with never more than three rhyme sounds. To duplicate this pattern in English is more difficult, since there are fewer rhyming words for any given sound than in Italian. Nevertheless, Sidney does so in many of the sonnets: Even when he varies the *abba* pattern with alternating rhyme, he still uses only one rhyme sound—*abababab*—in the octave. Within the basic two-part structure of the Petrarchan sonnet, however, Sidney introduces an innovation that anticipates the Shakespearean form: The octave divides further into two quatrains (sets of four lines), and the sestet is often yet another quatrain followed by a couplet (a rhymed pair).

The first *Astrophel and Stella* sonnet serves as an introduction to the whole, being a sort of sonnet on how to write a sonnet. Anxious to please Stella, the speaker decides to send her poetry but cannot decide how to go about writing it. After all his ideas are exhausted, the poet-lover finds his answer in the last line: "'Fool,' said my Muse to me, 'look in thy heart and write.'" The second sonnet then flashes back, revealing the course of his love for Stella, which develops gradually, "Not at first sight." After a few more sonnets declaring his love for Stella, Astrophel admits in sonnet 5 that reason is better than love, that love is an illusion, that true beauty is the eternal beauty of virtue—and yet he still loves Stella.

The sonnet 6 is another sonnet about sonnets. Like the first, it contrasts the imitative nature of other lover-poets with the honest simplicity of the heart that the muse advises Astrophel to consult in sonnet 1. Sidney returns to this topic in sonnet 15, where he lists types of bad poets and contrasts them to himself, whose only muse is Stella. The muses, or goddesses of inspiration in classical mythology, appear in seven of the sonnets (1, 3, 6, 55, 60, 77, and 84) and are contrasted to Stella, who is Astrophel's muse.

The fact that Stella is married, and thus that Astrophel's love for her is adulterous, was a long-standing Petrarchan tradition: It allows for an idealization of the lady and of the love, which is usually presented as unconsummated. The troublesome husband is usually not acknowledged in Petrarchan sonnets. In *Astrophel and Stella* the husband is referred to directly in only three sonnets. All three, however, contain puns on the name of Penelope's real-life husband, Lord Rich. In the first of these, sonnet 24, "rich" is the first and the last word of the sonnet: "Rich fools there be," it opens, and after discussing rich fools in general, and the rich fool who happens to be married to Stella in particular, Astrophel curses the fate that made this fool rich in Stella's love and cries in the last line, "Let him . . . grow in only folly rich." The pun on Lord Rich's name recurs in sonnet 35 ("Fame/ Doth grow ever rich, naming my Stella's name") and in sonnet 37, which laments that, though Stella is rich in everything, she "Hath no misfortune, but that Rich she is"—that is, that her name is Rich.

Despite these broad hints, the major conflict in the sonnet sequence is not between the two rivals for Stella's heart; since he is not much of a presence in the sonnets, the husband is not much of a threat to Astrophel there, whatever his status outside the world of the sonnets might be. What stands between Astrophel and Stella is not so much a real husband as the idea of a husband—or, to put it in the terms used in the sequence, the conflict is between Love and Virtue. Both Love and Virtue appear as allegorical characters, or personified abstractions. Love, in fact, appears under two names, Love and Cupid. Since Love is often referred to in *Astrophel and Stella* as the blind boy with the bow, the reader can properly consider them two names for the same character.

Love personified appears in 44 out of 108 (more than 40 percent) of the sonnets and in six out of eleven (more than half) the songs. The characterization of Love as a supernatural being influencing Astrophel is one of Sidney's triumphs, and it allows him to analyze and record the complex psychology of love in the poetry. Love is in turn a "Lieutenant" in the wars of passion (sonnet 36), a military conqueror (42, 43), a scholar (46), and an eternal boy (sonnet 73 and song 2).

The conflict between Love and Virtue is the subject of sonnet 52, but it appears explicitly in six other sonnets, 5, 25, 31, 48, 62, and 72. The first time Virtue and Love are mentioned together, the conflict is not seen: Virtue is embodied in Stella, who engenders Love in Astrophel. However, the power of Virtue to make Astrophel "burn in love" (sonnet 25) produces an irony: that very Virtue will not allow Stella, while another man's wife, to return Astrophel's love. Astrophel turns this moral irony into a sophistical seduction poem in sonnet 52. He argues that, while Stella's "fair outside" belongs to Love, her soul belongs to Virtue. Until the final couplet, it sounds as if Astrophel is making the argument of traditional morality: The spiritual beauty that is the stuff of Virtue outweighs the merely physical beauty that is the stuff of Love. Then come the last two lines: "Let Virtue have that Stella's self; yet thus/ That Virtue yet that body grant to us." Thus Astrophel tries to have his cake and eat it, too, to satisfy both Virtue and Love.

A memorable element of the *Astrophel and Stella* sonnets is the striking physical description of Stella. Not that description itself is unusual; the "vertical description" of the beloved, from head to toe, is a hallmark of the Petrarchan sonnet tradition. What is unusual is Sidney's departure from the Petrarchan cliché of the blue-eyed blonde as the feminine ideal to that of a dark beauty. The minor poet Henry Constable, to whom Lady Rich was later a patron, confirmed Astrophel-Sidney's description when he wrote of Penelope's "black sparkling eyes."

In *Astrophel and Stella*, Sidney extended the range of the Petrarchan sonnet sequence and led the way for other English imitators of the Italian sonneteers. They transcended imitation by inverting many of the conventions and probing various psychological states of the lover. Moreover, they are the first English sonnets to include the voice of the woman, thereby forcing the character of the lover to display greater subtlety than had prevailed before in English verse.

John R. Holmes

Further Reading

Berry, Edward. *The Making of Sir Philip Sidney*. Toronto, Ont.: University of Toronto Press, 1998. A combination of biography, literary criticism, and social history, in which Berry describes how Sidney created himself as a poet by creating depictions of himself in some of his characters, including Astrophel in *Astrophel and Stella*.

Hamilton, A. C. *Sir Philip Sidney: A Study of His Life and Works*. New York: Cambridge University Press, 1977. A critical biography based on original sources, which also analyzes Sidney's works in the probable order of their composition and provides insight into his development as a poet.

Kalstone, David. *Sidney's Poetry: Contexts and Interpretations*. Cambridge, Mass.: Harvard University Press, 1965. A specialized study focusing on the way Sidney reinvented the Italian poetic genres in English. Offers excellent analyses of the *Astrophel and Stella* sonnets in a form accessible to the general reader.

Kay, Dennis, ed. *Sir Philip Sidney: An Anthology of Modern Criticism*. New York: Oxford University Press, 1987. A collection of essays, most of them previously published, that concern all aspects of Sidney's writings, among them several dealing exclusively with the *Astrophel and Stella* sonnets.

Parker, Tom W. N. "Philip Sidney and Proportional Form: *Astrophel and Stella*, *Certaine Sonets*, and Bruno's *De gli eroici furori*." In *Proportional Form in the Sonnets of the Sidney Circle: Loving in Truth*. New York: Oxford University Press, 1998. A study of *Astrophel and Stella* and the other sonnet sequences that were popular in the late sixteenth century. Analyzes the work of Sidney, Giordano Bruno, and other poets, describing the patterns of their sonnet sequences. Argues that their arrangement of sonnets enabled the poets to use the "hymns of love" as a vehicle for expressing broader cosmological issues.

Rudenstine, Neil L. *Sidney's Poetic Development*. Cambridge, Mass.: Harvard University Press, 1967. A chronological study of Sidney's poetic works, which includes a detailed discussion of the *Astrophel and Stella* sonnets.

Stewart, Alan. *Philip Sidney: A Double Life*. London: Chatto & Windus, 2000. The title of this biography refers to the fact that the handsome, well-born, and talented Sidney was belittled in England by Elizabeth I, while he was acclaimed for his writing and statesmanship on the Continent.

Weiner, Andrew D. *Sir Philip Sidney and the Poetics of Protestantism*. Minneapolis: University of Minnesota Press, 1978. Provides helpful readings of Sidney's poetry, though limited by a critical theoretical approach, then in vogue, that connects sixteenth and seventeenth century theology and poetry. In the case of the *Astrophel and Stella* sonnets, this critical approach is quite illuminating, though a bit specialized for the general reader.

Atala

Author: François-René de Chateaubriand (1768-1848)
First published: 1801 (English translation, 1802)
Type of work: Novel
Type of plot: Philosophical realism
Time of plot: Early eighteenth century
Locale: Louisiana

Principal characters:
ATALA, an Indian maiden
CHACTAS, the beloved of Atala
FATHER AUBREY, a missionary

The Story:

Chactas is an old, blind, and wise Indian of the tribe of Natchez, whose hunting ground is in the territory of Louisiana. Because of his great age and deep wisdom gained through countless years of tragic misfortune, Chactas is the patriarch of the tribe. Thus it is that when a young Frenchman named René presents himself for membership in the tribe in the year 1725, it is Chactas who questions him to determine his fitness to join the Natchez nation. Finding René fixed in his determination to become one of the tribe, Chactas accepts him. As the Indians prepare for a beaver hunt, Chactas—even though he is blind—is made the leader of the party. One night as they lie in their canoes, Chactas recites the story of his adventures to René.

When Chactas had lived but seventeen summers, his father was killed in battle and he himself was taken prisoner by the enemy and led away by the Spaniards to St. Augustine. There he was befriended by an old Castilian named Lopez and his sister. The two white people cared for the young man and tried to educate him as their son. After thirty moons had passed, however, Chactas tired of this civilized life and begged Lopez to allow him to return to his people. Lopez, knowing the dangers awaiting a lonely youth in the forests, at first tried to dissuade Chactas. At last, seeing that the youth was firm in his resolve, the old man sent him on his way with his blessing.

The warning given by the good Lopez soon proved correct. Chactas, having lost his way in the woods, was captured by an enemy tribe and taken to their village to await death by burning. Because of his youth and bravery, the women of the tribe took pity on him. One night, as he sat by the campfire, he heard a rustling and then felt the presence of a woman beside him. In low tones, she told him that she was Atala, daughter of the chief and his wife, now dead. She asked Chactas if he was a Christian, and when he told her that he had not forsaken the gods of his father, she departed.

For many days the tribe marched, taking Chactas with them, and each night Atala visited him by the fire. One night, after Chactas was tied to a tree, Atala appeared and told his guard that she would watch the prisoner for a time. Since she was the daughter of the chief, the guard gladly gave her his place. She quickly untied the cords and gave Chactas his freedom, but, just as quickly, he placed the cords in her hand, telling her that he wanted to be chained to her forever. She cried out in anguish that their religions separated them. She also seemed to have some other terrible secret that she feared he would learn. Atala begged him to flee without her, but Chactas said that he would rather die by fire than leave her. Neither would change, and so Atala tied Chactas again, hoping that soon he would change his mind. Each night they slipped off into the woods together, but Chactas did not possess her, for her God helped her to deny her passion for Chactas. She prayed that the young man might give himself to her God so that one barrier to their love would be broken.

One night, her father's warriors discovered them together. Chactas was returned to the camp and placed under heavy guard. The tribe marched on and came at last to the place where Chactas was to be burned at the stake. Indians gathered from far and near to witness his torture and death at a Feast of the Dead. Chactas was prepared for his ordeal, his body painted and then laid on the ground with guards lying across the ropes so that they might feel the slightest movement of the prisoner's body. Despite the great precautions, however, Atala again freed him by a ruse, and they made their escape into the forest. Although they were pursued, the Indians were so drunk from celebrating the Feast of the Dead that the pursuit was only halfhearted, and the lovers had little trouble in eluding them.

Nevertheless, the wilderness almost conquered the fugitives, who were ill-prepared for the hardships they now had to endure. Their fates joined, Atala proclaimed her love for Chactas but said that they could never marry. Although she gave their differences in religion as the only reason, Chactas felt that there was more she feared to tell him. At last, upon his urging, she told him her secret. She was not the daughter of the chief, but the illegitimate child of a white man and the chief's wife. When Chactas learned that the white man was his old friend Lopez, he loved her as a sister as well as a lover. It was through Lopez that she had gained her Christian faith, transmitted to her by her mother.

A terrible storm drove them to the shelter of a tree, and while in that refuge, they saw a dog and an old hermit approaching. The hermit was a missionary, Father Aubry, who took them to his grotto and gave them food and shelter. Chactas feared to go, for he was not a Christian, but Father Aubry said that he was one of God's children and made him welcome. When he promised to instruct Chactas in Christianity so that he and Atala could be married, the girl paled at his words.

They learned that Father Aubry spent almost his entire life among the natives, although he could have had a more comfortable life in Europe. A good man, he considered it a privilege and not a sacrifice to endure the hardships and dangers of the wilderness. Atala and Chactas became a part of the little community of Christian natives over whom the good priest presided. After a time, Chactas began to feel the spirit of God in his heart.

One day, returning from a pilgrimage with Father Aubry, Chactas found Atala apparently dying from a mysterious fever. Then they learned what her true secret was. On her deathbed, Atala's mother took the girl's vow that she would always remain a virgin. Her own sin made her want to protect her daughter, and Atala, knowing nothing of real love, gave her vow, which could never be broken. When Father Aubry told the lovers that the bishop in Quebec could release her from her vow, Chactas's heart grew light. In real anguish, Atala then told them that she took poison because she believed Chactas was forever denied to her. There were no remedies for the poison. After receiving the blessing of the priest and the promise of Chactas that he would embrace the Christian religion so that they could be joined in heaven, the poor virgin died. With the priest's aid, Chactas buried his beloved. Then he said good-bye to Father Aubry and once more began his wanderings. Many years passed before he received baptism in the faith of his beloved Atala.

Many years more pass before the daughter of René, whom Chactas adopted, takes the bones of Atala and Father Aubry and Chactas to the land of the Natchez for burial. Chactas and Father Aubry are killed by enemies. The daughter of René tells a curious traveler that he should not grieve. The three friends are together with God.

Critical Evaluation:

A tale of passionate but pure love, *Atala* is another of the stories using the image of the noble savage, which began to find favor in the early nineteenth century. Against a background of the primitive American wilderness, the two lovers and the gentle priest wage a winning battle against sin and paganism. Simplicity and complexity of character are vividly contrasted, the two meeting in Christian faith in the goodness of God. *Atala* was the first of François-René de Chateaubriand's romances to be published, and the book had a tremendous vogue in its own day. The novel was originally planned as part of a much longer work, *The Natchez*, based on Chateaubriand's travels on the American frontier and influenced by his Romantic philosophy.

Atala is one of the significant literary expressions of the Romantic movement which developed essentially in France, Germany, and England in the latter part of the eighteenth century and constituted a revolution in thinking about virtually every phase of life. The aspects of the movement given literary expression in *Atala* include an awareness of the distinction between the true nature of human beings and the apparent or superficial nature that society imposes on them or which they adopt because of the expectations of those around them. The "true self" of Atala is that of a young woman with a natural warmth, compassion for the sufferings of others, and a readiness to love and to be loved. A vow that has societal but not natural force is imposed upon her by her mother; this and a misunderstanding of true religion make it impossible for her to be her natural self.

A second aspect of Romanticism—the "blue flower" concept expressed by Novalis in his *Heinrich von Ofterdingen* (1802; *Henry of Ofterdingen*, 1842—is a recognition that sensitive people may catch glimpses of an ideal (often an ideal love) but that the full ideal is never completely attainable except through intuition or imagination. Love, then, may remain in a pure or ideal state only if it cannot become actual marriage. Chactas's love for Atala remains pure throughout his long life, colored by a tint of sadness for "what might have been," even while it remains more beautiful than it could have been in the realities of marriage, work, home, and children. It is somewhat in this vein that the noble savage is idealized; this image can be idealized by Europeans, because it is known to them almost exclusively through their imaginations.

With nature, it is not the same. European civilization has "tamed" nature. The Romantics (William Wordsworth and Chateaubriand are prime examples) discover and deeply feel the beauties of uncontrolled nature, and *Atala* gives excellent testimony to the harmony of the receptive human spirit with that love of unspoiled nature, even with the hardships it may impose.

Chateaubriand does not represent the full range of Romantic thought; perhaps no single author incorporates all aspects of any literary period, but he is one of France's best prose representatives of European Romanticism.

Further Reading

Call, Michael J. "Atala's Body: Girodet and the Representation of Chateaubriand's Romantic Christianity." In *Comparative Romanticisms: Power, Gender, Subjectivity*, edited by Larry H. Peer and Diane Long Hoeveler. Columbia, S.C.: Camden House, 1998. Discusses *The Burial of Atala*, a painting by Anne-Louis Girodet de Roussy-Trioson, which depicted the burial of Chateaubriand's heroine. Call describes how Girodet's painting represented the Romanticism and religiosity of the novel.

Moscovici, Claudia. "Hybridity and Ethics in Chateaubriand's *Atala*." *Nineteenth Century French Studies* 29, no. 3/4 (2001): 197-216. An analysis of *Atala*, focusing on Chateaubriand's depiction of the Native American, "noble savage" characters and the more "civilized" Europeans. Moscovici maintains that Chateaubriand did not believe that "primitive" and "civilized" societies were "ethical opposites," and by the end of the novel he had transformed "this polarity into a more complex model of hybrid cultural identity."

Nemoianu, Virgil. "The Absent Center of Romantic Prose: Chateaubriand and His Peers." In *The Triumph of Imperfection: The Silver Age of Sociocultural Moderation in Europe, 1815-1848*. Columbia: University of South Carolina Press, 2006. This study of Romantic literature includes an analysis of Chateaubriand's work. Nemoianu argues that in dealing with the revolutionary changes of the nineteenth century, writers, philosophers, and statesmen sought a reconciliation between radical new ideas and past intellectual philosophy.

Porter, Charles A. *Chateaubriand: Composition, Imagination, and Poetry*. Saratoga, Calif.: Anma Libri, 1978. This brief monograph focuses on *Atala* and its companion piece, *René* (1802), discussing their portrayals of and interactions with Christianity.

Porter, Laurence M. "Writing Romantic Epiphany: Atala, Seraphita, Aurelia, Dieu." *Romance Quarterly* 34, no. 4 (November, 1987): 435-442. This article compares the heroine of *Atala* to characters in works by other French Romantics, including Honoré de Balzac, Gérard de Nerval, and Victor Hugo.

Smethurst, Colin. *Chateaubriand: Atala and René*. London: Grant & Cutler, 1995. A concise introductory overview and survey of the two novels' critical reception.

Switzer, Richard. *Chateaubriand*. New York: Twayne, 1971. This book-length study approaches Chateaubriand's literary output from a primarily biographical position. Switzer places *Atala* within the context of Chateaubriand's body of work, relating the text to trends in literature and thought.

Wakefield, David. "Chateaubriand's *Atala* as a Source of Inspiration in Nineteenth-Century Art," In *The French Romantics: Literature and the Visual Arts, 1800-1840*. London: Chaucer, 2007. Focuses on the manner in which Chateaubriand's works revived the French Catholic monarchist tradition, and how painters of the period represented this revival in their art.

Atalanta in Calydon

Author: Algernon Charles Swinburne (1837-1909)
First published: 1865
Type of work: Drama
Type of plot: Tragedy
Time of plot: Antiquity
Locale: Greece

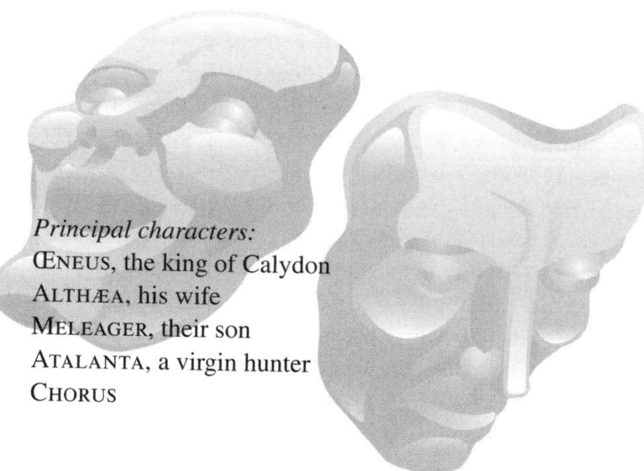

Principal characters:
ŒNEUS, the king of Calydon
ALTHÆA, his wife
MELEAGER, their son
ATALANTA, a virgin hunter
CHORUS

The Story:

Œneus, father of Meleager, offends Artemis, goddess of the hunt, by offering sacrifices to all the gods except her. As a punishment for his negligence, Artemis sends into Calydon a wild boar that ravages the land and the crops.

Althæa, embittered by the curse, refuses to pay homage to Artemis and rages against the gods. Althæa is a woman of strong will and determination. Years before, when her son Meleager was born, she had a strange dream concerning his birth. In the dream, three spinning women, the Fates, visited Althæa and promised that Meleager would have strength, good fortune, and a bounteous life, until the brand on the hearth burned completely. On hearing the last part of the prophecy, Althæa sprang from her bed, grasped the burning brand, and smothered the heat from it with her bare hands and feet. Then, to guard Meleager's life, she hid the brand.

She also dreamed that the heatless brand burst into flame as a bud bursts into flower; with this strange phenomenon, Death came to blow charred ash from the brand into her breast, but there Love quenched the flame. The omen presaged for Althæa the security of her family; but in spite of her great pride, she was not unmindful of the lots that the gods might cast for mortals. These thoughts are in her mind as she goes to arm Meleager for the boar hunt. Never was there so strong a man of royal birth as Meleager. The Chorus, reviewing the life span of human beings, sums up this existence as a passing between a sleep and a sleep.

The warriors of Arcadia join the Calydonians in the hunt, and Meleager and Althæa discuss the qualities and characteristics of these men, among them the valiant sons of Leda, Althæa's sister. Meleager describes Toxeus and Plexippus, Althæa's brothers, as undoing their deeds with too much talk. Althæa counsels her son against having too great pride in earthly accomplishments and advises him to submit his soul to fate. The Chorus admonishes Meleager to follow his mother's counsel.

Recounting the many tumultuous battles he experienced, Meleager points out to his mother that in all these frays he never saw evidence of the infallible gods to whom she and the Chorus would have him submit. Œneus reports the coming of the Arcadians and says that among them is a woman armed for the hunt. Although Œneus wishes to have this woman shown great respect because of her favor from the gods, he warns Meleager against becoming infatuated with her beauty. Althæa, recalling the prophecies of the Fates regarding Meleager's career, adds to her husband's warning against earthly love. Again imploring her son to give himself to fate, she tells him that he will not die as ordinary men die and that his death will be her death as well. Meleager declares his boundless love for his mother and expresses respect for her teaching. Ever faithful to Zeus, the sole determiner of things, he prepares for the hunt.

The Chorus, philosophizing on Love, sees her blind as a flame, covered by earth for hiding, and fronted by laughter to conceal the tears of desire. According to the portent of the Chorus, man and maid will go forth: the maid's name is Fate, the man's name is Death. The Chorus laments also the meagerness of life's span. This futility, an evil blossom born of sea foam and blood froth, came into existence with Aphrodite, goddess of love. Before, there was joy upon the earth, but Aphrodite's influence resulted in suffering, evil, and devastation.

In the hunt, as predicted, Meleager meets the Arcadian maiden. She is Atalanta, the virgin priest of Artemis, whom Œneus neglected in his sacrifices and who sent the wild boar to ravage Calydon. Atalanta invokes Artemis to favor Meleager that he might be victorious in the hunt. Meleager, confessing his love for Atalanta, is taunted by his uncles, Toxeus and Plexippus. Althæa pleads for peace among her kinsmen lest words become snakes and poison them against each other.

The hunt proceeds. According to a message sent by Œneus to Althæa, the expedition demands energy, courage, and hunting strategy. The boar, crazed by the chase and by the numerous wounds inflicted, charges Meleager, who with all daring and skill slays the animal, thereby ridding Calydon of its curse. Althæa offers praise to the gods. The messenger who had brought the message to Althæa adds that pride in earthly accomplishments will bring about destruction. The Chorus, chanting a song of thanksgiving to the gods, is hushed by the messenger, who orders them to change their songs to wails of pity because Toxeus and Plexippus were slain.

Althæa, lamenting the death of her brothers, finds comfort in the thought that Meleager will avenge them. The messenger questions whether her son should slay himself. When Althæa threatens him for his ambiguity, the messenger bluntly informs her that Meleager slew his uncles.

After the boar was killed, Toxeus and Plexippus requested that the head and the hide be kept as a monument in Calydon; but Meleager, enamored of Atalanta, gave her the spoils of the hunt. Pleased with this token of his devotion, Atalanta laughed. The Calydonians construed her reaction as a taunt and sought to destroy her. In furious fighting to protect the maiden, Meleager killed his uncles. Althæa recalls her brothers' kindnesses in their childhood, anticipates her sister's scorn for Meleager's crime, and accepts her fate as a victim of many curses.

The Chorus, endeavoring to comfort Althæa for the loss of her brothers, is rebuked. Had Toxeus and Plexippus died in sacrifice or battle, Althæa maintains, their lives would not have been in vain; but knowing that they were slain by her son, she can never become reconciled to their deaths or to his crime.

In Meleager's deed, caused by excessive earthly pride and undue desire for attainment, Althæa senses her error in taking the burning brand from the fire at the time of his birth.

Stoically, she thrusts the brand into the fire that it might be consumed at last. Althæa suffers with torment and anguish as the Chorus describes the burning, which results in Meleager's death after his return from the hunt.

Meleager reviews his existence without remorse and beseeches Œneus and Althæa not to let his name die. He describes his passing as an empty night harvest in which no man gathers fruit. Althæa dies of sorrow. Atalanta, hailing Meleager's greatness, returns to Arcadia. Œneus rules alone in Calydon.

Critical Evaluation:

Atalanta in Calydon was Algernon Charles Swinburne's first successful work. It was followed in 1866 by the first volume of his *Poems and Ballads*, which contains the shorter poems reckoned to be among his best. *Atalanta in Calydon* is a curiously anomalous work, whose form and manner seem to fly in the face of the aesthetic theories that had possessed Swinburne for five years previously: the theories of the Pre-Raphaelites, as explained to him by Dante Gabriel Rossetti and William Morris. Although it does not represent a frank refusal of the central doctrine of art for art's sake that the Pre-Raphaelites imported from France, *Atalanta in Calydon* departs markedly from their ideas. As an exercise in classical pastiche, it seems to qualify as a deliberate step backward: a temporary but determined retreat toward artistic conservatism.

Swinburne adopted the story of Meleager from Ovid's *Metamorphoses* (before 8 C.E.). There is an older version briefly recounted in Homer's *Iliad* (c. 750 B.C.E.), in which a war between the Calydonians and the Curetes is nearly lost because Meleager refuses to fight after being cursed by his mother, who was angered by the loss in battle of her brother. In the version in the *Iliad*, there is no mention of Atalanta; Meleager is married to a woman named Cleopatra. He also is married in Ovid's version, in which his presentation of the boar's hide to Atalanta—after insisting that she be allowed to join the hunt, against his uncles' wishes—seems to be motivated by simple courtesy. Ovid also added the legend of the symbolic brand, of which Swinburne makes so much—Swinburne's version is shot through with images of life as a consuming fire that ultimately makes ashes of the flesh.

Swinburne did the bulk of the work on *Atalanta in Calydon* at Northcourt, the home of Mary Gordon, with whom he went riding in his spare time. When he returned to London following this interlude, he composed his finest poetry in a hectic rush but also suffered a precipitous decline into alcoholism. Some of his biographers have speculated that he fell in love with Gordon and perhaps proposed to her as a last desperate attempt at heterosexuality. After she decided to marry another man, he rebounded to the dissolute lifestyle that scandalized London society.

However tempting it may be to assume that Swinburne's Atalanta is in some sense an image of Gordon—that its powerful sense of tragedy is simply her rejection of his love—the text does not sustain such an interpretation. Although Swinburne's Meleager is unmarried and strongly attracted to Atalanta, he is determined to suppress his attraction in order to concentrate his mind on the hunt. There seems to be no real need for his father to warn him that the gods have designed Atalanta for celibacy and that she will not make a suitable wife, still less for his mother to complain that his pursuit of strange loves will be the death of her unless he gives it up. In fact, these passages raise the suspicion that in Swinburne's mind, if not in the literal wording of the poem, Atalanta might not be female.

Such a suspicion is intensified by the passage in which Plexippus and Toxeus attempt to bar Atalanta from the hunt. They seem to be ready enough to accept her masculinity; what they attack is the implied femininity of Meleager's fondness for her. Plexippus sneers at Meleager, calling him a "man grown girl" and "woman-tongued," although Meleager already distinguished himself as one of the Argonauts. Atalanta closes the argument by insisting on her "iron maidenhood," winning the right to accompany Meleager on the hunt by insisting on her absolute celibacy. When the messenger tells how Meleager presented the spoils of the hunt to her, however, he describes her response in terms of an explicitly sexual metaphor.

If Atalanta were male in the private arena of Swinburne's imagination, then the anger of the uncles against her and Althæa's wrath against Meleager are cast in a different light. In this way, so is the dying Meleager's final speech, in which he demands that Atalanta "let no man/ Defile me or Despise me, saying, This man/ Died woman-wise, a woman's offering, slain/ Through female fingers in his woof of life,/ Dishonourable." He then begs her to kiss him once and twice.

The prime mover in this particular tragedy, as the Chorus loses no opportunity to remind the reader, is the sadistically insistent fate that has made both Atalanta and Meleager what they are. In an imitation Greek drama, Swinburne certainly would have the option of referring to this fate as Nemesis, or as the manifold gods of the classical pantheon, but he does not. In the remarkable passage that begins, "Who hath given man speech?" the Chorus concludes, after five full pages, with the final question, "Who makes desire, and slays desire with shame?" and the answer, "the supreme evil, God." It then proceeds to rage against that hateful God for three more pages. The Greek setting may have served to veil this calculated blasphemy from the eye of his critics, but Swinburne certainly seems to be addressing the God of the Victorians rather than the obsolete Zeus.

It is hard to see all this as the disappointment of a young man whose proposal to a female lover has been rejected; it makes more sense to construe it as the angry lamentation of a young man cursing nature that forced upon him a pattern of desire that his society, and by extension his God, will not sanction. If this is so, the use of Greek myth and a form approximating that of Greek drama may be explicable in other terms than a temporary reconciliation of the poet with the aesthetic ideals of classicism that the Pre-Raphaelites so disliked. The Greeks were, after all, famed for their tolerance of homosexuality and for encoding homosexual ideals within their myths.

Whatever the reason, *Atalanta in Calydon* was the first work in which Swinburne found an authentic depth of feeling to energize his poetic fluency; it is a pity that the imaginative fuel it provided lasted only a few short years before Theodore Watts-Dunton took Swinburne in hand, putting the brake on his melodramatic self-assassination, and securing for him a long life of physical and creative impotence.

"Critical Evaluation" by Brian Stableford

Further Reading

Cassidy, John A. *Algernon C. Swinburne*. New York: Twayne, 1964. A comprehensive study of Swinburne's life and work. Part 3 of chapter 5 posits that *Atalanta in Calydon* is a response to Mary Gordon's rejection of the marriage proposal that Swinburne may have made.

Henderson, Philip. *Swinburne: The Portrait of a Poet*. London: Routledge & Kegan Paul, 1974. Chapter 6 deals with various works, including *Atalanta in Calydon* and *Poems and Ballads*.

Hyder, Clyde K., ed. *Algernon Swinburne: The Critical Heritage*. New York: Routledge, 1995. A compilation of contemporary reviews and later criticism, tracing the critical reception of Swinburne's work. Includes an introductory essay providing an overview of his life and career.

Louis, Margot Kathleen. *Swinburne and His Gods: The Roots and Growth of Agnostic Poetry*. Montreal: McGill-Queen's University Press, 1990. Tracks the changes in Swinburne's attitude toward fate, in which context *Atalanta in Calydon* is a key work.

Maxwell, Catherine. "Beneath the Woman's and the Water's Kiss: Swinburne's Metamorphoses." In *The Female Sublime from Milton to Swinburne: Bearing Blindness*. New York: Manchester University Press, 2001. Traces John Milton's influence on Swinburne and other Victorian male poets. Argues that these poets attain vision at the cost of "symbolic blindness and feminization."

Rooksby, Rikky, and Nicholas Shrimpton, eds. *The Whole Music of Passion: New Essays on Swinburne*. Brookfield, Vt.: Ashgate, 1993. Collection of essays interpreting Swinburne's poetry, including discussions of Swinburne and Romantic authority, dramatic monologue, and the 1890's, and comparisons of his work with that of George Eliot and Percy Bysshe Shelley.

Rutland, William R. *Swinburne: A Nineteenth Century Hellene*. Oxford, England: Basil Blackwell, 1931. Proposes that Swinburne is an authentic tragedian in the classical tradition. Offers a comprehensive dissection of *Atalanta in Calydon*. Contains a useful appendix on various versions of the story of Meleager.

Atlas Shrugged

Author: Ayn Rand (1905-1982)
First published: 1957
Type of work: Novel
Type of plot: Philosophical realism
Time of plot: The future
Locale: United States

Principal characters:
JOHN GALT, an engineer, inventor, and philosopher
DAGNY TAGGART, a railroad company vice president and heir
JAMES TAGGART, her brother, a railroad company president
HANK REARDEN, a steel magnate and inventor
FRANCISCO D'ANCONIA, a wealthy copper industrialist

The Story:

"Who is John Galt?" asks a man who is walking along the streets of New York City, noticing the grime on the buildings and the cracks in the skyscrapers. Every fourth store is out of business, with windows dark and empty. For some unknown reason, talented people are retiring and disappearing. Pessimism and hopelessness rule.

Dagny Taggart, vice president of Taggart Transcontinental Railroad (TTR), aims to repair the crumbling Rio Norte line that serves the booming industrial area of Colorado. The state is one of the few places in not only the United States but also the world that is still prosperous, largely because of Ellis Wyatt's innovative ideas about extracting oil from shale. Other countries have become socialist states and are destitute.

James Taggart, Dagny's brother and president of TTR, tries to prevent his sister from getting new rail from Rearden Steel, the last reliable steel manufacturer. Industrialist Hank Rearden has developed a promising new alloy, but one that does not have the approval of most metallurgists. James would rather give the business to his friend, Orren Boyle, head of the inefficient Associated Steel. TTR's financial problems worsen when its San Sebastian line is nationalized by the Mexican government. The line, which had cost millions of dollars to construct, had been expected to serve copper mines that are run by an Argentine, Francisco d'Anconia, the world's wealthiest copper industrialist and a former lover of Dagny. D'Anconia, a dissolute playboy, has led his investors astray, thereby contributing to the general unrest.

James, in an effort to revive his company, uses his political clout to persuade the National Alliance of Railroads to pass a rule prohibiting competition. The legislation puts the well-run Phoenix-Durango Railroad, Taggart's competition, out of business. D'Anconia tells Dagny that he deliberately mismanaged his Mexican copper mines to damage d'Anconia Copper and TTR. Dagny is baffled, since d'Anconia had been a brilliant and productive leader.

Rearden and wife celebrate their wedding anniversary. Rearden's mother, brother, and wife argue that the strong are morally obliged to support the weak. Although Rearden regards the three of them with contempt, he goes along and provides for them.

Dagny and Rearden manage to build the Rio Norte line, despite an incompetent contractor and an overwhelming climate of pessimism. Rearden uses his metal to build an innovative bridge, but the State Science Institute tries to bribe him to keep the metal off the market. In retaliation for Rearden's refusal to cooperate, the institute issues a statement alleging possible weaknesses in the structure of Rearden's metal. Taggart's stock crashes, the contractor walks off the job, and the union forbids its members to work on the Rio Norte line.

Dagny decides to take a leave of absence from TTR and build the Rio Norte line on her own. She renames it the John Galt line, in a spirit of optimism. The government passes the Equalization of Opportunity law that prevents an individual from owning a company that does business with another company owned by that same person. Rearden, who has invested in the Galt line, is now prohibited from owning the mines that supply him with the raw materials needed to make his metal. Dagny finishes the line, ahead of schedule, and celebrates with Rearden.

Dagny and Rearden, now a couple, vacation by looking at abandoned factories around the country. At the ruins of the Twentieth Century Motor Company factory in Wisconsin, they find a motor that has the potential to revolutionize the world; but the motor is a wreck. When it worked, it pulled static electricity from the atmosphere and converted it to energy. Dagny determines to find the inventor and help the transportation industry. However, she is forced to devote her energies to opposing proposed government legislation that would force successful businesses to share their profits. Dagny realizes that the law would drive these companies into bankruptcy.

Continuing her quest to find the motor's inventor, Dagny finds the widow of the Twentieth Century Motor engineer who ran the company's research division. The woman tells Dagny that the inventor is a scientist who had worked under her husband. She has forgotten his name but directs her to a cook, who in turn warns Dagny that the inventor will not be found until he wants to be found. Dagny hurries back to Colorado when she learns that Wesley Mouch, the government's economic coordinator, has issued a series of directives that will destroy Colorado's industry. Oilman Wyatt, in response to the dictates, sets fire to his oil wells and retires. With the Wyatt oil wells gone, Colorado's economic climate crumbles. Other major industrialists retire and then vanish. Between cutting rail service, Dagny continues to search for the mysterious inventor.

Rearden sells his metal to another company, but sells more than the government permits and is brought to trial. Rearden refuses to recognize the court's right to try him because he does not consider his business transaction a criminal act. He tells the court that a person has the right to own the product of his or her efforts and to trade it. The government has no moral basis for outlawing the voluntary exchange of goods and services. By attempting to seize his metal, the government is, in effect, robbing him. The crowd applauds

Rearden. The judges acknowledge the truth of his argument and suspend Rearden's sentence.

Even though TTR is losing money, Dagny's brother, James, is persuaded by the government to raise workers' wages. Rumors swirl that the government also might force the railroad to cut shipping rates. A massive train wreck destroys a tunnel and halts all transcontinental train movement.

While heading back to Colorado, Dagny meets a hobo riding the rails. He had once worked for Twentieth Century Motor and tells Dagny that the company followed a communist belief: "From each according to his ability, to each according to his need." This belief, many say, tied the able to the unable, prompting a young engineer to quit the company and to vow to destroy the system. The engineer was named John Galt. Dagny's train stops because of a labor dispute, so she gets on a plane. The plane crashes in the Rocky Mountains, and Dagny finds herself in Atlantis, where the great intellectuals have escaped a dictatorship. She meets Galt and learns that the great minds are all on strike, refusing to participate in forced self-sacrifice.

Dagny falls in love with Galt. He asks her to join the strike, but she feels obligated to return to the railroad. A deeply conflicted Dagny leaves Atlantis, and Galt joins her. He expects that she will soon realize the error of her choice. Upon her return, Dagny discovers that the government has nationalized the railroad industry. Decisions are no longer made on the basis of profit or loss but according to government whims. Forced to go on the radio to express support for nationalization, Dagny tells the public about the dangers of the government takeover before being cut off from speaking further.

As the economy collapses because of the government's socialist policies, politicians put their own interests before those of the public. Railroad cars needed to haul wheat are diverted. Farmers riot in response and abandon their crops. The food supply collapses, leading to starvation.

In a speech, Galt announces that he has taken the "men of the mind" on strike, and he defends his decision to do so. He connects the collapse of the world to the dominance and implementation of a philosophy that is "antimind." Government thugs battle workers loyal to Dagny, but the loyal TTR employees win. Mr. Thompson, head of the state, is just about to speak to the public when a motor of incredible power cuts him off. Galt begins a thirty-five-thousand-word oration on the radio, now in his hands.

Galt asks his listeners who wish to live and recapture honor to choose a pro-life code instead of a philosophy that is antimind. He tells them that they had never truly believed in the dominant philosophy. He argues that the less people feel, the louder they proclaim their selfless love and servitude to others. Existence has become a giant pretense, he says, with everyone lying to everyone else about how they truly feel. Morality and practicality are opposites, and there is no ability to compromise.

Galt then asks his listeners to break this vicious circle. They have betrayed themselves, he says, and have sacrificed their self-esteem. He asks them to embrace an independent, rational consciousness and to glorify thinking. He then tells them how to implement a positive philosophical code and urges them to withdraw from the world, thereby avoiding any further harm to themselves and speeding the return of the workers who think. He says, in elaborating a new society, "I swear by my life and my love of it that I will never live for the sake of another man, nor ask another man to live for mine." Galt's speech brings the strike to a climax.

Critical Evaluation:

In a postscript to *Atlas Shrugged*, Ayn Rand presents her philosophy of objectivism:

> My philosophy, in essence, is the concept of man as a heroic being, with his own happiness as the moral purpose of his life, with productive achievement as his noblest activity, and reason as his only absolute.

The novel presents Rand's philosophical ideas in the form of a mystery.

It is impossible to separate Rand's personal history from the themes in *Atlas Shrugged.* Born Alisa Rosenbaum in St. Petersburg in 1905, Rand experienced first-hand the communist takeover of Russia before emigrating to the United States in 1926. In her youth, she concluded that individual freedom had to be the basis for any moral system of government. A fierce individualist, she saw communism as a sacrifice of the good and best to the mediocre and commonplace. This theme would echo in all of her writings, including her last work of fiction, *Atlas Shrugged.*

Rand has described John Galt's radio speech as her explanation of objectivism, or rational self-interest. Urged by one editor to cut the sixty book pages that make up the speech, she refused to do so, citing the speech's critical importance to the novel. Rand's philosophy, as expressed in *Atlas Shrugged*, still exerts a strong influence upon the political culture of the United States, particularly among free-market conservatives.

The philosophical themes of the book inspired the development of the objectivist philosophical school. Alan Greenspan, part of this school and a key member of Rand's inner circle, effectively became the leading economist of the United States when he became chair of the Federal Reserve Board in 1987. (He served in that position until 2006.) *Atlas Shrugged*, which remains the bible of economic conservatives, is arguably one of the most influential novels ever published.

Caryn E. Neumann

Further Reading

Binswanger, Harry, and Leonard Peikoff, eds. *Ayn Rand: Introduction to Objectivist Epistemology.* 2d ed. New York: Penguin Books, 1990. This second revised and expanded edition reprints a series of articles in which Rand discusses her reasoning processes. Also, more fully describes the philosophy of objectivism.

Gladstein, Mimi Reisel. *"Atlas Shrugged": Manifesto of the Mind.* New York: Twayne, 2000. Essentially a reader's guide to *Atlas Shrugged*, this work examines the book's literary and historical contexts as well as its plot, characters, and themes.

Gladstein, Mimi Reisel, and Chris Matthew Sciabarra, eds. *Feminist Interpretations of Ayn Rand.* University Park: Pennsylvania State University Press, 1999. Rand expressed hostility to feminism in several articles in her own newsletter. Nevertheless, feminist scholars have found Dagny Taggart to be one of the strongest women represented in Western literature and *Atlas Shrugged* to be a celebration of meritocracy.

Mayhew, Robert, ed. *Essays on Ayn Rand's "Atlas Shrugged."* Lanham, Md.: Lexington Books, 2009. Essays cover Rand's character development and the publication history of the novel, its reception, and its adaptation to film. Two essays on John Galt's speech demonstrate the integral role that it plays in the story and how it contributes to the theme.

Pierpont, Claudia Roth. *Passionate Minds: Women Rewriting the World.* New York: Alfred A. Knopf, 2000. Evocative, interpretive essays on the life paths and works of twelve women, including Rand, connecting the circumstances of their lives with the shapes, styles, subjects, and situations of their art.

Rand, Ayn. *For the New Intellectual: The Philosophy of Ayn Rand.* New York: Signet, 1963. Presents arguments for a philosophy based on rational self-interest rather than self-sacrifice. It is essentially a nonfiction companion to *Atlas Shrugged.*

Sciabarra, Chris M. *Ayn Rand: The Russian Radical.* University Park: Pennsylvania State University Press, 1995. Sciabarra charts the evolution of the author as a philosopher, of her dialectics, and of her philosophy, beginning with her early years. Includes a bibliography and photographs.

Walker, Jeff. *The Ayn Rand Cult.* Chicago: Open Court, 1999. Provides a chronology of the objectivist movement as well as a discussion of the effect of Rand's philosophy on her followers, including former Federal Reserve chair Alan Greenspan.

Younkins, Edward W., ed. *Ayn Rand's "Atlas Shrugged": A Philosophical and Literary Companion.* Burlington, Vt.: Ashgate, 2007. Collection of essays discussing *Atlas Shrugged* as a work of literature and philosophy. Includes discussions of the novel's ideas about aesthetics, economics, and human relationships; the novel as a work of science fiction; and its characterization.

Atonement

Author: Ian McEwan (1948-   )
First published: 2001
Type of work: Novel
Type of plot: Psychological realism
Time of plot: 1935, 1940, 1999
Locale: English countryside and London; French countryside and Dunkirk, France; Ireland

Principal characters:
BRIONY TALLIS, a thirteen-year-old girl, later a nurse and novelist
CECILIA TALLIS, her older sister
LEON TALLIS, her older brother
EMILY TALLIS, her mother
JACK TALLIS, her father
LOLA QUINCY,
JACKSON QUINCY and PIERROT QUINCY, visiting cousins of the Tallises
ROBBIE TURNER, the son of the Tallis family's cleaning lady, educated at Cambridge by the Tallises
PAUL MARSHALL, a wealthy friend of Leon from London

The Story:

Briony Tallis, age thirteen, wants her Quincy cousins to perform in a play she has written to celebrate her brother Leon's visit from London with his friend, Paul Marshall. Cecilia Tallis and Robbie Turner, formerly childhood friends, are both back from Cambridge, where they have become distant. When he tries to help her fill a valuable vase with water at a fountain, it breaks; in frustration, Cecilia strips to her underwear in front of him and dives in to recover the pieces. Briony observes this scene from the house and is troubled by what she sees. Meanwhile, her cousin Lola, age fifteen, undermines Briony's plans for the play, and rehearsals are abandoned. Briony walks out to the grounds in frustration.

Leon and Paul arrive from London and, meeting Robbie on the way in, invite him to dinner that night. At his mother's cottage, Robbie writes to Cecilia to apologize about the vase and explain his feelings for her. In one hastily written draft, he describes his desire in explicitly sexual terms; he abandons that version and writes a more appropriate one. On his way across the grounds, he encounters Briony and asks her to take his letter to Cecilia. Only as she reaches the house does he realize he put the sexually explicit letter in the envelope. By the time Cecilia meets him at the door with the letter in her hand, Briony has already read it.

Briony shares the information in the letter as well as the scene by the fountain with Lola; they decide Robbie is dangerous and Cecilia needs protection. Cecilia confronts Robbie in the library, and after they confess their affection for each other, they make love. Briony finds them and believes Robbie is attacking her sister. They all go down to dinner without speaking.

The meal is interrupted by the news that Jackson and Pierrot have run away; everyone disperses to look for them. In the darkness, Briony comes across a man and Lola having sex in the grass. The man sneaks off, and Briony believes it was Robbie; Lola does not contradict her. By the time Robbie returns to the house in the early dawn, bringing the two boys with him, the police are waiting to arrest him. He is convicted of rape and sent to prison; only Cecilia and his mother believe he is innocent.

Five years later, Robbie is in the British army in France, retreating after the fall of the Maginot line. He hides a wound in his side from his two comrades as they make their way to Dunkirk for evacuation. On the way, they dodge attacks by German bombers and attempt to help refugees. For comfort, Robbie thinks about Cecilia and their single meeting between his release from prison and basic training; Cecilia has cut herself off from her family and become a nurse in London, where they met for tea. They made plans to visit a cottage together, but war was declared and Robbie was shipped to France. In the chaos of Dunkirk, he and his comrades wait for the boats to evacuate them to England. His wound grows worse, and he becomes delirious.

Briony, now eighteen, has also entered nursing studies. She has begun to understand that she was mistaken about Robbie and Cecilia, and her doubts are confirmed when she learns that Paul Marshall and Lola Quincy are getting married. Her studies are accelerated when the evacuees begin arriving from France, and she experiences the horrors of nursing wounded soldiers.

On her day off, Briony walks across London to witness Lola and Paul's wedding. In their refusal to acknowledge her, she sees confirmation of her suspicions that Paul was guilty, not Robbie. She continues on to her sister's flat and explains that she wants to recant her earlier testimony. Robbie is visiting Cecilia as well. They are pleased that she will tell the truth about Lola and Paul but show no signs of forgiveness. Briony returns to the hospital determined to write a story that will atone for what she did.

Half a century later, Briony has just finished the novel which forms the earlier portions of *Atonement*. She knows that it cannot be published until after Paul and Lola are dead because they would sue her if it were. She has also just learned that she is losing her memory to vascular dementia. She returns to the Tallis country home, now a hotel, for a family reunion in honor of her birthday. After the party, she stays up late writing and thinking about her attempts to atone for her crime by writing Cecilia and Robbie's story; she admits that she has changed their ending to bring them together, when in fact they both died without seeing one another, or her, ever again.

Critical Evaluation:

Ian McEwan is widely considered to be one of the most important novelists writing in English. He studied with Malcolm Bradbury and August Wilson at the University of East Anglia, and he began winning awards early in his career. These included the 1976 Somerset Maugham Award for his first collection of short stories, *First Love, Last Rites* (1975); the 1987 Whitbread Novel Prize for *The Child in Time* (1987); and the 1998 Man Booker Prize for *Amsterdam* (1998). *Atonement* won the W. H. Smith Literary Award and the National Book Critics' Circle Fiction Award, among others. McEwan has also written children's books, screenplays, and librettos.

McEwan's earlier works earned him the nickname Ian Macabre for their graphic depictions of violence and sex. His work later shifted from elaborately detailed settings and scenes to extensive exploration of characters' thoughts and emotional states. He became interested in language as a medium of both communication and miscommunication, declaring that he wanted to "explore all the comic and tragic possibilities that occur when perfectly well-meaning people can fall foul of each other, simply through misunderstanding."

Atonement hinges on just such misunderstandings. Part 1 of the novel shifts back and forth between Briony's, Cecilia's, and Robbie's perspectives. By showing how each character perceives the events of the day, and how each event leads to further developments and greater misunderstanding, McEwan achieves a remarkable sense of realism both in each individual character and in the unfolding of rather extreme circumstances. In doing so, one reviewer writes, he has created the perfect fictional medium for showing trauma's "blind spots and sneaky obliquities." The central trauma is effaced by the ways the characters deal with its aftermath.

McEwan's interest in language and writing comes through in Briony, the aspiring writer. She is very conscious, at age thirteen, of being on the cusp of adult knowledge and experience, and the danger she thinks Robbie poses to her sister challenges her writerly desire to make her world orderly and clear; she is suddenly aware of "the strangeness of the here and now, of what passed between people, the ordinary people that she knew" and how easy it might be to misunderstand. In casting herself as the heroine who will protect her sister, it is Briony herself who gets it tragically wrong.

Briony's meeting with Cecilia and Robbie in her sister's flat five years later forms a potential turning point in all their lives; however, the jump to 1999 undercuts the sense of closure. Some critics see Briony's afterword as a bit of postmodern sleight of hand, but it continues McEwan's theme of the power and limitations of language. Briony's novel (parts 1 through 3 of the novel) gives her partial atonement by providing space for her sister and Robbie to be together, but as she still worries, "how can a novelist achieve atonement when, with her absolute power of deciding outcomes, she is also God?" She is able to write a happy ending for Robbie and Cecilia, but she is unable to make them forgive her, even in her novel.

The novel's lovers are equally interesting in their own right, negotiating issues of sexual and romantic attraction amid class tensions. Cecilia's higher class status has been upstaged by Robbie's superior performance at Cambridge. Additionally, their time at school together has distanced them from the childhood friends they once were, and they do not immediately recognize their own mutual attraction.

McEwan presents Robbie and Cecilia's scenes with great detail and subtlety, both interior and exterior. Robbie is aware of his feelings for Cecilia first, and as he dresses for dinner he frames his feelings for her in terms of the Freudian theory he read at college. His mistake in sending the sexually explicit letter represents a classic Freudian moment when a repressed desire escapes into expression. The scene in which Cecilia chooses a dress for the dinner party, her feelings for Robbie not yet clear to her, similarly ties physical action to barely acknowledged mental and emotional states.

Atonement is also a historical novel, most dramatically so in the second half of the novel. Robbie's experience of the British retreat to Dunkirk—the culmination of an early, disastrous campaign in France—reflects the futility of his relationship with Cecilia once the series of misunderstandings has been set in motion. Briony's nursing training and role in treating those first waves of casualties similarly casts the uselessness of her actions (attempting to atone by becoming a nurse like Cecilia) in the face of an overwhelming historical event. The scope of the events unfolding around Briony and the lovers in the second half has the effect of elevating their own personal tragedies to the level of the historical.

Ann M. Tandy

Further Reading

Concha, Ángeles de la. "Unravelling Conventions: Or, The Ethics of Deconstruction in Ian McEwan's *Atonement*." In *The Ethical Component in Experimental British Fiction Since the 1960's*, edited by Susana Onega and Jean-Michel Ganteau. Newcastle, England: Cambridge Scholars, 2007. Discusses *Atonement* as an ethical act of moral reparation that is dependent upon its experimental form. Part of a volume of essays on postmodern ethics, traditional morality, and the novel's ability to balance experiment with realism in such as way as to become a space for ethical consciousness.

Finney, Brian. "Briony's Stand Against Oblivion: The Making of Fiction in Ian McEwan's *Atonement*." *Journal of Modern Literature* 27, no. 3 (2004): 68-82. An analysis of the self-conscious fiction-making deployed throughout the novel (not just in Briony's coda at the end) and of the work's many intertextual elements.

Groes, Sebastian, ed. *Ian McEwan: Contemporary Critical Perspectives*. London: Continuum, 2009. Collects a range of scholarly essays addressing McEwan's entire body of work through *On Chesil Beach* (2007). Includes an interview with McEwan and a list of suggested readings.

Head, Dominic. "Ian McEwan." In *Contemporary British Novelists*, edited by Daniel Lea. New York: Manchester University Press, 2007. Analyzes McEwan's entire body of work, particularly addressing themes of morality, feminism, colonialism, and class structure, as well as narrative theories of consciousness. Includes discussion of his connections with and distinctions from other British novelists.

McEwan, Ian. "A Conversation with Ian McEwan." Interview by David Lynn. *Kenyon Review* 29, no. 3 (2007): 38-51. A discussion on topics ranging from the relationship between fiction and history to McEwan's writing process and thoughts on readers.

_______. "Zadie Smith Talks with Ian McEwan." Interview by Zadie Smith. In *The Believer Book of Writers Talking to Writers*, edited by Vendela Vida. San Francisco: Believer, 2005. The authors talk about novels and the power and importance of empathy, the challenges of writing about gender, the novel as a vehicle for investigation, and the ways in which the irrational imposes itself onto the rational.

Malcolm, David. *Understanding Ian McEwan*. Columbia: University of South Carolina Press, 2002. An introduction to shifts in McEwan's works prior to *Atonement* with particular attention to issues of feminism, morality, and fragmentary narratives. Includes a brief but useful section on his less studied works (his children's books, screenplays, and libretto).

Margaronis, Maria. "The Anxiety of Authenticity: Writing Historical Fiction at the End of the Twentieth Century." *History Workshop Journal* 65 (2008): 138-160. An astute consideration of *Atonement* (along with Toni Morrison's *Beloved*, 1987) as a historical novel and the problems of authority.

Mathews, Peter. "The Impression of a Deeper Darkness: Ian McEwan's *Atonement*." *English Studies in Canada* 32, no. 1 (2006): 147-160. Analysis of the issues of knowledge, innocence, secrets, and mysteries in relation to Briony's guilt and atonement.

Aucassin and Nicolette

Author: Unknown
First published: Aucassin et Nicolette, early thirteenth century (English translation, 1880)
Type of work: Novel
Type of plot: Romance and lyric
Time of plot: Twelfth century
Locale: Provence, France

Principal characters:
COUNT GARIN DE BEAUCAIRE
AUCASSIN, his son
NICOLETTE, a slave

The Story:

Count Bougars de Valence and Count Garin de Beaucaire are at war. Count Garin has one son, Aucassin, who is so smitten by love that he will neither accept the duties of knighthood nor participate in his father's quarrel, unless his father consents to his love for Nicolette. She is a slave, bought by a captain of the town from the Saracens and reared as his own daughter. Count Garin agrees to the marriage of Aucassin to any daughter of a king or count but not to Nicolette. He goes to see the captain and tells him to send Nicolette away. The captain says that he will keep Nicolette out of sight, and she is imprisoned in the high chamber of a palace with an old woman to keep her company. Rumors speed through the countryside: Nicolette is lost; Nicolette fled the country; Nicolette was slain by order of Count Garin.

Meanwhile, the war between the two counts grows more fierce, but Aucassin still refuses to fight. Father and son then make a covenant: Aucassin will go into the battle, and if God wills that he should survive, the count must agree to allow him two or three words and one kiss from Nicolette. Aucassin rides into the fray, but thoughts of Nicolette so distract him that he is captured. Then Aucassin reflects that if he is slain, he will have no chance at all to see Nicolette. Therefore, he puts his hand on his sword and begins fighting with all of his strength. He kills ten knights, wounds seven, and takes Count Bougars prisoner. When Count Garin refuses to keep the covenant, Aucassin releases Count Bougars. Aucassin is cast into a dungeon.

Nicolette, knowing her companion to be asleep, escapes from her prison by a rope made of bed linen and goes to the castle where Aucassin lies. While they exchange lovers' vows, the guards came searching for Nicolette, as her escape has been discovered. A friendly sentinel, however, warns Nicolette of their coming. She leaps into the moat and, bruised and bleeding, climbs the outer wall.

Nicolette falls asleep in a thicket near the castle. The next day, she sees some shepherds eating their lunch at a fountain nearby. She asks them to take a message to Aucassin, saying there is a beast in the forest and that he should capture this beast and not part with one of its limbs for any price. Nicolette builds a lodge within the forest and waits to prove her lover's faith.

Aucassin is taken from his prison and allowed to attend a great feast, but he finds no joy in it. A friendly knight offers his horse to Aucassin and suggests that he ride into the forest. Aucassin is only too happy for a chance to get away. He meets the shepherds by the fountain and hears what Nicolette told them. Aucassin prays to God that he will find his quarry.

He rides in haste through the thorny forest. Toward evening, he begins to weep because his search was fruitless. He meets a huge, ugly fellow, leaning on a terrible cudgel. Aucassin tells him that he mourns for a white hound he lost. The burly fellow scornfully replies that he lost his best ox and searched fruitlessly for three days without meat or drink. Aucassin gives the man twenty sols to pay for the beast. They part and go their separate ways.

Aucassin finds the lodge built by Nicolette and rests there that night. Nicolette hears Aucassin singing and comes to him. The next day, they mount Aucassin's horse and journey until they come to the seas. Aucassin and Nicolette board a ship, and a terrible storm carries them to Torelore. First, Aucassin fights with the king of that strange land and then frees the king from his enemies. He and Nicolette live happily in Torelore until Saracens besiege the castle and capture all within it. Aucassin is put in one ship and Nicolette in another. A storm scatters the ships, and that in which Aucassin is a prisoner drifts ashore at Beaucaire. He is now the Count of Beaucaire, since his parents died.

Nicolette is in the ship bearing the king of Carthage, who is her true father. They do not recognize each other because Nicolette was a small child when she was stolen. When she sees the walls of Carthage, however, memory comes back to her, and she reveals her identity in a song. The king gives her great honor and desires to marry her to a king of the Saracens, but Nicolette remains steadfast in her love for Aucassin. She disguises herself as a minstrel and takes ship for Provence, where she travels from castle to castle until she comes to Beaucaire.

In the great hall, Nicolette sings of her adventures. When Aucassin hears her song, he takes her aside and inquires concerning Nicolette. He asks her to return to the land where Nicolette lives and to bring her to him. Nicolette returns to the captain's house, and there she clothes herself in rich robes and sends for Aucassin. At last, they are wed and live long years with great joy.

Critical Evaluation:

Aucassin and Nicolette is a unique text from roughly the first half of the thirteenth century. It is a textbook example of the generic transformation and experimentation that characterize thirteenth century French literature. Classified as a *chante-fable* or song-story, the work, whose author remains anonymous, advances the plot by alternating prose and assonanced, seven-syllabic verse passages. The prose sections of *Aucassin and Nicolette* primarily move the plot, while the verse passages deliver material of more emotionally charged interest. In addition to the combination of prose and verse passages, the work embodies features from a wide variety of literary genres. It exhibits mainly the characteristics of the courtly romance and the chivalric epic, but it also includes elements borrowed from the *pastourelle*, the saint's life, the Byzantine adventure romance, troubadour lyric poetry, and the fabliau. Because of its compound nature, *Aucassin and Nicolette* is also referred to as a hybrid text. This composition was probably intended for public recital, possibly accompanied by musical instruments. While it is unique because it is the only existing example of this type of composition in French medieval literature, it was probably modeled after the Latin *prosimetrum* (prose-verse) tradition.

Besides its unique format, the text is curious in its treatment of subject matter and themes. While it is easily accessible and seemingly transparent, the intent of the author regarding his treatment of subject matter and themes remains rather elusive. The large number of differing interpretations brought forth by various scholars as to the underlying meaning of the work in general, and specific episodes such as the sojourn in Torelore in particular, attest to this. It can safely be stated, however, that one of the most striking characteristics of *Aucassin and Nicolette* is the theme of reversal. The author takes great delight in the reversal of the traditional chivalric romance elements, starting with the names of the protagonists: Aucassin, a French noble, carries a name that conjures up a Saracen theme, whereas his Carthaginian-born lover, Nicolette, has a French one. After both lovers have separately been incarcerated, it is not Aucassin but Nicolette who succeeds in escaping in order to seek out her beloved, and it is her shrewdness and cunning that bring about their reunion in the woods. The reversal of roles and themes continues throughout the work, culminating with Nicolette's disguise as a male minstrel in order to effect her final reunion with Aucassin.

Aucassin and Nicolette parallels many other thirteenth century works in its experimentation with both form and content. The parodic treatment and literary subversion of traditional subjects such as war, duty, and love are found in many other contemporary romances. Nicolette's resourcefulness and proactive ways cast familiar echoes of other such heroines who surmount social constraints and who emerge as brave and adroit in obtaining their heart's desire. Lïenor, the female protagonist of the early thirteenth century *Le Roman de la rose: ou, de Guillaume de Dole* comes to mind. In this story, the young woman devises a trick in order to disprove a cowardly attack on her reputation. Through courage and a clever mind, she ensures that her marriage with the emperor Conrad will be allowed to proceed.

Above all, *Aucassin and Nicolette* seems to indicate that the twelfth century literary models, whose generic codification and chivalric value system it subverts through the introduction of incongruous and farcical elements, do not correspond any longer to the reality or to the needs of the thirteenth century. It is this questioning and reworking of traditional subjects and structures that lie at the heart of *Aucassin and Nicolette*.

"Critical Evaluation" by Geert S. Pallemans

Further Reading

Cobby, Anne Elizabeth. *"Aucassin et Nicolette."* In *Ambivalent Conventions: Formula and Parody in Old French.* Amsterdam: Rodopi, 1995. Cobby's study of Old French literature includes an analysis of *Aucassin and Nicolette*, describing how the work alters the conventions of the fabliau to create its parody.

Ferrante, Joan M. "Courtly Literature." In *Woman as Image in Medieval Literature: From the Twelfth Century to Dante.* New York: Columbia University Press, 1975. Ferrante describes *Aucassin and Nicolette* as a "parody romance" in which the usual role expectations of men and women are reversed.

Kay, Sarah. "Genre, Parody, and Spectacle." In *The Cambridge Companion to Medieval French Literature*, edited by Simon Gaunt and Kay. New York: Cambridge University Press, 2008. Kay's discussion of parody in French medieval literature includes a detailed analysis of *Aucassin and Nicolette*.

Loomis, Laura Hibbard. Foreword to *Aucassin and Nicolette*. In *Medieval Romances*, edited by Roger Sherman Loomis and Laura Hibbard Loomis. New York: Random House, 1957. Loomis emphasizes the dramatic and performance qualities of this *chante-fable*. She discusses the characterizations of Aucassin and Nicolette and the linkings of music to lyrics, lyrics to prose, and romance to fables.

Mason, Eugene. Introduction to *Aucassin and Nicolette and Other Medieval Romances and Legends*. New York: E. P. Dutton, 1951. Mason places *Aucassin and Nicolette* and the other romances within a historical perspective, emphasizing the contradictions inherent in an understanding of the Middle Ages and its literature.

Pensom, Roger. *"Aucassin et Nicolete": The Poetry of Gender and Growing up in the French Middle Ages*. Bern, Switzerland: Peter Lang, 1999. Pensom's interpretation of *Aucassin and Nicolette* focuses on the work's poetic and narrative structures and how they relate to the work's depiction of the processes which create social and personal identity.

Stevens, John. "Man and God: Religion and Romance." In *Medieval Romance: Themes and Approaches*. New York: W. W. Norton, 1973. In this chapter in an illuminating study of medieval romance, Stevens discusses the complex relationship between romantic and religious ideals. He posits that the author uses Aucassin's blasphemous speech about preferring Hell to Heaven as an illustration of the hyperbolic absurdity of young love.

Tattersall, Jill. "Shifting Perspectives and the Illusion of Reality in *Aucassin and Nicolette*." *French Studies* 38, no. 3 (July, 1984): 257-267. Tattersall describes how the author deliberately works against the audience's expectations by using a multiplicity of perspectives, switches in narrative viewpoints, and a variety of types of characterization.

August 1914

Author: Aleksandr Solzhenitsyn (1918-2008)
First published: Avgust chetyrnadtsatogo, 1971; expanded 1983 (English translation, 1972; expanded 1989, as *The Red Wheel*)
Type of work: Novel
Type of plot: Historical realism
Time of plot: Early twentieth century
Locale: Russia

Principal characters:
SANYA, a young man who enlists in the army
VARYA, a young intellectual, and Sanya's former girlfriend
GENERAL SAMSONOV, a general who is forthright but incapable
COLONEL VOROTYNTSEV, an army staff officer
ARSENY BLAGODARYOV, an enlisted man
PYOTR STOLYPIN, a former Russian prime minister
DMITRI BOGROV, a Russian police agent and a secret assassin

The Story:

Russia has just entered World War I. Sanya, a young university student at home for the summer in his provincial town, boards a train for Moscow to enlist in the army. Sanya has been inspired by Russia's emperor, Czar Nicholas II, who has become a hero to his country by declaring war on Germany and Austria. Filled with patriotism, Sanya rejects his former pacifism and secretly vows to fight for his country.

On the train to Moscow, Sanya runs into a former girlfriend, Varya, who since the days when Sanya knew her at school has become educated and grown into an intellectual. Armed with radical opinions from speeches she has heard shouted on street corners, Varya questions Sanya's patriotism and challenges his desire to join the army, saying that he has denied his support of the common people's revolution in giving that support to the wealthy czar and his family. Sanya, defeated by her arguments, can only say that he is headed for battle because "I feel sorry for Russia."

In 1914, as the war begins, Nicholas paces the floor in a room in his palace one day in July, while his generals urge him, against his better judgment, to mobilize the Russian army. Nicholas lashes out at the generals and berates them for their incompetence; he wishes that Prime Minister Pyotr Stolypin were still alive, for he would have known what was best for Russia.

Stolypin had been murdered at a performance at the Kiev Opera House by police agent and secret assassin Dmitri Bogrov, scion of a prominent and wealthy family and a privileged and idle son intent on securing a place in the ruling class. Refusing to obey any agenda except his own, his allegiance is only to himself, even as he prepares for a career in the army. To further his career, Bogrov conspires with the czar's secret police to acquire an entrance pass to the exclusive opera house. The police intentionally overlook the revolver hidden in his pocket. Bogrov then assassinates Stolypin and thereby halts the prime minister's program of modernization. Bogrov is thereupon betrayed by the police, who secretly try and execute him to prevent his testifying at a public trial.

Meanwhile, on the battlefield at Tannenberg, Colonel Vorotyntsev, a graduate of a Russian military academy, and his friend Arseny Blagodaryov, an enlisted man, find themselves surrounded by advancing German troops. Rallying his men, Vorotyntsev leads a successful charge through enemy lines.

The colonel's small victory grew out of his excellent training as a soldier and his devotion to the military. After eight years of marriage with his wife, Alina, he has become disenchanted with her and finds himself troubled by dreams of adultery. In one dream, his wife turns down the covers of the bed they were to share and finds another woman's nightgown under the covers. Haunted by this vision of dishonor, the colonel decides that a military life holds more dignity than a domestic one.

Despite the colonel's break through enemy lines, the Russian army, betrayed by the incompetence of the czar's generals, is doomed. General Samsonov's Second Army is defeated by German general Hindenburg and his soldiers. Colonel Vorotyntsev retreats from the battlefield and reports to the grand duke, the supreme commander of Russia's armies. The colonel tells him that defeat is inevitable, that old Russia would be destroyed. The general staff refuse to believe him and cling instead to the lie that the war could still be won.

Sanya reflects on the early days of the war and longs to return with Varya to the places they had known and loved when they were young. The war has aged them, however, and Sanya is too patriotic to waste his life indulging himself. Instead, he will continue to serve the people of his mother Russia.

Critical Evaluation:

Aleksandr Solzhenitsyn, who was awarded the Nobel Prize in Literature in 1970, used his writing to confront the oppression of the former Soviet Union and the weight of its cruel bureaucracy, whereby individuals were lost and destroyed inside Siberian prisons, cancer wards, and insane asylums. Solzhenitsyn depicts simple human qualities and creates realistic portraits that bear witness to the incredible strength of the human spirit while undergoing intense suffering.

Best known for the novella *Odin den' Ivana Denisovicha* (1962; *One Day in the Life of Ivan Denisovich*, 1963) and for the novel *Arkhipelag GULag, 1918-1956: Opyt khudozhestvennogo issledovaniya* (1973-1975; *The Gulag Archipelago, 1918-1956: An Experiment in Literary Investigation*, 1974-1978), Solzhenitsyn had been a prisoner as well. In 1941, after earning degrees in mathematics and physics, he had begun teaching, but by 1945 he was the commander of a Soviet army artillery battery. That was when he wrote a personal letter criticizing Communist leader Joseph Stalin. The Soviet police and counterintelligence agents arrested Solzhenitsyn, and after a hasty trial he was found guilty of conspiring against the state and sentenced to a series of brutal prisons.

It was during his confinement, in prison amid the frozen wasteland—where the petty theft of a slice of bread or a pair of work boots could mean death—that the author had the transformative experiences that were to form the core of *One Day in the Life of Ivan Denisovich*. His experiences included a diagnosis of cancer, from which he miraculously recovered and which forms the basis of *Rakovy korpus* (1968; *Cancer Ward*, 1968). Freed from exile in central Asia in 1956, Solzhenitsyn returned to Russia, but he was arrested again when *The Gulag Archipelago* was published in France. In 1974, the Soviet Union finally expelled Solzhenitsyn and forced him into exile in the United States, where he remained until his triumphant return to Russia following the collapse of the Soviet Union in 1991.

August 1914 is the first volume of *The Red Wheel*, a series of novels in which Solzhenitsyn intended to present a sweeping view of twentieth century Russia and to correct the falsifications imposed on Russian history by the Soviet regime. Borrowing different styles from fiction, journalism, and film, Solzhenitsyn conveys the intricacy of political movements by using every literary and rhetorical technique at his disposal to unravel what he sees as the grossly misinterpreted "knot" of Russian history.

Solzhenitsyn's mastery of narration has been noted by numerous literary critics, and *August 1914* has been favorably compared to Leo Tolstoy's *Voyna i mir* (1865-1869; *War and Peace*, 1886) for its broad scope and detailed and accurate descriptions of battle scenes. While the core action of Solzhenitsyn's work takes place during twelve days of August,

1914, the author employs flashbacks, a pastiche of items from newspapers, advertisements, military documents, and camera-eye descriptions of events (all reminiscent of similar devices used by John Dos Passos in his trilogy *U.S.A.*, 1937), and other narrative artifices with great effect to widen the compass of the novel's social, political, and moral concerns.

Also noted by many who read Solzhenitsyn's works in the original is the author's exhaustive use of the enormous resources of the Russian language, which Solzhenitsyn acquired through attending to the speech of people of all levels and geographical areas of Soviet society. He had met diverse peoples in his native southern Russia, in school, in the army, and in the camps and places of exile scattered throughout the vast expanse of the Soviet Union. He also read widely in Russian literature and had closely studied Vladimir Dal's classic dictionary of the Russian language. The delicacy of Solzhenitsyn's exposition of character in *August 1914* invites comparison to the works of Anton Chekhov.

On the political level, *August 1914* attacks czarism for its reliance on favoritism and for using a biased system of advancement, including bribery and nepotism. These practices led to the appointment of incompetent generals whose blunders cost the lives of thousands. Solzhenitsyn views the czar's weakness and corruption as catalysts that started the terrible and bloody revolution that destroyed Russia's potential. In his books, Solzhenitsyn tried to explain why a great vision of Russia that included a well-developed and prosperous Siberia never materialized. For Solzhenitsyn, the dream died in the bloodbath of 1917, for which he sees two causes: the assassination in 1911 of prime minister Pyotr Stolypin, whose attempts to modernize Russia were cut short, and more specifically, the failure of General Samsonov, who had represented traditional Russia—forthright and sincere but incapable and unable to adapt.

Solzhenitsyn splits the blame for Russia's economic and ethical poverty between two opposing camps, the backward-looking officials known as the Black Hundreds, who were drawn from the wealthy upper class, and the forward-looking revolutionaries known as the Red Hundreds, impoverished insurgents from the lower classes. According to the author, both groups prevented Russia from fulfilling its destiny and leading the world, for as the two sides attempted to vanquish each other, the country decayed around them and the dignity and the rights of people were needlessly sacrificed. This is the tragedy at the core of *August 1914*.

In 1983, Solzhenitsyn published an expanded edition of *August 1914* that included three-hundred pages of additional text dealing with one of Communism's founders, Vladimir Ilich Lenin, and with Stolypin, the assassinated prime minister. Solzhenitsyn held that Stolypin's death stopped Russia's peaceful political development and removed a deterrent to the Bolshevik Revolution. Many historians and critics disagree, calling *August 1914* more of a personal political treatise than a serious dramatic novel.

In all his work, Solzhenitsyn advances his view of the human being as a noble animal, one capable of transcendence and dignity even in the most degrading and depersonalizing circumstances. Solzhenitsyn had described his job as a writer by saying that he had "to treat universal and eternal themes: the mysteries of the heart and conscience, the collision between life and death, the triumph over spiritual anguish."

August 1914 is an example of a writer's use of the novel to rewrite history. By seducing the reader with the familiar devices of fiction—story, character, plot, and imagery—Solzhenitsyn creates a reality in which events are seen from all sides, as opposed to the simplified, and biased, version provided in state-sanctioned textbooks. Accordingly, Solzhenitsyn describes his novel as a fascicle, which he defines as a "dense, all-round exposition of the events of a brief time span."

While Solzhenitsyn may not be entirely accurate historically, he nevertheless establishes that the form in which history is presented—be it journalistic, cinematic, or fictive—is in large measure responsible for determining its "truth" for the people reading it. In this way, *August 1914* seeks to remedy the distortions of the past established by the Soviet regime.

Solzhenitsyn's thesis is that the suffering and endurance and triumph experienced by individuals at the hands of human institutions ought not to be forgotten or misinterpreted. As a result, *August 1914* stands as the author's testament to the continued vitality of what is past and to its relevance to the ongoing struggle for freedom and equality.

David Johansson; revised by Carl Moody

Further Reading

Bloom, Harold, ed. *Aleksandr Solzhenitsyn*. Philadelphia: Chelsea House, 2001. A collection of critical essays, including comparisons of Solzhenitsyn's work with that of Leo Tolstoy and Boris Pasternak, an analysis of the representation of detention in the works of Solzhenitsyn and Fyodor Dostoevski, and a discussion of Solzhenitsyn's experiences as a creative artist in a totalitarian state.

Dunlop, John B., Richard Haugh, and Alexis Klimoff, eds. *Aleksandr Solzhenitsyn: Critical Essays and Documentary Materials*. Belmont, Mass.: Nordland, 1973. The essays in this collection interpret numerous aspects of Solzhenitsyn's work. Includes a bibliography of works by and about Solzhenitsyn.

Ericson, Edward E., Jr. *Solzhenitsyn and the Modern World.* Washington, D.C.: Regnery Gateway, 1993. Examines Solzhenitsyn in light of the collapse of Communism in Russia. Answers some of the common criticisms that are leveled at his writing.

_______. *Solzhenitsyn, the Moral Vision.* Grand Rapids, Mich.: William B. Eerdman, 1980. Analyzes Solzhenitsyn's work from the perspective of his Christian vision. Discusses Solzhenitsyn's theory of art as enunciated in his Nobel Prize lecture. Includes chapters on the major novels, as well as the short stories and prose poems.

Ericson, Edward E., and Alexis Klimoff. *The Soul and Barbed Wire: An Introduction to Solzhenitsyn.* Wilmington, Del.: ISI Books, 2008. Two major Solzhenitsyn scholars provide a detailed biography of the writer and analyses of his major fiction, including *August 1914.*

Kohan, John. "Peasants, Proverbs, and Problems of Historical Narrative in *August 1914.*" In *Proverbs in Russian Literature: From Catherine the Great to Alexander Solzhenitsyn*, edited by Kevin J. McKenna. Burlington: University of Vermont Press, 1998. Analyzes the novel's use of language and narrative structure. Part of a larger collection on the use of the proverb by Russian writers.

Mahoney, Daniel J. *Aleksandr Solzhenitsyn: The Ascent from Ideology.* Lanham, Md.: Rowman & Littlefield, 2001. Focuses on Solzhenitsyn's political philosophy and its effect on twentieth century thinking. Analyzes Solzhenitsyn's writings to demonstrate how they represent the political condition of modern humans.

Pearce, Joseph. *Solzhenitsyn: A Soul in Exile.* New York: HarperCollins, 1999. Generally uncritical biography chronicles Solzhenitsyn's evolution from pro-Marxist youth to anti-Soviet writer and, finally, to literary anachronism after the demise of the Soviet Union. Features exclusive personal interviews with Solzhenitsyn, previously unpublished poetry, and rare photographs.

Thomas, D. M. *Alexander Solzhenitsyn: A Century in His Life.* New York: St. Martin's Press, 1998. A personal portrait of Solzhenitsyn, providing insights into his struggle with the Soviet authorities and his relationship with the two women who provided strong support for his efforts to expose the evils of the Communist regime. An imaginative, well-documented, and at times combative biography, which includes a discussion of Solzhenitsyn's return to Russia in 1994.

Aurora Leigh

Author: Elizabeth Barrett Browning (1806-1861)
First published: 1856
Type of work: Poetry and verse novel
Type of plot: *Künstlerroman*
Time of plot: Mid-nineteenth century
Locale: Italy and England

Principal characters:
AURORA LEIGH, the protagonist, a poet
ROMNEY LEIGH, her cousin
LADY WALDEMAR, who wishes to marry Romney
MARIAN ERLE, whom Romney wishes to marry

Aurora Leigh blends the genres of poetry and the novel and is, at the same time, a bildungsroman (a novel that traces the development of a young person to maturity) or, more properly, a *Künstlerroman*, in which a young artist struggles to create an artistic identity despite adverse conditions. The work is innovative both in its blend of poetry and the novel form and in its focus on a woman as an artist.

As befitting a developmental novelist, Elizabeth Barrett Browning proceeds chronologically, from Aurora's childhood in Italy to her triumph as a mature artist. The child of a British father and an Italian mother, who dies when Aurora is only four years old, she grows up bereft of maternal nurturing, which she pursues throughout her life. Her sorrowing father leaves Aurora to the care of a servant until his own death when she is thirteen. She is whisked away to "frosty" England, in contrast to the "green reconciling earth" of Italy, the latter country being, in all senses, her "motherland." She is placed with her father's sister, who lives a "caged life," a life which, in turn, encases Aurora. Her education now emphasizes useless facts and accomplishments such as "spinning glass" and the need to be "womanly," or submissive, as her aunt defines it. Aurora befriends her cousin, Romney Leigh, master of Leigh Hall, only a few years older than she. She escapes into her father's stored library and discovers poetry, finding her life's work by beginning to write poetry and to receive inspiration from England's natural world.

The narrative distance of book 1, which recalls Aurora's childhood, yields to the immediacy of the focus in book 2 on her twentieth birthday, a beautiful June day. Thrilled with her life among poets, Aurora crowns herself with ivy leaves and is embarrassed to be discovered by Romney, who is amused at her pretension. He has come to propose marriage (without any mention of love) because he assumes she will join him in his dedication to solving the problems of the poor. He derides her poetic ambitions and prophesies failure since, as a woman, she cannot "generalize." Women are "personal and passionate," fit to be "doting mothers and perfect wives." She refuses his offer by saying, "What you love,/ Is not a woman, Romney, but a cause." The two have contrasting views on bettering humanity. Romney wants to extend personal charity or espouse one of the current social schemes, such as that proposed by Charles Fourier (a system based on cooperation rather than on capitalism). Aurora insists that reform must come from within the individual and that "high-souled men . . . move masses." While poetry has excited her, he offers her only the chance to "sweep my barns and keep my hospitals." When her aunt dies shortly afterward, Aurora refuses a "bequest" that Romney invents, leaving for London to ensure independence in pursuing her career.

As book 3 opens, three years have passed, and Aurora has found lodging in Kensington, supporting herself with freelance prose writing. Lady Waldemar calls to enlist Aurora's aid in diverting Romney's plan to marry a seamstress, Marian Erle. Waldemar plans to marry Romney herself and insists that his gracious effort to save Marian from poverty will demean him. Aurora refuses to interfere and decides to visit Marian, allowing Barrett Browning to give her readers a glimpse of the wretched conditions that the poor endured. As the reader progresses into book 4, Marian describes her miserable past and her rescue by Romney; she is totally indebted to him and willing to be his "handmaid and wife." Romney still scorns love and insists that he and Marian will be partners in his work.

Aurora interrupts the narrative for a novelistic foreshadowing of events, regretting that she did not protect Marian or advance the wedding. In this way, Barrett Browning builds suspense for further developments. When the actual wedding day arrives, the reader gets a glimpse of hell, both in the author's description of the mob attending the wedding and of the languid upper-class guests gossiping about the mismatched couple. A riot breaks out with the announcement that Marian will not appear; Marian has sent Romney a letter explaining that she has become convinced (through her conversations with Lady Waldemar) that their marriage will discredit Romney.

Book 5 may seem a digression from the main narrative, but it is crucial to the development of Aurora's poetic career. Romney's last words to her make her feel inconsequential, so the meditations in this book encourage her to evaluate her commitment. She exhorts herself to be humble as she strains toward producing some epic work; she questions that her efforts can sustain the weight of inspiration. She has not been satisfied with her apprenticeship in poetry and wonders if the poet needs someone to approve her efforts. Does she need the approbation of a man? She refuses to accept her dependence and decides to "affect no compromise." Next she contemplates whether epic heroes are still to be found. Homer's heroes are not "twelve feet high"; they are simply human. Thus, her contemporary world can provide epic material; a poet can see heroes in her own age. Poets should work to "represent" their own era, "the full-veined, heaving, double-breasted Age," which serves as a nurturing bosom for future generations. Art requires sacrifice, chiefly that of commitment to one ideal; thus Barrett Browning allies herself to the Romantic concept that a poet cannot have both life and art, that art is "intellectual" and denies "feeling." Aurora is lonely; poignant lines describe her desolation: "How dreary 'tis for women to sit still/ On winter nights by solitary fires/ . . . [with] unkissed lips/ And eyes undried." She is "hungry" for love and approval, love and approval from her dead parents and from Romney. She resolves to ignore her pain and renews her commitment to poetry. When Aurora visits Lord Howe's home, she finds Lady Waldemar among the guests. Gossip reveals that Lady Waldemar has been assisting Romney in his work, particularly at Leigh Hall, and that the two will marry soon. Pained by the news, Aurora decides to leave for Italy, hailing it as a nurturing mother drawing her "home."

As book 6 opens, however, Aurora's journey has taken her through France, giving her the opportunity to locate Marian. In her bare lodgings, Marian reveals her secret, "a yearling creature," a baby boy. Aurora is sympathetic to the "fallen" Marian, who begins to tell of her journey through her own hell. Lady Waldemar had convinced Marian to leave Romney and immigrate to Australia, a trip which she would arrange. Instead of escorting Marian to a ship bound for Australia, however, Lady Waldemar's servant brings her to a brothel in Paris; Marian is raped and turned out on the streets. Marian's saga continues into book 7, where she finds that she is pregnant and is taken in by a seamstress who allows her to work to support herself and her son. Moved by Marian's suffering, Aurora greets her as "sister" and offers to take her to Italy as her companion. She debates about writing to Romney about her discovery but is reluctant to ruin his supposed happiness. Calling upon "the man in me," she decides to write to Lord Howe and enclose a letter for Lady Waldemar, denouncing her evil machinations. The two travel on to Italy, but Aurora finds that she cannot recapture her childhood feelings for her "motherland." She also realizes that "The end of woman . . . /Is not a book"; she misses Romney and finds herself dissolving into "nothing" without love.

The last two books present the denouement; Aurora is surprised one evening to find that Romney has arrived. Because a letter went undelivered, she still assumes he has married Lady Waldemar; she also neglects to notice the signs that Romney is now blind. He admits that he has been wrong about his social programs and about her success as a poet. Aurora confesses that she is not the same person she was at twenty years old, and both agree that the Victorian principle, "Let us work," can solve their problems. Romney has experienced the death of his dreams for social reform and the loss of Leigh Hall in a fire set by a mob. He has come to make another grand gesture: marrying Marian to restore her reputation. He had never intended to marry Lady Waldemar, who has sent a letter to Aurora revealing her punishment for her treatment of Marian, her loss of Romney. She thinks she might have become a better person through this marriage and insists that she never meant Marian to be treated as she was. Marian now rejects Romney's proposal, revealing that she probably never loved him but instead was grateful for his generosity. She will not encumber him with "a bastard child/ And married harlot." She intends to dedicate her life to her child and may later help Romney in his work by caring for outcasts. Aurora finally realizes that Romney is blind and refuses to allow him to leave without telling him of her love. The two lovers agree to share their life's work; Aurora apparently succumbs to a compromise between art and life. She does, however, triumph; the marriage is based on her terms. She wins love, a poetic career, fame, independence, and power.

Following the acknowledged example of Lord Byron's *Don Juan* (1819-1824), Barrett Browning creates an exuberant epic, monumental in size and in scope, incorporating discussions of class struggle, social programs, politics, religion, the status of women, poetic theory, the glories of nature, and contemporary life, among other topics. She uses epic conventions introduced by Homer and Vergil (announcement of theme, an elevated style through epic similes and antiquated word choice, formal speeches, descents into Hades, and an evil manipulator) and creates a significant heroine employed in a noble quest. Like her predecessors, Barrett Browning tries to establish a new society, based on the inspiration of poetry, giving women a respected citizenship.

Aurora Leigh's faults are the reversals of its virtues, since it crosses the genre boundaries of poetry (written entirely in blank verse and including brilliant imagery and careful word choice), the novel, and the epic. The novel's demands for "realism" and "real" dialogue are negated by an epic's large scope and, at times, long-winded, heroic speeches. However, the narrative structure remains intact: exposition, complication (her digressions help to build suspense), immediacy of action, and a welcome denouement. *Aurora Leigh*, extremely popular at its publication and newly restored by feminist critics to its proper status after years of neglect, is Barrett Browning's masterpiece.

Elizabeth R. Nelson

Further Reading

Avery, Simon, and Rebecca Stott. *Elizabeth Barrett Browning*. London: Longman, 2003. A biography and critical assessment of Barrett Browning's poetry and her influence on later poets. Dispels the myth that Barrett Browning was reclusive and disabled, depicting her as one of the great intellectuals of her time.

Browning, Elizabeth Barrett. *Aurora Leigh: Authoritative Text, Backgrounds and Contexts, Criticism*. Edited by Margaret Reynolds. New York: W. W. Norton, 1996. In addition to the text of the poem, this volume includes materials providing background and context for the work, including correspondence between Robert and Elizabeth Barrett Browning and Victorian-era articles about women. The book also contains contemporary reviews, as well as numerous modern essays examining the lyrical philosophy, depiction of gender, idea of the mother, and other aspects of the poem.

Gilbert, Sandra, and Susan Gubar. *The Madwoman in the Attic*. New Haven, Conn.: Yale University Press, 1979. Feminist reading with emphasis on discussing Barrett Browning's solution to the contemporary conflict between "woman" and "poet." Clarifies maternal imagery in the poem.

Kaplan, Cora. Introduction to *Elizabeth Barrett Browning: Aurora Leigh, and Other Poems*. London: Women's Press, 1978. Provides an excellent starting point for comprehending the scope of *Aurora Leigh*; the editor's comments are often cited to support other readings of the poem. Good notes and a bibliography of critical material available at the time.

Lawson, Kate, and Lynn Shakinovsky. "Rape, Transgression, and the Law: The Body of Marian Erle in Elizabeth Barrett Browning's *Aurora Leigh*." In *The Marked Body: Domestic Violence in Mid-Nineteenth-Century Literature*, by Lawson and Shakinovsky. Albany: State University of New York Press, 2002. This chapter analyzing Barrett Browning's poem is included in the authors' feminist and psychological examination of the depiction of discarded and violated bodies in nineteenth century literature.

Leighton, Angela. *Elizabeth Barrett Browning*. Bloomington: Indiana University Press, 1986. A useful reading of *Aurora Leigh* as a feminist poem, especially in its defiance of patriarchal dominance of women and poetry.

Mermin, Dorothy. *Elizabeth Barrett Browning: The Origins of a New Poetry*. Chicago: University of Chicago Press, 1989. A biographical study emphasizing the female in *Aurora Leigh*, its position as a novel, maternal images, and its heroine's defiance of traditional attitudes toward women. Includes an excellent, comprehensive bibliography.

Moers, Ellen. *Literary Women*. Garden City, N.Y.: Doubleday, 1976. Focuses on the influence of Mme de Stael, George Sand, and Elizabeth Gaskell on Barrett Browning and her influence on later writers, especially Emily Dickinson. Moers suggests that Dickinson's poems be read along with *Aurora Leigh*. Cites epic features and establishes it as "*the* feminist poem."

The Autobiography of Alice B. Toklas

Author: Gertrude Stein (1874-1946)
First published: 1933
Type of work: Memoir
Type of plot: Historical realism
Time of plot: 1903-1932
Locale: Paris

Principal characters:
GERTRUDE STEIN, an artist
ALICE B. TOKLAS, her companion

The Story:

Alice is born in San Francisco, California. It is quite by accident that, shortly after the great San Francisco earthquake (April 18, 1906), Alice meets Michael and Sarah Stein, Gertrude's older brother and his wife. They have just returned from Paris to tend to their real estate holdings damaged by the earthquake. Sarah brings with her three small paintings by Henri Matisse. She shows them to Alice and her friends, tells them about her exciting life in France, and invites them all to visit her in Paris. In less than a year Alice goes to Paris and meets Gertrude Stein.

Alice makes her first visit to the already-famous Saturday-evening dinners at 27 rue de Fleurus, home of Gertrude. Of great significance to Alice is what she sees and whom she meets. She gives an account of the apartment and the extensive art collection, including paintings by Paul Cézanne, Pierre-Auguste Renoir, Matisse, and Pablo Picasso, with special attention given to Picasso's portrait of Gertrude Stein (which now hangs in New York's Metropolitan Museum). The list of the people in attendance on that and the many other Saturday evenings makes up a veritable who's who of European art and American literature during the early decades of the twentieth century. The most important person Alice meets that first evening is Pablo Picasso, the artist for whom Gertrude Stein has the greatest affinity.

Alice's experiences continue on the next day and include her first vernissage—a preview of an art exhibition—where she is further introduced to the art and artists of Paris. The third instance of Alice's introduction is a walk with Gertrude through various artists' studios in Montmartre, then the artists' quarter of Paris.

In the following chapter, "Gertrude Stein in Paris: 1903-1907," Gertrude details her formative years as a writer and one involved in the development of modern art, with specific reference to Cézanne, Matisse, and Picasso. In 1903, Gertrude begins writing *The Making of Americans*, an immense work that she regards as her major literary accomplishment at that time. It is finished in 1911 but is not published until 1925. During these years she also writes *Three Lives* (1909), her first published book.

In these years Gertrude and her brother Leo start buying

the paintings that make up their vast and valuable art collection, and, in this way, they meet the major artists working in Paris. Of greatest consequence to Gertrude's writing are Matisse and Picasso, whose paintings are in many ways the visual counterparts of her literary style.

In the next chapter, "Gertrude Stein Before She Came to Paris," a few high points of her early life are recounted, such as her travels with her parents and brother, studying psychology with William James at Radcliffe, and studying medicine at Johns Hopkins University. When she eventually loses interest in her medical studies she travels with Leo in Europe and settles in London for a winter, spending most days reading English literature at the British Museum. Gertrude returns to America for a brief stay and writes her first short novel (*Quod Erat Demonstrandum*, written 1903, "rediscovered" 1932, published as *Things as They Are*, 1950).

In "1907-1914," the story of Gertrude's and Alice's lives together begins again. The Saturday evenings at home continue on a regular basis, allowing further discussion about the famous artists, or those who are well known at the time. There are, however, also many minor figures, such as the maidservant Hélène, their Moroccan guide Mohammed, and a host of unnamed people. Virtually all these visitors become subjects of the portraits Gertrude writes during these years. One visitor is Carl Van Vechten, author and music critic for *The New York Times*. His early essay on Gertrude included the quotation from her portrait "Sacred Emily" that was to become her most famous motto: "A rose is a rose is a rose is a rose."

Two important events in Gertrude's life occur during these years. In 1909, Alice moves to 27 rue de Fleurus and becomes Gertrude's lifelong companion. In 1913, Gertrude's brother Leo, who was such an important influence on her early life, moves to Florence, Italy. They divide their art collection: She keeps the Cézannes and Picassos and he takes the Matisses and Renoirs.

"The War" reports the events that engage Gertrude and Alice during World War I (1914-1918). In addition to continued writing, the two women perform volunteer work, driving a supply truck for the American Fund for the French Wounded.

The final chapter, "After the War: 1919-1932," describes a very different life. The exciting crowd from before the war, by and large, disappeared from the Saturday-evening gatherings. It is, however, replaced by a new group that Gertrude labels "the lost generation" of American writers. Among the best known are Sherwood Anderson, Ernest Hemingway, and F. Scott Fitzgerald. Gertrude provides an extensive discussion of her relationship with Hemingway, suggesting that she not only influenced him to become a writer but also taught him how he should write.

The composer Virgil Thomson encourages Stein to write the libretto for the opera *Four Saints in Three Acts* (written 1927-1928; first performed 1934). It includes another famous Stein motto with Saint Ignatius and a chorus of saints singing "Pigeons on the grass alas."

Personally most satisfying for Gertrude is the public recognition she receives for her work in these years. The literary societies of Cambridge and Oxford universities invite her in 1926 to present her lecture "Composition as Explanation" to great acclaim. She realizes then that she has become a writer of distinction.

The last page of the book answers the question of its authorship. It begins with Gertrude's effort to persuade Alice to write the book, but Gertrude finally admits that the only way the autobiography will ever be written will be if she writes it.

Critical Evaluation:

The title of this book is misleading. Alice B. Toklas did not write it. The book is more the autobiography or memoirs of Alice and Gertrude Stein, as written by Gertrude.

Gertrude wrote more than two dozen books and plays, but most people have read only *The Autobiography of Alice B. Toklas* and, perhaps, *Three Lives*. Of course, many can quote "A rose is a rose is a rose is a rose," frequently forgetting the fourth rose, and "pigeons on the grass alas." As one of the preeminent authors of twentieth century American literature, she was the creator of a new literary style that had a profound influence on many younger novelists, poets, and dramatists.

Even though Gertrude's writings at the time were known to only a small group of readers, the publication of *The Autobiography of Alice B. Toklas* made her an international celebrity. *The Autobiography of Alice B. Toklas* was a great success, even making the best-seller list. Following its publication she was persuaded to give lectures and readings throughout the United States, and she became one of the best-known writers of her day. Contributing to her renown was her association with the new school of contemporary painting in Paris—Pablo Picasso, Henri Matisse, Paul Cézanne, Pierre-Auguste Renoir, and all the other modernists.

Two types of readers were attracted to *The Autobiography of Alice B. Toklas*: the serious reader, who recognized it as a more accessible example of her unique literary style, and the general reader, who saw the book as a report on bohemian life in Paris. The latter took delight in a chatty, gossipy account of the lives of the more than four hundred people mentioned. Some of these people were to become famous artists of the twentieth century, others were well known at the time but soon faded into obscurity, while many belonged to neither group. Several people whose names appear in *The Autobiography of Alice B. Toklas* objected to Stein's account of the Paris art scene and even wrote rejoinders trying to set the record straight.

The originality of Gertrude's work can be observed in the way in which she transcribes banal daily speech, exactly as she hears it, into her literature. In her early study of psychology she observed that the brain does not always operate on a sequential or logical level and that conversation is frequently made up of repetitions reflecting digressing or associative thoughts. From the French Symbolist poets she learned how the imagination can create linguistic images without having the brain serve as mediator to establish logical order. She believed that the mind could assign meanings to words that are unrelated to their dictionary meaning, especially when dealing with words describing emotions or remembering specific sounds.

To appreciate Gertrude's unique literary style the reader may wish to consider *The Autobiography of Alice B. Toklas* as a book of portraits. Stein wrote hundreds of portraits in her life, but these are unlike the traditional verbal or visual portraits found in art and literature. If one were to compare portraits written or painted in the eighteenth or nineteenth century with those, for example, painted by Picasso or Matisse in the early years of the twentieth century, one would note immediately that the former attempted to present a likeness that was as close as possible to the subject. In a Picasso or Matisse portrait, however, the painter does not strive for the representational correctness of a photograph and the viewer observes an abstract essence of the subject. In Picasso's *Portrait of a Young Girl*, for example, the subject has a head represented by numerous green shapes and a blue arm that seems to extend below the leg. Matisse's *Landscape at Collioure* is made up of no more than a series of different colored brushstrokes. Although painters can find such new and different ways to express themselves by varying colors and shapes, writers are much more limited by the boundaries of language.

In many of her portraits, Gertrude rejects the use of traditional narrative prose with all its complicated grammar rules, conventions, and limitations. She also discards the artificial ways in which discourse has been recorded in written form over the centuries. What she does is to present a verbal portrait of an individual based on the way in which that person thinks and speaks, using words unique to the speaker, with variations and permutations. Speaking about language, Stein stated that "it does not make any difference to me what language I hear, I don't hear a language, I hear tones of voices and rhythms." Her portraits are as complicated and difficult to understand as the paintings of the modernist artists working in Paris at that time. *The Autobiography of Alice B. Toklas*, however, utilizes the least radical form of Stein's literary style. *The Autobiography of Alice B. Toklas* is written in the way in which Alice would have written or spoken the story. Even though the plot traces Gertrude's life from her birth until 1932, when she finished writing this book, the reader has more of an understanding of the essence of Gertrude than an awareness or knowledge of her life. Gertrude has the character of Alice tell the story in her "rambling" speech, constantly interrupting herself to refer to a specific time, place, or person, and gradually painting the complete portrait as Gertrude wants to be seen. References to artists or writers of her time, whether praising or blaming, ultimately serve only to complete that picture.

The last paragraph in *The Autobiography of Alice B. Toklas* provides an important statement. It suggests that the book is like Daniel Defoe's fictional biography of Robinson Crusoe—a complete literary work of fiction.

Thomas H. Falk

Further Reading

Bloom, Harold, ed. *Gertrude Stein*. New York: Chelsea House, 1986. Contains fifteen essays on Stein, a chronology, and a bibliography. The selection is astute, although there is no specific essay on *The Autobiography of Alice B. Toklas*.

Bridgman, Richard. *Gertrude Stein in Pieces*. New York: Oxford University Press, 1970. A carefully conceived and clearly presented study that offers a full analysis of the overall structure and style of Stein's writing.

Curnutt, Kirk, ed. *The Critical Response to Gertrude Stein*. Westport, Conn.: Greenwood Press, 2000. A collection of contemporary and modern reviews and essays about Stein's works and persona. While including quintessential pieces on Stein by Carl Van Vechten, William Carlos Williams, and Katherine Anne Porter, this guide also includes previously obscure estimations from contemporaries, such as H. L. Mencken, Mina Loy, and Conrad Aiken.

Greenfeld, Howard. *Gertrude Stein: A Biography*. New York: Crown, 1973. A brief introduction to Gertrude Stein, well suited for the general reader.

Hoffman, Michael J. *Gertrude Stein*. Boston: Twayne, 1976. A balanced, critical study identifying Stein's work as the most important source and influence on modernism.

Malcolm, Janet. *Two Lives: Gertrude and Alice*. New Haven, Conn.: Yale University Press, 2007. An account of Stein's relationship with Alice B. Toklas, in which Malcolm provides new information about the couple's lives during the German Occupation of France. She explains how Stein and Toklas were allowed to survive because of their friendship with Bernard Faÿ, a wealthy, anti-Semitic Frenchman.

Mellow, James R. *Charmed Circle: Gertrude Stein and Company*. New York: Praeger, 1974. This book, rich with illustrations, captures the vibrant spirit of the exciting circle of painters, sculptors, writers, and fascinating passersby who came within the Stein-Toklas social orbit before and after World War I.

Simon, Linda. *The Biography of Alice B. Toklas*. Garden City, N.Y.: Doubleday, 1977. A fine biography of Toklas, especially for the reader interested in seeing the life and times from Toklas's perspective. Can serve as a valuable companion volume to Stein's book.

Sloboda, Noel. *The Making of Americans in Paris: The Autobiographies of Edith Wharton and Gertrude Stein*. New York: Peter Lang, 2008. Describes the personal and cultural contexts in which Stein created *The Autobiography of Alice B. Toklas*. Examines subjects common to that book and to Edith Wharton's *A Backward Glance* (1934).

Souhami, Diana. *Gertrude and Alice*. London: Pandora, 1991. The most thorough account of Stein's long lesbian relationship with Toklas, this book shows how strong Toklas was and how she dominated many aspects of her forty-year association with Stein.

The Autobiography of an Ex-Coloured Man

Author: James Weldon Johnson (1871-1938)
First published: 1912
Type of work: Novel
Type of plot: Psychological realism
Time of plot: Early twentieth century
Locale: Southern United States, New York City, and Europe

Principal characters:
ANONYMOUS NARRATOR, a mulatto who decides to pass for white
THE MILLIONAIRE, the narrator's patron

The Story:

Born in Georgia a few years after the American Civil War, the narrator, in comparison with other blacks, lives in a comfortably furnished little house. Thinking her son superior to other children in his neighborhood, the narrator's mother is particular about his dress and his associates. Later, the narrator remembers scenarios of familial bliss that centered on a "tall man with a small, dark moustache" who visited them in the evenings several times a week. Because he admires the man's shiny boots and his gold watch and chain, the narrator develops a subconscious identification with the white man that helps give him a sense of freedom and self-confidence. He later learns that this man is his father. Whereas he identifies with the tall, white man, the narrator's fondness for the black keys on the piano in his parlor represents his identification with that part of himself that is black. When he hears his mother playing old southern songs on the piano, the narrator feels happiest. By the time he is seven, he can play all the songs his mother knows.

Eventually, the narrator and his mother move from Georgia to Connecticut because the tall, white man is getting married and it would not be appropriate for his black mistress and his illegitimate son to live in the same town with his white wife. In Connecticut, the narrator learns that he is black and what that means. One day, the white students in his class are asked to stand. When he rises, his teacher asked him to wait and rise with the nonwhites. For the first time, the narrator recognizes differences between himself and his classmates. He also notices differences in the way he looks and the way his mother looks. He sees beauty in his features and defects in his mother's darker features. The narrator's heightened sense of difference forces him to adjust, temporarily, to the "dwarfing, warping, distorting influence" of America on the lives of blacks. After he becomes interested in reading the Bible and history books, the narrator's vicarious identification with heroic men of action such as King David, Samson, and Robert the Bruce emphasizes the narrator's early, intellectual separation from the masses of black people who are powerless in American society.

Despite his unassuming nature, the narrator is pleased with the applause he receives after playing the piano at his graduation. However, he wishes to receive the even greater enthusiasm aroused by the speech given by Shiny, a dark-skinned classmate who is the class orator. What Shiny said and how he said it reflects not only upon himself but on the whole race of black people.

Not long after the narrator graduates, his mother dies, and he decides to attend Atlanta University rather than Harvard, which would have been more expensive. The narrator never matriculates at Atlanta University because his money is stolen and he is too embarrassed to tell anyone at the school about his predicament. Instead, he catches a train for Jacksonville, Florida, where he earns money giving piano lessons and working in a cigar factory and where he earns the privileged position of "reader." Although he seems relatively satisfied with his life in Jacksonville, the narrator longs to see the North again. When the cigar factory closes, he moves to New York City.

Enticed by the less-than-commendable features of the city's attractions, the narrator discovers a gambling-house where the clientele can drink, play pool, and shoot dice. Caught up in the heady experience of gambling, the narrator decides that this will be his occupation. Because his winning streaks are sporadic, however, he masters the technique of playing ragtime music. A millionaire becomes his patron and introduces him to a world where rich, blasé, cynical whites pay him to entertain them with ragtime tunes. Attracted by the millionaire's "stamp of culture," the narrator agrees to play at dinners and parties. "Occasionally [the millionaire] 'loaned' me to some of his friends. And, too, I often played for him alone at his apartments."

Frightened out of New York by the prospect of being murdered by a jealous lover, the narrator accepts the millionaire's invitation to accompany him on an extended European tour. They spend weeks in London, Paris, Amsterdam, Luxembourg, Brussels, and Berlin, where the narrator's cosmopolitan sensibilities are refined. He discovers that the stereotyped descriptions of the natives of the different countries are false and that assumptions about an entire race or ethnic group cannot be determined from generalizations. He enjoys the freedom of not having to contend with constant reminders that he is a black man, and he learns something of the culture and languages of the different countries. His travels are rather aimless, however, until, while in Germany, he realizes the artistic possibilities of making black music an accepted part of American culture. He decides to take ragtime music and make it classical. The millionaire argues against this resolve, but the narrator reasons that he will have a better future as a composer.

As he makes his way into the Deep South, the narrator thinks about the complexities of the race question. While making his musical notations, he notices that "the Negroes themselves do not fully appreciate these old slave songs. The educated classes are rather ashamed of them and prefer to sing hymns from books." For all of its attractions and special cultural significance, the South is chaotic. It defies all attempts to make it orderly. Already predisposed to choose the kind of life that will lift the burden of race from his shoulders, a lynching of a black man makes the narrator finally decide to pass for white. As the narrator, transfixed, watches the horribly mechanical spectacle of the lynching, he does not identify with the man's predicament. The black man's fate can never be his own. The lynching forces the narrator to make a resolution he is able to keep. With his physical characteristics, speech patterns, and knowledge no one will believe he is black.

Critical Evaluation:

The Autobiography of an Ex-Coloured Man is the account of a mulatto who decides, after a series of experiences and revelations beginning in his childhood and stretching into adulthood, to "pass" for white. The mulatto narrator remains anonymous, and the tone of the book suggests that the story is based on fact. In the first paragraph the narrator professes to know his identity. He states that his autobiography is the complete expression of his "sort of savage and diabolical desire to gather up all the little tragedies of my life, and turn them into a practical joke on society."

When the novel was published anonymously in 1912, readers speculated about its verisimilitude. Anonymity, a common feature of the slave narratives that had lent support to the abolitionist movement, forms the foundation of the African American literary tradition. Just as anonymity had protected the identity of slaves and lessened the chance of reprisals from slave masters, it is not difficult to assume that this author chose anonymity to avoid answering questions or compromising his status. The book also reveals the trickster aspect of black-white relations: Readers cannot be certain that what the narrator says is precisely what he is thinking.

Some critics judged the narrator to be a moral coward because he chose to live his life as a white man. This criticism makes the assumption that choosing to be black would have been better than choosing to be white. If, however, the making of money is not innately immoral, it does not follow that the narrator's decision to function as a white businessman necessarily means that he is a moral coward. The narrator is criticized because he looks to material comfort for self-aggrandizement rather than to Christianity for spiritual growth in suffering. However, as a self-described agnostic, the narrator does not have any use for a religion that restricts people to emotionalism and numbs their impulse to strike back at avowed enemies. His willingness to suffer the millionaire's apparent ennui and homosexual overtures suggests an inability to demand respect when his physical comfort might be jeopardized.

Johnson explores the ambivalence that troubles mulattoes who have some of the "best" and some of the "worst" blood in the South coursing through their veins. More than once, the narrator decides to live as a black man and be an exemplar of his race, but he finds he cannot do it. He has not grown up with a reason to fight against social or economic injustices. He has had to develop an awareness of his ethnic relationship with black people and invent ways to give expression to his ethnicity. His intellectual attachment to biblical and historical figures provides a release for the psychological struggle that mirrors the plight of many light-skinned blacks, but he is physically detached from the majority of blacks.

Shamefully naïve about black folk culture, the narrator is repulsed by unkempt and loud lower-class blacks. For a short time, he appreciates the beauty of African American culture as lower-class blacks express it. His appreciation for black folk music wanes, though, as he becomes aware that black music outside black society is not accepted as authentic art. The popular attitude of the time is that black people are fundamentally incapable of creating anything that can be considered artistic. The narrator adopts this view as his own.

Johnson's use of anonymity to reveal the novel's complexities accentuates the narrator's sense of isolation from himself and from others, whether black or white. Having the narrator pass through rural, urban, and international environments suggests that a cosmopolitan experience can stimulate the development of art forms. However, the reaction to skin color, itself a rather ill-defined measure of personal identity, prevents the growth of artistic expression and an awareness of self.

Judith E. B. Harmon

Further Reading

Ahlin, Lena. *The "New Negro" in the Old World: Culture and Performance in James Weldon Johnson, Jessie Fauset, and Nella Larsen*. Lund, Sweden: Department of English, Centre for Languages and Literature, Lund University, 2006. An analysis of *The Autobiography of an Ex-Coloured Man* and books by the other two authors to demonstrate how these books reflected the emerging African American consciousness of the early twentieth century.

Bell, Bernard W. "James Weldon Johnson (1871-1938)." In *The Afro-American Novel and Its Tradition*. Amherst: University of Massachusetts Press, 1987. Bell argues that the psychological impact of color and class has turned the mulatto narrator from the majority of black Americans and toward an identity with white Americans that subverts his self-worth.

Davis, Arthur P. *From the Dark Tower: Afro-American Writers 1900-1960*. Washington, D.C.: Howard University Press, 1981. Contains a chapter devoted to a general discussion of Johnson's works. Pays some attention to character and theme in *The Autobiography of an Ex-Coloured Man*, which the author sees as a departure from the norm in African American fiction.

Fleming, Robert E. "Irony as a Key to Johnson's *The Autobiography of an Ex-Coloured Man*." *American Literature* 43, no. 1 (March, 1971): 83-96. Espouses the theory that to accept the unreliability of the narrator is essential to comprehending Johnson's novel.

Gates, Henry Louis, Jr. Introduction to *The Autobiography of an Ex-Coloured Man*, by James Weldon Johnson. New York: Vintage Books, 1989. An excellent discussion of Johnson's life and work. Focuses on the elements of structure and theme that make *The Autobiography of an Ex-Coloured Man* a signal accomplishment in African American fiction.

O'Sullivan, Maurice J. "Of Souls and Pottage: James Weldon Johnson's *The Autobiography of an Ex-Coloured Man*." *College Language Association Journal* 23 (September, 1979): 60-70. Examines Johnson's protagonist from a standpoint different from that of most critics. Contends that the book's narrator is "richly complex," not merely weak and vacillating, and that it is in the character's ambivalence that this complexity is centered.

Price, Kenneth M., and Lawrence J. Oliver. *Critical Essays on James Weldon Johnson*. New York: G. K. Hall, 1997. Includes reviews of *The Autobiography of an Ex-Coloured Man* that appeared when the book initially was published, other previously published pieces, and three new essays. Many of the essays examine *The Autobiography*, including discussions of irony, symbolic action, and subversion in the book and a comparison of Johnson's book to *Invisible Man* by Ralph Ellison.

Rosenblatt, Roger. "*The Autobiography of an Ex-Coloured Man.*" In *Black Fiction*. Cambridge, Mass.: Harvard University Press, 1974. Argues that Johnson's protagonist is yet another example of the "vanishing hero" in black fiction. Suggests that in trying to beat the system by accommodating to it, Johnson's narrator disappears into that system, losing all sense of himself in the process.

Ross, Joseph T. "Audience and Irony in *The Autobiography of an Ex-Coloured Man.*" *College Language Association Journal* 118 (December, 1974): 198-210. Asserts that the ambivalence of Johnson's protagonist is not so much a natural weakness of character but rather a studied attempt by the author to dramatize the effects of betrayal by a white upper-class value system from which the protagonist cannot escape.

Stepto, Robert. "Lost in a Guest: James Weldon Johnson's *Autobiography of an Ex-Coloured Man.*" In *From Behind the Veil: A Study of Afro-American Narrative*. Urbana: University of Illinois Press, 1979. A thorough examination of Johnson's novel within the context of other literary forms of the period, specifically the autobiography and the slave narrative. Concludes that although Johnson used many of the techniques of these forms, he produced something new and different.

Autobiography of Benjamin Franklin

Author: Benjamin Franklin (1706-1790)
First published: 1791, as *Mémoires de la vie privée de Benjamin Franklin* (English translation, 1860)
Type of work: Autobiography

The first part of the *Autobiography of Benjamin Franklin* (also known as the *Autobiography*) was begun in 1771. In the work, Benjamin Franklin first addresses his adult son, William. After a few pages about his ancestry and his own birth in Boston as the fourteenth of his father's seventeen children (and the seventh by his second wife), Franklin tells of being taken from grammar school at the age of ten and put to work for his father, a maker of candles and soap. The young Franklin did not enjoy this work but found consolation in being a leader among the boys in his neighborhood and in being an omnivorous reader.

At the age of twelve, Franklin was apprenticed to his printer brother, James. When the latter started his own newspaper, *The New England Courant*, Franklin not only worked at printing and delivering the newspaper but also made anonymous contributions, usually of a satirical nature, to the publication.

Franklin had been physically abused by his older brother, who had benefited from Franklin more than he realized. In 1723, Benjamin decided, without consulting his family, to leave home and live on his own. He traveled to New York but found no jobs for a printer. He continued to Philadelphia, where he found work with a printer named Keimer. He lived with the Read family and soon fell in love with young Deborah Read. He also made the acquaintance of Governor William Keith, who suggested that he travel to London for printing supplies. While Franklin was away, Deborah had married another man who, within a few months of their marriage, deserted her.

Franklin returned from London as a clerk for a merchant named Thomas Denham but later worked again for Keimer, from whom he bought a newspaper, the *Pennsylvania Gazette*. Franklin also adopted the philosophy of Deism, and undertook one of the first of his cultural enterprises: He started the Library Company of Philadelphia, the first circulating library in America. In 1730, he married Deborah, whose marital status was unclear at this time. They had two daughters together and raised Franklin's son, William.

After a break of seventeen years, Franklin wrote the second part of his *Autobiography*, turning to an examination of his religious and moral life. Raised as a Presbyterian, he came to believe some of its doctrines "unintelligible, others doubtful" and found greater satisfaction with the principles of Deism. These principles did not, however, provide him with a key to good conduct.

In an attempt to reach "moral perfection," Franklin consulted his wide range of readings and employed his own judgment to establish a list of thirteen virtues: temperance, silence, order, resolution, frugality, industry, sincerity, justice, moderation, cleanliness, tranquility, charity, and humility. He made charts for each virtue and recorded his daily progress in his pursuit of them. He found the third virtue, order, difficult to obtain but also felt that his efforts made him a better person. The last of his virtues, humility, he added after a Quaker friend told him that he was generally considered proud. Humility, too, proved a difficult virtue, for even if he obtained it, he observed that he would "probably be proud of my humility."

In the third part of his work, Franklin recounts many of the achievements of his middle years. He learned French, Italian, and Spanish. He filled a number of posts in Pennsylvania's general assembly. He established a philosophical society and an academy. He became the postmaster of the American colonies. He devised the Franklin stove and conducted many "electrical experiments," although he does not provide any details about his famous lightning-rod experiments. He studied the causes of fires and established a company to battle them. He devoted considerable time to military preparedness and offered a plan to unify the defenses of the colonies. Despite his dislike of organized religion, he admired the most famous traveling evangelist of his time, George Whitefield, and formed a "civil friendship" with him. He also was able to cooperate with Quakers in forwarding his defense measures.

In the fourth part, which he wrote in the last year of his life, Franklin tells of being sent by the Pennsylvania assembly as an agent to England, where he learned how Americans differed from the English in assessing their relationships, particularly those involving taxes. The scope of the *Autobiography* stops short of Franklin's part in the controversy over the Stamp Tax. The work thus contains nothing about his crowning work as a diplomat abroad or his contribution to the Constitutional Convention of 1787.

Although written in the last twenty years of a long life, Franklin's *Autobiography* covers only a little more than Franklin's first forty-plus years and omits much of importance in that period. Also, the integration of the work is hampered because the manuscript had been written at four different times, sometimes without other parts of the work at hand. The work's unity is hampered as well: The first part had been written for his son, the second part in response to a request by a friend for an account of Franklin's moral philosophy, and the last parts in response to requests for a memoir that he was, by this time, too old and too ill to complete.

Despite these intervals and shifts in motivation, the *Autobiography* reflects the consistency of Franklin himself. He was a native New Englander, and this work reflects a Puritan sense of duty and the influence of a tradition of personal narratives, such as those by Jonathan Edwards and John Woolman, which trace their respective struggles for moral progress. The Puritans had interpreted such progress as evidence that they might be spared God's wrath. At the end of every year, Puritans reckoned their economic success, mainly as evidence of divine favor; Franklin favored frugality because it would lead to wealth and freedom from social fears that arise from want. His economic influence is much more profound. Social philosopher Max Weber, in his book *Die protestantische Ethik und der Geist des Kapitalismus* (1904-1905; *The Protestant Ethic and the Spirit of Capitalism*, 1930), argues that Franklin's assertions about time, credit, and investment display the essential spirit of capitalism.

Franklin had left New England because of his dislike for authority. Also, he began to doubt some of the doctrines of congregational Presbyterianism. Offenses against the Puritan moral code were considered sins; Franklin spoke of errata, or mistakes, instead. To this day, Americans are more likely to follow Franklin in labeling their moral deviations "errors" or "mistakes" rather than sins. Franklin sought to arrange his moral life not by reference to doctrine but by his own reflections on the best advice he could find in his readings. One of the works most valued in colonial New England was John Bunyan's *Pilgrim's Progress* (1678, 1684). Franklin characteristically sold his copy to purchase historical works that would broaden his knowledge. His reading included periodical literature, and he admired Joseph Addison and Richard Steele's *Spectator*, whose title reflects an interest in the goings-on of any given moment—what was to be seen—rather than in the abstract spiritual realm that preoccupied preachers and theologians. His affinity with periodical literature helped him develop the plain, unadorned style that made the *Autobiography* understandable and stimulating to the reader of his day.

The first building that Franklin visited in Philadelphia was a Quaker meeting house. The meeting he first attended there was a typically quiet one—it even put him to sleep. It is significant that he had no interest in Quaker worship, but it is even more significant that the Quaker meetings reflected the religious toleration that he respected. As his stay in his new town continued, he perceived more of its advantages. Philadelphia, more so than Boston, was cosmopolitan, worldly, and involved with such topics as government, finance, and social welfare. He settled in Philadelphia.

Franklin's list of thirteen virtues, which would have puzzled a more typical New Englander, proved to be compatible with his new surroundings. Many of them—silence, order, and resolution, for instance—are not theological but philosophical. For Franklin, doing good was not an act of worship but a way of serving the community; the *Autobiography* describes many of his countless activities toward that end. He gave his new home a library and several educational institutions to educate his fellow citizens. He founded newspapers and published almanacs to keep citizens informed. He built a militia to keep them safe, a hospital to heal their wounds, a stove to warm them, a fire department to protect their lives and homes, pavements for their roads, and an improved postal service. His academy became the University of Pennsylvania. Many of these local improvements reached beyond Philadelphia; for example, his organization for philosophy became the American Philosophical Society. People found his inventions and creations empowering, and adopted them gratefully.

Some of his achievements led to advances he could never have predicted. Could he have imagined an institution like the present University of Pennsylvania, or the proliferation of great institutions of higher learning across the United States? His work in electricity contributed to an almost unimaginable and yet unceasing flow of improvements in everyday life. Some critics—novelist D. H. Lawrence in particular—found Franklin deficient in spirituality and even responsible for a deplorable spiritual decline in American life, but few people have complained about his contributions to social welfare.

It has often been said that Franklin's life mirrors American life, especially its concern for civic and social improvement. Indeed, his writing and the nature of his achievements exemplify a powerful sense of duty to form a prosperous and enjoyable society. J. A. Leo Lemay, an important editor and critic of Franklin's work, has argued that it was Franklin who formulated the idea of the American Dream. Franklin's conceptions of frugality and industry—the fifth and sixth of the virtues listed in the second part of the *Autobiography*—laid the path by which the common man (Franklin has little to say about women) could prosper in life. Lemay also points out that Franklin valued as more important not the attainment of wealth but the rise from helplessness to power. Another aspect of the American Dream is the philosophy of individualism, which allows for any person to succeed in life, if that person believes in the "possibility of accomplishment." Finally, "the fictive world of Franklin's *Autobiography*," Lemay argues, "portrays the first completely modern world that I know in Western literature: nonfeudal, nonaristocratic, and nonreligious."

Robert P. Ellis

Further Reading

Brands, H. W. *The First American: The Life and Times of Benjamin Franklin.* New York: Random House, 2000. This full biography relates Franklin's life to the birth of the United States.

Breitweiser, Mitchell Robert. *Cotton Mather and Benjamin Franklin: The Price of Representative Personality.* New York: Cambridge University Press, 1984. This study of the relationship of Franklin's thought with that of a highly influential New England clergyman of his time, Cotton Mather, clarifies Franklin's place in a developing American culture.

Campbell, James. *Recovering Benjamin Franklin: An Exploration of a Life of Science and Service.* Peru, Ill.: Carus, 1999. A study of Franklin's thinking on science, religion, morality, and politics as well as his ideas on public service.

Cohen, I. Bernard. *Science and the Founding Fathers: Science in the Political Thought of Jefferson, Franklin, Adams, and Madison.* New York: W. W. Norton, 1995. Cohen's chapter on Franklin explains how Franklin, who had only a few years of formal education, was able to become a distinguished scientist.

Cullen, J. P. "Benjamin Franklin: 'The Glory of America.'" *American History Illustrated* 6, no. 1 (1971): 40-47. Cullen's description of Franklin's early years as a printer is a valuable resource both for understanding Franklin's ideas and for tracing his early development.

Franklin, Benjamin. *Benjamin Franklin's Autobiography.* Edited by J. A. Leo Lemay and P. M. Zall. New York: W. W. Norton, 1986. A critical edition of the *Autobiography* that presents the authoritative text of Franklin's *Memoirs of the Life*. Particularly useful are thirty pages of biographical notes concerning the contemporary and historical figures mentioned in the *Autobiography*. Other valuable sections contain relevant extracts from Franklin's letters and selected commentaries by outstanding critics from Franklin's times to the mid-1980's.

Isaacson, Walter. *Benjamin Franklin: An American Life.* New York: Simon & Schuster, 2003. This biography reveals much about Franklin's family life and achievements that are not revealed in the *Autobiography*.

Lemay, J. A. Leo, ed. *Benjamin Franklin: Writings.* New York: Library of America, 1987. Features the text of the *Autobiography* and a selection of Franklin's other writings, including his satires, speeches, letters, and the popular *Poor Richard's Almanack.* Contains a useful chronology, notes, and an index of topics.

Lynch, Jack, ed. *Benjamin Franklin.* Pasadena, Calif.: Salem Press, 2009. A thorough critical analysis of Franklin and his multifaceted career. Includes essays on the *Autobiography.* Also includes suggested further readings. Part of the Critical Insights series.

Van Doren, Carl. *Benjamin Franklin.* 1938. Reprint. Birmingham, Ala.: Palladium Press, 2001. One of the most readily obtainable and most comprehensive biographies of Franklin accessible to the general reader. Extensive quotations from Franklin's works provide a "speaking voice" for both the historical figure and the human personality.

Autobiography of Benvenuto Cellini

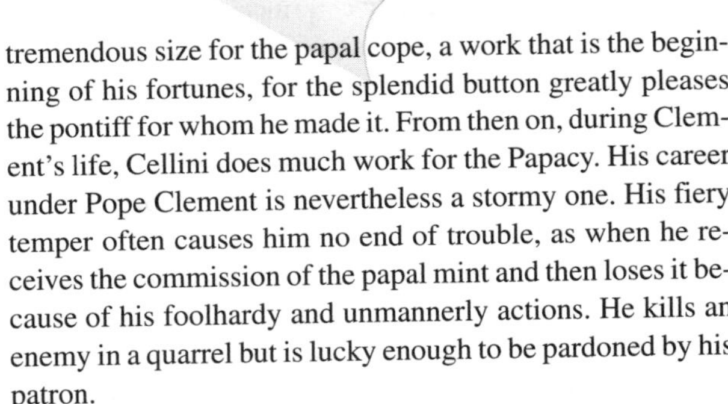

Author: Benvenuto Cellini (1500-1571)
First transcribed: La vita di Benvenuto Cellini, 1558-1562; first published, 1728 (English translation, as *The Life of Benvenuto Cellini, a Florentine Artist*, 1771)
Type of work: Autobiography

The Story:

At the age of fifty-eight, Benvenuto Cellini begins to set down his memoirs. After relating a fictional version of the founding of Florence by his ancestors, he starts the story of his life. Benvenuto's father plans for his son to be a musician, and as a boy Benvenuto is taught to play the flute and sing. His father's lessons in music fail to interest him, however, and at the age of fifteen Cellini apprentices himself to a goldsmith. Cellini says of himself that he has a natural bent for the work and in a few months he has surpassed men long in the trade. As an apprentice and, later, as a journeyman goldsmith, Cellini travels through Italy doing fine work and acting the part of a bravo. He becomes an excellent swordsman and handler of the poniard, as he proves when he kills an enemy in a street brawl.

In 1527, the constable of Bourbon marches on Rome and besieges Pope Clement VII in his fortress. Cellini, then in Rome and in sympathy with the pope, serves the pontiff valiantly as an artillerist and as a goldsmith, having been commissioned by the besieged prelate to melt down jewelry and turn it into a more transportable form. Later, Cellini boasts that during the siege he killed the constable of Bourbon and wounded the prince of Orange.

After the siege is lifted and a truce declared, Cellini returns to Florence and kills the murderer of his brother. He later goes to Mantua. After falling ill with fever in that city, he returns to Florence. When Pope Clement declares war on Florence, however, Cellini leaves his shop and trade to enter the papal service. While in Rome, he makes a medallion of tremendous size for the papal cope, a work that is the beginning of his fortunes, for the splendid button greatly pleases the pontiff for whom he made it. From then on, during Clement's life, Cellini does much work for the Papacy. His career under Pope Clement is nevertheless a stormy one. His fiery temper often causes him no end of trouble, as when he receives the commission of the papal mint and then loses it because of his foolhardy and unmannerly actions. He kills an enemy in a quarrel but is lucky enough to be pardoned by his patron.

Cellini's greatest commission from Pope Clement is for a gold chalice. The chalice is never finished, for Clement dies. During the last years of his life, however, the chalice is a matter of contention between the pope and his goldsmith. Cellini tends to work too slowly to suit the pope, and the pope, according to Cellini's account, often forgets that gold is needed to make the vessel.

Upon the accession of Cardinal Farnese as Pope Paul III, Cellini goes into his service for a time. He is away from Rome a great deal, however, at one time taking service with Cosimo de' Medici, the duke of Florence. Upon his return to Rome, Cellini is imprisoned on a charge of homicide. The pope grants him safe conduct for a time, but eventually he is imprisoned. Only after many difficulties does he receive a pardon.

Cellini comes to the notice of Emperor Charles V when that monarch visits Rome and is presented by the pope with a book of hours bound into a gold cover encrusted with jewels, the work of Cellini. A short time later, Cellini is sent for by Francis I, the king of France, but before he can leave Rome he is accused of theft and thrown into prison by the pope's *bargello*, or police force. Cellini clears himself of the charge, but he has made so many enemies that he is kept in prison for many months and suffers, at times, cruel punishment.

Action on Cellini's behalf by King Francis only serves to make his lot harder. At last, Cellini manages to escape by using bedsheets to lower himself from the prison tower and over the prison walls. Having broken his leg in flight, he is recaptured. Released after a long period of confinement, he finds asylum with a French cardinal and, with the aid of Cardinal d'Este of Ferrara, makes his way to France.

In France, with King Francis as his patron, the goldsmith and artist turns to sculpture. He executes an amazing statue of Jupiter for the king and also constructs a large statue of a nymph at Fontainebleau. However, Cellini makes an enemy of Madame d'Étampes, the king's mistress, and she makes his career difficult and his life dangerous. In addition, the cardinal of Ferrara does not fulfill the promises he has made to Cellini. Cellini's amorous adventures also get him into many difficulties.

In desperation, and hoping for a better future, Cellini leaves France and returns to his native Florence in 1545, there to find protection under the patronage of Cosimo de' Medici. In Florence, he makes an enemy of the duchess of Florence and a famous sculptor, Bandinello, whose work Cellini reviles in public and to the sculptor's face. As in France, a woman's enmity, the dislike of fellow artists, the pettifogging of minor officials, and small commissions use up Cellini's valuable time in Florence. Nevertheless, while there, in the years after 1545, Cellini does his greatest works, among them a bronze Perseus of which he is extremely proud. Following the completion of that statue, Cellini goes to work on other pieces, including a tremendous crucifix with a mausoleum at its base to hold his body when he dies.

While working in Florence for the duke, Cellini buys some farmland that fails to bring him the revenues he is promised and embroils him in lengthy and upsetting litigation. That trouble, plus the enmity of the duchess, finally drives him from Florence. In 1562, while the duke and his family are away on a journey, Cellini leaves Florence and heads for Pisa. Cellini ends his autobiography with his departure for Pisa, though he lived for eight more years.

Critical Evaluation:

The Florentine Benvenuto Cellini—contemporary of Michelangelo, Titian, Tintoretto, and Jacopo Sansovino—was a completely natural man of his time. Utterly unselfconscious and uncritical, he presents himself through his *Autobiography* in the context of the Italian Renaissance, totally involved in its art, its politics, its religion, and its culture. His was the life *engagée*, and his *Autobiography* reflects what Italian Renaissance life was really like.

Characteristically, Cellini's temper and temperament were, by later standards, a mixture of extremes. He loved and he hated; he concentrated intensely and he wasted time. In his lifetime, he killed several men, yet he was at the same time tender, compassionate, and concerned about both men and women when he was convinced they were in need of succor. His love affairs were equally extravagant. He loved many women, produced at least six offspring out of wedlock (some of whom were legitimated), but married only once, from which union issued two legitimate children. He frequently offended powerful men in high positions, and, as a consequence, he spent some time in prison and at other times was banished or exiled from his home, wherever it happened to be. At still other times, he was richly rewarded. He was obsessed with vengeance and honor. He killed his brother's murderer and took revenge for other outrages. He insisted on maintaining his honor, regardless of how onerous the circumstances might be. In fact, honor and revenge were the key concepts in his life and, in turn, keys to the Renaissance mind.

This Renaissance fusion of apparent contradictions also delineates the versatility of the period. As a man of letters, Cellini wrote his autobiography (most of it dictated to a scribe), valuable treatises on goldsmithery and sculpture, and other discourses on art. Some of his letters and his petitions survive. He also produced some poetry, which has been largely ignored. He wrote in the lusty Tuscan dialect, more vital than other conventional modes of communication. Cellini is best known, deservedly, as a goldsmith and a sculptor, but he was also an adept swordsman and a diligent soldier, and his engineering skills—particularly in the martial sphere—should not be underrated. This range of accomplishments was typical of cultured men of Cellini's time.

Despite his talents, Cellini was dependent on patronage and relied for his livelihood on commissions for artistic works from wealthy patrons. Hence, among other works, he executed vases and other vessels and plates as well as a variety of medals and jewelry for popes and prelates, royalty and nobles; busts and statuary for the Medici and for King Francis I of France; a crucifix for the Medici; and a famous salt cellar for Francis I. His irascible temper constantly brought him into conflict with his patrons, but Cellini was nevertheless honored, respected, and rewarded in his own time.

Artists of Cellini's time did not necessarily have to cater

to the tastes of their patrons. Cellini conceived his ideas first and then convinced his patrons that the ideas were worthy of support for their execution. Likewise, artists were not required to live morally or legally exemplary lives. They tended to live boisterous, disorderly lives in bohemian quarters wherever and whenever they congregated in urban centers. Their idiosyncrasies and eccentricities were tolerated by their patrons and by the general public because of their overriding contribution to culture. Rebellious religious and political activities were severely punished, however, as Cellini learned from his many imprisonments and exiles. Private immorality, however, was more leniently viewed.

It was under such circumstances as these that Cellini produced his masterworks of art. Categorization of these works is difficult. The sculptures have about them certain qualities of realism, even naturalism, yet they, like Cellini's goldsmithery, are more often placed by art critics in the mannerist school. In fact, such facile classification does injustice to precisely the quality that distinguishes Cellini's artistry, for Cellini was above all the epitome of the Renaissance man. His very versatility defies conventional classification. It is therefore more appropriate to say what he did and how he did it than to apply labels.

Among the works in gold, the jewelry, always with gold settings that Cellini himself cast, was often enameled, encrusted with precious and semiprecious gems, and occasionally embellished with exquisitely intricate filigree work, which Cellini also used to decorate a variety of vessels and small casks. Other works—rings, medals, clasps, breviary covers, buckles, crucifixes—were done in gold leaf delicately beaten to form high- or low-relief designs or figures. Among the most famous of such works is the elegant salt cellar created for Francis I, a large vessel, nearly twelve inches high, featuring the figures of Neptune and Mother Earth set on an elaborately embossed base. Cellini also cast seals for the bulls of cardinals and for official documents of state, made dies for the stamping of coins, and struck medals. In addition, he designed plates for engraving and etching, and he produced larger metal works, both hammered and cast, such as ornate vases, chalices, and life-size cast figures.

As for sculpture, Cellini was adept in several media. He chiseled, for example, from white Carrara marble a life-size Christ crucified and set the figure upon a cross of black Carrara marble to create a tremendous sculpture, a study in contrasts between stark white and stark black. (This crucifix now hangs in the Church of San Lorenzo in El Escorial.) For the gateway to Francis I's palace at Fontainebleau, he cast in bronze a reclining nymph—now known as the Nymph of Fontainebleau—more than ten feet long, surrounded by animals and flanked by two figures symbolizing Victory. For sheer elegance, however, the Nymph is outshone by Cellini's silver Jupiter, also executed for Francis I, a gorgeous statue set on a gilded pedestal that conceals hard wooden ball bearings that allow the statue to be moved with no more than a touch of the hand. A "colossus"—a sixty-foot statue of Mars—that Cellini planned for Francis I's fountain at Fontainebleau was never brought to fruition.

Cellini is perhaps best known and most admired for the slightly larger-than-life-size cast bronze Perseus with the Head of Medusa that he made for Cosimo de' Medici and that still stands in the Loggia de' Lanzia. Using methods similar to those he employed in creating the Nymph of Fontainebleau, he cast the figure of Perseus all in one piece, an amazing achievement of both art and craft. Cellini's description of the process forms one of the high points in his autobiography.

"Critical Evaluation" by Joanne G. Kashdan

Further Reading

Gallucci, Margaret A. *Benvenuto Cellini: Sexuality, Masculinity, and Artistic Identity in Renaissance Italy.* New York: Palgrave Macmillan, 2003. Critical biography places Cellini's life and works within the context of his time, focusing on contemporary discourses about law, magic, masculinity, and honor. Chapter 4 discusses *The Autobiography.*

Gallucci, Margaret A., and Paolo L. Rossi, eds. *Benvenuto Cellini: Sculptor, Goldsmith, Writer.* New York: Cambridge University Press, 2004. Collection of essays examines Cellini's life and work, including discussions of the history and reception of *The Autobiography.*

Howarth, William. "Some Principles of Autobiography." In *Autobiography: Essays Theoretical and Critical*, edited by James Olney. Princeton, N.J.: Princeton University Press, 1980. Discusses Cellini's autobiography as one of several works that attempt in prose what painters do on canvas: the creation of a self-portrait. Maintains that Cellini provides a straightforward account of his life.

Pascal, Roy. "The Early History of Autobiography." In *Design and Truth in Autobiography.* 1960. Reprint. New York: Garland, 1985. Includes a discussion of Cellini's *The Autobiography* in a general assessment of works that emerged during the Renaissance. Asserts that Cellini is truthful in the way he presents the facts of his life, and that he was confident of his greatness.

Pope-Hennessy, John W. *Cellini.* New York: Abbeville Press, 1985. Comprehensive biography of the artist uses *The Autobiography* as a principal source but highlights the differences between Cellini's account of his life and the records of events in other sources. Profusely illustrated.

Weintraub, Karl Joachim. "Benvenuto Cellini: The Naïve Individuality." In *The Value of the Individual: Self and Circumstance in Autobiography*. Chicago: University of Chicago Press, 1978. Provides an excellent scholarly examination of *The Autobiography*, analyzing the themes of self-aggrandizement and Cellini's self-confident belief that the story of his life was worth telling. Argues that the work is a significant document in the development of the concept of human personality.

Autobiography of John Stuart Mill

Author: John Stuart Mill (1806-1873)
First published: 1873, as *Autobiography*
Type of work: Autobiography

The *Autobiography* is a unique and fascinating book, one of a handful likely to be read as long as nineteenth century Britain is remembered. It bears witness to the intellectual ferment that was part of the industrial and democratic revolutions of the time. Wider suffrage led to state-supported education in Britain and debate about its proper content. These circumstances supplied Mill's chief motives for recording his life. He wished to recount his own intellectual development and mission in a period of cultural transition and to describe his remarkable education.

Mill, better than anyone, articulated the outlook of nineteenth century liberalism, and so, more than any other intellectual, shaped thinking about politics and society in English-speaking countries in the twentieth century. His interests included political philosophy, ethics, economics, psychology, logic, the scientific method, religion, liberty, the prejudice suffered by women. His ordered, lucid prose helped guarantee that his books would long be read. Generous by nature and fair-minded in considering the views of others, he was, as British Prime Minister William Gladstone declared, a "saint of rationalism."

The book recounts in detail a truly remarkable instance of home schooling, through which Mill acquired by his middle teens knowledge and analytical skills far superior to those of most university graduates—to say nothing of a phenomenal capacity for work. Mill missed a real childhood, however, suffering emotional disabilities that led to a severe psychological crisis and lifelong insecurity. The *Autobiography* reveals and conceals the emotional dimension of a committed rationalist.

Mill's education was provided by his father, James Mill, a gifted Scotsman of modest birth who had been sponsored at university by a squire, John Stuart. Trained in the classics and living by his pen in London, James commenced his eldest son's education at the age of three with Greek. Beginning with *Aesop's Fables* (fourth century, B.C.E.), Mill later read the historian Herodotus, the philosopher Plato, and numerous other works. Mill was tutored several hours each morning, then worked at his father's table, asking for definitions when necessary. He also read modern histories of Greece and Rome, typically—as he remembered it—on his own initiative, discussing them from his notes on long daily walks with his father. James gave explanations his son was required to restate in his own words; this introduced him to the analysis of institutions and the biases of historians. He also studied math and wrote poetry.

Mill began Latin at eight, also teaching it to his sister. He studied Greek and Latin poets, the historian Thucydides, and the philosopher Aristotle, and he commenced geometry, algebra, and calculus. His "private reading" was still mainly historical, and at eleven he wrote a long history of Roman government (his father did not intervene in any way). By this time he was reading Greek philosophers "with perfect ease," learning not just another language, but how to think critically. He was asked to explain and draw inferences. At about age ten he read aloud the entire manuscript of his father's ten-volume *History of British India* (1818), helping correct the proofs. At twelve he commenced logic with Aristotle and later writers. The heavily classical training raised no religious doubts: "I never threw off religion because I never had any."

Two friends of his father were important in his education.

He learned economics from his father's exposition, on walks, of David Ricardo's thought. Mill took daily notes, which his father used when writing a book on political economy. Mill later made marginal summaries on the manuscript so the order of ideas could better be assessed. Philosopher Jeremy Bentham was James's mentor. Bentham took a strong interest in Mill, and, via James, shaped his philosophical outlook.

By age fourteen most of Mill's formal education was complete. He had no idea he was exceptional. When he learned otherwise, he judged his abilities average at best and credited his father. He spent a year, 1820-1821, in France with Bentham's brother's family. There he acquired excellent French, learned dancing and piano, and displayed little aptitude for fencing and riding. He learned to love mountain scenery and botany, studied at the University of Montpellier, and later described this breath of "free continental air" as the happiest year in his childhood.

James's *History of British India* secured him a high bureaucratic position in the East India Company, which governed the colony of India. Mill studied law and German and became the chief teacher of his eight siblings until he was forty-five. At eighteen he also began working for his father and continued to do so for thirty-five years, seeking to achieve, as drafter of correspondence to India's administrators, beneficial government.

Mill, diligent and committed to ideas and reform, found time for another life in the world of ideas. While still a teenager he had edited Bentham's five-volume *Rationale of Judicial Evidence* (1825), a daunting task which required reconciling three complete manuscripts. He continued to write, publishing more than fifty letters, reviews, and articles before reaching age twenty. He formed groups, including the Utilitarians (short-lived, but the group's name would come to denote a branch of philosophy), a self-study group, and a debating society. Though not eloquent, he impressed others with his precision and relentless logic. He was likened by a friend to a "great steam engine."

In his early twenties a mental crisis came that he judged a reaction to his intellectually rich but emotionally starved upbringing. Mill came to say that fear, not love, characterized the relationship between James and his older children. Mill sank into depression after realizing that even if he achieved all of his reform goals he would not be happy. Distraught, he concluded that the analytical emphasis of his father's teaching had stifled his emotional development. He seemed to take pleasure in nothing, not even long-cherished books. The pathos of a French playwright's description of his father's death brought tears and released Mill's pent-up feelings. The poetry of William Wordsworth, evoking pleasure in nature's beauty, was another source of emotional renewal.

The depression, which he thought fruitless to discuss with his father, led Mill to new friends and new ideas, all of which were part of the cultural reaction against the eighteenth century. Some, such as poet Samuel Taylor Coleridge, historian Thomas Carlyle, and their German mentors, emphasized feeling and intuition. Others, such as Auguste Comte, propounded something quite new to Mill: the notion that cultural history necessarily follows a particular pattern, from theological to metaphysical to positive (scientific) thinking.

One friendship was to prove especially significant for the emotionally fragile Mill—one with a beautiful, intelligent, intense young woman, Harriet Taylor (1807-1858). They met in 1830; he was twenty-five, she twenty-three. She was also a married mother of two, soon to be three, and divorce was not then accepted. What ensued was an ardent but platonic relationship beset by gossip, a shrinking circle of friends, and prolonged public embarrassment for all concerned. The pair saw each other frequently, even traveling together. This lasted two decades, until Mr. Taylor died and they could wed in 1851. Mill saw Harriet as his coworker and emotional lodestone. The *Autobiography*'s dumbfoundingly extravagant praise of her superiority in character, feeling, intellect, and judgment reveals by implication that he was dominated by her emotionally. She chilled his relations with his family. Mill, who lived at home until forty-five, the last fifteen years of which time he was the head of his dead father's household, makes no mention of his mother in the *Autobiography.* Equally strange was Harriet's failure to protest in the slightest his ludicrously exaggerated praise of her. One must look beyond the *Autobiography*, or read between the lines, to understand their relationship.

The unusual nature of Mill's private and emotional life, however, did not deflect him from his sense of mission, his commitment to enlightening the public and giving voice to liberal elements in Parliament. The *Autobiography* recounts his work in detail. *A System of Logic* (1843), his first major work, defends empiricism against intuitionism, which he saw as a bulwark for reactionary political and religious thinking. *Principles of Political Economy* (1848) defends free market production but holds that no economic laws determine how wealth is distributed; by concerted action workers can alter their share of the wealth labor creates. This view, expressed in the third edition of the book, contributed much to the rise of socialism in England. *On Liberty* (1859), a joint work with Harriet, defends free thought and the sovereignty of the individual, and proclaims the social value of letting people develop in diverse ways. It emphasizes—as had historian Alexis de Tocqueville's *Democracy in America* (1835-1840), a book Mill esteemed highly—the danger of intolerant public opinion in a democracy. Mill hoped that *On Liberty* would be his most enduring work. *The Subjection of Women* (1869) combats the disenfranchisement of women.

Mill's liberalism is also evident in his numerous articles, many of which were later published as a book: *Dissertations and Discussions* (1859). His support for self-rule in Canada sped its achievement there. During the American Civil War he held that Union victory was vital to progress throughout the world and hoped it would destroy slavery, the "accursed thing" that violated America's constitution. He spoke for the exploited, be they landless Irish peasants or brutalized former slaves in Jamaica. His commitment to putting liberal ideas before the public is revealed not only by his many articles but also by his work as editor of the *London and Westminster Review* and his financial support of that and other journals.

In 1858, Parliament decided, over his able protest, to abolish the East India Company and rule directly. Mill received a generous position. He and Harriet planned a lengthy trip in southern Europe, but she suddenly died of consumption in Avignon, France. Much of his remaining fifteen years was spent living there, within sight of her grave. He continued to work productively, writing many of his books during the years in Avignon. Evidence of his apparent emotional need for a strong personality to fill the place first occupied by his father, then Harriet, is the fact that he elevated his stepdaughter Helen, who lived with him until his death in Avignon, to a similar position.

In the mid-1860's, Mill was asked to represent Westminster in Parliament. Though declaring that he would not campaign, he was victorious. His actions there were consistent with his principles. He sought land reform and the restoration of habeas corpus in Ireland, judicial action against those who violated the rights of Jamaicans, an end to election bribery, proportional representation for minorities, and enfranchisement of women. This last, surprisingly, was supported by eighty other members of Parliament, marking the effective beginning of the women's suffrage movement in England.

R. Craig Philips

Further Reading

Barros, Carolyn A. *Autobiography: Narrative of Transformation*. Ann Arbor: University of Michigan Press, 1998. Analyzes autobiographies by Mill and several other prominent Victorians, describing how these authors relate tales of major transformations in their lives; Mill's autobiography recounts a significant change in his philosophy.

Mazlish, Bruce. *James and John Stuart Mill, Father and Son in the Nineteenth Century*. New York: Basic Books, 1975. The material on James Mill adds much to one's understanding of his more famous son. The book has a strong "social science/psycho-history" perspective that is predicated on the validity of Freudian theory.

Mill, John Stuart. *The Early Draft of John Stuart Mill's Autobiography*. Edited by Jack Stillinger. Champaign: University of Illinois Press, 1961. Reveals differences between early drafts and the published versions of the *Autobiography*.

________. *John Stuart Mill and Harriet Taylor: Their Correspondence and Subsequent Marriage*. Edited by F. A. von Hayek. London: Routledge & Kegan Paul, 1951. A study of an important relationship in Mill's adult years. Drastically alters the glowing image of Harriet Taylor created by the *Autobiography*.

Packe, Michael. *The Life of John Stuart Mill*. New York: Macmillan, 1954. The standard biography. Comprehensive, intelligent, and elegantly written, setting many aspects of Mill's career in historical context.

Reeves, Richard. *John Stuart Mill: Victorian Firebrand*. London: Atlantic Books, 2007. An authoritative and well-received biography that recounts Mill's life, philosophy, and pursuit of truth and liberty for all.

The Autobiography of Malcolm X

Author: Malcolm X (1925-1965)
First published: 1965
Type of work: Autobiography

The Autobiography of Malcolm X, edited by Alex Haley, is an extended monologue by Malcolm X in which he recounts his life story, shares the dramatic changes that occurred in his life and thinking, and addresses the reader about the values he holds as if he were a moral philosopher or a member of the clergy. Although the book is edited, it is written in the first person, communicating with readers as if no second party or editor interfered with Malcolm X's direct connection with his reading audience. The exception to this style is the epilogue, which was written by the editor after Malcolm X's death. It is a record of the assassination of Malcolm X and reveals how the spirit of the man in life appears to continue after his death. It emphasizes the impact of Malcolm X's life and the number of people who have assessed his contribution, whether they agreed with his ideas or not. Malcolm X claimed that he would never live to see his autobiography published; because he was killed before it was printed, the epilogue by the editor is important as a conclusion to the life story of Malcolm X and as an analysis of his impact.

The Autobiography of Malcolm X has been so widely read and the interest in Malcolm X as a leader in American life in the 1950's and 1960's is so broad that many authors have written about his life and his speeches. *Malcolm X: A Selected Bibliography*, published in 1984, includes more than one hundred pages of listings of works by other authors about Malcolm X, including dissertations and theses. Among all of his speeches and other writers' critiques, however, *The Autobiography of Malcolm X* remains the most complete and direct communication of his life experiences and changing ideas. It is in some ways a traditional conversion narrative, showing how a man alters his perceptions and values. It is in other ways an admonition to a general audience of that which Malcolm X considered to be wrong with his time and place. It is in still other ways an explanation by the author of how he, as one African American male, experienced rejection and found ways to address and repudiate the discrimination against him. Although Malcolm X's words often imply that he had a sense of contentment toward the end of his life and that he could share that completed sense of self with others, *The Autobiography of Malcolm X* also has a continuing theme of change. The author shows not only how he has changed throughout his life but also how he is open to further change toward the end of his life. Thus, it is a narrative told by and about a man "in process." The epilogue raises questions about the direction Malcolm's life took in his later years and whether these challenged earlier directions he had promoted.

Malcolm X was born Malcolm Little in 1925 in Omaha, Nebraska. From an early age, he had knowledge both of white discrimination against blacks and of black separatist reactions. His father was a Baptist minister and follower of the black nationalist Marcus Garvey. When the family moved to Mason, Michigan, his father was murdered by white supremacists. Malcolm's mother found the care of the dependent children such a strain that she was placed in a mental hospital, and Malcolm and his siblings were placed in foster homes. Malcolm succeeded, however, in his largely white environment and was elected president of his seventh-grade class. At the same time, however, his English teacher advised him not to attempt to become a lawyer but to be content with being a carpenter because he was black. The suggestion devastated Malcolm, and he moved to Boston to live with his half sister. He stopped attending school after the eighth grade, held some menial jobs, and became involved in illegal acts. He later moved to Harlem, where he was known as Detroit Red because he had a fair complexion and reddish hair. He had also become successful as a hustler, pimp, and drug dealer. By the time he was twenty-one years old, Malcolm had been sentenced to prison for ten years.

The autobiography becomes far more than a "slice of life" ethnic history of one man when Malcolm describes the changes in his thinking in prison. These changes were not just mental; his style of life was altered and became consistent with the new ideas he encountered and embraced while incarcerated. Some of his brothers and sisters had become followers of Elijah Muhammad, the leader of the Nation of Islam (sometimes named the "Black Muslims"), and they sent him literature by Muhammad. Malcolm wrote to this leader daily and, when he was released from prison in 1952, became a follower of Elijah Muhammad and took the name Malcolm X in place of his birth name, which he now rejected as a slave name. Malcolm embraced the ideas of the Nation of Islam: that the black race was the original race, that blacks must develop pride in themselves by separating themselves from whites, and that blacks would enter a new age in which their race would rule the world. Malcolm felt the appeal of this theology and value system for himself but, more important, believed that black men would find this thought acceptable because they had historically experienced the "devil-nature" of white people. Malcolm agreed with Elijah Muhammad that attempting to change a white-dominated society was useless and was not the mission of blacks. Instead, black people would always be victimized by the inferior whites, and their only recourse was to depend on themselves and their own community to realize their innate purity partly by disassociating from whites. In 1953, Malcolm X was appointed the assistant minister of Detroit's Temple Number One of the Nation of Islam and later became Elijah Muhammad's national representative. By 1954, Malcolm was the head of a major mosque in Harlem in New York City. He had become Elijah Muhammad's main spokesperson throughout the country.

The autobiography makes it clear that Malcolm revered Elijah Muhammad for giving him the greatest gift of all, a new identity. The name change symbolized what had happened to Malcolm's perspectives and values. He had become a full man, worshiping a relevant god, finally understanding the way out of his plight of oppression. He was obedient to the Nation of Islam's doctrines and morality, abstaining from liquor and drugs, refusing to exploit other blacks, honoring black women, and accepting full responsibility for the roles of husband and father in a secure family life. At the same time, Elijah Muhammad had found in the gifted Malcolm a spokesperson who would obediently follow Muhammad's direction and an appealing, an articulate, but a street-smart voice who could generate and maintain the interest of masses of black people in the ideas of the Nation of Islam. It appeared to be, and was for several years, a productive relationship between the leader and his main representative in which both found ways to meet the other's needs. Under Malcolm's skilled presentation, the Nation of Islam grew from a very small cult of several hundred persons to a major religious organization in the black community with thousands of followers in all fifty states.

Malcolm's successes, however, were not appreciated by some of Elijah Muhammad's other assistants and, eventually, Elijah Muhammad reprimanded Malcolm for remarks he made about former president John Kennedy's assassination. Finally, Malcolm was removed from all responsibilities and expelled from the organization. This became one more decisive change in Malcolm's life and an opportunity to expand his own thinking, beyond the strict ideologies of the Nation of Islam. He made a pilgrimage to Mecca, where he took the name El-Hajj Malik El-Shabazz and announced that he had altered his views on integration. This was partly because of his experience in Mecca of perceiving brotherhood among Muslims of many nationalities, races, and ethnic groups. He also began working closely with Africans internationally who were seeking to unite blacks throughout the world. In order to process this work, he established a new organization, the Organization of Afro-American Unity, in the United States with headquarters in New York City.

Malcolm was assassinated while speaking to an audience of this organization in Harlem on February 21, 1965. Three persons were convicted of the crime, two of whom were members of the Nation of Islam. Malcolm had predicted his death through violence but had suspected that the action would require more than Black Muslim involvement, implying that other institutions such as governmental agencies would be part of the scheme.

The Autobiography of Malcolm X shows that Malcolm was a person always in transition and that the changes in his life were a series of dramatic conversions and reconversions. He was not content to keep fixed ideas for long periods of time without exploring options. Even as a member of the Nation of Islam, he applied thoughts he had read in the great works of Western culture from Georg Hegel, Immanuel Kant, and Friedrich Nietzsche. He also relied on traditional African American intellectuals, including W. E. B. Du Bois, whom the Nation of Islam did not consider among its teachers. He could use philosophical images when speaking with the uneducated. He could also use the shrewdness, competitive instinct, and wariness of his ghetto experiences when talking with reporters. Malcolm had the ability to expand his own universe by expanding that of others, and the autobiography is an elongated sermon that takes the reader from small-town America to urban poverty through universal religion and, eventually, into international concepts and organizations. Each of his several conversions and new experiences broadened his world, and readers are compelled to make their own changes and transitions.

Malcolm's autobiography is a document of spiritual growth and changing commitments that may encourage some to embark on a similar journey. It appeals to both theologians and sociologists as a pilgrim's progress, a study of conversions. It is also a depiction of the emotional structure of a leader who had a great impact on twentieth century America. As such, it appeals to psychologists and literary critics. It conveys a continuing struggle of a charismatic figure whose words are meant to mold and direct readers' thoughts, even though this struggle is not finalized and not absolute. It is also a personal testimony of a major player in the social revolutions of the mid-twentieth century United

States, one who encouraged his readers to think about and to act out justice. Because of this encouragement, it appeals to many who remain dissatisfied with the status quo, although their plans for restructuring society may differ from those proposed by Malcolm.

The epilogue by editor Alex Haley helps the reader to understand the ways in which Malcolm's life evolved and how unexpected the changes in his life were to many who knew him well, including Haley. It makes clear that this autobiography is not a final testament but rather the words of a man whose evolution was never final. By the end of his life, Malcolm was questioning the earlier criticisms he had made of the 1960's Civil Rights movement. He was meeting cordially with Martin Luther King, Jr., whom he had earlier demeaned, and he was becoming resistant to the authority of Elijah Muhammad, who had been his spiritual leader. He rejected the theology of a pure black race and expanded his commitment to the oppressed to include groups of all colors and ethnic backgrounds. He evolved from a national leader to an international figure who was attempting to unite African and developing world peoples from all continents. The epilogue assesses Malcolm as a pilgrim who did not know what his future thoughts, acts, and commitments would be, but who remained open to more conversions and transitions.

The Autobiography of Malcolm X has sold millions of copies and has received critical acclaim by readers who sometimes take issue with Malcolm's philosophy. Nevertheless, it remains a great work as the testimony of a leader for social change whose appeal extends far beyond the groups he formed and the people he directly represented. Many readers may be disturbed by some of the ideas he promotes, but all readers remain fascinated by the honesty, integrity, and humanity evident in this book.

William Osborne and Max Orezzoli

Further Reading

Bloom, Harold, ed. *The Autobiography of Malcolm X*. New York: Chelsea House, 2008. A guide for high school and college students. Includes critical excerpts analyzing the book, a description of the circumstances under which the book was written, a list of characters, a plot summary, and an annotated bibliography.

Evanzz, Karl. *The Judas Factor: The Plot to Kill Malcolm X*. New York: Thunder's Mouth Press, 1992. The author accuses the federal government of harassing Malcolm X and suggests that intelligence agencies were behind the assassination plot because they were concerned about the international aspects of Malcolm X's movement.

Friedly, Michael. *Malcolm X: The Assassination*. New York: Carroll & Graf, 1992. Describes the assassination and the trial of three accused Black Muslims. Analyzes various conspiracy theories, concluding that no U.S. government agency was involved in the assassination plot.

Gallen, David. *Malcolm X: As They Knew Him*. New York: Carroll & Graf, 1992. A collection of memoirs and interviews describing the life and times of Malcolm X from personal observations and recollections. Contains a good chronological chart of important events in Malcolm X's life and in the sentencing of his three assassins.

Karim, Benjamin, with Peter Skutches and David Gallen. *Remembering Malcolm*. New York: Carroll & Graf, 1992. The story of Malcolm X as told by his assistant minister, focusing on the religious aspects of Malcolm's career as a Black Muslim leader and the inner politics of the Black Muslim organization.

Lee, Spike, with Ralph Wiley. *By Any Means Necessary: The Trials and Tribulations of the Making of "Malcolm X."* New York: Hyperion Books, 1992. A famous African American filmmaker describes his experiences in making a screen adaptation of *The Autobiography of Malcolm X*. Lee's brilliant adaptation revived interest in Malcolm X for a whole new generation. Contains the film script.

Malcolm X. *Malcolm X Speaks: Selected Speeches and Statements*. Edited and with prefatory notes by George Breitman. New York: Merit, 1965. A collection of eloquent speeches mostly made during the last eight months of Malcolm X's life, while he was earnestly seeking new directions for himself and for his movement.

Perry, Bruce. *Malcolm: The Life of a Man Who Changed Black America*. Barrytown, N.Y.: Station Hill Press, 1991. A full-length scholarly biography of Malcolm X. Especially valuable because it contains 126 pages of detailed endnotes referring to newspaper articles, published interviews, books, speeches, and legal documents.

Wainstock, Dennis. *Malcolm X, African American Revolutionary*. Jefferson, N.C.: McFarland, 2009. Biography that begins with Malcolm X's imprisonment when he is 21 and continues until his death, with a particular emphasis on the eleven-month period from March 8, 1964, when he officially left the Nation of Islam, to February 21, 1965, when he was assassinated

Wood, Joe, ed. *Malcolm X: In Our Own Image*. New York: St. Martin's Press, 1992. An anthology of writers, including Amiri Baraka and Angela Davis, each of whom addresses a subject related to Malcolm, such as black rage, philosophy, the allure of Malcolm, and *The Autobiography of Malcolm X*.

The Autobiography of Miss Jane Pittman

Author: Ernest J. Gaines (1933-)
First published: 1971
Type of work: Novel
Type of plot: Historical realism
Time of plot: Mid-1860's to early 1960's
Locale: Rural southern Louisiana

Principal characters:

MISS JANE PITTMAN, a black plantation worker
CORPORAL BROWN, a Yankee soldier who inspires Jane to replace her slave name
NED DOUGLASS, Jane's adopted son
JOE PITTMAN, Jane's common-law husband
ROBERT SAMSON, SR., a plantation owner
ROBERT "TEE BOB" SAMSON, JR., Robert's legitimate son
TIMMY, Robert's illegitimate son
MARY AGNES LEFABRE, the plantation schoolteacher Tee Bob loves
JIMMY AARON, a young black civil rights leader

The Story:

Before Miss Jane Pittman agrees to give a tape-recorded account of her more than one hundred years of life—from before the end of slavery to the Civil Rights movement of the 1960's—the editor, a history teacher, has to convince her to do so in order to better teach African American history from the perspective of a black woman who experienced it first-hand. Miss Jane's story begins at the end of the American Civil War on a southern Louisiana plantation, when she is about ten or eleven. While bringing Yankee soldiers a drink, Miss Jane, then called Ticey, befriends a Yankee named Corporal Brown, who influences her to replace her slave name with that of Jane. Miss Jane decides to adopt the new name and the corporal's surname. Miss Jane reveals her pride for the first time when she refuses to accept her old slave name ever again, although her mistress whips her until she bleeds.

After the war ends a year later, Miss Jane, determined and proud, decides she is leaving the plantation for Ohio, in search of Corporal Brown, although she does not know the way or what she will eat along the way. When the two dozen other former slaves Miss Jane leaves with begin their journey north, they decide to change their slave names, as Miss Jane did, to declare their independence. They are soon to find out, however, that although they are legally free, they are to be treated no better and perhaps even worse than they had been during slavery. Soon after they leave, they are brutally attacked by a group of patrollers and former Confederate soldiers, who use sticks to beat to death all of those in the group except Miss Jane and a young boy, Ned, who are undetected in the bushes.

The two children bravely continue on alone for what they think is Ohio. The determined children journey until they eventually find themselves back on a southern Louisiana plantation that is very much like the one they fled. On the plantation, Miss Jane works in the field, lives in the old slave quarters, and takes care of Ned as if he were her child. For a short time everything seems to go well: The children and some adults are educated. White hate groups terrorize and kill blacks across the state, but the Yankee who temporarily owns the plantation has the plantation guarded by black troops to protect his workers. Soon, however, the original Confederate owner gets his land back during the deals the North and South are making in an attempt to reunite the country. Life on the plantation returns much to the way it was back in the days of slavery. The black politicians, troops, and teacher are all forced to leave, and the children are educated only a couple of months out of the year, when they cannot be used in the fields. Racist hate groups terrorize and kill blacks more than ever.

Blacks flee the terrorism, leaving the South in droves. Miss Jane and Ned, however, decide to stay, and Ned matures into a political advocate of black rights. The Ku Klux Klan then begins harassing him, so he leaves the plantation for Kansas. After Ned leaves, Miss Jane becomes the common-law wife of a widowed horse breaker, Joe Pittman. Joe soon finds work on another plantation. He and Miss Jane have to borrow money and sell everything they own to pay the plantation owner one hundred fifty dollars plus thirty dollars interest to leave the plantation. The money is what they supposedly owe for past protection against the Ku Klux Klan. Although the plantation owner is clearly embezzling their money, they pay out of fear. On the new plantation, Jane works as a house servant, and the two live there until Joe is killed while breaking a wild horse.

After twenty years of separation, Miss Jane reunites with

Ned and his new family. Ned establishes a school to teach the local black children and preach the politics of Frederick Douglass, until a Cajun hit man, who has a contract out on Ned's life, kills him.

After Ned is murdered, Miss Jane moves to the Samson plantation to work in the fields and later in the house as a servant. The paternalistic owner, Robert Samson, treats the black employees well but does not see them as the equals of whites. He has two sons, one, Tee Bob, the legitimate son of his wife, Miss Amma Dean, and the other the illegitimate son of the black worker, Verda. He treats his illegitimate son, Timmy, better than most black employees living on the plantation, letting him get away with many boyish pranks and letting him become a close friend with his white half brother.

Eventually, however, Timmy learns his place will never be equal to that of whites in Louisiana during the 1920's. When a poor white man named Tom Joe decides to harass Timmy and accuse him of breaking his half brother's arm, Timmy disputes the charge, and when he refuses to call the man "mister," Tom Joe beats him unconscious. Because this time Timmy has a run-in with a white person, Robert will not defend him. Instead, Robert gives Timmy money and tells him to move away for his own safety. No one on the plantation, including Robert, can explain to Tee Bob why his beloved half brother is being sent away when he did nothing wrong. Robert accepts these double standards as "part of life, like the sun and rain was part of life," and he assumes "Tee Bob would learn them for himself when he got older." Tee Bob never does learn, however, to accept racial segregation. He falls in love with a beautiful mulatto Creole schoolteacher named Mary Agnes LeFabre, who looks white, but when he comes to realize that the society in which he lives will never accept his marriage to her, he commits suicide.

Miss Jane Pittman's remembrances end during the Civil Rights movement, with an episode in which a young black man named Jimmy is killed for his involvement in planning a protest against the arrest of a black woman for drinking out of the whites-only fountain. The novel ends on a defiant note when Miss Jane stands up to Robert for the first time, leading the black community in protest against legal segregation: "Me and Robert looked at each other there a long time, then I went by him."

Critical Evaluation:

Ernest Gaines was one of the first authors to attempt to present African American history from the perspective of a black person. Until the 1970's, when it became popular to capture the lifestyle and dialect of the average black American in such novels as Alex Haley's *Roots* (1976), it was difficult to find fiction that presented African American history from the common person's perspective, especially from the perspective of a black woman. In *The Autobiography of Miss Jane Pittman*, Gaines uses the framing device of a history teacher who tape-records an interview. Although Miss Jane is actually a fictional character, she is based on the women who lived on the southern Louisiana plantation on which Gaines was raised. The novel depicts southern Louisiana plantation life, the dialect of the people, and history of the area accurately. Gaines, who was working as an English professor and not as a history teacher, accomplishes the fictional history teacher's goal of teaching black history more accurately through presenting it from the black perspective. The framing device is designed to make Miss Jane seem more real and make her autobiography more believable. It is not really important that she is fictional because her story is not fictional. Black women and men lived through the racism, hard labor, and poverty described in the novel. Thus, as the fictitious editor states in the introduction, "Miss Jane's story is all of their stories, and their stories are Miss Jane's."

In addition to re-creating a more personal depiction of African American history from a poor black woman's perspective, *The Autobiography of Miss Jane Pittman* also establishes two important themes: the determination and pride of African Americans in the face of seemingly unconquerable racism and the destructive effects of racism on all of society, including whites. Throughout the novel Miss Jane is a proud individual who has the courage to face the consequences of standing up for herself and for others in a racist society. She endures a harsh whipping as a young adolescent in order to reject her slave name, and as a ninety-year-old woman stands up to her white employer and landlord, risking the loss of her home, source of income, and perhaps even her life in order to partake in a demonstration against segregation. Although Miss Jane clearly suffers in the novel, she and other blacks are not the only people who suffer from racial discrimination and social and legal segregation. The white plantation owner's son Tee Bob is deprived of a loving and productive marriage to a beautiful and intelligent woman simply because she is part black. He decides killing himself is a better alternative than living by the hypocritical standards of his father and his father's society.

Another important detail in the novel is the naming of Miss Jane. One way former slaves declared their independence from slavery and rejected the subservient status associated with slave names was by giving themselves new names. In the novel, former slaves decide to rename themselves after Frederick Douglass, Abraham Lincoln, and other abolitionists or Union soldiers who helped them obtain their freedom. Miss Jane not only names herself after a Yankee corporal who first acknowledges her worth as an individual by telling her to reject her slave name, but she also is referred to as Miss, which connotes her dignity as a lady. *The Autobiography of Miss Jane Pittman* is revolutionary in its presentation of a black woman who is a realistic, multidimensional individual who cannot be classified as a stereotype.

Suzanne Obenauer Shaut

Further Reading

Babb, Valerie Melissa. *Ernest Gaines*. Boston: Twayne, 1991. A clear, critical analysis that devotes one chapter to each of Gaines's major works, including a detailed chapter on *The Autobiography of Miss Jane Pittman* that discusses the novel's historical and cultural accuracy, use of oral history, themes, and character development.

Beavers, Herman. *Wrestling Angels into Song: The Fictions of Ernest J. Gaines and James Alan McPherson*. Philadelphia: University of Pennsylvania Press, 1995. Analyzes the work of the two African American writers, whom Beavers maintains are following in the tradition of Ralph Ellison by exploring the complexity of American identity and citizenship. Chapter 5 includes a lengthy discussion of *The Autobiography of Miss Jane Pittman*, and the numerous other references to the novel are listed in the index.

Bell, Bernard W. "The Contemporary Afro-American Novel, Two: Modernism and Postmodernism." In *The Afro-American Novel and Its Tradition*. Amherst: University of Massachusetts Press, 1987. Examines Gaines's fiction as an example of African American postmodernism, which differs from white postmodernism by exploring the power in folk tradition rather than rejecting fictional tradition.

Callahan, John F. "A Moveable Form: The Loose End Blues of *The Autobiography of Miss Jane Pittman*." In *In the African-American Grain: The Pursuit of Voice in Twentieth-Century Black Fiction*. Urbana: University of Illinois Press, 1988. Focuses on the novel's use of the teacher as an oral historian editing his material. Callahan analyzes the art of the novel with reference to historiography and folk autobiography.

Carmean, Karen. *Ernest J. Gaines: A Critical Companion*. Westport, Conn.: Greenwood Press, 1998. Incisive introduction to Gaines's life and works. Chapter 5 focuses on *The Autobiography of Miss Jane Pittman*, discussing the plot, character development, themes, and other elements of the novel. Includes bibliography.

Doyle, Mary Ellen. *Voices from the Quarters: The Fiction of Ernest J. Gaines*. Baton Rouge: Louisiana State University Press, 2002. A close reading of Gaines's work, focusing on his skill at adapting oral tales into written fiction. Chapter 6 is devoted to *The Autobiography of Miss Jane Pittman*.

Estes, David C., ed. *Critical Reflections on the Fiction of Ernest J. Gaines*. Athens: University of Georgia Press, 1994. Collection of essays analyzing Gaines's work. Includes two discussions of *The Autobiography of Miss Jane Pittman*: "*The Autobiography of Miss Jane Pittman* as a Fictional Edited Autobiography" by Mary Ellen Doyle and "A 'Slow-to-Anger' People: *The Autobiography of Miss Jane Pittman* as Historical Fiction" by Keith E. Byerman.

Gaudet, Marcia, and Carl Wooton. *Porch Talk with Ernest Gaines: Conversations on the Writer's Craft*. Baton Rouge: Louisiana State University Press, 1990. A brief introduction to Gaines's life and works and a lengthy series of interviews of Gaines, with a heavy emphasis on *The Autobiography of Miss Jane Pittman*.

Hogue, W. Lawrence. "History, the Black Nationalist Discourse, and *The Autobiography of Miss Jane Pittman*." In *Discourse and the Other: The Production of the Afro-American Text*. Durham, N.C.: Duke University Press, 1986. Examines the novel as a product of the black nationalist movement of the 1960's. Sees Gaines as celebrating black history and correcting literary caricatures of blacks by such white writers as Mark Twain and Harriet Beecher Stowe.

Wertheim, Albert. "Journey to Freedom: Ernest Gaines' *The Autobiography of Miss Jane Pittman* (1971)." In *The Afro-American Novel Since 1960*, edited by Peter Bruck and Wolfgang Karrer. Amsterdam: B. R. Grüner, 1982. An analysis of the novel's theme of finding freedom. Contains a detailed review of the book's narrative structure.

The Autobiography of W. E. B. Du Bois
A Soliloquy on Viewing My Life from the Last Decade of Its First Century

Author: W. E. B. Du Bois (1868-1963)
First published: *Vospominaniia*, 1962 (English translation, 1968)
Type of work: Autobiography

The Autobiography of W. E. B. Du Bois, first published in Russian as *Vospominaniia* in 1962, tells the impressive and inspiring story of an individual's struggles, defeats, and accomplishments, as well as his major ideas developed during ninety years of a life dedicated to promoting racial equality and the sociological study of African American realities in the United States. *The Autobiography of W. E. B. Du Bois* presents a view of American life distilled through the perceptive, analytical eyes of one who may have been the foremost African American intellectual. Progressing from the Reconstruction era at the end of the American Civil War, through World Wars I and II, to the height of the Cold War and the atomic age, Du Bois's personal reflections provide a critical, panoramic sweep of American social history. *The Autobiography of W. E. B. Du Bois* is simultaneously a history of a personal and a social struggle, seen from the perspective of a central participant.

Du Bois is not simply an observer of the American scene. He contributes instrumentally to American history in his role as a leading architect of African American thought during the growth of the American Civil Rights movement in the twentieth century. Thus, *The Autobiography of W. E. B. Du Bois* is an important documentary piece of American history. From the inception of the National Association for the Advancement of Colored People (NAACP) in 1909, Du Bois was, as editor of its journal, *The Crisis*, its conscience and spokesperson. Du Bois opposed the influential policies of Booker T. Washington, creating a vital dialogue within the African American community. Much of Du Bois's vision of racial equality and African American achievement remains unfulfilled, and thus his autobiography is necessarily as much a blueprint for continued action as it is a historical narrative.

The chronological structure of the autobiography is purposefully transposed. Du Bois begins not with his childhood but with five brief chapters on his travels, starting in 1958, to Europe, the Soviet Union, and China. After seeing the accomplishments of socialist organization firsthand, Du Bois reaches the crowning ideological decision of his life: his conversion to communism. The remainder of the autobiography is fundamentally an embroidery on the question: How and why did Du Bois arrive at this crucial decision in the last years of his life? This chronological device focuses the entire work on Du Bois's inexorable move toward communist ideals in a way that starting simply with his birth and youthful years in Massachusetts could not accomplish.

Du Bois's chronicle of his childhood and early education is surprising precisely for its small-town conventionality and relative lack of racial conflict. Du Bois, it is crucial to remember, was born a Northerner, in rural Massachusetts. Despite Du Bois's African American heritage and the close temporal proximity of his birth to the end of the Civil War, Du Bois neither came from a slave family nor had direct childhood experience with the aftermath of slavery that characterized the southern United States. Du Bois excelled in a predominantly white school and had white playmates. The strict norms of the time and region minimized opportunities for contacts with the opposite sex, black or white, and thus Du Bois not only grew up ignorant of sexual biology but also escaped the sanctions so ruthlessly imposed in southern states, where whites' exaggerated fears of miscegenation ran rampant.

The autobiography is replete with instances that illustrate Du Bois's hard work, thrift, diligent study, and persistent planning. Were it not for the fact that Du Bois's story ends with his expatriation, the narrative reads often like an African American version of a Horatio Alger story. Du Bois, ultimately, avoids the trap that captures the self-made man, asking instead: "Was I the masterful captain or the pawn of laughing sprites?" Du Bois does not trust his life to luck; he "just went doggedly to work" and let the consequences fall where they might.

Du Bois learns concretely about racial bigotry during his college years at Fisk University in Tennessee, prior to his return to Massachusetts, where he continues his academic studies at Harvard University. Du Bois learns from notable scholars (including William James) at Harvard, earns a second bachelor's degree and, eventually, earns a doctorate in

1895. His doctoral program includes a hiatus for two years of study in Germany, where Du Bois comes to appreciate high standards of scholarship and listens to the stimulating lectures of the sociologist Max Weber. Following a year-long appointment at the University of Pennsylvania, where Du Bois completes a landmark sociological investigation, *The Philadelphia Negro: A Social Study*, he spends from 1897 to 1910 at Atlanta University as the nation's leading African American sociologist. If the black experience in America is to be investigated objectively and scientifically, Du Bois observes, it must be studied by astute, well-trained, African American sociologists such as himself.

As a result of the national importance of Du Bois's role in the NAACP, his considerable stature as an author and influential editor, and the problematic political legacy of the Du Bois-Washington debate—all of which are detailed in the autobiography and about which many critics and historians have commented—it is important to emphasize that a constant theme of the autobiography is Du Bois's work. Du Bois worked to initiate, foster, produce, and plan an extended series of erudite, systematic sociological investigations of African American life. It is Du Bois's unrelenting drive to live an intellectual life, to teach the "talented tenth" of black America, and to destroy white myths and misapprehensions about African Americans by means of careful research that gives coherence to his autobiography and meaning to his accomplishments.

Du Bois's many trips from North to South, to Europe and beyond, stand as metaphors for his complex, ninety-year intellectual journey from naïve schoolboy to sage, idealistic communist. Along the way, Du Bois enriches the sociological vocabulary with insightful concepts, including "the color line," "the veil," "the talented tenth," "double consciousness," and many others. All find ready use and illustration in his autobiography. Du Bois revels in the active, disciplined application of the mind. Philosophically and organizationally, Du Bois accomplishes what is beyond the grasp of most mortals. His grand sociological project is possible yet visionary; his communism is inclusive, liberating, and cooperative—never totalitarian or dictatorial. The temporary denial by the American government in 1951 of Du Bois's passport, ostensibly limiting his ability to travel outside the United States, propelled Du Bois toward a future unbounded by petty nationalisms, military-industrial excesses, or governmental oppression of the citizenry.

Perhaps the most gripping and instructive section of the autobiography is Du Bois's straightforward account of his indictment and persecution by the U.S. government on trumped-up charges, allegations infused with insinuations of treason and disloyalty. Du Bois's trial and acquittal in 1950 and 1951, for alleged failure to register as an agent of a foreign government, is a scary, sobering illustration of democratic institutions gone seriously awry. Du Bois is cleared of all charges, but the trial costs him his savings and his reputation. His fundamental faith in American institutions, already strained by years of racist oppression, crumbles completely. If Du Bois is sometimes angry, he often has justification.

Du Bois's autobiography is, from his perspective, a final reckoning and laying to rest of long-fought battles. Du Bois outlived most of his enemies and thereby won the satisfaction of the last word. It is on this personal level that the autobiography is least satisfying. The veracity of Du Bois's recollections concerning old animosities and interpersonal power struggles cannot be decided on the basis of his book alone. Du Bois leaves readers with selected, carefully crafted impressions of himself, his foes, and his intellectual journey. This book, he states with candor, is "a theory of my life"; it "is the Soliloquy of an old man on what he dreams his life has been . . . and what he would like others to believe."

Du Bois refers pointedly to his autobiography as a soliloquy. The soliloquy is a venerable technique in Western literature, especially in drama, reaching its classic form in William Shakespeare's plays and, more recently, in stream-of-consciousness writing typified by James Joyce's novel *Ulysses* (1922). Readers of Du Bois's autobiography will likely conclude, however, that Du Bois clearly speaks not to himself but rather to posterity.

Du Bois's choice of "soliloquy" to categorize his work reflects the political realities of 1960 more than it does a specific literary form. At the time Du Bois finished writing his autobiography, he had been persecuted by the American government, many of his well-educated African American friends had deserted him, and Du Bois had lived in exile in the newly independent nation of Ghana. Thus, Du Bois had reasons for thinking that he was talking primarily to himself. He may well have wondered who, in the United States at least, would ever read his autobiography.

Deepening the possibility that few Americans might see or read his final autobiographical statement is the fact of its first publication not in English but in a 518-page translated edition in Russian, printed in Moscow. When the autobiography finally appeared, posthumously, in English in 1968, it was published by International Publishers, a publishing house well known for its Marxist and Soviet-oriented books. In 1991, *The Autobiography of W. E. B. Du Bois* enjoyed its eleventh printing, but it remains the least read of Du Bois's autobiographical works.

There are several reasons why Du Bois's autobiography

still creates controversy in the United States. First, Du Bois enthusiastically endorses a radical, communist political perspective that many liberal and conservative Americans find unacceptable. Second, Du Bois levels stinging criticism at middle-class African Americans, who, in Du Bois's view, value their own economic security more highly than the worldwide struggle for racial equality and freedom of expression. Third, Du Bois praises the former Soviet Union for its opposition to organized religion. Finally, Du Bois transcends his previous, sharp critiques of whites, placing him at odds with separatist and some pluralist African American scholars who are more comfortable with Du Bois's earlier views. Nevertheless, Du Bois's autobiography is an engaging exposition in which Du Bois addresses his critics directly and usually with fairness, recounts his failures with dignity and humility, expounds his views with clarity and reason, and shares his hopes for a collective future with courage, conviction, and good will.

Michael R. Hill

Further Reading

Bloom, Harold, ed. *W. E. B. Du Bois*. Philadelphia: Chelsea House, 2001. Collection of essays focusing on Du Bois's ideas and literary works. Some of the essays examine Du Bois as a man of literature, his theory of a Black aesthetic, his literary Black nationalism, and his vision of the *Encyclopedia Africana*.

Blum, Edward J. *W. E. B. Du Bois: American Prophet*. Philadelphia: University of Pennsylvania Press, 2007. Focuses on Du Bois's spiritual ideas and temperament, tracing the religious meanings and biblical references in his writing. Du Bois's autobiography is discussed in chapter1, "The Hero with a Black Face: Autobiography and Mythology of Self."

Butterfield, Stephen. *Black Autobiography in America*. Amherst: University of Massachusetts Press, 1974. Explicates the autobiographical works of Du Bois, Richard Wright, Langston Hughes, and others as concerted attempts to unite the pieces of divided selves. Concludes that Du Bois's autobiographical works provide the most conscious and explicit examples in African American literature of this struggle.

DeMarco, Joseph P. *The Social Thought of W. E. B. Du Bois*. Lanham, Md.: University Press of America, 1983. An incisive exploration of Du Bois's philosophy.

Duberman, Martin. *The Uncompleted Past*. New York: Random House, 1969. Praises the characterization of Du Bois's childhood, but dismisses—rather too curtly—Du Bois's discovery and embrace of communist principles. Emphasizes Du Bois's pursuit of what Duberman presents as conflicting goals.

Howe, Irving. *Celebrations and Attacks*. New York: Horizon Press, 1979. Presents a concise summary of Du Bois's autobiography and a useful discussion of the deeper complexities in his controversial debate with Booker T. Washington. Fails, however, to distinguish between totalitarian Stalinism and the broader democratic principles that Du Bois championed.

Marable, Manning. *W. E. B. Du Bois: Black Radical Democrat*. New updated ed. Boulder, Colo.: Paradigm, 2005. Comprehensive biography, in which Marable charts the connections and consistency of Du Bois's life and writings. Originally published in 1986, this updated edition includes a new introduction focusing on Du Bois's advocacy of women's suffrage, social, and peace.

Turner, Jonathan H., Royce Singleton, Jr., and David Musick. *Oppression: A Socio-History of Black-White Relations in America*. Chicago: Nelson-Hall, 1984. Classifies Du Bois, along with Frederick Douglass, A. Philip Randolph, and Martin Luther King, Jr., as a "protest integrationist," or someone who attempts to work within the political system in order to change it. In this regard, Du Bois was the intellectual heir to Frederick Douglass, becoming the recognized leader of the Civil Rights movement and expanding the movement into the international arena before he was succeeded by Martin Luther King, Jr., in the mid-1950's.

The Autocrat of the Breakfast-Table

Author: Oliver Wendell Holmes (1809-1894)
First published: serial, 1857-1858; book, 1858
Type of work: Essays

Principal characters:
THE AUTOCRAT
THE SCHOOLMISTRESS,
THE DIVINITY-STUDENT,
THE OLD GENTLEMAN, and THE YOUNG FELLOW CALLED JOHN, the Autocrat's fellow boarders
THE LANDLADY
THE LANDLADY'S DAUGHTER
BENJAMIN FRANKLIN, the Landlady's son
THE PROFESSOR and THE POET, friends of the Autocrat who, though never present, contribute to the discussion

At one point in the recounting of his breakfast-table experiences, the Autocrat observes that, since medieval times, the reputation of Aristotle had passed through two stages and is just entering its third. First came the period of idolization, when everything attributed to the Greek sage was accepted not only as scientifically sound but as absolute and ultimate truth. Then came the period of critical examination, the stage at which his scientific inaccuracies were discovered and consequently all his ideas belittled and discredited. Finally, there was the third stage, the enlightened period when the scientific inaccuracies were excused, being viewed in historical perspective as unavoidable, and the value of his philosophical insights restored.

On a smaller time scale, the reputation of Oliver Wendell Holmes, along with that of his Cambridge-Boston group (as opposed to the Concord group), had gone through the first two of these stages but showed no signs, as yet, of entering the third. Although few, and certainly never Holmes himself, believe that Boston is the hub of the universe, Harvard Yard and the eastern end of Beacon Street (including the first eight doors on Arlington Street so as to take in the offices of the *Atlantic Monthly*) had been for more than half a century regarded as the dual nerve center, the cerebrum and cerebellum, as it were, of American culture. A Cambridge-born Harvard professor of anatomy, a member of the Saturday Club, a resident of Beacon Street, Holmes does not merely share in such regard, he helps to create it. It is he, in fact, who coined the term "The Hub." (The original statement, however, as it appears in chapter 6 of *The Autocrat of the Breakfast-Table*, is made not by a Bostonian but by an outlander who remarks, "Boston State-House is the hub of the solar system.") As lecturer, poet, novelist, biographer, and, most of all, perhaps, as the author of *The Autocrat of the Breakfast-Table* and, later, *The Professor at the Breakfast-Table* (1860) and *The Poet at the Breakfast-Table* (1872), Holmes helps to establish in the public mind a concept of Bostonian wit, sensibility, and culture.

Gradually—not suddenly as did the Wonderful One-Hoss Shay in chapter 11 of *The Autocrat of the Breakfast-Table*—the reputations of many of the New England writers become autumnal and dry, and a season of critical neglect sets in before the situation reverses itself again. Nathaniel Hawthorne is resurrected by the New Critics; the cautiously radical Ralph Waldo Emerson is turned into a spokesman for the Neoconservatives; and Henry David Thoreau, in conformist times, becomes a pet of nonconformists. The Concordians thus enter their third stage, but this does not happen with the Cambridge-Bostonians. Granted, their poetry is a mixture of neoclassic moralizing and a nostalgic and academic romanticism, but it should be remembered that Henry Wadsworth Longfellow has a gift for storytelling, that Robert Lowell is a sprightly satirist, and that Holmes possesses wit, urbanity, a background of knowledge, and a tolerant, all-encompassing view of life, the like of which has not appeared in English letters on either side of the Atlantic since his death.

It can be argued that in regard to Holmes such qualities do not produce the reputation but are deduced from it, that the alleged wit and urbanity are really provincial smugness, and that what passes for a tolerant and total worldview is in reality a carefully cultivated dilettantism. Such arguments have been made, but they neglect both the facts provided by history and the literary evidence provided by *The Autocrat of the Breakfast-Table*. The facts show that Holmes is learned in both science and humane letters and that he is one of the foremost advocates of technological progress in the nineteenth century United States. One English critic said that Holmes, rather than Emerson, deserves the title the "American Montaigne."

It is on an objective reading of *The Autocrat of the Breakfast-Table* that the case for Holmes must finally rest. The work appeared originally in the first twelve issues of the *Atlantic Monthly* (1857-1858) and was directly afterward published in book form. Its plan is simple: The Autocrat lives in a Beacon Hill boarding house; the essays are characterized as somewhat condensed reports, interlarded with the Autocrat's comments, of the conversations that take place each morning at the breakfast table around which a heterogeneous collection of boarders gathers. Each occasionally has a say but collectively their main purpose is to provide a sounding board for the wit and philosophizing of the Autocrat. There is conversation, but mostly there is monologue. The varied responses of the boarders allow Holmes's wit to play over a wide range of subjects, to jump easily from point to point, and to juxtapose ideas that have no apparent relevance.

The result may seem chaotic at first. The bubbling cleverness runs along easily enough but apparently to no particular place. The topics of the first chapter are, for example, in order of appearance: the algebraic classification of minds; the value of mutual admiration societies; the meaninglessness of brute fact; the typing of various kinds of speakers; the dangers of specialized learning; an attack on the use of puns (Holmes deplores the use of them here but cannot always resist them, as when he speaks of the landlady's economically minded poor relation as standing by her guns, "ready to repel boarders"); the poverty of pure logic as opposed to common sense; the foibles of young poets; the superiority of men of family over self-made men, "*other things being equal*" (Holmes's italics); and the rendering of a pair of poems. Holmes makes each of these points interesting, but there seems to be little connection between one and another. Gradually, however, it becomes evident that certain ideas recur; certain themes are announced and dropped but then repeated later with variations, and there are psychological connections in the apparently chance juxtapositions of ideas. The entirety develops in a geometric, not in an arithmetic, progression.

Holmes was a Bostonian, a Victorian American, and it has been said that his sympathies lay with the eighteenth century and that he was at heart a Neo-Johnsonian. If, however, his conscious affinities turned back one hundred years, his unconscious ones turned back even further. Andrew Lang noted "a fleeting resemblance to Sir Thomas Browne" based on "a community of professional studies," but this similarity between Holmes and the author of *Religio Medici* (written 1635; published 1642) and *Hydriotaphia, Urne-Burial* (1658) is not explained simply by the fact that both were medical men. Holmes possessed the divided sensibility found also in the metaphysical school; and Browne, it is now acknowledged, was a metaphysical poet writing in prose. This division in Holmes, which is obscured by his neoclassical pose, is often neglected.

Holmes was divided along a different axis than was Browne, for he lived under different conditions. The religious division results from the fact that though Holmes had disavowed the Puritanism of his fathers, he never completely lost the scars of his youthful indoctrination. More important, perhaps, at least as far as its reflection in *The Autocrat of the Breakfast-Table* is concerned, is his divided allegiance between Brahminism on the one hand, which for him stands for all the deeply rooted elements of the good life, and on the other science, which means technology and with it the unleashing of forces, both human and mechanical, that would destroy Brahminism. The division could not exercise itself in Holmes's poetry because the moralizing-romantic tradition is too binding. However, when Holmes has at his disposal a form free from restrictions with which he can experiment as he wishes, the essay, he is able to express his divided sensibility through the use of what closely resembles metaphysical techniques.

These techniques include the juxtaposition of topics, which is reflected most extremely in chapter 9. Here, anticipating the much later reflection of the metaphysical, Holmes presents a series of childhood reminiscences, the stuff of poems:

> Many times I have come bearing flowers such as my garden grew; but now I offer you this poor, brown, homely growth, you may cast it away as worthless. And yet—and yet—it is something better than flowers; it is a seed-capsule.

There is also the shift in prose style from the colloquial or scientific to the lofty and poetic, a device that hearkens back to the style of Browne. Most important, however, are the similitudes, the similes, metaphors, and extended analogies, which abound in *The Autocrat of the Breakfast Table*. What is important here is that they are functional, not decorative; they are the very fabric of the work. Holmes uses them to bring into focus the two parts of his divided world. Science and beauty stand for the two parts of the central dichotomy, representing Holmes's own two alter egos as the professor and the poet, and they play their dual parts in all the analogies:

> We get beautiful effects from wit—all the prismatic colors—but never the object as it is in fair daylight. A pun, which is a kind of wit, is a different and much shallower trick in mental optics; throwing the shadows of two objects so that one overlies the other. Poetry uses the rainbow tints for special effects, but always keeps its essential object in the purest white light of truth.

Through the interplay of these two conflicting worlds and by means of analogy and opposition of character, Holmes brings out the themes of the work. They appear as questions, not as answers, for awareness of the divided world permits no dogmatic assertions. He asks what love is and what beauty is; how human communication and expression are achieved; what, after all, is really important; and how can that be found—whether it is by sculling beneath the bridges of the Charles, searching for seed capsules of poetry in one's memory, or counting the rings of an elm that stood when Shakespeare was a boy.

To bring out these questions in a meaningful way is a decided literary achievement. *The Autocrat of the Breakfast-Table* is not an entirely great literary work. Holmes does not maintain his metaphysical detachment, he becomes too concerned with his characters, and in the end he reduces the Autocrat and the Schoolmistress into the principal figures of a rather sentimental romance. These are weaknesses, but with respect to the strengths demonstrated in *The Autocrat of the Breakfast-Table* Holmes deserves to have his reputation advanced to the third stage.

Further Reading

Dowling, William C. *Oliver Wendell Holmes in Paris: Medicine, Theology, and "The Autocrat of the Breakfast Table."* Durham: University of New Hampshire Press, 2006. Dowling describes how Holmes's experiences as a medical student in Paris provided the material for *The Autocrat of the Breakfast-Table* and the two other books in the Breakfast-Table trilogy.

Gibian, Peter. *Oliver Wendell Holmes and the Culture of Conversation*. New York: Cambridge University Press, 2001. Examines Holmes's role in creating and analyzing a new form of conversation, or "table-talk," that became popular in nineteenth century America.

Grenander, M. E. "Doctors and Humanists: Transactional Analysis and Two Views of Man." *Journal of American Culture* 3, no. 3 (Fall, 1980): 470-479. Contends that Holmes paved the way for transactional analysis theory, for in *The Autocrat of the Breakfast-Table* he discussed the factors considered—consciously and subconsciously—by two people when they speak to each other.

Hoyt, Edwin P. *The Improper Bostonian: Dr. Oliver Wendell Holmes*. New York: William Morrow, 1979. Chapter 16 describes Holmes's relationship with James Russell Lowell, the editor of *The Atlantic Monthly*, and other notable Boston literati. Explains the appeal of *The Autocrat of the Breakfast-Table* to educated readers and delineates Holmes's literary prominence.

Small, Miriam Rossiter. *Oliver Wendell Holmes*. New York: Twayne, 1962. Chapter 3, "The Breakfast-Table Series," discusses the style and theme of *The Autocrat of the Breakfast-Table* and obliquely compares it to Holmes's succeeding works. Small asserts that readers of the essays derive pleasure from recognizing experience, thought, and emotions as they are couched in Holmes's apt and winning style.

Tilton, Eleanor M. *Amiable Autocrat: A Biography of Dr. Oliver Wendell Holmes*. New York: Henry Schuman, 1947. Reports the contemporary reception of *The Autocrat of the Breakfast-Table* and traces the essays from their serialized appearance to their publication in book form.

Weinstein, Michael A. *The Imaginative Prose of Oliver Wendell Holmes*. Columbia: University of Missouri Press, 2006. Weinstein analyzes *The Autocrat of the Breakfast-Table* and Holmes's other prose works to trace the writer's development over the course of his lifetime. Weinstein refutes other critics who have dismissed Holmes as a dilettante, arguing that Holmes was a serious writer whose works displayed a deep understanding of the American national character.

The Awakening

Author: Kate Chopin (1851-1904)
First published: 1899
Type of work: Novel
Type of plot: Psychological realism
Time of plot: Late nineteenth century
Locale: New Orleans, Louisiana; Grand Isle, Gulf of Mexico

Principal characters:
EDNA PONTELLIER, an upper-class housewife who is not satisfied to be someone's property
LÉONCE PONTELLIER, her husband, a wealthy businessman
ROBERT LEBRUN, a young man who becomes romantically involved with Edna
ALCÉE AROBIN, an experienced playboy who seduces Edna
ADÈLE RATIGNOLLE, Edna's friend
MADEMOISELLE REISZ, a pianist who inspires Edna
DOCTOR MANDELET, a physician and adviser to the Pontelliers

The Story:

The Pontelliers, residents of New Orleans, are vacationing at Grand Isle, a resort in the Gulf of Mexico. The Lebrun and Ratignolle families, also Creoles of New Orleans, are companions of Edna, who is unhappy with the limited role dictated to her by her husband Léonce. Madame Lebrun's caged parrot symbolizes Edna's feeling of being trapped in a loveless marriage and in an economically oriented social system in which women are only wives and mothers. Her husband expects her to be like Adèle Ratignolle, who exemplifies the type of submissive and sacrificial wife that Léonce expects and thinks he deserves. Edna, however, is not willing to submit to such traditions or to sacrifice herself for the sake of her husband and their two sons.

When Léonce notices that Edna was sunburned after spending a time on the beach with Robert Lebrun, his main concern is that a "valuable piece of personal property . . . suffered some damage." In contrast to her husband's business-based value system, Robert offers her companionship and sympathy. She talks to him of her girlhood in Kentucky. Meanwhile, Léonce complains about her "habitual neglect of the children." Edna realizes that she can never be a good mother like Adèle if it means stifling her independence. "A certain light was beginning to dawn" in Edna that nurtures her dissatisfaction with her life and leads her to recognize that her marriage to the forty-year-old businessman (twelve years her senior) is a mistake. She was flattered by Léonce's devotion to her, but the violent opposition to the marriage by her father and her sister Margaret (because Léonce was a Catholic) may have been Edna's prime motive in marrying. Léonce belongs to another culture, a French American society quite different from the strict Presbyterian environment of Kentucky. One thing, however, is the same in both worlds. Women are regarded as necessary but inferior beings whose place is in the home.

Edna, who is interested in the arts, is introduced to Mademoiselle Reisz, a noted pianist. While the latter plays, Edna envisions a naked man in an attitude of resignation as he watches a bird fly away from him. The music inspires Edna to a sense of power, and, when the party moves to the beach, she overcomes her fear of the water and learns to swim. Gaining confidence, Edna challenges her husband by refusing his sexual entreaty. By withholding herself sexually, she feels that she is in possession of her body.

One Sunday, Edna asks Robert to attend church with her on a neighboring island. During the service, however, she flees from the stifling atmosphere of the church, much like the time in Kentucky when as a child she ran away from the Presbyterian prayers that were "read in a spirit of gloom" by her father. She believes that the churches are part of the status quo that keep women in their places. At the end of the Grand Isle vacation, Robert goes to Mexico. His departure depresses Edna, but it does not impair her rebellious nature. She tells Mademoiselle Reisz that she will not sacrifice herself for anyone, even her children. When the family returns to New Orleans, Edna's first act of nonconformity is to ignore Reception Day. Léonce is amazed that his wife does not observe the tradition. It is not just a social convention, it is business. He angrily leaves to have dinner at his club. Edna throws her wedding ring on the carpet and breaks a vase on the hearth. In a rebellious mood, Edna visits Mademoiselle Reisz. Edna discusses her attempt to paint, to become an artist. The pianist declares that an artist needs a courageous soul, a "soul that dared and defied."

Meanwhile, Léonce complains to Dr. Mandelet about the

change in Edna, particularly her sexual withdrawal. She even refuses to go to her sister's wedding. The doctor advises him to let Edna have her way for a while. Edna's father, a Kentucky colonel, arrives in New Orleans to buy a wedding present for Janet, his daughter. The real purpose for the visit is to coerce Edna into attending Janet's wedding, but Edna still refuses to go. Fond of bourbon, of horses, and of women who know their domestic duties, Edna's father angrily leaves. Soon after, Léonce leaves on one of his many business trips, and his mother takes the children to Iberville. Edna is happy to be alone. For inspiration, she reads Ralph Waldo Emerson, the famous champion of self-reliance and nonconformity. Edna, in a bold act of independence, decides to move out of her husband's house, ignoring his letter of disapproval in which he claims he is "simply thinking of his financial integrity." Before she leaves, she has a dinner party. One of the guests, Alcée Arobin, begins to court Edna. In the absence of Robert, Edna responds to Arobin's sexual advances. She had not heard from Robert since he went to Mexico. When Robert returns, he avoids her. One day, they meet accidentally, but he seems distant and uninterested. Arobin, on the other hand, continues to visit her. Another chance meeting with Robert occurs, however, and he confesses that he loves her and that he avoids her because she belongs to another. Edna says that she is no longer one of Mr. Pontellier's possessions. They make plans to meet again.

In the meantime, Edna helps Dr. Mandelet while Adèle is giving birth, an act that gives Edna a sense of dread. She explains to Mandelet that she wants nothing but her own way, even if it means trampling on the hearts and prejudices of others. He is unable to understand the depth of her commitment to finding a life of her own. Edna goes to her little house, around the corner from the big house on Esplanade Street, expecting Robert to be there. Instead, she finds a note: "I love you. Good-bye—because I love you." She realizes that the man she loves is not as brave as she is. She also realizes that she has another major decision to make. Grand Isle beckons to Edna again. She walks to the beach, to the seductive voice of the sea. She sees a bird with a broken wing descend to the water. She thinks about the courageous soul and about Robert's note and his failure to understand. Edna swims far into the ocean until her strength is gone. It is too late to go back.

Critical Evaluation:

When it was published in 1899, *The Awakening* was considered vulgar by most critics. The inferior social status of women was firmly entrenched, especially in the South. An accompanying concept was the assumed moral superiority of women, at least in sexual matters. Upper-class ladies such as Edna Pontellier were ornaments, displays of their husband's wealth. A book that challenged the traditional roles of women was likely to be controversial. The public was not ready to accept a liberated woman, even if she did commit suicide in the end. Kate Chopin disappeared from the literary world when her book was critically attacked and banned from libraries. Not all critics gave negative reviews. Willa Cather, later a famous novelist herself, praised *The Awakening*. Cather acclaimed the style of Chopin and also compared the protagonist to Emma Bovary and Anna Karenina, heroines of classic European fiction. From the mid-twentieth century on, critics, especially feminists, have raised the status of the novel to an American masterpiece. It has been celebrated as an important literary document in the history of women's rights and as an artistic success.

Chopin tells Edna's story without comment; the action and dialogue present ambiguities. Various schools of criticism have interpreted *The Awakening* from diverse views. Feminist critics have promoted it as a neglected text that should rightly be placed among the outstanding novels of the nineteenth century. It presents the plight of a woman who cannot accept the idea of being limited to a socially defined role. Edna rejects the economic and social success that her marriage to Léonce gives her in favor of working out her own destiny. She prefers to define her role actively rather than to be a passive object. Her awakening is sexual in part, but it is also a search for creativity, as suggested by her attempt to paint. She seeks the advice of the only artist she knows—Mademoiselle Reisz. She reads Emerson, the voice of individualism. From these sources, she gains the courage to challenge the authority of her husband. In her fight for independence, Edna becomes a threat to the values of a society.

Feminist critics also recognize other elements of the book relating to psychoanalytic theory, mythology, linguistics, and cultural studies. Critics from different fields saw it as naturalistic, an extended work of local color, or as a conflict between Creole and American cultures. A major emphasis, however, was the consideration of the novel as a work of art, which often involved an examination of patterns of imagery that tie the novel together.

One example is how Chopin uses birds to help define Edna's situation. On the first page, the caged parrot suggests her feeling of being trapped by traditions. The mockingbird, on the other side of Madame Lebrun's door, further illustrates her passive role, in which a voice of her own is not expected. Edna, however, speaks for herself by moving out of Léonce's house into what she calls her pigeon-house, suggestive of both a dependent domestic bird and a wild bird that has found its own nest. The advice that Edna gets from the pianist includes a reference to a bird that will have wings strong enough to fly above traditions and prejudices. Also, when the pianist plays for Edna, the latter envisions a naked man looking toward a distant bird in "hopeless resignation." Finally when Edna decides on suicide as a final act of free will, she watches a broken-winged bird descend into the sea. Edna breaks free from her cage, but she flounders in an alien environment. The story of her brief flight, however, has become a celebrated novel.

Noel Schraufnagel

Further Reading

Bloom, Harold, ed. *Kate Chopin*. New York: Chelsea House, 1987. A collection of ten critical essays on Chopin's works, with considerable discussion of *The Awakening*. Bloom's introduction contains a thought-provoking comparison of *The Awakening* with the poetry of Walt Whitman.

_______. *Kate Chopin's "The Awakening."* New York: Chelsea House, 2008. A student guide to the novel, featuring a biographical sketch of Chopin, a list of characters, plot summary, analysis, and a selection of critical essays. The essays discuss Chopin's virtues as a writer, the character of Edna Pontellier, white liberation and black oppression in the novel, and the novel's social and historical background, among other topics.

Chopin, Kate. *The Awakening: Complete, Authoritative Text with Biographical, Historical, and Cultural Contexts, Critical History, and Essays from Contemporary Critical Perspectives*. Edited by Nancy A. Walker. 2d ed. Boston: Bedford/St. Martin's, 2000. In addition to the text of *The Awakening*, this volume contains articles placing the novel within its cultural, historical, and biographical contexts, articles and advertisements from women's magazines and other journals that appeared around the same time as the novel's publication, and contemporary reviews. There are also several essays that approach the novel from modern critical perspectives, including that of feminism, gender studies, new historicism, deconstructionism, and reader-response theory.

Ewell, Barbara C. *Kate Chopin*. New York: Frederick Ungar, 1986. A biography of Chopin which surveys her writings in their entirety. Ewell emphasizes that *The Awakening* is Chopin's best-known and most important creation but represents only a portion of her total achievement as a writer. This excellent study also contains a chronology, a bibliography, and comprehensive endnotes.

Fryer, Judith. *The Faces of Eve: Women in the Nineteenth Century Novel*. New York: Oxford University Press, 1976. A chapter describes Edna Pontellier as the first woman in American fiction who is a fully developed character.

Keesey, Donald, Comp. *Contexts for Criticism*. 2d ed. Mountain View, Calif.: Mayfield, 1994. Considers *The Awakening* from the perspectives of historical, formal, reader response, mimetic, intertextual, and poststructural criticism.

Martin, Wendy, ed. *New Essays on "The Awakening."* New York: Cambridge University Press, 1988. A collection of four essays about Chopin's novel with a lengthy introduction by the editor, who provides an overview of Chopin's life and work. Each essay offers a distinct point of view; together they are intended to represent the best contemporary ideas about *The Awakening* by the so-called New Critics.

Sasa, Ghada Suleiman. *The Femme Fatale in American Literature*. Amherst, N.Y.: Cambria Press, 2008. Analyzes the character of Edna Pontellier and other women in works of American naturalist literature. Argues that these women are femme fatales who deliberately use their feminine power to overcome the world in which they are trapped.

Seyersted, Per. *Kate Chopin: A Critical Biography*. Baton Rouge: Louisiana State University Press, 1969. Reprint. New York: Octagon Books, 1980. An excellent biography by an authority on the author who served as editor of *The Complete Works of Kate Chopin*, published by Louisiana State University Press in 1970. Seyersted was influential in bringing Chopin back into the literary spotlight as a feminist writer of the first rank.

Toth, Emily. *Kate Chopin*. New York: William Morrow, 1990. An exhaustively researched book regarded by many critics as the definitive biography of Chopin. Toth identifies real-life models for Chopin's literary characters. Includes many photographs.

The Awkward Age

Author: Henry James (1843-1916)
First published: serial, 1898-1899; book, 1899
Type of work: Novel
Time of plot: 1890's
Locale: London and outlying estates

Principal characters:

FERNANDA BROOKENHAM (MRS. BROOK), the leader of a smart London set
EDWARD BROOKENHAM, her husband and a government employee
NANDA, their daughter
HAROLD, their son
MR. LONGDON, an elderly gentleman and a former suitor of Mrs. Brook's mother, Lady Julia
GUSTAVUS VANDERBANK (VAN), a member of Mrs. Brook's circle and a government employee
MR. MITCHETT (MITCHY), a wealthy young man who belongs to the circle
THE DUCHESS (JANE), the widow of an Italian duke, also a member of the circle
LITTLE AGGIE, her niece
TISHY GRENDON, a young married woman and a friend of Nanda
CARRIE DONNER, her sister
MR. CASHMORE, Mrs. Donner's lover
LADY FANNY CASHMORE, his wife
LORD PETHERTON, Lady Fanny's brother and Mitchy's friend

The Story:

For the sophisticated conversationalists of Mrs. Brookenham's social set, innuendo and the hinted nuance are a way of life. Indeed, their lives reside largely in talk. After Mr. Longdon spends his first evening at Mrs. Brookenham's, he has a long conversation with Gustavus Vanderbank, a remarkably handsome and imposing member of the set. Van is taken with the older man, whose manner contrasts charmingly with that of the set, and Mr. Longdon, despite misgivings about that set, is similarly pleased. Mr. Longdon confides to Van that he was a suitor to both Van's mother and Mrs. Brook's mother, Lady Julia, and that he never forgot his feelings for the latter, who is dramatically different from her daughter. Upon seeing a picture of Nanda, Mr. Longdon exclaims on her similarity to Lady Julia. The conversation ends with Mr. Longdon's revealing that the conversational tone of Mrs. Brook's evening indeed shocks him.

When she catches her son Harold in the act of stealing a five-pound note, Mrs. Brook has a colloquy with him. She is in her family mode, a studied and languorous melancholy quite at odds with her public manner, and her conversation turns on the problem of getting Harold invited to house parties and the family's financial straits. Harold leaves when the duchess enters, and the talk turns to Nanda, who is visiting her married friend Tishy Grendon. The duchess chides Mrs. Brook for allowing her daughter to mingle with such questionable associates; in the European manner, she is carefully sheltering her niece, Little Aggie, from any possible contaminations and preserving her as a perfect little *tabula rasa* until the time of her marriage. She urges Mrs. Brook to snare Mitchy as a husband for Nanda, adding that his ugliness and his being the son of a shoemaker render him an impossible mate for Aggie. After a brief conversation between Mrs. Brook and her husband, Mitchy and Petherton enter the room. Despite his outrageous talk, Mrs. Brook attributes to Mitchy a gentleness and "niceness" lacking in the others. The duchess reenters the room, this time with Aggie, followed by Carrie Donner and Lady Fanny, and the talk turns to the erotic entanglements of the Grendon-Donner-Cashmore set. The duchess informs Mitchy that Nanda is her mother's source on the degree of intimacy between Mrs. Donner and Mr. Cashmore.

When they meet, Nanda and Mr. Longdon sense an immediate rapport. Mrs. Brook sounds Van on the subject of Mr. Longdon's fortune and what he might do for Nanda, and at the same time she indicates that she might possibly be in love with Van. At a weekend party given by Mitchy, Mr. Longdon urges Nanda to marry, but she confides to him that she will probably never marry. The duchess tries to persuade Mr. Longdon to settle a sum on Van that will allow him to marry Nanda, which will leave Mitchy free for Aggie, who is in love with him. Mr. Longdon makes his offer to the uncertain Van, who requests time to consider the proposition and refuses to allow his prospective benefactor to name a sum.

When Van reveals Mr. Longdon's generous offer to Mrs. Brook, that lady enigmatically hints that he will refuse it. Against Van's wishes, Mrs. Brook tells Mitchy what she just learned and suggests that Van will pass up the chance to propose to Nanda rather than appear to have accepted a bribe. She justifies passing on the information as being in accordance with that principle of openness and honesty that marks their society. When Nanda enters shortly after the departure of her mother's guests, Mrs. Brook questions her about her relationship with Mr. Longdon and mentions the possibility and advisability of his adopting her.

Later, at Mr. Longdon's house, Nanda tells Mitchy, who she knows is in love with her, to marry Aggie. To please Nanda and to continue to enjoy at least the intimacy of sharing this plan with her, Mitchy acquiesces. He tells Van of his intentions, indicating that he will no longer be a rival for Nanda. Van remains uncommitted and indecisive, however.

Several months later, everyone is gathered at Tishy's estate. Nanda is Mr. Longdon's guest for several months; Harold ably distracts Lady Fanny from her design to run off with another gentleman; and Little Aggie, having married and lost her innocence, takes up with her aunt's lover, Petherton. In a tremendous scene in which she demands Nanda's return from Mr. Longdon, Mrs. Brook brings about public exposure of the group. She climaxes her performance with the revelation that Nanda read a scabrous French novel, lent to her by Vanderbank, which is pronounced unfit even for the presumably far more experienced Tishy. As a result, Vanderbank learns the depths of knowledge already open to Nanda, depths in the unveiling of which was instrumental but which, with cruel irony, now make her an impossible choice to be his wife.

The scene at Tishy's estate destroys the solidarity of the group. It is months before Van returns to Mrs. Brook's house, and though he supposedly comes to see Nanda, he ultimately avoids the chance to do so. Mrs. Brook interprets this to mean that he finally gives Nanda up, and she enjoins Mitchy to tell Mr. Longdon. As she explains to her remarkably obtuse husband, her purpose in creating the scene at Tishy's was simply to confirm Mr. Longdon's belief that she and her world are impossible for Nanda and to ensure his taking care of the girl.

Two weeks later, the overwrought and embarrassed Van makes what is presumably his final visit to Nanda. Nanda, however, lets the now awkward young man off easily by herself assuming the false position, and she generously entreats him not to desert her mother, a plea she also makes to Mitchy. Once only Mr. Longdon remains, she breaks down in the fullness of her suffering. They agree that Vanderbank ought to have married Aggie. Only her kind of innocence could have met his measure, an innocence capable of becoming its own obverse at the first taste of experience. Even under such a circumstance, however, Mitchy would still have been totally out of the question for her; it is his fate, as it is Nanda's, to love only the person who is out of the question. Nanda's thoughts revolve around the suffering Mitchy as she makes preparations for being taken away the following day by Mr. Longdon.

Critical Evaluation:

As he does in so much of his fiction, Henry James in *The Awkward Age* focuses his attention on the nature of social relationships in his adopted homeland, England. In this work, he does not, however, contrast the sophistication of European society with the more naïve, but at times morally superior, American scene. Instead, *The Awkward Age* is a scathing portrait of the hypocrisy and self-interest of British society, where young women, at that "awkward age" between girlhood and full-fledged adulthood, are especially vulnerable to the machinations of older women and men who wish to use them for their own purposes.

The unlikely hero of the story, Mr. Longdon, is not a member of the London society that James castigates. Well into middle age, Mr. Longdon returns to London from his country estate to reacquaint himself with the family of a woman he once loved deeply, whose memory he still cherishes though she is long dead. The society he finds is far different from the one he remembers from his youth. The contrast between past and present and the loss Mr. Longdon feels for the values he holds sacred are themes James plays upon throughout the work. Mr. Longdon, too, is at an "awkward age," too old to pursue amorous relationships with women but young enough to be stirred by the beauty of a girl such as Nanda. His solution is to become a kind of surrogate father for her, a knight who will rescue her from the metaphorical dungeon in which she is trapped by her scheming mother and the men who want her for all the wrong reasons.

Three women dominate the novel: Mrs. Brookenham, her daughter Nanda, and the shadow of Lady Julia. Mr. Longdon's reaction to each of them is a spur for what little action the novel contains. For the aging hero, the grace, poise, and moral rectitude he associates with Lady Julia have degenerated into Mrs. Brookenham's scheming and corruption. In Nanda, Mr. Longdon sees the reincarnation of her grandmother, and he believes it is his mission in life to save the young woman from the life she is destined to lead if she remains in the social circle dominated by her mother and her father's cousin, the duchess. These two femmes fatale, who are constantly working both as matchmakers and go-betweens for themselves and others in liaisons outside marriage, strike the man from an earlier generation as reprehensible and as a violation of the principles that governed relations between the sexes in an earlier era.

From Mr. Longdon's efforts to wrest Nanda away from her mother, and from the efforts of Mrs. Brookenham and the duchess to guide various other characters into and out of relationships, a central theme of the novel emerges: power and control in social situations. For James, the question is not simply one of gender domination: The women in this novel seem to exercise as much power over men as men do over women. The unusual arrangement, which often blurs the line between traditional qualities associated with males and females, arises from all of the characters' acquiescence in the social strictures that, by common assumption, should govern the lives of people in the higher social sets. Those standards involve a view of marriage as a financial and social arrangement rather than as a bond between two individuals deeply in love. Hence, both men and women in the novel are constantly concerned with improving their status in society by seeking the partner who will bring them money or position or both. Because her fortune seems assured, the duchess's niece Aggie is a more attractive catch than Nanda. Even Mr. Longdon, whom James seems to intend as the moral arbiter in the work, places a monetary value on Nanda when he makes the proposal that if Vanderbank will marry Nanda, he will settle a small fortune on her to assure the couple's financial independence. What emerges from this web of posturing and negotiating is a portrait of a society in which genuine concern for human feelings is subordinate to self-interest.

Such attitudes are only suggested, however. James's fiction rarely states a moral position directly. However, even within the James canon, *The Awkward Age* is a particularly difficult novel. Eschewing conventional methods of storytelling in fiction, James instead imposes dramatic principles on his story. Almost the entire novel is cast in the form of dialogue and conversation, and readers are left to discern characters' motives and moral qualities from the remarks they make about themselves and others. Often information is conflicting, even contradictory. It is never entirely clear whether such figures as Mrs. Brookenham and Vanderbank are simple seekers after pleasure or more complex personalities who recognize that living in the world of high society places extraordinary demands on individuals. It is never certain whether Mitchy is so devoted to Nanda that his marriage to Aggie is an act of self-sacrifice, or whether he is simply another of the dissolute men who populate Mrs. Brookenham's salon, willing to do whatever he is told rather than cause a scene. It is not even clear how Mr. Longdon and Nanda feel about each other when she agrees to leave her mother's home to live with him in the country. James has allowed readers to observe the characters and to listen to them for a while. How to judge the characters, however, remains a constant enigma, akin to the situation everyone faces daily in trying to judge those who are only known through what they say and do.

"Critical Evaluation" by Laurence W. Mazzeno

Further Reading

Coulson, Victoria. *Henry James, Women, and Realism*. New York: Cambridge University Press, 2007. Examines James's important friendships with three women: his sister Alice James and the novelists Constance Fenimore Woolson and Edith Wharton. These three women writers and James shared what Coulson describes as an "ambivalent realism," or a cultural ambivalence about gender identity, and she examines how this idea is manifest in James's works, including *The Awkward Age*.

Edel, Leon. *Henry James: A Life*. New York: Harper & Row, 1985. Abridgment of Edel's definitive study of the novelist. Includes comments about the writing and publication of *The Awkward Age*; discusses James's handling of character development, especially that of the middle-aged Longdon and the two young women whose stories are central to the plot.

Freedman, Jonathan, ed. *The Cambridge Companion to Henry James*. New York: Cambridge University Press, 1998. A collection of essays that provides extensive information on James's life and literary influences and describes his works and the characters in them.

Gard, Roger, ed. *Henry James: The Critical Heritage*. London: Routledge & Kegan Paul, 1968. Includes excerpts from four reviews of *The Awkward Age* by James's contemporaries. Cites both British and American sources and records the mixed success of the work among nineteenth century readers.

Jones, Granville H. *Henry James's Psychology of Experience: Innocence, Responsibility, and Renunciation in the Fiction of Henry James*. Paris: Mouton, 1975. Uses *The Awkward Age* to explore "the position of innocence in the structure, form, style, and substance of James's fiction." Claims that the novel shows James's attempt to explore the ramifications of change and loss of innocence.

Macnaughton, William R. *Henry James: The Later Novels*. Boston: Twayne, 1987. A chapter on *The Awkward Age* provides commentary on the genesis of the novel, examines James's sources, and discusses the ambiguities created by the author's use of dramatic form for his story. Also explores James's development of the central characters.

Pippin, Robert B. *Henry James and Modern Moral Life*. New York: Cambridge University Press, 2000. A look at the moral message James sought to convey through his writings. Pippin interprets several of James's works, including *The Awkward Age*.

Sicker, Philip. *Love and the Quest for Identity in the Fiction of Henry James*. Princeton, N.J.: Princeton University Press, 1980. Studies the "evolving conception of romantic love" in James's fiction. The extended discussion of *The Awkward Age* focuses on the inability of the middle-aged protagonist to adjust to changes wrought by time.

B

Baal

Author: Bertolt Brecht (1898-1956)
First produced: 1923; first published, 1922; revised, 1926 (English translation, 1963)
Type of work: Drama
Type of plot: Tragedy
Time of plot: c. 1911
Locale: Augsberg, Germany, and environs

Principal characters:
BAAL, a poet
MECH, a wealthy timber merchant
EMILY, his wife
JOHANNES SCHMIDT, Baal's friend
JOHANNA REIHER, Johannes's fiancé
EKART, a composer
SOPHIE BARGER, Baal's lover

The Story:

After taking the seat of honor in a dining room filled with admirers, the indigent poet Baal shows more interest in the food on his plate than he does in the praise of his poetry. Mech, a timber magnate, offers to publish Baal's work, but when Baal makes a pass at his wife, Emily, Mech is offended and leaves—as does everyone else.

Back in Baal's attic, Johannes asks Baal if he should try to have sex with his fiancé, Johanna. Baal tells him to avoid it because he will not have the toughness to abandon her when his passion dissipates.

Later, Johannes and Johanna meet Baal in a cheap bar, where Baal tells a group of truckers how Emily sought him out. Now Baal is sick of her. When Emily shows up, Baal tells her to drink and then grabs a waitress. Emily threatens to leave. When Johanna offers to accompany her, Emily bursts into tears and explains that Baal always behaves this way, yet she loves him. After Baal sings a song about how much he loves using the men's room, the truckers cheer. Ekart, a composer, invites Baal to take the party outside, but Baal declines. After Ekart leaves, Emily begs Baal to stop flirting with the waitress. Baal responds by demanding that Emily kiss a trucker. Crying, she consents and the truckers laugh. Johannes and Johanna scold Baal and leave. Emily sobs, and the truckers congratulate Baal for treating her roughly.

Johanna is in Baal's bed. She is distraught. Baal tells her to wash herself. When she asks him if he still loves her, he says his appetite is satisfied. She leaves. Later, two sisters come to Baal's room and begin undressing. When one mentions that a girl named Johanna had thrown herself into the river, Baal sends them away.

In the evening, Baal gets drunk and goes looking for a woman. When he returns with a woman named Sophie Barger, a disconsolate Johannes is waiting in his room. Baal sends him away. Sophie prepares to leave too. When she hesitates, Baal grabs her, kisses her, and takes her to his bed. She tells him it is her first time. On a spring night several weeks later, Baal and Sophie lie under the trees. Baal tells Sophie he loves her. She is afraid her mother will think she has drowned.

Baal shows up next in a grimy nightclub where he exchanges songs for drinks. When his request for more gin is refused, he sneaks out before completing his performance. Later, to amuse Ekart, Baal promises a group of farmers his brother will pay a high price for the bull with the strongest legs. Ekart wants to leave before the joke is exposed (there is no prize money). A good-natured parson convinces Baal to leave before the farmers return with their bulls.

Baal turns up next in a forest with a group of lumberjacks standing over a dead coworker. He scolds them for resolving to drink their fallen comrade's remaining gin. The lumberjacks discover the gin is gone, and they accuse Baal of drinking it. Baal, drunk, says they have no proof and encourages them to join him as he marvels at the darkening sky.

Later, Baal complains to Ekart about the way Sophie has been running after them. Then Sophie shows up. She is pregnant with Baal's baby. Ekart chastises Baal for mistreating her. When Ekart threatens to leave Baal and stay with Sophie, she confesses she cannot help loving Baal. Baal calls Ekart a simpleton, and Ekart attacks him. Holding Ekart close, Baal tells him they do not need women. They leave Sophie behind, screaming Baal's name.

Ekart and Baal approach sick beggars awaiting treatment in a hospital tavern. One gives a speech celebrating the freedom that comes with having no feelings or desires. Ekart complains that Baal has corrupted his soul and that he will go with him no farther. Baal responds by drinking to Ekart's health and telling him he loves him. Shortly after, Baal denounces the beggars as swine, and he and Ekart leave.

Sitting in a thicket near a river, Baal reaffirms his love for Ekart and adds that he no longer cares for women. That night, Baal wakes up Ekart to sing him a song about a woman's pale body that decays in the water until God forgets it. Baal calls the world God's excrement and praises its beauty. Ekart tells Baal he has not finished his quartet because he has been having sex with a redhead. When Baal asks Ekart if the redhead is more beautiful than he is, Ekart does not answer.

Later, Baal ambushes the redhead, takes her in his arms, and drags her into a thicket.

Some time afterward, when Baal asks Ekart what happened to the girl, Ekart intimates that she had drowned. Baal then shares his new song, "Death in the Forest," about a sick man who would rather die of exposure than be carried home.

Eight years later, Ekart shares a drink with Johannes, who is now a shameless drunk. Ekart professes his love for Baal, whom he likens to a child. Baal shows up and sings about a man who dreams of a lost childhood. Jealous of the waitress in Ekart's lap (she looks like Sophie), Baal leaps at Ekart, chokes him, and finally stabs him.

Back in the forest, Baal, alone, walks into the distance, singing about the vultures waiting to see him die. While hiding in the bushes, he overhears two police officers discussing his case. He learns from them that Ekart has died from his stab wounds.

Baal is next found lying in a dirty bed. Nearby, lumberjacks play cards and make offhand remarks about his impending death. When they get up to leave, Baal implores them to stay, but they laugh and leave anyway. Baal compels himself to crawl out the door. Some other lumberjacks later complain that Baal had stolen eggs from them while he was on his deathbed. They do not know his name.

"The Story" by Steve Benton

Critical Evaluation:

The twenty-year-old Bertolt Brecht began writing *Baal* in 1918 as a response to Hanns Johst's drama *Der Einsame: Ein Menschenuntergang* (1917; the lonely one: a human decline), an expressionist work about the nineteenth century poet Christian Dietrich Grabbe. Brecht had seen a production of Johst's play and discussed it in a seminar led by Arthur Kutschler at Ludwig Maximilian University in Munich, Germany. Brecht despised the play for its idealism—the notion that artists are different from other people—and for its sentimentality. He set out to write an antithetical play, using as his models for the protagonist the fifteenth century French poet François Villon, German expressionist balladeer and playwright Frank Wedekind, and Brecht's own bohemian experiences.

Suggestions of the relationship between the French poets Paul Verlaine and Arthur Rimbaud also appear in the play. Brecht's first draft, written in 1918, closely follows the structure and episodes of Johst's play; later drafts move away from his antimodel, de-emphasizing Johst's influence.

As Brecht's first mature play (he had written a short play during his school years), *Baal* is "indispensable reading for anyone who would understand Brecht's development," according to critic Ronald Speirs. The play is a heady brew of disparate influences and impulses that continued to be played out in many guises throughout Brecht's career. The tension of the play is dialectical: Decay is linked to existence, destruction to productive energy, and Eros to Thanatos. Brecht allows no triumphant rebirth or transcendence.

The paganism implied in the protagonist's name is not simply a reflection of a naïve and innocent longing to return to nature. Baal is the Semitic-Phoenician fertility god, associated with storms and the figure of the bull. His attraction for Brecht, no doubt, in part derives from the knowledge that in the Judeo-Christian tradition, Baal is the embodiment of evil. Brecht's character has strong associations also with philosopher Friedrich Nietzsche's Dionysian principle and with Wedekind's neopagan, antiheroine Lulu.

Although the action of the play takes place over many years, the essential movement is seasonal, as befits its roots in a mythic paganism. The play begins in spring with an emphasis on Baal's erotic desires. He successively seduces Emily, Johanna, and Sophie. The friendship between Ekart and Baal ripens through the summer until the autumnal harvest is signaled by Sophie's pregnancy. The fall's torrential rains drive Ekart and Baal from the woods into inns and taverns inhabited by worn-out social pariahs. Death marks the winter—first Baal's enraged murder of Ekart and then Baal's own lonely death under the starry sky.

Baal is seduced by nature, "that girl the world, who gives herself and giggles/ If you only let her crush you with her thighs,/ Shared with Baal who loved it, orgiastic wriggles," but he suffers no spiritual or metaphysical illusions. Nature will abandon him as easily as he abandons the lovers of which he has tired. Brecht's vision of nature incorporates a Darwinian materialism that does not deny the inevitability of death.

> In the dark womb of the earth the rotting Baal did lie.
> Huge as ever, calm, and pallid was the sky,
> Young and naked and immensely marvelous
> As Baal loved it when Baal lived among us.

As an amoral child of nature, Brecht's protagonist is lusting, romping, scratching after life, gobbling it up in great mouthfuls, all the while trying to survive in a world that is consuming and mad in itself.

Baal also belongs to the satiric tradition, contemptuous of established institutions and sanctioned morality. Baal's lust is voracious, and his teeth are sharp. When Baal insists that one must have teeth to reach love's ecstasy, "like biting into an orange when the juice squirts in your teeth," his friend Johannes observes, "Your teeth are the teeth of an animal: grayish-yellow, massive, uncanny."

Amid a society rotted with corruption and offering no meaning, the poet exults in motiveless pranks. Baal's trickery may be illustrated by the episode with the peasants and their bulls—he desires to create a divine spectacle but is thwarted by a well-intentioned and unimaginative parson. Baal celebrates life despite, or perhaps because of, being inextricably caught in the web of nature. This inevitability of death and decay is something that Brecht tried to overcome in his later plays. The atmosphere of *Baal* is one in which God is dead and nihilism is rampant. God is not dead in the medieval beast epic, to which *Baal* owes much, but God might as well be, for in such an epic nature reigns, the Church is useless, and the court is incapable of dispensing justice. In both worlds—that of the medieval beast story and that of *Baal*—one has only oneself to depend upon or worry about. When asked if he believes in God, Baal answers "I always believed in myself. But one *could* become an atheist."

Although the older Brecht, committed to the optimistic hope that the world could be improved through dedication to Marxism, repudiated the nihilism of his first play, it was from the writing of *Baal* that many of the playwright's techniques and themes evolved. The method of welding together multiple sources fused with a heightened poetic lyricism became his standard procedure in crafting a drama, as did his reliance on multiple collaborators. In the case of *Baal*, he relies upon the illustrations of Caspar Neher for visual inspiration and scenic decoration, on playwright Lion Feuchtwanger for editing help in the second draft, and on the actors, including Oskar Homolka, in the 1926 revision produced in Berlin and Vienna.

Baal was not produced again until the 1965 Off-Broadway production (of the 1963 English translation by Eric Bentley and Martin Esslin) with James Earl Jones as Ekart. Since that production, it has often been revived in university and alternative theaters and occasionally even in more mainstream venues as a seminal work not only in the evolution of Brecht's theater but also in the development of contemporary drama.

Jane Anderson Jones

Further Reading

Bentley, Eric. "*Baal*." In *The Brecht Commentaries, 1943-1980*. New York: Grove Press, 1981. Describes Baal as a pleasure-seeker and part monster and part martyr in a world of nothingness. Suggests that the mythic elements in the play will become increasingly important to a critical understanding of the play.

Blackadder, Neil. "'Pfui!' Disdaining Experimentation." In *Performing Opposition: Modern Theater and the Scandalized Audience*. Westport, Conn.: Praeger, 2003. Discusses how audience members who were scandalized by Brecht's experimental theater protested performances of *Baal* and other plays.

Brecht, Bertolt. *Baal*. Translated by Peter Tegel. Edited by John Willett and Ralph Manheim. New York: Arcade, 1998. In addition to an English translation of the play, this volume includes Brecht's own notes and variant scenes. There is also an introduction, editorial notes, and information about the various versions of the play that were performed and published between 1918 and 1926.

Hayman, Ronald. *Brecht: A Biography*. New York: Oxford University Press, 1983. Hayman intertwines a study of Brecht's life with a critical view of his work. He traces the inception of *Baal*, Brecht's collaboration with Caspar Neher, and the subsequent revisions of the play.

Hill, Claude. "Praise Ye the Cold, the Darkness, and Corruption." In *Bertolt Brecht*. Boston: Twayne, 1975. In this chapter, discussing *Baal* and five other early works, Hill reveals the influences that led Brecht to write the play and points out that there were multiple drafts, resulting in three distinctly different versions.

Speirs, Ronald. "*Baal*." In *Critical Essays on Bertolt Brecht*, edited by Siegfried Mews. Boston: G. K. Hall, 1989. Speirs connects Baal with the cult of vitality and modern paganism as represented by philosopher Friedrich Nietzsche's Dionysus and playwright Frank Wedekind's Lulu.

He explores how Baal experiences life's transience as both a threat of death and a source of pleasure.

Thomson, Peter, and Glendyr Sacks, eds. *The Cambridge Companion to Brecht*. 2d ed. New York: Cambridge University Press, 2006. Collection of essays offering numerous interpretations of Brecht's work, including examinations of Brecht and cabaret, music, and stage design; discussions of his work with the Berliner Ensemble; and a list of key words used in his theory and practice of theater. Chapter 4 discusses *Baal* and other early plays.

Unwin, Stephen. *A Guide to the Plays of Bertolt Brecht*. London: Methuen, 2005. Contains analyses of many of Brecht's plays, and discusses his theories of drama, the cultural effect of his work, and his legacy. Designed as an accessible introduction to Brecht for students, teachers, and general readers.

Babbitt

Author: Sinclair Lewis (1885-1951)
First published: 1922
Type of work: Novel
Type of plot: Social satire
Time of plot: 1920's
Locale: Zenith, Midwestern United States

Principal characters:
GEORGE F. BABBITT, a middle-age real estate broker
MYRA, his wife
TED, their son
VERONA, their daughter
PAUL RIESLING, Babbitt's friend
ZILLA, Paul's wife

The Story:

George F. Babbitt is proud of his house in Floral Heights, one of the most respectable residential districts in Zenith. Its architecture is standardized; its interior decorations are standardized; its atmosphere is standardized. Therein lies its appeal for Babbitt. He bustles about in a tile and chromium bathroom during his morning ritual of getting ready for another day. When he goes down to breakfast, he is as grumpy as usual. It is expected of him. He reads the dull real estate page of the newspaper to his patient wife, Myra. Then he comments on the weather, grumbles at his son and daughter, gulps his breakfast, and starts for his office.

Babbitt is a real estate broker who knows how to handle business with "zip and zowie." Having closed a deal whereby he forced a poor businessman to buy a piece of property at twice its value, he pockets part of the money and pays the rest to the man who had suggested the enterprise. Proud of his acumen, he picks up the telephone and calls his best friend, Paul Riesling, to ask him to lunch. Paul should have been a violinist, but he has gone into the tar-roofing business in order to support his shrewish wife, Zilla. Lately, she makes it her practice to infuriate doormen, theater ushers, or taxicab drivers and then asks Paul to come to her rescue and fight them like a man. Cringing with embarrassment, Paul pretends that he did not notice the incident. Later, at home, Zilla accuses him of being a coward and a weakling.

Paul's affairs seem so sad to Babbitt that he suggests a vacation to Maine together—away from their wives. Paul is skeptical, but with magnificent assurance, Babbitt promises to arrange the trip. Paul is humbly grateful. Back in his office, Babbitt refuses a raise for one of his employees. When he gets home, he and his wife decide to give a dinner party with the arrangements taken from the contents of a woman's magazine and everything edible disguised to look like something else.

The party is a great success. Babbitt's friends are exactly like Babbitt. They all become drunk on Prohibition-period gin, are disappointed when the cocktails run out, stuff themselves with food, and go home to nurse headaches.

Some time later, Babbitt and Myra pay a call on the Rieslings. Zilla, trying to enlist their sympathy, berates her husband until he is goaded to fury. Babbitt finally tells Zilla that she is a nagging, jealous, sour, and unwholesome wife, and he demands that she allow Paul to go with him to Maine. Weeping in self-pity, Zilla consents. Myra sits calmly during the scene, but later she criticizes Babbitt for bullying Paul's wife. Babbitt tells her sharply to mind her own business. On the train, Babbitt and Paul meet numerous businessmen who loudly agree with one another that what this country needs is sound business administration. They deplore the price of motor cars, textiles, wheat, and oil; they swear that they have not an ounce of race prejudice; they blame communism and socialism for labor unions that get out of hand. Paul soon tires of the discussion and goes to bed. Babbitt stays up late, smoking countless cigars and telling countless stories.

Maine has a soothing effect upon Babbitt. He and Paul fish and hike in the quiet of the north woods, and Babbitt begins to realize that his life in Zenith is not all it should be. He promises himself a new outlook on life—a more simple, less hurried way of living.

Back in Zenith, Babbitt is asked to make a speech at a convention of real estate men, which is to be held in Monarch, a nearby city. He writes a speech contending that real estate men should be considered professionals and called realtors. At the meeting, he declaims loudly that real estate is a great profession, that Zenith is God's own country—the best little spot on earth—and to prove his statements, he quotes countless statistics on waterways, textile production, and lumber manufacture. The speech is such a success that Babbitt instantly wins recognition as an orator.

Babbitt is made a precinct leader in the coming election. His duty is to speak to small labor groups about the inadvisability of voting for Seneca Doane, a liberal, in favor of a man named Prout, a solid businessman who represents the conservative element. Babbitt's speeches help to defeat Doane. He is very proud of himself.

On a business trip to Chicago, Babbitt spies Paul sitting at dinner with a middle-aged and pretty woman. Later, in his hotel room, Babbitt indignantly demands an explanation for Paul's lack of morality. Paul tells Babbitt that he can no longer stand living with Zilla. Babbitt, feeling sorry for his friend, swears that he will keep Paul's secret from Zilla. Privately, Babbitt envies Paul's independence. Babbitt is made vice president of the Booster's Club. He is so proud of himself that he brags loudly when his wife calls him at the office. It is a long time before he understands what she is trying to tell him: Paul shot his wife, Zilla is still alive, and Paul is in prison.

Babbitt's world collapses about him. He begins to question his ideas about the power of the dollar. Paul is perhaps the only person Babbitt ever loved. Myra long since became a habit, and the children are too full of new ideas to be close to their father. Babbitt suddenly feels alone. He begins to criticize the minister's sermons. He no longer visits the Athletic Club and rarely eats lunch with any of his business acquaintances. One day, the pretty widow Mrs. Judique comes to his office and asks him to find her a flat. Babbitt joins her circle of Bohemian friends. He drinks more than ever. He spends money wildly. Two of the most powerful men in town request that he join the Good Citizen's League—or else. Babbitt refuses to be bullied. For the first time in his life, he is a human being. He makes friends with his archenemy, Doane, and discovers that he likes his liberal ideas. He praises Doane publicly. Babbitt's new outlook on life appeals to his children, who at once began to respect him as they never have before. Babbitt, however, becomes unpopular among his business-boosting friends. When he again refuses to join the Good Citizen's League, he is snubbed in the streets. Gradually, Babbitt finds that he has no real resources within himself. He is miserable.

When Myra becomes ill, Babbitt suddenly realizes that he loves his colorless wife. He breaks with Mrs. Judique and joins the Good Citizen's League. By the time Myra is well again, there is no more active leader in the town of Zenith than George F. Babbitt. Once more he announces his distrust of Doane. He becomes the best booster the club ever had. His last gesture of revolt is private approval of his son's elopement. Outwardly he conforms.

Critical Evaluation:

Zenith, "the Zip City—Zeal, Zest, and Zowie," is Sinclair Lewis's satirical composite picture of the typical progressive American "business city" of the 1920's, and middle-aged, middle-class midwesterner George F. Babbitt is its average prosperous citizen. Everything about Zenith is modern. A few old buildings, ramshackle witnesses of the city's nineteenth century origins, are embarrassing, discordant notes amid the harmony of newness produced by shining skyscrapers, factories, and railroads. One by one, the old buildings are surrounded and bulldozed. The thrust of all energies in the city is toward growth: One of Zenith's most booming businesses is real estate; one of its favorite occupations is the religious tallying and charting of population increase.

As Lewis presents his characters, however, the reader discovers that the prosperity and growth of Zenith are inversely proportional to the intellectual bankruptcy and spiritual stagnation of its inhabitants. They subscribe to the values of Zenith's culture, which are all based on the "Dollar Ethic"; Lewis's characters think in terms of production and consumption, judge people on the grounds of their purchasing power, and seek happiness in the earning and spending of money. This creed of prosperity permeates every aspect of society. It is evident not only in political and economic beliefs (discussion between Babbitt and his friends about government affairs is limited to the monotonous refrain, "What this country needs is a good, sound business administration") but also in moral and religious attitudes. Thus, Dr. Drew attracts followers to his "Salvation and Five Percent" church with a combined cross-and-dollar-sign approach. Even more sinister is the facility with which the upright Babbitt carries through crooked deals in his real estate business. In one maneuver, he plots with a speculator to force a struggling grocer to buy the store building (which he has been renting for years) at a scalper's price. The money ethic is so elemental to Babbitt's conscience that he honestly feels nothing but delight and pride when the deal is completed; his only regret is that the speculator carries off nine thousand dollars while Babbitt receives a mere four hundred and fifty dollar commission. At the same time, Babbitt—with no inkling of his hypocrisy—discourses on his virtue to his friend Paul Riesling, touting his own integrity while denigrating the morality of his competitors.

The value placed on money also determines Zenith's aesthetic standards. There is no frivolity about the city's architecture; the most important structures are the strictly functional business buildings. Other structures, such as the Athletic Club—where the businessmen go to "relax" and discuss weighty matters of finance—are gaudy, unabashed copies of past styles; the club's motley conglomeration includes everything from Roman to Gothic to Chinese. The culmination of literary talent in Zenith is the work of Chum Frink, whose daily newspaper lyrics are indistinguishable from his Zeeco car ads. He comes to Babbitt's dinner party fresh from having written a lyric in praise of drinking water instead of poison booze; with bootleg cocktail in hand, he identifies the American genius as the fellow who can run a successful business or the man who writes the Prince Albert Tobacco ads.

Most important, the prosperity ethic is at the heart of social norms in Zenith; it is the basis upon which each citizen judges his individual worth. Lewis's novel includes caricatures of men in every major field of endeavor: Howard Littlefield is the scholar; T. Cholmondeley Frink, the poet; Mike Monday, the popular preacher; Jake Offut, the politician; Vergil Gunch, the industrialist. Despite their various professions, however, these men are identical in their values; they are united in their complacent pride in their own success and in their scorn for those who have not "made it." A man is measured by his income and his possessions. Thus, Babbitt's car is far more than his means of transportation, and his acquisition of gimmicks like the nickel-plated cigar cutter more than mere whim; both car and cigar cutter are affirmations of competence and virility. The more Babbitt and his peers strive to distinguish themselves through ownership, however, the more alike they seem. Thus, the men of Zenith, since they are saturated day after day with the demands of the business life and its values, are even more alike than the women, who are not as immersed in the rat race as their husbands.

Mercilessly revealing and minutely detailed as the portrait of Zenith is, however, *Babbitt* would not be the excellent novel it is if Lewis had stopped at that. In addition to being an exposé of shallowness, the novel is the chronicle of one man's feeble and half-conscious attempt to break out of a meaningless and sterile existence. In the first half of the book, Babbitt is the Zenithite par excellence; but in the realtor's sporadic bursts of discontent, Lewis plants seeds of the rebellion to come. Babbitt's complacency is occasionally punctured by disturbing questions: Might his wife be right that he bullied Zilla only to strut and show off his strength and virtue? Are his friends really interesting people? Does he really love his wife and enjoy his career? These nagging questions and the pressures in his life finally build sufficient tension to push Babbitt to the unprecedented step of taking a week's vacation in Maine without his wife and children. The trip relieves his tension and dissolves the questions, and he returns to another year in Zenith with renewed vigor and enthusiasm for Boosters, baseball, dinner parties, and real estate.

It takes the personal tragedy of his friend Paul to shock Babbitt out of his routine way of life; Paul's shooting of his wife and consequent imprisonment, which occur approximately midway in the novel, shake Babbitt to his foundations. The Babbitt of the first half of the story is a parody; the Babbitt of the second half is a weak and struggling human being. After Paul goes to prison, Babbitt, to all appearances, throws over his whole previous lifestyle: He drinks, smokes, and curses; he frequents wild parties, befriends the city's bohemian set, adopts radical opinions, and has a love affair. All these things are part of his rebellion against stifling circumstances and his attempt to escape into individuality. The attempt fails because he lacks the inner strength to be independent, and his revolt is ultimately little more than a teapot tempest. Whether preaching the philosophy of the Elks or rebelliously praising the radical politics of Doane, whether giving a dinner party with his wife or sneaking out to see Mrs. Judique, Babbitt never truly acts on his own.

Thus, by the end of the novel, Babbitt has "returned to the fold," joining the Good Citizen's League and redoubling his zeal on behalf of Zenith Booster activities. Even though Babbitt lacks the strength to break out of his mold, Lewis does not imply that he is unchanged by his experience. On the contrary, Babbitt rediscovers his love for his wife and learns something about himself. The Babbitt at the close of the novel has grown in awareness, even if he has proven himself incapable of essentially changing his life. If he has lost his own individuality, he is still able to hope for better things for his son, Ted, of whose elopement he secretly approves.

"Critical Evaluation" by Nancy G. Ballard

Further Reading

Bloom, Harold, ed. *George Babbitt.* Philadelphia: Chelsea House, 2004. A collection of essays about Lewis's best-known fictional character, including reprints of older essays by H. L. Mencken, Rebecca West, Sherwood Anderson, and Gore Vidal.

Bucco, Martin, ed. *Critical Essays on Sinclair Lewis.* Boston: G. K. Hall, 1986. Collection of criticism on Lewis's works. Begins with early interviews and goes on to include contemporary critics. Many of the articles contain discussion of *Babbitt,* with one essay devoted solely to this novel.

Dooley, D. J. *The Art of Sinclair Lewis.* Lincoln: University of Nebraska Press, 1967. Discusses *Babbitt* as the first novel to represent what would become Lewis's characteristic method—the intensive study of a subject. Discusses the novel's strengths and weaknesses and explores the significance of *Babbitt* in American life.

Grebstein, Sheldon Norman. *Sinclair Lewis.* Boston: Twayne, 1962. Makes a useful distinction between Lewis's novels, including *Babbitt,* which were written in the 1920's, and the rest of his works. Argues that *Babbitt* created an image of America that continues to be influential.

Hutchisson, James M. *The Rise of Sinclair Lewis, 1920-1930.* University Park: Pennsylvania State University Press, 1996. Focuses on Lewis's career in the 1920's, when he wrote *Babbitt* and the other novels that earned him the Nobel Prize in Literature. Hutchisson examines the techniques Lewis used to create his novels, devoting chapter 2 to an analysis of *Babbitt.*

_______, ed. *Sinclair Lewis: New Essays in Criticism.* Troy, N.Y.: Whitston, 1997. Includes Clare Virginia's essay "'Extremely Married': Marriage as Experience and Institution in *The Job, Main Street,* and *Babbitt,*" as well as essays on many of Lewis's other novels and an annotated bibliography of Lewis studies from 1977 through 1997.

Lingeman, Richard R. *Sinclair Lewis: Rebel from Main Street.* New York: Random House, 2002. A critical biography that includes analysis of Lewis's novels. Lingeman provides a detailed description of Lewis's unhappy life.

Love, Glen A. *Babbitt: An American Life.* Boston: Twayne, 1993. Places *Babbitt* in its historical and literary context. Includes chronology, critical analysis, and bibliography.

Schorer, Mark. *Sinclair Lewis: An American Life.* New York: McGraw-Hill, 1961. Indispensable. Discusses *Babbitt* from its inception to its reviews, and includes an analysis of the novel, concluding that *Babbitt* was published with timing perfectly suited to match the national mood.

Thompson, Graham. "The Businessman and the Fairy Child in Sinclair Lewis's *Babbitt.*" In *Male Sexuality Under Surveillance: The Office in American Literature.* Iowa City: University of Iowa Press, 2003. Examines the boundaries of male friendship in the novel.

The Bacchae

Author: Euripides (c. 485-406 B.C.E.)
First produced: Bakchai, 405 B.C.E. (English translation, 1781)
Type of work: Drama
Type of plot: Tragedy
Time of plot: Antiquity
Locale: Thebes, in Boeotia

Principal characters:
DIONYSUS, the god of the vine
PENTHEUS, the king of Thebes
CADMUS, the grandfather of Pentheus and the former king
TIRESIAS, a Theban seer
AGAVE, Pentheus's mother

The Story:

Semele, the daughter of Cadmus, the king of Thebes, is visited by Zeus and conceives a child. While she still carries her unborn child, she prays to see Zeus in all his splendor. Zeus accordingly appears to her in the form of a bolt of lightning, and Semele is killed instantly. Zeus takes the prematurely born child he fathered and places him within himself. At the proper time, the child is born again and named Dionysus. When he grows up and becomes the god of revelry and wine, men establish a cult for his worship. The cult of Dionysus spreads throughout western Asia but does not initially gain a foothold in Europe. Dionysus, the god-man whom his devotees associate with the vine and with the ecstasies derived from the juice of the grape, decides that Thebes, home of his ancestors, will be the logical place to initiate his cult in the West. At first, Theban resistance to Dionysian behavior encumbers his efforts, and many Thebans refuse to believe that he is a son of Zeus. Pentheus, the king of Thebes and grandson of Cadmus and cousin of Dionysus, dreads the disorders and madness induced by the new cult, and he stubbornly opposes its mysteries, based on orgiastic and frenzied rites of nature.

A group of eastern women, devotees of Dionysus, call on the Theban women to join them in the worship of their beloved god. During the ceremonies, blind Tiresias, an ancient Theban prophet, summons old Cadmus, now withdrawn from public life, to the worship of Dionysus. While performing the frenzied rites, the two old men miraculously regain youthful vigor.

Pentheus, enraged when some of his people turn to the new religion, imprisons all women who are seen carrying bacchic symbols such as wine, an ivy crown, or a staff. He rebukes his aged grandfather and accuses Tiresias of spreading the cult in Thebes. Tiresias champions Dionysus, declaring that wine provides men with a temporary release from the harshness and miseries of life. The Theban maidens, he says, are exalted and purified by the bacchic ecstasies. Old Cadmus seconds the words of Tiresias and offers to place an ivy wreath on Pentheus's brow. Pentheus brushes it aside and orders some of his soldiers to destroy Tiresias's house; others he directs to seize a mysterious stranger, a priest of Dionysus, who has a remarkable influence over Theban women.

When the stranger, Dionysus in disguise, is brought before the king, all the Theban women who were jailed suddenly and mysteriously find themselves free in a forest, where they proceed to worship Dionysus. Meanwhile, in the city, Pentheus asks the prisoner his name and his country. Dionysus refuses to give his name but says that he is from Lydia, in Asia Minor, and that he and his followers received their religion from Dionysus. When Pentheus asks to know more about the strange religion, Dionysus says that this knowledge is reserved for the virtuous only. Pentheus impatiently orders a soldier to cut off Dionysus's curls, which the prisoner says are dedicated to his god. Then Pentheus seizes Dionysus's staff and orders him to be imprisoned. Dionysus, calm in spite of these humiliations, expresses confidence in his own welfare and pity at the blindness of Pentheus. Before the guards take Dionysus to be imprisoned in the royal stables, he predicts catastrophe for Pentheus. The king, unmindful of this prophecy, directs that the female followers of Dionysus be put to practical womanly labors.

From his place of imprisonment, Dionysus calls out encouragement to his devotees. Then he invokes an earthquake, which shakes the foundations of Pentheus's fortress. Flames dance on Semele's tomb. Dionysus appears, mysteriously freed from his prison, and rebukes his followers for any doubts and fears they expressed. He casts a spell on Pentheus, who in his mad frenzy mistakes a bull for Dionysus and chains the animal in its stall while the god-man looks on. Another earth tremor transforms the royal fortress into ruins.

Pentheus, enraged at seeing Dionysus free, orders his guards to shut the gates of the city. A messenger reports that many Theban women, among them Pentheus's mother, Agave, are on nearby Mount Cithaeron observing Dionysian rites that combine a dignified and beautiful worship of nature with the cruel slaughter of cattle. A battle takes place between the women and Boeotian peasants, but the frenzied women, although victorious over the peasants, do not harm them. Pentheus orders the immediate suppression of the cult. Dionysus offers to lead the women back to the city, but he declares that if he does so the women will only grow more devoted to the man-god.

When Pentheus imperiously demands that his orders be obeyed, Dionysus casts a spell over him that makes the king express a desire to see the women at their worship. In a trance, he resists only feebly when Dionysus dresses him in women's clothes so that he might not be detected by the women, who are jealous of the secrecy of their cult. Pentheus, in fact, is almost overcome by Dionysus's charms as the god leads him to Mount Cithaeron.

On the mountain, Pentheus complains that he cannot see the rites because of the thick pine forest. Dionysus immediately bends a large pine tree to the ground, sets Pentheus in its topmost branches, and gently lets the tree return to its upright position. At that moment, the man-god disappears, but his voice booms out to his ecstatic devotees that a great enemy of the cult is hidden in the tall tree. The women, wild with fury, fell the tree with Pentheus in it. Agave, in a Dionysian frenzy, stands over her son. He frantically throws off his feminine dress and pleads with her to recognize him, but in her bacchic trance she imagines him to be a lion. With prodigious strength she tears off his left arm at the shoulder. Her sisters, Ino and Autonoe, join her and together the three women break Pentheus's body to pieces. Agave places his severed head on her wand and calls upon the revelers to behold the desert-whelped lion's head.

Cadmus and his attendants carry the maimed body of Pentheus back to the city. The old man feels the deepest pity for his daughter in her blindness. When Agave awakens from her trance and recognizes the head of her beloved son on her wand, she is bewildered and grief-stricken. Cadmus, mourning the violence that occurred, urges all men to comply with the wishes of the Olympian deities.

Dionysus returns in his divine form and prophesies that Cadmus and his wife, Harmonia, transformed into dragons, will overcome many Grecian lands before they die. He shows no sympathy for Agave, who cries out that she is guilty of sinning against him. He dooms her and her sisters to wander without respite until death overtakes them.

Critical Evaluation:

The Bacchae, written in Macedonia after the author's voluntary exile from Athens and produced posthumously, is one of Euripides' most poetically beautiful as well as thematically difficult dramas. The play abounds in passages of nature description unsurpassed in any of the playwright's other works, and the lyrics of the chorus in praise of Dionysus and his gifts of wine and sensuality are particularly fine. The vivid descriptions of landscape and the hymns to bacchanalian pleasure in the first part of the play are so intriguing, in fact, that Pentheus seems a combined brute and prude for opposing the spread of the Dionysian cult in Thebes. In the second half of the play, Euripides' descriptive talent turns, with equal effectiveness, to a different purpose as he presents the grisly scene of Pentheus's slaughter by the revelers, terrifying in their mindless, maddened frenzy.

The fact that *The Bacchae* has been alternately interpreted as Euripides' approval of the Dionysian nature-worship cult and as his condemnation of religious excess attests to the play's thematic complexity. Critics of the first persuasion cite the undeniable fact that the chorus, which traditionally functions as the upholder of moral values and as the mouthpiece of social standards, aligns itself with Dionysus and supports his attempt to introduce his cult into Thebes. Another follower of the god-man is Tiresias, the familiar blind prophet of Greek tragedy, who vehemently exhorts Pentheus to accept the new cult and accompany him—along with Pentheus's grandfather, Cadmus—to the worship rites. Perhaps the strongest evidence that can be used to support this interpretation is that the doom foretold by the chorus for Pentheus, if he persists in opposing what they view as the unquestionable right of the gods to demand worship, comes true: The king of Thebes is killed by his own mother in a most savage and gruesome manner. However, critics who feel that the play is Euripides' condemnation of excessive emotionalism and religious fanaticism can interpret the same event, Pentheus's cruel death, as the author's portrayal of the king as a victim of an unnecessary, unreasoning frenzy. This reading is also supported by the fact that Pentheus is not an evil character but a king who feels it is his duty to protect the city from disruptive social influences. This second interpretation would explain Agave's sentence of lifelong exile at the close of the play.

In view of Euripides' rational and humanistic stance in all his dramas, it would seem most likely that each interpretation contains some amount of truth but that both are oversimplified. It is true, for example, that Pentheus is not an evil king, but he is certainly unwise in his rejection of advice from his elders and in his total reliance on his own reason. His insistence that the cult be destroyed is a denial of one powerful aspect of human nature; Dionysus represents the animal nature in human beings, which is a strong force and must be reckoned with. It is also true that Agave is banished, but she is banished by Dionysus himself, against whom she sinned not in worshiping him but in perverting her worship to such excessive lengths as to kill her own son. It would seem that in *The Bacchae*, as elsewhere, Euripides is arguing for moderation in all things: Pure reason that denies the animal element in human beings leads to destruction just as surely as does pure sensuality unleashed without reasonable control.

Further Reading

Bloom, Harold, ed. *Euripides: Comprehensive Research and Study Guide*. Philadelphia: Chelsea House, 2003. Includes a biography of Euripides and a plot summary, list of characters, and eight critical essays providing various interpretations of *The Bacchae*.

Euripides. *The Bacchae of Euripides*. Translated by C. K. Williams. New York: Farrar, Straus & Giroux, 1990. This version of the play is useful primarily for Martha Nussbaum's introduction, which presents an alternative view of the play and sets it in relief against another Greek tragedy.

Grene, David, and Richmond Lattimore, eds. *Greek Tragedies*. Vol. 3. Chicago: University of Chicago Press, 1960. Lattimore is a scholar known for his work on Euripides. A faithful translation includes, in addition, contextual notes and a clear view to an understanding of Euripides at the end of his career.

Mills, Sophie. *Euripides: "Bacchae."* London: Duckworth, 2006. In addition to an analysis of the play, Mills provides information about Euripides and Greek theater, the role of Dionysus in Athenian religion, Euripides' characterization of Dionysus, and the play's critical reception.

Morwood, James. *The Plays of Euripides*. Bristol, England: Bristol Classical, 2002. Morwood provides a concise overview of all of Euripides' plays, devoting a separate chapter to each one. He demonstrates how Euripides was constantly reinventing himself in his work.

Segal, Charles. *Dionysiac Poetics and Euripides' "Bacchae."* Princeton, N.J.: Princeton University Press, 1983. Provides contextual background for *The Bacchae* and explains why it is such a radical text. Also discusses other works that deal with Dionysus and speculates on Euripides' response to those texts.

Soyinka, Wole. *The Bacchae of Euripides: A Communion Rite*. New York: W. W. Norton, 1974. Nobel Prize-winning African author Wole Soyinka provides a new interpretation of *The Bacchae* that brings to the fore important questions in the original text. Soyinka uses a communion rite to explain the death of Pentheus and the need to spread his body across the countryside.

Thumiger, Chiara. *Hidden Paths: Self and Characterization in Greek Tragedy: Euripides' "Bacchae."* London: Institute of Classical Studies, University of London, 2007. Focuses on the depiction of character in the play. Thumiger argues that Euripides' characterization demonstrates how Greek tragedy developed a view of self that culminated in the ignorance and miscommunication that led to Pentheus's death.

The Bachelors

Author: Muriel Spark (1918-2006)
First published: 1960
Type of work: Novel
Type of plot: Social satire
Time of plot: Mid-twentieth century
Locale: London

Principal characters:

RONALD BRIDGES, the assistant curator at a London museum of graphology and an epileptic
MARTIN BOWLES, a barrister
PATRICK SETON, a spiritualistic medium charged with fraudulent conversion
ALICE DAWES, his pregnant mistress and a diabetic waitress
ELSIE FORREST, her friend
MRS. FREDA FLOWER, a wealthy widow interested in spiritualism
MRS. MARLENE COOPER, the patron of a spiritualistic group
TIM RAYMOND, her nephew
EWART THORNTON, a teacher
WALTER PRETT, an art critic
MATTHEW FINCH, the London correspondent of *The Irish Echo*
DR. MIKE GARLAND, a clairvoyant
FATHER T. W. SOCKETT, a spiritualistic clergyman ordained by Fire and the Holy Ghost
THE HONORABLE FRANCIS ECCLES, a British Council lecturer
MR. FERGUSON, a detective inspector of police

The Story:

London is home to many bachelors, including Ronald Bridges, a thirty-seven-year-old epileptic who works as an assistant curator at a small handwriting museum. One Saturday morning, he meets his friend Martin Bowles, a thirty-five-year-old lawyer. After completing some shopping, they stop at a coffeehouse, where they spot a thin, anxious-looking man of about fifty-five talking with a young girl. Martin tells Ronald not to stare at the couple because next week he will be prosecuting the man, whose name is Patrick Seton. Patrick, a spiritualistic medium, is charged with fraudulent conversion and forgery and is under orders to report to the police daily. Ronald looks slightly ill and says that he wants to search for his newspaper, so Martin leaves. Actually, Ronald thinks he recognizes Patrick from somewhere and is trying to assure himself that his epilepsy is not causing him to lose his memory. Experimental treatment in America was not successful, but he learned to control his attacks, even to the point of being able to order a beer when his bachelor friends Walter Prett, Matthew Finch, and Ewart Thornton gather at a pub.

In addition to the legal charges, Patrick has personal problems. Alice, his girlfriend, is pregnant. Despite her friend Elsie's admonishments, she steadfastly defends Patrick and wants him to divorce his wife and marry her before the baby is born. Alice is a dependent person and believes that Patrick, by taking charge of her insulin injections, has only her best interests in mind.

The next evening, at a meeting of the spiritualist group where he is holding a séance, Patrick encounters more difficulties. Freda Flower, the wealthy widow who charged him with bilking her out of a sum of money by forging a letter, appears for the séance. Tossing his body about and groaning, Patrick works himself into a heavy trance and succeeds in contacting the spirit of Freda's husband despite the presence of another spiritual medium, Dr. Mike Garland, who tries to interrupt. It is a tricky situation, but with clever manipulations Patrick manages to get through the séance unscathed.

The competition between the two mediums polarizes the group members and causes quite a stir among them. Several meet over lunch to discuss the matter. Some plan to create an Inner Spiral of the most faithful members while others pursue less spiritual interests. After talking with Elsie about the beautiful Alice and her attachment to Patrick, Matthew spends the night with her. In his own rooms, Patrick thinks over his statement to the police and his plan to get rid of Alice if he is acquitted. His discussion with Ferguson, the policeman, did not reassure him. To set up a potential alibi for himself, he goes to see Dr. Lyte to get advice about giving insulin to Alice. At Alice's apartment, he convinces her of his solicitous nature.

To solidify the prosecution's case against Patrick, Martin elicits Ronald's handwriting expertise on the allegedly forged letter. He gives the letter to Ronald, who hides it in his apartment. In the coffeehouse later, Ronald and Matthew discuss the evidence with Alice, but she continues to believe Patrick innocent of everything, despite some suspicious information on his background. Matthew, who loves Alice, is ready to sacrifice his longtime bachelor status to marry her. Ronald promises to get more information on the case to relieve her worries. All the talk about marriage appears to trigger an epileptic fit. Luckily, Ronald has his medication with him and quickly recovers.

While these various people discuss his case, Patrick is not idle. He returns to Dr. Lyte's office and reminds the doctor about a forgotten incident involving spiritualism and séances. He then demands that the doctor lend him his chalet in the Alps so that he and Alice can go there for a secluded honeymoon. That is where he plans to implement his plan for Alice's demise. The doctor agrees and, feeling secure in his escape plans, Patrick confidently makes his daily report to the police. He even gives Ferguson some details about the appearance and background of his rival, Garland.

When Ronald returns home, he discovers that the letter he is examining for forgery is stolen from his apartment. Later, at a party, members of the group discuss the matter. Feelings run high both for and against Patrick. Ronald suspects that Elsie, pretending to be a cleaning lady, stole the letter. Elsie sometimes does secretarial work for the Reverend T. W. Sockett, another of Patrick's rival spiritualists, and she believes that he will fall in love with her if she has something valuable to offer him. When she brings the letter to his apartment, however, she sees Garland there dressed in women's clothes. Realizing that there is something going on between the two men, she takes the letter and runs out. When she fails to appear at the café, Matthew, who is hanging around Alice, begins to understand what happened. The next day, he tells Ronald that Elsie does in fact have the letter but will give it to him only if he sleeps with her that night. At her apartment, Ronald manages to convince her to return the letter and to tell Alice what she did. Alice, however, remains convinced of Patrick's spiritual claims and of his intentions to make a life for her and the baby. Meanwhile at the spiritualist group's meetings, gossip continues. Some think Freda and Patrick are lovers and that maybe she wrote the letter. Sockett, learning that Garland is a fake clairvoyant, goes over to Patrick's side. At one meeting the group closely monitors Patrick's writhing to make sure he is really in a trance. The next day, when the court case is to begin, several witnesses against him leave town, but the experts are ready with their testimony.

In court, Ronald, the star witness for the prosecution, as well as Freda and others, give testimony about Patrick's capabilities as a medium and a forger. In the middle of a debate over what constitutes a genuine trance, Ronald has an epileptic attack in the courtroom. The defense brings in another graphologist, but Ronald takes his medication and recovers. The surprise comes when Sockett testifies in favor of Patrick. The trial proceeds, with one witness discrediting the other. Through it all, Matthew stays by Alice's side.

At the end of all the testimony, Patrick believes himself to be safe and envisions himself away from London, giving Alice the fatal insulin injection in a remote region of the Alps. When the judge sentences Patrick to no less than five years, even after he pleads that he is about to become a father, the prosecution reveals his past as a con man. The next morning, as the sun rises over London and all the sleeping bachelors, Ronald ponders it all and wonders when Matthew will marry Alice.

"The Story" by Louise M. Stone

Critical Evaluation:

There are times when the novels of Muriel Spark suggest a mildly hallucinatory card game in which the dealer declares the trump suit only after the last card has been played and then proceeds to take all the tricks. This is not to say that Spark cheats or ignores the rules of the fictional game she is playing; however, she does add to her picture of the world some element of unearthly surprise, and she presents her people from an odd angle of vision, throwing an oblique light on the troubled condition of human beings—and, since she is a Christian writer, on their relation to God or the devil. All of her novels deal in one degree or another with the problem of faith: the grace with which people accept it or the ways by which they try to evade it. The result is an original body of work that cannot be mistaken for that of anyone else.

Satire is the literary climate in which her lively art appears to flourish best. Nevertheless, satire, touched with fantasy or the supernatural, is always a risky business. It demands, among other things, a sharp wit and a spirited style. The reader must also be sufficiently involved in order to go along with the game of pretense, and the story must make its point if the reader is to accept the satire as an insightful comment on the absurdities of the material world or the mysteries of the soul.

Spark takes on the risks deliberately. Her first novel, *The Comforters* (1957), relied for much of its effect on ghostly presences and double identities. In one scene, a character hears the clatter of the author's typewriter at work on the book. *Robinson* (1958) brought into congruous relationship such disparate elements as a desert island, a murder, and a spiritual dilemma resolved in a rather bizarre fashion. *Memento Mori* (1959) was the novel in which Spark revealed to the fullest that audacity, altogether her own, which became the guiding principle of her fiction. In this book, Death is a disembodied voice on the telephone making calls to a group of old people and reminding them that they must die; what this chilling fable offers is a contrast between the selfish, trivial concerns of these people's lives and the inescapable fact of their mortality. *The Ballad of Peckham Rye* (1960) brings to the pubs and rooming houses of a London suburb a devil incarnate who provides the people of Peckham with opportunities to display humankind's natural capacity for error and evil. By means of devices such as these, Spark shows a critical and moral imagination at work among observations of the clutter and waste of the contemporary scene.

The Bachelors is more restrained. It contains no open struggle with otherworldly forces, whether of God or of the devil. The only touch of the supernatural comes when a quack spiritualistic medium does, apparently, establish communication with the dead in an episode so briefly presented that it gives little weight to Spark's swiftly paced and crowded narrative. In this novel, her focus is on bachelordom, the noncommunity of the unattached, uncommitted male. The bachelor state is viewed as damnation, and for the ten examples presented, the writer provides an atmosphere of fearful reality. The lodgings in which they live, the pubs they frequent, the stores where they shop, their problems with meals, mothers, and women—all are images of the private hells of loneliness and trivial self-preoccupation in which each separately revolves. This vision is one that the more discerning of her bachelors share with their creator. Matthew Finch, who is Irish, Catholic, and plagued by sex, says that one's duty is to marry, to choose between Holy Orders and Holy Matrimony. Anything else—and he speaks from experience—is an unnatural life for a Christian. Ronald Bridges, a graphologist who is unable to fulfill his desire to become a priest because he is an epileptic, claims that he is a confirmed bachelor, but at the end of the novel he experiences a vision of the bachelor's selfish and uneasy life on the fringes of society: He imagines 17.1 bachelors in each of London's 38,500 streets, restless, awake, active with their bed partners, or asleep.

In this noncommunity, the solitary individuals try to find substitutes for solidarity and faith. Some, such as Ronald, find another vocation. Others, such as Martin Bowles, become social and moral hypocrites. Still others, such as Walter Prett, revile the world out of drunken self-pity. A few, such as Patrick Seton, prey on human credulity. Most, like Matthew, simply struggle; his predicament, trapped between spirit and flesh, is amusing and nevertheless real.

The uses to which Spark puts her social outsiders are crafty and entertaining. Patrick, the fraudulent medium, is charged with converting to his own needs two thousand pounds that Freda Flower, a rich widow, gives him for the work of The Wider Community, a spiritualistic group. Freda and another patron of the circle, Mrs. Marlene Cooper, are already rivals for the place of leadership within the group, and the charge against Patrick further widens the split. Marlene sees in the division an opportunity to direct the Inner Spiral, a secret group within The Wider Community; Freda hopes to bring the members under the influence of Mike Garland, a clairvoyant of notorious reputation, and of his friend Father Sockett. Ronald becomes involved because he is the friend of Tim Raymond, Marlene's nephew, and because, as a handwriting expert, he is asked to testify to the authenticity of a letter forged by Patrick. Other complications include the fact that Martin, who is also Ronald's friend, is the prosecuting counsel against Patrick, and that Matthew falls deeply in love with Alice. Through information innocently supplied by Matthew, Elsie Forrest, Alice's friend, is able to steal the letter from Ronald's lodgings. Meanwhile, Mike and Sockett are also after the letter for reasons of their own.

Spark handles this complicated material with skill and dash. After Patrick is convicted and sentenced, Matthew will marry Alice, and Ronald will continue to suffer from the nightmares of his epileptic seizures. They are his cross, but because of them he achieves a kind of wisdom and insight into the need of faith and the grace of compassion. This, the reader senses, is the meaning of Spark's conclusion, but she is too much an artist to flog a thesis or to point to a moral. Her characters are good, foolish, sinister, and kind. They exist larger than life and are illuminative of life, because they are self-contained in a world where sin and salvation coexist in precarious balance. It is a world where a man must earn the right to share commitment to his fellows or to God. This writer handles serious matters with a light but sure touch.

Spark's novels create an effect of wild improvisation, but actually the opposite is true. These works have been carefully planned and are cleanly structured and lucidly styled. Few writers have had a surer hold on the comic convention of the English novel, which brings the fantastic and the real together in a coherent whole.

Further Reading

Apostolou, Fotini E. *Seduction and Death in Muriel Spark's Fiction*. Westport, Conn.: Greenwood Press, 2001. A postmodernist and poststructuralist analysis of Spark's fiction. Argues that Spark's work often considers the seductive and destructive power of education, religion, and other social structures.

Bold, Alan, ed. *Muriel Spark: An Odd Capacity for Vision*. Totowa, N.J.: Barnes & Noble, 1984. A collection of essays by critics who investigate Spark's self-conscious style in portraying a sense of spiritual presence behind physical reality. Explores the novel as a sustained prose poem that uses poetic conventions in an unusual way.

Cheyette, Bryan. *Muriel Spark*. Tavistock, England: Northcote House/British Council, 2000. Examines common elements in all twenty of Spark's novels, including *The Bachelors*. Argues that Spark should not be categorized as a Catholic writer; her hybrid background—English, Scottish, Protestant, and Jewish—makes her a "diasporic writer with a fluid sense of self" and a limitless imagination.

Hynes, Joseph. *The Art of the Real: Muriel Spark's Novels*. London: Associated University Presses, 1988. An interesting source with a good bibliography and notes section. A long section on *The Bachelors* explains its investigational motifs. Discusses how Spark's work conveys her unusual sense of reality.

Kemp, Peter. *Muriel Spark*. New York: Barnes & Noble, 1975. A long discussion of *The Bachelors*' spiritual themes and the way it deals with materialism. Places the work within the perspective of Spark's other novels and themes.

McQuillan, Martin, ed. *Theorizing Muriel Spark: Gender, Race, Deconstruction*. New York: Palgrave, 2002. Collection of essays analyzing Spark's work from numerous perspectives, including feminism, queer theory, psychoanalysis, postcolonialism, and deconstructionism. Includes an interview with Spark.

Malkoff, Karl. *Muriel Spark*. New York: Columbia University Press, 1968. Discusses Spark's use of poetic techniques in *The Bachelors* to expose the commonplace from a transfigured point of view. Asserts that cataclysmic events force a reexamination of the ordinary. Analyzes the characters in terms of their solitary explorations to find new ways of knowing.

Stanford, Derek. *Muriel Spark*. Fontwell: Centaur Press, 1963. A memoir rather than a biography, presenting one person's image of Spark and her work. An interesting look at an unusual writer.

Back to Methuselah
A Metabiological Pentateuch

Author: George Bernard Shaw (1856-1950)
First produced: 1922; first published, 1921
Type of work: Drama
Type of plot: Play of ideas
Time of plot: From the beginning of time to 31,920 C.E
Locale: The Garden of Eden, the Middle East, and Great Britain

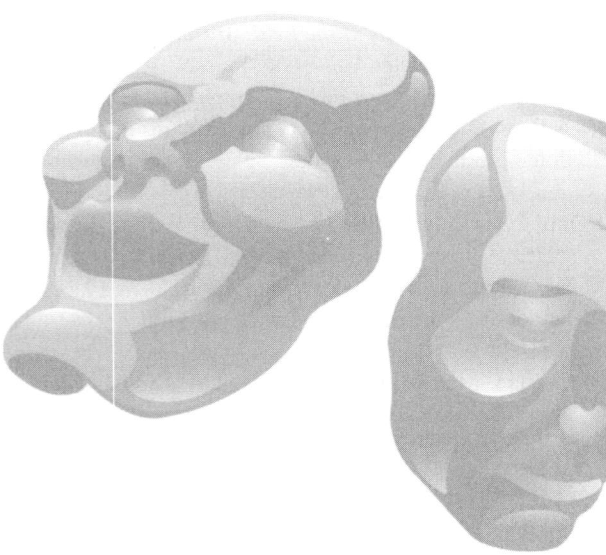

Principal characters:
ADAM, the first man
EVE, the first woman
CAIN, their son
THE SERPENT, not the traditional tempter
FRANKLYN BARNABAS, a former cleric
CONRAD BARNABAS, his brother, a biologist
A PARLORMAID in the Barnabas household
WILLIAM HASLAM, a young cleric
CYNTHIA BARNABAS (SAVVY), Franklyn's daughter
JOYCE BURGE, a British politician
LUBIN, a British politician
BURGE-LUBIN, president of the British Islands
BARNABAS, the accountant-general
CONFUCIUS, the chief secretary
MRS. LUTESTRING, the domestic minister
ELDERLY GENTLEMAN, a visitor to Ireland
ZOO, a young long-liver, his escort
GENERAL AUFSTEIG, a combination of Napoleon and Cain
AMBROSE BADGER BLUEBIN, the prime minister of the British Islands
ORACLE
CHLOE, a young girl entering adolescence
HE-ANCIENT, eight hundred years old
SHE-ANCIENT, a midwife
AMARYLLIS, the newly born
ARJILLAX, a sculptor
MARTELLUS, a sculptor
PYGMALION, a scientist
GHOST OF LILITH, the mother of creation

The Story:

Act 1: In the Beginning. In Eden, Adam discovers a dead fawn; he and Eve now understand that death must come to them, but Adam is also bored by the idea of eternal life. Adam disposes of the fawn, and the Serpent awakens and tells Eve that birth can overcome Death. She also tells Eve of Lilith, who gave birth to Adam and Eve by tearing herself apart, and that it takes two to give birth. Adam leaves and the Serpent tells Eve of the great secret of love and birth.

Several centuries later, in Mesopotamia, Adam is digging and Eve spinning. Cain enters and taunts Adam; Adam replies that Cain murdered his brother. Cain wants Eve to create more men so he can fight them. When Cain claims that he is a higher thing than man, Eve says he is simply Anti-Man. Cain wants martial glory and activity. Eve regards Lua, Cain's wife, and her daughter as good-for-nothing. Eve worries that already her grandchildren are dying before they learned to live, and she thinks there must be something better than digging, spinning, and killing.

Act 2: The Gospel of the Brothers Barnabas. After World War I, the brothers Barnabas discuss their theory of Creative Evolution and their belief that for humans to develop completely they need to live at least three hundred years; they believe that nature will work on the imagination and will accomplish this result. The brothers are joined by Franklyn's daughter and a young clergyman, and the parlormaid says that if she were to live several hundred years, she would hesitate to marry her fiancé, the cook.

The brothers are visited by two politicians who think that

the brothers have a scheme for winning the next election. They demonstrate their political stupidity and lose interest but still wish to exploit the theory. Haslam and Savvy are told that anyone might be the one to make this "evolutionary leap" yet they have no idea that it is to happen. Haslam laughs at this.

Act 3: The Thing Happens. Burge-Lubin, the president of the British Islands in 2170, wants Barnabas to attend a film on a system for breathing under water. The state is really run by a wise Chinaman named Confucius. Barnabas sees the film of high officials who drowned over the last several centuries and reports that four people from the past are the present archbishop of York. He turns out to be Haslam, who looks to be forty-five years old but admits to being 283 years old; he is forced to stage "deaths" because of bureaucratic rules and pension problems. Mrs. Lutestring enters and turns out to be the Barnabases' parlormaid, now 275. She and Haslam realize that they can produce more long-livers and leave to discuss marriage. The others now believe the theory.

Act 4: Tragedy of an Elderly Gentleman. In 3000, an Elderly Gentleman is on a visit to the lands of his ancestors on the Galway coast, accompanied by his son-in-law, the British prime minister, and General Aufsteig, who is much like both Cain and Napoleon. The Gentleman has been warned by a long-liver that this is a dangerous place for short-livers because of the disease of discouragement. He is given a companion, Zoo, a young girl of fifty-six; he is shocked when Zoo claims that long-livers are superior; she believes short-livers should be killed, like bad children. Leading the Gentleman to the temple of the Oracle, she says that the prime minister only pretends to consult the Oracle. The general confronts the veiled Oracle and says that he is the Man of Destiny, a military genius who has no talent except for war. Since he will be dethroned if he goes on making war, he asks the Oracle for a way out of this problem. Telling him he should die, she shoots him—but misses.

The Gentleman arrives with the British Envoy. After a talk with Zoo and others, the Gentleman becomes more discouraged. The Envoy wants to know whether he should call an election in August or in the spring. The Oracle tells him what she told his predecessor fifteen years before: "Go home, poor fool." He leaves and decides to tell the people that he got the same answer as his predecessor. The Gentleman is left alone and begs the Oracle for help; he wants to stay. She kills him, saying that she can do nothing else for him.

Act 5: As Far as Thought Can Reach. The children of A.D. 31,920, who are born at the age of eighteen and become adolescents four years later, are playing and making love. Chloe realizes that art and pleasure no longer interest her and that she wishes only to think of mathematics. Today is a Festival of the Arts and a birth. A He-Ancient of eight hundred years comes by; the children are appalled at his way of life. A She-Ancient comes and breaks the giant egg shell and Amaryllis is born; she tells Amaryllis that she will live long but eventually die accidentally.

Arjillax makes statues of the Ancients, showing their maturity; the children dislike them. Martellus makes two life-size statues, Man and Woman, for a scientist named Pygmalion, who manages to infuse them with life. Everyone is disgusted with them because they are like Man of thousands of years before. They die of discouragement, and the Ancients warn the children against making "dolls"; the only things they can really make are themselves. Eventually there will be only thought, not people.

Night comes and the ghosts of Adam, Eve, Cain, and the Serpent appear. The ghost of Lilith, the mother of creation, appears and ends the play with a long speech about the constant attempts of the Life Force to create new and better forms of life.

Critical Evaluation:

Because *Back to Methuselah* is made up of five full-length plays, it is extremely difficult to produce. Its first full production was at the Garrick Theatre in New York, with acts 1 and 2 being done on February 27, 1922, acts 3 and 4 on March 6, and act 5 on March 13. This first production resulted in a budget deficit of twenty thousand dollars. Obviously, a play that demands three long nights in the theater is unlikely to be produced often, both because of the expense and because of the demands on the audience.

The play presents the most complete representation of George Bernard Shaw's mature thought. In addition to its main themes of Creative Evolution and the Life Force, the work embraces many other typically Shavian beliefs and themes. It is Shaw's most profound statement and at the same time often almost unactable.

The point of the play is simple enough: For humans to profit from their experience, they must learn to live longer and gain wisdom. Shaw believed that the human race had rarely, if ever, demonstrated that it had learned from the past or that it had made any progress in moving beyond the mundane passions of individuals. As a noted socialist, Shaw had spent many years on the public platform, written many pamphlets and books arguing for a socialist society, and composed many plays that presented the virtues of a socialist view of life and the vices of capitalism. Shaw believed, however, that socialism was only a short-term solution to such problems of life as evil, the organization of society, and equality. In *Back to Methuselah*, he does not deny socialism or give up on it, but turns instead to the possibility of a long-term solution. Socialism may be said to be a political solution, while Creative Evolution is a spiritual, even religious, solution. Socialism, Shaw believed, could prepare the way for the type of humans and society able to progress to the basic lessons of Creative Evolution.

The pattern presented in the play and reflected, for example, in the character of Eve in act 1, is that something higher is desired, taken into the imagination, and finally willed to happen. This pattern is Shaw's answer to Darwin, whose idea on the origin of species Shaw detested for its mindless mechanism and for its dependence on chance. In opposition to this, Shaw set up the centrality of the will.

In terms of Shaw's thought, the play should be read in conjunction with *Man and Superman* (1903) and *Saint Joan* (1923). Together, these three plays present Shaw's most concentrated efforts to supply humankind with a new creed and a new theology. *Man and Superman* presents the ideas of the Life Force (a force that has faith in itself though it may have no relation to humankind) and of Creative Evolution. The woman will, by nature, select the best mate for her children; woman is the huntress, man the quarry. In *Saint Joan*, the reader sees an advanced human (though she is not allowed to live long) who is superior to the ordinary desires and social practices of human life. Shaw believed in the force of will, in human ability to create a thing if it were willed hard enough.

Shaw's visionary fable must not be taken too literally. It is a myth or a metaphor, an imaginative vision of what might or could be, but it is not a literal plan or program for the future. Shaw's faith is in life, not necessarily in human beings. The specifics of the play are only imaginings, a way of suggesting possibilities, and an attempt to present to the audience the glorification of the will and of the Life Force. In each of the five acts, there is at least one spokesman for the Life Force: In act1 it is the Serpent; in act 2, the brothers Barnabas; in act 3, the archbishop (and Mrs. Lutestring); in act 4, the Oracle (and Zoo); and in act 5, it is the Ancients (and Lilith).

Just as a number of the characters appear and reappear under various names and offices, so do a number of themes recur. The theme of war and the soldier occurs in acts 1, 2, and 4, as Shaw makes some of the same points about military matters as in *Arms and the Man* (1894). The theme of discouragement reappears in acts 2 and 4, after having been introduced by Eve in act 1. Discouragement, as Shaw sees it, is the recognition of a sense of futility in human life, and it is strong enough to kill. In acts 2, 3, and 4, one can see political themes, but overriding all—in every part of the play—there is the triumph of life over death and matter. In the final act, the condition of the Ancients, who aspire to become pure thought (though they have not as yet done so), represents the triumph over matter, the ability to put aside the things of children, such as art and pleasure, and to arrive at mature contemplation.

Shaw's philosophy and dramatic practice do not always coincide, however. Shaw insists, for example, that humans can choose to live longer, yet in acts 2 and 3, where the first "leap" is made to long-living, it is the parlormaid and the Reverend William Haslam, who think little of the idea of living longer, who become the first of the long-livers, apparently chosen by chance. Shaw always extolled the idea of living longer so that humans could accomplish better and more work, especially in social organization and politics. In the play, however, the state and any sort of social organization seems to have withered away. The Ancients do nothing but think, which issues in no more than a kind of self-gratification.

The play presents other dramatic difficulties. Act 1 seems to be the most dramatic and playable. The other parts are often dull, as Shaw admitted. Shaw was always known for the extended use of discussion in his plays, but this discussion seems to be indulged in for its own sake. Despite the frequent prosiness of the play, however, there are many entertaining comic scenes and acts, especially in the political commentary in acts 2, 3, and 4, in the character of Eve in act 1, and in the confrontation of the short-livers with the long-livers in act 4. The play has probably to be regarded more for its thought and content than for its innate dramatic qualities. Nevertheless, the final scene, where, on a darkened stage, Lilith in a poetic soliloquy delivers Shaw's summation of the past and future possibilities of humans, is a triumph of the fusion of thought and language.

Gordon N. Bergquist

Further Reading

Crompton, Louis. *Shaw the Dramatist*. Lincoln: University of Nebraska Press, 1969. Includes an excellent chapter on *Back to Methuselah*, which discusses Shaw's debts to the thinkers and writers of his time.

Dukore, Bernard F. *Shaw's Theater*. Gainesville: University Press of Florida, 2000. Focuses on the performance of Shaw's plays and how *Back to Methuselah* and other plays call attention to elements of the theater, such as the audience, characters directing other characters, and plays within plays. Includes a section on "Bernard Shaw, Director" and another section in which Shaw describes how a director should interpret *Pygmalion* for theatrical production.

Gahan, Peter. *Shaw Shadows: Rereading the Texts of Bernard Shaw.* Gainesville: University Press of Florida, 2004. Reexamines Shaw's work from the perspective of modern critical theory and argues that his writings anticipated many of the elements of poststructuralism. Includes an analysis of *Back to Methuselah.*

Innes, Christopher, ed. *The Cambridge Companion to George Bernard Shaw.* New York: Cambridge University Press, 1998. Collection of scholarly essays examining Shaw's work, including discussions of Shaw's feminism, Shavian comedy and the shadow of Oscar Wilde, his "discussion plays," and his influence on modern theater. The references to *Back to Methuselah* are listed in the index.

Pagliaro, Harold E. *Relations Between the Sexes in the Plays of George Bernard Shaw.* Lewiston, N.Y.: Edwin Mellen Press, 2004. Demonstrates how the relationship between men and women is a key element in Shaw's plays. Notes a pattern in how Shaw depicts these relationships, including lovers destined by the "life force" to procreate; relations between fathers and daughters, and mothers and sons; and the sexuality of politically, intellectually, and emotionally strong men.

Shaw, George Bernard. "Preface: The Infidel Half Century." In *Bernard Shaw: Collected Plays with Their Prefaces.* Vol. 5. New York: Dodd, Mead, 1972. Indispensable. Shaw's own lengthy and discursive discussion of *Back to Methuselah*, why he wrote it, and how it should be understood.

Whitman, Robert F. *Shaw and the Play of Ideas.* Ithaca, N.Y.: Cornell University Press, 1977. Emphasizes how *Back to Methuselah* presents and resolves contradictions. Deals with the importance of hope in this play and in the Shavian philosophy.

Badenheim 1939

Author: Aharon Appelfeld (1932-   )
First published: Badenheim, 'ir nofesh, 1975 (English translation, 1980)
Type of work: Novel
Type of plot: Parable
Time of plot: 1939
Locale: Badenheim, Austria

Principal characters:
DR. PAPPENHEIM, the impresario
MARTIN, the pharmacist
TRUDE, his wife
FRAU ZAUBERBLIT, a guest
LEON SAMITZKY, one of the musicians
PETER, the pastry shop owner
MANDELBAUM, a performer
SALLY and GERTIE, prostitutes

The Story:

In early spring, the impresario Dr. Pappenheim returns to the Austrian resort town of Badenheim. As usual, he worries whether the performers, especially Mandelbaum, will appear as promised, and whether the festival will be successful. Soon, guests begin to arrive. To Trude, the pharmacist's wife, they look pale, like patients in a sanatorium. To her, everything looks "poisoned and diseased."

The next day, a sanitation department inspector visits the pharmacy. Although Martin, the pharmacist, does not know why the inspector is there, he feels guilty. All over Badenheim, investigators from the sanitation department measure things, erect fences, and put up flags. Porters unfold rolls of barbed wire and put up cement pillars. People take off winter clothes and put on sportswear.

At April's end, the twins, who recite from the works of Rainer Maria Rilke, arrive. Dr. Shutz begins following a schoolgirl. Frau Zauberblit, who has left a tubercular sanatorium, talks with Leon Samitzky, a musician who is homesick for Poland. Professor Fussholdt stays in his room reading proofs of his latest book while his wife sunbathes and hunts for amorous adventures. The twins rehearse. Dr. Pappenheim receives a telegram announcing that Mandelbaum is ill and will not arrive.

In mid-May, an announcement demands that all Jewish citizens register with the sanitation department before the end of the month. A rumor circulates that they are being sent to Poland. Samitzky is happy to be going to Poland. Dr. Pappenheim, however, explains that the sanitation department makes the guests write their names in its "Golden Book" because it wants a record of its attractiveness to tourists. Dr. Pappenheim, Frau Zauberblit, and Samitzky register. Frau Zauberblit praises the sanitation department for "order and beauty."

The sanitation department begins to look like a travel agency. Its posters carry such slogans as "Labor Is Our Life" and "The Air in Poland Is Fresher." The department stays open at night. The band conductor carries his baptismal certificates in his pocket. Dr. Pappenheim tells him that he can "join the Jewish order." When the conductor says that he does not believe in religion, Dr. Pappenheim invites him to become "a Jew without religion."

Frau Zauberblit's daughter arrives with a document stating that her mother renounces her maternal rights; Frau Zauberblit signs it and her daughter leaves. That evening, the twins perform. They recite poems about death. They seem to have "visited hell," of which they are "no longer afraid."

The long-awaited child prodigy arrives. Because his name is not on the hotel register, the doorman will not admit him. Dr. Pappenheim tells the doorman to let him in, asking whether he cannot see that the prodigy is a Jew. The half-Jewish waitress asks Samitzky if she can come to Poland too, although she is not fully Jewish. Samitzky replies that even though both his parents converted to Christianity, he will be going.

The sanitation department is now "the center," and it spreads its nets in every direction. A barrier is erected to keep people from leaving or entering Badenheim. Milk is still being delivered, fruit is still being brought into town, and the band continues to play. However, the people are confined to the hotel, the pastry shop, and the swimming pool. At the sanitation department, Dr. Langmann is angry with Dr. Pappenheim. The people are registering for Poland. Dr. Pappenheim jokes that it makes no difference whether they are here or there.

A banquet is held to honor the child prodigy. The band conductor says that the people are going to their "native land." Dr. Langmann tells Frau Milbaum that he is leaving the next day. She asks whether he has registered with the sanitation department. He replies that he believes he is "a free Austrian citizen" and that they can "send the Polish Jews to Poland; they deserve their country."

After midnight, the child prodigy sings in Yiddish. Sally, the prostitute, asks Dr. Pappenheim if she can come to Poland too. He replies that "All the Jews and . . . everyone who wants to be a Jew" can come.

Summer arrives. The sanitation department closes the water supply. People who spent their time swimming now stand on the tennis court. Dr. Pappenheim says that now everyone will have time to study. Swearing loyalty to "Dr. Pappenheim's Jewish Order," the half-Jewish waitress says that her thighs are Austrian meat, and she offers everyone a taste. She saws on her legs with a knife and, bleeding, screams that when they leave for Poland they dare not go without her.

Letters stop arriving. The weather gets cold. Dr. Langmann asks the sanitation department to reexamine his case; he tells them that he is an Austrian. When he is told that he is also a Jew, he asks what that means.

The schoolgirl is pregnant. Dr. Shutz writes his mother that he is getting married. He asks for money, but the post office is shut. Frau Zauberblit runs a temperature of 101.2° and spits blood. Samitzky drinks steadily. In the pharmacy, Martin stops two men from poisoning themselves. People start buying poisonous drugs. Martin locks the pharmacy, but people break in and steal all the drugs.

Mandelbaum arrives. He says that where he comes from, the Jews were put in quarantine, but a young officer helps him escape so that he can get to the festival. Because Dr. Pappenheim was trying to get Mandelbaum to come for years, he is happy.

The telephone lines are cut. The non-Jewish employees leave. Dr. Langmann calls the Jews "an ugly people" and says that he cannot see "any use" in them. Supplies do not arrive. The hotel owner opens the storeroom. The twins grow thin.

Summer ends. The hotel serves golden cider. Usually, this is the time for leaving. Peter, the pastry shop owner, says, "Let Pappenheim emigrate, not us." Strangers fill the town. The two prostitutes, Sally and Gertie, offer them soup. Dr. Pappenheim tells the strangers about Poland.

In the hotel, people stop serving meals. People line up for barley soup and dry bread. The old rabbi appears in a wheelchair. Everyone thought he was dead. A Christian lady cared for him, he says, but suddenly she left.

The musicians want to go home, but the roads are blocked. New supplies do not arrive. Stocks run low. Peter vows to kill Dr. Pappenheim. Dr. Pappenheim receives a letter from the sanitation department requiring that the artists be placed "at their disposal." Delighted, he knows that a concert tour is coming.

The town runs out of cigarettes. People secretly swallow drugs stolen from the pharmacy. The child prodigy performs only for boxes of candy and grows fat. The people want the festival to be held.

Two men come from the sanatorium to take Frau Zauberblit back. They tell her that the Jewish patients are all emigrating; they tell her that she needs to return before the patients can leave. She agrees to go. The pastry cook buries the dead at night at the back of the Luxembourg Gardens. Every day, more people die.

On the last night, the people celebrate Gertie's fortieth birthday. At the celebration, Dr. Pappenheim announces that the emigration procedures are posted. Gertie apologizes for having nothing to offer her guests. Dr. Pappenheim tells them that they will hold a party later in Warsaw.

The next day, the Jews of Badenheim walk to the train station, but Peter refuses to leave. As the people walk, they discuss things such as wages in Poland, retirement, and vacations. Policemen walk behind, but they do not hurry the people. At the station, the people bring newspapers, lemonade, cigarettes, and sweets. Two armed policemen arrive, escorting Peter. An engine approaches, pulling "four filthy freight cars." As everyone is sucked into the cars, Dr. Pappenheim remarks: "If the coaches are so dirty it must mean that we have not far to go."

Critical Evaluation:

Badenheim 1939 was originally published as a story in a collection entitled *Shanim Ve'shaot* (years and hours), but it was not published as a separate novel until 1980, when it appeared both in Hebrew and in English translation. The Hebrew title, literally "Badenheim, Resort Town," is less revealing of the novel's meaning than the English title, which indicates that the story occurs after the Nazis had taken over Austria. Aharon Appelfeld based the book, he said, on his experiences as a young child at resorts to which his parents had taken him and on his personal knowledge of the Holocaust.

Appelfeld survived the Holocaust. At the age of eight, he escaped from the Transnistria labor camp in Ukraine and survived for three years in forests and villages. He said that his blond hair and ability to speak Ukrainian helped him avoid capture. In 1944, he was liberated by the Red Army, after which he worked for them as a messenger boy. After a stay in Italy, he went to Israel in 1946.

The novel has been called a fable, a parable, and a comedy. Appelfeld uses dramatic irony, satire, and allegory, and the novel is alternately dreamlike, surrealistic, and nightmarish. The Holocaust is never mentioned. Appelfeld assumes that the readers have the necessary historical knowledge to recognize that the Holocaust is part of the story. Many critics feel that the omission of explicit references to the Holocaust adds to the book's power.

Critics often compare Appelfeld to the Jewish Austrian-Czech writer Franz Kafka, whose works have a similar nightmarish quality. In Kafka's works, the reader feels a vague anxiety that things are not what they seem and that all is not right. The same kind of feeling pervades *Badenheim 1939*. The vacationers and the workers at Badenheim, especially Dr. Pappenheim, expend tremendous energy denying the reality of their situation. Even when he sees the freight cars, Dr. Pappenheim does not accept the horror that awaits him.

The freight cars are the final symbol of the destruction awaiting the Jews of Badenheim. There are, however, many earlier signs that things are not as good as Dr. Pappenheim asserts, beginning with the fact that all Jews must register with the sanitation department. Putting up fences, unrolling barbed wire, and erecting cement columns could be interpreted as preparation for the festival, but in this context the preparations point to concentration camps. Trude's feeling that something is wrong with the guests foreshadows the moment when the guests are loaded into freight cars.

Badenheim 1939 depicts the assimilated Jews of Germany and Austria who, like the poet Rilke, whose works the twins recite, believed that they had become part of the culture of the nations in which they lived. Often, however, they still found themselves living, working, and vacationing almost exclusively among Jews. The novel captures the awakening that occurred to many of them when they discovered that no matter how assimilated they may have felt, the preponderance of the non-Jewish citizens of their nations did not consider them part of their culture. The Nazis decided that outright extermination was appropriate. Appelfeld's Austrian Jews, like Dr. Langmann and Peter, attribute their problems to such Polish Jews as Dr. Pappenheim. Appelfeld has created a terrifying novel about humankind's inhumanity and about people's inability to recognize that inhumanity, or its source, even when they are its victims.

Richard Turek

Further Reading

Bernstein, Michael André. *Foregone Conclusions: Against Apocalyptic History*. Berkeley: University of California Press, 1994. Describes the way in which three historical periods—Austria before the Nazi rule, Austria during the Nazi rule, and the world after the Holocaust—are interrelated simultaneously in the novel.

Budick, Emily Miller. "Literature, Ideology, and the Measure of Moral Freedom: *Badenheim 1939*." In *Aharon Appelfeld's Fiction: Acknowledging the Holocaust*. Bloomington: Indiana University Press, 2005. Budick analyzes several of Appelfeld's works, including *Badenheim 1939*, focusing on how he depicts the experiences of

European Jewish life before, during, and after World War II.

Fridman, Lea Wernick. "The Silence of Historical Traumatic Experience: Aharon Appelfeld's *Badenheim 1939*." In *Words and Witness: Narrative and Aesthetic Strategies in the Representation of the Holocaust.* Albany: State University of New York Press, 2000. Fridman analyzes *Badenheim 1939* and other Holocaust literature to demonstrate how Appelfeld and other writers invent techniques to represent this "unrepresentable" tragedy.

Langer, Lawrence I. "Aharon Appelfeld and the Uses of Language and Silence." In *Remembering for the Future*, edited by Yehuda Bauer et al. 3 vols. Elmsford, N.Y.: Pergamon Press, 1989. Discusses Appelfeld's irony and ambiguity. The set also includes articles on Aharon Appelfeld by Nurit Govrin, A. Komem, Gila Ramraz-Raukh, and Lea Hamaoui.

Ramraz-Raukh, Gila. *Aharon Appelfeld: The Holocaust and Beyond.* Bloomington: Indiana University Press, 1994. Speaks of the novel's "cold horror." Sees the end as having been foreshadowed in the beginning.

Roth, Philip. "A Conversation with Philip Roth." In *Beyond Despair*, by Aharon Appelfeld. Translated by Jeffrey M. Green. New York: Fromm International, 1994. First published in *The New York Review of Books*, February 28, 1988. Roth, the American novelist, talks with Appelfeld about his life and works. Roth calls *Badenheim 1939* "vexing." The interview gives insight into the novel's autobiographical and historical background.

Schwartz, Yigal. *Aharon Appelfeld: From Individual Lament to Tribal Eternity.* Translated by Jeffrey M. Green. Hanover, N.H.: University Press of New England, 2001. Schwartz focuses on three major themes in Appelfeld's work: the recovery of childhood and memory, the creation of place, and the religious views of the Holocaust writer. He maintains that Appelfeld's underlying concerns transcend his experiences as a Holocaust survivor to include larger issues of Jewish identity.

The Bald Soprano

Author: Eugène Ionesco (1909-1994)
First produced: La Cantatrice chauve, 1950; first published, 1954 (English translation, 1956)
Type of work: Drama
Type of plot: Absurdist
Time of plot: Mid-twentieth century
Locale: London

Principal characters:
MR. SMITH, the owner of the house where the play is set
MRS. SMITH, his wife
MR. MARTIN, their guest
MRS. MARTIN, his wife
MARY, the Smiths' maid
THE FIRE CHIEF, an old family friend

The Story:

After dinner, the Smiths sit down in the sitting room of their typically English home. Mr. Smith smokes his pipe and reads the newspaper. Mrs. Smith, insisting that they are a typically English couple, speak of what they ate and what the children did. Mr. Smith clicks his tongue.

When Mrs. Smith remarks that Dr. Mackenzie-King had his own liver removed before operating on Mr. Parker's liver, Mr. Smith argues that if Mackenzie-King was really a good doctor, he should have taken his own life when Parker did not survive the liver operation; he asserts that a doctor should perish with a patient just as a captain goes down with the ship. Mr. Smith then changes the subject, mentioning that he read that their friend Bobby Watson died. The couple speaks about Bobby but quickly become lost in a confused conversation; because all of Bobby Watson's relatives are also named Bobby Watson, they are unable to figure out whom they are talking about, who died, and who is still alive.

Mary, the Smiths' maid, returns from her day off and announces that the Martins, whom they invited to dinner, were waiting for a long time downstairs. The Smiths, before leaving the room, instruct her to bring them up. Mary shows the Martins into the sitting room, then leaves. As if they never saw each other before, Mr. and Mrs. Martin begin to question each other, wondering where and when they previously met. Gradually, they are able to deduce that they both took the same train from Manchester and that they both live in the same room and sleep in the same bed. Moreover, both have a daughter who seems to be the same child. Therefore, they conclude, the two of them must be married. As they kiss, thrilled to have found each other again, Mary comes in and announces to the play's audience that Mr. and Mrs. Martin reasoned incorrectly, that the daughter they think they have in common is really two different children, and that they are not in fact husband and wife. Mary tells the audience that she is Sherlock Holmes; then she leaves.

The Smiths return, welcoming the Martins and yelling at them for arriving so late. They sit and attempt to make conversation but are unable to say much. Mrs. Martin is prompted to describe an incident that shocks her: She saw a man on the street who bent down to tie his shoelace. Mr. Smith, in an attempt to outdo her, recounts a tale that they find even more bizarre, of a man on the subway who is reading a newspaper.

Their interchange is interrupted by the doorbell. When Mrs. Smith opens the door, there is no one there. Again the bell rings, Mrs. Smith goes to the door, and no one is there. When the bell rings a third time, Mrs. Smith refuses to answer the door because she learned that when the bell rings, there is never anyone there. Mr. Smith disagrees, and the Martins join the fight. Finally, Mr. Smith goes to the door and opens it to discover the Fire Chief standing on their doorstep.

The Fire Chief, an old family friend, played a prank by ringing the bell and hiding. He is looking for fires. Even though Mr. Smith insists that there has not been a fire at their house for years, the Fire Chief is happy just to stay for a visit. They welcome him in and ask him to join them in telling amusing stories. Although the stories they tell sound like fables, they are all meaningless, pointless, and nonsensical. The conversation is interrupted by Mary, who wants to read them her own poem. Before she can begin, however, she and the Fire Chief recognize each other. They were sweethearts once and are glad to meet again. She then begins to recite her poem, which is about different things catching on fire. Mr. and Mrs. Smith push her out of the room.

The Fire Chief, very pleased with the poem, asks if anyone heard of the bald soprano. For some reason, the Smiths and the Martins become very embarrassed. The Fire Chief then tactfully departs, and the Smiths and Martins begin an angry discussion. Once again, what they say sounds as if it ought to make sense, but it does not. Nevertheless, they pursue the argument until their enraged chatter builds to a climax, during which they throw words and sounds meaninglessly at each other. In the short scene that follows, the Martins appear after dinner, sitting down in the same sitting room. Mr. Martin smokes his pipe and reads the newspaper. Mrs. Martin, insisting that they are a typically English couple, speaks of what they ate. Mr. Martin clicks his tongue.

Critical Evaluation:

Eugène Ionesco was born in Romania and eventually moved to France, where he was educated and where he remained during World War I. With *The Bald Soprano*, his first play, and those that followed—including *La Leçon* (1951; *The Lesson*, 1955), *Les Chaises* (1952; *The Chairs*, 1958), and *Rhinocéros* (1959; English translation, 1959)—he became internationally famous, and his plays were produced all over the world. Although his international success gradually declined, in France Ionesco continued to be highly respected, and his works are often revived there.

The name given to the style of Ionesco's plays (and to the plays of Samuel Beckett, Jean Genet, and Arthur Adamov) is absurdist. *The Bald Soprano*, which is frequently regarded as the first absurdist play, is typical of the theater of the absurd for its absence of plot and a circular trajectory that ends where it began. Absurdist characters tend to be broad, generalized, two-dimensional figures, while settings are nondescript and vague. Moreover, what the characters say is rather insignificant; they tend to communicate not through what they mean but through how they speak the words and how the reader or audience associates meanings with those words.

Little happens in an Ionesco play. Readers and audiences who feel that they can find little in *The Bald Soprano* that makes any sense have probably discovered an essential ingredient of this one-act absurdist classic. Long after the play opened in Paris, Ionesco revealed that he got the idea of writing it when he tried learning English from an old textbook. The book, written in dialogue form, introduced members of a typical British family who conversed almost meaninglessly about themselves and the world in which they lived. This may be the strongest clue that the play is a satire of the British—and, by extension, the middle-class—way of life. With its parody of conventional characters and conventional settings, the play clearly also makes fun of middle-class theater. The recognition scene between Mr. and Mrs. Martin, which is highly reminiscent of nineteenth century melodrama, becomes comedic when the audience realizes that this married couple cannot remember that they share the same bed and that this is a fact they can only deduce intellectually. Ionesco called *The Bald Soprano* an anti-play, which is doubly appropriate because the piece is so deliberately unlike any plays that came before it and because it draws on traditional drama in order to make fun of it.

The fact that there is no conflict in the play reflects the nature of the people in the play: They want nothing and nothing can occur to them. These middle-class characters, the Smiths and the Martins, use language as a means not to communicate with each other but to compete and put down their adversaries. Language becomes a weapon for them. They are so far from being alive that when the Fire Chief comes looking for fires they laugh at the notion that anything could be warm and burning at their house. Mary's poem, which describes different objects going up in flames, suggests a passion alien to them, and they are so offended by her recitation that they shove her offstage. Unlike the Martins, who must reason who they are before they can recognize each other, Mary and the Fire Chief (both driven by fiery passion) know each other on sight.

The two middle-class couples—in contrast to the more easygoing working-class maid and fireman—are fierce defenders of their respectable way of life, but as Ionesco presents them, their lives are amazingly empty, their stories are nonsensical, and their words ultimately amount to nothing more than angry sounds. There is much to laugh at here, and the comedy in *The Bald Soprano* is brilliantly funny. Many of the fables that precede Mary's poem and the fractured clichés exchanged at the end of the play are such outrageously illogical parodies of familiar, everyday speech that the only way to respond to them is with laughter.

Kenneth Krauss

Further Reading

Bloom, Harold, ed. *Eugène Ionesco*. Philadelphia: Chelsea House, 2003. Collection of essays providing critical interpretations of Ionesco's plays, including *The Bald Soprano*.

Bradby, David. *Modern French Drama 1940-1990*. 2d ed. New York: Cambridge University Press, 1991. In his discussion of the New Theatre, which flourished in France after World War II, Bradby suggests that *The Bald Soprano* is the "ultimate form of audience aggression." Bradby beautifully contextualizes Ionesco's first effort with those of other absurdists.

Cohn, Ruby. *From "Desire" to "Godot": Pocket Theater of Postwar Paris*. Berkeley: University of California Press, 1989. In examining some of the great plays that opened in some of the tiniest theaters in Paris after World War II, Cohn describes the original production of *The Bald Soprano*, including curious and often funny backstage details. An illuminating appreciation of the script and its performance.

Dobrez, L. A. C. *The Existential and Its Exits: Literary and Philosophical Perspectives on the Works of Beckett, Ionesco, Genet, and Pinter.* New York: St. Martin's Press, 1986. Emphasizing the philosophical aspects of absurdist theater, Dobrez explores Ionesco's most successful dramatic works. Addresses *The Bald Soprano*'s peculiar mixture of tragedy and comedy.

Esslin, Martin. *The Theatre of the Absurd*. 3d ed. rev. New York: Methuen, 2001. A pioneering critique that views Ionesco's work as basic to the absurdist repertory and provides fascinating information on how and why Ionesco wrote *The Bald Soprano*. A definitive work on absurdism. Includes useful biographical and production data.

Gaensbauer, Deborah B. *Eugène Ionesco Revisited*. New York: Twayne, 1996. Reevaluation of Ionesco's life and work published two years after his death. Gaensbauer analyzes all of the plays and Ionesco's other writings and concludes that each work was a piece in a long autobiography in which Ionesco sought to understand himself and humankind.

Holland, Michael. *Ionesco: "La Cantatrice chauve" and "Les Chaises."* London: Grant & Cutler, 2004. A concise introductory overview and survey of the plays' critical reception.

Lane, Nancy. *Understanding Eugène Ionesco*. Columbia: University of South Carolina Press, 1994. A reexamination of the playwright's career and works.

Bambi
A Life in the Woods

Author: Felix Salten (1869-1945)
First published: Bambi: Eine Lebensgeschichte aus dem Walde, serial, 1922; book, 1923 (English translation, 1928)
Type of work: Children's literature
Type of plot: Fable
Time of plot: Indeterminate
Locale: A forest

Principal characters:
BAMBI, a deer
THE OLD PRINCE, a stag who befriends Bambi
BAMBI'S MOTHER
FAMINE, Bambi's cousin
GOB, her brother
HE or HIM, the enemy of forest creatures

The Story:

Bambi is born in a thicket in the woods. While he is still an awkward young fawn, his mother teaches him that he is a deer. He learns that deer do not kill other animals nor do they fight over food as jaybirds do. He learns, too, that deer should venture from their hiding places to go to the meadow only in the early morning and late in the evening and that they must rely on the rustle of last year's dead leaves to give them warning of approaching danger. On his first visit to the meadow, Bambi has a conversation with a grasshopper and a close look at a butterfly.

One evening Bambi and his mother go to the meadow again. On his second visit, he is introduced to the hare, an animal with big, soft eyes and flopping ears. Bambi is not impressed. The little deer is considerably happier to meet his cousins, Gob and Famine, and their mother, End. The two families are about to separate when two stags with spreading antlers on their heads come crashing out of the forest. Bambi's mother explains that the larger, statelier stag is Bambi's father.

As he grows older, Bambi learns the sounds and smells of the forest. Sometimes his mother goes off by herself. Missing her one day, Bambi starts out to look for her and comes upon his cousins in the meadow. Famine suggests that both their mothers might have gone to visit their fathers. Bambi decides to continue his search by himself. As he stands at the edge of a clearing, he sees a creature he never saw before. The creature raises what looks like a stick to its face. Terrified, Bambi runs back into the woods as fast as he can go. His mother appears suddenly, and they both run home to their glade. When he and his mother are safe again, Bambi learns that the creature he saw is Man.

On another day, he begins to call for his mother. Suddenly, a great stag stands before him. He coldly asks Bambi why he is crying and tells him that he ought to be ashamed of himself. Then he is gone. The little deer does not tell his mother of his experience nor does he call her anymore. Later, he learns that he met Old Prince, the biggest and wisest stag in the forest. One morning Bambi is nibbling in the meadow with his mother when one of the stags comes out of the forest. Suddenly, there is a crash. The stag leaps into the air and then falls dead. Bambi races away after his mother. All he wants is to go deeper and deeper into the forest until he can feel free of that new danger. He meets Old Prince again. When Bambi asks him who Man is, the stag replies that he will find out for himself. Then he disappears.

The forest gradually changes as summer passes into fall and then into winter. Snow falls, and grass is not easy to find. All the deer become more friendly during the cold months. They gather to talk, and sometimes even one of the stags joins them. Bambi grows to admire the stags. He is especially interested in Rondo, the stag who escaped after a hunter wounded him in the foot. The constant topic of conversation is Man, for none of the deer understands the black stick he carries. They all are afraid of it.

As the winter drags on, the slaughter of the weaker animals in the forest begins. A crow kills one of the hare's children, a squirrel races around with a neck wound a ferret gives him, a fox murders a pheasant. A party of hunters comes into the woods with their noise-making sticks and kills many of the animals. Bambi's mother and his cousin Gob are not seen again.

That spring, Bambi grows his first pair of antlers. With his mother gone, he spends most of his time alone. The other stags drive him away when he tries to approach them, and Famine is shy with him. Deciding one day that he is not afraid of any of the stags, Bambi charges at what he thinks is one of his tormentors in a thicket. The stag steps aside, and Bambi charges past him. It is Old Prince. Embarrassed, the young deer begins to tremble when his friend comes close to him. With an admonishment to act bravely, the older deer disappears into the woods.

A year later, Bambi meets Famine again, and once more they play as they did when they were very young. Then an older stag named Karur appears and tries to block Bambi's way. When Bambi attacks him, Karur flees, as does the stag named Rondo, who was pursuing Famine.

Famine and Bambi venture into the meadow one day and there see a stranger nibbling the grass. They are surprised when he comes skipping up to them and asks if they know him. It is Gob. Hunters caught him and kept him until he was full-grown. Then he was sent back to join his family in the forest. His mother is delighted to see him once more. Gob explains his absence to an admiring audience and praises Man for his kindness. While he is talking, Old Prince appears and asks Gob about the strip of horsehair around his neck. Gob answers that it is a halter. Old Prince remarks pityingly that he is a poor thing and vanishes.

Gob will not live as the other deer in the forest do. He insists on going about during the day and sleeping at night. He has no fear about eating in the meadow, completely exposed. One day, when a hunter is in the woods, Gob declares that he will go talk to him. He walks out into the meadow. Suddenly there is a loud report; Gob leaps into the air and then dashes into the thicket, where he falls, mortally wounded.

Bambi is alone when he meets Old Prince for the first time since Gob's death. They are walking together when they find a hare caught in a noose. Old Prince carefully manages to loosen the snare with his antlers. Then he shows Bambi how to test tree branches for a trap. Bambi realizes for the first time that there is no time when Man is not in the woods. One misty morning, as Bambi stands at the edge of the clearing, a hunter wounds him. He races madly for the forest and in its protection lies down to rest. Soon he hears a voice beside him, urging him to get up. It is Old Prince. For an hour, the veteran leads Bambi through the woods, crossing and redressing the place where he laid down, showing him the herbs that will stop his bleeding and clear his head. He stays with Bambi until the wound heals. Before he goes off to die, the old stag shows Bambi a poacher who was killed. He explains that humans, like animals, must die. Bambi understands then that there is someone even more powerful than he.

Walking through the forest one day, Bambi spies a brother and a sister fawn crying for their mother. As Old Prince spoke to him so many years before, he asks them if they cannot stay by themselves. Then, as his friend did, he vanishes into the forest.

Critical Evaluation:

The first widely acclaimed work by the Austrian novelist Felix Salten (born Sigmund Salzmann), *Bambi* not only has remained a classic of children's literature but also has earned the discriminating approval of writers such as John Chamberlain, Alfred Werner, and John Galsworthy. It has been reprinted often, even before Walt Disney's sentimentalized film version extended its popularity, and has been translated into most modern languages, including Hebrew and Chinese. However, unlike many other children's favorites adapted by Disney, *Bambi* is a story of neither comfortable sentimentality nor whimsical humor. Instead, it is a touching, lyrical, sometimes gently melancholy romance of growth and developing awareness.

Possibly the melancholy of the novel springs in part from the writer's own childhood experiences. Salten suffered early in life from rootlessness and poverty. Until a relative discovered him destitute, friendless, and nearly famished and offered him employment, he despaired ever of surviving in a world of cruel indifference. To repay his benefactor, Salten, whose formal education was meager, began to write sketches at first, then longer pieces influenced by Guy de Maupassant and Gottfried Keller. The success of *Bambi* established for Salten a demand for more children's nature books that were to include, among his best, *Fifteen Rabbits* (1929) and *Perri* (1938). In addition to juvenile fiction, Salten wrote excellent criticism and travel literature, mostly revealing his appreciation for the United States (his adopted home after 1939) and Israel.

To the child's imagination, *Bambi* treats human experiences in the form of an animal fable. Young readers learn from the book the lessons of growing up, attaining independence, enduring the sorrows of loss, and meeting the challenges of change, from youth to maturity. Although many children's fairy tales resolve conflicts in the plot through wonderful interference, in *Bambi* life experiences are treated as natural, without the interference of magic or chance. On the contrary, the book deals honestly with two of the most terrible emotional crises a child can face: the estrangement of a father and the death of a mother. Bambi learns to become self-reliant and to earn from other forest creatures the respect deserved by the powerful and fully matured.

At the same time, Bambi comes to understand the weaknesses of his eternal enemy (Man); he masters his sexual rivals (Karur and Rondo), wins his mate Famine, and sires her young; and, above all, he comes to terms with the Old Prince—the father figure that has always protected and, from a distance, sustained him. Bambi learns the great lesson of resolute independence from the Old Prince. Whereas Gob tries to live with Man and dies from his trusting mistake, the old stag lives alone, true to the challenge he once gave Bambi: "Can't you stay by yourself?" Bambi learns to stay free, indifferent to comfort, even to friendship. He protects himself from dangers, yet he is sensitive to the need of protecting the weak who cannot defend themselves. Thus, he provides for children—and perhaps for their parents too—Salten's message of survival in a hostile world.

Further Reading

Blount, Margaret. *Animal Land: The Creatures of Children's Fiction*. New York: William Morrow, 1975. Brief discussion of *Bambi* as a great example of "animal biography," avoiding its predecessors' and imitators' tendency to caricature. Argues that the poignant and poetic account of animal life and death compensates for the novel's failings, chiefly its excessive anthropomorphism.

Cartmill, Matt. *A View to a Death in the Morning: Hunting and Nature Through History*. Cambridge, Mass.: Harvard University Press, 1993. Focuses primarily on Walt Disney's film as a piece of antihunting propaganda, but discusses Salten's novel at greater length than most sources. The novel exudes violence and death, influenced by the pessimism of post-World War I Austria and an intense misanthropy; the intrusion of human beings in the forest corrupts innocence and destroys life.

Egoff, Shirley A. *Thursday's Child: Trends and Patterns in Contemporary Children's Literature*. Chicago: American Library Association, 1981. Brief discussion of *Bambi* as the first significant European children's novel in the twentieth century. The novel was popular in its time, but the modern reader may find it overly sentimental; however, its negative view of humanity is quite modern and echoed by subsequent children's books about animals.

Guroian, Vigen. "Friends and Mentors in *The Wind in the Willows*, *Charlotte's Web*, and *Bambi*." In *Tending the Heart of Virtue: How Classic Stories Awaken a Child's Moral Imagination*. New York: Oxford University Press, 1998. Focuses on the relationship between Bambi and the old stag, who chooses Bambi to be his protégé and successor and teaches the young deer how to survive in the forest. Describes their relationship as a model of both friendship and mentorship for children who read the novel.

Meigs, Cornelia, et al. *A Critical History of Children's Literature*. Rev. ed. New York: Macmillan, 1969. Identifies *Bambi* as the most significant fact-based animal story in children's literature; its beautiful passages may appeal to readers despite their tone of sentimentality.

Pouh, Lieselotte. *Young Vienna and Psychoanalysis: Felix Doermann, Jakob Julius David, and Felix Salten*. New York: Peter Lang, 2000. Describes how Sigmund Freud was influenced by Jung-Wien (Young Vienna), an Austrian literary movement active between the end of the nineteenth and the beginning of the twentieth centuries; describes how Salten and two other members of the movement were influenced by Freud's ideas about psychoanalysis. Includes chapters summarizing Salten's life and works, "Salten, Freud, and Psychoanalysis," and an analysis of Salten's children's book *Der Hund von Florenz* (1923; *The Hound of Florence*, 1930).

Barabbas

Author: Pär Lagerkvist (1891-1974)
First published: 1950 (English translation, 1951)
Type of work: Novel
Type of plot: Moral
Time of plot: First century C.E.
Locale: Palestine, the Near East, and Rome

Principal characters:

BARABBAS, the robber freed in Christ's stead
A GIRL, formerly an intimate of Barabbas
SAHAK, a fellow slave of Barabbas and an Armenian Christian
THE ROMAN GOVERNOR
MARY
PETER
LAZARUS

The Story:

At Golgotha, Barabbas, watching the Crucifixion from which he was suddenly saved, is startled by the words uttered by the figure on the cross: "My God, my God, why hast thou forsaken me?" Even stranger to him is the darkness that seems to come over the world. As he is leaving the scene, he is also disturbed by the look of silent reproach directed at him by the dead man's mother.

Back in Jerusalem, he meets and walks with a young girl, whom he knew before. The girl, who has a harelip, goes with him to a dive where some of his low companions are gathered. Barabbas and the people there discuss Barabbas's rescue and the strange rabbi who made such extreme claims and yet permitted himself to be crucified like a criminal. Barabbas is considerably relieved that the people in the café do not believe in the rabbi's divinity, although he is troubled that they did not notice the darkness that for a while hung over the land. After the young girl leaves the dive, Barabbas indulges, as a kind of escape from his worries, in a drunken debauch with one of the patrons of the café—a fat, crude woman.

Later, Barabbas meets a red-bearded follower of Christ who expects Christ to rise from the dead the next day. He explains some of Christ's teachings to Barabbas but shamefacedly admits that before the end he denied Christ. The girl with the harelip, to whom Barabbas also talks about Christ, says that she met him. She is wilder in her predictions than is the red-bearded man; she expects the millennium and divine miracles at any moment. Superstition does not blur everything, however, for she tells Barabbas that Christ's message is one of love. Barabbas thereupon goes to the grave; he watches all night but sees nothing. The next day, however, the stone is gone from the entrance. He believes that the followers of Christ have taken the body; the girl thinks he had risen.

Barabbas asks the followers of Christ about these events but finds little satisfaction in their answers. He cannot understand one who uses his power by refraining from using it. Barabbas is later taken to a man who was dead four days and was raised again by this rabbi. This man tells Barabbas that death is nothing; it is there, but it signifies nothing. He adds that after one experiences death, life also is as nothing. As Barabbas further questions the followers of Christ, it becomes clear that although they are believers, they are quite confused as to the meaning of all of these happenings. When the followers learn Barabbas's identity, they naturally hate him.

About this time, Barabbas becomes estranged from his fellows in the low life of Jerusalem—so much so that he resigns himself from sensual life. The fat woman, his sometime lover, thinks that Christ's soul has possessed Barabbas. One day, by accident, Barabbas is present at a church meeting and hears a rather disappointing sermon by the red-bearded man who denied Christ. He finds the snuffling testimony of witness given by the harelipped girl even more distasteful. Later, when a blind man denounces the girl as a Christian, Barabbas nevertheless knifes the first person who stones her. She dies a humble martyr, but one who sees Christ as she dies. Barabbas carries her body to the grave of a baby she had; Barabbas was the father of that child.

A short time later, Barabbas leaves Jerusalem and returns to the robber band that he at one time led. The robbers are distressed by his seeming character change: Formerly the boldest of all—he fought, killed, and supplanted the bandit leader, earning the scar on his face—he now is apathetic. What none of the characters knows is that Eliahu, whom Barabbas killed, was his own father. Sensing that he no longer fits in with the robber band, Barabbas silently steals away from the camp.

For an indeterminate period, Barabbas wanders the earth. Later, he is enslaved and put to mining for the Romans. There he meets Sahak, a slave who is thrilled by the knowledge that Barabbas saw Christ. Without revealing to Sahak the true nature of his relationship with Christ, Barabbas increases the details of Sahak's belief by telling him things about Christ. Some of these are lies, such as that he saw an angel come down from the sky on the night that he watched outside Christ's tomb. After a time, Barabbas apathetically suffers Sahak to enter into Christian observances with him. He even permits Sahak to draw Christ's symbol on his slave's disk, and for a time he prays with him. Years later, a new mine overseer, attracted to Christianity but mystified by its doctrine of love, notices the two slaves, bound to each other by a chain. The overseer, having talked to them about Christianity, is moved to secure positions above ground for the two men. Although still slaves, Sahak and Barabbas are at least free of the deadly conditions of primitive mining.

Matters soon change when the Roman governor of the territory learns through another slave that both men are Christians. Sahak refuses to renounce his faith. Barabbas, who by this point would have liked to believe in Christ but cannot, readily renounces his. He lets the governor scratch through the sign that Sahak put on his disk. He then witnesses Sahak's crucifixion. He is relieved when no miraculous occurrences accompany the death of Sahak.

When the pagan but kindly Roman governor retires to Rome, he takes Barabbas with him. Once, Barabbas goes to the catacombs to see a Christian religious service, but no worshiper is there. In the darkness of the catacombs, he feels very much alone. He also feels that, as he dreamed one night, he is still chained to Sahak, just as he was during the days when he pretended to believe.

After he leaves the place of the dead, he smells fire; flames are everywhere. He thinks that Christ is returned to save the world, the first step of which will be to destroy Rome—for Rome considers Christ the enemy. Barabbas seizes a burning brand and begins to set everything afire that he can; he wildly thinks that he is helping the Christians and his Savior.

Thrown into prison with the Christians, Barabbas learns that there is no service in the catacombs because the followers were forewarned that an attack is to be made on them. The fires were probably set by agents or spies to further discredit the Christians.

The Christians in the prison naturally deny that Barabbas, who was caught in the act, is one of them. When they protest to the jailer, the man shows Barabbas's disk, which still has the Christian symbol dimly scratched on it, as evidence. A venerable old man among the Christians turns out to be one whom Barabbas met before, the man who denied Christ. Now he explains to Barabbas that it is Caesar who set the fires, not Christ; it is Caesar, therefore, whom Barabbas helped by trying to burn Rome. Christ's message is still that of love.

To the others, the old man adds that they must not condemn Barabbas. He continues that Barabbas is unhappy and that he has to wear his crossed-out disk. The others are also weak and full of faults; their belief comes from God. They must not condemn a man who has no god in whom to believe. Soon the Christians are led out in pairs to be crucified, but Barabbas is taken alone. When death comes, he speaks rather ambiguously into the darkness, saying that he delivers up his soul "to thee."

Critical Evaluation:

The transformation of a soul is the subject of *Barabbas*. Pär Lagerkvist's novel has the tone and manner of an ancient, oft-told story, recounted simply but with feeling. The tale is told with an austerity that renders it all the more moving for being pared down to essentials. The poetic prose is precise and vivid, despite its leanness; at the end of the book, the reader realizes with amazement how clearly the author has pictured by means of a word here and a phrase there the ancient, biblical world. *Barabbas* is a superbly written, enigmatic novel, open to many possible interpretations. If it possesses any fault, it is only that occasionally the prose is almost self-consciously understated, that the sophistication underlying the simplicity of the narration seems to peek through. This is a minor flaw and in no way detracts from the power of the book.

The question raised by *Barabbas* is that which haunts humanity, the question of what lies beyond life. Barabbas is compelled by his fate to question the universe in a manner that he does not understand or desire. Ordinarily such an uneducated thief would not have concerned himself with philosophical and moral issues, but the fact that he is acquitted and Jesus is crucified in his stead turns his world upside down. The book traces his wandering, both physically and spiritually, until his own end, also upon a cross. It is not the end that is important in this novel but rather the struggle. Lagerkvist leaves the ending ambiguous when he states that Barabbas's words were "as though" spoken to the darkness. The stages of this struggle are poignantly portrayed, from the initial confusion and wonderment through the denial to the final reassessment. Barabbas wants to believe, as so many human beings hunger for belief, but he cannot deceive himself; his belief must be hard-won, or it is meaningless and false.

The novel is rich with symbols, but the symbols never intrude; rather, they enrich the tale and serve to give it an added resonance. Most of the men and women who pass through the story are scarred, including Barabbas himself, who was at an early age scarred by his own father (whom he later unwittingly kills). These marked and deformed human beings seem to represent all of humanity, the battered multitudes who stare into the darkness, as does Barabbas, and wonder what is out there waiting for them. Love is the answer, Barabbas is told, but he finds it hard to believe. However, the fat woman and the girl with the harelip both find momentary happiness because he seems briefly to love them. The slave's badge that he wears around his neck becomes a double symbol, representing both the bondage of humanity to the earth and its powers and, after it is engraved with the name of the Savior, possibilities of freedom and happiness. Christian symbols are woven into the narrative, but they seem to arise naturally from the gradually developing Christian religion, to appear as they are needed, to help the followers keep faith.

Although the short novel seems simple, it is amazingly intricate, probing the human mind and the human spirit. Like so much of the best literature, *Barabbas* can be read and appreciated on several different levels and reread from time to time with pleasure and profit. In 1951, shortly after the appearance of this novel, Lagerkvist was awarded the Nobel Prize in Literature.

Further Reading

Brantly, Susan. "Tradition Versus Innovation: The Cradle of Swedish Modernism—Pär Lagerkvist." In *A History of Swedish Literature*, edited by Lars G. Warme. Vol. 3. Lincoln: University of Nebraska Press, 1996. A general overview of Lagerkvist's work, placing it within the context of Swedish modernism.

Gustafson, Alrik. *A History of Swedish Literature*. Minneapolis: University of Minnesota Press, 1961. Traces the evolution of Lagerkvist's prose style to its maturity in *Barabbas*. Examines the novel in terms of Lagerkvist's search for expressive form and his grappling with the problem of evil.

Polet, Jeff. "A Blackened Sea: Religion and Crisis in the Works of Pär Lagerkvist." *Renascence* 54, no. 1 (2001):

47-67. Polet focuses on the reality of human freedom, which Lagerkvist locates in the space between silence and the voice of God. He also explains why Lagerkvist's works only have marginal popularity among English readers.

Scobbie, Irene, ed. "Pär Lagerkvist." In *Aspects of Modern Swedish Literature*. Rev. ed. Chester Springs, Pa.: Dufour Editions, 1999. Scobbie devotes an entire chapter to Lagerkvist, providing an in-depth study of his work. Includes notes, bibliographies, select list of translations, and index.

Sjoberg, Leif. *Pär Lagerkvist*. New York: Columbia University Press, 1976. Argues that *Barabbas* is a modern rather than a historical novel. Relates the controversial ending to Lagerkvist's stated religious views.

Spector, Robert Donald. "*Barabbas*: The Bible as Modern Literature." In *Pär Lagerkvist*. New York: Twayne, 1973. Convincingly demonstrates how the novel reflects the dualism Lagerkvist saw in life. Spector's is the first full-length book in English devoted to Lagerkvist's work.

Swanson, Roy A. "Evil and Love in Lagerkvist's Crucifixion Cycle." *Scandinavian Studies* 38 (November, 1966): 302-317. Considers the novel's place in a series focusing on the event and significance of Jesus' crucifixion. Determines myth to be Lagerkvist's point of departure.

Weathers, Winston. "Death and Transfiguration: The Lagerkvist Pentalogy." In *The Shapeless God: Essays on Modern Fiction*, edited by Harry J. Mooney, Jr., and Thomas F. Staley. Pittsburgh, Pa.: University of Pittsburgh Press, 1968. Assesses the novel as one of five by Lagerkvist that explore the meaning of death and the escape from death. Writing from a Christian perspective, Weathers appraises the novel as a portrait of the secular person.

The Barber of Seville
Or, The Useless Precaution

Author: Pierre-Augustin Caron de Beaumarchais (1732-1799)
First produced: Le Barbier de Séville: Ou, La Précaution inutile, 1775; first published, 1775 (English translation, 1776)
Type of work: Drama
Type of plot: Comedy
Time of plot: Eighteenth century
Locale: Seville, Spain

Principal characters:
FIGARO, the barber of Seville
COUNT ALMAVIVA, a grandee of Spain
BARTHOLO, a doctor
ROSINE, his ward
DON BAZILE, Rosine's singing-master

The Story:

Count Almaviva is so much in love with Rosine, Dr. Bartholo's ward, that even though he never speaks to her, he leaves Madrid and the pleasure of the court in order to be near her in Seville. Her guardian desires to marry her himself, however, and he keeps the young girl locked in her room. To help him in his suit, the count enlists the aid of Figaro, the barber and apothecary of Bartholo.

A note Rosine throws from her window convinces the count that she returns his love. At Figaro's suggestion, the count disguises himself as a soldier seeking quarters for the night. He calls himself Lindor, the name Figaro used in telling Rosine of her unknown lover. When Bartholo, suspicious of everyone who might come near Rosine, refuses to give the disguised count lodging, the count manages to slip a note to Rosine before Bartholo orders him from the house. Bartholo forces Rosine to show him the note, but she cleverly tricks him into reading another note she has in her pocket. Nevertheless, his suspicions are not allayed.

Figaro learns that Bazile is a party to Bartholo's plot to force Rosine to marry him the next day. The count thereupon disguises himself as a student and, calling himself Alonzo, tells Bartholo that he was sent by Don Bazile, Rosine's music teacher, who, so the count says, is ill and has been asked to take his place. The count thinks that by pretending to help Bartholo he can be alone with Rosine and tell her his plans to rescue her from the old man. He gives Bartholo a letter that he claims will help Bartholo in his suit. The letter implies that there is another woman with whom Lindor is in love. Bartholo refuses to leave Rosine alone with the count until Figaro manages to trick him into leaving the room. Figaro takes the opportunity to steal the key to Rosine's room from the old man's key ring. When Bartholo returns to the room, the music lesson seems to be in progress. Suddenly Don Bazile is announced. It takes all of Figaro's ingenuity to keep him from exposing the count as an impostor. Figaro and the count at last manage to get Don Bazile out of the house before Bartholo learns the truth, but Bartholo, suspicious of everyone, sneaks behind the count and Rosine and overhears enough to make him decide to investigate Don Bazile's strange behavior and apparent bewilderment.

Don Bazile confesses that he knows nothing of his supposed illness and never before saw the so-called Alonzo. This confirmation of his suspicions makes Bartholo uneasy. Although he fears that Alonzo is Lindor's friend, he does not suspect that Alonzo is Lindor himself. He tells Don Bazile to arrange to have the notary come at once to perform his marriage to Rosine.

Immediately afterward he goes to the young girl's room and shows her the letter the count gave him. Instead of helping the count, however, it works against him, for Rosine believes Bartholo when he tells her that her young lover will pretend to rescue her but is in reality planning to pass her on to Alonzo. Because Rosine does not know the real identity of the man she calls Lindor, she believes Bartholo and promises to marry him at once. She also tells him of Alonzo's plan to steal into her room that night and carry her off. Bartholo leaves her to arrange for the police to come and apprehend the kidnapper.

While Bartholo is gone, the count and Figaro climb up a ladder and enter Rosine's room. Rosine accuses the count of a plot to pass her on to someone else. The count then throws aside his disguise. He tells her he is Count Almaviva and that in his love for her he followed her hopelessly for the past six months. Rosine is so overcome that she faints. When she revives, she admits that she doubted him and that she promised to marry Bartholo. She also says that Bartholo knows of the plan to carry her away. Already the ladder had been removed from her window and the police are on the way.

When all looks blackest, Don Bazile appears with a notary, as Bartholo instructed him to do. The notary knows only that he is to perform a marriage here and another marriage at the home of Figaro. Here he is to marry Bartholo and a young lady named Rosine. At Figaro's home he is to marry Count Almaviva and a young lady named Rosine. By some clever and rapid talking, the count and Figaro are able to convince the notary that he is merely confused. Don Bazile is more difficult, but he finally decides the money the count slipped into his hand is more important than loyalty to Bartholo. He signs the marriage contract as a witness just before Bartholo bursts into the room with many policemen and a justice of the peace.

Bartholo orders the justice of the peace to arrest the count, but that civil servant is too much impressed with Count Almaviva's high position to risk offending him. Bartholo, anxious to marry his ward, then orders the count out of the house. When he learns that the count and Rosine have just been married and that the contract is legally signed, he is infuriated and tries in vain to keep Rosine from leaving with her husband. By threatening Bartholo with a demand for an exact accounting of his ward's property, which Bartholo dares not allow, the justice of the peace is able to persuade the old man to sign the marriage certificate that gives his consent to Rosine's marriage. Bartholo cannot understand how his plans failed. Figaro tells him that youth and love can always defeat an old man's schemes.

Critical Evaluation:

Although the plot of *The Barber of Seville* has been used many times by dramatists and composers, Pierre-Augustin Caron de Beaumarchais took a fresh approach to the story. The play, fast-moving and brisk, has all the necessary ingredients for a sentimental comedy: intrigue, wit, clear-cut characterizations, satire, and a well-defined plot. Indeed, the plot is more important than the actors themselves, even though Figaro, the barber, has become famous in the literature of all countries.

Beaumarchais's *The Barber of Seville* displays wit, humor, and gaiety, and its structural ingenuity—the sheer fun of the piece—assures its immortality, just as in Gioacchino Antonio Rossini's opera of the same name and Wolfgang Amadeus Mozart's *The Marriage of Figaro*, which is based on Beaumarchais's sequel to the play.

Probability and depth of character are sacrificed to the plot, but the superbly constructed plot is well worth the sacrifice. It is a masterpiece of ingenuity and invention. Bartholo, the antagonist, and the protagonists Rosine, the count, and Figaro are expert in their attempts to outwit one another.

In the best tradition of farce, particularly French farce, the action never seems to flag. Even the catching songs that seemingly interrupt the action are, in fact, organic parts of it. Beginning somewhat slowly in the first act, much of which is necessary exposition, the action gathers momentum, twists and turns, moves from climax to higher climax, and ends abruptly in a quick denouement. The characters are confronted with one obstacle after another; there is withheld information revealed at crucial points in the play; and, finally, there is the big scene, or *scène à faire*.

Equally entertaining is the play's humor, which ranges from broad burlesque and farce to sophisticated comedy of manners. Slapstick is punctuated with brilliant wit and trenchant observations about people and society. However, Beaumarchais's touch is always light. Though Bartholo is ridiculed as the stock jealous cuckold pursuing a lady young enough to be his daughter, the satire stops short of bitterness or vituperation. His only punishment is that he loses Rosine, whom he never possessed in the first place. Seriousness and heavy-handed moralizing are also averted. There is, of course, the underlying moral that youthful lovers can always outwit a foolish old man, but that moral is absorbed in the rollicking dialogue and madcap antics of Figaro and the count. Here, nevertheless, the conquest of innocence is less offensive or cynical than in earlier neoclassical plays dealing with the same theme: Count Almaviva does not seduce Rosine but marries her. Not only love but also good will and lighthearted humor triumph.

Further Reading

Brown, Gregory S. *Literary Sociability and Literary Property in France, 1775-1793: Beaumarchais, the Société des auteurs dramatiques and the Comédie Française*. Burlington, Vt.: Ashgate, 2006. A history of the Société des auteurs dramatiques, the first professional association for creative writers in Europe. The organization was founded by Beaumarchais in 1777, and its members were the playwrights most closely associated with the Comédie Française. Brown traces the group's conception, founding, eventual demise, and its efforts to acquire increased remuneration and societal prestige for its members.

Cox, Cynthia. *The Real Figaro: The Extraordinary Career of Caron de Beaumarchais*. London: Longmans, 1962. Focuses primarily on Beaumarchais's many other activities, particularly diplomacy. Places *The Barber of Seville* in the context of Beaumarchais's traumatic trial. Provides much information on early performances, such as the one in which Marie-Antoinette played Rosine. Includes illustrations and bibliography.

Grendel, Frédéric. *Beaumarchais: The Man Who Was Figaro*. Translated by Roger Greaves. New York: Thomas Y. Crowell, 1977. Interprets the figure of Figaro as Beaumarchais's complete alter ego, the two having a similar ability to keep reinventing themselves for new situations. The complicated plot of *The Barber of Seville* demonstrates this ability at its best. Includes illustrations and selected bibliography.

Howarth, William D. *Beaumarchais and the Theatre*. New York: Routledge, 1995. A critical biography. After recounting the events of Beaumarchais's life and career, Howarth places his work within the broader context of dramatic writing and the theater in the eighteenth century and within the culture of theatergoing in prerevolutionary France. Chapter 12 provides an analysis of *The Barber of Seville*, which includes information about the play's critical reception, influence on contemporary drama, and the operatic adaption by Gioacchino Rossini.

Lever, Maurice. *Beaumarchais: A Biography*. Translated from the French by Susan Emanuel. New York: Farrar, Straus and Giroux, 2008. Instead of a strict chronological biography, Lever provides an entertaining, and detailed account of the many fascinating episodes in Beaumarchais's life. Describes his many occupations, including espionage, watchmaking, pamphleteering, and international trade, as well as his support of the American Revolution.

Ratermanis, J. B., and W. R. Irwin. *The Comic Style of Beaumarchais*. New York: Greenwood Press, 1961. Interesting scene-by-scene analysis of *The Barber of Seville* and *The Marriage of Figaro* and discussion of what makes the comedy work on stage. Stresses that Figaro, as the central character, sets the plot of *The Barber of Seville* in motion without being affected by the consequences himself, unlike the situation in *The Marriage of Figaro*.

Sungolowsky, Joseph. *Beaumarchais*. New York: Twayne, 1974. Concise biography, including an account of the development of *The Barber of Seville* from a *parade* (brief comic sketches) through an *opéra comique* to its present form. Stresses Beaumarchais's honing of his playwriting skills and his ability to reinvent comic traditions and character types.

Wood, John. Introduction to *"The Barber of Seville" and "The Marriage of Figaro."* London: Penguin Books, 1964. Excellent concise discussion of the plays and their social context. Sees *The Barber of Seville* as more concise and "manageable" than *The Marriage of Figaro*. Edition includes Beaumarchais's own notes on the characters and their costumes.

Barchester Towers

Author: Anthony Trollope (1815-1882)
First published: 1857
Type of work: Novel
Type of plot: Social satire
Time of plot: Mid-nineteenth century
Locale: Barchester, England

Principal characters:
BISHOP PROUDIE, the bishop of Barchester
MRS. PROUDIE, his wife
THE REVEREND OBADIAH SLOPE, his chaplain
THE REVEREND SEPTIMUS HARDING, a member of the cathedral chapter
MRS. ELEANOR BOLD, his daughter
DR. GRANTLY, the archdeacon of Barchester
CHARLOTTE STANHOPE, Mrs. Bold's friend
LA SIGNORA MADELINE VESEY NERONI, née Stanhope, Charlotte's sister
ETHELBERT STANHOPE (BERTIE), Charlotte's brother
MR. QUIVERFUL, Mrs. Proudie's candidate for warden of Hiram's Hospital
THE REVEREND FRANCIS ARABIN, the vicar of St. Ewold's

The Story:

After the death of Bishop Grantly of Barchester, there is much conjecture as to his successor. Bishop Grantly's son, the archdeacon, is ambitious for the position, but his hopes are defeated when Dr. Proudie is appointed to the diocese. Bishop Proudie's wife is of Low Church propensities as well as being a woman of extremely aggressive nature, who keeps the bishop's chaplain, Obadiah Slope, in constant tow.

On the first Sunday of the new bishop's regime, Mr. Slope preaches in the cathedral. His sermon concerns the importance of simplicity in the service and the consequent omission of chanting, intoning, and formal ritual. The cathedral chapter is aghast. For generations, the services in the cathedral were chanted; the chapter can see no reason for discontinuing the practice. In counsel, it is decreed that Mr. Slope never be permitted to preach from the cathedral pulpit again.

The Reverend Septimus Harding, who resigned from his position as warden of Hiram's Hospital because of moral scruples, now has several reasons to believe that he will be returned to his post, although at a smaller salary. Mr. Harding, however, is perturbed when Mr. Slope tells him that he will be expected to conduct several services a week and to manage Sunday schools in connection with the asylum. Such duties will make arduous a preferment heretofore very pleasant and leisurely.

Another change of policy is effected in the diocese when the bishop announces, through Mr. Slope, that absentee clergymen should return and help in the administration of the diocese. For years, Dr. Vesey Stanhope left his duties to his curates while he remained in Italy. Now he is forced to return, bringing with him an ailing wife and three grown children: spinster Charlotte, exotic Signora Madeline Vesey Stanhope Neroni, and ne'er-do-well Ethelbert (Bertie). Signora Neroni, who is separated from her husband, is disabled and passes her days on a couch. Bertie studied art and was at varying times a Christian, a Muslim, and a Jew. He amassed sizable debts.

The Proudies hold a reception in the bishop's palace soon after their arrival. Signora Neroni, carried in with great ceremony, captures the group's attention. She has a fascinating way with men and succeeds in almost devastating Mr. Slope. Mrs. Proudie disapproves and does her best to keep Mr. Slope and others away from Signora Neroni.

When the living of St. Ewold's becomes vacant, Dr. Grantly makes a trip to Oxford and sees to it that the Reverend Francis Arabin, a High Churchman, receives the appointment. With Mrs. Proudie and Mr. Slope advocating Low Church practices, it is necessary to build up the strength of the High Church forces. Mr. Arabin is a bachelor of about forty years. The question arises as to what he will do with the parsonage at St. Ewold's.

Mr. Harding's widowed daughter, Mrs. Eleanor Bold, has a good income and is the mother of a baby boy. Mr. Slope attempts to interest her in the work of the Sunday schools. At the same time, he asks Mr. Quiverful of Puddingdale to take over the duties of the hospital. Mr. Quiverful's fourteen children are reason enough for his being grateful for the opportunity. Mrs. Bold, however, learns how her father feels about the extra duties imposed upon him, and she grows cold toward Mr. Slope. In the end, Mr. Harding decides that he simply cannot undertake the new duties at his age, so Mr. Quiverful, a Low Churchman, is granted the preferment, much to Mrs. Proudie's satisfaction.

Mr. Slope is not the only man interested in Mrs. Bold. The Stanhope sisters, realizing that Bertie can never make a living for himself, decide that he should ask Mrs. Bold to be his wife. Meanwhile, Mr. Slope is losing favor with Mrs. Proudie. She is furious that he would throw himself at the feet of Signora Neroni, and his interest in Mr. Harding's daughter, who refuses to comply with her wishes, is disgraceful.

At a large gathering one day at the Thornes of Ullathorne, an old and affluent family, Mrs. Bold finds herself in the same carriage with Mr. Slope, whom by this time she greatly dislikes. Later that day, as she is walking with him, he suddenly puts his arm around her and declares his love. She rushes away and tells Charlotte, who suggests that Bertie speak to Mr. Slope about his irregularity; but the occasion for this discussion never arises. Bertie himself tells Mrs. Bold that his sister Charlotte urges him to marry Mrs. Bold for her money. Naturally insulted, Mrs. Bold is angered at the entire Stanhope family. That evening, when Dr. Stanhope learns what happened, he insists that Bertie go away and earn his own living or starve. After Bertie leaves, Signora Neroni writes a note asking Mrs. Bold to come to see her. When Mrs. Bold enters the Stanhope drawing room, Signora Neroni tells her that she should marry Mr. Arabin. With calculating generosity, she decided that he will make a good husband for Mrs. Bold.

The Dean of Barchester, who suffered a stroke of apoplexy, is not expected to recover. It is understood that Dr. Grantly will not accept the deanship. Mr. Slope wants the position, but Mrs. Proudie refuses to consider him as a candidate. When the dean dies, speculation runs high. Mr. Slope feels encouraged by the newspapers, which say that younger men should be admitted to places of influence in the church.

Mr. Slope is sent off to another diocese, for Mrs. Proudie can no longer bear having him in Barchester. Mr. Arabin, through Oxford influences, is appointed to the deanship, which is a victory for the High Churchmen. With Mr. Slope gone, the Stanhopes feel safe in returning to Italy.

Miss Thorne asks Mrs. Bold to spend some time at Ullathorne. She also contrives to have Mr. Arabin there. It is inevitable that Mr. Arabin will fall in love with Mrs. Bold and ask her to be his wife. Dr. Grantly is satisfied. He threatened to forbid the hospitality of Plumstead Episcopi to Mrs. Bold had she become the wife of a Low Churchman. In fact, Dr. Grantly is moved to such generosity that he furnishes the deanery and gives wonderful gifts to the entire family, including a cello to his father-in-law, Mr. Harding.

Critical Evaluation:

As a young man, Anthony Trollope, son of a ne'er-do-well barrister of good family, seemed destined to continue the decline of the family. An undistinguished student in two distinguished public schools, he had no hopes for university or career. His mother persuaded a family friend to find work for him in the London Post Office, where his performance as a clerk was eventually rated as "worthless." Indeed, the burdens of supporting the family fell on his indefatigable mother, who converted a family business failure in Cincinnati, Ohio, into a literary career with her satiric study *Domestic Manners of Americans* (1832). Like his mother, the son found his path in life after a change of scenery. When the Post Office sent him to the south of Ireland to assist in a postal survey, his career in the postal service began to advance, he married happily, and he began to write.

Success as a writer came after the Post Office sent Trollope to survey southwest England. A midsummer visit to the beautiful cathedral town of Salisbury produced the idea for *The Warden* (1855) and, more important, furnished the outlines for a fictional county, Barsetshire, which became as impressive as Thomas Hardy's Wessex or William Faulkner's Yoknapatawpha. When Trollope returned to the same milieu in *Barchester Towers*, he achieved resounding acclaim. Later he wrote four more novels to create what became known as the Barsetshire Novels. This series was set in a chiefly agricultural county with its seat of Barchester, a quiet town in the West of England, which was noted for its beautiful cathedral and fine monuments rather than for any commercial prosperity. Thus at middle age began the career of one of the most prolific of the Victorian novelists, who also remained, until his last years, one of the most popular.

In his day, Trollope was admired as a realist. He was delighted with Nathaniel Hawthorne's appraisal that his novels were "just as real as if some giant had hewn a great lump out of the earth and put it under a glass case, with all its inhabitants going about their daily business, and not suspecting that they were being made a show of." Some have also viewed Trollope's series as comic works and his characters as being in the grip of a firmly controlled irony. The irony that Trollope perceives in the affairs of the people of Barchester arises from discrepancies between the ideals they uphold and the means by which they uphold those ideals. A lay person with no special knowledge of the Church of England, Trollope vividly depicts the internecine war between the party of the new bishop of Barchester and that of the former bishop's son, Archdeacon Grantly. Both parties intend to preserve the integrity of the Church. With the Church vested in buildings, furnishings, and livings, these clergymen end up fighting for power over the appurtenances and worldly forms of the Church.

Barchester Towers includes a number of subplots, all of which are related to the ecclesiastical power struggle. Since buildings, furnishings, and livings are occupied by human beings, the clerics who guard the Church must also dispose over the lives of human beings. Some of the characters—Mr. Harding and the Quiverfuls in the competition for wardenship of Hiram's Hospital or Eleanor Bold in the rivalry of two clergymen for her hand in marriage—become mere objects in the disputes over power. Episodes not directly related to the ecclesiastical battles serve to underscore them, as in the parallel between the rivalry of Mrs. Lookaloft and Mrs. Greenacre and the absurd ploys of the higher orders that abound in the novel.

The main conflicts of the novel are those that engage the high and mighty of Barchester. The strength of Trollope's satire lies in his refusal to oversimplify the motives of these Church worldlings or to deny them sincerity in their defense of the Church. Even as Slope genuinely believes Grantly and his type to be the enemies of religion, so also does the archdeacon honestly believe that Slope is the kind who could well ruin the Church of England.

One of Trollope's devices for deflating these militant clerics is to treat their wars in the mock-heroic vein. After the first meeting between the archdeacon and the Proudies, the author declares, "And now, had I the pen of a mighty poet, would I sing in epic verse the noble wrath of the archdeacon." In time, Mrs. Proudie is ironically compared to Juno, Medea, even Achilles, while the archdeacon's extravagance in celebrating Mrs. Bold's marriage to his champion, Arabin, is suggestive of a glorious warrior returning from the fields with his spoils.

The reduction of marital glory is furthered by a recurrent analogy with games, underscoring the truth that Barchester's leadership is really concerned with social rather than spiritual or moral issues. Slope's major defeats arise from his indecorous behavior with Madeline Neroni, who is alert to every possible move. Worse, he underestimates his opponent, Mrs. Proudie, and at the end discovers that "Mrs. Proudie had checkmated him."

Human strife is incongruous with the idealized setting of peaceful Barchester, its venerable church and close, and its rural villages round about, all endowed with a loveliness suggestive of the age-old pastoral tradition. The cathedral itself seems to judge the folly of its worldly champions. As the battles commence, Archdeacon Grantly looks up to the cathedral towers as if evoking a blessing for his efforts. However genial the comedy played out beneath the Barchester towers, the outcome is not without serious import, for the ultimate result is the further separation of human beings from their ideals. In the end, the bishop's wife finds that her "sphere is more extended, more noble, and more suited to her ambition than that of a cathedral city," and the bishop himself "had learnt that his proper sphere of action lay in close contiguity with Mrs. Proudie's wardrobe." As Mr. Slope makes his ignominious final departure from the city, "he gave no longing lingering look after the cathedral towers." As for the archdeacon, it is sufficient for him to "walk down the High Street of Barchester without feeling that those who see him are comparing his claims with those of Mr. Slope."

Despite the futility of its human strivings, *Barchester Towers* is a cheerful novel, not merely because the satire provokes laughter but also because occasionally, briefly, the real and the ideal meet. Mr. Harding is too peaceable, too naïve, too reticent to be effective in the world; nevertheless, when prompted by his dedication to simple justice, he personally introduces Mr. Quiverful to his own former charges at Hiram Hospital. This act, representing the union of his profession and practice, creates a consequence greater than the act would suggest, for it causes the Barchester world to treat Mr. Quiverful with more respect as he assumes his duties. Quite appropriately, Trollope brings the novel to its close with pastoral serenity by offering a word of Mr. Harding, who functions not as a hero and not as a perfect divine but as a good, humble man without guile.

"Critical Evaluation" by Catherine E. Moore

Further Reading

Booth, Bradford A. *Anthony Trollope: Aspects of His Life and Art*. London: Edward Hulton, 1958. A study of Trollope's religious beliefs and their impact on *Barchester Towers*. Examines the differences between high and low church clergy and the nature of the Church of England in general.

Bridgham, Elizabeth A. *Spaces of the Sacred and Profane: Dickens, Trollope, and the Victorian Cathedral Town*. New York: Routledge, 2008. Describes how Trollope and Charles Dickens use the setting of Victorian cathedral towns to critique religious attitudes, business practices, aesthetic ideas, and other aspects of nineteenth century English life.

Bury, Laurent. *Seductive Strategies in the Novels of Anthony Trollope, 1815-1882*. Lewiston, N.Y.: Edwin Mellen Press, 2004. A study of seduction in all of Trollope's novels. Argues that seduction was a survival skill for both men and women in the Victorian era and demonstrates how Trollope depicted the era's sexual politics.

Clark, John W. *The Language and Style of Anthony Trollope*. London: André Deutsch, 1975. An excellent study of Trollope's use of language and his recourse in *Barchester Towers* to English dialects, foreign phrases, euphemisms, and church language.

Glendinning, Victoria. *Anthony Trollope*. New York: Alfred A. Knopf, 1993. An excellent biography of Trollope. Provides interpretations of the characters of Bishop and Mrs. Proudie, Signora Neroni, and Mr. Slope. Connects several scenes in *Barchester Towers* to events in Trollope's life.

Markwick, Margaret. *New Men in Trollope's Novels: Rewriting the Victorian Male*. Burlington, Vt.: Ashgate, 2007. Examines Trollope's novels, tracing the development of his ideas about masculinity. Argues that Trollope's male characters are not the conventional Victorian patriarchs and demonstrates how his works promoted a "startlingly modern model of manhood."

_______. *Trollope and Women*. London: Hambledon Press, 1997. Examines how Trollope could simultaneously accept the conventional Victorian ideas about women while also sympathizing with women's difficult situations. Demonstrates the individuality of his female characters. Discusses his depiction of both happy and unhappy marriages, male-female relationships, bigamy, and scandal.

Mullen, Richard, and James Munson. *The Penguin Companion to Trollope*. New York: Penguin, 1996. A comprehensive guide, describing all of Trollope's novels, short stories, travel books, and other works; discusses plot, characters, background, tone, allusions, and contemporary references and places the works in their historical context.

Sadleir, Michael. *Trollope: A Commentary*. New York: Farrar, Straus, 1947. Uses Trollope family papers and letters, as well as contemporary reviews of *Barchester Towers*, to identify some of Trollope's sources and to discuss the book's initial reception. Employs original documents to show the cuts in *Barchester Towers* that were demanded by the publisher.

Skilton, David. *Anthony Trollope and His Contemporaries: A Study in the Theory and Conventions of Mid-Victorian Fiction*. New York: St. Martin's Press, 1972. Discusses Trollope and *Barchester Towers* in the mid-Victorian context. Examines the relationship between Trollope and such contemporary authors as Charles Dickens and William Makepeace Thackeray.

Barnaby Rudge

A Tale of the Riots of '80

Author: Charles Dickens (1812-1870)
First published: 1841
Type of work: Novel
Type of plot: Historical
Time of plot: 1775-1780
Locale: England

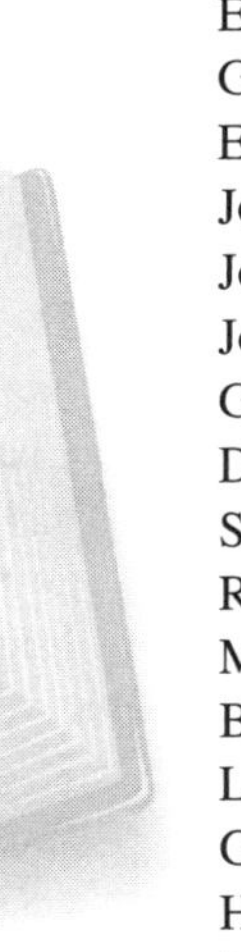

Principal characters:

EMMA HAREDALE, an heiress
GEOFFREY HAREDALE, her bachelor uncle
EDWARD CHESTER, a young man in love with Emma
JOHN CHESTER, his father
JOHN WILLET, the landlord of the Maypole Inn
JOE, his son
GABRIEL VARDEN, a London locksmith
DOLLY, his daughter
SIMON TAPPERTIT, Varden's apprentice
RUDGE, a fugitive from justice
MRS. RUDGE, his wife
BARNABY RUDGE, their half-witted son
LORD GEORGE GORDON, a fanatic
GASHFORD, his secretary
HUGH, a hosteler at the Maypole Inn
DENNIS, the hangman

The Story:

At twilight on a wild, windy day in March, 1775, a small group of men sits in the bar parlor of the Maypole Inn, an ancient hostelry situated in Chigwell parish on the borders of Epping Forest. Two guests in particular engage the attention of John Willet, the proprietor. One is a well-dressed young gentleman who seems preoccupied. The other, a traveler, sits huddled in an old riding coat, his hat pulled forward to hide his face from the landlord's curious gaze. After the young gentleman, Edward Chester, leaves the inn, Joe Willet, the landlord's son, informs the others that Edward, whose horse went lame, intends to walk the twelve miles to London despite the stormy weather because he is hoping to see Emma Haredale at a masquerade she is attending in town.

The name Haredale seems to interest the stranger, and he listens intently when Solomon Daisy, the parish clerk, tells the story of a murder that shocked the neighborhood twenty-two years before to the day. Mr. Reuben Haredale, Emma's father, was at that time owner of The Warren, a great house near the village. One morning, he was found murdered in his bedroom. His steward, a man named Rudge, and a gardener were missing. Several months later, Rudge's body, identified by the clothing he was wearing, was recovered from a pond on the estate. There was no trace of the gardener, and the mystery remains unsolved. Since her father's violent death, Emma lives at The Warren with Mr. Geoffrey Haredale, her bachelor uncle.

The stranger calls abruptly for his horse and gallops away, almost colliding with a chaise driven by Gabriel Varden, the Clerkenwell locksmith. By the light of a lantern, Varden sees the traveler's scarred, scowling face. On his way back to London that same night, Varden finds Edward lying wounded on the highway. About the fallen man capers the grotesque figure of Barnaby Rudge, son of the Rudge who was Reuben's steward. The boy was born half-witted on the day the murder was discovered. Helpless, loved, and pitied, he lives on a shabby street nearby with his mother and his tame, talking raven, Grip. Aided by Barnaby, Varden takes the wounded man to the Rudge house and puts him to bed.

The next morning, Varden tells the story of his night's adventures to Dolly, his daughter, and Simon Tappertit, his apprentice. Dolly, who knows of Emma's affection for Edward, is deeply concerned. When Varden goes to the Rudge house to inquire about Edward, he finds him greatly improved. While he is talking with Mrs. Rudge, whose face clearly reveals the troubles and sorrows of her life, a soft knocking sounds at the closed shutter. When she opens the door, Varden sees over her shoulder the livid face and fierce eyes of the horseman he encountered the night before. The man flees, leaving the locksmith convinced that he is the highwayman who attacked Edward. Mrs. Rudge, visibly upset by the man's appearance on her doorstep, begs Varden to say nothing about the strange visitor.

John Chester, Edward's father, is a vain, selfish man with great ambitions for his son. Shortly after his son's mysterious attack, he and Geoffrey meet by appointment in a private room at the Maypole. Although the two families were enemies for years, John knows that they at last have a common interest in their opposition to a match between Emma and Edward. John confesses frankly that he wishes his son to marry a Protestant heiress, not the niece of a Catholic country squire. Geoffrey, resenting John's superior airs, promises that he will do his best to change his niece's feelings toward Edward. The meeting of the two men causes great interest among the villagers gathered in the bar parlor of the inn.

The mysterious stranger comes again to Mrs. Rudge's house. When permitted to enter, he demands food and money. Frightened by the threats of the sinister blackmailer, she and her son move secretly to a remote country village.

Geoffrey, true to his promise, refuses Edward admittance to The Warren. When the young man confronts his father to demand an explanation for the agreement between him and Geoffrey, John sneers at his son for his sentimental folly and advises him not to let his heart rule his head. Edward, refusing to obey his father's commands, asks Dolly to carry a letter to Emma, who entrusts Dolly with a return note. Hugh, the brutish hosteler at the Maypole, takes the letter from Dolly by force and gives it to John, who is using every means to keep the lovers apart. Before long, he involves Mrs. Varden, Simon, and John Willet in his schemes.

Joe Willet becomes resentful when his father, trying to keep Joe from acting as a go-between for the lovers, begins to interfere with his son's liberties. Meanwhile, Joe has troubles of his own. He apprenticed himself to the locksmith in order to be near Dolly, but Mrs. Varden favors Simon's suit. Joe, annoyed by what he considers Dolly's fickleness, trounces his rival and declares that he will go off to fight the rebels in America. Dolly weeps bitterly when she hears of his enlistment.

Five years later, John Willet again presides over his bar parlor on the tempestuous nineteenth of March, the anniversary of Reuben's murder. Only Solomon is needed to make the gathering of cronies complete. When he appears, he tells the others that in the village churchyard he saw one of the men believed murdered years before. John Willet, disturbed by the clerk's story, carries it that same night to Geoffrey, who asks that the report be kept from his niece.

On the way home, John Willet and the hosteler who accompanied him on his errand are stopped by three horsemen. The travelers are Lord George Gordon, leader of an anti-Catholic crusade; Gashford, his secretary, and John Grueby, a servant. They stay overnight at the Maypole.

Lord Gordon is a fanatic. Gashford, his sly, malevolent helper, is the true organizer of the No-Popery rioters, a rabble of the disaffected and lawless from the London slums. Geoffrey gains Gashford's enmity when he publicly reveals his past. John, on the other hand, now a baronet, takes an interest in the Gordon cause. Among Gashford's followers are Simon, Hugh from the Maypole, and Dennis, the public hangman.

By chance, Barnaby and his mother journey to London on the day the Gordon riots begin. Separated from her by a yelling, roaming horde, Barnaby finds himself pushed along in a mob led by Hugh and Simon. Catholic churches, public buildings, and the homes of prominent Papists are sacked and burned. Later, Barnaby is among those arrested and thrown into Newgate prison.

Gashford, wishing to be revenged on Geoffrey, sends part of the mob to destroy The Warren. On the way, the rioters, led by Simon, Dennis, and Hugh, plunder the Maypole and leave the landlord bound and gagged. Geoffrey is not at home; he went to London in an attempt to learn the whereabouts of Barnaby and his mother. Fearing the destination of the mob headed toward Chigwell and alarmed for the safety of his niece and Dolly, her companion, he rides home as fast as he can. Solomon joins him on the way. Upon their arrival at the Maypole, they release John Willet and hear his account of a strange face, which peered through the window a short time before. Geoffrey and Solomon ride on to The Warren, a heap of smoking ruins. While they stir among the ashes, they spy a man lurking in the old watchtower. Geoffrey throws himself upon the skulking figure. His prisoner was Barnaby, the double murderer.

Geoffrey has Barnaby locked in Newgate. A few hours later, rioters fire the prison and release the inmates. The mob is led by Hugh, who learned of Barnaby's imprisonment from a one-armed stranger. The same armless man saves Varden from injury after the locksmith refused to open the door of the prison. Simon and Dennis, meanwhile, take Emma and Dolly to a wretched cottage in a London suburb.

In an attempt to take refuge from the mob, Geoffrey goes to the home of a vintner, but rioters attack the house. Escaping through a secret passage, they encounter Edward, just returned from abroad. With him is Joe Willet, who lost an arm in the American war. Edward and Joe succeed in taking Haredale and the vintner to a place of safety.

Betrayed by Dennis, Barnaby, his father, and Hugh are captured and sentenced to death. Having learned where the young women are being held, Edward and Joe lead a party to rescue them. The riots in the city were quelled, and Gashford, hoping to save himself, betrays Lord Gordon. Dennis is also under arrest. Simon, wounded and with his legs crushed, is discovered in the house where Emma and Dolly were held. Mrs. Rudge vainly tries to get her husband to repent before he and Dennis die on the scaffold. Hugh, who is John's natural son, meets the same end. After much effort, Varden is able to secure the release of innocent, feebleminded Barnaby.

Geoffrey withdraws all objections to a match between Edward and Emma. He plans to leave England, but before his departure, he revisits the ruins of The Warren. There he meets John and kills his old enemy in a duel. He flees abroad that same night and dies several years later in a religious institution. Gashford survives Lord Gordon and dies at last by his own hand.

These grim matters are of little concern to Dolly, mistress of the Maypole, or to Joe Willett, the beaming landlord; nor do they disturb the simple happiness of Barnaby, who lives many years on Maypole Farm, in company with his mother and Grip, his talking raven.

Critical Evaluation:

Barnaby Rudge is Charles Dickens's first attempt at writing a historical novel, something he accomplished with greater success in *A Tale of Two Cities* (1859). *Barnaby Rudge* ambitiously treats such matters as parental relationships (especially father-son relationships) and complex political situations. All too often, however, critics have ignored it or else attempted to excuse it as a misguided attempt at historical drama in the style popularized by Sir Walter Scott. Other criticisms of the novel have included unsatisfactorily developed female characters (a common criticism of Dickens's work) and the fact that so much of its purposes are enmeshed strongly with complex, contemporary political issues of Dickens's time.

Dickens's main subject in the novel is the Gordon Riots, which took place in the 1780's. The riots were a misguided movement, largely motivated by religious bigotry with no particular social grievance, and were one of the last great shows of anti-Catholic sentiment in England. When Dickens was writing *Barnaby Rudge*, he was perhaps motivated in part by his own fears about the potentially revolutionary situation existing in England at the time, a result of a clash between Chartism and Unionism. The novel's riots might be said to represent that most explosive of all political situations and the direst threat imaginable to Dickens and his middle-class audience: an alliance between the two political extremes, radical and reactionary. However, in the novel, the riots are brought about more by the collision of various personal motives on the parts of its leaders than by any political or revolutionary motive. Each of the mob's leaders has his own differing personal motives, which are only momentarily submerged in a common cry, in this case "No Popery."

One of the great strengths of the novel is in the descriptions of its crowd scenes, as the mob sweeps from the pastoral landscape of the Maypole Inn to London's Newgate prison. The riot offered Dickens the opportunity to explore the way in which an explosive social situation can come into existence. He shows how intolerable social conditions can produce fuel for riot, destruction, and social chaos and how the social evil of the riots was primarily caused by those who saw no common human bond between themselves and those economically less fortunate. Dickens attributes much of the willful destruction of the existing order to selfish indifference or ignorance about the part on the past of such characters as Simon Tappertit, John Chester, Gashford, Hugh, and Barnaby Rudge. In some way or another, they all are alienated from an identity grounded in the social structure they want to smash.

Dickens uses the riots to expose a fundamental sickness in society, the mindless urge to destroy. He forces himself and his readers to confront the harsh realities of riot and revolution through the great detail in which he presents scenes of destruction. These scenes forcefully bring home to his readers, almost in a cautionary manner, the reality of what revolution means. The looting of The Warren, Geoffrey Haredale's home, for example, which takes place over the course of several pages in the novel, shows in its remorseless attention to detail how determined Dickens was that his readers be spared nothing of the pain of this destruction. Likewise, in his description of the destruction of the Maypole Inn, Dickens's prose takes on a note of recognizable rage at what he sees as an offense against nature. He is determined to show his readers that the average as well as the exceptional must suffer from revolution. The inn represents a modest way of life that is just as susceptible to the madness of revolution as the great house.

Barnaby Rudge presents the causes and conditions that made the riots possible through a series of dramatic oppositions. The most notable opposition that Dickens sets up is that of the influence of the past on the present, of the old order against the new. The pastoral world, represented by the Maypole Inn at Chigwell, just outside London, is an obvious image of a stable social order rooted in the past. The opening sentences of the novel, however, suggest that this is a way of life that has grown old and apparently deserves to die.

In part, in these opening scenes, Dickens seems to be implicating the landed aristocracy, which gave up its age-old responsibility to provide governance and guidance to its tenants. This is represented in the character of Sir John Chester, one of the driving background forces of the mob violence. Through John, Dickens also explores a familiar topic of great concern to him, that of parenthood, in this case the relationships between fathers and sons. By disowning his sons Edward and Hugh, John does not merely threaten his way of life by irresponsibility but brings about its downfall by the willful destruction of his lineage. His son Hugh is the final product of a way of life that falls into decay; allowed to live as an animal, he is quite willing to help destroy the society that created and disowned him.

Barnaby, the title character, is similar to Hugh in that he, too, is the son of a wicked father. Simple-minded and ready to believe what people tell him without question, Barnaby is caught up in the riots as their revolutionary leader. Barnaby complements Hugh well, since the situation of the riots in which they both willingly participate is, in part, brought about by the actions of fathers such as theirs who selfishly destroy the traditional order of society. This selfishness damages the future, through their sons, as much as it destroys the past.

Barnaby is also an obvious image of the irrationality of violence, perhaps too obvious an image (although Dickens originally planned to have three escapees from the Bedlam asylum lead the mob). However, virtually no one connected with the riots has any more idea than Barnaby as to why he is where he is.

Often overlooked among Dickens's many novels, *Barnaby Rudge* certainly deserves more serious consideration. The novel is a complex treatment of the conditions that give rise to political disorder, coupled with a detailed treatment of one of Dickens's favorite themes, the relationship between parents and children.

"Critical Evaluation" by Craig A. Larson

Further Reading

Adrian, Arthur A. *Dickens and the Parent-Child Relationship*. Athens: Ohio University Press, 1984. Explores the effect of the cruelty of parents who withhold their love and ignore their children's feelings. Views *Barnaby Rudge* as a study of "father-son friction."

Hardy, Barbara. *Dickens and Creativity*. London: Continuum, 2008. Focuses on the workings of Dickens's creativity and imagination, which Hardy argues is at the heart of his self-awareness, subject matter, and narrative. *Barnaby Rudge* is discussed in chapter 3, "The Awareness of Art in *Sketches by Boz*, *Pickwick Papers*, *Oliver Twist*, *Barnaby Rudge*, *The Old Curiosity Shop*, *A Christmas Carol*, and *The Chimes*."

Jordan, John O., ed. *The Cambridge Companion to Charles Dickens*. New York: Cambridge University Press, 2001. Collection of essays with information about Dickens's life and times, analyses of his novels, and discussions of Dickens and language, gender, family, domestic ideology, the form of the novel, illustration, theater, and film.

Kincaid, James R. *Dickens and the Rhetoric of Laughter.* Oxford, England: Clarendon Press, 1971. Includes an excellent chapter on *Barnaby Rudge* that explores the nature of the humor in the novel. Suggests that Dickens wants the reader to laugh at tyranny.

Lindsay, Jack. "*Barnaby Rudge*." In *Dickens and the Twentieth Century*, edited by John Gross and Gabriel Pearson. New York: Routledge, 1962. Reconsiders *Barnaby Rudge*, treating the novel as a study of the nature of social change.

Newman, S. J. *Dickens at Play*. New York: St. Martin's Press, 1981. A good treatment of *Barnaby Rudge* that interprets the riots as a vision of the nature of anarchy. Focuses on the "unwilling collusion between madness and creativity" in the character of Lord Gordon.

Parker, David. *The Doughty Street Novels: "Pickwick Papers," "Oliver Twist," "Nicholas Nickleby," "Barnaby Rudge."* New York: AMS Press, 2002. Parker, the longtime curator of the Dickens House, traces Dickens's work on four early novels during the period when the writer lived on Doughty Street in London.

Paroissien, David, ed. *A Companion to Charles Dickens*. Malden, Mass.: Blackwell, 2008. Collection of essays providing information about Dickens's life and work, including Dickens as a reformer, Christian, and journalist and Dickens and gender, technology, America, and the uses of history. Also includes the essay *"Barnaby Rudge"* by John Mee.

Paz, D. G. *Dickens and "Barnaby Rudge": Anti-Catholicism and Chartism*. Monmouth, Wales: Merlin Press, 2006. Analyzes the novel from the perspective of Dickens's involvement in the Chartist reform movement and his efforts to warn readers of the dangers of Evangelicalism.

Rice, Thomas J. "The Politics of *Barnaby Rudge*." In *The Changing World of Charles Dickens*, edited by Robert Giddings. New York: Barnes & Noble, 1983. An excellent essay that firmly grounds the writing of *Barnaby Rudge* in the political situation of its time.

Baron Münchausen's Narrative of His Marvellous Travels and Campaigns in Russia

Author: Rudolf Erich Raspe (1737-1794)
First published: 1785
Type of work: Novel
Type of plot: Picaresque
Time of plot: Eighteenth century
Locale: The world and Moon

Principal character:
HIERONYMUS VON MÜNCHAUSEN, a German nobleman

The Story:

Baron Münchausen relates a history of his adventures. He once set out on horseback on a journey to Russia in midwinter. He ties his horse to a stump projecting from the snow and goes to sleep. When he awakens he finds that the abundant snow has melted and that his horse is dangling from the weather vane of a church steeple. He is subsequently pursued by a wolf that begins to devour his horse as it flees; when he attacks it with his whip, it eats the entire horse and ends up in harness itself.

While waiting to receive a commission in the Russian army, the baron hurries from his bedroom to shoot at a flock of ducks, but he strikes his head on the doorpost, which causes sparks to fly from his eyes. This experience proves useful when he finds that he has lost the flint from his flintlock; he has only to raise the musket to his face and punch himself in the eye to bag sixteen birds. He is not so lucky with a stag that he tries to bring down by spitting a cherry stone at it, but he later encounters a fine specimen with a cherry tree growing between its antlers.

His aim is just as true when he throws two flints at a pursuing bear; they strike fire in the creature's stomach and blow it up. He has no such armaments when he encounters a wolf, so he thrusts his arm into the beast's mouth, lays hold of its entrails, and turns it inside out. He dares not do the same to a rabid dog and throws his cloak over it instead; unfortunately, the cloak picks up the infection and passes it on to other suits in his wardrobe.

He possesses a greyhound so fast that it outruns its own legs and must thereafter be employed as a terrier. Another greyhound, a bitch, is determined to course even while heavily pregnant. One day when she chases a hare in a similar condition, the exertion leads them both to give birth, and instinct leads their respective offspring immediately to continue their mothers' chase.

Once the Russian army's campaign against the Turks begins, the baron's horse suffers the indignity of being cut in two by a portcullis, but his farrier manages to sew the two halves together with sprigs of laurel that eventually sprout to form a bower over the saddle. He is captured soon after and sets to work as a slave to drive the sultan's bees to their pasture every day. One day, when he throws his silver hatchet at bears that are attacking a bee, the hatchet carries the bee all the way to the Moon. To fetch it back, he climbs a gigantic beanstalk; then, while he is searching for it on the Moon, the Sun dries up the beanstalk, whereupon he has to make a rope out of straw to climb back down to Earth. He is still two miles up when he has to let go of the rope, and when he lands he makes a hole nine fathoms deep.

Although the baron's original account of his adventures ends at this point, he—or someone pretending to be him—continues to add more episodes to this remarkable career. After the war, he goes to sea, where he has many adventures of a similarly preposterous but rather more complicated nature.

His adventures at the Siege of Gibraltar involve the cunning use of colliding cannonballs, the total destruction of the British artillery, and the employment of a slingshot to cut down two prisoners of war from a scaffold. The sling in question is a family heirloom once used by William Shakespeare for poaching deer and since employed in various other exploits, including the launching of a balloon. The baron saves other prisoners of war by making wings for them.

Later, the baron travels to Ceylon, Sicily, the South Seas, and many other places, everywhere accomplishing extraordinary feats of ingenuity. He visits the Moon again, this time as a passenger on a ship lifted up to it by a hurricane, but he finds it to be very different from his first visit. Inside Mount Etna he converses with the Roman god Vulcan. He and his companions are swallowed by a huge fish, and he is carried across the American continent by eagles.

His account continues to grow longer in subsequent versions, which become many and various. The most familiar English-language version continues with an expedition into the heart of Africa, a visit to an island of ice, a new expedition to Africa in the company of the Sphinx and the giants Gog and Magog, and an eventual triumphant return to England. These later adventures also involve him with Don Quixote. After journeys to America and Russia, he rediscovers the lost library of Alexandria, meets the legendary magician Hermes Trismegistus, and eventually liberates France from its revolutionaries, freeing Marie-Antoinette and her family from their imprisonment.

Critical Evaluation:

The first edition of *Baron Münchausen's Narrative of His Marvellous Travels and Campaigns in Russia* was a rather brief document, almost certainly written in English by Rudolf Erich Raspe, a German satirist forced to seek refuge in England in 1775 after allegedly stealing gems from an employer. He never formally admitted authorship of the work but was named as the original author by Gottfried Bürger, who translated the work into German. Its great success in England prompted the publisher to add more material to subsequent editions issued during 1786, which might have been by Raspe, although a marked difference in style makes it more probable that another writer was responsible.

Late in 1786, a new publisher, G. Kearsley, produced his own rival version of Münchausen's narrative. All the pirated material in this edition was considerably rewritten in a more pompous and cumbersome fashion, and much more of a similar stripe was added by an unknown hand. It is this text, originally titled *Gulliver Revived: Or, The Singular Travels, Campaigns, Voyages and Adventures of Baron Munikhouson, Commonly Called Münchausen*, that virtually all later editions follow in their early phases, although it ought properly to be regarded as a corrupt version of Raspe's text.

Kearsley added yet more new material to his text between 1786 and 1792, at which point a new rival issued *A Sequel to the Adventures of Baron Münchausen*, whose substance was quickly coopted and added into Kearsley's text. The author of these new materials remains unknown, but it certainly was not Raspe. To add to the complications, editions of

Münchausen issued in France and Germany were augmented by native writers, thus diverging markedly from the parent text. In effect, the baron became common property and was adopted as a source and an authority for all manner of tall tales. The real Baron Münchausen thus found himself briefly notorious, somewhat to his surprise and much to his chagrin. He did not take kindly to being made to look a fool and deeply resented the fact that his reputation as a raconteur had been blackened by the utter absurdities and veiled obscenities favored by Raspe's successors.

Raspe's own version of the original anecdotes is much preferable to the Kearsley version. The improbabilities therein are modest enough to be amusing rather than appalling, and they are relayed in a delightfully laconic manner that suits their content well. The writers who added to Raspe's work were decidedly inferior in both these respects, and they may fairly be said to have ruined his work, no matter how little damage they did to its salability.

What survives their mutilations, however, is the idea of Münchausen: the comical, yet somehow towering, figure of the teller of tales who insists that the most astonishing improbabilities are records of actual events. Münchausen is the incarnation of the power that stories have to grip and involve those who hear and read them, and the narrative draws on the remarkably rich "urban folklore" that is passed on by word of mouth, concerning events which—the tellers insist—actually happened to "a friend of a friend." However unlikely these made-up tales might be, there is something about them that seduces belief and generates passionate insistence if a subsequent teller is challenged. Münchausen's narrative is not a collection of such tales, for they are not of a kind that easily survives writing down, but Raspe's original jottings are a deft literary parody of them and of the manner of their telling.

The transformation and growth of the Münchausen narrative once it was out of Raspe's control is a curious phenomenon. The additional material is so bad, for the most part, that it is hard for later readers to understand how the book retained its popularity. The incidents became sillier and sillier and all topical material was soon outdated. Perhaps the work would have been forgotten, save as an example of eighteenth century grotesquerie, had it not been for several excellent film versions; the likelihood, however, is that it was sustained in spite of its inadequacies by the one great asset handed down by Raspe to his feeble imitators. Everyone understands Baron Münchausen and recognizes him because there is a little of Münchausen in everyone.

All human beings exaggerate when they relate the funny or horrible things that happened to them, all make their accomplishments slightly more "marvellous," their escapes slightly more hairsbreadth, and their observations slightly more bizarre than they were in actual fact. This is a natural way of making the narratives of ordinary lives authentically dramatic. Baron Münchausen's narrative pokes fun at one of the absurd necessities of everyday social intercourse and points up the fact that although social life would not be possible without trust, the insistence that people tell the truth at all times makes it necessary that they constantly tell lies.

Brian Stableford

Further Reading

Carswell, John. *The Prospector: Being the Life and Times of Rudolf Erich Raspe, 1737-1794*. London: Cresset Press, 1950. A useful biography of Raspe, including a commentary on his most famous invention.

Green, Roger Lancelyn. *Into Other Worlds: Space-Flight in Fiction, from Lucian to Lewis*. 1958. Reprint. New York: Arno Press, 1975. Cites Raspe's narrative in chapter 5, "A Lunatick Century," in the context of other fictional lunar voyages.

Raspe, R. E., et al. *Singular Travels, Campaigns, and Adventures of Baron Münchausen*. Introduction by John Carswell. London: Cresset Press, 1948. An edition of Raspe's original text and its earliest embellishments, together with the first version of the sequel that was later integrated with Kearsley's text. The introduction provides an invaluable history of the text.

Rose, William, ed. Introduction to *The Travels of Baron Münchausen; Gulliver Revived: Or, The Vice of Lying Prophecy Exposed*. London: G. Routledge & Sons, 1923. Provides a brief history of the work and a commentary on its genesis.

Sigurdsson, Haraldur. "Baron Münchausen in the Volcano." In *Melting the Earth: The History of Ideas on Volcanic Eruptions*. New York: Oxford University Press, 1999. Sigurdsson's history includes this chapter describing how Baron Münchausen's adventures at Mount Etna reflects eighteenth century geological concepts.

Welcher, Jeanne K., and George E. Bush, Jr. Introduction to *Gulliveriana IV*. Delmar, N.Y.: Scholars' Facsimiles & Reprints, 1973. Discusses the fifth edition (Kearsley's), which is here reproduced in facsimile, with particular reference to its contemporary critical reception.

Barren Ground

Author: Ellen Glasgow (1873-1945)
First published: 1925
Type of work: Novel
Type of plot: Social realism
Time of plot: Late nineteenth and early twentieth centuries
Locale: Rural Virginia

Principal characters:
DORINDA OAKLEY, the daughter of a poor white Virginia farmer
JOSIAH and RUFUS, her brothers
JASON GREYLOCK, the last member of an old Virginia family
GENEVA ELLGOOD, who becomes Jason's wife
NATHAN PEDLAR, a country farmer and merchant

The Story:

Late one cold winter day, Dorinda Oakley walks the four miles between Pedlar's Mill and her home at Old Farm. The land is bleak and desolate under a gray sky, and a few flakes of snow are falling. For almost a year, she worked in Nathan Pedlar's store, taking the place of his consumptive wife. Her brisk walk carries her swiftly over the rutted roads toward her father's unproductive farm and the dilapidated Oakley house. On the way, she passes Green Acres, the fertile farm of James Ellgood, and the run-down farm of Five Oaks, owned by dissolute old Doctor Greylock, whose son, Jason, gave up his medical studies to take over his father's practice and to care for his drunken father.

As she walks, Dorinda thinks of young Jason Greylock, who overtakes her in his buggy before she reaches Old Farm. During the ride to her home, she remembers the comment of old Matthew Fairlamb, who told her that she ought to marry Jason. The young doctor is handsome and represents something different from Dorinda's drab, struggling life. Her father and mother and her two brothers are unresponsive and bitter people. Mrs. Oakley suffers from headaches and tries to forget them in a ceaseless activity of work. At Old Farm, supper is followed by prayers, prayers by sleep.

Dorinda continues to see Jason. Taking the money she is saving to buy a cow, she orders a pretty dress and a new hat to wear to church on Easter Sunday. Her Easter finery, however, brings her no happiness. Jason sits in church with the Ellgoods and their daughter, Geneva, and afterward, he goes home with them to dinner. Dorinda sits in her bedroom that afternoon and meditates on her unhappiness.

Later, Jason unexpectedly proposes, confessing that he, too, is lonely and unhappy. He speaks of his attachment to his father that brought him back to Pedlar's Mill, and he curses the tenant system, which he says is ruining the South. He and Dorinda plan to be married in the fall. When they meet during the hot, dark nights that summer, he kisses her with half-angry, half-hungry violence.

Geneva, meanwhile, tells her friends that she is engaged to Jason. In September, Jason leaves for the city to buy surgical instruments. When he is overlong in returning, Dorinda begins to worry. At last she visits Aunt Mehitable Green, an old black conjuring woman, in the hope that she heard some gossip from the Greylock servants concerning Jason. While there, Dorinda becomes ill and learns that she is to have a child. Distressed, she goes to Five Oaks and confronts drunken old Dr. Greylock, who tells her, cackling with sly mirth, that Jason married Geneva in the city. The old man intimates that Jason is white-livered and was forced into the marriage by the Ellgoods. He adds, leering, that Jason and his bride are expected home that night.

On the way home, Dorinda, herself unseen, sees the carriage that brings Jason and Geneva to Five Oaks. Late that night, she goes to the Greylock house and tries to shoot Jason, who is frightened and begs for her pity and understanding. Despising him for his weakness and falseness, she blunders home through the darkness. Two days later, she packs her suitcase and leaves home. By accident, she takes the northbound train rather than the one to Richmond, and so changes the course of her life.

Dorinda arrives in New York in October, frightened, friendless, and with no prospects of work. Two weeks later, she meets a kindly middle-aged woman who takes her in and gives her the address of a dressmaker who might hire her. On the way to the shop, however, Dorinda is knocked down by a cab. She awakens in a hospital. Dr. Faraday, a surgeon who saw the accident, is able to save her life but not that of her baby. Dr. Faraday hires her to look after his office and children.

Dorinda lives in New York with the Faradays for two years. Then her father has a stroke, and she returns home. Her brother Josiah is married, and Mrs. Pedlar is dead. Dorinda is now a woman of self-confidence and poise. She sees Geneva, who already looks middle-aged, and has only pity for the woman who married Jason. Her brother Rufus says Jason is drinking heavily and losing all his patients. Five Oaks Farm looks more run-down than ever. Determined to make the Oakley land productive once more, Dorinda borrows enough money to buy seven cows. She finds Nathan Pedlar helpful in many ways, for he knows good farming methods and gives her advice. When she sees Jason again, she wonders how she could ever have given herself to such a husk of a man.

After Mr. Oakley's death, Josiah and his wife Elvira go to live on their own land. Rufus, who hates the farm, wants to go to the city, but before he can leave, he is accused of murdering a neighboring farmer. Dorinda is convinced that he committed the murder, but Mrs. Oakley swears under oath that her son was at home with her at the time of the shooting. Her lie saves Rufus, but Mrs. Oakley's conscience begins to torment her and she takes to her bed. Her mind broken, she lives in dreams of her youth. When she dies in her sleep, Dorinda weeps. It seems to her that her parents' lives were futile and wasted.

During the next ten years, Dorinda works hard. She borrows more money to improve the farm and, although she saves and scrimps, she is happy. Geneva is losing her mind. One day she tells Dorinda that she bore a child but that Jason killed it and buried it in the garden. Geneva drowns herself the same day that Nathan asks Dorinda to marry him.

Together Dorinda and Nathan prosper. She is now thirty-eight and still feels young. John Abner Pedlar, Nathan's crippled son, looks to her for help, and she gives it willingly. Nathan's other children mean less to her, and she is glad when they marry and move away. When Five Oaks is offered for sale, Dorinda and Nathan buy it for six thousand dollars. As Jason signs over the papers to her, Dorinda notices that he is his dirty, drunken old father all over again.

Dorinda devotes the next few years to restoring Five Oaks. John Abner is still her friend and helper. There are reports that Jason is living in an old house in the pine woods and drinking heavily. Dorinda, busy with her house and dairy farm, has little time for neighborhood gossip. One day, Nathan takes the train to the city to have a tooth pulled and to attend a lawsuit. The train is wrecked, and Nathan is killed while trying to save the lives of the other passengers. He is given a hero's funeral. The years following Nathan's death are Dorinda's happiest, for as time passes, she realizes that she regained, through her struggle with the land, her own integrity and self-respect.

One day, hunters find Jason sick and starving in the woods. Her neighbors assume that Dorinda will take him in. Unwillingly, she allows him to be brought to Old Farm, where she engages a nurse to look after him. In a few months, Jason dies. Many of the people at the funeral come only out of curiosity, and a pompous minister says meaningless things about Jason, whom he never knew. Dorinda feels nothing as she stands beside the grave, for her memories of Jason outlived her emotions. She senses that, for good or ill, the fervor and the fever of her life, too, are ended.

Critical Evaluation:

Barren Ground is a disturbing novel because it represents the ways life can be lived under the most harrowing of circumstances. Ellen Glasgow writes about farmers faced with the difficulties of making an unwilling earth—a wasteland, in fact—yield a living. A few triumph against the odds; some do their best and barely survive; others give up and die early. All except those who give up work exceedingly hard. Glasgow believes, as she says in the 1933 preface to *Barren Ground*, that "the novel is experience illumined by imagination." In this novel, as in much of her work, she is faithful to her own experience in her native Virginia but colors that experience with a dark imagination that views human life as a constant struggle in which even the strong do not always survive. Those who do survive must adjust their idealism to fit reality.

The main theme of the novel is stated by its main character, Dorinda Oakley, who thinks that for the majority, life is "barren ground where they have to struggle to make anything grow." Dorinda has experienced more than the hardships of making a living from the soil of rural Virginia. At the age of twenty, she has the seed of love planted in her heart, only to have it uprooted by her lover's weakness. After that, as regards passion, her heart is indeed barren ground. Glasgow seems to suggest that Dorinda's life is also barren ground as far as happiness is concerned. To women, Glasgow writes, "love and happiness [are] interchangeable terms." After Jason jilts her, Dorinda spends the rest of her life distrusting men and building emotional, mental, physical, and financial walls to protect herself from them. She marries Nathan Pedlar only because she fears loneliness and because he is submissive to her and willing to live without physical intimacy. Dorinda becomes a cynic about love and marriage, believing that they seldom, if ever, go together; even when they do, the love does not endure.

Dorinda, like the characters of Thomas Hardy's novels, is driven by forces beyond her control, by the "eternal purpose." She feels that the trivial incidents in life are the crucial ones. Those incidents—Nathan's train trip that results in his heroic death, her meeting with Jason in the road, her poor aim when the gun goes off, the particular place and moment when she falls on Fifth Avenue—change the course of her life, yet none of them could have been foreseen or prevented. Dorinda believes that only once, in the hospital in New York, has the incident or device of fortune been in her favor. Much like Theodore Dreiser's Carrie Meeber or Hurstwood, she is "a straw in the wind, a leaf on a stream."

Glasgow, as she says in her preface, believes, however, that "character is fate," and that the individual destinies of her characters are partly determined by the nature they inherit, by, that is, their blood: Destiny is in the genes. The "vein of iron" that keeps Dorinda struggling (and that helps her to succeed) is a product of the "sense" of her great-grandfather, a member of the Southern upper class, and the physical strength of her father, a member of the "poor white" class. Jason fails, like his father had, because of "bad blood." Even though unforeseen events control individual destiny, character determines what an individual does in the circumstances.

As an archetype, Dorinda is at first a Medea figure who falls in love with a Jason who will forsake her for another. She becomes, however, an Artemis or an Atalanta, the devouring female who remains estranged from the male physically and psychologically. In the final analysis, Glasgow shows that all individuals are always isolated from their fellow creatures. Beyond that, Dorinda is also, paradoxically, an earth mother, who causes the soil to be productive and who keeps the best cows in the state. Her maternal instinct is satisfied by this bond with the soil and by her adoption through marriage of Nathan's children, in particular John Abner. Although she is never psychologically a whole person, Dorinda does her best given her character and experience. She achieves a wholeness that most never achieve. Although she is a woman, she farms better than most of the men in her rural community. Her black hair symbolizes her relationship with the earth, as its opposite, the sky, is symbolized in her blue eyes. Her experiences are much like her mother's (an early separation from a lover, a loveless marriage), but she manages to combine her mother's habit of hard work with a contentment her morally repressed mother never had. Jason goes away to New York and comes back to a dying father just as Dorinda does. However, Jason allows life to conquer him. Dorinda does not.

Further Reading

Donovan, Josephine. *After the Fall: The Demeter-Persephone Myth in Wharton, Cather, and Glasgow.* University Park: Pennsylvania State University Press, 1989. Donovan describes Glasgow's use of the resurrection myth in the mother-daughter relationship in *Barren Ground*, which reflects a shift from a traditional southern view of male supremacy to a woman-identified world, both for Dorinda and for the author, in which "green world" values and the ethos of Demeter the Mother are affirmed.

Godbold, E. Stanly, Jr. *Ellen Glasgow and the Woman Within.* Baton Rouge: Louisiana State University Press, 1972. A biography that describes Glasgow's writing process and her efforts to give life meaning, establishing a code for living that enabled her to survive, but perhaps drained her humanity.

Harrison, Elizabeth Jane. *Female Pastoral: Women Writers Re-Visioning the American South.* Knoxville: University of Tennessee Press, 1991. Considers Dorinda as a new type of pastoral heroine for her time. Suggests that she steals the role of hero from male characters in the novel and atones for this at the end.

Levy, Helen Fiddyment. *Fiction of the Home Place: Jewett, Cather, Glasgow, Porter, Welty, and Naylor.* Jackson: University Press of Mississippi, 1992. Discusses the place of *Barren Ground* in Glasgow's personal and literary development. Connects the author's rejection of her female destiny and her desire for the independence and achievement allowed males with her heroine's.

Nicolaisen, Peter. "Rural Poverty and the Heroics of Farming: Elizabeth Madox Roberts's *The Time of Man* and Ellen Glasgow's *Barren Ground*." In *Reading Southern Poverty Between the Wars, 1918-1939*, edited by Richard Godden and Martin Crawford. Athens: University of Georgia Press, 2006. Argues that many of the southern writers, social scientists, activists, and others who professed to be progressive actually upheld the traditional economic and social systems which allowed for the continued existence of poverty. The essay on Glasgow analyzes her novel to demonstrate how it fits this description

Patterson, Martha H. "Mary Johnston, Ellen Glasgow, and the Evolutionary Logic of Progressive Reform." In *Beyond the Gibson Girl: Reimagining the American New Woman, 1895-1915.* Urbana: University of Illinois Press, 2005. At the end of the nineteenth and beginning of the twentieth centuries, an image emerged of the "New Woman" who was well-educated, progressive, and white. Patterson's book describes how Glasgow and other writers challenged this image, creating women characters who were African American, southern, and in other ways different than the popular conception of womanhood.

Raper, Julius Rowan. *From the Sunken Garden: The Fiction of Ellen Glasgow, 1916-1945.* Baton Rouge: Louisiana State University Press, 1980. A follow-up to his earlier book, *Without Shelter: The Early Career of Ellen Glasgow.* Raper examines the second half of Glasgow's writing life, analyzing her concern with the evolution of the spirit and heredity. Explores her use of traditional devices, such as the foil, the double, and projection to create the psychologically rich inner lives of her characters.

________. *Without Shelter: The Early Career of Ellen Glasgow.* Baton Rouge: Louisiana State University Press, 1971. Examines the early writings in which Glasgow searched for what was enduring and universal in the face of the changing values and dying traditions of the post-Civil War South.

Santas, Joan Foster. *Ellen Glasgow's American Dream.* Charlottesville: University Press of Virginia, 1965. Extrapolates from her novels Glasgow's discovery of a newly envisioned but southern-based American Dream, focused not on acquisitiveness but on the creation of a blessed, ideal community which valued an inner civilization, fortitude, a sense of duty, classlessness, and acceptance of the weak.

Taylor, Welford Dunaway, and George C. Longest, eds. *Regarding Ellen Glasgow: Essays for Contemporary Readers.* Richmond: Library of Virginia, 2001. Collection includes examinations of Glasgow and southern history, Glasgow and Calvinism, her depiction of southern women, and the feminist elements in her work. Includes chronology, bibliography, and index.

Thiebaux, Marcelle. *Ellen Glasgow.* New York: Frederick Ungar, 1982. Discusses three themes developed in *Barren Ground:* the feminist theme of the protagonist's independent life; the Calvinist theme of her inheritance from her Scotch-Irish ancestors; and the agrarian theme of her attachment to the land.

Weaks-Baxter, Mary. "Veins of Iron: Ellen Glasgow's Virginia Farmers." In *Reclaiming the American Farmer: The Reinvention of a Regional Mythology in Twentieth-Century Southern Writing.* Baton Rouge: Louisiana State University Press, 2006. Weaks-Baxter analyzes works by Glasgow and other southern authors in the years from 1900 until 1960, focusing on how their works replaced idealized descriptions of the plantation system with a new agrarian mythology that glorified the "yeoman farmer."

Barrio Boy
The Story of a Boy's Acculturation

Author: Ernesto Galarza (1905-1984)
First published: 1971
Type of work: Autobiography
Type of plot: Historical
Time of plot: 1910-1920
Locale: Mexico and California

Principal personages:
ERNESTO GALARZA, the narrator
HENRIQUETA, his mother
AUNT ESTHER, his guardian
UNCLE JOSÉ, his closest companion
UNCLE GUSTAVO, another guardian

The Story:

Ernesto is born in an adobe in a small Mexican village that is hidden away in a mountainous region. It is so small that the town has only one street, no police, no fire department, and no mayor. The village belongs to everyone.

Ernesto's parents are divorced, so Ernesto lives with his mother, Henriqueta, as part of the property settlement. He also is reared by his Uncle Gustavo, his aunt Esther, and his Uncle José. Part of his daily chores is to watch over his pets: Coronel, his rooster; Nerón, his watchdog; and Relámpago, a burro who really does not belong to anyone.

Ernesto does not attend school so he does not know how to read or write well. Having a career is not as important as being able to prove his manhood through hard manual labor. Beginning at age seven, Ernesto learns that being a man means working day and night without pay.

One summer day, a great hurricane showers the village. The street is flooded, and everyone works together to save what is left of houses and corrals. Before the stories of the flood can be talked about, the *rurales*, special government police, enter the town looking for young men to be drafted in the army for the revolution. They do not allow anyone to leave. Fearing the worst, Henriqueta decides the family must escape. The night before the family slips away north, Halley's comet appears in the sky. According to Don Cleofas, the oldest person in the village, this is an omen of something serious.

After a day and a half traveling on horseback, Ernesto and his family arrive in Tepic and settle in their new home. Life is different. Uncle Gustavo and José now work for pay, and the marketplace becomes an adventure for Ernesto. He even begins to be educated at home. The problems of the revolution his mother thought she left behind at the old village (which people called Jalco) follow them to Tepic. Good news, however, arrives in the form of jobs on the Southern Pacific Railroad. The family again travels north to Acaponeta. Living there, close to the railroad station, means that revolutionaries often come to the family's door. With every grace, Henriqueta serves the men. Soon, a letter from Uncle Gustavo orders them to leave Tepic for Urias to get away from the violence. The stay in Urias does not last long, as the revolution soon enters Urias.

Ernesto and his family move farther north to Leandro Valle, Mazatlán. Living there, Ernesto soon begins to work, to earn money, and to become part of a gang. He also starts first grade. However, life in Leandro Valle does not last long either, and they leave for the United States.

After many weeks in Tucson, Ernesto and his mother travel by train to Sacramento to meet with Uncle Gustavo and José. With his limited English, Ernesto and his mother find their way in Sacramento, where they live in an apartment at 418 L Street. Ernesto encounters many nationalities, including Japanese, Chinese, and Filipino. The stay in the United States is to remain permanent. Whether it be by season or not, José finds work. Their homes in run-down places are always temporary.

Life in the United States is different for Ernesto. There are no marketplaces, no plazas, no close neighbors. Living in the United States also changes the way some Mexicans behave. For Ernesto, who enters first grade and works odd jobs, his English becomes better. Still, Ernesto and his family remain a Mexican family. *Pocho*, the unflattering name for an Americanized Mexican, is what Henriqueta jokingly calls Ernesto.

With the remarriage of his mother, the family decides to move into a new house in Oak Park, a house outside the barrio surrounded by English-speaking neighbors. Ernesto makes friends with a neighborhood boy, Roy, and soon buys a secondhand bicycle. He explores his new neighborhood and gets a job as a carrier for the city's newspaper. Enrolled at Bret Harte School, Ernesto's knowledge of English develops quickly. His family is impressed by his education and a phone is installed for his use.

Homesickness becomes a problem for his family, but for Ernesto the problem is his responsibility of taking care of his younger sisters. This ordinary daily routine ends when an influenza epidemic spreads into the city. Uncle Gustavo dies, then Ernesto's mother.

With the advice of Mrs. Dodson, the landlady, José and Ernesto look toward the future. They move to a rented basement room on O Street, on the edge of the barrio. Ernesto continues his education and works odd jobs with José. He is hired as a farmhand, and he learns how to drive a tractor. He works as a drugstore clerk, then finds a job as a delivery boy and later as a Christmas card decorator.

During his summer vacation, Ernesto works with other barrio people in the labor camps. He sees how the laborers are mistreated by the contractors, and he goes to the state authorities for help. The laborers do not appreciate his efforts. Summer ends, so Ernesto returns home, bikes his way to the high school, and thinks of his future.

Critical Evaluation:

Barrio Boy is aptly subtitled *The Story of a Boy's Acculturation*. Ernesto Galarza recounts his immigration northward from a small village in Nayarit, Mexico, to the edge of the barrio in Sacramento, California. His adjustments in a new country, a new language, a new lifestyle bring many changes for Galarza. Small town life does not prepare Galarza for the differences he encounters in the cities of Mazatlán and later Sacramento. Ernesto's tenacity and strength, however, allow him not only to survive but also to maintain his sense of identity as a Mexican. Acculturation, then, for Galarza, is not the process of abandoning one's culture but rather is the process of adaptation. This autobiography speaks to those who have traveled to the United States and who have faced the challenges of acculturation.

The autobiography is structured into five sections. Each part confronts Galarza's step-by-step process from being a Mexican to becoming a Mexican American. The first section, "In the Mountain Village," is a study in provincial Mexican life. Everyday mannerisms, traditions, and roles are poignantly played out. The lyrical description of the village and its people reads like a pastoral. One of the longest sections of the autobiography, the first section provides a clear and distinct portrait of Galarza's life before his move north.

When the family leaves the village, life becomes much less idyllic. Being able to settle down proves difficult during a revolution. "Peregrinations," the longest section of the book, tells this part of Galarza's story. Galarza also speaks sincerely of the struggles of the people, whether on burros or on foot, who move northward seeking refuge.

Realizing their best hope lies in emigrating to the United States, the family, in "North from Mexico," makes the decisive journey. Galarza details the train ride he and his mother endure. The train creates in him a discomfort and an uneasiness toward the American people, whom he finds both "agreeable and deplorable."

"Life in the Lower Part of Town" reflects the determination of Galarza and his family to benefit from the opportunities afforded to them. He begins his journey toward acculturation as he learns English and studies in school. He also acknowledges the differences in lifestyle between the Mexican and the Anglo American. He also points out his poverty.

The acculturation of Galarza becomes complete in "On the Edge of the Barrio." Having to learn on his own, Galarza works toward a promise of success. He participates, in his education, in society, and he becomes part of the American working class. His new identity as a Mexican American, because of his social participation, illustrates the positive balance Galarza maintains as a Mexican living in an Anglo American society.

With his life story set against the historical background of the Mexican revolution, Galarza becomes a representative of his era. In essence, *Barrio Boy* offers him a forum to express, to share, and to educate his readers to undiscovered events in history on a personal level. In fact, Galarza seems to want his readers to participate fully in his journey, for he provides a glossary of the Spanish words he believes he could not translate.

Historically speaking, then, *Barrio Boy* is significant in three ways. First, in the recounting of his migratory travels, Galarza exemplifies the immigrant who is uprooted by a social or political event. The long journey to safety and rest is poignantly depicted in the actions of his uncles Gustavo and José. Second, *Barrio Boy* reveals the destitute conditions of the farm laborer. Galarza learns through personal experience the disgusting working conditions and inhumane treatment of migrant workers. Galarza allows his autobiography to become a voice for the oppressed farmworkers. Finally, to acknowledge that in his case the process of acculturation does not psychologically damage him illustrates Galarza's theme for his autobiography: To be able to maintain a cultural identity in a world that focuses on individuality is a social triumph. Certainly, many times in the narrative, Galarza notes homesickness and the comfort of being surrounded by people who speak his language. Yet, he is also able to participate outside the security of his barrio. Accordingly, then, *Barrio Boy* is more than just an immigrant story. Galarza demonstrates the potential of many immigrant Americans who seek new opportunities.

Carmen Carrillo

Further Reading

Flores, Lauro. "Chicano Autobiography: Culture, Ideology and the Self." *The Americas Review* 18, no. 2 (Summer, 1990): 80-91. Explores the style, characterization, and structure of the autobiography. Asserts that *Barrio Boy* shows how society influences the individual.

King, Rosemary A. "*Barrio Boy*: Ernesto Galarza." In *Border Confluences: Borderland Narratives from the Mexican War to the Present*. Tucson: University of Arizona Press, 2004. King's examination of works set on the border between the United States and Mexico includes an analysis of *Barrio Boy*. She focuses on the way Galarza and other writers describe their characters' reactions to cultural differences.

Márquez, Antonio C. "Self and Culture: Autobiography as Cultural Narrative." *Bilingual Review* 14, no. 3 (September-December, 1987/1988): 57-63. Focusing on the theme of acculturation and adaptability, Márquez examines *Barrio Boy* as a celebration of individuality and culture. The themes of self-motivation and cultural pride are emphasized.

Pitti, Stephen J. "Ernesto Galarza, Mexican Immigration, and Farm Labor Organizing in Postwar California." In *The Countryside in the Age of the Modern State: Political Histories of Rural America*, edited by Catherine McNicol Stock and Robert D. Johnston. Ithaca, N.Y.: Cornell University Press, 2001. Galarza was a professor and labor organizer, as well as a writer. Pitti's essay focuses on Galarza's attempts to organize Mexican farm workers.

_______. "Ernesto Galarza Remembered: A Reflection of Graduate Studies in Chicano History." In *Voices of a New Chicana/o History*, edited by Refugio I. Rochín and Dennis N. Valdés. East Lansing: Michigan State University Press, 2000. Focuses on Galarza's scholarly activities.

Robinson, Cecil. *Mexico and the Hispanic Southwest in American Literature*. Rev. ed. Tucson: University of Arizona Press, 1977. Offers an analysis of *Barrio Boy* as an autobiography and social commentary. The place and contribution of *Barrio Boy* to the Hispanic literary tradition also is examined.

Rocard, Marcienne. *The Children of the Sun: Mexican-Americans in the Literature of the United States*. Translated by Edward G. Brown, Jr. Tucson: University of Arizona Press, 1989. Analyzes the internal struggles and conflicts in *Barrio Boy*, as well as other Hispanic novels and autobiographies. *Barrio Boy* is examined as the portrayal of acculturation from the immigrant's point of view. Also examines the politics of acculturation.

Saldîvar, Ramón. "Ideologies of the Self: Chicano Autobiography." *Diacritics* 15, no. 3 (Fall, 1985): 25-34. Analyzes the language and characterization of *Barrio Boy*. Examines individuality and the problems associated with moving from one culture to another. Compares *Barrio Boy* to other Chicano autobiographies.

Barry Lyndon

Author: William Makepeace Thackeray (1811-1863)
First published: serial, 1844; book, 1852
Type of work: Novel
Type of plot: Picaresque
Time of plot: Eighteenth century
Locale: England, Ireland, and continental Europe

Principal characters:
REDMOND BARRY, a braggart and a bully
LADY HONORIA LYNDON, his wife
LORD BULLINGDON, her son

The Story:

Deprived of wealth and estates by relatives, Widow Barry devotes herself to the careful rearing of her son Redmond. Uncle Brady takes a liking to the lad and asks the widow for permission to take the child to his ancestral home, Brady Castle. While there, Barry is treated kindly by his uncle. One of his cousins, Mick, persecutes him, however, and Mrs. Brady hates him. Aggressive by nature, Barry invites animosity; his landless pride in his ancestral heritage leads him into repeated neighborhood brawls until he fights every lad in the area and acquires the reputation of a bully. At age fifteen, he falls in love with twenty-four-year-old Nora Brady, who is in love with Captain John Quinn, an Englishman. Deeply in debt, Uncle Brady hopes that Nora will marry the captain, who promises to pay some of the old man's debts. Thoroughly unscrupulous and lacking in appreciation for his uncle's kindness, Barry insults Quinn in a fit of jealousy and wounds him in a duel.

Believing the captain dead, Barry hurriedly sets out on the road to Dublin. On the way, he befriends Mrs. Fitzsimons, the victim of a highway robbery. She takes him to her castle where Barry spends some of his own money in a lavish attempt to create a good impression. When he loses all his money through high living and gambling, Mrs. Fitzsimons and her husband are glad to see him leave.

Barry next takes King George's shilling and enlists for a military expedition in Europe. Boarding the crowded and filthy ship, he learns that Quinn did not die after all but married Nora Brady; the pistols were loaded only with tow. Detesting service in the British army, Barry deserts to the Prussians. At the end of the Seven Years' War, he is garrisoned in Berlin. By that time, he is known as a thorough scoundrel and a quarrelsome bully. Sent by Frederick the Great to spy on the Chevalier Balibari, suspected of being an Austrian agent, Barry learns that the officer is his own father's brother, Barry of Ballybarry. This elderly gentleman actually made his way by gambling, rising and falling in wealth as his luck ran. When the gambler decides to leave Berlin, Barry, eager to escape from Prussian service, disguises himself and flees to Dresden. There he joins his uncle, who is high in favor at the Saxon court.

Barry, living like a highborn gentleman, supports himself by operating a gambling table. At the court of the duke of X—, he pursues Countess Ida, one of the wealthiest heiresses in the duchy. Disliking the countess personally but greatly admiring her fortune, he ruthlessly sets about to win her from her fiancé, the Chevalier De Magny. Gambling with the hapless man, Barry wins from him all he possesses. At last, De Magny agrees to play for the hand of Countess Ida and loses. Barry's scheme might have succeeded if had he not become involved in a court intrigue. He is forced to leave the duchy.

Roaming through all the famous cities of Europe, Barry acquires a wide reputation as a skillful gambler. At Spa, he meets Lord Charles and Lady Honoria Lyndon, who hold the former Barry lands, and he decides to marry Lady Lyndon following the death of her sick husband. A year later, hearing that Lord Charles died at Castle Lyndon in Ireland, he sets out to woo Lady Lyndon. Employing numerous underhanded devices, including blackmail, bribery, dueling, and intimidation, Barry forces himself upon Lady Lyndon, who at first resists his suit. Barry, however, pursues the lady relentlessly, bribing her servants, spying on her every move, paying her homage, and stealing her correspondence. When she flees to London to escape his persistent attentions, he follows her. At last, he overcomes her aversion and objections, and she agrees to become his wife. Adding her name to his own, he becomes Barry Lyndon, Esq.

Although she is haughty and overbearing by nature, Lady Lyndon soon yields to the harsh dominance of her husband, who treats her brutally and thwarts her attempts to control her own fortune. After a few days of marriage, the Lyndons go to Ireland, where he immediately assumes management of the Lyndon estates. Living in high fashion, he spends money freely in order to establish himself as a gentleman in the community. When Lady Lyndon attempts to protest, he complains of her ill temper; if she pleads for affection, he calls her a nag. The abuse he showers upon her is reflected in the way he uses her son, Lord Bullingdon, who, unlike his mother, does not submit meekly to Barry's malice.

The birth of Bryan Lyndon adds to Barry's problems. Since the estate is entailed upon Lord Bullingdon, young Bryan will have no rights of inheritance to Lady Lyndon's property. To provide for his son, Barry sells some of the timber on the estates over the protests of Lord Bullingdon's guardian. Barry gives the money obtained to his mother, who uses it to repurchase the old Barry lands, which Barry intends to bequeath to his son. Barry is actively despised in the community, but through foul means and cajolery, he wins a seat in Parliament and uses his victory to triumph over his enemies.

Barry makes no attempt to disguise his contempt and his disgust for his wife, who under his profligacy becomes petulant. When she rebels against his conduct, he threatens to remove Bryan from her; she is subdued many times in this manner. Little Bryan is completely spoiled by his father's indulgence. Barry also contrives to rid himself of his stepson, who finally obliges by running off to America to fight against the rebels. Barry's enemies use Lord Bullingdon's flight to slander the Irish upstart, and the young man's legal guardians continue their efforts to curb the wasteful dissipation of Lady Lyndon's wealth, which is dwindling under Barry's administration. In the end, Barry's unpopularity causes him to lose his seat in Parliament.

Heavily in debt, he retires to Castle Lyndon. When Lord Bullingdon is reported killed in America, young Bryan becomes heir to the estates. Soon afterward, the boy dies when thrown from his horse. His death causes Lady Lyndon such anguish that a report spreads that she is mad. Barry and his mother, now the mistress of Castle Lyndon, treat Lady Lyndon shabbily. Keeping her virtually a prisoner, spying on her every move, and denying her intercourse with her friends, they almost drive her mad. Under the necessity of signing some papers, she tricks Barry into taking her to London. There her indignant relatives and Lord George Poynings, Lady Lyndon's former suitor, gather to free the unhappy woman from his custody; Barry is trapped.

Offered the alternative of going to jail as a swindler or of leaving the country with an annuity of three hundred pounds, he chooses the latter. Later, he returns secretly to England and nearly succeeds in winning back his weak-willed wife. His attempt is foiled, however, by Lord Bullingdon, who reappears suddenly after he was reported dead. Barry is thrown into the Fleet Prison, where he dies suffering from delirium tremens.

Critical Evaluation:

Published three years before *Vanity Fair* (1847-1848, serial; 1848, book), William Makepeace Thackeray's *The Luck of Barry Lyndon: A Romance of the Last Century*, as it was titled in serial presentation, is a minor masterpiece of classic comedy, and it embodies many of the same concerns with sham, materialistic values, and egoism found in the later novel. Both novels feature the kind of antihero more familiar, perhaps, to later readers than to Thackeray's contemporaries. In fact, there are distinct resemblances between *Vanity Fair*'s picara, Becky Sharpe, whose sharp practices, manipulation, and emotional blackmail arouse ambivalent delight in readers, and Barry, the appealing rogue who, reprehensible as his values may be, is yet true to his own code. His autobiography, cast in the form of an adult's remembrance of about forty years of his life, shows Thackeray's skillful handling of time and his imaginative creation of picaresque episodes, in the course of which Barry ingenuously, naïvely, yet arrogantly reveals his vices and ambiguous virtues.

Thackeray is much more than a social historian in *Barry Lyndon*. The three-part arrangement of the novel shows Barry as an adolescent in Ireland, where he falls in love for the first time; then abroad in English and Prussian military service, gambling in Europe; and finally, upon his return to England, having become militarily and financially successful, making a marital conquest as well. In the tradition of Daniel Defoe, Tobias Smollett, and Henry Fielding, Thackeray presents a picaro who reveals the tawdriness of empire and gaming as well as reflects the kinds of truths by which all people deceive themselves.

The tone of *Barry Lyndon*, with its combination of the conversational and the confessional, may not seem all that close to the tone of the author's mature fiction. However suited to the character the unselfconscious admissions of the narrative are, there is an air of levity and inconsequence about them that is missing from Thackeray's later works. However, the reader will not have read very much of *Barry Lyndon* before realizing that the hero's unaffected air of candor and completeness is being used to highly ironic purposes by the author. The result is that the novel may be thought to consist of two narratives: that of the hero and that of the author. The latter undermines the former, and the causes of this disruption are the result of nothing more than the hero's excesses. This complicated narrative interplay has a number of noteworthy consequences.

On one hand, it suggests that the author's intent is not to indulge his hero's narrative or to let it stand on its own account. Barry's amoral, improvised, opportunistic existence is not merely a colorful yarn or an episodic tissue of adventures. Its excesses produce their own moral counterpoint. This anticipates the situation in *Vanity Fair*, where Becky's unprincipled behavior calls forth the author's most stringent moral irony. In that novel, Thackeray contrasts a world of dazzling extravagance and exploitation with the virtues of domesticity and conjugal love. Thackeray's moral vision is not yet as comprehensively laid out in *Barry Lyndon*, but its origins are clearly visible, lacking only a medium other than the author's implicit critique of his hero to articulate them.

The issue of tone and of its implications is not confined to aesthetic considerations alone but pertains also to the question of genre. It is known from the publication of Thackeray's own nonfictional writings that he had a strong interest in English eighteenth century fiction and that one of his main interests was the manner in which he maintained lines of continuity with earlier novelistic practices.

It is a common critical practice to relate *Barry Lyndon* to Henry Fielding's *The History of the Life of the Late Mr. Jonathan Wild the Great* (1743). Fielding's novel, however, was a satirical adaptation of a popular genre literature of roguery. Works in this category depicted the brazen, criminal, and generally subversive careers of adventurers, men and women without attachment, commitment, or consistency, whose behavior represented a form of freedom as dangerous for the settled citizenry who came their way as for the protagonists themselves. This category owes much to picaresque fiction, one of the formative imaginative influences on the development of the novel. In *Barry Lyndon*, Thackeray reveals the intersection of an eighteenth century form with a nineteenth century sensibility, allowing on the one hand the protagonist's extemporaneous existence but ensuring on the other hand that such an existence is being depicted to exemplify a code of values that is the antithesis of those with which the protagonist identifies. Thackeray was by no means the only author of his day to adapt the literature of roguery to contemporary purposes—evidence of similar interests may be found in the work of Charles Dickens, and another contemporary of theirs, Harrison Ainsworth, made a successful career from the same practice.

Although Thackeray fully engages his moralizing imagination in *Barry Lyndon*, he appears also to distance himself from his own effects by permitting Barry to tell his own story—so that his own words will condemn him—and by conceiving his narrative in terms of an already existing genre. A further, and equally revealing, distancing tactic is the work's Irish dimension. If Thackeray were interested merely in drawing a moral lesson by depicting the counterproductive career of a picaresque hero, there would be no need to invoke an Irish element. The fact that one exists may be attributed to the commercial success achieved by Irish novelists in the early Victorian literary marketplace with their own picaresque works. Many of these works placed their protagonists in the setting of the Napoleonic wars, in which the improvisations and quirks of fortune endemic to the picaresque hero's career became identified with a positive, and even virtuous, historical outcome. In *Barry Lyndon*, Thackeray undoes such possibilities, for Barry's military service is not with the forces of the Crown. By this means, as well as by depicting Barry's empty social pretension and his generally amoral behavior, Thackeray presents him as retaining a stereotypical Irishness. Thackeray uses this ethnic label as a synonym for Barry's failure to integrate himself with the morality, decorum, laws of property, and codes of gentlemanliness that a responsible member of British society must observe. Thackeray ultimately presents the reader with an ideological and a political judgment as well as a moral one.

"Critical Evaluation" by George O'Brien

Further Reading

Altinal, A. Savkar. *Thackeray and the Problem of Realism.* New York: Peter Lang, 1986. Includes a chapter in which *Barry Lyndon* is discussed within the context of Thackeray's beginnings as a novelist; the discussion focuses mainly on the hero's character. Assesses the novel's artistic achievements and its place in Thackeray's development.

Clarke, Micael M. *Thackeray and Women.* DeKalb: Northern Illinois University Press, 1995. Examines Thackeray's life, novels, and other works from a feminist-sociological perspective to analyze his treatment of female characters, demonstrating how his writings critique the position of women in Western culture. Includes bibliographical references and an index.

Colby, Robert. "*Barry Lyndon* and the Irish Hero." *Nineteenth Century Fiction* 21 (September, 1966): 109-130. Locates the novel in the Thackeray canon and identifies sources for the story. Discusses Thackeray's narrative method as well as relevant contextual matters. The main emphasis is on the ways in which the novel reveals Thackeray's creative rereading of contemporary Irish fiction.

Fisher, Judith L. *Thackeray's Skeptical Narrative and the "Perilous Trade" of Authorship.* Burlington, Vt.: Ashgate, 2002. An analysis of Thackeray's narrative techniques, describing how he sought to create a "kind of poised reading which enables his readers to integrate his fiction into their life."

Harden, Edgar F. *Thackeray the Writer: From Journalism to "Vanity Fair."* New York: St. Martin's Press, 1998.

_______. *Thackeray the Writer: From "Pendennis" to "Denis Duval."* New York: Macmillan, 2000. Two-volume biography chronicling Thackeray's development as a writer, beginning with his experiences as a book reviewer and culminating in the creation of *Vanity Fair.* Traces how Thackeray became an increasingly perceptive social observer.

Hardy, Barbara. *Forms of Feeling in Victorian Fiction*. London: Peter Owen, 1985. Contains a chapter on Thackeray that makes a number of pertinent observations about *Barry Lyndon*. Analyzes the novel's comic character and the hero's emotional nature. Notes the relation between these features and the novel's structure.

Parker, David. "Thackeray's *Barry Lyndon*." *Ariel* 6 (October, 1975): 68-80. Relates the novel to eighteenth century literature of roguery. Examines Thackeray's tonal and formal adaptations of that literary model as well as his moralistic approach to his material.

Shillingsburg, Peter. *William Makepeace Thackeray: A Literary Life*. New York: Palgrave, 2001. An excellent introduction to the life of the novelist, thorough and scholarly, but accessible. Includes a chapter on reading *Vanity Fair,* notes, and index.

Taylor, D. J. *Thackeray: The Life of a Literary Man*. New York: Carroll and Graf, 2001. A lengthy biography that argues for Thackeray's preeminence among nineteenth century English novelists. A generally comprehensive study of the man that sheds much light on his work.

Bartholomew Fair

Author: Ben Jonson (1573-1637)
First produced: 1614; first published, 1631
Type of work: Drama
Type of plot: Satire
Time of plot: Early seventeenth century
Locale: Smithfield, London

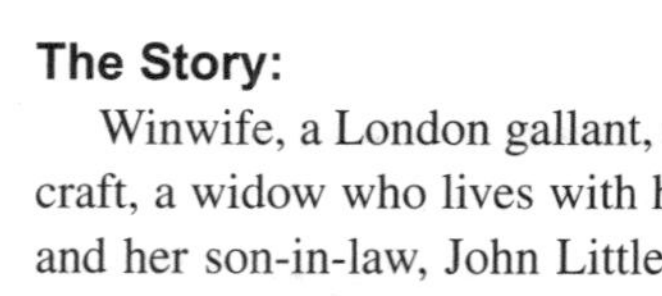

Principal characters:
JOHN LITTLEWIT, a minor city official
WIN-THE-FIGHT or WIN, his wife
DAME PURECRAFT, her mother, a widow
ZEAL-OF-THE-LAND BUSY, a Puritan, suitor of Dame Purecraft
WINWIFE, Busy's rival, a London gallant
QUARLOUS, Winwife's friend, a gamester
BARTHOLOMEW COKES, a foolish young squire
GRACE WELLBORN, Cokes's fiancé
HUMPHREY WASPE, Cokes's servant
ADAM OVERDO, a justice of the peace
DAME OVERDO, his wife
URSULA, owner of a booth at Bartholomew Fair
TROUBLE-ALL, a madman

The Story:

Winwife, a London gallant, comes courting Dame Purecraft, a widow who lives with her daughter, Win-the-Fight, and her son-in-law, John Littlewit, a proctor. Littlewit discloses to Winwife that Dame Purecraft was told by fortune-tellers that she will marry, within a week, a madman. In this connection, Littlewit suggests to Winwife that he deport himself in the manner of his companion Tom Quarlous, a city madcap.

Quarlous, entering in search of Winwife, kisses Win-the-Fight several times until Winwife cautions him to desist. Littlewit, who is not too acute, actually encourages Winwife and Quarlous to be free with his wife. Littlewit also reveals to his visitors that Dame Purecraft has a new suitor, one Zeal-of-the-Land Busy, a Puritan from Banbury. Busy has taken lodgings in Littlewit's house.

Humphrey Waspe, the testy old servant of young Bartholomew Cokes, a foolish gentleman of the provinces, comes to Littlewit to pick up a marriage license for his master. Soon afterward, Cokes appears in company with two women. One is Mistress Overdo, his natural sister and the wife of Justice Adam Overdo; the other is Grace Wellborn, Cokes's fiancé and Overdo's ward. It is clear that Waspe is the servant of an extremely light-headed young man. Cokes declares his intention of squiring Grace to Bartholomew Fair before they return to Middlesex. Waspe objects but finally resigns himself to the inevitable. Winwife and Quarlous, sensing fun at hand, decide to go along. Not wishing to miss the fun, Littlewit declares that he will go too. Dame Purecraft and Busy both rationalize Puritan strictures against attending fairs and give the young couple permission to go so that Win might eat roast pig; Busy and the widow declare their intention of going with them to Bartholomew Fair.

In disguise and with a notebook in his pocket, Justice Overdo goes to the fair to seek out criminals and to record lawlessness. Suspecting Ursula, a seller of beer and roast pig, Overdo stops at her booth to test her. As he drinks, various shady personalities enter the booth. He asks Mooncalf, Ursula's handyman, for information about them all, but Mooncalf's replies are always vague. Overdo conceives a feeling of sympathy for one Edgeworth, a young cutpurse, although not suspecting Edgeworth's profession. Overdo decides he should rescue the young man from such knavish company.

At Ursula's booth, where Winwife and Quarlous condescendingly stop for a drink, Quarlous becomes involved in a fight with Knockem, a horse trader. Ursula, running from her kitchen to throw hot grease on Winwife and Quarlous, stumbles, and the grease burns her leg. Knockem declares that he will operate her booth while she sits by to oversee the business.

Cokes and his party arrive at the fair and make their way to Ursula's booth, where Overdo warns them against the evils of tobacco and ale. Edgeworth steals Cokes's purse and gives it to his confederate, Nightingale, a ballad monger. Mistress Overdo observes that Overdo, who is in disguise, speaks much in the manner of her own husband, Justice Adam Overdo. Missing his purse, Cokes declares indiscreetly that he has another one and that he defies cutpurses by placing it on his belt where the other one had been. Waspe, suspecting Overdo to be the cutpurse, thrashes the justice. As Overdo cries for help, Cokes and his party leave Ursula's booth.

Busy leads Littlewit, Win, and Dame Purecraft into the fair, after cautioning them to look neither to left nor right and to avoid the sinful booths as they march toward Ursula's booth to get roast pig. While they wait to be served, Overdo reappears, still determined to observe the goings on, but without preaching. Cokes and his party, burdened with trinkets, also return to the booth. Waspe is miserable because Cokes is spending his money on every foolish article offered him. When a toyman and a gingerbread woman argue over customer rights, Cokes buys the wares of both and even retains the toyman to provide entertainment at the forthcoming marriage. Nightingale and Edgeworth fear that Cokes will spend all of his money before they can get at him again. Nightingale sings a ballad while Edgeworth lifts the second purse from the enchanted Cokes's belt. Winwife and Quarlous look on with amusement. When Cokes realizes his loss and cries out, Overdo, who is standing nearby, is seized as a suspect. Waspe, sure that Cokes will lose everything he possesses, takes into his care a black box containing the marriage license.

Quarlous, meanwhile, discloses to Edgeworth that he has been detected stealing Cokes's purse. In exchange for secrecy, Edgeworth promises to steal the contents of the black box.

Busy and his friends eat pork at Ursula's booth. Encountering the toyman and the gingerbread woman, Busy, in a moment of religious zeal, attempts to seize the wicked toys and upset the tray of gingerbread figures. The toyman calls police officers, who take Busy, followed by Dame Purecraft, away to be put in the stocks. Littlewit and Win are now free to enjoy the fair as they choose.

Overdo, also in the stocks, overhears to his shame that he has a reputation for harshness in meting out justice. He does not reveal himself when the officers take him and Busy away to face Justice Overdo.

While Cokes is looking for the toyman and the gingerbread woman, in hopes of getting his money back from them, he is intercepted by Nightingale and Edgeworth, who trick him out of his hat, jacket, and sword. Wretched Cokes begins to understand at last that he was grievously abused at the fair.

In another part of the fair, Winwife and Quarlous, who attract Grace away from her group, draw swords to decide a dispute as to who should have Cokes's attractive young fiancé. Grace bids them not to fight; at her suggestion, each writes a word on a tablet. The first passerby is to choose the word he likes the better. The one whose word is thus chosen will win the hand of Grace, who decides that Cokes is not the man for her. This business is interrupted, however, when Edgeworth urges both men to watch him steal the marriage license from Waspe, who is with the crowd in Ursula's booth.

Waspe and his companions, including Mistress Overdo, are drinking ale; all are quite intoxicated. When Waspe gets into a scuffle with Knockem, Edgeworth takes the license from the black box. Quarlous laughs at the drunken antics of one of the group and has to fight. Officers enter and seize Waspe for disturbing the peace.

Littlewit, who has written the story of the puppet show, leaves Win at Ursula's booth while he joins the puppeteers. While she waits, Win meets Captain Whit, a bawd, who tells her that he knows how she can live a life of endless pleasure and wealth.

Unable to find Justice Overdo at his lodgings, the officers return their prisoners to the stocks. Waspe, brought to the stocks, manages to escape before his legs can be confined. When a madman engages an officer in a scuffle, Overdo and Busy also escape, the lock of the stocks being left unclasped. Dame Purecraft suddenly falls in love with the madman Trouble-All, a lawyer who is distracted because of a past misunderstanding with Justice Overdo.

Later Quarlous, disguised as the madman and pursued by Dame Purecraft, returns to Winwife and Grace. Meanwhile, the real madman chooses Winwife's word, "Palemon." Grace then declares that she will become Winwife's spouse. Overdo, disguised as a porter, comes upon Quarlous. Anxious to help the man whom he brought to distraction, Overdo gives him a seal and warrant for anything within reason that he might desire.

Cokes finds his way to the puppet theater, where he borrows money from Littlewit. When Captain Whit, Knockem, and Edgeworth come to the theater, they have with them Win, masked, and Mistress Overdo, who is sick from too much ale. Captain Whit offers Win to Overdo for his pleasure. Waspe also comes to the theater and joins his young master. The play is presented; it is an idiotic blending of the legends of Hero and Leander and Damon and Pythias. During the showing, Busy enters and threatens to break up the theater. Persuaded to argue the sinfulness of the puppet theater with one of the puppets, he is soundly defeated in the argument.

Quarlous, still disguised as the madman, comes with Grace to the theater. Littlewit, who went in search of Win, returns without her. The true madman and Ursula enter. When all are together, Overdo declares his intention of punishing all who engaged in rascality. When Quarlous questions his judgment and reveals Edgeworth as a cutpurse and not an innocent youth, as the justice supposed, Overdo decides there is such a thing as false judgment and that humanity is weak. Quarlous wins the hand of Dame Purecraft. Reassured that restitution will be made all around, Overdo invites everyone to his house for dinner.

Critical Evaluation:

Two years after the first performance of *Bartholomew Fair*, Ben Jonson published his accumulated plays in a folio volume entitled *Works*. Such an act was as unprecedented as it was audacious, because it implied both that Jonson considered himself worthy of serious attention as a writer and that the stage drama of the time should be considered an important part of literature.

Bartholomew Fair comes from Jonson's greatest period as a comic dramatist. It is one of Jonson's most direct defenses of drama (and art in general), a form that, although illusory, is a means to the truth. The play is also a clear portrayal of the reality of the world's evil and a plea for a sober appreciation of the depth of that evil. Like Jonson's *Volpone* (1605), *Epicœne* (1609), and *The Alchemist* (1610), *Bartholomew Fair* is characterized by a remarkable unity provided by a particular event or location. Plot and character are thus focused around a prevailing mania or social evil particular to that event or place. Jonson, in all these plays, makes an incisive analysis of the social scene and shows his opposition to humanity's acquisitive tendencies.

Bartholomew Fair teems with life and is probably unsurpassed for its delineation of English types—especially the low types—of the period. Jonson also holds the society of his day up for criticism in such figures as Zeal-of-the-Land Busy, the Puritan; Adam Overdo, the zealous justice of the peace; and Bartholomew Cokes, the well-to-do simpleton from Middlesex. That no great evil is done in the play and that no one comes to any grief indicates that Jonson, although a satirist, feels a real affection for all people in his beloved London.

Bartholomew Fair's main plot, if there can be said to be one, is the story, reminiscent of *The Arabian Nights' Entertainments* of Harun-al-Rashid, of Adam Overdo's mingling, in disguise, among people to whom he metes out justice. The other plots are hinted at rather than developed. The play is framed by an "induction" given by the stagekeeper and the bookholder, in which the illusory character of drama as reality is raised for the audience's consideration. The induction includes an agreement between the audience and the author about what the audience can and cannot expect in the forthcoming drama, with a reminder that the audience should not look for real persons in the characters on stage, nor should it expect to see the Smithfield fair presented there. This disclaimer is ironic, because Jonson intends that his audience see itself in his characters. At the end of the play, the audience is invited to participate in the final celebration at Overdo's house, thus bringing the convention of life-as-drama full circle by drawing the audience into the world of the fair.

The puppet play that occurs in act 5 is the center of Jonson's statement about drama and art. The puppet play is referred to in each act, since Littlewit has written the script and several characters look forward to attending the production. It is the climax of *Bartholomew Fair*; in the puppet play, the various characters' delusions are torn away. The range of possible aesthetic reactions to the illusion of drama is nicely detailed by the play-within-a-play. There is Cokes's naïve belief, Busy's Puritan denunciation of the theater, and

Leatherhead's manipulation (as puppetmaster) of the audience's sensibilities. Grace, Winwife, and others in the audience not only watch the puppet show but also comment on Cokes's and Busy's comments, while Jonson's audience or reader observes those observers. Cokes worries about the injury one of the puppets may have received with a blow on the head and naïvely repeats all the puppets' lines as truth. Busy carries on the traditional Puritan argument against theater with the puppet Dionysius, charging that actors are unnatural since in theater, males dress up as females. The puppet answers that puppets are neither male nor female and lifts his garment to prove it. Busy, so gullible as to believe he is seriously arguing with a person, accepts the puppet's refutation.

The puppet show reduces the two greatest myths of Renaissance literature—the Hero and Leander ideal of love and the Damon and Pythias ideal of friendship—to the story of Hero the whore and the alehouse rowdies Damon and Pythias. The obscenities and scatological references in the puppet play are appropriate in the context, in which humanity is reduced to that most elemental level at which even sexual differences disappear, as in the puppets themselves.

The protagonist of the play is the fair itself, and Bartholomew Fair becomes a metaphor for the world. The two sets of characters—the respectable fairgoers and the disreputable fair employees—are seen to be essentially alike. They come together in the common acts of buying, drinking, and eating. Finally, there is no difference between them. The madness of the fair is the madness of the world. Certain words recur as motifs in the play, and the action comes to reflect these words: "vapours," meaning a game of arguing or irrational whims; "mad" and "madness"; "enormity"; and "warrant," meaning license. For Jonson, the whole world is regarded as mad, governed by follies and vapours, committing enormities of one sort or another, entirely governed by irrationalities, and seeking warrants of various kinds to justify its behavior.

Different characters refuse to accept the fair for what it is or to acknowledge the reality of the world's madness. Overdo disguises himself in order to catch troublemakers and mete out justice; instead, he is always too late and is mistaken for a criminal himself. Cokes is blinded by his innocent country origins and duped over and over again. Busy deceives himself by equating the fair not with the world but with sin. He reduces himself to an animal by closing his eyes to keep out the corruption of the fair and sniffing his way to Ursula's tent for roast pig. Dame Purecraft goes to the opposite extreme by embracing madness; falling in love with the madman Trouble-All is a way out of the madness of the world. As she says, "Mad do they call him! the world is mad in error, but he is mad in truth." Ursula is the only one who accepts her role without illusion or inhibition. She is a caricature of an earth mother—fat and gross, but honest.

Each of these characters, with the exception of Ursula, makes elaborate attempts to disguise from himself or herself the true nature of humanity; humanity's animal nature is fully expressed at the fair. Justice Adam Overdo is gently chastened at the end of the play by Quarlous with a line that can stand for Jonson's reminder to his audience: "Remember you are but Adam, flesh and blood." In *Bartholomew Fair*, Jonson does not try to change the world; instead he urges acceptance, without illusion, of the corruption of the world.

"Critical Evaluation" by Margaret McFadden-Gerber

Further Reading

Barish, Jonas. *Ben Jonson and the Language of Prose Comedy*. Cambridge, Mass.: Harvard University Press, 1960. A masterful discussion of Jonson's comic language and an important starting point for study of Jonson's dramatic works. Convincingly argues for *Bartholomew Fair* as Jonson's masterpiece.

Barton, Anne. *Ben Jonson, Dramatist*. New York: Cambridge University Press, 1984. Compelling discussion of Jonson's interests in chaos and order. Offers an important chapter on the use of names and naming—an obsessive interest of Jonson's across his career—in the context of discussions of names and language from Plato to historian William Camden, Jonson's contemporary and teacher.

Bowers, Rick. *Radical Comedy in Early Modern England: Contexts, Cultures, Performances*. Burlington, Vt.: Ashgate, 2008. Applies the theories of Mikhail Bakhtin and other philosophers to analyze early modern English comedies, describing the types of humor employed in these plays and how they satirize political, religious, and medical authority. Chapter 8 discusses *Bartholomew Fair* and several of Jonson's other plays.

Donaldson, Ian. *Jonson's Magic Houses: Essays in Interpretation*. New York: Oxford University Press, 1997. Donaldson, a Jonson scholar, provides new interpretations of Jonson's personality, work, and literary legacy.

________. *The World Upside Down*. Oxford, England: Clarendon Press, 1970. Views the play as festive in its forms and themes, and explores the anthropology of festivity. Excellent insights into the play's relevance to the court of James I.

Harp, Richard, and Stanley Stewart, eds. *The Cambridge Companion to Ben Jonson*. New York: Cambridge University Press, 2000. Collection of essays about Jonson's life and career, including analyses of his comedies and late plays, a description of London and its theaters during Jonson's lifetime, and an evaluation of his critical heritage.

Loxley, James. *A Sourcebook*. New York: Routledge, 2002. An introductory overview of Jonson's life and work, particularly useful for students. Part 1 provides biographical information and places Jonson's life and work within the context of his times; part 2 discusses several works, including *Bartholomew Fair*; part 3 offers critical analysis of the themes in his plays, the style of his writing, and a comparison of his work to that of William Shakespeare.

McEvoy, Sean. *Ben Jonson, Renaissance Dramatist*. Edinburgh: Edinburgh University Press, 2008. McEvoy analyzes all of Jonson's plays, attributing their greatness to the playwright's commitment to the ideals of humanism during a time of authoritarianism and rampant capitalism in England. Chapter 7 focuses on *Bartholomew Fair*.

Mardock, James D. *Our Scene Is London: Ben Jonson's City and the Space of the Author*. New York: Routledge, 2008. Describes how *Bartholomew Fair* and some of Jonson's other plays dealt with Londoners' conceptions of their city and the space in which they lived.

Martin, Mathew R. *Between Theater and Philosophy: Skepticism in the Major City Comedies of Ben Jonson and Thomas Middleton*. Newark: University of Delaware Press, 2001. Martin provides deconstructionist and other modern critical interpretations of *Bartholomew Fair* and several other Jonson plays.

Batouala

Author: René Maran (1887-1960)
First published: Batouala, véritable romannègre, 1921 (English translation, 1922; definitive edition, 1972)
Type of work: Novel
Type of plot: Social realism
Time of plot: c. 1910
Locale: Ubangi-Shari and French Equatorial Africa

Principal characters:
BATOUALA, the chief of many villages
YASSIGUI'NDJA, the first and favorite of Batouala's nine wives
BISSIBI'NGUI, a handsome young man who seduces Batouala's wives
I'NDOUVOURA, another of Batouala's wives

The Story:

At the start of the day, the great chief Batouala arises at dawn to his usual morning ritual of scratching himself, yawning, rubbing his eyes with the back of his hand, and making love to his sleeping wife—all mundane acts he performs daily and mindlessly. His days consist of a morning smoke, his favorite pastime; breakfast with Yassigui'ndja, his first and favorite but childless wife; and disdainful reflections on how the whites' way of life is different from his. Because his thoughts and actions are tradition-inspired, he rejects anything that opposes custom. He muses disdainfully on the ridiculousness of whites, the *boundjous*, who are "the vilest and most perfidious of men" and therefore worthy of contempt. Their "witches' inventions"—from shoes and the radio to the telescope and the bicycle—their proud claim of knowing "everything and then some," their atrocities and exploitation of the natives in the name of civilization, their paternalism and enslavement of the black people, and their "malignity and omniscience" make them "terrifying." Unlike the Banda concept of life and work, the *boundjous'* concept of work means fatigue without immediate or tangible remuneration. More important to Batouala, the guardian of obsolete customs, the *boundjous* robbed the villagers of their dances and songs, their whole life. Batouala vows that he will not tire of telling about the *boundjous'* cruelty, duplicity, and greed until his last breath.

Batouala begins his formal duties by summoning the villagers, among them Bissibi'ngui, to remind them of the approaching feast of the Ga'nza, three days hence. Unbeknown to Batouala, Bissibi'ngui, a young, handsome, muscular womanizer, popular among the village women, slept with eight of Batouala's nine wives. The exception is Yassigui'ndja, to whom Bissibi'ngui is attracted but whom he did not yet seduce. Feeling young and "rich in unused passion," particularly since Batouala is beginning to grow old and seems mostly interested in smoking his pipe, Yassigui'ndja is tempted to and does finally accept Bissibi'ngui's advances, intimating through her musings that Batouala, although a good husband, no longer satisfies her sexually.

Batouala's suspicions about Yassigui'ndja and Bissibi'ngui are aroused, and shortly thereafter confirmed, during the climax of the fertility dance of the Ga'nza ceremony, when "all things are permitted, even perversions and sins against custom." Seized with the drunkenness of the dance, Yassigui'ndja and Bissibi'ngui fall to the ground entwined, but they are soon separated by the enraged, knife-wielding Batouala, who swears to skin his wife and emasculate her seducer. The feverish festival of the Ga'nza ends abruptly, but not until Batouala's drunken father dies from a heavy dose of Pernod, "foreign kene" (the white man's liquor). Because the villagers' dances and songs are forbidden by the colonial administration, Batouala's people are able to satisfy their customs only in the absence of the French commandant. At his approach, however, the drunken villagers flee, leaving behind the dead body of Batouala's father.

After the customary two-week ritual burial of Batouala's father, Batouala begins planning his revenge on Bissibi'ngui. While the men are out burning the bush and arranging the nets for the great annual hunt, Yassingui'ndja and Bissibi'ngui pledge their desire to possess each other. The villagers hold Yassigui'ndja responsible for the death of Batouala's father, and they threaten to ascertain her guilt by subjecting her to a series of violent tests. Bissibi'ngui agrees to leave the village and become a soldier, but not until after the great annual hunt. Joining Batouala and his hunting party, wily Bissibi'ngui schemes to kill Batouala, the renowned hunter warrior. The hunt begins, but not before a panther bounds into their midst, causing confusion. Taking advantage of the pandemonium, Batouala aims his lance at Bissibi'ngui, his *ouandja* (enemy), but misses. Disturbed by the confusion and Batouala's flying spear, the enraged panther mauls and disembowels Batouala, the great chief and celebrated warrior, whose exploits in love and in war are unparalleled.

Chaos prevails for two weeks of exorcism, fetishes, and incantations, and the villagers finally give up all hope of saving their chief. While Batouala lies dying, the villagers plunder his belongings, raid his flock, and steal his weapons. In his delirium, Batouala reproaches the whites. Emboldened, Yassigui'ndja and Bissibi'ngui make love in his hut. Suddenly, in one final defiant gesture, the chief rises from his bed and lunges at the pair, causing them to flee into the night. Batouala collapses and dies. The great chief is felled by *Mourou*, the panther, and by the implacable witchcraft of *Do'ndorro*.

"The Story" by Pamela J. Olubunmi Smith

Critical Evaluation:

Batouala is important not as a story—although within its modest limits it provokes suspense and sustains interest in the affairs of its characters—but as a sensitive evocation of the experience of being an African native in the French Congo. René Maran, who was born in Martinique, served from 1909 until 1925 as a member of the diplomatic service of the French government in French Equatorial Africa. His novel, the result of six years of study and writing, is an attempt to render in a thoroughly objective manner the thoughts, beliefs, and attitudes of an African chief.

The attempt to be objective in the presentation of thoughts and attitudes necessarily involves the author's sympathetic extension of his imagination. Maran's work rings true not because he is a black man—for the knowledge of the temperament and the customs of the black Africans is not inherited with skin color—but because he is concerned about the people of whose lives he writes and because, like them, he has come to love life and to condemn the French colonialism that did so much to destroy the values of life for the African natives.

The technique of the novel can be described as stream of consciousness, supplemented to some extent with descriptive passages that maintain the perspective of the African. At the same time, the persons whose experiences are being evoked are not of the same society as their author but removed, both spatially and in terms of culture, from the world of this stranger who is attempting to reconstruct the tenor of their days. To overcome the distance between himself and his subjects, Maran adopts a modification of the speech of the Africans; he writes as if their minds were speaking, and he retains their native phrasing. More important, he manages to express the smoldering, helpless anger that is part of the daily experience of Africans dominated by the white invaders. Such writing is objective in the sense that it communicates what is, in fact, part of someone's experience; but it is passionate and subjective because the reader can sense that the author shares the anger and, by sharing it, throws in his lot with that of his characters.

This brief novel, which does no more than tell how a young man's desire for the favorite wife of his chief is finally satisfied as the chief lies dying from the wound of a panther's bite, succeeds remarkably well in immersing the reader in a complete and foreign world. Considered didactically, the novel is powerfully effective because of its success representing the experiences of the African.

Maran's indictment of the colonial administrators in the introduction to his novel speaks of the vileness of colonialization and of civilization built on corpses. He calls on his fellow writers to correct France's brutal policies. These remarks, however impassioned, do not compete in persuasive power with the sparse, bitter comments of the Africans themselves in the novel. The characters refer to the way they are treated like slaves, punished unreasonably, and used as police to keep their own brothers in line; the whites are indicted for lying, for believing lies, and for callously dismissing the suffering and death of the natives. One incident in the novel tells of the French commandant who, upon hearing of Batouala's imminent death, cheerfully replies that Batouala can rot to death and all the others with him.

The natives confuse conventions and objects they do not understand with magic, and in their reflections on that magic Maran depicts the natives' contempt for the white usurpers as well as their awe. In his reflections, Batouala thinks of white people's stench, particularly of their foul-smelling feet encased in skins; he marvels at the white people's ability to remove their teeth or even an eye; he thinks of white people who can look through tubes at objects far away, and he remembers the white "doctorro" who can make anyone urinate blue. At other moments, however, he remembers the colonials' drunkenness, their disregard for his children born of black women, and their promises never kept.

If the novel expresses nothing more than the bitterness of a subjugated people, it would not be convincing and would fail to achieve its revolutionary intention. The main character, however, Batouala, is a living man and a convincing tribesman, not a mouthpiece for Maran. He knows the value of doing nothing and distinguishes between resting for the joy of it and sheer laziness. When he discovers that the young man, Bissibi'ngui, wants to possess his favorite wife, he does not accept the fact of desire, as most do in his tribe; he determines to pursue Bissibi'ngui and pounce on him like a panther, tearing him to bits. Bissibi'ngui was already successful with eight of Batouala's nine wives, but his attempt to add Yassigui'ndja to his list of conquests is frustrated by Batouala's pride. Only an accident of the hunt, brought about by Batouala's act of hurling a javelin at Bissibi'ngui instead of at a charging panther, brings about his downfall and death. Ironically, the chief who would kill like the panther dies by the panther.

Not these events alone, but, more important, the characters' thoughts and responses intrigue the reader. While they are alive, they glory in life; the men think there is nothing better in all the world than to be strong, to run with the hunters, to be in danger, to kill the beasts that are hunted. They also delight in calling friends together, as in the circumcision ceremony, and the rhythm of their drumming conveys not only the invitation but also the spirit of it—the anticipatory joy of good food, drink, dancing, and riotous lovemaking. When a man dies from too much drink at the circumcision festival, however—as Batouala's father died—he is soon forgotten; he is no longer useful to anyone, and only convention prompts the mourning that extends over eight days in order to make sure that the man is truly dead, not merely sleeping. Death, to the native, is a sleep so profound that a man never wakes again. The references to the gods are more conventional than pious; the concerns of the day, the joy and sorrow of it, are too compelling to leave time for either religion or metaphysics.

Batouala comes to a strange conclusion. The natives are not romanticized: They are not noble savages, but they are nevertheless noble in their direct acceptance of the needs and conventions of their lives. Even in their acceptance of superstition and in their giving way to the lust of the native dance, they seem to relate themselves more honestly to the earth about them than do the white administrators who fortify their fancied superiority with alcohol, brutality, and disdain. The problem for the white colonials becomes that of using their knowledge and power to develop something more respectable than human meanness.

There is more than truth and power to *Batouala*; there is poetry, the rhythmical expression of jungle images and jungle emotions. This dimension of style gives the novel a beauty that makes the crime it depicts even more reprehensible. As long as one people suffer under another, *Batouala* will continue to be not only a work of art but also an indictment.

Further Reading

Cameron, Keith. *René Maran*. Boston: Twayne, 1985. A critical overview of Maran, providing analysis of his fictional and nonfictional works and an appraisal of the controversial French reception of *Batouala*. Chapter 1 offers general background about Maran's life and work; chapter 2 sketches the genesis, structure, style, and reception of *Batouala*.

Coundouriotis, Eleni. "The Traditional Cultures of René Maran and Chinua Achebe." In *Claiming History: Colonialism, Ethnography, and the Novel*. New York: Columbia University Press, 1999. A postcolonial analysis of African novels written in both French and English, describing how these novels were an African response to European colonialism. The first chapter compares *Batouala* to Achebe's *Things Fall Apart* and *Arrow of God*, focusing on the writers' descriptions of traditional culture.

Ikonné, Chidi. *Links and Bridges: A Comparative Study of the Writings of the New Negro and Negritude Movements*. Ibadan, Nigeria: University Press PLC, 2005. The first two chapters, "René Maran and the New Negro" and "*Batouala*: A Pacesetter for the New Negro and Negritude Writings," focus on Maran and his importance within the Negritude movement.

Irele, Abiola. *The African Experience in Literature and Ideology.* London: Heinemann, 1981. Contains a short but informative essay establishing *Batouala* as the likely precursor of French African prose and Maran as an important forerunner of the Negritude movement.

James, Charles. "*Batouala:* René Maran and the Art of Objectivity." *Studies in Black Literature* 4, no. 3 (1973): 19-23. Commemorates the fiftieth anniversary of Maran's 1921 Prix Goncourt for *Batouala*. Revisits its controversial reception and affirms the novel as "the very epitome of Maran's subtle and overt rebelliousness," noting its success in objectivity.

Marriott, David. "En moi: Frantz Fanon and René Maran." In *Frantz Fanon's "Black Skin, White Masks": New Interdisciplinary Essays*, edited by Max Silverman. New York: Manchester University Press, 2005. Describes how both writers shared a view that black people were forced to wear existential disguises and live a double life in order to survive in a white culture.

Ojo-Ade, Femi. *René Maran, the Black French Man: A Bio-Critical Study.* Washington, D.C.: Three Continents Press, 1984. Comprehensive, well-documented, critical study. Critiques Maran's passionate crusade to denounce victimization, injustice, and the evils of a colonial system. Questions the morality of Maran's stance and concludes that Maran's claim to "help the negro cause" is ambiguous and his reputation as "promoter of negro culture" paradoxical.

The Bay of Silence

Author: Eduardo Mallea (1903-1982)
First published: La bahía de silencio, 1940 (English translation, 1944)
Type of work: Novel
Type of plot: Existential
Time of plot: 1930's
Locale: Buenos Aires and Europe

Principal characters:
MARTÍN TREGUA, a young aspiring writer
JIMÉNEZ and ANSELMI, Martín's close friends
MERCEDES MIRÓ, a rich woman
GLORIA BAMBIL, a young librarian

The Story:

Martín Tregua is an aspiring writer in Buenos Aires who believes that he has to enjoy life to the fullest to improve his literary craft. Although he is an aloof young man and a newcomer to the city, he is constantly surrounded by young people who enjoy the active night life of Buenos Aires as he does. His favorite pastime is to take long walks through the city, which exerts a passionate attraction over him that he cannot understand.

Martín lives in a boardinghouse, where he meets his best friends: Jiménez, a government bureaucrat, and Anselmi, a law student. Another resident is Doctor Dervil, a well-read intellectual who engages Martín in philosophical arguments on the purpose of life. Mercedes Miró is another close friend, a rich woman who gives Martín opportunities to meet interesting people from the Argentine upper classes.

Martín's life changes on the day he sees a woman come into a flower shop as he is finishing a purchase. He dares not speak to her, although her striking beauty and her absent-minded manner cause him to remember having seen her thirteen years earlier, shortly after his arrival in Buenos Aires as a law student. On that day he fell in love with her beauty and followed her home. Eventually he found out her name and other information: She was well-born but married a poor lawyer in rebellion against her family. Her husband became rich, however, through dubious financial arrangements with international investors.

Unable to concentrate on writing his novel but eager to keep busy, Martín joins Jiménez and Anselmi in publishing a newspaper for radical young people. Other young intellectuals join the group, which becomes quite heterogeneous, and their newspaper, *El Navío* (the ship), achieves great success. The newspaper opens doors in the intellectual world of Buenos Aires to Martín. This comes at a very good time because Mercedes Miró, with whom Martín is in love, asks that he stop seeing her. As a result, he loses contact with the social class to which she has access.

Martín's fame is short-lived, however. Because of irreconcilable ideological differences, Martín's group decides to stop publication of *El Navío*. Even his close friends find themselves too busy with their personal problems to spend time with him. Jiménez falls in love with Inés Boll, a young woman who takes a room in his boardinghouse in the hope of escaping the physical abuses of her husband. When Jiménez starts dating her, he disappears from Martín's life.

After the newspaper's demise, Martín's existentialist crisis becomes more acute. He cannot stop thinking about the mysterious woman, who one night strikes him with her car. Martín is not hurt. His monotony comes to a sudden end the day that Jiménez is attacked by Inés's husband. The fight leaves Jiménez blind. In terror, Martín leaves for Europe.

His trip takes him through several European countries. His final destination is Brussels, where his friend Ferrier is a physician. Ferrier is a well-read intellectual who, like Martín, enjoys the night life of bars and nightclubs, and he introduces Martín to a number of interesting people. In Brussels, Martín seems to recover from his depression; he starts to enjoy life again and finally finishes writing his novel. His knowledge of philosophy is enriched through his contact with political thinkers, vocal antifascists, and budding communists. Homesick for Buenos Aires, however, Martín returns to Argentina.

There Martín is depressed again for several months until he meets Gloria Bambil. Gloria is a reserved young librarian, but eventually she shows some interest in Martín. When he discovers that Gloria read his first novel, he convinces her to go out with him. They become very dependent on each other, despite Gloria's insistence that she cannot love anyone. Martín confronts her with his love, swearing that he can sense that they are in love. Gloria gives up and becomes his lover. She finally opens her heart to Martín and tells him her personal background, including the fact that she was abused by her father.

The mysterious woman comes into Martín's life again. One night, as Gloria and Martín are having dinner, Gloria sees the woman and comments on her beauty. Martín, who did not forget the woman, remembers having read that she recently lost one of her teenage sons in a riding accident. Several days later, he sees her in the same florist shop as twelve years before. As a tribute to her inexplicable influence on him, he decides to dedicate his story to her. That story is the plot of *The Bay of Silence*.

Critical Evaluation:

Eduardo Mallea is considered one of the promoters of vanguardism in Latin American literature. Extremely well read, he produced works that reflect multiple influences from European writers and intellectuals, especially from existentialist thinkers. In his own country, he was respected for his many articles as an editor of the literary section of *La Nación*, Argentina's major newspaper. It is said that his positive recommendation of a young writer resulted in that individual's immediate success.

Mallea's literary production reflects his strong inclination to the contemplative essay, in which he often explores two favorite themes: the purpose of human existence and Argentina's role in the twentieth century. Early in his career, with the publication in 1937 of *Historia de una pasión argentina* (*History of an Argentine Passion*, 1983) Mallea demonstrates interest in the existential quest in a systematic analysis of the history of Argentina in a worldwide context. In this autobiographical essay, Mallea brings forward issues relevant to pre-World War II society, such as social alienation and its related existential angst.

Unlike other existentialists, however, Mallea displays hope for the resolution of his characters' anguish. Following in the footsteps of the Spanish philosopher Miguel de Unamuno y Jugo (1864-1936), Mallea offers in his philosophical analysis a new historical perspective by bringing a new point of view to the national history experienced by the common citizen. Mallea evaluates Argentine history by means of characters who, affected by everyday occurrences, take a closer look into those events that appear harmless but directly affect their existence. That untold history—what Mallea refers to as "the invisible Argentina"—is the core of Mallea's sociopolitical existentialism. His characters, true existential protagonists, accept the limitations of reason and view their experiences, however unimportant they may at first seem, as an intricate part of the natural or instinctual learning process. The protagonists soon learn that these experiences are not coincidental, and they start viewing them as part of the larger concept of life.

A novel of thesis, or *novela de conciencia* (novel of the conscience) to use Mallea's label, *The Bay of Silence* presents an intimate picture of the existential conflicts experienced by Martín Treba, an aspiring young writer. This strongly autobiographical novel is a fictional account of Martín's desire to document his existence, moved by an inexplicable need to address his memoirs to a mysterious woman, known throughout the novel simply as "you." Although a shadow character, the unnamed woman contributes to his existential crisis because the encounter triggers his exploration of his existential questioning. The unusual interpersonal dynamic of their casual meetings creates in Martín a feeling of aloofness or isolation, which leads him to leave the country.

The influence of the German bildungsroman is obvious here. A young character feeling alienated from society leaves it for other environments and eventually returns home a mature adult. Unlike the traditional bildungsroman, however, Mallea's work places the protagonist as the axis of the plot. Martín exemplifies the existentialist's efforts to use systematic analysis of his own experiences to articulate the essential isolation of the individual in a purposeless society. That fact is stressed by frequent interruption of the plot line by philosophical comments of a purely didactic nature. The lengthy novel subordinates the minimal action to the message, a constant attack on the dehumanizing influence of modern social structures.

Mallea is a literary figure, however, not a philosopher or a politician in the conventional sense. His interest in literature is evident in his vanguardist preference for spontaneous or unconscious thinking. The automatic thought, expressed in literature by means of stream of consciousness, verbalizes Martín's existentialist conflicts in a consciousness of existence. That consciousness conveys strong political convictions, that are related to Mallea's involvement in Argentine politics. After his existential crisis is over, Martín has gained a special knowledge, the so-called existential truth that affirms his natural freedom and his refusal to submit to repressive social structures.

Mallea's work may be considered a precursor of the highly experimental movement of the 1960's in Latin American literature. His literary style is an example of the influence of European literature in Latin America after World War II, a period that shaped later twentieth century literature. The fact that his characters are individuals who respond to human needs not necessarily limited to their Latin American locale makes Mallea one of the first Latin American writers of the twentieth century attractive to international readers. An intellectual with foreign connections, Mallea offers a production free of geographical boundaries. His work is the mature product of a threefold purpose of literature: personal, political, and aesthetic.

Rafael Ocasio

Further Reading

Foster, David William, and Virginia Ramos Foster. "Mallea, Eduardo." In *Modern Latin American Literature*, edited by David William Foster and Virginia Ramos Foster. New York: Frederick Ungar, 1975. Surveys Mallea's production by providing excerpts from critical studies written by various critics. A good introduction to Mallea's most famous works.

Gertel, Zunilda. "Mallea's Novel: An Inquiry into Argentine Character." In *Retrospect: Essays on Latin American Literature*, edited by Elizabeth Rogers and Timothy Rogers. York, S.C.: Spanish Literature, 1987. A short analysis that concentrates on Mallea's oeuvre and indicates his contribution to the formation of contemporary Argentine society. Focuses on Mallea's literary and political importance.

Levine, Suzanne Jill. "The Latin American Novel in English Translation." In *The Cambridge Companion to the Latin American Novel*, edited by Efraín Kristal. New York: Cambridge University Press, 2005. Levine includes three of Mallea's novels—*The Bay of Silence*, *Fiesta in November*, and *All Green Shall Perish*—in her discussion of Latin American novels that have been translated into English.

Lewald, H. Ernest. *Eduardo Mallea*. Boston: Twayne, 1977. Excellent introduction to Mallea's life and works. Provides an overview of his works and gives strong biographical and historical background.

Lichtblau, Myron I. *The Argentine Novel: An Annotated Bibliography—Supplement*. Lanham, Md.: Scarecrow Press, 2002. Lichtblau, who has critiqued and translated Mallea's work, has compiled bibliographies of all editions, reprintings, and translations of Argentine novels published from 1788 through the end of the twentieth century. The book also includes critical commentary about the novels that originally appeared in American and Argentine newspapers and journals. This supplement expands the original 1997 edition.

Mallea, Eduardo. *History of an Argentine Passion*. Translated by Myron Lichtblau. Pittsburgh, Pa.: Latin American Literary Review Press, 1983. Mallea's autobiography relates to the history of Buenos Aires and to his own literary works. Essential for readers interested in the influence of Mallea's autobiographical writings on his fictional works.

Polt, John Herman Richard. *The Writings of Eduardo Mallea*. Berkeley: University of California Press, 1981. In-depth analysis of Mallea's literary production. Places strong emphasis on contemporary literary theories. A good source for advanced readers of Mallea's works.

The Bean Trees

Author: Barbara Kingsolver (1955-)
First published: 1988
Type of work: Novel
Type of plot: Social criticism
Time of plot: 1980's
Locale: Arizona, Kentucky, and Oklahoma

Principal characters:
MISSY "TAYLOR" GREER, a new mother
TURTLE GREER, Taylor's acquired daughter
LOU ANN RUIZ, a single mother
MATTIE, a woman who boards political refugees
ESTEVAN, a Guatemalan refugee
ESPERANZA, Estevan's wife, also a refugee

The Story:

Missy Greer has grown up in Kentucky. She does not consider herself smart, but she knows that she needs to get out of Kentucky before she gets pregnant and suffers a life of poverty. She buys a 1955 Volkswagen and takes off for the West. She also takes a new name, Taylor.

As Taylor drives west, her car breaks down in the Cherokee Nation in Oklahoma. While the car is being fixed, she goes to a bar to get something to eat. As she is leaving the bar, a Cherokee woman places a baby girl in her car and, before leaving, tells Taylor to take the girl. At a motel that evening, Taylor sees that the girl is badly bruised over most of her body. Taylor names her Turtle.

Taylor leaves the motel and begins her drive, headed toward Tucson, Arizona. She stops in a hail storm and finds she has two flat tires. Now at Jesus Is Lord Used Tires in Tucson, she meets the owner, Mattie, who is kind to her and Turtle. A priest shows up while Mattie is getting juice for Turtle. He leaves with what looks like American Indians in his car. Mattie shows Taylor the purple bean plants behind the tire shop.

Lou Ann Ruiz is another woman from Kentucky. She lives in Tucson and is married to Angel, who leaves her when Lou Ann is pregnant. Lou Ann soon gives birth to a boy and names him Dwayne Ray.

Answering a classified ad in the local newspaper, Taylor meets and then moves in with Lou Ann, who lives across the street from Jesus Is Lord Used Tires. The two of them become friends immediately. Taylor gets a job working with Mattie. She is learning a lot but fears exploding tires. She has been haunted by tires ever since, as a child, she saw a friend's father get blown to the top of a sign by an overfilled tractor tire. Mattie helps Taylor get over her fears.

Taylor, Lou Ann, Mattie, the kids, and a couple from Guatemala (Estevan, an English teacher, and his wife, Esperanza) go on a picnic by a creek. Esperanza seems to be thinking about some child she once knew when she first sees Turtle. As the picnickers start driving back, Estevan stops quickly for several quail crossing the road. As Taylor slams on the breaks as well, she hears a voice from the back seat. The voice belongs to Turtle, who is laughing. Taylor hears Turtle's voice for the first time. Later, as they are out in Mattie's garden, Turtle says her first word: bean.

Two elderly neighbors, Edna and Virgie Mae, visit Mattie's house and bring a portable television so they can all see Mattie being interviewed. It takes a while to get the television to work, so they see only the last part of the interview. Mattie is talking about illegal immigrants, although she does not use that term. Estevan and Esperanza are at Mattie's house, too. They introduce themselves to Edna and Virgie Mae as Steven and Hope. The older women are upset about illegal immigrants in the United States. Taylor learns that Mattie has Central American refugees living in a room above the tire shop.

Estevan comes over one night and tells Taylor that Esperanza has tried to kill herself. Mattie has taken her to a hospital that does not demand identity papers. He tells Taylor that Turtle reminds Esperanza of Ismane, their daughter, who was taken by Guatemalan authorities who wanted Estevan to give up the names of other members of the teacher's union. Ismane, he believes, has probably been given to a government official. Estevan talks of torture in his home land. Taylor tells him a little about growing up as a poor kid (a Nutter) in Kentucky. Nutters are social outcasts. The two fall asleep together on the sofa.

Taylor and Lou Ann take the kids out to a park with wisteria trees, which are seeding. Turtle, who still thinks of most everything in terms of vegetables, calls them "bean trees."

Taylor visits Esperanza, who turns out to be okay after her suicide attempt. Taylor has never been upstairs at Mattie's house. There she finds striking artwork—especially pictures by children that feature guns and blood. In a one-sided conversation with Esperanza, Taylor tells her how much Estevan loves her and how much she hopes that Esperanza will not lose either hope or patience. It now appears that Estevan and

Esperanza must move from Tucson before they are caught and deported to Guatemala, where they face imprisonment and possible death. Taylor is horrified that such a thing could happen. She does not want to believe that the world could be so unjust.

Taylor, Mattie, Estevan, and Esperanza go out to the hills above town to celebrate New Year's Day—July 12 this year—the day that the first rain of summer falls. Taylor realizes that she is in love with Estevan, even knowing that he is unavailable.

When she gets home, Taylor finds that Turtle has gone back to a vegetative state. A man had grabbed her in the park and had been fought off by Edna. Taylor is devastated and talks about how horrible it is that people pick on the weak—meaning not just Turtle, but Mattie's refugees as well. Soon, Turtle starts talking again, and the two of them meet with a social worker. The social worker notices that Taylor has no legal rights to guardianship of Turtle. She says that the government will soon take Turtle away. Later, the worker tells Taylor what sort of papers she will need to keep Turtle, and she refers her to a lawyer in Oklahoma City.

Despite Mattie's reservations, Taylor makes plans to go to Oklahoma to take Estevan and Esperanza to a safe house and to get custody papers signed by Turtle's parents. Their first hurdle is getting through an immigration checkpoint, and they do. Taylor wonders how someone can call another person "illegal." When they get to Oklahoma, Taylor cannot find anything about Turtle's parents. She does not know what to do. They all go out and spend a day and night at the Lake of the Cherokee, where Taylor and Estevan get increasingly close, and Esperanza and Turtle do the same. While the adults eat at a picnic table, Turtle takes her doll and buries it. Taylor then realizes that Turtle's mother is dead.

Taylor comes up with a plan, and Estevan and Esperanza say they will help, even though it might be dangerous for them. They go to the lawyer's office in Oklahoma City. There they play an amazing game in which Estevan and Esperanza (as Steve and Hope) act as if they are Turtle's parents and say they want to give her to Taylor. Taylor is overwhelmed by the good acting of Estevan and Esperanza and grateful for their willingness to take such a risk. Taylor gets Estevan and Esperanza to the safe house. Taylor has an intimate moment with Estevan before he leaves. He says that "in a world as wrong as this one, all we can do is make things as right as we can."

Taylor and Turtle cannot leave Oklahoma until all the papers are finalized. As they wait, they go to the library and find a book about plants. They find out that wisteria is a legume and that all beans are supported by rhizobia, microscopic bugs that live around the roots of the plant. Taylor tells Turtle that the invisible network of support is needed for humans, too. Taylor gets the papers and heads back to her family in Arizona—as Turtle's legal mother.

Critical Evaluation:

The Bean Trees, Barbara Kingsolver's first novel, set the standard for her works that follow. In the novel, Kingsolver addresses three main themes: parenthood, friendship, and social injustice.

The parenthood theme centers on the experiences of Taylor and Turtle and Lou Ann and Dwayne Ray. Both Taylor and Lou Ann are single moms struggling with raising a child in a world where there is no support for them. Taylor had grown up trying at all costs not to become a mother, only to have that responsibility thrust upon her in Oklahoma. Lou Ann is abandoned by her husband just before she gives birth, and suddenly is on her own. Neither young woman knows what to do with her new responsibilities. It is a dilemma that haunts both of them, and their working through and coming to terms with the dilemma are central to the novel.

The theme of friendship includes the stories of many relationships, all with different innuendos. The most prevalent friendship is that between Taylor and Lou Ann. Still, all of the main characters are intertwined in one way or another. Taylor and Estevan have a complicated relationship. She loves him and wants him, but her respect for Esperanza keeps her from acting upon that desire. Mattie becomes somewhat of a maternal figure to everyone.

Finally, and perhaps most important, the novel explores the problems of Central American refugees in the 1980's as they flee from tyranny and look for asylum in the United States. However, no asylum is offered, and despite the terrors they have endured, they are not wanted in the United States.

Estevan and Esperanza come from Guatemala. At the time of the novel, the country was controlled by a military dictator, José Efraín Ríos Montt, who committed acts of genocide, among other acts of violence and torture. Thousands of people were killed, more were arrested, and more than four hundred villages were destroyed. This is the type of society from which the refugees in *The Bean Trees* are fleeing.

Steve Hecox

Further Reading

DeMarr, Mary Jean. *Barbara Kingsolver: A Critical Companion*. Westport, Conn.: Greenwood Press, 1999. This study is a detailed overview of Kingsolver's works, through the late 1990's. The chapter on *The Bean Trees* concentrates on various approaches to the novel, with detailed analyses of plots, characters, and genre readings.

_______. "Mothers and Children in Barbara Kingsolver's *The Bean Trees*." In *Women in Literature: Reading Through the Lens of Gender*, edited by Jerilyn Fisher and Ellen S. Siller. Westport, Conn.: Greenwood Press, 2003. This is a short piece that summarizes *The Bean Trees* and mentions briefly some of the novel's concerns. DeMarr also discusses issues the novel might bring up for students.

Himmelwright, Catherine. "Gardens of Auto Parts: Kingsolver's Merger of American Western Myth and Native American Myth in *The Bean Trees*." *Southern Literary Journal* 39, no. 2 (Spring, 2007): 119-139. A discussion of *The Bean Trees* as a regional novel. Himmelwright argues that Kingsolver brings girls and women into the traditionally masculine Western novel.

Ryan, Maureen. "Barbara Kingsolver's Lowfat Fiction." *Journal of American Culture* 18, no. 4 (Winter, 1995): 77-123. Ryan examines the ways Kingsolver addresses the problems of women and children, both in *The Bean Trees* and its sequel, *Pigs In Heaven*. Argues that while Kingsolver addresses important issues, she does so in a superficial way, one that makes the reader feel good rather than concerned.

Snodgrass, Mary Ellen. *Barbara Kingsolver: A Literary Companion*. Jefferson, N.C.: McFarland, 2004. Alphabetical entries include analyses of characters, dates, historical figures and events, allusions, literary motifs, and themes from Kingsolver's work. Excellent resource for any study of Kingsolver.

Wright, Charlotte M. "Barbara Kingsolver." In *Updating the Literary West*, edited by scholars of the Western Literature Association. Fort Worth: Texas Christian University Press, 1997. Informative essays reconsider the subjects of Western literature, taking into account a newly emerging canon that includes children's literature, ethnicity and race, environmental writing, gender issues, and more. Kingsolver's novels are discussed in the context of this changing genre.

The Beaux' Stratagem

Author: George Farquhar (1677/1678-1707)
First produced: 1707; first published, 1707
Type of work: Drama
Type of plot: Comedy of manners
Time of plot: Early eighteenth century
Locale: Lichfield, England

Principal characters:
AIMWELL, a poor younger brother of Lord Aimwell
ARCHER, his friend
DORINDA, an heiress
LADY BOUNTIFUL, Dorinda's mother
MRS. SULLEN, Dorinda's sister-in-law
SULLEN, Dorinda's brother, a drunkard and a brute
FOIGARD, an Irishman disguised as a French priest

The Story:

Aimwell and Archer, two younger sons who are down to their last two hundred pounds, leave London and travel to Lichfield, where they hope that Aimwell will marry an heiress and thus make their fortunes. Aimwell poses as his older brother, Lord Aimwell, and Archer assumes the livery of a servant. Arriving in Lichfield, they go to an inn, where the innkeeper at first mistakes them for highwaymen traveling in disguise.

In Lichfield they learn that Dorinda, sister of Sullen, the local squire, is an heiress in her own right. Aimwell goes to church on Sunday to call himself to her attention and to see her for himself. Back at the inn, Archer makes advances to the innkeeper's daughter, Cherry. He finds her ready to marry him and bring him a dower of two thousand pounds. Despite the fact that she is pretty and well-dowered, he cannot, as a gentleman, make up his mind to marry her.

After church, Dorinda and her sister-in-law, Mrs. Sullen, talk about the gentleman they saw at the service. Dorinda decides that she is in love with him. Citing her own unhappy marriage to the brutal and drunken Sullen, Mrs. Sullen urges her not to hurry into matrimony. Mrs. Sullen also discloses that she is enjoying a flirtation with Bellair, a French officer held prisoner in Lichfield. Dorinda agrees to help Mrs. Sullen in her flirtation as long as Mrs. Sullen retains her honor.

At the inn, the landlord, who is in league with a gang of robbers, talks with the highwayman Gibbet about Aimwell and Archer. The evasiveness of Archer and Aimwell, when questioned, make the innkeeper and Gibbet even more certain that the two are also highwaymen. The innkeeper's daughter, overhearing the conversation, resolves to help Archer.

Meanwhile Dorinda and Mrs. Sullen try to learn more about Aimwell. They have their servant invite his supposed servant, Archer, to the house so that they can question him about his master. While the two women make their plans, Gibbet introduces himself to Aimwell and tries to find out who Aimwell might be. They are both introduced to Foigard, who claims to be a French priest but is actually an Irishman in disguise.

At the Sullen house, Dorinda and Mrs. Sullen question Archer about his master. Mrs. Sullen, seeing through his disguise as a servant, becomes infatuated with him. Dorinda and Mrs. Sullen later agree that Aimwell and Archer must be hiding after a duel, since both of them are obviously gentlemen. Later in the day, Bellair comes to the house. While he and Mrs. Sullen talk, Sullen enters and threatens to kill the Frenchman, even though the visitor bears no arms. Mrs. Sullen intervenes, threatening her husband with a pistol.

Late in the afternoon, Aimwell pretends to take ill in front of the Sullen house. Carried inside for treatment, he takes the opportunity to get better acquainted with Dorinda and her sister-in-law. Both Aimwell and Dorinda are soon convinced that they are in love, and Mrs. Sullen finds herself more and more infatuated with Archer. While in the house, Archer discovers from the servants that Foigard, the pretend Frenchman, plotted to introduce Bellair into Mrs. Sullen's bedroom that night.

On their return to the inn, Aimwell and Archer make Foigard acknowledge his plot against Mrs. Sullen. Rather than be taken to law, he agrees to help them. While they speak, in another part of the inn, the landlord, Gibbet, and other highwaymen are plotting to rob the Sullen house that night. They plan to leave the country afterward.

Early in the evening, Sir Charles Freeman, Mrs. Sullen's brother, arrives at the inn. Just returned to England, he is furious to learn that his sister is married to Sullen. Sir Charles, knowing what a brute Sullen is, hopes to secure his sister's release from the marriage.

With the help of Foigard, Archer hides himself in Mrs. Sullen's bedroom. When he reveals himself to Mrs. Sullen, they talk until the robbers enter the house. Gibbet, entering Mrs. Sullen's room, is overpowered by Archer, who then goes in pursuit of the other rogues. As he engages two of them, Aimwell, aroused by the innkeeper's daughter, arrives and aids his friend in subduing the robbers.

Archer, slightly wounded in the fray, is taken away and treated by Mrs. Sullen and her mother-in-law, Lady Bountiful. Aimwell proposes to Dorinda and is accepted. As Foigard is about to begin the impromptu ceremony, Aimwell becomes conscience-stricken at the thought of marrying the girl under false pretenses. When he reveals that he is not Lord Aimwell but only a poor younger brother, the ceremony is postponed.

Sir Charles Freeman arrives from the inn to visit his sister. Archer and Aimwell, who know him well, realize that he will penetrate their disguises immediately. Dorinda puts an end to their worries when she returns to tell Aimwell that his brother died. He is now Lord Aimwell and a rich man. Aimwell cannot believe the news until Sir Charles Freeman confirms the story. Aimwell agrees quickly to give an amount equal to Dorinda's dower, ten thousand pounds, to Archer, who helped him win her hand.

Sullen, entering on this scene of happiness, demands to be told what Aimwell and Archer are doing in his home. He softens somewhat when told that they rescued his family and property from robbers. Then Sir Charles Freeman questions Sullen and discovers that he is as unhappy as Mrs. Sullen in their marriage. Sullen agrees to a separation, but he refuses to give up her dower. Archer then produces some papers he took from the robbers, including the marriage documents and Sullen's titles to property, and gives them to Sir Charles Freeman. Faced with the loss of the documents, Sullen agrees to give up both his wife and her dower.

Everyone except Sullen joins hands and dances their celebration of the approaching marriage of Dorinda and Aimwell and Mrs. Sullen's separation from her husband. Sullen glumly sends for a drink of whiskey.

Critical Evaluation:

Restoration comedy has been condemned as immoral and superficial, but neither the moral indignation of its critics in centuries past nor the cool contempt of later commentators has diminished its appeal to audiences. Despite its carefree attitude toward moral conventions and its willingness to indulge in trivial humor, comedy written at the end of the seventeenth and in the very early eighteenth centuries continues to enjoy a theatrical and literary life.

George Farquhar's plays were written at a time when the early exuberance and rakish irreverence of Restoration comedy were beginning to give way to a more sentimental and moralized comedy. Farquhar's heart was with his Restoration masters, particularly Sir George Etherege, whose comedies from thirty years earlier reveled in cynicism, wit, and the ridicule of pretentious, dandified behavior. Farquhar knew, however, that his audiences wanted to "feel" rather than to "think," so he curbed his natural bent toward wit and tried to develop a sentimental side. His Dorinda is compassionate enough, but one has the impression Farquhar would have preferred to make her more like Etherege's Harriet in *The Man of Mode* (1676)—a woman possessing no less charm and far more wit and worldly wisdom.

If Farquhar had to soften his satire, he managed to direct some of the energy that his precursors would have used for purposes of ridicule toward social criticism. It is one of the ironies of literary and dramatic history that a dramatist less comfortable with sentiment and feeling than with contempt and ridicule should have launched what has come to be known as the theater of social protest—ironic because ordinarily contempt is not associated with caring.

The cause that Farquhar championed was divorce. Here, too, there is delicious irony. The prevailing theme of Restoration comedy is seduction; its favorite butt is the cuckold. Infidelity was the fuel on which the cavalier engines ran. Happiness in marriage was as rare in fact as it was naïve in principle. For the famous Restoration rakes of Etherege and William Wycherley, marriage was a trap to be avoided at all cost; its greatest danger was that it exposed the husband to the risk of cuckoldry. (Sullen, at one point, even tells his wife "if you can contrive any way of being a whore without making me a cuckold, do it and welcome.") That is one danger a bachelor escaped. When Farquhar makes an eloquent case for Mrs. Sullen's liberation from marriage, this is in one sense only to free her and her husband from the dangers of social embarrassment. Divorced, Mrs. Sullen is free to love Archer without cuckolding her husband.

Nevertheless, Farquhar's bid for divorce involves more than the oddity of Restoration manners. It is obvious that he has drifted far enough from Restoration cynicism to believe in the unnaturalness of a forced, unhappy marriage. Although he admired Restoration sophistication and the stylish cultivation of a studied and brilliant artificiality, Farquhar was enough of a child of the dawning age of sentiment to sympathize with the cry for nature and the plea for true sentiment. At the end of act 3, Mrs. Sullen is eloquent in her desperate assertions to Dorinda regarding the emotional suffering attendant on an unhappy marriage: Who can prove "the unaccountable disaffections of wedlock? Can a jury sum up the endless aversions that are rooted in our souls, or can a bench give judgment upon antipathies?" Such speeches open the floodgates to truly serious feeling, and they open the play's action to problems wit alone cannot solve. There is no clever answer—nor did Farquhar intend that there should be—to Mrs. Sullen's question, "Can radical hatreds ever be reconciled?" When she closes the act with the famous exclamation, "No, no sister, nature is the first lawgiver," Farquhar shows that he has left the ranks of Restoration dramatists. That exclamation is followed by a rhymed closing epilogue that contrasts the harmony of the earth's elements with the agonizing disharmony of a bad marriage. Mrs. Sullen becomes reminiscent of Ulysses in William Shakespeare's *Troilus and Cressida* (pr. 1601-1602, pb. 1609); when the perspicacious Greek hero analyzes the disunity of the Greeks, he makes similar allusions to the harmony of the spheres. There can be no victory for the Greeks unless all men and all factions take their proper place in the ranks of the Greek host. Mrs. Sullen sounds no less noble when she insists that without harmony and understanding between a husband and wife the marriage can have no center—nor tolerate a master: "Omnipotence is just, were man but wise."

The divorce theme is treated seriously, but Farquhar will not follow through on the sublime note of Mrs. Sullen's epilogue. Her husband finally agrees to a separation, but if Archer did not secure the papers from the robbers and place them in Sir Charles Freeman's hands, Sullen would never have agreed to a divorce. He is tricked, then, in the spirit of Restoration foolery, into agreeing to the divorce on which Mrs. Sullen lavishes so much sincere emotion. However, the charm of their brisk repartee at parting redeems the tone of Restoration theater. As the two adversaries shower barbs of polite insult in taking leave of each other, audiences have as their final impression the brilliance of Farquhar's benevolent satire.

Farquhar's closing tone is a reminder that he has been writing a Restoration comedy, not a sentimental domestic problem play. The happiness of the separated couple is as great as that of the united lovers, Dorinda and Aimwell. The Restoration rake-heroes, Archer and Aimwell, out-thieve the thieves and steal their way into the hearts, and fortunes, of their ladies. Mrs. Sullen is freed by Archer's trickery only to fall into the hands of a fortune hunter, though a charming one. The wry note on which the play ends reestablishes the "way of the world" as Restoration comedy conceived it. Farquhar may have tipped his hat to sentimental values, but the buttons of his costumes are firmly snapped by the same tailors who fashioned the theater of Etherege and Wycherley, Sir John Vanbrugh and William Congreve. The divorce theme lingers in the mind, but the antics of Archer and Aimwell, the disguises, the "catechisms" of love, and the farcical confrontation of Count Bellair and Sullen all distinguish Farquhar as the last of the Restoration comic dramatists.

"Critical Evaluation" by Peter A. Brier

Further Reading

Bull, John. *Vanbrugh and Farquhar.* New York: St. Martin's Press, 1998. Examines the plays of Farquhar and of Sir John Vanbrugh, whose work appeared at the end of the period of post-Restoration comedy. Places Farquhar's work within the context of his times and of theatrical production. Chapter 7 focuses on *The Beaux' Stratagem* and *The Recruiting Officer.*

Burns, Edward. *Restoration Comedy: Crises of Desire and Identity.* New York: St. Martin's Press, 1987. Burns's central premise is that Restoration comedy was shaped by the pastoral mode that was popular in sixteenth and seventeenth century literature. His treatment of individual plays and playwrights includes an interesting discussion of *The Beaux' Stratagem.*

Heard, Elisabeth J. *Experimentation on the English Stage, 1695-1708: The Career of George Farquhar.* Brookfield, Vt.: Pickering & Chatto, 2008. Examines how Farquhar and his contemporaries experimented with characters, plot lines, and dialogue to create a new type of English comedy. Chapter 4 examines the success of these experiments in *The Beaux' Stratagem* and *The Recruiting Officer.*

Milhous, Judith, and Robert D. Hume. *Producible Interpretation: Eight English Plays, 1675-1707.* Carbondale: Southern Illinois University Press, 1985. Two of the leading scholars in the field of Restoration and eighteenth century drama outline the production history of *The Beaux' Stratagem* and discuss interpretive problems.

Rothstein, Eric. *George Farquhar.* New York: Twayne, 1967. An excellent study of Farquhar and his work. Includes a short biographical sketch, followed by a solid discussion of the works, including a chapter on *The Beaux' Stratagem.*

The Beaver Coat

Author: Gerhart Hauptmann (1862-1946)
First produced: Der Biberpelz, 1893; first published, 1893 (English translation, 1912)
Type of work: Drama
Type of plot: Satire
Time of plot: Nineteenth century
Locale: The outskirts of Berlin

Principal characters:
FRAU WOLFF, a washerwoman and a seller of stolen goods
JULIUS WOLFF, her husband, a poacher
LEONTINE, their older daughter
WULKOW, a buyer of stolen goods, a boatman
KRÜGER, the well-to-do victim of the thieves
DOCTOR FLEISCHER, his friend, a liberal
VON WEHRHAHN, a justice of the peace
MOTES, an informer

The Story:

To the suburban shack of the Wolff family, which Julius and Frau Wolff are paying off on the installment plan, their older daughter Leontine returns with complaints that her employers, the Krügers, sent her out for wood late at night. Leontine was hired out to the rich family in the neighborhood to earn enough money to start a stage career, because Frau Wolff thinks that her appearance will assure her success. Although Julius wants to send the girl back to the Krügers immediately, Frau Wolff seizes the opportunity to devise a plan to steal the wood that her rebellious daughter refuses to carry. If the older daughter has delusions of grandeur, the younger one, Udelheid, does not.

Julius manufactures boats and runs the local ferry as a kind of front for his real profession, the illegal snaring of game. He returns with his shipwright's tools and oars, and Frau Wolff completes butchering a stag in preparation of the arrival of a boatman, Wulkow, who deals in plundered goods. The family, which thrives by trickery, wit, and chance, just then has a supply of firewood and a stag ready for market.

Wulkow seems reluctant to pay more than thirteen shillings for the meat, but Frau Wolff, the real ringleader in the family dealings, bargains him up to seventeen. The important sale, however, is that Wulkow declares himself willing to pay sixty or seventy crowns for a good fur coat to relieve his rheumatism during the cold days on the barge. Frau Krüger bought just such a coat for her husband's Christmas present. Their bargaining is interrupted by the appearance of Motes and his wife, who obtain eggs and bread from Frau Wolff in return for an uneasy truce over several snares they found. Motes, who lost an eye in a hunting accident and thereupon his job as a ranger, sometimes remedies his misfortunes by informing on poachers in the neighborhood.

After this encounter, Frau Wolff fortifies her husband with whiskey for the midnight excursion to load wood. Their friend, the policeman who on his nightly rounds wheedles drinks, innocently helps the Wolffs prepare for the task ahead. He is several days late in delivering a message that Frau Wolff is to appear at Justice von Wehrhahn's house on the following morning.

In the justice's court the next day, Krüger lodges a complaint that his wood was stolen, but the justice is not at all interested in the theft. He hears that Krüger's friend and boarder, Doctor Fleischer, a notorious liberal democrat and freethinker, said slanderous things about a certain official newly arrived in town, and von Wehrhahn is certain that he is the official to whom Fleischer referred. He is therefore preoccupied with a plan to rig circumstantial evidence to press charges against Doctor Fleischer. When Krüger insists that his hired girl be forced to return, Frau Wolff is brought in, dripping from her work at the von Wehrhahn tubs, to settle the dispute. She announces that she refuses to send her daughter back to a house where she is forced to carry wood in the middle of the night. Krüger, who is partially deaf, becomes angry and accuses the justice of shouting and the court of incompetency. As Frau Wolff returns with injured pride to her washing and Krüger storms out, von Wehrhahn is left with Motes, who gives him reassurance.

Several days later, a beaver coat is delivered to Wulkow for ninety-nine crowns (when new, the coat cost about one hundred crowns). Frau Wolff counts her money carefully, claiming that the boatman cheated her of one crown. In spite of Julius's wish to pay the final installment on their house, his wife insists on burying the money until things blow over. Udelheid, the younger daughter, busily building a fire of stolen wood, is sent to study confirmation verses for the coming celebratory season. Doctor Fleischer and his little boy, great favorites of the family, stop by for a boat ride, a whimsical midwinter wish of the delicate child. Udelheid is taking them out when Krüger arrives with lamentations and apologies. He emphasizes his lamentations by waving a stick of stolen wood and denouncing the security system for the loss of both his wood and his beaver coat. He apologizes for the way he treated Frau Wolff and pleads for Leontine to return to work at higher pay. Frau Wolff assures him that jail is the place for scoundrelly thieves.

In an effort to deceive the authorities, Frau Wolff declares that a waistcoat, a note, and a key have been found by her daughter near the railway station. Her theory is that the thief left them behind when he took the beaver coat to Berlin. However, she seems willing to believe that the thief might still be in the vicinity, all the more so after Wulkow appears in the courtroom to register the birth of a daughter. So many petitioners show up simultaneously that Justice von Wehrhahn cannot get on with his plans to indict Doctor Fleischer for slander on the false testimony of Motes's landlady, who is quite gullible and ignorant of Motes's habit of avoiding any kind of payment whatsoever. Doctor Fleischer, however, has knowledge of a beaver coat. While out on the river he saw a boatman—the unfortunate Wulkow, who could not get his boat free of the ice in time to get his wife to Berlin for the expected event—sitting on deck in a new fur coat. This evidence makes no impression on von Wehrhahn; anyone can own a fur coat, he insists, even a boatman. Wulkow assures him that boatmen could easily afford such a coat and that he himself has one. Krüger, not hearing all that was said, criticizes the justice severely for not allowing the good washerwoman to present her daughter's evidence. He also rebukes the magistrate for consorting with Motes, a man who never pays his bills, who informs on others, and who is even now rigging false evidence. Doctor Fleischer presents documentary proof that Motes extracted evidence from his landlady against himself. All this the justice waved aside.

Wulkow finally succeeds in registering the birth of his daughter. The incriminating evidence against him is thrown out, von Wehrhahn saying that he would have to search every house in the area—Frau Wolff suggests that he start with hers—if such flimsy stories were to be believed. Krüger states that he will not rest until the coat and his stolen wood are found. Von Wehrhahn sends away Motes and his star witness. Frau Wolff, true to her sense of honor, refuses to say anything good of Motes or anything bad of Doctor Fleischer, even though the justice is more than willing to hear such information. He admires her feelings but begs to differ with the honest lady, one whom everyone admires and with whom no one finds fault. To his pronouncement that as sure as she is an honest woman, Doctor Fleischer is a thoroughly dangerous person, Frau Wolff says only that she does not know what to think.

Critical Evaluation:

The Beaver Coat is one of Gerhart Hauptmann's earliest comedies, written at a time when the young author was under the influence of such intellectual movements sweeping Europe as social determinism, which is epitomized in the writings of Karl Marx and Friedrich Engels, and naturalism, a literary movement begun in France and codified by Émile Zola. Although most of the works produced by naturalist authors, including those of Hauptmann, tend toward tragedy, *The Beaver Coat* is exceptional in that the playwright here applies the principles of naturalism to a decidedly comic plot. Hauptmann abandons the strict demands of the well-made play, made popular in the nineteenth century by contemporary European writers and by the theories of Hauptmann's countryman Gustav Freytag, and relies instead on sharp characterization and the repetition of stock events to create humor and to mask the more serious social satire that the play embodies. Hauptmann's decision to cast his satire in the form of a comedy was fortuitous; despite a lackluster initial reception, *The Beaver Coat* came to be ranked with Gotthold Ephraim Lessing's *Minna von Barnhelm* (1767) and Heinrich von Kleist's *The Broken Jug* (1808) as one of the greatest comedies in German literature.

Central to the success of the drama is his depiction of the inventive and irrepressible Frau Wolff, whose attempts to outwit the officials of the Prussian government are the main source of comedy. She dominates both her family and her friends, and she enlists their aid in outwitting the pompous justice of the peace who threatens her schemes for increasing the family's wealth. The other characters, often little more than types drawn from comic tradition as old as Aristophanes, allow playgoers to see the folly of a government so intent on rooting out political opposition that it permits criminal activity to occur right under the noses of the local magistrates.

Beneath its comic surface, *The Beaver Coat* offers a serious critique of nineteenth century Prussian society. Hauptmann achieves this by applying naturalism and realism to the play's comic conventions. Modeling his work on the theories of the naturalist movement most forcefully expounded by Zola, Hauptmann emphasizes details of everyday life and meticulously chronicles the speech and action of characters from the lower social classes. Using realistic techniques pioneered in drama by Henrik Ibsen, whom he greatly admired, Hauptmann in *The Beaver Coat* introduces a cast of characters from the working and criminal classes, presenting them sympathetically and with appreciation for their situation. This is no drawing-room comedy; instead, it shares many characteristics of the proletariat literature that had begun to appear in Europe during the final decades of the nineteenth century, inspired by the theories of Marx and Engels. The men and women in Hauptmann's comedy are engaged in a struggle that parallels the one described in the works of Charles Darwin and Herbert Spencer; their world clearly embodies the principle of "survival of the fittest." The animal imagery that dominates the play, especially in the naming of characters, reinforces this image. It should be no surprise to readers that the "wolf" (Frau Wolff) bests the blustering, militaristic "hen" (Wehrhahn). What is ironic, of course, is that the tables are turned in this portrait of society, and that the criminals are able to better the authorities even within the confines of the law.

Not surprisingly, Hauptmann was criticized by some of his contemporaries and by later audiences and readers because the comic resolution of *The Beaver Coat* leaves justice—at least legal justice—unserved and suggests that the criminal behavior of Frau Wolff and her family may be pardoned. The authorities in his own day found Hauptmann's treatment of government officials offensive; questions even arose regarding the way the playwright was able to get his play passed by the government censor, who judged the work to be so insignificant that it could not possibly have any adverse impact on audiences. In later years, when the aging Hauptmann became a darling of the Nazi regime, producers of *The Beaver Coat* found it necessary to sanitize the drama so that it would not lead German audiences to think ill of Hitler's regime.

That the play seems to condone immorality may be explained by appealing to the tradition Hauptmann is following. As a naturalist work, *The Beaver Coat* depicts, but does not judge, a slice of life the author knows well and presents without commentary. Hauptmann is quite familiar with both the characters and the situations he dramatizes, and most of the men and women in *The Beaver Coat* are modeled on people he knew. Frau Wolff, for example, is a fictional portrait of his laundress, Marie Heinze; von Wehrhahn is drawn from Hauptmann's memories of an encounter with Oscar von Busse, who had harassed the young writer when he was living in Erkner, the town outside Berlin that serves as the setting for *The Beaver Coat*. Hauptmann is suggesting in his play that sometimes criminals do escape; sometimes justice is represented by people who do not uphold the concepts of law and equity in totally admirable ways. He makes no attempt to condone Frau Wolff's behavior or her cause, nor does he condemn it. Like all good practitioners of naturalism, Hauptmann is interested primarily in placing before his audience an accurate portrait of life among common people, whose struggle to get ahead in a society insensitive to their needs sometimes places them at odds with the law. Judgments are left to the audience, who may sympathize with the playwright's spunky and industrious heroine or condemn her for her actions as they see fit.

"Critical Evaluation" by Laurence W. Mazzeno

Further Reading

Gassner, John. Introduction to *Five Plays by Gerhart Hauptmann*, translated by Theodore H. Lustig. New York: Bantam, 1961. A general introduction that sketches Hauptmann's achievement as a dramatist, highlighting his contributions to the naturalist movement. Comments on the topicality of *The Beaver Coat* but claims that it is an "outstanding character comedy" that transcends the limitations of the time and place of its initial production.

Guthke, Karl S. "The King of the Weimar Republic: Hauptmann's Role in Political Life." In *Trails in No-Man's-Land: Essays in Literary and Cultural History*. Columbia, S.C.: Camden House, 1993. Guthke views Haputmann's literary works from the broader context of his role in German politics.

Maurer, Warren R. *Gerhart Hauptmann*. Boston: Twayne, 1982. Overview of Hauptmann's life and work intended for the nonspecialist. Organized chronologically, it shows the development of Hauptmann's theory of drama. Discusses the principal themes of *The Beaver Coat*, highlights its politically charged undertone, and cites the author's use of imagery and dramatic structure.

_______. *Understanding Gerhart Hauptmann*. Columbia: University of South Carolina Press, 1992. Excellent overview of Hauptmann's works. Discussion of *The Beaver Coat* focuses on the comic aspects of the play and on the character of Mrs. Wolff.

Osborne, John. *Gerhart Hauptmann and the Naturalist Drama*. 2d rev. and updated ed. Amsterdam: Harwood Academic, 1998. Discusses *The Beaver Coat* as a naturalist comedy, citing various devices Hauptmann uses to achieve comic effect. Points out parallels to Molière's plays. Originally published in 1971 as *The Naturalist Drama in Germany*.

Sinden, Margaret. *Gerhart Hauptmann: The Prose Plays*. Toronto, Ont.: University of Toronto Press, 1957. Studies the major dramas, including *The Beaver Coat*, which Sinden calls a work of great vigor. Discusses the play as an exploration of the impact of the modern era on a traditional rural settlement.

Bech
A Book

Author: John Updike (1932-2009)
First published: 1970
Type of work: Short-story sequence
Type of plot: Comic realism
Time of plot: 1960's
Locale: Russia; Romania; Bulgaria; Martha's Vineyard, Massachusetts; Virginia; London; New York City

Principal characters:
HENRY BECH, a middle-aged Jewish writer suffering from writer's block
EKATERINA "KATE" RYLEYEVA, Russian translator-guide
ATHANASE PETRESCU, Rumanian literary translator
VERA GLAVANAKOVA, Bulgarian poet
WENDELL MORRISON, Bech's former student
NORMA LATCHETT, Bech's mistress
BEA COOK, Norma's sister and Bech's subsequent mistress
RUTH EISENBRAUN, college English professor
TUTTLE, British interviewer
MERISSA, British gossip columnist
BECH'S MOTHER

John Updike's *Bech: A Book* is composed of loosely related stories featuring Updike's fictional literary alter ego Henry Bech, a Jewish novelist from Manhattan who diverges from his creator in numerous significant ways, chief among them his religion and persistent writer's block. Bech first appeared in "The Bulgarian Poetess" and subsequently became the vehicle through which Updike wrote about his literary travels and satirized the publishing industry. Although the stories were originally published separately, Updike arranged them in a loose picaresque series and added other unpublished material to create a short-story sequence similar to his *Olinger Stories* (1964) and *Too Far to Go* (1979). Updike's assignment of the subtitle "a book" indicates the volume's intermediate status between a novel and a miscellaneous story collection.

The volume begins with a foreword purportedly written as a letter by Bech to Updike. Bech parses his own literary resemblance to other famous living Jewish writers, as well as to Updike himself, praises Updike for treating the oppression of writers by the publishing industry, criticizes him for his prose, and ultimately bestows his blessing on Updike's representation of him. This device hints slyly at the volume's overall themes, establishes its pervasive satirical tone, and provides an ironic critique of Updike's portrait of the artist while establishing the main character's voice. Through Bech's analysis, Updike anticipates some of the critical reviews of his work and introduces the volume's thematic focus on the writer as self-created character whose life becomes a consumable public fiction that consumes his literary talent.

The picaresque chronicle of Henry Bech's literary travels opens with three stories that take place in Eastern Europe, returns to the United States for two stories, and then moves back across the Atlantic to England before returning Bech home to Manhattan. The book concludes with two appendixes: excerpts from Bech's Russian journal and a fictional bibliography of literary criticism on Bech. Bech is a blocked writer who seeks to escape his creative problems by embracing literary celebrity, repeatedly reinforcing and sometimes exacerbating his situation. Updike's use of the short-story sequence is therefore apt, as each individual story repeats Bech's dilemma and the overall form depicts a discontinuous life rather than advancing a novelistic plot.

The book's opening story, "Rich in Russia," recounts Bech's ambivalent acquisition of a large sum of rubles, showered on him by the Soviet government as royalties for recent translations of his work. The behavior of the Soviets stands in contrast to that of the American publishing industry, which has taken advantage of Bech's poor business sense to keep most of the profits from his best-selling novel *Travel Light*. Experiencing feelings of guilt about taking money from the proletariat, Bech determines to spend the money in Russia, enlisting the aid of Kate, his devoted guide and translator, who is eager to spend time with him.

Obsessed with spending, Bech fails to recognize Kate's feelings for him until her moist farewell kiss at the airport alerts him to the missed opportunity. As he rushes to his plane, his suitcase bursts open on the runway; though he recovers his purchases—furs and now-cracked watches—he is forced to leave behind copies of his translated books. These lost books represent the excess baggage of a cumbersome literary reputation, and they help Bech understand that he leaves Russia without having experienced it fully. The story's narrative frame, a college professor relating this episode while lecturing on Bech, provides commentary on Bech's subject position and highlights the role of literary biography in constructing a character, paralleling Bech's self-conscious creation of a literary persona.

The next story, "Bech in Rumania," opens with Bech wearing an astrakhan hat purchased in Russia, alerting readers to the stories' progressive, interrelated nature. This story also concerns missed connections, signaled by the American Embassy personnel's failure to recognize Bech at the airport and by the Rumanian Writers' Union's attempt to keep him away from the Rumanian literati, who the Americans hope will be stirred up by his presence. Bech accidentally meets one of these writers—a friend of Petrescu, the admiring guide whose devotion to reading and writing causes Bech to realize that his own passion has waned. However, little meaningful exchange occurs between the mutually disinterested writers. They are unable to find common ground, since the Rumanian writes about peasants while Bech's work portrays the bourgeoisie. While Bech fails to understand the country through his muddled experiences, he nonetheless discovers some glimmer of truth about himself through an encounter with a reticent Rumanian chauffer who embodies the country's enigma. His reckless driving evokes Bech's memories of fearing a childhood tormenter and triggers Bech's epiphany that—unlike his literary hero Melville—he fails to face fear with courageous diffidence and has squandered his talent.

Vera Glavanakova, the title character of the 1965 O. Henry First Prize-winning story "The Bulgarian Poetess," has a much more profound effect on Bech than his previous guides. Arriving in Bulgaria in the midst of anti-American turmoil, Bech retreats to his hotel room and reads Nathaniel Hawthorne for comfort. Instead, Hawthorne's "Roger Malvin's Burial" (1846) sets off a mild panic attack akin to one that Bech experiences in a later story, as Malvin's solitary death seems parallel to Bech's feeling of being cut off behind the Iron Curtain. Bech nonetheless begins to emerge from the pose of ironic weariness that masks his inner emptiness when he encounters Vera, whose beauty and devotion to her art reawaken him emotionally and intellectually.

On a trip with Vera to the Rilke monastery, Bech understands the extent to which she has stirred his spirit when his dormant writerly eye recognizes beauty in simplicity. While Bech perceives Vera as his soul mate, their brief liaison consists of three short meetings and an exchange of inscribed books, illustrating to him that "actuality is a running impoverishment of possibility"—a theme that resonates through much of Updike's work. After Vera and Bech separate reluctantly at the airport, he studies her inscription and concludes that a word that looks like "leave" must be "love"—ironically linking the two and connecting with the reiterated Updike theme that love's strength and purity often grow from separation, mystery, and unfulfilled longing.

"Bech Takes Pot Luck" is set in Martha's Vineyard, where the restless writer hopes to rub elbows with fashionable celebrities and to find female adulation. Traveling with his mistress Norma, her sister Bea, and Bea's three children, Bech meets Wendell Morrison, a former student from a creative writing course at Columbia, who joins the group uninvited. When Wendell shares marijuana with them, the results are comic and somewhat disastrous: Norma greedily partakes and belittles Bech; Bea sees threatening shapes outside the window as guilt about her divorce emerges; and Bech becomes increasingly pompous as he gets higher, although he does experience a fleeting moment of clarity before succumbing to nausea and vomiting. As he subsequently becomes disconsolate about his failure to emulate past literary greats, Bea comforts him by praising his work, and they begin the affair that will eventually end Bech's relationship with Norma.

"Bech Panics," composed as a bridge between the previous story and the next, is the volume's most serious story, climaxing with Bech's severe existential dread. The narrative voice, reminiscent of that in "Rich in Russia," presents the action as a speculative commentary on a series of slides—a form that parallels the book's separate stories—highlighting the fiction-making process and the conjecture necessary to fill in gaps within a loosely connected sequence. The roots of Bech's panic derive from his anxiety about his developing relationship with Bea, especially the domestic life he fears being drawn into and her challenges to his literary stagnation.

Fleeing the domestication that seems to him inevitable, Bech impulsively accepts a telephone invitation to speak at a Virginia women's college, tempted by the speaker's fee and fantasizing about adulation by nubile Southern girls. Playing the role of visiting author, he maintains surface composure but is haunted by the hollowness of his performance and by visions of an abyss of meaninglessness. At the height of his panic, during a forest walk, Bech throws himself on the damp ground and prays. This epiphanic moment is undercut when ants bite him, but the small surge of faith Bech experiences serves as a prelude to the fuller respite from panic that he achieves when he sleeps with Ruth Eisenbraun, the Jewish literature professor from New York behind his invitation. With his panic at an ebb, Bech judges a poetry contest before leaving, finding some consolation in the winning poem's brave and gracious acceptance of life's frailty. He returns to Bea spiritually enervated but temporarily purged of his anxieties.

"Bech Swings?" finds Bech promoting a British collection of his works. Arriving in London as daffodils bloom, he hopes for a corresponding renewal of his ebbing creativity. After a brief fling with Merissa—who he later discovers is a gossip columnist—his dormant artistic spirit is briefly awakened: Bech sees Merissa as a potential prototype for a character in an ambitious new novel, aptly titled *Think Big*. At his publisher's behest, he undergoes a grueling three-day interview conducted by Tuttle, an American graduate student, who ultimately uses few of his actual words. The interview, however, saps Bech of the energy to launch his new novel and to continue his sexual exploits with Merissa, who—like the Bulgarian poet Vera—tries to provide him with advice that will help him understand how to replace ardor with art and who portrays him with gentle fondness in her gossip column.

"Bech Enters Heaven," written specifically to round out the volume, begins with a flashback to Bech's trip to a Manhattan honorary literary society with his mother, who serves in a capacity similar to the other stories' female guides as she tries to inspire and reorient her precocious son. Although the young Bech observes that fame has crystallized the writers enshrined there, he idealizes this haven of art and years later returns to the literary society to be admitted as a member. His induction, however, proves disillusioning when the ceremony degenerates into contentious posturing and his fellow inductees—youthful literary idols—seem seedy and inattentive. When Bech believes he sees his deceased mother in the audience, he perceives a metaphoric connection between the induction ceremony and death. What should be a milestone in his career thus provides the same ambivalent satisfaction as his travels had in the preceding stories.

While Updike may not have been hinting at a sequel in the book's purposefully anticlimactic words—"Now what?"—Bech's literary and amorous misadventures continued in subsequent short fiction and were gathered in similarly structured volumes of integrated stories: *Bech Is Back* (1982) and *Bech at Bay: A Quasi-Novel* (1998). *The Complete Henry Bech* (2001) united the stories from all three books, together with a subsequent Bech story, "His Oeuvre."

Robert M. Luscher

Further Reading

Bech, Henry [John Updike]. "Henry Bech Redux." *The New York Times Book Review*, November 14, 1971, p. 3. A self-interview by Updike, indulging in mild self-satire in the voice of Henry Bech critiquing and interrogating his creator.

Detweiler, Robert. *John Updike*. Rev. ed. New York: Twayne, 1984. Analyzes *Bech: A Book* in the context of Updike's overall canon, noting its unique comedy and overall themes while explicating individual stories in a chapter titled "The Protestant as Jew."

Greiner, Donald. *John Updike's Novels*. Athens: Ohio University Press, 1984. Places *Bech* in the context of Updike's remarks on the American writer's situation and provides analysis of Bech's artistic plight and Updike's satiric stance.

Hamilton, Alice, and Kenneth Hamilton. "Metamorphosis Through Art: John Updike's *Bech: A Book*." *Queen's Quarterly* 77 (1970): 624-636. Early study of the volume's themes, emphasizing Bech's plight as a struggling artist.

Luscher, Robert M. *John Updike: A Study of the Short Fiction*. New York: Twayne, 1993. Focuses on the volume as a short-story sequence, emphasizing the overall themes and the stories' interrelatedness in a chapter titled "Blocked Art and Bygone Ardor: Bech's Burden."

Ozick, Cynthia. "Bech, Passing." In *Art and Ardor: Essays*. New York: Knopf, 1983. Notes shortcomings of Updike's depiction of a Jewish protagonist who mostly resembles the author but is surrounded by ethnic trappings.

Pinsker, Sanford. "Updike, Ethnicity, and Jewish-American Drag." In *The Cambridge Companion to John Updike*, edited by Stacey Olster. New York: Cambridge University Press, 2006. Analyzes how Updike's portrayal of Bech as a Jewish writer evolved during Updike's career, specifically within the context of Jewish American literature.

Siegel, Lee. "Updike's Bech." In *Falling Upwards: Essays in Defense of the Imagination*. New York: Basic Books, 2006. This chapter in a larger study of the literary imagination focuses on Updike's act of imagining himself as a (Jewish) other in the person of Henry Bech.

Taylor, Larry E. *Pastoral and Anti-pastoral Patterns in John Updike's Fiction*. Carbondale: Southern Illinois University Press, 1971. Remarks on Bech's appearance as a different direction for Updike, with special attention to tying the stories' pastoral themes to Updike's other fiction.

Becket
Or, The Honor of God

Author: Jean Anouilh (1910-1987)
First produced: Becket: Ou, L'Honneur de Dieu, 1959; first published, 1959 (English translation, 1960)
Type of work: Drama
Type of plot: Historical
Time of plot: Twelfth century
Locale: England, France, and Rome

Principal characters:
THOMAS À BECKET, archbishop of Canterbury
HENRY II PLANTAGENET, king of England
GILBERT FOLLIOT, bishop of London
THE QUEEN, Eleanor of Aquitaine
THE QUEEN MOTHER, the king's henpecking parent
GWENDOLEN, Becket's former mistress, a suicide

The Story:

King Henry is doing ritual penance for his suspected role in the assassination of Thomas à Becket, archbishop of Canterbury, formerly his friend and chancellor of England. While the king wonders aloud where their friendship went wrong, Thomas's ghostly presence appears before him, telling him to pray instead of talk. The scene then shifts to the early days of the two men's boon companionship. Henry makes an impulsive appointment of Becket to the position of chancellor, a move intended to give the king more control of a rebellious clergy. Equally mistrusted by the bishops and by the king's own henchmen, Becket nevertheless performs his duties with grace and skill, earning the grudging respect of both sides.

The king, however, fails to understand his friend's true motivations. While riding through the woods shortly after Becket's appointment as chancellor, the two are caught in a downpour. The king's questions to Becket show the king to be quite ignorant regarding his own subjects and the laws that govern them. The king then becomes enamored of the young peasant girl in the shack where they take cover. Becket pretends to want the girl for himself in order to parry the king's indiscretion. Becket soon thereafter loses his mistress to the king's misguided playfulness: The king decides that Becket should return the favor that the king granted Becket in the shack. Specifically, the king should sleep with Becket's mistress. Becket, circumspect as ever, agrees to share Gwendolen's favors in exchange for those of the peasant girl. Gwendolen stabs herself rather than sleep with the king. Henry, oblivious as ever, concludes that he has survived an assassination attempt on Gwendolen's part.

As chancellor, Becket finds himself obliged to educate and civilize the king and his henchmen-barons, instructing them in manners and in enlightened self-interest, especially when dealing with conquered enemies such as France. Becket also perceives a growing domestic threat from the British clergy. Upon learning of the death of the archbishop of Canterbury, Henry decides to move against that threat by naming his friend Becket to the post, much against Becket's wishes and better judgment. Becket, a former candidate for the priesthood, resolves to do, as usual, the best possible job of whatever is handed to him, giving away all of his possessions to the poor. The king, meanwhile, faces trouble in his household as well as in his reign. He is henpecked by his wife and mother, both of whom envy his friendship with Becket, and he is unable to control his adolescent sons.

Becket's resignation as chancellor, on the grounds that he cannot serve God and king at once, drives the king to the desperate act of plotting against Becket with Gilbert Folliot, bishop of London and chief among Becket's enemies within the church. Soon Becket, condemned on patently false charges of embezzlement and witchcraft, seeks refuge, going first to France and then as far as Rome for an audience with the pope. Becket then returns to France. The French, however, find him too worrisome a fugitive for permanent asylum. The king of France, seeking compromise, arranges for Becket to meet with King Henry on neutral ground in an effort to reconcile their differences. Both men still care about each other, but neither will abandon his principles and the meeting fails. Returning from France, knowing his life to be in danger, Becket waits at Canterbury for the inevitable, a murderous assault by the henchmen of the king. The play's final scene, replicating the first, portrays the king's ritual flagellation for his part in the assassination plot. Such penance is in fact a deft political move, defusing a revolt mounted against the king by his own sons. The king is showing, in his canny statecraft, how much he has learned from Becket. A final irony is that Becket, from the grave, manages at last to transform Henry II from a petty tribal chieftain into a true monarch.

Critical Evaluation:

As in his earlier *L'Alouette* (1953; *The Lark*, 1955), about Joan of Arc, Anouilh, in *Becket*, treats the life and death of a martyred Christian saint through the eyes of a nonbeliever who is less concerned with faith than with human character and motivation. What matters to Anouilh is the legendary figure of Becket as recalled and reconstructed over the centuries in history and literature. As had the Greek myth that he had exploited earlier in his *Antigone* (1944; English translation, 1946), the lives of the saints provided context for psychological and social commentary. What Anouilh does in *Becket* is demystify the saint under consideration, presenting him to the audience in straightforward human terms.

The legend of Thomas à Becket has appealed frequently to playwrights, most notably T. S. Eliot, whose *Murder in the Cathedral* (1935) is often revived. Eliot's play, however, takes the point of view of a believer, with emphasis on theological debate. Anouilh, well acquainted with Eliot's version, attempted some twenty-five years later to expand the scope of Eliot's inquiry, opening the exposition to include not only the outdoors (through the use of costly stage sets) but also a full range of European history and politics. For Eliot, Thomas's life is exemplary and inspirational; for Anouilh, it is legendary and symbolic, illustrative of problems that continue to plague the human race. Borrowing freely from the conventions of murder mystery, spy fiction, and broad political satire, as well as from cinematic technique, Anouilh creates in *Becket* a highly convincing and entertaining portrayal of a close friendship in decline. The text of *Becket* often reads more like a screenplay than a stage play, with frequent flashbacks, rapid scene changes, and highly specific instructions about how a particular line is to be delivered. A 1964 film version, featuring Richard Burton as Becket and Peter O'Toole as the king, was extremely faithful to the text and remained in circulation for years afterward. By the time he addresses himself to Becket, Anouilh is well aware that the martyred bishop was no Saxon, as supposed by the historian Augustin Thierry (1795-1856), whose works Anouilh had read as a boy, but rather a Norman like the king himself. Thus deprived of a possible dramatic theme, Anouilh, in *Becket*, derives considerable rhetorical and dramatic effect at the level of character from the political interplay between the king and the pragmatic Becket (who does not, in fact, represent the compromising spirit of the conquered Saxon people). Inner-directed, secretive, at times seemingly heartless, Anouilh's Thomas is a shrewd political manipulator, yet it is impossible for him to believe in anything except the strict code of personal conduct that somehow, until the end, ensures his survival. In *Becket*, Anouilh continues an exposition, begun before *Antigone* and sustained through subsequent plays, of the inevitable conflict between idealism and realism. Antigone chooses death over compromise, but Thomas is a survivor, an unlikely candidate, until his last principled stand, for martyrdom. Forced, by his father's supposed collaboration with the occupying Norman army, to invent his own values, Thomas goes even so far as to deny his evident love for the unfortunate Gwendolen in favor of his newly contracted loyalty to the king. Still improvising, Becket becomes a martyr only when his contract to defend the "honor of God" as archbishop conflicts with his previously sworn loyalty to the king.

Fifteen years after the first performances of *Antigone* and the subsequent liberation of France by Allied forces, the divided moral choices of World War II were still quite fresh in Anouilh's memory. No doubt he had also not forgotten the accusations of political ambiguity that had been leveled against *Antigone*. Thomas, at least as much a pragmatist as Antigone's antagonist, Creon, emerges as a more affirmative character than Creon or Antigone. Thomas substitutes in all of his actions an aesthetic standard for the religious conviction that he lacks. Even at the end, for Anouilh's Thomas, certain actions are simply more beautiful or appropriate than others. He shows, for example, an instinctive feel for the uses and abuses of political power, based upon his grasp of individual and group psychology. The king, a slow but generally receptive learner until the friendship goes sour, allows his cleverer, subtler friend ample opportunity to explain and to test his theories. At no point, however, does Anouilh allow content to intrude upon the play's intended entertainment value. His realized ambition, in Becket as in most of his other plays, is the creation of a playable, engrossing drama with a number of memorable lines and scenes.

Among Anouilh's best-known dramatic efforts (although expensive to mount and therefore seldom revived in production), *Becket* was written at the approximate midpoint of a distinguished, sometimes controversial dramatic career spanning more than fifty years and nearly as many plays. Among French playwrights of his generation, Anouilh is perhaps the most concerned with great theater rather than great ideas or great experiments. He shunned, however, such traditional classifications as comedy and tragedy, preferring to label his plays as black, pink, or grating, the last designed to set one's teeth on edge. Another of Anouilh's classifications is costume plays such as *Becket* and *The Lark*.

Many of the black plays are rich in comic elements, just as most pink plays carry tragic undertones beneath a comic surface. *Becket*, perhaps the most accomplished of the costume plays, combines comic and tragic elements in approximately equal portion, steering clear of melodrama in such scenes as that of Gwendolen's suicide. As a product of the author's full maturity, preceded by several lesser efforts, *Becket* displays a sure touch and a depth of vision absent from such earlier efforts as *Antigone*. At the same time, its monumental scope and glossy surface relate it closely to the commercial theater that Anouilh had long been accused of courting, especially by those who preferred to see him as a literary playwright. As Albert Camus had in his Caligula, Anouilh found in Becket a legendary historical figure subject to interpretation. Anouilh, following the lead of Jean Giraudoux and other French playwrights, found in classical mythology a rich context for the analysis of contemporary problems. Anouilh's Thomas emerges as a model hero for the latter half of the twentieth century. Unable or unwilling to believe in a higher power, Becket constantly improvises in search of values that might lead him toward himself.

David B. Parsell

Further Reading

Della Fazia, Alba. *Jean Anouilh*. Boston: Twayne, 1969. A thoughtful examination of Anouilh's theater, with good consideration of the costume plays. Discussion of Becket is brief but perceptive.

Falb, Lewis W. *Jean Anouilh*. New York: Frederick Ungar, 1977. Good overview of Anouilh's theater, yet slights *Becket* in favor of *The Lark*.

Harvey, John. *Anouilh: A Study in Theatrics*. New Haven, Conn.: Yale University Press, 1964. Correctly distances Anouilh from the thinker-playwrights of his generation, situating him within the tradition of theatricality along with Molière and William Shakespeare. Good analysis of the costume plays.

McIntyre, H. G. *The Theatre of Jean Anouilh*. London: Harrap, 1981. Prepared with Anouilh's life work all but complete, McIntyre's study is perhaps the most useful. It finds continuity where others have seen only confusion.

Pronko, Leonard C. *The World of Jean Anouilh*. Berkeley: University of California Press, 1961. Perhaps the strongest earlier study of Anouilh's theater, including the costume plays. Authoritative on theme and structure in the plays it covers.

The Bedbug

Author: Vladimir Mayakovsky (1893-1930)
First produced: Klop, 1929; first published, 1929 (English translation, 1931)
Type of work: Drama
Type of plot: Satire
Time of plot: 1929 and 1979
Locale: Tambov, Soviet Union

Principal characters:
IVAN PRISYPKIN, a former Party member and a worker
ELZEVIR DAVIDOVNA, a manicurist and cashier at a beauty parlor
ROSALIE PAVLOVNA, her mother
ZOYA BERYOZKINA, a working girl
OLEG BARD, a house owner

The Story:

In a State Department store in Tambov, a central Russian town, in 1929, Ivan Prisypkin (otherwise known as Pierre Skripkin), a former Party member, former worker, and now the fiancé of Elzevir Davidovna Renaissance, accompanies her mother, Rosalie Pavlovna, and a neighboring house owner, Oleg Bard, on a shopping spree in preparation for the wedding. Salespeople are hawking their wares, and Prisypkin is buying everything because his house must be like a horn of plenty and his future children must be brought up to be refined. His future mother-in-law worries about splurging, while Bard supports Prisypkin's extravagance, pointing out, clearly in jest, that the triumph of the victorious proletarian class must be symbolized by a ravishing, elegant, and class-conscious wedding. Prisypkin comes face-to-face with Zoya Beryozkina, his former girlfriend, who demands an explanation for the shopping spree and, more important, for his abandoning her. "Our love is liquidated," he proclaims, using a current official phrase mockingly, while Rosalie calls her a pregnant slut. A militiaman finally breaks up the confrontation.

In a hostel for young workers, there is lively talk about Prisypkin's impending wedding and about the thorough change of his behavior. One of the workers, looking for his boots, is told that Prisypkin took them—for the last time, he swore—to impress his fiancé. They all criticize Prisypkin's betrayal of his class, making fun of his awkward attempts to act like a member of high society. They also make fun of his mother-in-law, saying that her breasts weigh eighty pounds each. Some workers, however, chastise their colleagues for jealousy, noting that most of them would do the same thing if they had a chance.

Prisypkin shows up in brand-new shoes and tosses back the pair of worn-out boots he "borrowed." The workers turn their backs to him, making all kinds of derisive gestures and performing mocking dances. Bard advises Prisypkin to ignore these vulgar manifestations, complaining that a man of great talent has no elbow room in Russia, what with capitalist encirclement and the building of socialism happening simultaneously in one country (again mocking common official phrases). Instead, he ought to learn more refined dances, such as the foxtrot, and endeavor to rise above the riffraff. As the workers continue to harass Prisypkin, he angrily retorts that they all are fighting for a better life, after all. By bettering himself materially, he now firmly believes, he will raise the living standards of the whole proletariat. At that moment a voice announces that Zoya tried to kill herself.

Undeterred, Prisypkin proceeds with the wedding, assisted ably by Bard. The festivities take place with all the pomp of the rich. The wedding guests frolic, utter snide remarks, and act according to their nature. When the ushers try to calm them, a fire starts, and many guests perish in the fire. The firemen find only charred corpses, with one person unaccounted for.

The scene shifts to an undetermined place fifty years later. In 1979, much is changed. There is an amphitheater set in modernistic surroundings. All persons are nameless, clad in sterile white attire, communicating with each other in a manner typical of a futuristic society. They are puzzled by a discovery of a frozen male body, and they have no idea who it might be. All they can see, after an X-ray examination, is that he had calloused hands. They decide to thaw out the body. It turns out that it is Prisypkin, the only person who survived the wedding fire fifty years before. Doused by plenty of water, he was able to survive half a century in a frozen state.

Prisypkin is bewildered by the people around him and by the state in which he finds himself. He is filthy. His corner is like a pigsty, littered with cigarette butts and overturned bottles, recalling a carousing wedding celebration. The only person he can vaguely recognize now is Zoya, who survived her suicide attempt. She brings him some books he requested, but he rejects them as crude propaganda, wanting something "to pluck at his heartstrings." He finally finds something to his liking, while Zoya remarks that she might have died for this skunk.

Because of enormous public curiosity about the discovery, Prisypkin is placed in a zoo cage. The spectacle is replete with musicians, spectators, and many reporters. When the cage is opened to view, the zoo director explains that they found two bugs on the thawed-out body—*Bedbugus normalis* and *Bourgeoisius vulgaris*. The only difference is that the first gorges on a single human being, while the latter gorges on all of humanity. While the proletariat is writhing and scratching itself to rid itself of filth, its parasites build their nests and make their homes in the dirt. Prisypkin is used as an exhibit of the bygone era of filth. The era and the *Bourgeoisius vulgaris* are totally extinct. The signs on the cage—Caution: It Spits! No Unauthorized Entry! and Watch Your Ears: It Curses!—delight the crowd.

When Prisypkin looks at the audience, he expresses his bewilderment and asks heart-rending questions, such as why is he alone and why is he suffering, calling upon the spectators to join him. To forestall possible harm to them, especially to children, the cage is covered again and the director calms the spectators by explaining that the insect (Prisypkin) is tired and is having hallucinations because of the lights. He will recover tomorrow and they can come and view him again.

Critical Evaluation:

Vladimir Mayakovsky wrote *The Bedbug* as a satire on the Soviet society in the late 1920's. This is evident from many aspects of the play and from his biography. Mayakovsky was a staunch supporter of the communist system throughout his life. During the revolution, he willingly lent his services to the revolutionary cause, "setting my heel on the throat of my own song," as he said in one of his poems. He was displeased with the New Economic Policy established by Vladimir Ilich Lenin in 1921 to bring Russia back from the ruins of the revolution and civil war. He was even more displeased with the First Five-Year Plan, instituted in 1928 by Joseph Stalin after the country had recovered economically. The worst aspect of that plan, according to Mayakovsky, was the establishment of a huge army of bureaucrats, who were always a thorn in his side. It should be kept in mind that when the play premiered in Moscow on February 13, 1929, most of the audience consisted of exactly the kind of bureaucrats Mayakovsky satirized. The official reaction to the play was highly critical, and the author was accused of being against the state. Had he not committed suicide on April 14, 1930—caused in part by the "failure" of *The Bedbug* and other works—many believe that he might have become a victim of the purges.

The main source of his disillusionment and bitterness was his fear that the proletariat, for whose sake the revolution was fought, was being betrayed. The betrayal is embodied in the characters of Ivan Prisypkin and Elzevir Davidovna. Both belong to the working class, but during the New Economic Policy they want to join the more affluent society that was created by the freer economic policies. The couple pretends to belong still to the workers' union, which is Mayakovsky's way of criticizing the entire leadership. As a member of the victorious class, Prisypkin demands the benefits of victory ("what did I fight for?"): more and better material goods, a wife above a regular worker status, and "a horn of plenty." At the high point of his and Elzevir's rise, he changes his name to Pierre Skripkin (alluding to French culture and to a Russian name for a violin player) and adds Renaissance to Elzevir's last name. The wedding, opulent and ostentatious, mirrors their nouveau riche status. That almost all the wedding guests perish during the merrymaking is poetic justice.

The satire becomes more serious in the second half of the play. On the one hand, Mayakovsky criticizes the future Soviet society as sterile, nameless, devoid of love and compassion. On the other hand, the resurrected Prisypkin stands as a museum exhibit, filthy and utterly disoriented, to be feared and shunned in the advanced society for which he was supposed to have fought. Mayakovsky makes it clear that in such society there is no room for people of lower classes and workers. Prisypkin's painful cries—"Where am I?" and "Why am I alone in the cage?" and "Why am I suffering?"—underscore the betrayal of the working class. Addressing the audience made up of the people who should have guaranteed the victory of the working class, Mayakovsky is posing a disturbing question about who are the real traitors in the struggle. Although one may call Mayakovsky an early dissident, it must be pointed out that he satirized his society not as an opponent but as an idealistic believer in the cause. He remained true to his belief; he was shunned and presumably would have been killed.

The play is written in a modernistic style, fashionable in the 1920's. It features fast-moving scenes instead of acts, a film technique of which Mayakovsky was fond. The characters are not individuals but types, expressing ideas and slogans rather than individual experience. Satire is the strongest thrust of the play. Mayakovsky uses satire unsparingly, often in a pungent, racy language that never misses its mark. As in his poetry, he frequently plays on words and phrases, always reaching for the strongest effect. For example, Oleg Bard, playing on Prisypkin's desire for his home to be a horn of plenty, solemnly declares that Comrade Prisypkin's "pants must be like a horn of plenty." That *The Bedbug* must have delighted many spectators the first time around, despite official disclaimers, is evident from the success of the play when it was staged again in the late 1950's and later, running simultaneously in two Moscow theaters.

Vasa D. Mihailovich

Further Reading

Brown, Edward J. *Mayakovsky: A Poet in the Revolution*. Princeton, N.J.: Princeton University Press, 1973. A seminal study of Mayakovsky as a man and a writer by a leading American scholar of Soviet literature. Mayakovsky's role in the revolution, as reflected in his works, is emphasized.

Cassiday, Julie A. "Flash Floods, Bedbugs, and Saunas: Social Hygiene in Maiakovskii's Theatrical Satires of the 1920's." *Slavonic and East European Review* 76, no. 4 (October, 1998): 643. Examines the contextual complexity of *The Bedbug* and Mayakovsky's other theatrical satires of the 1920's, discussing the themes and characters of these works.

Metchenko, Alexei, ed. *Vladimir Mayakovsky: Innovator*. Translated by Alex Miller. Moscow: Progress, 1976. Twenty-six articles, mostly by Russian scholars, about Mayakovsky's innovations in his poetry and plays. Of special interest is Valentin Pluchek's article "The New Drama."

Moore, Harry T., and Albert Parry. "Soviet Theatre to the Second World War." In *Twentieth Century Russian Literature*. Carbondale: Southern Illinois University Press, 1974. Provides an overview of theatrical works by Mayakovsky and other Soviet playwrights.

Porter, Robert, ed. *Seven Soviet Poets*. 2d ed. London: Bristol Classical, 2002. Provides biographical information about Mayakovsky and an analysis of his poetry.

Russell, Robert. "Mayakovsky's *The Bedbug* and *The Bathhouse*." In *Russian Drama of the Revolutionary Period*. Totowa, N.J.: Barnes & Noble, 1988. Argues that in these plays Mayakovsky combines satirical condemnation with utopian idealist fantasies, making both works "problem plays."

Segel, Harold B. "The 1920's and the Early 1930's: Social Comedy, Absurd and Grotesque NEP Satire, Melodrama." In *Twentieth-Century Russian Drama: From Gorky to the Present*. Updated ed. Baltimore: Johns Hopkins University Press, 1993. Includes information about Mayakovsky's plays during this period.

Shklovskii, Viktor B. *Mayakovsky and His Circle*. Edited and translated by Lily Feiler. New York: Dodd, Mead, 1972. Recollections and critical remarks about Mayakovsky, including his plays, by one of the most respected modern Russian critics and Mayakovsky's contemporary.

Terras, Victor. *Vladimir Mayakovsky*. Boston: Twayne, 1983. Analysis of Mayakovsky's poetry and plays as well as of his role in literature and events of his time. One of the best brief English-language introductions to his works.

Woroszylski, Wiktor. *The Life of Mayakovsky*. Translated by Bołesław Taborski. New York: Orion Press, 1970. An objective biography by a Polish poet, based on documents and opinions of Mayakovsky's contemporaries. Mayakovsky's contributions to theater and to cinema are discussed at length.

The Beet Queen

Author: Louise Erdrich (1954-)
First published: 1986
Type of work: Novel
Type of plot: Domestic realism
Time of plot: 1929-1972
Locale: Argus, North Dakota; Prairie Lake, Minneapolis, and Blue Mound, Minnesota

Principal characters:
MARY ADARE, an abandoned girl
KARL ADARE, Mary's brother, also abandoned
JUDE MILLER, Mary and Karl's brother, abandoned as an infant
ADELAIDE ADARE, Mary, Karl, and Jude's mother
FRITZIE ADARE KOZKA, Mary's aunt
SITA KOZKA TAPPE, Fritzie's daughter
CELESTINE JAMES, Jude's wife
WALLACETTE "DOT" ADARE, Jude and Celestine's daughter
RUSSELL KASHPAW, Celestine's half brother
WALLACE PFEF, lover of Karl and Dot's adoptive uncle

The Story:

Eleven-year-old Mary Adare and her brother, Karl, who is fourteen years old, are left penniless with their mother, Adelaide, after her married lover dies. It is 1932, and many people are suffering through the Great Depression. Adelaide tries to keep the family together by pawning her few bits of jewelry, but this fails to bring in enough money. In desperation, she leaves Mary, Karl, and her newborn baby to fend for themselves, leaving them for stunt pilot Omar. Adelaide and Omar fly off in his barnstorming plane, never to return. The children are left to care for the baby. When things get even more desperate, Mary and Karl give their unnamed baby brother to the Millers, Catherine and Martin.

Mary and Karl hop a freight car for Argus, where their aunt, Fritzie Adare Kozka, runs a butcher shop. Mary arrives safely with a little box containing her mother's garnet necklace, but Karl, after arriving with Mary in Argus, jumps back on the train. Fritzie and her husband take Mary in, give her a bed in their daughter Sita's room, and give her some of Sita's old clothes, sparking a lifelong jealousy in Sita.

Mary discovers that the necklace box contains only a pawn ticket. She puts this disappointment behind her and busies herself with the butcher shop and with school. She becomes friends with Celestine James, once Sita's closest friend. Celestine is more like Mary—competent and practical—than like Sita—who has romantic notions about herself. When Fritzie shows Mary a postcard from her mother in Florida, Mary sends the card back to her mother, with a note that her (her mother's) three children have died.

Mary had made a new life in Argus after traveling there by train with Karl. Her brother, however, broke both legs after jumping again from the train. Fleur Pillager, a Chippewa woman, helped him to heal. After recovering, Karl begins to fantasize about rescuing his mother from Omar, who is now married to her. Eventually, Karl enters a Catholic orphanage in Minneapolis and plans to become a priest. His vocation is mostly self-preservation, however, and he leaves the seminary in early adulthood, returning just long enough to recognize a young seminarian as his lost brother—the abandoned baby, now known as Jude Miller.

It is now 1941, and Mary is running the butcher shop for her aunt, whose health is failing. Mary, who knows that she is not attractive, makes a play for Celestine's half brother Russell, who bluntly resists her advances. Fritzie and her husband retire to Arizona, and Sita moves to Fargo, North Dakota, to model for a local department store. There, Sita puts most of her energies into preserving her looks and angling for an advantageous marriage. She receives a forwarded letter from Jude's adopted mother that tells the story of how she raised him and announces his ordination in Minneapolis. Sita goes to the ceremony and later redeems Adelaide's ancient pawn ticket for the old garnet necklace. She keeps the garnets and writes Jude's mother that she is unable to identify Jude.

Meanwhile, Karl, selling farming implements, meets a young man named Wallace Pfef at an agricultural show and learns that Pfef is from Argus. Karl takes him to dinner and later seduces him. Back in Argus, living safely in the proverbial closet, Pfef is stunned by his sexual experience with Karl. He moves on with his plans to promote sugar-beet farming in the area.

By 1953, Russell has returned from service in Korea as a decorated but seriously wounded soldier. In a burst of generosity, Mary, Russell, and Celestine attend the opening of

Sita's pretentious new restaurant and salvage the opening by taking over the cooking; the restaurant seems as doomed as Sita's marriage to Jimmy. Back in Argus, Karl, now selling cheap knives, arrives at the butcher's shop and begins an affair with Celestine. She takes him home, displacing Russell, who now must spend time in his fishing shack. Karl lives with Celestine until she tires of his sponging, and she sends him away just as she discovers she is pregnant. A little later, Russell has a serious stroke and leaves town to live with his Chippewa relatives.

When Karl leaves Celestine, he goes to Sita's house in Blue Mound to sell Bibles. During a strained lunch with Karl and Louis, Sita's new husband, she develops the delusion that Karl has robbed her and then begins a mental breakdown that eventually leads to her hospitalization.

Karl moves on to Pfef's welcoming house, stays for a time, and then disappears. Pfef salves his painful loneliness by adopting a stray dog. That winter, Celestine arrives in a blizzard and is about to give birth. Pfef helps deliver the baby, a girl whom Celestine names Wallacette Adare. Mary nicknames her Dot. All three adults adore the child, indulge her constantly, and compete for her affection. Dot becomes a stubborn, selfish, assertive child, much like Mary. She bullies other children and even falsely accuses a teacher of abusing children.

It is now 1964, and the butcher shop burns down. Mary moves in with Dot and Celestine temporarily, but she is a difficult houseguest, constantly telling fortunes. Dot plays the biblical Joseph in the school Christmas play, but the event ends in disaster when, out of frustrated infatuation, she hits the boy who plays the donkey. Humiliated, she flees to Pfef. Later, in an effort to make Mary popular, Pfef plans an elaborate birthday party for her; this, too, ends in disaster as Mary gets extremely drunk.

Sita, now almost a decade older, is widowed and becomes ill; for the first time in years she asks for Mary. With Celestine, Mary arrives to help. Sita's illness is mostly caused by an addiction to pain pills. Weeks pass, then Mary and Celestine find the letter from Jude's mother amid Sita's hoarded junk. Sita dies from an overdose, wearing the garnet necklace.

Mary and Celestine bring Sita's body back to Argus, fearful of missing the Argus Beet Festival and the crowning of the Beet Queen. Pfef, now a civic leader, has rigged the competition to ensure that Dot wins the crown. Despite a serious drought, Pfef has hired a skywriter to announce her reign. Russell is at the festival as well, in a wheel chair and wearing his medals. He has a fatal stroke before the judging begins. Karl attends, too. Even Jude, now a priest, arrives to seek his lost siblings.

Mary leaves Sita's body in the truck because time is tight. Mary alone imagines that Dot can win the crown fairly, but Dot has learned of Pfef's vote rigging. Furious, she knocks him out cold with a softball in the fair's dunking tank. Karl arrives in time to save Pfef from drowning.

After Dot is proclaimed queen, she climbs into the skywriter's plane. The plane takes off, and the pilot spells out "Queen Wallacette" in the sky. Dot returns long after the event has ended. Only Celestine still waits. As the two go home, they see Karl's car at Pfef's house. Celestine fixes supper, and a long rain begins.

Critical Evaluation:

The Beet Queen demonstrates techniques and themes that readers have come to associate with Louise Erdrich's work. The book's large cast of characters is a feature of her first novel, *Love Medicine* (1984), and it continues to characterize her later works. Her later novels also include the use of multiple voices, American Indian elements, and comedy; an examination of gender roles; and themes that insist on the power of love.

Erdrich's use of multiple viewpoints is a technique that links her with other postmodern writers. As the various characters relate parts of the narrative, the author establishes their separate voices and attitudes. Erdrich sometimes lets characters retell events that others have already narrated, creating ambiguities and allowing the contradictions to illuminate the characters. Thus, when Sita speaks about her courtship with Jimmy, the reader understands that her claims about her career and good looks are mostly products of her own vanity. Not all chapter titles indicate a given chapter's speaker; in some cases, the titles simply suggest a shift in point of view. "The Passenger," for instance, uses third-person narration to focus on Jude's arrival in Argus. Although Dot dominates the second half of the novel, she has a voice only in the last chapter.

Gender, too, is an important theme in *The Beet Queen*. Mary, and later Dot, are masculine in their pugnacity and stubborn insistence on having their own way. In later life, Mary wears outlandish clothes with no concern for her public image. Her fondness for palm reading and fortune-telling suggests that she would be glad to control the future as thoroughly as she does the present. She simply learns to forget the parts of reality she cannot control, such as her unappealing looks. She does not worry about Sita's jealousy or Russell's rejection.

Dot is much like her aunt in looks and personal style. When in grade school she tries to get the attention of a boy who interests her, she can only hit him. Her adolescent rebellion is intensified by her frustration at her failure to connect with others. At the beet festival, she knows that she looks ridiculous in traditional beauty-queen clothes.

Wallace Pfef, on the other hand, who hides his homosexuality behind vague references to a dead sweetheart, is portrayed as feminine in his devotion to homemaking and his adopted niece. Erdrich does not stereotype Pfef, who is also a well-respected town leader and founder of Argus's sugar-beet industry. Karl seems to claim both genders in his bisexuality. As Celestine's lover, he had been much more passive; with Pfef, he had been a seducer. Significantly, he saves Pfef's life at the festival, and his car is in Pfef's driveway at the end of the story.

Celestine, on the other hand, though not traditionally feminine (she is six feet tall), seems to share Pfef's impulse to nurture at the same time she manages her own life. She enjoys her affair with Karl but is able to send him away; she is strong enough to rescue her paralyzed brother, but she also knows how to salve Dot's humiliation at the novel's end. Sita is the novel's most stereotypically feminine character; she is also the one who is least able to shape her own life.

In this novel, the American Indian elements seem muted, but they are certainly present. The irony of the marginalized Indian leaves Russell, who is part Chippewa, paralyzed and voiceless in his medal-adorned military uniform in the beet-festival parade. A similar irony underscores adolescent Karl's fantasies about his mother (who abandoned him) while Fleur, a Chippewa woman, goes to considerable trouble to rescue and heal him. Significantly, Celestine is the most self-realized American Indian in the novel.

In Erdrich's fictional world, there exists plenty of suffering, but love and family loyalties have the last voice. In *The Beet Queen*, families are marked by blood relationships (like the Chippewa relatives who take in Russell and the impulse that sends Mary to help Sita in her last days), but they are also created by other bonds, like Pfef's devotion to Dot. Indeed, even some of the suffering takes a comic turn, as when Dot's birthday party disintegrates after Mary drunkenly overwinds the spring-powered cake stand and sends cake flying through the room. Dot calls it the best party ever.

Despair had made Adelaide Adare try to fly away from her troubles when she abandoned her children, and rage made Dot try a similar escape at the novel's end. Unlike Adelaide, however, Dot returns to earth, where she finds her mother waiting to help her home while a healing rain ends the drought.

The Beet Queen is the second book of the tetralogy that makes up Erdrich's early work; the others are *Love Medicine*, *Tracks* (1988), and *The Bingo Palace* (1994). Together, the tetralogy has ensured Erdrich's place as a major contemporary novelist and an important American Indian voice.

Ann D. Garbett

Further Reading

Barak, Julie. "Blurs, Blends, Berdaches: Gender Mixing in the Novels of Louise Erdrich." *Studies in American Indian Literature* 8, no. 3 (Fall, 1996): 49-62. Examines manly women, feminine men, and cross-dressing in *The Beet Queen*. Relates gender-bending (and gender-blending) to American Indian themes.

Beidler, Peter G., and Gay Barton. *A Reader's Guide to the Novels of Louise Erdrich*. Columbia: University of Missouri Press, 1999. An informative handbook for students of Erdrich's fiction that covers geography, chronology, and character relationships in her novels through 1998.

Meisenhelder, Susan. "Race and Gender in Louise Erdrich's *The Beet Queen*." *Ariel* 25, no. 1 (January, 1994): 45-57. A consideration of Erdrich's themes of gender roles, gender expectations, and race as they relate to American Indian identities.

Stookey, Lorena Laura. *Louise Erdrich: A Critical Companion*. Westport, Conn.: Greenwood Press, 1999. This study of Erdrich's works presents biographical information, an examination of Erdrich's place in the literary tradition, and an analysis of each novel through 1998. Includes bibliographical references and an index.

Tharp, Julie. "Women's Community and Survival in the Novels of Louise Erdrich." In *Communication and Women's Friendships: Parallels and Intersections in Literature and Life*, edited by Janet Doubler Ward and JoAnna Stephens Mink. Bowling Green, Ohio: Bowling Green State University Popular Press, 1993. In this general study of women's friendships and everyday communication, Tharp pays particular attention to the friendship between Mary and Celestine in *The Beet Queen*.

The Beggar Maid
Stories of Flo and Rose

Author: Alice Munro (1931-)
First published: 1978, as *Who Do You Think You Are?*
Type of work: Short fiction
Type of plot: Domestic realism
Time of plot: 1940's-1970's
Locale: Ontario and British Columbia, Canada

Principal characters:
ROSE, the protagonist
FLO, her stepmother
BRIAN, her half-brother
ROSE'S FATHER
PATRICK BLATCHFORD, her husband
ANNA, her daughter
JOCELYN,
CLIFFORD, and
SIMON, her friends

The Story:

Rose lives in Hanratty, Ontario. Her father repairs furniture while Flo, Rose's stepmother, runs the family store. One day, Flo wants Rose punished for teaching her little brother, Brian, a crude childish rhyme. Rose's father loosens his belt, signaling the familiar struggle of whipping and protest. Eventually, the wounded Rose escapes to her room, where Flo brings food as a peace offering.

Later, Rose's father comments on the ignoramuses in the neighborhood, those men who are fool enough to believe that the bright western star, visible over Michigan, is really a mysterious airship. (Years later, Rose hears a radio interview featuring one of those local ignoramuses on his one-hundredth birthday. His countrified storytelling amuses Rose, and she wishes she could tell Flo about it, but Flo has grown too old to care.)

Rose finds the country-school outhouses filthy and repulsive. She avoids them all day and then wets her pants on the way home. Flo, disgusted by Rose's accidents, mocks the child. At school, older students abuse the defenseless children, yet the teacher ignores the cruelty. She locks the school door, leaving the students unsupervised outside during recesses. As protection, Rose seeks the friendship of Cora, an older girl who wears bright lipstick and frilly dresses. Cora accepts Rose, then coddles her and paints her fingernails red. Rose steals candy from the family store as a present for Cora. In an effort to feel grown-up herself, Cora returns the candy to the store. Rose is not punished for stealing, but Flo teases her stepdaughter for admiring Cora, a girl whose curvaceous hips will eventually become womanly fat. Flo distrusts the idea of love, hopefulness, and need.

Rose's father dies of lung cancer, leaving the girl in the care of her stepmother until she leaves Hanratty for college. In college, Rose is mentored by Dr. Henshawe, a female English professor who praises Rose's intellect. Rose meets Patrick Blatchford, a pale, serious graduate student, in the university library. He finds her as lovely as the woman in *King Cophetua and the Beggar Maid* (1884), a painting by Edward Burne-Jones depicting a legendary king who transforms a beggar into a queen. Rose both craves and disdains Patrick's devotion. When she takes him to Hanratty, the disparity between his affluent life and her coarse world are magnified. Rose marries Patrick but never allows herself to love him fully. (Decades later, she spies Patrick in an airport coffee bar. She hopes he will admire her as her audiences do. However, he looks at her with loathing.)

Rose befriends artists and free thinkers, people opposite Patrick and his provincial family. She becomes infatuated with Clifford, a talented violinist who is married to her friend Jocelyn. Years later, Rose visits the couple again. Clifford and Jocelyn have grown conventional. They possess objects they once disdained, like color televisions and waffle irons. Their rebellion has given way to complacency.

Rose divorces Patrick, works as an actor, and finds work at a radio station in central Canada; she takes their daughter, Anna, with her. Eventually, Rose realizes that she cannot simultaneously care for her daughter, pursue her career, and find love. She sends Anna back to live with Patrick and his new wife. To supplement her acting career, Rose teaches university classes. At a party, she meets Simon, a classics professor, and they go to Rose's house. They plan a garden for her country cottage, and Simon promises a return visit. Rose never sees him again. Later, she learns that Simon had died of pancreatic cancer.

Rose returns to Hanratty. Flo has become too old to live alone, so Rose takes her to the county home. The hometown crowd recognizes Rose from her work on television. She is a local success. People no longer ask her, "Who do you think you are?" Times have changed for her and the town. As she interacts with the people from her childhood, she realizes that she is connected to them in an inexplicable way. For once, she belongs.

Critical Evaluation:

The Beggar Maid comprises ten stories, many of which were initially published in *The New Yorker* and other literary and popular magazines between 1977 and 1978. *The Beggar Maid* was released first in Canada as *Who Do You Think You Are?* (1978). Some critics view the compilation as a loose-fitting novel. The stories are arranged chronologically, beginning with Rose's recollections of childhood.

In each story, the action focuses on Rose at a certain stage in her life but ends with a reflection that Rose has gained from a distance. Thus, the story "Royal Beatings" begins by recounting the whippings Rose received as a child but ends with Rose describing Flo's old-age decline. Munro says that her process for writing a story is not like following a road, but like building a house. The action goes back and forth like movement from room to room in a fictional dwelling, allowing Munro to connect past and present seamlessly.

The title story, "The Beggar Maid," marks the center of the collection. Rose leaves home to experience university life. When she meets Patrick Blatchford, she accepts the young man's admiration but feels she cannot adequately return his love. She resents his upper-class status as much as she wants to escape her impoverished roots. In this relationship, as with others in the story cycle, Rose finds that she does not trust people. Her attempts to achieve a better life are often stymied by her own shortcomings. She fails to value and accept others as they are, and she often puts on an act as though her life were a stage play or radio drama.

Early on, Rose realizes that she is different. She has aspirations far beyond the confines of Hanratty, Ontario. Like Francie Nolan, in Betty Smith's *A Tree Grows in Brooklyn* (1943), Rose faces brutality in school and rock-hard poverty in her neighborhood, but she still dreams of a better life. However, Munro's heroine is less hopeful than Nolan. Rose realizes that Hanratty's poverty is not just wretchedness and deprivation, but a setting for things ugly, cheap, or crude, without knowing any better. *The Beggar Maid* reflects a 1970's disillusionment that combines the desire to break free of social restraints with the fruitless pursuit of the unattainable.

Munro asserts that behaving like a nice girl while she was growing up meant she had to abdicate her own self. This conflict is similarly reflected in Rose's struggle: Who does she think she is? She searches for the answer in every story. In the closing chapter, "Who Do You Think You Are?," Rose returns to Hanratty. A stranger says Rose looks "better in person" than she does on television. Although Rose considers that "everything she had done could sometimes be seen as a mistake," she seems at peace. She realizes that she cannot abandon the part of her that poverty and suffering have created. Flo may have meted out royal beatings, but she also taught Rose storytelling. The challenge for Rose is to determine when to tell the story and when to face the truth. Because of her journey, Rose realizes she has become "better in person."

Paula M. Miller

Further Reading

Fowler, Rowena. "The Art of Alice Munro: *The Beggar Maid* and *Lives of Girls and Women*." *Critique* 25, no. 4 (1984): 189-199. Compares the development of female characters in Munro's works. Demonstrates how narrative style and theme reinforce the coming-of-age elements of the women characters and Munro's interest in blending the past and the present.

Martin, W. R., and Warren U. Ober. "Alice Munro as Small-Town Historian: 'Spaceships Have Landed.'" *Essays on Canadian Writing* 66 (1998): 128-147. Essay explores the importance of setting in Munro's works. The rural landscapes of Ontario and the tales of local historians have influenced the author's own storytelling and myth creation.

Mazur, Carol, and Cathy Moulder. *Alice Munro: An Annotated Bibliography of Works and Criticism.* Lanham, Md.: Scarecrow Press, 2007. A comprehensive source listing works by and about Munro through 2005. Sources include articles of criticism as well as author interviews.

Munro, Sheila. *Lives of Mothers and Daughters: Growing Up with Alice Munro.* Toronto, Ont.: McClelland & Stewart, 2001. This memoir by Munro's daughter discusses how Munro managed home and career. Also details how real events and locations found their way into her mother's stories. Readers may gain insight into the autobiographical elements of *The Beggar Maid.*

Redekop, Magdalene. *Mothers and Other Clowns: The Stories of Alice Munro.* New York: Routledge, 1992. Chapter 9, "Who Do You Think You Are? Blaming the King of the Royal Beatings," focuses on the symbolic nature of female characters in *The Beggar Maid.*

Warwick, Susan J. "Growing Up: The Novels of Alice Munro." *Essays on Canadian Writing* 29 (1984): 204-226. An insightful analysis of the protagonists in *The Beggar Maid* and *Lives of Girls and Women* (1971). Warwick considers the works as novels, focusing on the development of the characters and their failings and epiphanies.

The Beggar's Opera

Author: John Gay (1685-1732)
First produced: 1728; first published, 1728
Type of work: Drama
Type of plot: Social satire
Time of plot: Early eighteenth century
Locale: London

Principal characters:
CAPTAIN MACHEATH, a highwayman
MR. PEACHUM, a receiver of stolen goods and an informer
POLLY PEACHUM, his daughter, who is in love with Macheath
MR. LOCKIT, the warder of Newgate
LUCY LOCKIT, his daughter, who is also in love with Macheath

The Story:

Mr. Peachum, reckoning up his accounts, declares that his is an honest employment. Like a lawyer, he acts both for and against thieves. That he should protect them is only fitting, since they afford him a living. In a businesslike manner he decides who among some arrested rogues should escape punishment through bribes and who are so unproductive as to deserve deportation or the gallows. Though Mrs. Peachum finds a favorite of hers on his list, she makes no effort to influence her husband's decision, for she knows that the weakness of her sex is to allow emotions to dominate practical considerations. She does say, however, that Captain Macheath, a highwayman, stands high in her regard, as well as in that—so she hints to Mr. Peachum—of their daughter Polly. The news upsets her spouse. If the girl marries, her husband might learn family secrets and gain power over them. Peachum orders his wife to warn the girl that marriage and a husband's domination will mean her ruin. Consequently they are dismayed when Polly announces her marriage to Macheath. They predict grimly that she will not be able to keep Macheath in funds for gambling and philandering, that there will not even be enough money to cause quarrels, that she might as well have married a lord.

The Peachums' greatest fear is that Macheath will have them hanged and so gain control of the fortune that is intended for Polly. They decide it will be best to dispose of him before he can do that, and they suggest to Polly that she inform on him. Widowhood, they tell her, is a very comfortable state. The girl stubbornly asserts that she loves her dashing highwayman, and she warns Macheath of her parents' plan to have him arrested. They decide that he should go into hiding for a few weeks until, as Polly hopes, her parents relent.

Parting from his love, Macheath meets his gang at a tavern near Newgate to tell them that for the next week their rendezvous will have to be confined to their private hideout, so that Peachum will think the highwayman is deserting his companions. After his men leave to go about their business, some street women and female pickpockets enter. Two of them cover Macheath with his own pistols as Peachum, accompanied by constables, rushes in to arrest him. When Macheath is carried off to spend the night in Newgate, some of the women express indignation at not having been among those chosen to spring the trap and share in the reward Peachum offers for the highwayman's capture.

Though Macheath has funds to bribe his jailer to confine him with only a light pair of fetters, it is another matter to deal with Lucy Lockit, the jailer's daughter. As Macheath freely admits, she is his wife but for the ceremony. Lucy hears of his gallantry toward Polly and can only be convinced of his sincerity by his consenting to an immediate marriage.

Peachum and Lockit, meanwhile, agree to split the reward for Macheath. As he goes over his accounts, however, Peachum finds cause to question his partner's honesty. One of his men was convicted, although he bribed Lockit to have the man go free. Peachum's informer, Mrs. Coaxer, was likewise defrauded of information money. The quarrel between Peachum and Lockit is short-lived, however, as they are well aware that each has the power to hang the other. After his talk with Peachum, Lockit warns his daughter that Macheath's fate is sealed. He advises her to buy herself widow's weeds and to be cheerful; since she cannot have the highwayman and his money, too, she might as well make use of the time that is left to extract what riches she can from him.

There is no clergyman to be found that day, but Lucy softens toward her philandering lover so far as to agree to see if her father can be bought off. She just consents to help him when Polly appears in search of her husband. Macheath manages to convince Lucy of his faithfulness by disowning Polly, who is carried off by the angry Peachum. After they leave, Lucy agrees to steal her father's keys so that her lover might escape. Macheath, free once more, joins two of his men at a gambling house. There he makes arrangements to meet them again that evening at another den, where they will plan the next robbery.

Peachum and Lockit are discussing the disposal of assorted loot when they are joined by Mrs. Trapes, a procurer who innocently tells them that Macheath is at that moment with one of her girls. While Peachum and Lockit go off to recapture him, Polly pays a visit to Lucy. Together they bewail their common fate—Macheath's neglect. Lucy tries to give Polly a poisoned drink. When the suspicious girl refuses to accept it, Lucy decides that perhaps Polly is too miserable to deserve to die.

When Macheath is brought back to prison once more by Peachum and Lockit, both girls fall on their knees before their fathers and beg that his life be spared. Neither parent is moved. Lockit announces that the highwayman will die that day. As he prepares to go to the Old Bailey, Macheath says that he is resigned to his fate, for his death will settle all disputes and please all his wives.

While Macheath in his cell reflects ironically that rich men can escape the gallows but the poor must hang, he is visited by two of his men. He asks them to make sure that Lockit and Peachum are hanged before they themselves are finally strung up. The thieves are followed by the distraught Polly and Lucy, come to bid Macheath farewell. When the jailer announces that four more of his wives, each accompanied by a child, have appeared to say good-bye, Macheath declares that he is ready to meet his fate.

The rabble outside, believing that the poor should be allowed their vices just like the rich, raises so much clamor for Macheath's reprieve that charges are dropped and he is released in triumph. In the merrymaking that follows, he chooses Polly as his partner, because, he gallantly announces, she is really his wife. From that time on he intends to give up the vices—if not the follies—of the rich.

Critical Evaluation:

The Beggar's Opera, one of the finest plays written in English in the early eighteenth century, follows in the satiric tradition of Jonathan Swift and Alexander Pope. John Gay's purpose is likewise to ridicule the corrupt politics of his day and the follies of polite society. His depiction of crime and vice in all strata of society and his shrewd, humorous characterizations give the play universality. *The Beggar's Opera* has remained popular since its first performances, both in its original version and in such reworkings as those by composers Benjamin Britten and Arthur Bliss; Bertolt Brecht's adaptation of the original with music by Kurt Weill, *The Threepenny Opera*; and a fine British film version made in 1953.

The Beggar's Opera was written as a satire of the government of King George II, represented by Macheath, and the Whig prime minister, Robert Walpole, represented by Peachum. Gay also satirizes the contrived but popular Italian operas and the simpler English alternative to them. The work features well-known English and Scottish ballads and airs to which Gay added his own lyrics.

Colley Cibber, whom Pope satirized in *The Dunciad* (1728-1743) and who managed the Drury Lane Theatre, unwisely declined to produce *The Beggar's Opera* when Gay submitted it to him. At length a reluctant John Rich, of the Theatre Royal, agreed to produce the play. His fears of failure proved unwarranted, for the play became a great financial success. It was said at the time that *The Beggar's Opera* made Gay rich and Rich gay.

Gay's achievement and the reason for the play's continued success is the fact that the work can be enjoyed without a knowledge of the contemporary political and theatrical milieu that it satirizes. The tone is jocular and bawdy, but it never lapses into bitterness or mere vulgarity. The diction is simple, the satire sharp, but the message is neither overly subjective nor acidic. The play may be considered as one long song, for it has that lyrical, bell-like quality of its finest airs. The plot, unlike the comedies of manners, the burlesques, and the farces popular at the time, is extremely simple, with no complicated and intertwining subplots to divert attention.

Like a song or ballad, *The Beggar's Opera* has several refrains. One of these is the cynical view of love and marriage, a favorite theme of the comedy of manners. There is, too, the typical strain of antifeminism ("Tis woman that seduces all mankind," sings Filch in act 1, scene 2). As Gay makes clear, however, neither sex is faultless when it comes to romance. "Love," says Lucy, "is so very whimsical in both sexes, that it is impossible to be lasting" (act 3, scene 8). That Macheath and Polly will at least attempt a lasting relationship is suggested by the song he sings to Polly in act 1, scene 13:

> My heart was so free,
> It rov'd like the bee,
> 'Till Polly my passion requited;
> I sipt each flower,
> I chang'd ev'ry hour,
> But here ev'ry flower is united.

Not the least aspect of this song's effectiveness lies in its sexual imagery, which is typical of the play.

Two other refrains are the plays Gay makes on the words "duty" and "honor." Polly, say her parents, must have her husband "peach'd" (impeached, given to the authorities for reward money) because it is her "duty" thus to obey her parents—a subversion of the biblical commandment to honor one's parents. It is also the "duty" of the thieves to rob, of the whores to "love," and of Polly to stand by her husband, who is anything but faithful.

Another refrain, the pun on the word "honour," effectively criticizes the manners of the court. Thus the honor of the Peachums (that is, the Walpoles) is in question if Polly makes an unsuccessful marriage, one that is not remunerative. However, Polly insists: "I did not marry him (as tis the fashion) coolly and deliberately for honour or money. But, I love him." The thieves are "men of honour" in name only, just as are the courtiers, and Lockit, with heavy irony, declares to his fellow mobster, Peachum: "He that attacks my honour, attacks my livelyhood."

One of Lockit's songs advises: "When you censure the age,/ Be cautious and sage." Yet, subtle and sophisticated as his censure of the court and Walpole's government is, the prime minister sees through it and refuses to allow the production of *Polly* (1729), Gay's sequel to *The Beggar's Opera*. By 1737, the Licensing Act was in effect and the theaters had been closed, ending dramatic criticism of the government. (*The Beggar's Opera* and the plays of Henry Fielding are in fact largely credited with having brought on the 1737 act.) Gay's masterpiece, however, not only survived but also thrived.

"Critical Evaluation" by Clifton M. Snider

Further Reading

Armens, Sven. *John Gay, Social Critic*. 1954. Reprint. New York: Octagon Books, 1966. This full-length critical examination of Gay and his work deals in depth with *The Beggar's Opera*.

Atkins, Madeline Smith. *The Beggar's "Children": How John Gay Changed the Course of England's Musical Theatre*. Newcastle, England: Cambridge Scholars, 2006. Recounts the significant impact of *The Beggar's Opera* on London's musical theater. The success of Gay's work spurred the creation of numerous ballad operas, and this form of musical theater dominated the stage from 1728 through the mid-eighteenth century. Discusses *The Beggar's Opera* and the other ballad operas produced in those years.

Bronson, Bertrand H. "*The Beggar's Opera*." In *Studies in the Comic*. Los Angeles: University of California Press, 1941. A fine critical study of *The Beggar's Opera*, particularly valuable for placing the work in the context of its time and exploring the links to Italian opera that Gay so skillfully exploited.

Dugaw, Dianne. *"Deep Play": John Gay and the Invention of Modernity*. Newark: University of Delaware Press, 2001. Examines how Gay used ballads, songs, country dances, fables, stories, legends, and other forms of popular culture to comment on opera, drama, and literature.

Gay, John. *The Beggar's Opera*. Larchmont, N.Y.: Argonaut Books, 1961. This edition of the play, a reproduction of the 1729 version, contains the lyrics to all the tunes that Gay adapted.

Irving, William Henry. *John Gay: Favorite of the Wits*. Durham, N.C.: Duke University Press, 1940. Considered one of the best treatments of Gay's life and works.

Noble, Yvonne, ed. *Twentieth Century Interpretations of "The Beggar's Opera."* Englewood Cliffs, N.J.: Prentice-Hall, 1975. Comprises a series of nine critical and informative essays on Gay's masterpiece, as well as an informative introduction by the editor.

Nokes, David. *John Gay, a Profession of Friendship*. New York: Oxford University Press, 1995. Biography of Gay containing updated information about his life and work. Analyzes Gay's work and compares it to the work of his contemporaries.

Spacks, Patricia Meyer. *John Gay*. New York: Twayne, 1965. An excellent introduction to Gay's life and works.

Being and Nothingness

Author: Jean-Paul Sartre (1905-1980)
First published: L'être et le néant, 1943 (English translation, 1956)
Type of work: Philosophy

The French philosopher Jean-Paul Sartre has become widely identified with twentieth century existentialism as its most popular and well-known proponent and as a lucid and gifted writer of both philosophy and literature. Although existentialist tenets had been expressed in the thought of such previous philosophers as Søren Kierkegaard and Martin Heidegger, the mood of alienation and despair evoked by existentialism found its greatest response in the post-World War II circumstances in which Sartre lived and worked. As the leading French intellectual movement of the era, Sartrean existentialism infiltrated virtually every form of thought and artistic achievement, including literature, the theater, the visual arts, and theology. *Being and Nothingness*, Sartre's major philosophical work, is considered to be one of the most influential texts of this movement, as well as being an important work in the history of philosophy as a whole.

Born in Paris in 1905, Sartre was educated at the École Normale Supérieure, where he graduated at the age of twenty-two with a degree in philosophy. "Philosophy is absolutely terrific," he said later of his early educational experience. "You can learn the truth through it." In 1929, having completed his studies, Sartre began teaching in French secondary schools. Throughout this period (1929-1934), Sartre also traveled extensively in Greece, Italy, Egypt, and especially Germany, where he studied under the German philosophers Edmund Husserl and Heidegger, both of whom greatly influenced his work. In 1935, Sartre began teaching at the Lycée Condorcet, where a following of young intellectuals soon gathered around him.

Although Sartre wrote throughout this time, his breakthrough to the larger world came in 1938 with the publication of *La Nausée* (*Nausea*, 1949), his first novel. A year later, he published a collection of short stories entitled *Le Mur* (*The Wall, and Other Stories*, 1939). Both books emphasized the themes of loneliness, despair, and the anxiety of personal freedom, themes that recurred throughout Sartre's later work. In 1943, these themes were given large-scale, systematic philosophical expression with the publication of *Being and Nothingness*.

The book is divided into an introduction and four main parts. Sartre opens with a challenging discussion of pure Being, one of the central preoccupations of the metaphysical tradition of philosophy. Although he rejects the Kantian "thing-in-itself" (*das Ding an sich*), that aspect of pure Being that lies behind the phenomenal appearances of being, Sartre maintains that pure Being, when considered as a whole, always lies outside the realm of human perceptibility. The abundance of Being, in all its manifestations, cannot be specifically described or categorized by our consciousness of it. According to Sartre,

> Being is simply the condition of all revelation. It is being-for-revealing [*être-pour-dévoiler*] and not revealed being [*être dévoilé*]. . . . Certainly I can pass beyond this table or this chair toward its being and raise the question of the being-of-the-table or the being-of-the-chair. But at that moment I turn my eyes away from the phenomenon of the table in order to concentrate on the phenomenon of being. [Being becomes] an appearance which, as such, needs in turn a being on the basis of which it can reveal itself.

This pure Being of which Sartre writes is manifested primarily as a split between "Being-in-itself" [*en-soi*] and "Being-for-itself" [*pour-soi*]. The examination of these two concepts forms the bulk of the first half of the book.

Being-in-itself may be described as that mode of being that is complete in itself, which does not choose what it may become. It corresponds to the realm of physical objects and phenomena, the universe of "things." Being-in-itself is causally predetermined by the nature of its own being; as Sartre writes, "Being-in-itself is never either possible or impossible. It *is*." Being-in-itself contains the realm of absolutes, the realm of "facticity" in which choice is impossible and Being simply exists without alternative.

On the other hand, Being-for-itself is not causally predetermined by anything. Being-for-itself may be defined as the realm of human consciousness, the realm of subjectivity and choice, and the realm of freedom within alternatives. It is the mode of being that cannot simply be, but must always be becoming; it can never be "complete in itself."

Being-in-itself is prior to Being-for-itself; that is, Being-for-itself depends on the existence of Being-in-itself for its own existence. As one of Sartre's more famous slogans has it, "Existence precedes essence." The existential choices a human makes every moment of life ("existence") determine that human's "essence," which Sartre defines simply as the past or what has already occurred in a person's life. These past occurrences or choices, taken together, make up the essential self, the Being-for-itself. Sartrean existentialism thus eliminates any idea of a human self or "human nature" imposed by God or by genetics; in Sartre's view, the essence of an individual human is only what he or she has chosen that essence to be.

Human consciousness itself exists only by the act of "nihilation" (*néantisation*), a word coined by Sartre: The consciousness causes a "nothingness" to arise between itself and the objects of consciousness, that Being-in-itself of which Being-for-itself is the consciousness. A wall of alienation or separation must always and necessarily exist between consciousness and its objects; since this separation distances individuals from Being itself, Sartre calls consciousness "a hole of being at the heart of Being," that is, a nothingness. Since Being-for-itself is indeterminate, unfixed, and always in the state of "becoming" rather than in the state of "being" possessed by Being-in-itself, human consciousness exists only by virtue of its incompleteness, its separation from Being-in-itself. Alienated from Being, consciousness must then be considered a "privation," or a form of nothing.

This condition irresistibly produces a deep and profound anxiety (another key Sartrean term) in the person aware of this alienated status, an anxiety that may be defined as "a continual awareness of one's own freedom." Humans are free to become, to choose; humans are "condemned to be free," in Sartre's famous phrase. Humanity finds itself in an existence filled with alternatives and must face these alternatives at every moment; humans must choose, commit, and move on, without complete knowledge of the consequences of these choices. Humans themselves, then—not God, genetics, "human nature," or any other such predetermining factor—are responsible for their own being.

Although humanity knows this terrifying freedom to be its nature, its deepest desire lies in the realm of solidity and certainty, the realm of Being-in-itself. Being-for-itself seeks the impossible: to be united with Being-in-itself to form "Being-in-itself-for-itself," a state of being that is self-contained and self-existent, such as the state of Being-in-itself, but also self-conscious and free to choose, such as the state of Being-for-itself. Sartre calls this, humanity's deepest desire, the "Desire to Be God"; since this deepest desire of humanity is logically contradictory and so is inevitably frustrated, humanity is condemned to a tragic existence: "Man is a useless passion."

Because of this, human existence is revealed as "absurd" and meaningless. Life contains no external purpose or justification; humans' pitiful attempts to become God are directed toward an unattainable goal, the goal to exist simultaneously as free in choice (Being-for-itself) and absolute in nature (Being-in-itself).

In part 3, it is shown that Being-for-itself involves Being-for-others (*pour-autrui*) as well. This is the state of interpersonal relations, in which the Being-for-itself exists as an object for others. Conflict arises as the Being-for-itself seeks to recover its own being by making an object out of the others; however, the two (self and others) are inseparable, as the Being-for-itself can only know itself fully by means of Being-for-others.

What sort of life could be made out of such a seemingly gloomy philosophy? According to Sartre, humans are yet capable of "authentic existence"; this type of existence comes about by the willingness to stand by one's choices and face their consequences unflinchingly. This is the closest Sartre comes to an affirmation of human existence, thereby avoiding a complete abandonment to pessimism and despair: Humans may redeem themselves, at least from self-deception, by recognizing and acknowledging their position as "a quite unjustifiable creature in a groundless universe," to quote the critic Margaret Walker. By accepting complete responsibility for their own existence, people may "climb out of the abyss of despairing awareness to achieve some form of self-affirmation." This "authentic existence" is the goal of existential psychoanalysis, which is discussed in part 4 of the book.

Those who busy themselves with the day-to-day flurry of life merely to avoid facing the terrifying responsibility of choice exhibit what Sartre calls "bad faith" (*mauvaise foi*). Bad faith is a self-deception, in that the Being-for-itself seeks to objectify its own body as Being-in-itself; responsibility for actions or choices is thus evaded or postponed. Sartre gives the example of a woman who is being courted by a suitor. Her own desires are contradictory: She does not want to give in to his advances, nor does she want to reject him and possibly end the relationship. Therefore, she objectifies herself into a "thing," merely being acted upon rather than acting; if the suitor, for instance, holds her hand (and by doing so implicitly asks for a rational decision), she deceives herself into not noticing that he is holding her hand. Her hand, her body, become "objects"; she seeks to postpone her own existence as Being-for-itself by wrongfully seeing herself as Being-in-itself. This is a display of bad faith.

In the realm of Being-for-itself, bad faith is always a possibility. Sartre describes a waiter in a cafeteria to illustrate this point: By his overly precise and meticulous actions, the waiter seems robotlike; those who watch him realize that he is "playing at being" a waiter. The human consciousness, then, becomes an affectation of consciousness; bad faith becomes an ever-present possibility when it becomes clear that humans cannot simply "be who they are" apart from choice (Sartre's "principle of identity"), as this is possible only for Being-in-itself. The activity of consciousness is itself a choice, so any attempt to evade responsibility for one's existence is illusory.

No brief summary can do full justice to the complexity of Sartre's thorough and systematic treatise. *Being and Nothingness* must stand as one of the most ambitious and influential philosophical works of the twentieth century and certainly as Sartre's philosophical magnum opus. In his work, Sartre's existentialist concepts capture, probably to a greater degree than any other modern philosophy, the angst of the twentieth century mind.

Craig Payne

Further Reading

Caws, Peter. *Sartre*. Boston: Routledge & Kegan Paul, 1979. Presents an overview of Sartre's philosophical writings. Chapters 4-6 discuss ideas from *Being and Nothingness* and examine the concepts of being, negation, subjectivity, and "bad faith." Points out the roots of *Being and Nothingness* in Sartre's earlier writings and especially highlights his ideas regarding interpersonal emotional relationships.

Danto, Arthur C. *Jean-Paul Sartre*. 2d ed. London: Fontana, 1991. A good introductory overview to Sartre's life and thought.

Fournay, Jean-François, and Charles D. Minahen, eds. *Situating Sartre in Twentieth Century Thought and Culture*. New York: St. Martin's Press, 1997. Sartre scholars offer varied interpretations on the significance of Sartre's philosophical and literary works.

Grene, Marjorie G. *Sartre*. New York: New Viewpoints, 1973. Contains a helpful discussion of Sartre's philosophical predecessors and an analysis of his place among twentieth century thinkers. Chapters 4-5 specifically discuss the ideas of *Being and Nothingness*, which Grene calls "one of the treasure-houses" of philosophy. This view does not, however, prevent her from strongly criticizing the role of Cartesian dualities in Sartre's thinking, such as the division of body and mind. Recommended for more advanced readers of Sartre.

Kerner, George C. *Three Philosophical Moralists: Mill, Kant, and Sartre—An Introduction to Ethics*. New York: Oxford University Press, 1990. A comparative study of three of the most influential ethical thinkers in modern Western philosophy.

McBride, William L. *Sartre's Political Philosophy*. Bloomington: Indiana University Press, 1991. A thoughtful interpretation of the main points in Sartre's political theory and their implications for the future.

Murdoch, Iris. *Sartre: Romantic Rationalist*. New Haven, Conn.: Yale University Press, 1959. A well-written introduction to Sartre's thought. Discusses *Being and Nothingness* thoroughly and, to a lesser degree, Sartre's fiction and politics. Critical of existentialism's "deficiencies," but presents Sartre's views fairly.

Reisman, David. *Sartre's Phenomenology*. London: Continuum, 2007. An examination of *Being and Nothingness*, describing Sartre's ideas about consciousness; the relationship of consciousness to the body, the external world, and other minds; and how individuals perceive themselves as full persons. Compares Sartre's thought to other philosophers' ideas about the philosophy of mind.

Van den Hoven, Adrian, and Andrew Leak, eds. *Sartre Today: A Centenary Celebration*. New York: Berghahn Books, 2005. A collection of essays published during the centenary of Sartre's birth. Includes two essays on *Being and Nothingness*: "Sartre's Ontology from *Being and Nothingness* to *The Family Idiot*" by Joseph S. Catalano and "Freedom, Nothingness, Consciousness: Some Remarks on the Structure of *Being and Nothingness*" by Reidar Due.

Wider, Kathleen Virginia. *The Bodily Nature of Consciousness: Sartre and Contemporary Philosophy of Mind*. Ithaca, N.Y.: Cornell University Press, 1997. Underscores the emphasis that Sartre places on the embodied nature of human consciousness and relates Sartre's views to important contemporary theories about the mind-body relationship.

Being and Time

Author: Martin Heidegger (1889-1976)
First published: Sein und Zeit, 1927 (English translation, 1962)
Type of work: Philosophy

Martin Heidegger exerted a strong influence on philosophy, theology, and politics. His most important works include *Was ist Metaphysik?* (1929; *What Is Metaphysics?*, 1949), a political treatise *Vom Wesen der Wahrheit* (1943; *The Truth from One Being*), and his collected essays, entitled *Wegmarken* (1967; *Pathmarks*, 1968). A complete edition of his works, published in 1975, consists of seventy volumes.

Heidegger's *Being and Time* is a conception of philosophy based on Franz Brentano's *Von der mannigfachen Bedeutung des Seienden nach Aristoteles* (1862; *On the Manifold Meaning of Being According to Aristotle*). The premise from which Heidegger analyzes the world around him, metaphysics, is a philosophy concerned with the study of the ultimate causes and the underlying nature of things. *Being and Time* is based on Aristotle's study of philosophy, which he wrote after his studies related to physics. The entire text provides a linguistic study of language meaning and usage, in the course of which Heidegger creates new words and assigns new meaning to existing words. His goal is to interpret the meaning of existence concretely in accordance with the way people live and with what influences them.

Being and Time is divided into two major parts. In the first part, Heidegger seeks to define the temporality of existence. In the second, he explores the idea of time as the transcendental limit for questioning the meaning of being.

Heidegger sees words as a metaphorical pathway that proceeds without people knowing where it came from or where it is going. In his view, the manner of questioning is an integral part of seeking answers. Depending on how questions are asked about a tree—for example, What is that over there in the distance? and What is that which we call a tree?—each question evokes different answers even though both concern the same object. The essence of existence focuses on asking the correct questions. It is not enough merely to ask What?; one must also ask How?

Since no two human beings are totally alike and all humans question their existence individually, people learn to function in the world by communicating. Communication involves formulating meaningful questions and listening in order to formulate more questions. Heidegger labels thoughts that are "self-evident" (*selbstaugenscheinlich*) as false-consciousness because those who stop asking questions acquire false notions.

Heidegger believes that language gives meaning to life. Humans are created by language, since humans are defined by consciousness. The bond between human beings and nature is broken by consciousness. Since animals and plants are part of each other in nature, consciousness and language are the alienation of nature. Speech and language produce dance, poetry, painting, and music, which are the foundation for culture within human society. Culture distances people from nature.

The experience of living suffices to enable people to understand the complex language of philosophers as well as the simple language of their contemporaries. Heidegger defines dialogue as "co-responding." According to Heidegger, it is irrelevant to know philosophy as long as people are in a dialogue with their own existence. In order to "co-respond," people should not answer, for when there are answers people stop listening. Philosophy is tuned co-respondence, in which vibrations from one thinker harmonize with the thinking of others. Heidegger is the first to see that being with others (*Mitsein*) evokes a question of existence rather than a question of knowing.

In contrast to the existentialist thought prevalent in his time, Heidegger focuses on considering ways in which humanity exists concretely. Existentialism centers on the analysis of existence and stresses freedom, responsibility, and usually the isolation of the individual. In metaphysics, however, in order to find meaning for self, people must look directly at humanity in the world. The only reality is concrete.

Metaphysics theorizes that the individual is the source of all values and responsible for his or her own development. In order to be part of humanity, individuals must be inseparable from the world. Being involves being "with"; however, individuals can learn about themselves even if they are not physically free. Espousing an affirmation of mystical self-liberation, Heidegger defines knowing as the ability to discuss the world.

Humankind has overemphasized knowing and become too technological. Heidegger criticizes science and technology, which he associates with nihilism. Knowing is grounded in existing. Being in the world is a necessary condition for knowing. Heidegger feels that people cannot learn anything they do not care about; without some type of fascination, there can be no knowledge.

Heidegger envisions the entire world as "being" or "existing," and he defines "existing" as that which is part of humanity's system of questioning. According to Heidegger, human beings are not physical structures but fluctuating series of possibilities (*Seinkönnen*) that constitute their existence.

Part of unconscious knowledge relates to an awareness of entities (*Zeug*). People are not necessarily conscious of their awareness. Heidegger defines "everydayness" (*Alltäglichkeit*) as the connection of humans with entities. The world is only authentically ready-to-hand as it "comes before us." People can form questions and listen for responses only as they experience life. It is the experience of individuals that offers development, not the body of historical knowledge that people have relied on before each individual experienced it.

When experiencing the world around the self, the primary concern is not what various things "are" but what they "do." Equipment is meaningless without knowing what the equipment can do. There are three areas, called deficient modes, that interfere with a person's ability to understand what things do in the world. The conspicuous mode relates to those situations in which an object cannot be used for its original purpose. In the obtrusive mode, understanding is interrupted when something is missing; when an item is needed and fails to be ready-at-hand, its obtrusiveness interferes with understanding. Last, in the obstinate mode, one item obstructs the ability to use another. If a lock on a box prevents someone from reaching a necessary object such as a hammer, the box is obstinate; a person who is obstinate cannot fully experience the world because the mind refuses to question what things do and dwells instead on what they are.

The concept of Being can be understood more fully when the relationship of Being and Being-there (*Dasein*) becomes disturbed. In order to see things ontologically, people must experience a disturbance. Heidegger claims that part of people's daily routine is filled with emptiness, which constitutes part of human suffering. Through experience with the deficient modes of concern, Heidegger circumvents understanding nature. With positive modes, people would never go beyond childhood concepts of concern that are rooted in nature. Existentialism is based on positive modes that, according to Heidegger, will lull people into ontological sleep. Heidegger views nature as a dark covering over the world that traps human beings into accepting answers without having voiced proper questions. Heidegger's approach to humanity's attempt to understand itself is through questioning and listening and further questioning. The essence of the world has no meaning apart from humanity; therefore, understanding nature stops the thought process that Heidegger sees as a necessary manifestation of understanding people's place in the world.

Besides knowing their place in the world, human beings must also be involved with the world. While artists must accept their medium as it is, they are also deeply involved with their medium and must continue to question, observe, and listen to the medium's properties. Artists deal with the limits of their medium because, in spite of the artist's involvement, the medium will go its own way. Artists are thus involved in the world by being active and participatory, according to Heidegger. Without such involvement, Being-there, or existence, becomes deficient. Being-there must give itself the task of understanding its Being-there.

The key to Heidegger's premise is his focus on humanity. Among the major points of Heidegger's concept of existence is its uniqueness. Existence is noncategorized, unstable, unpredictable, and therefore free. It is centered on the individual and has no specified behavior patterns, since it is in constant change. It is focused on potential. People are equated with their possibilities. Adventure, accomplished through constant questioning and the search for new pathways, is a key point to evolving. People continually challenge, question, and make their own decisions; however, humans can never truly know who they are, only who humanity was. People cannot project into the future, nor can human progress be scientifically measured.

Heidegger describes phenomena as the totality of what lies in the light of day or can be brought to light. The essence of humanity consists of its definition according to each individual and the freedom of mind of each individual. Humanity always precedes itself on the path to understanding. The origin or upheaval, as realized in the position of humanity, is the Heideggerian description of *eksistence*.

Annette M. Magid

Further Reading

Biemel, Walter. *Martin Heidegger: An Illustrated Study*. Translated by J. L. Mehta. New York: Harcourt Brace Jovanovich, 1976. Biemel, a student of Heidegger, elucidates the philosopher's concern for being and truth in an accessible analysis of seven works, including *Being and Time*. Dozens of black-and-white photographs of Heidegger and his contemporaries, a five-page chronology, and a twenty-page bibliography, including English translations and important secondary works, contribute to this introduction to Heidegger's thought.

Blattner, William D. *Heidegger's "Being and Time": A Reader's Guide*. London: Continuum, 2006. Discusses the themes of the work, its historical and philosophical context, and its critical reception and influences. Contains a detailed explanation of the philosophical concepts in the text. Designed for students and general readers.

Dastur, Françoise. *Heidegger and the Question of Time*. Translated by François Raffoul and David Pettigrew. Atlantic Highlands, N.J.: Humanities Press, 1998. Referencing more than twenty works by Heidegger, this book is a clear and insightful introduction to Heidegger's question of time and being. Useful for the expert, as well as the novice.

Glazebrook, Trish. *Heidegger's Philosophy of Science*. New York: Fordham University Press, 2000. A thoughtful and carefully documented explication of the philosopher's works.

Gorner, Paul. *Heidegger's "Being and Time": An Introduction*. New York: Cambridge University Press, 2007. An accessible introduction providing a detailed examination of the work's philosophical concepts, including being-in the world, being-with, truth, and authenticity.

Guignon, Charles, ed. *The Cambridge Companion to Heidegger*. London: Cambridge University Press, 1993. A collection of thirteen essays by highly respected scholars, published for the first time, on a variety of aspects of Heidegger's philosophy, including the influence of his thinking on psychotherapy, ecology, and theology. A valuable part of this collection is its bibliography, which contains a list of the publication schedule for the more than one hundred volumes of Heidegger's collected works in German, along with a list of secondary sources in English for students and others interested in Heidegger's writings.

Large, William. *Heidegger's "Being and Time*." Bloomington: Indiana University Press, 2008. Guides readers through Heidegger's work, section by section, idea by idea.

Poggeler, Otto. *Martin Heidegger's Path of Thinking*. Translated by Daniel Magurshak and Sigmund Barber. Atlantic Highlands, N.J.: Humanities Press, 1987. Originally published in German in 1963, Poggeler's work is the most renowned critical study of the development of Heidegger's early metaphysical work into his later, nonmetaphysical thinking. For this translation of the text of the second German edition, Poggeler wrote a helpful preface and afterword.

Rée, Jonathan. *Heidegger*. New York: Routledge, 1999. An excellent biographical introduction to the thoughts of the philosopher, clearly presented and requiring no special background. Includes a bibliography.

Steiner, George. *Martin Heidegger*. New York: Viking Press, 1978. Intended for the general reader, Steiner's short work, published soon after Heidegger's death, intertwines a short biography of the philosopher and an exposition of *Being and Time*, with a nod toward Heidegger's later works. Clarifies the central themes of Heidegger's philosophy. A brief chronology of Heidegger's life, a bibliography of English titles, and an extensive index supplement a helpful text.

Wolin, Richard. *The Politics of Being: The Political Thought of Martin Heidegger*. New York: Columbia University Press, 1990. Motivated by the increased recognition in the 1980's of Heidegger's involvement with Nazism, Wolin seeks here to unearth political themes in Heidegger's philosophy from *Being and Time* through his later critiques of technology and humanism. From this perspective, he argues that Heidegger's involvement with National Socialism was not a "momentary lapse" of thinking but reflective of an endemic blindness to the concrete specifics of modern social life.

Being There

Author: Jerzy Kosinski (Josek Lewinkopf, 1933-1991)
First published: 1971
Type of work: Novel
Type of plot: Comic satire
Time of plot: Early 1970's
Locale: New York City

Principal characters:
CHANCE, mistakenly called Chauncey Gardiner
THE OLD MAN, owner of the house in which Chance grows up
THE MAID, who cleans the Old Man's house
THOMAS FRANKLIN, the lawyer handling the Old Man's estate
BENJAMIN RAND, a wealthy financial consultant
ELIZABETH EVE "EE" RAND, his wife
PRESIDENT OF THE UNITED STATES, a friend of Benjamin Rand
VLADIMIR SKRAPINOV, Soviet ambassador to the United States
O'FLAHERTY, a political party leader

The Story:

Chance tends the garden in the house of the Old Man, where he has lived for as long as he can remember. His mother died in childbirth and his father was unknown, and, although there is no record of any arrangement, the Old Man took him in. Chance never had any real contact with the Old Man, however, especially during his later years, when he was bedridden. Chance is cared for by the maid of the house, but he needs very little: whatever time he does not spend in the garden he spends in front of the television, which is his major source of information about the world. He is illiterate, but gains whatever education and manners and knowledge of social behavior he has from the programs he watches on television.

When the Old Man suddenly dies, Chance is turned out of the house by Thomas Franklin, the lawyer in charge of the estate, who can find no record of Chance's existence. Bewildered by being in the outside world for the first time, he walks aimlessly in the street and is unable to avoid being hit by the limousine of Elizabeth Eve Rand when it backs toward him. Chance is not seriously hurt, but Elizabeth and her chauffeur are concerned and take him to the Rands' house to have him checked out thoroughly. She introduces herself as EE, and as he fumblingly explains that he is Chance, the gardener, she mishears this as Chauncey Gardiner, the name by which he is referred to from that point on.

Chance settles in to his new home very quickly, as both EE and Mr. Rand become very attached to him. EE finds him charming because, although he is simple and utterly without experience or intelligence, he perfectly mimes the behavior of characters he has seen on television. Mr. Rand, the shrewd and powerful chairman of the board of the First American Financial Corporation, is equally charmed by Chance and also impressed by what he takes to be his deep insights into the contemporary economic crisis. Rand interprets his trite mundane and literal comments about plants, flowers, trees, and roots as penetrating wisdom that supports his own conservative thoughts about the need for patience, strong and steady leadership, and support for the established business and political authorities who are a bulwark against those arguing for change.

It never crosses Chance's mind that he is anything but a simple gardener, but everyone around him quickly adopts him as a charismatic adviser. The president of the United States visits Rand, and he too is impressed by Chance's apparent optimistic philosophy of soil and seasons, so much so that he mentions Chance's name in a major speech he delivers later that night. More than an adviser to business leaders and the president, Chance quickly becomes a celebrity. He is referred to and quoted in newspapers and magazines and asked to appear on a popular television show. He is perfectly suited for the latter, having been almost completely raised by watching television, and he immediately becomes quite literally the talk of the town.

By this time, EE is fully in love with Chance and attempts to seduce him. Chance has had no real experience of love but, although the garden offers him no help in this case, television once again does. It has acquainted him with some romantic gestures that he can imitate. Ironically, it has also rendered him completely devoid of emotion, which EE takes as admirable restraint and respect. Later, when EE approaches him again, more fully committed to making love to him, Chance responds with what he has learned from years of television. "I like to watch," he says, which leads to mutual satisfaction: She is free to satisfy herself physically, and he is free to watch—not her, but the television that is almost always on wherever he is.

As Chance becomes increasingly famous, people in power, including not only the president but also the Russian ambassador, want to learn about his past, but no one can find out anything: Neither the American nor the Russian secret services can discover any trace of the man they know they will have to acknowledge as a major force. The fact that Chance is a blank slate, that he has no background, no identity, and no history of a lived life, turns out to be an asset: It means that he has no demonstrable blemishes and that he can be what people want him to be. As the story concludes, Chance is being seriously considered for high political office, and this vision of him as the ideal candidate, indeed, the ideal office-holder, is slyly juxtaposed with a final view of Chance walking out alone from a dinner party, completely thoughtless and yet completely at peace, into a garden that is beautiful but insensate.

Critical Evaluation:

Amid the calm beauty portrayed at the novel's end, as in a Zen parable, or koan, a reader is left to ponder the far-reaching implications of Jerzy Kosinski's softly stated but disturbing suggestion that at the heart of both the media-obsessed culture and nature is a fundamental absence. What is missing from both, in Kosinski's estimation, is a fully developed—that is, a thinking, feeling, and socially engaged—human being. The title, *Being There*, is never explained in the novel, but it is surely meant to be ironic. (*Blank Page*, one of the working titles for the novel, would have been more self-explanatory but somewhat less resonant.)

Being There tells the story of a displaced person, one disconnected from his environment, from the people around him, and ultimately even from himself. Chance is in many respects never really "there," never at home or fully engaged anywhere, and he takes this as normal, never questioning or complaining. Although the style of the novel is realistic throughout, it is meant to be a fable on several levels. It is, like so much modern literature, an existential fable, a portrait of a man exemplifying what many consider to be the fundamental human condition—alienation—gliding through a world of which he is not truly a part. It is also a historical fable, rooted in the conditions of contemporary times.

In a previous novel, *The Painted Bird* (1965), based at least in part on some of his own experiences as a refugee, Kosinski had already written about a dispossessed and wandering person, strikingly akin to Chance in these respects, although in much different circumstances: That character was traumatized by life in the shadow of concentration camps and almost unspeakable horrors during World War II. *Being There* takes place decades after the war, which is never alluded to, but the world in which Chance lives has found a new way to create nonpersons: by omnipresent technology, television in particular. Such technology is represented as pleasurable and entertaining rather than painful and brutal, but as nevertheless powerfully dehumanizing.

During the 1960's and 1970's, the general time period of *Being There*, the media and cultural analyst Marshall McLuhan was very prominent and influential. He argued that the ongoing electronic revolution was one that people should welcome. He warned that the transition from print to electronic culture, from books to television and computers, would be a difficult one, as people clung to the mental habits, morals, and values reinforced by older media. He believed, however, that the inevitable acceptance of new ways of thinking and acting, conditioned by new media, would be liberating: Defining media as extensions and magnifications of humankind's physical and mental abilities, he argued that humanity's powers would be expanded by the new media. The sense of place would be altered, as humans would find their home less in the limited realm of physical space and more in the free, disembodied realm created by new media and later referred to as cyberspace. The enhanced individuals of this future society would be members of an electronically connected global village.

Being There offers almost a point-by-point rebuttal of McLuhan's key arguments and paints a picture of a society and a species—humankind—endangered by new media. Chance represents the other side of McLuhan's optimism. He is literally raised, educated, and socialized by television, and he lives his life either watching television, watching life as though it is on the screen, or modeling his behavior after what he has seen on television. The result is that he turns out to be barely human, at least as that term has been defined in preelectronic cultures: He is illiterate, thoughtless, emotionless, and uninvolved with others. He lives his life watching rather than doing. Rather than giving him what McLuhan spoke about as a "depth experience," activating his senses and intelligence, Chance's detachment keeps him from having real experiences at all. He follows the lives and actions of the people he sees on television, but this fascination with televisual reality keeps him disengaged from the real people that he occasionally meets.

Chance knows how to garden, but this activity also keeps

him in an enclosure removed from human contact, and if his gardening represents an immersion in life, the life-forms he is surrounded by, plants, are lower ones. In making the garden a central image in the book, Kosinski may be doubly allusive: Chance's "back to the earth" lifestyle and philosophy, treated as deep wisdom by many people who listen to his simple-minded comments about the seasons and growing and watering, associates him with the "flower children" of the late 1960's and early 1970's, who Kosinski presumably thinks of as ill-equipped to face the challenges and complexities of the real world. The activity of cultivating one's own garden inevitably identifies Chance as a modern-day version of the title character of Voltaire's *Candide: Ou, L'Optimisme*, 1759 (*Candide: Or, All for the Best*, 1759) Like Candide, Chance is disarmingly naïve and charming but by no means a model of a fully evolved and capable human being.

While he focuses primarily on Chance, Kosinski also satirizes society at large. Chance is, after all, not entirely different from everyone else; he is only an extreme form of what characterizes the entire culture. Everyone in one way or another relies heavily on the media, ostensibly for information about reality but ultimately as a substitute reality. Television may have initially been a representation of reality, but now it is the primary mode of experience, and it creates and ratifies celebrities who control not only entertainment but also government. Kosinski depicts a media-driven society that has passed beyond the stage where presidents become celebrities to one where being a celebrity is the primary qualification for being president.

Kosinski does not make any direct comments about his message and his warning, relying instead on irony—in fact, a carefully established double irony—to speak for him. Chance, for all his deficiencies, is not only happy and peaceful but also successful. A reader of *Being There* should be alert enough to recognize without specific statements by Kosinski that this happiness and success are not signs of a life well led and a properly functioning society but of someone who has not evolved into a full human being, in large part because he lives in a culture that has gone dangerously off track.

While Chance is cultivating his garden, his society is not properly cultivating him. Kosinski does not show any of the bitterness often associated with satirists, and his novel is not written to generate violent outrage. It provides, however, a penetrating analysis and a powerful dramatization of a society that manufactures what the classical world defined as idiots: that is, fundamentally private people, disconnected from the real world and from interaction with real people. "Videots," to borrow a term Kosinksi used in interviews, abound. Immersion in electronic media, an emphasis on detachment rather than emotional engagement, the cult of celebrity, and the reliance on spectacle and images rather than reason and substance have intensified enormously in the decades since *Being There* was published. The novel can thus help address the extent to which a technology- and media-saturated society conspires to make people less, rather than more, human.

Sidney Gottlieb

Further Reading

Ferrell, William K. *Literature and Film as Modern Mythology*. Westport, Conn.: Praeger, 2000. Study of ways in which contemporary film and literature function analogously to myths of the past. Includes a chapter on *Being There* as a myth of contemporary life.

Kosinski, Jerzy. *Passing By: Selected Essays, 1962-1991*. New York: Random House, 1992. Collects nonfiction by Kosinski. Particularly relevant to *Being There* are "Gog and Magog: On Watching TV," "TV as Baby-Sitter," "Against Book Censorship." and "Dead Souls on Campus."

Lavers, Norman. *Jerzy Kosinski*. Boston: Twayne, 1982. Introductory overview of Kosinski's life and career up to 1982, with a brief chapter on *Being There* that focuses on its biblical motifs and critique of television.

Lilly, Paul R., Jr. *Words in Search of Victims: The Achievement of Jerzy Kosinski*. Kent, Ohio: Kent State University Press, 1988. Concentrates on Kosinski's works as reflexive analyses of the art of writing fiction. Brief treatment of *Being There* focuses on Chance's use of language.

Lupack, Barbara Tepa, ed. *Critical Essays on Jerzy Kosinski*. New York: G. K. Hall, 1998. Includes reviews of *Being There* by William Kennedy and John W. Aldridge, as well as Lupack's essay "Chance Encounters: Bringing *Being There* to the Screen," a detailed comparative analysis of the novel and its 1979 film adaptation.

Sloan, James Park. *Jerzy Kosinski: A Biography*. New York: Dutton, 1996. Pays substantial attention to autobiographical elements of *Being There* and its resemblances to a popular Polish novel from 1932.

Teicholz, Tom, ed. *Conversations With Jerzy Kosinski*. Jackson: University of Mississippi Press, 1993. Scattered comments throughout these interviews help place *Being There* in the context of Kosinski's other writings. Particularly relevant is the interview "A Nation of Videots."

Bel-Ami

Author: Guy de Maupassant (1850-1893)
First published: 1885 (English translation, 1889)
Type of work: Novel
Type of plot: Naturalism
Time of plot: c. 1885
Locale: Paris and Cannes, France

Principal characters:
GEORGES DUROY, later GEORGES DU ROY DE CANTEL, a newspaperman
MADELEINE FORESTIER, the wife of Duroy's benefactor and later Duroy's wife
CLOTILDE DE MARELLE, Duroy's mistress
CHARLES FORESTIER, Duroy's former brother officer and the editor who befriends him
MONSIEUR WALTER, the owner of the newspaper for which Duroy works
BASILE WALTER, Monsieur Walter's wife
SUZANNE WALTER, Monsieur Walter's daughter

The Story:

Georges Duroy, a former soldier, has only three francs in his pocket when he meets his brother officer, Charles Forestier, in Paris one evening. Forestier, an editor of the daily newspaper *La Vie française*, unhesitatingly loans Duroy money to buy suitable clothes and invites him to dinner the following evening to meet the owner of the paper. The Forestiers' party is a success for Duroy. M. Walter hires him as a reporter to write a series of articles on his experiences in Algeria.

It is not easy for Duroy to adapt himself to his new job. His first article is due the day following the dinner party. Unable to write it in the proper form, he is forced to hurry to the Forestier home early in the morning to seek stylistic advice. Forestier, just leaving, refers Duroy to Mme Forestier for help. Together they turn out a successful piece. With her help, Duroy slowly builds a reputation as a clever reporter, but his salary remains small.

Two months after the Forestiers' dinner party, Duroy calls on Mme de Marelle, who was among the guests that evening. Duroy's acquaintance with Mme de Marelle quickly develops into an intimate friendship. Because M. de Marelle is often away from home, his wife has ample time to see her lover, at his lodgings at first and then at an apartment that she rents. Duroy objects mildly to having Mme de Marelle bear this expense, but it is not long before he finds himself regularly accepting small sums of money from her. It is Mme de Marelle's daughter Laurine who first calls him "Bel-Ami," a nickname gradually adopted by most of his friends.

M. Forestier suffers from a bronchial ailment. As his health grows worse, his disposition becomes unbearable at the office. Duroy determines to avenge himself by attempting to seduce Mme Forestier. She gently rebuffs him but agrees that they could be friends. Duroy is brash enough to propose that she become his wife if she is ever widowed.

At Mme Forestier's suggestion, Duroy begins to cultivate Mme Walter. The week following his first visit to her, he is appointed editor of the "Echoes," an important column. He has barely assumed this position when the editor of a rival newspaper, *La Plume*, accuses him falsely of receiving bribes and suppressing news. To uphold the honor of *La Vie française*, Duroy is forced to challenge his disparager to a duel. Though neither man is injured, M. Walter is pleased with Duroy's spirit.

Duroy moves into the apartment that Mme de Marelle has rented for their meetings after promising that he will never bring anyone else there. Shortly afterward, Forestier becomes seriously ill, and Duroy receives a telegram asking him to join the Forestiers in Cannes, where they went for his health. After Forestier's death, as he and Mme Forestier keep a vigil over the corpse, Duroy proposes once more. The widow makes no promises, but the next day she tells him that she might consider marrying him, though she warns him that she will have to be treated as an equal and her conduct left unquestioned.

Mme Forestier returns to Paris. A year later, she and Duroy, or Georges du Roy de Cantel, as he now calls himself at his wife's suggestion, are married. They agreed to spend their honeymoon with his parents in Normandy, but Mme de Cantel refuses to spend more than one day with his simple, ignorant peasant family in their tiny home.

The newspaperman finds in his wife a valuable ally who not only aids him in writing his articles but also, as the friend of influential men, helps him to find a place in political circles. Nevertheless, friction soon develops between them.

After he moves into his wife's home, de Cantel finds that its comforts were designed to please its old master and that he is expected to fill the niche his friend occupied. Even the meals are prepared according to Forestier's taste. To pique his wife, de Cantel begins to call Forestier "poor Charles," always using an accent of infinite pity when he speaks the name.

Not long after his marriage, de Cantel resumes his relationship with Mme de Marelle and at the same time begins an affair with Mme Walter. He briefly bemoans the fact that he did not marry wealthy young Suzanne Walter, but he soon becomes intrigued with the idea of seducing her mother, a pillar of dignity. His conquest is not a difficult one. Mme Walter begins to meet her lover at his rooms and to shower so much affection and attention upon him that he quickly becomes bored.

Among Mme de Cantel's political acquaintances is the foreign minister, Laroche-Mathieu, who supplies news of government activities to *La Vie française*. Because the minister is also a close friend of M. Walter, it is not difficult for de Cantel's new lover to learn a state secret, namely that France will soon guarantee the Moroccan debt. Mme Walter plans to buy some shares of the loan with the understanding that de Cantel will receive part of the profit. While Mme Walter is carrying on her speculations, the de Cantels receive a windfall in the form of a bequest from the late Count de Vaudrec, an old family friend of Mme de Cantel. De Cantel objects to the count's bequest of one million francs on the grounds that appearances will compromise her. He allows her to accept the money only after she agrees to divide it equally with him, so that it will seem to outsiders as if they have both received a share.

De Cantel profits handsomely when France assumes the Moroccan debt, but his gains are small compared to those of Laroche-Mathieu and M. Walter, who have become millionaires as a result of the intrigue. One evening, he and his wife are invited to view a painting in the Walters' magnificent new mansion. There de Cantel begins a flirtation with Suzanne Walter; his own wife and Laroche-Mathieu have become intimates without attempting to conceal their friendship. That evening, de Cantel persuades Suzanne to agree never to accept a proposal without first asking his advice. At home after the reception, he receives with indifference the cross of the Legion of Honor that the foreign minister gives him. He believes that he is entitled to a larger reward for concealing news of the Moroccan affair from his readers. That spring, he surprises his wife and Laroche-Mathieu at a rendezvous. Three months later, he obtains a divorce, causing the minister's downfall by naming him correspondent.

A free man again, de Cantel is able to court Suzanne. It is simple for him to persuade the girl to tell her parents she wishes to marry him and to have her go away with him until they give their consent to the match. Mme Walter is the only one at the magnificent church wedding to show any signs of sadness. She hates the daughter who has taken her lover, but she is powerless to prevent the marriage without compromising herself. M. Walter manages to resign himself to having a conniving son-in-law and, in fact, recognizes his shrewdness by making him chief editor of the newspaper. Suzanne is innocently happy as she walks down the aisle with her father. Her new husband is also content. Greeting their well-wishers in the sacristy after the ceremony, he takes advantage of the occasion to reaffirm, with his eyes, his feelings for Mme de Marelle. As he and his wife leave the church, it seems to him that it is only a stone's throw from that edifice to the chamber of deputies.

Critical Evaluation:

Bel-Ami is the story of an intriguer who climbs to a position of wealth and power by publishing the story of his first wife's disgrace and later cheating her of part of her fortune. The unscrupulous parvenu and the women he dupes are among the masterpieces of characterization produced by the French realistic school to which Guy de Maupassant belongs.

In the novel, Georges Duroy, who might be considered the male counterpart of William Makepeace Thackeray's Becky Sharp, represents the restlessness of a certain class at a time when the once-frozen class system slowly begins to thaw. He illustrates the morally debilitating nature of poverty. Although Maupassant scrupulously avoids comment, he seems to be suggesting that while it is easy enough to be moral with enough money in one's pocket, society should hesitate to condemn those who must use their wits to survive (and are not too particular about how they do it). Duroy automatically looks for prey (as he did when stationed in Africa) to help him get ahead, and if confronted he would respond, what else could a man in his position do?

Duroy's essential laziness prevents him from taking advantage of all the opportunities that open before him, but a natural shrewdness and ruthlessness carry him along far enough to be within sight of his goal. He is a man who never can be satisfied. Neither his background nor his instincts have given him a moral base on which to conduct his life; to him, "honor" is a catchword, not a code that touches him to the core. In fact, nothing touches him deeply. Pleasure, for him, equals happiness.

Ambition and death alternate as themes in the novel, the

latter showing the ultimate futility of the former. The long and painful death of Charles Forestier provides Duroy with a greater opportunity for advancing in the world with the aid of Madeleine Forestier, but it also foreshadows the end that awaits Duroy and everyone else. A sense of terror crushes Duroy when he sits by the body of Forestier, and he wonders what the difference is between flies who live a few hours and men who live a few years. He has no ideals, no purpose to his life other than temporary physical sensations, and he can even see how meaningless they are. He is not, however, a profound enough thinker to pursue this train of thought. Soon, he is back at his usual scheming and plotting. With superb understatement, Maupassant says at this point: "Duroy returned to all his old habits."

The young Maupassant considered himself a disciple of Gustave Flaubert. Certainly, the supple prose and carefully selected details, as well as the understated irony of the novel, are true to Flaubert's literary teachings. Maupassant also belonged to the circle of realists that included Émile Zola and Ivan Turgenev. He presents his characters in *Bel-Ami* with strict objectivity, noting always the word or gesture that betrays the essential personality of each one. Conciseness and a rigorous economy of words and images underlie the art of the novel. He gives in *Bel-Ami* a true picture of the society of his time. Every detail is precise and factual, yet the view of humankind is powerfully universal.

Further Reading

Bloom, Harold, ed. *Guy de Maupassant*. Philadelphia: Chelsea House, 2004. Although most of the essays in this collection focus on Maupassant's short stories, some of the essays also can pertain to his novels, including a discussion of the influence of Maupassant's realism and critiques by Anatole France and Joseph Conrad.

Donaldson-Evans, Mary. "The Harlot's Apprentice: Maupassant's *Bel-Ami*." *The French Review: Journal of the American Association of Teachers of French* 60, no. 5 (April, 1987): 616-625. An examination of the hero and of sexual identity in Maupassant's novel. Discusses the novel in the context of nineteenth century naturalistic literature.

Duffy, Larry. "Maupassant, *Doxa*, and the Banalisation of Modern Travel." In *Le Grand Transit Moderne: Mobility, Modernity, and French Naturalist Fiction*. New York: Rodopi, 2005. Argues that in *Bel-Ami* and in other fiction, Maupassant attacks romanticized views of travel while ridiculing the fears and superstitions of middle-class travelers. Many of the quotations cited in the text are in French.

Gregorio, Laurence A. *Maupassant's Fiction and the Darwinian View of Life*. New York: Peter Lang, 2005. Maupassant, like other naturalist writers, believed in Charles Darwin's theory of evolution. Gregorio describes how evolutionary theory and social Darwinism figure significantly in Maupassant's fiction, demonstrating how these writings reflect the concepts of natural selection, heredity, and materialism.

Hamilton, James F. "The Impossible Return to Nature in Maupassant's *Bel-Ami* or the Intellectual Heroine as Deviant." *Nineteenth-Century French Studies* 10, no. 3 (Spring/Summer, 1982): 326-339. Considers Maupassant's novel in terms of his conceptualization of female characters. The examinations of Madeleine Forestier and Clotilde de Marelle are rigorous and insightful. In dealing with the issue of heroine and intellect, the article elucidates Maupassant's use of naturalistic and realistic literary devices.

Lethbridge, Robert. "Maupassant's *Bel-Ami* and the Art of Illusion." In *Studies in French Fiction in Honour of Vivienne Milne*, edited by Robert Gibson. London: Grant & Cutler, 1988. Explores duplicity in *Bel-Ami*. Considers the work as an example of nineteenth century French literature.

Lloyd, Christopher. *Maupassant: "Bel-Ami."* London: Grant & Cutler, 1988. Examines the novel's philosophy and style and offers a thorough overview of the work as a study of social position and ambition.

Prince, Gerald. "*Bel-Ami* and Narrative as Antagonist." *French Forum* 11, no. 2 (May, 1986): 217-226. A study of the character of Georges Duroy in terms of Maupassant's development of narrative and of his construction of an antagonist.

Belinda

Author: Maria Edgeworth (1768-1849)
First published: 1801
Type of work: Novel
Type of plot: Social realism
Time of plot: Late eighteenth century
Locale: London and southern England

Principal characters:
BELINDA, a young woman
LADY DELACOUR, a lady of fashion
LORD DELACOUR, her husband
HELENA DELACOUR, their daughter
CLARENCE HERVEY, a wealthy young man
VIRGINIA ST. PIERRE (RACHEL HARTLEY), his ward
MR. VINCENT, Belinda's suitor
MRS. SELINA STANHOPE, Belinda's aunt
HARRIET FREKE, Lady Delacour's former friend
MR. PERCIVAL and LADY ANNE PERCIVAL, friends to Helena and Belinda
DR. X——, a physician

The Story:

Belinda's aunt, wishing Belinda to acquire a husband of wealth and social position, sends her to live with Lady Delacour, a leading figure in fashionable London. At first Belinda is dazzled by Lady Delacour's wit and elegance and by the glamour of her world. Quickly, however, Belinda becomes disgusted by the shallow frivolity that permeates this world and by the manipulative jockeying for social position that drives its players. In particular, she realizes that Lady Delacour's social brilliance disguises a deeply unhappy woman who despises her husband and marriage, fears the aging of her body, and conceals a mysterious personal secret known only to her maid, Marriott.

Belinda's aunt hopes to match her with Clarence Hervey, one of London's eligible young men, who is not only wealthy but also clever. Lady Delacour, too, encourages Belinda's interest in Hervey, though she considers him one of her own admirers. To Belinda, Hervey initially seems foppish and conceited, and Hervey is on his guard against Belinda because he assumes she shares the goals of her aunt, a notorious matchmaker. At a masked ball, a disguised Belinda overhears Hervey denigrating her before his male friends as a "composition of art and affectation." Belinda is mortified and resolves to take no interest in Hervey.

After the ball, Lady Delacour reveals to Belinda the true misery of her life. To hurt her husband, whom she thinks an alcoholic fool, she encouraged a beau, Colonel Lawless; Lord Delacour shot Lawless in a duel, and Lady Delacour still suffers from guilt over his death. Motherhood means little to her, and her surviving daughter, Helena, is someone she thinks little about and seldom sees. Lady Delacour is obsessed by a rivalry with another London host, Mrs. Luttridge, and her best friend, Harriet Freke, joined Mrs. Luttridge's camp. Finally, a breast injury she received in a duel with another woman, she thinks, became a disease that is killing her. Nevertheless, she feels compelled to keep her sickness hidden from the world and continue her life of social gaiety as long as possible.

Belinda is both horrified by Lady Delacour's story and moved by it. She wants to help Lady Delacour. Hervey, who soon revises his opinion of Belinda, wishes this as well. They becomes friends in an effort to bring Lady Delacour closer to her daughter Helena. Helena was cared for on school holidays by Mr. Percival and Lady Anne Percival, whom Hervey meets when Mr. Percival saves him from drowning. Seeing Helena's longing for her mother, Hervey maneuvers a meeting between Helena and Belinda, and Hervey and Belinda arranged a visit from Helena to Lady Delacour. Lady Delacour is stirred by Helena's love and vows to reform.

When Belinda attempts to reconcile Lady Delacour and her husband, Lady Delacour becomes suspicious that Belinda is pursuing Lord Delacour, so Belinda goes to stay with the Percivals at Oakly-park, their country home. Before she leaves London, Belinda, who rejected a proposal from the stupid and pretentious Sir Philip Baddely, becomes more interested in Hervey, but when she sees a painting said to be a portrait of his mistress, she tries to stop thinking of him. At the Percivals' she meets a new suitor, Mr. Vincent, heir to West Indian wealth. Belinda refuses his first proposal, but she is influenced by Lady Anne's praise of his virtues to allow his continued courtship. Belinda also rejects Harriet's efforts to alienate her from the Percivals and Lady Delacour, and she defeats the practical joke with which Harriet tries to persuade Mr. Vincent's black servant, Juba, that he is haunted by a ghost.

Lady Delacour fears she is dying and summons Belinda back to London. In the hope that an operation might save her, she reveals her disease to her husband. She is spared the operation when Dr. X—— informs her that her illness is caused not by breast disease but by the opium she is taking.

Lady Delacour is convinced that Belinda still loves Hervey and tries to persuade her not to marry Mr. Vincent. Hervey, however, announces he will marry Virginia St. Pierre, the original of the portrait Belinda saw earlier. Hervey is the guardian of Virginia (then named Rachel Hartley, but renamed by Hervey) since her grandmother died. He planned to marry her, and, influenced by the theories of the French philosopher Jean-Jacques Rousseau, directed that she be kept as nearly as possible a "child of nature," protected from exposure to frivolous social sophistication. He prefers Belinda's strong, socially educated mind and character to Virginia's ignorance and passivity, but he thinks that Virginia is in love with him and he is obligated to marry her. On the verge of marrying Mr. Vincent, Belinda discovers he is a gambler (though he was temporarily saved from ruin by the generous Hervey), and she ends the engagement. After further entanglements and disentanglements, Belinda and Hervey are free to marry each other.

Critical Evaluation:

During the first two decades of the nineteenth century, Maria Edgeworth was among the most popular and most critically admired of contemporary English novelists. Her reputation declined later in the century as standards of realism changed, although her novels helped to develop such standards. The novels of Jane Austen and Sir Walter Scott came to eclipse Edgeworth's in the public eye, but Austen and Scott admired Edgeworth's fiction and were influenced by it.

Edgeworth herself came to dislike *Belinda*, particularly its title character, whom she called "cold" and "tame"; she preferred her novels with Irish settings, such as *Castle Rackrent* (1800) and *The Absentee* (1812). As a story about a young woman who must navigate social perils on her way to the choice of a suitable husband, *Belinda* is in many respects a conventional novel of its time. Its structure and manner show the influence of Fanny Burney and Elizabeth Inchbald, both well-regarded late eighteenth century novelists. Belinda is distinctive, though, in her combination of virtue and independent thought and in her refusal to submit to the authority of others. She can appreciate and act on wise advice from a friend, such as that of Lady Anne Percival, but she makes her own decisions. In the novel's last scene, the stage is set for Belinda's acceptance of Clarence Hervey, but she delays her acceptance, reinforcing the reader's sense that Belinda is as much her own woman at the end of the story as she was at the beginning.

Edgeworth emphasizes Belinda's independence by juxtaposing her against three other female characters: Harriet Freke, Lady Delacour, and Virginia St. Pierre. The outrageous Harriet—cross-dressing, proclaiming women's superiority to men, and involving herself and Lady Delacour in an attempt to influence a political campaign—is a parody of a late eighteenth century feminist. She perhaps made a contemporary reader think of the scandals that had collected by 1801 around the pioneer feminist Mary Wollstonecraft. It became known that Wollstonecraft, the author of *A Vindication of the Rights of Woman* (1792), openly bore a child out of wedlock. Harriet's characterization seems to support the most conservative patriarchal ideology of the period by illustrating the chaos produced by women who discard the rules of female propriety, who are not subservient to men, and who act in the public sphere. In fact, Edgeworth's thinking about women's intellectual and moral equality to men and the importance of educating women to develop their capacity for reasoned judgment was actually close to Wollstonecraft's.

Belinda comprises two major interpolated tales. One is about Lady Delacour, and the other is about Virginia St. Pierre. They serve as object lessons in the value of women's rights. Lady Delacour's life history is introduced near the beginning of the novel, Virginia's near the end. These histories develop perspectives, on the one hand, on the pitfalls of a woman's life that is apparently independent but in truth so out of control as to be prey to the whims of others, and, on the other hand, on the dangers of a woman's life subject to rigid control by protective guardians. Lady Delacour seeks worldly power and evades the dictates of a moral code that would have her obey her husband. Fearing the loss of worldly gratifications and subjection to her husband that may come if she admits her illness, she begins to be destroyed by the opium she takes to ameliorate the pain of her imagined breast disease. She becomes the prey of her own compulsions and of a quack doctor. Virginia, on the other hand, is the epitome of an overly sheltered young girl. During her childhood she is shielded from society because of her grandmother's fears about female vulnerability to seduction and unfaithful men, and as an adolescent she is kept isolated because of Hervey's enthusiasm for Jean-Jacques Rousseau's romantic ideas about the moral purity of a life close to nature. He also accepts uncritically Rousseau's ideas on the corrupting effects on women of an education that exposes them to worldly complexities. Whereas Lady Delacour is prey to her fears of loss of power and to the quack doctor's opium, the barely educated Virginia is prey to the fantasies encouraged by the romances to which she has become addicted. Neither is able to think clearly about her situation.

Set against these two interpolated tales as well as the dramatization of Harriet, Belinda's story is Edgeworth's effort to define a mode of female behavior that is neither submissive to external authority nor willfully given over to excitements. Belinda's name recalls the vain, frivolous heroine of Alexander Pope's satire *The Rape of the Lock* (1712, 1714). Edgeworth's Belinda, however, is not frivolous; she can make her way toward reasoned judgments without depending on the guidance of a "superior" masculine vision.

That Belinda's character seems dull to her author and that the more dramatic assertions of the unreformed Lady Delacour sometimes threaten to take over the novel suggest that for Edgeworth herself there were tensions between the domestic ideology her novel advocates and her own resistance to the restrictions it places on women's lives. Nevertheless, the model of egalitarian marriage and devotion to family represented by the Percivals and the reformed Delacours points toward the dominant middle-class domestic ideal of the nineteenth century. *Belinda* shows clearly how Edgeworth believed this model to be empowering for women.

Anne Howells

Further Reading

Butler, Marilyn. *Jane Austen and the War of Ideas*. New York: Oxford University Press, 1975. The chapter on Edgeworth is a good introduction to *Belinda*'s treatment of women's lives.

_______. *Maria Edgeworth: A Literary Biography.* Oxford, England: Clarendon Press, 1972. One of the best biographies of Edgeworth. Has an extensive and thoughtful treatment of Edgeworth's relationship with her father, which was very influential for her writing. Discusses *Belinda*'s place in Edgeworth's canon.

Johnson, Claudia L. *Jane Austen: Women, Politics, and the Novel*. Chicago: University of Chicago Press, 1988. Places *Belinda* in the context of the politics of the 1790's and other novels of the period.

Kaufman, Heidi, and Chris Fauske, eds. *An Uncomfortable Authority: Maria Edgeworth and Her Contexts*. Newark: University of Delaware Press, 2004. The editors have collected essays examining Edgeworth's works within various cultural and ideological contexts. Includes an analysis of *Belinda*.

Kowaleski-Wallace, Elizabeth. *Their Fathers' Daughters: Hannah More, Maria Edgeworth, and Patriarchal Complicity.* New York: Oxford University Press, 1991. Investigates issues raised by Edgeworth's representation of women's rationality and irrationality and argues that her treatment of Lady Delacour and motherhood is the core of the novel.

Mellor, Anne K. *Romanticism and Gender.* New York: Routledge, Chapman & Hall: 1993. Reads *Belinda* as a presentation of "the new feminine Romantic ideology" of "balanced feminism." Includes an extensive bibliography emphasizing women writers of the period, including Edgeworth.

Nash, Julie. *Servants and Paternalism in the Works of Maria Edgeworth and Elizabeth Gaskell*. Burlington, Vt.: Ashgate, 2007. Examines the servant characters in Edgeworth's stories and novels, including *Belinda*, to show how her nostalgia for a traditional ruling class conflicted with her interest in radical new ideas about social equality.

_______, ed. *New Essays on Maria Edgeworth*. Burlington, Vt.: Ashgate, 2006. A collection of essays examining Edgeworth's work from a variety of perspectives, including analyses of *Belinda*.

A Bell for Adano

Author: John Hersey (1914-1993)
First published: 1944
Type of work: Novel
Type of plot: Social realism
Time of plot: 1943
Locale: Adano, Italy

Principal characters:
MAJOR VICTOR JOPPOLO, the American military governor of Adano
SERGEANT BORTH, Major Joppolo's subordinate
CAPTAIN PURVIS, the head of the military police
GENERAL MARVIN, the commander-in-chief of the American invasion troops and Major Joppolo's superior

The Story:

When the U.S. Army invades Sicily, Major Victor Joppolo is placed in command of Adano. He sets up his office in the city hall, rehires the janitor, and investigates the records left by the Fascist mayor, who has fled to the hills. Soon after his arrival, Major Joppolo summons the leading citizens of the town and asks them, through Giuseppe, his interpreter, what they consider the most important thing to be done. Some answer that the shortage of food is the most pressing problem. Others insist that what the town needs most is its bell, which was removed by the Fascists. The bell, it seems, had a soothing tone and it regulated the lives of Adano's residents. The major promises every effort to recover the bell. Meanwhile, the problem is to obtain food and to have produce brought into the town. In order that his directives will be understood and carried out, the major issues proclamations that the town crier, after being silent for so long, hastens to shout in the village.

On Sunday morning, when the major attends mass at one of the churches, he notices a blond girl sitting in front of him. When he later asks Giuseppe about her, the interpreter assumes that the American's interest has nothing to do with official business. Major Joppolo's primary interest, however, is the girl's father, Tomasino, owner of a fishing fleet. He has Giuseppe ask Tomasino to come to see him, but Tomasino, distrustful of authority, refuses to come to the headquarters. The major therefore goes to Tomasino, followed by practically all the townspeople. The old Italian is defiant, sure that the major comes to arrest him. Major Joppolo finally convinces him that he means neither to arrest him nor to ask for a cut in the proceeds from the sale of the fish but rather wants him to go out with his fishing fleet, despite the danger of mines.

The major and his policies are the subject of much discussion among the people. The Fascist mayor provides a great deal of amusement because he comes out of hiding and is paroled into Sergeant Borth's custody. Every morning, the mayor goes to Sergeant Borth and publicly confesses a Fascist sin. Giuseppe is astonished to discover that the major means what he says when he tells him to report for work at seven in the morning. Gargano, the former Fascist policeman, learns that he can no longer force the others to make way for him when they stand in line at the bakery.

While driving through Adano one day, General Marvin finds the road blocked by a mule cart. The driver, having had his daily quota of wine, is sleeping peacefully. When the mule refuses to budge, the general orders the vehicle thrown into the ditch. Reluctantly, the soldiers dump the cart, mule, and sleeping driver. Swearing furiously, the general drives to the city hall, where he confronts Major Joppolo and orders that all carts be forbidden to enter Adano.

The next day, a group of townspeople besiege the major to explain that the carts are essential, for they bring food and water into the town. Major Joppolo countermands the general's order and telephones Captain Purvis that he will accept full responsibility. Captain Purvis, anxious to keep out of trouble, orders Lieutenant Trapani to make a memorandum and send it to General Marvin. The lieutenant, out of regard for Major Joppolo, puts the memorandum among Purvis's papers in the hope that the captain, who rarely looks through his files, will never find it.

Major Joppolo's efforts to restore the bell are not successful, for it has been melted down by the Fascists. A young naval officer in charge of a nearby station promises to obtain a ship's bell for him.

In the meantime, Captain Purvis goes through the papers on his desk and finds the memorandum for General Marvin. He orders it forwarded at once. Lieutenant Trapani mails it, but addresses it to the wrong person at headquarters in Algiers. From there, it is forwarded to the general's aide, Colonel Middleton. Every day the colonel meets with General Marvin and goes over important communications. Accordingly, he is halfway through Purvis's letter before he realizes what it is. He tries to go onto the next letter, but it is too late. The general hears Major Joppolo's name and that of Adano, and he remembers both.

The bell arrives in Adano. It is touched, prodded, sounded by the experts, and admired by everybody. When it peals forth, the townspeople declare that its tone is even better than that of the old bell. The major is a hero. To show their appreciation and affection, the townspeople take him to a photographer. A local artist paints his portrait from the photograph. At the celebration that night, Sergeant Borth becomes very, very drunk. He refuses to take orders from Major Joppolo, saying that the major is no longer in any position to give orders. Captain Purvis, says the sergeant, almost sobbing, received a letter from General Marvin, ordering Major Joppolo back to Algiers. The next morning, the major says good-bye to Borth, who apologizes for his conduct of the previous night. The major asks him to help his successor make the people happy. As he drives away from the town, he hears in the distance the tolling of a bell, the new bell for Adano.

Critical Evaluation:

John Hersey's *A Bell for Adano*, which was published in 1944 and for which the novelist was awarded the Pulitzer Prize the following year, achieved enormous popularity in its day and was seen as a classic war novel. Because Hersey had experienced the war as a correspondent, the novel was thought to be considerably more realistic than it actually is. With some qualifications, the work can, however, be placed in that genre of American fiction called realism.

The situation of an Italian-speaking American officer, Major Joppolo, serving as administrator of the small Sicilian village of Adano allows Hersey to set out his beliefs about the primacy of democracy over Fascism, the duty of leaders to serve the people, the need for administrative control, and the disasters that result when people are left to their own devices. These beliefs coincided with the opinions held by many Americans at the close of World War II. It was consequently the perfect reading material for Americans who needed to believe that war was necessary and that the United States was helping the rest of the world by occupying Italy. It was also pleasant to believe that amid the difficulties of war there could be moments of humor and that one could encounter good simple folk. The novel is optimistic, often comic in tone, and ultimately romantic in its conclusion: When Major Joppolo is ordered by General Marvin to leave the town, he stops for one final time to hear the ringing of the bell that his efforts had brought the people. "It was a fine sound on the summer air," the novel maintains, and the reader is left with the image of Joppolo as a decent man who has done his best. That the town has little future is immaterial; the residents of Adano will simply continue their bungling ways. The main conflict in the novel stems from the clashes between Major Joppolo, who believes in democracy and servant leadership, and General Marvin, whose selfishness and cruelty in shooting the mule and ordering carts out of the village make him the symbol of American arrogance and lack of consideration for the native population. There is additional conflict and satire in Joppolo's struggles with postwar bureaucracy; his reaction to his "Instructions to Civil Affairs Officers," which is to tear up the pages and use his own judgment, affords both humor and commentary on the unrealistic, theoretical approach to occupying a small town.

That General Marvin, who has the right to order Joppolo to leave Adano, is ultimately the victor suggests that Hersey believes that it is important for individuals to do something good, even if it is only a small gesture. No one in the novel changes or develops; the soldiers continue to be superficial, the townspeople petty, the Army bureaucracy uncaring. Life goes on, but it is vital that individuals do good deeds and therein find satisfaction.

Most of the Italian villagers are depicted as foolish, nostalgic, and opportunistic. Hersey achieves some of his best humor at their expense, frequently using caricature and such tags as "lazy Fatta" and "formidable Margherita." Hersey also gives some of the townspeople dignity, however. Old Cacopardo's reproach of General Marvin's lack of appreciation of the antique mahogany table on which the general and his aide are playing mumblety-peg shows the clash of cultures and allows Hersey to point out the inability of most Americans to realize the richness of other histories and cultures. This same theme is echoed in the earliest conversations about the village bell when "small Zito" maintains that the bell will be of greater significance than additional food would be. Zito rejects a replica of the American Liberty Bell: "I do not think the people of Adano want any liberty that has a crack in it."

In his depictions of the soldiers Chuck and Polak, who seek only drink and sexual escapades and who destroy the art objects in the house where they are billeted, Hersey provides a biting commentary on the behavior of American soldiers abroad. Some reviewers in fact questioned Hersey's accuracy, particularly regarding the language he ascribes to the soldiers, which was considered shocking at the time.

The novel is more a series of vignettes than a complex narrative; there is little if any interior action. Hersey is at his best in depicting isolated incidents: Major Joppolo's arrival in Adano, the first visit with Tomasino and his family, the Hemingway-inspired dialogue between Chuck and Polak, the conversations about the crack in the American Liberty Bell, the final moments when Major Joppolo stops to hear the bell.

A Bell for Adano has an important history and keeps a

secure place in American popular fiction and war literature. The novel eventually became both a Broadway play and a motion picture. Hersey's subsequent publication of *Hiroshima* (1946) further solidified the critical reputation of *A Bell for Adano* and gave it additional credibility.

"Critical Evaluation" by Katherine Hanley

Further Reading

Bradbury, Malcolm. *The Modern American Novel.* New York: Oxford University Press, 1984. A helpful summary of twentieth century American fiction, which places *A Bell for Adano* in the mainstream of conventional realism and naturalism.

Buchanan, Andrew. "'Good Morning, Pupil!': American Representations of Italianness and the Occupation of Italy, 1943-1945." *Journal of Contemporary History* 42, no. 2 (April, 2008): 217-240. This discussion of American images of "Italianness" in novels, films, and the news media during World War II includes an analysis of *A Bell for Adano*. Buchanan argues that Italians generally were depicted "as an infantile, emotional and largely apolitical people whose character was marked by cowardice and unpredictable violence."

Gemme, Francis. *John Hersey's "A Bell for Adano," "Hiroshima," and Other Works: A Critical Commentary.* New York: Monarch Press, 1966. A brief survey for beginning students. Good cursory treatment of Hersey's works and an overview of the initial reception of his novels.

Huse, Nancy Lyman. *John Hersey and James Agee: A Reference Guide.* Boston: G. K. Hall, 1978. Extremely helpful compilation of materials for research. Includes reviews from the time of initial publication.

Sanders, David. *John Hersey.* New Haven, Conn.: College and University Press, 1967. Excellent overview of Hersey and his work. Traces significant themes and beliefs. Provides a good treatment of Hersey's life, with critical attention to his literary output.

_______. *John Hersey Revisited.* Boston: Twayne, 1990. A competent survey of Hersey's life and works, updating the previous information on the critical estimate of Hersey and of *A Bell for Adano*. Includes bibliography.

The Bell Jar

Author: Sylvia Plath (1932-1963)
First published: 1963
Type of work: Novel
Type of plot: Psychological realism
Time of plot: 1953
Locale: New York City and New England

Principal characters:
ESTHER GREENWOOD, a college student
DOREEN, a friend and guest editor
MRS. GREENWOOD, Esther's widowed mother
BUDDY WILLARD, a boyfriend of Esther
DOCTOR NOLAN, a psychiatrist
JOAN GILLING, Esther's colleague

The Story:

Esther Greenwood is in New York City the summer that Julius and Ethel Rosenberg are to be executed (1953). Ecstatic over having won a position as guest editor on the college board for a well-known magazine for young women, she is puzzled that she is not having the time of her life.

On the face of it, she has everything going for her. She is attractive, intelligent, and talented. She is a straight-A student. The magazine arranges concerts, dances, celebrity interviews, fashion shows, and luncheons galore for the twelve college student women who won positions as guest editors. Why is she feeling depressed? Esther's boyfriend Buddy is in a sanatorium recovering from tuberculosis. She is discovering that her feelings for him are lukewarm. She feels free to date other men, but somehow those dates are not turning out as well as she expects.

She and the eleven other young women from colleges across the United States are living in a hotel for women. Doreen, who is cynical and audacious, particularly appeals to Esther. One night on their way to a party, they let themselves be picked up by a disc jockey, Lenny Shepherd. After drinks he asks them to his apartment. After more drinks, Doreen and Lenny dance lasciviously. Esther is disgusted. She leaves Doreen and walks back to the hotel disillusioned with Doreen and later with herself for abandoning Doreen.

Doreen is not the only reason Esther is disillusioned. The city glamour she expected manifests itself as a series of shoddy episodes. Behind the glittery surfaces she sees a world of competition, meanness, fakery, and backbreaking work leading to some trivial end.

Esther and the other young women are invited to a "ladies' magazine" luncheon. Beautifully presented crabmeat salad is served, but later they are all violently sick. The crabmeat was tainted. Another event in New York City that was supposed to be wonderful is spoiled.

Another spoiled event for Esther is the work she is assigned at the magazine. She is a perfectionist, an overachiever, and always anxious about deadlines. Stress becomes apparent during a photography session. Esther, told to hold a paper rose and smile (to represent her dream to be a poet), bursts into tears.

Later, however, she lets Doreen talk her into going out on another date. It is another fiasco. Ripping Esther's dress and throwing her in the mud, calling her a slut, the "country-club gentleman" date, Marco, tries to rape her. She escapes and once again flees back to her hotel.

Her stint as guest editor over, in a gesture of her feelings, Esther throws all of her new clothes off the roof of the hotel. In the morning she leaves for home. Her mother meets her at the train station. Esther hates their small house and the suburbs and plans to escape by attending a creative writing seminar at Harvard. She is not accepted. The rejection, in addition to her recent experiences, sends her into depression. She cannot concentrate on writing her honors thesis. She tries to work on a novel, but disappointment and despondency lock her in lethargy. Esther's apathy worries her mother who, at her wits' end, suggest they see a psychiatrist.

Unfortunately, the psychiatrist, Doctor Gordon, is the wrong doctor for Esther. She finds him insensitive and patronizing. In addition, the shock treatments he prescribes for her not only frighten her but also send her into a deeper depression. Esther begins to dwell on suicide even though she attempts to do normal things, such as double-dating and hospital volunteer work.

One rainy day, after visiting the grave of her father, she returns home, leaves a note that she is going for a walk, takes a bottle of sleeping pills and a glass of water, and goes to the basement. Hiding herself in a crawl space behind some firewood, she swallows the pills. She takes too many, causing her to vomit, which saves her life. Now desperate, her mother sends Esther to a state mental institution.

At this point Esther's benefactress, Philomena Guinea, proposes that Esther be sent to a private hospital. Philomena will finance it. At the new institution Esther begins to improve. Doctor Nolan, her psychiatrist, an intuitive woman, gains Esther's trust. Intuitive people gain Esther's approval. Esther learns that it is all right to say that one hates one's mother. She also learns that her need to be sexually active is not only normal but also feasible. Doctor Nolan prescribes birth control. Under compassionate supervision and carefully conducted shock treatments, Esther begins to improve.

One of Esther's college friends, Joan Gilling, is also at the hospital. Joan, like Esther, tried to kill herself. In addition, like Esther, Joan dated Buddy Willard, but at the hospital Joan confesses that she prefers women to men. Initially disgusted with Joan's homosexuality, Esther nevertheless continues to befriend Joan. Eventually, Esther and Joan are allowed town and overnight privileges from the hospital. On one of these outings, Esther has her first sexual experience with a professor she meets. Esther's experience is another misadventure. She begins to hemorrhage. The professor, in a panic, takes her to the apartment where Joan is staying. Joan, upset, takes Esther to an emergency ward, and a doctor repairs the damage. One in a million, he says.

A few days later, Joan hangs herself. Doctor Nolan, worried that Joan's suicide will throw Esther back into despair, assures her that no one is to blame. A sign of Esther's newly gained stability is that neither her sexual misadventure nor Joan's suicide casts her into depression. Buddy then visits Esther at the sanatorium and tells her that she is no longer a suitable marriage prospect. Esther is not disturbed. In fact, his pompous announcement frees her. Buddy, from then on, is out of her life. It is another sign of her recovery that she responds in a healthy way to his announcement. Esther is well. She has the strength to face the panel of doctors, who, if she passes their examinations, will discharge her from the hospital. She will take charge, once again, of her destiny.

Critical Evaluation:

The Bell Jar is the only novel by Sylvia Plath, who is best known as a poet. Her novel was published in England in January, 1963, under the pseudonym Victoria Lucas. Plath committed suicide in February of the same year. Since its publication, *The Bell Jar* has received steady acclaim. Critics first viewed it as a fine first novel in the style of J. D. Salinger's *The Catcher in the Rye* (1951). *The Bell Jar* was published in the United States in 1971. Critics in the United States also praised the novel. It was a complex psychological portrayal of a young woman of the early 1950's. Esther Greenwood, in her search for self-determination, is a prototype heroine of the mid-century women's movement, a movement heralded by the publication of Betty Friedan's *The Feminine Mystique* in 1963.

Plath had written a rough draft of *The Bell Jar* by 1960, and she won a grant to finish it from the Eugene F. Saxton Foundation. In a letter to her brother, she called the work a "pot-boiler." Her prose, however, took a turn from the mediocre to the remarkable; her poetry had already taken this turn. The poet Ted Hughes, Plath's husband, described Plath's rather sudden change from talent to genius as a "plunge into herself," into the subjective, the imaginary. That the novel contains so much of "herself" was her reason for publishing it under a pseudonym. She did not want to offend anyone she knew; the characters in the novel had their counterparts in life.

The protagonist, Esther, is a young woman who sees life as if from within a bell jar. Her experiences are askew, not what they are supposed to be. There is always "a worm in the rose." She has a "perfect" boyfriend, but rather than finding him romantic she finds him dull, pilloried by mother's maxims. She watches a baby being born and instead of seeing a miracle, she sees brutality. She goes to New York City to have the time of her life, but the time of her life is overshadowed by the execution of the Rosenbergs. She discovers that the job of her dreams is contrived; she sees that the woman's world of fashion, romance, and domesticity is a sham.

What Plath learned when she wrote her honors thesis, "The Magic Mirror: A Study of the Double in Two of Dostoevski's Novels," was "stuff about the ego as symbolized in reflections (mirror and water), shadows, twins." She wrote that "recognition of our various mirror images and reconciliation with them will save us from disintegration." *The Bell Jar* is, to some degree, a fictional account of this study. Throughout the novel, Plath shows the double, "the various mirror images" of the ego. Images of the double resonate throughout the narrative.

Esther's face is an example of the double. After traumatic episodes, Esther sees her face mirrored as some kind of blotched, distorted, bloated image—an icon, she thinks, to her dark nature. Her "good" face is restored only after she undergoes a purging ritual, one that can be as simple as a hot bath, as radical as throwing her new clothes off the rooftop of a hotel or as desperate as a suicide attempt. The double is not only associated with Esther's face but also associated with the faces of other people. The other face of Hilda, a guest editor, a young woman of high fashion, impeccably dressed, appears when she tells Esther that she is "so glad" the Rosenbergs are going to die. Out of her mouth echoes the voice of a demon. "Fashion" and "devil" are doubles of Hilda. Joan Gilling's suicide and lesbian sexuality is the other side of the face of the privileged American girl. In addition to people, events also have double faces. A ladies' luncheon, put on by a glossy magazine epitomizing the glamorous "face" of feminine dreams, is elegantly presented, but the plates of crabmeat and avocado are poisonous.

The double motif exposes the hypocrisy that lies beneath the glamorous, glitzy surfaces of a mercantile society. The result is a densely packed, quickly paced novel, one that, in spite of its youthful tone, is complex. It describes the journey of a young woman undergoing trials and pitfalls in her search for an authentic life.

Alice L. Swensen

Further Reading

Alexander, Paul, ed. *Ariel Ascending: Writings About Sylvia Plath*. New York: Harper & Row, 1985. The essays in this volume concentrate on Plath as a craftsperson. Two of the essays, "Esther Came Back Like a Retreaded Tire" by Robert Scholes and "Victoria Lucas and Elly Higginbottom" by Vance Bourjaily, deal solely with interpretations of *The Bell Jar*.

Axelrod, Steven Gould. *Sylvia Plath: The Wound and the Cure of Words*. Baltimore: Johns Hopkins University Press, 1990. In the preface, the author describes his work as "a biography of the imagination." The chapter "A Woman Famous Among Women," proposing Virginia Woolf's influence on Plath, offers an interesting contrast and comparison between Clarissa Dalloway, from Woolf's 1925 novel *Mrs. Dalloway*, and Esther Greenwood. Includes a portrait of Plath and an extensive bibliography.

Badia, Janet. "*The Bell Jar*, and Other Prose." In *The Cambridge Companion to Sylvia Plath*. New York: Cambridge University Press, 2006. In addition to Badia's analysis of Plath's prose, this collection includes essays on Plath and psychoanalysis and the problem of biography when dealing with Plath's work.

Bundtzen, Lynda K. *Plath's Incarnations: Women and the Creative Process*. Ann Arbor: University of Michigan Press, 1983. Combines psychological and feminist criticism in a critical biography. Bundtzen traces Plath's personal development as an artist and relates that development to the image of women in society and the world of art. The index provides topical guidance for information on *The Bell Jar*, and the chapter "*The Bell Jar*: The Past as Allegory" offers an interpretation of the novel as feminist allegory. Includes a bibliography.

Gentry, Deborah S. *The Art of Dying: Suicide in the Works of Kate Chopin and Sylvia Plath*. New York: Peter Lang,

2006. Analyzes the motif and theme of suicide in *The Bell Jar*, applying theories that divide women literary characters who commit suicide into angels or monsters.

Hall, Caroline King Barnard. *Sylvia Plath, Revised*. Boston: Twayne, 1998. A revised edition of the introductory overview originally published in 1978. Contains an expanded discussion of *The Bell Jar* and updated information about Plath scholarship.

MacPherson, Pat. *Reflecting on "The Bell Jar."* New York: Routledge, 1991. Focuses on the social context of *The Bell Jar*, including examinations of postwar life in the suburbs, the hatred of one's mother expressed in films of the 1950's, and homosexuality. Discusses how the era's Cold War paranoia, introduced in the novel by the execution of Julius and Ethel Rosenberg, affects the protagonist personally. The bibliography contains relevant sociological and political entries.

Wagner-Martin, Linda. *"The Bell Jar": A Novel of the Fifties*. Boston: Twayne, 1992. An excellent analysis of the novel in the context of its times and the author's life.

_______, ed. *Sylvia Plath: The Critical Heritage*. New York: Routledge, 1988. Reprints reviews of Plath's work at the time it was published, including ten reviews and essays on *The Bell Jar*.

La Belle Dame sans Merci

Author: John Keats (1795-1821)
First published: 1820; collected in *Life, Letters, and Literary Remains of John Keats*, 1848
Type of work: Poetry

The first three stanzas of "La Belle Dame sans Merci" pose the speaker's questions to a melancholy knight who looks lonely, listless, and ill. The sedge, a grasslike plant that thrives in wetlands, has dried up, and the knight, as if in sympathy with this arid setting, appears depleted both physically and emotionally.

In stanza four, the knight begins to answer the speaker's questions, reporting that he met a beautiful, fairylike lady in the meads (meadows). Enchanted by this beautiful figure, the knight describes her graceful movement, her alluring long hair, and her lively appearance, apparent in her wild eyes.

In stanza five, he makes a garland (a wreath of intertwined flowers) for her head and bracelets that enhance her natural perfume. She is responsive to his loving tribute, and her sweet moaning signals that she is falling in love with him. In stanza six, enraptured with his newfound love, the knight places her on his horse and follows her all day as she looks down as him and sings a fairy song, while in stanza seven she gathers and feeds him sweet roots and delectable foods to express her true love for him.

In stanza eight, the mood of the poem shifts back toward melancholy, when the knight relates how the woman took him to a grotto, a sort of magical space the knight associates with fairy creatures such as elves. In this setting, the delicate, fleeting nature of the lady's feelings suddenly erupts with her tears, which the knight tries to soothe with his kisses that shut her "wild wild eyes"—words that suggest he has fallen in love with a creature that he cannot possess.

It is the lady who lulls the knight to sleep, however. In stanzas nine to eleven, he is engulfed in a dream of kings and princes who are pale (as he is at the beginning of the poem) and who warn him that he has become enslaved by the beautiful lady without mercy. When he awakes, the knight finds himself on the cold hillside, feeling the deathlike cold of his dream and looking like the sad figure the speaker first encountered. Coming full circle in stanza twelve, the knight notes that his experience with the lady is why he remains in this bleak setting, alone and feeling that he has lost the love of this beautiful figure that haunts and blights not only his life but also the world in which he finds himself.

This deceptively simple tale written in a ballad style, featuring short lines and romantic longings, evokes the human yearning for an eternal, imperishable love, a bond that outlasts death and that conquers mortality. To lose the lady is tantamount to a kind of death for the knight. Thus, John Keats uses the medieval setting as a kind of allegory, a symbolic representation of what love represents. To the lover, the beloved is a fairy creature usually associated with perfection and with the desire to do good and to protect the loved one.

The knight is at the mercy of his love, meaning both the lady and the knight's feelings for the lady. When she withdraws her love, she is portrayed as without mercy. The heat of passion vanishes, and this is why the knight feels cold and why the world itself seems frigid.

Keats differs from his medieval sources insofar as he is conscious of a psychological dimension in the knight's suffering. In other words, "La Belle Dame sans Merci" is as much about the knight's state of mind as it is about the lady that he meets. The grotto to which they retire can be viewed as a sort of underworld of the mind, the "gloam," the twilight world in which dreams occur and reveal the deepest origins of human apprehensions.

Like many of his contemporaries—Romantic poets such as Samuel Taylor Coleridge and Sir Walter Scott—Keats was drawn to medieval poems, romances, and stories because he believed this literature expressed an emotional truth that needed to be recovered and cherished rather than diminished by those who saw the late eighteenth and nineteenth centuries as the Age of Reason. Reason seemed to its proponent to relegate the fairy tales and fables of the past to the "dark ages" when human beings were prey to their fears and anxieties. To Keats, the older forms of poetry such as the ballad should be resurrected so as not to ignore the vital—indeed inescapable—role that human emotions play in human affairs.

Keats biographer Robert Gittings notes that the poem's use of archaic words and constructions, such as "meads," "grot," "withereth," and "woe-betide," as well as the ballad structure itself, recalls *Lyrical Ballads* (1798), the joint work of Coleridge and William Wordsworth that heralded the great age of Romantic poetry. Indeed, as Gittings notes, when Keats accidentally met Coleridge on Hampstead Heath, the latter spent an hour discoursing on the nature of dreams, perhaps thus contributing to the role dream plays in "La Belle Dame sans Merci." Morever, as Gittings also notes, Coleridge later remembered grasping Keats's hand, which seemed as cold as death. Keats, who would die of tuberculosis in agony over his unfulfilled love for Fanny Brawne, found a way, Gittings implies, of projecting his own anguish into this antique form of poetry.

Another interpretation of the poem—suggested by a passage in Aileen Ward's biography of Keats—emphasizes the theme of betrayal, that love will not last, and that the knight suffers because of the lady's withdrawal of her affections. After all, the knight is warned by princes and kings who are deathly pale and who appear with the gaping visages of corpses. The grotto in the poem could then be viewed as the grave of love with the lady already mourning her knight's decease. At the very least, there is a foreboding atmosphere in the poem that Ward associates with Keats's own distraught reflections on his love for Fanny Brawne.

Like Keats's other biographers, Walter Jackson Bate notes that the poem may stem from but it also transcends Keats's biography. Bate sees the poem as a "distillation of diverse feelings," an apt way of suggesting the poem's universality, its ability to evoke the conflicting emotions that love can arouse from intense attachment, euphoria, and devotion to alienation, depression, and disaffection. Bate questions the knight's behavior, wondering whether the poem is more about his persistence than it is about the lady's rejection of him. What does it mean, for example, that the lady looks "sidelong" at the knight? The word implies that she is not straightforward or fully committed to him, especially since, as Bate notes, she expresses her love in "language strange." The lady is not entirely human, the biographer notes, and therefore she may be misinterpreted by the knight as well as being a projection of his imagination, of what he wants to come true.

Carl Rollyson

Further Reading

Bate, Walter Jackson. *John Keats*. Cambridge, Mass.: Harvard University Press, 1964. Includes a very shrewd and suggestive interpretation of "La Belle Dame sans Merci" that looks carefully at what Keats himself said about it as well as comparing it with other Keats poems.

Gittings, Robert. *John Keats*. London: Heinemann, 1968. Perceptively describes the autobiographical sources of the poem.

Kelly, Theresa M. "Poetics and the Politics of Reception: Keats's 'La Belle Dame sans Merci.'" In *John Keats*, edited and with an introduction by Harold Bloom. Updated ed. New York: Chelsea House, 2007. Reads the poem as a response to the critical reception of Keats's earlier works, which shaped his attitude toward and use of poetic conventions.

Ward, Aileen. *John Keats: The Making of a Poet*. New York: Viking Press, 1963. Complements but also contrasts with Gittings's interpretation of the poem as Keats's personal statement.

Wells, Marion A. *The Secret Wound: Love-Melancholy and Early Modern Romance*. Stanford, Calif.: Stanford University Press, 2007. Extended study of the medieval tradition to which Keats's poem responds. Discusses the poem itself in the work's conclusion.

Whale, John. *John Keats*. New York: Palgrave Macmillan, 2005. Compares "La Belle Dame sans Merci" to three of Keats's other narrative romance poems.

Bellefleur

Author: Joyce Carol Oates (1938-)
First published: 1980
Type of work: Novel
Type of plot: Gothic
Time of plot: Mid-sixteenth to late twentieth centuries
Locale: Upstate New York

Principal characters:
JEAN PIERRE BELLEFLEUR, the American founder of the Bellefleur family
LOUIS and JEDEDIAH, his sons
RAPHAEL, Jedediah's son
GIDEON, Jedediah's great-great-grandson
LEAH, Gideon's first cousin and wife
GERMAINE, daughter of Leah and Gideon

The Story:

Jean Pierre Bellefleur, banished from his native France and cast out by his father, a duke, settles in the Lake Noir region of the United States in the mid-1700's and becomes a powerful force in the area. Notorious for his drinking, gambling, and shady business deals, Jean Pierre is impeached from Congress during his second term for scandal and corruption. When his wife, Hilda, flees his house, to the neighbors' horror, he brings an Onondagan Indian woman, Antoinette, to live with him.

His son Louis marries Germaine O'Hagan, a local woman, and has three children with her. Louis's family lives with Jean Pierre, and Louis participates in the family businesses with a disregard for the law that equals that of his father.

Jedediah Bellefleur, the less business-minded son, goes off to live in the nearby mountains to prove to himself that he can survive there for a year. The years begin to multiply, and Jedediah does not return. He becomes a hermit, religiously zealous, suspicious of the occasional trappers and hunters he encounters on the mountain, and paranoid that his family will have him forcibly removed back to their home. His mission is to see the face of God.

After nineteen years on the mountain, Jedediah is persuaded to return to his family home; Jean Pierre, Louis, Antoinette, and Louis's children were brutally murdered by vengeful neighbors. Only Germaine survived the midnight raid on the family home. In order to keep the family name alive, Jedediah marries Germaine and they have three children, including Raphael, who dedicates himself to building the family fame and fortune.

In addition to running for governor and losing three times, helping to found the Republican Party in the area, and creating a hops empire from nothing, Raphael builds Bellefleur Manor, a mammoth, Gothic castle that dominates the landscape in the Lake Noir region. There Raphael entertains numerous politicians, including senators, Supreme Court justices, a vice president, and dignitaries from overseas. He claims that he offered refuge to Abraham Lincoln at the manor when Lincoln, depressed and anxiety-ridden, according to Raphael, hired an actor and staged his own murder. Raphael is best known for having a provision in his will that he be skinned upon his death. He orders that the skin be stretched over a Civil War cavalry drum, that the drum forever reside in the Great Hall of Bellefleur Manor, and that it be "sounded each day to announce meals, the arrival of guests, and other special events." The drum mainly is used by the Bellefleur children to scare each other and unsuspecting friends.

Subsequent generations of Bellefleurs are punctuated by such members of the family as Jean Pierre II, who is convicted of murdering eleven people in an area tavern; Hiram, an irrepressible sleepwalker; and Vernon, a poet; but most prominent are Gideon and Leah Bellefleur, who live in the twentieth century.

Gideon and Leah are first cousins who marry and have three children. They are beautiful, powerful, and extreme. Anything Gideon drives—a car, a horse, a plane—he drives fast. He races for high stakes and always wins. Leah takes in and tames strays: a large, ferocious cat; a child; a baby that she forcibly removes from its own mother's care; a dwarf. Her children believe she has the power of foresight. After a lengthy and inactive pregnancy with her third child, she sets about to restore the Bellefleur fortune, which is a bit depleted, to its previous glory. For luck and inspiration in her business deals, Leah brings along her daughter Germaine, whom she believes has power of her own. Germaine is a quiet, precocious child who had been born with an extra torso and set of legs growing from her abdomen. These had been promptly cut off by her grandmother, but Germaine is characterized by a sadness that may have resulted from a sense of loss over the part of herself that was removed or may have resulted from the burden of knowing ahead of time what will happen to family members.

As Leah pursues her business interests and is away from home frequently, her relationship with Gideon, which once had been as passionate as all other aspects of their lives, begins to sour. He has numerous affairs with tawdry, uneducated women, the antitheses of Leah, and eventually becomes obsessed with flying planes. Leah has a number of affairs of her own, which she uses as a means to get business accomplished. They only bother to fight over the affections of Germaine, each claiming to be a more devoted parent to her than the other.

In an act that nullifies not only the accumulating successes of Leah's business ventures but also Bellefleur Manor and all but a few members of the family, Gideon crashes a plane loaded with explosives into the manor. Only Germaine, whom Gideon safely deposited with a distant aunt, and the Bellefleurs, who long since fled the manor and never returned, are spared.

Critical Evaluation:

Joyce Carol Oates had published more than sixty works—including novels, plays, and collections of stories, poems, and essays—by the mid-1990's, making her one of the United States' most prolific writers. *Bellefleur*, which is generally acknowledged as her masterpiece, characterizes Oates's tremendous output through its abundance of events, characters, pages, even words per sentence. A huge, sprawling novel of 558 pages, *Bellefleur* covers seven generations and more than fifty members of the Bellefleur family, which dominated a region of the eastern United States that resembles upstate New York. In addition to elements of gothicism and Magical Realism, the novel is characterized by its nonchronological approach to relating the Bellefleur saga, its overabundance of specific details, and Oates's unusual habit of undercutting the story's tension by mentioning hints regarding the outcomes of various events before those events have even been related.

The Bellefleur family history parallels that of the United States, operating sometimes within the context of American history and culture, but more often in the separate, parallel world of Bellefleur Manor. A sense of otherness is brought about largely by the massiveness of the manor and the miles of land surrounding it, including a range of mountains, all of which are owned or otherwise dominated by the Bellefleurs.

Increasing this sense of otherness is the fact that there are few details that reveal the particular time period of the novel's events. Oates does not provide birth and death dates for the characters beyond 1830 in the family tree found at the beginning of the novel. That readers are not able to pin a specific time to the events of the story makes the lives of the characters seem more fluid and adds to the novel's expansiveness. Not only do the Bellefleurs have an abundance of wealth, land, children, rooms in which to dwell, works of art, horses, and cars, they apparently live longer and more fully than the average human. The things that surround the Bellefleurs are carefully, specifically documented by Oates—one chapter is devoted to a history of the cars they have owned—but the timelessness of these items, their inability to date those surrounding them, increases the reader's sense of Bellefleur Manor as otherworldly and shows that the events of the past are inextricably bound up with the present.

Gothic elements—such as the stone castle with its several wings and towers and off-limits rooms, a would-be vampire, a family curse, and the vulture that steals a baby from the manor's garden—add an atmosphere of gloom and impending doom in the novel. Its elements of Magical Realism, however, create a sense of abundance and possibility that better capture the novel's feel. Young Raphael, whose only emotional connection is to a small, secluded pond, is absorbed into the pond that is, in turn, absorbed into the land. A deformed dwarf eventually straightens and grows tall after several years at the manor. One Bellefleur disappears into a mirror. The bigger-than-life passions of these characters have been so strong, they are transforming.

The sense of the possibility of the supernatural created by the Magical Realism pairs nicely with one of the novel's most striking characteristics, its nonchronological approach to the telling of the story. Despite elements of traditional, historic narratives in *Bellefleur*, Oates presents the events of the novel for effect. The frequent time shifting, which usually occurs at chapter breaks, enables Oates to juxtapose, for the sake of contrast, events from the past with events from the nearer present. The nonchronological approach adds to the reader's sense of the family as exerting a cumulative force on successive generations. The reader feels, along with the Bellefleurs, the power of their ancestry and the burden that is entailed in simply being born into the family. This burden is what drives many family members away and leads Gideon to finally destroy the family and the manor.

Oates's nonchronological approach is a useful device in another way: It allows her to hint at things to come, thereby undercutting any tension or suspense that might be building around certain events in the novel. Readers know ahead of time about the murders of Jean Pierre, Louis, and their families; about Raphael's being skinned; that Gideon will destroy the family; and other things. By undercutting much of the suspense or tension in the novel, Oates distances the reader from individual characters and maintains the focus on her more prevailing concern: the Bellefleur family. She uses the

Bellefleurs to track both the ingenuity and potential that the United States represents, and the violence, lust, greed, and eventual destruction contained within the nation as well.

Bellefleur is a work remarkable in its scope, its vision, and its ability to work within, yet turn on, conventional storytelling devices. Events of the story are presented in waves, and the tension of the work is developed around seemingly insignificant events, while major plot points are frequently glossed over. At times, the reader is presented with pages-long lists of the things that surround the Bellefleurs. All these unconventional choices provide a multilayered, profound perspective on power and the American family.

Michelle Fredette

Further Reading

Bender, Eileen T. "History as Woman's Game: '*Bellefleur*' as *Texte de Jouissance*." *Soundings: An Interdisciplinary Journal* 76, nos. 2/3 (Summer/Fall, 1993): 369-381. Argues that "unshapely, fueled by waves of ungratified desire, *Bellefleur* is an audacious and revisionary model of historical fiction."

Cologne-Brookes, Gavin. *Dark Eyes on America: The Novels of Joyce Carol Oates*. Baton Rouge: Louisiana State University Press, 2005. Traces the evolution of Oates's novels, demonstrating how she moved from abstract introspection to a more pragmatic concern with understanding personal and social problems and possibilities.

Creighton, Joanne V. *Joyce Carol Oates: Novels of the Middle Years*. New York: Twayne, 1992. A critical analysis of Oates's novels and essays published between 1977 and 1990. Calls *Bellefleur* Oates's "most impressive reworking" of the nineteenth century gothic genre.

Daly, Brenda. *Lavish Self-Divisions: The Novels of Joyce Carol Oates*. Jackson: University Press of Mississippi, 1996. Traces the development of Oates's female characters from father-identified daughters in the 1960's to self-identified women in the 1980's.

Johnson, Greg. *Invisible Writer: A Biography of Joyce Carol Oates*. New York: Dutton, 1998. Johnson recounts the events of Oates's life and describes how she transforms them in her fiction.

Nodelman, Perry. "The Sense of Unending: Joyce Carol Oates's *Bellefleur* as an Experiment in Feminine Storytelling." In *Breaking the Sequence: Women's Experimental Fiction*, edited by Ellen G. Friedman and Miriam Fuchs. Princeton, N.J.: Princeton University Press, 1989. Argues that *Bellefleur*, in its nonchronological approach to storytelling, is especially feminine in its experimentation because it transcends "the limitations of both conventional and conventionally innovative forms of fiction" represented by the traditional narrative form of conflict, crisis, and resolution.

Oates, Joyce Carol. *The Faith of a Writer: Life, Craft, Art*. New York: Ecco, 2003. Reprints twelve essays and an interview in which Oates discusses the writing life.

_______. *Joyce Carol Oates: Conversations, 1970-2006*. Edited by Greg Johnson. New York: W. W. Norton, 2006. In this collection of reprinted interviews, Oates discusses literature, her work, and her life.

_______. *(Woman) Writer: Occasions and Opportunities*. New York: E. P. Dutton, 1988. A collection of Oates's own musings on writing and the woman writer. Contains the preface to *Bellefleur*, in which Oates discusses the classification of the novel as gothic and reveals the one image from which the novel grew.

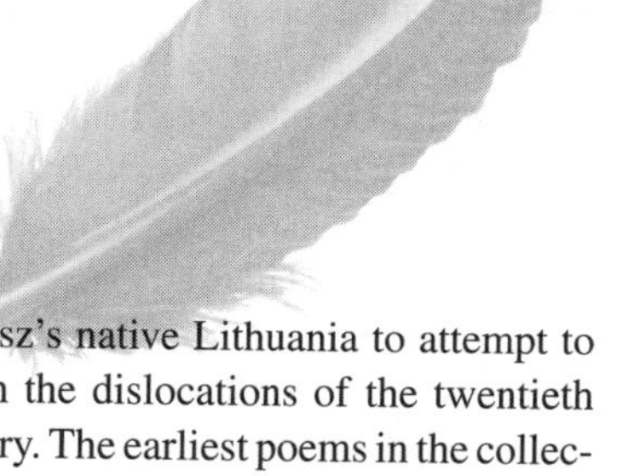

Bells in Winter

Author: Czesław Miłosz (1911-2004)
First published: 1978
Type of work: Poetry

Czesław Miłosz's *Bells in Winter* is a book of short lyric poems, an extended historical poem, and one long poem made up of six sections. The lyric poems are various, since some deal with nature and religion and others with the social and historical losses of the mid-twentieth century. The long poem goes back to Miłosz's native Lithuania to attempt to come to terms with both the dislocations of the twentieth century and his own history. The earliest poems in the collection were written in 1936 and 1944 in the midst of the destruction of World War II in Eastern Europe. Miłosz is a poet who writes in Polish but was born in Lithuania, and he saw the destruction of his country and the slaughter of millions. In this way the context of history frames the rest of the poems, which were written in the 1970's.

The first poem in the collection is called "Encounter." It begins with a pastoral landscape with a hare and a man who perceives it. The poem then contrasts that pastoral scene with death and destruction. "Today neither of them is alive,/ Not the hare, nor the man who made the gesture." The speaker asks where are they going, but there is no answer. Instead, the sense of loss is modulated by placing it in another emotional context: "I ask not in sorrow, but in wonder." The poem was written in 1936, a time when the beginnings of World War II were becoming apparent. Wonder is the appropriate emotion to the cataclysm that was to take place; it is literally beyond sorrow.

In contrast, "A Frivolous Conversation," written in 1944, provides a positive vision that can come into being when "mutability ceases." The vision is of a blessed earth filled with marvels and "tranquil glory." However, the speaker of the poem only contemplates these wonders; he does not desire and is "content." The speaker is free from desire, and the time is free from the destruction that change brings. It is a rare moment of pure contemplation and stasis. Thus, the first two poems contrast and represent the dual vision on which Miłosz's art insists.

"Tidings" clearly contrasts to "A Frivolous Conversation." It seeks to define "earthly civilization," asking if it is "a system of colored spheres cast in smoked glass" or a "golden fleece,/ In a rainbow net." After such glorious but fantastical images, the answer is much different. "Or perhaps we'll say nothing of earthly civilization./ For nobody really knows what it was." This suggests that the various positive formulations of civilization are merely illusions, and the reality of human life is far different and more terrible.

"How It Was" also deals with civilization. The poem portrays a journey deep "into the mountains" where the speaker sees only "absence." There was "No eagle-creator . . . protective spirits hid themselves in subterranean beds of bubbling ore." In this poem, there is no God the Father and no Son of God: "This time it was really the end of the Old and the New Testament." The poem concludes with the speaker described as among those who "longed for the Kingdom" and took refuge "in the mountains to become the last heirs of a dishonored myth." Miłosz often writes about Christianity and its history. In this poem, the Christian era has come to an end and the poet-speaker is one of the few to remain loyal to a myth that no longer has the power to compel belief or reverence. Miłosz often sees the modern world as embracing nihilism; he understands its sources and context, but he can never give his assent to it.

"Not This Way" is a poem of self-accusation, one of many in the book. The poet-speaker describes himself as a "schemer" who uses language in a "childish" manner to transform "the sublime into the cordial." His voice "always lacked fullness." He desires a new language of the elements of "fire and water" to "render a new thanksgiving." In this vision, poetry must reduce itself to the essentials and to a language of utter simplicity in order to fulfill its mission.

"Study of Loneliness" portrays one man alone in the daily glories of nature who begins to question for whom those splendors exist. "For me alone?/ Yet it will be here long after I perish." Nature will go on, apparently indifferent to the fate of humanity. The resolution of the poem is a recognition that it is hopeless to complain: "And he knew there was no use in crying out, for none of them would save him." Salvation cannot come from humanity or from nature, even though Miłosz writes some of his most moving poems on the power within nature.

"A Felicitous Life" is one of the most interesting lyrics in the collection. It first portrays the blessed life of a man who dies in a time of peace without any disturbances in nature. He feels a pang of loss in his death: "It was bitter to say farewell to the earth so renewed." However, the resolution of the poem is very different. "Two days after his death a hurricane razed the coast." Dormant volcanos erupt and "war began with a battle in the islands." The regret at losing the world and beneficent nature is ironically reversed as the transitory nature of everything is revealed. Peace gives way to war and nature turns upon itself.

"Temptation" is another poem of self-accusation. The poet-speaker is seen as "taking a walk" with "the spirit of desolation." This spirit is telling the poet that he is "not necessary," others would have done what he did. The poem, however, reverses itself as the poet responds by rejecting that spirit of desolation. "It's not up to me to judge the calling of men./ And my merits, if any, I won't know anyway." Reputation is not the poet's business. He will be judged in time by others after he is dead. His job is simply to create and to do what he can. Desolation only impedes that creation as does concern with reputation.

"The Chronicles of the Town of Pornic" is a historical poem of four sections. In the first section, it is the site of Bluebeard's Castle. Giles de Laval had "too much freedom" and fell in with the "courtly Falstaffs" of his region. The judgment on his actions, however, is divided in the poem. He either "violated all divine and human rights," or he was put to death "out of greed for his land." Miłosz does not settle the problem but lets the opposite views stand simultaneously.

The next section of this poem is called "The Owners." It is now the time of revolution, when aristocrats are beheaded and the lower classes take over the castle. First, it is occupied by a blacksmith and later a merchant who pays off the debt. "The castle was then inherited by Joubert, manufacturer of cloth." The decline in the inhabitants is ironic as the common and ordinary replace the aristocrats. The "Vandeans" portrays the revenge of those who were temporarily displaced. They murder 215 persons in their social rage. Knowledge of this atrocity is retained only in the memory of a "very old woman" who witnessed it at the age of four.

The last section of the poem is "Our Lady of Recovery." The statue in the "granite chapel" represents a resolution to the murder that social change brings. Our Lady is there to create a longing to return to "the dear earth." The end of this section suggests that a new cycle is to begin, a fruitful and benign one. "Later they drank, grew boisterous, their women conceived./ Her smile meant that it was all according to her will." The will of the Virgin stands for the creative, in contrast to the destructive, impulse in humanity. She can help humankind overcome the seemingly endless destruction caused by class and history.

"Ars Poetica" is a manifesto on the art of poetry. Miłosz sees poetry as involuntary and controlled by a "daimonion." Such an activity is not pleasant, and no sane person would wish to become "a city of demons." The best poetry, according to Miłosz, is without "irony" and morbidity. Finally, he asserts, poetry "should be written rarely and reluctantly . . . and only with the hope/ that good spirits, not evil ones, choose us for their instrument." Miłosz consistently sees an important role for poetry if only the poet can suspend his pride and desire for rewards.

The last poem in the collection, "From the Rising of the Sun," is a long poem that is divided into six sections. The first section is clearly an introduction to the poem. It contrasts Miłosz's life in California along the Pacific coast with his childhood in Lithuania. In his early years, he was "cuddled like a vegetal baby in a seed." In America, "I write here in desolation/ Beyond the land and sea."

The second section returns to his early years in Poland, where he was taught about nature by Stefan Baginski and Erazm Majewski. However, he turns away from "the profession of a traveler-naturalist" and makes a pilgrimage back to that earlier life and place. He returns to the chapel where a "wooden Madonna" is admired by art lovers. What is lost, however, can never be recovered again; his memory is "unfaithful." He hears "no call./ And the holy had its abode only in denial." "Over Cities" returns to that early world, but the poet-speaker finds loss and absence again. "Everything taken away. Crossed out. All our treasures." He recalls scenes of instruction with "Sir Hieronymus," but neither he nor that world can return. "And where is Sir Hieronymus? Where did I go? Here there is no one."

"A Short Recess" deals with the guilt of Miłosz at leaving his native land to go to Paris, here called "Megalopolis." "I wanted glory, fame and power. . . . So I fled to countries." The decision to seek glory means that he must break pledges and oaths made in and to his land. The result is not glory but doubt and self-recrimination. "Who can tell what purpose is served by destinies/ And whether to have lived on earth means little/ Or much."

The last section of the poem "Bells in Winter" returns triumphantly to the land that Miłosz abandoned for Paris and, later, California. He portrays a cold morning when he hears all of the church bells of the city peal "So that Lisbeth wrapped up in her cape could go to morning mass." (Lisbeth is an old servant woman who brought logs for the fireplace for the apartment that Miłosz occupied in his younger days.) He then contrasts that magical moment with the bells to his present residence in San Francisco and its "rusty fog." He sees, however, in this section, the possibility of restoration. "And the form of every single grain will be restored in glory./ I was judged for my despair because I was unable to understand this." The vision of the restoration of all things is evoked in the poem, even though the poet acknowledges that he is unable to affirm it in his life.

James Sullivan

Further Reading

Baranczak, Stanislaw. "Miłosz's Poetic Language: A Reconnaissance." *Language and Style* 18 (Fall, 1985): 319-333. Baranczak argues that the stylistic variety in Miłosz's poetry is a way of being both realistic and visionary at the same time.

Carpenter, Bogdana. "The Gift Returned: Czesław Miłosz and American Poetry." In *Living in Translation: Polish Writers in America*, edited by Halina Stephan. New York: Rodopi, 2003. Focuses on Miłosz's exile in the United States, describing his acculturation to his exiled country, the interaction of Polish and American culture in his work, and his influence upon American literature.

Fuit, Aleksander. *The Eternal Moment: The Poetry of Czesław Miłosz*. Berkeley: University of California Press, 1990. One of the best extended studies of Miłosz's poetry. Fuit discusses both the political and stylistic elements in the poetry.

Grosholz, Emily. "Miłosz and the Moral Authority of Poetry." *Hudson Review* 39 (Summer, 1986): 251-270. Grosholz discusses Miłosz's critique of current social and scientific theories that claim the place religion once held.

Jastremski, Kim. "Home as Other in the Work of Czesław Miłosz." In *Framing the Polish Home: Postwar Cultural Constructions of Hearth, Nation, and Self*, edited by Bozena Shallcross. Athens: Ohio University Press, 2002. Examines works by Miłosz and other Polish writers to describe how the concept of home is fundamental to Polish culture and national identity.

Malinowska, Barbara. *Dynamics of Being, Space, and Time in the Poetry of Czesław Miłosz. and John Ashbery*. New York: Peter Lang, 2000. Uses the philosophy of Martin Heidegger to describe how the two poets create their visions of reality.

Miłosz, Czesław. *Czesław Miłosz: Conversations.* Edited by Cynthia L. Haven. Jackson: University Press of Mississippi, 2006. Reprints interviews with and an article about Miłosz. Includes an interview conducted by poet Joseph Brodsky, a friend of Miłosz who also received the Nobel Prize in Literature.

Nathan, Leonard, and Arthur Quinn. *The Poet's Work: An Introduction to Czesław Miłosz.* Cambridge, Mass.: Harvard University Press, 1991. One of the best available introductions to Miłosz's work. The authors provide contexts for the poetry and are especially good in discussing the philosophical views that are such an important part of Miłosz's poetry.

Beloved

Author: Toni Morrison (1931-)
First published: 1987
Type of work: Novel
Type of plot: Psychological realism
Time of plot: Nineteenth century
Locale: Cincinnati, Ohio

Principal characters:
SETHE, a former slave
BELOVED, her first daughter
DENVER, her second daughter
HALLE SUGGS, her deceased husband
BABY SUGGS, her mother-in-law
PAUL D GARNER, her lover
HOWARD and BUGLAR, her sons

The Story:

In 1848, at the age of thirteen, Sethe is sold to Mr. Garner and his wife Lillian, who run a plantation in northern Kentucky called Sweet Home. Intended to replace Baby Suggs, whose freedom was purchased by her son Halle by renting out his labor on Sundays, Sethe marries Halle, one of five male slaves (the "Sweet Home men") owned by the Garners, in 1849. Each of the other Sweet Home men—Paul A Garner, Paul D Garner, Paul F Garner, and Sixo—wants Sethe for himself, but each accepts her choice and respects her position as Halle's wife.

Mr. Garner dies in 1853, and his financially strapped, cancer-ridden widow sells Paul F and then brings her cruel brother-in-law, "schoolteacher," and his equally cruel nephews to Sweet Home as overseers. Fearful that schoolteacher might sell them all, the remaining Sweet Home slaves begin planning an escape in 1855. Before the plan can be effected, the pregnant Sethe is attacked by schoolteacher's two nephews. One holds her down while the other sucks the milk from her breasts. Schoolteacher watches and takes notes. Unknown to Sethe, her helpless husband sees the entire "mammary rape" from the hayloft, and the event destroys his sanity. Determined to escape, Sethe sends her three children (Howard, age five; Buglar, age four; and Beloved, age nine months) to join the emancipated Baby Suggs in Cincinnati, planning to follow the next day. The four Sweet Home men fail to escape. Sixo is captured and burned alive, Paul A is hanged, Paul D is sold, and the broken Halle, who dies soon after, loses the will to escape. Only Sethe stumbles into the woods toward freedom.

Sethe nearly dies of exposure, but she is found by a runaway white girl, Amy Denver, who doctors her torn feet and helps her to the Ohio River, where they find an abandoned, leaking boat. Before they can cross, Sethe's water breaks and with Amy as midwife she gives birth prematurely to her second daughter, Denver, in the nearly swamped boat. Amy, also on the run, abandons Sethe and Denver. Stamp Paid, a black riverman, finds mother and daughter and ferries them across the Ohio to the Bodwins, Quaker conductors on the Underground Railroad. The Bodwins deliver Sethe and Denver to Baby Suggs's house on Bluestone Road outside Cincinnati, where Sethe is reunited with Howard, Buglar, and Beloved.

Sethe enjoys twenty-eight glorious days of freedom before the slave catchers track her down. When the slave catchers approach, Sethe tries to kill her children rather than allow them to be returned to slavery. Three miraculously survive, but Beloved dies. Sethe is arrested and sentenced to hang, but the Bodwins obtain a pardon for her and she is allowed to return to Bluestone Road. The ghost of the murdered Beloved also returns and haunts the house for eighteen years, during which it keeps away all visitors, drives away Howard and Buglar in 1865, and breaks the spirit of Baby Suggs, who takes to her bed and dies just months before the Civil War ends. Paul D, after escaping from a Georgia chain gang and wandering through much of the eastern United States, finds Sethe on Bluestone Road in 1873. He drives out the ghost and moves in with Sethe.

Just as Paul D, Sethe, and Denver begin to bond into a family, a young black woman, calling herself Beloved, appears from nowhere, seeking sanctuary. Sethe takes her in, and Beloved begins disrupting the new family by insinuating herself into the affections of Sethe and Denver and seducing Paul D. In 1874, Stamp Paid tells Paul D about Sethe's murder of her child nineteen years before, and Paul D leaves Sethe. Shunned by all as they had been since the murder in 1855, Sethe and Denver form a family with Beloved.

The following year Sethe comes to believe that Beloved is her own murdered child and gradually becomes obsessed with her, neglecting Denver as she tries desperately to make up for the murder. The diabolical Beloved soon consumes Sethe entirely. Sethe loses her job, and the starving Denver goes begging for work. Through Denver the community learns of Beloved's presence and determines to help the Bodwins, who had rescued Sethe in 1855, rescue Denver from Sethe and Beloved. The women of the community begin praying outside the house just as the elderly Mr. Bodwin arrives for Denver. The deranged Sethe, mistaking Mr. Bodwin for a slave catcher, tries to stab him with an ice pick. Denver and the other women stop her, and Beloved disappears. Broken in spirit by losing Beloved again, the twice-bereaved Sethe takes to her bed as the broken Baby Suggs had done in 1865. At the end of the novel Paul D, who has loved Sethe since she first arrived at Sweet Home twenty-five years before, returns to her. He refuses to let Sethe die and begins trying to heal her wounded heart.

Critical Evaluation:

In 1993, Toni Morrison became the first African American to receive the Nobel Prize in Literature. A great American novelist, Morrison has garnered numerous awards for her fiction, including a National Book Award nomination in 1975 for her second novel, *Sula*, the National Book Critics Circle Award in 1977 for her fourth novel, *Song of Solomon*, and the Pulitzer Prize in 1988 for *Beloved*. Morrison is responsible for helping bring African American literature and culture into the consciousness of the mainstream reader, not only through her fiction but also through an influential, best-selling volume of literary theory.

A modernist writer who has been compared to William Faulkner and James Joyce, Morrison crafts novels that are complex and absorbing. They are also difficult to categorize. Multiple narrators in *Beloved* give the novel a veneer of realism. They reveal Sethe's story in fragments, a technique that closely emulates reality in the way in which people ordinarily learn about each other. However, the novel includes two ghosts as main characters, the infant Beloved and the adult Beloved. Some readers consider it a bildungsroman, or coming-of-age novel, because at its close Sethe, with the help of Paul D, finally begins to discover a sense of self-worth. Still others consider it a historical novel because it is based on a historical incident, detailed in Middleton Harris's *The Black Book*, which Morrison edited in 1974, and because it examines the horrors of slavery and racism in excruciatingly frank detail.

Attempts to interpret Morrison strictly within the Western literary tradition, however, fail because Morrison is intent on building an African American canon of literature, perhaps influenced by the Western tradition but always in rebellion against it. Differentiation between physical ownership and psychological possession is a key theme; the characters in *Beloved*, particularly Sethe, must learn to judge themselves and each other according to their own values rather than those imposed on them by the dominant white culture. Few succeed. After Baby Suggs's feast, the community punishes her for being pretentious or "uppity," just as a white slave owner might have done, by refusing to warn her about the approaching slave-catchers. Stamp Paid, perhaps, is one who has been owned by the slavers but never possessed, who has performed their forced labor but has never internalized their forced values. However, even Stamp Paid gives in to the values of white society when he reveals Sethe's crime to Paul D.

Those white values, in a sense, are represented by the poltergeist, the tantrum-throwing ghost of the murdered baby, Beloved, because neither white society nor its courts can understand Sethe's crime, which springs from her deep conviction that her children are better off dead than enslaved. Her guilt haunts the house on Bluestone Road and demands that Sethe and her family appease it. Buglar leaves home when the ghost has achieved such power that he can no longer look into a mirror without shattering it. Metaphorically, the African American past, dominated by subjection, has forced the African American to internalize the white judgment of black inferiority. Howard departs when the baby's handprints appear in a cake; the past taints even the spirit of celebration represented by the cake. Baby Suggs, who consecrates her emancipation by preaching self-love and pride to the other freed slaves, takes to her bed the day after Beloved's death, dying some time later in the belief that all her preaching has been a lie, that black people deserve neither love nor pride. Sethe must remain, appeasing the guilt, vivified as a ghost, that haunts her life.

When Paul D arrives in 1873, Sethe begins to experience love and hope for the first time since Beloved's death in 1855. Paul D drives away the ghost, but she returns several days later as a young woman of nineteen or twenty—the age Beloved would have been—and disrupts the bonding process that has nearly made a family of Sethe, Paul D, and Denver. Upon seeing her, Sethe runs to the outhouse but does not make it; she finds herself urinating on the ground in a scene reminiscent of her water breaking at Beloved's birth. This symbolic rebirth of Beloved destroys Sethe's chance at happiness. This new Beloved—threatening, demanding, controlling, destroying—eventually possesses Sethe, enslaving her again. Once again, she must be emancipated.

Perhaps the most striking example of Morrison's genius in this novel is her treatment of the adult ghost. The reader naturally is suspicious of this new Beloved, who may be Sethe's slain infant somehow brought to life, but the characters treat her as real. The reader experiences vicariously what Sethe experiences. Fear, guilt, shame, and self-loathing live in Sethe's mind and heart, and Beloved lives for the reader. The reader can never be sure, even after Beloved vanishes, if she is flesh or spirit and so shares Sethe's self-doubt. Paul D's return reminds Sethe and the reader of that most Morrisonian of themes, self-affirmation as the key to life.

Craig A. Milliman

Further Reading

Bloom, Harold, ed. *Toni Morrison: Modern Critical Views.* New York: Chelsea House, 1990. Includes general essays on Morrison, plus Marilyn Sanders Mobley's essay identifying the source of Sethe's story and arguing that *Beloved*, rather than partaking of Western literary tradition, employs the "trope of memory to revise the genre of the slave narrative."

Evans, Mari, ed. "Toni Morrison." In *Black Women Writers, 1950-1980: A Critical Evaluation.* Garden City, N.Y.: Anchor Press/Doubleday, 1983. Two critics, Dorothy Lee and Darwin Turner, plus Toni Morrison herself discuss and evaluate Morrison's novels. In "Rootedness: The Ancestor as Foundation," Morrison discusses the traditional role of the African American ancestor and the folk tradition of orality in her fiction. In "The Quest of Self: Triumph and Failure in the Works of Toni Morrison," Lee reveals Morrison's consistency of vision about the human condition. In "Theme, Characterization, and Style in the Works of Toni Morrison," Turner comments on Morrison's style, images, and lyricism.

Ferguson, Rebecca Hope. *Rewriting Black Identities: Transition and Exchange in the Novels of Toni Morrison.* Brussels, Belgium: Peter Lang, 2007. Examines Morrison's first eight novels, including *Beloved*, focusing on her depiction of the complex layers of African American identity. Analyzes these novels from the perspectives of feminism, poststructuralism, and race-related theory.

Gates, Henry Louis, Jr., and K. A. Appiah, eds. *Toni Morrison: Critical Perspectives Past and Present.* New York: Amistad Press, 1993. In a notable essay in this useful collection, Trudier Harris discusses physical ownership versus psychological possession. Most of the former slaves in the novel, Harris argues, were both owned and possessed, accepting the dominant white culture's evaluation of them rather than developing their own sense of self-worth.

Harding, Wendy, and Jacky Martin. *A World of Difference: An Inter-Cultural Study of Toni Morrison's Novels.* Westport, Conn.: Greenwood Press, 1994. Argues that Morrison's fiction should be analyzed at the "cultural interface," the territory where the dominant culture and the dominated collide and a new culture arises.

Harris, Trudier. *Fiction and Folklore: The Novels of Toni Morrison.* Knoxville: University of Tennessee Press, 1991. Maintains that African American folklore is the basis for most African American literature and that Morrison transforms historical folk materials in her novels, creating what Harris terms "literary folklore," allowing no dichotomy between form and substance. The study examines *The Bluest Eye, Sula, Song of Solomon, Tar Baby*, and *Beloved* based on this theory.

Heinert, Jennifer Lee Jordan. "Re-Membering Race: Realism and Truth in *Beloved*." In *Narrative Conventions and Race in the Novels of Toni Morrison*. New York: Routledge, 2009. Explores the relationship between race and genre in selected novels, demonstrating how Morrison broke with traditional narrative forms in order to subvert and rewrite the American literary canon.

Peterson, Nancy J. *Beloved: Character Studies*. New York: Continuum, 2008. Aimed at students, this book offers a concise analysis of the novel's characters, themes, issues, historical context, and depiction of the mother-daughter relationship, black manhood, and whiteness.

Samuels, Wilfred D., and Clenora Hudson-Weems. *Toni Morrison*. Boston: Twayne, 1990. Argues that *Beloved* is a historical novel that reshapes the slave narrative for a modern audience, omitting the conventional antislavery polemics, now unnecessary, and delving more deeply into the horrors of slavery than nineteenth century slave narrators dared.

Simpson, Ritashona. *Black Looks and Black Acts: The Language of Toni Morrison in "The Bluest Eye" and "Beloved."* New York: Peter Lang, 2007. Analyzes how Morrison uses language to create the effect of "black English."

Spaulding, A. Timothy. *Re-Forming the Past: History, the Fantastic, and the Postmodern Slave Narrative*. Columbus: Ohio State University Press, 2005. Analyzes *Beloved* and other modern adaptations of the slave narrative that use elements of fantasy to redefine the historic and literary depiction of American slavery.

Tally, Justine, ed. *The Cambridge Companion to Toni Morrison*. New York: Cambridge University Press, 2007. Collection of essays examining all aspects of Morrison's career. In addition to analyses of individual novels, including "*Beloved* or the Shifting Shapes of Memory" by Claudine Raynaud, other essays provide more general discussions of the language and narrative technique in her novels, the critical reception for her work, and her works of social and literary criticism.

Ben-Hur
A Tale of the Christ

Author: Lew Wallace (1827-1905)
First published: 1880
Type of work: Novel
Type of plot: Historical
Time of plot: Time of Christ
Locale: Antioch and Jerusalem

Principal characters:
BEN-HUR, a Roman-educated Jew
BALTHASAR, an Egyptian
SIMONIDES, a Jewish merchant and a friend of Ben-Hur
ESTHER, his daughter, later Ben-Hur's wife
IRAS, the daughter of Balthasar
MESSALA, a Roman and an enemy of Ben-Hur

The Story:

In the Roman year 747, three travelers—an Athenian, a Hindu, and an Egyptian—meet in the desert, where they have been led by a new bright star shining in the sky. After telling their stories to one another, they journey on, seeking the newborn child who is King of the Jews. In Jerusalem, their inquiries arouse the curiosity of King Herod, who orders that they be brought before him. Herod then asks them to let him know if they find the child, for he, too, wishes to adore the infant whose birth has been foretold.

Arriving at last in Bethlehem, the three men find the newborn child in a stable. Having been warned in a dream of Herod's evil intentions, however, they do not return to tell the king of the child's whereabouts.

At that time, there lived in Jerusalem three members of an old and eminent Jewish family named Hur. The father, who had been dead for some time, had distinguished himself in service to the Roman Empire and had, consequently, received many honors. The son, Ben-Hur, is handsome, and the daughter, Tirzah, is likewise beautiful. Their mother is a fervent nationalist who has implanted in their minds a strong sense of pride in their race and national culture.

When Ben-Hur was still a young man, his friend Messala returned from his studies in Rome. Messala had become arrogant, spiteful, and cruel. Ben-Hur left Messala's home after their meeting, and was hurt, for he realized that Messala had so changed that their friendship must end.

A few days later, while watching a procession below him in the streets, Ben-Hur is implicated when a piece of tile, accidentally dislodged, falls on the Roman procurator. The Roman believes that the accident was an attempt on his life. Led by Messala, who has pointed out his former friend to the soldiers, the Romans arrest the Hur family and confiscate their property.

Ben-Hur is sent to be a galley slave. While he is being led away in chains, a young man takes pity on him and gives him a drink. One day, while he is rowing at his usual place in the galley, Ben-Hur attracts the attention of Quintus Arrius, a Roman official. Later, during a sea battle, Ben-Hur saves the life of Quintus, who adopts the young Jew as his son. Educated as a Roman citizen, Ben-Hur inherits his foster father's wealth when Quintus dies.

Ben-Hur goes to Antioch, where he learns that his father's old servant, Simonides, is now a prosperous merchant. In effect, the wealth of Simonides is really the property of the Hur family, for he has been acting as agent for his dead master. Simonides assures himself that Ben-Hur is really the son of his old master and begs that he be allowed to serve the son as well. Ben-Hur is attracted to Simonides's daughter, Esther.

In company with a servant of Simonides, Ben-Hur goes to see a famous well on the outskirts of Antioch. There an aged Egyptian is watering his camel, on which sits the most beautiful woman Ben-Hur has ever seen. While he looks, a chariot comes charging through the people near the well. Ben-Hur seizes the lead horse by the bridle and swerves the chariot aside. The driver is his false friend, Messala. The old Egyptian is Balthasar, one of the wise men who had traveled to Bethlehem. The beautiful woman is his daughter, Iras.

Learning that the arrogant Messala is to race his chariot in the games at Antioch, Ben-Hur wishes to defeat and humiliate his former friend. He has Simonides and his friends place large wagers on the race, until Messala has staked his whole fortune. The day of the race comes. At the turn, Messala suddenly strikes with his whip at the horses of the chariot Ben-Hur is driving. Ben-Hur manages to keep his team under control, and then in the last lap around the arena, he drives his chariot so close to Messala's vehicle that the wheels lock. Messala is thrown under his horses and crippled for life. Since Messala had attempted foul play earlier in the race, the judges allow Ben-Hur to be proclaimed the winner. Messala is ruined.

From Balthasar, Ben-Hur learns that the King of the Jews to whom the Egyptian and his companions had paid homage some years before is not to be the king of a political realm, but of a spiritual one. Simonides, however, convinces Ben-Hur that the promised king will be a real deliverer who will lead the Jews to victory over the Romans.

From Antioch, Ben-Hur goes to Jerusalem to search for his mother and sister. There he learns the part Messala had played in the ruin of his family. After Ben-Hur's arrest, his mother and sister had been thrown into prison, and Messala and the procurator had divided the confiscated property between them. Messala knew nothing of the fate of the two women after the procurator had ordered them confined to an underground cell. There they had contracted leprosy. When Pilate, the new procurator, arrived, he had ordered all political prisoners freed, so the two women had been set at liberty. There was no place for them to go except to the caves outside the city where the lepers were sent to die. A faithful old servant found them and carried food to them daily, under sacred oath never to reveal their names. When Ben-Hur meets the old servant, she allows him to believe that his mother and sister are dead.

Meanwhile, Simonides, acting for Ben-Hur, buys the Hur home. He, Esther, Balthasar, and Iras take possession of it. Ben-Hur himself can visit it only at night and in disguise. He is plotting to overthrow the Roman rule and is recruiting an army to follow the future King of the Jews. He goes one day near the place where the lepers usually gather on the hill beyond the city gates. On the way, he meets a young man whom he recognizes as the one who had given him a drink of water years before when he was being led away to slavery. The young man is the Nazarene. That day, the old servant persuades Tirzah and her mother to show themselves to the Nazarene as he passes. The women are cured, and Ben-Hur sees the two lepers transformed into his mother and sister.

Ben-Hur's attitude toward the King of the Jews is slowly changing. When he witnesses the crucifixion in company with Simonides and old Balthasar, any doubts that he might have had are removed. He is convinced then that Christ's kingdom is a spiritual one. From that day on, he and his family are Christians.

Some years later, in the beautiful villa at Misenum, Ben-Hur's wife, Esther, receives a strange visit from Iras, the daughter of Balthasar. Iras tells Esther that she has killed Messala for the misery he had brought her. When he learns of the visit, Ben-Hur is sure that on the day of the crucifixion, the day that Balthasar himself had died, Iras had deserted her father for Messala.

Ben-Hur is happy with Esther and their two children. He and Simonides devote their fortunes to the Christian cause. When Nero begins the persecution of the Christians in Rome, it is Ben-Hur who goes there to build the catacombs under the city, so that those who believe in the Nazarene can worship in safety and peace.

Critical Evaluation:

Lew Wallace was born in Indiana in 1827. His father, a West Point graduate who left the U.S. military for politics, was the state's sixth governor. Wallace's first career was in the military, serving but not seeing combat during the Mexican-American War (1846-1848). He then turned to law and local politics, but returned to the U.S. Army during the American Civil War (1861-1865), as a general. Afterward, he became the governor of New Mexico and then the U.S. ambassador to the Ottoman Empire.

Wallace and his wife, Susan, wrote during their travels. Wallace finished *Ben-Hur* while in Santa Fe, New Mexico, and continued his literary career while a diplomat, before retiring to Indiana to focus on writing. *Ben-Hur* was the most successful of his seven major works, which included two other historical novels and a Roman-themed play. *Ben-Hur* was the best-selling novel of the nineteenth century, and has remained in print.

Ben-Hur is not often regarded as a well-done literary piece. The plodding first section, the long descriptions of settings and characters, and the extensive historical notes belie the excitement promised by the chariot race made famous in the film adaptation of the story. However, the novel frequently appears on lists of significant literary works. For Wallace's early readers, the novel was their introduction to the historical events surrounding the birth of Jesus Christ, to the seemingly exotic Near East, and to novels themselves, accepted alongside the Bible in many American households.

The early twentieth century literary critic Carl Van Doren credited *Ben-Hur* with overcoming the nineteenth century American public's Puritan-inspired opposition to reading novels. Wallace reported that the novel was inspired by a personal quest for spiritual understanding. In the course of a conversation with a well-known atheist, Wallace became a believer in Christian doctrine and resolved to study the events of the Bible for himself, leading to his interest in the Christmas story. He was not conventionally religious, and he used the pseudepigrapha, some of nonbiblical books, as the basis for his later work, *The Boyhood of Christ* (1888). He feared that a novel with Jesus as protagonist would not be well received, so instead he told his story through a surrogate Jew, Judah Ben-Hur. The human Ben-Hur makes the mistakes of arrogance and anger that Jesus could not, making both characters more real.

It was the realism that made *Ben-Hur* appealing, and its religiousness that made it acceptable. Wallace's Jesus, a quietly strong, compassionate, tragic character, popularized the very human Jesus that was gaining attention in the 1880's, a characterization of Jesus that remains common. Ben-Hur ultimately becomes more Christ-like, dedicating himself to the faith, love, and good works that are recurring concepts in the narrative.

Before he became a pacifist, however, Ben-Hur was a warrior. He can be seen as a perfectly masculine man, a rugged fellow whose success is a challenge to the more urban, professional culture that developed with the Industrial Revolution. Ben-Hur is an early example of a man who led the strenuous life, an ideal that would be advocated and exemplified by U.S. president Theodore Roosevelt in the early twentieth century. Judah Ben-Hur was a vigorous, physically strong man, not someone dependent on the comforts of a decadent city. Unlike the effete and privileged Messala, Ben-Hur had to make his own way in the world. This success suggests a second comparison, to the rags-to-riches stories made popular by Horatio Alger just after the American Civil War. Ben-Hur's story of working himself up from the nothingness of slavery appealed to Americans who were heading West to new frontiers and new opportunities. The spiritual ideals of faith, love, and good works came with temporal rewards for those who embraced them.

The American West—where Wallace had lived when he was writing the novel—prompts a third comparison, to the Western. While the novel can be seen as a straightforward historical novel, a fictional work with a background of actual events and characters, Blake Allmendinger suggests it is a Western in Eastern clothes. The story of white civilization defeating Indian "savagery" is shifted in time and space, so that Christian civilization defeats Rome's pagan savagery, with the chariot race rather than a shootout as the climactic moment in the battle.

In his "savages," Wallace exemplifies nineteenth century Orientalism. Orientalism had been the American and European view of the Orient—of the East—as a mysterious, exotic, and corrupt Other, destined to be dominated by the West. This view would be famously criticized by literary theorist Edward Said beginning in the 1970's, but Wallace in his time was laying the groundwork for a fascination with the East. This fascination led to things such as Ben-Hur Flour in the markets and encouraged the making of a stage play and films based on the novel. Wallace does not quite follow the classic Orientalist trope, for in *Ben-Hur* the Romans are the depraved and decadent "Orientals" while the Jew stands in for Western Christianity. Wallace's depiction of Eastern settings is of an exciting but inferior land, against which the modern Western reader might define him- or herself.

Ben-Hur is most significant as an inspiration. It inspired a new interest in novel reading in the nineteenth century, along with a surge in interest in a Christianity that emphasized a personal relationship with a personable Jesus. However, *Ben-Hur*, subtitled *A Tale of the Christ*, may more accurately be subtitled "a tale with the Christ." Although the character of Jesus satisfied Wallace's spiritual quest, it also lent respectability to a story of sea battles and chariot races, giving religious, social, and literary weight to a novel that fit neatly into the popular literary traditions of its era.

"Critical Evaluation" by Laura Shumar

Further Reading

Allmendinger, Blake. "Toga! Toga!" In *Ten Most Wanted: The New Western American Literature*. New York: Routledge, 1998. Discusses the circumstances in which Wallace wrote *Ben-Hur*, making the case that the work is essentially a Western novel in an Asian setting.

Gutjahr, Paul. "'To the Heart of the Solid Puritans': Historicizing the Popularity of *Ben-Hur*." *Mosaic* 26, no. 3 (Summer, 1993): 53-67. Offers reasons for *Ben-Hur*'s pleasing even those readers mistrustful of novels. One reason mentioned is that the novel advocates feeling and faith to counter the scientific challenges to the Bible and to traditional Christianity.

Mayer, David, ed. *Playing Out the Empire: "Ben-Hur," and Other Toga Plays and Films, 1883-1908: A Critical Anthology*. New York: Oxford University Press, 1994. Includes introductory commentary and notes on Wallace's novel, William Young's 1899 play, and the 1907 Kalem Company film version.

Miller, Howard. "The Charioteer and the Christ." *Indiana Magazine of History* 104, no. 2 (June, 2008): 153-175. Examines the impact of *Ben-Hur* on American culture, focusing on the transformation of the charioteer and the Christ figures in the novel's many stage and screen adaptations. Explains how Wallace wrote the novel when his personal view of Christ was gaining popularity in the United States.

Pentz-Harris, Marcia L., Linda Seger, and R. Barton Palmer. "Screening Male Sentimental Power in *Ben-Hur*." In *Nineteenth-Century American Fiction on Screen*, edited by R. Barton Palmer. New York: Cambridge University Press, 2007. A detailed discussion of *Ben-Hur*, placing the work within the context of nineteenth century religion, society, and literature. Discusses the novel's influence on subsequent novels and films, and its immense popularity. According to the authors, "rarely, if ever, has a novel aroused such passion in the American public."

Quinn, Arthur Hobson. *American Fiction: An Historical and Critical Survey*. East Norwalk, Conn.: Appleton-Century-Crofts, 1936. Praises *Ben-Hur* for its magnificent opening, presentation of rival forces (Judaism, Christianity, Roman imperialism), key dramatic scenes (lepers' cell, naval battle, chariot race), absence of anti-Semitism, minor characters, and relation of all of the characters to Ben-Hur. Dated but still useful.

Wallace, Lew. *Lew Wallace: An Autobiography*. 2 vols. 1906. Reprint. New York: Harper and Brothers, 1969. Wallace's autobiography, completed posthumously. Includes a reprint of Wallace's 1895 interview, "How I Came to Write *Ben-Hur*."

A Bend in the River

Author: V. S. Naipaul (1932-)
First published: 1979
Type of work: Novel
Type of plot: Psychological realism
Time of plot: Early 1970's
Locale: African interior

Principal characters:

SALIM, a coastal Muslim who moves to the interior of Africa to open a business
INDAR, his childhood friend
ALI (METTY), Salim's servant
NAZRUDDIN, the family friend who sets up Salim in business
ZABETH, a woman from the bush
FERDINAND, her son
BIG MAN, the ruler of the Domain
RAYMOND, a white European who works for Big Man
YVETTE, his wife
FATHER HUISMANS, a teacher at the *lycée*

The Story:

Salim envies his well-to-do friend Indar, who informs him that he is going away to England to study at a famous university. Indar explains that one has to be strong to continue to live in Africa and that "We're not strong. We don't even have a flag." It is against such a backdrop of insecurity and fear that Salim decides to leave the coast and his Muslim community and head into the interior. "To stay with my community," Salim acknowledges, "to pretend that I had simply to travel along with them, was to be taken with them to destruction. I could be master of my fate only if I stood alone."

Nazruddin, a family friend, offers Salim his abandoned shop in the interior of Africa, at the bend of a river, in a settlement that has been half destroyed during the violence that preceded the area's political independence. Salim travels to the interior, takes over the small shop, and spends the next seven years attempting to establish himself before the violence and social chaos return.

He befriends some Indian families, trades with a mysterious character named Zabeth, a magician from downriver, and agrees to look after her son, Ferdinand, who attends school at the local *lycée*. He soon acquires a living companion when his family, which broke up and dispersed during a social revolution on the coast, sends him their slave, Ali, who takes the new name of Metty (a name that means "someone of mixed race"). Salim later befriends a white couple, Raymond and Yvette. Raymond works for the local ruler, Big Man (a character drawn after Joseph Mobutu, the king of Zaire); Big Man is the closest white personal friend of Raymond, who manages a university in the Domain, a group of new buildings in the town's former white suburb.

Father Huismans is a teacher at the *lycée*, where Ferdinand enrolls as a student. Although the *lycée* is a remnant of the colonial period, Father Huismans possesses a genuine love for Africa and its traditions. He amasses a large collection of African masks that are intended for specific religious purposes. Salim observes that, although Father Huismans knows a great deal about African religion, he does not seem concerned about the state of the country. During the subsequent revolution to purify Africa and cast off European influences, Father Huismans becomes a victim of his own purity, naïveté, and dedication to a religious-academic enterprise. His mutilated body is found among the thick water hyacinths that clot the river. His head is cut off and placed on a spike.

Ferdinand, schooled at the Domain, develops a powerful sense of self-importance and rebels against Salim's more temperate influence. He becomes an idealist who commits his life to a new Africa under the leadership of Big Man and his flag of "authenticity." Salim comes to realize that under the dictatorial powers of Big Man he is constantly surrounded by violence and by the threat of violence. The ancient tribes from the bush are displaced by the new army, which draws its authority from Big Man.

Salim's life takes a new turn when his childhood friend Indar comes from his home in England as a guest of the government to teach at the Domain for one term. Indar introduces Salim to Raymond and Yvette, a meeting that changes the course of Salim's life. Indar's philosophy asserts that the past is a death trap: "You see that the past is something in your mind alone, that it doesn't exist in real life. You trample on the past, you crush it."

Salim maintains many ties with his past; these ties include his servant Metty and his obsession with the mystery and security of tribal life in the bush, which are embodied in the person of Zabeth. The past reflects Salim's dream of a peaceful world whose customs and rituals are barriers to the present disorder. Salim comes to adopt Indar's philosophy, but he modifies it to suit his own temperament. He concludes that he cannot return to his home and that the idea is a deception that will weaken and destroy his reality. "We had to live in the world as it existed," he determines.

Salim's stoic philosophy is shaped partly by his experience with Yvette, which opens up to him a powerful new vision of sexuality and romance. His sexual adventure with this fascinating white European woman overwhelms Salim with a sense of fulfillment and unappeased pleasure. However, the romance soon gives way to bitter disillusionment and anger.

As the town and government experience new insurrections, Raymond and Yvette realize that their comfortable life is coming to an end. In the last meeting with Yvette, Salim explodes in a rage and beats her to the floor. Although he accuses her of seducing him with false promises, Salim's real contempt and anger are directed toward himself.

After he loses Yvette, Salim becomes increasingly frustrated with the moral and social decay of his violent surroundings. To escape the fate of those around him, he travels to London, as Indar did earlier. There, Salim becomes engaged to Nazruddin's daughter. When he returns to Africa, however, he gets caught up in the corruption and is imprisoned for smuggling ivory. Ferdinand releases him from prison and confesses to Salim his total disillusionment with the "new" Africa of Big Man. Salim finally comes to the conclusion that the best he can hope for is to follow in the stoic but optimistic path of the successful Nazruddin, to return to England, and to start again in a world where there is a stable culture and where he can explore and learn to accept a new interior.

Critical Evaluation:

A Bend in the River is based on V. S. Naipaul's observations during a 1975 visit to Zaire, a new African nation that had formerly been the Belgian Congo. In Zaire, Naipaul encountered several worlds at once: the Congo of Joseph Conrad, a writer whose clear insights into that country and into human character had fascinated Naipaul since childhood; the Africa of the bush, seemingly eternal and indomitable, despite Arab and Belgian attempts to civilize it; and the new Africa, the so-called authentic Africa of Joseph Mobutu. Naipaul quickly saw through the rhetoric and propaganda of the new government and of the ostentatious façades of Zaire's new art and architecture, and he exposed Mobutu's kingship as a temporary reign of self-aggrandizement, greed, and terror. In creating his novel, *A Bend in the River*, Naipaul combined his experiences in Zaire (which he documented in his critical essay on Mobutu, "A New King for the Congo: Mobutu and the Nihilism of Africa," 1975) with his personal preoccupation with such themes as the mingling of different cultures and the deterioration of dreams, sexuality, and personal and cultural security.

The hero of the novel, Salim, comes from a coastal Muslim family that in its customs is closer to the Hindus of northwest India, from which it had come centuries earlier. As the narrator, he is established both as an African and as an outsider, for, as he points out, the coast is not truly African but rather an area settled by Arabs, Indians, Persians, and Portuguese. This cultural background helps to explain Salim's growing sense of dislocation and alienation as he attempts to come to grips with the bush (represented by Zabeth), the "new" Africa of Big Man, the philosophy of his friend, Indar, and his sexual and cultural fantasies that center upon Yvette.

Corruption pervades the novel. Big Man ruthlessly asserts his control over the "new" Africa by fear and violence. He commands respect because of his wealth and power, and he undermines the ancient culture of the African bush by his campaigns of terror. Despite the trappings of a new cultural identity and "authenticity," Big Man and his followers are no better than the cultures they have nationalized in the name of African unity. The sensitive and intelligent Ferdinand represents the bright young African who emerges from the bush and is seduced by the promises of Big Man, who promises a radicalized Africa. By the end of the novel, however, Ferdinand has become totally disillusioned by the movement's hypocrisy and use of terror. The novel ends with an impending revolution that may again bring about massive killings and, perhaps, even the destruction of Big Man himself. Ferdinand, filled with rage that all he has studied and worked for has come to nothing, warns Salim to flee the country.

None of the characters in this novel succeeds in finding his or her identity in this violent country. Indar flees to London, where he becomes a failure at his work and turns to living in a past he can never reassume. Yvette and Raymond, whom Big Man uses to advance his policies, are discarded once their usefulness is over. Father Huismans, another European, is murdered, despite his dedication to the religious culture of Africa. Ferdinand has lost his ideals and hope yet cannot return to the bush from which he had come.

Salim and Nazruddin come close to attaining a degree of independence and self-fulfillment, Nazruddin by exchanging his African past for a life in London, and Salim by seeking refuge in England from the social and psychic disorder of his fractured and radicalized homeland. Salim opens his story with words of wisdom that he achieves only after his painful experiences in the interior of Africa: "The world is what it is; men who are nothing, who allow themselves to become nothing, have no place in it." The idea of going home, the idea of the other place, is a fiction that comforts only to destroy those who believe in it. There are no places to escape in this changing, dangerous, and disillusioning world, and this is especially true of people like Salim. He discovers that he must live in the world as it is, and that even his passage to England and his relationship with Nazruddin and his daughter will offer no more than a temporary respite from the relentless disorder that has shaped him.

Richard Kelly

Further Reading

Dooley, Gillian. "Sex and Violence: *Guerrillas* and *A Bend in the River*." In *V. S. Naipaul, Man and Writer*. Columbia: University of South Carolina Press, 2006. Dooley analyzes Naipaul's works in light of his stated intentions and beliefs, tracing the forty-year development of his literary style. She argues that Naipaul's refusal to compromise his vision has made him a controversial writer.

Feder, Lillian. *Naipaul's Truth: The Making of a Writer*. Lanham, Md.: Rowman & Littlefield, 2001. Feder analyzes Naipaul's major fiction and nonfiction, concluding that the search for truth is the common theme in his work. She describes his writings as narratives of self-creation that are told in the first or third person.

French, Patrick. *The World Is What It Is: The Authorized Biography of V. S. Naipaul*. London: Picador, 2008. French uses the opening words of *A Bend in the River* as the title for his brutally honest biography. He depicts Naipaul as a man and writer haunted by race, colonialism, and sex, who is both a racist and a victim of racism, and who treated his wives and other women despicably.

Hayward, Helen. "Images of Africa and Europe in *A Bend in the River*." In *The Enigma of V. S. Naipaul: Sources and Contexts*. New York: Palgrave Macmillan, 2002. Hayward traces common themes in Naipaul's work, such as cultural alienation, detachment, and anxiety, and relates them to his life.

Kelly, Richard. *V. S. Naipaul*. New York: Continuum, 1989. Analyzes Naipaul's novels, short stories, essays, and travel books through *The Enigma of Arrival* (1988).

King, Bruce. *V. S. Naipaul*. 2d ed. New York: Palgrave Macmillan, 2003. A thorough introduction to Naipaul's work.

McSweeney, Kerry. *Four Contemporary Novelists*. Montreal: McGill-Queen's University Press, 1983. Includes one chapter on Naipaul's novels, which provides an excellent discussion of the major themes in his oeuvre.

Nixon, Rob. *London Calling: V. S. Naipaul, Postcolonial Mandarin*. New York: Oxford University Press, 1992. Examines Naipaul's cultural conflicts as they are reflected in his fiction.

Ramchand, Kenneth. *The West Indian Novel and Its Background*. New York: Barnes & Noble, 1970. An invaluable source of information about the cultural background that shaped Naipaul's thinking.

Benito Cereno

Author: Herman Melville (1819-1891)
First published: serial, 1855; book, collected in *The Piazza Tales*, 1856
Type of work: Novella
Type of plot: Adventure
Time of plot: 1799
Locale: Harbor of St. Maria, off the coast of Chile; Lima, Peru

Principal characters:
AMASA DELANO, an American sea captain
DON BENITO CERENO, a Spanish sea captain
BABO, an African slave

The Story:

Captain Amasa Delano is commander of an American ship called *Bachelor's Delight*, which is anchored in the harbor of St. Maria, on an island off the coast of southern Chile. While there, he sees a ship apparently in distress, and, thinking it carries a party of monks, he sets out in a whaleboat to board the vessel and supply it with food and water. When he comes aboard, he finds that the ship, the *San Dominick*, is a Spanish merchant ship carrying slaves. The crew is parched and moaning; the ship is filthy; the sails are rotten. Most deplorable of all, the captain, the young Don Benito Cereno, seems barely able to stand or to talk coherently. Aloof and indifferent, Cereno seems ill both physically (he coughs constantly) and mentally. He is attended by Babo, his devoted slave.

Delano sends the whaleboat back to his ship to get additional water, food, and extra sails for the *San Dominick*, while he remains aboard the desolate ship. He tries to talk to Cereno, but the captain's fainting fits keep interrupting the conversation. The Spaniard seems reserved and sour, in spite of Delano's attempts to assure the man that he is now out of danger. Delano finally assumes that Cereno is suffering from a severe mental disorder. The captain does, with great difficulty and after frequent private talks with Babo, manage to explain that the *San Dominick* was at sea for 190 days. They started out, Cereno explained, as a well-manned and smart vessel sailing from Buenos Aires to Lima but encountered several gales around Cape Horn, lost many officers and men, and then ran into dreadful calms and the ravages of plagues and scurvy. Most of the Spanish officers and all the passengers, including the slave owner, Don Alexandro Aranda, died of fever. Delano, who knew that the weather in recent months was not as extreme as Cereno described it, simply concludes that the Spanish officers were incompetent and did not take the proper precautions against disease. Cereno continually repeats that only the devotion of his slave, Babo, kept him alive.

Numerous other circumstances on the *San Dominick* begin to make the innocent Delano more suspicious. Although everything is in disorder and Cereno is obviously ill, he is dressed perfectly in a clean uniform. Six black men are sitting in the rigging holding hatchets, although Cereno says they are only cleaning them. Two are beating up a Spanish boy, but Cereno explains that this deed is simply a form of sport. The slaves are not in chains; Cereno claims they are so docile that they do not require chains. This notion pleases the humane Delano, although it also surprises him.

Every two hours, as they await the expected wind and the arrival of Delano's whaleboat, a large African man in chains is brought before Cereno, who will ask him if he, Cereno, can be forgiven. The man will answer, "No," and be led away. At one point, Delano begins to fear that Cereno and Babo are plotting against him, for they move away from him and whisper together. Cereno then asks Delano about his ship, requesting the number of men and the strength of arms aboard the *Bachelor's Delight*. Delano thinks they might be pirates.

Nevertheless, Delano joins Cereno and Babo in Cereno's cabin for dinner. Throughout the meal, Delano alternately gains and loses confidence in Cereno's story. He tries, while discussing a means of getting Cereno new sails, to get Babo to leave the room, but the man and the master are apparently inseparable. After dinner, Babo, while shaving his master, cuts his cheek slightly despite the warning that was given. Babo leaves the room for a minute and returns with his own cheek cut in an imitation of his master's. Delano thinks this episode curious and sinister, but he finally decides that the man is so devoted to Cereno that he had punished himself for inadvertently cutting his master.

At last, Delano's whaleboat returns with more supplies. Delano, about to leave the *San Dominick*, promises to return with new sails the next day. When he invites Cereno to his own boat, he is surprised at the captain's curt refusal and his failure to escort the visitor to the rail. Delano is offended at the Spaniard's apparent lack of gratitude. As the whaleboat is about to leave, Cereno appears suddenly at the rail. He expresses his gratitude profusely and then, hastily, jumps into the whaleboat. At first Delano thinks that Cereno is about to kill him; then he sees Babo at the rail brandishing a knife. In a flash, he realizes that Babo and the other slaves were holding Cereno a captive. Delano takes Cereno back to the *Bachelor's Delight*. Later they pursue the fleeing slaves. The slaves, having no guns, are easily captured by the American ship and brought back to shore.

Cereno later explains that the slaves, having mutinied shortly after the ship set out, committed horrible atrocities and killed most of the Spaniards. They murdered the mate, Raneds, for a trifling offense and committed atrocities on the dead body of Don Alexandro Aranda, whose skeleton they placed on the masthead.

On his arrival in Lima, Cereno submits a long testimony, recounting all the cruelties the slaves committed. Babo is tried and hanged. Cereno feels enormously grateful to Delano, recalling the strange innocence that somehow kept the slaves from harming him, when they had the chance, aboard the *San Dominick*. Cereno plans to enter a monastery; however, broken in body and spirit, he dies three months after he completes his testimony.

Critical Evaluation:

Originally serialized in *Putnam's Monthly* in 1855, *Benito Cereno* first appeared, slightly revised, in book form as the first story in Herman Melville's *Piazza Tales* in 1856. It was not reprinted until 1924, when interest in Melville's writings was revived. Since then, it has often been praised as not only one of Melville's best fictional works but also one of the finest short novels in American literature.

Benito Cereno is Melville's version of a true story he read in Amasa Delano's *Narrative of Voyages and Travels in the Northern and Southern Hemispheres* (1817). Melville freely adapts Delano's account to his own fictional purposes. The court depositions, which make up a considerable part of the latter half of *Benito Cereno*, have been shown to be close to those in Delano's account, though Melville omitted some of the court material. In contrast, the creation of atmosphere, the building of suspense, the development of the three main characters—Delano, Cereno, and Babo—and the extended use of symbolism are among Melville's chief contributions to the original story. Also, the thematically important conversation between Delano and Cereno at the end of *Benito Cereno* was added by Melville.

The remarkable third paragraph of *Benito Cereno* illustrates Melville's careful combining of atmospheric detail, color symbolism, and both dramatic and thematic foreshadowing.

> The morning was one peculiar to that coast. Everything was mute and calm; everything grey. The sea, though undulated into long roods of swells, seemed fixed, and was sleeked at the surface like waved lead that has cooled and set in the smelter's mould. The sky seemed a grey surtout. Flights of troubled grey vapours among which they were mixed, skimmed low and fitfully over the waters, as swallows over meadows before storms. Shadows present, foreshadowing deeper shadows to come.

The description, with its repeated use of the color grey and the word "seemed," is important in setting the scene for a story the action of which will be, as seen through Delano's eyes, ambiguous and deceptive until the light of truth suddenly blazes upon the American captain's mind. Until that time, he will be seeing both action and character through a mist. The grey is symbolically significant also because Delano's clouded vision will cause him to misjudge both the whites and the blacks aboard the *San Dominick*. In the light of the final revelations of the story, the grey has a moral symbolism, too, perhaps for Melville and surely for the modern reader, since Cereno and Delano are not morally all good, nor is Babo all bad. The Spaniard is a slaver, and the American appears to condone the trade though he is not a part of it; the slave is certainly justified in seeking an escape from captivity for himself and his fellow slaves, though one cannot justify some of the atrocities consciously committed by Babo and his followers. The closing sentence of this mist-shrouded paragraph, "Shadows present, foreshadowing deeper shadows to come," not only looks forward to the mystery that so long remains veiled but also anticipates the final words of the two captains, words that partly suggest the great difference in their characters. Delano says, "You are saved: what has cast such a shadow upon you?" Cereno replies, "The negro."

In reading *Benito Cereno*, one is caught up in the same mystery that Delano cannot penetrate, and one longs for a final release of the suspense, a solution to the strange puzzle. Melville's hold upon the reader until the flash of illumination in the climax is maintained by his use of Delano's consciousness as the lens through which scene, character, and action are viewed. The revelation is so long delayed because of Delano's being the kind of man he is. His heart is benevolent, but his mind is slow to perceive through the dragging hours from his boarding the *San Dominick* until he is finally shocked into recognition of the truth when Babo prepares to stab Cereno with the dagger concealed in his hair. Delano is alternately repelled by Cereno's manner or suspicious of his intentions and then inclined to acquit Cereno of seeming rudeness because of his frail health or condemn himself for his suspicions with the excuse that "the poor invalid scarcely knew what he was about."

Just as Melville may have intended to portray Delano as representing a type of American—good-hearted, friendly, and helpful but rather slow-witted and naïve—so he may have delineated Cereno as emblematic of eighteenth century Spanish aristocracy—proud, enfeebled, and, finally, troubled in conscience over such moral crimes as slave trading. To Delano, he first appears as "a gentlemanly, reserved-looking, and rather young man . . . dressed with singular richness, but bearing plain traces of recent sleepless cares and disquietudes." Later, Cereno's manner "conveyed a sort of sour and gloomy disdain [which] the American in charity ascribed to the harassing effects of sickness." Further observation leads Delano to conclude that Cereno's "singular alternations of courtesy and ill-breeding" are the result of either "innocent lunacy, or wicked imposture." He is finally undeceived and apologizes for having suspected villainy in Cereno toward the end of the danger-filled encounter with the slaves. Delano is lighthearted and eager to dismiss the affair when the danger is over and his suspicions have been erased. Cereno's mind, however, is of a different cast. He broods on the results in human experience of the confusing of appearance and reality. "[Y]ou were with me all day," he says to Delano, "stood with me, sat with me, looked at me, ate with me, drank with me, and yet, your last act was to clutch for a monster, not only an innocent man, but the most pitiable of all men. To such degree may malign machinations and deceptions impose. So far may ever the best man err, in judging the conduct of one with the recesses of whose condition he is not acquainted."

The horrors resulting from the slave mutiny and the tensions and terror that follow Delano's kind offer to aid a ship in apparent distress leave an already ill man a dejected and broken one. The shadow of "the negro" is cast forever upon him. He retires to the monastery on the symbolically named Mount Agonia and, three months later, is released from his sufferings, in death.

Babo, the third major character in *Benito Cereno*, is unforgettable, one of the first important black characters in American fiction (Harriet Beecher Stowe's Uncle Tom had preceded him by only four years). He is one of the most striking of Melville's "masked" men who appear in his work from beginning to end, hiding their true selves behind the semblance they present to the world. Delano is completely deceived in his first sight of Babo with Cereno. "By his side stood a black of small stature, in whose rude face, as occasionally, like a shepherd's dog, he mutely turned it up into the Spaniard's, sorrow and affection were equally blended." His attentiveness makes him seem "less a servant than a devoted companion" to Cereno. Though he speaks little, his few brief speeches suggest the intelligence that enables him to lead the revolt on the *San Dominick*. He is capable of irony when Cereno explains that it is to Babo that he owes his preservation and that Babo pacifies "his more ignorant brethren, when at intervals tempted to murmurings." "Ah, master," he sighs, "what Babo has done was but duty." The remark is as masked as Babo's bowed face, and the American is so completely taken in that, "As master and man stood before him, the black upholding the white, Captain Delano could not but bethink him of the beauty of that relationship which could present such a spectacle of fidelity on the one hand and confidence on the other."

With its many ironies—an aristocratic Spanish slaver captured by his slaves, a murderous man posing as a faithful servant, a naïve American protected from violent death through his own innocence and uncovering villainy by accident—*Benito Cereno* may be read as a magnificently contrived parable of limited, rational, well-ordered humanity struggling against evil in the social and natural universe and achieving at least a partial victory.

"Critical Evaluation" by Henderson Kincheloe

Further Reading

Bloom, Harold, ed. *Herman Melville's "Billy Budd," "Benito Cereno," "Bartleby the Scrivener," and Other Tales*. New York: Chelsea House, 1987. Collects some of the best in late twentieth century views of Melville's tale, with emphasis on postmodernist approaches to the interweaving of fiction and history and to the different types of documentation represented in the narrative.

Burkholder, Robert E., ed. *Critical Essays on Herman Melville's "Benito Cereno."* New York: G. K. Hall, 1992. Contains indispensable essays on *Benito Cereno* in relation to nineteenth century expansionism, slavery, and other topics.

Delbanco, Andrew. *Melville: His World and Work*. New York: Knopf, 2005. Delbanco's critically acclaimed biography places Melville in his time, including information about the debate over slavery and details of life in 1840's New York. He also discusses the significance of Melville's works at the time they were published and in the twenty-first century.

Gross, Seymour, ed. *A "Benito Cereno" Handbook*. Belmont, Calif.: Wadsworth, 1965. Still one of the most comprehensive texts for understanding Melville's short novel. Reprints Melville's source, a chapter in the travel narrative of the eighteenth century ship captain Amasa Delano, as well as eleven critical articles offering historical points of view and discussions of narrative mode, style, symbolism, and theme.

Newman, Lea Bertani Vozar. *A Reader's Guide to the Short Stories of Herman Melville*. Boston: G. K. Hall, 1986. The section on *Benito Cereno* is indispensable, with sections on publication history, sources and influences, relationship to Melville's other works, a summary of criticism, and a comprehensive bibliography of related works.

Rollyson, Carl E., and Lisa Paddock. *Herman Melville A to Z: The Essential Reference to His Life and Work*. New York: Checkmark Books, 2001. Comprehensive and encyclopedic coverage of Melville's life, works, and times; the 675 detailed entries provide information on the characters, settings, allusions, and references in his fiction, his friends and associates, and the critics and scholars who have studied his work.

Runden, John P. *Melville's "Benito Cereno": A Text for Guided Research*. Boston: D. C. Heath, 1965. An overview of responses to the story from early reviews to mid-twentieth century interpretations. Includes discussion of Melville's source in a biography of Charles V. The text of *Benito Cereno* is reprinted with original pagination.

Stuckey, Sterling. *African Culture and Melville's Art: The Creative Process in "Benito Cereno" and "Moby-Dick."* New York: Oxford University Press, 2009. A new interpretation of the two works in which Stuckey argues that Melville's worldview and his literary innovations were shaped by African cultural forms.

Spanos, William V. "*Benito Cereno*: The Vision of American Exceptionalism." In *Herman Melville and the American Calling: Fiction After "Moby-Dick," 1851-1857*. Albany: State University of New York Press, 2008. Analyzes the major works that appeared after the publication of *Moby-Dick*. Argues that these works share the metaphor of the orphanage: a place that represents both estrangement from a symbolic fatherland and the myth of American exceptionalism.

Beowulf

Author: Unknown
First transcribed: c. 1000
Type of work: Poetry
Type of plot: Epic
Time of plot: Sixth century
Locale: Denmark and southern Sweden

Principal characters:
BEOWULF, a Geat hero
HROTHGAR, the king of the Danes
UNFERTH, a Danish warrior
WIGLAF, a loyal noble of Beowulf's court

The Poem:

Once, long ago in Hrothgar's kingdom, a monster named Grendel roamed the countryside at night. Rising from his marshy home, Grendel would stalk to the hall of the king, where he would seize fifteen of Hrothgar's sleeping warriors and devour them. Departing, he would gather fifteen more into his huge arms and carry them back to his watery lair. For twelve years this slaughter continues.

Word of the terror spreads. In the land of the Geats, ruled over by Hygelac, lives Beowulf, a man of great strength and bravery. When he hears the tale of Hrothgar's distress, he sets sail for Denmark to rid the land of its fear. With a company of fourteen men he comes ashore and asks a coast watcher to lead him to Hrothgar's high hall. There he is feasted in great honor while the mead cup goes around the table. Unferth reminds Beowulf of a swimming contest that Beowulf was said to have lost. Beowulf says only that he has more strength and that he also slaughtered many deadly monsters in the sea. At the close of the feast, Hrothgar and his warriors go to their rest, leaving Beowulf and his band in the hall. Then the awful Grendel comes to the hall and seizes one of the sleeping warriors. He is fated to kill no more that night, for Beowulf without shield or spear seizes the dreaded monster and wrenches off his right arm. Thus maimed, Grendel flees to his marshland home. His bloody arm is hung in Hrothgar's hall.

The next night Grendel's mother comes to avenge her son. Bursting into the great hall, she seizes one of the warriors, Aeschere, Hrothgar's chief counselor, and flees with him into the night. She also takes with her the prized arm of Grendel. Beowulf is asleep in a house removed from the hall and not until morning does he learn of the monster's visit. Then, with Hrothgar leading the way, a mournful procession approaches the dire marsh. At its edge they see the head of the ill-fated Aeschere and see the stain of blood on the water. Beowulf prepares for a descent to the home of the foe. Unferth offers Beowulf the finest sword in the kingdom and thus forfeits his own chance of brave deeds.

As Beowulf sinks beneath the waters of the marsh, he is beset on every hand by prodigious monsters. After a long swim he comes to the lair of Grendel's mother. Failing to wound her with Unferth's sword, he seizes the monster by the shoulder and throws her to the ground. During a grim hand-to-hand battle, in which Beowulf is being worsted, he sights a famous old sword of the giants, which he seizes and thrusts at Grendel's mother, who falls in helpless death throes. Then Beowulf turns and sees Grendel lying weak and maimed on the floor of the lair. Quickly he swings the sword and severs Grendel's head from his body. As he begins to swim back up to the surface of the marsh, the sword with which he has killed his enemies melts until only the head and hilt are left. On his return, the Danes rejoice and fete him with another high feast. He presents the sword hilt to Hrothgar and returns Unferth's sword without telling that it failed him.

The time comes for Beowulf's return to his homeland. He leaves Denmark in great glory and sails toward the land of the Geats. Once more at the court of his lord Hygelac, he is held in high esteem and is rewarded with riches and position. After many years, Beowulf himself becomes the king of the Geats. One of the Geats accidentally discovers an ancient hoard of treasure and, while its guardian dragon sleeps, carries away a golden goblet that he presents to Beowulf. The discovery of the loss causes the dragon to rise in fury and to devastate the land. Old man that he is, Beowulf determines to rid his kingdom of the dragon's scourge. Daring the flames of the dragon's nostrils, he smites his foe with his sword, but without effect. Once more Beowulf is forced to rely on the grip of his mighty hands. Of all his warriors only Wiglaf stands by his king; the others flee. The dragon rushes at Beowulf and sinks its teeth deeply into his neck, but Wiglaf smites the dragon with his sword, and Beowulf with his war-knife gives the dragon its deathblow.

Weak from loss of blood, the old hero is dying. His last act is to give Wiglaf a king's collar of gold. The other warriors now come out of hiding and burn with pagan rites the body of their dead king. From the dragon's lair they take the treasure hoard and bury it in the great mound they build over

Beowulf's ashes. Then with due ceremony they mourn the passing of the great and dauntless Beowulf.

Critical Evaluation:

Beowulf is the earliest extant heroic poem in any modern European language. The poem has come down through the centuries in a single manuscript, which was damaged and almost destroyed in the 1731 fire in the Cotton Library. Although the manuscript dates from the tenth century, the poem was probably composed in the eighth century and deals with sixth century events, before the migration of the Germanic tribes to Britain.

The poem was composed and performed orally. Old English bards, or scops, most likely began by piecing together traditional short songs, called heroic lays; they then gradually added to that base until the poem grew to its present size. The verse form is the standard Old English isochronic in that each line contains four stresses; there is a strong caesura in the middle of the lines, and the resultant half lines are bound together by alliteration. Although little Old English poetry survives, *Beowulf*'s polished verse and reflective, allusive development suggest that it is part of a rich poetic tradition.

Besides having unusual literary merit, *Beowulf* also provides information about and insight into the social, political, and ethical systems of Anglo-Saxon culture. There is a strong emphasis on courage in battle, fidelity to one's word, and loyalty to kinsmen. This is a violent but highly principled society in which struggle is everywhere and honor is everything. The hero, bound by family ties, by his own word, and by a strict code of revenge, is surrounded by his comitatus, his band of devoted comrades in arms. Judeo-Christian elements enter into the poem and into the society, but these aspects of the poem bear more resemblance to the philosophical systems of the Old Testament, stressing justice rather than love. There is controversy about whether these elements are intrinsic or are interpolations by a tenth century monastic scribe. In any case, it does not much resemble the Christianity of the High Middle Ages or of the modern world. Frequently the poem seems a reflection on the traditional pagan value system from the moral point of view of the new, incompletely assimilated Christianity.

Despite the fact that the heroic poem centers on valorous exploits, *Beowulf* contains curiously little action. The plot is embedded in a mass of other materials that some critics have seen as irrelevant or peripheral. However, the poem is basically reflective and ruminative, and the digressive materials provide the context in which the action of the poem is to be seen and interpreted. Consequently, *Beowulf* contains historical information, ceremonial descriptions, lengthy genealogies, elaborate speeches, and interspersed heroic songs that reveal much about the world in which *Beowulf* is set. For example, it is important that the action is entwined in a historical sequence of events, because complex loyalties and responsibilities are thereby implied. Beowulf helps Hrothgar because of the past links between their families, and, much later, when Beowulf succumbs to the dragon, it is clear that the future of his whole people is in jeopardy. In addition, the songs of the scop at Hrothgar's court indicate the value of poetry as a means of recording the past and honoring the brave. In like manner, the genealogies dignify characters by uniting them with revered ancestors, and the ceremonies underscore the importance of present deeds and past worth. Through these apparently extrinsic materials, the poet builds a continuity between past and present and extends the significance of his poem and characters to the whole of society.

In this context, Beowulf meets a series of challenges embodied in the poem's three monsters. That Beowulf battles imposing monsters rather than human adversaries suggests that his actions bear larger meanings. The hero arrives at the court of Hrothgar at the height of his youthful abilities. Not a neophyte, he has already fought bravely and demonstrated his preternatural power and charisma. He has no doubts or hesitancies as he prepares to fight. Grendel, a descendant of the line of Cain, is hateful to God, a lonely and vicious outcast, who hates light and joy and exacts bloody vengeance on man. All the more fearful because of his vague but imposing physique, Grendel is a representative of the physical evil that was so present in the lives and imaginations of the Anglo-Saxons. Beowulf confronts that physical evil and, bolstered by lineage and loyalty, routs the inimical force with which all people must contend.

However, Grendel, mortally wounded, escapes to his undersea lair, a submerged area devoid of light and appropriate to his joyless evil. Beowulf must, as a result, trace evil to its source if he is to be truly victorious. He ultimately returns with Grendel's head as a sign of victory, but to do that he must descend to the depths and exterminate the source of evil figured in Grendel's mother. This battle is more difficult and ominous: Beowulf doubts his capacities, and his men almost give up on him. Naturally this battle is more arduous, because he is facing the intellectual or moral evil that is at the root of the physical evil that threatens human life and joy. The poem is not a moral allegory in which Beowulf roots evil out of the world, but an exemplum of how each person must face adversity.

One greater challenge remains for Beowulf, and it is significant that it is separated by space and years from these youthful encounters. As a young warrior, Beowulf faces evil in vigorous foreign exploits; as an old king in his own country, he faces the dragon, the ultimate test of his courage. The dragon is at once less horrible (he does not have a distorted human form) and more fearsome. Beowulf, as the representative of his society, must enter the battle in which he knows he will die. The nonhuman dragon is a figure of the metaphysical evil that is woven into the fabric of the universe. Physical and moral evil can be challenged and overcome, but the ultimate evil (perhaps, at its extremity, age and death) cannot be avoided. Beowulf slays his antagonist and transcends his own death. By dying as he lived, he is a model for triumph in the last struggle every human must face.

"Critical Evaluation" by Edward E. Foster

Further Reading

Bloom, Harold, ed. *Beowulf.* New York: Chelsea House, 2007. A collection of essays analyzing various aspects of the epic, including discussions of its structure and unity, the monsters and other characters, and how to locate the work within literary history.

Brodeur, Arthur G. *The Art of "Beowulf."* Berkeley: University of California Press, 1960. From the starting point of belief in a singular author having written *Beowulf*, this volume provides a structural and thematic criticism of the work. Brodeur discusses diction, unity, setting, and Christian elements. A landmark reference.

Goldsmith, Margaret E. *The Mode and Meaning of "Beowulf."* London: Athlone Press, 1970. Goldsmith's book revises earlier discussions of Christian allegory in *Beowulf* and attempts to prove that the text is an extended Christian allegory. She provides a classic examination of the manuscript's Christian hero pitted against evil.

Hill, John M. *The Narrative Pulse of Beowulf: Arrivals and Departures.* Toronto, Ont.: University of Toronto Press, 2008. Hill disagrees with scholars who maintain that *Beowulf* lacks a steadily advancing narrative and that its structure is complicated by numerous digressions. He argues that the epic's scenes of arrival and departure provide a "narrative pulse" that structures the work.

Joy, Eileen A., Mark K. Ramsey, and Bruce D. Gilchrist, eds. *The Postmodern Beowulf: A Critical Casebook.* Morgantown: West Virginia University Press, 2006. A collection of essays, in which twenty-three scholars and critics, including Michel Foucault, John M. Hill, and John D. Niles, analyze *Beowulf* from a postmodern perspective.

Nicholson, Lewis E. *An Anthology of "Beowulf" Criticism.* Notre Dame, Ind.: University of Notre Dame Press, 1963. This early volume saves hours of searching through scholarly journals by presenting a comprehensive collection of widely recognized articles. It covers more than two dozen aspects of the text from allegory to zoology.

North, Richard. *The Origins of Beowulf: From Vergil to Wiglaf.* New York: Oxford University Press, 2006. Based on his extensive research, North suggests that *Beowulf* was written in the winter of 826-827 by an abbot named Eanmund as a requiem for King Beornwulf of Mercia on behalf of Wiglaf, the elderman who succeeded him.

Ogilvy, Jack D. A., and Donald C. Baker. *Reading "Beowulf."* Norman: University of Oklahoma Press, 1983. This work provides a modern and thorough view of the poem. After providing the historical background for the piece, it focuses on a two-part summary of the story and a subsequent analysis of theme, versification, and style. Includes an extensive annotated bibliography as well as many illustrations.

Staver, Ruth Johnston. *A Companion to Beowulf.* Westport, Conn.: Greenwood Press, 2005. A basic guide to *Beowulf* designed for students and other nonspecialists. Includes a detailed plot summary and analysis of the work's language and style, treatment of religion, and relation to both Anglo-Saxon and popular culture.

Whitelock, Dorothy. *The Audience of "Beowulf."* Oxford, England: Clarendon Press, 1951. A transcription of a series of lectures that concentrates on the poet and audience of *Beowulf* in their context of early Christianity. There are several references to other scholarly works as well as translations of the actual text. Includes an extensive index.

Bérénice

Author: Jean Racine (1639-1699)
First produced: 1670; first published, 1671 (English translation, 1676)
Type of work: Drama
Type of plot: Tragedy
Time of plot: 79 C.E.
Locale: Rome

Principal characters:
TITUS, the emperor of Rome
BÉRÉNICE, the queen of Palestine
ANTIOCHUS, the king of Comagene
PAULIN, Titus's confidant
ARSACE, Antiochus's friend and confidant
PHÉNICE, Bérénice's confidant

The Story:

The period of official mourning for the Emperor Vespasian ends. His son Titus is to succeed to the throne, and the rumor is that he will marry Bérénice, the queen of Palestine, with whom he was long in love. Antiochus, the war companion of Titus and a close friend, is also Bérénice's faithful friend. Although he was in love with her for five years, she never responded to his feeling.

Antiochus, who hopes that Titus will not marry Bérénice, goes to see her for the last time before he leaves Rome. He gives orders to his confidant Arsace to prepare everything for his departure. Arsace is surprised that Antiochus is preparing to leave when Titus is rising to great honor and will, in all probability, want his friend close by.

Bérénice, confident that the rumor of her marriage with Titus is true, is expecting a confirmation at any moment. When Antiochus appears to bid her farewell, she cruelly reproaches him for declaring his love at that time. She declares that she enjoyed his friendship and is depending on him to stay as a witness to her happiness.

Titus, aware that his love for Bérénice is a cause of concern to the Roman Empire, asks Paulin, a faithful confidant, his opinion of the emperor's suit. Paulin says frankly that the court will approve anything Titus might do, but that the Roman people will never be willing to have Bérénice as their empress. Although Titus realizes this fact only too well, he tries desperately to cling to his hope that somehow he can make her his wife without arousing public indignation and protest. Meanwhile, he sends for Antiochus and asks him to take Bérénice back to her own country.

When Bérénice arrives, full of love and joy and believing that she will soon marry Titus, the emperor, unable to tell her the truth, blames his father's death for the restrictions imposed upon him. She misunderstands him, however, and with all her passion reaffirms her love, saying that he can never miss his father as she will miss him if he does not love her. Overwhelmed, Titus finds it impossible to tell her that he cannot make her his empress.

Left alone with Phénice, Bérénice shows some concern over Titus's actions and speech. Then, remembering that Titus is to see Antiochus, she imagines that he is jealous of Antiochus and therefore really in love with her, and that soon everything will be all right.

When Antiochus arrives, Titus asks him to talk to Bérénice in his place, as a friend, and to assure her that Titus is sacrificing their love only out of the demands of duty. Left alone with Arsace, Antiochus does not know whether to rejoice for himself or grieve for his friend. Although his heart is filled with renewed hope, he does not want to be the one to tell Bérénice of Titus's decision. In spite of his reluctance Bérénice persuades him to reveal what Titus told him. On hearing his story she refuses to believe him and says that she will see Titus herself. In a painful interview she declares that she will kill herself. Paulin has a difficult time keeping Titus from following her when she leaves. Antiochus, alarmed, comes to beg Titus to save her life.

Titus meets with the representatives of the senate. Meanwhile, he asks Antiochus to reassure Bérénice of his love. Arsace comes looking for Antiochus with the news that Bérénice, about to leave Rome, wrote a letter to Titus. Antiochus announces that he is going to commit suicide and leaves. Bérénice, coming out of her apartment, meets Titus and tells him she is leaving immediately. When Titus declares that he loves her now more than ever, she pleads with him to show mercy and love her less when he orders her to leave. He finds the letter, which announces her decision to die since she cannot stay with him. Saying that he cannot let her go, he calls for Antiochus. When Bérénice collapses, Titus, in despair, assures her that he loves her to such a degree that he is willing to give up the empire for her sake, even though he knows that she will be ashamed of him if he would do so. If she will not promise to stay alive, he declares, he will kill himself. When Antiochus arrives, Titus tells him to be a witness to how weak love makes his friend. Antiochus replies that he always loved Bérénice and that he was preparing to commit suicide when Titus called him back.

Moved by so much grief on all sides, Bérénice accepts Titus's decision. Leaving, she asks Antiochus to pattern his decision on theirs. The three go their different ways.

Critical Evaluation:

In his preface to *Bérénice*, Jean Racine writes about the originality of this powerful tragedy, in which the plot is very limited. Racine explains that a tragedy need not include death. He argues that it is the "majestic sadness" expressed by the three principal characters in *Bérénice* that creates the aesthetic pleasure for theatergoers and readers alike. Racine understands that readers of tragedies are moved to tears by the restrained dignity and the profound sentiments expressed by characters—and not by the deaths of sympathetic characters. In *Bérénice*, no one dies, but readers are moved by the self-sacrifice and humanity shown by Emperor Titus and Queen Bérénice.

Bérénice was the fifth of eleven tragedies that Racine wrote between 1664 and 1691. It stands out from his other tragic masterpieces because of the stark simplicity of plot and the small number of principal characters. In *Bérénice*, the only major characters are the Roman emperor Titus, his fiery queen Bérénice from Palestine, and King Antiochus from the Middle Eastern kingdom of Comagena. Many years before, Antiochus fell in love with Bérénice, but as this tragedy begins, Antiochus realizes that Bérénice loves only Titus. Unlike many of Racine's tragedies, *Bérénice* has no villains.

The tragic conflict in *Bérénice* is quite simple. The newly crowned Roman emperor Titus and the Palestinian queen Bérénice loved each other for several years, and they wish to get married. In his preface, Racine stresses that their mutual love is so pure that they have not yielded to the temptation to make love before marriage. There is little or nothing in *Bérénice* that could offend the moral or religious sensitivities of a reader. The passion that Titus and Bérénice feel for each other becomes more intense because they did not yet consummate their love. Although Titus and Bérénice are kind and moral characters, there is an insurmountable obstacle to their happiness: Roman law does not permit an emperor to marry a woman who is not Roman or a woman who is a queen. Many Roman historians have explained that Rome was ruled by tyrannical kings before the creation of the Roman Republic. No real difference existed between the absolute power of Roman emperors and that of Roman kings. It was only a question of terminology. Racine suggests throughout this tragedy that xenophobia is the only possible explanation for the Roman tradition that prevents an emperor from marrying a foreigner. When Racine wrote *Bérénice*, King Louis XIV of France was married to Queen Maria Teresa of Spain. No one in France would have dared to criticize the king's decision to marry a foreigner; such criticism would have been viewed as unacceptable interference with the king's freedom of action. Despite the irrational nature of his subjects' hatred of foreigners and queens, Titus knows that he will have to resign if he marries Bérénice, and he believes that it will be dishonorable for him to resign from his position. Fate weighs heavily on the three principal characters as they come to understand that none of them can ever attain true happiness in life. As this tragedy begins, however, Bérénice has not yet discovered this. Bérénice tells Antiochus of her profound love for Titus; she considers Antiochus to be a countryman and a friend. Although she and Antiochus were once attracted to each other, she believes that neither still feels any passion for the other.

She is, however, mistaken. When Antiochus tells her that he still loves her, Bérénice restrains herself and tells him that she can love only Titus. In her mind, she is not free to love anyone other than her fiancé, Titus. Titus is also so emotionally committed to Bérénice that he could never love another woman.

Titus and Bérénice try to persuade themselves that Romans will not oppose their marriage. Not one of the three wants to recognize that social prejudice dooms his or her love to failure. Titus tries to believe that it will somehow be possible for him to reconcile his passion for Bérénice with his duty to uphold Roman laws and traditions, but he soon realizes that no such compromise exists. In many scenes in this tragedy, Titus and Bérénice agonize about what they should do, and they ask themselves whether they possess the inner strength to renounce their personal happiness in order to ensure peace and tranquillity in Rome. Bérénice becomes very angry and questions the sincerity of Titus's passion for her. At first, she cannot believe that Titus, who claims to love her, could decide not to marry her because of political pressure, but she comes to realize that his decision not to marry indicates, paradoxically, the depth of his passion for her. If he were to resign as emperor, Bérénice would someday be unable to respect a man who had shown so little respect for his social duty. The profound psychological insights into the nature of passion and the exquisite quality of the poetry in *Bérénice* continue to move readers and theatergoers centuries after its first performance.

"Critical Evaluation" by Edmund J. Campion

Further Reading

Abraham, Claude. *Jean Racine*. Boston: Twayne, 1977. An excellent general introduction to Racine's plays, as well as an annotated bibliography of important critical studies. Examines the psychological depth of *Bérénice* and develops the not totally convincing argument that Bérénice is a "self-centered" and "arrogant" character.

Barthes, Roland. *On Racine*. Translated by Richard Howard. New York: Hill & Wang, 1964. Examines the importance of love, violence, and heroism in Racine's tragedies. Argues persuasively that Bérénice is consumed by her love for Titus, whereas the emperor is unwilling to accept the dominance of passion in his life.

Campbell, John. *Questioning Racinian Tragedy*. Chapel Hill: University of North Carolina Press, 2005. Analyzes individual tragedies, including *Bérénice*, and questions if Racine's plays have common themes and techniques that constitute a unified concept of "Racinian tragedy."

Cloonan, William J. *Racine's Theatre: The Politics of Love*. University, Miss.: Romance Monographs, 1977. Examines the political motivation for Titus's decision not to marry Bérénice and suggests that the emperor no longer loves Bérénice as passionately as he once did. Argues that Bérénice is a much more sympathetic character than Titus.

Knapp, Bettina L. *Jean Racine: Mythos and Renewal in Modern Theater*. Tuscaloosa: University of Alabama Press, 1971. Contains a fascinating Jungian interpretation of Racine's tragedies. Describes the extraordinary psychological complexity of Titus and Bérénice.

Racevskis, Roland. *Tragic Passages: Jean Racine's Art of the Threshold*. Lewisburg, Pa.: Bucknell University Press, 2008. Examines *Bérénice* and Racine's other secular tragedies, demonstrating how these works construct space, time, and identity. Argues that the characters in these plays are in various stages of limbo, suspended between the self and the other, onstage and offstage, life and death, and the plays emphasize this predicament of being "in-between."

Weinberg, Bernard. *The Art of Jean Racine*. Chicago: University of Chicago Press, 1963. Analyzes the evolution of Racine's skill as a tragic playwright. The chapter on *Bérénice* explores the evocative power of Racine's refined verse and his artistry in using a simple plot.

Berlin Alexanderplatz

Author: Alfred Döblin (1878-1957)
First published: Berlin Alexanderplatz: Die Geschichte vom Franz Biberkopf, 1929 (*Alexanderplatz, Berlin*, 1931)
Type of work: Novel
Type of plot: Social realism
Time of plot: 1928-1929
Locale: Berlin

Principal characters:
FRANZ BIBERKOPF, an ex-convict
EMILIE (MEIZE) PARSUNKE, his girlfriend
REINHOLD, his betrayer
EVA, his ex-girlfriend
HERBERT WISCHOW, Eva's pimp
FATTY PUMS, criminal overlord
OSKAR FISCHER, member of Pums's gang

The Story:

Franz Biberkopf is released from Tegel prison, where he served four years for killing his girlfriend in a drunken rage. Back in Berlin, he decides to go straight. He begins to peddle bow ties on a street corner and drifts into selling other merchandise. At the same time, he starts an affair with Polish Lina and gets involved fleetingly with a bewildering series of political movements, ranging from homosexual rights to the Nazi Party. His wearing of the Nazi armband angers his worker friends, who expel him from his favorite pub. However, his real troubles begin after he enters in a partnership with Otto Lüders. After Lüders robs and assaults one of his customers, to whose apartment he gained access by using Franz's name, Biberkopf is forced to flee to an obscure part of the city to avoid complications.

A few weeks later, Franz returns to his usual haunts and takes up a job as a newspaper vendor. He also begins to consort with the flashy miscreant Reinhold. Reinhold is adept at making women fall in love with him, but he tires quickly of each new conquest and devises a system for Franz to help him. Each time Reinhold tires of a girlfriend, Franz throws off his current mistress and takes Reinhold's latest castoff. When Franz becomes sincerely attached to Cissy, one of Reinhold's rejects, he refuses to comply further. Indeed, he tells Reinhold's girlfriend how things stand. This infuriates Reinhold, though he pretends to acquiesce in Franz's attempt to reform him.

Through a mix-up, Franz is recruited by Fatty Pums, a so-called fruit vendor, who wants his men to collect some "produce." It soon becomes clear that Pums heads a criminal gang, which includes Reinhold. The gang is closely pursued as they drive away from a robbery, and Reinhold, given to psychotic rages and remembering Franz's interference with his social life, pushes him from the speeding automobile. Franz is run over by the chasing car.

He awakens in a hospital, missing one arm. Bedridden, he is taken in by the pimp Herbert Wishchow and his companion, Eva, friends from his criminal days. Once Franz feels better, Eva sets him up with the young prostitute named Emilie (Meize) Parsunke, who begins to support him. With time on his hands, Franz starts dropping in for friendly chats with Reinhold. At first, the members of Pums's gang fear the crippled Franz, thinking he will betray them to the police. When they find that he bears them no grudge—though his forbearance is inexplicable—they include him in a few jobs. Reinhold does not trust Franz, however, and decides to push him away by taking Meize away from him. Meize is secretly seeing another gang member, Oskar Fischer, to learn more about the gang's activities so that she can protect Franz. Oskar passes her to Reinhold, after the couple meet him "by chance" at a pleasure resort. Reinhold and Meize thereupon go for a walk in the woods and Reinhold turns on his charm. He is on the point of seducing her when he tactlessly begins running down her lover. This makes Meize's blood boil and she breaks away. Reinhold, mad with lust, drags her to the ground and, attempting to rape her, ends by killing her. He gets Oskar to help him bury the body.

When Meize does not return, Franz is distraught. Reinhold is not afraid of retribution because he concealed his crime well. Oskar, who decides to rob without the gang, is arrested. Because he believes, erroneously, that Reinhold warned the police, he tries to retaliate by confessing to being an accessory to Reinhold's murder of Meize. Reinhold, however, moved the corpse, putting it in a trunk that he asks Franz to buy in a conspicuous manner. When the body is found in its new berth, both Reinhold and Franz are suspected. The police put out a dragnet for them.

Franz learns of Meize's death and the hunt for him through the newspapers. Disguised with a false arm, he sets off to track down Reinhold. For a while, he is protected by two talkative good angels—one of the novel's many brief departures from realism. Eventually, tired and confused, Franz wanders into a nightclub that is in the process of being raided by the police. He is arrested. Reinhold, who got himself jailed under an assumed name, thinking prison is an ideal hiding place, is betrayed by a young man he befriended.

Franz has a mental breakdown and is placed in the Buch Asylum, where he lies as if dead. In his mind, he is undergoing a violent confrontation with Death, who recalls to Franz his misdeeds and charges him to start a new life. When he comes out of his stupor, he is changed. After he is released, he quietly becomes a gatekeeper, refuses to incriminate Reinhold at the killer's trial, and avoids any bad associations. From then on, he is known by the new name Franz Karl Biberkopf, for he is a remade man.

Critical Evaluation:

Berlin Alexanderplatz is an unusual twentieth century, avant-garde novel in being both a popular and a critical success. Readers liked the book's cynical, acid portrayal of Berlin's underworld as well as its happy ending, and the critics were enthusiastic about Alfred Döblin's use of montage techniques to create an electrifying portrait of a metropolis.

The breezy, hard-boiled tone, which characterizes much of the book, is a hallmark of Berlin's interwar writing. Germany's premier playwright of the time, Bertolt Brecht, perfected this tone in such works as *The Threepenny Opera* (1928). Works of this type depict the world of small-time criminals, shysters, prostitutes, and other outcasts and deviants. Their lives, like those of gamblers, are filled with abrupt rises and falls. Relationships are unstable and unpredictable, passions hot, and loyalties only for the short term. To these characters, highly industrialized, modernized Berlin seems to be governed not by rational procedures but by a whimsical, inscrutable fate. The only way to live in such a world is with a shield of knowing cynicism. In Döblin's book, characters such as Herbert and Eva have adopted this cynical attitude, and Franz acquires it in modified form at the conclusion. He learns about the mysteriousness of fate when he is repeatedly laid low by such unexpected disasters as Meize's disappearance.

However, Franz's outlook at the end is not purely cynical but includes a more positive element. This element, which accompanies the book's fatalism throughout, is the celebration of primal, resilient vitality. Döblin reflects this vitality both in the ongoing nascence of the city—a city that is constantly being demolished and reconstructed—and in the ingenuity of its inhabitants, who invent innumerable dodges to survive and strive in the difficult conditions. In his 1924 essay "The Spirit of the Naturalistic Age," Döblin asserted that the twentieth century would produce improved humans, who would arise from the energy of people living in giant collectives. The massification of humans, which many writers deplored, represents for Döblin the staging ground for the emergence of a happier, more fraternal, humanity. In *Berlin Alexanderplatz*, he points to this new spirit by frequently departing from his narrative to present a collage of the components of urban life that testify to the vitality of the metropolis and in his description of Franz's regeneration. In the asylum, Franz feels his body dissolve and flow out to take sustenance from the age's massed energy. This leads him to a nondenominational religious exaltation wherein he is healed through connection to the inner principle of his age.

Critical enthusiasm for *Berlin Alexanderplatz* focused on the author's use of montage, that is, the juxtaposition of heterogeneous materials. While working on his book, Döblin had been reading the Irish novelist James Joyce's *Ulysses* (1922), in which the montage method is extensively utilized. However, where Joyce deploys a different battery of devices in each major section of his text, Döblin takes the single tool of montage and uses it in various ways for varied effects. One is to interrupt his narrative by a cascade of facts and observations about Berlin life. He quotes advertisements and public notices, catalogs streetcar stops and the departments in a giant corporation, and chronicles the weather and stock market prices. The cumulative effect of such information is to lend immediacy to the novel's setting, Berlin. A second type of montage uses the thumbnail sketch. When Franz is hiding out after the Lüders disaster, for example, Döblin goes through his apartment building, room by room, and briefly describes each resident. Each life holds a spark of interest, and this is another indication of the city's fertility. Last, Döblin mixes in tales taken from the Bible and heroic sagas to deepen the novel's perspective. In *Ulysses*, Joyce uses the parallels between his story and the Greek myth referred to in his title to cast a dual light on his characters and to suggest both that they are degraded in relation to the classical prototypes and that their survival in the city demands a degree of heroic mettle. By contrast, when Döblin compares his protagonist's betrayal by Reinhold to the classical precedent of Orestes, who is betrayed by his mother, he does not use the parallel to imply connections between the times. Instead, the author explicitly declares that the Greek tale can no longer have anything but picturesque value once the classical style of life is surpassed.

James Feast

Further Reading

Barta, Peter I. "Walking in the Shadow of Death: *Berlin Alexanderplatz*." In *Bely, Joyce, and Döblin: Peripatetics in the City Novel*. Gainesville: University Press of Florida, 1996. An analysis of three novels about cities—Döblin's *Berlin Alexanderplatz*, James Joyce's *Ulysses*, and Andrei Bely's *Petersburg*. Barta argues that these novels juxtapose descriptions of the city with descriptions of the characters' rambling thoughts in order to show how the city creates a sense of psychic displacement and tension in its residents. Includes notes and a bibliography.

Berman, Russell A. *The Rise of the Modern German Novel: Crisis and Charisma*. Cambridge, Mass.: Harvard University Press, 1986. Concludes that Weimar literature often ties political progressivism to a mystical faith in humanity, a linkage the author considers central to *Berlin Alexanderplatz*.

Boa, Elizabeth, and J. H. Reid. *Critical Strategies: German Fiction in the Twentieth Century*. Montreal: McGill-Queen's University Press, 1972. In this survey of twentieth century German literature, Döblin's book is discussed as regards its plastic rendering of space and its thematic insistence on the inseparability of the individual and an individual's milieu.

Dollenmayer, David B. *The Berlin Novels of Alfred Döblin: "Wadzek's Battle with the Steam Turbine," "Berlin Alexanderplatz," "Men Without Mercy," and "November 1918."* Berkeley: University of California Press, 1988. Indicates how *Berlin Alexanderplatz* was quite a departure for Döblin, who until then had focused on intellectual protagonists and usually set his books in earlier times or in foreign lands.

Durrani, Osman. *Fictions of Germany*. Edinburgh: Edinburgh University Press, 1994. A quarter of this book is devoted to *Berlin Alexanderplatz*, concentrating especially on Döblin's masterful use of Berlin slang and on his montage techniques.

Koepke, Wulf. *The Critical Reception of Alfred Döblin's Major Novels*. Rochester, N.Y.: Camden House, 2003. This critical study examines the reviews of Döblin's novels that were written before and after 1933—the year he went into exile. Koepke also analyzes the scholarly articles that were written about the novels, placing them in historical context. Chapter 9 is devoted to a discussion of *Berlin Alexanderplatz*.

Kort, Wolfgang. *Alfred Döblin*. New York: Twayne, 1974. Includes a valuable chapter on the author's thoughts on the twentieth century epic, noting that Döblin considered *Berlin Alexanderplatz* an epic, not a novel. Kort argues that the book calls into play the creative power of the reader, who must help construct the text.

Midgley, David. "Radical Realism and Historical Fantasy: Alfred Döblin." In *German Novelists of the Weimar Republic: Intersections of Literature and Politics*, edited by Karl Leydecker. Rochester, N.Y.: Camden House, 2006. Döblin is one of the twelve German writers whose work is analyzed in this study of Weimar Republic literature. The essays focus on the authors' response to the political, social, and economic instability of the era.

Sander, Gabriele. "Döblin's Berlin: The Story of Franz Biberkopf." In *A Companion to the Works of Alfred Döblin*, edited by Roland Dollinger, Wulf Koepke, and Heidi Thomann Tewarson. Rochester, N.Y.: Camden House, 2004. This analysis of *Berlin Alexanderplatz* is included in a collection of essays interpreting Döblin's works.

The Berlin Stories

Author: Christopher Isherwood (1904-1986)
First published: 1945; includes *The Last of Mr. Norris*, 1935; *Goodbye to Berlin*, 1939
Type of work: Novel
Type of plot: Suspense and narrative
Time of plot: 1930-1933
Locale: Berlin, Paris, Switzerland, and London

Principal characters:
WILLIAM BRADSHAW, a young writer
ARTHUR NORRIS, his new friend, a double agent
SCHMIDT, Norris's secretary
BARON VON PREGNITZ, a wealthy Berliner
SCHROEDER, Bradshaw's landlady
CHRISTOPHER ISHERWOOD, a young writer
SALLY BOWLES, a young nightclub singer
NATALIE LANDAUER, Christopher's pupil
BERNHARD LANDAUER, her cousin, a department-store manager

Christopher Isherwood's *The Berlin Stories* consists of two popular books, loosely based upon his own experiences in Germany. These books first appeared separately as short novels: *The Last of Mr. Norris*, essentially a strongly plotted thriller, and *Goodbye to Berlin*, a roughly continuous narrative comprising six stories set in the early 1930's, during Nazi dictator Adolf Hitler's rise to power.

The Last of Mr. Norris introduces narrator William Bradshaw (Isherwood's middle names), a young writer who encounters a bewigged fellow Englishman named Arthur Norris on a train bound for Berlin. As they converse, Bradshaw, despite his companion's nervousness at the German border, agrees to meet for tea at Norris's Berlin flat. At the flat, he is briefly confused by two entrances, one marked as an office and the other marked private. Once inside, he sees that the office is separated from the living quarters only by a heavy curtain, a confusing duplicity.

Bradshaw encounters Herr Schmidt, Norris's sinister secretary, who controls his employer by confronting creditors and doling out Norris's pocket money. Bradshaw also discovers that Norris, a masochist, enjoys pornography, but he refuses to judge him. Together they spend New Year's Eve amid Berlin's notorious nightlife with the wealthy baron von Pregnitz; they also visit a brothel.

Fraulein Schroeder, Bradshaw's aging landlady, is impressed whenever Norris calls, but other friends advise Bradshaw not to trust him. However, Bradshaw likes him and is stirred when Norris speaks passionately at a communist meeting. Later, they meet with Ludwig Bayer, the Communist Party leader in Berlin, who asks Bradshaw to translate a manuscript into English.

Norris invites Bradshaw to his birthday celebration. In the meantime he pawns his rug for additional funds. Schmidt objects because Norris owes him nine months' wages and is already five thousand pounds in debt. He refuses to give Norris the cash, and the party is canceled. When Norris's phone is disconnected, Bradshaw realizes that he has left Berlin, perhaps for Paris. Schmidt follows, seeking his wages.

Bradshaw visits London in the spring of 1932, but when he returns that autumn he finds an economic depression, joblessness, and more Nazi uniforms on the street. Schroeder, noticeably older and thinner, greets him, as does a newly prosperous Norris, who now rents a room from her. Norris is generous, pays his rent promptly, and invites Bradshaw to an expensive dinner with the baron, who has acquired a post in the new government. When Norris arrives late, the baron is obviously offended, but Bradshaw makes a joke, the ice is broken, and the dinner goes well. Afterward, Norris abruptly excuses himself, leaving the other two alone. The baron nudges Bradshaw's foot, but Bradshaw deflects his advances, and they part politely.

Norris asks Bradshaw to accompany the baron to Switzerland, ostensibly for winter sports but actually to allow Norris and Margot, his connection in Paris, to elicit information from the baron. Over dinner, the baron admits that he enjoys boys' adventure books and confides his recurring dream of seven youths on an island. After he offers to teach Bradshaw to ski, they encounter a Dutch youth and his uncle, who turns out to be Margot, the Paris connection.

The baron shifts his attention from Bradshaw to the boy, while the uncle and Bradshaw talk at teatime. Then a telegram urges Bradshaw to return to Berlin immediately. Bayer warns that Margot is an unofficial police agent who collects and sells political information and has already sent Norris money from the French secret service. The baron, a politician, now has access to Germany's secrets. Bradshaw must urge Norris to leave Germany before he is arrested. Norris, it turns out has also double-crossed the Communist Party by gathering and selling information about them. The next day, Norris plans his escape to Mexico and then disappears.

Needing cash, the baron eventually agrees to sell information to Paris, but police decipher the code and arrest him. He flees but not fast enough. Cornered, he shoots himself. Bradshaw is terrified that he, too, will be arrested and questioned for working with Bayer and for his friendship with Norris. Meanwhile, Norris escapes from Schmidt to Mexico City, then California, then Costa Rica. Apparently, he tries to have Schmidt murdered.

Norris, who primps routinely, employing makeup, powder, and an ever-changing wig, is clearly not who he seems. He is the treacherous double agent, betraying everyone—Bradshaw, the baron, the government, and the Communist Party. In contrast, Schmidt reveals his inner truth openly, without disguise. He is Norris's negative, an unholy double; his malice is always visible. He follows Norris relentlessly, blackmailing him, withholding his funds; he and Norris seem inextricably linked forever.

In *Goodbye to Berlin*, the narrator, another young English writer, is Christopher Isherwood—not the author himself, but "a convenient ventriloquist's dummy," who famously describes himself as "a camera with its shutter open, quite passive, recording, not thinking." The first four words compose the title of John van Druten's 1951 play *I Am a Camera*, which subsequently reappeared as the stage and film musical *Cabaret*. The stories that follow reveal different facets of life in the doomed Weimar Republic.

"A Berlin Diary (Autumn 1930)" introduces several characters. Christopher is again Fraulein Schroeder's tenant and, like Bradshaw, he supports himself by teaching English to private pupils. His landlady, however, has metamorphosed. Previously tiny and delicate, Schroeder is now a strong, earthy woman who waddles about, gossiping enthusiastically. She sleeps in the living room behind a screen and rents the rooms in her flat to four other lodgers. To Christopher, a former medical student, she freely complains about her heavy bosom.

Christopher takes careful note of whatever he sees: He is recording. The narration includes considerable impressionistic detail. He observes the heavy furniture, the smell of the room, the young men in the street whistling for their sweethearts, the three motherly prostitutes on the corner. Little mention is made of politics, but its hostilities are symbolized by the friction between two tenants: the Bavarian yodeler Fraulein Mayr, a loyal Nazi supporter, and the Jewish frau Glanterneck, who lives below.

Sally Bowles is a rebellious young female who sings none too well at a local club. Her story spans the following year. When a mutual friend introduces her, Christopher notes her green fingernails, dirty hands, and heavily powdered face. An English girl, she soon telephones to invite Christopher to tea. They become good friends; she will become an actor, he a novelist. Sally obtains a cheaper room with Schroeder and, happily promiscuous, has an affair with her pianist, who soon abandons her.

Later, Sally and Christopher befriend a wealthy American at the Troika bar. They assume he is serious when he invites them both to travel the world with him, and Sally thinks she is in love. Then he departs Berlin for Budapest without notice, leaving them an indifferent message. When she discovers she is pregnant, Sally asks Schroeder to arrange an abortion. Christopher finally decides to start writing and leaves Berlin for Ruegen Island. While he is gone, Sally moves out and, after another unfortunate deception, disappears.

"On Ruegen Island (Summer 1931)" offers a brief pastoral interval in which Christopher again is more an observer than a participant. He rents a summer house with two others: Peter Wilkinson, a moody, gay, English intellectual, and a German working-class boy named Otto Nowak. These two share a bed but are an uneasy couple. Tensions escalate as the bisexual Otto goes dancing at night with local girls, making Peter jealous. Otto returns to the mainland early, leaving Christopher a note promising to visit him in Berlin.

"The Nowaks," set in the following winter, somewhat resembles an unfinished draft, with disjointed scenes and a great deal of dialogue. After the British pound is devalued, Christopher visits Otto, seeking a cheaper room in their district. Frau Nowak, a charwoman, politely urges him to live with her dysfunctional family in their leaky attic, and he accepts. She misses the kaiser, while her alcoholic husband supports the Nazis; Otto is a communist. Amid all this, Christopher attempts to write. Finally, he locates a new room and a new job, but just after Christmas he returns to the Nowaks with small presents. Frau Nowak, who has tuberculosis, is now in a sanatorium. Christopher's tender visit to her is the most effective scene in this story.

The poverty of the Nowaks is balanced by Christopher's view of "The Landauers," which spans the years covered by the book. They are a wealthy, educated Jewish family, owners of a major department store. Natalia Landauer, intelligent and well read, is his private pupil. She does not wish to attend a university, and would rather travel to Paris to study art and cooking so that she could earn a living if necessary. Her family includes her older cousin, Bernhard, manager of the Berlin store, who invites Christopher to his flat and greets him wearing a kimono over street clothes. Polite but enigmatic, Bernhard speaks intimately of his early life, his sense of alienation, and his love of Asia.

Christopher and Bernhard meet again many months later, and Bernhard looks ill. He is receiving anonymous threats because he is Jewish. Christopher is going to England for the summer, although Bernhard suggests that they both leave immediately for Peking. Christopher assumes he is joking, but when he returns in the fall of 1932, they have lost contact, and he assumes Bernhard is abroad. Meanwhile, the store is surrounded by Nazi storm troopers, ordering customers not to buy from Jews.

Christopher hears his final news of the Landauers while in Prague. Bernhard has died of a heart failure, prompting a man to announce, "There's a lot of heart failure . . . in Germany these days," implying that he has been murdered. Natalia and her parents are safe for the moment in Paris.

In the final "Berlin Diary (Winter 1932-3)," the city has become more somber and squalid, "a skeleton which aches in the cold." Violence is closer to the surface, and fear is infectious. Houses are searched, and people are imprisoned. Hitler becomes chancellor, and the Reichstag burns. Brown shirts and black uniforms attack a young boy in the street and stab him to death as police look on. Berlin is undergoing a terrible transformation, but Fraulein Schroeder, like many others, has adapted to the new regime. In May, Christopher leaves Berlin for good, for "Hitler is master of this city."

The Berlin Stories was originally part of an unfinished novel called *The Lost*, and Isherwood's Berlin, at the heart of Germany, remains here a city of the lost, as is Christopher himself. While exploring many levels of the culture, Isherwood offers a compelling, historically accurate portrait of Germany in the 1930's with surprising wit and humor. The threat of Nazism deepens with the ominous presence of Hitler looming in the background, especially in *Goodbye to Berlin*, which has been viewed as "more complex and . . . symbolic, denser in texture" than *The Last of Mr. Norris*. Readers, already aware of the war and the deaths to come, experience the powerful effect of dramatic irony. One critic has called *The Berlin Stories* "the best rendering of early Hitler Germany we have."

Joanne McCarthy

Further Reading

Finney, Brian. *Christopher Isherwood: A Critical Biography.* New York: Oxford University Press, 1979. Offers a chapter on each book of *The Berlin Stories* as well as the real background that inspired them and the inherent structure that links the stories.

Heilbrun, Carolyn G. *Christopher Isherwood.* New York: Columbia University, 1970. Compares Isherwood with his narrators, and classifies both books as "documentaries" in which the narrator serves as a camera, maintaining a necessary distance from the action.

Schwerdt, Lisa M. *Isherwood's Fiction: The Self and Technique.* New York: St. Martin's Press, 1989. Examines Isherwood as Bradshaw, contending that *The Last of Mr. Norris* is really Bradshaw's story because the reader is always aware of how Bradshaw feels while seeing Norris only from the outside.

Shuttleworth, Anthony. "In a Populous City: Isherwood in the Thirties." In *The Isherwood Century: Essays on the Life and Work of Christopher Isherwood*, edited by James J. Berg and Chris Freeman. Madison: University of Wisconsin Press, 2000. Presents a detailed analysis of Norris as a corrupted aesthete who believes in his devotion to art and is blind to his parallels with Hitler and the Nazis. Identifies Isherwood's Berlin as "a city populated by appearances" and filled with pretense and delusion, as are many of the characters and Nazism itself.

Wilde, Alan. *Christopher Isherwood.* New York: Twayne, 1971. Offers a symbolic interpretation of *The Berlin Stories*, with extensive analyses of the double in *The Last of Mr. Norris* and of the role of animal imagery.

The Betrothed

Author: Alessandro Manzoni (1785-1873)
First published: I promessi sposi, 1827 (English translation, 1828)
Type of work: Novel
Type of plot: Historical
Time of plot: Seventeenth century
Locale: Milan, Italy

Principal characters:
LORENZO, a young Italian peasant
LUCIA, his betrothed
DON RODRIGO, an arrogant nobleman
THE UN-NAMED, a powerful outlaw nobleman
DON ABBONDIO, a parish priest
FRA CRISTOFORO, a Capuchin and a friend of the betrothed couple

The Story:

On the day before he is to perform the marriage ceremony for Lorenzo and Lucia, two young peasants, Don Abbondio, parish priest at Lecco, is warned by two armed henchmen of Don Rodrigo, a tyrannical noble, not to marry the pair. In fear for his life, Don Abbondio refuses to perform the marriage when asked to do so by the young couple. When they try to trick him into being present while they exchange vows, he dashes away into hiding.

The reason for the warning given to the priest is that Don Rodrigo wishes to seduce Lucia. He is not in love with the young woman, but he wagered his cousin that he can have her for his enjoyment while she is still a virgin. Toward this end, he sends a crew of his henchmen to abduct the girl from her home. Appearing at Lucia's home, they are frightened away by the tumult aroused when the priest causes the alarm to be sounded by tolling the church bell.

Frightened, Lucia seeks aid from a saintly Capuchin, Fra Cristoforo, who gives her, her mother, and Lorenzo temporary haven within the walls of the monastery while he makes arrangements for the safety of all three, away from the wrath and wickedness of Don Rodrigo. He sends the girl to seek sanctuary with a Capuchin chapter at Monza, along with her mother. He sends Lorenzo to another monastery in Milan.

Arriving at Monza, Lucia is put under the care of a nun who belongs to a noble family that placed her in the convent rather than pay a dowry. The nun is a headstrong woman and, in some ways, wicked, but the Capuchins think Lucia will be safe under her care. Lucia remains hidden for some weeks.

Don Rodrigo initiates a search for her until his henchmen discover her place of refuge. Fearing that he can never take her from the sanctuary, Don Rodrigo enlists the aid of a powerful noble called the Un-named. The Un-named, grateful for past services by Don Rodrigo, agrees to aid his vassal in abducting the woman and in teaching a harsh lesson to peasants who think they can defy the nobility.

The Un-named learns that one of his men living near the convent is to murder a nun who displeased the woman to whom the Capuchins sent Lucia. As a result of the murder committed for her benefit, the nun is forced to enter into the scheme and send Lucia out of the convent. Once out of the sanctuary, Lucia is kidnapped by the Un-named's men and taken in a coach to his mountain retreat.

Meanwhile, Lorenzo fails to reach the Capuchin monastery in Milan. Upon his arrival in the city, he finds the populace in turmoil because of a shortage of bread. He takes part in a riot, and afterward he becomes drunk in a tavern. While drunk, he babbles to a police spy that he incited a crowd to riot, and the spy has him arrested by the police. Another mob releases Lorenzo from the police. With a price on his head, he flees from the Duchy of Milan into territory controlled by Venice. There he locates a distant relative who finds work for him in a silk mill. When the authorities of Milan try to have him returned to that city, Lorenzo flees again and assumes a fictitious name in another Venetian community.

The Un-named is moved by Lucia's beauty and innocence and refuses to turn her over to Don Rodrigo. Instead, he goes to Cardinal Federigo and announces that he suffered a change of conscience and wishes to end a career of tyranny and oppression. The churchman welcomes him as an erring parishioner. Lucia is released from her imprisonment in the noble's mountain castle and returns once again to the keeping of her mother. Rather than send the woman to her home and the persecution of Don Rodrigo, Cardinal Federigo sends Lucia and her mother to the home of a noblewoman known for her charity. There Lucia will be safe.

Don Rodrigo, angry because Fra Cristoforo aids the young woman and so preserves her honor, causes the removal of the Capuchin to Rimini. More than a year passes; Lorenzo is unable to return to the Duchy of Milan because of his banishment. Corresponding with Lorenzo through letters, Lucia tells him that in her period of duress she vowed to the Virgin that she will never marry if released from the clutches of the ruffians. Finally, because of the time that intervenes and the confusion that arises because of a plague, Lorenzo decides to return to Milan, where Lucia is staying with the charitable noblewoman. While searching for her in a city desolated by the plague, he contracts the disease. After his recovery, he continues his search, only to learn that Lucia is ill and was sent to the pesthouse, along with thousands of other unfortunates who contract the disease.

At the pesthouse, he finds Fra Cristoforo, who went to Milan to aid the sick. Among his patients the Capuchin has Don Rodrigo, who catches the plague and is near death. Fra Cristoforo makes Lorenzo pardon Don Rodrigo and promise to pray for his soul. Continuing his search for Lucia, Lorenzo finds her convalescing in the women's section of the pesthouse. After their reunion, Fra Cristoforo tells Lucia that her vow to the Virgin is not valid, inasmuch as she previously exchanged betrothal vows with Lorenzo.

When the plague subsides, Lorenzo goes back to their village and finds that the plague almost wiped out its population, although sparing Don Abbondio and Lucia's mother. While he is there, the new heir to the estate arrives, Don Rodrigo having succumbed to the plague. With the new incumbent's aid, for he is a friend of the cardinal who befriended Lucia, the betrothed couple return to Lecco and are at last married by Don Abbondio.

After their marriage, the couple move, again with the nobleman's aid, to a new home in the Venetian territory, where Lorenzo plies his trade in a silk mill, and he and Lucia rear a large and healthy family.

Critical Evaluation:

The Betrothed, one of the world's great historical novels, established its author as the leading Italian Romantic novelist of the nineteenth century. It is the work of Alessandro Manzoni, and *The Betrothed* in particular, that raised Italian fiction from the low estate to which it had fallen and made it, in the nineteenth century, assume a high place in European fiction. The simple, adventurous story that Manzoni tells has captivated readers ever since it first appeared. In the best tradition of historical fiction, Manzoni presents many facets of life and culture in Milan during the 1620's, when much of Italy was under Spanish domination. In this novel, there are not only peasants and villainous nobles, who are the chief characters, but also the bravos, citizens, nuns, petty officials, churchmen, and scores of other types typical of seventeenth century Italy.

The complex and involuted history of Manzoni's revisions of his work and the drama of his artistic self-consciousness in their elaboration are as Romantic, in essence, as the story itself. *The Betrothed* underwent its first massive revision from 1823, the date of its first completion, until its eventual publication in 1827 as *Fermo e Lucia*, a revision overseen by the author's friend and adviser, Flauriel. The revision witnessed changes in the names and roles of most of the major characters, the modification of their motivation and psychology, and the excision of numerous digressions, such as the story of Gertrude, as well as endless linguistic and stylistic changes. Nevertheless, a second major revision of the retitled novel took place between its publication as *Fermo e Lucia* and its definitive form as *I promessi sposi*, which reflects not only Manzoni's concern about such issues as the work's commitment to doctrinal and historical truth but also his scrupulousness toward the language of the novel, down to its spelling, typography, and punctuation. The work underwent changes not only from edition to edition but also from copy to copy within the edition as whole pages were removed and reinserted. It would seem that the arbitrariness of time, more than artistic inevitability, governed the novel's final form. Manzoni did not stop revising it until he died.

Manzoni's Milan is alive with new ideas largely imported from France but lacks commanding figures to propound them. Milanese culture was undergoing a tumultuous change from the ideals of the Enlightenment to those of Romanticism, as the last waves of the French Revolution and the Napoleonic era ebbed. The Italians of Manzoni's time were painfully aware of their disunity, which found its most potent symbol in the absence of a national language. The creation of this national language became one of Manzoni's goals in writing *The Betrothed*, and both literary and ethical concerns would converge on it. The novel demanded a language that would be current, literary, and rich enough to express the most profound values and ideas of seventeenth century Italy. The language also needed to remain accessible to the common reader, for whom it was intended. Manzoni found this language in Florentine during his 1827 sojourn in Florence. Thus began the linguistic revision that would eliminate from his novel the archaisms, stilted literary language, and regionalisms that impeded his goal for a national language.

Many of Manzoni's revisions illustrate his personal rejection of the Enlightenment literary tradition and his espousal of Romanticism. The first version of *The Betrothed* yokes much of the picaresque violence of Voltaire to the rustic idylls popular at the time. These passages were fated for early excision. Sir Walter Scott's *Ivanhoe* (1819) replaced the influence of Voltaire's *Candide* (1759) in the later versions. Scott's conception of the use of poetic invention for a better understanding of history impressed Manzoni. However, history in Scott's work is essentially the picturesque background for tales of adventure, but in Manzoni's it becomes the means to an essentially moral end: understanding the limits of human freedom in the struggle between good and evil, and the particular nature of that struggle in a given age. Manzoni made the historical novel illuminate the nature of being in the world; the novel concerns itself with particular men and women and with minutely studied historical situations. If Manzoni appears obtuse about the larger historical and political implications of a major event, such as, for example, the siege of Casale, it is largely because of his concern with the individual.

Manzoni's Romanticism and his Catholicism dictated the democratic ends and themes of the work. The novel is for and about the humble folk of the world—artisans, peasants, and laborers. Such an audience conditioned both the choice of spoken Florentine as the language of the novel as well as the characterization of the protagonists. They represent their class well in their spontaneity, naturalness, thirst for justice, and sincere religiosity. By making the poor the heroes of moral struggle, Manzoni shows that they need not merely suffer history, but, by realizing the Christian message, create it. The social and ethical struggle of the work is accordingly the central struggle of Christianity: the struggle between pride and humility. In Christianity, Adam falls in pride and, in so doing, damns humanity, which has to await its redemption in the humble Christ. In *The Betrothed*, pride is represented by Don Rodrigo and the Governor of Milan, whose lives are circumscribed by an irrationality that their high positions seem to impose on them. This is typified by their code of honor, which leads them to seek Lorenzo's destruction. Humility is virtually personified by Lorenzo, Lucia, and Fra Cristoforo, who realize in their lives the values of gentleness, charity, and brotherhood. On a higher level, the struggle between pride and humility translates itself for Manzoni into the struggle between the oppressive Austrians and the subjugated Italians.

Criticism of *The Betrothed* centered about the degree to which the novel can be said to create new values and meanings that are not reducible to a simplistic catechism. The question for critics has often been, then, whether the novel does or does not have a Christian moral. An event such as the conversion of the Un-named would then display the violence of the miraculous on the development of plot and character. Others have argued that it is the extraordinary coherence of character that is at issue, since the Un-named's fear of death and damnation conform perfectly to his previous behavior and virtually assure his conversion. Manzoni's choice of weak characters such as Don Abbondio and ultimately perhaps the Un-named himself sets into relief Manzoni's concern with the loneliness of moral choice. The authorial voice that tells the story and is aware of its outcome is unavailable to the character who must make his choice in anxiety. Manzoni's Christianity may moralize reality and offer itself as the ultimate key to the understanding of human nature, but it does so only in the end; the novel is also artistically whole, independent of Christian doctrine.

"Critical Evaluation" by James Thomas Chiampi

Further Reading

Barricelli, Gian Piero. *Alessandro Manzoni*. Boston: Twayne, 1976. A thorough introduction to Manzoni. Provides a biography that focuses more on his life after his conversion to Catholicism in 1810 than on his life preceding the conversion. Analyzes *The Betrothed*'s characters, styles, and themes.

Chandler, S. B. *Alessandro Manzoni: The Story of a Spiritual Quest*. Edinburgh: Edinburgh University Press, 1974. An insightful investigation of Manzoni's works, describing how his writings demonstrate Manzoni's spiritual development and his movement toward a spiritual view of life.

Ferlito, Susanna F. "Fear of the Mother's Tongue: Secrecy and Gossip in Manzoni's *I promessi sposi*." *MLN* 113, no. 1 (January, 1998): 30-51. Discusses how Manzoni's representation of the mother-daughter bond in *The Betrothed* implicitly recognizes and keeps at bay the critical potential of that bond and, by extension, a female alliance among the peasants.

________. *Topographies of Desire: Manzoni, Cultural Practices, and Colonial Scars*. New York: Peter Lang, 2000. Drawing upon a wide range of current disciplinary debates in the fields of comparative politics, anthropology, cultural studies, and comparative literature, Ferlito examines how Manzoni's French and Italian works produced differences between cultural discourses in a nineteenth century Europe that did not consider itself to be naturally divided between nation-states. Includes bibliography and index.

Godt, Clareece G. *The Mobile Spectacle: Variable Perspective in Manzoni's "I promessi sposi."* New York: Peter Lang, 1998. Describes how Manzoni consistently represents what the eye sees (landscape, cityscape) and the mind conceives (characters' plans, history) under different and often paradoxical aspects. Includes notes and comprehensive bibliography.

Matteo, Sante, and Larry Peer, eds. *The Reasonable Romantic: Essays on Alessandro Manzoni*. New York: Peter Lang, 1986. A collection of critical essays on the range of Manzoni's works.

Pierce, Glenn. *Manzoni and the Aesthetics of the Lombard Seicento: Art Assimilating into the Narrative of "I promessi sposi."* Lewisburg, Pa.: Bucknell University Press, 1998. Pierce examines *The Betrothed* in terms of seventeenth century aesthetics, demonstrating how Manzoni used artistic and dramatic works from that period as historical documents with which to create his novel. Contains numerous illustrations.

Ragusa, Olga. "Alessandro Manzoni and Developments in the Historical Novel." In *The Cambridge Companion to the Italian Novel*, edited by Peter Bondanella and Andrea Ciccarelli. New York: Cambridge University Press, 2003. Ragusa's essay is included in this historical overview of the Italian novel. While referring to many of his works, she focuses on *The Betrothed* and provides a broader context of his place in Italian literature.

Wall, Bernard. *Alessandro Manzoni*. New Haven, Conn.: Yale University Press, 1954. Provides an overview of Manzoni's life and his role as poet and dramatist before examining *The Betrothed*, its place in literature, and the controversies of Manzoni's religion, his use of the Italian language, and the novel's relationship to Romanticism.

Betsey Brown

Author: Ntozake Shange (1948-)
First published: 1985
Type of work: Novel
Type of plot: Bildungsroman
Time of plot: 1959
Locale: St. Louis, Missouri

Principal characters:
BETSEY BROWN, a thirteen-year-old girl
JANE BROWN, her mother, a social worker
GREER BROWN, her father, a doctor
ALLARD, her younger brother
CHARLIE, her cousin
VIDA MURRAY, her grandmother
BERNICE CALHOUN, a a nanny
EUGENE BOYD, a friend of Charlie
REGINA JOHNSON, a nanny-housekeeper
MRS. MAUREEN, a beautician
CARRIE, a nanny-housekeeper
MR. JEFF, a gardener

The Story:

Betsey Brown is at the awkward junction between childhood and womanhood, torn between the everyday life of home and school and her dreams of romance and accomplishment. Often drawn into the schemes of her contentious younger siblings, she is also becoming aware of the complexities of the adult world, but not yet sure how to sort these realities out. The Brown's rambling Victorian home is full of nooks and hideaways, and Betsey often retreats to one of them to think, and to observe the neighborhood's activities unseen.

On a typical weekday morning, Betsey stands on a terrace watching the sun rise over the city's rooftops. Soon the rest of the family is stirring, with the children squabbling over bathroom access, mother Jane and father Greer claiming a brief respite for lovemaking before the day's duties set in, and Grandma Vida Murray, Jane's mother, brewing coffee and checking out the children's school gear. Betsey reluctantly comes inside, practicing a selection by composer Paul Laurence Dunbar that she is scheduled to recite in school today. Dr. Greer, an early advocate of African American pride, lines the children up and conducts a daily quiz. Each child fields a question on black leaders, culture, or geography. A correct answer wins them an extra nickel. They start for school as the parents leave for work. The neighborhood falls quiet. Vida goes outside to admire her beloved flower beds.

Despite the comforting routine of daily life, both Betsey and her world are on the cusp of change. Her mother feels overwhelmed by the multiple demands of her own life: raising five spirited children, working with crazy patients at the "colored" hospital, and Greer's loud and heartfelt advocacy of African American music and causes.

One day, a weirdly dressed woman named Bernice Calhoun comes to the door, looking for work. Jane hires her and hopes Bernice will be a big help with the children. Vida, however, deplores her uncouth speech and manner. Betsey is hiding in her favorite retreat—the big oak tree in the front yard—when her mother calls the children to come meet their new nanny. No one before has discovered Betsey's tree perch, but Bernice spots her there and reveals Betsey's secret to the whole family. Betsey is quietly furious at having her hideaway revealed. It does not take much persuasion to organize her siblings into staging an especially chaotic morning for the next day. The morning includes widespread damage from spilled grease and from swinging on the curtains. Bernice quits her job on the spot.

Betsey brags at school about the episode, horrifying her friend Veejay. She tells Betsey that her mother makes her living looking after bratty white kids. Bad behavior like this is expected from whites, but she had thought Betsey would treat a black woman better.

Stung by Veejay's comments, Betsey dashes home to make amends with Bernice, but she has gone. Jane and Vida do not blame Betsey for the morning disaster, but Betsey herself still feels guilty. Her longtime friendships at school are fraying under the stress of adolescent cliques and romance. Betsey herself is mightily interested in kisses. When cousin Charlie's friend Eugene Boyd comes over to shoot baskets, her interest turns into reality. They share two gentle lip touches, but though Betsey imagines Eugene as her boyfriend, their kisses fail to enlighten her about the whole man-woman thing.

The adults of the family have their own preoccupations. Jane, still bothered by the constant noise and confusion of family life, hires a young woman named Regina Johnson as a nanny and housekeeper. The girls love Regina's fashion consciousness and high spirits, but Vida views her as a bad influence. In the meantime, court-ordered busing has begun in St. Louis, Missouri, and Greer insists his children take part. Jane fears for their safety, but Greer stays adamant. They must do it for their own future and for the future of their race, he says.

The children are nervous, too, but Charlie reminds them that Emmett Till was the same age as him when he was brutally murdered. At the new school, Betsey's experience is not so bad. At worst, some of her new classmates ignore her. Charlie comes home with a black eye; he had to defend himself against a gang of five. Greer offers to go with him to school tomorrow, reassuring Charlie. He knows that Greer had been a boxing champion in his youth. The family settles into a new schedule, with the children commuting uneasily between their safe neighborhood and the white world.

One day the stress becomes too much for Betsey. Her mother yells at her for her low-class taste in music and dancing, and her teacher refuses to let her report on composer Dunbar. Everyone distrusts Betsey's interest in boys. Finally, Betsey realizes that she does not fit in with her family. After some thought she decides to go work at Mrs. Maureen's beauty salon and make her way in the world.

Betsey's appearance at the salon shocks Mrs. Maureen, whose evening work as a madam is just winding up when Betsey appears. Maureen brings Betsey into the beauty shop, treats her to a luxurious makeover, and explains that she cannot hire her. She gives Betsey money for a cab ride home. Betsey dallies on the way, immersed in daydreams. Her family does not know she is safe until the police take her to the hospital, where a distraught Dr. Greer is making rounds.

The next day, Greer and Jane quarrel over Greer's plan to take the children to a street demonstration. To Jane, this is tantamount to child abuse. Greer will not back down, so Jane leaves. In her absence, Greer hires a woman named Carrie to look after the house and children. Carrie is competent but strange, and her colorful vocabulary and relationship with Mr. Jeff, the gardener, alarm Vida, the family's moralist. Late one evening, Jane returns home. She fires Carrie, who has just been arrested for knife-fighting. The family is overjoyed with their mother's return and the return of normal life. Betsey climbs back into her tree and broods about all she has learned.

Critical Evaluation:

Ntozake Shange first won recognition for her dazzling choreopoem, *for colored girls who have considered suicide/ when the rainbow is enuf*, which debuted on Broadway in 1974. A choreopoem is an innovative combination of poetry, drama, music, and dance. Her subsequent writings continue to impress critics and readers with their unique imagery, use of language, and tough-but-tender explorations of what it means to be a black woman in the United States.

Shange is best known for her poetry and plays. Of her published novels, *Betsey Brown* is probably least known to the reading public, yet it is a little gem of a novel. In it, Shange combines her extraordinary gifts for dialogue and image to build a story that sensitively treats family life, growing up, and the impact of the very early days of the Civil Rights movement on an African American family.

A typical young teenager, Betsey Brown is filled with longings. She wants to experience life in all its "thickness" and "heat," to understand the world, and to find her place in it, claiming the fame and romance she deserves. Betsey is a good girl, and her upbringing has been a protected one in many ways, so her transgressions are minor. Still, her mother deplores her taste in music and dance, her new teacher does not recognize her heroes, and everyone looks askance at her interest in boys. Along with all this she must struggle to keep a secret place for herself amid the ongoing circus of family life. No wonder Betsey feels like she does not fit in.

Betsey's mother, Jane, also feels besieged. In many ways she and husband Greer balance each other well, as spouses in successful marriages often do. Greer's unabashed embrace of African American culture—down to the loud conga drums he plays every morning—clashes with her more ladylike sensibilities, even though there is no doubt the two have a strong and sensual bond. Jane feels the frustrations of any multitasking mother, and the lack of any time for herself. The tension-relieving remedies she does use—like solitaire games and nail polish—do not quite help. Ultimately, after her "time-out" from the family, she returns because, in spite of it all, she realizes she really does belong with them.

Betsey's and Jane's dilemmas are widely shared by American women of almost every ethnic background, but society's institutionalized segregation and racism adds another dimension to their life experiences. For black girls and women, the stakes are higher. This is signaled in a telling incident, when two white police officers catch cousin Charlie and Betsey's brother Allard recklessly careening around an all-white Catholic girls' school campus on their bicycles. The police bring the boys home to Jane, but only "on accounta you special," and they do not know local customs. It is clear that any repeat offense will be punished severely. The officers' disrespectful attitude enrages and terrifies Jane. She knows that boisterous behavior by white boys would be treated much more leniently.

Likewise, the lures of "low-class" black music and ardent young males send danger signals to Betsey's mother and grandmother. The fates of Regina Johnson, whom Betsey last meets pregnant and deserted at Mrs. Maureen's salon, and of Carrie, whose loss of impulse control with a friend is about to send her to jail, highlight that Betsey has little leeway to make mistakes; and what will her innocent flirtation with Eugene Boyd, or even her spats with school friends, lead to?

The Browns enjoy a certain degree of safety and status within the African American community. They live in a sedate neighborhood where women cultivate roses and hire maids. To most whites in the years just before the Civil Rights movement, however, all this hardly matters; all "Negroes" are just "those people." In view of what he risks, Greer's willingness to confront the white establishment on its own territory seems little short of heroic.

Altogether, the novel is notable for the way it illuminates the impact of racism on middle-class African Americans, and for showing, as few contemporary novels do, that black women, too, can be innocent and fragile.

Shange's work has been criticized for presenting an unduly negative image of black men. This is perhaps inevitable, considering her overall literary focus on women, but is not the case in *Betsey Brown.* Greer is a good man and an admirable father and role model. The other significant adult male character, Mr. Jeff, the family's gardener, is a quiet and reliable presence, whose inexplicable attraction to the eccentric Carrie only makes him more interesting.

Betsey Brown is not, primarily, an autobiographical novel. However, the author has drawn on her own childhood experiences for much background to Betsey's story. Shange was the oldest daughter of Paul T. Williams and Eloise Williams, a surgeon and a psychiatric social worker, respectively. The family first lived in St. Louis, until Shange was thirteen years old. Also, as a child, she took part in court-ordered busing, which desegregated the city's schools. Her parents knew such African American luminaries as musicians Dizzy Gillespie and Miles Davis and writer W. E. B. Du Bois, who appears in a family story in *Betsey Brown.* Altogether, the novel gives a unique and insightful portrayal of growing up black in America.

Emily Alward

Further Reading

Ryan, Judylyn S. *Spirituality as Ideology in Black Women's Film and Literature*. Charlottesville: University Press of Virginia, 2005. This study of the spiritual in the creative work of African American women includes a chapter comparing Shange's use of spirituality to that of writer Zora Neale Hurston and playwright Ama Ata Aidoo.

Shange, Ntozake. "Catching up with Ntozake Shange." Interview by Will Power. *American Theatre* 24 (April, 2007): 30-33. A transcript of an interview, with added notes. Shange speaks of the influence of place on her plays, pointing out how, for example, highway-building breaks up urban neighborhoods to create a sense of loss for residents.

________. "In the Heart of Shange's Feminism: An Interview." Interview by Neal A. Lester. *Black American Literature Forum* 24 (Winter, 1990): 717. Shange explains the roots of her feminism in this interview. She also discusses her thoughts on the different ways that men and women respond to novels.

Tate, Claudia. *Black Women Writers at Work.* New York: Continuum, 1983. In her essay in this collection, Shange explains how and why she is "writing for little girls coming of age."

Whitson, Kathy J. *Encyclopedia of Feminist Literature*. Westport, Conn.: Greenwood Press, 2004. This article reads Shange from the point of view of her feminism as well as her race. Places her alongside feminist writers of all races and nationalities.

Willard, Nancy. "Life Abounding in St. Louis." *The New York Times Book Review*, May 12, 1985, p. 12. A lengthy review of *Betsey Brown*. Praises Shange's use of dialogue to convey character, and the evocative quality of her descriptions of place and atmosphere.

Between the Acts

Author: Virginia Woolf (1882-1941)
First published: 1941
Type of work: Novel
Type of plot: Psychological realism
Time of plot: June, 1939
Locale: England

Principal characters:
BARTHOLOMEW OLIVER, the owner of Pointz Hall
GILES, his son
ISA, his daughter-in-law
MRS. LUCY SWITHIN, his widowed sister
MRS. MANRESA and WILLIAM DODGE, the guests at the pageant
MISS LA TROBE, the writer and director of the pageants

The Story:

Pointz Hall is not one of the great English houses mentioned in the guidebooks, but it is old and comfortable and pleasantly situated in a tree-fringed meadow. The house is older than the name of its owners in the county. Although they hang the portrait of an ancestor in brocade and pearls beside the staircase and keep, under glass, a watch that stopped a bullet at Waterloo, the Olivers lived only a little more than a century in a district where the names of the villagers go back to the Domesday Book. The countryside still shows traces of the ancient Britons, the Roman road, the Elizabethan manor house, and the marks of the plow on a hill sown in wheat during Napoleon's time.

The owner of the house is Bartholomew Oliver, retired from the Indian Civil Service. With him lives his son Giles, his daughter-in-law Isa, two small grandchildren, and his widowed sister, Mrs. Lucy Swithin. Bartholomew, a disgruntled old man who lives more and more in the past, is constantly snubbing his sister, as he did when they were children. Mrs. Swithin is a woman of careless dress, good manners, quiet faith, and great intelligence. Her favorite book is an *Outline of History*; she dreams of a time when Piccadilly was a rhododendron forest in which the mastodon roamed. Giles is a London stockbroker who wanted to be a farmer until circumstances decided otherwise. A misunderstanding lately developed between him and his wife Isa, who writes poetry in secret. She suspects that Giles is unfaithful and fancies herself in love with Rupert Haines, a married gentleman farmer of the neighborhood. Isa thinks that Mrs. Haines has the eyes of a gobbling goose.

On a June morning in 1939, Pointz Hall awakens. Mrs. Swithin, aroused by the birds, reads again in the *Outline of History* until the maid brings her tea. She wonders if the afternoon will be rainy or fine, for this is the day of the pageant to raise funds for installing electric lights in the village church. Later, she goes to early service. Old Bartholomew walks with his Afghan hound on the terrace where his grandson George is bent over a cluster of flowers. When the old man folds his newspaper into a cone to cover his nose and jumps suddenly at the boy, George begins to cry. Bartholomew grumbles that his grandson is a crybaby and goes back to his paper. From her window, Isa looks out at her son and the baby, Caro, in her perambulator that a nurse is pushing. Then she goes off to order the fish for lunch. She reads in Bartholomew's discarded newspaper the story of an attempted assault on a girl in the barracks at Whitehall. Returning from church, Mrs. Swithin tacks another placard on the barn where the pageant will be given if the day turns out rainy; regardless of the weather, tea will also be served there during the intermission. Mocked again by her brother, she goes off to make sandwiches for the young men and women who are decorating the barn.

Giles is expected back from London in time for the pageant. The family decides not to wait lunch for him when Mrs. Manresa and a young man named William Dodge arrive unexpectedly and uninvited. They intended, Mrs. Manresa explains, to picnic in the country, but when she saw the Olivers' name on the signpost, she suddenly decided to visit her old friends. Mrs. Manresa, loud, cheerful, and vulgar, is a woman of uncertain background married to a wealthy Jew. William Dodge, she says, is an artist. He is, he declares, a clerk. Giles, arriving in the middle of lunch and finding Mrs. Manresa's showy car at the door, is furious; he and Mrs. Manresa are having an affair. After lunch, on the terrace, he sits, hating Dodge. Finally, Mrs. Swithin takes pity on Dodge's discomfort and takes him off to see her brother's collection of pictures. The young man wants to tell her that he is married, but that his child is not his child, that he is a pervert, that her kindness heals his wretched day; but he cannot speak.

The guests, arriving for the pageant, begin to fill the chairs set on the lawn, for the afternoon is sunny and clear. Behind the thick bushes that serve as a dressing room, Miss La Trobe, the author and director of the pageant, is giving the last instructions to her cast. She is something of a mystery in the village, for no one knows where she came from. There are rumors that she kept a tea shop and was an actress. Abrupt and restless, she walks about the fields, uses strong language, and drinks too much at the local pub. She is a frustrated artist. Now she is wondering if her audience will realize that she is trying to give unity to English history in her pageant and to give something of herself as well.

The pageant begins. The first scene shows the age of Chaucer, with pilgrims on their way to Canterbury. Eliza Clark, who sells tobacco in the village, appears in another scene as Queen Elizabeth. Albert, the village idiot, plays her court fool. The audience hopes he will not do anything dreadful. In a play performed before Gloriana, Mrs. Otter of the End House plays the old crone who saves the true prince, the supposed beggar who falls in love with the duke's daughter. Then Miss La Trobe's vision of the Elizabethan age ends, and it is time for tea during the intermission.

Mrs. Manresa applauds; she sees herself as Queen Elizabeth and Giles as the hero. Giles glowers. Walking toward the barn, he comes on a coiled snake swallowing a toad, and he stamps on them until his tennis shoes are splattered with blood. Isa tries to catch a glimpse of Rupert Haines. Failing, she offers to show Dodge the greenhouses. They discover that they can talk frankly, like two strangers drawn together by unhappiness and understanding.

The pageant begins again. This time the scene shows the Age of Reason. Once more, Miss La Trobe wrote a play within a play; the characters have names such as Lady Harpy Harraden, Sir Spaniel Lilyliver, Florinda, Valentine, and Sir Smirking Peace-be-with-you-all, a clergyman. After another brief interval, the cast reassembles for a scene from the Victorian Age. Mr. Budge, the publican, is made up as a policeman. Albert is in the hindquarters of a donkey, while the rest of the cast pretends to be on a picnic in 1860. Then Mr. Budge announces that the time is come to pack and be gone. When Isa asks Mrs. Swithin what the Victorians were like, the old woman says that they were like Isa, Dodge, and herself, only dressed differently.

The terrace stage is left bare. Suddenly, the cast comes running from behind the bushes, each holding a mirror in which the men and women in the audience see themselves reflected in self-conscious poses. The time is the present of June, 1939. Swallows are sweeping homeward in the late light. Above them twelve airplanes flying in formation cut across the sky, drowning out all other sounds. The pageant is over; the audience disperses. Mrs. Manresa and Dodge drive away in her car. Miss La Trobe goes on to the inn. There she drinks and sees a vision and tries to find words in which to express it—to make people see once more, as she has tried to do that afternoon.

Darkness falls across the village and the fields. At Pointz Hall, the visitors are gone, and the family is alone. Bartholomew reads the evening paper and drowses in his chair. Mrs. Swithin takes up her *Outline of History* and turns the pages while she thinks of mastodons and prehistoric birds. At last, she and her brother go off to bed.

Now the true drama of the day is about to begin, ancient as the hills, secret and primitive as the black night outside. Giles and Isa will quarrel, embrace, and sleep. The curtain rises on another scene in the long human drama of enmity, love, and peace.

Critical Evaluation:

Between the Acts was completed without final revision before Virginia Woolf's suicide in 1941; in it, she returns to the tightly controlled structure, the classical unities of time and place, used before in *Mrs. Dalloway* (1925). *Between the Acts* takes place in a single day, the day of the annual village pageant, and in the house or on the grounds of Pointz Hall.

In the novel, Woolf presents a critique of patriarchy, militarism, and imperialism, themes familiar from her earlier fiction and nonfiction. Woolf's critique of male socialization becomes clear when George, Isa's small son, searches the flowerbeds and grasps a flower "complete," only to have his moment of being with the natural world shattered by the insistent presence of his grandfather Bartholomew, "a terrible peaked eyeless monster." George must identify with the patriarchal forces embodied in his Grandfather, who waves the same newspaper in which Isa will later read of the rape of a young girl carried out by soldiers.

Isa's husband, Giles, and Bartholomew are particularly identified with the powers of imperialism and male dominance, especially when Giles stamps on the snake eating a toad in a moment of parody of the militaristic man-of-action. To Woolf, the cult of masculinity contributes to the causes of war. It is against the background of a possible German invasion of England that Woolf sets the central event of the novel: Miss La Trobe's historical pageant.

Like Lily Briscoe in *To the Lighthouse* (1927), Miss La Trobe represents Woolf's ideal of the androgynous artist, a creator who is "woman-manly." As a lesbian, however, Miss La Trobe knows a level of personal frustration and artistic anguish over the success of her pageant that is foreign to the more tranquil and asexual Lily Briscoe.

Struggling to impose an artistic unity on the chaos around her and on the tendency of the audience to "split up into scraps and fragments," Miss La Trobe's vision of history seeks to show how the past informs and shapes the present. At the pageant's conclusion, she has her actors flash mirrors before the audience in which they glimpse their own faces and forms. This suggests that the present can only be understood in the context of the past. Miss La Trobe's project in presenting her pageant is strikingly similar to Woolf's own project in all her fiction, which is to insist on the world's being both unified and fragmentary, on the persistence of the past in the present, and on an understanding that only through art can the world become conscious of itself.

The title of the novel suggests some of the ironic possibilities Woolf thought existed in the interplay between art and life. *Between the Acts* refers to the precarious time between World War I and World War II. It also refers to the events, relationships, and conversations that take place between the acts of the village pageant. Finally, the story occurs between the times when the estranged couple Giles and Isa truly communicate. Significantly, the novel's last lines are: "Then the curtain rose. They spoke." The couple's performance together merges with Miss La Trobe's artistic vision to suggest that all human lives are concerned with role playing and illusion.

The impending war, although seldom mentioned directly, is always in the background in the novel; it is briefly referred to in the spectators' conversations and more directly in the sound of airplanes at the end. The reality of war does not trivialize the efforts of the villagers to put together their amateur pageant, but instead stresses the power of art to give humanity order and meaning in times of crisis.

World War I fragmented Western civilization both socially and psychologically, and the spectators see themselves in the pageant's mirrors as fragmented and isolated. For a moment, however, Miss La Trobe creates a unity in the audience by means of music. A state of harmony is reached wherein male and female, the one and the many, the silent and the speaking, are joined. Woolf was always searching for such a unity in her art, a way to reconcile opposites.

The novel is filled with cryptic and portentous symbolism. Written during the early years of World War II, it presents with poetic and fragmentary vision an outline of stark human drama against the backdrop of history. In Woolf's handling of background there is always an awareness of the primitive and historical past, conveyed in images of the flint arrowhead, the Roman road, or the manor house, which is the scene of the novel. England, rather than time, gives the novel its underlying theme. The pageant that presents a picture of English history from the Middle Ages to 1939 is only an interlude between the acts. The true drama is found in the lives of the trivial, selfish, stupid, frustrated, and idealistic people who watch the pageant and in the end are brought face-to-face with themselves. These people are actors in a drama that is older than Miss La Trobe's pictures out of the past. They are more important than the threat of war to come in the planes droning overhead. The novel represents Woolf's final affirmation of the artist's vision, the ability to distinguish between the false and the true.

"Critical Evaluation" by Roberta Schreyer

Further Reading

Barrett, Eileen, and Patricia Cramer, eds. *Virginia Woolf: Lesbian Readings*. New York: New York University Press, 1997. Part 2 of this collection of conference papers focuses on the novels, with lesbian interpretations of *Between the Acts* and six other books.

Briggs, Julia. *Virginia Woolf: An Inner Life*. Orlando, Fla: Harcourt, 2005. Focuses on Woolf's work and her fascination with the workings of the mind. Traces the creation of each of Woolf's books, from *The Voyage Out* through *Between the Acts*, combining literary analysis with details of Woolf's life.

De Gay, Jane. "Bringing the Literary Past to Life in *Between the Acts*." In *Virginia Woolf's Novels and the Literary Past*. Edinburgh: Edinburgh University Press, 2006. Examines Woolf's preoccupation with the fiction of her predecessors. Analyzes eight novels and other works to explore her allusions to and revisions of the plots and motifs of earlier fiction.

Goldman, Jane. *The Cambridge Introduction to Virginia Woolf.* New York: Cambridge University Press, 2006. Provides a wealth of information designed to help students and other readers better understand Woolf, including biographical details and discussions of the novels and other writings. One section of the book places Woolf's life and work within its historical, political, and cultural context, including information about the Bloomsbury Group; another section focuses on critical reception, featuring contemporary reviews and explanations of how Woolf's work was received from the 1940's through the 1990's.

Gordon, Lyndall. *Virginia Woolf: A Writer's Life.* New York: W. W. Norton, 1984. An analytical biography that integrates events in Woolf's life with a thematic study of her works.

Hanson, Clare. *Virginia Woolf.* New York: St. Martin's Press, 1994. A sophisticated study of gender in Woolf's novels with specific attention to her feminism and its consequences for her works. An unusual reading of *Between the Acts* focuses on gender tensions in the novel.

Reid, Panthea. *Art and Affection: A Life of Virginia Woolf.* New York: Oxford University Press, 1996. Drawing on the vast amount of material available about Woolf and her circle, Reid's biography focuses on Woolf's desires to write and to be loved. The book is especially strong in providing a psychological explanation for Woolf's artistic choices, such as her decision to abandon conventional representation in her fiction.

Roe, Sue, and Susan Sellers, eds. *The Cambridge Companion to Virginia Woolf.* New York: Cambridge University Press, 2000. A collection of essays by leading scholars that address Woolf's life and work from a range of intellectual perspectives. Includes analyses of her novels and discussions of Woolf and modernism, feminism, and psychoanalysis. References to *Between the Acts* are listed in the index.

Rose, Phyllis. *Woman of Letters: A Life of Virginia Woolf.* New York: Oxford University Press, 1978. A critical biography of Woolf, with extended discussions of all of her works.

Rosenman, Ellen Bayuk. *The Invisible Presence.* Baton Rouge: Louisiana State University Press, 1986. Informed by psychological theory, this study examines the bonds between mothers and daughters in Woolf's novels and her representations of the female artist. Includes a detailed chapter on Miss La Trobe in *Between the Acts.*

Rosenthal, Michael. *Virginia Woolf.* New York: Columbia University Press, 1979. Focuses on Woolf's preoccupation with form. Includes an excellent chapter on *Between the Acts.*

Bevis of Hampton

Author: Unknown
First transcribed: c. 1200-1250
Type of work: Poetry
Type of plot: Romance
Time of plot: c. tenth century
Locale: England, the Holy Land, and Western Europe

Principal characters:
BEVIS, a knight, heir to the estate of Hampton
JOSYAN, a Saracen princess
SIR MURDOUR, the usurper of Hampton
ASCAPARD, a giant
SABER, a knight, Bevis's uncle
ERMYN, a Saracen king, Josyan's father
INOR and BRADMOND, Saracen kings and enemies of Bevis

The Poem:

The bold spirit of Bevis is first displayed when he is only seven years old. His father was treacherously murdered, and now his mother and the assassin are engaged in shameless revelry. Bursting into the castle hall, Bevis cudgels his mother's paramour, Sir Murdour, into senselessness. The mother, fearing future outbursts, sells Bevis into slavery.

Honor, not slavery, awaits the courageous youth. Taken by slave merchants from England to a Saracen court, Bevis so impresses the king, Ermyn, that the monarch makes the youth a chamberlain. After holding this position for eight uneventful years, Bevis begins a series of remarkable exploits. The first is his single-handed slaughter of sixty Saracen warriors who make the error of deriding his Christianity. Next, he attacks and kills a man-eating boar and, to retain his trophy, beats out the brains of twelve keepers of the forest. These successes of the fifteen-year-old boy lead Ermyn to place him in charge of a small troop that defends the kingdom against the aggression of Bradmond, a rival king. Bevis, astride his incomparable horse Arundel and wielding his good sword, Morglay, lays waste to the enemy forces. To his later misfortune, however, he spares Bradmond's life.

Bevis's valor does not escape the attention of Josyan, the king's daughter. In fact, this fair young girl becomes so enamored of him that she agrees to renounce her religion and become a Christian if he will marry her. Hitherto reluctant, Bevis, under this condition, consents. When news of his daughter's apostasy reaches Ermyn, the incensed king determines to get rid of her corrupter. To accomplish this task, he sends Bevis unarmed to the court of Bradmond with a sealed letter requesting the bearer's execution. Only after a considerable number of men are slain is Bevis subdued and thrown into a dungeon.

For seven long years Bevis remains in the dungeon, and during that time he grows in Christian virtue. At last divine intercession, as a reward for his piety, and his own initiative lead to an escape in which Bevis kills two jailers and a dozen grooms. Immediately, he heads for Jerusalem to confess his sins and give thanks to God. Killing a sturdy knight and a thirty-foot giant on the way, he reaches the Holy City and there receives absolution, accompanied by an injunction never to marry a woman who is not a virgin.

Then, in order to be reunited with Josyan, he starts toward Ermony, but on the way he learns that the maid, during his imprisonment, married King Inor of Mounbraunt. To have one last look at his beloved, he dresses himself as a palmer and goes to Mounbraunt. There Josyan, discovering his true identity, implores him to take her away. He at first refuses; but when she reveals that, though seven years married, she has by magic avoided defloration, he relents.

After they escape from the city by trickery, Bevis turns his thoughts toward returning to England and avenging his father's death. Several years before he learned that Saber, his uncle, was waging war against Sir Murdour and needed his nephew's help to gain the victory. Imprisonment, however, detained Bevis, and he was to encounter other obstacles before he again saw England.

Killing two lions with one blow and subduing a thirty-foot giant, Ascapard, who then becomes his page, the indomitable Bevis, accompanied by his mistress, makes his way to the coast. In a ship taken from the Saracens, they set sail for Germany. In Cologne, Josyan is at last baptized. Near this city, Bevis has the most perilous adventure of his life. A burning dragon is his opponent on this occasion. Only after suffering a broken rib, being knocked unconscious, and falling into a miraculous healing well is Bevis able to defeat his enemy.

Leaving Ascapard to protect Josyan and taking with him a hundred men, Bevis finally sails to England. Posing as a French knight, he tricks Sir Murdour, who is now his stepfather, into providing him with arms and horses. These supplies he then carries to his uncle and they prepare to make war on Sir Murdour.

Back in Cologne, meanwhile, Josyan is in trouble, for a German earl has conceived a great lust for her. After tricking the giant into leaving, he fancies that she is at his mercy. The resourceful Josyan insists that he marry her; then on the wedding night she calmly makes a slipknot in her girdle, strangles the unsuspecting German, and hangs the corpse over a beam. The next day, when the deed is exposed, the unrepenting widow is sentenced to be burned; but before the sentence can be carried out, Ascapard and Bevis arrive, rescue her from the stake, and kill all who oppose them.

Taking Josyan and Ascapard with him this time, Bevis returns to England to pursue his war against Sir Murdour. Although Sir Murdour has a large army from Germany and another from Scotland, Bevis, assisted by Ascapard, Saber, and a moderate number of knights, wins the battle. Sir Murdour is thrown by the victors into a cauldron filled with boiling pitch and molten lead; Bevis's mother, on hearing the news, throws herself from a lofty tower.

Bevis has now avenged his father's death and regains his heritage. To complete his happiness, he marries Josyan. He is not destined, however, to settle down in peace. In London, where he goes to receive investiture, an event occurs that leads him into further adventures after the son of King Edgar tries to steal Bevis's horse and has his brains knocked out by the animal's sudden kick. King Edgar is inconsolable over the loss of his son and intent on revenge, so Bevis proposes, in expiation of the crime, to settle his land on Saber and to banish himself and his horse from England.

Ascapard, after pondering this change in his master's fortunes, decides to betray him. Hastening to Mounbraunt, he makes an agreement with King Inor to bring back Josyan. When the giant discovers her in a forest hut, she has just given birth to twin boys. Leaving the babies, he seizes Josyan and starts for Mounbraunt. Bevis, returning to the hut, takes up the children and begins searching for Josyan. Arriving at a large town, he decides to stay there and await news of his wife. While waiting, he enters a tournament and overcomes all adversaries. The prize is the hand in marriage of a young lady, daughter and heiress of a duke. Bevis agrees to wed her after seven years, if Josyan does not by then appear.

Saber, meanwhile, learns, through a dream, of Josyan's plight. Accompanied by twelve knights, he overtakes the giant on the road to Mounbraunt, kills him, and frees Josyan. Then begins a long search for Bevis. After nearly seven years of wandering, they come to the town where Bevis resides, and Josyan is reunited with her husband and children. Presently, news arrives that Josyan's father is in trouble: King Inor is attacking his kingdom. Bevis goes to his rescue, defeats King Inor, and reaches a reconciliation with his father-in-law. When Ermyn dies a short time later, Bevis's son Guy becomes king of Ermony. A second empire comes to the family soon after; in another fight with King Inor, Bevis kills him and becomes the ruler of Mounbraunt. To both these countries, Bevis, by the method of rewarding converts and butchering recalcitrants, brings Christianity.

Again he is not destined to rule in peace. News comes that his uncle's lands have been taken by King Edgar. Hurrying to the assistance of Saber, Bevis and his two sons lead an attack on the city of London in which sixty thousand men are killed. To end the slaughter, Edgar agrees that his only daughter should marry Mile, son of Bevis.

Guy, Bevis's other son, resumes his rule of Ermony, and Bevis and Josyan return to Mounbraunt. There Josyan, stricken by a mortal disease, dies in her husband's arms. A few minutes later the peace of death descends also on that incomparable knight, Sir Bevis of Hampton.

Critical Evaluation:

Readers accustomed to the tightly constructed plots of modern novels and narrative poems may find the plethora of action, the wandering story line, the frequent digressions, and the disregard for verisimilitude that characterize *Bevis of Hampton* strange, and even disturbing. The hero of this thirteenth century metrical narrative is able to slay men and monsters alike with virtual impunity; a one-man army, he appears invincible against forces considerably larger and often better armed. He engages frequently in adventures that can only be classified as fantastic. His unswerving devotion to his beloved Josyan and to his Christian faith survive every test. There seems to be nothing he cannot accomplish to rectify the wrongs done to him and to his family.

Such are the elements of the medieval romance, and *Bevis of Hampton* is typical of the genre. Its appearance in numerous manuscript versions and in a number of languages, as well as its presence among the first printed texts in England in the late fifteenth century, attest to its popularity among audiences for over three centuries. The poem is one of the most important of those that celebrate Britain in describing the exploits of heroes such as King Horn, Guy of Warwick, and King Arthur and the knights of his Round Table. While most versions treat Bevis as an English hero, some scholars have noted parallels between his story and that of a number of Continental figures; it may be that earlier stories were recast by an Anglo-Norman scribe to create a heroic story that would satisfy audiences in the land conquered by French invaders little more than a century before *Bevis of Hampton* was composed. Such an explanation would be consistent with the pattern followed by many authors of medieval works, who placed less value on invention than on pleasing audiences with variations on well-known stories about characters with whom they could identify.

The adventures Bevis experiences are typical of those described in romances of the period: He is wrongfully denied his patronage and inheritance, he is exiled from his homeland, he overcomes monumental odds in battle, he falls in love with a beautiful maiden from whom he is separated and whom he must win by force of deeds. Like so many of the knights celebrated in romances of the period, Bevis is engaged, throughout his many adventures, on a quest—here, the quest to regain his rightful place as head of his family and lands, and to claim as his bride the woman he loves. Thirteenth century audiences seem to have been less concerned about unity of plot than they were in hearing about the adventures of individuals engaged in exploits of personal daring.

One of the principal distinguishing characteristics of *Bevis of Hampton* is the hero's devotion to his Christian faith. It is not uncommon for heroes in romances to struggle against pagan infidels; the real-life exploits of European knights in the various Crusades provided an abundance of material for the fertile imagination of scribes and storytellers wishing to please audiences made up of the nobility by creating an ancestry for them that included heroic figures both real and fictional. Unfortunately, many modern readers may find the attitude expressed in the poem disturbing, since the non-Christians are presented in a highly unfavorable light. The hero's exploits in slaying Saracen warriors are treated with great relish and presumably were met with great approval by medieval audiences. The hatred with which Christian Europe looked upon the Islamic nations, which in the European view had transgressed on the most holy lands of Christendom, was a commonplace on which authors could count to evoke feelings of admiration and sympathy for knights who furthered the cause of Christianity and who remained constant to their faith. Unquestionably, the bounds of realism are strained in this poem, since the young Bevis is snatched away from his Christian home when he is only seven, yet he remains constant to the tenets of his faith while living among people who have only disdain for that creed. Even after he has committed himself to Josyan and demonstrated his determination to maintain his fidelity to her despite temptation and hardship, his commitment to his faith holds a higher place in his system of values, as he makes clear when he insists that she must convert to Christianity before he can marry her.

Like the young hero of Wolfram von Eschenbach's *Parzifal* (c. 1200-1210), a work contemporary with *Bevis of Hampton*, the title character of this romance is presented as a model of the Christian knight, fighting not only for himself but also for his Church, exhibiting the virtues one should emulate. The audiences of romance expected such instruction, and the entertainment they gained from hearing of the knight's exploits simply reinforced the lesson they gained from seeing Christianity triumph over other religions. The ability of knights such as Bevis to overcome great odds in serving his faith simply gave evidence to them that God, who had come down to earth to establish the Christian faith, would always support those who fought for His cause. This theme explains both the action and motivation of heroes who were much beloved by audiences of centuries ago.

Bevis of Hampton is of special importance because it also contains typically English elements and thus serves as a fine example of the transition from the rude Anglo-Saxon tales to the more refined French romances that prevailed after 1066. This quality of the poem may be seen by the later additions of much foreign material to a typically English celebration of a local hero. Although early romances are seldom found to have great unity of plot, *Bevis of Hampton* probably violates this principle as much as such a form can. As a metrical romance, *Bevis of Hampton* is not a success, but it is historically significant and contains that most common charm of early tales: the exuberant force of great events told in a fast-moving, sometimes even humorous, fashion.

Bevis of Hampton is often spoken of and linked together with Guy of Warwick: both English heroes upholding the Christian faith in Saracen lands, valiant youths from a very early age. They are both Crusades knights, although the romance of *Bevis of Hampton* is far more Christian in theme and characterization.

The story of Bevis probably originated in France; there are three different versions in verse and one in prose. The poem was translated into Italian, Scandinavian prose, Dutch verse, and Celtic versions. Its popularity is further attested to by the numerous references in other medieval works.

From studies of the dialect, it appears that the work was composed in the south of England, probably near Southampton, where Bevis is supposed to have been born.

The narrative encompasses a longer period of time than many medieval romances; it begins when Bevis is sold into slavery at the age of seven, continues through the time when his grown sons fight alongside him, to the moment when both he and his faithful wife die within a few minutes of each other, presumably at a mature age.

Although there is little character differentiation, there are realistic touches such as detailed description of hand-to-hand combats, of weapons, and of military engines. The author also shows his knowledge of London in the passages where Bevis and his sons resist the inhabitants aroused by the king's evil steward.

The author uses an entire arsenal of the material of romance: typical expressions of grief, pious benedictions, greetings, oaths, similes, transitional phrases, promises, character traits, methods of wounding and slaying enemies. Much of this repetition is necessitated by demands of the rhyme scheme of metrical romance. *Bevis of Hampton* begins with the oral formula of the typical metrical romance, probably used by traveling minstrels to gather crowds in a marketplace: "Lordinges, herkneth to me tale!" This tale moves rapidly, has a Christian theme carefully adhered to, and, not unlike other such romances, has comic touches in several scenes. It celebrates one of England's earliest and most stalwart heroes.

"Critical Evaluation" by Laurence W. Mazzeno

Further Reading

Billings, Anna Hunt. *A Guide to the Middle English Metrical Romances*. New York: Haskell House, 1965. Although it is dated in its commentary, this study contains useful details about the date of composition, authorship, and poetic qualities of *Bevis of Hampton*. Helpful as a starting point for further scholarly study.

Fellows, Jennifer, and Ivana Djordjevic, eds. *Sir Bevis of Hampton in Literary Tradition*. Rochester, N.Y.: D. S. Brewer, 2008. Collection of essays considering the work within its historical and literary contexts and analyzing its Anglo-Norman, Welsh, Irish, and Icelandic versions. Some of the essays examine the work's narrative structure, representation of gender, and reception in the Renaissance. Includes a bibliography of Bevis scholarship.

Field, Rosalind. "Romance in England, 1066-1400." In *The Cambridge History of Medieval English Literature*, edited by David Wallace. New York: Cambridge University Press, 1999. Field's essay includes a discussion of both the English and French versions of the Bevis romances.

Holmes, U. T. *A History of Old French Literature from the Origins to 1300*. New York: F. S. Crofts, 1938. Discusses *Bevis of Hampton* as one of several *chansons de geste* that were immediately popular and that influenced subsequent literature in a number of countries. Believes the work is misclassified as a romance.

Loomis, Laura Alandis Hibbard. *Medieval Romance in England: A Study of the Sources and Analogues of the Non-cyclic Metrical Romances*. Rev. ed. New York: Burt Franklin, 1963. Discusses the sources of *Bevis of Hampton* and its international flavor, achieved through the wanderings of the hero. Includes a bibliography of secondary sources.

Mehl, Dieter. *The Middle English Romances of the Thirteenth and Fourteenth Centuries*. London: Routledge & Kegan Paul, 1968. Describes the form of the work and traces its popularity with medieval audiences. Mehl notes that the writer achieves unity by focusing on the hero; the emphasis throughout is on action rather than ideology.

Rickard, P. *Britain in Medieval French Literature, 1100-1500*. New York: Cambridge University Press, 1956. Links the Continental version of *Bevis of Hampton* with other French works dealing with the theme of "rebellion against English domination."

Beyond Freedom and Dignity

Author: B. F. Skinner (1904-1990)
First published: 1971
Type of work: Psychology

In *Beyond Freedom and Dignity*, behavioral psychologist B. F. Skinner summarized his ideas about the nature of science, the techniques for controlling human behavior, and the possibility of building a happier and more stable society. Convinced that all human behavior is determined by environment and biology, he denied the existence of free will (or freedom) and moral autonomy (or dignity). Indeed, he held that illusions about their existence are harmful, because they militate against the establishment of an effective technology to eliminate harmful forms of behavior. Skinner had already discussed his theories in previous publications, but *Beyond Freedom and Dignity* had the advantages of being more readable and relatively concise, comprising 215 pages of text. When published in 1971, the book created a great deal of interest and controversy, and it remained on the *New York Times* best-seller list for eighteen weeks—an unusual occurrence for a theoretical work of this kind.

More than two decades earlier, Skinner had published his utopian novel, *Walden Two* (1948), in which protagonist T. E. Frazier told about a happy community that utilized Skinnerian principles of control to produce a way of life inspired by Henry David Thoreau's writings. As was true of many persons in the early 1970's, Skinner had become alarmed about population growth and environmental degradation, and he wrote *Beyond Freedom and Dignity* with the goal of providing an additional theoretical explanation about how to design and operate the kind of culture that his character Frazier had described.

Skinner confidently proclaimed that, because of modern science, engineering a better society is entirely possible and that, once established, such a society would produce people who voluntarily pursue policies that promote survival. In particular, citizens would embrace limitations on population growth and restrictions on practices that damage the environment. With confidence in the engineering skills of those who would design and control the community, he was happy to give these benevolent engineers the power to change "the conditions under which men live and, hence, [to engage] in the control of human behavior." With Frazier-like optimism, Skinner appeared to see no need to put any limitations on the powers of the new, enlightened leadership.

Skinner's psychological system, which is commonly called "radical behaviorism," included three major components. First, he focused exclusively on behaviors that can be observed and measured empirically, and he argued that it was unscientific (or prescientific) to investigate "mentalist" phenomena such as thoughts, cognitions, and intentions. Second, he concentrated on behaviors that are learned (or conditioned) as a result of reinforcements, with an emphasis on the benefits of positive reinforcements rather than those that are negative. Third, in contrast to Pavlovian conditioning (also called "classical conditioning"), which was directed at involuntary reflexes, as in Ivan Pavlov's experiments with the salivation of dogs, Skinner called his approach "operant conditioning," which referred to the teaching of voluntary behaviors that interact with the environment, as in his experiments in teaching mice to push levers to obtain food.

The key term for Skinner was "operant," by which he referred to any nonreflexive behavior that reacts to the environment and produces reinforcing effects. Although every operant exists naturally, it tends to remain weak or inert without reinforcement. With effective reinforcements it becomes activated and powerful. Often referring to the learning of "organisms," Skinner held that operant conditioning works with humans in the same way that it does with other animals, and he rejected the concept of an "autonomous inner man" (or mind) controlling the behavior of a human being. Particularly critical of cognitive psychology, he insisted that no account of what happens inside the body can ever explain the origins of human behavior.

In arguing against any consideration of mentalist concepts, Skinner used an analogy to the sciences of physics, chemistry, and astronomy. For many centuries, progress in these fields was held back by beliefs in mysterious forces such as indwelling spirits, but significant advances occurred after scientists began to concentrate exclusively on phenomena that could be observed and measured. Likewise, Skinner argued, a scientific approach to psychology must look only at external behavior that can be observed; thus it may not rely on subjective methods such as introspection that are not amenable to objective measurement. Although Skinner did not deny that human beings might experience cognitions, intentions, and other functions of the brain, he found that consideration of such phenomena was unnecessary to account for human behavior, and, furthermore, that reliance on these internal processes would make it impossible to develop psychology into a scientific disciple.

Relying on the premise that no phenomenon can occur without sufficient causes, Skinner insisted that modern science is inherently deterministic. Asserting that the traditional concepts of free will and human autonomy imply that human behavior is "uncaused," he found that a person's behavior is determined entirely by two causative variables: "genetic endowment" and "environmental circumstances." Skinner does not appear to have considered the compromise position of soft determinism, which recognizes some margin of choice, even if it is greatly limited. Since he would not concede even this limited degree of free choice, moreover, he logically concluded that a scientific analysis is incompatible with the notion of individual responsibility, which has traditionally been the justification for punishing people who disobey societal rules.

Without expressing concern about whether punishments are ever morally justified, Skinner found that punishment is not very successful at controlling behavior. A competent parent learns that rewarding a child for desired behavior is much more likely to result in the desired result than is punishing undesired behavior. An even more effective strategy is to change the environment, utilizing "contingencies of reinforcement" that maximize desirable behavior and achievement.

Observing that modern societies already control the behaviors of babies and persons with disabilities, Skinner advocated the application of such controls to everyone. Once an appropriate "technology of contingent reinforcements" was institutionalized, he asserted, the members of the new society would enjoy the kind of existence described in *Walden Two*. They would live in harmony with one another, take pleasure in music and literature, and consume only a bare minimum of resources. In addition, Skinner asserted that "it should be possible to design a world in which behavior likely to be punished seldom or never occurs." Convinced that behavior has almost nothing to do with attitudes, he wrote: "The problem is to induce people not to be good but to behave well."

Skinner recognized that controlling a population would require a very sophisticated "science of behavior" (which he also called a "technology of technology"). Although admitting that behaviorism was still only "a science in progress," he insisted that it continued to develop and was "much further advanced than its critics usually realize." The lack of further development, in his opinion, was largely attributable to the desire to maintain traditional views about the existence of free will, dignity, and individual responsibility. This was his justification for holding that the literature of human freedom and dignity "stands in the way of further achievements." In several places, Skinner writes that "man" will be controlled by "an environment which is largely of his own making." By using the same word to refer to both the designers and the population of the utopia, Skinner appeared to obscure the likelihood that the population would be controlled by an environment that would be under the control of a small ruling elite. Skinner, therefore, saw no urgent need to explain how this elite would be selected.

Almost all psychologists agree that Skinner's techniques of operant conditioning are at least partially effective and useful in the training of animals and young children. It is also possible, moreover, that a few small voluntary communities might operate according to some of the principles of *Beyond Freedom and Dignity*, even though Hilke Kuhlmann has shown that almost all such efforts have failed, usually because everyone wanted to be the Frazier of the group. In the early twenty-first century, very few social and behavioral scientists maintain that it will ever be possible to organize and control a large society, such as the United States, along Skinnerian lines. It is difficult to deny that there are limits to the extent that operant conditioning can be successfully applied to large groups of adult humans, who are already products of socialization. While admitting the importance of environmental and genetic influences, cognitive psychologists have made a strong case for the view that complex processes in the human brain play a causative role on human behavior. Noam Chomsky, moreover, has observed that Skinner wrote his books with the goal of convincing readers to agree with his behavioral theories, utilizing arguments that appeal to readers' cognitions, with the tacit assumption that changes in their cognitions would result in behavioral changes.

Thomas Tandy Lewis

Further Reading

Chomsky, Noam. "The Case Against B. F. Skinner." *The New York Review of Books* 17 (December 30, 1971): 18-24. A classic review of *Beyond Freedom and Dignity*, arguing that its theories are unscientific, dogmatic, and sometimes incoherent.

Ellis, Albert, Mike Abrams, and Lidia D. Abrams. *Personality Theories: Critical Perspectives.* Thousand Oaks, Calif.: Sage, 2009. In addition to providing a good summary of Skinner's theories, this text allows for a comparison with Ellis's synthesis of "cognitionism" and behaviorism.

Ferguson, Kyle E., and William T. O'Donahue. *The Psychology of B. F. Skinner.* Thousand Oaks, Calif.: Sage, 2001. A comprehensive work that clarifies Skinnerian ideas in their historical and philosophical contexts.

Kuhlmann, Hilke. *Living Walden Two: B. F. Skinner's Behavioral Utopia and Experimental Communities.* Urbana: University of Illinois Press, 2005. Sympathetic study of several small communities inspired by Skinner, including analysis about why all but one in Mexico failed after a short time.

Machan, Tibor. *The Pseudo-Science of B. F. Skinner.* Washington, D.C.: University Press of America, 2007. A provocative but polemical analysis of Skinner's ideas about science, particularly rules of evidence, experiments, inferences, and the construction of theories.

Sagal, Paul T. *Skinner's Philosophy.* Washington, D.C.: University Press of America, 1981. A concise analysis of Skinner's ideas about determinism, free will, morality, and the nature of science.

Skinner, B. F. *Recent Issues in the Analysis of Behavior.* Columbus, Ohio: Merrill, 1989. Includes summaries of major concepts, responses to critics, and a new preface to *Beyond Freedom and Dignity.*

Beyond Good and Evil

Author: Friedrich Nietzsche (1844-1900)
First published: Jenseits von Gut und Böse: Vorspiel einer Philosophie der Zukunft, 1886 (English translation, 1907)
Type of work: Philosophy

In *Also sprach Zarathustra* (1883-1885; *Thus Spake Zarathustra*, 1896) Friedrich Nietzsche proclaims in parable and pseudo-prophetical cries the philosophy of the Superman, the being who would transcend humanity in having the will to power, going beyond conventional morality, and making one's own law. *Beyond Good and Evil* carries forward, in a somewhat more temperate style, the same basic ideas, but with particular attention to values and morality. The central thesis of the book is that the proud, creative individual goes beyond good and evil in action, thought, and creation.

Ordinary people are fearful, obedient, and slavelike. The true aristocrat of the spirit, the noble, is neither slave nor citizen, but rather is a lawmaker, the one who determines by acts and decisions what is right or wrong, good or bad. The aristocrat is what the novelist Fyodor Dostoevski in *Prestuplenya i nakazaniye* (1866; *Crime and Punishment*, 1886) calls the "extraordinary" person. To sharpen his image of the noble, Nietzsche describes two primary types of morality: master-morality and slave-morality. Moral values are determined by either the rulers or the ruled. Rulers naturally regard the terms "good" and "bad" as synonymous with "noble" and "despicable." They apply moral values to the individual, venerating the aristocrat; but those who are ruled apply moral values primarily to acts, grounding the value of an act in its utility, its service to them. For the noble, pride and strength are virtues; for the "slaves," patience, self-sacrifice, meekness, and humility are virtues. The aristocrat scorns cowardice, self-abasement, and the telling of lies; as a member of the ruling class he or she must seek the opposite moral qualities. According to Nietzsche,

> The noble type of man regards himself as a determiner of values; he does not require to be approved of; he passes the judgment: "What is injurious to me is injurious in itself"; he knows that it is he himself only who confers honour on things; he is a creator of values. He honours whatever he recognizes in himself: such morality is self-glorification.

Those who are ruled, the slaves, construct a morality that will make their suffering bearable. They are pessimistic in their morality and come to regard the "good" person as the "safe" person, one who is "good-natured, easily deceived, perhaps a little stupid, un *bonhomme*."

Nietzsche concludes that in slave morality "language shows a tendency to approximate the significations of the words 'good' and 'stupid.'" Perhaps because Nietzsche regards love considered "as a passion" as of noble origin, he maintains in the chapter titled "Apophthegms and Interludes" that "What is done out of love always takes place beyond good and evil."

A proper interpretation of Nietzsche's work is possible only if one remembers that Nietzsche is not talking about actual political rulers and the ruled, although even in this particular case something of his general thesis applies. He is speaking instead of those who have the power and will to be a law to themselves to pass their own moral judgments according to their inclinations, and of those who do not: The former are the masters, the latter, the slaves. A revealing statement of the philosophical perspective from which this view becomes possible is the apophthegm: "There is no such thing as moral phenomena, but only a moral interpretation of phenomena."

Nietzsche must be given credit for having anticipated to a considerable extent many of the prevailing tendencies in twentieth century philosophy. He is sophisticated about language: He understands the persuasive function of philosophy, and he is unrelenting in his naturalistic and relativistic interpretation of human values and moralities. If he errs at all in his philosophic objectivity, it is in endorsing the way of power as if, in some absolute sense, that is the way, the only right way. This flaw in Nietzsche's disdain of dogmatism, this capitulation to dogmatism in his own case, is one cause of the ironic character of his book.

Another weakness in the author that makes something of a mockery out of his veneration of the Superman is his fear of failure and rejection. The fear is so strong that it comes to the surface of certain passages despite what must have been the author's desire to keep it hidden. Certainly he would not have appreciated the irony of having others discover that he himself is the slave he so much despises. For example, in the last few pages of the book Nietzsche writes that "Every deep thinker is more afraid of being understood than of being misunderstood." A little later, in describing the philosopher, he writes: "A philosopher: alas, a being who often runs away from himself, is often afraid of himself." He ends the book with a passage that begins, "Alas! what are you, after all, my written and painted thoughts!" and ends, "but nobody will divine . . . how ye looked in your morning, you sudden sparks and marvels of my solitude, you, my old, beloved-evil thoughts!" Although in context such passages seem to be part of Nietzsche's pose of superiority, it is interesting that out of context they take on another, revealing meaning.

Nietzsche begins his book with a chapter on the "Prejudices of Philosophers." He claims that philosophers pretend to doubt everything, but in the exposition of their views they reveal the prejudices they mean to communicate. Philosophers of the past have tried to derive human values from some outside sources; the result has been that what they reveal is nothing more than their own dogmatic "frog perspective." Nietzsche prides himself on being one of the "new" philosophers, one who suggests that the traditional values may be intimately related to their evil opposites.

Nietzsche chides traditional philosophers for scurrying after Truth as if she were a woman. He argues that false opinions are often better than true ones, that the only test of an opinion is not whether it is true or false but whether it is "life-furthering, life-preserving, species preserving, perhaps species-rearing." This is the point at which his own dogmatism shows itself: In making "species-rearing" the criterion of a worthy idea, he shows his own prejudice in favor of the man of power. He is unabashed in his preference and argues that the recognition of the value of untruth impugns the traditional ideas of value and places his philosophy beyond good and evil. Nietzsche, declaring himself one who wishes to bring about a transvaluation of all values, argues that there is no more effective way than to begin by supposing that conventional morality is a sign of slavery and weakness. The free person, the one strong enough to be independent, sees through the pretenses of philosophers and moralists; such a person laughs and creates a new world.

According to Nietzsche himself, there is danger in his philosophy. In fact, he takes pride in that danger. He identifies himself with the "philosophers of the dangerous 'Perhaps'"—that is, with philosophers who insist that "perhaps" everyone else is mistaken. He offers certain "tests" that one can use to determine whether he is ready for independence and command, and he says that one should not avoid these tests, "although they constitute perhaps the most dangerous game one can play." He chooses a dangerous name for the new philosophers: "tempters."

Speaking for the "philosophers of the future," the "opposite ones," Nietzsche writes,

> We believe that severity, violence, slavery, danger in the street and in the heart, secrecy, stoicism, tempter's art and deviltry of every kind—that everything wicked, terrible, tyrannical, predatory, and serpentine in man, serves as well for the elevation of the human species as its opposite.

Considered coolly, what is this danger and deviltry of which Nietzsche is so fond? It is nothing more than the possibility of new lines of development for the human spirit. The danger and the deviltry are such only in relation to the rule-bound spirits of conventional people. Nietzsche is philosopher enough to know that the human being is too complex an organism ever to have been confined or exhausted by ways of life already tried and endorsed. He calls attention to the value of revolt by playing the devil or tempter. The "most dangerous game," or the "big hunt," is humanity's free search for new ways of being. The hunting domain is extensive; it is the entire range of human experience, both actual and possible. Furthermore, there is no need or use in taking "hundreds of hunting assistants," Nietzsche points out, for each person must search alone; people must do everything for themselves in order to learn anything.

Nietzsche's objection to Christianity is that it has been a major force in limiting humanity by imposing a static morality. Since Nietzsche thinks of humanity's most important creative function as the creation of a new self, since he would urge each person, as an artist, to use himself or herself as material and fashion a new self, he rejects as life-defeating any force that works against such a creative function. He argues that people with neither the strength nor the intelligence to recognize the differences among people, to distinguish the nobles from the slaves, have fashioned Christianity with the result that humanity has become nothing more than "a gregarious animal, something obliging, sickly, mediocre."

Whether one agrees with Nietzsche in his estimate of Christianity and philosophy, no one can justifiably deny his claim that to look beyond good and evil, to throw away conventional modes of thought, is to provide oneself with a challenging, even a liberating, experience. The old "tempter" tempts readers into a critical consideration of their values, and that is all to the good.

Further Reading

Berkowitz, Peter. *Nietzsche: The Ethics of an Immoralist.* Cambridge, Mass.: Harvard University Press, 1995. Shows how Nietzsche's attacks on conventional and traditional morality entail a distinctive ethical outlook.

Burnham, Douglas. *Reading Nietzsche: An Analysis of "Beyond Good and Evil."* Montreal: McGill-Queen's University Press, 2007. Explains the central concepts of this work and places them within the broader context of Nietzsche's overall philosophy.

Chessick, Richard D. *A Brief Introduction to the Genius of Nietzsche.* Lanham, Md.: University Press of America, 1983. One section deals specifically with *Beyond Good and Evil.* A wonderful primer for understanding the concepts of nihilism and eternal recurrence.

Hayman, Ronald. *Nietzsche.* New York: Routledge, 1999. An excellent biographical introduction to the thoughts of the philosopher, clearly presented and requiring no special background. Includes bibliography.

Kaufman, Walter Arnold. *Nietzsche: Philosopher, Psychologist, Antichrist.* 4th rev. ed. Princeton, N.J.: Princeton University Press, 1974. Underscores the radical nature of Nietzsche's philosophy, especially given the Christian focus of the European literary world of his time.

Klein, Wayne. *Nietzsche and the Promise of Philosophy.* Albany: State University of New York Press, 1997. Discusses Nietzsche's vision of what philosophy should and should not be and traces the implications of his analysis.

Lampert, Laurence. *Nietzsche's Task: An Interpretation of "Beyond Good and Evil."* New Haven, Conn.: Yale University Press, 2001. A section-by-section interpretation of the work, explaining its philosophical concepts.

Lomax, J. Harvey. *The Paradox of Philosophical Education: Nietzsche's New Nobility and the Eternal Recurrence in "Beyond Good and Evil."* Lanham, Md.: Lexington

Books, 2003. Detailed textual analysis of the work, with special attention focused on Nietzsche's concept of nobility.

Mencken, H. L. "Beyond Good and Evil." In *Friedrich Nietzsche*. New Brunswick, N.J.: Transaction, 1993. A sympathetic treatment of Nietzsche's work. Probes his attacks on conventional morality.

Solomon, Robert C., ed. *Nietzsche: A Collection of Critical Essays*. Garden City, N.J.: Anchor Press, 1973. A valuable collection of essays by such prominent writers as Thomas Mann, George Bernard Shaw, and Hermann Hesse. Discusses Nietzsche's views on nihilism, moral change, and eternal recurrence.

Stack, George J. *Nietzsche: Man, Knowledge, and Will to Power.* Durango, Colo.: Hollowbrook, 1994. A modern and critical analysis of the major tenets of *Beyond Good and Evil*. Easy to follow, and illuminating. Contains extended bibliography, detailed index, and footnotes.

The Big Rock Candy Mountain

Author: Wallace Stegner (1909-1993)
First published: 1943
Type of work: Novel
Type of plot: Historical realism
Time of plot: 1905-1932
Locale: North Dakota, Washington, Saskatchewan, Montana, Utah, and Nevada

Principal characters:
HARRY (BO) MASON, a bootlegger
ELSA (NORGAARD) MASON, his wife
CHESTER (CHET) and BRUCE, their sons
LAURA BETTERTON, Chet's wife

The Story:

After Elsa Norgaard's mother dies and her father marries her best friend, Elsa, not yet nineteen, leaves her home in Minnesota to live with her uncle in Hardanger, North Dakota. In 1905, Hardanger is a little town on the edge of the frontier. There she meets Harry Mason, better known as Bo, who runs a combination bowling alley, pool hall, and blind pig (an illegal bar).

Several years older than Elsa, Bo ran away from his abusive father when he was fourteen. Restless and ambitious, he was looking for a place that was just opening up where he could make his fortune. Elsa is attracted to Bo, who can be charming. Despite misgivings about his temper, when Bo proposes, Elsa accepts. Bo and his partner buy a hotel in Grand Forks, North Dakota, and run it for seven years. Bo and Elsa have two boys: Chester (Chet) and Bruce.

When a customer pays his bar bill with gold dust from the Klondike, Bo and his partner decide to move to Alaska. While in Seattle waiting to sail, Chet and Bruce come down with scarlet fever. The partner goes while Bo, impatient, stays. Bo and Elsa buy a café near a lumber camp. After Elsa's arm is injured, Bo is increasingly restless at the café, which makes little money, and short with Bruce, who clings to his mother. When Bo loses his temper and mistreats Bruce, Elsa locks him out.

Elsa cannot run the café by herself. She places Chet and Bruce in an orphanage, swallows her pride, and moves back to her father's home.

Bo goes to Canada and opens a boardinghouse for railroad workers, selling them bootleg liquor at night. Prospering but lonely, he begs Elsa to come back to him. In 1914, Elsa and the boys go with him to Whitemud, Saskatchewan. For the next five years, they live in town during the winters and on their homestead during the summers. The price of wheat is high but yields are low. In 1918, they end the summer without enough money to live on that winter.

In late October, there are rumors of a flu epidemic. Alcohol, although illegal, is considered good medicine. Bo drives to Montana on primitive roads and buys enough to fill his car. On the way back, a blizzard hits. Badly frostbitten, he soon has pneumonia as well. When Elsa and Bruce get the flu, Chet sells the liquor. Profits are good, and Bo goes into bootlegging on a steady basis.

The next year, with Prohibition in effect in the United States, Bo buys a faster car and they move to Great Falls, Montana. When a large operation pressures Bo into working for it, he moves his family to Salt Lake City. Here Chet and Bruce attend high school. A gifted athlete, Chet excels at baseball. Bruce is more academically inclined. He skips a couple of grades and graduates from high school with Chet.

At seventeen, Chet hopes to play professional baseball and is increasingly serious about a young woman, Laura Betterton, who is twenty-one. Concerned, Bo and Elsa arrange for Chet to work for a local semipro team in the hope that he will eventually play for them. One evening the police raid the house. Chet is home alone but Bo soon arrives. Both are taken to the police station, though Chet is not charged. Embarrassed, Chet gives up hopes for a baseball career and elopes with Laura. Both fathers insist on an annulment, but Chet and Laura soon run off again and move to Rapid City, South Dakota.

After completing college, Bruce goes to law school at the University of Minnesota. Elsa is stricken with breast cancer and has a mastectomy. In 1931, Chet loses his job and moves home with Laura and their child. Chet is washed up at twenty-three, and even Laura leaves him. Shortly after, he succumbs to pneumonia.

Bo invests in a casino in Reno, Nevada, his most profitable venture ever. Afraid that it will not last, he sells his share after a few months. When Elsa's cancer returns, they move back to Salt Lake City. Bruce leaves school to help take care of her. Bo, unable to deal with her illness, is gone much of the time. When Elsa dies, they bury her beside Chet.

Bruce returns to the University of Minnesota. Bo invests the last of his money in a mine deal that does not pay off. Old and lonely, his money gone, Bo has no more grand schemes for the future, no more places to move toward. As Bruce graduates from law school, he learns that his father shot the mistress who spurned him and then shot himself. While arranging the funeral, Bruce tries to make sense of his father's life and death. Although he hated Bo and revered Elsa, he realizes that both parents are a part of him.

Critical Evaluation:

The Big Rock Candy Mountain, Wallace Stegner's fifth novel, was his first commercial success. All of Stegner's fiction starts from his own experience, but *The Big Rock Candy Mountain* is the most autobiographical. Bo Mason is modeled after Stegner's father, Elsa after his mother, Chet after his older brother, and Bruce after himself. Stegner, who did not finish the book until after his father's death, says that writing about the father-son relationship was a way to exorcise his father.

Often categorized as regional literature, *The Big Rock Candy Mountain* is set in the West, in places in which Stegner had lived and which he knew intimately. His is an accurate, detailed picture of the language, the customs, and the psychology of the people who lived there. A major theme of the book is the attraction of the mythic West, the place where a person can start over and build a new, more prosperous life. The Big Rock Candy Mountain, described in an old song, is a symbol of such a place, and Bo's whole life is devoted to finding it.

The novel depicts a period of time between the old days, when the West was still a frontier, and the modern period, which had not yet begun. Bo comes from a long line of pioneers who had been moving farther west with each generation. Like his ancestors, he is born with an "itch in his bones" to find a place where he can realize the great American dream of success and independence, but he is born too late and the best opportunities have been taken. Many who migrated west did so to homestead farmland, and Bo does homestead in Canada, but the only land left is marginal and produces a good crop only occasionally. The only real opportunities Bo finds are outside the law.

Elsa's father also feels the lure of the frontier. He leaves Norway because he hopes to do better in America, but he wanders only as far as Minnesota and settles down. Elsa rejects her father and his way of life because his marrying her best friend is intolerable. Perhaps she finds Bo attractive because he is different from her own father, and when her father objects to the match, she plunges ahead with the marriage. Although she rejects her father, what Elsa wants most is a home and a family and roots. The desires of the restless man and the nesting woman will always be in conflict.

As a result of their vagabond existence, the Mason family is doomed to be rootless. Toward the end of the book, Bruce realizes that having lived so many places, he does not know where home is, but it is someplace west of the Missouri River. The Mason family is isolated socially because Bo's bootlegging activities keep them outside respectable society. They have broken the ties with their own families. Bo, Elsa, Chet, and Bruce have only one another—and the relationships in this family are uneasy. Bo loves Elsa and the boys but believes his family obligations are holding him back from realizing his dream. Elsa loves Bo but believes she is a burden to him. Just as Bo and Elsa leave home at a young age, so, too, do Chet and Bruce escape from their parents' way of life as soon as possible. The Mason family is like many other American families: The urge to move ever westward results in the social disruption of the family and the absence of community.

At the beginning of the book, Elsa's and Bo's points of view dominate. As Chet and Bruce grow up, their voices are heard as well, and the relationship between father and sons is another important theme. Chet is more like Bo, athletic, a man of action, independent. Embarrassed by Bo's bootlegging activities, he runs away from home at seventeen but cannot make it on his own. A failure, he dies at twenty-three.

Bruce, who is small, unathletic, and bookish, has mixed feelings about his father. As a boy, he admires some of Bo's talents, but he is most often the target of Bo's temper when things go wrong. The only time he feels close to his father is in Saskatchewan when Bo kills a snake: Death is the one thing they share. As he grows older, he escapes to school and books. Eventually he chooses to study law—a direct rejection of Bo's lifelong habit of living outside it. When Elsa is dying, Bruce cannot understand Bo's self-centeredness, and his hatred grows more intense. After Elsa dies and he discovers that Bo has given her clothes to his mistress, he walks out. He never sees Bo alive again.

Elsa's and Bo's points of view dominate the first three-fourths of the book, dramatizing the conflict between the restless man and the nesting woman. Bruce's point of view, which controls the latter one-fourth, is much more reflective and tends toward a stream-of-consciousness narration. Bruce's sections, the ones most associated with Stegner's own voice, are more authoritative. Much of his perspective makes Elsa seem like a saint while Bo is condemned for his shortcomings.

Only when Bruce is making arrangements for Bo's funeral does he take a more enlightened view of his father. He acknowledges that Bo was a competent carpenter, mechanic, and storyteller, that "his qualities were the raw material for a notable man," and that in an earlier time he might have been great. He also realizes that family was important to Bo. Bruce comes to understand that he is the product not only of Bo and Elsa but of all his other ancestors. He cannot disown any part of himself. Instead, he must find a way to synthesize the restless chaser of dreams with the socially responsible person to become a complete man.

Eunice Pedersen Johnston

Further Reading

Arthur, Anthony, ed. *Critical Essays on Wallace Stegner.* Boston: G. K. Hall, 1982. Includes two reviews of *The Big Rock Candy Mountain* written when it was first published and several critical essays that analyze themes, point of view, and autobiographical influences.

Benson, Jackson J. *Down by the Lemonade Springs: Essays on Wallace Stegner.* Reno: University of Nevada Press, 2001. Collection of essays by a Stegner biographer (below). The essays include examinations of Stegner's fiction, the writer as an environmentalist, and Stegner's friendship with poet Robert Frost.

_______. *Wallace Stegner: His Life and Work.* New York: Viking Press, 1996. A biography that argues against pigeonholing Stegner as a Western writer. Focuses largely on the people and events that most influenced Stegner's art, including Robert Frost and Bernard DeVoto; covers Stegner's teaching career and his influence on such writers as Ken Kesey, Edward Abbey, Wendell Berry, and Larry McMurtry.

Fradkin, Philip L. *Wallace Stegner and the American West.* New York: Alfred A. Knopf, 2008. A detailed, astute biography, describing how Stegner transformed the failure of his father's homestead and other incidents of his father's life into his fiction about the American West.

Lewis, Merrill, and Lorene Lewis. *Wallace Stegner.* Boise, Idaho: Boise State College, 1972. A brief overview of Stegner's life and work.

Meine, Curt, ed. *Wallace Stegner and the Continental Vision: Essays on Literature, History, and Landscape.* Washington, D.C.: Island Press, 1997. A collection of papers presented at a 1996 symposium in Madison, Wisconsin. Includes essays on Stegner and the shaping of the modern West, the art of storytelling, history, environmentalism, politics, and bioregionalism.

Rankin, Charles E., ed. *Wallace Stegner: Man and Writer.* Albuquerque: University of New Mexico Press, 1996. A collection of essays by various critics on Stegner's life and art. Includes discussion of Stegner as a Western humanist; Stegner, the environment, and the West; and Stegner, storytelling, and Western identity.

Robinson, Forrest Glen, and Margaret G. Robinson. *Wallace Stegner.* Boston: Twayne, 1977. Includes biographical information and a discussion of Stegner's fiction and nonfiction, including *The Big Rock Candy Mountain.*

Stegner, Wallace, and Richard W. Etulain. *Conversations with Wallace Stegner on Western History and Literature.* Rev. ed. Salt Lake City: University of Utah Press, 1990. Stegner discusses his life and his writing, as well as his views on literature and history.